CONVEYANCING

CONVEYANCING

Editors

Dr Gabriel Brennan
Nuala Casey

OXFORD
UNIVERSITY PRESS

OXFORD

UNIVERSITY PRESS

Great Clarendon Street, Oxford, OX2 6DP,
United Kingdom

Oxford University Press is a department of the University of Oxford.
It furthers the University's objective of excellence in research, scholarship,
and education by publishing worldwide. Oxford is a registered trade mark of
Oxford University Press in the UK and in certain other countries

© Law Society of Ireland 2016

The moral rights of the authors have been asserted

Fifth edition 2011
Sixth edition 2012
Seventh edition 2014
Impression: 4

Public sector information reproduced under Open Government Licence v3.0
(http://www.nationalarchives.gov.uk/doc/open-government-licence/open-government-licence.htm)

Published in the United States of America by Oxford University Press
198 Madison Avenue, New York, NY 10016, United States of America

British Library Cataloguing in Publication Data
Data available

Library of Congress Control Number: 2016944785

ISBN 978–0–19–877841–7

Printed in Great Britain by
Bell & Bain Ltd., Glasgow

PREFACE

Our aim in writing this book is to provide trainee solicitors with a comprehensive text dealing with all the fundamental aspects of conveyancing practice and procedure. The primary focus of the text is to prepare trainee solicitors for practice. Where necessary academic law is referred to; however, it is assumed that readers have a basic knowledge of land law and contract law, upon which the practice of conveyancing rests.

This text is designed for the guidance of trainee solicitors attending the Law Society's Law School. It is anticipated that the text will provide a foundation for their learning and also assist them once their traineeship period is concluded and they have entered the solicitor's profession. Indeed, it is hoped that the text will provide assistance to all practitioners in the conveyancing field. If utilised in practice, the sample forms and precedents included in the text should be adapted as appropriate to the transaction in question.

It is recognised that conveyancing practice and procedures throughout Ireland vary and, while acknowledging these variations, the text reflects Law Society recommended practice, which, like all aspects of law, is constantly evolving. The law and practice are stated as at 1 May 2016.

While every effort has been made to ensure that the text is accurate, the authors would be grateful to learn of any errors or omissions. Any comments or queries on this Manual should be sent to the editors at the Law Society.

Thanks to all our colleagues who gave their support and special thanks to our wonderful families.

Dr Gabriel Brennan
Nuala Casey
May 2016

AUTHORS

Dr Gabriel Brennan is a solicitor with the Law Society. She is Course Manager with the Law School for Applied Land Law and Senior Advisor to the Society's eConveyancing Project. She is editor and co-author of the Law Society's *Landlord and Tenant Law* manual and co-editor and co-author of this and other property law manuals. She lectures on the Law Society's Professional Training and Diploma courses. She is a member of the Law Society Conveyancing Committee, eConveyancing Task Force, and the PRA eRegistration Project Board. Gabriel was formerly in practice with Abercorn Solicitors.

Sean Brodie has lectured on the Law Society's VAT and Landlord and Tenant Law modules on the Professional Practice Courses and on the Law Society's Diploma in Commercial Conveyancing. He has also lectured on VAT for the Irish Tax Institute and is co-author of *Value Added Tax* published by the Irish Tax Institute. He is currently a partner with PricewaterhouseCoopers where he advises on all aspects of VAT. Prior to joining PricewaterhouseCoopers he worked in the office of the Revenue Commissioners.

Nuala Casey (BCL, TEP) is a Consultant Solicitor with Shiel Solicitors. She has extensive experience in the areas of conveyancing and probate practice. She is a lecturer and tutor for the Law Society Professional Practice Courses and lectures on probate and conveyancing topics for the Law Society. She is a registered Trust and Estate practitioner and has lectured and tutored on the Law Society/Society of Trust & Estate practitioners (STEP) Diploma in Trust and Estate Practice. She is co-editor and co-author of the Law Society's *Complex Conveyancing Manual* and co-author of the Law Society's *Wills Probate and Estate* manual. She is a committee member of Solicitors for the Elderly.

Deirdre Fox has lectured extensively on conveyancing practice both to students on the Law Society's Professional Practice Courses and to members of the profession. Deirdre has been a member of the Law Society Conveyancing Committee since 1996. In September 2006 she left *eircom* Limited, where she had been the head of the Conveyancing Department in the legal office for the previous nine years, in order to set up her own practice, Deirdre Fox and Associates, in Aughrim, Co Wicklow. In August 2011, Deirdre was appointed by the Minister for Justice and Equality as the Law Society's representative on the Property Registration Authority.

Rachael Hession qualified as a solicitor in 1997. She is a Course Manager on the Law Society's Professional Practice Courses and is a Programme Manager with Law Society Professional Training. She is secretary to the Law Society Taxation Committee. She lectures and tutors on the Professional Practice Courses and is co-editor and co-author of the *Law Society Complex Conveyancing* manual. She was previously in practice with Ronan Daly Jermyn Solicitors and Henry P.F. Donegan Solicitors. She is an associate of the ITI and a member of STEP. She holds an MA in Higher Education, Professional Legal Education and Skills and is currently studying for a Doctorate in Education.

Barry Magee qualified as a solicitor in 2000 and initially practised with Maurice E. Veale & Co. Solicitors. He joined the Office of the Chief State Solicitor in 2001 where he worked in the State Property Division. In 2008 he joined the Railway Procurement Agency which is the State Agency tasked with the provision of Luas light rail, metro infrastructure, and integrated ticketing. He has lectured and tutored on the Law Society Professional Practice Courses in conveyancing and landlord and tenant law. He became Chairperson of the Refugee Appeals Tribunal in 2013.

John Murphy is a solicitor and Deputy Registrar in the Property Registration Authority (PRA). He has worked in the Land Registry and Registry of Deeds since 1980 and has broad experience in all aspects of registration of title. John lectures on PRA-related matters on the Law Society's Professional Practice Courses, on the Professional Training program, and to various Bar Associations.

Anne Stephenson is the principal of Stephenson Solicitors. She is a member of STEP, Solicitors for the Elderly, the DSBA Probate and Taxation and Mental Health and Capacity Committees, the Probate Liaison Committee, and the Law Society's Probate Administration and Trust Committee and is a member of the Committee of the Solicitors for the Elderly. She lectures, examines, and tutors on the Law Society's Professional Practice Courses and on the STEP Diploma in Wills, Trust & Estate Planning. She also lectures on the Law Society's Professional Training Courses and to the DSBA and numerous other professional bodies. She is co-author of the Law Society's manual on *Wills, Probate and Estates*, this manual, and the *Capital Taxation for Solicitors* manual.

ACKNOWLEDGEMENTS

While the individual authors are, of course, solely responsible for the contents of the manual, we would like to express our gratitude to the many colleagues who so ably assisted us in this project. Grateful acknowledgements are due to the many members of the profession who helped bring this manual about by reading individual chapters at various stages, offering invaluable advice and judicious improvements. In particular, thanks is due to Pat O'Brien and Rory O'Donnell for their contributions.

OUTLINE CONTENTS

DETAILED CONTENTS

TABLE OF STATUTES

TABLE OF EUROPEAN LEGISLATION

TABLE OF SECONDARY LEGISLATION

TABLE OF CASES

CHAPTER 1

INTRODUCTION TO CONVEYANCING AND SYSTEMS OF REGISTRATION

1.1   What is Conveyancing?

Put very simply, conveyancing is the process of transferring ownership of immovable property from one person to another.

Conveyancers are the qualified professionals retained by the parties to a transaction to ensure the proper disposal and acquisition of the title to the property involved and to secure the mortgage or charge of any lending institution involved. In Ireland conveyancing for reward can only be carried out by qualified solicitors.

Conveyancing is the generic term used to describe property transactions whether they be in respect of a commercial property, a residential property, an agricultural property, or a mix of all or any of them. The basic rules and principles of conveyancing apply with equal force irrespective of the nature of the property. However, the practice may vary somewhat in respect of the different types of properties, eg if the property in question was a commercial property, such as licensed premises, there are certain essential pre-contract enquiries and requisitions that will be raised which would not be relevant to the acquisition of a title to a residential property.

Likewise, there are certain pre-contract enquiries and requisitions that might be raised if the property being acquired was an agricultural holding.

1.2   Objectives of the Manual

The general objective of this Manual is to:

   (a)   explain a conveyancer's role and function in acquiring and disposing of an interest in immovable property (property meaning both buildings and lands) and how this is achieved;

   (b)   establish the basic principles involved in passing both good title and good marketable title;

   (c)   identify and explain the two systems of registration in operation in Ireland, viz the Registry of Deeds and the Land Registry (now both under the auspices of the Property Registration Authority), and how they work;

   (d)   establish the documentation and evidence required for a good marketable title and, in particular, identify what is a good root and what is not a good root of title;

   (e)   clarify the length of title required;

   (f)   advise on and outline current practice in conveyancing and in particular Law Society of Ireland recommended practice;

   (g)   identify standard documentation currently in use;

(h)   identify current legislation, ie within the past 30 years or so, which has had a sub-stantial impact on conveyancing practice;

(i)   identify and explain the terminology used by conveyancers; and

(j)   deal with any other matter generally arising.

The particular focus is on residential conveyancing transactions but it should be noted, given the complexity of property transactions, that the text offers guidance on practice which is not absolutely applicable in every case.

1.3   Major Reforms and Modernisation

The Land and Conveyancing Law Reform Act, 2009 ('the 2009 Act') is the most important piece of legislation passed in this area in decades, if not centuries. Prior to this Act convey-ancers had to consult a myriad of legislation dating from previous centuries. The 2009 Act both consolidates the existing conveyancing statute book and modernises certain areas of the law. This Act, together with the Registration of Deeds and Title Act, 2006 ('the 2006 Act'), now provide a comprehensive body of legislation.

One practical feature of the 2009 Act that is of particular benefit to conveyancing practi-tioners is that the corresponding section of the old legislation is listed in the margin. This is of benefit when consulting cases or textbooks which deal with the old legislation. For ex-ample we can see that s 51 of the 2009 Act re-enacts the provisions of s 2 of the Statute of Frauds (Ireland) Act, 1695. Another extremely useful feature of the 2009 Act is the Ex-planatory Memorandum which accompanies the Bill. This provides a simple explanation of the intention of the various sections and outlines how this alters the previous provision.

A few notes of caution must be sounded that will arise in practice:

• the 2009 Act is mainly prospective (not retrospective) in effect. This means that the ef-fectiveness of any particular deed or event on title should be judged according to the law as it stood at the relevant date of the deed or event, and not under the 2009 Act, if the deed or event precedes 2009;

• students and practitioners must therefore be aware of the law as it stood prior to the 2009 Act, when investigating a title; and

• when consulting older case law or textbooks, the legal basis of the issue being discussed may have been amended by the 2009 Act.

The Act came into force on 1 December 2009 save for s 132 which came into force on 28 February 2010.

The next major proposal for the modernisation of conveyancing is the introduction of electronic conveyancing (eConveyancing). In 2002 the Law Reform Commission estab-lished a working group to look at the introduction of such a system. The group identi-fied three main areas that required examination. These were: changes to the existing law; changes to the conveyancing process; and changes required to State services as-sociated with this process. The 2009 Act has largely dealt with the first of these areas. The Law Reform Commission asked all stakeholders, including the Law Society, to de-vise a plan for eConveyancing. The Law Society published its vision of an electronic system of conveyancing ('eVision') entitled *eConveyancing: Back to Basic Principles* in March 2008. It can be seen from this document that substantial changes to both practice and systems are required to fully implement eConveyancing. Changes to systems have already commenced with the Land Registry now being fully online, and the Rev-enue Commissioners introducing online stamping of documents from 1 January 2010. The Government recently committed to reviewing and reporting on the steps required to deliver a system of eConveyancing in Ireland as part of its Construction 2020 strategy published in May 2014.

1.4   Role of Conveyancers

A conveyancer's role generally falls under one of three headings:

(a)   representing a vendor on the sale or transfer of an interest in property;

(b)   representing a purchaser on the purchase or acquisition of an interest in property; or

(c)   representing a lending institution which is advancing money by way of a charge or mortgage on the security of a property.

Occasionally a solicitor will also be asked to give independent legal advice to a party who is asked to execute a document relating to a conveyancing transaction, eg to advise a spouse on the legal significance of executing a consent under the provisions of the Family Home Protection Act, 1976 as amended, or advising a life tenant or a person with a right of residence in a property who is asked to sign a document, ie a deed of postponement, postponing that interest in favour of a lending institution so as to give that lending institution a first charge on the property involved.

To properly fulfil this role a modern conveyancer must be conversant with several areas of the law. In particular a solid knowledge of the following areas is required:

1.   land law;

2.   planning law;

3.   tax law;

4.   contract law;

5.   equity;

6.   family law;

7.   environmental law;

8.   succession law.

It is also vital to keep abreast of all developments in law or practice as any change can affect property and must be considered in any transaction. A useful list of relevant texts and websites is provided at the end of this chapter.

1.5   The Conveyancing Process

While there is no legal requirement that a conveyancing transaction follow a particular set of steps it has become standard practice for every conveyancing transaction to consist of the following phases:

1.   pre-contract;

2.   contract;

3.   post contract/pre-closing (Objections and Requisitions on Title);

4.   closing;

5.   post-closing.

During each of these stages the solicitors on either side must carry out various tasks to ensure that their client is properly protected. These steps are explained fully in **chapter 2**. This chapter should be read in conjunction with each of the other chapters which explain many of the steps in more specific detail.

The core concept of a conveyancing transaction is that the vendor offers title to a property to a purchaser by way of a Contract for Sale. If the purchaser is satisfied that the title on offer is a good title the purchaser enters into the contract with the vendor agreeing to purchase the property at the agreed price. Once the contracts are exchanged and binding on both parties the purchaser then further investigates the title on offer, by raising what are known as Objections and Requisitions on Title. Once satisfactory replies are furnished a closing takes place on an agreed date. At the closing the deed transferring ownership from the vendor to the purchaser is exchanged for the balance of the purchase price. After the closing the purchaser's solicitor attends to having their client's title registered and payment of whatever taxes are due, eg stamp duty, and the vendor's solicitor may have to pay off/redeem any mortgages registered against the property out of the purchase monies.

This process is the same no matter how large or small the transaction and regardless of the type or nature of the property being sold.

1.5.1 WHY THIS PROCESS?

Apart from having the advantage of age this process also has the advantage that the purchaser is not obliged to go to the expense of having to carry out a full investigation of the title on offer before the vendor is legally bound to sell to them. The purchaser merely has to investigate the root of title, a concept dealt with in **chapter 4**, as set out in the contract. Once the vendor has signed the contract and is bound to complete the transaction the purchaser can then proceed to carry out a full investigation confident in the knowledge that they have secured the property.

In modern residential conveyancing the certificate of title system, as detailed in the next section, certifies that the purchase was effected on foot of the current standard Law Society Contract for Sale and/or Building Agreement and that an investigation of title was made in accordance with the current Law Society Objections and Requisitions on Title. Therefore, while in theory the process described previously need not be used, in practice it always is. Further developments on the path to eConveyancing are likely to lead to substantial changes in this process as a process improvement exercise forms a key part in the development of such a system.

1.5.2 CERTIFICATE OF TITLE SYSTEM

In a conveyancing transaction involving the purchase of a residential property it is now standard practice for lending institutions to allow the purchaser's solicitor exclusively to investigate the title and, on completion of the purchase, to allow the purchaser's solicitor to take responsibility for having the mortgage duly executed by the borrowers, stamping and registering the borrower's title and furnishing a certificate of title together with the title documents/deeds to the lending institution. This practice was adopted some years ago as a result of public pressure on lending institutions, in particular building societies, as purchasers at that time were obliged not only to pay their own solicitor on the purchase of the property but also to pay the building society's solicitor who independently investigated the title. The objective in introducing the certificate of title procedure was to save the purchaser the expense of having to pay fees to two solicitors for performing what, in the view of the public, was the same work.

This certification of title procedure is confined exclusively to residential property transactions. Since it was first introduced the system has been refined by the Conveyancing Committee of the Law Society in conjunction with the representatives of the lending institutions. The current format of the certificate of title and guidance notes relating to it are those issued by the Conveyancing Committee in April 2012. It is the view of the Conveyancing Committee that this current form of certification should not be departed from by a solicitor acting for a purchaser of residential property under any circumstances.

Solicitors are prohibited by law from giving undertakings to lenders in commercial property transactions, save in very limited circumstances, by SI 366/2010, see **3.2.4**.

1.5.3 SECTION 51 2009 ACT AND CONTRACTS FOR THE SALE OF LAND

Another reason for the use of a contract to purchase land is to be found in s 51 of the 2009 Act. Section 51 provides that, in order to be enforceable, the Contract for Sale of land must be in writing or there must be a note or memorandum of the agreement.

Section 51 states:

> . . . *no action shall be brought to enforce any contract for the sale or other disposition of land unless the agreement on which such action is brought, or some memorandum or note of it, is in writing and signed by the person against whom the action is brought or that person's authorised agent.*

This is subject to s 51(2) which provides that s 51(1) does not affect the law relating to part performance or other equitable doctrines. Section 51(3) provides that payment of a deposit is not necessary for an enforceable contract unless the contract expressly states otherwise.

If the section is not complied with, the agreement, while valid, is unenforceable.

The memorandum or note must contain the following details:

(a)   parties (and their capacities);

(b)   price;

(c)   property; and

(d)   particulars, ie statement of material terms.

See **2.2.1.15** for a full discussion of the case law in this area.

1.6   Law Society Standard Documentation

1.6.1   CONTRACTS

For many years there was a substantial variety of contracts in use for the purchase and sale of land and, likewise, building contracts in respect of the construction of new houses. Practically every auctioneer had his or her own conditions of sale and every law stationer also had its own conditions of sale. This was a most unsatisfactory situation which persuaded the Law Society to produce its first edition of a standard Contract for Sale in 1976. This Contract for Sale was introduced to give a fair balance of rights between a vendor and a purchaser and proved extremely successful. It has been revised from time to time and the current edition is the 2009 edition. This form of Contract for Sale has now become the standard Contract for Sale used by the legal profession in all types of sales and purchases. It incorporates terms and conditions which are appropriate to both a sale by auction, as well as a sale by private treaty.

Likewise, in the private house building sector, a standard Building Agreement was developed and its current edition issued in 2001 is now recommended for use in the purchase and sale of new houses.

In the standard certificate of title for private dwellings referred to earlier, the certificate provides that the standard Contract for Sale issued by the Law Society has been used or if the property is a new house, the standard Building Agreement has been used.

The Law Society periodically issues updated and revised versions of these standard documents and thus attention should be paid to ensure that the most current version is being used in any particular transaction. The 2009 edition of the Contract for Sale is currently in use. At the time of writing work is ongoing on a revised Contract for Sale. It should be noted that this standard Contract for Sale is often referred to as the General Conditions of Sale.

As in all of these cases it should never be overlooked that these contracts are standard contracts for use in general conveyancing practice and regard must always be had to variations which may be required from time to time in respect of any particular transaction. Particular attention must be paid to the nature of any amendments that are made or proposed in the standard Building Agreement. In or about the mid 1990s, during the building boom, many amendments to the terms of the standard Building Agreement were made by some solicitors acting for builders in various parts of the country. These amendments were considered to be very unfair and unreasonable to the purchaser who had little or no bargaining power. Attempts to negotiate fairer and more reasonable terms by a purchaser's solicitor were usually met with a blank refusal and a 'take it or leave it' attitude prevailed.

In 1997 the Law Society Conveyancing Committee, recognising the onerous and unfair burden placed on purchasers and their solicitors by these amended terms and conditions, urged the Director of Consumer Affairs to take action under the European Communities (Unfair Terms in Consumer Contracts) Regulations, 1995. This incorporated the relevant European directive on unfair terms and conditions in consumer contacts into Irish law. In May 2001, the Director issued proceedings using 15 sample conditions provided mainly by the Law Society in which various 'interested parties' as provided by the Regulations filed affidavits, viz the Law Society, the Construction Industry Federation/Irish Home Builders Association, and the Department of the Environment. The application for a declaratory order was heard by the High Court on 5 December 2001 and the terms of an agreed order were ruled on 20 December 2001. The order not only prohibited the use of, or if appropriate, the continued use in building agreements of any of the 15 terms listed in the schedule to the order, but it also prohibited the use of 'any term that is intended to, or does, in fact, have like effect'. The 15 terms are set out in **chapter 12**.

It is, therefore, vital that solicitors acting for both builders and purchasers of new houses must examine each and every special condition in the building agreement and test it for compliance with this court order. The exact details of the terms and the overall nature of this order are set out in a comprehensive article entitled 'Safe as houses?' written by Patrick Dorgan, then chairman of the Law Society's Conveyancing Committee, and published in the Law Society *Gazette* in January/February 2002.

This has resulted in the issuing of a Practice Note by the Conveyancing Committee in the July 2014 edition of the *Gazette* which outlines the many problems encountered by practitioners in dealing with restrictive conditions included in Contracts for Sale by solicitors acting for receivers or mortgagees.

Finally it must be emphasised that the certificate of title given by a purchaser's solicitor to their client's lending institution is based on the use of the standard Building Agreement and Contract for Sale and any significant change in these documents raises a serious question mark over the validity of the certificate.

1.6.2 OBJECTIONS AND REQUISITIONS ON TITLE

Objections and Requisitions on Title are the queries raised by the purchaser's solicitor in all conveyancing transactions in respect of the vendor's title and many ancillary matters relevant to the property in question. The requisitions cover a multitude of matters, not all of which may be relevant to the particular transaction being dealt with. The form of requisitions on title has again been standardised by the Law Society and the current edition of them, viz the 2015 edition, is now in general use in all conveyancing transactions.

Because of the multiplicity of additional factors which all conveyancers now have to take into account, a substantial number of requisitions have been added to the standard ones. These are incorporated in the printed forms issued by the Law Society but are to be excluded in cases to which they do not apply, eg there are separate requisitions on title covering matters like licensing, second-hand apartments, etc. This topic is fully explored in **chapter 15**.

1.6.3   FAMILY LAW DECLARATIONS

Because of the development since 1976 of legislation dealing with family law, it has become essential for conveyancers to have regard to a number of legislative provisions which may affect property transactions, ie Family Home Protection Act, 1976, Family Law Act, 1981, Judicial Separation and Family Law Reform Act, 1989, Family Law Act, 1995, Family Law (Divorce) Act, 1996, and Civil Partnership and Certain Rights and Obligations of Cohabitants Act, 2010.

In order to deal with this developing branch of conveyancing, standard declarations recommended for use by the solicitors' profession have been prepared and issued by the Law Society. These have been updated and amended from time to time and the declarations are recommended for standard use as being adequate to deal with the various matters raised in the legislation. It is important to emphasise, however, that they should not be used without giving proper consideration to the contents thereof to ensure that, where necessary, relevant amendments are made to cover any particular situation that may arise. This is still a developing area of law and these standard declarations may require amendment from time to time.

The reader is referred to **chapter 7**, which deals with this topic, for further details of the particular elements of the legislation to which conveyancers must have regard.

1.7   Systems of Registration

1.7.1   GENERALLY

Once a conveyancing transaction is completed it is vital for the change of ownership to be properly registered. To fully understand the practice of conveyancing one must first of all become familiar with the two systems of registration currently in operation in Ireland, the Registry of Deeds and the Land Registry.

1.7.2   REGISTRY OF DEEDS

The first system of registration introduced in Ireland was the Registry of Deeds. It was originally established under the Registration of Deeds (Ireland) Act, 1707 ('the 1707 Act'), which was established for the purpose of giving priority to registered deeds and the prevention of fraud in dealing with the transfer of ownership of land. It is now under the control of the Property Registration Authority since 4 November 2006. It is the registration system which is most frequently encountered in dealing with titles in urban areas, particularly Dublin and Cork. Most of the titles outside these areas are dealt with in the Land Registry.

While the Registration of Deeds and Title Act, 2006 has now repealed the 1707 Act, and subsequent amending legislation, the effect of the 2006 Act is substantially the same.

There are a number of points to be noted in respect of the Registry of Deeds system:

(a)   It deals with the registration of documents, not the registration of the title dealt with by the documents.

(b)   Registration in the Registry of Deeds is not compulsory. It is, however, obligatory for a solicitor to ensure the registration of a purchase deed or a mortgage deed for the purpose of obtaining the priority afforded by the legislation.

(c)   Registration is not necessary to transfer the title as title passes when the deed is delivered and the purchase money is paid.

(d)   While the Acts are entitled Registration of Deeds Acts, the Registry will accept the registration of other documents that are not deeds, eg a Contract for Sale or an option to buy land. In fact any type of document in writing relating to a transaction in respect of land duly executed and witnessed and with the appropriate form duly completed will be accepted by the Registry and registered.

(e)   The registration of a deed or other document in the Registry of Deeds is not notice under the doctrine of notice. The effectiveness of the registration is governed by the statutory provisions which grant priority to a registered deed.

(f)   The Registry of Deeds has no responsibility for the effectiveness of the deed or other document being presented to it for registration. This remains the sole responsibility of the parties preparing the document.

(g)   The Act grants priority because of registration, ie the first registered of two registered deeds gets priority. Therefore:

   (i)   a registered deed gains priority over an unregistered deed;

   (ii)   the Act has no application as between two unregistered deeds;

   (iii)   the Act has no application as between a registered deed and an unregistrable transaction, eg the equitable deposit of title deeds with a lending institution. In this instance there is no document capable of registration.

(h)   It should be noted that in respect of the statutory protection afforded by the actual registered deed against an unregistered deed the courts of equity have intervened to make it clear that they will not allow statute to be used as an instrument of fraud. A party cannot claim the protection of the Act on foot of a registered deed when that party has actual notice of an unregistered deed. What is required is actual notice not actual knowledge. Constructive notice is not sufficient. The case of *O'Connor v McCarthy* [1982] IR 161 demonstrates this principle. There is a very detailed and well-written judgment of Costello J in that case which not only deals with the priority granted under the 1707 Act but also looks very fully at the whole question of notice. That case incidentally also turns on the registration of a Contract for Sale which was not a deed.

   This protection for an unregistered deed of which a claimant under a registered deed has notice is preserved in s 38(3) of the Registration of Deeds and Title Act, 2006.

(i)   Priority is determined by the time of registration. Under the 1707 Act the exact time and date of registration were endorsed on the deed. Under ss 37 and 38 of the 2006 Act a serial number is allocated to each deed, and that serial number will determine the order of priority. This does not affect rules of law and equity regarding the doctrine of notice.

(j)   Section 17 of the 1707 Act and now s 32 of the 2006 Act provide that a lease for a term not exceeding 21 years, where actual possession goes with it, is not registrable. In such a case possession is considered notice to a purchaser to make enquiries. It is interesting to note that a similar provision to the same effect is contained in the Registration of Title Act, 1964, s 69 in respect of similar leases in Land Registry cases.

1.7.2.1   Formalities for registration

Prior to the 2006 Act the registration of a deed or other document in the Registry of Deeds was achieved by the completion of a memorial. A memorial was an extract from the deed or other document containing the date of the deed, the names and addresses of the parties to the deed, the nature of the deed, the effect of the deed, and a full description of the property affected by it. Details of the due execution of the deed or other document by the parties was noted with the full names and addresses of the witnesses. The memorial was then executed by the party disposing of the interest in the land, eg in the case of a sale of property by the vendor, in the case of a mortgage by the mortgagor, or in the case of a lease by the lessor. A memorial executed in this fashion was accepted as evidence against the parties to the deed of the contents thereof. It had become commonplace for the memorial to be executed by any of the parties to the deed and this was accepted for registration purposes.

One of the advantages of the Registry of Deeds system was that if a deed or other document which is registered was lost or mislaid, a certified copy of the memorial could have been obtained which would prove the existence of the deed, the execution of the deed by the parties to it, the property affected and the parties to the deed and, possibly, a description of the title and the effect of the deed. This was of considerable help in reconstituting a title if an original deed was lost or destroyed. Such certified copy memorials remain secondary evidence of the existence of the deed and, where a deed has been lost, are generally accepted as sufficient evidence of the existence and execution of the original deed, coupled with a properly completed statutory declaration dealing with the loss of the original.

However the memorial has now been replaced. The Registration of Deeds Rules, 2008 (SI 52/2008) now prescribe the forms to be used on an application for registration of a deed. While the new forms are undoubtedly easier to use than memorials, they provide much less information about the deed being registered. They are therefore of considerably less assistance when trying to reconstruct a title where the original title deeds are lost. A copy of the memorial or application form (post 1 May 2008) is the fullest statement of the contents of a deed the Registry of Deeds can supply.

1.7.2.2   Index of names and lands

The Registry of Deeds today functions on an Index of Names only. Up to 1947 the Registry of Deeds also kept an Index of Lands but that Index has not been kept up to date and lapsed in 1947. Section 46 of the 2006 Act deemed the Index of Lands to have been closed on 31 December 1946. It is, however, still available if endeavouring to trace registered documentation prior to 1947 in respect of a particular piece of land where precise information as to the parties involved in any particular deed is not available.

The Index of Names is maintained under the name of the person or party disposing of or granting an interest under the registered document, eg a lease will be registered under the name of the lessor, a conveyance or assignment under the name of the vendor, and a mortgage under the name of the mortgagor. The only variation in that practice is that since the introduction of vesting certificates, ie a document issued by the Land Registry under the Landlord and Tenant (Ground Rents) (No 2) Act, 1978 vesting the freehold in a lessee, the Registry of Deeds index maintains such vesting certificates in the name of the person acquiring the freehold title rather than in the name of the person disposing of it.

Care must be taken when searching against names on the Index of Names as the Names Index is kept very precisely on the basis of the spelling contained in a particular deed. This name may have many variations in practice, eg the common practice with Irish surnames spelt with or without 'Mc' or a surname with or without an 'O', eg McGee or Magee or Connor or O'Connor. It is accordingly important when making the search to check the deeds to ascertain the spelling of the name used and also to check the signature to see if the individual signed his or her name differently from the spelling on the deed itself.

Any alternative spelling should always be included to ensure that the search made is accurate. It should also be noted that requisition 13.2 of the Law Society Objections and Requisitions on Title, under the heading 'Searches' asks whether the vendor has ever executed any document in the Irish version of their name. This is of crucial importance when searching the Index of Names as the Irish and English versions of a name can be significantly different.

1.7.2.3   **Searches**

Why make searches?

The key to the operation of the Registry of Deeds is the system of searching on the Index of Names. This search is required because there is no other way for a purchaser to know whether they have been furnished with all of the title deeds that affect the property or informed about all the transactions that affect the property. There could be additional deeds or acts that the vendor is not aware of, eg a judgment mortgage, or there is always the possibility that the vendor is concealing some deed from the purchaser. By carrying out proper searches a purchaser can discover all deeds and acts which affect the property which have been registered in the Registry of Deeds.

Formal searches

The Registry of Deeds itself provides one official search. An official search is made by an official Registry of Deeds searcher and the results are certified by the Registry. The application form is prescribed as is the certificate of the result. These are Forms 11 and 12 in the Schedule to the Registration of Deeds Rules, 2008 (SI 52/2008). When perusing a title to determine what searches are to be made, first of all check to see what searches are already made on the title, as searches should have been made when each transaction on the title was taking place and the results of such searches should be with the title deeds. It is common practice now not to go back more than 15 years with searches but this may prove inadequate on an application for first registration as full searches against all parties on the title will be required to be produced to the Land Registry.

The searches are made in the Registry of Deeds against a party from the time that party acquired the property until such time as the deed under which they parted with their interest in the property is registered in the Registry of Deeds. Full details and examples are given in **chapter 10**. The reason for this is that the date of registration of the deed is the key date in the Registry of Deeds which gives priority to the deed over any other unregistered deed or a later registered deed, even if the other deed was executed earlier in time. Searches may also be carried out by professional law searchers, of whom there are a number of firms operating, and any firm used should be checked regularly to ensure that it has proper insurance cover against any claims. All of the firms concerned provide a very speedy and reliable service and are an essential part of the conveyancing process.

In addition to covering gaps in Registry of Deeds searches, these professional searchers also deal with additional searches required on the closing day of the sale in the Land Registry, the Companies Registration Office, the Bankruptcy Office, the Judgments Office, and the Sheriff's Office, but more information on this aspect of conveyancing is furnished in **chapter 10**.

Rectification of errors in the Registry of Deeds

Section 40 of the 2006 Act allows for the rectification of errors by the Registry of Deeds either with the consent of the applicant and other interested parties, or if satisfied that no loss will be suffered by any person, on giving such notices as may be prescribed or by application to the Circuit Court if the court is satisfied that there will be no injustice done to any person and on such terms as it may decide in relation to costs or otherwise as it thinks just.

1.7.3   **LAND REGISTRY**

1.7.3.1   **Generally**

Chapters 13 and **14** deal fully with the Land Registry and this section will only give a brief introduction and overview.

1.7.3.2   Registry of deeds distinguished

The second system of registration in Ireland is the Land Registry and this system is the alternative registration system to the Registry of Deeds. The two systems are mutually exclusive. The crucial and essential difference between the two systems is that in the Registry of Deeds system all that is registered is the document, whereas in the Land Registry it is the title itself that is registered. Thus conveyancers, when they talk about the Registry of Deeds, talk about an 'unregistered title', whereas in Land Registry cases they talk about a 'registered title'. This terminology is strictly speaking correct but should not be confused with the phrase 'unregistered' in the Registry of Deeds system as registration of deeds is still required. The registration of title system operated by the Land Registry is now under the control of the Property Registration Authority which was established on 4 November 2006 under the provisions of the Registration of Deeds and Title Act, 2006. See the Registration of Deeds and Title Act 2006 (Establishment Day) Order, 2006 (SI 512/2006).

1.7.3.3   Establishment

The Land Registry was formally established in Ireland under the Local Registration of Title Act, 1891 ('the 1891 Act'). Prior to that there was the Record of Title Act, 1865. This earlier Act, however, provided only for a voluntary registration system and no more than 700 to 800 titles were registered under it. For the first time under the 1891 Act registration in the Land Registry was compulsory in certain cases. It was introduced originally to deal with the vast volume of titles that were being transferred under the major land reforms at the end of the nineteenth century when substantial government funds were provided to purchase agricultural land. It was felt that a proper registration system was needed for these titles to protect the State's investment and hence the Land Registry was established. Land acquired by the Land Commission had to be registered under the compulsory registration system introduced under the 1891 Act. The legislation was eventually extended to cover labourers' cottages and dwellings purchased under the Small Dwellings Act, 1899 and the Labourers Act, 1906 by local authorities. It also allowed for voluntary registration of a title.

The 1891 Act was replaced by a modern statute which is the Registration of Title Act, 1964 ('the 1964 Act') which came into effect on 1 January 1967. Its operation coincided with the coming into operation of the Succession Act, 1965 and both pieces of legislation were brought into operation contemporaneously. Changes to the 1964 Act have been made by the Registration of Deeds and Title Act, 2006 and these are dealt with in **chapters 13** and **14**.

1.7.3.4   Registration of Title Act, 1964

Under the 1964 Act compulsory registration was extended under ss 23 and 24. Section 23 provided for compulsory registration in the following cases:

(a)   where the land has been or is deemed to have been at any time sold and conveyed to or vested in any person under any of the provisions of the Land Purchase Acts or the Labourers Acts, 1883 to 1962;

(b)   where the land is acquired after the commencement of the 1964 Act (ie 1 January 1967) by a statutory authority (this includes a local or public authority); and

(c)   in any case to which s 24(2) applies.

Section 23 further provides that the registration of the ownership of a leasehold interest is compulsory in the following cases:

(a)   where the interest is acquired after the commencement of the Act by a statutory authority; or

(b)   in any case to which s 24(2) applies.

Section 24 was intended to be the key section in the Act under the terms of which compulsory registration would be extended to all land in the State, both urban and rural. It was intended that this would be achieved by designating areas in the State as being liable to compulsory purchase under s 24(2). This has occurred for the following counties and cities from the following dates:

Counties Affected	Effective Date
Carlow, Meath, and Laois	1 January 1970
Longford, Westmeath, and Roscommon	1 April 2006
Clare, Kilkenny, Louth, Sligo, Wexford, and Wicklow	1 October 2008
Cavan, Donegal, Galway, Kerry, Kildare, Leitrim, Limerick, Mayo, Monaghan, North Tipperary, Offaly, South Tipperary, and Waterford	1 January 2010
Cities of Galway, Limerick, and Waterford, as defined in s 10 of the Local Government Act, 2001	1 January 2010
Counties of Cork, Fingal, Dun Laoghaire-Rathdown and South County Dublin, and cities of Dublin and Cork	1 June 2011

In these areas, the registration of ownership, if not already compulsory, became compulsory in the following circumstances:

(a) in the case of freehold land upon conveyance on sale; and

(b) in the case of a leasehold interest on the grant or assignment on sale of such an interest.

'On sale' means for money or money's worth and accordingly would not apply to a voluntary transfer of title by way of gift or a title transferred on death for example assents.

As all areas of Ireland are now compulsorily registrable the consequence of this will be the eventual registration of all titles in the Land Registry.

Section 52 of the 2006 Act provides that compulsory registration of land purchased under the Irish Church Act, 1869 shall be deemed never to have been required under s 23. This section is of considerable assistance in practice, as several titles that should have been registered under the Irish Church Act, 1869 were not registered, giving rise to considerable difficulty in practice.

Section 25 of the 1964 Act provides that where registration becomes compulsory it must be carried out within six months of the relevant document becoming operative, otherwise no title passes to the transferee. The Registrar has power to extend this period of six months. The section does not clarify where ownership of the title goes after the six-month period has expired without an application being made for registration. The Registrar of Titles will generally extend the six-month period for registration but if for any reason they should refuse then the court has power to do so.

A much more detailed examination of the Land Registry system is dealt with in **chapters 13** and **14** but the following is a brief explanation of how the system works in practice.

1.7.3.5   **Documents**

The map (known as a title plan)

The entire system is based on the boundaries of the particular property in respect of which the title is registered being shown on an ordnance survey map. This digital OS map is not part of the register and is accordingly not automatically issued with a copy of the folio and must be specifically requisitioned. However, as the map or the title plan (previously called the file plan) is a key part to identifying the land covered by the title registered it should always be obtained as part of the documentary evidence of the title and should bear a date contemporaneous with the copy folio.

However, it is one of the drawbacks of the Land Registry system that the official map or title plan is not conclusive of the extent of the land or the boundaries shown and this is provided for in the 1964 Act, s 85.

This provision is said to be consistent with an unregistered title where the description of the land is often described as 'more or less' or 'thereabouts'. Accordingly, it is important that the client is shown any such map and asked to confirm or check that the boundaries shown are correct. It is possible under the 1964 Act, s 86 and rules 139 to 142 of the Land Registration Rules, 2012 for adjoining owners to agree on the precise location of their boundaries and to have this agreement recorded on their respective folios. The case of *Tomkins Estates Ltd v O'Callaghan*, 16 March 1995, McCracken J (29 May 1995 ITLR) highlighted the problem that this lack of conclusiveness in the boundaries of Registry maps can cause. The case involved a dispute relating to a laneway at the rear of No 1 Merrion Square, Dublin, the ownership of which was claimed by the owner of No 3 Merrion Square, Dublin on whose Land Registry map the laneway was clearly shown as part of the land in respect of which his title was registered. However, the owner of No 1 had an unregistered title which also showed ownership of the laneway. McCracken J held that as the 1964 Act, s 85 made it clear that the Registry map was not conclusive of the boundaries shown, the registered owner of the land could not rely on it and accepted the evidence of the title deeds of the owner of No 1 as having a freehold title to the laneway in question.

The folio

The folio is the actual register of the title and is set out in three parts. The heading on the folio shows the folio number and the county to which it relates and which register the title is on, viz freehold, leasehold, or subsidiary.

- *Part 1* gives details of the property and specifies the map reference on the Registry map. It also sometimes specifies the area of the land. If it does specify the area, it usually includes one-half of any adjoining roadway. One should be careful of this in rural areas particularly, as a large farm might have extensive road frontage which could account for several acres of the area shown on the folio thus reducing the actual area of the farm land.

- *Part 2* shows the class of title and ownership and who is the registered owner.

- *Part 3* shows the burdens and notices of burdens.

Each registered title has a separate folio number under the relevant county in which it is situated. If it is a freehold title it merely bears a reference number but in modern folios has the letter 'F' after the relevant number. If the title is a leasehold folio then the letter 'L' is appended to the folio number.

There are various categories of title which would be registered either in the freehold register or the leasehold register. There is also a third register, known as a Register of Subsidiary Interests, and if there is a folio issued under that category the letter 'S' is appended to the folio number. These are, however, rare. They would cover such matters as the ownership of a rent payable out of a freehold title, eg a fee farm rent which would rarely be registered. They would also include interests such as an inchoate interest, eg an interest vested in a Minister for State to supervise from the bank of a river fisheries under the control of the State.

The land certificate

Prior to 1 January 2007 the Land Registry would on request issue a land certificate in respect of a folio. A copy of the folio issued by the Land Registry and certified by it as a true copy of the folio was sufficient evidence of the title to that particular land on the date the folio was issued. However, if a land certificate issued it was noted on the front of the folio that it issued and was then an important document of title. It was required to be produced in respect of any transaction under which title was being transferred. Section 73 of the 2006 Act, which came into effect on 1 January 2007, provided that the Property Registration Authority shall cease to issue land certificates. All land certificates still in existence ceased to have effect from 1 January 2010 and in the intervening three-year period a person who held a lien through deposit or possession of such certificate could apply to the Registrar to have a lien registered as a burden on the folio.

Certificates of charge

Again prior to 1 January 2007 the Land Registry issued certificates of charge under rules 156 or 157, these being the relevant rules under the 1972 Land Registration Rules, which are the basic rules under which the Land Registry functioned with some small subsequent amendments. A rule 156 charge was an endorsement on the deed of the charge itself and was not a separate document. A rule 157 charge, however, was a certificate of the ownership of the charge and was the equivalent of a land certificate and was required to be produced when the charge was being cleared off or being otherwise dealt with.

Similarly, s 73 of the 2006 Act, which came into effect on 1 January 2007, provided that from 1 January 2007 no new certificates of charge be issued. All existing certificates ceased to have effect from 1 January 2010 and in the intervening three-year period a person who held a lien through deposit or possession of such certificate could apply to the Registrar to have a lien registered as a burden on the folio.

Transfers

In Land Registry titles ownership is dealt with under the forms provided for in the 1972 Rules, as amended. The latest amendments are to be found in SI 349/2009 and 456/2009. There is one form only used for the transfer of title inter vivos, namely a deed of transfer and this is used both for freehold and leasehold titles. It is important to note that title in a Land Registry case only passes when the title has been registered (see Registration of Title Act, 1964, s 51). The 2012 Rules provide a substantial variety of forms to be used in virtually all cases that will be experienced in dealing with registered land and if the rules are followed and the documentation properly completed, then the transaction will be registered without any query. Transactions which may take several weeks to complete will gain priority from the time they are lodged in the Land Registry and registration will relate back to the date of lodgement assuming that no query has been raised or that the dealing is not subsequently rejected by the Land Registry. If the dealing is rejected and sent back then priority will only arise again from the date of re-lodgement of the dealing with the queries discharged.

1.7.3.6   Effect of registration in the Land Registry

The effect of registration of a title in the Land Registry is that such title falls out of the Registry of Deeds system. The two systems are mutually exclusive. The title in the Land Registry carries with it a State guarantee that it is valid. It is, however, crucial to remember that they are mutually exclusive only in respect of the same title and not in respect of the same property. It is commonplace to find property with several titles affecting it, eg a freehold title, a leasehold title, and possibly a sub-leasehold title. The freehold title may be registered in the Land Registry, while the documents relating to the leasehold and the sub-leasehold title may be registered in the Registry of Deeds. The crucial difference here is that they are different titles affecting the same property and each title coexists quite happily with the other in a different registration system. If those titles should merge at any stage, eg if the sub-leasehold interest was enlarged under the Landlord and Tenant (Ground Rents) (No 2) Act, 1978 into a full freehold by the sublessee acquiring the superior leasehold and the registered freehold, then it would be advisable to take the entire leasehold and sub-leasehold title into the Land Registry and convert the entire title into a registered freehold, at which stage the leasehold and the sub-leasehold would cease to exist and thereafter, the entire remaining freehold title would be dealt with in the Land Registry system.

1.8   Systems Contrasted

The essential differences between the two systems are set out in the following table.

Registry of Deeds (Unregistered Title)	Land Registry (Registered Title)
• Existence of documents noted	• The effect of document noted
• Registration gives no validity except in case of a judgment mortgage	• Registration gives validity to the effect of a document
• Title must be fully investigated—not conclusive	• Title and folio conclusive (except for s 72 burdens and boundaries)
• Title not guaranteed by the State	• Title guaranteed by the State
• Property is identified by the description contained in various title deeds	• Property identified by official Land Registry Ordnance Survey map

1.9   Words and Phrases Commonly Used

As in all professions, words and phrases are used that are meaningless to a lay person, particularly when an abbreviation is used. The following is a list of the most commonly used terms in conveyancing and its associated field of landlord and tenant:

Alienation: the transferring of immovable property from one person to another. It is often interchangeable with the word 'assignment'.

Appurtenant: attaching to land, eg an easement.

Assent: describes the document under the terms of which a legal personal representative vests title to a property in a beneficiary under the will or on the intestacy of a deceased.

Assign: the act of transferring unregistered leasehold title.

Assignee: the person to whom an assignment of a lessee's interest in a lease is made.

Assignment: describes the deed transferring unregistered leasehold title.

Assignor: the person who assigns the lessee's interest.

Assurance: a generic term for any document transferring title.

CAT Cert: a clearance certificate from the capital taxes branch of the Revenue Commissioners certifying that all capital acquisitions tax on a property has been discharged where there is a death or a gift on title. Now abolished by the Finance Act, 2010, retrospectively since 3 April 2010, except in the case of applications for registration based on adverse possession, where a form CA12 may be required.

Certificate of compliance: used to describe a certificate endorsed on a lease by the lessor to confirm that a particular covenant in a lease has been complied with, usually a covenant to build. Also used to describe a certificate from an architect or an engineer confirming that a property or a development to a property has been built in accordance with the relevant planning permission and the building regulations or that the development is exempt. This is now usually done by way of an opinion rather than a certificate.

Certificate of title: certificate given by a purchaser's solicitor to a lending institution that the title over which they are taking a charge or mortgage is a good marketable title. There is a standard form used, the terms of which have been agreed between the Law Society, the building societies, and the banks and which is used only in respect of residential properties.

CGT (CG50A) Cert: exemption certificate issued by the Revenue Commissioners under the capital gains tax legislation exempting a purchaser from making any deduction from the purchase monies on closing when the consideration exceeds the relevant current threshold set by the legislation, which is usually updated on an annual basis. This certificate is required for all sales which exceed the relevant threshold, irrespective of whether there is capital gains tax payable on the disposal or not, and if not available on closing, the purchaser must deduct 15 per cent of the purchase price in a relevant case from the full purchase price on closing and forthwith remit it to the Revenue Commissioners.

Convey: the act of transferring an unregistered freehold title.

Conveyance: describes the deed transferring an unregistered freehold title.

Deed: a document executed under seal.

Demise: used as a noun to describe a lease and as a verb to describe the act of leasing.

Demised premises: the property which is let or leased.

Engrossment: final version of a deed for execution by the parties.

Equity note: a note entered on pre-1967 Land Registry folios to protect any interest prior to the registered owners, which are not shown on the face of the folio (if any). In post-1967 folios, such titles are shown as possessory.

Family law declarations: statutory declaration by a vendor (and spouse if married) to establish whether the property being sold is or is not a family home as defined in the Family Home Protection Act, 1976 as amended. Such declarations also deal with the provisions of the Family Law Act, 1981, the Judicial Separation and Family Law Reform Act, 1989, the Family Law Act, 1995, the Family Law (Divorce) Act, 1996, and the Civil Partnership and Certain Rights and Obligations of Cohabitants Act, 2010 and any matters arising thereunder.

Fee farm grant: fee simple estate (subject to a rent). This estate can no longer be created since s 12 of the Land and Conveyancing Law Reform Act, 2009 was passed.

Fee simple: the largest estate in land that a person can have.

Fee tail: freehold estate of inheritance confined to descendants of the initial grantee. Section 13(1) of the 2009 Act provides that the creation of a fee tail of any kind at law or in equity is prohibited.

Freehold: the general term used to describe a fee simple, fee tail, fee farm grant, life estate, and lease for lives renewable forever. Section 11(1) of the 2009 Act provided that the only legal estates in Ireland which may be created or disposed of are the freehold and leasehold estates specified by s 11. It goes on to define 'freehold estate' as a fee simple in possession and includes a further three variations.

Gale day: is the day on which a periodic payment of rent is due.

Graft: in equity the profit or asset obtained by a person acting as a trustee is deemed to be grafted upon the original trust property and thereby held upon the same trusts.

Grantee: the person to whom the transfer is made.

Grantor: the person who transfers property by deed in writing.

Habendum (*Habere*: to have): the clause in a deed which defines the estate to be taken by the purchaser.

Hereditament: a parcel of freehold land.

Indenture: deed to which there are two or more parties. The origin of the word arose due to the freehand indentation of the paper in early times.

Land purchase annuity: the sum advanced by the Irish Land Commission which is repaid by the purchaser over an agreed period of years by means of a yearly payment called an annuity.

Lease: the giving by a lessor to a lessee of possession of property for a certain period of time. It is defined by s 3 of the 2009 Act as a noun meaning an instrument creating a tenancy; and as a verb meaning the granting of a tenancy by an instrument. The expression 'lease' denotes an interest for a longer period of time whereas 'letting agreement' or 'tenancy agreement' is used in the context of a shorter period, eg one year. The term 'lease' also tends to be used in the context of commercial property versus a 'letting agreement' for residential property.

Lease for lives renewable forever: a lease granted for the term of certain lives, usually three, which contains a condition that when any of the lives 'dropped out', ie died, the grantor would grant a renewal of the lease for a new life/lives on payment of a sum of money called a renewable fine. Section 14 of the 2009 Act prohibits the future creation of various categories of leases for lives or for a combination of lives and a period of years.

Lessee/tenant: person to whom a lease/tenancy agreement is granted. 'Lessee' is defined by s 3 of the 2009 Act as meaning the person, including a sublessee, in whom a tenancy created by a lease is vested and the word 'tenant' means the person, including a subtenant, in whom a tenancy is vested.

Lessor/landlord: person who grants a lease/tenancy agreement. Section 3 of the 2009 Act defines 'lessor' as meaning the person, including a sublessor, entitled to the legal estate immediately superior to a tenancy created by a lease. The word 'landlord' means the person, including a sublandlord, entitled to the legal estate immediately superior to a tenancy.

Life estate: an interest in land for the period of the lifetime of a named party. The interest determines (ie ends) on the death of that life. Section 11(6) of the 2009 Act provides that life estates will no longer be legal estates and will vest as equitable interests only.

Mortgage: transfer or lease of property as security for a debt. It is defined in s 3 of the 2009 Act as including any charge or lien on any property for securing money or money's worth.

Outgoings: necessary expenses and charges affecting a property, eg rates.

Parcel: a separately identified plot of land either by reason of its boundaries or it having a separate or distinct title.

Parcels: the part of a deed setting out the description of the property/land, its location, physical extent, and dimensions.

Per Reps (Personal Representatives): a generic term used to describe executors and administrators of an estate.

Possessory title: a term used to describe a title in the Land Registry post 1967 (see *Equity note* earlier in this list) or an unregistered title unsupported by documentary evidence commonly known as a 'squatters title'.

Recital: clause in a deed which recounts the previous ownership of the land and explains the context of the present transaction.

Reddendum: ('that which is to be paid') the clause in the lease/tenancy agreement which specifies the rent which is payable and the time and manner of its payment.

Redemption: discharging an encumbrance affecting property.

Reversionary lease: a lease granted during the currency of an existing lease for a term of years, which commences on the expiration of the current lease.

Section 72 declaration: statutory declaration by the registered owner of a title registered in the Land Registry to confirm that none of the burdens which can affect registered land without registration as set out in s 72 of the Registration of Title Act, 1964 as amended affect the subject property and usually includes a paragraph stating that there are no deaths or voluntary dispositions on title in the last 12 years.

Seisin: this comes from the French 'saisine'. It defies precise definition but is the feudal concept involving the notion of possession of land but is not synonymous with possession—only a freeholder holding under freehold tenure had seisin.

Sub-letting/Underletting: a lease created by a lessee out of his leasehold interest for a period less than the period held by him under his lease.

Tenure: the manner whereby tenements were held. In feudal times land was held by the tenure of a particular service to be given to the owner and non-performance of that service would entitle the owner/lord to forfeit the lands. Today it is the relationship between one person and his reversioner, eg tenant and landlord.

Term: a fixed period of time for which an interest in land is granted.

Terms: the covenants and conditions of the agreement (whether oral or written).

Transfer: used as a term to describe the deed used for passing both freehold and lease-hold registered titles.

Vesting cert: document issued by the Registrar of Titles in the Land Registry vesting the freehold and all superior leasehold title in a lessee under the provisions of the Landlord and Tenant (Ground Rents) (No 2) Act, 1978.

Wayleave: the right over another's land to facilitate the supply of utility services, eg gas, water, electricity.

For further definitions relevant to landlord and tenant matters, and more detailed explanations of some of these terms, the Law Society's Manual on Landlord and Tenant Law, paragraph 1.2 should be consulted.

1.10   Useful Legal Texts

1.10.1   GENERAL LAND LAW

Fiona De Londras, *Principles of Irish Property Law* (2nd edn, Clarus Press, 2011).

Andrew Lyall with Albert Power, *Land Law in Ireland* (3rd edn, Dublin Round Hall, 2010).

J.C.W. Wylie, *Irish Land Law* (5th edn, Dublin Bloomsbury Professional, 2013).

1.10.2   SPECIALIST TITLES

Peter Bland, *Easements* (3rd edn, Roundhall, 2015).

John Deeney, *Registration of Deeds and Title in Ireland* (Bloomsbury Professional, 2014).

Barry Magee, *Investigating Unregistered Title* (Bloomsbury Professional, 2012).

Albert Power (ed), *Intangible Property Rights in Ireland* (2nd edn, Bloomsbury Professional, 2008).

Margaret Walsh (ed), *Irish Conveyancing Precedents* (Bloomsbury Professional, 2016).

J.C.W. Wylie and Una Woods, *Irish Conveyancing Law* (3rd edn, Bloomsbury Professional, 2015).

1.11   Useful Websites

- Conveyancing Handbook.

  This contains all the Conveyancing Committee's practice notes up to July 2006. http://conveyancinghandbook.lawsociety.ie/

- Online Practice Notes.

  All practice notes since 1986 in a searchable database.

  www.lawsociety.ie/Solicitors/Practising/Practice-Notes/

- Conveyancing Committee.

  Extensive information, precedents, forms, and resources.

  www.lawsociety.ie/Solicitors/Representation/Committees/Conveyancing/About/

- Property Registration Authority of Ireland.

Contains practice directions and forms on all aspects of Land Registry and Registry of Deeds practice. Landdirect.ie is the Property Registration Authority's subscription-based online service which gives authorised users access to all Land Registry folios and the online map.

www.prai.ie/

• British and Irish Legal Information Institute (Bailii).

Full text of Supreme Court, Court Of Appeal, High Court, and Court of Criminal Appeal judgments since 2000 and selected pre-2000 judgments.

www.bailii.org/

• Law Reform Commission—Revised Acts.

The Commission produces Revised Acts which are administrative consolidations of Acts with amendments incorporated, to allow the legislation to be read seamlessly as amended. This site contains over 200 Revised Acts and is growing. The Law Reform Commission website also contains a number of consultation papers and reports on land and property law.

www.lawreform.ie/restatement.84.html

• Revenue Commissioners.

This website contains a wide range of materials relating to tax practice including statements of practice, guidance notes, precedents, details of double taxation treaties, and access to all revenue forms.

www.revenue.ie

• Houses of the Oireachtas.

This contains the Acts of the Oireachtas, Bills, and explanatory memoranda to Bills in pdf form since 1997. It also has a link to the Irish Statute Book. It also includes all Dáil and Seanad parliamentary debates from 1919 to date and also Select Committee debates from 1999 to date.

www.oireachtas.ie

• Irish Statute Book.

It contains all the Acts of the Oireachtas and Statutory Instruments from 1922. Also the chronological tables of the Statutes show how Acts have been subsequently affected (Legislation Directory).

www.irishstatutebook.ie

CHAPTER 2

STEPS IN A CONVEYANCING TRANSACTION

2.1 Introduction

The purpose of this chapter is to set out in chronological order the various steps in a conveyancing transaction, and what a vendor's solicitor and a purchaser's solicitor does at each stage of the process. As mentioned in **chapter 1** there will occasionally be a third solicitor involved, ie a solicitor acting for a lending institution. In modern conveyancing practice solicitors acting for lending institutions usually become involved only in commercial lending transactions as practically all domestic conveyancing transactions involve only the vendor and the purchaser's solicitor with the purchaser's solicitor certifying the title to the lending institution and ensuring that all of the relevant mortgage documentation is signed by the borrower.

The process may be usefully broken down into three stages:

(a) pre-contract: the steps prior to the formation of a formal contract between the parties;

(b) contract to completion: the steps from when a formal contract has been entered into until the completion of the transaction between the parties; and

(c) post completion: the steps to be taken by each side after the transaction has been completed.

2.2 Steps Prior to Formalising a Contract

It is essential for both the solicitor for the vendor and the purchaser to ensure they have the necessary procedures in place to comply with their obligations under anti-money laundering legislation. These obligations are comprehensively dealt with by a Law Society publication entitled 'Guidance Notes for Solicitors on Anti-Money Laundering Obligations'. This is available on the members section of the Law Society website which also provides links to various updates and developments in the area.

Particular attention should be paid to the Practice Note issued in September 2013 which reminded solicitors that there is no exemption provided by the anti-money laundering regulations for existing clients.

2.2.1 VENDOR'S SOLICITOR

2.2.1.1 Checking vendor's title

The primary matter which concerns the vendor's solicitor is the nature of the vendor's title to the particular property and unless the vendor's solicitor is familiar with the title, eg he or she may have acted for the vendor when the vendor purchased the property originally, the first thing a vendor's solicitor must do is to obtain the vendor's documents of title. These are either furnished to him or her by the vendor or are taken up by the vendor's solicitor on accountable trust receipt from a lending institution from whom the vendor may have taken a loan when the property was purchased. Deeds taken up on accountable trust receipt from a lending institution impose upon a vendor's solicitor serious obligations and responsibilities to the lending institution, eg he or she must ensure that the property is being sold for a sum sufficient to enable him or her to discharge the amount due on the loan or alternatively he or she must obtain clear authority from the lending institution if the proceeds of sale will not be sufficient to discharge the loan as a purchaser of the property will require the loan to be released or discharged on or immediately following the completion. The emergence of negative equity in recent years makes this step in the transaction all the more important to be considered and dealt with at an early stage and, as recommended by the Law Society Conveyancing Committee, should be dealt with before allowing the vendor to sign the contract. See the January/February 2010 Law Society *Gazette*.

If the property is subject to a charge or mortgage in favour of the National Asset Management Agency (NAMA) reference should be made to the Practice Note issued in September 2013 (Law Society *Gazette*) that gives detailed guidance on the specific steps required to be undertaken by the vendor's solicitor.

2.2.1.2   Nature of property

The second matter to be considered by the vendor's solicitor is the nature of the property being sold, eg whether it is a dwellinghouse, a commercial property such as licensed premises, an agricultural holding, a hotel, a commercial property with multi- or mixed use, etc. If, for example the property is a licensed premises then the vendor's solicitor must obtain very detailed instructions on the nature of the licence and whether there have been any prosecutions for breaches of the licensing laws and whether there have been any convictions endorsed on the licence. Likewise an enquiry should be made as to whether the original licensed premises were ever extended and if so whether there was an appropriate court order made extending the licence. Similar detailed enquiries need to be made in relation to other types of properties, eg in an agricultural holding it is necessary to research the question of whether the property has any milk quota attached and if so, how it is to be dealt with on the sale. It is a useful exercise for the vendor's solicitor at this stage to look at the particular requisitions on title that will be raised by the purchaser's solicitor in respect of a specific property and to obtain from the vendor specific instructions as to how each of these requisitions is to be dealt with and what documentation is available to support the answers. The Law Society has produced a pre-contract check list for purchase and sale that can be sent to the client.

2.2.1.3   Planning laws

The third area which modern-day conveyancers must now give particular attention to is the question of the planning laws in respect of developments after 1 October 1964 and the regulations made under the Building Control Act, 1990 in respect of developments that have taken place since 1 June 1992. It is important for the vendor's solicitor at this stage to clarify the position in respect of the relevant property and to ensure that if the full provisions of general condition 36 of the Law Society Contract for Sale are to remain in place without any variation or alteration, he or she is satisfied that he or she can support the provisions of that condition with relevant documentation and if necessary certification from the vendor's architect or engineer. If there is any doubt or difficulty in respect of the planning aspect it may be necessary to insert special conditions in the contract for sale. Any such special conditions should specifically deal with the manner in which the provisions of condition 36 of the Contract for Sale are to be amended. See **chapter 11** for a full discussion of this area.

2.2.1.4   The family home/shared home

The fourth matter which is important at this stage arises under the provisions of the Family Home Protection Act, 1976 and the Civil Partnership and Certain Rights and Obligations of Cohabitants Act, 2010 ('the 2010 Act'). If the property being sold is a family home/ shared home within the meaning of that term in the 1976 Act as amended and the 2010 Act, the vendor's solicitor will need to ensure that if the property is held in the sole name of one of the vendors and that vendor is married or has a registered civil partnership, the prior consent of that vendor's spouse or civil partner will be forthcoming to the sale. It would be prudent for the vendor's solicitor to obtain a State copy of the marriage certificate or copy of the certificate of civil partnership as difficulties may sometimes arise under this legislation if either of the vendors was previously married, eg there may be some doubt cast on the validity of a divorce obtained outside this jurisdiction. Likewise the vendor's solicitor should satisfy himself or herself that no difficulties would arise under other family law legislation, ie the Family Law Act, 1981, the Judicial Separation and Family Law Reform Act, 1989, the Family Law Act, 1995, and the Family Law (Divorce) Act, 1996. See **chapter 7** for a full discussion of this area.

2.2.1.5   Satisfying contractual conditions

If there are any matters affecting either the vendor and spouse or either of them or the property under any of this legislation then the vendor's solicitor should obtain all relevant documentation or any court orders that there may be so as to ensure that he or she may satisfy the legitimate requisitions and requirements of the purchaser's solicitor. Leaving aside the question of the formation of the contract between a vendor and purchaser before either of them go to their legal advisors (a matter which is quite rare nowadays), the sale of a property takes place either by public auction or private treaty. If it is by public auction, the vendor's solicitor will normally have three to four weeks' notice of the vendor's intention to auction the premises and has a reasonable length of time within which to obtain the documents and prepare a contract. In the matter of a public auction the premises are offered for sale on the terms and the conditions set out by the vendor's solicitor in the conditions of sale.

Unless a prospective purchaser can negotiate an amendment of those conditions prior to the auction then the property is bought subject to those conditions without any negotiations or amendments of the conditions prior to the sale. Once a purchaser has been declared a successful bidder at an auction then the terms of the contract are binding. The format of the conditions of sale for an auction are the same as that for a sale by private treaty in that the standard printed form of contract issued by the Law Society is used in all cases, the only difference being the general conditions relating to the conduct of the auction itself. A contract in respect of a sale by public auction will not be in any way conditional, ie it will not be made subject to the purchaser obtaining loan approval or subject to the purchaser obtaining a survey of the property or any other such condition which is fairly common in private treaty contracts. There is always a temptation in a sale by auction for a vendor's solicitor to impose terms in respect of the title which a vendor's solicitor would not insert in a contract for a sale by private treaty, but always bear in mind the vendor's obligation to give a good title and the purchaser's entitlement to get one and that contracts with conditions drawn unfairly in favour of a vendor may be construed against the vendor if an issue arose as to the enforceability of the contract.

It is important for a vendor's solicitor to clarify at this stage whether the vendor has received any notices affecting the property for sale, eg a notice of intention to compulsorily acquire part or all of the property, a demolition notice to demolish the property, a notice from a local authority alleging a nuisance in respect of the property, a notice from a landlord of an alleged breach of the terms of the lease, and such like notices which would affect the premises or the title to them. Any such notices should be brought to the attention of the proposed purchaser, should be specified in the contract, and a special condition inserted specifying as to how such notices are to be dealt with between the parties prior to completion.

2.2.1.6   Outgoings

Clarification should be sought from the vendor at this stage in respect of any outgoings or income which may affect the property such as rates, local authority charges, environmental waste charges, non-principal private residences charge, local property tax, water charges, septic tank levy, ground rent, fee farm rents, income from tenants, etc. It is necessary to take instructions from the vendor as to whether these have been paid up to date and the necessity to produce receipts to vouch for their payment on closing, as such charges, if unpaid by the vendor, may become the responsibility of the purchaser. In addition the PPS number, tax status, and local property tax ID number of the vendor will be required to enable the stamping of the purchase deed.

2.2.1.7   Tax

Depending upon the sale price of the property consideration is to be given at this stage to an application for a certificate under the capital gains tax legislation. The relevant figure under this legislation is currently €1,000,000 in the case of residential property (houses and apartments) and €500,000 for all other properties. Thus, if the sale price in respect of any property depending on its nature exceeds €1,000,000 or €500,000 an application must be made by the vendor to the vendor's tax office for a certificate under the capital gains tax legislation absolving the purchaser from making a deduction on closing. It is prudent at this stage to obtain details of the vendor's PPS or tax reference number, tax type, and his or her inspector of taxes for the purpose of these applications and also to clarify if any difficulty is likely to be experienced in obtaining them. As from February 2007 residential property tax clearance certificates are no longer required. And as from 3 April 2010, certificates of discharge from CAT are no longer required. However a form CA12 may be required in relation to a s 49 application or application for first registration in the Land Registry. Full consideration of the tax implications of a conveyancing transaction is provided in **chapter 16**.

2.2.1.8   VAT

It is now recommended practice that the issue of VAT be considered and dealt with pre-contract. This is because under the current VAT system, it is now open to the parties to choose whether VAT is to be charged on the purchase price in certain circumstances. The Law Society have issued pre-contract VAT enquiries to be raised by purchasers. A vendor's solicitor must therefore be in a position to furnish correct responses. It should always be remembered that if a vendor's solicitor does not consider him- or herself to have the necessary tax knowledge to deal properly with these enquiries they should advise their client to have an accountant, or other suitably qualified tax practitioner, advise on the appropriate VAT treatment of the sale.

2.2.1.9   Title flaws

If there are any flaws in the title or if there should be some deficiency in the documentation, eg there may be a deed or deeds missing or, in a Land Registry title, the title is qualified in some respect, it is at this stage of the transaction that consideration should be given as to how that particular problem will be dealt with. For example, if it is an unregistered title then the purchaser will have to be given some explanation as to the reason for the document or documents being missing and will have to be satisfied that same have not been lodged or pledged as security for a loan or otherwise. Consideration might have to be given to providing an insurance bond by way of an indemnity to the purchaser in respect of the missing documents.

2.2.1.10   Advising on vendor's risk

The vendor should at this stage be advised that the property will remain at the vendor's risk until the actual day of the completion of the sale in accordance with the current Law Society contract. The vendor should be strongly advised that if he or she does not have insurance cover or if the insurance cover is not adequate he or she should immediately arrange to take out insurance or to increase it to an adequate sum. Likewise, if contents are included in the sale these should be specifically set out in the special conditions to the contract and if necessary a value apportioned to them and, likewise, the vendor remains responsible for them until the actual completion of the sale.

2.2.1.11   Closing date

Instructions should be sought from the vendor as to a closing date. This may have already been agreed between the vendor and the purchaser but, if not, special attention should be paid to this, particularly if another transaction is depending upon the completion of this one going through on time, eg a vendor may be purchasing an alternative dwellinghouse to the one being sold and may wish to have the two transactions completed simultaneously. There may also be circumstances in which the vendor may wish to make time of the essence in respect of the closing date. This is a matter which should be treated very cautiously as it can operate both against and in favour of a vendor, depending on the circumstances.

2.2.1.12   Special requisitions

Depending on the type of property being sold it may be useful at this stage to go through with the vendor some of the special requisitions from the purchaser's solicitors that will have to be dealt with, eg requisitions relating to a licensed premises or relating to a second-hand apartment or to a farm with a milk quota attached. If detailed instructions are taken at this stage then the vendor's solicitor will be in a position to assess whether any special conditions should be inserted in the contract dealing with any particular difficulty that may arise.

2.2.1.13   Costs and outlays

Finally at this stage the vendor's solicitor must furnish to the vendor a notice under the Solicitors (Amendment) Act, 1994, s 68 dealing with the question of the costs and outlay involved in the transaction. See the recent Practice Note issued by the Law Society Guidance and Ethics Committee in January 2015 (*Gazette*) on 'the dos and don'ts of section 68 – re-visited'. At the same time it may also be prudent for the vendor's solicitors to furnish to the vendor a detailed analysis not only of the costs and outlay involved but also the finances of the entire transaction particularly if the transaction is one which is dependent upon the completion of another one, eg the sale and purchase of dwellinghouses contemporaneously.

2.2.1.14   Preparing the contract

When the vendor's solicitor having regard to the foregoing matters feels or believes that he or she is in a position to draft and furnish a Contract for Sale then he or she does so. This is usually done in duplicate and it is furnished in duplicate to the purchaser's solicitor with copies of the relevant documentation where the sale is by private treaty. When sending the contract it is now accepted practice for the vendor's solicitor to formally state that the letter is sent 'subject to contract' (see *Boyle v Lee* [1992] 1 IR 555) that is to say that the solicitor forwarding the contract has no authority to bind the vendor and that the letter sending the contract is not to be taken as a memorandum which might bind the vendor under the provisions of s 51 of the Land and Conveyancing Reform Act, 2009 ('the 2009 Act'). It is also commonplace now for such a letter to formally declare that there is no contract in existence between the parties and that a formal contract shall come into existence only when the contracts have been signed by both parties and exchanged and a full deposit paid.

If the sale is by public auction then the vendor's solicitor will prepare a contract, generally described as conditions of sale for the auction, which on the front page will briefly identify the property for sale, who the auctioneers are and the date, time, and location of the auction. The remainder of the conditions will follow the same formula as that for a sale by private treaty. Any purchaser who is interested in bidding at the auction will either personally or through his or her solicitor contact either the auctioneer or the vendor's solicitors for copies of the conditions of sale and the relevant documents and the auction will proceed on the basis of the conditions of sale as prepared by the vendor's solicitor.

2.2.1.15   The creation of a binding and enforceable contract

The creation of a valid and binding contract for the sale and purchase of land between a vendor and a purchaser arises in the same way as the creation of a valid contract in respect of matters other than the purchase and sale of land. However, a rule as to the enforceability of such a contract was introduced in 1695 by s 2 of the Statute of Frauds and which has been the cause of a huge volume of litigation and resulting case law over the intervening centuries up to the present day. The most recent major review of the operation of this statute was undertaken by a full Supreme Court in *Boyle v Lee* [1992] 1 IR 555.

This rule is now expressed in a slightly amended format in s 51 of the 2009 Act; however, the case law and application of s 2 can assist in providing guidance on how s 51 will operate.

The basic rules for the formation of a contract apply, the primary ones being offer and acceptance. There must also be the intention to create legal relationships, consideration, form, reality of consent, and legality of the object. The Statute of Frauds overlaid a probative element or requirement in s 2, now restated in s 51 of the 2009 Act which provides that:

> *no action shall be brought to enforce any contract for the sale or other disposition of land unless the agreement on which such action is brought, or some memorandum or note of it, is in writing and signed by the person against whom the action is brought or that person's authorised agent.*

It should be noted that while s 51 presupposes the existence of a contract in which the relevant terms have been agreed (although not specifying any particular format), it does not, contrary to a common misconception, say that the contract must be in writing. What it does say is that the contract will not be enforced unless the agreement or some note or memorandum thereof is in writing and signed by the party against whom the action is brought or that person's authorised agent. The section does not lay down any conditions as to the formation of a contract, only its enforceability. It is not proposed to deal here with what constitutes a note or memorandum in writing to satisfy the statutory provisions of this Act but rather to deal with the issue of whether there is in existence any contract between the parties which may have been formed by the actions or lack of actions of the respective solicitors for the vendor and the purchaser.

For the purpose of avoiding the creation of a legally binding contract for the sale and purchase of land which might be caught by the provisions of s 51 before the solicitors acting for the parties have the opportunity of preparing and agreeing the terms of the contract to be signed by the parties, the practice has become established in modern conveyancing whereby both the solicitor for the vendor and the solicitor for the purchaser, and indeed the auctioneer representing the vendor, will state in their initial letters and all subsequent letters prior to the formation of the contract, that any agreement is 'subject to contract' and denying that any contract exists between the parties. Most solicitors will in addition formally state that they have no authority to bind their clients, that their letter is not a note or memorandum for the purposes of the 2009 Act, and that a binding contract shall not come into existence until the terms of the contract, as prepared by the vendor's solicitor, have been agreed, signed by both parties, and exchanged and a full deposit paid. The assumption underlying such correspondence is that no completed contract exists between the parties and that no note or memorandum sufficient to satisfy the 2009 Act exists. If a payment has been made to the vendor's auctioneer by the purchaser, it is usually categorised as a booking deposit which is now generally accepted as not sufficient to formally bind the parties provided that any note or receipt or memorandum in respect of the payment contains the disclaimers referred to previously.

In *Boyle v Lee* (referred to earlier), all five judges held that the 'subject to contract' element was fatal to the plaintiff's claim. Finlay CJ approved the principle that no note or memorandum which contains any term or expression such as 'subject to contract' can be sufficient even if it is established by oral evidence that the term or expression was not part of the originally concluded agreement. However, some members of the court were not as positive in their view as the Chief Justice in relation to the use of the term 'subject to contract' and seemed prepared to follow some earlier cases where the term had been considered superfluous as the evidence showed that an earlier concluded oral agreement had been entered into by the parties and a sufficient note or memorandum to satisfy the Statute of Frauds existed which allowed the court to make an order for specific performance. These earlier cases were *Kelly v Park Hall School* [1979] IR 340 and *Casey v Irish Intercontinental Bank* [1979] IR 364. O'Flaherty J said in *Boyle v Lee* that 'he regarded them as exceptional and confined to the peculiar facts found in each case and as properly confined to the era in which they were decided'. Also in *Boyle v Lee*, Egan J accepted that only in rare and exceptional circumstances could the words 'subject to contract' be treated as of no effect.

If in fact a concluded agreement has been reached between the parties containing what are generally regarded as the four essential elements viz the parties, the property, the price, and the essential provisions (sometimes called 'the four Ps'), and that these are contained in a note or memorandum sufficient to satisfy the 2009 Act, then what one has is a classic 'open' contract, to which will be applied the provisions as to title contained in the 2009 Act. Conveyancers do not favour this type of contract because of its informality, the lack of legal knowledge usually existing between non-professional parties, but principally because there are often many additional provisions which need to be inserted in the more formal written contracts and agreed between the parties and their solicitors before the transaction becomes binding on both parties.

It is important to be aware of the legal status of each step taken by a vendor's solicitor and a purchaser's solicitor in the initial preparation and submission of a contract by a vendor's solicitor, the signing by the purchaser, its return to the vendor's solicitor, and the signing of it by the vendor and its return to the purchaser's solicitor. Reference has been made earlier to the exchange of contracts between the parties and/or their solicitors. In Ireland, this rarely happens, although perhaps some thought should be given to adopting it as a practice. In the UK, it is standard practice. In that jurisdiction, initially one copy of the contract is issued to the purchaser's solicitor and the other copy kept by the vendor's solicitor. When the terms of the contract have been agreed and all other pre-contract enquiries completed, the vendor and the purchaser each sign one copy of the contract and the solicitors then exchange the signed contracts and each party then becomes simultaneously bound.

The uncertainty in Ireland inherent in the current practice as to when both parties can be said to be bound by the contract was considered by the Supreme Court in the more recent case of *Embourg Ltd v Tyler Group Ltd* [1996] 3 IR 480. The court consisting of Hamilton CJ, Blayney J, and Barrington J confirmed the order of the learned President of the High Court dismissing the plaintiffs' claim for specific performance and dismissed the plaintiffs' appeal. The judgment of the court was delivered by Blayney J. The facts of the case are as follows.

McLoughlin was interested in purchasing property at 55 Mary Street, Dublin which was owned by the defendant. On 20 September 1994 agreement was reached on price between the defendant's auctioneer, Messrs Lisney & Son, and McLoughlin's accountant. Lisneys sent a letter to McLoughlin's accountant headed 'Subject to Contract', proposing a closing date of six months from exchange of contracts and denying any binding contract. The letter referred to 'Proposed purchaser' and 'Proposed purchase price' and named the solicitors for both parties. The next day, McLoughlin sent a cheque for £5,000 to the vendor's solicitor who acknowledged it saying that no binding contract is to be deemed to exist until such time as a contract herein has been executed by all the parties, that they did not have authority to bind their client (the vendor), and that the booking deposit was accepted 'subject to contract'. On 28 September 1994, McLoughlin's solicitor wrote to the vendor's solicitor in a letter headed 'Subject to Contract/Contract denied', saying that they did not have authority to bind their clients and that no binding contract would be deemed to exist between the parties until contracts were executed and exchanged.

When sending the contract on 3 October 1994, the vendor's solicitor again stated that 'no binding contract shall be deemed to exist until such time as the contracts herein in all cases have been executed by all parties and the full deposits accepted by you' (sic). The contract signed by McLoughlin in trust for Embourg Ltd was returned on 25 January 1995 and six queries on title were raised. In reply, on 1 February 1995 the queries were dealt with in a letter from the vendor's solicitor who stated that he was arranging to have the contract executed by his client.

Up to this point, the transaction was proceeding along fairly predictable and standard lines. However, the next step was a letter from the vendor's solicitor on 25 April 1995 returning the deposit of £5,000 as the vendor was not proceeding with the sale, which letter crossed with a letter from the purchaser's solicitor stating that he presumed the contract had been signed by the vendor and returned from England and asking that one part be furnished to him without further delay, in order that he might proceed with his requisitions on title.

A plenary summons was issued by the plaintiffs on 27 April 1995. This was followed by a statement of claim on 14 June 1995 claiming that there was a written agreement between the parties and that the agreement was contained in the correspondence between the respective solicitors and in particular in an open letter from the plaintiff's solicitor dated 25 January 1995, enclosing the contract executed by the plaintiff and the reply from the defendant's solicitor of 1 February 1995. In its defence of 20 June 1995, the defendant denied that any enforceable contract had ever come into existence. It was agreed that the case would be heard on affidavits. It came before the President of the High Court on 3 July 1995. In the defendant's affidavit sworn by one of its directors, he stated that although he had returned a signed contract to his (the vendor's) solicitor, duly signed, the solicitor was not to release it unless and until he had the director's prior written authority in that regard. No such authority was ever given.

In his judgment, Blayney J made the following findings:

(a) The claim that there was a contract in the correspondence was not sustainable and this had been conceded by counsel for the plaintiff (purchaser) in the course of his submissions to the court and this point was not pursued. Apart from the fact that the solicitor for the defendant (vendor) had no authority to enter into a contract, they had done nothing that could be construed as an acceptance of the offer to purchase.

(b) There was no acceptance of the plaintiff's offer to purchase made when the contracts signed by the plaintiff were returned to the defendant's solicitor.

(c) It was the clear intention of the parties that no binding contract would exist until contracts were exchanged and this had never occurred.

(d) The case was not a case in which it was claimed that there ever was an oral agreement for the sale of the property.

(e) The despatch of the two contracts by the defendant's solicitor could not be construed as an offer to sell on the terms set out in the contract. This sending of contracts was merely an indication to the plaintiff that these were the terms on which the defendant was prepared to negotiate with him.

(f) The return of the contracts signed by the plaintiff was an offer to purchase.

(g) While the contracts were signed by the defendant, the acceptance of the offer by the defendant was never communicated to the plaintiff, an essential part of the process to conclude a binding contract. He quoted Lindley J who said in the course of his judgment in a leading case, *Carlill v Carbolic Smokeball Co* [1893] 1 QB 256:

> 'Unquestionably, as a general proposition, when an offer is made, it is necessary in order to make a binding contract, not only that it should be accepted but that the acceptance should be notified.'

(h) He dealt extensively with the significance in general in construing correspondence and other documents between the parties as to the parties' intentions which may be significant in deciding whether their subsequent actions are binding. In this case the intention of the parties clearly was that there would be no binding contract until signed contracts were exchanged and, as this never happened, the plaintiff could not succeed in the action for specific performance.

(i) He noted that the conclusion he had reached was determined by the special facts of the case and it did not follow that whenever there is a sale 'subject to contract', no binding contract comes into existence until contracts have been exchanged. Each case must be decided on its own merits.

The following general conclusions can be arrived at from a consideration of the foregoing cases and the general law of contract:

(a) the use of the term 'subject to contract' in correspondence will, except in rare and exceptional cases, establish the non-existence of a previously concluded oral contract for the purpose of excluding the provisions of s 51 of the 2009 Act;

(b) the issue of a contract by a vendor's solicitor under the protection of the term 'subject to contract' is an invitation to treat only and not an offer to sell;

(c) the return of this contract signed by the purchaser is an offer to purchase and is not an acceptance of an offer from the vendor;

(d) the return of this contract signed by the vendor is an acceptance of the offer to purchase by the purchaser;

(e) a concluded contract binding on both parties will come into existence when all of the steps at (b), (c), and (d) have taken place;

(f) the vendor is not bound until he or she has returned the contract to the purchaser or his or her solicitor duly signed;

(g) the purchaser is not bound until the vendor has signed the contract and returned it as it would be open to the purchaser to withdraw the offer prior to its acceptance by the vendor, provided such withdrawal is notified to the vendor before the vendor accepts the offer and notifies the purchaser of the acceptance. This will only apply if the purchaser's offer is not made or deemed to be irrevocable until accepted or rejected by the vendor, a practice that is unknown in this jurisdiction;

(h) the uncertainty as to when the parties on both sides become contractually bound would be removed if the practice of exchanging contracts became the norm. If that had been the practice in 1995, the case of *Embourg* would never have arisen.

2.2.1.16 Heading letters in conveyancing transactions 'without prejudice'

The Law Society in a Practice Note in the June 2011 *Gazette* expressed the view as to the significance of correspondence passing between solicitors during the negotiation of contracts for the sale of land being headed 'without prejudice' in addition to or in substitution for 'subject to contract'. The Conveyancing Committee advised that they could not see any justification for the use of these words when negotiating a contact for the sale of land. In addition, the use of the words 'without prejudice' being added to solicitors' replies to pre-contract enquiries is entirely inappropriate. A prospective purchaser is entitled to get clear and unequivocal replies from a prospective vendor to such enquiries.

2.2.2 PURCHASER'S SOLICITOR

2.2.2.1 Nature of purchaser's agreement

The purchaser's solicitor may have received, prior to getting a contract and documents from the vendor's solicitor, some instructions from his or her client and, as with the vendor's solicitor, he or she will go into some detail with the purchaser as to the type of property, the contract price, the closing date, etc. The purchaser's solicitor should clarify with the purchaser how the purchase is to be financed and how and when the finance will be available on completion. In the vast majority of cases, purchasers will be borrowing from some lending institution to finance the purchase and it will be necessary for the purchaser's solicitor to obtain full and specific details of this borrowing as the solicitor may be obliged to advise the purchaser on the terms of the loan, compliance with any of the conditions attached, and the completion by the purchaser's solicitors of undertakings and certificates for the benefit of the lending institution.

2.2.2.2   Perusing contracts and other documentation

The purchaser's solicitor will obtain contracts and copy documents from the vendor's so-licitor. If the property is being sold by auction, the purchaser may require his or her solici-tor to bid for him or her at the auction and, if so, a purchaser's solicitor should not do so without getting specific written instructions from the purchaser as to the limit up to which he or she may bid and discuss specific arrangements with the purchaser as to how the purchase is to be financed. The solicitor should arrange, prior to the auction, details of how he or she is to be financed if he or she should be successful in the bidding. If the sale is by private treaty, then he or she will receive the documents from the vendor's solicitor in the post. In either case he or she will immediately embark upon a perusal of the contract and documents furnished to establish the nature of the title being offered, a full description of the property, whether it includes any contents and what, if any, special conditions the vendor's solicitor seeks to impose. The question of the title and the nature of the title is a matter for the purchaser's solicitor to clarify and satisfy himself or herself on before the purchaser is allowed to sign the contract. However, the question of the identity of the property is also crucial as is the type of property and any rights attached to it, eg a licensed premises where it may be necessary to embark upon further detailed pre-contract enquiries, as has been previously indicated.

2.2.2.3   Advising on purchaser's risk

It is important to emphasise at this stage to the purchaser that the principle of caveat emp-tor applies save where the property being purchased is a new premises where there will inevitably be a building contract and Contract for Sale under the terms of which the pur-chaser will have certain rights in respect of the standard of the building being constructed and purchased. However, in a straightforward purchase of second-hand premises it is crucial for the purchaser's solicitor to advise the purchaser to have a full structural survey carried out. This survey should be a structural survey and not a valuation survey. All lend-ing institutions will carry out a valuation survey but this does not necessarily involve a detailed structural survey. It is important that a purchaser's solicitor emphasises this matter to a purchaser. If the purchaser decides that he or she is not going to have a survey carried out then the purchaser's solicitor should write to the purchaser advising him or her of the consequences of failing to do so (see *O'Connor v FNBS* [1991] ILRM 208).

2.2.2.4   Tax

There can be a variety of tax relief schemes available for the purchase of various different types of properties. These schemes are many and are confusing and the ground rules in respect of many of them change from time to time. Unless the purchaser's solicitor has a particular expertise in this area it would be prudent to advise a purchaser in such circum-stances to consult with his or her accountant to satisfy himself or herself that the tax relief which he or she hopes to obtain will in fact be available to him or her. There may be some documentation which a purchaser's solicitor will need to obtain for the purpose of ensur-ing that the purchaser will get the necessary tax relief and these are matters to which very careful consideration should be given by a purchaser's solicitor.

The purchaser's solicitor should also address the question of stamp duty. Again, this is an area which has become much more complex than it used to be. There are now different rates of stamp duty for residential property and non-residential property. Where there is mixed residential and non-residential property very careful attention should be paid as to how the stamp duty will be assessed and apportioned. If an apportionment is necessary between the residential and non-residential elements then either these should be agreed between the vendor and the purchaser at the time the contracts are signed or valuations obtained and some endeavour made to clarify the valuations. The Revenue Commission-ers will require an agreement between the parties on the apportionment and will also require a valuation in support of the apportionment.

The issue of VAT will also need to be addressed with the purchaser. Given the system of VAT that has applied to property since July 2008, it is vital that the various options be discussed with the purchaser. The new Law Society condition dealing with VAT in the Contract for Sale requires certain choices to be made by the parties before the contract becomes binding. If these choices are not agreed pre-contract considerable conflict could arise between the parties in how the transaction should be treated for VAT purposes.

2.2.2.5   Potential problems with title

The purpose for which the purchaser is acquiring the property should be considered. Questions may arise as to whether the title to the property may inhibit or, indeed, prohibit the use that the purchaser has in mind or the existing planning for the property may not permit the proposed user. In particular, covenants and conditions contained in a leasehold title that will bind the purchaser should be identified to the purchaser. For example, a purchaser may wish to run a business from the property, or part of it. It is common for leasehold titles in residential areas to contain a covenant in the lease restricting use of the property to residential only.

2.2.2.6   Insurance

The purchaser should be advised also of the position in respect of insurance. Notwithstanding that the contract will provide that the risk in respect of the property remains with the vendor until the actual completion date, a purchaser should be advised to take out insurance on the property from the time the contract is signed as the property may be under insured by the vendor or not insured at all. In particular, if the purchaser is borrowing, he or she should be advised to liaise with his or her lending institution as to how the insurance is to be effected and for how much, as the lending institution will require evidence that the insurance is in place for an amount acceptable to it and its interest noted on the policy before advancing the loan cheque.

It is not the practice in this jurisdiction to obtain confirmation that the vendor has insurance cover in place or to seek to have the purchaser's interest in the property noted on any such policy.

2.2.2.7   Pre-contract enquiries

The full extent of the pre-contract enquiries and searches to be made will depend entirely upon the nature of the property and careful consideration should be given to this aspect of the matter. The whole issue of raising pre-contract enquiries or requisitions and obtaining replies which may or may not be binding on the vendor should be considered very carefully, bearing in mind that the vast majority of purchasers will have little or no experience in property transactions and will be relying almost exclusively upon their solicitors to advise them properly in the matter and to ensure that the purchaser gets what the purchaser believes he or she is entitled to. For example, a planning search, which is an essential prerequisite to having the contract signed, should be made by the purchaser's solicitor. However, such planning search will only glean from the local authority information concerning the particular property being purchased and will not disclose any development that may be due to take place in the immediate neighbourhood.

Accordingly, it is necessary to advise a purchaser to make his or her own enquiries with the local authority as there may be a development due to take place in the immediate area of which the purchaser is unaware, but which might have some detrimental effect on his or her user or enjoyment of the premises, and which he or she may believe is a matter that his or her solicitor would ascertain for him or her in due course of investigating the title. Potential difficulties may not arise if, for example, the property being purchased is a residential property in the middle of an established housing development, but it could be a matter of some consequence if the property being purchased is a green field site on the outskirts of an urban area where there may be a potential for a variety of different types of development in the immediate neighbourhood.

2.2.2.8   Obtaining loan approval

If the contract is to be made subject to loan approval or survey very careful attention should be paid to the precise terminology being used. If it is being made subject to loan approval, then a simple clause to that effect of itself may not be sufficient. All loan approvals of themselves contain conditions and if the contract is being signed before the formal loan approval document has issued then it is of critical importance that the contract is made subject, not only to loan approval, but to the purchaser being in a position to comply with any conditions attached, or that there are no conditions attached which the purchaser is unable or unwilling to comply with. A particular problem that may arise in these circumstances is where a purchaser is obliged under the terms of the loan approval to get a life insurance policy and, because of some health problem, may not be in a position to do so or may only be in a position to do so on the payment of a very heavily loaded premium which he or she may not be able to afford. Likewise, if the contract is to be made subject to a survey, very careful attention should be paid to the precise wording being used. The better advice in terms of surveys is that the survey should be carried out before contracts are signed so that the purchaser is fully aware before he or she signs the contract of any problems that the survey may identify with the particular property.

As a result of the recent property 'bust' a particular problem has emerged with contracts for the purchase of properties with long closing dates. A loan offer will only hold good for a specific period of time. This is the case even if it has been accepted but funds have not yet been drawn down. If the purchaser is intending to contract for the purchase of a property that will not close for a long time, it is important to advise the client to ascertain whether the loan offer/approval will still be valid when they seek to draw down funds. Cases have recently emerged where banks are no longer willing to provide funding for a purchase due to a change in the circumstances of the borrower, or the market, from the time when the loan offer was accepted. This has left some purchasers in the position where they are bound by a contract to purchase a property but they have no way to finance the purchase.

2.2.2.9   Costs and outlays

In accordance with the provisions of the Solicitors (Amendment) Act, 1996, s 68, the purchaser's solicitor should issue a statement to the purchaser setting out the basis upon which his or her professional fee will be charged or calculated, together with items of outlay, stamp duty, etc so that the client is aware before the matter proceeds what the extent of his or her liability will be. To assist practitioners in dealing with this section, the Law Society has issued standard forms of letters for use by solicitors.

2.2.2.10   Effects of delay

The purchaser's solicitor should also at this stage advise the purchaser of the position if there is a delay in completion which may give rise to a potential liability for interest on the balance of purchase money.

2.2.2.11   Signing the contract

Assuming that everything is in order and that all questions or queries raised have been satisfactorily dealt with, the contract at this stage is signed by the purchaser and returned to the vendor's solicitor with a remittance for the deposit which will normally amount to 10 per cent of the purchase price. If a booking deposit has already been paid, credit will be taken against the 10 per cent for any such payment. If any amendments have been made to the contract which have not been agreed with the vendor's solicitor (and it is good practice to try to agree any such amendment before contracts are signed and sent back) then they should be brought specifically to the attention of the vendor's solicitor in the covering letter returning the contracts so that he or she would be aware of the basis upon which the transaction between the parties is to proceed. Technically, the issue by the vendor's solicitor of the contracts is not an offer to sell but is an invitation to treat under contract law. Accordingly, sending back the signed contract by the purchaser's solicitor will amount to an offer by the purchaser and the vendor's solicitor should be aware of any change in the terms of the invitation to treat. If the changes in the contract are material, obviously the vendor's solicitor will take full instructions from the vendor and there may be further negotiations between the parties before the final terms of the contract are agreed. In any event, any change should be brought to the attention of the vendor before the contracts are signed by the vendor. If it is a family home which requires the spouse's prior consent then the spouse should sign his or her consent to the sale before the contract is signed by the vendor.

When the contracts have been signed by the vendor one copy is retained by the vendor's solicitor and the other copy is returned to the purchaser's solicitor. At this stage the vendor's solicitor will furnish to the purchaser's solicitor the balance of the title documents to complete the chain of title from the documentation specified in the contract down to the last document or event showing how the vendor acquired the premises. There is now in existence between the parties a binding contract.

2.3 From Exchange of Binding Contracts to Completion of Transaction

2.3.1 PURCHASER'S SOLICITOR

2.3.1.1 Raising requisitions on title

After binding contracts have been exchanged the main work initially falls on the purchaser's solicitor. The purchaser's solicitor will have obtained all the balance of vendor's title which requires him or her to embark upon a careful perusal of the title and to raise requisitions and objections (if any). As covered in **chapter 15** there are standard requisitions on title issued by the Law Society, not all of which apply to every case. First of all, when raising requisitions the solicitor should take out or exclude from the printed form those which do not affect the particular property. Secondly, he or she should then add in any particular objections or requisitions that he wishes to raise outside of the standard printed ones. Finally, the requisitions are finished off by putting in a list of closing documentation which will be required by the purchaser's solicitor on completion. These requisitions are sent in duplicate to the vendor's solicitors within the time limit specified in the contract.

2.3.1.2 Lending institution requirements

If the purchaser is borrowing for the transaction it is at this stage that the purchaser's solicitor may have to complete and furnish documentation to the lending institution or the lending institution's solicitors to satisfy their particular requirements. Compliance with any terms and conditions in a loan approval should not be left in abeyance until the last minute and a purchaser's solicitor should, in so far as he or she is responsible to do so, complete any documentation at his or her end of the transaction that the lending institution requires so that there will ultimately be no delay in issuing the loan cheque when it is requisitioned.

2.3.1.3 Draft deed

It was formerly the practice not to draft the purchase deed until such time as full replies to requisitions were received, as it might be necessary to join some other parties in the deed if the replies to the requisitions disclosed that some other party had an interest. However, it has now become common practice that with the requisitions on title the draft deed is also furnished for approval to the vendor's solicitor. It should be sent 'without prejudice' to the replies to the requisitions.

2.3.1.4 Rejoinders

The purchaser's solicitor, having received the replies to the requisitions, should check the replies carefully and, if any further questions or queries are required, then he or she will raise what are called rejoinders on title, which are effectively further requisitions or clarification sought as to the replies already given. Again, these should be furnished to the vendor's solicitor within the time limited by the contract for him or her to deal with them. This process will continue until such time as the purchaser's solicitor receives satisfactory replies to all of his or her requisitions. He or she will at this stage also prepare an engrossment of the deed and return the draft deed with the engrossment for execution by the vendor.

2.3.1.5   Finance

The purchaser's solicitor at this stage will be liaising with the purchaser and with the vendor's solicitor with a view to closing and, once he or she is satisfied that all matters are in order then, if there is a loan involved, he or she should give the lending institution adequate notice to requisition the loan cheque so that it is available on the date the sale is due to be closed. At this stage he or she will require from the purchaser all the necessary finance to complete the transaction. He or she will in particular require funding to pay the stamp duty, and normally at this stage he or she would ask the purchaser to furnish him or her with funds to cover not only the balance of purchase money (over and above the amount of the loan) and the stamp duty, but also his or her fees and outlays as well.

2.3.1.6   Searches

Having made an appointment with the vendor's solicitor to complete, usually at the office of the vendor's solicitor as provided for in the contract, the purchaser's solicitor will requisition all searches required by him or her for the closing and in that respect the reader is referred to **chapter 10** as to what is required in any particular case.

2.3.2   VENDOR'S SOLICITOR

2.3.2.1   Tax

Prior to the receipt of the requisitions on title one matter, which arises under the capital gains tax legislation, the vendor's solicitor may have to deal with immediately upon the exchange of binding contracts. In order to deal with an anti-avoidance measure in this legislation, any property sold for a sum in excess of €1,000,000 in the case of houses and apartments and €500,000 in all other cases, requires the issue of a certificate from the Revenue Commissioners exempting the purchaser from making a deduction amounting to 15 per cent of the proceeds of sale from the sale price on closing. If the vendor himself or herself or his or her accountant is not applying for this certificate then the vendor's solicitor should immediately do so and a copy of the signed contract will need to be furnished to the Revenue Commissioners with the application form duly signed by the vendor.

Great care must be taken in dealing with the sale of property belonging to a non-resident vendor. The Finance Act, 1997, ss 1042 and 1034 provides that capital gains tax must be paid by a non-resident vendor or his or her agent within three months of the sale of the property. A solicitor acting for such a vendor will be regarded by the Revenue Commissioners as the agent liable to pay the tax. It is important to remember that the exemption certificate referred to earlier is not a tax clearance certificate but is one issued for the benefit of the purchaser only which absolves the purchaser from making any deduction from the proceeds of sale on closing.

Accordingly, irrespective of the amount of the consideration, which may well be below the threshold amount requiring the issue of an exemption certificate, a solicitor acting for a non-resident vendor, even if the property is a residential property, must retain from the proceeds of sale a sum sufficient to pay any capital gains tax liability arising from the sale and make a full return to the Revenue Commissioners for the purpose of determining the correct amount of tax due on the sale and discharge the tax from the funds retained. If the purchaser has already made a deduction and furnished the proper deduction certificate on closing, credit will be given for that amount. There is no procedure for obtaining a clearance certificate from the Revenue Commissioners prior to completion of the sale.

2.3.2.2   Replying to requisitions on title

When he or she receives the requisitions, the vendor's solicitor must reply to them fully. A vendor's solicitor should never assume that he or she knows the correct answer to a requisition and, if there is any requisition that he or she has any doubts about, then he or she should send a query to his or her client and get the client's written instructions to reply. It has now become commonplace for solicitors to do a précis of the requisitions and send them to the vendor and get the client's written replies duly signed by the client to ensure the solicitor has a record from the client as to what the correct replies are. He or she then replies to the requisitions, furnishes any additional documentation that may be required, and returns them to the purchaser's solicitor, usually with the draft deed approved.

2.3.2.3   Draft family law declaration

It is now common practice at this stage to furnish a draft of the declaration to be made dealing with the relevant provisions of the Family Home Protection Act, 1976 and the subsequent other pieces of family law legislation but again there are standard declarations prepared by the Law Society, which have become accepted as covering the vast majority of cases, and these forms should always be used or adapted for use to the particular transaction.

2.3.2.4   Outgoings

At this stage also the vendor's solicitor should be checking with his or her client in relation to any vouchers that may be required for outgoings, eg for rates, ground rent, fee farm rent, service charges, water charges, etc. If it is a property which is producing an income then the position in respect of the payment of the income should also be clarified as it will be necessary to vouch all the outgoings and income to the purchaser's solicitor on closing. The preparation of an apportionment account apportioning the outgoings and the income between the vendor and the purchaser will be necessary.

2.3.2.5   Closing date

Arrangements should also be put in train at this stage with the vendor to ensure that whatever closing date was agreed between the parties can now be met and confirming that the vendor is in a position to complete on the agreed closing date. If any difficulties arise in this respect then the sooner the purchaser's solicitor is made aware of this the better so that alternative arrangements, if necessary, may be made to meet the needs of the parties.

2.3.2.6   Preparation for closing

The vendor's solicitor having received the engrossed deed will have brought his or her client into his or her office to have the deed signed and also if necessary to have his or her spouse's prior consent endorsed on it. While such consent would have been endorsed on the contract where necessary, the practice is that it should also be endorsed on the deed as contracts are normally not kept with the documents of title, whereas the consent on the deed prevents any difficulty or query arising at a later stage. In addition any declarations that require to be completed by the vendors should be sworn at this stage. Where vacant possession is being furnished the vendor's solicitor should collect the keys from the vendor and ensure that on the closing date the property has been vacated.

It is usually not necessary for the vendor to attend at the closing once all the documentation has been signed beforehand. It is, however, commonplace for the purchasers to be in attendance not only to sign the purchase deed but also, usually, to sign any mortgage documentation where there is a loan involved as these are normally done contemporaneously with the closing and, of course, to collect the keys.

2.4   Closing

2.4.1   VENDOR'S SOLICITOR

On closing it is of the utmost importance that the vendor's solicitor receives payment of the balance of the purchase money by way of banker's draft or electronic bank transfer. He or she will be handing over on closing the purchase deed which contains an acknowledgement by the vendor that he or she has received the purchase money and the vendor's solicitor is authorised under the Land and Conveyancing Law Reform Act, 2009, s 77, to hand over the deed on behalf of the vendor as a receipt. Consequently, a vendor's solicitor is under an obligation to ensure that the payment he or she receives is negotiable and an ordinary cheque should never be accepted. Again, it has become commonplace for cheques from lending institutions to be tendered duly endorsed by the purchaser in lieu of a bank draft. Strictly speaking, these should not be accepted by the vendor's solicitor and it is a recommended practice of the Law Society that if such cheques are to be accepted that the vendor's solicitor obtains written instructions from the vendor to do so.

If there is an existing mortgage on the premises it is common practice for a vendor's solicitor to undertake to discharge this mortgage from the proceeds of sale and to furnish the mortgage duly vacated or released or evidence that this has occurred as soon as possible after completion. The recommended practice of the Law Society is that the contract should provide that prior to closing a statement is produced from the lending institution of the amount necessary to redeem the mortgage on the closing date and that on closing the purchaser's solicitor provides the purchase money in two lots, first by way of a bank draft payable to the lending institution and, secondly, a bank draft for the balance of the purchase monies due. The bank draft payable to the institution is handed over to the vendor's solicitor against a written undertaking that he or she will immediately use that bank draft to pay off the amount of the loan.

There may be other matters in respect of which undertakings are given and practitioners should always be extremely careful about either giving or accepting undertakings. It is a fundamental rule that an undertaking should never be given unless the solicitor giving it is satisfied that he or she can comply with it. An undertaking should never be accepted if the purchaser's solicitor has any doubts as to whether it can be implemented. Undertakings should really be given only in respect of minor matters. However, the practice of conveyancing demands that undertakings remain an integral part of the system and conveyancing on a practical basis simply would not work without the exchange of solicitors' undertakings. Solicitors should remember that a breach of an undertaking will leave them open not only to a civil claim but also a complaint to the Law Society as breach of an undertaking is regarded as a serious disciplinary matter by the Law Society. Hence, when undertakings are given, they should be properly recorded by both parties and the solicitor giving the undertaking should ensure that it is complied with as quickly as possible.

If difficulties arise between the parties to the contract before the sale is formally completed it may be necessary to consider what rights the parties have under the terms of the contract and in that respect the reader is referred to **chapter 6** dealing with the Law Society formal contract. Suffice to say at this stage that the remedies available may amount to specific performance proceedings, a vendor and purchaser summons to clarify some issue in relation to the title, service of a notice to complete making time of the essence, or service of a notice forfeiting the deposit paid. The various options will depend upon the remedy sought by the party seeking to avail of the remedy.

2.4.2 PURCHASER'S SOLICITOR

The purchaser's solicitor will attend the closing usually at the office of the vendor's solicitor but occasionally at the office of a lending institution's solicitor, usually with the purchaser present. He or she will ensure that all matters covered by the requisitions on title are fully dealt with on closing and that all relevant documentation duly executed and witnessed or signed and sworn are handed over to him or her. In particular, he or she will ensure that he gets all documents of title as specified in the contract and requisitions on title, together with all clearance certificates, discharges of mortgages, capital gains tax clearance certificate, etc so as to give his or her client a good marketable title. He or she will also require the vendor's solicitor to explain and discharge any acts on the closing searches. If the purchaser is closing with the aid of a loan cheque he or she will need to have all the necessary mortgage documentation signed by the purchaser after fully explaining same to the purchaser before parting with the loan cheque.

He or she should also receive the keys of the premises if buying with vacant possession. It is only when he or she is fully satisfied that all his or her requirements have been fully met that he or she will pay over the balance of purchase money.

2.5 After Completion of the Sale

2.5.1 VENDOR'S SOLICITOR

The first responsibility of the vendor's solicitor is to ensure that he or she discharges any undertakings he or she had given on completion. In particular, if he or she has taken the deeds up from a lending institution on accountable receipt, then he or she should immediately upon completion discharge the amount due to that lending institution from the proceeds of sale. He or she should prepare and furnish to the vendor a full statement involving all finances involved in the transaction and how they were dealt with and remit to the vendor any balance remaining in his or her hands as quickly as possible. He or she should also notify any local authority of the change of ownership and, if there are tenants involved, the tenants should be formally notified of the change of ownership. Likewise, if there is a landlord involved, the landlord should also be notified of the change of ownership.

2.5.2 PURCHASER'S SOLICITOR

The obligation of the purchaser's solicitor is to have the documentation completed by the purchaser, have the deed stamped and obtain a stamp certificate and then lodge the relevant documentation either in the Registry of Deeds or the Land Registry for registration. If the title is currently registered in the Registry of Deeds, an application for first registration with the Land Registry will now also be required due to the extension of compulsory registration to all counties in Ireland. He or she should also at this stage report back to the lending institution that the transaction has been completed and, when registration of the title has taken place, he or she should furnish all of the title deeds with a certificate of title to the lending institution. If, in fact, a separate solicitor represents the lending institution on the closing then the matters post completion of stamping and registration will be done by the lending institution's solicitors and not by the purchaser's solicitors.

Finally, the purchaser's solicitor should then send a full detailed statement to the purchaser and fully account to the purchaser for all funds involved in the transaction.

2.6   How Long Should a Solicitor Keep a File in a Conveyancing Transaction?

The most recent Practice Note on this point, April 2005, noted that most solicitors keep files for at least 12 years before disposing of them. This is because most solicitors take the view that the doctrine of adverse possession would sort out any difficulties that might necessitate reference to the file. With the degree of paperwork involved in modern transactions this has presented, and continues to present, storage problems. The Practice Note also notes that it is valid to argue that 12 years may be too long as the purchaser's solicitor is precluded from raising title queries post closing save in cases of fraud or misrepresentation. Each individual solicitor must make his or her own decision on this aspect of the matter but prudence would suggest that they should at least observe the 12-year period for a retention of papers.

2.7   Time Landmarks

The following are just some of the significant time landmarks that are of relevance to conveyancers:

(a)   Written assents became necessary in respect of deaths on or after 1 June 1959 (Administration of Estates Act, 1959).

(b)   Planning Act, 1963 came into operation on 1 October 1964.

(c)   Land Act, 1965 came into operation on 9 March 1965.

(d)   Registration of Title Act, 1964 came into operation on 1 January 1967.

(e)   First registration for the following counties became compulsory from the dates listed in the following table:

Counties Affected	Effective Date
Carlow, Meath, and Laois	1 January 1970
Longford, Westmeath, and Roscommon	1 April 2006
Clare, Kilkenny, Louth, Sligo, Wexford, and Wicklow	1 October 2008
Cavan, Donegal, Galway, Kerry, Kildare, Leitrim, Limerick, Mayo, Monaghan, North Tipperary, Offaly, South Tipperary, and Waterford	1 January 2010
Cities of Galway, Limerick, and Waterford, as defined in s 10 of the Local Government Act, 2001	1 January 2010
Counties of Cork, Fingal, Dun Laoghaire-Rathdown, and South County Dublin and cities of Dublin and Cork	1 June 2011

(f)   Succession Act, 1965 came into operation on 1 January 1967.

(g)   Family Home Protection Act, 1976 operates from 12 July 1976.

(h)   Landlord and Tenant (Ground Rents) Act, 1978 came into operation on 17 May 1978.

(i)   Family Law Act, 1981 came into operation on 23 June 1981.

(j)   Judicial Separation and Family Law Reform Act, 1989 came into operation on 19 October 1989.

(k)   Family Law Act, 1995 came into operation on 1 August 1996.

(l)   Family Law (Divorce) Act, 1996 came into operation on 27 February 1997.

(m)   Building Control Act, 1990 came into operation on 1 June 1992.

(n)   Local Government (Planning and Development) Regulations, 1994 (main provisions) came into force on 16 May 1994.

(o)   Certificates under the Capital Gains Tax Acts now apply to sales in excess of €500,000 that have taken place since 5 April 2000 (increased to €1 million in 2016).

(p)   Planning and Development Act, 2000 came into force on 28 August 2000.

(q)   Local Government (Planning and Development) Regulations, 2001 came into force on 21 January 2002 and 11 March 2002.

(r)   Registration of Deeds and Title Act, 2006 came into force on various dates, ie 7 May 2006, 26 May 2006, 4 November 2006, 1 September 2007, and 1 May 2008.

(s)   Land and Conveyancing Law Reform Act, 2009 came into force on 1 December 2009, save for s 132 which came into force on 28 February 2010.

(t)   Civil Partnership and Certain Rights and Obligations of Cohabitants Act came into force on 11 January 2011.

(u)   Land Registration Rules 2012 commenced on 1 February 2013.

2.8   Purchase of Property—Financial Memo

This is an example of a financial memo prepared by the solicitor for a purchaser of an unregistered property:

Purchase price		€400,000.00
Less deposit		€40,000.00
Balance		€360,000.00
Amount of loan		€180,000.00
Final balance		€180,000.00
Costs & Outlay		
Stamp duty		
€400,000 @1%	€ 4,000.00	
Application Form 1	€ 50.00	
Assignment of life policy	€_____	€4,050.00
Land Registration Fees		
1. Registration of		
(i) Transfer	€_____	
(ii) Charge	€_____	
(iii) Discharge	€_____	
2. Copy instrument	€_____	
3. Copy folio and title plan	€ 40.00	
4. First Registration application using Form 3 (alternatively fee will be €500.00 if using Form 1 or 2)	€ 130.00	€170.00
Miscellaneous		
1. Certificates		
(i) Marriage/Death	€_____	
(ii) Services in charge	€_____	
(iii) Valuation	€_____	

2. Commissioner for Oaths	€ 12.00	
3. Searches (estimated) and other petty outlay (estimated)	€ 150.00	€162.00
Professional fees		
Purchase/mortgage/charge	€ 4,000.00	
Consent of lessor	€ 0	
	€ 4,000.00	
Postage, telephone and		
Photocopying	€ 50.00	
	€ 4,050.00	
VAT at 23%	€ 931.50	€4,981.50
TOTAL		€9,363.50

Notes

1. Check if payment of VAT arises.

2. Check on possible exemptions or reduction from stamp duty, eg if purchaser is a charity.

3. Verify that CGT clearance certificate is available and that no deductions arise.

4. If split draft re vendor's mortgage—get details.

2.9   Chart of Basic Steps in a Residential Conveyancing Transaction

The following flowchart shows the basic steps involved in a residential conveyancing transaction.

BASIC STEPS IN A RESIDENTIAL CONVEYANCING TRANSACTION

Vendor's Solicitor   Purchaser's Solicitor

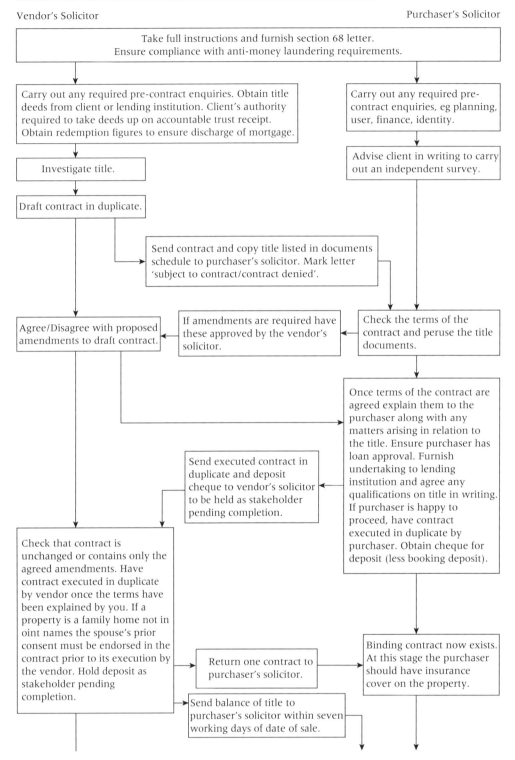

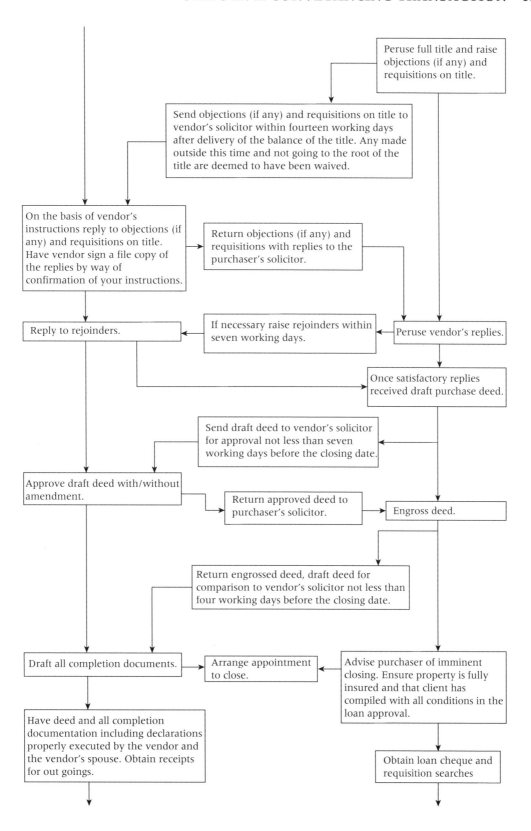

Peruse full title and raise objections (if any) and requisitions on title.

Send objections (if any) and requisitions on title to vendor's solicitor within fourteen working days after delivery of the balance of the title. Any made outside this time and not going to the root of the title are deemed to have been waived.

On the basis of vendor's instructions reply to objections (if any) and requisitions on title. Have vendor sign a file copy of the replies by way of confirmation of your instructions.

Return objections (if any) and requisitions with replies to the purchaser's solicitor.

Reply to rejoinders.

If necessary raise rejoinders within seven working days.

Peruse vendor's replies.

Once satisfactory replies received draft purchase deed.

Send draft deed to vendor's solicitor for approval not less than seven working days before the closing date.

Approve draft deed with/without amendment.

Return approved deed to purchaser's solicitor.

Engross deed.

Return engrossed deed, draft deed for comparison to vendor's solicitor not less than four working days before the closing date.

Draft all completion documents.

Arrange appointment to close.

Advise purchaser of imminent closing. Ensure property is fully insured and that client has compiled with all conditions in the loan approval.

Have deed and all completion documentation including declarations properly executed by the vendor and the vendor's spouse. Obtain receipts for out goings.

Obtain loan cheque and requisition searches

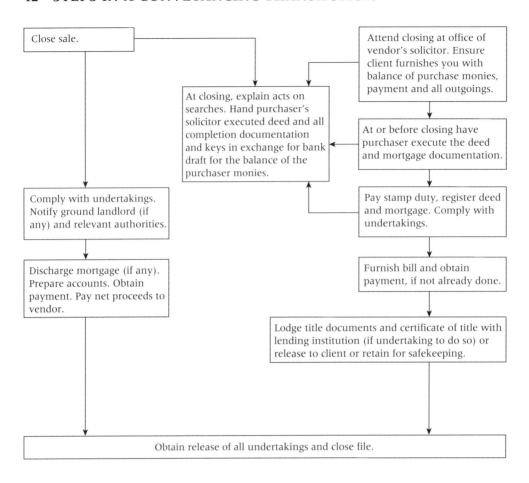

Close sale.

Attend closing at office of vendor's solicitor. Ensure client furnishes you with balance of purchase monies, payment and all outgoings.

At closing, explain acts on searches. Hand purchaser's solicitor executed deed and all completion documentation and keys in exchange for bank draft for the balance of the purchaser monies.

At or before closing have purchaser execute the deed and mortgage documentation.

Comply with undertakings. Notify ground landlord (if any) and relevant authorities.

Pay stamp duty, register deed and mortgage. Comply with undertakings.

Discharge mortgage (if any). Prepare accounts. Obtain payment. Pay net proceeds to vendor.

Furnish bill and obtain payment, if not already done.

Lodge title documents and certificate of title with lending institution (if undertaking to do so) or release to client or retain for safekeeping.

Obtain release of all undertakings and close file.

CHAPTER 3

ETHICS

'In a society founded on respect for the rule of law, solicitors fulfil a special role. Their duties do not begin and end with the faithful performance of what they are instructed to do so far as the law permits. Solicitors must serve the interests of justice as well as the rights and liberties of their clients. It is their duty not only to plead their clients' cause but also to be their adviser.'

A Guide to Professional Conduct of Solicitors in Ireland (3rd edn, 2013)

3.1 Ethics and Conveyancing

In conveyancing, there are professional codes of practice that fall directly under the heading of ethics and that must be followed as a matter of course by all solicitors and their staff in dealing with their colleagues and other parties and institutions engaged in conveyancing, eg banks, building societies, lending institutions, and local authorities. Any behaviour considered to be a breach of ethical conduct may lead to disciplinary proceedings by the Law Society. The following is a short list of some of the more obvious matters:

(a) fair dealing and courtesy with your colleagues, avoiding any sharp practices or dishonesty;

(b) all dealings for or with your client to be honest and above board;

(c) full observance and performance of any undertakings. Failure to do so may lead to civil litigation against you as well as disciplinary proceedings by the Law Society;

(d) proper files and books of account to be kept, the latter to conform fully with the solicitor accounts regulations;

(e) all correspondence and enquiries from the Law Society relating to the conduct of a client's affairs to be dealt with immediately; and

(f) to ensure that all actions taken by you are in the client's best interest and are in accordance with the client's instructions.

The Law Society has published *A Guide to Professional Conduct of Solicitors in Ireland* (3rd edn, 2013). This is essential reading for any practitioner.

3.2 Undertakings

3.2.1 WHAT IS AN UNDERTAKING?

An undertaking is a trust that professionals are bound to honour—a professional promise. The consequences of not complying include loss of trust amongst colleagues, appearance before the disciplinary committees of the Law Society, enforcement by the High Court, and ultimately, dipping into one's own pocket. It is regrettable to note that due to an 'unprecedented number of complaints relating to undertakings' the Law Society felt compelled to publish a Practice Note in the December 2009 *Gazette* reminding practitioners of the principles governing undertakings. This Practice Note was stated to be in addition to the principles as set out in the *Guide to Professional Conduct of Solicitors in Ireland* (3rd edn, 2013) ('the Guide'). In Appendix 3.1 a Practice Note from 1996 is reproduced in full. This is an excellent statement of the principles governing undertakings and should be read in conjunction with the Guide and the December 2009 Practice Note. Further more recent guidelines were provided by the Guidance and Ethics Committee in the January/February 2016 edition of the Gazette and this should also be consulted.

It is noticeable that recent years have featured a steady stream of cases before the Solicitor's Disciplinary Tribunal relating to the failure of solicitors to comply with their undertakings. This has led to constant reminders by the Registrar of Solicitors, most recently in the August/September 2013 *Gazette*, of the need for solicitors to check if they have any overdue undertakings and the potentially severe consequences of failure to comply with an undertaking.

The Guide was built on the principles governing undertakings noted earlier. In particular at paragraph 6.5., it defines an undertaking:

> 'An undertaking is any unequivocal declaration of intention addressed to someone who reasonably places reliance on it which is made by a solicitor in the course of his practice, either personally or by a member of the solicitor's staff, whereby the solicitor, or in the case of a member of his staff, his employer, becomes personally bound.'

3.2.1.1 An unequivocal declaration of intention

Undertakings are often conditional on the occurrence of a given event and, if so, the contingency on which the performance of the undertaking relies must be spelt out and the undertaking diluted accordingly.

3.2.1.2 Addressed to someone who reasonably places reliance on it

Normally only the giver of an undertaking will be expected to honour it and only the recipient may complain of a breach.

3.2.1.3 Made by a solicitor or a member of a solicitor's staff in the course of practice

Where a solicitor in partnership gives an undertaking in the course of his practice, all partners are responsible for its performance. This responsibility enures beyond leaving a firm and lives while a solicitor is still on the roll, even if not holding a practising certificate. For obvious reasons many firms restrict the autonomy of assistant solicitors or paralegals to give undertakings without the imprimatur of a partner.

3.2.1.4 Whereby he or she becomes personally bound

Do not give an undertaking if it relies on other people who may fail to deliver. There is no obligation on a solicitor to give or accept an undertaking and it is binding even if it is to do something outside the solicitor's control. A solicitor who fails to honour an undertaking is *prima facie* guilty of professional misconduct.

3.2.2 UNDERTAKINGS AND CONVEYANCING

In the area of conveyancing one of the most important and frequently used undertakings is the undertaking to a lending institution in connection with residential mortgage lending. Full details of how this system works are given in **chapter 9**, but it is worthwhile dealing with the ethical aspects of this system here.

A solicitor's obligations under this undertaking are:

1. to carry out a full and proper investigation of title and obtain a good and marketable title to the property;

2.   to attend to the execution of the purchase and mortgage documentation;

3.   to stamp and register the purchase and mortgage deeds;

4.   to ensure that the lender has a first fixed charge on the property; and

5.   to furnish a properly completed certificate of title to the lender together with the relevant title documents.

A solicitor in giving the eventual certificate of title does not in any way act on behalf of the lending institution. He is merely giving a certificate of good and marketable title, though in reality any matter that may adversely affect the lender's interests will have been covered by way of qualification.

Some essential points to remember when giving this undertaking are as follows and it should be noted that many of these points equally apply to all undertakings.

1.   A solicitor must seek a client's written irrevocable authority to give an undertaking, having explained the implications to the client. This authority and retainer, whereby the client undertakes not to revoke their instructions in relation to the transaction without releasing the solicitor from his undertaking, is contained within the undertaking he gives to the lending institution.

2.   A solicitor needs to get the consent of a spouse where appropriate and make sure that the spouse understands the nature and effect of the giving of such consent, if necessary ensuring that they get independent legal advice.

3.   A solicitor needs to ensure, before giving an undertaking, that he is either in a position to perform the task he has undertaken or that his undertaking is sufficiently qualified, highlighting matters which are not within his direct control. Any such qualifications must be agreed in writing with the lending institution. If a matter arises after a solicitor has given an undertaking but before negotiating the loan cheque, he must inform the lending institution and agree a course of action, as otherwise the lender is relying on his unqualified undertaking.

4.   A solicitor needs to ensure when giving an undertaking to a lending institution that the monies or deeds, the subject matter of the undertaking, actually pass through his hands. If for instance the loan cheque is given to the borrower and he absconds with it, the solicitor is still bound by his undertaking to ensure that the lender gets a first fixed charge over the property in question, which he cannot now do without the money. If the money cannot be recovered the solicitor may have to use his own money to compensate the lending institution.

5.   A solicitor should not give or accept undertakings in ambiguous or obscure terms. They may well be construed against him. It is much better to delay closing until the appropriate paperwork is in order, even though this may inconvenience the client. If a thorough investigation of title has been carried out the surprise element of something unexpected appearing for the first time on closing is minimised.

6.   A solicitor should not give or accept undertakings from a colleague where neither party is personally capable of performing them. Take the scenario where the solicitor is completing the purchase of a property on behalf of a client and the planning search he has commissioned on closing reveals a permission granted for an extension to the property of which the vendors' solicitor was unaware. He contacts the vendors, establishes that the extension was built, contacts the architect who supervised construction and establishes that the architect is prepared to give a certificate of compliance with planning permission and building regulations. Should the solicitor hand over the money, complete the purchase, and rely on an undertaking to furnish the certificate? What if the architect was subsequently unable to provide the certificate? It would be preferable to wait until the certificate is available for closing.

7.   A solicitor should not give undertakings in terms which are too general, such as to discharge a client's general indebtedness or to discharge any specific sum of money on behalf of a client, unless he has a clear picture of the sum involved and the funds are within his unlimited control.

8. If a solicitor is undertaking to furnish a good marketable title to a lending institution in a situation where the necessary funds have been provided to acquire a property, he should ensure that the client lodges funds to pay such things as stamp duty and registration fees as are necessary to enable the completion of the registration of the client's title and the security, as this is a fundamental element of the undertaking. Most borrowers are aware that the deeds do not have to be stamped for 30 days, but if the money is not available upfront, the solicitor is relying on a third party who may not perform.

9. A solicitor should not take over an undertaking given by a colleague without as full an investigation of the matter as they would carry out if they themselves had been giving the undertaking in the first place. See the Practice Note from the Guidance and Ethics Committee of November 2014 (Law Society *Gazette*).

The High Court emphasised the severe consequences that can attend on failure to comply with the terms of an undertaking. In the case of *AIB Plc v Maguire & ors* [2009] IEHC 374 (28 July 2009), AIB sued on foot of an undertaking given by a firm of solicitors in the usual terms in relation to the financing of a purchase. Peart J found as a matter of fact that the solicitor in question, who was not a partner of the firm, had deliberately breached the undertaking given. He then considered the previous case law in the area being the judgment of Geoghegan J in the Supreme Court in the case of *Bank of Ireland Mortgage Bank v Coleman* [2009] IESC 38 (5 May 2009), and in the judgment of Laffoy J in the High Court in the same case. (See [2006] IEHC 337 (6 November 2006).) Peart J summarised the principles that emerged from the *Coleman* case as follows:

1. The court has an inherent jurisdiction in matters concerning the conduct of solicitors, being officers of the court, including but not confined to compliance with their undertakings.

2. It is both a punitive and compensatory jurisdiction.

3. It is discretionary and unfettered in nature requiring each case to be considered on its own facts and circumstances.

4. In its exercise, the court is concerned to uphold the integrity of the system, and the highest standards of honourable behaviour by its officers—a standard higher than that required by law generally.

5. The order made by the court can take whatever form best serves the interests of justice between the parties.

6. In the matter of undertakings, the court must consider the entire undertaking in order to reach a conclusion as to its real ultimate purpose.

7. The court may order compliance with the undertaking, though late, where there remains a reasonable possibility of so doing.

8. Even where the undertaking may still be complied with, the court may nevertheless order the solicitor to make good any loss actually occasioned by the breach of undertaking, which may or may not be the entirety of the sum which was the subject of the undertaking.

9. Where compliance is not possible to achieve by the time the court is deciding what order, if any, to make, it may order the solicitor to make good any loss actually occasioned by the breach of undertaking.

10. Carelessness or other form of negligence on the part of the person affected by the undertaking, and in relation to the matter the subject thereof, may be a factor which the court will have regard to when determining what order may be fair and just.

11. Any order the court may make ought not be oppressive on the solicitor. Nevertheless, gross carelessness or other conduct considered sufficiently egregious by the court, though falling short of criminal behaviour or even professional misconduct, will entitle the court, should it consider it just to do so, to order payment of the

entire sum which was the subject of the undertaking, and not simply a lesser sum in respect of loss actually occasioned by the breach of undertaking.

To these principles Peart J added a further principle as follows:

12. 'The special supervisory jurisdiction being exercised by the Court in these matters is not unlike an equitable jurisdiction, given the wide discretionary nature thereof, and its objective of ensuring that justice is done between the parties in a broad sense. In my view, therefore, it seems to me that it is not inappropriate or otherwise wrong for a Court to have regard to the overall behaviour of the solicitor, somewhat akin to seeing whether a person who is claiming an equitable relief has come to court with clean hands, even where the undertaking may be still reasonably capable of being completed, and even where the loss actually occasioned and sustained by the claimant may be less than the entire sum which was the subject of the undertaking.'

Peart J went on to state that:

'In cases of deliberate, conscious or reckless breach of an undertaking by a solicitor, and not one resulting from mere mistake, oversight, inadvertence or other human frailty, a situation cannot be allowed to exist whereby the Court is seen to tolerate less than honourable and professional behaviour, by permitting a solicitor who has acted thus, egregiously, and in a way that is deliberate and utterly reprehensible, to simply walk away from that with permission to comply late with his undertaking, and pay whatever sum has resulted directly from the breach, and perhaps leave the other party with a substantial loss to bear. To my mind, such an order may be appropriate where the breach has been accidental or otherwise not deliberate, or through inadvertence or other human frailty, but that an egregious, deliberate and fundamental breach must be treated differently in order to take account of and mark its distinct character, and the court's absolute disapproval and condemnation thereof.

To do otherwise would be to fall short of what is necessary under the supervisory element of the Court's inherent jurisdiction—a jurisdiction which exists to uphold honourable conduct by solicitors—and would overly emphasise the compensatory element of the jurisdiction at the expense of the supervisory element of the jurisdiction.'

Peart J granted judgment **personally** against the solicitors named, ie the partners, in the amount of the funds drawn down, being some €3,000,000 together with any interest due to date of payment.

Peart J expressed sympathy for the predicament of the partners and specifically found that 'as soon as the defendants discovered the awful truth of what had happened they acted promptly, professionally and honourably in the only way they could'.

While this case specifically deals with the deliberate breaching of an undertaking, the principles previously listed are equally applicable to all undertakings furnished by a solicitor.

3.2.3 EXAMPLES

Some common examples that arise in giving and receiving undertakings are set out in this section. These are typically things that arise in the course of ordinary conveyancing transactions but ultimately also have an impact on the undertaking that is given to a lending institution.

3.2.3.1 To explain and discharge acts appearing on searches

This undertaking should never be given or accepted. Searches should be produced on closing and explained on the spot. What happens if this undertaking is given and it turns out that a charge of which the vendors' solicitor is unaware has been registered against the property, and there are no funds to discharge it? The purchasers' solicitor has already negotiated the funds but has not gained a clear title. He has breached his undertaking to his *client's* lender and purchased an encumbered title for his client.

3.2.3.2   To discharge Land Registry queries

This undertaking should never be given or accepted. The vendor's solicitor is paid to sell the title not to guarantee it. It is up to the purchaser's solicitor to get sufficient documentation on closing to enable him to complete registration of his client's title.

3.2.3.3   To discharge Land Registry mapping queries

This undertaking should never be given or accepted. This undertaking arises when a folio is being subdivided. Although great care may have been taken in commissioning the appropriate professional to prepare a map acceptable to the Land Registry for registration purposes, errors do occur. The best a solicitor should undertake is to use his best endeavours to assist with mapping queries as he is not qualified to redraw a map and is dependent on a third party.

3.2.3.4   Compulsory registration

The Conveyancing Committee of the Law Society has confirmed that a vendor's solicitor *is not* obliged to give an undertaking to discharge Land Registry queries in the context of compulsory registration. An undertaking should be given by the vendor pursuant to the provisions of general conditions 28 and 29 of the Law Society Contract for Sale.

3.2.3.5   To discharge an existing mortgage and furnish a release when received

This undertaking should never be given unless the solicitor has received definitive redemption figures from the lender. If the statement is provisional or hedged in any way then a solicitor leaves himself open to having to discharge any additional sums in order to comply with an undertaking to furnish a release of the mortgage. See the Practice Note published in the Law Society *Gazette* in November 1999.

3.2.3.6   To furnish a statutory declaration of the vendor

This undertaking, similar to the previous example regarding the architect's certificate, should never be given or accepted. All relevant declarations should be approved and agreed before closing and handed over on closing. A client could refuse to swear the declaration for some reason or due to unforeseen circumstances may be unable to sign on the dotted line.

3.2.3.7   To furnish a certificate of title

No money received by a solicitor from the lender should be handed over until the title to the property is received, save in the case of a property in the course of construction covered by HomeBond or Premier, whereby stage payments up to the limits covered by the HomeBond or Premier schemes can be released in advance of the title vesting in the borrowers. See the Practice Note published in the Law Society *Gazette* in April 1998.

A solicitor must consider carefully before he gives or accepts an undertaking, unless he is happy to discharge the obligation from his own personal funds.

3.2.3.8   To lodge net proceeds of sale

Guidelines in relation to giving undetakings to lodge net proceeds of sale are outlined in a Practice Note in August/September 2011 *Gazette*. In such undertakings the following issues should be addressed:

1. Has the full (and irrevocable) written authority of the client been obtained?

2. In a probate/administration case, what is to happen if the instructing executor/administrator dies?

3. Is the undertaking worded so as to apply only 'if and when the property is sold'?

4. Is the undertaking stated to be subject to the solicitor having carriage of sale and subject to the sale proceeds coming through the solicitor's office?

5. If the undertaking relates to the sale of property does the solicitor have possession of the title deeds and control of the deeds?

6. 'Net proceeds' should be clearly defined and quantified and the undertaking should be to pay the exact agreed figure rather than the 'net proceeds of sale'.

7. Do not give the undertaking where a sale has not already been agreed and carry out searches against the client and the property in advance of giving the undertaking.

3.2.3.9   Irish Banking Federation Undertakings

Four forms of undertaking were agreed between the Law Society and the Irish Banking Federation in the late 1970s and early 1980s. These were:

- Form 1—Inspection and Return of Documents.

- Form 2—Sale or Mortgage and Account for Net Proceeds.

- Form 3—Delivery of Deeds to Bank Following Purchase or Refinancing.

- Form 4—Bridging Finance.

Due to changes in banking practice the Conveyancing Committee recommended, in a Practice Note published in the August/September 2012 *Gazette*, that such undertakings should no longer be given.

3.2.4   RESTRICTIONS ON UNDERTAKINGS

The Solicitors (Professional Practice, Conduct and Discipline—Secured Loan Transactions) Regulations, 2009 (SI 211/2009) came into force on 1 September 2009. This restricts the giving of undertakings to mortgagees in secured loan transactions in which the solicitor, or a person closely connected, is beneficially interested. This restriction will apply unless the solicitor has given specified notice and the bank or other person has both acknowledged receipt of the notice and consented to the solicitor providing the undertaking. A solicitor cannot avoid the requirements of the Regulations by arranging his or her interests so that they are held through the means of a company, a partnership, or a trust. See the Practice Notes in the Law Society *Gazette* of July 2009 and August/September 2009.

The Solicitors (Professional Practice, Conduct and Discipline—Commercial Property Transactions) Regulations, 2010 (SI 366/2010) prohibit the giving of undertakings to lenders in commercial property transactions except in very limited circumstances. These regulations apply from 1 December 2010.

3.2.5   CONCLUSION ON UNDERTAKINGS

Undertakings bind the solicitor and his firm until they are discharged. Each firm should ensure that a system is put in place in the office alerting anybody who comes into contact with a file that there is an outstanding undertaking. This may take the form of a note written on the front of the physical file, a flagging system on the computer system, a central 'diary' of undertakings given and received by the firm, a monthly review of completed transactions to check compliance with undertakings, or all of the above. Each office will have a different practice but it is imperative that some system is in place. When sending documents to a third party discharging an undertaking the solicitor must be sure to include a request for an acknowledgement of the discharge of that undertaking.

3.3   Voluntary Conveyances

3.3.1   INTRODUCTION

Voluntary deeds are normally deeds between related parties where one owner transfers a property to another for 'natural love and affection'. There is no formal consideration in money terms paid. These deeds are perfectly valid but they are liable to be set aside. Voluntary conveyances are considered in **chapter 5** at **5.8.2**.

3.3.2   UNDUE INFLUENCE

Many practitioners are unaware that, in a voluntary transfer situation, there may be a presumption of undue influence in relation to the transaction. What this means is that if the transaction is challenged it fails unless the donee is in a position to rebut the presumption of undue influence. In itself the fact that there was no undue influence is not sufficient. The presumption must be rebutted.

Where a solicitor acts on both sides of a voluntary transfer, it has been held by the courts that, as he is not independent of either party, he cannot give evidence, which will rebut the presumption. Thus in order to rebut the presumption, independent advice, usually, but not necessarily, independent legal advice, must be obtained.

3.3.3   SIGNED ACKNOWLEDGEMENTS

Some solicitors get the donor to sign an acknowledgement that the donor has been offered independent advice but has declined the offer. This is not sufficient, as it does nothing to rebut the presumption of undue influence.

3.3.4   SETTING UP THE INDEPENDENT ADVICE

When organising the independent advice it is good practice to do a letter to the person giving the independent advice setting out all the facts relative to the transfer. In particular, the letter should set out details of the property being transferred (its market value based on a professional valuation), details of the donor's other assets, and full details of the family situation, identifying the educational and financial circumstances of each family member. When giving independent advice, a full attendance note should be done and this attendance note should be sent to the solicitor doing the transfer so that it can be stored on the main transfer file. By doing this the donor's solicitor is setting out that he has knowledge of all of the facts and it also shows that the person giving the independent advice has been made aware of these facts.

Undue influence is divided into categories—actual and presumed. Actual undue influence is where a person benefits from a transaction by influencing a donor into a course of action. In doing a voluntary transfer a solicitor should take all steps necessary to minimise the risk of actual undue influence. For example, the donee should not be present when the donor is instructing the solicitor in relation to the proposed transaction.

Presumed undue influence arises where there exists a relationship of trust and confidence between the parties. There has been no limit put on the range of relationships where the presumption might arise but case law has shown that transactions between family members are within this category. Elements which cause the presumption to arise are a significant imbalance in the relationship between the parties and any transaction which is under value and thus disadvantageous to the weaker party, while creating a substantial benefit for the stronger party. Where a donee derives a benefit from a donor with no particular benefit going to the donor, then the donee must be in a position to rebut the presumption of undue influence, if challenged, by establishing that the gift was a free exercise of the donor's will. It is not required that actual undue influence be expressly exercised or that the donor be mentally incapable, or that there be any improper conduct on the part of the donee.

The case *Carroll v Carroll* [1999] 4 IR 243, [2000] 1 ILRM 243 indicated that the reason the equitable law intervenes to protect a frail person is 'one of public policy'. The Supreme Court held in dismissing the appeal that the relationship between the donor and the donee was such as to raise a presumption that the donee had influence over the donor and that the onus was on the donee to establish that the transfer was the free exercise of the will of the donor. This presumption was not rebutted. Equity comes to the rescue whenever parties to a contract have not met on equal terms. The case of undue influence was upheld. It was stated that in the circumstances assiduous care should have been taken not to take advantage of Mr Carroll senior who gave away practically his sole asset (a pub and premises).

With regard to rebutting the presumption of undue influence in *Gregg v Kidd* (1956) IR 183 Budd J approved certain principles from the judgment of Farwell J in *Powell v Powell* [1900] 1 CH 243 as follows:

- a solicitor who acts for both parties cannot be independent of the donee in fact;

- to satisfy the court that the donor was acting independently of any influence from the donee and with full appreciation of what he was doing, it should be established that the gift was made after the nature and effect of the transaction had been fully explained to the donor by some independent and qualified person;

- further, the advice must be given with knowledge of all relevant circumstances and must be such as a competent advisor would give if acting solely in the interests of the donor.

These principles were also followed in *O'Carroll v Diamond*, High Court, 31 July 2002 (unreported) and Supreme Court [2005] 4 IR 41, [2005] 2 ILRM 219 where the defendant, a solicitor, found himself in difficulty.

The Conveyancing Committee of the Law Society issued a Practice Note in the December 2001 *Gazette* which dealt with the inherent dangerous and legal complexities involved in acting for a donor and donee in a voluntary transfer. The presumption of undue influence is merely the first hurdle. In all cases where a solicitor is acting for both parties in relation to a voluntary transaction the following practices should be followed:

- The clients should be seen separately.

- Should either the donor or donee be independently advised? A solicitor who has previously acted for a member of a family and who is asked to act for the first time for a prospective donor would do well to have the donor separately advised. Equally, a solicitor who has previously acted for the donor should consider advising the donee, in a situation where the transfer will impose obligations on the donee, to be independently advised. They should be advised in writing to obtain independent legal advice.

- All relevant family and family relationships should be noted.

- Full details of the donor's other assets must be obtained to decide whether the donor is in a financial position to carry out his desires.

- A decision on the donor's mental capacity must be taken. Is the proposal a free exercise of the donor's will or should medical opinion be sought?

- Does the donor's physical situation allow the gift to be made? What are his future requirements? Does the proposal put in jeopardy his financial independence? Does he appreciate the situation?

- Does the proposal imperil the financial independence of other members of the family? Have other members of the family been made promises or relied on arrangements, which will be affected by what is proposed? Do the proposals contradict any previous drawn wills or other documents?

- Is the solicitor aware from dealings with other members of the family that this proposal will surprise other family members?

- Does the donor need accommodation and maintenance?

- Are the full implications of the transaction understood? Even if independent advice is not required, care must be taken to explain the consequences of the proposed transaction to both donor and donee.

Careful notes of all attendances on both parties should be taken and kept. Full written advice should be given to both parties on all aspects of the transaction. Any documents requiring execution must be given to the parties in advance for perusal and must be read and explained to them.

In *Carroll v Carroll* [1999] 4 IR 243, [2000] 1 ILRM 243, referred to earlier, the transfer deed was not read to the transferor by the solicitor in question or by anybody else.

In view of the matters outlined in this section, care must be taken by practitioners to ensure that when instructed to act on behalf of both parties in relation to a voluntary transaction they will not be found guilty of negligence in a claim of undue influence.

3.3.5 CONTENT OF THE ADVICE

A recent Supreme Court decision, *Whelan & ors v Allied Irish Bank Plc & ors* [2014] IESC 3, provided a useful reminder of the law on the duties of a solicitor when giving advice, sometimes unwelcome, to a client. The relevant paragraph, 67, in the decision of O'Donnell J. is worth quoting at some length:

> '... it seems clear that the law has consistently and correctly held that an advisor such as a solicitor will owe a duty of care when giving advice to a client on an area within his or her expertise and where the request for the advice, and provision of it, is neither in casual circumstances nor entirely separate from the business then being transacted. It is not necessary that a client make very clear that the advice is critical to any decision which he or she might make, or that it be the sole or decisive factor. The obligation of a professional person is to give advice some of which may be unwelcome. Clients may be slow to appreciate advice, which they are paying for, but which warns them against a course of action which they wish to follow. The practice of law and other professions have developed considerably, and in many cases for the better, but there can be strong pressures on lawyers and other advisors to take a "commercial" view of matters, and to bring only the good news to a client. It remains very important that advisors give independent advice which, in an appropriate case, may counsel caution. The obligation to give independent and professional advice which is important not just to clients but to society more generally, is reinforced if solicitors and other advisors understand that they have a duty to be careful in the content of the advice which they give to clients.'

3.4 Acting for a Vulnerable Client

The Law Reform Commission Consultation Paper on The Law and the Elderly (LRC CP 23–2003) recommends that a potential reform option would be to create a category of agreements called 'care agreements' whereby a person gives property or other assets to another person in return for care in old age. It also proposed a new independent Office of Public Guardian to protect vulnerable adults and suggested that there could be an obligation on solicitors to inform the Office in any case where concerns arose and to inform the people concerned of the existence of the Office and the assistance it would provide.

The Consultation Paper recommends that detailed guidelines be considered to assist solicitors in dealing with financial and property transactions including gifts of property for vulnerable elderly people. These guidelines should be formulated in consultation with the proposed Office of the Public Guardian and should deal with the following issues:

1. Who is the client?

   Solicitors should not act for donor and donee unless the issue of conflict of interest is clearly explained and each agrees separately to use the same solicitor. Clients should be interviewed alone even if they wish to have another person present.

2. Is the gift appropriate in the client's circumstances?

   Clients are entitled to make inappropriate gifts provided this is done freely and with an informed understanding of the situation. The solicitor should find out as much as possible about the client's circumstances and try to establish *inter alia* if the gift is being made in the expectation that care will be provided. If so, can this arrangement be made legally enforceable? Are all details of care arrangements clarified between the parties? Is there provision for resolution of disputes?

3. Alternative measures.

   Solicitors should investigate whether the client's intentions could be equally well effected by making a will or an enduring power of attorney.

4. Record of advice.

   A record of instructions and advice given should be kept and a copy sent to the client.

5. Legal capacity.

   The solicitor should make an assessment of the legal capacity of the client and, if in doubt, should arrange for a medical assessment.

6. Office of the Public Guardian.

   The solicitor should inform the client of the existence of, and services provided by, the Office of Public Guardian.

The recent case of *Keating v Keating & Anor* [2009] IEHC 405 (24 August 2009) highlights the care that must be taken when dealing with a vulnerable client. In that case Laffoy J set aside the transfer of lands on the basis that it was an improvident transaction. The solicitor in that case acted on behalf of both sides. Of particular interest is that Laffoy J specifically found that the transfer was not procured by duress or undue influence. Laffoy J quoted with approval the decision of Peter Millett QC, as he then was, in *Alec Lobb (Garages) Ltd v Total Oil (Great Britain) Ltd* [1983] 1 WLR 87 (at pp 94/95) in which the essential pre-conditions for setting aside a transaction on the grounds of unconscionability were set out as follows:

> 'First, one party has been at a serious disadvantage to the other, whether through poverty, or ignorance, or lack of advice, or otherwise, so that circumstances existed of which unfair advantage could be taken. Second, this weakness of the one party has been exploited by the other in some morally culpable manner . . . And thirdly, the resulting transaction has not merely been hard or improvident, but overreaching and oppressive . . . In short, there must, in my judgment, be some impropriety, both in the conduct of the stronger party and in the terms of the transaction itself . . . which in the traditional phrase "shocks the conscience of the court" and makes it against equity and good conscience of the stronger party to retain the benefit of a transaction he has unfairly obtained.'

The case is somewhat complicated by the fact that there were also findings of forgery and assault as against the defendants, but on the key question Laffoy J found that the transaction was improvident on the part of the plaintiff and should be set aside.

The Law Society issued a Practice Direction in February of 2011 to the effect that firms should not act on both sides of property transactions where one party is vunerable. In particular they approved the following three guidelines:

1. A solicitor or firm of solicitors should not act for both parties to a property transaction where one or both of the parties is a vulnerable person.

2. Practitioners should note that the characteristics of vulnerability are not exhaustive and include a person who, by reason of age, infirmity, mental illness, mental

incapacity, or physical disability, lacks the ability to make an informed or independent decision regarding the acquisition or disposal of property.

3. A property transaction includes a mortgage, lease, transfer, disclaimer, release, easement, and any other disposition of property, otherwise than by will or *donatio mortis causa*, and also includes an enforceable agreement (whether conditional or unconditional) to make any of the foregoing dispositions.

This must now be read in conjunction with the prohibition on acting for both a vendor and purchaser or donor and donee, irrespective of vulnerability, outlined in **3.5.2**.

3.5   Conflicts of Interest

3.5.1   CONFLICTS OF INTEREST

A solicitor should give careful consideration to the difficulties and possible conflict of interest that may arise if both parties to a transaction require the same solicitor, or firm, to act. Prior to the certificate of title procedure referred to earlier, and which is dealt with in detail in **chapter 9**, a practice had emerged of certain lending institutions requiring the purchaser's solicitor to act for the lending institution as well as the purchaser in connection with his or her mortgage and security on the property being purchased. In so doing it became clear that a conflict of interest could arise and, accordingly, the current certificate of title procedure makes it clear that a purchaser's solicitor does not act for a lending institution as well as a purchaser but should merely represent the purchaser and certify the title on the basis of the normal conveyancing practice and procedures adopted on behalf of a purchaser.

A conflict of interest may arise if a spouse's prior consent is required for the sale or a mortgage of a property governed by the provisions of the Family Home Protection Act, 1976 as amended. It is imperative that the spouse who is asked to sign such a prior consent fully understands the nature and implication of what is being signed. The Supreme Court ruled in *Bank of Ireland v Smyth* [1996] 1 ILRM 241 that what is required in such cases is a fully informed consent. If there is any doubt in the matter such a spouse should be separately advised by another independent solicitor.

3.5.2   ACTING FOR BOTH PARTIES

The position since 1 January 2013 is set out in the Solicitors (Professional Practice, Conduct and Discipline—Conveyancing Confliction of Interest) Regulation, 2012 (SI 375/2012). As a general principle there is a total prohibition on a solicitor or a firm acting on both sides in a conveyancing transaction regardless of whether the transaction is a voluntary transfer or a transfer for value, subject to the following limited exceptions:

1. The transfer is the voluntary transfer of a family/shared home (as defined in the respective legislation) from the owner into the joint names of the owner and their spouse/civil partner (as defined in the respective legislation); note that the exception does not include the transfer from joint names into a sole name which will be a prohibited transaction.

2. The vendor and the purchaser are associated companies, as defined by s 432 of the Taxes Consolidation Act, 1997, or where one party is a company and the other is an individual who holds the entire issued equity share capital of that company.

3. Where the property is held under a bare trust and is being transferred by existing trustees to new trustees, or to a beneficiary.

4. In a transaction for value the parties are qualified parties under the Prospectus Directive (2003/71/EC) Regulations, 2005 (SI 324/2005).

The situation of acting for both parties in a given case which does not involve the transfer of property is dealt with by a Practice Note of the Guidance and Ethics Committee published in the March 2013 *Gazette*. This relates to the principles surrounding the use of socalled 'Chinese walls' within firms.

APPENDIX 3.1

Principles Relating to Undertakings

INTRODUCTION

Undertakings have become a very important aspect of the practice of law in the jurisdiction. In conveyancing, they are used to expedite matters which, in the absence of undertakings, would cause considerable delay and inconvenience to the client and the practitioner. The use of undertakings in litigation, particularly personal injury litigation, while perhaps ill-advised, has become widespread. The undertaking invades practically every area of practice and it is seen as unlikely that its use will be reduced.

From the point of view of the profession and their members, undertakings are to be viewed under two headings. Primarily, the undertakings may create a legal obligation upon the solicitor which is enforceable by, for example, mandatory injunction. The ability to enforce compliance is vested in the courts and the Society has no role. Secondly, the giving of an undertaking places on the solicitor an ethical obligation to comply with same. It is this area which concerns the Society, which has to date, and it is hoped for the foreseeable future, treated failure to comply as misconduct. To do otherwise, would considerably devalue undertakings.

Over the years, the Professional Guidance and Registrar's Committees have been obliged to deal with complaints against solicitors in respect of alleged failure to comply with undertakings. The profession at large are entitled to receive some guidance in relation to the topic of undertakings and are also entitled to receive some definite indications from the Society of its views. The long-standing rule 'undertakings are sacrosanct' can hardly be felt to be the definitive work on the subject. Over the years, the Society has issued to the profession guidelines, drafts, warnings and advice on the subject of undertakings. It is felt that it is reasonable that the profession receive from the Society general guidelines which can be applied to any undertaking rather than specific commentary on particularly unwise practices. In May and July of 1987, the newsletter gave exceedingly good advice to the profession and no doubt, in an effort to make sure it sank in, a substantial portion of the advice was repeated in September of the same year. Unfortunately, difficulties arise with regularity and it is presumed that this unhappy situation will continue.

The primary concern of the Professional Guidance Committee is to alert the profession to the requirement of having the client's prior authority before the issue of the undertakings. Of equal importance, the giver of the undertaking must be satisfied of his or her ability to comply with his undertaking and be alert to the outside agencies or events which may affect this ability. It is also felt necessary to alert the profession to the Society's role in relation to undertakings.

The proposed guidelines are merely a codification of the policy or philosophy of the Society in relation to undertakings and do not constitute a departure from present practice or imposition of new standards.

Thirteen principles, which are applicable to all undertakings, are set out in the following pages. It is felt that the principles as presented are clear and informative. Any further commentary may tie the hands of committees in particular cases and a certain amount of discretion and/or right of interpretation needs to be retained by the Society.

Some general comments follow the main text.

Niall Casey,
July 1996

PRINCIPLES

1.   Definition.

2.   Breach of undertaking is *prima facie* evidence of misconduct, consequently the Law Society can require implementation.

3.   Undertaking to be honoured as between giver and recipient only.

4.   If undertaking ambiguous, to be construed in favour of recipient.

5.   Undertaking does not have to constitute legal contract.

6.   Undertaking is binding even if outside solicitor's control.

7.   Solicitor is responsible for undertakings of staff.

8.   All partners responsible for all undertakings.

9.   Undertaking must be honoured even if breach of duty to client.

10.   If undertaking is contingent, must notify recipient if contingency fails.

11.   Court can enforce undertakings also, as solicitors are officers of the court.

12.   Undertaking not to be given as inducement to secure business.

13.   Undertaking which should not be given should not be sought.

PRINCIPLES RELATING TO PROFESSIONAL UNDERTAKINGS

1.   **An undertaking is any unequivocal declaration of intention addressed to someone who reasonably places reliance on it and made by a solicitor in the course of his practice, either personally or by a member of the solicitor's staff whereby the solicitor (or in the case of a member of his staff, his employer) becomes personally bound.**

Commentary

1.01   There is no obligation on a solicitor either to give or accept an undertaking, nor can a solicitor be required to stand guarantor for a client by way of an undertaking.

1.02   The Society does not recommend the giving or accepting of oral undertakings. Oral undertakings can lead to uncertainty as to the nature and extent of the undertaking. Evidential problems may arise. When oral undertakings are given, the lack of formality detracts from the gravity which should be attendant on the giving of any undertaking.

The Society recognises that an oral undertaking given by one person to another may be enforceable at law, but the Society will not render assistance to a party seeking to enforce that undertaking as a matter of conduct. (This commentary does not apply to oral undertakings given to a court.)

2.   **Failure by a solicitor to honour the terms of a professional undertaking is *prima facie* evidence of professional misconduct. Consequently, the Society will require its implementation as a matter of conduct.**

Commentary

2.01   The Society has no power to order payment of compensation or to procure the specific performance of an undertaking if a solicitor declines to implement it. The Society will proceed by way of disciplinary action for failure to honour the undertaking.

2.02   The Society will require an undertaking to be honoured by solicitors for so long as their names remain on the roll and regardless of whether they hold current practising certificates or not.

2.03 The Society has no power to order the release of a solicitor from the terms of an undertaking. This is a matter for the court, or the person entitled to the benefit of the undertaking.

3. **An undertaking will normally be required to be honoured only as between the giver and the recipient.**

Commentary

3.01 The Society will normally require compliance with an undertaking only at the instance of a recipient.

3.02 A solicitor cannot assign the burden of an undertaking (and thus claim to be released from its terms) without the express approval of the recipient.

4. **An ambiguous undertaking is generally construed in favour of the recipient.**

5. **An undertaking does not have to constitute a legal contract to be enforceable in conduct.**

Commentary

5.01 No consideration is necessary for an undertaking to be enforceable in conduct.

6. **An undertaking is still binding even if it is to do something outside the solicitor's control.**

Commentary

6.01 Before giving any undertaking a solicitor must carefully consider whether it will be possible to implement it. It is no defence to a complaint of professional misconduct that the undertaking was to do something outside the solicitor's control.

7. **A solicitor is responsible for honouring an undertaking given by a member of the solicitor's staff, whether admitted to the Roll of solicitors or not.**

Commentary

7.01 Where an assistant solicitor gives an undertaking, the conduct of the assistant may also be called into question by the Society.

8. **Where a solicitor in partnership gives an undertaking as a solicitor in the course of practice, all partners are responsible for its performance.**

Commentary

8.01 A partner remains responsible for the firm's undertakings even after that solicitor leaves the firm or the partnership is dissolved.

9. **A solicitor cannot avoid liability on an undertaking by pleading that to honour it would be a breach of duty owed to the client.**

Commentary

9.01 Since a solicitor will be personally bound to honour his undertakings, it is essential for the solicitor's protection that the client's authority to do so is given before the undertaking is furnished.

10. **A solicitor who gives an undertaking which is expressed to be dependent upon the happening of a future event must notify the recipient immediately if it becomes clear that the event will not occur.**

11. **In addition to the Society's power to enforce undertakings as a matter of conduct, the court, by virtue of its inherent jurisdiction over its own officers, has power of enforcement in respect of undertakings.**

Commentary

11.01　Where undertakings are given by solicitors to the court, the Society takes the view that enforcement is a matter for the court; for this reason the Society will not normally intervene.

12.　**An undertaking should not be given by a solicitor as an inducement to a client to secure that client's business.**

13.　**The seeking by a solicitor of an undertaking from another solicitor which the first solicitor knows, or ought to know, should not be given, may be deemed to be professional misconduct.**

3.2　GENERAL COMMENTS ON PRECEDING PRINCIPLES

1.　This principle is a general definition of undertakings. It is important to emphasise that the solicitor is personally liable on foot of the undertaking and it is hoped consequently that he would consider initially whether he has control of compliance and secondly, what conditions should be inserted to protect himself against frustration by outside agencies or events. An undertaking, however ill-advised, is still an undertaking, and the fact that there is no possibility of the giver being in a position to comply with the same should not prevent the recipient who relied upon it from maintaining a complaint.

The Society's view in relation to oral undertakings should be noted in particular. Oral undertakings are recognised in law and will be enforced by the courts. However, the Society wishes to promote the better practice of always seeking a written undertaking. The Society's policy now, is not to assist the enforcement of oral undertakings as a matter of conduct.

2.　This principle merely confirms the position that 'undertakings are sacrosanct'. It also clarifies the Society's position by advising that failure to comply may be deemed to be misconduct but we cannot enforce implementation. The principle is required so as to impress upon the profession the serious view taken by the Society of a solicitor's obligations arising from undertakings.

3.　Undertakings are not a saleable commodity and the Society is anxious to prevent complaints by parties who may have a consequential interest in performance of the solicitor's obligation but were not the receivers of the undertaking.

4.　The Committee has had several cases where two, or indeed more, interpretations could be given to an undertaking. It is intended to alert the profession that in the event of same occurring, the interpretation most favourable to the recipient will be preferred. This is merely inserted to prevent reconstruction by the giver of the undertaking in an effort to avoid the liability or obligation arising thereunder.

5.　This principle is inserted to alert the profession to the fact that while the legal pre-requisites of a contract may be absent from the undertaking, compliance with the terms of same may be required by the Society as a matter of conduct. It prevents the giver of an undertaking avoiding compliance by arguing that it was not a legally enforceable contract. It was felt, that this principle retains within the Society the right to expect of the profession standards of ethics and conduct beyond those which may be enforceable in a court of law.

6.　This principle is inserted to clarify the obligations of the giver of an undertaking. It should also alert the giver to the dangers of flippant or ill-advised undertakings. It is hoped that the profession will think before they dictate the undertaking and that they will consider its contents carefully when they are proof-reading the resulting document.

7.　This principle is inserted to impress upon the members their vicarious liability for undertakings given in their name. It is hoped that it will alert the profession to the necessity of good practice management in relation to the stringent regulation of the giving of undertakings and alert the membership to the obligation of ensuring that all members of staff are aware of the serious nature of same. It restates the solicitor's obligation to properly supervise staff and it is hoped will prevent undertakings which are ill-advised 'sneaking out' from the firm.

8. This principle is self-explanatory and highlights the fact that the motto of the three musketeers has its drawbacks as well as its advantages.

9. An undertaking given by a solicitor is personal to that solicitor and is not subject to the whim of the client. The recipient who has placed reliance on it, cannot be frustrated by subsequent events affecting the client of the giver which events are entirely beyond the control of the recipient. The principle highlights the absolute necessity of obtaining the client's authority and explaining to the client the solicitor's own obligations which arise from same. It should discourage the flippant giving of undertakings.

10. This principle is self-explanatory and is there to extend to the recipient of an undertaking a courtesy to which the recipient is entitled.

11. This principle is self-explanatory, although it is felt that should the court make a complaint to the Society on foot of a non-compliance, the Society would not be precluded from considering such a complaint.

12. This principle is self-explanatory.

13. This principle is self-explanatory.

In the foregoing, the words 'Society', 'profession' and 'membership' are interchangeable. The Society merely represents the profession and all their members and the principles as drafted are considered to be for the benefit of all. They give guidance to the profession on the topic of undertakings in general.

This appendix is reproduced with permission of Niall Casey.

CHAPTER 4

TITLE

4.1 Introduction

A person who is either disposing of or acquiring a property generally describes their disposal or acquisition as the purchase/sale of a house, a factory, a farm, etc. In legal terms what that person is doing is disposing of or acquiring a particular title to the property in question. The nature of the title being disposed of or acquired may vary from a simple weekly tenancy to a full unencumbered fee simple. In between those two extremes of title may be a variety of different types, eg short leaseholds, long leaseholds, fee farm grant interests, life estates, leases for lives renewable forever, etc. Some of the titles concerned may impose severe restrictions on the use of the property or may impose substantial conditions on the person holding the current interest in the property, eg there may be a very severe repairing clause imposed upon a lessee in a leasehold title. Irrespective of the nature of the title to the property, a conveyancer is obliged to ensure that what is being disposed of and what is being acquired is a good marketable title (see **4.4**).

4.2 What is 'Title'?

'Title' is essentially the evidence of the ownership of a person to an estate in property. In the case of unregistered land it takes the form of a deed or series of deeds and other documents. With registered land it consists of a folio.

A vital point in understanding title and conveyancing is that a person's title to property provides evidence of ownership, not of the property itself, but of that person's interest or estate in the property. We know from land law that several legal estates can exist in the same piece of property at the same time. Take the example of a person, A, who holds the fee simple estate in a piece of property. A grants a lease of this property to B for 900 years. There are now two people with an interest in the property. This does not cause any difficulties as they both own different estates in the same property. A is the freehold owner and B is the leasehold owner. But in everyday language, who can we say 'owns' the property? A non-conveyancer may say that the freehold owner is the true owner as B only has a lease. But the lease is for 900 years and there is little chance of A getting the property back in their lifetime. Possession of the property rests with B for 900 years and this is the much more valuable interest. So should we say that B is the 'owner' of the property as they hold the more valuable interest?

The correct legal answer is that neither A nor B 'owns' the property because in our legal system no one actually 'owns' property at all. All that A and B 'own' is an 'estate' in the property. A 'owns' the fee simple estate and B 'owns' the leasehold estate. Each estate has rights and obligations attaching to it. B's leasehold estate carries the right for B to keep possession of the property for the length of the lease, but also obliges B to comply with the covenants and conditions contained in the lease including the payment of a rent to A.

A's fee simple estate carries the right for A to receive the rent and have the covenants and conditions performed by B but obliges A to allow B to have possession of the property for the term of the lease.

'Title' is therefore evidence of a person's ownership of a particular estate in property.

4.3   Good Title

If a vendor can satisfactorily prove to a purchaser that they are the legal owner of a certain estate in property we can say that the vendor has a 'good title' to that property. Essentially the concept of a good title rests on the root of title (see **4.7.1**). However, the quality of the estate itself is a different matter. In our previous example, B held the property on foot of a 900-year lease. If 895 years of the term had elapsed we could say that B had good title to the leasehold estate of the property. However, the quality of that estate would not be very good as B is only entitled to possession of the property for a further five years, after which the lease runs out and the property reverts to A, the owner of the fee simple estate.

From a conveyancing perspective what a purchaser wants to acquire is not merely a good title to the property but what is known as a 'good marketable title' to the property.

4.4   Good Marketable Title

4.4.1   GENERALLY

A 'good marketable title' is a term adopted over many years and is understood by conveyancers to mean the standard of title which is given and accepted by conveyancers following what are regarded as good conveyancing rules and practice. There is no statutory definition of a good marketable title and hence conveyancers have determined their own code of practice supported by the views of the courts as to what constitutes a good marketable title.

The introduction by the Law Society of a standard Contract for Sale, standard requisitions on title, practice recommendations on issues that arise in practice from time to time, and the preparation of standard documentation dealing with the provisions of the Family Home Protection Act, 1976, as amended, have been decisive matters in establishing an acceptable balancing of the conflicting rights that arise between vendors and purchasers. These documents, when used in conjunction with such statutory provisions as there are, dealing with the length of title to be furnished, have established a clearly understood concept of what is a good marketable title in modern conveyancing.

Most conveyancers will come across the phrase 'good marketable title' in the context of the certificate of title system used for residential conveyancing and which is detailed in the next section.

4.4.2   CERTIFICATES OF TITLE

In residential conveyancing matters the approved form of certificate of title (being the 2011 edition approved by the Law Society) states that a good marketable title within that system means a title of a quality commensurate with prudent standards of current conveyancing practice in Ireland. These standards require, *inter alia*, that the purchase be effected on foot of the current Law Society Contract for Sale and/or Building Agreement. They also require that the investigation of title to the property is made in accordance with the current Law Society Requisitions on Title together with any additional requisitions appropriate to the property and that satisfactory replies have been received. Where the property is already owned by the borrower, title shall be so investigated that if the said requisitions had been raised, satisfactory replies would have been obtained.

In the guidelines issued with the certificate of title, it is stated at paragraph 7 that title must be:

- freehold; or

- leasehold with an unexpired term of at least 70 years (unless a statutory right to purchase the fee simple exists);

- if Land Registry leasehold it must be either absolute or good leasehold (see **4.9.4**).

The certificate goes on to provide that any dispute with regard to the quality of any title (within the foregoing definitions) may be referred for a ruling to the Conveyancing Committee of the Law Society but without prejudice to the right of either party to seek a determination by the court on the issue. Thus, within conveyancing of residential property using the certificate of title system, there is a facility whereby any dispute may be dealt with, if agreed between the parties, without going to court. The alternative in residential conveyancing and in any other type of conveyancing is to go to court on foot of a vendor and purchaser summons. This is a summons issued under the provisions of s 55 of the Land and Conveyancing Law Reform Act, 2009 ('the 2009 Act') which enables parties to go to court for a ruling where a dispute has arisen under the terms of the contract in respect of the title and it is a relatively quick and cheap way of resolving any disputes. The appendix to **chapter 9** on mortgages reproduces the certificate of title documentation.

4.4.3   COURTS OF EQUITY

The ultimate test as to what is a good marketable title is that a court of equity will not enforce a contract against a purchaser unless the vendor makes out and shows a good marketable title in accordance with the contract. The courts of equity will not force a purchaser to take a bad title. It is a well-settled principle that, in so far as the enforcement of a contract for a sale of property is concerned, a purchaser is entitled to a good title and that, accordingly, a vendor must give one and that, in addition, a vendor must make out or show his or her title. This broad principle has been stated by judges over the years in different cases. For example in *Re Flynn and Newman's Contract* [1948] IR 104, Kingsmill Moore J stated:

> 'in the absence of any express provision to the contrary the vendor undertakes and is bound in law to show a good title to the property to be sold and to convey land corresponding substantially in all respects with the description contained in the contract'.

Whether this right arises as an implied term of the contract or exists as a rule of law was at one stage considered to be of some consequence but the distinction now seems to be purely academic.

4.5   Open Contracts

The many statutory provisions and common law rules relating to the title to be shown on a sale relate mainly to open contracts. An open contract is one which does not contain any restrictions on the purchaser's right to investigate the title of the vendor. This is very rare in practice and usually arises where an enforceable contract has been entered into without legal advice. A good example would be the proverbial 'contract written on the back of an envelope'. This usually arises where a court finds that there is sufficient evidence of the contract available in writing to satisfy the provisions of s 51 of the 2009 Act. The decision of the Supreme Court in *Boyle v Lee* [1992] 1 IR 555 delivered on 12 December 1991, discussed further in **chapter 2**, in which the court fully reviewed the manner in which the Statute of Frauds (Ireland) Act, 1695 should be applied, makes it even less likely that an open contract will be encountered in practice.

A closed contract will limit what title the purchaser can investigate.

The duty to provide, and the entitlement to receive, a good marketable title is said to have two aspects:

(a) to *show* good title in the sense of stating all matters essential to the title contracted to be sold; and

(b) to *make* good title in the sense of proving by proper evidence those matters.

The full force of this duty arises only in open contracts. In everyday conveyancing a vendor's solicitor will restrict the purchaser's enquiry into the title being offered and, in some very limited circumstances, may in fact exclude the purchaser's normal right by appropriate conditions in the Contract for Sale. This is a practice which should create no difficulty provided that the vendor's solicitor imposes conditions on the purchaser's solicitor's right to investigate the title in terms which are considered to be fair and reasonable and which are not fraudulent or ambiguous. If in fact conditions are inserted which are considered by the courts to be unduly onerous, then the contract will be construed against the vendor and specific performance will be refused.

4.5.1 STATUTORY PROVISION GOVERNING OPEN CONTRACTS

4.5.1.1 Generally

There were old common law rules that a good root of title must be at least 60 years old. These common law rules were first amended by the Vendor and Purchaser Act, 1874 and then by the Conveyancing Act, 1881. These Acts reduced the period of time to 40 years for freeholds and introduced special rules for leaseholds.

The current statutory position is to be found in Part 9 of the 2009 Act.

4.5.1.2 Land and Conveyancing Law Reform Act, 2009

Section 56:

1. reduces the period of title a purchaser may call for in an open contract to 15 years;

2. provides that where the title commences with a fee farm grant or a lease, the grant or lease must be produced;

3. confirms that these provisions apply only to an open contract.

Section 57:

1. provides that under a contract to grant or assign a tenancy or subtenancy of land, the intended grantee, ie tenant, is not entitled to call for the fee simple or any tenancy out of which the subtenancy is to be derived;

2. on a contract to grant a tenancy or subtenancy for a term exceeding five years, the intended grantee may call for a copy of the conveyance or in the case of a subtenancy a copy of the superior lease out of which the tenancy is to be immediately derived. Where the tenancy is granted for full market rent, the grantee may also call for 15 years' title as a purchaser under s 56(1);

3. no preliminary contract for or relating to the tenancy forms part of the title for the purposes of deducing that title;

4. this subsection abolishes what was known as the rule in *Patman v Harland* (1881) 17 Ch D 353, by providing that a purchaser is not affected by notice of any matter or thing which exists in the title which subsection (1) prevents them from seeing;

5. subsections (1) and (2) take effect subject to the terms of any contract for the grant or assignment of the tenancy.

It must be emphasised that these provisions relate only to open contracts. In the normal course of events a formal Law Society Contract for Sale will be entered into dealing with the length of title being offered, ie a closed contract.

4.6   Defective Titles

It should also be remembered that a condition in the contract restricting investigation of a particular part of a vendor's title does not relieve the vendor from disclosing latent defects in title of which the vendor is, or ought to have been, aware. Furthermore, s 60 of the 2009 Act makes it both a criminal offence and a civil wrong actionable in damages by the purchaser or persons deriving title under him or her for the vendor or his or her solicitor or other agent to conceal *with intent to defraud* from the purchaser any instrument or encumbrance material to the title or to falsify any pedigree upon which the title may depend in order to induce the purchaser to accept the title offered or produced.

It must be remembered that there will always be titles which fall short both in their nature and documentation of what would normally be sought and given. One of the prime examples of this type of title is what is known as a 'squatters' title', ie a title acquired under the Statute of Limitations, 1957 where somebody has entered into possession of a property adverse to the owner's title and occupied it for more than 12 years without acknowledging the true owner's title. In such a case, if the vendor is proposing to dispose of the interest that he or she has established in the property, he or she will have no documentary evidence whatsoever other than providing a statutory declaration made by himself or herself and any other party who may have knowledge of the length and nature of his or her occupation. In very many cases he or she may not even be able to establish the nature of the title that he or she is barring. In such a case, if a vendor fairly discloses all the facts surrounding the nature of the title he or she is offering for sale, and if a purchaser, having been given all of the relevant information, contracts to purchase such an interest, then the courts will enforce the contract.

Likewise, while good conveyancing practice insists upon a title starting with a good root of title (a concept which is dealt with later), it is always open to a purchaser to accept what is considered to be a bad root of title. In considering this proposition it is important to distinguish between a valid deed and a defective deed. A bad root of title may of itself be a perfectly valid deed but for other reasons which are explained later is not acceptable as a good root. In a leading case on this point, *Marsh v Earl of Granville* (1882) 24 Ch D 11, it was stated in the contract that the title to a certain freehold property would commence with a deed of conveyance less than 40 years old. After the contracts had been exchanged and title furnished it transpired that the deed referred to was a voluntary deed, ie one in which there was no valuable consideration paid for the transfer of ownership, but this was not stated in the contract. It was held in that case that the purchaser was justified in refusing to complete and was entitled to assume, as nothing had been stated to the contrary in the contract, that the deed was a conveyance for value which would have been accepted as a good root of title.

Accordingly, if intending to furnish a contract starting with a document which would be classified as a bad root of title then the nature of that document should be clearly specified in the special conditions of the contract so that the proposed purchaser is put on full notice of the nature and content of it.

4.7   Roots of Title

4.7.1   INTRODUCTION

All titles must start somewhere. For a leasehold title it can be simply stated that title starts with the lease itself. However, where does a freehold title start?

In theory one could trace a modern freehold title back through the feudal titles of free and common socage, frankalmoigne or perhaps even knight's service, and ultimately back to a Crown grant of lands by Henry II sometime in the twelfth century. However, it would obviously be unfair to ask a vendor to produce the freehold title from the twelfth century to the present. Instead it is accepted that if a vendor can produce a deed which has certain characteristics, this will be acceptable as the root, or beginning, of the title on offer. The concept of a good title essentially hangs on the quality of the root of title offered and its age.

A good root of title is the document from which the vendor proposes to show that his or her title starts. The rest of his or her title from that time onwards is literally rooted in that document. It is accordingly an essential prerequisite to a good marketable title that what has become accepted as a good root of title is used by a vendor to commence his or her title.

The rules set out in the following paragraph relating to roots of title arise for unregistered titles where the title is based on a series of sequential documents. The 'root of title' for registered titles will, in effect, be the folio. If a registered freehold title is based on a fee farm grant then this must also be produced or if it is a leasehold folio then the lease must be produced.

4.7.2 DEFINITION

There is no statutory definition of a 'good root of title'. The 2009 Act chooses not to offer a definition while using the phrase itself; see s 56. Many years of conveyancing practice and court decisions have laid down the guidelines which must be followed in identifying a good root.

One of the classic textbooks, *Williams on Title* (4th edn), p 574, gives a good definition of what is required in a good root of title which covers all the essential ingredients as follows:

> 'a document purporting to deal with the entire legal and equitable estate and interest in the property, not depending for its validity upon any previous instrument, and containing nothing to throw any suspicion on the title of any of the disposing parties'.

This can be divided up into the following requirements:

1. a document or instrument of disposition;

2. dealing with the ownership of the whole legal and equitable estate in the property sold;

3. without the aid of extrinsic evidence; and

4. showing nothing to cast a doubt on the title of the disposing parties.

We can also add the following additional requirements that:

5. it must contain a description by which the property can be identified; and

6. it must be of a certain age.

4.7.3 BASIC PRINCIPLE

The basic principle involved in selecting the appropriate type of deed suitable to constitute a good root is that any investigation of the title by a purchaser's solicitor will establish that the title is a good title and the contract would thus be enforced by the courts. In relation to bad roots of title, these would perhaps be deeds or documents in which no prior investigation of title would have taken place, say, for example, a voluntary deed where there was no valuable consideration passing, or a deed which relied upon the content and existence of an earlier document for its validity. An example would be a deed of assent which relies on the grant of representation or a conveyance under a power of sale.

It should always be remembered that the purpose of the root of title is to establish the nature of the title/what the title on offer is, ie freehold or leasehold, registered or unregistered. Subsequent deeds merely transfer ownership of that same title; they do not change it.

4.7.4 AGE OF ROOTS OF TITLE

The next important matter to be considered in connection with roots is their age.

4.7.4.1 Law Society guidelines

The Law Society Conveyancing Committee previously recommended that, in general, a minimum period of 20 years' title should be provided and sought in closed contracts. This means that the root of title should be at least 20 years old and comply with the definition of a 'good root of title' detailed earlier in this chapter. In many cases it will be necessary, because of the nature of the title being dealt with, to start with a root that is much older than 20 years. This Law Society recommendation of 20 years' title being shown leaves practitioners in the somewhat unusual position that a purchaser on an open contract is entitled to less title than that they might expect to obtain in a closed contract. Because of this, it is anticipated that, based on the provisions of ss 56 and 57 of the 2009 Act, the Law Society recommended period will be reduced to 15 years, but no such formal recommendation has yet been made. As a matter of standard practice, however, conveyancers are now accepting 15 years' title unless there is some reason to seek a longer period.

4.7.4.2 Current practice

The basic reason for adopting the 20-year rule was the frequency with which property changes hands compared to the situation in 1874 and 1881 when the previous Acts relating to open contracts were passed. With the huge increase of the development of urban land which took place in Ireland in the 1950s and 1960s and which continues to this day, it became commonplace for large tracts of land for housing and for commercial use to be developed. Each such tract of land would have a single title from which the title for each individual property was carved. Such titles were read and accepted by a substantial number of different solicitors acting for each individual purchaser as well as the solicitors acting for each lending institution who advanced money on the security of each title. Thus, each such title was scrutinised many times and, if any defects were found, such defects were corrected at that time. As the properties and the titles aged it was felt that adherence to a longer period was unnecessary.

Accordingly, in order to simplify conveyancing practice and to reduce the volume of paperwork each time a property changed hands, the period of time to be shown for the root gradually shortened to the recommended 20 years. This was a *recommended period only* and had no force of law although it did have the support of the Law Society's Conveyancing Committee as good practice in modern conveyancing. As already stated practitioners are now adhering to a 15-year period as a matter of practice in line with the provisions of the 2009 Act.

It should also be noted that on a subsequent application for first registration in the Land Registry, under rule 18 of the Land Registry Rules 2012, no evidence of title shall be called for that could not be required on a sale of the property under an open contract. As we have seen this period is now 15 years under s 56 of the 2009 Act. However, as a conveyancer gains experience they will be better able to assess those titles where it is advisable to go beyond the recommended 15-year period.

4.7.4.3 Leases and fee farm grants

With a leasehold or fee farm grant (a hybrid freehold containing many of the characteristics of a leasehold), title always starts with the original lease or fee farm grant irrespective of how old it is as the purchaser will be bound by the covenants and conditions contained in it. The purchaser will always want to know what these are even if the deed is 500 or 900 years old as they will be bound by them. If it is necessary to go back for a substantial period of time to find a good root, the vendor of a leasehold title is then entitled to skip to an assignment for value or, if freehold (ie a fee farm grant), the vendor can skip to a conveyance for value more than 15 years old. The document skipped to is called the document from which title is deduced.

There is no need to investigate the title during the intervening period, ie the skipped period, as title will be deduced from this more recent assignment or conveyance. The intervening title is known as intermediate title.

The title intervening between the root and the subsequent deed for value (the document from which title is deduced) is not investigated, nor are any of those deeds furnished to the purchaser's solicitor during the course of the transaction. Instead this intermediate title is handed over on closing on a without prejudice basis. The object of this skipping is to reduce as much as possible the necessity to investigate unnecessarily all of the title prior to contracts being exchanged. The reason to skip to a deed for value more than 15 years old is on the understanding and belief that the purchaser's solicitor at that time would have investigated the intervening title.

If the title is based on a lease for lives renewable forever that has been converted to a fee farm grant under the Renewable Leasehold Conversion Act, 1849, then the lease for lives is where the title must start and not the fee farm grant, as the covenants and conditions in the lease are grafted onto the grant and are preserved. This means that the covenants and conditions are carried forward and in effect incorporated into the fee farm grant.

If the lease for lives is dated earlier than 1 August 1849 and has not been converted under the 1849 Act, it is automatically converted to a freehold title under the Landlord and Tenant (Amendment) Act, 1980, s 74 and that freehold title is deemed to be a graft on the previous interest and is subject to any rights or equities arising from its being such a graft. In such a title, the lease for lives will be the starting point for the title.

Section 12 of the 2009 Act now prohibits the creation of fee farm grants at law or in equity. The effect of a deed which purports to create a fee farm grant or a lease for lives renewable forever or for any period which is perpetually renewable is that it vests in the purported grantee or lessee a legal fee simple or as the case may be an equitable fee simple, and any contract for such a grant entered into after the commencement will operate as a contract for such vesting. Existing fee farm grants and contracts to grant one which pre-date the commencement of the Act, 1 December 2009, will not be affected. Section 12(3) provides that any such fee simple when vested 'is freed and discharged from any covenant or other provision relating to rent but all other covenants or provisions continue in force so far as consistent with the nature of a fee simple'.

Section 14 of the 2009 Act also provides that the grant of a lease for a life or lives and any contract for such a grant made after its commencement will be void both at law and in equity.

4.7.5 EXAMPLES

4.7.5.1 Good roots

The following documents are examples of, and have become accepted as being, good roots of title:

(a) where land is vested by the Crown (pre-1922) or by an Act of the Oireachtas;

(b) a conveyance or a lease for value;

(c) a sealed and certified copy Land Registry folio with title absolute;

(d) a landed estates court conveyance;

(e) a settlement in consideration of marriage;

(f) an ante-nuptial settlement, the consideration being marriage;

(g) a legal mortgage in fee simple;

(h) a fee farm grant (distinguished from a fee farm conversion grant) (see **4.7.4.3**);

(i) a fee farm conversion grant converted under the Renewable Leasehold Conversion Act, 1849 converting a lease for lives into a freehold title. Note that this form of grant was previously considered to be a bad root as it relied for its validity upon the converted lease but, in modern conveyancing practice, it is now generally accepted as a good root, particularly if the original lease for lives is available. However, in a substantial number of cases these leases for lives are not available, but because of their antiquity and if the property concerned has been used for the same purpose for a substantial number of years without any notices from the grantor, they are generally accepted; and

(j)   a specific devise in a will of a person who died prior to 1 June 1959. Note that this form of root is not acceptable for any person who died on or after 1 June 1959. The Administration of Estates Act, 1959 provided that, on or after 1 June 1959 a written assent to a beneficiary in a will is required. Thus after 1 June 1959 what is required is not one, but three documents, namely a specific devise in a will, the grant of representation, and the subsequent assent from the personal representative in favour of the beneficiary.

4.7.5.2   Bad roots

The following is a non-exhaustive list of examples of bad roots of title:

(a)   general devise in a will;

(b)   voluntary conveyance;

(c)   deed of appointment of trustees;

(d)   conveyance under a power of sale;

(e)   post-nuptial settlement;

(f)   post-1959 will on its own;

(g)   possessory title in the Land Registry;

(h)   legal mortgage by demise;

(i)   disentailing deed; and

(j)   deed of assignment.

4.8   The Chain of Title

The 'chain of title' is the term used to describe all of the connected acts and events on a title from the root of title down to the document or event that vested the ownership of the property in the current vendor. This chain of title may consist of a variety of documents or events, eg conveyances or assignments, wills, grants of representation, assents, court orders, transfers, deaths, bankruptcies, liquidations, etc. These documents should provide evidence of an unbroken chain of ownership, starting with the root of title and ending with the current vendor.

However, a vendor is not always obliged to produce the entire chain of title from the root. As noted earlier at **4.7.4.3** special rules apply to cases involving a leasehold title, or that of a fee farm grant. These rules are synopsised in the next paragraph.

4.8.1   DEVOLUTION OF UNREGISTERED TITLE FROM THE ROOT

4.8.1.1   Devolution of a leasehold or fee farm grant title from the root

We know that the root of title will always be the lease, or the fee farm grant, no matter how old it is, as the terms, conditions, and covenants contained therein will always continue to affect the subject property. However, it is considered unfair on a vendor to have to produce the whole chain of title, particularly when the root may be several hundred years old. Instead the vendor is entitled to skip to a second document, eg a conveyance or assignment for value at least 15 years old, from which the chain of title can then be shown. This is the document from which title is deduced.

Ideally any such document should have the characteristics of a good root of title as described earlier at **4.7.2**. In particular a purchaser would want such a document to be at least 15 years old so that they can rely on the contents thereof due to the provisions of s 59 of the 2009 Act, the relevant part of which reads as follows:

> *Recitals, statements and descriptions of facts, matters and parties contained in instruments, statutory provisions or statutory declarations 15 years old at the date of the contract are, unless and except so far as they are proved to be inaccurate, sufficient evidence of the truth of such facts, matters and parties.*

A document which is less than 15 years old is likely to meet with an objection that its recitals do not prove themselves by virtue of the section and thus this puts the onus on the purchaser's solicitor to seek further evidence of such recitals.

4.8.1.2   Devolution of a freehold title from the root

Where the title consists of a series of conveyances, ie there is no fee farm grant, there is no need to skip and the root of title will be a conveyance for value more than 15 years old. This will also be the document from which title is deduced.

4.9   Registered Titles

4.9.1   GENERALLY

The foregoing observations in respect of roots and lengths of title apply mainly in respect of unregistered titles, ie titles which are in the Registry of Deeds system and are not in the Land Registry system. We saw in **chapter 1** that it is a fundamental principle of the Land Registry system that the State guarantees the title registered and relieves the purchaser from having to carry out any further investigation. At **4.7.5.1** a Land Registry folio with title absolute was given as an example of a good root of title. The classes of title that are registered in the Land Registry are covered in detail in **chapters 13** and **14** and **4.9.4**. In respect of two of these classes, namely absolute freehold and absolute leasehold, the earlier observations in respect of roots of title and lengths of title have no application. The effect of the registration of these two classes of title is as later stated and a conveyancer is spared any further investigation beyond what is stated on the register *irrespective of the date of registration of the registered owner*. The 15-year rule has no relevance and one is entitled to rely on the register without looking behind it and the State guarantee that the register is correct.

However, there are certain circumstances where a conveyancer must look behind the folio to satisfy themselves fully that a good marketable title has been shown.

4.9.2   THE REGISTERS

The Land Registry maintains three registers:

- freehold;
- leasehold;
- subsidary.

Freehold and leasehold are self-explanatory. The subsidiary register deals with such matters as rentcharges, fee farm rents, and fishing rights. This subsidiary register is rarely encountered in practice and is not considered here in any detail but the same principles apply to it as to the other registers.

4.9.3   CLASSES OF OWNERSHIP

The Land Registry can register a person with different classes of ownership.

There are currently two classes of ownership:

1.   full freehold owner; and

2.   full leasehold owner.

Previously there were two additional classes of ownership: limited freehold owner and limited leasehold owner. The most common example of a limited owner was a tenant for life or a person having the power of a tenant for life. A sale by a limited owner required evidence of the nature of their power of sale and may have required the consent or joinder of some third party in the deed as rights of third parties under the settlement on foot of which the limited owner was registered may have been protected by an inhibition registered on the folio. Students are referred to Fitzgerald, *Land Registry Practice* (2nd edn, 1995) for a more detailed discussion on these classes of ownership.

4.9.4   CLASSES OF TITLE

Within the classes of ownership are classes of title for freehold and leasehold respectively. These classifications identify the quality of the title registered. There are seven classes of title:

1.   absolute freehold;

2.   possessory/subject to equities freehold;

3.   qualified freehold;

4.   absolute leasehold;

5.   possessory/subject to equities leasehold;

6.   qualified leasehold; and

7.   good leasehold.

4.9.4.1   Absolute

This means that the folio is conclusive as to its contents and is a good root of title no matter how recently the folio was opened. This applies to both freehold and leasehold folios.

4.9.4.2   Subject to equities/possessory

Where the title is registered subject to equities or, in modern folios, registered with a possessory title in both freehold and leasehold titles, evidence must be obtained to enable the purchaser to apply to have the equity note discharged or the possessory note converted to absolute or good leasehold title. With a possessory folio the Land Registry is not satisfied that good title was shown in the application for first registration and is not prepared to guarantee the title as absolute. If the purchaser can now show good title the Land Registry will convert the title to absolute or good leasehold.

4.9.4.3   Good leasehold

This class of title means that the Land Registry has not investigated the title of the lessor to grant the lease but only investigated the title of the lessee. If the Land Registry has investigated the title of the lessor to grant the lease, and is satisfied with that title, an absolute leasehold folio will be opened.

Accordingly, with a good leasehold folio the State guarantee does not extend to the title of the lessor. In such cases one must apply the 15-year rule to the lease. If the lease is less than 15 years old then one should look for the title of the lessor to grant the lease. If the lease is more than 15 years old then, if it is acceptable as a good root, it is not necessary to enquire beyond the register and the 15-year rule may be applied.

Always remember, even in Land Registry cases, that a copy of the lease must be obtained by the purchaser who will be bound by its covenants and conditions.

4.9.4.4   Qualified

A qualified title is the same as an absolute title but it will be qualified in some way by excepting from the effect of registration any right:

    (a)   arising before a specified date; or

    (b)   arising under a specified instrument; or

    (c)   otherwise particularly described in the register.

Therefore, depending on the nature of the qualification a purchaser may be obliged to carry out further investigations.

4.9.5   COMPULSORY FIRST REGISTRATION

When a purchaser is obliged to make an application for first registration in the Land Registry, due to the title becoming compulsorily registrable, they need only seek 15 years' title. The Land Registration Rules 2012 state, at rule 18, that on such an application for first registration no evidence of title shall be called for that could not be required on a sale of the property under an open contract. Under s 56 of the 2009 Act this period is now 15 years.

4.10   Summary Checklist

4.10.1   UNREGISTERED FREEHOLD TITLE

Root *must*:

1.   deal with the ownership of the whole legal and equitable estate in the property sold;

2.   not rely on extrinsic evidence, ie it must not depend on another document for its validity, eg a power of sale;

3.   contain a description by which the property can be identified;

4.   show nothing to cast a doubt on the title of the disposing parties; and

5.   be at least 15 years old.

4.10.2   UNREGISTERED LEASEHOLD/FEE FARM GRANT TITLE

The root of title is *always* the lease or the fee farm grant and *must* be at least 15 years old. If the fee farm grant is a conversion grant, the lease for lives must also be shown. If the lease is less than 15 years old, title to the superior interest *must* be shown.

Title can then skip to a deed or document that should, if possible:

1.   deal with the ownership of the whole legal and equitable estate in the property sold;

2.   not rely on extrinsic evidence, eg a power of sale;

3.   contain a description by which the property can be identified;

4.   show nothing to cast a doubt on the title of the disposing parties; and

5.   be at least 15 years old.

4.10.3   REGISTERED TITLE

1. Freehold/leasehold folio of a registered full owner with ***absolute*** title requires no further investigation. If leasehold a copy of the lease is required.

2. ***Limited*** owner requires investigation of the nature of the limitation.

3. ***Possessory*** requires investigation of additional title/evidence to enable conversion to absolute/good leasehold.

4. ***Qualified*** requires investigation depending on the nature of the qualification.

5. ***Good leasehold*** requires investigation of lessor's title if the lease is less than 15 years old.

CHAPTER 5

INVESTIGATION OF TITLE

'There is nothing which so generally strikes the imagination, and engages the affections of mankind, as the right of property; or that sole and despotic dominion which one man claims and exercises over the external things of the world, in total exclusion of the right of any other individual in the universe. And yet there are very few that will give themselves the trouble to consider the origin and foundation of this right. Pleased as we are with the possession, we seem afraid to look back to the means by which it was acquired, as if fearful of some defect in our title.'

Blackstone *Commentaries on the Laws of England*, Vol II (18th edn, 1829) p 2

5.1   Why Investigate Title?

This chapter considers matters relevant to the actual investigation of a title. It deals with the type of documentation that will be encountered in various types of titles and the main points to have regard to when reading a title. It is worth stating at this stage that reading a title is just as important for a vendor's solicitor as for a purchaser's solicitor as it is the duty of the vendor's solicitor to prepare the Contract for Sale, and to enable him or her to do that properly on behalf of the vendor he or she must first read the title to determine the manner in which the contract is to be drawn and, indeed, to identify precisely the nature of the title that the vendor is contracting to sell.

Having said that, however, the main onus thereafter is on the purchaser's solicitor to read the title and satisfy himself or herself that he or she can acquire a good marketable title on behalf of the purchaser, that the title being provided is that contracted for in the Contract for Sale, and that the property contracted to be sold is properly and adequately identified in the title deeds.

5.2   Notice

It is a well-settled principle of law that a bona fide purchaser for value without notice acquires a good title to property unaffected by matters of which they had no notice. The question of notice may arise either by some matter arising from the documentation contained in the title deeds themselves or given in response to replies to requisitions on title or that may be apparent from an inspection of the premises.

It must be remembered that the Contract for Sale also deals with the issue of notice, at general conditions 15 and 16. See **6.3.7.1** and **6.4.4.7** for a further discussion of these conditions.

5.2.1   TYPES OF NOTICE

There are three types of notice:

1. *Actual* where the person knows the relevant fact.

2. *Constructive* where the person does not know the relevant fact, but would know it if they made the proper enquiries.

3. *Imputed* where the person does not know the relevant fact but some person acting on their behalf had actual or constructive notice of it.

For a solicitor it is therefore vitally important that proper enquiries are made as failure to do so could put the client on notice of some relevant fact relating to the property. If a solicitor does not make the proper enquiries and some fact later comes to light that results in a loss to their client, the solicitor could face a negligence action from their client.

Section 86 of the Land and Conveyancing Law Reform Act, 2009 provides a statutory basis for this doctrine. It provides that a purchaser is on notice of any instrument, fact, matter, or thing if:

1. it is within their own knowledge; or

2. it would have come within their knowledge if such inquiries and inspections were made as ought reasonably to have been made.

'Purchaser' includes their solicitor or other agent or counsel in the same transaction.

In the case of *Northern Bank v Henry* [1981] IR 1, the Supreme Court considered what a 'reasonable man' might enquire into. It held that 'constructive notice could be found only when the lack of knowledge was due to such careless inactivity as would not be expected in the circumstances from a reasonable man'. A reasonable man was to be distinguished from a mere prudent one. The key difference is that a reasonable man would look beyond the impact on his own affairs and consider the impact on his neighbour.

5.2.2   BONA FIDE—GOOD FAITH

The other requirement of the rule is that a purchaser act *bona fides* or in good faith. The broad basis upon which the principle works was well stated by Henchy J in the case of *Somers v Weir* [1979] IR 94. This case was the first major case dealing with the notice provisions contained in the Family Home Protection Act, 1976 ('the 1976 Act') and in that case Henchy J stated that the nub of the case was whether the purchaser was 'an assignee who in good faith acquires an estate or interest in property'?

Henchy J stated the law as follows:

'The question whether a purchaser has acted in good faith necessarily depends on the extent of his knowledge of the relevant circumstances. In earlier times the tendency was to judge a purchaser solely by the facts that had actually come to his knowledge. In the course of time it came to be held in the Court of Chancery that it would be unconscionable for the purchaser to take a stand on the facts that had come to his notice to the exclusion of those which ordinary prudence or circumspection or skill should have called to his attention. When the facts at his command beckoned him to look and enquire further and he refrained from doing so, Equity fixed him with constructive notice of what he would have ascertained if he had pursued the further investigation which a person of reasonable care and skill would have felt proper to make in the circumstances. He would not be allowed to say "I acted in good faith in ignorance of those facts of which I learned only after I took the conveyance", if those facts were such as a reasonable man in the circumstances would have brought within his knowledge.'

Accordingly, in this case it was held unanimously by the Supreme Court that the purchaser did not acquire a good title as the purchaser failed to satisfy the court that he had acted in good faith within the meaning of the 1976 Act, s 3, in the purchase of the property.

5.2.2.1   *O'Connor v McCarthy*

There is another more recent Irish case of *O'Connor v McCarthy* [1982] IR 161 in which the entire question of notice was considered in detail by Costello J (see also **1.7.2 (h)**). That case turned upon the registration of a Contract for Sale in the Registry of Deeds which was the second contract signed in respect of the sale of the same premises. As the first contract (though valid and enforceable) was not registered, the purchaser under the second contract claimed that his contract had priority under the Registration of Deeds (Ireland) Act, 1707 ('the 1707 Act') as it was registered, whereas the first contract, although dated earlier, was not registered. It was sought to upset this claim by establishing that the purchaser under the second contract had notice of the existence of the first contract. Costello J deals fully with the question of constructive notice, actual notice, and whether the 'flying rumours' in respect of the first sale which it was claimed circulated in the district where the property was situate were sufficient to defeat the second purchaser's claim. In that case on the facts determined by Costello J he held in favour of the purchaser under the second contract and declared that as the second purchaser did not have actual notice of the first contract, he was entitled to purchase the property by virtue of the priority which the registration of the contract gave him under the 1707 Act.

5.2.2.2   **Family law matters**

This concept of a purchaser for valuable consideration in good faith without notice has been further extended in family law matters and incorporated into the Judicial Separation and Family Law Reform Act, 1989, s 29, the Family Law Act, 1995, s 35, and the Family Law (Divorce) Act, 1996, s 37, in the context of a reviewable disposition under those three pieces of legislation: see **chapter 7**.

5.2.2.3   **Putting yourself on notice**

There is an ongoing debate among conveyancers on the question of notice arising from a practice which is becoming more common among solicitors of furnishing all the vendor's title documents to the purchaser's solicitor with the draft contract before a binding contract between the parties comes into existence. This is regarded as a bad practice and further comments are made upon this matter in **chapter 2**.

5.3   Pre-Contract Enquiries

5.3.1   GENERALLY

As a result of the increasing complexity in respect of all matters relating to property transactions in recent years it has become necessary for conveyancers to consider the extent and nature of which pre-contract enquiries should be made by a purchaser's solicitor before allowing a purchaser to sign a contract. In England the practice is that all enquiries in relation to title matters are dealt with before binding contracts come into existence and the sale is completed more or less contemporaneously with the exchange of signed contracts. This is not the practice in Ireland, but there are a number of areas where a strong view has developed for pre-contract enquiries to be made, eg apartments. The Conveyancing Committee took this factor into account some years ago and in the current requisitions on title there are several areas where separate pages are printed as part of the requisitions which may be extracted and furnished as pre-contract enquiries rather than left to be dealt with after binding contracts have been exchanged. If any such pre-contract enquiries are made and answered by the vendor's solicitor they should be repeated as formal requisitions on title after the exchange of binding contracts so as to legally bind the vendor to the replies given. Set out in the following paragraphs are some of the areas which would be covered by these pre-contract enquiries.

Since the decision of the Supreme Court in the case of *Frescati Estates Ltd v Walker* [1975] IR 177, decisions affecting premises under the Planning Acts and the various amendments and regulations are now matters of title. Many practitioners consider the warranties under condition 36 of the general conditions of sale in the Law Society contract to be too wide-ranging. It has now become commonplace for the vendor's solicitor in the special conditions of the contract to restrict, or in some cases delete completely, the provisions of general condition 36 by providing specifically for the documentation that will be furnished by a vendor in respect of any developments that have taken place on the property since 1 October 1964 when the first Planning Acts came into operation. Planning law is an entire branch of law which has developed its own expertise and **chapter 11** deals with the matters under planning law that should concern a purchaser's solicitors. Planning permissions may sometimes be very complex and lengthy documents, particularly where the property being purchased is a large and perhaps multi-user property, eg a combined shopping centre cum office cum residential dwelling, and particular attention should be paid to this aspect of a property before contracts are signed. This view has been endorsed by the Law Society in its Practice Notes (Law Society *Gazette*, May 2000).

VAT on property is another area of conveyancing law that has become increasingly complex. See **chapter 16** for a detailed treatment of the subject. A new VAT regime on property was introduced in July 2008. Prior to this, special condition 3 of the Law Society Contract for Sale fully dealt with the potential for VAT to be charged on a purchase. This is no longer sufficient as it may now be open to the parties to choose whether to charge VAT on the purchase price or not. This decision must be taken prior to contracts being executed. The Conveyancing and Taxation Committees of the Law Society have issued a standard set of pre-contract VAT enquiries.

5.3.2   SPECIFIC EXAMPLES

The following types of properties will also, in the majority of cases, require pre-contract enquiries to be raised and satisfied:

(a)   licensed premises be they public house, restaurant, hotel, or off-licence;

(b)   a commercial property where there may be many enquiries to be made in respect of planning, building control regulations, and fire regulations and user;

(c)   investment properties, eg an office block containing multi-user tenants all with separate leases perhaps for different lengths of time and subject to rent reviews;

(d)   new or second-hand apartments or flats. The Law Society has published pre-contract enquires to deal with the provisions of the Multi-Unit Developments Act, 2011. This Act, which was enacted on 24 January 2011, established a new statutory framework for multi-unit developments. See chapter 6 of the Law Society *Complex Conveyancing Manual* (2nd edn) published by Bloomsbury Professional;

(e)   agricultural properties where there may be a milk quota or where there may be problems arising under environmental legislation; and

(f)   premises being sold with the benefit of a special tax incentive. However, it is again emphasised that a purchaser's solicitor should not rely exclusively on replies to such pre-contract enquiries and should repeat the enquiries as requisitions on title after the parties are contractually bound.

Each of the foregoing requires a particular expertise because of the type and nature of the property. The title itself may in fact be quite simple and very often a conveyancer has to spend far more time dealing with planning matters, registration matters, fire safety requirements, etc than with the actual title to the property itself. It is important for conveyancers to recognise areas of special difficulty and they should not hesitate to seek the assistance of specialists in any particular area to ensure that the purchaser is adequately protected.

5.4   Types of Title

The type of title that a solicitor will be dealing with will determine the investigations that a solicitor will be obliged to carry out. As was seen in **chapter 4**, titles are basically either a freehold or a leasehold title and this applies to registered and unregistered titles.

5.4.1   LEASEHOLD UNREGISTERED TITLES

We know that in cases involving a leasehold title, the root of title will always be the lease, no matter how old it is, as the terms and conditions and covenants contained therein will always continue to affect the subject property. It may seem an obvious point, but it is always vital for a purchaser's solicitor to investigate what the covenants and conditions in the lease are, and to inform the purchaser of them. It is quite likely that in a lease of a house there would be a covenant not to use the property otherwise than as a private residential dwelling. This could cause a purchaser problems if they were planning to run a business from the property, eg a vet or doctors surgery.

It is important to recognise that while the lease under which the vendor holds the property will always be the root, provided the rules relating to good roots of title are observed it may be necessary to seek copies of any head leases as the terms, covenants, and conditions contained in any of the head leases may in fact continue to affect the property. While most of these terms, covenants, and conditions will usually be reflected, if not actually repeated, in the vendor's lease, it is important for a purchaser to at least be aware of the nature of the superior covenants and as to whether or not any of such covenants may impose restrictions which he or she might otherwise not be aware of.

With a leasehold title the concern for a purchaser is always that the covenants and conditions have been complied with. This is because failure to comply with the covenants and conditions is a breach of the terms of the lease and would enable the landlord to take action to force compliance. In theory a landlord could seek to forfeit the lease, but in the case of a residential dwellinghouse held on foot of a long lease, it is highly unlikely that a court would grant such a remedy. This is because the value of the landlord's reversion is extremely small and therefore the landlord will suffer little damage to their reversion by virtue of the breach. However, it is still a possibility and so a purchaser is concerned that the covenants and conditions have been complied with.

Section 59(2) of the 2009 Act provides that the production of the last receipt for rent is conclusive evidence that there are no breaches of the covenants and conditions in the lease unless the contrary is proven.

With long leaseholds it is frequently impossible to identify the landlord. Often the rent reserved under the lease is a small amount and has not been collected for many years. A purchaser may not be able to rely on s 59(2) where the rent has not been demanded. In those circumstances it is usual to obtain a declaration that the rent has not been demanded for a period of 12 years and that the vendor is not aware of any breaches of the terms of the lease. This does not relieve a purchaser from making a proper inspection of the property and if they discover that part of the property is being used as a business in breach of a covenant in the lease, s 59(2) or a declaration does not remedy the breach.

5.4.2   FEE FARM GRANTS UNDER THE RENEWABLE LEASEHOLD CONVERSION ACT, 1849

Fee farm grants have already been discussed in **chapter 4**. If the title is based on a lease for lives renewable forever that has been converted to a fee farm grant under the Renewable Leasehold Conversion Act, 1849 ('the 1849 Act') then the lease for lives is where the title should start and not the fee farm grant as the covenants and conditions in the lease are grafted on to the grant and are preserved.

If the lease for lives is dated earlier than 1 August 1849 and has not been converted under the 1849 Act it is automatically converted to a freehold title under the Landlord and Tenant (Amendment) Act, 1980, s 74. That freehold is deemed to be a graft on the previous interest and is subject to any rights or equities arising from its being such a graft. In such a title the lease for lives will be the starting point for the title. In practice the lease for lives may not be available and is not available in many titles. Consequently the fee farm grant may be the only document upon which the title can be based. In such cases it has become accepted practice to treat the fee farm grant as a good root even though technically it does not conform to the definition of a good root set out in **chapter 4**. In many cases this will not create any problems for a purchaser if the property has been continuously used for the same purpose for a substantial number of years without any notices having been served or any other action taken by the superior owner of the rent for a breach of any of the terms, covenants, and conditions contained in the lease for lives which have been grafted onto the fee farm grant. However, if the purchaser intends to materially change the established use or carry out a major development of the property then the terms of the lease for lives would have to be established or alternatively the interest of the superior owner may have to be bought out.

The devolution of this type of title will follow the same format as that for leases.

Bear in mind the provisions of s 12 of the 2009 Act which prohibits the creation of new fee farm grants.

5.4.3 FREEHOLD UNREGISTERED TITLES

In freehold titles the normal root of title is a conveyance for value but may also be one of the documents specified in **chapter 4** as a good root of title. In unregistered freehold titles commencing with a fee farm grant the devolution of the title will follow the same format as for leases, namely that the vendor would be entitled to skip down to a document for valuable consideration, ie a conveyance more than 15 years old, and deduce title from that document down to the present vendor. Where the title consists of a series of conveyances, ie there is no fee farm grant, there is no need to skip and the root of title will be a conveyance for value more than 15 years old.

5.4.4 REGISTERED TITLES

In a registered title that is registered with title absolute the only document of title required is an official copy of the Land Registry folio on which the title is registered, together with a copy of the map or title plan issued in respect of the lands registered. If it is a leasehold title then again, if the title is absolute, the original lease and an up-to-date copy of the folio and map or title plan consist of the title. In such cases there is no need to have any other documentation produced as one of the primary aims of the Land Registry is to take out of the conveyancing system all documents of title other than the Land Registry folio. Section 73 of the Registration of Deeds and Title Act, 2006 provides that since 1 January 2010 land certificates ceased to have any effect. It is therefore irrelevant whether a land certificate has issued in respect of a folio or not.

However, as previously discussed, if the title is either registered subject to equities or is a possessory title then the vendor should produce documentary evidence to enable such titles to be converted to absolute or to have the equity note discharged. If registered as good leasehold, then evidence of the lessor's title to grant the lease should be obtained if the lease is less than 20 years old. If qualified, the nature of the qualification must be investigated.

5.5   Documents Produced with the Contract

In terms of the documentation that should be produced at the initial stage of the transaction, ie when contracts are being prepared and issued, the recommended practice of the Conveyancing Committee of the Law Society is that the only documents that should be produced at that stage are the root of title, any document from which title is being deduced, ie the conveyance or assignment for value being skipped to in unregistered titles (that is a conveyance or assignment for value at least 15 years old), any document referred to in the special conditions, and planning documentation (see Law Society *Gazette*, May 2000). If there are no documents referred to in the special conditions which are required to be produced, then the only documents that should be listed and produced at the contract stage are the root of title, the document from which title is being deduced, and the planning documentation. In the case of a registered title a copy of the folio with the map or title plan is the relevant document and the lease, if leasehold, or fee farm grant if the freehold is based on this. It is only after contracts have been signed and exchanged and become binding that the balance of the title is furnished.

The Law Society's Conveyancing Committee has issued, on three occasions (see Law Society *Gazette* Practice Note, January/February 1991, March 1995, and May 2000) a Practice Note emphasising the importance of following this recommended practice as a contrary practice had become commonplace of vendors' solicitors issuing at the contract stage copies of the entire title to the property for sale. This raised difficult questions of practice because by doing so the vendor is putting the purchaser on notice of the contents of all of the documents and may oblige the purchaser to raise requisitions on title before any binding contract comes into existence. This is a practice which is commonplace in England, but is not the practice here and it is a practice which the Conveyancing Committee strongly discourages. Indeed, it is an open question as to whether pre-contract queries may be raised as requisitions and whether any replies given bind the vendor as there is no legal relationship between the parties until they are contractually bound to each other.

5.6   Important Statutory Provisions

When investigating any title the following statutory provisions may be of tremendous assistance in overcoming difficulties which arise. The following sections of the Land and Conveyancing Law Reform Act, 2009 are of particular importance:

- **Section 59(1)** *Recitals*

  Enables conveyancers to accept recitals statements and descriptions of facts contained in instruments, statutory provisions, or statutory declarations 15 years old as sufficient evidence unless proven to be inaccurate.

- **Section 59(2)** *Rent receipt*

  Production of the last receipt for rent payable under a lease is acceptable as conclusive evidence of compliance with the terms of the lease unless the contrary is proven.

- **Section 76** *All estates clause*

  Known as the 'all estates clause' it provides that a conveyance shall be effectual to pass all the estate, right, title, and interest vested in the conveying party to a purchaser unless a contrary intention is expressed in the conveyance. This section was intended to catch any interest inferior to the freehold which was vested in the vendor without the necessity of having to have full recitals in the deed.

- **Section 77** *Receipt clause*

  A receipt clause in a deed of assurance, apart from giving a discharge to the person paying the consideration, entitles a solicitor acting for a vendor to collect the consideration in exchange for the deed and to give a valid receipt for it.

- **Section 80** *Implied covenants*

  In a conveyance for value if the vendor is selling as 'beneficial owner' certain covenants are implied: that the vendor has full right to convey the property; the vendor warrants a covenant for quiet enjoyment; the vendor warrants that the property is free from encumbrances; and that the vendor will execute further assurances to vest the interest contracted to be sold in the purchaser if necessary. (See Parts 1 and 2 of Schedule 3 of the 2009 Act.)

- **Section 84** *Statutory acknowledgement and undertaking*

  Statutory acknowledgements and undertakings in respect of original documents which are retained by the vendor impose obligations upon the vendor to produce the documents for inspection, to produce them in court on a hearing to establish title, and to furnish copies on request and also oblige the vendor to keep the documents safe and whole unless destroyed by fire. The section states that the obligation attaches to the documents themselves and binds the person in possession of them. The benefit is exercisable by a person claiming any interest, right, or estate through the person to whom the original undertaking was given. In practice this means that the benefit or burden does not have to be assigned in every subsequent deed.

5.7   The Chain of Title

The 'chain of title' is the term used to describe all of the connected events on a title from the root of title down to the document or event that vested ownership of the property in the current vendor or owner. This chain of title may consist of a variety of documents or events, eg conveyances, assignments, wills, grants of representation, assents, court orders, transfers, deaths, bankruptcies, liquidations, etc. The conveyancer's task is to ensure that from the root of title down to the document or event that vested title in the current vendor or owner there is an unbroken series of documents or events, not only marking the change of ownership, but also ensuring that the document or event properly transfers title from one owner to another. See **4.8** for a more detailed explanation.

5.8   Events on Title

There are some events on the title which a conveyancer will commonly come across as set out in the following paragraphs.

5.8.1   DEATHS ON TITLE

Prior to 1 June 1959 a devise of freehold property vested directly in the beneficiary and not in the executor or administrator. Pure personalty, ie a leasehold interest, vested in the personal representative, but on completion of the administration the beneficiary assumed occupation and ownership without any further formal documentation. In respect of all deaths on or after 1 June 1959, under the Administration of Estates Act, 1959, all titles vested in the personal representative and thereafter no interest passed to a beneficiary without a written assent from the personal representative.

Thus, if a beneficiary wished to pass title in respect of an interest acquired under a death which occurred on or after 1 June 1959, the paper documentation required to establish the title was the grant of probate incorporating the original will, or a grant of administration with the will annexed incorporating the original will, or a grant of letters of administration intestate coupled with the assent or assignment or conveyance from the personal representative formally vesting title to the property in the beneficiary.

Alternatively the property could be sold by the personal representative and this power of sale is now contained in the Succession Act, 1965. In such cases the purchaser from a personal representative is relieved of the responsibility of having any beneficiary join in the sale.

The case of *Mohan v Roche* [1991] 1 IR 560 may prove useful in certain limited circumstances where no assent has been obtained. It was held in that case in the High Court by Keane J, that upon construction of ss 52 and 53 of the Succession Act, 1965, where property had devolved and was vested in the personal representative and was to be distributed to him he became beneficially entitled to it and therefore an assent was not required. The Law Society issued a Practice Note on this decision in December 1997 and has pointed out that this decision is limited to the following scenarios:

1. where the administrator alone is beneficially entitled to the estate of an intestate deceased and evidence is forthcoming that all the liabilities of the estate have been discharged or have become statute-barred;

2. where the executor alone is beneficially entitled to the unadministered part of the estate of a testate deceased and evidence is forthcoming that all the liabilities of the estate have been discharged or have become statute-barred and that all legacies, devises, and bequests have been satisfied in full.

The Practice Note points out that the decision should not be taken to alter the general practice of obtaining assents to the vesting of land. Rather the decision may be of assistance in dealing with a title, or an estate, where an assent was not applied for and it may be possible to rely on the decision rather than apply for de bonis non grant.

Where the property is held jointly, the title automatically devolves on the surviving joint owner on the death of one or more of the other joint owners and the only evidence required in respect of the passing of the title is a copy of the deceased joint owner's death certificate exhibited in a statutory declaration identifying the deceased joint owner as the person named in the death certificate with a confirmatory declaration by the surviving joint owner that the joint tenancy was never severed.

Where the property is held in common ownership, as tenants in common then each owner has a separate interest in the property which does not devolve upon the survivors when one tenant in common dies. In such a case the title will have to be traced through his or her will or on intestacy.

Prior to the Finance Act, 2010 it was necessary to produce a certificate of discharge from CAT for all gifts or inheritances in the previous 12 years. This requirement is now abolished and the Revenue will not issue any such certificates as they are no longer required.

5.8.2   VOLUNTARY CONVEYANCES

Voluntary conveyances are normally conveyances between related parties where one owner transfers a property to another for 'natural love and affection'. There is no formal consideration in money terms paid. These deeds are perfectly valid but they are liable to be set aside. If the donor is made a bankrupt within three years of the deed, then the deed is void as against the official assignee (this was previously two years). If after three years and still within five years the donor is made bankrupt, the deed is void unless the donor can establish that he or she was solvent at the time of the deed without relying on the property (Bankruptcy Act, 1988, s 59 as amended by s 154 of the Personal Insolvency Act 2012). A deed of this nature will accordingly require a statutory declaration by the donor (referred to in practice as a declaration of solvency) confirming that the transfer to the donee was effected for natural love and affection without any intent to defraud his or her creditors and for the purpose of conferring a benefit upon the donee and that in doing so the donor was solvent and able to meet his or her other creditors without the benefit of the property transferred. In addition a bankruptcy search will be required. See **10.2.3**.

If, in fact, a transfer from the donee to another party has taken place within three years then previously an indemnity bond for the value of the property from an insurance company was required to protect the purchaser from the possibility of the original donor becoming bankrupt within the three-year period. However, a Practice Note in the April 1998 Law Society *Gazette* advises that a bond should not now be required once a declaration of solvency is produced by the donor. This Practice Note is based on case law on the 'old' bankruptcy rules, to the effect that within the three-year period the deed is void only as against the official assignee: see *Re Carter and Kenderdine's Contract* [1897] 1 Ch 776 and *Re Hart* [1912] 3 KB 6. Until the official assignee is appointed on the bankruptcy of the donor, the deed is merely voidable. A purchaser from a donee, within this three-year period, is protected provided they have no notice of the bankruptcy of the original donor. This is accomplished by carrying out a bankruptcy search. Therefore, a purchaser from a donee is protected, even within the three-year period, provided that the donor was not bankrupt at the time of the deed from the donee to the purchaser.

It should be noted that the Personal Insolvency Act, 2012 increased the previous period of two years in s 59 of the Bankruptcy Act, 1988 to three years, from 3 December 2013 (see SI 462/2013).

5.8.3   LOST DEEDS

It is not uncommon to come across cases where either an entire set of documents of unregistered title or some of the documents in the chain of title have been lost. What is required to perfect the chain of title are certified copies of the missing deeds or official copies of the memorials of any deeds registered in the Registry of Deeds. The copy memorials are readily procurable from the Registry of Deeds once the names of the parties and the approximate dates of the deeds are known. Apart from production of copies of the relevant documents a full detailed statutory declaration should be obtained from the vendor and, if necessary, confirmed by any other party who may have knowledge, fully setting out the circumstances in which the deeds were lost and, most importantly, confirming that the deeds were not pledged or lodged in any way as security for a loan or otherwise. Appropriate searches must also be conducted for the entire period covered by the title to ensure that there are no outstanding charges registered which have not been cleared off.

In some cases it may be necessary to obtain an insurance company indemnity bond for the value of the premises to protect the purchaser against any claim that might be made if the deeds should turn up in the hands of some person who has a sustainable claim against the property, but such bonds are quite expensive. If a satisfactory explanation is forthcoming, supported by sworn declarations, and copies of the relevant deeds are made available, then a bond should not be necessary but this is a matter which can only be judged in each individual case.

5.8.4   CERTIFIED COPY DEEDS

It is commonplace in urban areas for the root of title, eg a lease, to cover a number of properties. As these properties are sold off individually, some of the property owners will get only certified copies of the original deeds and the original owner will normally retain possession of the originals. This is a perfectly acceptable practice provided that contained in each deed, where a part of the property is sold off, there is a statutory acknowledgement by the vendor at the time, who retains possession of the original deeds acknowledging the right of the purchaser to the production of the original deeds and undertaking for their safe custody. Such documents would normally be listed in the deed and the benefit of this would pass to all subsequent owners. See s 84 of the 2009 Act.

5.8.5   DEEDS OF RECTIFICATION

Deeds of rectification may turn up on the title occasionally where there has been some error in an earlier deed which has been identified and the relevant parties would join in for the purpose of correcting the error.

5.9 Capacity of Vendors

It is important to appreciate that the mere fact that a person or body makes a contractual commitment to sell a particular property does not automatically mean that such a person or body has any legal title to do so. An ordinary individual, if he or she buys a property, would have legal entitlement to subsequently sell it. However, there are a number of categories of persons in respect of whom further enquiries must be made and documentation obtained to establish that they do have a legal title and the following is a non-exhaustive list of those to which special attention must be paid.

5.9.1 TRUSTEE

Section 20 of the 2009 Act provides that a trustee has the full power of an owner to convey or otherwise deal with land. This is subject to the duties of the trustee and any restrictions imposed by statute, the general law of trusts, or by any instrument or court order relating to the land. This section simplifies the law in this area. Prior to the Act, a trustee did not have an automatic power of sale. The power to sell the land could, however, have been granted under a power of sale contained in a trust document or a trust for sale or under a settlement inter vivos or under a will. Section 21 of the 2009 Act now provides protection for purchasers from a trust from any person with an equitable interest in the land even where the purchaser was on notice of such an interest. This is called overreaching and essentially means that the purchaser takes the land free from such equitable interest. The equitable interest that is overreached now attaches to the proceeds arising from the sale and not to the land itself.

When investigating a title it is important to ascertain whether the deed was executed prior to the commencement of the 2009 Act, ie 1 December 2009. If it was executed prior to the Act then evidence of the trustee's power of sale must be shown. If it is post the 2009 Act, it is sufficient that satisfactory evidence be obtained that the restrictions on the power of sale, as set out in s 20(1)(a) and (b), do not affect the land. Thus, it would be prudent to obtain a statutory declaration from the trustee that no restrictions to his or her powers apply along with a copy of the trust deed. Section 86 of the 2009 Act sets out the principles governing whether a purchaser is on notice of any fact, instrument, matter, or thing.

If a trust is not shown on the title furnished, the solicitor should not raise any specific requisitions enquiring if such trust exists as he or she may be creating difficulties by putting himself or herself on notice of the trust where the title furnished does not so disclose.

If the trust is a charitable trust then the trust does not come within the provisions of the 2009 Act by virtue of s 18(9). Charities are now governed by the Charities Acts, 1961–2009. Of particular relevance is s 34 of the Charities Act, 1961, which allowed the Commissioners for Charitable Donations and Bequests to authorise the sale of lands held under a charitable trust. This function now vests in the Charities Regulatory Authority under the Charities Act, 2009.

5.9.2 A COMMITTEE OF A WARD OF COURT

A committee of a ward of court is a person appointed by the court to look after the person and property of a person taken into wardship. A committee has no authority to sell the property belonging to a ward of court without a court order. The requisite documents that are necessary are a copy of the order appointing the committee and a copy of the order authorising the committee to sell the ward's property. Probably the production of the second order would be adequate as the court undoubtedly would not make any such order unless the committee was properly appointed. The order permitting the committee to sell will also contain detailed provisions as to how the property is to be sold and the various steps to be taken in respect of lodgement of the deposit, purchase money, etc.

5.9.3   A COMPANY

In the case of a company the first matter to be checked is that the company was properly registered and this is done by the production of a certified copy of the certificate of incorporation. It is also very important in modern day conveyancing, having regard to the powers now vested in the Registrar of Companies, to ensure that the company is still on the register of companies. If it is not, then it would either have to be restored to the register before the sale may proceed or, alternatively, it is necessary to investigate the operation of the statutes under the terms of which the assets of all companies struck off the register are vested in the Minister for Finance. In such cases, if a restoration to the register of companies is not possible, then the only party who may have any title to transfer may be the Minister for Finance. In addition, the memorandum of the company, ie the objects for which it was founded, should include an entitlement, first to acquire property and, secondly, to sell property. Finally, the articles of association should always be checked to see in what way the company is authorised to affix the seal to the purchase deed. If the company was incorporated under the Companies Act, 1908 then the sealing requirements under that Act were for the seal to be countersigned by two directors and the secretary, whereas in most modern companies it is one director and the secretary, or two directors, or one director and a nominated person.

If the company is one not registered in this jurisdiction then be particularly careful in determining the company's authority to sell and, in particular, the manner in which the company is authorised to execute documents as some foreign companies do not have a seal. Section 64(2)(b)(iv) of the 2009 Act now provides that a foreign company can validly execute a deed in this jurisdiction if it is executed in the manner provided for in the jurisdiction where it is incorporated.

5.9.4   RECEIVERS—CONTRACTUAL AND STATUTORY

A receiver is a person appointed to seize, maintain, and dispose of property as a result of the insolvency of the debtor or due to litigation. The receiver receives the assets of the debtor for and on behalf of a creditor in satisfaction of obligations owed to the creditor. The receiver has a duty to preserve the assets, collect any income coming from those assets, and to sell them to discharge money owing to the owner of the charge. A receiver can be appointed by the court or by deed, eg on foot of a debenture entered into by a company. The appointment by deed is the more common procedure. To be properly appointed there must first be an act or event of default by the debtor. What constitutes an act or event of default is usually set out in the debenture. The receiver must also be appointed in accordance with the terms of the debenture.

The recent case of *McCleary v McPhillips & Ors* [2015] IEHC 591 shows the importance of checking the debenture to ensure that the receiver has been properly appointed in accordance with its terms. Cregan J held that the receiver had not been validly appointed as the mortgage required that he be appointed by the bank 'in writing under its hand'. The deed of appointment was done under seal. It was held that this was not sufficient. The persons who signed the deed of appointment as witnesses of the sealing were not authorised by the bank to sign a document in writing under hand on behalf of the bank. At the time of writing this decision is under appeal.

Generally contractual receivers' powers are specified in the mortgage or charge and also, in the case of a company receiver, in the Companies Acts, 1963–2010. The vast majority of receivers appointed are contractual receivers. Sometimes a receiver is appointed by a court order, under the Conveyancing Acts, 1881–1911 or more commonly by NAMA (the National Assets Management Agency). See s 147 of the National Asset Management Act, 2009 which provides for the appointment of statutory and contractual receivers. See also chapters 2 and 11 of the Law Society *Complex Conveyancing Manual* (2nd edn) published by Bloomsbury Professional.

Once validly appointed a receiver is entitled to sell the assets of a company affected by the debenture and so a purchaser may find themselves purchasing from a receiver. From a conveyancing perspective a receiver acts on behalf of the company and usually executes documents with the benefit of a power of attorney contained in the instrument under which they are appointed and will sign the purchase deed as such.

The Law Society Practice Directions from the *Gazettes* of September 1986, April 1987, and December 1994 detail the documentation that should be sought when purchasing from a receiver. The contents of these directions are summarised at **5.14**.

5.9.5 LIQUIDATOR

A liquidator is a person appointed to wind up a company, realise its assets, and distribute them in accordance with the law.

A company can be wound up either voluntarily or involuntarily. A liquidator can be appointed by the members, a creditor, or the court. A full examination of the different types of liquidation are beyond the scope of this chapter and it is suffice to say that once appointed a liquidator takes over the functions and powers of the directors of the company. A liquidator has a power of sale over the property of the company and will affix the company seal to the purchase deed. The liquidator will also enter into the deed as liquidator, to confirm the sale. A Law Society Practice Direction in the *Gazette* of September 1986 details the documentation that should be sought when purchasing from a liquidator and it is summarised at **5.14**.

5.9.6 STATUTORY BODY

In the case of statutory bodies it is necessary to check the relevant statute under which the body was founded to establish the statutory authority of the body to sell and also whether there are any prior consents required, eg from the Minister for Finance, before a valid conveyance may be executed. With a sale by local authority, evidence must be produced of compliance with the Local Government Act, 2001, s 183.

5.9.7 LIFE TENANT

Previously under the provisions of the Settled Land Acts, 1882–90 a life tenant had an inherent power of sale. However, such a life tenant did not have any entitlement to receive the proceeds of sale which had to be paid to two trustees of the settlement. If a valid receipt was not obtained in the deed witnessed by two trustees, the deed was void. It was essential that there were two trustees, unless the trust authorised the payment to one trustee as sufficient discharge. In cases where an infant in his or her own right was seised of or entitled in possession to land, the land was deemed settled land and the infant a tenant for life. In such a case the trustees of the settlement, or if there were no such persons, whoever the court ordered, could exercise the statutory power of sale of the tenant for life on behalf of the infant, this being one of the rare cases in which the trustees did have a power of sale although not specifically conferred upon them by the instrument setting up the trust (see Trustee Act, 1882, ss 59 and 60). Further provisions were contained in the Succession Act, 1965, ss 57 and 58, giving powers of sale to trustees of an infant's property.

The 2009 Act greatly simplifies the law in this area by providing in s 19(1)(a) that a tenant for life is now a trustee together with the trustees of the settlement. Therefore a tenant for life will now be selling as trustee. The old law in this area is, however, still relevant for deeds on title executed prior to the commencement of the 2009 Act.

5.9.8   PERSONAL REPRESENTATIVE

A personal representative is authorised to sell the property of a deceased under the provisions of the Succession Act, 1965, s 50. There is a protection contained in the Act for bona fide purchasers for value who do not have to enquire as to whether the personal representatives have followed all the statutory provisions contained in the Act in respect of consulting with the beneficiaries. It is not necessary in a sale by a personal representative to join any of the beneficiaries in the deed. A purchaser from a personal representative is protected from any action by any person entitled to a share in the estate by s 51 of the Act. This relieves a purchaser from enquiring as to whether a personal representative is acting properly in the administration of the estate. The grant of representation (ie grant of administration intestate, will annexed, probate, or de bonis non) is a necessary document of title to evidence the appointment of the personal representative.

5.9.9   A BENEFICIARY UNDER A WILL

As previously stated at **5.8.1** if the vendor is a beneficiary under a will in respect of a death which occurred on or after 1 June 1959 then, in addition to the grant of probate which contains a copy of the will, a formal assent from the executor is required and this must be in writing. Any such vendor is selling as full beneficial owner. Similarly, a beneficiary under an intestacy will be required to furnish a copy of the grant of administration intestate and the assignment, conveyance, or assent vesting title to the property in him or her.

5.9.10   ATTORNEY

Originally powers of attorney were dealt with under the provisions of the Conveyancing Act, 1881 and a properly drawn power of attorney was declared to be irrevocable for a period of 12 months. Accordingly, a purchaser from an attorney under such a power did not have to make any enquiries if the power was no more than 12 months old. If the power, however, was older than 12 months then a purchaser was put on notice to make enquiries as to the fact that the donor of the power was still alive and that such donor was capable. The death of a donor or his or her incapacity rendered such a power of attorney invalid.

There are now two new forms of power of attorney under the Enduring Power of Attorneys Act, 1996. The first type, namely the enduring power of attorney, only comes into operation under this Act when the donor of the power becomes incapable, from mental incapacity, of conducting his or her own affairs and not otherwise. Such a power of attorney must then be registered in the Wards of Court Office and the persons specified in the power formally notified that it has come into operation before it becomes effective.

In addition, this Act introduces in s 16 a very short form of power of attorney which gives extremely wide powers to the donee of the power. Under any other form of power of attorney it is crucial to check and ensure that the power gives the grantee of the power the right to sell. The original power is normally retained by the vendor and a certified copy only is produced. If the original is registered in the Central Office then an attested copy from the Central Office is normally furnished.

5.9.11   SURVIVING JOINT TENANT

The first matter to check in the case of a surviving joint tenant is that the original deed did in fact create a joint tenancy and not a tenancy in common. If the surviving joint tenant is selling, then evidence is required as stated at **5.8.1** that the other joint tenant is deceased by exhibiting a death certificate in a statutory declaration and confirming that the joint tenancy was not severed prior to the death.

Alternatively in advance of the sale an application for registration of the surviving joint tenant as sole owner can be made to the Land Registry. In effect this is a form of removal of the name of the deceased from the folio on the basis of Form 47 which exhibits the death certificate.

Section 30 of the 2009 Act contains important provisions regarding the unilateral severance of a joint tenancy. Part 7 of the Act deals with co-ownership. One joint tenant is no longer able to sever the joint tenancy by disposing of their interest or acquiring a further interest in the land. Any such disposal or acquisition will require the consent of all the joint tenants. The vesting of property in an official assignee in bankruptcy or the registration of a judgment mortgage against the interest of one joint tenant no longer severs the joint tenancy after 1 December 2009. Any agreement of the joint tenants to sever the joint tenancy does not necessarily have to be in writing although clearly this would be preferable. Nothing in the 2009 Act affects the jurisdiction of the courts to find that all the joint tenants by mutual agreement or by their conduct have severed the joint tenancy in equity.

A recent decision of the High Court has clarified the position in respect of the registration of a judgment mortgage against the interest of one joint tenant. In the case of *Judge Mahon & ors v Lawlor & ors* [2008] IEHC 284 (30 July 2008), Laffoy J held that the registration of judgment mortgages against the interest of one joint tenant, as burdens on the lands, had not given rise to a severance of the joint tenancy and had not created a tenancy in common. In those circumstances on the death of that joint owner, the lands accrued to the surviving joint tenant by right of survivorship freed from the judgment mortgages.

5.9.12   MORTGAGEE IN POSSESSION

Mortgage documents are highly technical and there are a number of steps which mortgagees must follow before they are entitled to exercise their powers of sale. In particular, Chapter 3 of Part 10 of the 2009 Act now sets out the obligations, powers, and rights of a mortgagee under any mortgage created after 1 December 2010. A purchaser from a mortgagee in possession is relieved from the responsibility of ensuring that all of the necessary technical steps have been taken and accordingly a purchaser from a mortgagee in possession need only satisfy himself or herself on the following points:

(a)   obtain a copy of the mortgage deed to ensure that the mortgagee did have a right of re-entry and sale;

(b)   evidence that the amount due on foot of the mortgage became due and payable;

(c)   evidence that the mortgagee properly obtained possession of the property either by way of a surrender to it by the mortgagor or on foot of a court order;

(d)   if on foot of a court order, a copy of the ejectment decree showing it having been executed by the sheriff should be obtained; and

(e)   if the property is a residential property, then it is necessary to ensure that the mortgage was properly executed in full compliance with the provisions of the Family Home Protection Act, 1976.

5.9.13   COURT ORDER

There are circumstances in which the court will order a sale of a particular property and a purchaser is entitled to rely exclusively upon the terms of the court order as sufficient evidence that the person designated in the order as the person entitled to sell the property has a proper title to do so. An attested copy of the court order and compliance with any of the terms and conditions set out in the court order is all that is required.

5.9.14   CHARITABLE ORGANISATION

In the case of a charitable organisation, if there is no power of sale contained in the document establishing the trust, then the consent of the Commissioners for Charitable Donations and Bequests was previously required. Under the Charities Act, 2009 the consent of the Charities Regulatory Authority is now required. If there is a power of sale in the document establishing the trust no such consent is required.

5.9.15   THE COUNTY REGISTRAR

There are provisions in the Landlord and Tenant (Ground Rents) Act, 1967 that where a superior owner cannot be identified or located, the county registrar has power to appoint a person (or on an appeal from the county registrar the court may so order) to sign the deed in respect of the transfer or conveyance of the freehold on behalf of the unknown person and all that is required as evidence in this case is a certified copy of the relevant court order or the order of the county registrar, appointing a party to execute a deed on behalf of the unknown owner.

5.9.16   UNINCORPORATED BODY

The category of unincorporated bodies would include, for example, a club. In such a case it is necessary to look to the club rules to see what provision is made by them for the sale. The procedures laid down must be carefully followed and documented by the club secretary and the actual parties entitled to convey (usually the club trustees) identified and the necessary resolutions by the club members (a common enough requirement) authorising the sale must be passed and authenticated by the club secretary.

5.10   Investigation of Unregistered Title (Notes on Title)

As an unregistered title will consist of a bundle of title documents, eg a fee farm grant with subsequent conveyances, a series of conveyances, or a lease with subsequent assignments, the investigation of this title will necessarily be much more complex than the investigation of a registered title. Each deed in the chain of title will need to be examined and there are various matters which a conveyancer will need to check in order to ensure that the title is a good marketable title. **5.12** contains a sample chart which can be used to assist in this investigation of unregistered title, otherwise known as doing notes on title. A detailed explanation of some of these matters is dealt with in the following paragraphs.

It is very important to realise that the provisions of the 2009 Act in respect of the content of deeds and their operation are not retrospective in their effect. This means that, when investigating a title the provisions of the 2009 Act, in so far as they amend the law, are only of relevance for deeds executed after 1 December 2009. In this respect Chapters 3 and 4 of Part 9 of the 2009 Act, ss 62–85, are of paramount importance. For all other deeds, the old law continues to apply.

5.10.1   REVENUE STAMP

Previously the Revenue stamp was impressed on the front page of each deed showing the stamp duty paid in respect of that particular deed. Now all deeds executed on or after 30 December 2009 will have a stamp certificate—with a unique ID number—attached to the front of the deed as evidence that the deed is stamped. It is important to check that the correct amount of stamp duty relevant at the date of the deed was properly impressed. In the case of registered land s 64 of the Registration of Deeds and Title Act, 2006 ('the 2006

Act'), commenced by SI 511/2006, amends s 104 of the Registration of Title Act, 1964 in so far as the Registrar no longer has a 'duty' to check the stamp duty on each deed but may now proceed to register a deed unless there are reasonable grounds for suspecting that stamp duty or the correct amount of stamp duty has not been paid.

5.10.2   DATE AND TIME OF REGISTRATION

On the front page of each deed in an unregistered title will be imprinted the details of the date and time of registration of the deed in the Registry of Deeds and it is important to check that the deed has been registered and that the deed has been registered in its correct priority. For deeds registered after the commencement of the 2006 Act a serial number is allocated to each deed. The date of registration is also stamped on the front of the deed. The actual deed itself will be headed with the date of the deed and again it is important to check that this date is in the correct date order with the remainder of the documents of title.

5.10.3   THE PARTIES

The next part of the deed contains the names and addresses of the parties and, again, these should be carefully checked and compared with deeds prior and subsequent to it so as to ensure that the parties are correctly identified and are the correct parties who are either transferring or receiving the title, or who are required to join in the deed for the purpose of ensuring that a full title passes to the purchaser.

5.10.4   RECITAL OF TITLE

The next part of the deed normally contains recitals, eg this part normally recites the root of title be it a conveyance for value or a lease with which the title starts. It also very often gives a detailed description of the property for sale as contained in the earlier deed or a description of the property from which it is carved. It may also be necessary here to trace the title in some detail from the root if its devolution is not straightforward. This part of the deed can be of considerable importance to later conveyancers who may be entitled to rely upon the recitals contained if they are more than 15 years old in accordance with the provisions contained in s 59 of the 2009 Act.

5.10.5   RECITAL OF CONTRACT

The Contract for Sale is then recited between the parties to the deed and the purchase price specified. It is also important at this stage that if there are any other parties to the deed, apart from the vendor and the purchaser, that the reason for their joining in the deed should be set out here, and their function, and the particular interest that they may be joining in the deed to convey or assign.

5.10.6   TESTATUM, CONSIDERATION, RECEIPT CLAUSE

The deed then recites the conveyance or assignment of the property for the specified consideration and at this point must contain a receipt clause by the vendor acknowledging receipt of the agreed purchase money. If no receipt clause is included there is the possibility that all of the purchase monies were not paid to the vendor. Unpaid purchase monies are a lien on the property. The receipt clause acts as a discharge to the person paying the consideration (see **5.6**).

5.10.7 OPERATIVE WORDS AND CAPACITY

It is important that the deed uses words appropriate to the nature of the title being passed. If the deed does not contain the correct operative words then some interest, other than that intended, may have passed. In a conveyance the correct words are 'grant' or 'convey' and in an assignment the correct word is 'assign'. A more detailed explanation of these and other operative words is contained in **chapter 8**. The vendor should convey or assign as beneficial owner which implies all the relevant covenants as outlined in **5.6**. If the vendor is not selling as beneficial owner then the capacity in which the vendor is selling should be specified. Such alternative capacity may imply covenants less extensive than those of a beneficial owner.

5.10.8 DESCRIPTION OF PROPERTY

A full description of the property being conveyed or leased or assigned should be next and this will very often be taken first from earlier documents, eg from the original lease if it is a leasehold title, and then go on to describe the property by reference to its modern description. It may be necessary in some cases to properly identify it by reference to a map attached to the deed. It is important to remember that the basic principle is that the words of the deed will be relied upon for the description of the property in preference to the map attached and it is only if such description of the deed is ambiguous that the map may be relied upon.

5.10.9 HABENDUM

The habendum marks out or defines the quantum of the estate being taken and it commences with the words 'TO HOLD'. To do this, appropriate words of limitation were previously required. There are no words of limitation required in a transfer of registered land and s 67 of the 2009 Act has now abolished the need for words of limitation in a conveyance of unregistered land. Such a conveyance now passes the fee simple or the other entire estate or interest which the grantor had power to create or convey, unless a contrary intention appears in the conveyance.

5.10.10 EXCEPTIONS AND RESERVATIONS

In a leasehold assignment the deed will contain covenants by the purchaser to observe and perform all the covenants and conditions in the lease and to pay any rent reserved and to indemnify the vendor against any claims in respect of any breach, non-performance, or non-observance of the covenants or the non-payment of the rent. Such covenants obviously will not appear in a conveyance of a freehold. However, at this stage there may be further provisions incorporated such as exceptions and reservations in favour of the vendor, eg a reservation of a right of way or right of access to and the use of sewers or water pipes or something of that nature and this is the place in which it would be contained.

If the original deeds are not being handed over then the acknowledgement and undertaking in respect of safe custody of the original deeds would be contained here.

5.10.11 FINANCE CERTIFICATES

For deeds executed after 7 July 2012 there is no longer any requirement to insert any finance certificates. For deeds executed prior to this date it was necessary to insert the correct certificate in order to identify the correct rate of stamp duty to be paid.

5.10.12 CERTIFICATES OF CITIZENSHIP

It was previously necessary to check for certificates of citizenship or other qualification to acquire the property under the Land Act, 1965, depending upon where the property was located and who the purchaser was. While the relevant provisions of the Land Act, 1965 are now repealed compliance should be checked for in previous deeds on title. This is dealt with in more detail at **5.15**.

5.10.13 EXECUTION OF THE DEED

Finally the deed will then be executed by the parties and should be signed and delivered by the vendor and purchaser or executed by a company or statutory body under its corporate or common seal. Previously a deed needed to be sealed and delivered to validly pass title. Section 64 of the 2009 Act removes the sealing requirement and provides that execution by an individual by signing and having their signature witnessed will be sufficient.

If the property is a family home or shared home where the spouse's/civil partner's prior consent is required this consent appears at the end of the deed. It must be remembered that it is of crucial importance that such consent be signed by the spouse/civil partner prior to the deed being executed by the vendor; otherwise the consent is totally ineffective.

It is, of course, of crucial importance that the execution by any of the parties to the deed should be properly witnessed and the name, address, and occupation of the witness inserted in the appropriate place beside the execution of the parties. It is useful to remember that any signatures which are difficult to decipher should be printed so as to assist any future parties who may require to identify the witness in the event of any dispute arising over the contents or execution of the deed.

5.11 Approach to Investigating a Title

When faced with investigating title the following queries may assist in identifying the matters which should be investigated:

1. What is the tenure and nature of the title on offer, ie freehold or leasehold, registered or unregistered?
2. If leasehold/fee farm grant, which covenants and conditions affect the property?
3. Will these affect the purchaser's intended use of the property?
4. Are there any patent defects affecting the property?
5. Does the nature of the property require any pre-contract enquiries to be raised?
6. Has a good root of title been offered?
7. Is the age of the root of title sufficient, ie 15 years or over?
8. In the case of a leasehold title, are there more than 70 years to run on the lease, thus ensuring that it is a good marketable title?
9. Has a full chain of title been shown?
10. Are there any events on title requiring additional documentation?
11. Does the capacity of the vendor in any deed require additional documentation?
12. Are the necessary and correct parties included in each deed?
13. Is the property properly described in each deed?
14. Is there a receipt clause in each deed?
15. Are the words of limitation correct in previous deeds?
16. Is each deed properly stamped and registered?
17. Are the proper certificates present?
18. Is the deed properly executed?

5.12   Example Notes on Title

For each deed on title that is examined it is important to make proper notes of the key features. This will be of great assistance when reviewing the title, and will also provide a framework to identify any potential defects on title. The following table provides a framework for doing this exercise.

Type of Deed:	Date:	Parties:	
Query:	Yes/No Correct/ incorrect?	Additional documents required or need to be checked?	Statutory provision to assist? Follow up actions?
Stamped/Stamp certificate?			
Registration details			
Voluntary deed?			
Receipt clause?			
Words of grant?			
Capacity?			
Description of lands?			
Words of limitation?			
Covenants?			
Acknowledgements and undertakings?			
Statutory certificates?			

5.13   Dealing with Defects on Title

Inevitably solicitors will be faced with defects on a title. How should these be dealt with and can they be fixed? Often the textbooks are of little help as they tend to describe how things ought to be and give little or no guidance as to what to do if there is a problem.

A suggested method of dealing with such problems is to ask the following questions:

1.   What is wrong?

2.   Why is that important?

3.   What is the worst case scenario?

4.   How would a purchaser be prejudiced?

5.   Is there any statutory provision that would assist?

6.   What can be done to protect the purchaser?

7.   Will the passing of time solve the problem (statute barred)?

If these questions are asked, often a solution can be found which will enable the transaction to proceed. It is very rare that a flaw on title will be so serious that some solution cannot be found.

Take the following example.

Problem:	A conveyance forming part of the chain of title has not been registered in the Registry of Deeds.
1. What is wrong?	Deed has not been registered.
2. Why is that important?	It does not affect the validity of the deed but does affect priority.
3. Worse case scenario?	Another deed, eg a judgment mortgage or another conveyance, could be registered thereby securing priority.
4. Is purchaser prejudiced?	Title might be vested in someone else or a charge registered against the property.
5. Statutory provision to assist?	Searches should be made up to date against the vendor of the unregistered deed to disclose whether any other deeds have been registered in priority. The deed should be registered now to secure priority.
6. What can be done?	Nothing to protect purchaser.
7. Will time solve the problem?	No, the deed must be registered to secure priority.

5.14 Summary Events on Title

The following chart sets out some of the common issues and events on title that need to be addressed in the course of investigation of title. It will act as an aide-memoire to assist in ensuring that an unbroken chain of title is established. The right-hand column lists the evidence that should be obtained in each specific instance in order to protect the purchaser.

Death on Title	For Deaths Pre 1 June 1959: 1. Devise of freehold sufficient to vest property in beneficiary. 2. Personalty vested in personal representative but on completion of administration, beneficiary assumed occupation and ownership.
	For Deaths Post 1 June 1959: 1. Grant of administration/probate/will annexed/de bonis non. 2. Assent (if sale by beneficiary).
	If Joint Tenancy: 1. Evidence by way of statutory declaration of surviving joint tenant that joint tenancy was not severed prior to death. 2. Evidence by way of statutory declaration, exhibiting death certificate that deceased is same as person on title.
Voluntary Conveyances	1. Statutory declaration of disponer that disposition made bona fide for the purpose of benefiting the donee and without intent to defraud creditors. If made within past five years: 1. Statutory declaration of disponer that at date of disposition disponer was solvent and able to meet debts without recourse to the property (ie statutory declaration of solvency). 2. Bankruptcy search against disponer.

Lost Deeds	1. Official copies of memorials or application forms.
	2. Statutory declaration setting out how deeds were lost and were not pledged as security.
	3. Insurance bond, depending on circumstances of case.
Certified Copy Deeds	1. Statutory acknowledgement and undertaking given for originals.
Trustee	1. Trust instrument providing power of sale or trust instrument and evidence for purposes of s 20 of the 2009 Act (if applicable).
	2. Deed of appointment of trustees.
	3. If charity and no power of sale in trust instrument, consent of the Commissioners of Charitable Donations and Bequests for Ireland/Charities Regulatory Authority.
Committee of a Ward of Court	1. Copy order appointing committee.
	2. Copy order ordering sale.
Company	1. Certified copy of certificate of incorporation.
	2. Certified copy of memorandum and articles of association.
Statutory Body	Statute establishing body and governing its powers.
Life Tenant	Receipt of two trustees for purposes of Settled Land Acts if pre 2009 Act.
	Post 2009 Act life tenant is a trustee, s 19.
Power of Attorney	Certified copy of the power of attorney.
Mortgagee in Possession	1. Mortgage deed.
	2. Evidence that amount was due and owing.
	3. Evidence that possession properly obtained.
	4. Copy of ejectment order, if any.
Court Order	Copy court order.
County Registrar	Copy order.
Unincorporated Body	Copy constitution/rules.
Court Liquidation	1. Official copy of winding up order from High Court.
	2. If 1. does not contain appointment of liquidator, copy of order of appointment.
	3. Copy of order for sale, if applied for.
Creditors Liquidation	1. Copy ordinary resolution of company as to winding up as lodged in Companies Registration Office.
	2. Copy resolution appointing liquidator.
	3. Copy notice of appointment of liquidator with acceptance as filed in Companies Registration Office.
	4. If directors joining in, copy authority of committee of inspection sanctioning continuance of powers of directors under s 269(3) of the Companies Act, 1963.

Members Liquidation	1. Copy special resolution of company as to winding up as filed in Companies Registration Office.
	2. Copy resolution of company appointing liquidator.
	3. Copy notice of appointment of liquidator with acceptance endorsed as filed.
	4. If directors joining in, copy liquidator's authority sanctioning continuance of powers of directors, s 258(2) of the Companies Act, 1963.
Receiver Unregistered land	1. Satisfactory documentary evidence that right to appoint receiver has been made but not met.
	2. Certified copy appointment of receiver.
	3. Original mortgage if all property in mortgage is being released.
	4. Certified copy mortgage if only partial release.
	5. Original release and application form.
Receiver Registered land	1. Satisfactory documentary evidence that right to appoint receiver has been made but not met.
	2. Original deed of appointment of receiver.
	3. Receiver appointed in accordance with the terms of the debenture.
	4. Original instrument creating charge if fully discharged.
	5. Certified copy instrument creating charge if partial discharge.
	6. Original deed of discharge.

5.15 The Land Act, 1965

5.15.1 INTRODUCTION

Brought into operation on 9 March 1965, the Land Act, 1965 ('the 1965 Act') is one in a long series of Land Acts, Settled Land Acts, and Land Purchase Acts. Until the enactment of the Land Act, 2005 it was not possible to practise as a conveyancing solicitor within the State without coming across the provisions of the 1965 Act on a regular basis. Of the Act's 48 sections, there were four with which the conveyancer was required to be particularly familiar. These were ss 12, 13, 18, and 45.

Sections 12 and 45 were repealed by s 12 of the Land Act, 2005 which came into operation on 4 November 2005. The text of these sections is reproduced below, for information purposes only. Sections 13 and 18 remain in force and are dealt with at **5.15.3** and **5.15.4**.

By virtue of the Irish Land Commission (Dissolution) Act, 1992, the Irish Land Commission, the body in which many of the powers under the 1965 Act had been vested, was dissolved and its powers devolved to the Minister for Agriculture and Food ('the Minister'). In addition, with the exception of fishing rights and fisheries, all property and rights in respect of property, formerly vested in the Land Commission, are now vested in the Minister. Fishing rights and fisheries are vested in or reserved to the Central Fisheries Board. Finally, the jurisdiction of the Judicial Commissioner and Appeal Tribunal of the Commission is now vested in the High Court. The Irish Land Commission (Dissolution) Act, 1992 came into operation on 31 March 1999, by virtue of the Irish Land Commission (Dissolution) Act, 1992 (Commencement) Order, 1999 (SI 75/1999).

5.15.2   REPEAL OF SS 12 AND 45

Section 12(1) of the Land Act, 1965 provided:

An Agricultural Holding shall not be let, sub-let or sub-divided without the consent in writing of the Land Commission which may be either general or particular or subject to conditions.

Section 45(2)(a) provided:

Notwithstanding any other enactment or any rule of law but subject to paragraph (b) of this section and to subsection (3) of this section, no interest in land to which this section applies shall become vested in a person who is not a qualified person except with the written consent (whether general or particular) of the Land Commission and subject to any conditions attached to the consent having been complied with, and the determination of the application for such consent shall be an excepted matter for the purposes of section 12 of the Land Act, 1950.

Sections 12 and 45 were fully repealed with effect from 4 November 2005. Section 12 of the Land Act, 2005 contains the specific repeal provision. Thus the consent of the Land Commission, and subsequently the Minister for Agriculture and Food, as previously required, are no longer necessary for the subdivision of holdings (s 12) or the purchase of land by non-qualified persons (s 45) and these certificates are no longer required in every deed. See Practice Note in the Law Society *Gazette* in December 2005.

5.15.3   PROVISIONAL LIST OF LAND FOR COMPULSORY PURCHASE: S 13

Although s 13 should not trouble the practitioner very often, it is important that a solicitor acting for the purchaser of agricultural land is aware of its application and makes appropriate enquiries. The section applies only to lands appearing on the Minister's provisional list for compulsory purchase. Any land appearing on this list may not be sold, let, sublet, or subdivided without the written consent of the Minister, until such time as the proceedings for the acquisition of the lands, under the Land Purchase Acts, have been terminated (s 13(1)).

This provisional list is transmitted to the Registrar of Titles, who will make appropriate entries in the register. These entries are deleted when they cease to have effect. In the case of registered land, therefore, the usual search in the Land Registry will disclose whether or not a property is affected by the provisional list. In the case of unregistered land, the usual searches will not make a similar disclosure. It is, therefore, imperative for the solicitor acting for the purchaser of unregistered agricultural land to pay particular attention to the reply furnished by the vendor to requisition 12 of the requisitions on title. This requisition includes the Land Acts in its list of notices to be disclosed. Also helpful is requisition 19.3, which calls for the production of 'any Vesting Order made to provide for consolidation with the property sold'.

From the perspective of the solicitor acting for the vendor of agricultural land, it is extremely important to make careful enquiry of the vendor, to ascertain whether any notices, relating to compulsory purchase under the Land Purchase Acts, have been served on him. In this regard, the vendor's solicitor must note carefully the provisions of s 40(6) of the Land Act, 1923 and s 13(2) of the 1965 Act. The former provision enables any person appointed by the Minister to enter upon any lands to inspect them, once notice in writing has been served upon the owner or occupier of such lands. By virtue of the 1965 Act, s 13(2), any sale, letting, subletting, or subdivision of land, within three months of service of such a notice, is void as against any person. This period of three months may be extended to six months by the Minister. When taking instructions in relation to the sale of agricultural land, therefore, the vendor's solicitor must bear in mind the provisions of general condition 35 of the Contract for Sale, relating to the disclosure of notices.

5.15.4   SPORTING RIGHTS: S 18

Section 18 applies only to registered land and deals with sporting rights reserved to a person other than the registered owner of the lands affected by the rights. Where the sporting rights have not been exercised for a period of 12 years ending on 9 March 1965 (the effective date of the 1965 Act), or for any subsequent 12-year period, s 18 provides that these rights shall cease to exist.

In the context of s 18, sporting rights exclude (a) fishing rights and (b) sporting rights reserved to the Land Commission (now the Minister).

Where the sporting rights have ceased to exist by operation of s 18, the registered owner or occupier of the property is entitled to make an application to the Land Registry to have the reference to the sporting rights removed from the register. The application is made on foot of an affidavit sworn by the interested party, a notice having first been placed in a local newspaper.

It is also possible to have the burden removed by consent. A letter from the National Parks and Wildlife Service should be obtained confirming that they have no objection to the removal. This is then sent to the Department of Agriculture, Food and Marine who will consent to the removal as the statutory successor to the Land Commission.

When acting for the purchaser of such sporting rights, a solicitor should take care to ascertain whether the rights have been exercised within the 12 years prior to the transaction. If they have not, the rights will cease to exist by operation of s 18. Where the sporting rights have been exercised within the relevant period, an affidavit to that effect should be obtained from the vendor.

CHAPTER 6

CONTRACT FOR SALE

6.1   Introduction

6.1.1   THE FORM OF THE CONTRACT

In order to be enforceable, a contract for the sale of land, in common with all other types of contract, must comply with the general principles of contract law. These are:

(i)   the parties to the contract must have the legal capacity to enter into it;

(ii)   the parties must have sufficient intention to create legal relations;

(iii)   the terms of the contract must be certain;

(iv)   there must be a valid offer and acceptance; and

(v)   there must be consideration.

In addition to the foregoing general principles of contract law, prior to the introduction of s 51(1) of the Land and Conveyancing Law Reform Act, 2009 ('the 2009 Act'), which came into effect on 1 December 2009, a contract for the sale of land also had to comply with the requirements of s 2 of the Statute of Frauds (Ireland) Act, 1695 which provided,

> *no action shall be brought whereby . . . to charge any person . . . upon any contract for sale of lands, tenements or hereditaments, or any interest in or concerning them . . . unless the agreement upon which such action shall be brought, or some memorandum or note thereof, shall be in writing, and signed by the party to be charged therewith, or some other person thereunto by him lawfully authorised.*

The effect of s 2 of the Statute of Frauds (Ireland) Act, 1695 was tempered by the development of the equitable doctrine of part performance. By virtue of this doctrine an oral contract for the sale of land may be upheld on the basis that the party, seeking to enforce the oral contract, has partly performed its obligations under the said oral contract and the other party, against whom enforcement of the contract is being sought, has acquiesced in those acts of part performance.

Section 2 of the Statute of Frauds (Ireland) Act, 1695 was repealed by the 2009 Act, and was restated in modern wording in s 51(1) which provides:

> *. . . no action shall be brought to enforce any contract for the sale or other disposition of land unless the agreement on which such action is brought, or some memorandum or note of it, is in writing and signed by the person against whom the action is brought or that person's authorised agent.*

This is subject to s 51(2) which provides that s 51(1) does not affect the law relating to part performance or other equitable doctrines. Section 51(3) provides that payment of a deposit is not necessary for an enforceable contract unless the contract expressly states otherwise.

A full discussion of the exact requirements, which must be satisfied, before a memorandum for the purposes of the 2009 Act can be said to have come into existence, is outside the scope of this book. However, it is accepted case law that the following elements must be present:

(i)   the parties to the contract must be identified;

(ii)   the property, the subject matter of the contract must be described;

(iii) the consideration for the sale must be set out; and

(iv)   any other provisions, which the parties consider germane to the contract, should also be included.

Where both the requirements of contract law and the 2009 Act are satisfied an enforceable contract for the sale of land will come into being. Such a contract is termed an 'open contract'. It is open in the sense that the terms of the contract, other than those recorded in the memorandum, are not specified. For example, the precise title being produced by the vendor may not be set out. In this instance, the parties must rely upon the general principles of common law and precedent to determine those terms not dealt with in the memorandum itself.

Where the parties seek to set out all of the terms of the agreement between them in a formal agreement, the resulting contract is said to be 'closed'. So long as the basic principles of contract law and the requirements of the 2009 Act are satisfied, such a formal agreement may take any form agreed by the parties. Since 1976, however, it has become standard conveyancing practice for the parties to record their formal agreement using the standard form of Contract for Sale produced by the Law Society of Ireland. For a further examination of open and closed contracts see **4.5**.

6.1.2   STANDARD LAW SOCIETY CONTRACT/CONDITIONS FOR SALE

Prior to 1976, where the parties to a contract for the sale of land wished to record the agreement in a closed contract, it was standard practice that one of the solicitors, usually the solicitor acting for the vendor, would draft a contract ab initio. In reality, most firms of solicitors had their own standard form of contract, with which the solicitors in that firm were very familiar, but which, for the purchaser's solicitor, was unknown territory. Transacting business in this manner resulted in additional work on the part of both the vendor's and the purchaser's solicitor, which in turn led to delays. In addition, the drafting party ran the risk of having ambiguous conditions or clauses interpreted against him or her.

In order to alleviate this situation, in 1976 the Law Society introduced the prototype of its standard Contract for Sale. The purpose of the standard Contract for Sale was to give a fair balance of rights between the vendor and the purchaser. The standard Contract for Sale has been through many iterations since 1976. As the standard Contract for Sale is revised on a regular basis by the Conveyancing Committee of the Law Society, practitioners are reminded to ensure that they use the most up-to-date edition for each transaction. The Law Society recommended contract is entitled the 'General Conditions of Sale' but it is more commonly referred to as the Contract for Sale.

The standard Contract for Sale is in a pre-printed form and comprises the following elements:

(i)   memorandum of agreement;

(ii)   particulars and tenure;

(iii) documents schedule;

(iv)   searches schedule;

(v)   special conditions;

(vi)   non-title information sheet; and

(vii) general conditions of sale.

The current Contract for Sale (the 2009 edition) contains 51 general conditions, three special conditions, a memorandum page, particulars and tenure, a documents schedule, a searches schedule, and space to include any additional special conditions which the parties wish to insert in the contract together with a two-page query sheet for non-title information. It reflects all legislative changes up to 31 December 2009 including the Land and Conveyancing Law Reform Act, 2009 and eStamping requirements which came into effect on 30 December 2009.

This chapter deals exclusively with the standard Contract for Sale and references to the 'Contract for Sale' refer to the Law Society standard Conditions of Sale 2009 edition. Reference to the 'general conditions' or to any specific general condition refers to the general conditions of sale numbering 1 to 51 attached to this edition of the Law Society Contract for Sale. Any amendment to these general conditions must be dealt with by way of special condition inserted in the Contract for Sale.

This 2009 edition of the standard Contract for Sale is currently under review by the Law Society Conveyancing Committee.

6.1.2.1 Definitions and interpretation

Definitions and interpretation are covered by general conditions 1 to 3. The closing date and the interest rate will be dealt with later in this chapter. The other definition requiring comment is that of the 'purchase price'. This definition provides that where goodwill, crops, or purchased chattels are included, the purchase price extends to the money payable for these. Thus, by virtue of general condition 24(a), which provides for the payment of the balance of the purchase price on closing, the purchaser is liable on the closing date not only for the balance of the monies due in respect of the property being purchased but also for any sums payable in respect of goodwill, crops, or purchased chattels.

In the 2001 edition of the contract, general condition 3 was expanded to cover the situation where the contract included a special condition which was void, illegal, or invalid. General condition 3 now provides that so long as the void, illegal, or invalid condition does not go to the root of the contract, such a special condition shall be deemed to have been severed and omitted from the Contract for Sale.

6.2   The Situation Pre-Contract: Pre-Contract Enquiries— Preparation of the Contract for Sale

In a standard conveyancing transaction, it is the vendor's solicitor who drafts the Contract for Sale. In order to properly draft the Contract for Sale, the vendor's solicitor must:

(a) take comprehensive instructions from his or her client;

(b) investigate the vendor's title to the subject property; and

(c) have a working knowledge of the general conditions of the standard Contract for Sale.

When investigating the title to the subject property, the vendor's solicitor must scrutinise the title by the light of the same standards, which he would apply if he were purchasing the subject property. In other words, the vendor's solicitor must establish the type of title being offered by the vendor, the root of title, and any defects affecting the title. For a more detailed discussion on investigation of title and roots of title generally, see **chapter 4** and **chapter 5**. The necessity for the vendor's solicitor to take detailed instructions and to carefully investigate his client's title prior to the preparation of the Contract for Sale becomes clearer with a fuller understanding of the elements, which comprise the standard Contract for Sale as set out in the rest of this chapter.

To assist both the vendor's and purchaser's solicitor in taking proper instructions from their clients, the Law Society and the Dublin Solicitors Bar Association have produced useful pre-contract questionnaires. These list the type of pre-contract information required in ordinary residential transactions. As the questionnaires are updated from time to time, practitioners are reminded to ensure that they use the most up-to-date version.

The following checklists might also provide assistance when taking instructions in a residential conveyancing transaction:

Checklist for the vendor. Sale of premises; pre-contract information (**6.2.1**).

Checklist for the purchaser. Purchase of premises; pre-contract information (**6.2.2**).

Particulars of vendor (**6.2.3**).

Particulars of purchaser (**6.2.4**).

6.2.1 CHECKLIST FOR THE VENDOR

SALE OF PREMISES: PRE-CONTRACT INFORMATION

1. Boundaries

    (i) which are shared and which are in common

    (ii) any special agreements

    (iii) all maps and identity to be checked

2. Services

    (i) drainage

    (ii) water

    (iii) electricity

    (iv) telephone

    (v) gas

    (vi) alarm system—number/code

3. Services

    (i) in charge

    (ii) private—details/indemnity

    (iii) if the property is serviced by water treatment system has it been registered? —produce Certificate—any issues regarding effectiveness of treatment system?

4. Easements

    (i) right of way/light

    (ii) services

    (iii) others

    (iv) if prescriptive, need to apply for court order or register in Land Registry?

5. Forestry/fishing/sporting

6. Tenancies/vacant possession

7. PLV

8. Outgoings

    (i) ground rent

    (ii) rates

    (iii) water rates/water charges/environmental waste charges/NPPR charge/-household levy

    (iv) service charge

    (v) insurance contribution

    (vi) receipts and vouchers

9. Notices

   (i) served

   (ii) given

   (iii) CPO

10. Encumbrances/proceedings

    (i) mortgage of vendor—negative equity?—transferred to NAMA?

    (ii) litigation/disputes (including family)

    (iii) grants—are they repayable?

11. Voluntary dispositions

12. Taxation

    (i) Probate tax—certificate of discharge

    (ii) Capital gains tax—clearance certificate

    (iii) CA12 in applications for adverse possession (s 49 applications)

    (iv) VAT

    (v) Tax number, and appropriate documentation vouching same. Details of PPS number and details of inspector of taxes (name and address and dis-trict no), details of PPS number of purchasers for the Contract for Sale and for Stamp Duty Returns. Local authority levy in respect of second residential properties (non principal private residence). Certificate of Discharge/Certificate of Exemption

    (vi) Household charge/Certificate of Discharge/Certificate of Exemption/Certifi-cate of Waiver

    (vii) Confirmation of payment of Local Property Tax for all relevant years—evidence of value band declared for the property by the Vendor in mak-ing returns/property identifier number. Is Special Clearance from Revenue required? LPT id number is required for stamping a residential property.

13. Body corporate/trustee

    (i) memorandum and articles of association

    (ii) Companies Registration Office search

    (iii) rules

    (iv) trust instrument

14. Family law

    (i) all relevant State certificates

    (ii) is the property a 'family home' or 'shared home'?

    (iii) is the property anybody else's 'family home' or 'shared home'?

    (iv) other information

15. Planning/building bye-law approval/building regulations/fire certificate/Fire Ser-vices Act/environment

16. Landlord and tenant/lease

    (i) consent to assign

    (ii) consent to change of use

17. Fee simple—acquired?

18. First Registration—required/ triggered by current transaction. (If so, Land Registry compliant map is necessary)

19. Inventory

20. Insurance

Increase to full replacement value if necessary and advise in writing pre-contract

21. BER Certificate and Advisory Report

6.2.2   CHECKLIST FOR THE PURCHASER

PURCHASE OF PREMISES: PRE-CONTRACT INFORMATION

1. DETAILS OF VENDOR

(i)   name

(ii)   address

(iii)   price

(iv)   deposit

(v)   loan clause

(vi)   solicitors for vendor

(vii)   PPS/tax number

2. FINANCE

(i)   deposit/equity from sale of house

(ii)   loan—amount €

(a)   name of lending institution

(b)   branch/address

(c)   position of loan application

(d)   survey/fire cover/life cover

(iii)   bridging accommodation

(iv)   undertaking and irrevocable authority

(v)   prepare and furnish financial memo

3. ITEMS INCLUDED IN SALE

(i)   inventory

(ii)   value

4. PURCHASE OF PART

(i)   map

(ii)   easements including:

(a)   right of way/light

(b)   services

(c)   maintenance

5. STRUCTURE/SURVEY

(i)   inspection by expert independent of lending institution

(ii)   check re survey/valuer's report for lending institution (advise in writing)

6. PLANNING

(i)   planning search (pre-contract)

(ii)   any change in planning unit/division

(iii)   any change in use/intensification

(iv)   fire certificate/building regulations

7. INSURANCE

(i)   cover from date of contract/roofing if new building

(ii)   life cover/mortgage protection

6.2.3 PARTICULARS OF VENDOR: CHECKLIST

DATE

GENERAL

1. CLIENT
   - (i)   name
   - (ii) address and occupation
   - (iii) status/age—married/single/separated/divorced
   - (iv) telephone/fax
   - (v)   PPS/tax number

2. SPOUSE/CIVIL PARTNER/COHABITING PARTNER
   - (i)   name
   - (ii) other details
   - (iii) PPS/tax number

3. BANK
   - (i)   name
   - (ii) address
   - (iii) contact (name)
   - (iv) undertaking
   - (v)   financial arrangements

4. CLOSING DATE
   - (i)   desired closing date
   - (ii) alternative

5. DETAILS OF PURCHASERS
   - (i)   names
   - (ii) address
   - (iii) price
   - (iv) deposit
   - (v)   loan clause
   - (vi) PPS/tax number of purchasers
   - (vii) solicitors for purchaser

6. MORTGAGOR OF VENDORS
   - (i)   name of lending institution
   - (ii)   branch/address
   - (iii) amount due
   - (iv)   authority re deeds
   - (v)   any other encumbrances
   - (vi)   undertaking—retainer and irrevocable authority
   - (vii) vendor in negative equity?
   - (viii) loan transferred to NAMA?

7. ITEMS INCLUDED IN SALE
   - (i)   inventory
   - (ii) value

8. SALE OF PART
   - (i)   map

        (ii)   easements including

             (a)   right of way/light

             (b)   services

             (c)   maintenance

  9. INSURANCE

        (i)   any general conditions re risk remaining

        (ii)   is property insured to full replacement value?

        (iii)   maintain insurance until completion

  10. INFORMATION—REPLIES TO REQUISITIONS

6.2.4 PARTICULARS OF PURCHASER: CHECKLIST

DATE: ....

PURCHASER'S NAME: ....

ADDRESS: ....

OCCUPATION: ....

HOME TELEPHONE NUMBER: .... OFFICE: ....

FAX NO: ....

PPS/TAX NUMBER: ....

MARRIED/SINGLE/DIVORCED/SEPARATED/ENGAGED/CIVIL PARTNER/COHABITING:....

IF MARRIED/CIVIL PARTNER NAME OF SPOUSE/CIVIL PARTNER AND DATE AND PLACE OF MARRIAGE/CIVIL PARTNERSHIP CEREMONY: ....

....

AGE:...

IF JOINT PURCHASE—IS PROPERTY TO BE TAKEN AS JOINT TENANTS OR TENANTS IN COMMON (EXPLAIN DIFFERENCE): ....

VENDOR'S NAME: ....

ADDRESS: ....

....

VENDOR'S SOLICITOR: ....

....

ADDRESS OF PROPERTY TO BE PURCHASED: ....

....

BORROWING ARRANGEMENT: ....

NAME AND ADDRESS OF BANK/BUILDING SOCIETY: ....

....

CHECK IF BRIDGING FINANCE WILL BE NECESSARY: ....

GET IRREVOCABLE AUTHORITY FROM THE PURCHASER AND HIS SPOUSE/CIVIL PARTNER, IF APPLICABLE, TO COMPLETE PURCHASE AND TO GIVE RELEVANT UNDERTAKING TO THE BANK:...

ITEMS AGREED WITH VENDOR TO BE INCLUDED IN THE PURCHASE: ....

DESIRED CLOSING DATE: ....

ADVISE CLIENT TO HAVE HOUSE CHECKED BY ARCHITECT: ....

ADVISE CLIENT TO HAVE HOUSE INSURED: ....

ESTIMATED COST OF TRANSACTION: ....

Stamp duty on assurance	€
Land Registry/Registry of Deeds etc.	€
First Registration (if necessary)	€
Marriage/Civil Partnership certificate	€
Searches	€
Surveyor's fees	€
Land Registry/Registry of Deeds fees on mortgage	€
Sundries	€
Own professional fee	€
VAT	€

6.2.5   VALUE ADDED TAX

The manner in which value added tax (VAT) is levied upon property transactions was dramatically altered with the introduction on 1 July 2008 of a new VAT on property system. The manner in which the new rules are applied to the sale of freehold and 'freehold equivalent interests' is examined in detail in **chapter 16**. Given the complexity of this new VAT on property system and its potential to affect fundamentally the financial position of the vendor *and* the purchaser, it is imperative that the solicitors acting for the vendor and the purchaser are appraised of the VAT position at a *pre-contract stage*. In order to assist practitioners in this regard, the Conveyancing and the Taxation Committees of the Law Society have jointly issued VAT pre-contract enquiries ('PCVE'). These enquiries are updated on a regular basis and may be accessed by logging onto the members' area of the Law Society website. Practitioners should ensure that the most up-to-date version available on the website is used in each individual transaction. Although the enquiries are to be raised by the purchaser's solicitor, in a joint Practice Note issued in the May 2009 *Gazette*, the Conveyancing and Taxation Committees stated that it was their view that the enquiries would prove a useful tool for the vendor's solicitor in establishing the VAT position in each individual transaction, thereby assisting the vendor's solicitor in correctly drafting special condition 3 of the Contract for Sale (discussed later). The PCVE incorporate a guide to completing special condition 3. It is, therefore, advisable that, on receiving instructions regarding the sale of the property, the vendor's solicitor would liaise with the vendor and, if necessary, the vendor's taxation advisor, in order to complete the questionnaire. Purchasers' solicitors should carefully consider the responses to the enquiries received from the vendor and ensure that the purchaser is fully aware of the VAT implications of the transaction. On completion, the purchaser's solicitor ought to seek confirmation from the vendor's solicitor that the replies to the enquiries are still accurate and correct. As the enquiries are comprised of a series of very detailed questions regarding the VAT history of the property, it is strongly advised that, unless the solicitor in question is an expert in VAT or the transaction is a straightforward one, the vendor should be advised to engage the services of a VAT specialist or a tax advisor. Equally, the purchaser's solicitor ought to advise the purchaser to seek specialist assistance, if he or she does not feel competent to analyse the information furnished by the vendor and advise on the consequences of the same for the VAT treatment of the transaction.

6.2.6   NEGATIVE EQUITY AND NAMA

General condition 8(c) of the Contract for Sale provides 'subject as stipulated in the special conditions the vendor shall, prior or at the completion of the sale, discharge all mortgages and charges for the payment of money (other than items apportionable under condition 27(b)) which affect the subject property'. In the January/February 2010 edition of the *Gazette*, the Conveyancing Committee of the Law Society issued a Practice Note reminding practitioners that they must not allow a vendor to enter into a binding Contract for Sale where the vendor only has negative equity in the property, without first making appropriate arrangements either with the vendor's lending institution or with the purchaser. Having made appropriate arrangements, the vendor's solicitor ought then address the issue with an appropriate special condition. Failure to do so will result in the vendor being contractually bound by general condition 8(c) to discharge the mortgage, even where the proceeds of sale will not be sufficient to do so. The Conveyancing Committee's Practice Note reminds practitioners that it is the responsibility of the vendor to make good title, which includes the obligation to discharge all mortgages and charges affecting the subject property. From the perspective of the vendor's solicitor he or she must also be careful not to put himself or herself in a position where an undertaking has been given to the vendor's lending institution regarding the discharge of the mortgage and any other charges affecting the property with which he or she is not able to comply by virtue of the fact that the vendor is in negative equity. Clearly, this is an issue which must be addressed at the earliest possible stage and the Conveyancing Committee has, therefore, recommended that redemption figures be obtained by the vendor's solicitor immediately upon receiving instructions for sale so that the vendor's solicitor may satisfy himself or herself as to the position. Obtaining redemption figures at an early stage will also alert the vendor's solicitor to potential difficulties arising from the subject property being used as cross security for another property.

The vendor's solicitor should also establish at an early stage whether any charge or mortgage affecting the property has been transferred to NAMA or if the charge or mortgage has been granted directly in favour of NAMA. The approval of NAMA to the transaction will be required and that approval should be obtained in writing in the form agreed between the Conveyancing Committee and NAMA (see Practice Note issued in September 2013 *Gazette*). This process may involve a period of negotiation between the vendor and NAMA and the approval which ultimately issues may have conditions attached, such as the requirement that the proceeds of sale be split to allow net sale proceeds to be paid directly to NAMA or the participating lending institution. As a result, it is advisable that the vendor await receipt of the written approval, prior to entering into a Contract for Sale and that the position, once clear, be addressed in an appropriate special condition.

6.2.7   NON PRINCIPAL PRIVATE RESIDENCE CHARGE (NPPR)

With effect from 31 July 2009, the Local Government (Charges) Act, 2009 ('the LG 2009 Act') required that the sum of €200 be paid to the relevant local authority by the owners of non-principal private residences (called the NPPR charge). The NPPR charge was levied in respect of the years 2009 to 2013. Since the LG 2009 Act provides that the NPPR charge is a charge upon the property to which it relates, which is enforceable for a period of 12 years from the date on which it falls due, it is covered by general condition 8(c) of the Contract for Sale. SI 278/2009 made under the LG 2009 Act nominated 31 July as the liability date for 2009. Thereafter, the LG 2009 Act provided that the liability date would be 31 March in each succeeding year. Thus, any person owning a non-principal private residence on the relevant liability date was liable to pay the charge. It is important that the vendor's solicitor establish prior to issuing the Contract for Sale whether or not the subject property was a non-principal private residence on any of the liability dates during the years 2009 to 2013. If the subject property was a NPPR on any one of the liability dates and none of the exemptions provided for in the LG 2009 Act applies, the position regarding payment of the charge should be ascertained. On the initial introduction of the NPPR charge, the Conveyancing Committee issued a Practice Note (August 2009) advising purchasers' solicitors that if it was claimed by the vendor that the property was not liable to the NPPR charge the purchaser's solicitor should seek confirmation of this by way of statutory declaration. This initial advice was revised by a Practice Note, issued in June 2013, which took account of the Local Government (Household Charge) Act, 2011 ('The LG (HC) 2011 Act') which inserted, *inter alia*, a new s 8A(4) into the LG 2009 Act. This provision requires that, on or before the completion of the sale of a residential property, the vendor shall give to the purchaser either: (a) a Certificate of Discharge; or (b) a Certificate of Exemption, as appropriate in respect of each year in which a liability date fell since the date of the last sale of the property. It is, therefore, necessary for the vendor to apply to the relevant section of the local authority to obtain either a Certificate of Discharge or a Certificate of Exemption, as the case may be. The maximum liability, including penalties and interest, which can be applied in respect of an unpaid NPPR charge has, with effect from 1 September 2014, been capped at €7,230.00.

Part 12 of the Local Government Reform Act 2014 deals with the collection of undischarged liabilities relating to the NPPR charge.

6.2.8   HOUSEHOLD CHARGE

With effect from 31 March 2012 a household charge set at €100 per annum was introduced in respect of residential properties. The household charge was introduced as an interim measure, which was ultimately replaced in 2013 by the Local Property Tax ('LPT'). The household charge was, therefore, only payable in respect of 2012. However, as it is a charge on property and remains so for a period of 12 years from the last due date, the owner of a residential property remains liable for any outstanding amounts and arrears for that period. The appropriate Certificates of Discharge, Exemption, or Waiver, establishing the position, must, therefore, be furnished to the purchaser on completion. Since the introduction of Local Property Tax, outstanding amounts and arrears in respect of the household charge are collected by the Revenue Commissioners through the Local Property Tax system and payments are recorded on certificates relating to LPT. See **chapter 16** for further details.

6.2.9   LOCAL PROPERTY TAX

As mentioned at **6.2.8**, the household charge was intended as an interim measure. An annual Local Property Tax ('LPT') came into effect in 2013. Save for those properties outside the scope of the LPT charge or which are exempt from the charge, LPT is charged on all residential properties in the State. Section 123 of the Finance (Local Property Tax), 2012 ('the LPT 2012 Act') provides that any LPT charge, interest, or other monetary penalty amount which is due and unpaid by a liable person shall remain a charge on the relevant property to which it relates. The LPT Act further provides at s 124 that this charge shall continue to apply without a time limit until such time as it is paid in full. It therefore follows that general condition 8(c) applies to LPT and the vendor is, consequently, under an obligation to transfer title free from encumbrances. Section 126(1) of the LPT 2012 Act (as amended by s 12(3) of the Finance (Local Property Tax) (Amendment) Act, 2013 ('The LPT 2013 Act)) provides that a vendor of residential property shall, before completion of the sale of the property pay any local property tax, penalties, and accrued interest due and payable in respect of that property. The liability date for LPT is 1 November every year (save for the year in which LPT was introduced, when the liability date was 1 May 2013). By virtue of s 126(2) of the LPT 2012 Act (as amended by s 12(f) of the LPT 2013 Act) the sale of a residential property essentially brings forward the date on which the tax becomes payable, so that, where a sale closes prior to 1 November in any year, the charge for the entirety of the succeeding year will become due on the date of sale and must be paid by the vendor. The effect of these statutory provisions prompted the Conveyancing Committee of the Law Society to issue a Practice Note in June 2013 recommending that in circumstances other than where an exemption from LPT applies, a special condition providing for the apportionment of the LPT between the vendor and the purchaser should be inserted into the Contract for Sale. The following is the recommended wording:

> 'The Vendor shall discharge all local property tax relating to the Subject Property in advance of the completion of the sale and furnish the Purchaser with confirmation of payment on completion of sale. The amount paid by the Vendor in respect of local property tax relating to the Subject Property shall be apportioned as between the Vendor and the Purchaser in accordance with the provisions of General Condition 27. General Condition 8(c) and General Condition 27 are amended accordingly.'

Where an exemption applies, the foregoing special condition is, of course not appropriate and a special condition, tailored to the specific circumstances, should be drafted and inserted. Where the exemption arises by virtue of the status of the purchaser, for example where the purchaser is a first-time buyer, the Conveyancing Committee has recommended that the vendor should seek evidence of entitlement to the exemption. Such evidence might, for example, take the form of a Statutory Declaration.

The confirmation of payment of LPT, referred to in the previously discussed special condition, should be in the form of a print out of the LPT history relating to the subject property. The LPT history may be obtained either by the vendor him or herself or by the vendor's solicitor by accessing the LPT online system. In order to do so, practitioners must obtain from their clients the property ID number, the client's PPSN or tax reference number, and the Property Access Number (PAN). The LPT history should be printed in landscape format in order to display all relevant information. The vendor's solicitor should also be provided with the market value or valuation band declared on each relevant return, together with the basis for the said valuation and details of any exemptions claimed by the vendor. As it will be necessary to establish whether there has been any under-declaration of LPT, which must be corrected by the vendor prior to completion, the vendor's solicitor should consult the guidelines issued by the Revenue Commissioners entitled 'Guidelines for the Sale or Transfer of Ownership of a Relevant Residential Property'. These guidelines which are updated from time to time and are available on the Revenue website set out the conditions which must be satisfied in order for a general clearance in respect of LPT to apply. In certain circumstances, the Revenue Commissioners will issue a specific clearance on request from a vendor. The procedure for requesting and obtaining a specific clearance is also set out in the Revenue guidelines. The application and operation of LPT is considered in further detail in **chapter 16**.

6.2.10 WATER SERVICES (AMENDMENT) ACT, 2012

The Water Services (Amendment) Act, 2012 ('the Water Services 2012 Act'), which came into operation on 26 June 2012, provides for the introduction of the registration and inspection of waste-water treatment systems, such as septic tanks. The Waste-Water Treatment Systems (Registration) Regulations, 2012 (SI 220/2012) appoint 1 February 2013 as the prescribed date for the registration of waste-water treatment systems. Section 70 of the Water Services Act, 2012 provides that a person who sells a property connected to a domestic water treatment system, will be obliged, on the closing of the sale, to furnish to the purchaser a valid certificate of registration in respect of the water treatment system. After the sale has completed the purchaser is obliged to notify the water services authority of the change of ownership. Section 70C places an obligation on property owners to ensure that water treatment systems do not constitute and are not likely to constitute a risk to human health or the environment. Specifically, the property owner must ensure that the treatment system does not create a risk to water, air, soil, plants, or animals. The section further imposes a duty not to create a nuisance through noise and odours. In its Practice Note issued in March 2013, the Conveyancing Committee of the Law Society advised purchasers' solicitors to query the position regarding both the registration and the efficacy of the water treatment system at a pre-contract stage. It follows that the vendor's solicitor must acquaint him- or herself of the position at an early stage. Any anomalies manifesting themselves at the pre-contract stage should be addressed by an appropriately drafted special condition.

6.2.11 BUILDING ENERGY RATING (BER) CERTIFICATES

The European Union (Energy Performance of Buildings) Regulations, 2012 (SI 243/2012) ('the BER 2012 Regulations') came into operation on 9 January 2013. These regulations revoke earlier regulations contained in SI 666/2006, SI 229/2008, and SI 591/2008. Part 3 of the BER 2012 Regulations sets out the requirements regarding production of Building Energy Rating (BER) Certificates. Section 10(1) obliges any person who commissions the construction of a new dwelling, the construction of which commences on or after 9 January 2013, to obtain a BER certificate and accompanying advisory report in relation to the building before such dwelling is occupied for the first time. Where a new dwelling, the construction of which commenced on or after 9 January 2013 or a dwelling which was in existence on or before 9 January 2013 is offered for sale or letting, the vendor or lessor or any agent acting on behalf of the vendor or lessor in connection with the sale or lease is obliged by virtue of s 10(2) to produce a printed copy of the BER certificate and accompanying advisory report to any person expressing an interest in purchasing or letting the dwelling. A dwelling offered for sale or letting on the basis of plans and specifications may only be so offered if accompanied by a provisional BER certificate and accompanying advisory report. The final BER certificate, taking into account any changes implemented to the plans and specifications, implemented during the construction of the dwelling, must be produced to the purchaser or the tenant prior to completion of the sale or letting (s 10(3)(b)). Similar provisions apply to buildings other than dwellings and are set out in s 11 of the BER 2012 Regulations. Sections 10(4) (dwellings) and 11(4) (buildings other than dwellings) provide that a person required to produce a BER certificate and accompanying advisory report in respect of any building shall warrant that the BER certificate and advisory report so produced corresponds to the current BER record for the building on the BER register. By virtue of s 12 of the BER 2012 Regulations it is mandatory to advertise the energy performance indicator of the BER certificate for that building in any advertisements relating to the sale or letting. Certain buildings are excluded from the application of the BER 2012 Regulations and these are set out in the Regulations. A person contravening any provision of Part 3 of the BER 2012 Regulations is guilty, by virtue of s 15, of an offence. It follows from the foregoing that the vendor's solicitor must ensure, prior to issuing the Contract for Sale, that the requirements of the BER 2012 Regulations have been satisfied.

6.2.12   GENERAL

In many specialist transactions it is necessary to raise the requisitions on title, in relation to that type of transaction, pre-contract. Properties to which this applies include:

(a)   licensed premises;

(b)   other commercial premises;

(c)   new apartments;

(d)   second-hand apartments; and

(e)   agricultural land.

The Conveyancing Committee of the Law Society has issued standard Pre-Contract Enquiries in respect of the Multi-Unit Developments Act 2011, which may be downloaded from the precedents section of the Law Society's website. As these Pre-Contract Enquiries are updated from time to time, practitioners should ensure that they use the most up-to-date version in each transaction.

A solicitor should not undertake the conveyancing of any of these listed properties without being fully familiar with all the legal implications of the transaction. For example, environmental law might play a major part in the purchase of a factory.

6.2.13   BENEFICIAL INTEREST

Since 1 December 2009, s 52 of the 2009 Act provides that the beneficial interest in land will pass to a purchaser upon the signing of an enforceable Contract for Sale without any need for consideration to be paid, therefore overturning the decision in *Tempany v Hynes* [1976] IR 101. In its December 2009 Practice Note the Taxation Committee of the Law Society advised that:

'. . . notwithstanding the coming into force of the section . . . Revenue does not regard the section as changing the existing position regarding the time of supply of immovable property for VAT purposes.'

6.3   Portions of a Contract for Sale to be Completed by Vendor

6.3.1   COVER PAGE

The cover page of the standard Contract for Sale has no legal effect but ought to be completed as it provides space for the insertion of some useful details such as the identity of the auctioneer and vendor's solicitor, and, in the case of an auction, the time, date, and venue for the auction.

6.3.2   MEMORANDUM OF AGREEMENT

6.3.2.1   General

In order to complete the memorandum of agreement, the vendor's solicitor must have the following information available to him or her:

(a)   vendor's name, address, and tax number;

(b)   purchaser's name, address, and tax number;

(c)   purchase price;

(d)   deposit payable on execution of the contract;

(e)   the closing date; and

(f)   the interest rate payable in the event of late closing.

In addition, it will be necessary for the vendor's solicitor to have investigated the situation regarding the family home. If the property is the family home or shared home of the vendor and his or her spouse/civil partner and that spouse/civil partner is not on the title, in order to satisfy the requirements of the Family Home Protection Act, 1976/Civil Partnership and Certain Rights and Obligations of Cohabitants Act, 2010, the consent of the non-owning spouse/civil partner should be endorsed on the Contract for Sale. The memorandum of agreement of the Contract for Sale provides a space at the top of the memorandum for the endorsement of the non-owning spouse/civil partner. For further discussion on this topic see **chapter 7**.

6.3.2.2   Deposit

Items (a), (b), and (c) of the preceding list can be easily ascertained from the vendor and/ or the auctioneer. The quantum of the deposit, payable by the purchaser on the execution of the contract, depends upon the transaction. As a general rule, ten per cent of the purchase price is considered appropriate, but there may be circumstances in which either a greater or a smaller sum might suffice. In guiding the vendor in this regard, the vendor's solicitor should bear in mind the purpose of the deposit. By virtue of general condition 41(a):

'If the purchaser shall fail in any material respect to comply with any of the Conditions, the vendor (without prejudice to any rights or remedies available to him at law or in equity) shall be entitled to forfeit the deposit and to such purpose unilaterally to direct his solicitor to release same to him . . .'

The function of the deposit is, therefore, twofold. Firstly, it is to serve to dissuade the purchaser from reneging upon his obligations under the contract. Secondly, in the event that the purchaser fails to fulfil his obligations, the deposit will be retained by the vendor as some modicum of compensation for the wasted effort and expense of the failed trans-action. It follows that the deposit must be sufficiently large to fulfil these two functions. Thus for example, if, the consideration for the sale were a modest one, the vendor might consider that only a deposit in excess of ten per cent would give him sufficient comfort.

In the case of an auction, general condition 4(d) expressly provides that the deposit shall be ten per cent of the purchase price. If either a greater or a smaller percentage is to be paid, a special condition, altering the general condition, ought to be inserted into the sec-tion of the Contract for Sale dealing with special conditions. General condition 4(d) also provides that the deposit, paid at auction, is to be held by the vendor's solicitor as stake-holder. A space is provided at the end of the memorandum of agreement for the vendor's solicitor to acknowledge receipt of the deposit and to confirm that he or she holds the deposit as stakeholder. The status of the vendor's solicitor with regard to the deposit pre-contract and post contract is discussed at **6.5** and **6.6** respectively.

6.3.2.3   Closing date

In the context of a sale by private treaty, the closing date will often have been agreed be-tween the vendor and the purchaser. In the case of a sale not by private treaty where there is no such agreement or where the property is sold by tender or at auction, the closing date should be stipulated by the vendor. If no date is specified in the memorandum of agree-ment, the definition of 'closing date' provided for in general condition 2 (Definitions) of the Contract for Sale applies. This general condition defines the closing date as:

> 'the date specified as such in the Memorandum, or, if no date is specified the first Work-ing Day after the expiration of five weeks computed from the Date of Sale'.

'Date of Sale' is defined in general condition 2 as:

> 'the date of the auction when the Sale shall have been by auction, and otherwise means the date upon which the contract for the Sale shall have become binding on the vendor and the purchaser'.

The five-week closing date, stipulated by general condition 2, was included in the 2001 edition of the Contract for Sale after it came to the attention of the Law Society Convey-ancing Committee that many vendors were stipulating unreasonably short closing dates in contracts for sale. When guiding their clients regarding an appropriate closing date, vendor's solicitors have a duty to advise their client regarding what is a realistic time frame for the completion of a conveyancing transaction. In the view of the Conveyancing Com-mittee a five-week period is reasonable in most transactions.

Frequently, the closing date is to be fixed by reference to some condition precedent to clos-ing. In this case it is usual for the vendor's solicitor to insert the words 'see special condi-tions' in the space provided for filling in the closing date and for the condition precedent to be described in a special condition.

6.3.2.4   Interest rate

As with the quantum of the deposit, when taking instructions from the vendor on the interest rate to be inserted, the vendor's solicitor ought to be mindful of the circumstances in which interest will become applicable. The application of the interest rate is set out in general condition 25(a) of the Contract for Sale, which provides:

> 'If by reason of any default on the part of the purchaser, the purchase shall not have been completed on or before the later of (a) the Closing Date or (b) such subsequent date where-after delay in completing shall not be attributable to default on the part of the vendor
>
> (i) the purchaser shall pay interest to the vendor on the balance of the Purchase Price remaining unpaid at the Stipulated Interest Rate for the period between the Closing Date (or as the case may be such subsequent date as aforesaid) and the date of the actual completion of the Sale. Such interest shall accrue from day to day and shall be payable before and after any judgment.'

Thus, the interest rate is to be used to calculate the penalty, payable by the purchaser, in the event of late closing caused by the default of the purchaser. It follows that the actual rate must be sufficiently penal to achieve this objective.

In the event that the vendor's solicitor fails to insert an actual interest rate into the memorandum of agreement, the definition of 'Stipulated Interest Rate', set out in general condition 2 shall apply. This definition provides:

'"Stipulated Interest Rate" means the interest rate specified in the Memorandum, or, if no rate is so specified, such rate as shall equate to four per cent per annum above the Court Rate obtaining pursuant to s 22, Courts Act, 1981 and ruling at the date from which interest is to run.'

It is useful to remember that the vendor never pays interest under the Contract for Sale. Interest is only payable by the purchaser.

6.3.3   PARTICULARS AND TENURE

6.3.3.1   General

In this section of the Contract for Sale, the vendor's solicitor is required to provide both a physical (the particulars) and legal (the tenure) description of the subject property. Clearly, neither can be furnished unless the vendor's solicitor is familiar with the vendor's title.

6.3.3.2   Particulars

The physical description must describe the subject property with sufficient certainty for a court to identify it in the event of a dispute. In the case of unregistered land and where the entirety of the property, acquired by the vendor, is the subject of the contract, it is customary to adopt the description of the subject property, contained in the deed to the vendor. Care must be taken, however, not to replicate errors or misdescriptions contained in previous transactions. In the case of registered property, the subject property is described by reference to the relevant folio. Where part only of the vendor's property is to be sold, it is usual to recite the area of the property being transferred, together with reference to a suitable map, which is then attached to the contract.

The doctrine of caveat emptor applies to the physical description of the subject property. Thus, it is the purchaser's responsibility to satisfy himself as to the boundaries, etc of the subject property and unless there has been a deliberate misdescription of the subject property on the part of the vendor, the vendor will be entitled to rely on this doctrine in the event of a dispute. This is reflected in general condition 14 of the Contract for Sale, which provides:

'The purchaser shall accept such evidence of identity as may be gathered from the descriptions in the documents of title plus (if circumstances require) a statutory declaration to be made by a competent person, at the purchaser's expense, that the Subject Property has been held and enjoyed for at least twelve years in accordance with the title shown. The vendor shall be obliged to furnish such information as is in his possession relative to the identity and extent of the Subject Property, but shall not be required to define exact boundaries, fences, ditches, hedges or walls or to specify which (if any) of the same are of a party nature, nor shall the vendor be required to identify parts of the Subject Property held under different titles.'

6.3.3.3   Tenure

The legal description of the title being offered must be accurate and must reflect what is evidenced by the documents of title being furnished with the contract. In this section of the Contract for Sale, the vendor's solicitor must state whether the nature of the subject property is freehold or leasehold.

It is also customary for the description of the tenure to include references to any appurtenant rights benefiting or any burdens affecting the subject property for example any rights of way.

6.3.3.4   Sample particulars and tenure

<u>Unregistered Freehold—entirety of vendor's property being sold</u>

(Particulars)

ALL THAT AND THOSE the dwellinghouse and premises known as No 196 Brownwood Avenue, Rathmines situate in the Parish of St. George formerly in the County but now in the City of Dublin more particularly delineated on map annexed hereto and thereon outlined in red.

(Tenure)

HELD in Fee Simple

<u>Unregistered Leasehold—entirety of vendor's property being sold</u>

(Particulars)

ALL THAT AND THOSE the dwellinghouse and premises known as No 41 Victoria Avenue, Ranelagh situate in the Parish of St. Paul formerly in the County but now in the City of Dublin

(Tenure)

HELD under an Indenture of Lease dated the 4th day of May 1900 and made BETWEEN Joseph Black of the One Part and Mary White of the Other Part for a term of Nine Hundred and Ninety Years from the 1st day of June 1900 subject to the annual rent of Ten Pounds Ten Shillings and Sixpence thereby reserved and to the covenants on the part of the lessee and conditions therein contained.

<u>Unregistered Freehold—entirety of vendor's property being sold and sitting tenant in possession</u>

(Particulars)

ALL THAT AND THOSE the dwellinghouse and premises known as No 21 Herbert Lane, Coolock situate in the Parish of St. Michael formerly in the County but now in the City of Dublin

(Tenure)

HELD in Fee Simple

SUBJECT TO AND WITH THE BENEFIT OF Indenture of Lease dated the 1st day of January 2006 and made between the Vendor of the One Part and Niall Murray of the Other Part for a term of Ten years from the 1st day of January 2006 subject to the annual rent of Twelve Thousand Euro thereby reserved and to the covenants on the part of the lessee and the conditions therein contained.

<u>Registered Freehold—part only of vendor's property being sold</u>

(Particulars)

ALL THAT AND THOSE part of the property comprised in Folio WW1234F more particularly delineated on the map annexed hereto and thereon outlined in red, measuring 5.14 hectares or thereabouts. (This folio may also be described using the following longer format '. . . comprised in Folio 1234F of the Register of Freeholders County Wicklow.' Either format is correct.)

(Tenure)

HELD in Fee Simple

(Note that, in the context of a registered property, where the particulars are furnished in the manner described here, the tenure has already been included in the particulars, so that the additional 'HELD in Fee Simple' is not strictly required. However for the avoidance of doubt it is preferable to set out the tenure separately.)

Registered Leasehold – entirety of vendors property being sold

(Particulars)

ALL THAT AND THOSE the property known as Apartment 5 Blackwater Court being the property comprised in Folio DN5678L. (Or '. . . the property comprised in Folio 5678L of the Register of Leaseholders County Dublin')

(Tenure)

HELD under Lease dated the 4th day of March 2003 and made between Blackwater Developments of the First Part, Blackwater Court Management Company Limited of the Second Part and Ursula and Stephen O'Halloran of the Third Part for a term of 999 years from the 1st day of January 2003 subject to the annual rent of Ten Euro thereby reserved and to the covenants on the part of the Lessee and the conditions therein contained.

6.3.4 THE DOCUMENTS SCHEDULE

The documents schedule identifies the documents which are being furnished by the vendor with the Contract for Sale. Copies only are furnished at this stage and the originals will only be handed over at completion. The Conveyancing Committee has issued Practice Notes (Law Society *Gazette*, March 1995 and May 2000) setting out what should be included and what should not be included in the documents schedule. The 1995 Practice Note referred to the practice of including all the documents of title in the documents schedule and states:

'the Conveyancing Committee disapproves of the foregoing practice and recommends that in accordance with established conveyancing practice, the documents listed in the Documents Schedule should be limited to:

(a) The root of title being shown.

(b) Any document to which title is stated to have passed under the Special Conditions.

(c) Any document which is specifically referred to in a Special Condition.'

The May 2000 Practice Note adds planning documentation to this list.

Thus the current recommended practice of the Law Society provides that the documents listed in the documents schedule should be limited to:

(a) the root of title (note s 56 of the 2009 Act which allows a root of title 15 years old);

(b) any document from which title is being deduced;

(c) any document referred to in a special condition;

(d) planning documents; and

(e) BER certificate and advisory report.

If we assume that there are no difficulties with the title or the property which need to be dealt with by way of special condition, ie there are no documents which fall within (c) above, and if we assume that there are no planning documents, ie there are no documents which fall within (d) above, then the following are the *only* documents to be listed in the documents schedule:

6.3.4.1 Unregistered leasehold title

(a) The root of title—this will always be the lease (provided of course that the lease is at least 15 years old and has all the characteristics of a root of title—if the lease is not 15 years old the head leasehold title or the freehold title must be investigated).

(b) The document from which title is being deduced, ie an assignment or conveyance for value that is at least 15 years old and has all the characteristics of a root of title; for example, it is not a voluntary deed.

The title between these two documents is called 'intermediate title'. The title prior to the root is called 'prior title'.

6.3.4.2   Unregistered freehold title

The root of title—this will be a conveyance at least 15 years old which has all the characteristics of a root of title. Title will also be deduced from this document. (Unless there is a fee farm grant. If there is a fee farm grant then this is the root of title and title will be deduced from a conveyance at least 15 years old.)

6.3.4.3   Registered leasehold or registered freehold title

The root of title—this will always be the folio. (It might be more accurate to say the root is the register but the evidence of the register is the folio.) If it is a leasehold folio a copy of the lease should be furnished so as to show the term and the covenants and conditions.

If it is a freehold folio based on a fee farm grant a copy of the fee farm grant should be furnished so as to show the rent and the covenants and conditions. Note that a fee farm grant can no longer be created after 1 December 2009; see s 12(1) of 2009 Act.

6.3.4.4   Furnishing of documents

Copies of the documents listed in the documents schedule are furnished to the purchaser's solicitor with the draft Contract for Sale.

In light of the statutory obligations to produce a BER certificate and advisory report placed upon agents of persons selling or letting or building (discussed at **6.2.11**) it is advisable that the BER certificate and advisory report also be furnished with the Contract for Sale. In addition, given the difficulties which may arise in respect of LPT Returns, it is also advisable that the printout of the LPT history, relating to the subject property, be furnished at this stage.

Under the provisions of general condition 7 of the Contract for Sale, copies of the documents of title, after the document from which title is being deduced *to* the present sale, are furnished to the purchaser's solicitor within seven working days from the date of the signing of the contract. An example of such a document might be the deed to the vendor.

All original title documents are furnished on closing, save where otherwise provided for in a special condition.

Intermediate title *must* also be furnished to the purchaser's solicitor on closing. This is done on a without prejudice basis.

Hence the title to be furnished with the draft contact for sale is limited; however the Conveyancing Committee is currently canvassing practitioners to see if this practice should be changed and to determine if a full investigation of title should be done pre-contract as a matter of standard conveyancing practice.

6.3.5   THE SEARCHES SCHEDULE

General condition 19 provides that the purchaser shall be furnished with the searches (if any) specified in the searches schedule and any searches already in the vendor's possession which are relevant to the title or titles on offer.

In the case of registered land, the folio will be furnished and it will be a matter for the purchaser to make any other searches which he or she wishes.

In some areas, it is not the practice for the vendor to seek an official search in the Registry of Deeds; instead, the purchaser will rely on a hand search. However, because of the computerisation of the Registry of Deeds, official searches are now available in shorter periods and they should be made available to a purchaser.

Searches are covered in detail in **chapter 10**.

6.3.6   THE SPECIAL CONDITIONS

6.3.6.1   Special conditions 1, 2, and 3

As mentioned at **6.1.2**, the current Contract for Sale contains three pre-printed special conditions. Special condition 1 in the pre-printed Contract for Sale provides that the definitions and provisions as to interpretation set forth in the general conditions shall be applied for the purposes of the special conditions. It is, therefore, important that, when drafting special conditions, practitioners take note of the definitions and interpretations set out in general conditions 1 and 2, and exclude their application, *as appropriate*, to any special conditions being inserted. Failure to do so may result in an unintended interpretation of the special condition. Equally, the effect of special condition 2, which provides that in the event of a conflict between the general conditions and the special conditions, the special conditions will prevail, should be borne in mind by practitioners when drafting special conditions.

Special condition 3 addresses the VAT treatment of the transaction. As mentioned in **6.2.5**, the vendor should ascertain the position in respect of VAT as early as possible in order to enable him or her to correctly draft special condition 3. Prior to the introduction of the new VAT on property system, the pre-printed form of Contract for Sale included the text of general condition 3 which was set out as a series of self-cancelling clauses. With the introduction of the new VAT regime the drafting of general condition 3 became a far more complex matter. In order to assist practitioners, the Taxation and Conveyancing Committees of the Law Society issued a joint Practice Note in April 2008 which set out guidelines to the new VAT on property system. In August 2011 the committees approved a revised version of special condition 3 and added a new section to the VAT pre-contract enquiries giving guidance on the manner in which the special condition is to be used. Having taken careful pre-contract instruction from the client, practitioners ought to consider in every case which of the standard clauses are appropriate and, indeed, whether any of the standard clauses require amendment in the context of the particular transaction. The text of the special condition no longer appears in the pre-printed version of the Contract for Sale which, instead, contains a direction, under special condition 2, to attach or insert the current recommended form of VAT special condition, amended as appropriate. Practitioners are directed to the Law Society website where the most up-to-date version of the special condition can be accessed. Great care should be exercised by practitioners in drafting special condition 3 and the assistance of specialist advisors retained if necessary. Equally, the purchaser's solicitor, in analysing the effect of special condition 3, as inserted by the vendor's solicitor, ought to consider whether it is appropriate to seek specialist advice.

6.3.6.2   General

Apart from the three special conditions, contained in the pre-printed Contract for Sale, the vendor and the purchaser are, subject to some legislative restrictions, free to insert such special conditions as may be agreed between them. Faced with such a blank canvas, however, the vendor's solicitor ought not to give way to the temptation to fill it with unnecessary or unreasonable special conditions. In drafting the special conditions, the vendor's solicitor ought always to be mindful of the purpose which they serve, namely:

(a)   to set out terms, agreed between the parties, which are specific to the transaction; and

(b)   to vary the respective rights and obligations, conferred and imposed upon both the vendor and the purchaser by the general conditions of the Contract for Sale.

In recent times, the practice of inserting special conditions which may be considered either unnecessary or unreasonable has manifested itself on a regular basis in a Contract for Sale where the vendor is a receiver or mortgagee in possession. The Law Society's Conveyancing Committee addressed this worrying trend in two separate Practice Notes issued in June 2012 and June 2014 respectively. In the later Practice Note the Conveyancing Committee set out examples of special conditions which are unlawful, as well as examples of conditions which may be unenforceable. In addition, the Practice Notes lists conditions which are not in accordance with good conveyancing practice or which are in conflict with recommendations issued by the Conveyancing Committee. In the Practice Note, the Committee reiterated its previous general recommendation that where a vendor's solicitor is seeking to vary a general condition by insertion of a special condition the reason for the variation should be disclosed. The earlier Practice Note considers the position of the purchaser's solicitor in respect of a Contract for Sale, where the general conditions and warranties have been restricted by special condition. In such circumstances, the purchaser's solicitor should carefully advise his or her client of the effect of such restrictions and should also consider whether amendment of his or her Certificate of Title to any lending institution is appropriate. While the Practice Note specifically addressed issues arising in the context of the sale of repossessed properties, the advice contained therein is equally applicable to other transactions where the vendor's solicitor seeks to limit or restrict the general conditions and warranties contained in the standard Contract for Sale.

As mentioned earlier, special condition 2 provides that, in the event of a conflict between the general conditions and the special conditions, the special conditions will prevail. Careful drafting is, therefore, a key element in the preparation of this section of the contract.

6.3.6.3   Sample special conditions

The following are some sample special conditions.

1. The title shall commence with Indenture of Lease dated the 1st day of January 1930 and made between John Smith of the One Part and Anthony Jones of the Other Part and shall then pass to an Indenture of Assignment made the 4th day of July 1994 and made between Tony Ryan of the One Part and James O'Reilly of the Other Part and shall be deduced therefrom. No objection, requisition or enquiry shall be raised in relation to the intermediate title but without prejudice the vendor will furnish all documents of intermediate title in his possession on closing.

   The purchaser shall conclusively assume that the said Indenture of Lease was validly granted and is a valid and subsisting lease and shall raise no objection, requisition or enquiry in relation to title prior thereto.

2. The title shall commence with Indenture of Conveyance dated the 2nd day of March 1995 and made between Martin O'Neill of the One Part and Maureen Hara of the Other Part and shall be deduced therefrom.

3. The title shall consist of official certified copy folio and file plan (map) of Folio 1705 of the Register of Freeholders County Dublin.

4. The title shall consist of official certified copy folio and file plan of Folio 2345L County Dublin. The Purchaser is referred to copy Indenture of Lease dated 21st day of March 1962 and made between John Smith of the One Part and Tom O'Flynn of the Other Part, furnished herewith and referred to at item 4 of the Documents Schedule. On completion, the purchaser shall be furnished with the original/an original Counterpart/a plain copy (delete as appropriate) of the said Indenture of Lease.

5. The title to the property shall commence with Indenture of Lease dated the 17th day of October 1958 and made between Joseph Flynn and Others of the One Part and Brigid Flynn of the Other Part and shall then pass without objection requisition or enquiry in relation to the intermediate title to Indenture of Assignment dated the 31st day of December 1992 and made between Gail Ward of the One Part and Francis Bouchier of the Other Part and shall be deduced therefrom. (This is a similar but shorter version of number 1.)

6. The title to the property shall commence with Indenture of Lease dated 4 March 2007 and made between George Russell of the one part and Pamela Walsh of the other part and shall be deduced therefrom. Without prejudice to the

foregoing, the purchaser is referred to Deed of Conveyance dated 10 January 1990 and made between Thomas Brennan of the one part and George Russell of the other part, a copy of which is furnished herewith and listed at item 2 of the documents schedule. On completion the purchaser shall be furnished with a certified copy of the said Deed of Conveyance. (Note that because the lease is less than 15 years old the vendor is providing a copy of the superior title ie the conveyance to the vendor.)

7. This contract shall be subject to the purchaser obtaining approval from a loan of €[ ] from (lender) on the security of the premises PROVIDED ALWAYS that if this loan has not been approved in writing within four weeks from the date hereof either party shall be entitled to rescind this contract and in such event the purchaser shall be refunded his deposit without interest costs or compensation thereon.

    If the loan approval is conditional on a survey satisfactory to the lending institution or a mortgage protection or a life insurance policy being taken out or the lending institution being satisfied at any time prior to drawdown of the loan that its valuation of the property has not changed since the date of loan approval or some other condition compliance with which is not within the control of the purchaser, the loan shall not be deemed to be approved until the purchaser is in a position to accept and draw down the loan on terms which are within his reasonable power or procurement.

8. Included in the contract price are the fitted carpets, curtains and light fittings presently in the premises for the sum of €4,000.

9. This contract is subject to and conditional upon the present Lessors, Irish Life Limited, consenting within four weeks from the date hereof to the assignment of the premises to the purchasers and to the premises being used as a retail shoe shop. The purchaser hereby agrees that he shall furnish without delay such references and reasonable information as may be required by the Landlord.

10. The sale is conditional upon the purchaser obtaining planning permission for the erection on the land described in the Particulars and Tenure of 72 houses in accordance with plans and specifications whereof details will be submitted to the Planning Authority for the purposes of obtaining such permission. If at the expiration of six months from the date hereof planning permission as aforesaid shall not have been granted or shall have been granted subject to conditions which are unacceptable to the purchaser and that fact shall have been notified to the vendor within seven days after the expiration of the said period then either party may be notified in writing in that behalf served upon the other to rescind this agreement whereupon the vendor shall return the deposit to the purchaser but without interest costs or compensation and the purchaser shall return the copy title deeds and any other papers furnished to him and neither party shall be entitled to any sum in respect of costs, compensation or otherwise.

11. This contract is conditional upon the vendor obtaining within three months from the date hereof planning permission for the retention of the kitchen recently built by the vendor. If the said planning permission is not obtained within the said period of three months the purchaser shall be refunded his deposit without interest costs or compensation and this contract shall be null and void. The purchaser shall accept the vendor's Architect's Certificate that the extension complies with all conditions (if any) in the retention permission and in his view would have complied with Building Bye Laws if they had been applied for at the time of the erection of the extension. General Condition 36 is hereby varied accordingly.

12. (a) The property being sold under this contract is at present subject to a mortgage in favour of [ ] bank/building society. Prior to completion the vendor shall inform the purchaser of the sum required to repay the mortgage and the balance purchase money shall be paid at the purchaser's expense to the vendor's solicitor in the following manner:

(i)   a bank draft in favour of [   ] bank/building society for the balance outstanding to the said bank/building society; and

(ii) a bank draft for the remaining balance of the purchase price in favour of the vendor's solicitor.

(b) The purchaser shall on closing accept the vendor's solicitor's undertaking to immediately forward the bank draft for the redemption monies to the bank/ building society and to furnish a vacate of the said mortgage duly registered in the Registry of Deeds as soon as possible thereafter.

Where the vendor's charge is registered in the Land Registry and the eDischarge system applies the following alternative paragraph should be inserted;

(c) The purchaser shall accept the vendor's solicitor's undertaking to redeem the mortgage in favour of [   ] bank/building society and to furnish a copy folio showing the cancellation of the mortgage as a burden at Entry Number [   ] at Part 3 of Folio [   ] County [   ] within one week of receiving notice of completion from the Property Registration Authority.

In many transactions funds are now being transferred by EFT (electronic funds transfer) and if this is being done this draft special condition will need to be adapted. Use of EFT often results in some delay in closing as the funds may take 3–5 days to clear. Regardless of the method being used to pay the balance of the purchase monies practitioners should take into account the time required to clear funds.

13. The purchaser shall raise no objection, requisition or enquiry regarding the fact that the Deed of Conveyance dated the 4th day of March, 1946 did not contain an express Declaration of Merger. The purchaser shall conclusively assume that the leasehold interest merged in the freehold reversion expectant upon the determination thereof by virtue of the said Deed of Conveyance of the 4th day of March 1946.

14. The vendor is selling in her capacity as personal representative of the estate of Bridget Maher deceased and will assure the property in such capacity.

15. The vendor will assign to the purchaser the benefit of the consent of the freehold owner to the acquisition of the fee simple under the provisions of the Landlord and Tenant (Ground Rents) (No 2) Act, 1978.

16. This sale is subject to the consent of Clare County Council being first had and obtained. The vendor will immediately apply for such consent and the purchaser will furnish the vendor with any information and comply with conditions required by Clare County Council in respect of such application. If such consent is not forthcoming within six weeks from the date hereof this agreement shall be rescinded and the purchaser's deposit shall be returned without interest costs or compensation. If such consent is forthcoming the sealing of the Deed of Assurance shall be the responsibility of the purchaser.

17. The purchaser is furnished with a letter dated 1 December 2009 from Dublin City Council confirming that the roads, footpaths and services abutting the premises are in charge of the local authority and will not raise any objection, requisition or enquiry in relation thereto.

18. The purchaser is referred to Voluntary Deed of Assignment dated 4 November 2004 and made between Francis J Bouchier of the One Part and his wife— Katherine Deirdre Bouchier of the Other Part affected under the provisions of Section 14 of the Family Home Protection Act, 1976. A Statutory Declaration re the Family Home Protection Act, 1976 and the Family Law Act, 1981 was not obtained at the date of this deed. The vendor relies on the provision of Section 54 of the Family Law Act, 1995 and no objection, requisition or enquiry may be raised as to the non-availability of this Statutory Declaration. However a Section 54 Declaration in the Law Society recommended format will be furnished on closing.

19. The Deed of Assent referred to at document number 3 of the Documents Schedule hereto was not registered in the Registry of Deeds. The purchaser will not raise any objection, requisition or enquiry regarding this and will not look for the registration of same. The purchaser is referred to Section 53(1)(c) of the Succession Act, 1965. (Registration of an Assent is not compulsory but if not registered the beneficiary runs the risk of losing his priority.)

20. The vendor has applied for a Grant of Probate in the estate of the deceased owner. The closing date hereof shall be seven days after the purchaser's solicitor has been notified by the vendor's solicitor that the said Grant of Probate has issued.

21. The vendors will forthwith apply to purchase the freehold interest in the premises from Pembroke Estates Holdings Limited, the party entitled to the said freehold interest. If the said freehold interest shall have been acquired at the time of completion of the sale herein then the vendors shall convey the freehold interest at the time of completion. If the freehold interest shall not have been acquired before completion of the sale then the vendors will convey the freehold interest to the purchaser as soon as possible thereafter. The vendors shall be responsible for the purchase price of the fee simple interest and also for any legal costs involved in the acquisition thereof.

22. The closing date is 1 December 2016 and in this respect time is deemed to be of the essence. (Exercise caution when inserting a special condition making time of the essence as it can be a double-edged sword.)

23. The Deed dated 5th day of May 2003 and made between A of the one part and B of the other part has been mislaid. On closing the vendor will furnish an attested copy Memorial/application form relating to the said deed together with Statutory Declaration of the vendor's solicitor regarding same in the form of the drafts referred to in the Documents Schedule herein. The purchaser shall accept said documentation and no further objection or requisition or enquiry shall be raised in relation to same. (Note that the memorial has now been replaced by a Registry of Deeds application form so a copy of this would need to be provided for more recent deeds.)

This last special condition is an example of a special condition inserted in a contract where a title document that forms part of the 'chain of title' is missing. The vendor's solicitor is aware of this at the time of drafting the contract and has made a search in the Registry of Deeds, has located the memorial/application form and obtained an attested copy. All due enquiries as to the whereabouts of the missing deed have been made and a draft statutory declaration has been prepared for completion by the vendor as well as a statutory declaration by the firm who acted at the time the vendor purchased. The attested copy memorial/application form and the draft statutory declarations should be exhibited in the documents schedule of the contract. Where all of the title documents are missing it may be possible to reconstruct the chain of title by means of attested copy memorials/application forms, possibly supported by copies of some of the deeds and an insurance company bond (see Law Society *Gazette* Practice Note, July 1997 in relation to bonds).

An example would be in the case of a leasehold interest where the original lease and subsequent assignments are missing or destroyed. Enquiries may be made to ascertain the party entitled to the lessor's interest and an approach made to them to obtain a certified copy of the counterpart lease which they would hold. Searches may then be made in the Registry of Deeds to try to trace the chain down. It is also possible, by checking the solicitors' files and papers at the time the vendor purchased, that copy documents may have been retained on the file which, backed up by attested copy memorials, would help. Again, the loss of the documents would be supported by statutory declarations from the last party who would have had them and from the solicitors acting for any lending institution who had held them as security pending the discharge of a mortgage.

6.3.6.4   Conveyancing Committee Practice Notes

Given the importance to both the vendor and the purchaser of correctly drafted special conditions, it is hardly surprising that the Law Society Conveyancing Committee has issued numerous Practice Notes in relation to this section of the Contract for Sale. Indeed, in the May 2005 *Gazette*, concerned about 'the growing tendency of including in contracts for sale special conditions that are unnecessary, badly drafted, unfair or unacceptable for some other reason' the Conveyancing Committee issued a Practice Note which offered guidance to vendor's solicitors on best practice in this area. This Practice Note states as follows:

'Amendments to general conditions

The General conditions of sale of the Law Society, as amended from time to time, have been accepted by the profession for a considerable time as, on balance, reasonable to both parties. Where special conditions are inserted for the purpose of amending the general conditions, there should be a particular reason as to why the general conditions cannot be adopted. The necessity for special conditions that conflict with the general conditions should be capable of being explained to the solicitor for the purchaser (unless this is obvious). Otherwise, considerable time can be wasted in negotiating conditions that are not necessary.

For example, special conditions requiring the purchaser to accept the boundaries of the property, and so on, may be unnecessary if this is already adequately covered by general condition 14 under the heading "Identity".

Similarly, clauses providing that the purchaser buys with full knowledge of the state of repair of a second-hand house are unnecessary, as this is covered by the caveat emptor rule and only leads to queries as to why the special condition has been inserted.

Special conditions re: title

Special conditions are typically used to preclude a purchaser from insisting on something relating to the title to which he would be otherwise entitled. The special condition should be specific as to what is missing or excluded from the title and should not mislead. If there is a defect on the title, a purchaser cannot be precluded from an investigation unless the condition contains a warning about the defect. It should not be stated that something is not known to the vendor if, in fact, it is.

Planning

Similarly, if there is any unauthorised development or other planning defect, this should be disclosed by special condition and an indication given as to what extent and why the warranty in general condition 36 is to be limited.

Drafting

Inserting special conditions may not always have the intended effect and regard should be had to a number of aspects:

1. Bad drafting may turn out to be a problem for the vendor, as any ambiguity will be construed in favour of the party whose rights are to be restricted. Usually this means that it will be construed against the party drafting the special condition.

2. The Law Society conditions provide that the special conditions shall prevail in case of any conflict with the general conditions.

3. In the case of new houses, a term that is found to be unfair within the meaning of the European Communities (Unfair Terms in Consumer Contracts) Regulations 1995 will be unenforceable. Certain terms found by the High Court in December 2001 to be unfair within the meaning of the Regulations may not be included in a building agreement.

4. Some conditions are, in any event, prohibited by statute, such as:

    (a) a condition precluding a purchaser from objecting to title on the grounds of absence or insufficiency of stamps on any instrument executed after 16 May 1888—section 131, Stamp Duties Consolidation Act, 1999

    (b) a term designed to prevent the raising of requisitions in relations to burdens generally or to any particular burden that, by virtue of section 72 of the

Registration of Title Act, 1964, may affect registered land—section 115 of the Act

(c)   a condition requiring one party to pay any of the legal fees incurred by the other party on the granting of a lease—section 32, Landlord and Tenant (Ground Rents) Act, 1967

(d)   a condition requiring a purchaser, lessee or tenant to pay the fees of an auctioneer or house agent employed by the vendor, lessor or landlord—section 2, Auctioneer's and House Agents Act, 1973.

Practitioners are requested to give some thought to special conditions and not to include them merely because they have been seen in contracts prepared by other solicitors or because they find they can impose them on purchasers regardless of their suitability or necessity.

The reputation of the profession depends on individual solicitors acting in a professional manner at all times.'

In an earlier Practice Note, issued in December 1994, the Conveyancing Committee expressed its disapproval of the practice of furnishing contracts for sale which refer to and incorporate the general conditions of the Contract for Sale, without actually attaching the pages of general conditions to the contract. It remains the view of the Committee that this practice is undesirable.

The Conveyancing Committee's views on the practice of some vendors' solicitors significantly restricting the general conditions and warranties contained in the standard contract of sale and the information which may be sought by the purchaser's solicitor in the context of sales by receivers or mortgagees in possession were considered by the Committee in its Practice Notes issued in June 2012 and June 2014 respectively. These Practice Notes have already been discussed in **6.3.6.2**.

The practice of including 'entire agreement' clauses in contracts for the sale of residential property was categorically condemned by the Committee in the May 2006 *Gazette*. Such clauses seek to preclude the purchaser from relying on any advertisement or statement, oral or in writing, made by the vendor or his agent in the course of the negotiation, leading up to the contract and provide that the Contract for Sale represents the entire terms and conditions of the agreement between the parties. Such a clause will not only prevent the purchaser from relying on any advertisement, brochure, or representation made or published by or on behalf of the vendor, but also any replies given to a purchaser in pre-contract enquiries. In the view of the Committee these clauses are not appropriate to residential conveyancing and should not be included in agreements for the sale of residential property, whether by auction or private treaty. A further practice note was issued in January/February 2016 re-iterating that these clauses are more suitable for commercial contracts.

The situation regarding time limits in loan approvals and the revaluation of security by lenders prior to drawdown was considered by the Conveyancing Committee in its Practice Note published in the June 2009 edition of the *Gazette*. The Committee drew to the attention of practitioners the necessity of carefully checking time limits imposed by letters of loan offer. The Committee also highlighted the practice of some lenders of revaluing security prior to drawdown. Due to such revaluations resulting in the loan offer being either withdrawn or significantly reduced the Committee recommended the insertion of the following special condition where appropriate:

'This contract shall be subject to the purchaser obtaining approval of a loan of [€] from [lender] on the security of the premises PROVIDED ALWAYS that if this loan has not been approved in writing within four weeks from the date hereof either party shall be entitled to rescind this contract and in such event the purchaser shall be refunded his deposit without interest costs or compensation thereon.

If the loan approval is conditional on a survey satisfactory to the lending institution or a mortgage protection or a life insurance policy being taken out or the lending institution being satisfied at any time prior to drawdown of the loan that its valuation of the property has not changed since the date of loan approval or some other conditions compliance with which is not within the control of the purchaser, the loan shall not be deemed to be approved until the purchaser is in a position to accept and draw down the loan on terms which are within his reasonable power or procurement.'

The Committee reiterated its advice regarding the inclusion of the above special condition in its Practice Note issued in July 2015. This Practice Note alerted practitioners to the impact of SI 47/2015—Central Bank (Supervision and Enforcement) Act 2013 (Section 48) (Housing Loan Requirements) Regulations, 2015. Essentially, these new regulations require that a lender carry out a market valuation of the residential property on which the loan is to be secured *not earlier* than a period of two months from the date on which the advance under the housing loan is made (Clause 7(3)). Where the housing loan is made for the purchase of land for the construction of a building Clause 7(4) requires the lender to undertake a valuation of the land within the same period. In transactions where a period in excess of two months elapses between the initial valuation and the drawdown of the loan, the Regulations have the effect of obliging the lending institution to obtain an updated second valuation. This has potentially serious consequences for a purchaser who has entered into a binding contract on the strength of the original loan approval, particularly if the revaluation results in a reduction of the loan. The Regulations came into effect on 9 February 2015.

As discussed at **6.2.9**, in April 2013 the Conveyancing Committee issued wording for a special condition providing for the apportionment of LPT as between the vendor and the purchaser.

On the issuing of the 2009 edition of the Contract for Sale, the Committee advised in its accompanying explanatory memorandum (*Gazette*, May 2010) that where the purchaser and vendor envisage that a deed of assurance will not be delivered on completion, the matter should be addressed by way of special condition.

In June 2012 the Conveyancing Committee advised caution to purchasers' solicitors where the vendor is selling a repossessed property and the vendor's solicitor seeks to significantly restrict the general conditions and warranties provided for in the Contract for Sale.

6.3.6.5   Contents of special conditions

Bearing in mind the guidelines as to best practice, provided by the Law Society Conveyancing Committee, the vendor's solicitor must frame special conditions specific to the subject property and specific to the transaction in question. For example, a special condition may be inserted identifying certain fixtures and fittings which are not to be included in the sale or making the contract conditional upon the purchaser obtaining planning permission or a loan offer. More often, however, the purpose of the special conditions will be to amend a general condition so as to limit or remove entirely either a warranty otherwise given or an obligation otherwise imposed upon the vendor. Clearly, in order to be effective in doing this, the vendor must be familiar with the relevant general conditions.

6.3.7   GENERAL CONDITIONS

6.3.7.1   Obligations placed upon the vendor by the general conditions

The obligations placed on the vendor by the Contract for Sale may be broken into two sections:

(a)   the formal warranties given by the vendor under the Contract for Sale; and

(b)   the other obligations placed on the vendor under the contract.

Registered land

Under general conditions 13(a) and (b) the vendor warrants, in respect of possessory title and title registered subject to equities, that he or she will furnish sufficient evidence to enable the purchaser to register his title as absolute.

Under general condition 13(d) the vendor warrants that a statutory declaration in respect of the non-existence of any burdens, which under the Registration of Title Act, 1964, affect registered land without registration (s 72: burdens), will be available on closing. Burdens specified or mentioned in the particulars or in the special conditions are excluded from this warranty.

Searches

Under general condition 19, the vendor warrants that he will be in a position to explain and discharge any acts appearing on the purchaser's searches covering the period from the date stipulated or implied from the commencement of title to the date of actual completion.

Under general condition 21, the vendor warrants that the purchaser will get vacant possession of the property in sale on closing. This warranty applies unless there is a contrary provision in the particulars or in the conditions or unless it is otherwise implied by the nature of the transaction that there will not be vacant possession.

Leases

Under general condition 23, the vendor warrants that in the case where the property sold is subject to any lease:

> 'that there has been no variation in the terms and conditions of said Lease (other than such as may be evident from an inspection of the Subject Property or apparent from the Particulars or the documents furnished to the purchaser prior to the sale), and that the said terms and conditions (save those pertaining to the actual state and condition of the Subject Property) have been complied with'.

Planning

Under general condition 36, the vendor gives a planning warranty. Planning is dealt with extensively in **chapter 11**.

Under condition 36 the vendor warrants there has been no development since 1 October 1964 or, alternatively, that there have been developments after that date but that all planning permissions and building bye-law approvals relevant to the property have been complied with substantially.

Under condition 36(b), the vendor warrants that in all appropriate cases, there has been substantial compliance with the Building Regulations made under the Building Control Act, 1990. This general condition now contains a proviso that the warranty will not extend to approvals under the Building Bye-Laws or compliance with such Building Bye-Laws in respect of development or works carried out prior to 13 December 1989. This proviso refers to non-conforming development which is development that, although enforcement proceedings may not be taken, remains unauthorised.

Chattels

Under general condition 46 the vendor warrants that all chattel property included in the sale is not 'subject to any lease, rental hire, hire-purchase or credit sale agreement or chattel mortgage'.

Title

Under general condition 8(b), if the title is based on possession, the vendor agrees to furnish a certificate from the Revenue Commissioners pursuant to the Finance Act, 1994, s 146 as amended by the Finance Act, 1996, s 128. This is now s 62(2) of the Capital Acquisitions Tax Consolidation Act, 2003. Under that section the certificate to be issued (namely CA12) is to the effect that the Revenue is satisfied:

(a)   that the property did not become charged with gift tax or inheritance tax during the relevant period; or

(b)   that any charge for gift tax or inheritance tax to which the property became subject during that period has been discharged or will be discharged within a time considered to be reasonable by the Revenue Commissioners.

Condition 8(c) was introduced in the 1995 edition of the Contract for Sale, and specifically states that the vendor is obliged to discharge all mortgages and charges for the payment of money affecting the property at or before completion of the sale.

Foreign vendor

General condition 9 provides that where the vendor is a company established outside the State, this should be disclosed in the special conditions. The purpose of the condition is to put the purchaser on notice so that the necessary enquiries can be made pre-contract. A Practice Note headed 'Foreign Lawyer's Opinion' in the Law Society *Gazette* of March 2001 sets out the intricacies of acting for a purchaser where the vendor is a foreign company.

Prior title

Condition 11(b) is again a provision introduced in the 1995 edition of the Contract for Sale.

Under general condition 11(a) there is the provision that the purchaser shall not object to or investigate the title prior to the date of the instrument specified in the special conditions of the Contract for Sale as the commencement of title, ie the root of title. However, in the case of registered land this condition is too restrictive and hence paragraph (b) puts the obligation on the vendor to deal with matters arising under the following:

(a)   the Registration of Title Act, 1964, s 52;

(b)   the Registration of Title Act, 1964, s 115; and

(c)   the Succession Act, 1965, s 121, as extended by the Family Law Act, 1995, s 25(5).

This condition was designed to meet difficulties arising on the investigation of registered titles in the area of capital acquisitions tax and voluntary dispositions.

(a) Registration of Title Act, 1964, s 52

Section 52(1) provides that on foot of a transfer of freehold land:

there shall be vested in the registered Transferee an estate in fee simple in the land transferred together with all implied or expressed rights, privileges and appurtenances, belonging or appurtenant thereto subject to (a) the burdens, if any, registered as affecting the land, and (b) the burdens to which, though not registered, the land is subject by virtue of Section 72, but shall be free from all other rights including rights of the state.

Section 52(2) provides that where the transfer is made without valuable consideration, it shall:

so far as concerns the Transferee and persons claiming under him otherwise than from valuable consideration, be subject to all unregistered rights subject to which the Transferor held the land transferred.

(b) Registration of Title Act, 1964, s 115

Section 115 states:

Every stipulation in a Contract for the Sale or Charge of registered land or for the Transfer of a registered charge whereby the purchaser or intending Chargeant or the intending Transferee (as the case may be), is precluded from making Requisitions in relation to burdens generally or any particular burden which, by virtue of Section 72, may affect the land shall be void.

(c) Succession Act, 1965, s 121

Section 121(1) states:

this Section applies to a disposition of property (other than a testamentary disposition or a disposition to a purchaser) under which the beneficial ownership of the property vests in possession in the Donee within three years before the death of the person who made it or on his death or later.

Section 121(2) provides that if a court is satisfied that the disposition was made for the purpose of defeating or substantially diminishing the share of the disponer's spouse,

purchaser's solicitor, it means that the information will be available to him or her without having to make enquiries in relation to the particular matters contained therein.

General condition 33(a) caters for the situation where the information contained in the non-title information sheet is inaccurate.

6.3.9 FURNISHING THE DRAFT CONTRACT TO THE PURCHASER'S SOLICITOR

Once the vendor's solicitor has drafted the Contract for Sale to the satisfaction of his client, the Contract for Sale, in duplicate, together with copies of the documents listed in the documents schedule, and the BER certificate and advisory report (if not already furnished to the purchaser) are forwarded to the solicitor acting for the purchaser. As the parties are still at the pre-contract stage, the covering letter, accompanying the contract and other documents, is usually headed 'Subject to Contract/Contract Denied'. In addition, it is customary for a paragraph to be included at the end of the letter in the following format:

'Please note that we have no authority, express or implied, to bind our client contractually and this letter shall not constitute a Memorandum for the purposes of s 51 of the Land and Conveyancing Law Reform Act, 2009. No contract shall exist or be deemed to exist until such time as a formal agreement has been executed by both parties and exchanged and any deposit payable has been paid by the purchaser to the vendor.'

The purpose of these precautions is to avoid the correspondence being construed as a memorandum for the purposes of the 2009 Act and an open contract coming into existence as a consequence (see *Boyle v Lee* [1992] 1 IR 555). In a Practice Note issued in June 2011, the Conveyancing Committee reminded practitioners that the use of the phrase 'without prejudice' in addition to, or in substitution for, 'subject to contract' as a heading on correspondence between solicitors negotiating the terms of a Contract for Sale is inappropriate.

6.4 The Situation Pre Contract—Purchaser's Pre-Contract Enquiries

6.4.1 INTRODUCTION

When acting for a purchaser, a solicitor has to be aware of the terms and conditions of the Contract for Sale, as drafted by the vendor's solicitor. The purchaser's solicitor has to decide what matters need to be dealt with before the contract is signed and what matters may be left outstanding until after the signing of the contract. These vary from case to case and may also depend on the actual purchaser. In order to identify those issues, which ought to be dealt with pre-contract, the purchaser's solicitor must:

(a) take comprehensive instructions from the client;

(b) examine the documents of title furnished with the Contract for Sale;

(c) carefully consider the special conditions, inserted by the vendor's solicitor; and

(d) have a good working knowledge of the general conditions of the Contract for Sale.

In order to assist the purchaser's solicitor in taking comprehensive instructions, a questionnaire or checklist such as those set out at **6.2.2** and **6.2.4** should be used.

This leads to the division between the pre-contract enquiries which must be made (ie before the purchaser has signed the contract) and the requisitions on title which must be raised after the contract has been signed by all necessary parties. Requisitions on title are dealt with in detail in **chapter 15**.

The purchaser's pre-contract enquiries may be broken into two categories:

(a)   those relating to the physical condition and location of the property; and

(b)   enquiries arising out of the documents including the contract furnished.

6.4.2   VALUE ADDED TAX

As discussed in **6.2.5** the position regarding the VAT treatment of the subject property must be clarified by both the vendor's and the purchaser's solicitors at the pre-contract stage. While the pre-contract VAT enquiries jointly issued by the Taxation and Conveyancing Committees may be used by the vendor's solicitor as a means of ascertaining the position with regard to VAT, they are, strictly speaking, to be issued by the purchaser's solicitor and they remain a purchaser's document. Prior to issuing the enquiries to the vendor's solicitor, the purchaser's solicitor should complete the statement on the purchaser's VAT status, contained in p 2 of the enquiries.

6.4.3   ENQUIRIES IN RELATION TO PHYSICAL CONDITION AND LOCATION OF PROPERTY

The basic legal rule which applies is caveat emptor, ie buyer beware. See general condition 16 of the Contract for Sale.

6.4.3.1   Physical state of the property

The purchaser buys the property as it stands. The vendor is not under a duty to disclose any physical defects in the property. A purchaser must be advised of this and must be advised that in order to protect himself or herself he or she should have the property fully surveyed before the contract is signed. The vast majority of buyers will have the property surveyed without question and will, in all probability, furnish a copy of the survey to their solicitor. Once the solicitor has the copy of the survey it is evidence in his or her file that he or she has given the buyer the necessary advice. However, if a client decides not to have the property surveyed then his or her solicitor needs to be extremely careful to ensure that the file is in order and that he or she is not leaving himself or herself open to a subsequent action for negligence. To protect himself, the purchaser's solicitor should ensure that he has on file a letter to the purchaser setting out the legal position, ie that the purchaser is advised to have an independent survey carried out, and an acknowledgement from the purchaser that he received this letter. The importance of advising a client in writing to have an independent survey carried out was discussed in the case of *O'Connor v FNBS* [1991] ILRM 208. See **2.2.2.3**.

A purchaser's solicitor should never put the following or similar terms in to the contract: 'The sale is subject to the purchaser obtaining a satisfactory survey of the property.' Only a court could determine what the words 'satisfactory survey' mean. If the timber in one of the windows has rotted does this entitle the buyer to rescind the sale?

Where the purchaser is buying a house in the course of construction the position is different. At the contract stage no building work may have commenced and therefore it would not be possible to have the property surveyed. In such cases the purchaser's rights are governed by the terms and conditions of the building agreement and the warranties given in the building agreement.

Occasionally, a vendor's solicitor will issue a Contract for Sale in respect of a house in the course of construction without including a building contract for the work which remains to be completed. A purchaser's solicitor should never accept this arrangement and should always insist on having a building contract as well.

6.4.3.2   General location of the property

A vendor gives no warranty as to the use or occupation of property adjoining the property he is selling. Accordingly, the purchaser should be advised to check out certain matters before he or she signs the contract.

Other planning permissions

Depending on the property in question, it may well be that planning permission has already been granted for development on the adjoining property which would affect the property in sale. For example, a purchaser might not be too happy to discover that a substantial factory could be looking into his or her back garden at a future date.

Road widening

With the current infrastructural developments which are taking place, it is very important that a purchaser checks to ensure that the building of a new road or the widening of an existing road will not have a negative impact on the property being bought.

The necessity for advising the client in relation to these matters depends on the location of the property. If a purchaser is buying a house within a cluster of 200 new houses in a housing estate, it is unlikely the local authority is going to consider building a new road through the existing development.

6.4.3.3 Access to the property

It depends on the circumstances of the transaction whether or not the purchaser requires access to the property being bought. The legal right to gain access to the property must be evidenced prior to the signing of the contract. It is too late to discover the problem when replies to the requisitions on title are returned to the purchaser's solicitor's desk. No purchaser wants to buy a landlocked site.

In many cases it is clear from a physical inspection of the property itself that it is abutting the public road. In the new development situation it is necessary to ensure that there is a grant of right of way contained in the deed of conveyance or deed of transfer. This grant of right of way must be from the property in sale to a roadway already taken in charge.

Access to the property in sale may be one of the following:

(a) by abutting the public highway;

(b) by an appurtenant right of way granted by deed;

(c) by an appurtenant right of way created by long usage; or

(d) by adjoining a public right of way not taken in charge by the local authority.

Most agricultural rights of way are not registered. When the Land Commission purchased the estates from the landlords and vested them in the existing tenants no references were made to rights of way. In the later years of the Land Commission, when it acquired land for redistribution, it did create registered rights of way.

A purchaser's solicitor will refer, in the first instance, to the replies given by the vendor to query 1(a) of the non-title information sheet attached to the contract.

6.4.3.4 Water supply

The Contract for Sale does not include a warranty that the subject property has a water supply. While this does not normally create a difficulty in the urban situation this is not necessarily so in rural areas. The property owner may have been allowed to take water from a well on an adjoining property on a temporary basis or may have been given permission, on a temporary basis, to place a waterline on an adjoining property. Accordingly, a purchaser must be satisfied that the necessary easements and wayleaves are in place to ensure a water supply to the property.

A purchaser's solicitor will refer, in the first instance, to the replies given by the vendor to query 1(a) of the non-title information sheet attached to the contract.

6.4.3.5 Other services

A purchaser's solicitor needs to be satisfied that the septic tank and its soakage area are within the site being purchased. If the subject property is served by the local authority sewer, do the pipes go directly from the property in sale to the local authority system? If they pass through intervening properties have legal wayleaves been created?

A purchaser's solicitor will refer, in the first instance, to the replies given by the vendor to query 1(a) of the non-title information sheet attached to the contract.

As mentioned at **6.2.10**, due to the obligations based on owners of property serviced by waste-water treatment systems, it is now recommended practice to raise enquiries regarding the registration and efficacy of the treatment system at the pre-contract stage.

6.4.3.6   BER certificate

As outlined in **6.2.11** the purchaser will either have received the BER certificate directly from the selling agent or auctioneer or a copy of it will be received by the purchaser's solicitor with the Contract for Sale and vouching title documentation. The purchaser's solicitor should ensure that the purchaser is made aware of the rating of the subject property prior to the execution of the contract and that the purchaser is given a copy of the accompanying advisory report.

6.4.3.7   Other pre-contract matters

The purchaser will be concerned with the outgoings in respect of the subject property. Information regarding this will be given on the non-title information sheet in reply to query 3(a). He or she may want to know about rents, rates, service charges, and the like.

While totally unconnected with title investigation, a purchaser's solicitor should advise the purchaser of the necessity of having finance arranged to enable the transaction to be completed.

6.4.4   ENQUIRIES ARISING OUT OF DOCUMENTS INCLUDING THE CONTRACT

6.4.4.1   The wording of the contract

If the title to be produced is limited under the contract then a purchaser's solicitor may need to raise pre-contract enquiries in relation to the title furnished before allowing the purchaser to sign the contract. If the title furnished was not limited then the same enquiries would be raised with the requisitions on title.

For example, if licensed premises are being sold with 'the ordinary seven-day publican's licence attached thereto', then it is a matter for requisitions on title for proof of the type of licence, whereas if the contract says the property 'together with the intoxicating liquor licence attached thereto' then, before the purchaser signs a contract, the purchaser's solicitor must ensure what type of licence is attached because the vendor has not warranted that it is a seven-day ordinary licence.

6.4.4.2   Purchaser on notice of certain documents

General condition 6 of the Contract for Sale states:

'The documents specified in the Documents Schedule or copies thereof have been available for inspection by the purchaser or his solicitor prior to the Date of Sale. If all or any of the Subject Property is stated in the Particulars or in the Special Conditions to be held under a lease or to be subject to any covenants, conditions, rights, liabilities or restrictions, and the lease or other document containing the same is specified in the Documents Schedule, the purchaser, whether availing of such opportunity of inspection or not, shall be deemed to have purchased with full knowledge of the contents thereof, notwithstanding any partial statement of such contents in the Particulars or in the Conditions.'

A purchaser's solicitor must satisfy himself that he has all the documents as listed in the documents schedule. He must read through these documents and satisfy himself that there is no matter contained therein which gives rise for concern. Because the purchaser is deemed to be on notice of the contents, it is too late to raise queries in relation to the contents of the documents produced after the contract has been signed.

Good conveyancing practice in preparing a contract is to provide the purchaser with:

(a)   the root of title;

(b)   any document to which title is stated to pass under the special conditions;

(c)   any document which is specifically referred to in the special conditions (see Law Society *Gazette*, January/February 1990 and March 1995); and

(d)   planning documentation (see Law Society *Gazette*, May 2000).

6.4.4.3   Prior leasehold title

Both under general conditions 10(a) and 16 of the Contract for Sale and by statute there is a restriction on the right of a purchaser to obtain evidence of the landlord's title. Where a property is held under lease if a purchaser's solicitor feels that, in the particular circumstances of the case, he or she should have evidence of the landlord's title then this must be done pre-contract or by amendment to the contract to provide for production of the landlord's title.

6.4.4.4   Restriction of purchaser's right to investigate certain matters in relation to leasehold title

General condition 10 of the Contract for Sale restricts the purchaser's right to raise any objection or requisition in relation to:

10(b)(i)   lack of consent of a superior owner to the apportionment of rent between sublessees, and

10(b)(ii)   by reason of any discrepancy between the covenants, conditions and provisions contained in any sublease and those in any superior lease (unless they were such as would give rise to forfeiture or a right of re-entry).

General condition 10(b)(iii) provides that the production of the receipt for the last gale rent reserved shall be accepted as conclusive evidence that all rent accrued and due has been paid and that all the covenants and conditions in the lease have been performed and observed.

General condition 10(b)(iv) provides that the vendor shall not be required to institute legal proceedings to obtain the landlord's consent to alienate where a landlord's consent is required but withheld. However, if this consent is not obtained 'either party may rescind the sale by seven days prior notice to the other'.

6.4.4.5   Investigating prior and intermediate title

Condition 11 of the Contract for Sale provides that the purchaser is not entitled to investigate or object to the title prior to the date of the instrument specified in the special conditions as the commencement of title.

General condition 12 prohibits the investigation of the intermediate title (ie where the title commences with a particular instrument and then passes to a second instrument or to a specified event).

A vendor's solicitor has a duty to his client to ensure that in preparing the contract he does not unnecessarily limit the title being furnished to a purchaser. Accordingly, in normal circumstances this condition will not create problems for a purchaser's solicitor. However, in the occasional case where a vendor's solicitor has unduly limited the title furnished, a purchaser's solicitor needs to be aware that it is too late to raise queries at the requisitions stage.

6.4.4.6   Identity of property in sale

Condition 14 limits the purchaser's right to evidence of identity of the property in sale. Once the contract has been signed the purchaser is entitled to the evidence of identity as may be gathered from the documents furnished together with, if circumstances require, a 'statutory declaration to be made by a competent person, at the purchaser's expense, that the Subject Property has been held and enjoyed for at least twelve years in accordance with the title shown'. There is no obligation to identify boundaries, party walls, or to identify parts of the property in sale held under different titles.

6.4.4.7 Disclosure of matters affecting property in sale

General condition 15 requires the vendor to disclose before the sale all easements, rights, privileges, taxes, and other liabilities, which are known by the vendor to affect the property or to be likely to affect it following the completion of the sale. Subject to this, condition 16 then states that the purchaser is deemed to buy with full notice of the actual state and condition of the property and subject to all leases mentioned in the particulars and special conditions and to all easements, rights, reservations, exceptions, privileges, covenants, restrictions, rents, taxes, liabilities, outgoings, and incidents of tenure.

Condition 35 provides that the purchaser may rescind the sale if he has not been furnished with notices given or otherwise known to the vendor at the date of sale which affect the property.

6.5 Execution of the Contract

Once the purchaser and his or her solicitor are satisfied in respect of the various matters referred to already, the contract should be executed, in duplicate, by the purchaser in the space provided in the memorandum of agreement. The purchaser's signature should be witnessed and the memorandum of agreement also provides a space for the witness to sign and insert his address and occupation. If the purchaser is a limited company, the contract may be executed, either by the common seal of the company being affixed to the memorandum in accordance with the articles of association of the company or by an officer of the company, with authority to do so. As a matter of company law, one does not need to look behind the assertion of an officer of a company that he or she has the requisite authority to bind the company. A Contract for Sale is, therefore, no less enforceable for having been executed by an individual 'for and on behalf' of the company, as opposed to under seal, the only real difference being that the applicable period for bringing claims in respect of instruments under seal is 12 as opposed to six years.

By virtue of general condition 30, where a person signs the memorandum of agreement 'in Trust', 'as Trustee', or 'as Agent' or with some similar qualification he shall be personally liable for the obligations of the purchaser under the contract until such time as he reveals the identity of the principal.

Once executed by the purchaser, the contract, in duplicate, is returned to the vendor's solicitor, accompanied by the deposit stipulated in the memorandum of agreement. Failure to pay the deposit provided for in the memorandum of agreement shall, according to general condition 31, entitle the vendor to terminate the sale and/or sue the purchaser for damages.

On receipt of the contract, duly executed by the purchaser, the vendor's solicitor should arrange for the execution by the vendor of both copies of the memorandum of agreement. While arranging this, the vendor's solicitor is entitled to negotiate the deposit cheque by lodging it into his client account. The status of the deposit during the period between same having been furnished to the vendor's solicitor and the coming into being of a binding Contract for Sale was considered in the High Court case of *Wallace v Rowley* [2013] IEHC 372. In that case the Contract for Sale had been executed by the purchaser and had been returned, together with the deposit payable, to the vendor's solicitor. The vendor company went into liquidation without a binding Contract for Sale having come into being and without the deposit monies having been returned to the purchaser. It was held by Judge Feeny that general condition 5(c), which states that the deposit is to be paid to the vendor's solicitor as trustee thereof for the purchaser, could not apply and would not bind the vendor until such time as the vendor had signed the contract and same was exchanged becoming a binding Contract for Sale. He further held that the deposit monies paid in this manner are paid to the vendor's solicitor as agent of the vendor and not as stakeholder. In light of this judgment, in its Practice Note issued in April 2013, the Conveyancing Committee of the Law Society recommended the inclusion of the following paragraph in the covering letter forwarded by the purchaser's solicitor, when returning the contracts, duly executed by the purchaser:

'The cheque for the deposit attached is sent subject to the following pre-condition namely, that it will be held by you (or your firm) in trust for the purchaser until contracts are exchanged in a manner acceptable to both vendor and purchaser, from which time the money can be held as stakeholder under the terms of the Contract. If you are not willing to accept payment of the deposit subject to this condition, please return it immediately.'

This paragraph will, of course, require amendment where the deposit is being furnished by electronic transfer funds. In December 2013, the Registrar of Solicitors and Director of Regulation issued a Practice Note stating *inter alia*:

'Where deposit monies in the normal course of a conveyancing transaction are paid by a purchaser to a vendor's solicitor, those funds are held by the vendor's solicitor:

(i) As a trustee for the purchaser pending the coming into being of a binding Contract for Sale (where so requested by the purchaser). While holding the deposit in trust for the purchaser, a vendor's solicitor, as trustee for the purchaser, cannot pay the deposit to the vendor or any other party without the consent of the purchaser.'

Note the wording in parenthesis, which reflects the Conveyancing Committee's Practice Note.

A cheque, presented by the purchaser, in respect of the deposit, which is not honoured when presented by the vendor, entitles the vendor, under general condition 32, to either rescind the contract by virtue of the purchaser's breach or to enforce payment of the deposit by suing on the cheque.

Once the memorandum of agreement has been executed by the vendor, one copy of the completed contract is returned to the purchaser's solicitor. At this point, the contract becomes effective and the vendor and the purchaser are both bound by the terms of the Contract for Sale.

6.6   The Situation Post Contract—The Deposit

In a sale by private treaty, general condition 5 of the Contract for Sale provides that, with effect from the date of sale (as defined), the deposit shall be held by the vendor's solicitor as stakeholder or, if the deposit or some portion thereof is being held by some other person, nominated by the vendor, eg an auctioneer, then that person shall hold the deposit as stakeholder.

Where the property is sold at auction, general condition 4 provides that the deposit shall be held by the vendor's solicitor as stakeholder and the memorandum of agreement provides a space for execution by the vendor solicitor, acknowledging receipt of the deposit and confirming that it is held by the solicitor as stakeholder.

The person holding the deposit as stakeholder is personally responsible to both the purchaser and the vendor for its safe-keeping. Unlike an agent, who must hand over the deposit to his principal on demand, the stakeholder may not hand the deposit over to the vendor until such time as the vendor is entitled to it.

Where a vendor's solicitor does not intend holding the deposit as stakeholder but instead will be passing the deposit to the vendor prior to completion, a special condition, amending general conditions 4 or 5, as appropriate, must be inserted into the Contract for Sale.

6.7 The Position Post Contract—Working Towards Completion

6.7.1 DELIVERY OF TITLE

General condition 7 provides that within seven working days from the date of sale, the vendor shall deliver or send by post to the purchaser or his solicitor copies of the documents which had not been furnished prior to the date of sale necessary to vouch the title to be shown in accordance with the conditions.

It is on receipt of these documents that the purchaser will raise requisitions on title.

6.7.2 REQUISITIONS ON TITLE

Under general condition 17, the purchaser shall, within 14 working days (as defined) after the later of the date of sale (as defined) or the delivery of copy documents of title in accordance with general condition 7, send to the vendor's solicitors his objections and requisitions on title. The vendor's replies to any objections or requisitions shall be answered by the purchaser in writing within seven working days after the delivery thereof. The purchaser has a right to raise rejoinders to the requisitions on title and likewise the seven-day time limit applies. All the time limits under this general condition are placed on the purchaser.

The Contract for Sale provides that time is of the essence in respect of the time limits for the raising of objections, requisitions, and rejoinders. General condition 17 states that 'any Objection or Requisition not made within the time aforesaid and not going to the root of the title shall be deemed to have been waived'. Therefore, the vendor is not obliged to reply to any requisition on title raised outside the time limit set in the condition unless the matter raised goes to the root of the title.

General condition 18 entitles the vendor to rescind the sale by giving not less than five working days' notice to the purchaser where the purchaser insists on any objection or requisition as to the title 'which the vendor shall, on the grounds of unreasonable delay or expense or other reasonable ground be unable or unwilling to remove or comply with'. The purchaser is entitled to withdraw the objection or requisition before the expiration of the five working days, in which case the sale is not rescinded.

The implications of general condition 18 are discussed at length in Wylie and Woods, *Irish Conveyancing Law* (3rd edn), paras 15.27 to 15.35. At para 15.30 Wylie and Woods state:

> 'This right of rescission constitutes a considerable restriction on the purchaser's rights and so it is not surprising that the courts have been alert to see that it is not abused. In fact the courts have laid down a number of qualifications to the vendor's right of rescission. First, it is settled that the vendor must exercise it in a reasonable manner or, as it is more usually put, he must not invoke it without reasonable cause. He must not act capriciously or arbitrarily and, if necessary, will have to convince the court that the objection or requisition which has caused him to invoke his right of rescission is one which will cause him substantial expense or involve him in litigation if he is to comply with it or remove it. Thus, he cannot use the right as a convenient method of getting out of his contract with the purchaser, eg, in order to be able to accept a higher offer for the property from a third party.'

6.7.3 THE ASSURANCE

General condition 20 provides that the purchaser shall submit a draft deed of assurance, ie the conveyance, transfer, or assignment, not less than seven working days, and the engrossment not less than four working days, before the closing date.

At common law, the production of a draft deed gives rise to the presumption of the acceptance of the title furnished. For convenience the purchaser's solicitor often delivers the draft deed at an early stage. Frequently, it is delivered with the requisitions on title. So as to negative the presumption of acceptance of title arising by virtue of the delivery of the draft deed of assurance, general condition 20 states: 'the delivery of the said draft or engrossment shall not prejudice any outstanding Objection or Requisition validly made'. General condition 20(c) provides that a completed Particulars Delivered (PD) form shall be handed over to the purchaser on or before handing over the assurance. However a PD form is no longer required since 30 December 2009 with the advent of eStamping (see **chapter 16**).

The 2009 edition of the Contract for Sale inserted a new general condition 20(b), which clarified that, on completion, a purchaser is required to accept delivery of an assurance of the property in favour of the purchaser or the purchaser's nominee. Any deviation from this arrangement should be dealt with by way of special condition.

In addition, general condition 20(d) provides that the vendor will on or before completion of the sale, if required by the purchaser, furnish the vendor's tax number 'appropriately vouched'. The Law Society suggests that vouching may be by way of an extract from correspondence with the Revenue or an accountant's certificate. It is recommended that all solicitors use this general condition and ensure that they obtain the tax number properly vouched before completion to avoid delays in having the deed stamped.

6.7.4 DOCUMENTS OF TITLE RELATING TO OTHER PROPERTY

Condition 34 deals with the situation where the documents of title relate to other property as well as the property in sale. It reflects the position outlined in s 84 of the 2009 Act dealing with the production and safe custody of documents. It provides that the vendor will give certified copies of the relevant documents, together with a statutory acknowledgement of the right of production and also an undertaking for safe custody of all documents retained by him. It also provides that the purchaser shall furnish a counterpart deed to the vendor after it has been stamped and registered. The purpose of giving the counterpart deed to the vendor is so as to enable him or her to use it for the purpose of explaining and discharging searches which will arise on subsequent transactions in respect of the balance of the property. General condition 34 does not deal with registered land. In the case of registered land the Land Registry will open a new folio for the portion being transferred.

6.7.5 RISK

General condition 43 deals with the passing of the risk in respect of the subject property to the purchaser. The current position is that the risk passes to the purchaser when the sale is closed. If the sale is closed at the office of the vendor's solicitor or is closed through the post on the basis set out in general condition 24, then it is quite clear when the risk has passed to the purchaser. The vendor must be advised to maintain insurance cover until the sale has been completed. In practice most lending institutions require the premises to be insured before issuing the loan cheque. Therefore, in most transactions the premises will be doubly insured for a certain period prior to the closing.

6.7.6 INSPECTION

General condition 47 gives the purchaser a right to inspect the subject property on a reasonable number of occasions and at reasonable times prior to the closing of the sale. Thus, if the purchaser wishes to inspect the property on the day of the closing, he has a right to do so under this condition.

6.7.7 NON-MERGER

General condition 48 is headed 'Non-Merger'. At common law the contract is deemed to merge with the conveyance. This means that once the sale is closed, the vendor's obligations under the contract cease and it is only those obligations, if any, contained in the conveyance which survive.

However, general condition 48 provides that notwithstanding delivery of the deed to the purchaser:

> 'all obligations and provisions designed to survive completion of the Sale and all warranties in the Conditions contained, which shall not have been implemented by the said Assurance, and which shall be capable of continuing or taking effect after such completion, shall enure and remain in full force and effect'.

Examples of this would be the planning warranty given under condition 36 and the warranty given in relation to chattel property under condition 46. Another area where it arises is where fencing is involved. In particular, if a purchaser has bought a site from a farmer, the contract may include a provision such as:

> 'prior to the commencement of any work on the site the purchaser shall erect a stock proof fence at least 4.5 feet high between the property sold and the property being retained by the vendor'.

If there was merger, the deed of conveyance would have had to include a covenant about fencing.

6.8   Completion

6.8.1   COMPLETION AND INTEREST

General conditions 24 to 26 deal with the completion of the sale and the payment of interest. As already mentioned the purchase price as defined by the definition section must be paid on or before the closing date.

General condition 24(b) provides that, unless otherwise agreed the sale is to be completed at the office of the vendor's solicitor. Where the parties agree to close, otherwise than at the offices of the vendor's solicitor, the procedure outlined in general condition 24(c) should be followed. This procedure is outlined in a Conveyancing Committee Practice Note in the Law Society *Gazette* of July 2006 which inserted a new general condition 24 into the Contract for Sale.

General condition 25 of the contract deals with the situation where there is default either by the purchaser or by the vendor.

General condition 25(a) provides that where there is default on the part of the purchaser in not closing the sale at the closing date, the purchaser shall pay interest at the contract rate and the vendor shall be entitled to the rents and profits of the property up to the actual date of closing.

Under general condition 25(b), if the vendor is in default and has not been ready, willing, and able to complete on the closing date, he is obliged to give the purchaser at least five working days' notice of any proposed new closing date.

General condition 25(c) provides that the vendor shall not be entitled to delay the closing of the sale solely because there is a dispute as to whether interest is payable or there is a dispute as to the amount of interest payable. However, the condition provides that the sale shall be closed without prejudice to the vendor's right to pursue his claim for interest.

6.8.2   COMPLETION NOTICES

This general condition covers all contracts for sale and deals with the issue of completion notices where one of the parties fails to complete the sale on the closing date.

General condition 40 deals with all contracts of sale where time is not of the essence in respect of the closing date. While, from a preliminary viewpoint, it may seem sensible to make time of the essence in the Contract for Sale, in practice this creates as many difficulties for the vendor as it does for the purchaser. If, for any reason, the vendor is unable to complete on the day, he will be bound by the terms of his own contract.

The purpose of general condition 40 is to enable either party to the contract to issue a notice making time of the essence, thereby creating a cut-off point.

The condition provides for the issue of 28-day notices (which are in reality a number of days longer). The period is 28 days after the service of the notice but excluding the date of service. Under general condition 49 the date of service is either the date of delivery or, when posted, the expiration of three working days after the envelope has been put in the post. (General condition 50 also deals with matters in relation to working days and in particular, where the last day for doing something is a day other than a working day, it extends the time to the next following working day.)

The 28-day notice does not terminate the contract but makes time of the essence and enables the party giving the notice to exercise his rights under the contract.

The requirement of general condition 40(b) is that notice be given to the other party. The service of this notice is governed by general condition 49. This condition provides for service of the notice by:

(a) delivery;

(b) post; and

(c) by facsimile transmission.

It should be noted that there is no provision for use of the Document Exchange, or email. It is imperative that the solicitor acting for the party serving a 28-day notice only does so when he or she is satisfied that the serving party is 'ready, willing and able to complete' the sale at the time of the service of the notice. The meaning of this phrase was considered in the case of *Mackin v Deane*, 20 May 2010, High Court.

6.8.3 SAMPLE NOTICES: GENERAL CONDITION 40

In the March 2009 issue of the *Gazette*, the Conveyancing Committee issued two new precedent completion notices.

A. VENDOR'S COMPLETION NOTICE FOR SERVICE ON THE PURCHASER COMPLETION NOTICE

Contract dated [   ] between the Vendor(s) and the Purchaser(s) in respect of the Property ("the Contract")

Vendor(s) and our clients(s):

Purchaser(s) and your client(s):

Closing Date:

Property: [Quote from particulars in the Contract]

TAKE NOTICE THAT, as the closing date in the Contract has passed without completion having taken place, we refer you to General Condition 40 of the Contract.

TAKE NOTE THAT the Vendor(s) is/are able, ready and willing to complete the sale of the above property to the Purchaser(s) or is/are not so able, ready and willing by reason of the default or misconduct of the Purchaser(s).

The Vendor(s) require(s) the Purchaser(s) forthwith to complete the sale and to pay the balance of the Purchase Price amount of €[   ] (with interest thereon calculated or otherwise determined in accordance with the Contract) within twenty eight days after the date of service hereof (as defined in Condition 49 of the Contract and excluding the date of service) and in this respect time is hereby made of the essence of the Contract.

If the Purchaser(s) does/do not comply with this notice before the expiration of the last date of the said period then General Condition 40(d) of the Contract shall immediately apply. The Purchaser(s) will be deemed to have failed to comply with the Contract and the conditions therein in the material respect and the Vendor(s) will enforce against the Purchaser(s), without further notice, such rights and remedies as may be available to him/them at law or in equity or (without prejudicate to such rights and remedies) may invoke and impose the provisions of General Condition 41 of the Contract.

Dated the [   ] day of [   ], 20[   ]

Signed:_____
Solicitors for the Vendor
Of:

To: Purchaser(s) Solicitor(s):_____
Of:

Note: There is no provision in general condition 49 of the contract for service by DX or email.

B. PURCHASER'S COMPLETION NOTICE FOR SERVICE ON VENDOR
COMPLETION NOTICE

Contract dated [   ] between the Vendor(s) and the Purchaser(s) in respect of the Property ("the Contract")

Vendor(s) and our clients(s):

Purchaser(s) and your client(s):

Closing Date:

Property: [Quote from particulars in the Contract]

TAKE NOTICE THAT, as the closing date in the Contract has passed without completion having taken place, we refer you to General Condition 40 of the Contract.

TAKE NOTICE THAT the Purchaser(s) is/are able, ready and willing to complete the purchase of the above property from the Vendor(s) or is/are not so able, ready and willing by reason of the default or misconduct of the Vendor(s).

The Purchaser(s) require(s) the Vendor(s) forthwith to complete the sale within twenty-eight days after the date of service hereof (as defined in Condition 49 of the Contract and excluding the date of service) and in this respect time is hereby made of the essence of the Contract.

If the Vendor(s) does/do not comply with this notice before the expiration of the last day of the said period then General Condition 40(e) of the Contract shall immediately apply. The Vendor(s) will be deemed to have failed to comply with the Contract and the conditions therein in a material respect and the Purchaser(s) will enforce against the Vendor(s), without further notice, such rights and remedies as may be available to him/them at law or in equity.

Dated the [   ] day of [   ], 20[   ]

Signed:_____
Solicitors for the Purchaser
Of:

To: Vendor(s) Solicitor(s):_____
Of:

Note: There is no provision in general condition 49 of the contract for service by DX or email.

These notices are also available on the members' areas of the Law Society website.

6.9   Problems—Resolution and Consequences

6.9.1   ARBITRATION

General condition 51 provides for arbitration between the parties. It sets out the mechanisms for the appointment of the arbitrator and lists the situations in which differences and disputes arising under the Contract for Sale will be referred to arbitration.

These are all differences and disputes between the vendor and purchaser as to:

'(a)   whether a rent is or is not a rack rent for the purpose of Condition 10(b)(iii), or

(b)   the identification of the Apportionment Date, or the treatment or quantification of any item pursuant to the provisions for apportionment in the Conditions, or

(c)   any issue on foot of Condition 33, including the applicability of said Condition, and the amount of compensation payable thereunder, or

(d)   the materiality of any matter for the purpose of Conditions 35(b)(iii) or 36(a)(ii), or

(e)   the materiality of damage or any other question involving any of the provisions in Conditions 43, 44 and 45 including the amount of compensation (if any) payable, or

(f)   whether any particular item or thing is or is not included in the Sale, or otherwise as to the nature or condition thereof.'

6.9.2   FORFEITURE OF DEPOSIT AND RESALE

General condition 41(a) provides for forfeiture of the deposit by the vendor and the resale of the property. This condition provides that if the property is resold within one year after the closing date:

'the deficiency (if any) arising on such re-sale and all costs and expenses attending the same or on any attempted re-sale shall (without prejudice to such damages to which the vendor shall otherwise be entitled) be made good to the vendor by the purchaser, who shall be allowed credit against same for the deposit so forfeited. Any increase in price obtained by the vendor on any re-sale, whenever effected, shall belong to the vendor.'

General condition 41(b) was inserted in the 2001 contract by way of protection of the solicitor who has held the deposit as stakeholder. It does not limit the purchaser's right to sue the vendor where it is claimed that the deposit has been wrongly forfeited.

6.9.3   DAMAGES FOR DEFAULT

General condition 42(a) provides that a purchaser who obtains specific performance is not precluded from an award of damages at law or in equity in the event of such order not being complied with.

General condition 42(b) excludes the application of the rule in *Bain v Fothergill* (1874) LR 7 HL 158. Previously that rule limited the damages that could be awarded to a purchaser in an action for breach of contract against a vendor who had failed to show good title. The exclusion of this rule placed an additional onus on the vendor's solicitor in respect of the preparation of the contract. This rule has now been abolished by s 53 of the 2009 Act.

6.9.4   RESCISSION

General conditions 37, 38, and 39 relate to the situation where the sale is rescinded in accordance with any of the provisions of the Contract for Sale. The conditions provide that, where there is rescission, the purchaser is entitled to a refund of his deposit without interest and the purchaser must submit to the vendor all documents in his possession belonging to the vendor and procure the cancellation of any entry relating to the sale in any register.

If the vendor does not return the deposit to the purchaser within five working days from the date upon which the sale has been rescinded, the purchaser is entitled to interest (at the rate specified at the definition section) from the expiration of a period of five days until actual payment.

6.9.5   REMEDIES AVAILABLE TO VENDOR/PURCHASER UNDER THE LAW SOCIETY CONTRACT FOR SALE

A brief description of the remedies available to both the vendor and purchaser are set out hereunder:

VENDOR	PURCHASER
General Condition 40	**General Condition 40**
1. Give 28 days' notice to complete and time is now made of the essence.	1. Give 28 days' notice to complete and time is now made of the essence.
2. Vendor may enforce such rights and remedies available at law or in equity: (a) sue for specific performance and damages—it is prudent in every case in which specific performance is sought also to seek damages in addition to or as an alternative to specific performance which is an equitable remedy; (b) forfeit deposit—invoke general condition 41 and resell; (c) rescind. Note general condition 40 applies where time is not of the essence in the contract.	2. Purchaser may enforce such rights and remedies available at law or in equity: (a) sue for specific performance and damages; or (b) ask the vendor to return the deposit.
General Condition 41	**General Condition 38**
In addition to the rights outlined in general condition 40 the vendor may resell the property with/without notice to the purchaser. In the event of the vendor reselling the subject property within one year after the closing date any deficiency on such resale and all costs and expenses relevant to the resale shall be paid by the purchaser who shall, however, be allowed credit against same for his forfeited deposit. Any increase in price obtained shall belong to the vendor.	Purchaser is entitled to the return of the deposit paid but without interest or costs where 'contractual' rescission occurs (ie rescission under the terms of the contract). Where 'traditional' rescission occurs (ie where the parties are restored to their original position before the contract was entered into) in cases where the purchaser rescinds he is entitled to recover not only the deposit with interest but also any legal expenses incurred in investigating title. However, to avail of 'traditional' rescission the would-be purchaser must apply to the court for an order of rescission.

Section 55 of the 2009 Act (which replaces s 9 of the Vendor and Purchaser Act, 1874) provides that any party to a contract for the sale of land may apply to court in a summary manner by way of vendor and purchaser summons for an order determining a question relating to the contract. A question referred under this section may relate to any requisition, objection, claim for compensation, or other question arising out of or connected with the contract but the parties may not apply under this procedure for an order affecting the existence or validity of the contract itself.

APPENDIX 6.1

General Conditions of Sale 2009 Edition

WARNING: IT IS RECOMMENDED THAT THE WITHIN SHOULD NOT
BE COMPLETED WITHOUT PRIOR LEGAL ADVICE

Law Society of Ireland

GENERAL CONDITIONS OF SALE 2009 EDITION

PARTICULARS
and
CONDITIONS OF SALE
of

*SALE BY PRIVATE TREATY
*SALE BY AUCTION

to be held at

on   the   day of,   20
at   o'clock

*Auctioneer:

*Address:

_____

* Delete, if inappropriate

Vendor:

Vendor's Solicitor:

Address:

Reference:

Law Society General Conditions of Sale
2009 Edition
© Law Society of Ireland

FAMILY HOME PROTECTION ACT, 1976 SPOUSAL CONSENT

I, ... being the Spouse of the under-named Vendor hereby, for the purposes of Section 3, Family Home Protection Act, 1976, consent to the proposed sale of the property described in the within Particulars at the price mentioned below.

SIGNED by the said Spouse ....
in the presence of: ....

....

MEMORANDUM OF AGREEMENT made this .... day of .... 20 ....
BETWEEN

....

of ....

("VENDOR")

(appropriate tax number(s) to be inserted)

AND

of ....

("PURCHASER")

(appropriate tax number(s) to be inserted)

whereby it is agreed that the Vendor shall sell and the Purchaser shall purchase in accordance with the annexed Special and General Conditions of Sale the property described in the within Particulars at the Purchase Price mentioned below.

REMINDER: Where appropriate, Vendor should insert an appropriate VAT Special Condition 3

Purchase Price □ ....   Closing Date: ....

less deposit □ ....   Interest Rate: .... per cent per annum

Balance □ ....

SIGNED ....   SIGNED ....

(Vendor)   (Purchaser)

Witness ....   Witness ....

Occupation ....   Occupation ....

Address ....   Address ....

....

....

(For Sale by Auction)

As Stakeholder I/We acknowledge receipt of Bank Draft/Cheque for □ .... in respect of deposit.

SIGNED ....

PARTICULARS AND TENURE

DOCUMENTS SCHEDULE

SEARCHES SCHEDULE

1. Negative Search in the Registry of Deeds on the Index of Names only for all acts affecting the Subject Property by the Vendor from the   day of

and

SPECIAL CONDITIONS

1. Save where the context otherwise requires or implies or the text hereof expresses to the contrary, the definitions and provisions as to interpretation set forth in the within General Conditions shall be applied for the purposes of these Special Conditions.

2. The said General Conditions shall:

   (a) apply to the sale in so far as the same are not hereby altered or varied, and these Special Conditions shall prevail in case of any conflict between them and the General Conditions

   (b) be read and construed without regard to any amendment therein, unless such amendment shall be referred to specifically in these Special Conditions.

3. *Attach/insert the current recommended format of VAT special condition (available on www.lawsociety.ie) amended as appropriate.*

NON-TITLE INFORMATION

Query		Reply (Please tick and / or insert comments as appropriate)		
		Yes	No	Comment
1.	**SERVICES**			
(a)	How is the Subject Property serviced as to: (i) drainage; (ii) water supply; (iii) electricity; (iv) gas; and (v) otherwise.			
(b)	Have the services (including roads, lanes, footpaths, sewers and drains) abutting or servicing the Subject Property been taken over by the Local Authority. Will a letter from the Local Authority or a solicitor's certificate to vouch the position be furnished on or before closing. If services are not in charge, are there appropriate easements and indemnities in existence.			
(c)	Is the Subject Property serviced by: (i) septic tank; or, (ii) private drainage scheme.			
(d)	Is the Subject Property serviced for television and if so is it by; (i) Cable T.V.; (ii) Satellite Dish; (iii) MMDF; (iv) TV aerial owned by Vendor; or (v) TV aerial owned by another. If (ii) or (iv) applies, will it be included in the Purchase Price.			
(e)	Is there a telephone line to be supplied with the Subject Property.			
(f)	Is there an ISDN line to be supplied with the Subject Property.			

2.	CONTENTS	Yes	No	Comment
(a)	Are there any contents included in the Purchase Price.			
	If so, give Vendor's estimate of value.			€
	Are there any fixtures, fittings or chattels included in this Sale which are the subject of any Lease, Rent, Hire Purchase Agreement or Chattel Mortgage.			
	If so, furnish now the Agreement and on closing proof of payment to date or discharge thereof.			

3.	OUTGOINGS	Yes	No	Comment
(a)	What is the Rateable Valuation of: (i) Lands; (ii) Buildings.			€ €
(b)	Give particulars of any other periodic or annual charge which affects the Subject Property or any part of it.			
(c)	Is the Vendor or any predecessor in title liable for any payments under the Local Government (Charges) Act 2009 in respect of the Subject Property?			
	If so, a letter of clearance from the local authority confirming no outstanding payment will be required on closing.			
	If not, please state why not.			
4.	**BUILDING ENERGY RATING ("BER")**			
	Furnish a copy of a valid BER certificate and related advisory report in respect of the Subject Property.			

NOTE: These General Conditions are not to be altered or deleted other than by way of Special Condition.

A Special Condition altering or deleting a General Condition should give the reason for such variation, unless manifestly evident.

Special Conditions should be utilised in instances where it is required to adopt recommendations or advices of the Law Society or of any committee associated with it, where such Recommendations or Advices are at variance with provisions expressed in the General Conditions.

General Conditions of Sale

DEFINITIONS

1. In these General Conditions:

    "Conditions" means the attached Special Conditions and these General Conditions

    "Documents Schedule", *"Searches Schedule"* and *"Special Conditions"* mean respectively the attached Documents Schedule, Searches Schedule and Special Conditions.

    "Memorandum" means the Memorandum of Agreement on Page 1 hereof

    "Particulars" means the Particulars and Tenure on Page 2 hereof and any extension of the same

    "Purchaser" means the party identified as such in the Memorandum

    "Sale" means the transaction evidenced by the Memorandum, the Particulars and the Conditions

    "Subject Property" means the property or interest in property which is the subject of the Sale

    "Vendor" means the party identified as such in the Memorandum.

2. In the Conditions save where the context otherwise requires or implies:

    "Apportionment Date" means either (a) the later of (i) the Closing Date (as defined hereunder) and (ii) such subsequent date from which delay in completing the Sale shall cease to be attributable to default on the part of the Vendor or (b) in the event of the Vendor exercising the right referred to in Condition 25 (a)(ii) hereunder, the date of actual completion of the Sale or (c) such other date as may be agreed by the Vendor and the Purchaser to be the Apportionment Date for the purpose of this definition

    "Assurance" means the document or documents whereby the Sale is to be carried into effect

    "Closing Date" means the date specified as such in the Memorandum, or, if no date is specified, the first Working Day after the expiration of five weeks computed from the Date of Sale

    "Competent Authority" includes the State, any Minister thereof, Government Department, State Authority, Local Authority, Planning Authority, Sanitary Authority, Building Control Authority, Fire Authority, Statutory Undertaker or any Department, Body or person by statutory provision or order for the time being in force authorised directly or indirectly to control, regulate, modify or restrict the development, use or servicing of land or buildings, or empowered to acquire land by compulsory process

    "Date of Sale" means the date of the auction when the Sale shall have been by auction, and otherwise means the date upon which the contract for the Sale shall have become binding on the Vendor and the Purchaser

    "Development" has the meaning ascribed to it by the Local Government (Planning and Development Act) 1963 or by the Planning and Development Act, 2000 which ever meaning shall be applicable to the circumstances

    "Lease" includes (a) a fee farm grant and every contract (whether or not in writing or howsoever effected, derived or evidenced) whereby the relationship of Landlord and Tenant is or is intended to be created and whether for any freehold or leasehold estate or interest and (b) licences and agreements relating to the occupation and use of land, cognate words being construed accordingly

    "Non-Title Information Sheet" means the Non-Title Information sheet attached hereto

"Planning Legislation" means the Local Government (Planning and Development) Acts 1963 to 1999, the Planning and Development Act, 2000, Building Bye Laws, the Building Control Act 1990, and all regulations made under those Acts

"Purchased Chattels" means such chattels, fittings, tenant's fixtures and other items as are included in the Sale

"Purchase Price" means the Purchase Price specified in the Memorandum PROVIDED HOWEVER that, if the Sale provides for additional moneys to be paid by the Purchaser for goodwill, crops or Purchased Chattels, the expression *"Purchase Price"* shall be extended to include such additional moneys

"Requisitions" include Requisitions on the title or titles as such of the Subject Property and with regard to rents, outgoings, rights, covenants, conditions, liabilities (actual or potential), planning and kindred matters and taxation issues material to such property

"Stipulated Interest Rate" means the interest rate specified in the Memorandum, or, if no rate is so specified, such rate as shall equate to 4 per centum per annum above the Court Rate obtaining pursuant to Section 22, Courts Act, 1981 and ruling at the date from which interest is to run

"Working Day" means any day other than a Saturday or Sunday or any Bank or Public Holiday or any of the seven days immediately succeeding Christmas Day.

INTERPRETATION

3.   In the Conditions save where the context otherwise requires or implies:

Words importing the masculine gender only include the feminine, neuter and common genders, and words importing the singular number only include the plural number and vice versa

The words "Vendor" and "Purchaser" respectively include (where appropriate) parties deriving title under them or either of them and shall apply to any one or more of several Vendors and Purchasers as the case may be and so that the stipulations in the Conditions contained shall be capable of being enforced on a joint and several basis

Any condition (or, as the case may be, any part of any condition) herein contained, not going to the root of the Contract, which shall be or become void, illegal or invalid or shall contravene any legislation for the time being in force, shall, while the same shall continue to be void, illegal, invalid, or so in contravention be deemed to have been severed and omitted from the Conditions PROVIDED HOWEVER that neither its inclusion in the first instance nor its deemed severance and omission as aforesaid shall prejudice the enforceability of the Conditions nor affect or curtail the other stipulations and provisions herein set forth

Unless the contrary appears, any reference hereunder:

(a)   to a particular Condition shall be to such of these General Conditions of Sale as is identified by said reference

(b)   to a Statute or Regulation or a combination of Statutes or Regulations shall include any extension, amendment, modification or re-enactment thereof, and any Rule, Regulation, Order or Instrument made thereunder, and for the time being in force

Headings and marginal notes inserted in the Conditions shall not affect the construction thereof nor shall the same have any contractual significance.

AUCTION

4.   Where the Sale is by auction, the following provisions shall apply:

(a)   the Vendor may divide the property set forth in the Particulars into lots and sub-divide, consolidate or alter the order of sale of any lots

(b) there shall be a reserve price for the Subject Property whether the same shall comprise the whole or any part of the property set forth in the Particulars and the Auctioneer may refuse to accept any bid. If any dispute shall arise as to any bidding, the Auctioneer shall (at his option) either determine the dispute or again put up the property in question at the last undisputed bid. No person shall advance at a bidding a sum less than that fixed by the Auctioneer, and no accepted bid shall be retracted. Subject to the foregoing, the highest accepted bidder shall be the Purchaser

(c) the Vendor may withdraw the whole of the property set forth in the Particulars or, where such property has been divided into lots, withdraw any one or more of such lots at any time before the same has been sold without disclosing the reserve price

(d) the Purchaser shall forthwith pay to the Vendor's Solicitor as stakeholder a deposit of ten per centum (10%) of the Purchase Price in part payment thereof, and shall execute an agreement in the form of the Memorandum to complete the purchase of the Subject Property in accordance with the Conditions.

PRIVATE TREATY SALE

5. Where the sale is by private treaty, the following provisions shall apply:

(a) the Purchaser shall, on or before the Date of Sale, pay to the Vendor's Solicitor a deposit of the amount stated in the Memorandum in part payment of the Purchase Price, which deposit is, with effect on and from the Date of Sale, to be held by the said Solicitor as stakeholder

(b) if notwithstanding Condition 5(a) a part of such deposit has been or is paid to any other person appointed or nominated by the Vendor, that other person, with effect as from the Date of Sale, shall be deemed to receive or to have received said part as stakeholder

(c) any moneys paid by way of deposit by or on behalf of the Purchaser prior to the Date of Sale to the Vendor's Solicitor or to any such other person as aforesaid shall, up to the Date of Sale, be held by the recipient thereof as trustee for the Purchaser.

The Following Conditions Apply Whether the Sale is by Auction or by Private Treaty

PURCHASER ON NOTICE OF CERTAIN DOCUMENTS

6. The documents specified in the Documents Schedule or copies thereof have been available for inspection by the Purchaser or his Solicitor prior to the Date of Sale. If all or any of the Subject Property is stated in the Particulars or in the Special Conditions to be held under a lease or to be subject to any covenants, conditions, rights, liabilities or restrictions, and the lease or other document containing the same is specified in the Documents Schedule, the Purchaser, whether availing of such opportunity of inspection or not, shall be deemed to have purchased with full knowledge of the contents thereof, notwithstanding any partial statement of such contents in the Particulars or in the Conditions.

DELIVERY OF TITLE

7. Within seven Working Days from the Date of Sale, the Vendor shall deliver or send by post to the Purchaser or his Solicitor copies of the documents necessary

to vouch the title to be shown in accordance with the Conditions which had not been furnished to the Purchaser or his Solicitor on or prior to the Date of Sale.

TITLE

8. (a) The Title to be shown to the Subject Property shall be such as is set forth in the Special Conditions

(b) Where the title to be shown to the whole or any part of the Subject Property is based on possession, the Vendor shall, in addition to vouching that title and dealing with such further matters as are required of him by the Conditions, furnish to the Purchaser on or before completion of the Sale a certificate from the Revenue Commissioners to the effect (i) that the Subject Property or (as the case may be) such part of the same as aforesaid is not charged with any of the taxes covered by the provisions of Section 146, Finance Act, 1994 as amended by Section 128 Finance Act, 1996 or (ii) that the Revenue Commissioners are satisfied that any such charge will be discharged within a time considered by them to be reasonable

(c) Save as stipulated in the Special Conditions the Vendor shall, prior to or at the completion of the Sale, discharge all mortgages and charges for the payment of money (other than items apportionable under Condition 27(b)) which affect the Subject Property.

FOREIGN VENDOR

9. Where the Vendor is a company, corporation, association or other similar entity incorporated, formed or established outside the State, the Vendor shall disclose this fact in the Special Conditions.

LEASEHOLD TITLE

10. (a) Where any of the Subject Property is held under a lease, the Purchaser shall not call for or investigate the title of the grantor or lessor to make the same, but shall conclusively assume that it was well and validly made, and is a valid and subsisting lease.

(b) Where any of the Subject Property is stated to be held under a lease or an agreement therefor then:

(i) no Objection or Requisition shall be made or indemnity required on account of such lease or agreement being (if such is the case) a sublease or agreement therefor, or on account of any superior lease comprising other property apart from the Subject Property or reserving a larger rent, or on the ground of any superior owner not having concurred in any apportionment or exclusive charge of rent

(ii) no Objection or Requisition shall be made by reason of any discrepancy between the covenants, conditions and provisions contained in any sublease and those in any superior lease, unless such as could give rise to forfeiture or a right of re-entry

(iii) the production of the receipt for the last gale of rent reserved by the lease or agreement therefor, under which the whole or any part of the Subject Property is held, (without proof of the title or authority of the person giving such receipt) shall (unless the contrary appears) be accepted as conclusive evidence that all rent accrued due has been paid and all covenants and conditions in such lease or agreement and in every (if any) superior lease have been duly performed and observed or any breaches thereof (past or continuing) effectively waived or sanctioned up to the actual completion of the Sale, whether or not it shall appear that the lessor or reversioner was aware of such breaches. If the said rent (not being a rack rent) shall not have been paid in circumstances where the party entitled to receive the same is not known to the Vendor, or if the Subject Property is indemnified against payment of rent, the production of a Statutory Declaration so stating shall (unless the contrary appears) be accepted as such conclusive evidence, provided that the Declaration further indicates that no notices or rent demands have been served on or received by the Vendor under the lease or agreement on foot of which the Subject Property is held; that the Vendor has complied with all the covenants (other than those in respect of payment of rent) on the part of the lessee and the conditions contained in such lease or agreement, and that he is not aware of any breaches thereof either by himself or by any of his predecessors in title

(iv) if any of the Subject Property is held under a lease or agreement for lease requiring consent to alienation, the Vendor shall apply for and endeavour to obtain such consent, and the Purchaser shall deal expeditiously and constructively with and shall satisfy all reasonable requirements of the lessor in relation to the application therefor, but the Vendor shall not be required to institute legal proceedings to enforce the issue of any such consent or otherwise as to the withholding of the same. If such consent shall have been refused or shall not have been procured and written evidence of the same furnished to the Purchaser on or before the Closing Date, or if any such consent is issued subject to a condition, which the Purchaser on reasonable grounds refuses to accept, either party may rescind the Sale by seven days prior notice to the other.

PRIOR TITLE

11. (a) The title to the Subject Property prior to the date of the instrument specified in the Special Conditions as the commencement of title, whether or not appearing by recital, inference or otherwise, shall not be required, objected to or investigated.

(b) In the case of registered freehold or leasehold land registered under the Registration of Title Acts, 1891 to 1942 or the Registration of Title Act, 1964 the provisions of subparagraph (a) of this Condition shall apply without prejudice to Sections 52 and 115 of the last mentioned Act and shall not disentitle the Purchaser from investigating the possibility of there having been a voluntary disposition on the title within the period of twelve years immediately preceding the Date of Sale or a disposition falling within Section 121, Succession Act, 1965 as extended by Section 25 (5), Family Law Act, 1995 and the Vendor shall be required to deal with all points properly taken in or arising out of such investigation.

INTERMEDIATE TITLE

12. Where in the Special Conditions it is provided that the title is to commence with a particular instrument and then to pass to a second instrument or to a specified event, the title intervening between the first instrument and the second instrument or the specified event, whether or not appearing by recital, inference or otherwise, shall not be required, objected to or investigated.

REGISTERED LAND

13. Where all or any of the Subject Property consists of freehold or leasehold registered land registered under the Registration of Title Acts, 1891 to 1942

("the Acts of 1891 to 1942") or the Registration of Title Act, 1964 ("the Act of 1964") then:

(a) if the registration is subject to equities under the Acts of 1891 to 1942, the Purchaser shall not require the equities to be discharged, but the Vendor shall, with the copy documents to be delivered or sent in accordance with Condition 7, furnish sufficient evidence of title prior to first registration or otherwise to enable the Purchaser to procure their discharge

(b) if the registration is with a possessory title under the Act of 1964 the Purchaser shall not require the Vendor to be registered with an absolute title, but the Vendor shall, with the copy documents to be delivered or sent in accordance with Condition 7, furnish sufficient evidence of the title prior to such registration or otherwise to enable the Purchaser to be registered with an absolute title

(c) the Vendor shall, with the copy documents to be delivered or sent in accordance with Condition 7, furnish to the Purchaser a copy of the Land Registry Folio or Folios relating to the Subject Property written up-to-date (or as nearly as practicable up-to-date), together with a copy of the relevant Land Registry map or file plan

(d) the Vendor shall furnish a Statutory Declaration, by some person competent to make it, confirming that there are not in existence any burdens which under the Act of 1964 affect registered land without registration, save such (if any) as are specifically mentioned in the Particulars or the Special Conditions

(e) if the Land Certificate has been issued to the Land Commission or if no such Certificate has been issued, the Purchaser shall not be entitled to require such Certificate to be produced, handed over on completion or issued

(f) the Purchaser shall procure himself to be registered as owner of the Subject Property at his own expense

(g) in the event of the Subject Property being subject to a Land Purchase Annuity the Vendor shall, prior to completion, redeem the same or (as the case may be) such proportion thereof as may be allocated to the Subject Property

(h) where the Subject Property is part only of the lands in a Folio, the Vendor shall (i) do everything within the reasonable power or procurement of the Vendor to satisfy within a reasonable time any Land Registry mapping queries arising on the registration of the Assurance to the Purchaser so far as it affects that land, and (ii) pay and discharge any outlay to the Land Registry which ought properly to be paid by the Vendor, including additional fees attributable to default on the part of the Vendor.

IDENTITY

14. The Purchaser shall accept such evidence of identity as may be gathered from the descriptions in the documents of title plus (if circumstances require) a statutory declaration to be made by a competent person, at the Purchaser's expense, that the Subject Property has been held and enjoyed for at least twelve years in accordance with the title shown. The Vendor shall be obliged to furnish such information as is in his possession relative to the identity and extent of the Subject Property, but shall not be required to define exact boundaries, fences, ditches, hedges or walls or to specify which (if any) of the same are of a party nature, nor shall the Vendor be required to identify parts of the Subject Property held under different titles.

RIGHTS—LIABILITIES—CONDITION OF SUBJECT PROPERTY

15. The Vendor shall disclose before the Date of Sale, in the Particulars the Special Conditions or otherwise, all easements, rights, reservations, exceptions, privileges, covenants, restrictions, rents, taxes and other liabilities (not already

known to the Purchaser or apparent from inspection) which are known by the Vendor to affect the Subject Property and are likely to affect it following completion of the Sale.

16.   Subject to Condition 15, the Purchaser shall be deemed to buy:

(a)   with full notice of the actual state and condition of the Subject Property and

(b)   subject to (i) all leases (if any) mentioned in the Particulars or in the Special Conditions and (ii) all easements, rights, reservations, exceptions, privileges, covenants, restrictions, rents, taxes, liabilities, outgoings and all incidents of tenure affecting the Subject Property.

REQUISITIONS

17.   The Purchaser shall, not later than fourteen Working Days after the Date of Sale or (where the Vendor is required to furnish copy of documents pursuant to Condition 7) the delivery of the copy documents of title in accordance with Condition 7, send to the Vendor's Solicitor a written statement of his Objections (if any) on the title and his Requisitions. Any Objection or Requisition not made within the time aforesaid and not going to the root of the title shall be deemed to have been waived. The Vendor's Replies to any Objections or Requisitions shall be answered by the Purchaser in writing within seven Working Days after the delivery thereof and so on toties quoties, and, if not so answered, shall be considered to have been accepted as satisfactory. In all respects time shall be deemed to be of the essence of this Condition.

18.   If the Purchaser shall make and insist on any Objection or Requisition as to the title, the Assurance to him or any other matter relating or incidental to the Sale, which the Vendor shall, on the grounds of unreasonable delay or expense or other reasonable ground, be unable or unwilling to remove or comply with, the Vendor shall be at liberty (notwithstanding any intermediate negotiation or litigation or attempts to remove or comply with the same) by giving to the Purchaser or his Solicitor not less than five Working Days notice to rescind the Sale. In that case, unless the Objection or Requisition in question shall in the meantime have been withdrawn, the Sale shall be rescinded at the expiration of such notice.

SEARCHES

19.   The Purchaser shall be furnished with the searches (if any) specified in the Searches Schedule and any searches already in the Vendor's possession, which are relevant to the title or titles on offer. Any other searches required by the Purchaser must be obtained by him at his own expense. Where the Special Conditions provide that the title shall commence with a particular instrument and then pass to a second instrument or to a specified event, the Vendor shall not be obliged to explain and discharge any act which appears on a search covering the period between such particular instrument and the date of the second instrument or specified event, unless same goes to the root of the title. Subject as aforesaid the Vendor shall explain and discharge any acts appearing on Searches covering the period from the date stipulated or implied for the commencement of the title to the date of actual completion.

ASSURANCE

20.   (a)   On payment of all moneys payable by him in respect of the Sale, and subject to the provisions of Section 980, Taxes Consolidation Act, 1997, and (if relevant) to those contained in Section 107, Finance Act, 1993 (in relation

to Residential Property Tax), the Purchaser shall be entitled to a proper Assurance of the Subject Property from the Vendor and all other (if any) necessary parties.

(b) On completion of the Sale the Purchaser shall accept delivery of the Assurance of the entire of the Subject Property in favour of the Purchaser or such other person(s) as the Purchaser shall nominate, such Assurance to be prepared by and at the expense of the Purchaser. The draft thereof shall be submitted to the Vendor's Solicitor not less than seven Working Days, and the engrossment not less than four Working Days, before the Closing Date. The delivery of the said draft or engrossment shall not prejudice any outstanding Objection or Requisition validly made.

(c) If the Stamp Duty (Particulars to be Delivered) Regulations, 1995 apply to the Sale, the Vendor shall, on or before handing over the Assurance, furnish to the Purchaser the Form referred to in such Regulations duly completed in accordance therewith.

(d) Where required by the Purchaser to enable the Purchaser to stamp the Assurance, the Vendor will furnish to the Purchaser the tax number of the Vendor prior to or on completion of the Sale, such tax number being appropriately vouched.

VACANT POSSESSION

21. Subject to any provision to the contrary in the Particulars or in the Conditions or implied by the nature of the transaction, the Purchaser shall be entitled to vacant possession of the Subject Property on completion of the Sale.

LEASES

22. Where the Subject Property is sold subject to any lease, a copy of the same (or, if the provisions thereof have not been reduced to writing, such evidence of its nature and terms as the Vendor shall be able to supply) together with copies of any notices in the Vendor's possession served by or on the lessee (and of continuing and material relevance) shall, prior to the Sale, be made available for inspection by the Purchaser or his Solicitor.

23. Unless the Special Conditions provide to the contrary, the Purchaser shall be entitled to assume that, at the Date of Sale, the lessee named in any such Lease (as is referred to in Condition 22) is still the lessee; that there has been no variation in the terms and conditions of said Lease (other than such as may be evident from an inspection of the Subject Property or apparent from the Particulars or the documents furnished to the Purchaser prior to the Sale), and that the said terms and conditions (save those pertaining to the actual state and condition of the Subject Property) have been complied with.

COMPLETION AND INTEREST

24. (a) The Sale shall be completed and the balance of the Purchase Price paid by the Purchaser on or before the Closing Date.

(b) Unless otherwise agreed, completion shall take place at the office of the Vendor's Solicitor.

(c) Where completion is to take place otherwise than at the office of the Vendor's Solicitor, then the following provisions shall apply:

(i) the Purchaser's Solicitor shall nominate seven days prior to closing the manner in which all completion documents are to be dispatched (registered post, courier, DX, collection or other agreed mode of dispatch).

The mode of dispatch will be at the Purchaser's Solicitor's sole risk and expense, provided that the Vendor's Solicitor uses the mode of dispatch nominated by the Purchaser's Solicitor or otherwise agreed

(ii)   not later than four days prior to closing the Purchaser's Solicitor shall send to the Vendor's Solicitor a list of closing requirements in accordance with the terms of the contract and as agreed in replies to Requisitions on Title and rejoinder on title (if any)(hereafter referred to as 'the completion documents'). It is the responsibility of the Purchaser's Solicitor to ensure that closing searches are furnished to the Vendor's Solicitor on or before the Closing Date, and failure to do so will not be a reason to postpone the completion of the Sale.

(iii) when the Vendor's Solicitor is immediately able to satisfy these closing requirements, then:

— where applicable, redemption figures for any mortgage or charge on the Vendor's title shall be furnished to the Purchaser's Solicitor

— the Vendor's Solicitor shall undertake with the Purchaser's Solicitor in the following form

"In consideration of the completion of the within sale and in consideration of your furnishing the balance of the Purchase Price to us (in the agreed manner), we hereby undertake with you to immediately furnish copies of all the completion documents to be signed by the Vendor properly executed and to act as your agent (without charge) in accepting delivery of the Deed of Assurance containing the receipt clause (thereby complying with Section 77(3) of the Land and Conveyancing Law Reform Act 2009) and immediately thereafter to dispatch to you all of the completion documents in accordance with the agreed list of completion documents and the mode of dispatch nominated or otherwise agreed".

(iv)   Completion shall take place at the office of the Vendor's Solicitor when the Vendor's Solicitor:

— has received the balance of the Purchase Price

and

— is in a position to satisfactorily explain all acts appearing on any closing searches received

and

— is in a position to satisfy all of the Purchaser's closing requirements, in accordance with the terms of the contract.

(d)   All of the completion documents shall thereupon be dispatched to the Purchaser's Solicitor by the mode of dispatch nominated or otherwise agreed to include satisfactory explanation of all acts appearing on searches and the property's keys or authority for their collection. The Vendor's Solicitor shall communicate with the Purchaser's Solicitor in a recorded form advising that completion has taken place, and thereupon the Vendor's Solicitor shall be entitled to release the purchase moneys and the Purchaser shall thereupon be entitled to vacant possession.

(e)   Pending completion in accordance with these Conditions, any moneys received in advance of completion by the Vendor's Solicitor, other than the deposit, shall be held by the Vendor's Solicitor as trustee for the Purchaser.

25. (a) If by reason of any default on the part of the Purchaser, the purchase shall not have been completed on or before the later of (a) the Closing Date or (b) such subsequent date whereafter delay in completing shall not be attributable to default on the part of the Vendor

(i)   the Purchaser shall pay interest to the Vendor on the balance of the Purchase Price remaining unpaid at the Stipulated Interest Rate for the period between the Closing Date (or as the case may be such subsequent date as aforesaid) and the date of actual completion of the Sale. Such interest shall accrue from day to day and shall be payable before and after any judgment and

(ii)   the Vendor shall in addition to being entitled to receive such interest, have the right to take the rents and profits less the outgoings of the Subject Property up to the date of the actual completion of the Sale.

(b)   If the Vendor by reason of his default shall not be able, ready and willing to complete the Sale on the Closing Date he shall thereafter give to the Purchaser at least five Working Days prior notice of a date upon which he shall be so able ready and willing and the Purchaser shall not before the expiration of that notice be deemed to be in default for the purpose of this Condition provided that no such notice shall be required if the Vendor is prevented from being able and ready to complete or to give said notice by reason of the act or default of the Purchaser.

(c)   The Vendor shall not be entitled to delay completion solely because of a dispute between the parties with regard to liability for such interest or as to the amount of interest payable PROVIDED ALWAYS that such completion and the delivery of any Assurance on foot of these Conditions shall be had strictly without prejudice to the right of the Vendor to pursue his claim for interest.

26.   The submission of an Apportionment Account made up to a particular date or other corresponding step taken in anticipation of completing the Sale shall not per se preclude the Vendor from exercising his rights under the provisions of Condition 25 and in the event of such exercise the said Apportionment Account or the said other corresponding step shall (if appropriate) be deemed not to have been furnished or taken, and the Vendor shall be entitled to furnish a further Apportionment Account.

APPORTIONMENT AND POSSESSION

27.   (a)   Subject to the stipulations contained in the Conditions, the Purchaser, on paying the Purchase Price shall be entitled to vacant possession of the Subject Property or (as the case may be) the rents and profits thereout with effect from the Apportionment Date

(b)   All rents, profits, rates, outgoings and moneys (including rent, outgoings and money payable in advance but not including impositions derived from hypothecation) referable to the Subject Property shall for the purpose of this Condition, be apportioned (whether apportionable by law or not) on a day to day basis as at the Apportionment Date, up to which the liability for or the entitlement to the same shall (subject to apportionment as aforesaid to accord with the position obtaining as to moneys paid or due at such date) be for the account of the Vendor and thereafter for that of the Purchaser provided that if completion shall have been delayed through the default of the Vendor the Purchaser may opt for apportionment under this Condition as at the Closing Date or at the date at which the Purchaser (if also in default) shall have ceased to have been so in default whichever shall be the later

(c)   In the implementation of this Condition the Vendor shall be regarded as being the owner of the Subject Property until midnight on such date as is appropriate for apportionment purposes

(d)   The balance of the Purchase Price shall (where appropriate) be adjusted upwards or downwards to accommodate apportionments calculated pursuant to this Condition and the expression "balance of the Purchase Price" where used in the Conditions shall be construed accordingly

(e)   To the extent that same shall be unknown at the Apportionment Date (or shall not then be readily ascertainable) amounts to be apportioned hereunder,

including any amount apportionable pursuant to Condition 27(f), shall be apportioned provisionally on a fair estimate thereof, and, upon ascertainment of the actual figures, a final apportionment shall be made, and the difference between it and the provisional apportionment shall be refunded by the Vendor or the Purchaser (as the case may be) to the other within ten Working Days of the liable party becoming aware of the amount of such difference

(f)   Excise and kindred duties payable in respect of the Subject Property or any licence attached thereto shall be apportioned on a day to day basis as at the Apportionment Date up to which the liability for the same shall be for the account of the Vendor and thereafter for that of the Purchaser and Condition 27 (c) shall apply for the purposes of such apportionment.

COMPULSORY REGISTRATION

28.   If all or any of the Subject Property is unregistered land the registration of which was compulsory prior to the Date of Sale the Vendor shall be obliged to procure such registration prior to completion of the Sale

29.   If all or any of the Subject Property is unregistered land, the registration of which shall become compulsory at or subsequent to the Date of Sale, the Vendor shall not be under any obligation to procure such registration but shall at or prior to such completion furnish to the Purchaser a Map of the Subject Property complying with the requirements of the Land Registry as then recognised and further the Vendor shall, if so requested within two years after completion of the Sale, by and at the expense of the Purchaser, supply any additional information, which he may reasonably be able to supply, and produce and furnish any documents in his possession that may be required to effect such registration.

SIGNING "IN TRUST" OR "AS AGENT"

30.   A Purchaser who signs the Memorandum "in Trust", "as Trustee" or "as Agent", or with any similar qualification or description without therein specifying the identity of the principal or other party for whom he so signs, shall be personally liable to complete the Sale, and to fulfil all such further stipulations on the part of the Purchaser as are contained in the Conditions, unless and until he shall have disclosed to the Vendor the name of his principal or other such party.

FAILURE TO PAY DEPOSIT

31.   The failure by the Purchaser to pay in full the deposit hereinbefore specified as payable by him shall constitute a breach of condition entitling the Vendor to terminate the Sale or to sue the Purchaser for damages or both but such entitlement shall be without prejudice to any rights otherwise available to the Vendor.

32.   In case a cheque taken for the deposit (having been presented and whether or not it has been re-presented) shall not have been honoured, then and on that account the Vendor may (without prejudice to any rights otherwise available to him) elect either:

(a)   to treat the Contract evidenced by the Memorandum, the Particulars and the Conditions as having been discharged by breach thereof on the Purchaser's part

or

(b)   to enforce payment of the deposit as a deposit by suing on the cheque or otherwise.

DIFFERENCES—ERRORS

33. (a) In this Condition "error" includes any omission, non-disclosure, discrepancy, difference, inaccuracy, mis-statement or mis-representation made in the Memorandum, the Particulars or the Conditions or the Non-Title Information Sheet or in the course of any representation, response or negotiations leading to the Sale, and whether in respect of measurements, quantities, descriptions or otherwise

   (b) The Purchaser shall be entitled to be compensated by the Vendor for any loss suffered by the Purchaser in his bargain relative to the Sale as a result of an error made by or on behalf of the Vendor provided however that no compensation shall be payable for loss of trifling materiality unless attributable to recklessness or fraud on the part of the Vendor nor in respect of any matter of which the Purchaser shall be deemed to have had notice under Condition 16(a) nor in relation to any error in a location or similar plan furnished for identification only

   (c) Nothing in the Memorandum, the Particulars or the Conditions shall:

   (i) entitle the Vendor to require the Purchaser to accept property which differs substantially from the property agreed to be sold whether in quantity, quality, tenure or otherwise, if the Purchaser would be prejudiced materially by reason of any such difference

   or

   (ii) affect the right of the Purchaser to rescind or repudiate the Sale where compensation for a claim attributable to a material error made by or on behalf of the Vendor cannot be reasonably assessed

   (d) Save as aforesaid, no error shall annul the Sale or entitle the Vendor or the Purchaser (as the case may be) to be discharged therefrom.

DOCUMENTS OF TITLE RELATING TO OTHER PROPERTY

34. (a) Documents of title relating to other property as well as to the Subject Property shall be retained by the Vendor or other person entitled to the possession thereof.

   (b) where the property is sold in lots, all documents of title relating to more than one lot shall be retained by the Vendor, until the completion of the Sales of all the lots comprised in such documents, and shall then (unless they also relate to any property retained by the Vendor) be handed over to such of the Purchasers as the Vendor shall consider best entitled thereto.

   (c) the Vendor shall give to the Purchaser (and where the property is sold in lots, to the Purchaser of each lot) certified copies of all documents retained under this Condition and pertinent to the title to be furnished (other than documents of record, of which plain copies only will be given).

   (d) subject as hereinafter provided, the Vendor shall give the usual statutory acknowledgement of the right of production and undertaking for safe custody of all documents (other than documents of record) retained by him under this Condition and pertinent to the title to be furnished. Such acknowledgement and undertaking shall be prepared by and at the expense of the purchaser.

   (e) if the Vendor is retaining any unregistered land held wholly or partly under the same title as the Subject Property, the Assurance shall be engrossed in duplicate by and at the expense of the Purchaser, who shall deliver to the Vendor the Counterpart thereof, same having been stamped and registered and (if appropriate) executed by the purchaser.

DISCLOSURE OF NOTICES

35.   Where prior to the Date of Sale

(a)   any closing, demolition or clearance order

or

(b)   any notice for compulsory acquisition or any other notice (other than such other notice, details of which are required to be entered on the Planning Register pursuant to the requirements of Planning Legislation)
made or issued by or at the behest of a Competent Authority in respect of the Subject Property and affecting the same at the Date of Sale has been notified or given to the Vendor (whether personally or by advertisement or posting on the Subject Property or in any other manner) or is otherwise known to the Vendor, or where the Subject Property is, at the Date of Sale, affected by any award or grant, which is or may be repayable by the Vendor's successor in title, then if the Vendor fails to show

(i)   that, before the Date of Sale, the Purchaser received notice or was aware of the matter in question

or

(ii)   that the matter in question was apparent from inspection of the Development Plan or the current or published Draft Development Plan for the area within which the Subject Property is situate

or

(iii)   that same is no longer applicable or material

or

(iv)   that same does not prejudicially affect the value of the Subject Property

or

(v)   that the subject thereof can and will be dealt with fully in the Apportionment Account

the Purchaser may by notice given to the Vendor rescind the Sale.

DEVELOPMENT

36.   (a)   Unless the Special Conditions contain a stipulation to the contrary, the Vendor warrants:

In cases where property is affected by an unauthorised development or a breach of Condition/ Conditions in a Permission/ Approval amounting to a non- conforming development or where the Bye-Law Amnesty covered by Section 22(7), Building Control Act, 1990 is relevant, it is recommended that same be dealt with expressly by Special Condition.

(i)   that there has been no Development of the Subject Property since the 1st day of October, 1964, for which Planning Permission or Building Bye-Law Approval was required by law

or

(ii)   that all Planning Permissions and Building Bye-Law Approvals required by law for the Development of the Subject Property as at the Date of Sale were obtained (save in respect of matters of trifling materiality), and that, where implemented, the conditions thereof in relation to and specifically addressed to such Development were complied with substantially

PROVIDED HOWEVER that the foregoing warranty shall not extend to (and the Vendor shall not be required to establish) the obtaining of approvals under the Building Bye-Laws or compliance with such Bye-Laws in respect of Development or works carried out prior to the 13th day of December, 1989 (this proviso being here inafter in Condition 36 referred to as the "Proviso")

(b)   Unless the Special Conditions contain a stipulation to the contrary, the Vendor warrants in all cases where the provisions of the Building Control Act, 1990 or of any Regulation from time to time thereunder apply to the design or Development of the Subject Property or any part of the same or any activities in connection therewith, that there has been substantial compliance with the said provisions in so far as they pertained to such design, Development or activities

(c) The warranties referred to in (a) and (b) of this Condition shall not extend to any breach of provisions contained in Planning Legislation, which breach has been remedied or is no longer continuing at the Date of Sale.

(d) The Vendor shall prior to the Date of Sale make available to the Purchaser for inspection or furnish to the Purchaser copies of:

    (i)   all such Permissions and Approvals as are referred to in Condition 36 (a) other than in the Proviso

    (ii)   all Fire Safety Certificates and (if available) Commencement Notices issued under Regulations made pursuant to the Building Control Act, 1990, and referable to the Subject Property (such Permissions, Approvals and Certificates specified in this Condition 36(d) other than those specified in the Proviso being hereinafter in Condition 36 referred to as the "Consents")

    and

    (iii) (Save where Development is intended to be carried out between the Date of Sale and the date upon which the Sale shall be completed) the documents referred to in Condition 36 (e).

(e) The Vendor shall, on or prior to completion of the Sale, furnish to the Purchaser

    (i)   written confirmation from the Local Authority of compliance with all conditions involving financial contributions or the furnishing of bonds in any such Consents PROVIDED HOWEVER that where

        the Development authorised by such Consents relates to a residential housing estate of which the Development of the Subject Property forms part

        and

        such Consents relate to the initial construction of a building on the Subject Property

        written confirmation from the Local Authority that the roads and services abutting on the Subject Property have been taken in charge by it shall be accepted as satisfactory evidence of compliance with such conditions, unless the said confirmation discloses a requirement for payment of outstanding moneys

    (ii)   a Certificate or Opinion by an Architect or an Engineer (or other professionally qualified person competent so to certify or opine) confirming that,

        — such Consents relate to the Subject Property

        — (where applicable) the design of the buildings on the Subject Property is in substantial compliance with the Building Control Act, 1990 and the Regulations made thereunder

        — the Development of the Subject Property has been carried out in substantial compliance with such Consents and (where applicable) the requirements of the Building Control Act, 1990 and Regulations made thereunder

        — all conditions (other than financial conditions) of such Consents have been complied with substantially

        and

        — in the event of the Subject Property forming part of a larger development, all conditions (other than financial conditions) of such Consents which relate to the overall development have been complied with substantially so far as was reasonably possible in the context of such development as at the date of such Certificate or Opinion

(f) (i) Where the Vendor has furnished Certificates or Opinions pursuant to Condition 36 (e), the Vendor shall have no liability on foot of the warranties expressed in Condition 36(a) or 36(b) or either of them in respect of any matter with regard to which such Certificate or Opinion is erroneous or inaccurate, unless the Vendor was aware at the Date of Sale that the same contained any material error or inaccuracy

(ii) if, subsequent to the Date of Sale and prior to the completion thereof, it is established that any such Certificate or Opinion is erroneous or inaccurate, then, if the Vendor fails to show

that before the Date of Sale the Purchaser was aware of the error or inaccuracy

or

that same is no longer relevant or material

or

that same does not prejudicially affect the value of the Subject Property

the Purchaser may by notice given to the Vendor rescind the Sale.

RESCISSION

37. Upon rescission of the Sale in accordance with any of the provisions herein or in the Special Conditions contained or otherwise:

(a) the Purchaser shall be entitled to a return of his deposit (save where it shall lawfully have been forfeited) but without interest thereon

(b) the Purchaser shall remit to the Vendor all documents in his possession belonging to the Vendor and the Purchaser shall at his expense (save where Special Conditions otherwise provide) procure the cancellation of any entry relating to the Sale in any register.

38. If any such deposit as is to be returned pursuant to Condition 37 shall not have been returned to the Purchaser within five Working Days from the date upon which the Sale shall have been rescinded, the Purchaser shall be entitled to interest thereon at the Stipulated Interest Rate from the expiration of the said period of five Working Days to the date upon which the deposit shall have been so returned.

39. The right to rescind shall not be lost by reason only of any intermediate negotiations or attempts to comply with or to remove the issue giving rise to the exercise of such right.

COMPLETION NOTICES

40. Save where time is of the essence in respect of the Closing Date, the following provisions shall apply:

(a) if the Sale be not completed on or before the Closing Date either party may on or after that date (unless the Sale shall first have been rescinded or become void) give to the other party notice to complete the Sale in accordance with this condition, but such notice shall be effective only if the party giving it shall then either be able, ready and willing to complete the Sale or is not so able, ready or willing by reason of the default or misconduct of the other party

(b) upon service of such notice the party upon whom it shall have been served shall complete the Sale within a period of twenty-eight days after the date of such service (as defined in Condition 49 and excluding the date of service), and in respect of such period time shall be of the essence of the contract but without prejudice to any intermediate right of rescission by either party

(c) the recipient of any such notice shall give to the party serving the same reasonable advice of his readiness to complete

(d) if the Purchaser shall not comply with such a notice within the said period (or within any extension thereof which the Vendor may agree) he shall be deemed to have failed to comply with these Conditions in a material respect and the Vendor may enforce against the Purchaser, without further notice, such rights and remedies as may be available to the Vendor at law or in equity, or (without prejudice to such rights and remedies) may invoke and impose the provisions of Condition 41

(e) if the Vendor does not comply with such a notice within the said period (or within any extension thereof which the Purchaser may agree), then the Purchaser may elect either to enforce against the Vendor, without further notice, such rights and remedies as may be available to the Purchaser at law or in equity or (without prejudice to any right of the Purchaser to damages) to give notice to the Vendor requiring a return to the Purchaser of all moneys paid by him, whether by way of deposit or otherwise, on account of the Purchase Price. Condition 38 shall apply to all moneys so to be returned, the period of five Working Days therein being computed from the date of the giving of such last mentioned notice. If the Purchaser gives such a notice and all the said moneys and interest (if any) are remitted to him, the Purchaser shall no longer be entitled to specific performance of the Sale, and shall return forthwith all documents in his possession belonging to the Vendor, and (at the Vendor's expense) procure the cancellation of any entry relating to the Sale in any register

(f) the party serving a notice under this Condition may, at the request of or with the consent of the other party, by written communication to the other party extend the term of such notice for one or more specified periods of time, and, in that case, the term of the notice shall be deemed to expire on the last day of such extended period or periods, and the notice shall operate as though such extended period or periods had been specified in this Condition in lieu of the said period of twenty-eight days, and time shall be of the essence in relation to such extended period

(g) the Vendor shall not be deemed to be other than able, ready and willing to complete for the purposes of this Condition:

  (i) by reason of the fact that the Subject Property has been mortgaged or charged, provided that the funds (including the deposit) receivable on completion shall (after allowing for all prior claims thereon) be sufficient to discharge the aggregate of all amounts payable in satisfaction of such mortgages and charges to the extent that they relate to the Subject Property

  or

  (ii) by reason of being unable, not ready or unwilling at the date of service of such notice to deliver vacant possession of the Subject Property provided that (where it is a term of the Sale that vacant possession thereof be given) the Vendor is, upon being given reasonable advice of the other party's intention to close the Sale on a date within the said period of twenty-eight days or any extension thereof pursuant to Condition 40 (f), able, ready and willing to deliver vacant possession of the Subject Property on that date.

FORFEITURE OF DEPOSIT AND RESALE

41. (a) If the Purchaser shall fail in any material respect to comply with any of the Conditions, the Vendor (without prejudice to any rights or remedies available to him at law or in equity) shall be entitled to forfeit the deposit and to such purpose unilaterally to direct his Solicitor or other stakeholder to release

same to him AND the Vendor shall be at liberty (without being obliged to tender an Assurance) to resell the Subject Property, with or without notice to the Purchaser, either by public auction or private treaty. In the event of the Vendor re-selling the Subject Property within one year after the Closing Date (or within one year computed from the expiration of any period by which the closing may have been extended pursuant to Condition 40) the deficiency (if any) arising on such re-sale and all costs and expenses attending the same or on any attempted re-sale shall (without prejudice to such damages to which the Vendor shall otherwise be entitled) be made good to the Vendor by the Purchaser, who shall be allowed credit against same for the deposit so forfeited. Any increase in price obtained by the Vendor on any re-sale, whenever effected, shall belong to the Vendor.

(b) A Solicitor or other stakeholder acting on any such direction as is referred to in Condition 41(a) shall have no further obligations as stakeholder or otherwise in respect of such deposit to the Vendor or to the Purchaser PROVIDED that he shall have given to the Purchaser notice of the receipt by him of the said direction and the Purchaser shall not within twenty one days of the giving of such notice have instituted and served proceedings disputing the rights alleged by the Vendor to forfeit the deposit.

DAMAGES FOR DEFAULT

42. (a) Neither the Vendor nor the Purchaser, in whose favour an order for specific performance has been made, shall be precluded from an award of damages at law or in equity, in the event of such order not being complied with.

(b) Notwithstanding any rule of law to the contrary failure on the part of the Vendor to show title to the Subject Property in accordance with the Conditions shall not per se preclude the making of an award for damages to the Purchaser for loss of bargain or otherwise in relation to the Sale.

RISK

43. Subject as hereinafter provided, the Vendor shall be liable for any loss or damage howsoever occasioned (other than by the Purchaser or his Agent) to the Subject Property (and the Purchased Chattels) between the Date of Sale and the actual completion of the Sale BUT any such liability (including liability for consequential or resulting loss) shall not as to the amount thereof exceed the Purchase Price.

44. The liability imposed on the Vendor by Condition 43 shall not apply:

(a) to inconsequential damage or insubstantial deterioration from reasonable wear and tear in the course of normal occupation and use, and not materially affecting value

(b) to damage occasioned by operations reasonably undertaken by the Vendor in his removal from, and vacation of the Subject Property, provided that the same are so undertaken with reasonable care

(c) where any such loss or damage has resulted from a requirement restriction or obligation imposed by a Competent Authority after the Date of Sale.

45. Nothing in Conditions 43 and 44 shall affect:

(a) the Purchaser's right to specific performance in an appropriate case

(b) the Purchaser's right to rescind or repudiate the Sale upon the Vendor's failure to deliver the Subject Property substantially in its condition at the Date of Sale (save where such failure shall have been occasioned by the Purchaser or his Agent)

(c) the operation of the doctrine of conversion

(d) the Purchaser's right to gains accruing to the Subject Property (or the Purchased Chattels) after the Date of Sale

(e)   the Purchaser's right to effect on or after the Date of Sale his own insurance against loss or damage in respect of the Subject Property or any part of the same (or the Purchased Chattels)

(f)   the rights and liabilities of parties other than the Vendor and the Purchaser

(g)   the rights and liabilities of the Purchaser on foot of any lease subsisting at the Date of Sale, or of any arrangement whereby the Purchaser shall prior to the actual completion of the Sale have been allowed into occupation of the Subject Property or any part thereof (or into possession of the Purchased Chattels).

CHATTELS

46.   Unless otherwise disclosed to the Purchaser prior to the Sale the Vendor warrants that, at the actual completion of the Sale, all the Purchased Chattels shall be his unencumbered property and that same shall not be subject to any lease, rental hire, hire-purchase or credit sale agreement or chattel mortgage.

INSPECTION

47.   The Vendor shall accede to all such requests as may be made by the Purchaser for the inspection on a reasonable number of occasions and at reasonable times of the Subject Property (and the Purchased Chattels).

NON-MERGER

48.   Notwithstanding delivery of the Assurance of the Subject Property to the Purchaser on foot of the Sale, all obligations and provisions designed to survive completion of the Sale and all warranties in the Conditions contained, which shall not have been implemented by the said Assurance, and which shall be capable of continuing or taking effect after such completion, shall enure and remain in full force and effect.

NOTICES

49.   Unless otherwise expressly provided, any notice to be given or served on foot of the Conditions shall be in writing, and may (in addition to any other prescribed mode of service) be given:

(a)   by handing same to the intended recipient, and shall be deemed to have been delivered when so handed

(b)   by directing it to the intended recipient, and delivering it by hand, or sending same by prepaid post to:

    (i)   such address as shall have been advised by him to the party serving the notice as being that required by the intended recipient for the service of notices

        or

    (ii)   (failing such last mentioned advice) the address of the intended recipient as specified in the Memorandum

        or

    (iii)   (in the event of the intended recipient being a Company) its Registered Office for the time being

        or

       (iv)   the office of the Solicitor representing the intended recipient in relation to the Sale

(c)   by facsimile transmission directed to the office of the Solicitor representing the intended recipient in relation to the Sale

and any such notice shall be deemed to have been given or served, when delivered, at the time of delivery, and, when posted, at the expiration of three Working Days after the envelope containing the same, and properly addressed, was put in the post and, when sent by facsimile transmission, at the time of its transmission.

TIME LIMITS

50.   Where the last day for taking any step on foot of the Conditions or any Notice served thereunder would, but for this provision, be a day other than a Working Day, such last day shall instead be the next following Working Day provided that for the purpose of this Condition the expression "Working Day" shall not be deemed to include (i) any Saturday, Sunday, Bank or Public Holiday nor (ii) any of the seven days immediately succeeding Christmas Day nor (iii) any day on which the registers or records wherein it shall be appropriate to make searches referable to the Sale shall not be available to the public nor (iv) any day which shall be recognised by the Solicitors' Profession at large as being a day on which their offices are not open for business.

ARBITRATION

51.   All differences and disputes between the Vendor and the Purchaser as to:

(a)   whether a rent is or is not a rack rent for the purpose of Condition 10(b)(iii)

     or

(b)   the identification of the Apportionment Date, or the treatment or quantification of any item pursuant to the provisions for apportionment in the Conditions

     or

(c)   any issue on foot of Condition 33, including the applicability of said Condition, and the amount of compensation payable thereunder

     or

(d)   the applicability or materiality of any matter for the purpose of Condition 35(b)(iii), or the effect on the value of the Subject Property of any matter pursuant to Condition 35(b)(iv)

     or

(e)   the materiality of any matter for the purpose of Condition 36(a)(ii), or the relevance or materiality, or effect on the value of the Subject Property, of any matter pursuant to Condition 36(f)(ii)

     or

(f)   the materiality of damage or any other question involving any of the provisions in Conditions 43, 44 and 45, including the amount of compensation (if any) payable

(g)   whether any particular item or thing is or is not included in the Sale, or otherwise as to the nature or condition thereof

shall be submitted to arbitration by a sole Arbitrator to be appointed (in the absence of agreement between the Vendor and the Purchaser upon such appointment and on the application of either of them) by the President (or other Officer endowed with the functions of such President) for the time being of the Law Society of Ireland or (in the event of the President or other Officer as aforesaid being unable or unwilling to make the appointment) by the next senior Officer of that Society who is so able and willing to make the appointment and such arbitration shall be governed by the Arbitration Acts, 1954 to 1998 provided however that if the Arbitrator shall relinquish his appointment or die, or if it shall become apparent that for any reason he shall be unable or shall have become unfit or unsuited (whether because of bias or otherwise) to complete his duties, or if he shall be removed from office by Court Order, a substitute may be appointed in his place and in relation to any such appointment the procedures hereinbefore set forth shall be deemed to apply as though the substitution were an appointment de novo which said procedures may be repeated as many times as may be necessary.

Law Society of Ireland

GENERAL CONDITIONS OF SALE 2009 EDITION

CHAPTER 7

THE FAMILY HOME, THE SHARED HOME, AND COHABITING COUPLES

7.1 Introduction

The Family Home Protection Act, 1976 is the first in a series of enactments dealing with matters of family law, which have impacted greatly on Irish conveyancing practice. The coming into force on 1 January 2011 of the Civil Partnership and Certain Rights and Obligations of Cohabitants Act, 2010 ('The Act of 2010') has, with the introduction of the two new concepts of 'shared home' and 'qualified cohabitant', extended the areas of inquiry to be undertaken by the practitioner. The purpose of this chapter is to examine the effects of these Acts and their sister enactments upon conveyancing practice and to explain the best practice to be followed in light of those effects.

7.2 Protection of Rights of Residence of Spouses and Civil Partners

7.2.1 FAMILY HOME PROTECTION ACT, 1976

The Family Home Protection Act, 1976 ('the 1976 Act') came into force on 12 July 1976. Prompted by a report published in 1972 by the Commission on the Status of Women, the purpose of the Act was to prevent one spouse, in whose sole name the family home (as defined in the Act) was vested, from dealing with the property without the knowledge and/or the consent of the non-owning spouse. The Act does not make any distinction between a wife and a husband and affords protection to all non-owning spouses, irrespective of gender.

That protection is contained in s 3(1), which provides as follows:

> *Where a spouse, without the prior consent in writing of the other spouse, purports to convey any interest in the family home to any person except the other spouse, then, subject to subsections (2) and (3) and section 4, the purported conveyance shall be void.*

Rather than conferring any interest in the property on a non-owning spouse, the 1976 Act seeks to protect that spouse's right to reside in the family home. It achieves this by declaring void any conveyance by the owning spouse, where the prior written consent of the non-owning spouse has not been obtained.

The operation of s 3(1) was discussed in *Barclays Bank Ireland Ltd v Carroll*, 10 September 1986, High Court (unreported). In that case, a husband transferred the family home to C, without having obtained his wife's prior consent to the transfer. The transferee subsequently mortgaged the property. When C went bankrupt, his assignee in bankruptcy sought to have the mortgage set aside on the basis that the original transfer was void for non-compliance with s 3(1) and, therefore, C did not have sufficient title to create the mortgage. Hamilton P stated, however, that, as the purpose of the section was the protection of the right of residence of the non-owning spouse, only he or she could invoke the section to have an offending conveyance declared void. In the instant case, as the wife had no desire to have the original transfer avoided, there was no other person entitled to do so.

There are two, interconnected, conclusions to be drawn from this decision. First, the protection afforded by s 3(1) is personal to a spouse whose right to reside in the family home is under threat. Secondly, the stipulation that any conveyance not complying with the provisions of s 3(1) is void is to be interpreted as meaning voidable at the instigation of such a spouse.

Clearly, the introduction of the 1976 Act impacted greatly on practitioners, who were, as a result of its introduction, obliged to ensure that the prior written consent of any non-owning spouse was obtained to any conveyance of the family home executed after 12 July 1976 (this is subject to the exception expounded in *Hamilton v Hamilton* [1982] IR 466 where the Supreme Court held that the Act did not apply to conveyances executed after 12 July 1976 where the relevant Contract for Sale had been executed prior to that date). The consequence, subject to certain exceptions, of failing to do so was the possibility that the conveyance in question could be declared void.

7.2.2   SECTION 54 OF THE FAMILY LAW ACT, 1995

The draconian effect of s 3(1) was tempered by the introduction of s 54(8)(b) of the Family Law Act, 1995 ('the 1995 Act') (the effective date of the Family Law Act, 1995 is 1 August 1995), which added a new subsection (8) to s 3 of the 1976 Act and which provides as follows:

> *Proceedings will not be instituted to have a conveyance declared void by reason only of sub-section (1) [of s 3 of the 1976 Act] after the expiration of six years from the date of the conveyance.*

The section effectively introduced a six-year time limit within which proceedings to have a conveyance declared void by a non-owning spouse could be brought. The section further provides that a conveyance will not be void by virtue of s 3(1) of the 1976 Act unless declared so by a court in proceedings instituted before the passing of the 1995 Act or, if after that date, within the six-year time limit introduced by the 1995 Act.

It should be noted that the six-year rule does not apply to a conveyance which is the subject of proceedings instituted prior to 1 August 1995. In addition, the six-year rule does not apply to proceedings instituted by a spouse who has been in actual occupation of the family home from immediately before the expiration of six years from the date of the conveyance in question until the institution of the proceedings. This exception is provided for in s 54(1)(b)(ii) of the 1995 Act. The operation of this exception is illustrated by the following example. In January 1990, a husband, the sole owner of a family home, executes a mortgage, without obtaining the prior written consent of his wife. Under the normal operation of the six-year rule, the time for instituting proceedings to have the mortgage declared void elapses in 1996. However, the wife has been in actual occupation of the property since before January 1990, so that when, in March 1997, she discovers the existence of the mortgage she is still entitled to bring proceedings to have the mortgage declared void. The Law Society has produced a sample declaration for the purposes of s 54(1)(b) of the 1995 Act and s 28(ii)(b) of the Act of 2010. This should be used when there is no family law declaration in relation to a prior deed which is over six years old.

7.2.3   EXCEPTIONS

There are four specific exceptions to the application of s 3(1) of the 1976 Act.

7.2.3.1   Agreements made in contemplation of marriage

Section 3(2) is self-explanatory and provides that s 3(1) does not apply to conveyances made in pursuance of an enforceable pre-nuptial agreement.

7.2.3.2   Conveyance to a purchaser for full value

Section 3(3) provides that 'No conveyance shall be void by reason only of subsection (1)(a) if it is made to a purchaser for full value'. Section 3(6) defines a 'purchaser' as 'a grantee, lessee, assignee, mortgagee, chargeant or other person who in good faith acquires an estate in property'. The exception contained in s 3(3) therefore applies only to a bona fide purchaser for value. Furthermore, s 3(5) provides that, for the purposes of s 3(3), 'full value' shall mean 'such value as amounts or approximates to the value of that for which it is given'.

Section 3(3) makes reference to the Conveyancing Act, 1882, s 3, which has now been repealed and replaced by s 86(1) of the Land and Conveyancing Law Reform Act, 2009 ('the 2009 Act'). Section 86(1) provides that a purchaser (defined in the 2009 Act as meaning 'an assignee, chargeant, grantee, lessee, mortgagee or other person who acquires land for valuable consideration') is not affected prejudicially by notice of any act, instrument, matter, or thing unless:

(a)   *it is within the purchaser's own knowledge or would have come to the purchaser's knowledge if such inquiries and inspections had been made as ought reasonably to have been made by the purchaser, or*

(b)   *in the same transaction with respect to which a question of notice to the purchaser arises, it has come to the knowledge of the purchaser's counsel, as such, or solicitor or other agent, as such, or would have come to the knowledge of the solicitor or other agent if such inquiries and inspections had been made as ought reasonably to have been made by the solicitor or agent.*

Section 3(3) of the 1976 Act will therefore operate to protect a purchaser where the vendor conceals the fact that the property for sale is his family home and the purchaser or his agents, having made due enquiry, do not discover this fact. In that situation, the non-owning spouse is precluded from instituting proceedings to have the conveyance declared void. However, the section will not protect the purchaser who is ignorant of the fact that the property is a family home by reason of his own failure to make proper enquiries.

A case in point is the decision in *Somers v Weir* [1979] IR 94. The property in question was a leasehold premises, the lease to which the husband of the defendant had taken in March 1961, five months before his marriage to the defendant. The defendant and her husband resided in the premises until October 1973, when the marriage broke down and the defendant left the family home and went to reside in accommodation rented from Dublin Corporation. A separation agreement was executed in November 1974, but the agreement was silent as to the ownership of the family home, which therefore remained in both the possession and ownership of the husband. On 2 August 1976 (ie after the coming into effect of the 1976 Act) the husband entered into an agreement with the plaintiff for the sale to the plaintiff of the premises. On 10 August, the plaintiff's solicitor wrote to the husband's solicitor, requesting sight of a copy of the separation agreement. The husband's solicitor replied, saying that he had not acted for the husband in relation to the separation, and, therefore, did not possess a copy of the agreement. The solicitor further stated that 'In view of the fact that the premises are not now a family home and your client is the purchaser for full value, we cannot see how your client is concerned with the matrimonial situation.' The plaintiff's solicitor completed the sale on 17 August 1976 on foot of a statutory declaration of the husband, stating that the defendant had not relied on the premises as her family home since the execution of the separation agreement and that, by virtue of the separation agreement, she now had no interest in the property. This declaration had been prepared by the plaintiff's solicitor, who had never seen the separation agreement.

The matter came to light when the plaintiff sought to resell the premises in 1977 and the lending institution for the new purchaser requested proof that the provisions of s 3 had been complied with. The plaintiff's solicitor sought the defendant's retrospective consent to the 1976 deed, which she refused. The plaintiff then applied to court to have the defendant's consent dispensed with under s 4 of the 1976 Act. On appeal to the Supreme Court, Henchy J found that the premises had, in fact, at all material times been the family home of the defendant and her husband. Having stated that a conveyance will be no less void if the purchaser for value takes a property, without having first made the proper enquiries, than if he had actual knowledge that the wife's prior consent was required and failed to obtain it, he went on to say:

> 'In this case, the inquiries and inspections which ought reasonably to have been made as a matter of common prudence were not made. Instead, a statement which was unwarranted by any document and which falsely swept aside the defendant's rights was presented to her husband for execution as a statutory declaration and, on the basis of that statutory declaration, the sale by him went through behind his wife's back. It was a transaction of the precise kind that s 3 of the Act of 1976 was designed to make void.'

From the practitioner's perspective, the clear implication of this decision is that the solicitor acting for the purchaser of any property is under a strict duty to carry out all necessary investigations to ascertain the position regarding the family home. Failure to do so will result in the conveyance to his client being vulnerable to challenge under s 3(1). The proper investigations to be carried out by purchasers' solicitors are discussed at **7.2.7** and **7.2.8**.

7.2.3.3   Conveyance of an interest by a person other than a spouse

Conveyances of an interest in the family home by a person other than a spouse are specifically excluded from the ambit of s 3(1) by s 3(3)(b). In other words, the only party obliged to obtain spousal consent when purporting to alienate his or her interest in the family home is a spouse. This means, for example, that the mortgagee of the family home may convey its interest in the property without requiring the consent of a non-owning spouse to the conveyance. (Note, however, the provisions of the Bankruptcy Act, 1988, s 61(4) which oblige the official assignee of a bankrupt to obtain the consent of the High Court before disposing of the interest of a bankrupt in the family home.)

7.2.3.4   Family Law Act, 1995, s 54(3)

Section 54(3) of the 1995 Act provides that where a court, when granting a decree of judicial separation, orders that the ownership of the family home shall be vested in one or other of the spouses, it shall, unless it sees reason to the contrary, order that s 3(1) shall not apply to any conveyance by that spouse of his or her interest in the family home.

7.2.4   CIVIL PARTNERSHIP AND CERTAIN RIGHTS AND OBLIGATIONS OF COHABITANTS ACT, 2010

The Civil Partnership and Certain Rights and Obligations of Cohabitants Act, 2010 ('The Act of 2010') creates two new legal relationships:

(i)   the civil partnership; and

(ii)   qualified cohabitants.

The rights and obligations relating to the qualified cohabitants are dealt with in **7.5**.

This section deals with the rights conferred upon 'civil partners' in respect of the 'shared home'. Section 3 of the Act of 2010 defines a civil partner as being:

> . . . *either of two persons of the same sex who are –*
>
> (a)   *parties to a civil partnership registration that has not been dissolved or the subject of a decree of nullity, or*
> (b)   *parties to a legal relationship of a class that is the subject of an Order made under s 5 that has not been dissolved or the subject of a decree of nullity.*

Section 5 of the Act of 2010 provides for the recognition in the State of foreign legal relationships between persons of the same sex subject to the four conditions, set out in subsection (1) of s 5, being satisfied. The requirements in respect of the annulment or the dissolution of civil partnerships are set out in Part 11 and Part 12 respectively of the Act of 2010, as amended by the Marriage Act, 2015.

The protections afforded civil partners in respect of their shared home is detailed in s 28. Subsection (1) to s 28 provides:

> *Where a civil partner, without the prior consent in writing of the other civil partner, purports to convey an interest in the shared home to a person except the other civil partner, then subject to sub sections (2), (3), and (8) to (14) and s 29, the purported conveyance is void. It will be noted that s 28 of the Act of 2010 mirrors the protection afforded a spouse under s 3 of the 1976 Act.*

For the purposes of s 28 an 'interest' means '. . . *any estate, right, title or other interest legal or equitable'*.

7.2.5   EXCEPTIONS

There are two specific exceptions to the application of s 28(1).

7.2.5.1   Conveyance made pursuant to an enforceable agreement between civil partners

Subsection (2) to s 28 provides for the possibility that the parties to a civil partnership may, prior to the registration of their civil partnership, enter into an agreement regulating matters between them. Where a conveyance is made pursuant to such an agreement, the provisions of subsection (1) will not apply. It should be noted that, by virtue of s 67 of the Act of 2010, any provisions contained in such an agreement purporting to exclude or limit the operation of any of the provisions of Part 5 (Maintenance of Civil Partner) or Part 6 (Attachment of Earnings) will be void.

7.2.5.2   Conveyance to a purchaser for full value

Subsection (3) provides:

> *A conveyance is not void by reason only of subsection (1) if –*
>
> (a)   *it is made to a purchaser for full value,*
> (b)   *it is made by a person other than the civil partner to a purchaser for value, or*
> (c)   *its validity depends on the validity of a conveyance in respect of which a condition mentioned in subsection (2), or*
> (d)   *(a) or (b) is satisfied.*

For the purposes of subsection (3) 'full value' is defined as '. . . *value that amounts or approximates to the value of that for which it is given'* and 'a purchaser' means a '*grantee, lessee, assignee, mortgagee, chargeant or other person who in good faith acquires an estate or interest in property'*.

With effect from the 16 November 2015 (the date of commencement of the Marriage Act, 2015) couples can no longer serve notice of intention to enter into a civil partnership. Section 59L(1) of the Civil Registration Act, 2004, as inserted by s 10 of the Marriage Act, 2015, provides that on the commencement of s 8 of the Marriage Act, 2015, a notification of an intention to enter into a civil partnership given under s 59B of the Civil Registration Act, 2004 and in force immediately before the commencement of the Marriage Act, 2015 may, if requested by the parties concerned, be taken to be and treated by a registrar as if it were a notification of their intention to marry under s 46 of the Civil Registration Act, 2004. Where a civil partnership registration form was duly completed under s 59C of the Civil Registration Act, 2004 and was validly served on the registrar immediately before the commencement of the Marriage Act, 2015, and the parties to the notification form do not wish to convert same to a notification of marriage, they may proceed with the civil partnership (s 59L(2) of the Civil Registration Act, 2004 as inserted by s 10 of the Marriage Act, 2015). As the civil partnership registration form is valid for a period of six months, it follows that the latest possible date on which a civil partnership may be solemnised is six months after the commencement of the Marriage Act, 2015. Hence after 16 May 2016, while existing civil partnerships continue, there will be no new civil partnerships created. Section 109A of the Act of 2010, as inserted by s 11 of the Marriage Act, 2015, provides that a civil partnership existing between two persons immediately before their marriage to each other shall stand dissolved on and from the date of that marriage. The registrar is directed to enter that dissolution as a particular in the entry concerning that civil partnership in the register of civil partnerships. When acting for a vendor or mortgagor whose civil partnership to their current spouse was dissolved by virtue of s 109A of the Act of 2010, practitioners should amend the statutory declaration relating to the family home to take account of the existence of a prior civil partnership and subsequent dissolution of that civil partnership.

7.2.6   THE MEANING OF 'CONVEYANCE'

In order for either the 1976 Act or the Act of 2010 to apply, there must be a 'conveyance' within the meaning of those Acts. 'Conveyance' is defined in s 1 of the 1976 Act as including:

> *a mortgage, lease, assent, transfer, disclaimer, release, and any other disposition of property otherwise than by a will or a donatio mortis causa and also includes an enforceable agreement (whether conditional or unconditional) to make any such conveyance, and 'convey' shall be construed accordingly.*

A similar definition of 'conveyance' is contained in s 27 of the Act of 2010.

Where any of the documents listed in the definition relates to a family home or a shared home, it is necessary to obtain the prior consent in writing of the spouse or civil partner to the proposed conveyance.

By virtue of these definitions, a contract for the sale of property is as much a conveyance as is the deed of assurance. Thus, where the transaction to which the contract relates is the disposal of one spouse's interest in the family home or one civil partner's interest in the shared home, strictly speaking, the prior written consent of the non-owning spouse or civil partner to both the contract and the deed is required in order to satisfy s 3(1) of the 1976 Act and s 28(1) of the Act of 2010. This point, as it applies to the 1976 Act, was discussed in the case of *Kyne v Tiernan*, 15 July 1980, High Court (unreported). In that case, the family home was registered in the sole name of the husband. The husband and the wife decided to put the property on the market. When a purchaser was found, the wife, although unwilling to sign a consent endorsed on the Contract for Sale in the usual manner, did sign an unequivocal consent to the sale, which had been printed on a separate sheet of paper. Prior to the completion of the sale, the couple experienced marital difficulties and the wife ultimately refused to endorse her consent on the deed of transfer. When the purchaser applied to court for an order for specific performance of the contract, the question arose as to whether the consent to the contract would also suffice as consent to the deed. McWilliam J was of the opinion that it would, stating 'I cannot imagine that it could have been the intention of the legislature to require two consents for the completion of one transaction, namely the sale of one house.'

Thus, it would seem that only the consent to the Contract for Sale is required. It is, nonetheless, good conveyancing practice to have the spouse's or civil partner's consent endorsed on the deed, as well as the contract. This avoids any difficulties arising, should the Contract for Sale be lost. An alternative solution would be to bind the contract to the back of the deed, for safekeeping.

The list of documents contained in s 1 of the 1976 Act and s 27 of the Act of 2010 is not conclusive. Thus, in the case of *Bank of Ireland v Purcell* [1989] 2 IR 327, it was held that an equitable deposit of deeds could constitute a conveyance within the meaning of s 3(1) of the 1976 Act. On the other hand, in both *Containercare (Ireland) Ltd v Wycherly* [1982] IR 143 and *Murray v Diamond* [1982] 2 ILRM 113, the court found that a judgment mortgage did not constitute a conveyance for the purposes of the Act. At p 115 of the judgment in *Murray v Diamond*, Barrington J stated:

> 'I do not think that the mere fact that a man has irresponsibly allowed himself to get into debt, or allowed a judgment to be obtained against him and thereby allowed a situation to develop in which his creditor registers a judgment against his interest in the

family home, would justify a court in saying that he has conveyed or purported to convey his interest in the family home to the judgment mortgagee.'

In April 2007 the Conveyancing Committee of the Law Society issued a Practice Note advising that, as an option to purchase land passes an equitable interest in the property to the prospective purchaser, it was the view of the Committee that such an option to purchase comes within the definition of 'conveyance' for the purposes of the 1976 Act. Best practice therefore requires that a non-owning spouse's consent and the usual supporting statutory declaration should be sought whenever any person who is married enters into an option to sell any interest in land. Presumably this advice now also extends to the consent of the non-owning civil partner in such cases.

7.2.7   THE MEANING OF 'FAMILY HOME' AND 'SHARED HOME'

7.2.7.1   Definition of 'family home' and 'shared home'

It is only the purported conveyance of an interest in the 'family home' to which s 3(1) of the 1976 Act applies and a conveyance of an interest in the 'shared home' to which s 28(1) of the Act of 2010 applies. In this regard, there are two questions, which should be asked:

(a)   whether the property is or was a family home or shared home for some period of time; and

(b)   whether there is a spouse or civil partner whose consent is necessary.

A 'family home' is defined in s 2(1) of the 1976 Act as meaning a dwelling in which a married couple ordinarily resides. Furthermore, the definition encompasses a *'dwelling in which a spouse whose protection is in issue ordinarily resides, or, if that spouse has left the other spouse, ordinarily resided before so leaving'*. Thus, as has been seen in *Somers v Weir* [1979] IR 94, where the spouse whose rights are vulnerable has been forced to leave the property in which he or she had formerly resided with his or her spouse, that former residence will remain the family home for the purposes of the 1976 Act. The rule of thumb to be followed in all cases of doubt is 'once a family home, always a family home'. The Act intends to protect the current residence of a married couple, who are living together, and the former residence of a couple, who are separated.

It should also be noted that this definition also encompasses a dwelling in which one spouse (but not both) is residing, having been forced by the other spouse to leave the family home.

A 'shared home' is defined in s 27 of the Act of 2010 as meaning

(a)   *subject to paragraph (b), a dwelling in which the civil partners ordinarily reside; and*

(b)   *in relation to a civil partner whose protection is in issue, the dwelling in which that civil partner ordinarily resides or, if he/she has left the other civil partner, in which he/she ordinarily resided before leaving.*

7.2.7.2   Definition of 'dwelling'

The definitions of family home contained in s 2(1) of the 1976 Act and of shared home contained in s 27 of the Act of 2010 both refer to a 'dwelling'. Section 2(2) of the 1976 Act, as amended by s 54(1)(a) of the 1995 Act, defines a dwelling as:

any building or part of a building occupied as a separate dwelling and includes any garden or other land usually occupied with the dwelling, being land that is subsidiary and ancillary to it, is required for amenity or convenience, and is not being used or developed primarily for commercial purposes, and includes a structure that is not permanently attached to the ground and a vehicle, or vessel, whether mobile or not, occupied as a separate dwelling.

A similar definition is contained in s 27 of the Act of 2010.

It follows from this definition that, for example, where an agricultural holding consists of both a farmhouse, which is a family home or a shared home, and land upon which the farming is carried out, it is possible to dispose of the farmland separately from the farmhouse, without the necessity of obtaining a spouse's or civil partner's consent. This is by virtue of the land being used primarily for commercial purposes and therefore not coming within the definition of 'dwelling'. On the other hand, if the land attached to the family home or shared home were merely a small garden, not used for any commercial purpose, it would not be possible to dispose of the garden separately, without obtaining the spouse's or civil partner's consent.

Another possibility, which stems from the definition, relates to the situation of an apartment above a shop or pub. Quite clearly, the apartment could be the ordinary residence of a married couple or civil partners. According to the preceding definition, it is possible to sever the commercial premises on the ground floor from the apartment above. Thus, if the entire premises were in the sole ownership of the wife, for example, it would be in order for her to sell the commercial premises separately from the residential premises, without obtaining the husband's prior consent to the conveyance.

7.2.7.3 'Ordinarily reside'

Apart from the situation outlined in **7.2.7.1**, namely where one spouse has been forced to reside in a dwelling other than the premises occupied by both spouses, a husband and wife must use a premises as their ordinary residence, in order for it to constitute a family home. Similar considerations apply in respect of a shared home. In *National Irish Bank v Graham* [1995] 2 IR 244, the Supreme Court made clear that the term 'ordinarily reside' did not apply to a premises in which a married couple *intended* to reside.

In most situations, the question of where a married couple or civil partners ordinarily reside is easily answered. Sometimes, however, the answer may not be so straightforward. Take, for example, the case of a married couple with two residences, one in the city, perhaps, and the other in the country. They spend an equal amount of time in each residence. Which is their family home? Or perhaps they do not spend exactly equal amounts of time in each premises. Is it now possible to say with certainty which property is the family home? In such a situation, by far the wisest course of action for a solicitor acting for the purchaser of either residence is to obtain the wife's consent.

7.2.8 THE MEANING OF 'CONSENT'

7.2.8.1 Generally

Where the premises for sale are a family home or shared home, but the vendors are the joint owners of the property and are married to each other, or are the civil partners of each other, no spousal or partner's consent is required to any conveyance of the property, as both spouses or civil partners (as the case may be) will be joining in the deed of assurance. Likewise, where the vendor is one spouse or civil partner only, but the property for sale is not the family home or the shared home of the vendor and his or her spouse or civil partner, the consent of the non-owning spouse or civil partner is not necessary. (In this case, however, solicitors acting for purchasers and lending institutions should be extremely careful to investigate the position regarding whether or not the premises are, in fact, a family home or shared home.)

In all other situations, where one spouse or civil partner is alienating his or her interest in the family home or shared home, the consent of the non-owning spouse or civil partner to at least the contract is required.

7.2.8.2 Consent must be prior and in writing

Both s 3(1) of the 1976 Act and s 28(1) of the Act of 2010 are very clear that the requisite consent must be given prior to the purported conveyance and it must be in writing. A solicitor acting for the vendor must therefore take every care to ensure that this has, in fact, been done. In the case of a Contract for Sale, for example, the current 2009 edition of the Law Society General Conditions of Sale includes the following endorsement at the top of the memorandum of agreement:

'I . . . being the Spouse of the undernamed vendor, hereby, for the purposes of Section 3, Family Home Protection Act 1976, consent to the proposed sale of the property described in the within particulars at the price mentioned below.

SIGNED by the said Spouse

in the presence of:'

At the time of writing, this endorsement had not been updated to take account of the coming into effect of the Act of 2010. It should, therefore, be amended appropriately where the consent of a civil partner rather than a spouse is being endorsed.

Solicitors should ensure that the consenting party does, in fact, sign the endorsement *before* the vendor. It is not necessary for the spouse or civil partner to sign the endorsement before the purchaser executes the contract; however, it is vital that it is done prior to the vendor executing the contract. In the case of a deed, it is also usual to have the consent endorsed on the actual document. Although most practitioners insert this endorsement paragraph after the space for the signatures of the parties to the deed, it is again *absolutely vital* that the consent is actually executed *prior* to the vendor executing the deed. It is good practice to recite this fact in the endorsement. Although this is the usual method of obtaining spousal consent, it is not absolutely necessary. A case in point is *Kyne v Tiernan*, discussed at **7.2.6**. Here, the wife had endorsed her consent on a separate sheet of paper and the court found that this was an acceptable consent to the deed of transfer. Note that the prior consent should be dated prior to the date of the deed of assurance.

Where the property is being sold at auction, the vendor's solicitor should arrange to have the non-owning spouse or civil partner present to endorse consent on the contract. Where this is not possible, it is necessary to have the spouse or civil partner execute a separate consent, prior to the auction. This consent should recite that the spouse or civil partner consents to the sale at auction of the property and should stipulate a minimum sale price. This price will, in fact, be the reserve agreed for the auction. Should the property not achieve this price, the spouse's or civil partner's consent will not be valid.

7.2.8.3   Consent must be informed

Apart from the requirement that consent be prior and in writing, the courts have made clear that the consent must also be informed. The question of informed consent was discussed by the Supreme Court in *Bank of Ireland v Smyth* [1996] 1 ILRM 241. Here, the wife had given her consent to what she believed to be a charge over the land attached to the family home. In fact, the charge included both the family home and the land. Mrs Smyth had executed her consent to the charge in the presence of an employee of the plaintiff bank. It transpired that the employee had not enquired of Mrs Smyth whether she understood what was being covered by the document to which she was consenting.

The bank contended that it was not required to take into account what was in Mrs Smyth's mind. Discussing the nature of spousal consent, however, Blayney J stated that the validity of Mrs Smyth's consent depended on whether she had full knowledge of what she was doing. At p 428 of the judgment he stated:

'The spouse giving it [consent] must know what it is he or she is consenting to. Since giving one's consent means that one is approving of something, obviously, a precondition is that one should have knowledge of what it is that one is approving of.'

In the instant case, Mrs Smyth could not give a valid consent to the conveyance in question, as she was not aware of its full import. Furthermore, the court found the bank to be on notice of Mrs Smyth's lack of knowledge, as it would have been apparent if the bank employee had made reasonable enquiry. The charge was therefore held to be invalid as no valid consent had been obtained.

Examining this judgment from the perspective of a solicitor acting for a lending institution, it should not be interpreted as placing upon banks a duty either to explain a charge fully to spouses or to advise them to seek independent legal advice. This suggestion was specifically rejected by Blayney J. However, he did state that it would have been good practice to have done so, not because the bank owed any duty to Mrs Smyth, but because, if these steps had been taken, the charge would not have been invalidated, as Mrs Smyth would have then been precluded from claiming that the exact import of the charge was unknown to her.

Although the issue of informed consent has yet to be tested in relation to the Act of 2010, it is likely that the courts will follow the line of precedent established in respect of spousal consent.

7.2.8.4   Consent of a minor

Although the 1976 Act does not stipulate an age limit below which a spouse cannot give a valid consent, the question as to whether a minor could give a valid consent was rendered academic by the introduction of the Age of Majority Act, 1985 and the Family Law Act, 1995. The former lowered the age of majority from 21 years to either 18 years or upon marriage. The latter, at Part V, rendered null and void any marriage contracted by a person under 18 years, unless a court exemption has been obtained. Section 7(3)(c) of the Act of 2010 stipulates that there shall be an impediment to a civil partnership registration if one or both of the parties to the intended civil partnership will be under the age of 18 years on the date of the intended civil partnership registration.

7.2.8.5   Dispensing with the consent of the non-owning spouse or non-owning civil partner

The requirement to obtain spousal consent in every case where there is a purported conveyance of one spouse's interest in the family home is somewhat tempered by the provisions of s 4(1) of the 1976 Act. Section 4(1) provides that '[w]here the spouse whose consent is required under s 3(1) omits or refuses to consent, the court may, subject to the provisions of this section, dispense with the consent'. The court's power to dispense with the consent of a civil partner is enshrined in s 29(1) of the Act of 2010, which mirrors the provisions of s 4(1) of the 1976 Act. Both s 4(1) and s 29(1) provide that the court may dispense with spousal or civil partner's consent in the following three circumstances:

1.   It is unreasonable of the spouse/civil partner to withhold consent.

2.   Due enquiry having been made, the spouse or civil partner cannot be located.

3.   The civil partner or spouse is, by virtue of unsoundness of mind or other mental disability, incapable of giving consent.

In addition, the 1976 Act allows for the spousal consent to be dispensed with where the spouse whose consent is required has deserted and continues to desert the other spouse. For these purposes, desertion includes conduct on the part of the spouse whose consent is required, which results in the other spouse, with just cause, leaving and living separately and apart from the first spouse.

Before considering the first situation in the preceding list (ie that it is unreasonable of the spouse or civil partner to withhold consent) in greater detail there are three preliminary points to be noted:

(a)   the application to the court to dispense with the consent may be made under the 1976 Act or the Act of 2010 as appropriate;

(b)   in the case of the 1976 Act at least, the application must be made prior to the conveyance in question. The court clearly stated in *Somers v Weir* [1979] IR 94 (discussed at **7.2.3.2** and **7.2.7.1**) that it had no jurisdiction to dispense with spousal consent retrospectively. This point has not yet come up for consideration by the court in relation to the Act of 2010; and

(c)   the application may be made by either the spouse or civil partner purporting to dispense with his or her interest in the family home or shared home, or by the intended transferee.

Turning to the circumstances in which the court may dispense with consent, the first relates to a situation where a spouse or civil partner unreasonably withholds consent. This situation is covered by s 4(2) of the 1976 Act, which provides:

The court shall not dispense with the consent of a spouse unless the court considers that it is unreasonable for the spouse to withhold consent, taking into account all the circumstances, including:

(a) *the respective needs and resources of the spouses and of the dependent children (if any) of the family, and*

(b) *in a case where the spouse whose consent is required is offered alternative accommodation having regard to the respective degrees of security of tenure in the family home and in the alternative accommodation.*

Similar wording is contained in s 29(2) of the Act of 2010, although the needs and resources of dependent children, referred to at subsection (b), are not a consideration in the corresponding subsection in the Act of 2010. In the case of *R v R*, December 1978 (unreported), the court refused to dispense with the wife's consent, on the basis that her refusal was not unreasonable. Here, the husband and wife had been married in 1960 and had three daughters. The couple experienced marital difficulties for a number of years and, for a year prior to the application to court, had slept apart in separate rooms within the family home.

Prior to the application, the husband had formed an attachment with another woman and had decided to leave the family home. As he had a number of outstanding debts and wished to make a fresh start, he proposed mortgaging the family home, hoping to raise sufficient funds to discharge his debts. The wife refused her consent to the mortgage, stating that, on the husband's salary, it would not be possible for him to make the mortgage repayments, while at the same time supporting two households. The husband therefore applied to the court to have his wife's consent dispensed with. The application was refused on the grounds that the court could not hold that the wife's refusal in this instance was unreasonable. McMahon J did comment, however, that the situation might be different if the husband were to succeed in paying off the short-term loans over the succeeding two years.

The decision in *R v R* should be contrasted with that in *S O'B v M O'B*, December 1981 (unreported). Here, a Roman Catholic Church decree of nullity was granted, with the concurrence of both the husband and the wife. The wife continued to reside with their two children in the family home, which was in the sole ownership of the husband. The husband moved to Hong Kong, where he subsequently remarried in a church ceremony. He had a third child out of this relationship.

Some time after his second marriage, the husband wished to return to Ireland, and decided to sell the family home in order to raise enough money to do so. As the original marriage had not been annulled by the State, the first wife was still his spouse for the purposes of the 1976 Act. The first wife refused her consent to the sale and the husband applied to the court under s 4. It was the husband's proposal that, once he had disposed of the family home, a portion of the proceeds, sufficient to set the first wife up in alternative accommodation, would be handed over to the first wife. On the facts, O'Hanlon J concluded that as both parties had been responsible for the break-up of the marriage, they both had suffered the consequences in terms of attempting to maintain two households on whatever resources were available. As the husband was willing to make as much as half of the proceeds of sale available to the wife, O'Hanlon J concluded that her refusal to give consent was unreasonable and granted an order dispensing with her consent.

The question of what constitutes an unreasonable refusal to grant consent was again considered in the case of *BM v AM*, 3 April 2003, High Court (unreported). In this case, the plaintiff sought an order for the sale of premises, occupied by the defendant, her husband, pursuant to ss 3 and 4 of the Partition Act, 1868. The plaintiff and the defendant had lived in the premises as husband and wife between 1966 and 1989. In 1989, due to unhappy differences between the plaintiff and the defendant, the plaintiff left the premises and moved to Great Britain. The defendant continued to live in the premises. Between 1996 and 2001 various correspondence passed between the plaintiff and the defendant, wherein the plaintiff sought the agreement of the defendant to the sale of the premises. In 2001, having failed to gain the agreement of the defendant to a sale, the plaintiff instituted proceedings, seeking an order for sale under the Partition Act, 1868 ('the 1868 Act'). The Circuit Court made an order that the premises be sold and the proceeds divided between the plaintiff and the defendant in the proportions of 60 per cent and 40 per cent respectively.

The matter was appealed to the High Court where the decision of the Circuit Court was set aside by Peart J. On the facts, Peart J found that the defendant, in opposing the plaintiff's application, had established to the satisfaction of the court that there was a good reason why the court ought not to exercise the wide powers of sale, granted to it under ss 3 and 4 of the 1868 Act. Having reviewed the evidence, Peart J noted that:

'. . . Mr. Hayden has submitted to the Court that if a sale were to be ordered and a division of the proceeds made, the defendant, bearing in mind the current property market and his age (in the context of his ability to obtain a loan) and the circumstances generally which include the fact that the plaintiff has a house in England, would effectively be left without a home'.

Turning to the effect of the 1976 Act on the powers conferred upon the court under the 1868 Act, Peart J stated that:

'It has been decided that any rights a party may have to seek relief under the Partition Acts must be tempered by the effect of the 1976 Act, section 4 of which provides that the court may dispense with the consent of a spouse if it is unreasonably withheld. In the present case, if this court was being asked to dispense with the defendant's consent to a sale, as being unreasonably withheld, it would not be prepared to do so in the circumstances of this case, as it would not have any sufficient evidence from which to conclude that any withholding of consent is unreasonable.'

It should also be noted that, in considering whether the court must dispense with the consent of the non-agreeing spouse before granting an order under the Partition Acts, 1863–1876, Peart J was following the reasoning of the court in *O'D v O'D*, 18 November 1983, High Court (unreported) and *AL v JL*, 27 February 1984, High Court (unreported). In the latter case, Finlay P (as he then was) had found that:

'Having regard to the provisions of the Family Home Protection Act, 1976, in the absence of an agreement between the parties, an order of sale cannot in my view be made under the Partition Acts unless the court is also satisfied that it should dispense with the consent of the non-agreeing spouse under section 4 of the 1976 Act.'

7.2.9   STANDARD QUERIES

7.2.9.1   Introduction

As has been seen, neither s 3(1) of the 1976 Act nor s 28(1) of the Act of 2010 will apply to a conveyance to a bona fide purchaser for value without notice. It has also been seen that, in order to qualify as such, a purchaser and/or his or her agents are under a duty to carry out reasonable investigations into the position regarding the family home or the shared home. The enquiries which are considered reasonable in particular circumstances are set out at **7.2.10**. However, there are some basic enquiries which must be made in every case.

7.2.9.2   Statutory declarations

Although the 1976 Act does not require the production of a statutory declaration by way of proof as to the situation regarding the family home, it is now standard practice to require a statutory declaration from the vendor and his or her spouse, evidencing the position. The practice has also been adopted by practitioners of seeking corroboration of certain matters. It is quite usual, for example, for a declaration to exhibit a marriage or death certificate as proof of marriage or death. Similarly, a declaration might exhibit an extract of the separation agreement or a divorce decree, where appropriate. This practice now extends to seeking the requisite averments in relation to the Act of 2010.

Note carefully that the statutory declaration should not be confused with the prior written consent of the spouse or the civil partner. As shall be seen, it is now normal practice to request a statutory declaration as corroborating evidence. However, this does not negate the necessity for the spouse's or civil partner's prior written consent to be obtained where there is a conveyance of the family home or shared home, and the spouse or civil partner in question is not a joint owner.

Although the practice of seeking a statutory declaration is now the norm, this was not the case immediately after the introduction of the 1976 Act. As a result, many solicitors, in and around 12 July 1976, failed to obtain such supporting evidence. To alleviate the confusion thus caused, the Conveyancing Committee of the Law Society issued a Practice Note in June 1981, advising that, where, in accordance with s 3(1), a spouse's consent is endorsed on a conveyance of the family home, executed prior to 1 January 1978, a purchaser's solicitor should seek no supporting evidence, where none is available. Examples of the current Family Law Statutory Declarations are available on the Law Society website. A schedule of the precedent declarations currently available, together with the additional jurats reflecting the changes introduced by s 49 of the Civil Law (Miscellaneous Provisions) Act, 2008, relating to the identification of the declarant by means of a 'relevant document', are also available on the Law Society website.

In March 2001 the Conveyancing Committee of the Law Society issued a Practice Note dealing with the practice of providing and accepting solicitors' certificates in relation to the 1976 Act and other related Acts. In its Practice Note, the Conveyancing Committee expressed the view that the practice of giving such certificates, simply because it is more convenient than obtaining an appropriate statutory declaration from the vendor, is to be discouraged. Best conveyancing practice requires that a purchaser's solicitor should always seek the best evidence in respect of the position pertaining to the family home or the shared home. Other than in exceptional circumstances, 'best evidence' is a statutory declaration of the vendor and, his or her spouse or civil partner, if appropriate, together with corroborating evidence. To quote the Practice Note, a vendor's solicitor's certificate should only be accepted 'where the best evidence is not reasonably available and where there is good reason for its nonavailability'.

Whether it is prudent for a purchaser's solicitor to seek a statutory declaration of a non-owning spouse, confirming the position, where it is alleged by the vendor that the property for sale is not a family home, was considered by the Conveyancing Committee in May 2006. In a Practice Note, issued in that month's *Gazette*, the Conveyancing Committee stated that best conveyancing practice required that a family law declaration, whether or not it relates to a family home, should, if the property is owned by an individual, be sworn both by the owner and his or her spouse. In the view of the Committee, best conveyancing practice requires that such a declaration be sought, irrespective of whether or not proceedings are in being under the Judicial Separation and Family Law Reform Act, 1989, the Family Law Act, 1995 or the Family Law (Divorce) Act, 1996. Where proceedings are in being, practitioners are advised that, as an alternative to obtaining a statutory declaration from the disinterested spouse (which may, in the circumstances, be impossible to obtain) the vendor must furnish the purchaser with the appropriate court order, entitling the vendor to deal with the property in question.

7.2.9.3   Searches

A conveyance shall be deemed not to be and never to have been void by reason of either s 3(1) of the 1976 Act or s 28(1) of the Act of 2010 unless it has been declared void by a court or the parties to the conveyance, or their successors in title, within six years from the date of the conveyance, make a statement in writing to the effect that the conveyance is void for lack of consent. A solicitor acting for a purchaser must therefore be satisfied both that no proceedings have been brought to have any conveyance pertaining to the property for sale declared void and that no statement declaring the conveyance void has been made. Although the precedent family law declarations contain an averment to the effect that no proceedings have been brought and the Law Society Standard Requisitions on Title also query the position, it is, nevertheless, necessary for a purchaser's solicitor (or, indeed, a solicitor acting for a lending institution) to make further enquiries. These take the form of searches to be made in either the Land Registry or the Registry of Deeds (whichever is appropriate) and in the Lis Pendens Register.

The search in the Registry of Deeds or the Land Registry will reveal whether a statement has been lodged in respect of any conveyance. This is because s 3(8)(c) of the 1976 Act (inserted by the 1995 Act, s 54) and s 28(12) of the Act of 2010 require that a certified copy of any statement declaring a conveyance to be void be lodged in the appropriate registry.

Section 3(8)(d) of the 1976 Act and s 28(13) of the Act of 2010 require that in order to have a conveyance declared void by reason of either s 3(1) of the 1976 Act or s 28(1) of the Act of 2010 a person who institutes proceedings shall, as soon as may be, cause relevant particulars of the proceedings to be entered as a lis pendens in accordance with the Judgments (Ireland) Act, 1844.

Where such searches reveal the existence of proceedings, the only course of action for the solicitor acting for a purchaser is to await the outcome of the proceedings.

7.2.9.4   Requisitions on title

The various provisions of the 1976 Act, the Family Law Act, 1981, the Judicial Separation and Family Law Reform Act, 1989, the 1995 Act and the Act of 2010, discussed in previous paragraphs, are covered by requisitions 23, 24, and 25 of the requisitions on title:

- requisition 23: the Family Home Protection Act, 1976, the Family Law Act, 1995, the Family Law (Divorce) Act, 1996, and the Civil Partnership and Certain Rights and Obligations of Cohabitants Act, 2010;

- requisition 24: the Family Law Act, 1981 and the Family Law Act, 1995; and

- requisition 25: the Judicial Separation and Family Law Reform Act, 1989, the Family Law Act, 1995, the Family Law (Divorce) Act, 1996, and the Civil Partnership and Certain Rights and Obligations of Cohabitants Act, 2010.

As a result of the effects of these and the other enactments, already discussed, it is extremely important, when acting for the vendor of property that a solicitor makes proper enquiry of the vendor, to be able to reply fully to these requisitions. As with replies to all other requisitions, the vendor verifies the replies, before they are forwarded to the solicitor acting for the purchaser. Likewise, when acting for the purchaser, a solicitor should ensure that complete responses to requisitions 23, 24, and 25, have been received and those responses should be forwarded to the purchaser, so that he or she may confirm that he or she is happy with same.

The following is a brief summary of requisitions 23 to 25.

Requisition 23 deals with whether or not the premises are the family home or shared home of the vendor or *any other person*. The requisition requires the vendor to confirm the position and to support that confirmation with a statutory declaration and appropriate corroborating evidence. The requisition also seeks evidence of spousal consent by way of a statutory declaration and exhibit in respect of conveyances of unregistered property on or after 12 July 1976 and the prior written consent, statutory declaration, and exhibit in respect of civil partners on title on or after 1 January 2011.

Requisition 24 queries the position in respect of the Family Law Act, 1981, as amended by the Family Law Act, 1995. The vendor is required to advise whether there have been any dispositions of the property to which ss 3, 4, and 5 of the 1981 Act apply. For further discussion of ss 3, 4, and 5 of the 1981 Act see **7.3**.

Requisition 25 deals with the Judicial Separation and Family Law Reform Act, 1989, the Family Law Act, 1995, the Family Law (Divorce) Act, 1996, and the Civil Partnership and Certain Rights and Obligations of Cohabitants Act, 2010. The requisition is aimed at ascertaining whether or not an order in respect of the property has been made by the court, using its powers under these Acts. A statutory declaration is required confirming that no application or order has been made under these Acts. The vendor is further required to confirm that the transaction is not for purposes of defeating a claim for financial relief. For further discussion of these property orders, see **7.4**.

7.2.10   PARTICULAR ENQUIRIES

7.2.10.1   Where the vendor sells as personal representative

In December 1981, the Conveyancing Committee recommended that it was not necessary for a solicitor purchasing a property from a personal representative, selling qua personal representative, to enquire into the position in relation to the 1976 Act. This recommendation did not receive widespread acceptance, as it did not deal with the (quite common) situation where the personal representative was selling, several years after the death, albeit in his capacity as personal representative. Having consulted senior counsel, the committee issued the following guidelines:

(a)   The facts in each case must ultimately determine the position.

(b)   Where there is no evidence to suggest that the personal representative and his or her spouse have resided in the property, no consent should be sought. However, a declaration confirming non-residency should be obtained from the personal representative.

(c)   Where there is some evidence to suggest that the personal representative and his or her spouse resided in the property for a short period, but there is evidence that the personal representative's family home is elsewhere, no consent should be sought. Again, a declaration confirming the situation should be obtained.

(d)   Where the personal representative and his or her spouse have lived in the property and there is no evidence to suggest that their family home is elsewhere, it is reasonable to require the consent of the spouse. This is particularly important where the personal representative and his or her spouse are beneficially entitled under the will or intestacy.

7.2.10.2   Where the vendor is a company

In 1980, the Joint Committee of the Law Society and the Building Societies issued a recommendation that solicitors acting for purchasers, where the vendor was a company, need not concern themselves with the provisions of the 1976 Act. This was simply because the vendor, being a company, could not have a spouse whose consent was required.

This position was significantly altered by the decision in *Walpole v Jay*, November 1980 (unreported). In that case, the vendor of the property was a company, but the purchaser was on notice that a director of the company and his wife had resided in the premises for a number of years. McWilliam J held that, while there was nothing in the 1976 Act which would invalidate a conveyance by a company, the purchaser was entitled to make enquiries as to the nature of any interest held by the director. If such an investigation revealed that an interest had vested in the director, then the consent of the director's spouse was required to any alienation of that interest.

As a result of this decision, the Conveyancing Committee issued a further Practice Note, published in the Law Society *Gazette*, October 1983, recommending that, where the purchaser after enquiry is aware that a director or other employee of the vendor company has been in occupation of the premises, additional requisitions should be raised.

In recent years it has become common practice for solicitors to furnish their own certificate that the property in question is not a family home. In this regard, however, it should be noted that the Law Society does not advise solicitors to give such a certificate lightly. It is strongly advised that solicitors only give such a certificate in cases of the clearest possible personal knowledge and not on the basis only of information given to him or her by the client.

7.2.10.3   In cases of disputes between spouses or civil partners

As may be seen from the cases discussed previously, the risk to purchasers/mortgagees/lessees is highest in cases where there is or has been a dispute between the spouses or civil partners. In a situation where such a dispute has not been resolved, either by a separation agreement, the granting of a decree of judicial separation or divorce, or the granting of a decree of nullity or dissolution of a civil partnership, a statutory declaration by the vendor only, without any corroboration, is not acceptable.

The extreme caution, which must be exercised by practitioners, in cases of dispute was made clear in the decision handed down by the High Court in *Tesco Ireland Ltd v McGrath*, 14 June 1999, High Court (unreported). This case related to the purchase of lands by the plaintiff from the defendants. The transaction proceeded in the normal course, with the plaintiff seeking and obtaining the usual confirmation, in compliance with requisition 25 of the Law Society Requisitions and Objections on Title, that the sale was not being made for the purpose of defeating any claim for financial relief. Prior to completion, however, the plaintiff became aware that the defendant and his wife had instituted proceedings for judicial separation. The plaintiff sought sight of the proceedings but the request was refused by the defendant's solicitor on the basis that the proceedings had been held in camera and to furnish copies would, therefore, have been in contempt of court. Having failed to satisfy himself as to the precise arrangements vis-à-vis the property as a result of the proceedings, the plaintiff sought to rescind the Contract for Sale. The matter was referred to the court by way of special summons. The court found that the plaintiff, having been put on notice of the existence of proceedings, could no longer rely on the statutory declaration furnished by the vendor, confirming that the disposal was not for the purpose of defeating a claim for financial relief. To do so would, in the view of the court, put the plaintiff in peril of a finding that it was not a bona fide purchaser for value without notice and, in the event of a finding of the court under s 35 of the 1995 Act that the disposition was for the purpose of defeating a claim for financial relief, the disposition to the plaintiff could be set aside by the court. Thus, the plaintiff could rescind the contract. The practical effect of this decision is to place a moratorium upon either spouse dealing with matrimonial property, once proceedings have been instituted, since any prudent purchaser, once put on notice of the proceedings, should withdraw from the transaction and await the outcome of the action.

Considerable caution should also be exercised in relation to cases where the vendor is stated to be either divorced or separated or to have obtained a decree of dissolution or nullity of a civil partnership. In such a situation, the vendor may either claim that the property was purchased subsequent to the court decree or separation agreement and his or her spouse or civil partner never resided in the premises or that the decree or separation agreement provided that the property be vested in the vendor. In the case of separation agreements, the Conveyancing Committee, in a Practice Note published in the Law Society *Gazette*, January/February 1985, recommended that a purchaser's/mortgagee's solicitor should seek a statutory declaration from the disinterested spouse confirming that the property is not a family home. This will, however, not prevent the court from subsequently looking at the transaction to see if it is a reviewable disposition under the Family Law (Divorce) Act, 1996. Where such a declaration is not available, the solicitor should seek either:

(a)   a corroborative declaration from the vendor's solicitor stating that he or she has read the separation agreement and quoting any relevant extracts therefrom; or

(b)   a declaration from a party to the separation agreement, exhibiting a solicitor's certified copy of the relevant extracts therefrom. The committee recommends that only those sections of the agreement relating to the property should be exhibited, as it would not be proper to exhibit the entire document. In this regard, it is good practice, when drafting separation agreements, to place the paragraphs dealing with the family home just above the signatures of the parties.

The same considerations apply in relation to divorce decrees, decrees of dissolution or nullity of civil partnership, and judicial separations and in those circumstances the appropriate court order and/or decree should be exhibited.

In relation to the drafting of separation agreements, practitioners should note that, since the introduction of s 3(9) of the 1976 Act, by s 54(1) of the 1995 Act, it is now possible for a spouse to give a general consent to any future conveyance of an interest in the family home, provided that the general consent is in writing. In drafting a separation agreement, which contains provisions relating to the family home, practitioners should be careful to include a general consent of the disinterested spouse. The issue of the exhibition of court orders and proceedings with statutory declarations has become a thorny issue since the decision in *Tesco Ireland Ltd v McGrath*, discussed earlier. In that case, the court held that the solicitors for the defendants had acted correctly in refusing to furnish the plaintiff with copies of the pleadings and orders relating to the case.

This issue was also discussed in the case of *RM v DM* [2000] 3 IR 373. In that case, one of the parties to proceedings under the Family Law (Divorce) Act, 1996 sought to adduce the proceedings relating to the family law hearing as evidence in an action brought against his barrister before the Barristers' Professional Conduct Tribunal. When the Circuit Court refused consent to allow the proceedings to be used in evidence, the matter was appealed to the High Court. In the High Court, Murphy J confirmed the decision of the lower court. Reviewing the decision of the Circuit Court, Murphy J stated:

> 'Having considered the authorities the court held, inter alia, that the primary reason for the in camera rule is to provide protection for minors from the harmful publicity arising out of the disclosure of evidence and other related matters in protected proceedings. There is no absolute embargo on disclosure of evidence in all circumstances.'

Whether or not the court would, in a particular case, grant consent for the dissemination of documentation relating to the proceedings, the subject of the in camera rule, depends upon whether or not the release of the information is in the interests of justice or it is crucial in the public interest that the information on the matrimonial proceedings be made public. In the instant case, neither requirement was satisfied. In the course of his judgment, Murphy J confirmed the decision in *Tesco Ireland Ltd v McGrath*, stating that he was in no doubt that solicitors for vendors are precluded by the in camera rule from furnishing copies of claims, orders, and pleadings made in family law proceedings.

In order to deal with the practical implications of these two decisions, many practitioners, involved in litigation under either the 1989 or the 1996 Act, request the court, as part of the proceedings, to make an order allowing the exhibition of any appropriate documentation in statutory declarations, relating to subsequent transactions. This issue has, however, become significantly more straightforward with the coming into effect of s 40 of the Civil Liability and Courts Act, 2004 ('the 2004 Act'). This section was included in the miscellaneous provisions part of the 2004 Act after much lobbying by the Law Society on behalf of the legal profession. Section 40(3) provides that:

Nothing contained in a relevant enactment shall operate to prohibit—

(a)   the preparation by a barrister at law or a solicitor or a person falling within any other class of persons specified in regulations made by the Minister and publication of a report of proceedings to which the relevant enactment relates,

or

(b)   the publication of the decision of the court in such proceedings,

in accordance with rules of court, provided that the report or decision does not contain any information which would enable the parties to the proceedings or any child to which the proceedings relate to be identified and, accordingly, unless in the special circumstances of the matter the court, for reasons which shall be specified in the direction, otherwise directs, a person referred to in paragraph (a) may, for the purposes of preparing such a report, attend the proceedings subject to any directions the court may give in that behalf.

Section 40(4) goes on to allow the supply, by a party to proceedings to which any relevant enactment relates, of copies of, or extracts from, orders made in the proceedings to such persons and in accordance with such conditions as may be prescribed by order of the minister. For the purposes of s 40, 'relevant enactment' includes certain sections of the Family Home Protection Act, 1976, the Judicial Separation and Family Law Reform Act, 1989, the Family Law Act, 1995, and the Family Law (Divorce) Act, 1996. Section 40 came into force on 31 March 2005. The class of persons, to whom extracts of court proceedings may be supplied, has now been set out in the Civil Liability and Courts Act, 2004 (Section 40(4)) Order, 2005 (SI 338/2005) and includes, *inter alia*, solicitors and the Land Registry. The order prohibits the prescribed person, to whom such an extract has been supplied, from showing or supplying the copy to any person other than a person to whom it is necessary to supply or show the copy for the purpose of enabling the prescribed person to perform his or her duties. It is, therefore, now possible for practitioners, acting for the vendors of properties, the subject of proceedings, to corroborate statements made by such vendors in family law declarations by exhibiting appropriate extracts from relevant court orders. Caution should be exercised in the preparation of such family law declarations to ensure that only relevant extracts of the court orders are exhibited.

The legal priority of a judgment mortgage where proceedings in respect of the land were commenced under the Family Law Act, 1995 prior to the registering of the judgment mortgage were considered in *Dovebid Netherlands BV v William Phelan, trading as the Phelan Partnership, and Denise O'Byrne* [2007] IEHC 131 (23 April 2007). In this case, the plaintiff had obtained judgment against the first-named defendant and the judgment was registered in December 2005 against the interest of the first-named defendant in certain lands and premises which the first-named defendant held jointly with the second-named defendant. The first and the second defendants were married but separated and family law proceedings had been instituted between them. These proceedings commenced prior to the judgment mortgage and resulted in a property adjustment order requiring the respondent to those proceedings (the first-named defendant) to transfer the entirety of the beneficial interest in the premises to the applicant (the second-named defendant). Dunne J found that the interests of the second-named defendant on foot of the property adjustment order ranked in priority to that of the plaintiff.

When purchasing unregistered property from a divorced or separated vendor who has acquired the property from his or her former or estranged spouse or civil partner on foot of a property adjustment order or separation agreement, care should be exercised to ascertain whether the conveyance to the vendor triggered compulsory first registration under s 24 of the Registration of Title Act, 1964. By virtue of SI 516/2010, registration of ownership of land became compulsory throughout the State in the case of freehold land, upon conveyance on sale and in the case of a leasehold interest on the grant or assignment on sale of such an interest. Subsection (3) of s 24 provides that 'conveyance on sale' and 'assignment on sale' mean an instrument made on sale for money or mony's worth by virtue of which there is conferred or completed a title in respect of which an application for registration as owner may be made, and include a conveyance or assignment by way of exchange where money is paid for equality of exchange and also include any contract, agreement, condition, or covenant affecting the property comprised in the conveyance or assignment and entered into or made as part of, or in association with, such conveyance or assignment. Where the property adjustment order or separation agreement provides for the transfer of an interest in property between divorced or estranged spouses or civil partners in consideration of money or money's worth, this will trigger compulsory first registration, which must be attended to before the vendor may dispose of his or her interest. Where the property adjustment order or separation agreement makes no provision for payment, then the deed of conveyance ought to recite that the property is assured 'in consideration of the premises', in order to avoid the categorisation of the assurance as a 'conveyance on sale', thus triggering first registration.

7.2.10.4   Where the property is registered property

Where the property is registered land, the Registrar of Titles is concerned with the application of both the 1976 Act and the Act of 2010, as the Registrar is under a general duty to register only valid transfers. In *Guckian v Brennan* [1981] IR 478, Gannon J stated that 'the provisions of s 31(1) of the Registration of Title Act, 1964 (establishing the conclusiveness of the register) afford a sufficient protection of the vendor and the intending purchaser in relation to all prior transactions affecting the registered ownership as appearing on title'. The court went on to hold that 'the duty of insuring that any instrument of transfer is valid and effective, so as to enable a transmission of ownership to be duly registered, falls upon the Registrar at the time of the registration'. Prior to March 2009, the Registrar interpreted this obligation as including a duty to require the production of the best evidence available as to the position regarding the family home at the time of registration. In March 2009, however, the Land Registry issued a new Practice Direction stating that, henceforth, in order to be satisfied that the instrument of transfer is valid and effective, the Property Registration Authority ('the Authority') need only ensure that no proceedings have been commenced and no statement made under s 3(8)(c) or (d) of the 1976 Act to the effect that the registered deed is void. Thus, before registration, the Authority will now check the following matters only:

1.   that there is no entry in part (III) of the relevant folio as to a statement of invalidity under s 3(8) of the 1976 Act, as amended, by the parties to the deed and no such dealing pending; and

2.   that there is no lis pendens on the folio as per s 3(8) of the 1976 Act, as amended, and no such dealing pending.

Apart from the foregoing, the Authority no longer requires consents, statutory declarations, or certificates to be lodged but, if lodged, these documents will be filed with the instrument. This position is reflected in the 2010 edition of Form 17. In May 2009 the Conveyancing Committee of the Law Society issued a Practice Note in the *Gazette* confirming that, notwithstanding the Authority's Practice Direction, it is proper practice to lodge family law declarations and corroborating documents with Land Registry dealings. The Authority has confirmed that staff, while no longer checking them, will continue to accept them.

A person, married to a party who has an interest in registered land, may, by virtue of s 12 of the 1976 Act, register a notice of the existence of the marriage, under the Registration of Title Act, 1964. Section 36(1) and (2) permits a civil partner to lodge with the Property Registration Authority a notice stating that he or she is a civil partner of a person having an interest in property or land. The notice will appear on Part 2 of the relevant folio. Clearly, the purpose of registering such a notice is to fix third parties with notice of the interest of the spouse. It is possible to remove the notice from the folio when the property ceases to be a family home or shared home or following the registration of the spouse or civil partner as sole owner. The Law Society has recommended that it is good practice to have such notices removed from the register when they no longer apply, eg on change of ownership (Practice Note, Law Society *Gazette*, December 2003). This can be done by lodging a form of application adapted from Form 71A where the spouse who registered the notice consents; in other cases Form 71B should be adapted and appropriate evidence of non-application of the notice adduced.

A comprehensive Practice Direction relating to the Act of 2010 was published by the Property Registration Authority in May 2011 and may be accessed on the Property Registration Authority website.

7.2.10.5   Where the property is unregistered property

Where the property is registered in the Registry of Deeds, the Registrar is not concerned with the validity of the deed and will register the priority of the deed, without enquiring into the position regarding the family home or shared home. Where the consent of the spouse or the civil partner to the conveyance has been required and obtained, it is normal to endorse that consent on the actual deed. There is, of course, always the possibility that the deed may be lost and with it the spouse's or civil partner's consent. It is therefore good practice to recite, in the Registry of Deeds application form for the registration of the deed, the fact that consent had been endorsed on the conveyance.

As with registered land, s 12 of the 1976 Act and s 36 of the Act of 2010 provides for the registration, in this case pursuant to the Registration of Deeds (Ireland) Act, 1707, of a notice of marriage or of the existence of a civil partnership in respect of unregistered land. It should be noted, however, that unlike registered land, it is not possible to remove the notice of marriage or of the existence of a civil partnership from the register, maintained by the Registry of Deeds.

7.2.10.6 Where vendor is selling under a power of attorney

The situation regarding the 1976 Act where the vendor is selling under a power of attorney is dealt with in a Practice Note published by the Conveyancing Committee in the Law Society *Gazette*, July 1997.

In relation to sales, mortgages, etc, where the vendor is acting under a power of attorney of the non-owning spouse, where the power of attorney either relates to a specific transaction or is more general in nature, the power of attorney if correctly drafted, will empower the donee to execute a consent on behalf of the donor. A solicitor acting for a purchaser in such a situation may be able to accept a conveyance with the consent of the donee endorsed thereon, provided that the solicitor has satisfied himself or herself that the power of attorney is appropriately drafted. The preference would be for the power of attorney to be specifically drafted to empower the donee to execute a consent for the specific transaction. If there is any doubt about the matter, evidence could be sought that the non-owning spouse was independently advised in relation to the granting of the power of attorney. For more detail see the Practice Note in the Law Society *Gazette* in July 1997.

The donee of a power of attorney is never empowered to complete a statutory declaration on behalf of the donor. A person may only make a declaration from his own personal knowledge. Thus, a solicitor acting for a purchaser, where the vendor is selling under a power of attorney, may never accept a declaration which the donee purports to make on foot of a power of attorney. A declaration of the donee, in his personal capacity, and declaring facts which are within his own personal knowledge, is acceptable, where there is no better evidence available.

These recommendations apply equally to a general power of attorney and to an enduring power of attorney, granted under the Powers of Attorney Act, 1996 with one slight difference. An enduring power of attorney will only come into effect once the donor has become mentally incapable and the power of attorney has been registered under s 10 of the Powers of Attorney Act, 1996. A solicitor acting for a purchaser/mortgagee must, therefore, check carefully that the power of attorney has, in fact, been so registered. If it has not, the donee will have no authority to execute a consent on behalf of the donor.

7.3 Family Law Act, 1981

The provisions of the Family Law Act, 1981 ('the 1981 Act') which impact most upon conveyancing practice are ss 3, 4, and 5.

7.3.1 ENGAGEMENT GIFTS: SS 3 AND 4

Under s 3, where two persons agree to marry, and are given any property by a third party as a wedding gift, there is a rebuttable presumption that such property was given to them as joint owners. There is a further presumption that the gift was made subject to the condition that it will be returned, should the engaged couple not marry. Section 4 deals with the situation where one party to the engagement makes a gift to the other party. Here, there is also a rebuttable presumption that the gift is made subject to the condition that it shall be returned if the marriage does not take place for any reason other than the death of the donor. Where the donor dies prior to the marriage, there is a rebuttable presumption that the gift was given unconditionally.

7.3.2   BROKEN ENGAGEMENTS: S 5

The effect of s 5 is to give parties to a broken engagement the same rights as those given to spouses in relation to property in which either or other of them has a beneficial interest. The section only relates to engagements terminated within the three years prior to the purported conveyance.

The extent to which the 'rules of law relating to the rights of spouses' pertain to engaged couples is rather uncertain. Probably, the presumption of advancement is included. By virtue of this presumption, if the property is bought in the joint names of the spouses, with money put forward by the husband only, there is a presumption of advancement in favour of the wife and she is thus entitled to half of the property.

Included also is the doctrine of resulting trust, whereby, if the property is bought in the sole name of one spouse, and there is a contribution towards the purchase price by the other spouse, the courts will apply the doctrine of resulting trust to give the contributing spouse a share based on the proportion of the contribution.

The normal conveyancing practice is to include a paragraph in the statutory declaration dealing with the Family Home Protection Act, stating that the provisions of s 5 of the Family Law Act, 1981 do not apply.

Where the vendors are joint owners, have been married to each other for more than three years and execute a statutory declaration to that effect, exhibiting a civil marriage certificate, it is not necessary to require a statement in relation to s 5: see Conveyancing Committee Practice Note, published in the Law Society *Gazette*, January/February 1986.

Where enquiries reveal that there is a broken engagement within the past three years and the other party did, indeed, make a contribution, two possible situations may arise. The most satisfactory, from the perspective of the purchaser, is to have the other party join in the deed of assurance. For obvious reasons, this might not always be possible. As the interest of the contributing party is equitable, it is not absolutely necessary to have them join in the deed of assurance. It is, however, essential that the fiancé(e) receive his or her share of the proceeds and that he or she provide a receipt for same. In circumstances such as these, the solicitor acting for the purchaser should not only request that the receipt, or a certified copy of same, be handed over on closing, but also that a separate statutory declaration, dealing solely with the 1981 Act, be furnished.

7.4   Power of the Court to Deal with Property

7.4.1   THE FAMILY HOME PROTECTION ACT, 1976 AND THE CIVIL PARTNERSHIP AND CERTAIN RIGHTS AND OBLIGATIONS OF COHABITANTS ACT, 2010

By virtue of s 5 of the 1976 Act and s 30 of the Act of 2010, the court is empowered to make any order, which it considers proper, where it is of the view that one spouse or civil partner is guilty of conduct which could lead to the loss of the family home or shared home. In addition, s 9 of the 1976 Act and s 34 of the Act of 2010 permit the court to restrict the disposal of any household chattels. Section 4 of the 1976 Act and s 29 of the Act of 2010 enables the court to make an order dispensing with the prior consent of the non-owning spouse or civil partner. Finally, s 7 of the 1976 Act and s 32 of the Act of 2010 empower the court to postpone proceedings brought by the mortgagor or lessor of the family home or the shared home, where those proceedings arise as a result of late payment under either a lease or mortgage. These basic powers, as they relate to the 1976 Act, have been expanded by the provisions of the Judicial Separation and Family Law Reform Act, 1989 ('the 1989 Act'), and the Family Law (Divorce) Act, 1996.

7.4.2 THE JUDICIAL SEPARATION AND FAMILY LAW REFORM ACT, 1989

The 1989 Act must be read in conjunction with the provision of the Family Law Act, 1995, which repealed and/or amended many of the provisions of the 1989 Act. With the introduction of the 1989 Act, the State recognised the necessity to put in place a framework, whereby spouses experiencing marital breakdown could bring proceedings for judicial separation.

Section 6 of the 1995 Act deals with the situation during the period after the institution of such proceedings and before the hearing of the action. By virtue of s 6, the court is empowered to make preliminary orders under ss 5 and 9 of the 1976 Act. Once made, such a preliminary order remains in force until the hearing of the action.

On granting a decree of judicial separation, at any time during the lifetime of the respondent spouse, the court is empowered by virtue of s 9 of the 1995 Act (replacing s 15 of the 1989 Act) to make a property adjustment order. A property adjustment order made subsequent to the granting of a decree of judicial separation may be made on the application of either spouse at any time during the lifetime of the other spouse. This entitlement to apply to the court for a property adjustment order ceases, however, in the event of the remarriage of either spouse (s 9 of the 1995 Act). The property adjustment orders, which may be made under s 9, deal with the following issues:

(a) the transfer of property from one spouse to the other spouse or to any dependent member of the family or to a third party for the benefit of such a member;

(b) the settlement of any property for the benefit of one or both spouses or for any dependent member of the family;

(c) the variation of a previous agreed settlement of any property; and

(d) the extinguishment or reduction of any interest held by either spouse held under any such settlement.

By virtue of s 10 of the 1995 Act, the court is empowered to make a variety of orders:

(a) s 10(1)(a)(i) order allowing one spouse to occupy the family home exclusively;

(b) s 10(1)(a)(ii) order for the sale of the family home; and

(c) s 10(1)(b) order determining any issue of ownership of property between spouses.

Like orders made under s 9, the foregoing orders may be made by the court either at the time of granting the decree of judicial separation or subsequently, on the application of either spouse during the lifetime of the other spouse.

Finally, s 18 provides for the variation by the court of any order made pursuant to ss 9(1)(b), (c), or (d) and 10(1)(a)(i) or 10(1)(a)(ii).

7.4.3 THE FAMILY LAW (DIVORCE) ACT, 1996

The Family Law (Divorce) Act, 1996 ('the 1996 Act') came into force 'on the day that is three months after the date of its passing', ie 27 February 1997. By virtue of s 5(1) of the 1996 Act, the court was empowered, on being satisfied in respect of certain matters, to grant a decree of divorce in respect of any marriage, the subject of an application under the Act. The effect of such a decree is set out in s 10, which states:

Where the court grants a decree of divorce, the marriage, the subject of the decree, is thereby dissolved and a party to that marriage may marry again.

Sections 14 and 19 of the 1996 Act grant the court power to make property adjustment orders and orders for the sale of property, respectively. Orders made under these sections may be subsequently varied by the court by virtue of s 22. In addition to ss 14 and 19, s 37 of the 1996 Act empowers the court to 'make such order as it thinks fit' in order to restrain one spouse from making a disposition of property, where the other spouse has instituted divorce proceedings and where the court is satisfied that the purpose of the disposition is to defeat the claim for relief of the applicant spouse. Under s 37(2)(a)(ii), the court is further empowered to set aside a 'reviewable disposition' where satisfied that the disposition has been made in order to defeat the claim for relief. 'Reviewable disposition' is defined by s 37(1) as meaning:

a disposition made by the other spouse concerned or any other person but does not include such a disposition made for valuable consideration (other than marriage) to a person who, at the time of the disposition, acted in good faith and without notice of an intention on the part of the respondent to defeat the claim for relief.

7.4.4   REGISTRATION OF COURT ORDERS

Where a property adjustment order has been made by a court in respect of property under either s 14 of the 1996 Act (in the case of divorce), s 9 of the 1995 Act (in the case of an order for judicial separation) or s 128 of the Act of 2010 (in the case of the dissolution of a civil partnership), the Registrar of that court is obliged by s 14(4) of the 1996 Act, s 9(4) of the 1995 Act, or s 118(4) of the Act of 2010 to lodge a certified copy of the order for registration as a burden under s 69(1)(h) of the Registration of Title Act, 1964 either in the Land Registry or the Registry of Deeds. In October 2001, the Conveyancing Committee issued a Practice Note on this topic, advising that, when instituting proceedings under either the 1995 or the 1996 Acts, practitioners ought to ensure that comprehensive details of the title are included in the civil bill or special summons. This is to ensure that, when the order is perfected, the Registrar has sufficient information to enable registration in the correct Registry.

The Acts did not originally provide for the automatic cancellation of the burden, once the terms of the order were satisfied. In an attempt to address this unsatisfactory position, the Conveyancing Committee of the Law Society issued a Practice Note in May 2000, recommending that the instrument implementing the terms of the order should contain the consent of the parties to the instrument to the cancellation of the burden. The situation was regularised by the introduction of ss 74 and 75 of the Civil Law (Miscellaneous Provisions) Act, 2008 which inserted new subsections into s 9 of the Family Law Act, 1995 and s 14 of the Family Law (Divorce) Act, 1996 respectively. These new subsections provide that the Authority, on being satisfied that a property adjustment order has been complied with or discharged, shall cancel the entry made in the register. The Practice Direction issued by the Authority to its staff stipulates the proofs to be lodged in order to cancel the entry.

By the insertion of a new subsection (8) into s 18 of the Family Law Act, 1995 and s 22 of the Family Law (Divorce) Act, 1996, the Civil Law (Miscellaneous Provisions) Act, 2008 provides for the amendment or cancellation of an entry made in the register where a property adjustment order which has been registered is subsequently varied, discharged, suspended, or revived by a subsequent court order and that subsequent order is duly lodged for registration. Section 118(5) of the Act of 2010 provides for the cancellation of an entry made in the Land Registry or the registration in the Registry of Deeds of a note of compliance with an order made and registered under s 118.

7.5   Qualified Cohabitants

As mentioned at **7.1**, in addition to dealing with the position of civil partners in relation to the shared home, the Act of 2010 introduced the concept of a 'qualified cohabitant' and sets out a scheme of redress available to such cohabitants. A cohabitant is defined by s 172(1) as follows:

For the purposes of this Part, a cohabitant is one of 2 adults, (whether of the same or opposite sex) who live together as a couple in an intimate and committed relationship and who are not related to each other within prohibited degress of relationship or married to each other or civil partners of each other.

Subsections (2), (3), and (4) further refine this definition by setting out the factors to be taken into account by the court in determining whether or not two adults are cohabitants for the purpose of the Act of 2010.

A 'qualified cohabitant' is defined by subsection (5) as meaning:

. . . an adult who was in a relationship of cohabitation with another adult and who, immediately before the time that that relationship ended, whether through death or otherwise, was living with the other adult as a couple for a period—

(a) *of 2 years or more, in the case of where they are the parents of one or more dependent children, and*

(b) *of 5 years or more, in any other case.*

A dependent child means:

. . . any child of whom both the cohabitants are the parents and who is—

(a) *under the age of 18 years, or*

(b) *18 years of age or over and is—*

      (i) *receiving full-time education or instruction at any university, college, school or other educational establishment and is under the age of 23 years, or*

      (ii) *incapable of taking care of his or her own needs because of a mental or physical disability.*

The meaning of 'qualified cohabitant' was considered by the High Court in the case of *D.C. v D.R.* [2015] IEHC 09.

In that case, the plaintiff, D.C. brought an application under s 194(1) of the Act of 2010, seeking that financial provision be made out of the estate of J.C. with whom he alleged he had been in an intimate cohabiting relationship. J.C. died intestate on 7 August 2014 and Letters of Administration intestate in her estate issued to D.R., the defendant in the case. D.R. who was a brother of the late J.C., denied that the plaintiff was a qualified cohabitant for the purposes of the Act of 2010 and further denied that if, in fact, the plaintiff was found by the court to be a qualified cohabitant, it was proper that provision be made for the plaintiff out of the estate of the late J.C. Having heard evidence from the plaintiff, the defendant and the witnesses called by each of them as to the nature of the relationship between D.C. and J. C., Baker J. considered the meaning of 'an intimate and committed relationship' for the purposes of s 172(1) of the Act of 2010 and noted the following:

'The Act offers no assistance as to what is meant by an intimate relationship, but having regard to s 172(3) it is clear that a relationship must have been at some point in time a sexual relationship for intimacy to be found. The intimacy that is intended is a sexual intimacy and not merely the intimacy of close friendship.'

She then went on to consider the factors, set out in s 172(2) of the Act of 2010, to be taken into account by the court in determining whether or not two adults are cohabitants. In this regard, she stated:

'The scheme of the Act envisages the Court looking at seven identified factors in s 172(2) not as conclusive as to the nature of the relationship but as indicative of that relationship and how it is to be properly categorised. I consider that the test requires the court to determine whether a reasonable person who knew the couple would have regarded them as living together in a committed and intimate relationship, and that the individual and many factors in how they are perceived must be taken into account.'

On the evidence before her, Baker J. concluded that the plaintiff and the late J.C. were, indeed, in an intimate and committed relationship at the date of J.C.'s death and had been so cohabiting in excess of five years prior to her death. Having thus concluded, Baker J then considered the provision, if any, which ought to be made out of the estate of the deceased and in particular considered the following factors which she considered to be relevant:

1. the nature of the relationship;

2. contribution made by the cohabitants to the welfare of either of them and their relative resources;

3. contributions made by the cohabitants in looking after the home;

4. the conduct of the cohabitants;

5. the financial circumstances of each cohabitant; and

6. the interests of others.

Having considered these factors, Baker J. found that provision for the plaintiff amounting to approximately 45 per cent of the estate of J.C. ought to be made.

By virtue of s 172(6) of the Act of 2010 an adult who would otherwise be a qualified cohabitant is excluded from the redress scheme if one or both of the cohabitants is or was married at any time during the cohabitation in question *and* at the time the cohabitation in question ends, each cohabitant who is or was married has not lived apart from his or her spouse for a period or periods of at least four years during the previous five years.

Any person who is a qualified cohabitant may apply to court for one or all of the following orders:

1. a property adjustment order relating to any property in which the cohabitant has an interest either in possession or reversion (s 174);

2. a compensatory maintenance order against the other cohabitant (s 175); or

3. a pension adjustment order in respect of the pension of the other cohabitant (s 187).

It should be noted that any matters regulated by the cohabitants in an agreement which satisfies the requirements of s 202 will not be addressed by the court under the redress scheme but will, instead, be dealt with in accordance with the terms of the cohabitants' agreement.

Since the redress scheme allows for property adjustment orders, solicitors acting for purchasers or mortgagees must now satisfy themselves of the position in relation to qualified cohabitants. The current editions of the family law declarations, available on the Law Society's website, address the situation.

7.6 Conveyancing Requirements Regarding Cohabitants: Deeds of Confirmation

The Law Society Conveyancing Committee in a Practice Note in the January/February 2014 issue of the Law Society *Gazette* have outlined the correct position regarding cohabitants executing deeds of wavier or deeds of confirmation in cases where they are not on title.

A cohabitant who has no equity in a property should make a family law declaration to this effect for a conveyancing transaction, including a mortgage transaction.

However, where a cohabitant who is not on title (whether a qualified cohabitant or not) has equity in a property, or if there is a doubt as to whether or not the cohabitant has such equity, the family law declaration should reflect this fact, and the cohabitant should execute a deed of confirmation in favour of either the purchaser or the mortgagee as appropriate.

It should be noted that, in circumstances where it is established that a cohabitant has equity in a property, it is not possible for them to 'waive' their interest: the appropriate deed is a deed of confirmation, as stated earlier.

The question arises as to how a solicitor can be certain that an equitable interest has not accrued in any particular situation and that, therefore, a deed of confirmation is not necessary. The view of the conveyancing committee is that, if a cohabitant cannot make a declaration that he or she has no equitable interest, he or she should sign a deed of confirmation. Where a deed of confirmation is to be signed by a cohabitant, he or she should be advised to obtain independent legal advice.

Even in a case where it is established that a cohabitant has no equitable interest, a family law declaration is required in any case in order to exclude the possibility of proceedings under the Civil Partnership and Certain Rights and Obligations of Cohabitants Act, 2010.

CHAPTER 8

DRAFTING

8.1 Introduction

This chapter deals primarily with the drafting of deeds in relation to unregistered title. It deals only briefly with the drafting of transfers in relation to registered titles as these are dealt with more fully in **chapter 14**.

This chapter also outlines the procedure for registering deeds in the Registry of Deeds. It does not deal with the procedure for registering deeds in the Land Registry as this is also dealt with in **chapter 14**.

Drafting is an important aspect of conveyancing practice as a poorly drafted deed may have serious consequences for the conveyancer. A deed of rectification may be required or, if the parties to the original deed cannot be located, the deed may remain a defect on the title. The deed could also be void with consequent implications for the client and the solicitor's professional indemnity insurance.

8.2 Drafting a Deed in Relation to Unregistered Title

8.2.1 INTRODUCTION

Save in certain exceptional cases (mortgage, lease, building estate grant) the deed of purchase is drafted by the purchaser's solicitor and furnished for approval to the vendor's solicitor. Its purpose is to give effect to the intention of the parties, as expressed in the Contract for Sale, to make, confirm, or concur in an assurance of some interest in property. The purchaser's solicitor must ensure that the deed provides for his or her client to obtain everything he or she is paying for and the vendor's solicitor must ensure that the deed does not give the purchaser more than he or she is paying for.

General condition 20 of the Contract for Sale provides that subject to the legislation listed therein:

> 'On payment of all moneys payable by him in respect of the Sale, and subject to the provisions of Section 980, Taxes Consolidation Act, 1997, and (if relevant) to those contained in Section 107, Finance Act, 1993 (in relation to Residential Property Tax), the Purchaser shall be entitled to a proper Assurance of the Subject Property from the Vendor and all other (if any) necessary parties.'

This assurance is to be prepared by and at the expense of the purchaser. This condition further provides that a draft of the deed shall be submitted to the vendor's solicitor not less than seven working days, and the engrossment (ie the final version for execution) not less than four working days, before the closing date. There are many books of precedents to assist practitioners with the drafting of deeds and many firms have, over time, built up their own precedents bank. The Land Registry has also set out precedent transfers in the Land Registration Rules, 2012. It should be noted, however, that over-reliance on precedents inevitably leads to errors. Every transaction is different and thus precedents should be used merely as a guide for even the most experienced of practitioners.

There are general rules of construction which govern all deeds. These provide guidelines to be followed when drafting a deed for a specific transaction and also when interpreting a deed drafted by someone else.

There are particular deeds used for particular transactions depending on the nature of the title being passed. These are given in the following list.

Conveyance	Sale of unregistered freehold interest
Fee farm grant	Creation of unregistered freehold interest subject to a rent (see following note re s 12 of the 2009 Act)
Lease	Creation of leasehold interest (term of years and subject to a rent and covenants and conditions) carved out of a freehold interest
Sublease	Creation of leasehold interest (term of years and subject to a rent and covenants and conditions) carved out of a leasehold interest (then called a head lease)
Assignment	Sale of unregistered leasehold interest (residue of a term of years and subject to a rent)
Transfer	Sale of registered land (both freehold and leasehold)

The generic words indenture/deed/assurance/purchase deed may be used in any given situation to refer to the purchase deed drafted by the purchaser's solicitor.

The Land and Conveyancing Law Reform Act, 2009 ('the 2009 Act'), s 12, has now prohibited the creation of a fee farm grant at law or in equity. Section 12 does, however, not affect fee farm grants or contracts to create fee farm grants entered into before the section came into force.

Both the purchaser's solicitor drafting the deed and the vendor's solicitor approving it should ensure that the deed correctly reflects the bargain between the parties. The essential elements of the transaction must be correctly reflected in the deed, eg the parties, the price, and the property. The nature of the title must also be looked at so as to determine the correct type of deed to be drafted. If more than one type of title is passing it may be necessary to use two separate deeds or, alternatively, one deed could be drafted dealing with both titles. For example, if both freehold and leasehold unregistered title is passing an amalgamated conveyance and assignment could be drafted. Alternatively it may be appropriate to merge the interests and thus draft a conveyance with a declaration of merger.

It is recommended by the Conveyancing Committee that it is good practice when lodging applications for first registration (whether same is compulsory or not) that the conveyance/assignment/other assurance of unregistered title would first be registered in the Registry of Deeds before lodging it in the Land Registry, in order to preserve priorities pending registration in the Land Registry. See Law Society *Gazette*, January/February 2012.

8.2.2   WHAT IS A 'DEED'?

Section 32(1) of the Registration of Deeds and Title Act, 2006 ('the 2006 Act') provides that a 'deed' means a document by which an estate or interest in land is created, transferred, charged, or otherwise affected and includes, *inter alia*, any of the following documents, whether under seal or not, affecting land: a conveyance, an assent under the Succession Act, 1965, a vesting certificate, and any other document as may be prescribed. It does not include any document affecting registered land, or a lis pendens or a caution as these are not registrable in the Registry of Deeds, or any lease for a term not exceeding 21 years where actual occupation is in accordance with the lease.

Section 62(1) of the 2009 Act affirms this by providing that, subject to s 63, a legal estate or interest in land may only be created or conveyed by a deed. The exceptions listed in s 63 include, *inter alia*, an assent, a disclaimer, a receipt, or any other conveyance which may be prescribed. Section 11(1) of the 2009 Act provides that the only legal estates in land which may be created or disposed of after 1 December 2009 are the freehold and leasehold estates specified in s 11.

Section 64 of the 2009 Act sets out three requirements for the creation of a deed. These relate to the description of the document, its execution, and its delivery. Section 64(2)(a) provides that an instrument is a deed if it is described at its head by words such as 'Assignment', 'Conveyance', 'Charge', 'Surrender', 'Deed', 'Indenture', 'Lease', 'Mortgage', or other heading appropriate to the deed in question, or it is otherwise made clear on its face that it is intended by the person making it, or the parties to it, to be a deed, by expressing it to be executed or signed as a deed. In order to be a deed the instrument must also be executed in accordance with s 64(2)(b) (see **8.2.5.16**) and must be delivered in accordance with s 64(2)(c) (see **8.2.5.16**).

8.2.3   PARTS OF THE DEED

In principle there are 15 parts to a deed though not all them appear in every deed.

1. Commencement and date.
2. Parties.
3. Recital of title (narrative).
4. Recital of Contract for Sale (connecting).
5. Testatum.
6. Consideration.
7. Receipt clause.
8. Operative words.
9. Parcels.
10. Habendum.
11. Covenants and conditions/Exceptions and reservations.
12. Acknowledgements and undertakings.
13. Statutory certificates.
14. Testimonium.
15. Attestation/Execution.

8.2.4   SPECIMEN DEED OF CONVEYANCE

This is an example of a deed of conveyance. The parts of the deed have been listed in the margin for illustration purposes only.

COMMENCEMENT AND DATE   **THIS CONVEYANCE** dated the first day of May Two Thousand and Fourteen

PARTIES   **BETWEEN JOHN CITIZEN** of Ballymurphy in the County of Dublin Soldier (hereinafter called 'the vendor' which expression shall where the context so admits or requires include his executors and administrators) of the one part and **PATRICK PENSIONER** of Ballymurphy in the County of Dublin Retired Sailor (hereinafter called 'the purchaser' which expression shall where the context so admits or requires include his executors, administrators and assigns) of the other part.

RECITAL OF TITLE	**RECITALS**
	(a) the vendor is seised of hereditaments and premises hereinafter more particularly described and intended to be hereby assured for an estate in fee simple in possession free from encumbrances.
RECITAL OF CONTRACT	(b) the vendor has agreed with the purchaser for the sale to the purchaser of the said hereditaments and premises for an estate in fee simple free from encumbrances for the sum of Five Hundred and Fifty Thousand Euro
TESTATUM	**NOW THIS CONVEYANCE WITNESSETH** that in pursuance of the said agreement
CONSIDERATION	And in consideration of the sum of Five Hundred and Fifty Thousand Euro (€550,000.00) paid by the purchaser to the vendor
RECEIPT CLAUSE	(the receipt whereof the vendor doth hereby acknowledge)
OPERATIVE WORDS	The vendor as **BENEFICIAL OWNER** hereby **CONVEYS** to the purchaser
PARCELS	**ALL THAT AND THOSE** that plot of land with the buildings thereon situate at Number One Main Street in the Village of Ballymurphy Townland of Greenacre Parish of All Saints Barony of Pale and County of Dublin as the same is more particularly delineated on the map or plan thereof attached hereto and thereon shown edged red
HABENDUM	**IN FEE SIMPLE**
STATUTORY CERTIFICATES	**IT IS HEREBY CERTIFIED...** (to be included if appropriate)
TESTIMONIUM	**IN WITNESS** whereof the parties hereto have hereunto set their hands the day and year first herein written.
ATTESTATION	**SIGNED** and **DELIVERED** by the said John Citizen in the presence of:
	SIGNED and **DELIVERED** by the said Patrick Pensioner in the presence of:

8.2.5 ANALYSIS OF DEED

8.2.5.1 Commencement and date

The general practice is to commence a deed with the words **'THIS ASSIGNMENT'** if the deed is an assignment and **'THIS CONVEYANCE'** if the deed is a conveyance. Section 64(2)(a) of the 2009 Act provides that an instrument is a deed if it is described at its head by words such as 'Assignment', 'Conveyance', 'Charge', 'Surrender', 'Deed', 'Indenture', 'Lease', 'Mortgage', or other heading appropriate to the deed in question. Section 64(2)(b) sets out the manner of execution (see **8.2.5.16**) and s 64(2)(c) provides that an instrument is a deed if it is delivered as a deed by the person executing it or by a person authorised to do so on that person's behalf.

When the deed is in draft form the date will be left blank. The appropriate date to insert on completion is the date of execution, that is when the deed is signed by the party giving effect to the transaction. This will usually be a vendor. Delivery may often occur after execution. In strict conveyancing theory no date is necessary provided there is alternate evidence of the date of execution. However, from a practical point of view the deed will not be stamped without the insertion of the date. A penalty is incurred for late stamping.

A deed may be delivered subject to some condition being fulfilled. The deed is then stated to be held in escrow. The deed does not become effective until the condition is fulfilled and that date is then the date of execution.

8.2.5.2   Parties

The names and addresses of the parties suffice to identify them. All persons necessary to enable the deed to achieve all its objects should be joined as parties to the deed. In a straightforward deed, the parties to be joined will be obvious. Examples include: vendor and purchaser; lessor and lessee; mortgagor and mortgagee. In some circumstances it may be necessary for a spouse's or civil partner's prior consent to be endorsed on a deed or for the deed to be executed by a third party. Examples include a lending institution to release a loan or a liquidator to confirm a sale.

If there are only two parties to the deed the first party is generally referred to as the party 'of the one part' and the second party is referred to as the party 'of the other part'. If there are more than two parties they are generally described as the party 'of the first part', the party 'of the second part', the party 'of the third part' and so on. It is also common, after stating the names and addresses of the parties, to provide that they shall thereafter be called not by their name but by the term which indicates their capacity, for example 'the vendor', 'the purchaser', or 'the mortgagee'. This is done by inserting after the parties' name and address the words '(hereinafter called "the vendor/purchaser/mortgagee")'. This practice may also be used to describe the term of a lease, ie 'the term', the lease itself, ie 'the lease', or even the description of the property, ie 'the property'.

When listing the parties to the deed the party granting the property should always be listed first and the party taking the property listed last.

8.2.5.3   Recitals of title

Recitals are not necessary to the validity of the deed but they are to be recommended provided they are not over-used. They are designed to make the title more intelligible as they provide a history of the property from the root to the present day showing how the vendor became entitled. In older deeds recitals have been introduced by the words WHEREAS/AND WHEREAS but Judge Laffoy has suggested that this be replaced with the word RECITALS. (See her paper on Deeds and Contents of Deeds delivered at the Law Society CPD seminar on the Land and Conveyancing Law Reform Act, 2009 held on 25 September 2009.)

In conveyances recitals may be abbreviated to recite merely that the vendor is seised of the property for the estate in question. In assignments, the person drafting the deed may skip from the root, that is the lease, to the assignment under which the vendor acquired title, but if anything unusual has occurred on title it is customary to recite this chronologically.

Recitals may provide assistance in terms of reconstructing the title in the event that any of the title deeds are lost or mislaid. Another advantage of recitals is that the party making the recital, usually the vendor, will subsequently be estopped from denying the truth of that recital.

Previously s 2 of the Vendor and Purchaser Act, 1874 provided that recitals in deeds 20 years old were sufficient evidence of the truth of what was recited unless it was proved to be inaccurate. This has now been repealed and replaced by s 59(1) of the 2009 Act. This similarly states that recitals, statements, and descriptions of facts, matters, and parties contained in instruments, statutory provisions, or statutory declarations 15 years old at the date of the contract are, unless and except so far as they are proved to be inaccurate, sufficient evidence of the truth of such facts, matters, and parties.

8.2.5.4   Recitals of contract

The practice is to recite the agreement between the parties in a general way. This introduces the rest of the deed by explaining the intention of the current deed.

8.2.5.5 Testatum

Testatum is the start of the most important part of the deed. The testatum is a declaration that what follows contains details of the operation of the deed.

8.2.5.6 Consideration

It is necessary to state the consideration in the deed in order to:

(a) show that it is not a voluntary deed;

(b) enable a receipt clause to be included; and

(c) enable the liability of the deed to stamp duty to be ascertained as required by law.

8.2.5.7 Receipt clause

A receipt clause is necessary in the body of the deed in order for the purchaser and his successors in title to avail of certain statutory protection. This statutory protection was previously provided by the Conveyancing Act, 1881.

Section 54 of the Conveyancing Act, 1881 made a receipt in the body of a deed a sufficient discharge for the purchase money. Section 55 of the same Act provided that a receipt in the deed was sufficient evidence of the payment of the purchase money in favour of a subsequent purchaser, provided he or she was a bona fide purchaser for value without notice. Payment of the purchase money to the vendor's solicitor in exchange for the deed was authorised by s 56.

These sections have been repealed by the 2009 Act and have been restated with some modification by s 77. Section 77(1) provides that a receipt for consideration in the body of a deed is sufficient discharge for the consideration to the person giving it, without any further receipt being endorsed on the deed. Section 77(2) provides that a receipt for consideration in the body of a deed is, in favour of a subsequent purchaser without notice otherwise, conclusive evidence of the giving of the whole consideration. Section 77(3) authorises payment of the purchase money to the vendor's solicitor in exchange for the executed deed.

8.2.5.8 Operative words

Words of grant

Words of grant are a statement as to what the vendor does by virtue of the deed. It is important to select the words of grant appropriate to the nature of the title being passed. Appropriate words of grant are:

'Grant' or 'Convey' = conveyance of an unregistered freehold interest.

'Demise' = creation of a leasehold interest.

'Assign' = assignment of an unregistered leasehold interest.

'Transfer' = all interests registered in the Land Registry (both freehold and leasehold).

'Surrender' = surrender of lease to reversioner.

'Release' = discharge of mortgage.

'Appoint' = exercise of power.

'Confirm' = confirmation of equitable interest supplemental to transfer of legal interest.

Capacity

It is also usual for the deed to state the appropriate capacity in which the vendor sells. If these words are omitted the validity of the deed is not affected, but the purchaser loses the benefit of various covenants for title that are implied into the deed. These covenants were previously implied by s 7 of the Conveyancing Act, 1881. This has now been repealed by the 2009 Act and the new covenants are set out in ss 80 and 81 and Schedule 3 of the 2009 Act.

When the correct words are used these covenants for title are automatically implied in the deed.

In a conveyance for value, if the vendor was selling 'as beneficial owner' and this was stated in the deed, four covenants were implied by virtue of s 7 of the Conveyancing Act, 1881. These were that:

(a)   the vendor had full right to convey the property;

(b)   the vendor warranted a covenant for quiet enjoyment;

(c)   the vendor warranted that the property was free from encumbrances (save and except for any encumbrances disclosed in the deed, such as that the property was subject to a leasehold interest); and

(d)   the vendor would execute further assurances to vest the interest in the purchaser if this was necessary.

Where the words 'as personal representative', 'as trustee', 'as mortgagee', or 'under order of court' were used only one covenant was implied, namely a covenant that the purchaser would receive the property free from encumbrances created by that party.

Section 7 of the 1881 Act continues to apply in relation to deeds executed prior to the commencement of the 2009 Act. For deeds after commencement the covenants for title will be as set out in ss 80 and 81 and Schedule 3 of the 2009 Act. These effectively restate the covenants for title and provide that they are deemed to be made by the person or by each person who conveys, to the extent of the estate or interest or share of the estate or interest expressed to be conveyed by such person. Sections 80 and 81 and Schedule 3 set out the implied covenants in respect of different classes of deed and thus the specific provisions should be examined in any action to enforce such covenants.

8.2.5.9   Parcels

'Parcels' is a technical term denoting a description in words of the property being assured. It should be strictly accurate and care should be taken that a map, if attached, does not conflict with the words. It should describe only the property which the vendor has contracted to sell and which the purchaser has contracted to buy. It should be sufficient so as to ensure that someone reading the deed will be able to correctly identify the property.

The parcels clause generally commences with the words **'ALL THAT AND THOSE'** followed by a clear and accurate description of the property. The description of the property may be contained in the body of the deed or alternatively the parcels clause may refer to a schedule to the deed containing the description. If a schedule is used it should be inserted after the testimonium and before the attestation clause.

If, for some reason, a map is being attached to the deed, eg there is a subdivision, then this should be drawn by a professional draftsman.

In the event that there was an error made in the description of the property s 6(1) and (2) of the Conveyancing Act, 1881 assisted. This section provided that a conveyance operated to convey with the land all buildings, fixtures, ditches, fences, easements, rights, etc appertaining to the land and all houses, outhouses, sewers, gutters, drains, etc. Section 6 has now been repealed by the 2009 Act and replaced by s 71 of that Act. Section 71(1) provides that a conveyance of land includes, and conveys with the land, all buildings, commons, ditches, drains, erections, fences, fixtures, hedges, water, watercourses and other features forming part of the land, advantages, easements, liberties, privileges, *profits à prendre* and rights appertaining or annexed to the land. This section takes effect subject to the terms of the conveyance.

Section 71(2) goes on to provide that a conveyance of land which has houses or other buildings on it includes, and conveys with the land, houses, or other buildings all:

(a)   areas, cellars, cisterns, courts, courtyards, drainpipes, drains, erections, fixtures, gardens, lights, outhouses, passages, sewers, watercourses, yards, and other features forming part of the land, houses or other buildings; and

(b) advantages, easements, liberties, privileges, *profits à prendre* and rights appertaining or annexed to the land, houses or other buildings.

Obviously, if a new easement is being created this must be expressly stated and, notwithstanding the benefits of these statutes, it is also the practice to refer to existing easements in the parcels clause.

It is worth noting that while s 71 and many other sections in the 2009 Act refer to 'conveyance' the definition of conveyance in s 3 of the Act includes *inter alia* assignment, charge, lease, mortgage, release, surrender, transfer, and every other assurance by way of instrument except a will.

8.2.5.10 Habendum

The main object of the habendum is to mark out, define, or specify the quantum of the estate being taken by the purchaser. In older deeds this part commences with the words 'TO HOLD'.

This is done by using appropriate words of limitation. It is important that the correct words of limitation are used as otherwise there will be a doubt as to the interest that passed. The correct words of limitation are:

Conveyance: 'in fee simple'

Section 51 of the Conveyancing Act, 1881 provided that 'in fee simple' were the only words of limitation required to convey a fee simple. Previously the words 'and his heirs' were essential. Section 51 has now been repealed by the 2009 Act and s 67(1) provides that a conveyance of unregistered land with or without words of limitation passes the fee simple or the other entire estate or interest which the grantor had power to create or convey, unless a contrary intention appears in the conveyance. Despite this section it is crucial to include the correct words of limitation so as to put the matter beyond doubt.

Lease: 'for the term of years'.

Assignment: 'for the unexpired residue of the term of years'.

Previously the habendum contained a conveyance to uses, ie the time-honoured formula 'unto and to the use of' the grantee. This was necessary in the case of a voluntary conveyance to prevent a resulting use in favour of the grantor coming into effect. These words were, however, not strictly necessary in the case of a conveyance for consideration, but it became common practice to include them in every deed. The 2009 Act has now repealed the Statute of Uses (Ireland) Act, 1634 which required this formula of words and s 62(2) provides that a deed is fully effective without the need for any conveyance to uses and will pass possession or the right to possession of the land, without actual entry, unless subject to some prior right to possession. Thus a conveyance to uses is no longer required. Section 62(3) affirms the position by providing that in the case of a voluntary conveyance a resulting use for the grantor is not implied merely because the land is not expressed to be conveyed for the use or benefit of the grantee. Therefore it is no longer necessary for a deed to contain the words 'unto and to the use of' after 1 December 2009.

Section 67(1) of the 2009 Act also provides that words of limitation in a conveyance of unregistered land are no longer required. A conveyance of unregistered land with or without words of limitation, passes the fee simple or the other entire estate or interest which the grantor had power to create or convey, unless a contrary intention appears in the conveyance. In addition, s 67(2) provides that the word 'successors' is no longer required in a conveyance to a corporation sole. This is without prejudice to any act or thing done or any interest disposed of or acquired before the commencement of the Act; s 67(4).

If there are two or more purchasers it should be stated in the habendum whether they are taking the property as joint tenants or as tenants in common. If no words of severance are included, such as 'in equal shares', 'equally', or 'as tenants in common', they will take as joint tenants. If the purchasers are taking the property as tenants in common, the respective shares of each party should be identified.

If the sale is subject to any existing encumbrances this must be disclosed at the end of the habendum by using the words 'SUBJECT TO' followed by a description of the encumbrances. An example would be a freehold interest sold subject to a lease or if, for example, the property is subject to a right of way.

Previously s 63 of the Conveyancing Act, 1881 provided that unless a contrary intention was expressed in the deed, a conveyance was effectual to pass all the estate, right, title, and interest vested in the conveying party to the purchaser. This has now been repealed and replaced by s 76 of the 2009 Act. Section 76 similarly provides that, subject to the terms of the conveyance, a conveyance of land passes all the claim, demand, estate, interest, right, and title which the grantor has or has power to convey in, to, or on the land conveyed or expressed or intended to be conveyed. This 'all estate clause' is extremely useful in a situation where the vendor holds a leasehold and freehold interest in the same property but forgets to assign the leasehold interest with the freehold.

While words of limitation are no longer required it remains prudent to include them so that there is no possible doubt about the nature of the interest being passed.

8.2.5.11   Covenants and conditions/Exceptions and reservations

These will depend on the circumstances of the particular transaction and could include a covenant to build or the reservation of a right of way.

The most frequent covenant arising is a covenant to pay rent contained in a deed of assignment as follows:

> 'THE PURCHASERS and each of them hereby covenant with the vendor that they the Purchasers will henceforth during the continuance of the said term pay the rent reserved by and observe the covenants on the part of the Lessee and conditions contained in the Lease and will at all times keep the vendor effectually indemnified against all actions and proceedings, costs, damages, expenses, claims, demands and liability whatsoever by reason or on account of the non-payment of the said rent or any part thereof or the breach non-performance or non-observance of the said covenants and conditions or any of them.'

Section 81 and Schedule 3 (Part 3) of the 2009 Act now provide that in the case of an assignment of a leasehold interest for valuable consideration this covenant will be implied. This, however, may be modified by the express provisions of the assignment; s 81(5).

While all covenants bind the parties to the deed, previously only negative covenants ran with freehold land so as to bind the successors in title of the covenantor (*Tulk v Moxhay* (1848) 2 Ph 774). A positive covenant is a covenant to do something while a negative covenant is a covenant not to do something.

Section 49(1) of the 2009 Act has now abolished the rule in *Tulk v Moxhay* and any other rules of common law and equity relating to the enforceability of a freehold covenant. Section 49(2) of the Act provides that any freehold covenant which imposes in respect of servient land an obligation to do or to refrain from doing any act or thing is enforceable by the dominant owner for the time being against the servient owner for the time being. Thus both positive and negative covenants now run with freehold land so as to bind the successors in title of the covenantor.

8.2.5.12   Statutory acknowledgement and undertaking

Where original documents of title are being retained by the vendor, under general condition 34 of the Contract for Sale, the vendor shall acknowledge the right of the purchaser to production of same and to delivery of copies thereof and undertakes to keep the documents in safe custody as provided for in the 2009 Act, s 84. This replaces s 9 of the Conveyancing Act, 1881 which has been repealed.

This usually arises where part only of a property is being sold. The purchaser will receive certified copies of the title documents and the following acknowledgement and undertaking will be included in the deed:

> 'The vendor hereby acknowledges the right of the purchaser to production of the title documents listed in the schedule hereto (possession of which is retained by the vendor) and to delivery of

copies thereof and hereby undertakes with the purchaser for the safe custody of the said documents.'

The acknowledgement imposes the following obligations on the vendor:

(a)   to produce the documents for inspection;

(b)   to produce the documents for demand for court hearings to establish title; and

(c)   to furnish copies of the documents on request.

The undertaking imposes an obligation on the vendor to keep the documents complete, safe, uncancelled, and undefaced (s 84(3)) unless destroyed by fire or other inevitable accident (s 84(6)). This acknowledgement and undertaking is prepared by and at the expense of the purchaser.

8.2.5.13   Statutory certificates

Statutory certificates relating to stamp duty, consanguinity relief (relationship certificate), and s 12 and s 45 of the Land Act 1965 are no longer required but will be seen in older deeds. These certificates often related to the location of the property, the consideration passing, or the relationship between the parties. Only two generally used certificates remain. These are:

Family Home Protection Act, 1976, s 14 certificate/Civil Partnership and Certain Rights and Obligations of Cohabitants Act, 2010, s 38

This certificate is required on a deed transferring a family home/shared home from one spouse/civil partner into the joint names of both spouses/civil partners in order to claim exemption from stamp duty, Land Registry fees, and Registry of Deeds fees. The certificate states:

'It is hereby further certified that the property hereby transferred is a family home/ shared home within the meaning of the Family Home Protection Act, 1976/Civil Partnership and Certain Rights and Obligations of Cohabitants Act, 2010 and that this Instrument creates a joint tenancy of a family home/shared home and is exempt from stamp duty, Land Registry fees and other Court fees by reason of Section 14 of the Family Home Protection Act, 1976/Section 38 of the Civil Partnership and Certain Rights and Obligations of Cohabitants Act, 2010.'

Companies Act, 2014, s 238 (previously Companies Act, 1990, s 29) certificate

This certificate should be included in transactions between natural persons and bodies corporate and in transactions between bodies corporate to show that the parties are not connected with one another or are connected with one another and the requisite resolution has been passed by the companies involved. Section 238 provides that a company may not enter into an arrangement with a connected person without the arrangement having been first approved by resolution of the company in general meeting. The recommended certificates (relating to the 1990 Act) are set out in a Practice Note, Law Society *Gazette*, December 1991.

Section 96 of the Stamp Duties Consolidation Act, 1999 exempts from stamp duty any transfer between spouses/civil partners. To obtain the benefit of this exemption this certificate must be inserted in the deed.

8.2.5.14   Stamp duty

As stamp duty certificates are no longer required in deeds it is important that solicitors have a record of the client's instructions as to the amount of stamp duty payable as the solicitor will be returning this information to the Revenue Commissioners via the e-stamping system. The Conveyancing Committee have drafted a precedent record sheet for use and retention on the solicitor's file in case the transaction is subsequently audited by Revenue. See Practice Note, Law Society *Gazette*, December 2015. The record sheet is available in the precedent area of the Law Society website.

8.2.5.15   Testimonium

This part of the deed links the body of the deed to the execution thereof. The words generally used are:

'*IN WITNESS whereof the parties hereto have hereunto set their respective hands the day and year first above WRITTEN.*

If the parties are companies then the testimonium will state that the parties have '*caused their common seals' to be affixed hereto the day and year first above **WRITTEN**.*'

If the deed refers to a schedule this should be inserted at this point, ie after the testimonium and before the attestation.

8.2.5.16   Execution/attestation

This is where the deed is signed and delivered. Delivery of the deed indicates an intention that the deed should become operative. A deed is deemed to be delivered on execution. Previously execution by an individual required the deed to be sealed. Section 64(1) of the 2009 Act now provides that any rule of law which requires a seal for the valid execution of a deed by an individual or authority to deliver a deed to be given by deed is abolished. Section 64(2)(b) provides that a deed may be executed in the following manner:

- if made by an individual:

  (a)   it is signed by the individual in the presence of a witness who attests the signature; or

  (b)   signed by a person at the individual's direction given in the presence of a witness who attests the signature; or

  (c)   acknowledged by the individual in the presence of a witness who attests the signature,

- if made by a company registered in the State, it is executed under the seal of the company in accordance with its Articles of Association;

- if made by a body corporate in the State it is executed in accordance with the legal requirements governing execution of deeds by such a body corporate;

- if made by a foreign body corporate it is executed in accordance with the legal requirements governing execution of the instrument in question by such a body corporate in the jurisdiction where it is incorporated.

Section 64(2)(c) of the Act provides that in order to be a deed the instrument must be delivered as a deed by the person executing it or by a person authorised to do so on that person's behalf.

Attestation means the proper witnessing of signatures.

The type of attestation clause will depend on the parties to the transaction. The correct attestation clause for a person is:

'*SIGNED and DELIVERED*

by the vendor in the presence of:'

The correct attestation clause for a body corporate is:

'*PRESENT when the common seal of*

the vendor was affixed hereto:'

8.3 Drafting a Transfer (A Deed in Relation to Registered Land)

In the case of both freehold and leasehold registered land the appropriate deed is a transfer. The Land Registration Rules, 2012 prescribe the forms of transfer to be used and the forms are set out in the attached Schedule of Forms. The correct form and wording must be used, otherwise the dealing will be rejected by the Land Registry. This is discussed in more detail in **chapter 14**.

8.4 Procedure for Registration of Deeds in the Registry of Deeds

The Registry of Deeds is under the control and management of the Property Registration Authority. The function of the Registry of Deeds is to provide a system of registration for deeds affecting unregistered land. Deeds which are registered in the Registry of Deeds have legal priority over unregistered deeds or deeds registered later in time.

When a deed is registered in the Registry of Deeds it is not filed there. Instead it is returned to the party who delivered it for registration. The document previously filed in the Registry of Deeds was a memorial which summarised the provisions of the deed. Since 1 May 2008 memorials are no longer required and applications for registration in the Registry of Deeds are made by way of a form set out in the Schedule of Forms to the Registration of Deeds Rules, 2008 (SI 52/2008). There is no statutory requirement to register but failure to do so may result in a loss of priority. The act of registration does not guarantee title to the land.

Section 32(1) of the 2006 Act provides a definition of a deed and thus a list of documents which may be accepted for registration as a deed. The list is wider than the normal, previously understood, definition of a deed, that is, a document under seal. In fact s 64(1) of the 2009 Act now provides that any rule of law which requires a seal for the valid execution of a deed by an individual is abolished. See **8.2.5.16**.

8.4.1 REQUIREMENT FOR REGISTRATION

Previously priority was conferred on a deed on the basis of the date and time of registration of that deed in the Registry of Deeds. Sections 37 and 38 of the Registration of Deeds and Title Act, 2006 ('the 2006 Act') now provide that priority is determined by the serial number allocated to every application for registration. This does not affect rules of law and equity such as the doctrine of notice.

Purchasers can protect themselves by searching the records to be satisfied that there are no registered deeds ranking in priority to their proposed purchase and by registering their deed to obtain priority. Registration gives statutory priority to the deed over other deeds affecting the same property that are either registered later or not registered at all. The application must consist of the prescribed application form duly completed, the original deed, and the prescribed fee. The current fees are set out in the Registry of Deeds (Fees) Order, 2008 (SI 51/2008). Forms completed by a solicitor need only be signed. Where a form is completed by any other person it must be sworn.

8.4.2 APPLICATION FORM

The application form must contain the following:

    (a)   name of deed ie whether conveyance, assignment, grant, assent, judgment mortgage, or other;

(b)   date of deed;

(c)   all grantors ie the names of all parties granting property in the deed;

(d)   all grantees ie the names of all parties obtaining an interest in the property;

(e)   a description of the property (to include the county and barony or the city or town and parish). Property details that are not in the deed should not be entered on the form;

(f)   details of the original lease when applying for registration of an assignment.

The application form will be compared with the deed to ensure that:

(a)   the form relates to the deed;

(b)   the form has been signed by the individual solicitor acting for the applicant;

(c)   the solicitor's details are on the form or applicant's details in the case of personal applications;

(d)   the form has been correctly sworn where appropriate;

(e)   the name of the deed has been inserted;

(f)   the date of the deed has been inserted;

(g)   the fee is endorsed thereon where payable;

(h)   all grantors in the deed are listed correctly on the form;

(i)   all grantees in the deed are listed correctly on the form; and

(j)   the property details are correct.

Once the application form correctly reflects the details from the deed registration can proceed. A serial number is allocated, details of the registration are recorded on the system, a certificate of registration stamp is endorsed on the deed, and the deed is returned to the lodging party.

If the application is not in order it is returned to the lodging party with the reasons for rejection. On re-lodgement the application is deemed to be a new application. For further information see the Registry of Deeds Practice Direction (1 December 2009) Registry of Deeds Procedures.

8.4.3   FUNCTION OF REGISTRAR

It is important to note the difference between the functions of the Registrar of Deeds in the Registry of Deeds and the Registrar of Titles in the Land Registry. The Registrar in the Registry of Deeds will register a deed provided the statutory particulars are present. The Registrar is not concerned with any question relating to the validity of the deed. This is the function of the purchaser's solicitor. By contrast the Registrar of Titles in the Land Registry must be satisfied that any transfer which is lodged for registration is a valid transfer and, consequently, must ensure that title is validly passing to the transferee on foot of the documents which are lodged for registration.

For example, a conveyance by a husband/wife of a property which is a 'family home' within the meaning of the Family Home Protection Act, 1976 without the consent of his or her spouse may be registered in the Registry of Deeds although it is void under the Family Home Protection Act, 1976. In the Land Registry, a transfer of the same property would not be registered by the Registrar of Titles without the prior consent of the spouse and verification of the marriage by statutory declaration.

This is due to the fact that title registered in the Land Registry is guaranteed by the State.

8.4.4 FIRST REGISTRATION

By virtue of rule 51 of the Land Registration Rules, 2012 until such time as an application for first registration of an unregistered title has been successfully completed by the settlement of a draft folio, or draft entry for a folio in the Land Registry, that title remains unregistered and must be treated as such. Therefore a purchaser of an unregistered title, which becomes compulsorily registrable by virtue of that acquisition, should ensure that the deed of assurance and any charge are registered in the Registry of Deeds as expeditiously as possible to secure priority. Once this registration is completed the application for first registration can be made. Where purchasing property that is awaiting first registration, the purchaser's solicitor must investigate the unregistered title in the usual manner and, it is recommended, have sight of the vendor's application for first registration together with any rulings on title raised by the Land Registry and responses thereto. Unless first registration has been completed in advance of closing, the deed to be drafted and executed is for an unregistered title and the appropriate words of limitation are required. The vendor may not be described as 'the person entitled to be the registered owner'. After completion the purchaser's deed must be registered in the Registry of Deeds and then lodged for first registration either taking account of the existing statement of title drafted by the vendor's solicitor or that application may be withdrawn and a new statement of title drafted. See Practice Note, December 2014, Law Society *Gazette*.

8.5 Sample Deeds

8.5.1 FREEHOLD CONVEYANCE

THIS CONVEYANCE made the   day of   Two Thousand and   BETWEEN   of   (hereinafter called 'the vendor(s)' which expression shall where the context so admits or requires include his/her/their executors and administrators/its successors) of the One Part and   of   (hereinafter called 'the purchaser(s)' which expression shall where the context so admits or requires include his/her/their executors administrators and assigns/its successors and assigns) of the Other Part.

RECITALS

1. The vendor(s) is/are seised of the hereditaments and premises more particularly described in the Schedule hereto (hereinafter called 'the scheduled property') and expressed to be hereby assured for an estate in fee simple in possession free from encumbrances.

2. The vendor(s) has/have agreed with the purchaser(s) for the sale to him/her/them of the scheduled property for an estate in fee simple in possession free from encumbrances for the sum of €

NOW THIS CONVEYANCE WITNESSETH that in pursuance of the said agreement and in consideration of the sum of € now paid by the purchaser(s) to the vendor(s) (the receipt whereof the vendor(s) hereby acknowledge(s)) the vendor(s) as beneficial owner(s) hereby CONVEY(S) to the purchaser(s) as joint tenants/as tenants in common (insert shareholding i.e. in equal shares) ALL THAT AND THOSE the scheduled property in fee simple.

IN WITNESS whereof the parties hereto have hereunto set their hands the day and year first herein WRITTEN.

SCHEDULE

(Description of premises)

SIGNED AND DELIVERED

by the vendor(s) in the
presence of:

SIGNED AND DELIVERED
by the purchaser(s) in the
presence of:

I,   being the lawful spouse/civil partner of the within named vendor in pursuance of the provisions of the Family Home Protection Act, 1976/Civil Partnership and
Certain Rights and Obligations of Cohabitants Act, 2010 HEREBY CONSENT to the assurance of the within property to the purchaser for the sum of €

SIGNED by the said
in the presence of:

Dated the   day of   20
One Part
And
Other Part
CONVEYANCE
Solicitors

8.5.2   ASSIGNMENT OF ENTIRE LEASEHOLD INTEREST

THIS ASSIGNMENT made the   day of   Two Thousand and
BETWEEN   of   (hereinafter called 'the vendor(s)' which
expression shall where the context so admits or requires include his/her/their executors and
administrators/its successors) of the One Part and   of   (hereinafter called 'the
purchaser(s)' which expression shall where the context so admits or requires include his/
her/their executors administrators and assigns/its successors and assigns) of the Other Part.

RECITALS

1. By Indenture of Lease (hereinafter called 'the Lease') dated   the day
    of   and made between   of the One Part and   of the Other
    Part the premises therein and in the Schedule hereto described and intended to be
    hereby assured (hereinafter called 'the scheduled property') were demised by the
    said   to the said for   a term of years from the   day of   sub-
    ject to the yearly rent of €   thereby reserved and to the covenants on the
    part of the Lessee and conditions therein contained

2. Pursuant to the covenant in that behalf contained in the Lease the Lessee duly
    erected the dwellinghouse and premises now standing on the scheduled property
    and intended to be hereby assigned.

3. By divers mesne assurances acts in the Law events and ultimately by Indenture of
    Assignment dated the   day of   and made between   of
    the One Part and the vendor of the Other Part the scheduled property became
    vested in the vendor for the residue of the term of years granted by the Lease subject
    to the yearly rent thereby reserved and to the covenants on the part of the Lessee
    and conditions therein contained.

4. The vendor(s) has/have agreed with the purchaser(s) for the sale to the purchaser(s)
    subject to the covenants and conditions in the Lease but otherwise free from en-
    cumbrances for the sum of €   of the scheduled property.

NOW THIS ASSIGNMENT WITNESSETH that in pursuance of the said agreement and in
consideration of the sum of €   paid by the purchaser(s) to the vendor(s) (the
receipt of which the vendor(s) hereby acknowledge(s)) the vendor(s) as beneficial owner(s)
HEREBY ASSIGN(S) to the purchaser(s) as joint tenants/tenants in common (insert shareholding i.e. in equal shares) ALL AND SINGULAR the scheduled property henceforth for
all the residue now unexpired of the said term granted by the Lease and subject to the

yearly rent thereby reserved and to the covenants on the part of the Lessee and conditions therein contained.

AND THE PURCHASER(S) hereby covenant(s) with the vendor(s) that he/she/they the purchaser(s) will henceforth during the continuance of the said term pay the rent reserved by and observe the covenants on the part of the Lessee and conditions contained in the Lease and will at all times keep the vendor(s) effectually indemnified against all actions and proceedings costs damages expenses claims demands and liability whatsoever by reason or on account of the non payment of the said rent or any part thereof or the breach non performance or non observance of the said covenants and conditions or any of them.

IN WITNESS whereof the parties hereto have hereunto set their hands the day and year first herein WRITTEN.

SCHEDULE

(Description of premises)

SIGNED AND DELIVERED
by the vendor(s) in the
presence of:

SIGNED AND DELIVERED
by the purchaser(s) in the
presence of:

I,   being the lawful spouse/civil partner of the within named vendor in pursuance of the provisions of the Family Home Protection Act, 1976/Civil Partnership and Certain Rights and Obligations of Cohabitants Act, 2010 HEREBY CONSENT to the assurance of the within property to the purchaser for the sum of €.

SIGNED by the said
in the presence of:

Dated the day of 20	
	One Part
	And
	Other Part
	ASSIGNMENT
	Solicitors

8.5.3 ASSIGNMENT OF PART OF A LEASEHOLD INTEREST

THIS ASSIGNMENT made the   day of   Two Thousand and   BETWEEN   of   (hereinafter called 'the vendor(s)' which expression shall where the context so admits or requires include his/her/their executors and administrators/its successors) of the One Part and   of   (hereinafter called 'the purchaser(s)' which expression shall where the context so admits or requires include his/her/their executors administrators and assigns/its successors and assigns) of the Other Part.

RECITALS

1. By Indenture of Lease (hereinafter called 'the Lease') dated the   day of   and made between   of the One Part and   of the Other Part the premises therein and in the First Schedule hereto described and portion of which is intended to be hereby assured more particularly described in the Second Schedule hereto were demised by the said   to the said   years from the day of   subject to the yearly rent of €   (hereinafter called 'the rent') thereby reserved and to the covenants on the part of the Lessee and conditions therein contained.

2. By divers mesne assurances acts in the Law events and ultimately by Indenture of Assignment (hereinafter called 'the Assignment') dated the   day

of   and made between   (hereinafter called 'the previous Assignor') of the One Part and the vendor of the Other Part the premises intended to be hereby assured more particularly described in the Second Schedule hereto became vested in the vendor for the residue of the term of years granted by the Lease subject to the apportioned yearly rent thereby reserved as hereinafter recited and to the covenants on the part of the Lessee and conditions therein contained but otherwise free from encumbrances.

3. By the Assignment the rent was apportioned so that €   portion thereof was charged exclusively on the premises intended to be hereby assured more particularly described in the Second Schedule hereto and the balance thereof amounting to €   was charged upon the remainder of the premises described in the Lease which was retained by the previous Assignor and the vendor and the previous Assignor mutually covenanted to pay the apportioned part of the rent which ought to be paid by each of them as set out in the Assignment and to perform and observe the covenants on the part of the Lessee other than the covenant for payment of the entire of the rent and the conditions contained in the Lease in so far as same relate to their portion of the premises and to indemnify each other in respect of the apportioned part of the rent borne by each of them and the previous Assignor and the vendor declared that all monies which might become payable to either of them under the respective covenants for indemnity contained in the Assignment were charged on the portion of the premises belonging to the other of them.

4. The vendor(s) has/have agreed with the purchaser(s) for the sale to the purchaser(s) subject to the apportioned yearly rent and to the covenants and conditions in the Lease but otherwise free from encumbrances for the sum of €   of the property in the Second Schedule hereto.

NOW THIS ASSIGNMENT WITNESSETH that in pursuance of the said agreement and in consideration of the sum of €   now paid by the purchaser(s) to the vendor(s) (the receipt of which the vendor(s) hereby acknowledge(s)) the vendor(s) as beneficial owner(s) HEREBY ASSIGN(S) to the purchaser(s) as joint tenants/tenants in common (insert shareholding i.e. in equal shares) ALL AND SINGULAR the property described in the Second Schedule hereto henceforth for all the residue now unexpired of the said term granted by the Lease and subject to the apportioned yearly rent of €   thereby reserved and to the covenants on the part of the Lessee and conditions therein contained.

AND THE PURCHASER(S) hereby covenant(s) with the vendor(s) that he/she/they the purchaser(s) will henceforth during the continuance of the said term pay the apportioned rent reserved by and observe the covenants on the part of the Lessee and conditions contained in the Lease and will at all times keep the vendor(s) effectually indemnified against all actions and proceedings costs damages expenses claims demands and liability whatsoever by reason or on account of the non payment of the said rent or any part thereof or the breach non performance or non observance of the said covenants and conditions or any of them.

AND THE VENDOR(S) hereby assign(s) the benefit of the indemnity in respect of the balance of the rent contained in the Assignment and the statutory acknowledgement and undertaking for production of the title documents contained in the Third Schedule of the Assignment TO HOLD the same unto the purchaser(s) absolutely.

IN WITNESS whereof the parties hereto have hereunto set their hands the day and year first herein WRITTEN.

FIRST SCHEDULE

(Description of premises in Lease)

SECOND SCHEDULE

(Description of premises being assigned)

SIGNED AND DELIVERED
by the vendor(s) in the
presence of:

SIGNED AND DELIVERED
by the purchaser(s) in the
presence of:

I,   being the lawful spouse/civil partner of the within named vendor in pursuance of the provisions of the Family Home Protection Act, 1976/Civil Partnership and Certain Rights and Obligations of Cohabitants Act, 2010 HEREBY CONSENT to the assurance of the within property to the purchaser for the sum of €   .

SIGNED by the said
in the presence of:

Dated the   day of   20

One Part

And

Other Part

ASSIGNMENT

Solicitors

8.5.4   SPECIMEN ASSIGNMENT AND CONVEYANCE (ASSURANCE)

THIS ASSIGNMENT AND CONVEYANCE made the   day of   Two Thousand and   BETWEEN   of   (hereinafter called 'the vendors' which expression shall where the context so admits or requires include their executors and administrators) of the One Part and of (hereinafter called 'the purchasers' which expression shall where the context so admits or requires include their assigns and the executors, administrators and assigns of the survivor of them) of the Other Part.

RECITALS

1.   By Indenture of Lease dated the   day of   and made between the   of the One Part and   of the Other Part (hereinafter called 'the said Lease') ALL THAT AND THOSE the premises described in the Schedule hereto and intended to be hereby assured (hereinafter called 'the premises') were demised unto the said for a term of   years from the day of   (hereinafter called 'the term') subject to the yearly rent of (hereinafter called 'the rent') thereby reserved and to the covenants on the part of the Lessee and conditions therein contained.

2.   By divers mesne assurances acts in the law and events and ultimately by Indenture of Assignment dated the   day of   and made between   of the One Part and the vendors of the Other Part the premises therein and hereinafter more particularly described in the Schedule hereto and intended to be hereby assured were assigned to the vendors for all the residue then unexpired of the term of years subject to the rent reserved by the Lease and to the performance and observance of the covenants and conditions contained therein.

3.   By Vesting Certificate dated the   day of   (Reference No. GR.) the Registrar of Titles in exercise of the powers conferred on him by Section   of the Landlord and Tenant (Ground Rents) (No. 2) Act, 1978 vested the fee simple in the   premises therein and hereinafter more particularly described in the Schedule hereto and intended to be hereby assured in the vendors free from encumbrances and any intermediate interests.

4.   The vendors have agreed with the purchasers for the sale to them at the price or sum of Euro (€   ) of all their interest in the premises described in the Schedule hereto and intended to be hereby assured.

NOW THIS ASSIGNMENT AND CONVEYANCE WITNESSETH as follows:

1. In pursuance of the said agreement and in consideration of the said sum of Euro (€   ) now paid by the purchasers to the vendors (the receipt whereof the vendors hereby acknowledge) the vendors as beneficial owners HEREBY FIRSTLY CONVEY to the purchasers as joint tenants/tenants in common (insert shareholding i.e. in equal shares) ALL THAT AND THOSE the premises comprised in and demised by the said Lease as described in the Schedule hereto in fee simple AND HEREBY SECONDLY ASSIGN to the purchasers as joint tenants/tenants in common ALL THAT AND THOSE the premises comprised in and demised by the said Lease as described in the Schedule hereto for all the residue of the term of years granted by the Lease subject to the covenants by the Lessee and conditions therein contained save for payment of the rent insofar as the Lease still subsists.

IN WITNESS whereof the parties hereto have hereunto set their hands the day and year first herein WRITTEN.

SCHEDULE

ALL THAT AND THOSE the premises comprised in the said Lease and therein described as.

SIGNED AND DELIVERED by
the said   in
the presence of:

SIGNED AND DELIVERED by
the said   in the
presence of:

SIGNED AND DELIVERED by
the said   in
the presence of:

SIGNED AND DELIVERED by
the said   in
the presence of:

Dated the   day of   20

One Part

And

Other Part

ASSIGNMENT AND CONVEYANCE

Solicitors

8.5.4.1   Declaration of merger

If the freehold and leasehold titles are to be merged the following paragraph should be included in the deed after the recital of title and before the recital of the Contract for Sale:

'In so far as the same has not already merged the vendors hereby declare that the term shall forthwith merge in the freehold reversion thereof and thereby become extinguished.'

The deed will then become a deed of conveyance and the only operative words required are those appropriate to a freehold title, ie 'GRANT' or 'CONVEY'.

8.5.5   LAND REGISTRY TRANSFER (FREEHOLD FOLIO)

LAND REGISTRY

County   Folio

TRANSFER dated the   day of   20   .   the Registered Owner(s) in consideration of €   (the receipt of which is hereby

acknowledged) as beneficial owner(s) HEREBY TRANSFER(S) all the property described in Folio   of the Register County   to as joint tenants/tenants in common.

The address(es) of the purchaser(s) in the State for the service of notices and his/her/their description(s) is/are:

SIGNED AND DELIVERED
by the said
in the presence of:

SIGNED AND DELIVERED
by the said
in the presence of:

I,   being the lawful spouse/civil partner of the within named   hereby give my prior consent to the sale of the within described premises at the price of €   and I hereby endorse my said consent pursuant to Section 3 of the Family Home Protection Act, 1976/Civil Partnership and Certain Rights and Obligations of Cohabitants Act, 2010.

SIGNED by the said
in the presence of:

8.5.6 LAND REGISTRY TRANSFER (TRANSFER OF PART OF FOLIO)

LAND REGISTRY

County   Part of Folio

TRANSFER dated the   day of   20   .   the Registered Owner(s) in consideration of €   (the receipt of which is hereby acknowledged) as beneficial owner(s) HEREBY TRANSFER(S) the property described in the Schedule hereto (hereinafter called 'the Scheduled Property') being part of the property described in Folio   of the Register County   to   as joint tenants/tenants in common.

The address(es) of the purchaser(s) in the State for the service of notices and his/her/their description(s) is/are:

SCHEDULE

(Description of premises)

SIGNED AND DELIVERED
by the said
in the presence of:

SIGNED AND DELIVERED
by the said
in the presence of:

I,   being the lawful spouse/civil partner of the within named   hereby give my prior consent to the sale of the within described premises at the price of €   and I hereby endorse my said consent pursuant to Section 3 of the Family Home Protection Act, 1976/Civil Partnership and Certain Rights and Obligations of Cohabitants Act, 2010.

SIGNED by the said
in the presence of:

8.5.7 LAND REGISTRY TRANSFER (LEASEHOLD FOLIO)

LAND REGISTRY

County   Folio

TRANSFER dated the   day of   20   .   the Registered Owner(s) (hereinafter called 'the Transferor(s)') in consideration of €   (the receipt of which is hereby acknowledged) as beneficial owner(s) HEREBY TRANSFER(S) the property described in Folio   of the Register   of Leaseholders County to   (hereinafter called 'the Transferee(s)') as joint tenants/tenants in common.

The Transferee(s) hereby covenant(s) with the Transferor(s) that he/she/they will henceforth during the continuance of the term pay the rent reserved by and perform and observe the covenants conditions and stipulations contained in the Lease dated the day of   made between   of the One Part and   of the Other Part and on the part of the Lessee to be performed and observed and will indemnify and keep indemnified the Transferor(s) from and against all actions and proceedings costs damages expenses claims demands and liabilities whatsoever by reason or on account of the non payment of the said rent or any part thereof or the breach non performance or non observance of the said covenants and conditions or any of them.

The address(es) of the Transferee(s) in the State for the service of notices and his/her/their description(s) is/are:

SIGNED AND DELIVERED
by the said
in the presence of:

SIGNED AND DELIVERED
by the said
in the presence of:

I,   being the lawful spouse/civil partner of the within named   hereby give my prior consent to the sale of the within described premises at the price of €   and I hereby endorse my said consent pursuant to Section 3 of the Family Home Protection Act, 1976/Civil Partnership and Certain Rights and Obligations of Cohabitants Act, 2010.

SIGNED by the said
in the presence of:

8.5.8   LAND REGISTRY TRANSFER (LEASEHOLD FOLIO WITH VESTING CERTIFICATE CONTAINING DECLARATION OF MERGER)

LAND REGISTRY

County   Folio

TRANSFER dated the   day of   20 .   the Registered Owner(s) in consideration of €   (the receipt of which is hereby acknowledged) as beneficial owner(s) HEREBY TRANSFER(S) all the leasehold interest and the freehold interest in the property described in Folio   of the Register of Leaseholders County   being the property also described in Vesting Certificate No.   dated the day of   to   (hereinafter called 'the Transferee(s)') as joint tenants/tenants in common and the Transferee(s) being the person(s) becoming entitled to the entire beneficial interest in the said property HEREBY DECLARE(S) that the leasehold interest in the said Folio   of the Register of Leaseholders County   shall merge with and be extinguished in the fee simple interest vested by the said Vesting Certificate.

The address(es) of the Transferee(s) in the State for the service of notices and his/her/their description(s) is/are:

SIGNED AND DELIVERED
by the said
in the presence of:

SIGNED AND DELIVERED
by the said
in the presence of:

I,   being the lawful spouse/civil partner of the within named   hereby give my prior consent to the sale of the within described premises at the price of €   and I hereby endorse my said consent pursuant to Section 3 of the Family Home Protection Act, 1976/Civil Partnership and Certain Rights and Obligations of Cohabitants Act, 2010.

SIGNED by the said
in the presence of:

8.5.9   LAND REGISTRY VOLUNTARY TRANSFER RETAINING RIGHT OF RESIDENCE

LAND REGISTRY

County   Folio

TRANSFER dated the   day of   20 .   the Registered Owner(s) in consideration of the natural love and affection which he bears towards his son as beneficial owner(s) HEREBY TRANSFER(S) all the property described in Folio   of the Register County   to the said subject to and charged with a right of residence maintenance and support in favour of the said (and his wife) for the duration of their natural lives.

The address of   in the State for the service of notices and his description is:

hereby assents to the registration of the aforementioned right of residence maintenance and support as a burden on the property hereby transferred.

IT IS HEREBY FURTHER CERTIFIED by the party (or parties) becoming entitled to the entire beneficial interest in the property that the person (or each of the persons) becoming entitled to the entire beneficial interest in the property is related to the person (or each of the persons) immediately theretofore entitled to the entire beneficial interest in the property as lawful son (for example).

SIGNED AND DELIVERED
by the said
in the presence of:

SIGNED AND DELIVERED
by the said
in the presence of:

I,   being the lawful spouse/civil partner of the within named   hereby give my prior consent to the transfer of the within described property pursuant to the Family Home Protection Act, 1976/Civil Partnership and Certain Rights and Obligations of Cohabitants Act, 2010.

SIGNED by the said
in the presence of:

8.5.10   LAND REGISTRY TRANSFER OF FAMILY HOME INTO JOINT NAMES OF SPOUSES

LAND REGISTRY

County   Folio

TRANSFER dated the   day of   20 .   the Registered Owner in consideration of the natural love and affection which he bears towards his wife as beneficial owner HEREBY TRANSFERS all the property described in Folio of the Register County   to the said   and himself as joint tenants.

The address of   and   in the State for the service of notices and their descriptions are:

IT IS HEREBY CERTIFIED that the property hereby transferred is a family home within the meaning of the Family Home Protection Act, 1976 and that this Instrument creates a joint tenancy of a family home and is exempt from stamp duty, Land Registry fees and other Court fees by reason of Section 14 of the Family Home Protection Act, 1976.

IT IS HEREBY FURTHER CERTIFIED by the party (or parties) becoming entitled to the entire beneficial interest in the property that the person (or each of the persons) becoming entitled to the entire beneficial interest in the property is related to the person (or each of the persons) immediately theretofore entitled to the entire beneficial interest in the property as lawful spouse.

SIGNED AND DELIVERED
by the said
in the presence of:

SIGNED AND DELIVERED
by the said
in the presence of:

8.5.11 LAND REGISTRY TRANSFER OF DUBLIN CORPORATION HOUSE HELD UNDER TRANSFER ORDER (LEASEHOLD FOLIO)

LAND REGISTRY

County   Folio

TRANSFER dated the   day of   20 .   the Registered Owner(s) in consideration of €   (the receipt of which is hereby acknowledged) as beneficial owner(s) with the consent of The Right Honourable The Lord Mayor Aldermen and Burgesses of Dublin (hereinafter called 'the Corporation') HEREBY TRANSFER(S) all the property described in Folio   of the Register of Leaseholders County   to   as joint tenants/tenants in common subject to the terms conditions and special conditions affecting the same contained in a Transfer Order dated the day of and   under the Housing Act, 1966.

The said   hereby covenant(s) with the said   that he/she/they will henceforth pay the rent reserved by the Transfer Order and will perform and observe all the covenants on the part of the Transferee and conditions therein contained and will indemnify and keep indemnified the said   his/her/their executors administrators and assigns from and against all actions and proceedings costs damages expenses claims demands and liabilities whatsoever by reason or on account of the non-payment of the said rent or any part thereof of the breach non performance or non observance of the said covenants and conditions or any of them. The address(es) of the said   in the State for the service of notices and his/her/their description(s) is/are:

SIGNED AND DELIVERED
by the said
in the presence of:

SIGNED AND DELIVERED
by the said
in the presence of:

The Right Honourable The Lord Mayor Aldermen and Burgesses of Dublin hereby consent to the within transfer.

8.5.12   CONVEYANCE OF A FAMILY HOME SUBJECT TO A MORTGAGE, BY A HUSBAND TO HIMSELF AND HIS WIFE AS JOINT TENANTS, THE MORTGAGEE PARTICIPATING TO RELEASE THE HUSBAND FROM HIS SOLE COVENANT TO PAY THE MORTGAGE DEBT AND TO OBTAIN A JOINT AND SEVERAL COVENANT FROM THE HUSBAND AND THE WIFE

THIS CONVEYANCE made the day   of   BETWEEN   of   (hereinafter called 'the Husband') of the first part a Building Society incorporated under the Building Societies Acts, 1976 to 1989 having its chief office at   (hereinafter called 'the Mortgagee') of the second part and the said   and   of   (hereinafter called 'the Wife') (both of whom are hereinafter collectively called 'the Husband and the Wife') of the third part.

RECITALS

A.   The Husband is seised of the premise described in the Schedule hereto (hereinafter called 'the Premises') for an estate in fee simple in possession subject to the Mortgage next hereinafter recited but otherwise free from incumbrances.

B.   By a Mortgage (hereinafter called 'the Mortgage') dated the   day of   made between the Husband of the one part and the Mortgagee of the other part the Premises were conveyed unto the Mortgagee in fee simple by way of Mortgage to secure payment to the Mortgagee of the principal sum of €   (hereinafter called 'the Mortgage debt') and interest thereon as therein provided.

C.   The Mortgage debt remains owing to the Mortgagee on the security of the Mortgage but all interest thereon accrued due at the date hereof has been paid.

D.   The Premises constitute the family home within the meaning of the Family Home Protection Act, 1976 (hereinafter called 'the Act of 1976') of the Husband and the Wife who are married to each other.

E.   The Husband is desirous of vesting the Premises in the Husband and the Wife as joint tenants subject to the Mortgage.

F.   The Mortgagee at the request of the Husband and the Wife and in consideration of the joint and several covenant by the Husband and the Wife with the Mortgagee hereinafter contained has agreed to join in these presents for the purpose of signifying its consent to the vesting in the Premises in the Husband and the Wife as joint tenants in the manner hereinafter appearing.

NOW THIS CONVEYANCE WITNESSETH as follows:

1.   For effectuating the said desire and in consideration of his natural love and affection for the Wife the Husband as settlor with the consent of the Mortgagee as signified by its execution of these presents hereby conveys unto the Husband and the Wife ALL THAT AND THOSE the Premises to the Husband and the Wife in fee simple as joint tenants subject to the Mortgage and the Mortgage debt and the interest hereafter to accrue due thereon.

2.   The Husband and the Wife hereby jointly and severally covenant with the Mortgagee to pay to the Mortgagee the Mortgage debt and interest thereon and all other monies now due or henceforth to become due to the Mortgagee under the Mortgage in the manner and at the times stipulated in the Mortgage and henceforth to perform and observe all covenants conditions provisos and agreements expressed or implied in or by the Mortgage and on the part of the Husband to be performed and observed as if the same were herein set forth at length and as if the names of the Husband and the Wife were substituted for the same of the Husband in the Mortgage.

3.   Nothing herein contained shall prejudice or affect the power of sale and the other powers contained or implied in the Mortgage or the remedies for recovering

payment of the monies thereby secured or any part thereof all of which powers and remedies shall continue in full form and effect.

IT IS HEREBY CERTIFIED for the purposes of Section 14 of the Act of 1976 that the Husband and the Wife are lawfully married to each other and that the Premises constitute their family home within the meaning of the Act of 1976.

IN WITNESS whereof the Husband and the Wife have hereunto set their respective hands and the common seal of the Mortgagee has been affixed hereto the day and year first above WRITTEN.

SCHEDULE

(The Premises)

ALL THAT AND THOSE

SIGNED and DELIVERED
by the HUSBAND
in the presence of:

SIGNED and DELIVERED
by the MORTGAGEE
in the presence of:

SIGNED and DELIVERED
by the HUSBAND
in the presence of:

SIGNED and DELIVERED
by the WIFE
in the presence of:

8.5.13 ASSIGNMENT OF AN UNENCUMBERED LEASEHOLD INTEREST IN A FAMILY HOME BY A HUSBAND TO HIMSELF AND HIS WIFE AS JOINT TENANTS

THIS ASSIGNMENT made the   day of   BETWEEN   of   (hereinafter called 'the Husband') of the one part and the said   and   of   (hereinafter called 'the Wife') (both of whom are hereinafter collectively called 'the Husband and the Wife') of the other part.

RECITALS

A. By a Lease (hereinafter called 'the Lease') dated the   day of   made between   of the one part and   of the other part the premises described in the Schedule hereto (hereinafter called 'the Premises') were demised to the said for the term of   years from the day of   (hereinafter called 'the term') subject to the yearly rent of €   (hereinafter called 'the rent') thereby reserved and the covenants on the part of the lessee and the conditions therein contained.

B. By divers mesne assignments acts in the law and events and ultimately by an Assignment dated the   day of   made between   of the one part and the Husband of the other part the Premises became and are now vested in the Husband for all the residue of the term subject to the rent and the covenants on the part of the lessee and the conditions contained in the Lease but otherwise free from incumbrances.

C. The Premises are the family home within the meaning of the Family Home Protection Act, 1976 (hereinafter called 'the Act of 1976') of the Husband and the Wife who are married to each other.

D. The Husband is desirous of vesting the Premises in himself and the Wife as joint tenants in the manner hereinafter appearing.

NOW THIS ASSIGNMENT WITNESSETH as follows:

1. For effectuating the said desire and in consideration of his natural love and affection for the Wife the Husband as settlor hereby assigns to the Husband and the Wife as joint tenants ALL THAT AND THOSE the Premises for all the residue now unexpired of the term subject to the rent and the covenants on the part of the lessee and the conditions contained in the Lease.

2. The Wife hereby covenants with the Husband that she the Wife will henceforth during the continuance of the term jointly with the Husband pay the rent and perform and observe the covenants on the part of the lessee and the conditions contained in the Lease and will at all times keep the Husband his executors and administrators effectually indemnified against all actions and proceedings costs damages expenses claims and demands whatsoever by reason or on account of her failure to pay the rent or any part thereof as aforesaid or the breach non-performance or non-observance by her of the said covenants and conditions or any of them.

IT IS HEREBY CERTIFIED for the purposes of Section 14 of the Act of 1976 that the Husband and the Wife are lawfully married to each other and that the Premises constitute their family home within the meaning of the Act of 1976.

IN WITNESS whereof the parties hereto have hereunto set their respective hands the day and year first above WRITTEN.

SCHEDULE

(The Premises)

ALL THAT AND THOSE

SIGNED and DELIVERED
by the HUSBAND
in the presence of:

SIGNED and DELIVERED
by the WIFE
in the presence of:

CHAPTER 9

MORTGAGES

9.1 Introduction

The most commonly used manner of raising money to buy any building or property is by arranging a loan from a bank or lending institution and securing that loan by way of mortgage over the asset to be acquired. Usually the loan cheque will be released, the purchase of the asset completed, and the mortgage put into place contemporaneously. In this way the lending institution knows that the day it releases the proceeds of the loan to the borrower it has secured the loan against a tangible asset of real value. Thus the lender can be satisfied that if the borrower defaults in terms of its commitment to repay, there will be a significant asset to be targeted in terms of a resale, in addition to all of the usual remedies which would lie directly against the borrower in terms of forcing him to repay the loan money and any interest accruing thereon. Although this is the most usual scenario it is certainly not the only instance under which a mortgage is put in place.

Mortgages also are widely used as a means of securing loans which have been sanctioned for other purposes, such as home improvements or extensions, car purchases, financing the education fees of children and so forth. Borrowers raise money for a variety of purposes and, if the amount of the loan is in any way significant, the lender invariably looks for some form of security by way of mortgage over land or buildings. Although a borrower is frequently reluctant to encumber assets in this way, the temptation to do so usually is that the rate of interest charged by the lender will be significantly lower on a loan which is secured by way of mortgage over real property than on a loan which is unsecured or secured over an asset through some form of leasing or hire-purchase agreement.

The term negative equity is used when the amount secured by the mortgage exceeds the value of the property.

This chapter primarily focuses on mortgages in the context of residential conveyancing (home loans) as it is this type of mortgage most often encountered by conveyancing practitioners.

9.2 What is a Mortgage?

9.2.1 INTRODUCTION

In legal terms there was previously a difference between 'mortgaging' a property the title to which was registered in the Land Registry and 'mortgaging' an unregistered property. An unregistered property was mortgaged and a registered property charged. This distinction has been removed by the Land and Conveyancing Law Reform Act, 2009. Section 89(1) provides that a legal mortgage of land may only be created by a charge by deed and such a charge is referred to as a mortgage. Thus the previous type 'mortgage' of unregistered property, ie 'conditional transfer' of property to a lending institution or bank that became absolute if the borrower/mortgagor fell into arrears and was unable to make the repayments which it had covenanted to make, is no longer possible. In that mortgage the property was conveyed, leased, or assigned by the borrower (the 'mortgagor') to the lending institution (the 'mortgagee') subject to the mortgagor's equity of redemption in the property. The equity of redemption was the right retained by the mortgagor in relation to the property and included the borrower's equitable right to get the title back and have it vested in him or her once more when the loan is repaid. This type of mortgage is no longer possible.

Section 89(1) of the 2009 Act commenced on 1 December 2009 provided that a legal mortgage of land may only be created by a charge by deed. The old methods of creating a legal mortgage over unregistered land, by conveyance or demise, in the case of freehold land, or by sub-demise or assignment, in the case of leasehold land, were abolished.

A legal mortgage of land may now only be created by a charge. Title to the land does not pass to the lender; instead the charge is a burden on the title which is retained by the owner. Thus, while the term 'mortgage' is not inaccurate it is more correct to refer to 'charges' when referring to land. In general usage however the term mortgage is still used when strictly speaking from a legal point of view what is happening is that the interest in land is being charged.

A mortgage may also be created by equitable deposit of title deeds with a bank or building society and s 89(6) confirms that these equitable mortgages of land remain unaffected.

9.2.2 CHARGES

The Law Society Conveyancing Committee reminded practitioners in a Practice Note in the Law Society *Gazette* in December 2009 that from 1 December 2009 all Land Registry charges must be in the form prescribed or approved by the Property Registration Authority. The forms of Land Registry charge are available on its website, www.prai.ie.

Under rules 52 and 105 of the LR Rules 2012, the forms of charge prescribed are as follows:

- Form 49 is a prescribed form of charge for a principal sum;

- Form 50 is a prescribed form of charge for future advances;

- Form 51 is a prescribed form of charge for present and future advances (this gives statutory effect to a form agreed with the Irish Banking Federation (IBF)) (the IBF has now become the Banking and Payments Federation Ireland (BPFI));

- Form 52 is the prescribed form for a specific charge for present and future advances arising on the creation of a commercial mortgage or debenture. Mortgage conditions are referred to and incorporated by way of a specific clause as if they were set out in the forms in full.

Practitioners should take care to ensure that the correct form of charge is used in any particular transaction. See the *Gazette*, March 2012 Practice Note and the joint article entitled 'Taking Charge' by William Prentice and Frank Treacy in the April 2012 *Gazette*.

Under the Registration of Title Act, 1964, s 62 registered land may be 'mortgaged' only by the registered owner by means of a registered charge. Section 89(1) of the 2009 Act now has the same effect for unregistered land. The old methods of creating mortgages by conveyance, demise, or assignment are abolished. Unlike these previous 'mortgages' a charge involves no transfer of ownership to the lender. Ownership remains with the registered owner and the lender only acquires rights over the property.

In this chapter the term 'mortgage' is used to denote a charge for both registered and unregistered property.

9.3   Discharge of a Mortgage

Previously the vacate or redemption of a mortgage and its removal from the title took the form of a release in the case of unregistered land and a discharge in the case of registered land. Since all mortgages are now charges the term 'discharge' will be used for both unregistered and registered land.

The discharge for unregistered land takes the form of a paper document sealed by the lender. The application for registration of this discharge will be in Form 6 of the Schedule of Forms to the Registration of Deeds Rules, 2008 (SI 52/2008).

In the case of registered land the lender continues to seal a paper document for partial discharges; however, a system of electronic discharge (eDischarge) is available in the case of entire discharges. eDischarge is the first phase in the development of a system of electronic registration (eRegistration) by the Property Registration Authority. This new system provides for the cancellation of a charge on a folio when an application in the form set out in the LR Rules, 2012 (SI 483/2012) is made directly by the lender. This collaborative initiative between the Property Registration Authority, Law Society, and Irish Mortgage Council has eliminated many of the inefficiencies and delays in the discharge of registered mortgages.

The eDischarge system was launched with three lenders on 30 March 2009 and was opened to other lenders on 14 April 2009. It does not apply to unregistered land or partial discharges. In these instances the lender continues to seal a paper discharge and forwards it to the solicitor who redeemed the mortgage for registration. For registered land, both residential and commercial, if the lender is signed up to the eDischarge system and the redemption is a full discharge of the mortgage no paper discharge is sealed. Instead the lender lodges an electronic application with the Land Registry within 21 days of receipt of the redemption figure and a request for the discharge. The Land Registry will cancel the entry of the charge on the folio within three days on foot of this application and a notice of completion will issue by e-mail to the lender and solicitor. A fully up-to-date list of participating lenders is maintained by the Land Registry at www.eregistration.ie. Practitioners are also advised of changes to the list by e-mail.

Given that a paper discharge will no longer issue where the eDischarge system is being used, practitioners will need to provide a different form of undertaking on closing. The following form of wording is suggested as appropriate to be furnished by the vendor's solicitor to the purchaser's solicitor on closing of a sale where the eDischarge system applies:

> 'We hereby undertake to redeem the mortgage in favour of . . . bank and to furnish a copy folio showing the cancellation of the mortgage as a burden at entry number . . . at part 3 of Folio . . . County . . . within one week of receiving notice of completion from the PRA.'

Further information on the eDischarge system is available at www.eregistration.ie or see the Practice Note in the March 2009 *Gazette*. In particular this Practice Note advised solicitors to nominate an appropriate e-mail address for communication of completion notices by the Land Registry. Such e-mail address should be checked regularly and, if a standard firm e-mail address is being used, the e-mails will need to be disseminated to the appropriate people within the firm.

The Law Society *Gazette* of March 2009 contains an article entitled 'New Conveyancing Initiatives—eDischarges and QeD Form' which should be consulted.

Under the Housing Act, 1988, s 18 the discharge may also take the form of a receipt endorsed on the back of the original mortgage. All lenders may issue a receipt but it is compulsory for local authority lenders. If such a receipt is provided it is sufficient for the purposes of registration both in the Land Registry and the Registry of Deeds. The application for registration in the Registry of Deeds will be in Form 7 to the 2008 Rules.

9.4 Content of the Mortgage Deed

9.4.1 INTRODUCTION

In general terms, the mortgage document is very simple. It recites the fact that the lender has made a loan available to the owner of the property and that the owner of the property has agreed to guarantee that the loan will be repaid by securing the loan against his or her property. This security is put in place by way of a charge over the property in question. The mortgage deed contains a recital by the borrower to:

(a) firstly abide by the mortgage conditions as if they were set out in the mortgage document. The mortgage conditions are contained in a separate document and the borrower acknowledges in the mortgage deed that he or she has been given a copy of the conditions and has read them and agrees to be bound by them. In the event of any conflict arising between the terms of the mortgage conditions and the mortgage deed it is agreed that the mortgage deed will prevail. The term 'total debt' is defined in the mortgage conditions. The borrowers covenant will always extend to repay the loan, that is the total debit, and any interest which accrues thereon, together with any costs associated with the repossession of the property and the ultimate enforcement of the security, if this proves to be necessary; and

(b) secondly, as security for the payment and discharge of the total debt, to charge the property in favour of the lender with payment of the total debt and assents to the registration of the charge as a burden on the mortgaged property.

9.4.2 ADDITIONAL COVENANTS

Although mortgage documents vary in substance and form from one institution to another, it is usual to find the following additional covenants in every mortgage document.

(a) There will be a covenant to the effect that the mortgaged property must be used by the borrower (in cases involving residential lending) as the borrower's principal private residence. The covenant will confirm that the property will not be rented or sublet and, in the event of the borrower breaking this covenant, the lending institution may elect between forfeiture on the one hand and charging a penalty rate or commercial rate of interest on the other hand. The commercial rate of interest which is applicable is normally somewhat higher than the residential lending rate.

(b) In addition, there will be a covenant by the owner of the property to the effect that he or she will not carry out any development whatsoever (as defined in the Local Government (Planning and Development) Act, 1963 and subsequent amendments thereto) without the consent in writing of the lender. In practice, this means that the borrower may not carry out any extension, improvements, or work to the property which would require planning permission or be an infringement of the building regulations without the lender's consent in writing. The lender will invariably have no difficulty with any work undertaken which enhances the value of the property. The lender will, however, strive to ensure that the work is done in a proper and workmanlike manner. Naturally, the lending institution will be anxious to ensure that the work is not done in a poor fashion or in a way which might result in difficulties in a sale in the event of a foreclosure situation arising.

(c) There will also be a covenant by the borrower to the effect that the property must be kept insured at all times and the interest of the lender is always noted on the insurance policy in question. The lender will frequently be given rights to insure the property and to charge the premium to the borrower in the event of the property owner/borrower allowing the existing policy of insurance to lapse or be cancelled.

In practice most mortgage documents have quite a number of additional clauses, principally comprising covenants by the mortgagor, such as a covenant to keep the property insured, a covenant to repay the money which he or she has obtained promptly and on time, a provision allowing the mortgagee to apply a variable interest rate to the loan, unless the rate of interest has been fixed by agreement between the parties, and covenants that the mortgagor may not deal with his or her property in any way without the prior consent in writing of the mortgagee and so forth. It is, however, very important to read every mortgage document carefully, particularly when dealing with lenders who are not market leaders. Some mortgage documents contain clauses incorporating very penal methods of computation of interest, penalties for early redemption and the like.

9.4.3 LETTER OF LOAN OFFER

A mortgage document frequently refers back to the letter of a loan offer, which has been issued by the lender and accepted by the borrower. The letter of loan offer frequently has many additional covenants, conditions, and assurances by the borrower. It also often has additional elements of default, most notably in commercial loan transactions. The letter of loan offer may also underline and set out the circumstances under which the lending institution has power to appoint a receiver and may contain provisions under which the borrower irrevocably appoints the lending institution as its attorney for certain purposes connected with the realisation of the security, should the need so occur. Solicitors are obliged under the Certificate of Title system (2011 edn) (see **9.7.2**) to ensure that the same consideration is expressed in the letter of loan offer as in the purchase deed/building agreement. Where there is any discrepancy, this must be notified to the lender prior to drawdown of the loan funds and may result in a reduction of the loan (see Practice Note, Law Society *Gazette*, August/September 2015).

In the June 2009 *Gazette* the Conveyancing Committee warned practitioners of the importance of checking certain matters in loan approvals in a timely fashion including time limits within which the letter of offer must be accepted, time limits for drawdown, etc. The Committee noted that some lenders are revaluing properties before the loan funds are drawn down and if the value of the property has fallen the lender is withdrawing the loan approval or is reducing the amount to be advanced. A borrower who has entered into a binding contract on the strength of the original loan approval will find possibly that the purchase cannot be completed resulting in a loss of deposit and an action for specific performance and/or damages for breach of contract. Solicitors were advised to warn clients about these dangers. The Committee recommended that a special condition be inserted in the contract providing that the contract and the completion thereof is subject to the purchaser's loan approval being in place at the date of completion in a sum sufficient to allow the purchaser to complete the contract. A sample special condition was provided. See **9.7.1** for the wording. See also the Practice Note in the summer 2009, *The Parchment*. See also 9.6.6 for the impact of the 2015 Regulations on the position.

In instances where property subject to a mortgage is being transferred from one spouse to another, whether on foot of a court order or otherwise, the consent of the mortgagee is required and a letter of loan offer will issue to the transferee unless the mortgage is being discharged during the course of the transaction. It is often the case that the transferee will be taking on sole obligation for meeting the terms of the mortgage. In that instance it is vital that the mortgagee is contacted at an early stage as it may take the view that the transferee does not have the necessary means to meet the repayments and thus may not consent to the transfer. Provided such consent is forthcoming the mortgagee should be joined as a party to the deed.

9.5 Types of Mortgages

9.5.1 'PRINCIPAL SUMS'

Historically, mortgages were always created to secure a fixed amount of indebtedness together with interest running on that particular loan and, if the borrower wanted a supplemental mortgage or a 'top-up' loan, he had to create a second mortgage over his property. However, the lending institutions are now generally using 'all sums due' mortgages.

9.5.2 'ALL SUMS DUE'

As a general rule the lending institutions are now writing into their mortgage document an 'all sums due' clause. This clause results in the mortgagor pledging his or her property to the lending institution, not only for the loan he or she is taking out at that time, but for all indebtedness which he might have to the lending institution at the time or which he or she may incur into the future, eg car loan or credit card bill. This clause covers potential indebtedness to the lending institution as well as actual indebtedness, including contingent liabilities, which may arise in the future on the strength of an obligation undertaken pursuant to a guarantee.

The existence of this type of charging clause is very significant. The clause must be explained in detail to potential purchasers who may not be aware of the impact of same. Many house buyers take the view that they do not want to have 'all of their lending eggs in one basket'. In other words, they want to have their indebtedness in relation to the house with one institution and their day-to-day indebtedness (such as overdraft facilities, term loan facilities, car loans, and so forth) with some other institution. However, if a borrower signs a mortgage which has an 'all sums due' charging clause in it, the property is charged to the lending institution not only to secure the repayment of the home loan but also to secure all of the borrower's indebtedness to that lending institution (or its subsidiaries) both actual and contingent and howsoever arising, for example the credit card bill or car loan.

9.5.3 THE ANNUITY MORTGAGE

The annuity mortgage is one which requires the borrower to repay the entire principal, which he or she is borrowing from the lending institution, and all of the interest throughout the term of the mortgage. The rate of repayment is set by the lending institution, having regard to the fact that both principal and interest are repaid over the term of years and the amount of the repayment is calculated to ensure that, at the end of the term, the entire amount of the principal and interest will have been repaid. Normally, the mortgage document provides for a variable rate of interest and allows the lending institution to increase and decrease the rate in line with mortgage interest changes in the mortgage market. Annuity mortgages are invariably backed up by a mortgage protection policy which is a life policy taken out by the lender at the borrower's cost on the borrower's life to secure the amount of the loan. In the event of the borrower dying 'in harness' during the currency of the mortgage, the life assurance policy falls into place and the amount due is paid by the insurance company to the lending institution whereupon the mortgage is immediately redeemed and the borrower's personal representative/beneficiary may take the mortgaged property freed and discharged from the mortgage. A mortgage protection policy is now a statutory requirement under the Consumer Credit Act, 1995, s 126 if the mortgagor is a 'consumer' and is obtaining a 'housing loan' as defined in the Act.

9.5.4 ENDOWMENT MORTGAGE

An endowment mortgage, by contrast, operates on the basis that the borrower will repay only interest on the money which he has borrowed from the lending institution and never pays a penny of the capital amount. In lieu of repaying the capital, the borrower takes out an endowment life policy on his own life with an insurance company. The mortgage is repaid out of the proceeds yielded by the insurance policy on its maturity or on the borrower's death. The policy itself is drafted to ensure that the amount of the loan will be paid to the lending institution on the occasion of the borrower's death (in harness) or on the occasion of the expiry of the term of years for which the loan was granted. The borrower will be allowed to complete the mortgage with the lending institution only when this policy has been taken out and when he or she has assigned the benefit of the life policy in question to the lending institution. Once the life policy has been signed over to the lending institution, it recovers the capital amount which it had advanced either on the occasion of the borrower's death during the currency of the loan or, in any event, on the last day of the term of the mortgage. Accordingly, there is no risk to the lending institution and it is quite happy to accept ongoing repayments of interest alone. Most endowment mortgages provide that in the event of the borrower failing to meet the repayments which he or she owes to the life assurance agency, the mortgage is automatically converted to an annuity mortgage whereupon the borrower becomes liable to the lending institution for principal and interest alike.

With an endowment mortgage there may be no guarantee that the proceeds of the insurance policy will be sufficient to repay the loan in full at the end of the term. The Consumer Credit Act, 1995 contains a number of provisions which attempt to protect consumers securing loans for the purchase of residential property. One of these provisions is s 133 which provides that the borrower must be warned that there is no guarantee that the proceeds of the policy will be sufficient to repay the loan in full when it becomes due for repayment. Section 133 sets out the specific text of a warning that must be included in the documentation issuing to the borrower. Endowment mortgages are volatile as the endowment policy is linked to performance of a portfolio of various stocks and shares; thus they are no longer commonly used.

9.6 Sale

9.6.1 ACCOUNTABLE TRUST RECEIPT (ATR)

Under normal circumstances, when a solicitor receives instructions in relation to the sale of a property, the first thing he or she does is obtain the client's retainer and authority so that he or she may apply to the lending institution holding the deeds and documents of title for permission to collect the same so as to peruse the title and draft the Contract for Sale. The deeds will be released to the solicitor subject to him or her signing an accountable trust receipt (ATR) and proving to the lending institution that he or she has the client's written authority to take up the title deeds on such ATR. The ATR is a commitment to the effect that the solicitor will hold the deeds safely, on trust and to the order of the lending institution and that he or she will not part with same or use the deeds in any way which might prejudice the lender until such time as he or she is in a position to repay all of the borrower's indebtedness as secured against the deeds themselves. Thus, a solicitor must not release the title deeds until he or she is in a position to comply with the trust. In default of honouring this commitment, the solicitor undertakes to be personally responsible for the indebtedness in question.

In 2014 the Law Society issued a Practice Note (Law Society *Gazette*, December 2014) in response to a large number of complaints it received from solicitors about the form and content of ATRs being used by some lending institutions. The Committee drafted a recommended form of ATR and negotiations are taking place to agree this format with the lending institutions. This recommended form is set out at **9.6.1.1**.

It is important for the solicitor to check that the sale proceeds, after payment of costs and outlay, are sufficient to cover the amount owing to the lending institution. Thus, the solicitor must determine the exact amount of indebtedness secured against the deeds and not simply the amount of the home loan which is outstanding. If the sale proceeds are not sufficient to discharge the mortgage the vendor will need to pay the difference prior to completion of the sale. If a shortfall arises after completion and after the title deeds are released and the vendor does not pay up then the solicitor may find themselves personally liable on foot of the ATR. Thus it is vital that the exact amount due to the lending institution on foot of the mortgage is determined at an early stage in the transaction.

In previous years solicitors found it difficult to obtain accurate figures for the total amount due from lending institutions. Solicitors who requested the total amount due from their client's local branch of the lending institution sometimes discovered that the information furnished did not include figures for loans held with other branches of the same lending institution. As a result the Law Society issued a Practice Note (Law Society *Gazette*, November 1999) setting out a standard letter to be used by solicitors when requesting redemption figures from lending institutions. In the opinion of the Conveyancing Committee a borrower is entitled to be given a redemption figure which the lender will stand over, ie one which is not stated to be provisional. This standard letter has now been replaced by the QeD form and the difficulties previously encountered by the lack of accurate redemption figures have now been resolved to some degree by this form and by the new guidelines and agreement forming part of the certificate of title documentation (2011 edn).

9.6.1.1   **Recommended form of ATR**

No alternations may be made to this form of undertaking

LAW SOCIETY APPROVED FORMAT OF ACCOUNTABLE TRUST RECEIPT

Undertaking by Solicitor where Title Documents are –

(1)   lent to Solicitor for purpose of inspection only and return

OR

(2)   furnished to Solicitor for purpose of sale or mortgage of property (or part of it) and to ac-count to Bank for net proceeds.

_____

My/Our Client: ....

Property: ....

Estimated Sale Price/Mortgage Proceeds: €............... (where property is being sold or mortgaged)

To: .... Name of Bank)

I/We hereby acknowledge that I/We have received on loan from you the documents of title relat-ing to the above property, which documents are set out in the schedule hereto, for the purpose of either the inspection and return of title deeds OR the sale/mortgage of the above property or part thereof as the case may be.

[STRIKE OUT WHICHEVER OF (1) OR (2) IS NOT APPLICABLE]

TAKING UP FOR INSPECTION:

(1)   I/We undertake to hold the said documents of title on your behalf and to return them to you on demand in the same condition in which they now are and not to do any act which would enable the property to become in any way charged, con-veyed, assigned, leased, en-cumbered or disposed of.

OR

TAKING UP FOR SALE OR MORTGAGE:

(2)   Pending completion of the sale/mortgage as the case may be, I/We undertake to hold the said documents of title on your behalf and to return them to you on de-mand in the same condition in which they now are and without the property to which they relate or any in-terest therein being to my/our knowledge in any way charged, conveyed, assigned, leased, encumbered, or disposed of save for the purpose of the said sale/mortgage of the above property or part thereof.

If the transaction is completed I/We undertake –

to pay to you either:

[STRIKE OUT WHICHEVER OF (A) OR (B) IS NOT APPLICABLE]

(A) the amount required to release the property from the bank's security;

OR

(B) €_____ being the agreed amount payable to you on completion of the transaction;

(C) If the documents of title relate to other property in addition to that which is the subject of the proposed sale/mortgage, to return them to you together with a copy or copies of the appro-priate instrument or instruments evidencing the transaction.

SCHEDULE

AUTHORITY

I/We confirm that I/we have my/our client's irrevocable authority to give this Undertaking and, where applicable, the prior consent of my/our client's spouse or civil partner to give this Undertaking.

Signature: ....

Name of Firm: ....

State whether Principal or Partner: ....

Address of Solicitor

Or Firm: ....

CLIENT'S AUTHORITY AND RETAINER

To .... Solicitor(s)

of ....

I/We hereby irrevocably authorise and direct you to give an undertaking in the form and contain-ing the information set out overleaf to _____ (Name of Bank)

I/We hereby irrevocably authorise and direct you, where you act in the sale or mortgage of the above property, to pay to _____ (Name of Bank) sufficient funds out of the net proceeds of the sale/mortgage, if such funds are adequate to discharge my/our indebtedness to the said Bank, but if such funds are not adequate to pay to the said Bank the net proceeds.

And in consideration of your giving the foregoing undertaking, I/We hereby undertake that I/We will not discharge your retainer as my/our solicitor(s) in connection with the foregoing matter unless and until I/We have procured from the Bank your effective release from the obligations imposed by such undertaking and l/We hereby indemnify you and all your partners and your and their executors, administrators and assigns against any loss arising from my/our act or default.

Dated this   day of   20

Signature(s): ....

CONSENT PURSUANT TO FAMILY HOME PROTECTION ACT, 1976 OR CIVIL PARTNERSHIP AND CERTAIN RIGHTS AND OBLIGATIONS OF COHABITANTS ACT, 2010

I, _____ the lawful spouse/civil partner of the above named client

DO HEREBY GIVE MY PRIOR IRREVOCABLE CONSENT for the purposes of the Family Home Protection Act, 1976 (as amended) or the Civil Partnership and Certain Rights and

Obligations of Cohabitants Act, 2010 to the foregoing retainer and authority of my said spouse/civil partner and to the within undertaking to be given by my spouse's/civil partner's solicitor(s).

I acknowledge that it has been recommended to me that I should obtain independent legal advice with regard to the legal implications of giving this irrevocable consent. Where I have chosen not to take such advice, I declare that I did so voluntarily.

The Property is not adversely affected by section 5 of the Family Law Act, 1981, the provisions of the Judicial Separation and Family Law Reform Act, 1989, the Family Law Act, 1995, the Family Law (Divorce) Act, 1996, or the Civil Partnership and Certain Rights and Obligations of Cohabitants Act, 2010.

Dated the _____ day of _____

Signature of Spouse or Civil Partner _____

Name of Spouse or Civil Partner in BLOCK CAPITALS _____

Witness _____

(Solicitor)

Address of Witness _____

NOTE: This undertaking should be signed by the solicitor in person or (in the case of a firm) by a partner or by an agent authorised in writing by such solicitor or firm.

December 2014

9.6.2   QED FORM

In conjunction with the launch of the eDischarge system (see **9.3**) a new streamlined procedure was agreed between the Law Society and lenders for solicitors requesting title deeds, redemption figures, and discharge of a mortgage. This procedure is based on a standard form called QeD ('Quick electronic Discharge') for residential property and it applies to all residential property, both registered and unregistered.

The procedure is designed to remove inefficiencies in communications between solicitors and lenders by adopting a standardised approach and by providing clarification on the appropriate channels for such communications.

All participating lenders have published the relevant addresses for receipt of the QeD form and the form itself is available at www.bpfi.ie/customer-assist/business-customers/qed-mortgage-conditions/. For some lenders the address is a central channel whilst for other lenders there are different channels depending on the nature of the request.

The standard deeds of charge and housing loan mortgage general conditions are also available at this web address.

Requests for title deeds, redemption figures, and discharge of a charge sent to the appropriate channel result in the quickest response. Lenders have requested that solicitors discourage the mortgagors from separately seeking a redemption figure as multiple requests delay the process. It is acknowledged that solicitors will of course have to seek redemption figures on receipt of the initial instruction to sell/re-mortgage and also for closing of the sale/re-mortgage. Indeed it may be necessary to seek updated redemption figures a number of times during the currency of a transaction particularly if delays arise between contract and completion.

Practitioners can download the QeD form and complete it at their desktop. A list of frequently asked questions is also available to assist practitioners in completing the form. Lenders have acknowledged to the Law Society that the timelines in the QeD form are upper limits and they will endeavour to process requests well within those timelines; however, this is dependent on the form being correctly completed and sent to the appropriate channel for that lender. The timelines are ten working days for redemption figures and ten working days for title deeds in the lender's possession (or ten working days of them coming into the lender's possession). These timelines correspond to those agreed as part of the certificate of title documentation (2011 edn).

It should be noted that interest continues to run on the secured debt pending clearance of funds and this should be taken into account when calculating the amount of redemption monies to be lodged with the lender. The QeD form requires the lender to quote figures for all sums secured by all mortgages against the property in its favour including:

- the amount of daily interest accruing and accrued;
- breakage costs (if applicable);
- all legal and/or other expenses, costs, or charges associated with the furnishing of the title deeds;
- all legal and/or other expenses, costs, or charges associated with the release/discharge of the security/ies; and
- all and any other applicable costs and charges.

This is called the 'redemption figure' and on receipt of this amount the lender must authorise an eDischarge or execute a (paper) discharge. If, after completion, the figure is found to be inadequate, the lender cannot withhold the discharge. See March 2009 *Gazette*. See also a reminder to solicitors to use this form in the May 2012 *Gazette*.

9.6.3   SPECIAL CONDITION

When drafting the Contract for Sale a vendor's solicitor will insert a special condition in the contract to the effect that the property is subject to a mortgage which will be discharged on closing. The Law Society has recommended the wording of this type of special condition (see Practice Note, Law Society *Gazette*, June 1979) which provides that prior to closing:

> 'the vendor's solicitors will furnish to the purchaser's solicitors a statement from the vendor's mortgagees setting out the amount required to redeem the mortgage as at the closing date together with the accruing daily rate of interest thereafter and, on closing, the purchaser will furnish to the vendor separate lending institution drafts for the amount required to redeem the vendor's mortgage and for the balance of the purchase monies respectively and the vendor will forthwith discharge the mortgage debt to the vendor's mortgagees and will furnish to the purchaser proper evidence of such discharge and will furnish to the purchaser such release of the mortgage as may be appropriate'.

See also Practice Notes, Law Society *Gazette*, September 1983 and July 1995. In this way the property is sold and the mortgage cleared from the title. It should be noted that this special condition does not state which party is to bear the cost, if any, of splitting the purchaser's loan cheque or of registering the discharge. The Law Society Conveyancing Committee takes the view that the vendor's mortgage is not discharged off the title until the discharge is registered and therefore the cost of registering same should be borne by the vendor.

The Law Society Conveyancing Committee in a Practice Note in the January/February 2010 issue of the *Gazette* dealt with the problems that may arise for solicitors when acting for a vendor where the vendor only has negative equity in the property being sold. The Committee advised that practitioners acting for vendors in this situation must not allow the vendor to enter into a contract without first making appropriate arrangements either with the vendor's lending institution or the purchaser. It is important for the vendor's solicitor to ascertain as early as possible whether the purchase price will be sufficient to redeem all charges affecting the property for sale. The Committee recommends that, as soon as is practicable after the receipt of instructions but, in any case, prior to the coming into being of a binding Contract for Sale, the vendor's solicitor would obtain redemption figures from the lending institution(s) in question. Where the vendor's solicitor discovers that the monies required to redeem the loan exceed the anticipated proceeds of sale, the vendor should be advised of the position immediately and instructions sought regarding the payment of the shortfall in the redemption monies. Alternatively, the vendor may be able to reach some arrangement with the lender. The vendor's solicitor must ensure that any such proposals or arrangements will enable him or her to comply with any undertaking given to the lender.

Once the solicitor is satisfied in this regard, a special condition, outlining the position, should be inserted in the Contract for Sale. In drafting the special condition, the vendor's solicitor should be cognisant that it is the vendor's responsibility to make good title and the special condition should, therefore, confirm that the vendor's solicitor will, prior to completion, demonstrate that he or she will, on completion, be in a position to clear all charges on the property. Where a feasible solution is not forthcoming and this would make it impossible for the vendor's solicitor to comply with his or her undertaking to the lender, the vendor should be advised that the solicitor is unable to act in the proposed transaction and the title documents should be returned to the lender.

In order that the amount of the lending institution drafts may be determined, the vendor's solicitor must obtain accurate details of the amount required to redeem the vendor's home loan and forward those details to the purchaser's solicitor. When the purchaser's solicitor receives the figures, he or she can obtain the lending institution drafts and proceed to close the sale. Subsequently the vendor's solicitor will pay the first lending institution draft to the lending institution requesting a discharge of the mortgage.

When a mortgage is redeemed, the solicitor is released from his ATR.

It should be noted that if the redemption is not occurring because of a sale and the title documents were not already released to the solicitor on ATR then, on redemption of the mortgage, the title documents will automatically be released to the mortgagor not to the solicitor. In these circumstances the solicitor should include with the redemption money an authority from his client authorising the release of the title documents to him or her (Practice Note, Law Society *Gazette*, October 1990).

Solicitors must be careful about the wording of ATRs and undertakings which they execute in relation to title deeds or discharges. A solicitor's undertaking is a personal obligation assumed by the solicitor or firm of solicitors in question to the effect that something will be done, irrespective of the wishes of the client. Once the solicitor, having received appropriate authority from his or her client, issues an undertaking to a colleague, he or she is bound by the terms of that undertaking. For example, an undertaking to procure a discharge in respect of a mortgage is binding on the solicitor even if the solicitor does not have adequate client funds available to redeem the mortgage in question. A solicitor can only be released from an undertaking by the party to whom the undertaking was given. Once the undertaking is given, and prior to it being released, the solicitor is still bound by it even if the client instructs otherwise.

General condition 15 of the Contract for Sale provides that the vendor shall disclose before the sale, in the particulars, the special conditions or otherwise, all easements, rights, reservations, privileges, taxes, and other liabilities (not already known to the purchaser or apparent from inspection) which are known by the vendor to affect the subject property or which are likely to affect it.

General condition 8(c) of the Contract for Sale provides that:

> 'Save as stipulated in the Special Conditions the vendor shall, prior to or at the completion of the Sale, discharge all mortgages and charges for the payment of money . . . which affect the Subject Property.'

The vendor is obliged to give an unencumbered title to the purchaser save and except where otherwise provided for in the Contract for Sale. He or she is obliged to ensure that all mortgages which affect the subject property are discharged and evidence of this handed over on closing.

9.6.4 MORTGAGEE SELLING UNDER POWER OF SALE

This obviously does not apply when a mortgagee is selling under a power of sale. This power of sale will arise under the terms of the mortgage and the mortgage deed will form part of the vendor's title. The mortgage will not be discharged and the original of the mortgage will be handed over to the purchaser.

If there is more than one mortgage on the property a purchaser need not concern himself with the other mortgages provided the power of sale is being exercised by the mortgagee holding in priority to the other mortgagees, ie the first mortgagee.

Section 104 of the Land and Conveyancing Law Reform Act, 2009 ('the 2009 Act') provides that a mortgagee exercising the power of sale conferred by the Act, or an express power of sale, has power to convey the property freed from all estates, interests, and rights in respect of which the mortgage has priority but subject to all estates, interests, and rights which have priority to the mortgage. This was previously set out in s 21 of the Conveyancing Act, 1881 but this has now been repealed by the 2009 Act.

Thus the first mortgagee will hold the proceeds of sale on trust for the subsequent mortgagees. The purchaser need not concern himself or herself with obtaining discharges in respect of the other mortgages and he or she obtains an unencumbered title.

The position is different if a subsequent mortgagee is selling under a power of sale. In that circumstance a purchaser will require that the prior mortgage be discharged and proof of this furnished on closing. Thus the mortgages which have priority to the mortgage under which the power of sale is being exercised (ie the mortgages above but not below) must be redeemed.

9.6.5 REQUISITIONS ON TITLE

Requisition 14 of the Law Society Requisitions on Title deals with proceedings and encumbrances including mortgages and charges. This requisition requires the vendor to confirm if the property is subject to any mortgage or charge. If there is a mortgage or charge full particulars must be furnished and the vendor is reminded that evidence of discharge must be furnished on closing.

9.6.6 CLOSING

In response to queries, the Conveyancing Committee prepared a sample letter of undertaking to be given on closing to redeem a mortgage/charge on the title (see Practice Note, Law Society *Gazette*, April 2014). The text of the proposed letter that should satisfy solicitors on both sides of a transaction is as follows:

Our ref:

Our clients:

Your client:

Premises:

Dear Sirs,

In consideration of you closing the sale of the above mentioned property, we hereby undertake to immediately redeem the mortgage(s) in favour of_____bank affecting the above mentioned property from that portion of the proceeds of sale provided for that purpose and to furnish you with one of the following together with the appropriate property registration fees (if any) as soon as possible:

1. Original Deed of Mortgage with vacate endorsed thereon,

2. Deed of Release,

3.   Deed of Discharge, or

4.   Evidence of eDischarge, for example, copy folio showing the relevant charge removed.

Residential property

In the event that the bank does not furnish us with one of the documents mentioned above, within the time limits agreed between the IBF and the Law Society under the Certificate of Title system for Residential Mortgage Lending, we confirm that we will promptly commence the consumer complaints process provided for in the Guidelines to the Certificate of Title system under Provision 10.9 of the Consumer Protection Code 2012 issued by the Central Bank of Ireland, and in accordance with the sample letters published by the Law Society.

Yours faithfully

See **9.7.2.6** for further details of the sample letters to be used in the complaints process.

In September 2015 the Conveyancing Committee issued another Practice Note concerning the closing of the transaction. This relates to the impact of the Central Bank (Supervision and Enforcement) Act, 2013 (Section 48) (Housing Loan Requirements) Regulations, 2015 (SI 47/2015) on residential conveyancing transactions where there is a secured loan. Under clause 7(3) a lender providing a housing loan is required to carry out a market valuation of the property not earlier than a period of two months before the date on which the advance is made. Clause 7(4) has a similar provision for the purchase of land for the construction of a building. Given the timelines in conveyancing transactions, in many cases lenders will now have to obtain a second valuation prior to drawdown of the loan cheque. This has serious consequences for a purchaser who has entered into a binding contract on the strength of the original loan approval. If the revaluation results in a reduction of the loan, or the withdrawal of loan approval entirely, the purchaser may not be able to proceed with the purchase, resulting in loss of the deposit and the possibility of an action for specific performance and/or damages for breach of contract.

The Committee advised practitioners to include a special condition in the Contract for Sale and to warn purchaser clients about this revaluation and its potential consequences. The Committee had previously issued a sample special condition which addresses any change in valuation of the property (see Law Society *Gazette*, June 2009) and this is set out at **6.3.6.4**. See also **9.4.3**.

9.7   Purchase

9.7.1   SPECIAL CONDITION

If a purchaser is obtaining a mortgage and using the loan cheque to make up the purchase money then he will need to make the Contract for Sale subject to him obtaining loan approval for the required amount. Loan approval of itself does not guarantee him or her the loan cheque as such approval will be subject to conditions. Thus, prior to entering into an unconditional contract to purchase the property, a purchaser must be sure not only that loan approval issues but also that he or she is in a position to comply with all of the conditions therein laid down by the lending institution. If a purchaser allows the contract to become unconditional and subsequently loan approval does not issue or the purchaser is unable to comply with the lending institution's requirements, then the loan cheque will not issue and he or she may be committed to a contract that he or she cannot complete.

The Law Society has recommended a standard special condition making a Contract for Sale subject to loan approval (see Practice Note, Law Society *Gazette*, December 1979). It provides for the Contract for Sale to be subject to the purchaser obtaining approval for a loan of a specified amount from a specified lending institution on the security of the premises within a certain period of time. It provides for the contract to be rescinded by either party if written loan approval does not issue within the time specified and the purchaser is to be repaid his or her deposit without interest, costs, or compensation.

The special condition also states that if

'the loan approval is conditional on a survey satisfactory to the lending institution or a mortgage protection or life assurance policy being taken out or some other condition compliance with which is not within the control of the purchaser the loan shall not be deemed to be approved until the purchaser is in a position to accept the loan on terms which are within his reasonable power or procurement'.

The wording of this special condition has been extended in view of the new practice by lenders of withdrawing loan approval where the value of the property to be offered as security is perceived to have fallen since the grant of loan approval. The recommended wording of this special condition as set out in the Law Society *Gazette* of June 2009 is now as follows:

'This contract shall be subject to the purchaser obtaining approval for a loan of € from (lender) on the security of the premises PROVIDED ALWAYS that if this loan has not been approved in writing within four weeks from the date hereof either party shall be entitled to rescind this contract and in such event the purchaser shall be refunded his deposit without interest costs or compensation thereon.

If the loan approval is conditional on a survey satisfactory to the lending institution or a mortgage protection or a life insurance policy being taken out or the lending institution being satisfied at any time prior to drawdown of the loan that its valuation of the property has not changed since the date of loan approval or some other condition compliance with which is not within the control of the purchaser, the loan shall not be deemed to be approved until the purchaser is in a position to accept and draw down the loan on terms which are within his reasonable power or procurement.'

Problems arise when the agreed time frame is about to pass and the purchaser has not yet received his or her loan approval or has received his or her loan approval but is in difficulty in relation to complying with the conditions set out therein. The vendor will seek to have the special condition deleted so as to make the contract unconditional and, in order to avoid losing the property, the purchaser may agree.

If the purchaser agrees to the deletion of the special condition, even though loan approval has not issued or has issued with onerous conditions attached, then it would be advisable to obtain his or her instructions in writing. It would also be wise to advise him or her in writing that the contract is no longer unconditional and he or she will be required to complete even if he or she cannot obtain a mortgage.

9.7.2   CERTIFICATE OF TITLE SYSTEM (2011 EDITION)

9.7.2.1   Introduction

In part due to the fact that lending institutions are unable to pass to the borrower any legal fees which they incur in connection with putting a mortgage in place (Consumer Credit Act, 1995), it is normal in the case of home loans for the lending institution not to engage its own solicitor to check the title. It should be noted that this applies only in the case of residential lending and does not prohibit lenders from 'charging on' security fees in the context of commercial lending.

In residential lending, the purchaser's solicitor is required to furnish an Undertaking and Certificate of Title in the format agreed by the Law Society with the legal advisors of the various financial institutions (2011 edn) (see March 2012 Practice Note, Law Society *Gazette*). See **Appendices 9.1–9.3**. This latest edition of the Undertaking and Certificate of Title is to be utilised for all residential property mortgage loan transactions approved on or after 2 April 2012. See Practice Note in the March 2012 *Gazette*. This documentation ensures that the obligation of the solicitor to the lending institution is confined to the terms agreed in the undertaking, certificate of title, guidelines, and agreement. No other documentation should be accepted or used by practitioners and solicitors should reject any documentation which does not conform with the agreed package. The purchaser's solicitor does not act for the lender (see Practice Note, Law Society *Gazette*, April 1998) and thus is not paid by the lender for this work as this would lead to a conflict of interest. The Undertaking and Certificate of Title reflect this by stating that both are given by the solicitor in his or her sole capacity as solicitor for the borrower and not as solicitor for, or as agent/quasi-agent of, the lender. The borrower's solicitor acts only for the borrower. The Irish Mortgage Council (IMC), representing the lending institutions, has confirmed that, in registering the lender's charge, the borrower's solicitor is discharging part of the undertaking under the Certificate of Title system, but is not specifically acting on behalf of the lender (see Practice Note, Law Society *Gazette*, June 2004).

The certificate of title and undertaking form part of the mortgage documentation which is sent by the lending institution to the purchaser's solicitor once the mortgage is approved. The pack also includes details of the terms of the loan offer and the mortgage deed. In recent years, lending institutions have used the terms of the loan offer to place additional obligations on the solicitor, for example to check the creditworthiness of the borrower. The solicitor should always check the terms of the loan offer so as to ensure that no such obligations are placed upon him or her. See the detailed Practice Note issued by the Law Society Conveyancing Committee in the June 2007 *Gazette*. The solicitor is, however, protected by the terms of the undertaking which provide that the undertaking relates to matters of title and represents the sum of the solicitor's obligations to the lender in relation to the loan transaction. It further states that the solicitor has no responsibility for any matter of a non-title nature except in so far as any of the matters set out in the undertaking may be deemed to be matters of a non-title nature. The solicitor should ensure that only the agreed mortgage package is used so as to avoid other obligations being placed on him or her.

In a Practice Note in the Law Society *Gazette* of January/February 2010 the Conveyancing Committee of the Law Society raised some concerns regarding the operation of the previous edition of the Certificate of Title system. It had come to their attention that certain lenders are raising requirements with borrowers' solicitors that are *inter alia* at variance with what was agreed with the lenders as part of the new system. These include a requirement that the borrower's solicitor certify to the bank that there has been compliance with the special conditions of the loan approval. The Certificate of Title system provides that the solicitor is responsible only for special conditions that relate to title. Special conditions in a loan approval might include conditions regarding life assurance, property insurance, matters of valuation of the security and so on—all of which are not matters of title and do not form any part of the Certificate of Title system. Solicitors should delete any non-title conditions from the lender's documentation before lodging the request for funds.

9.7.2.2 Undertaking

Having agreed the Contract for Sale and perused the title, the purchaser's solicitor completes the undertaking (having been authorised in writing to do so by the borrower/purchaser and having obtained the spouse's prior consent in writing (where applicable)) and returns this to the lender. The solicitor signing the undertaking should be a partner, principal, or other solicitor duly authorised in writing on behalf of the firm, though the firm would be liable on foot of an undertaking signed by an authorised member of staff even if the staff member was not authorised in writing. On foot of this signed undertaking, the lending institution will then release the loan cheque to the solicitor to enable him or her to complete the purchase transaction.

On foot of the undertaking and prior to negotiating, ie releasing the loan cheque, the solicitor must ensure that:

(a) the borrower is acquiring good marketable title (as defined in the Undertaking and Certificate of Title) to the property or the borrower has good marketable title, if the borrower already owns the property, save for any qualification on title as agreed in writing with the lender;

(b)   the mortgage documentation is completed and properly executed by the purchaser/borrower;

(c)   a deed of confirmation is executed by any other party perceived to have, possibly or actually having, an interest in the property;

(d)   the provisions of the Family Home Protection Act, 1976 as amended are complied with;

(e)   the mortgage ranks as a first legal mortgage/charge on the property;

(f)   the solicitor is put in sufficient funds to enable him or her to discharge all stamp duty and registration fees payable in connection with the purchase;

(g)   the borrower has executed the lender's standard form of life policy assignment, if furnished by the lender and specified in the loan offer (note that a solicitor is not required to insert the details of the policy in the assignment form; see Practice Note in the July 2010 *Gazette*); and

(h)   the borrower has executed the lender's standard guarantee, if furnished by the lender and specified in the loan offer.

Pending compliance with all of these requirements the solicitor holds the loan proceeds in trust for the lender.

If there is another interest in the property, eg a right of residence in favour of a parent or another charge on the property, the lender may also require the party holding that right or interest to execute a deed of postponement or deed of confirmation. This ensures that the right or interest will be postponed in favour of the lender in the event of a realisation of the asset. The lender will thus have priority in any enforcement of the terms of the mortgage. See **7.6** for the conveyancing requirements regarding completion of deeds of confirmation by cohabitants.

At closing the borrower/purchaser must execute the mortgage deed contemporaneously.

After releasing the loan cheque the solicitor must:

(a)   within the time prescribed by law pay the stamp duty on the purchase deed/transfer and deal expeditiously with all related queries and issues raised by the Revenue Commissioners;

(b)   as soon as practicable, but in any event within four months, following receipt of the purchase deed/transfer duly stamped:

(i)   lodge the purchase deed/transfer and the mortgage in the appropriate Registry so as to ensure that the lender obtains a first legal mortgage/charge on the property; and

(ii)   furnish the lender with the Land Registry dealing number and/or confirm to the lender in writing the date of lodgement in the Registry of Deeds,

(c)   ensure, where the borrower already owns the property, that the above is complied with in respect of the mortgage within four months of completion.

After completion, and pending the lodging of the documents with the lender, the solicitor holds the title documents in trust for the lender. During this time the solicitor is obliged, if requested by the lender, to advise in writing on progress concerning the stamping and registration of the purchase deed/transfer and the mortgage. If the time limits set out in the undertaking are not met the solicitor is obliged to furnish the lender with a certified copy of the executed mortgage within five working days of receipt of the lender's written request.

It should be noted that once this undertaking has been given to the lending institution the solicitor will be unable to exercise a lien over the title documents in the event of his or her fees not being paid.

As soon as practicable following registration the solicitor must furnish to the lender:

(a)   the certificate of title;

(b)   all deeds and documents registered with the stamp certificates;

(c)   the original mortgage or, if Land Registry title, the counterpart mortgage and an up-to-date copy folio showing the mortgage registered as a burden thereon; and

(d)   any deed of confirmation or life policy assignment and any guarantee.

In a Practice Note in the May 2012 *Gazette* the Conveyancing Committee confirmed that a plain copy or printout of a folio is sufficient for the purpose of complying with the solicitor's undertaking under the agreed system. This is an additional assurance to lenders that their mortgage is registered, the main evidence of registration being the counterpart charge document with the details of registration stamped thereon by the Land Registry.

Occasionally lenders may seek additional documentation or impose further obligations that have not been negotiated as part of the agreed system and the Law Society Conveyancing Committee will raise this with the lenders in order to cease such practices when they arise. See the Practice Note in the July 2013 *Gazette* for an instance of this.

Since the 2011 Certificate of Title system was agreed two small amendments have been made to the solicitor's undertaking to comply with new Single European Payments Area (SEPA) regulations (Practice Note in the March 2014 *Gazette*). These are:

1.   the insertion of 'BIC' instead of 'bank sort code', and

2.   the insertion of 'solicitor's client account IBAN' instead of 'solicitor's client account number'.

9.7.2.3   Qualifying the undertaking

It is important to note that the undertaking specifically provides for the possibility of the solicitor not being able to certify the title without qualification. This will arise where the purchaser is not obtaining good marketable title to the property; for example if there is an unauthorised development on the property or if the purchase is not effected on foot of the Law Society Contract for Sale. An additional example might be if the developer offers the Premier Guarantee Scheme on the purchase of a new house instead of HomeBond (see Practice Note, Law Society *Gazette*, May 2002). If qualifications are required to be made, they must be cleared in advance in writing with the lending institution. In such cases, the lending institution reserves the right to either withdraw the loan approval or to appoint its own solicitor to consider the matter.

After reading the draft contract furnished by the vendor's solicitor and after examining the title, it should be apparent to a purchaser's solicitor if he or she will be seeking to qualify the certificate of title. If a qualification is necessary the purchaser's solicitor should ensure, not only that the relevant qualification is notified to the lending institution at a very early date to give the lending institution time to consider the matter and comment thereon, but also that unconditional contracts are not exchanged until it is clear that the lending institution will accept the qualification on title. The lending institution has complete discretion as to whether or not it will accept a qualification on title. Particularly if the loan equity ratio is high, the lending institution may refuse to accept the qualification and may not proceed with the loan unless the title is absolutely in order.

An example of a qualification might be as follows: 'The property is subject to a right of way marked yellow on the attached map.' Many qualifications relate to planning problems and these qualifications would be similar to the wording used in the special condition in the Contract for Sale, but obviously without the amendment to general condition 36. See **chapter 11** for suggested wordings.

An example of issues that may not necessitate a qualification on title is a claim that is statute barred or a problem that will be resolved before closing.

9.7.2.4   Certificate of title

When the purchase has been completed and the mortgage documentation executed, there is an obligation on the solicitor to pay the stamp duty, register all of the documents, and thereafter to return the documents to the lending institution with the certificate of title confirming that the purchaser/borrower has good marketable title to the premises in question free from encumbrances.

In July 2004, the Law Society Conveyancing Committee reminded practitioners that the certificate of title should be dated as of the date of parting with the loan funds (Practice Note, Law Society *Gazette*). This is the date a solicitor can properly certify the title. This is also usually the date of the mortgage and of title searches. Such certificates of title certify the title to the property as of that date, and they speak only to circumstances that pertained as of that date. After this date some event or act might occur which would require the Undertaking and Certificate of Title to be further qualified. It would be too late at that stage to seek the approval of the lending institution to such qualification, so it is vital that the certificate is dated the day of parting with the loan funds or the first drawdown of loan funds where stage payments are involved (see Practice Note in the June 2013 *Gazette* relating particularly to the certificate of title in stage payment cases). If some title matter arises subsequent to that date, it does not impact on the certificate of title. Solicitors should not provide further certificates of title by way of update or otherwise and the Committee re-affirmed the position that a certificate of title should be dated as of the date of parting with the loan funds (Practice Notes in the January/February 2012 *Gazette* and June 2013 *Gazette*).

The solicitor for the purchaser is responsible to the purchaser who is acquiring the property and also to the lending institution on the strength of the certificate of title. In theory, this dual responsibility should not present a problem. After all, if the title to the premises which is being purchased is good and marketable, one can safely certify this to any party including the lending institution.

However, complications may arise where there is a fault or defect on the title being offered. When the fault or defect is brought to the attention of the purchaser he or she may instruct that the transaction proceed in any event, as he or she is acquiring the property at the 'right price'. In this event the solicitor must inform the purchaser that, as he or she is required to certify the title to the lending institution, the fault or defect must be brought to its attention and the certificate of title qualified accordingly. The purchaser may realise this could preclude him or her from getting the loan which he or she requires to complete the purchase. Clients have been known to exert pressure on solicitors to forgo mentioning or drawing attention to a problem and to issue a certificate of title in cases where an unqualified certificate should not be issued. To do this leaves the solicitor exposed to a negligence action at the hands of the lending institution. In the event that the client falls into arrears with his or her repayments and the property is repossessed, the problem with the title will come to light and the solicitor will be liable to the lending institution for any loss suffered as a result of the problem. This situation may also arise if a solicitor issues a certificate of title in reliance on a colleague's undertaking. If the colleague fails to comply with the undertaking then the solicitor is also in difficulty. Thus, undertakings given and received on the completion of a transaction should be scrutinised carefully.

Once the lender receives the title documents and the signed certificate of title the undertaking will be released and the lender will instead rely on the certificate of title. In the January/February 2011 *Gazette* the Law Society Conveyancing Committee noted the difficulties associated with getting lenders to acknowledge receipt of title deeds. A lender may not acknowledge receipt or may furnish a general letter of acknowledgement but not a signed schedule confirming receipt of the specific documents listed therein. The Committee pointed out that the onus is on the lender to ensure that the specific documents listed in the schedule are furnished. In order to avoid the implication that the solicitor may be responsible if any document is subsequently found to be missing the Committee advised the insertion of the following paragraph into correspondence:

'A duplicate schedule is attached for you to sign and return to us in order to acknowledge receipt of the enclosed title documents. In default of hearing from you within ten working days this firm will take it that you have received all the documents on the schedule and that it is released from any undertaking given in relation to this transaction and in relation to the title documents, and thereafter this firm disclaims all responsibility for the title documents. Our file will be closed and placed in storage and any query from you arising in relation to this matter after that date will incur a charge, details of which will be provided to you at the time of raising the query, and which charge will be payable in advance of replying to such query.'

The Practice Note recommended that a copy of the letter and schedule be retained on file and that delivery of the title documents should be by hand or some form of recorded delivery.

The lender or lender's solicitor, as the case may be, should not go behind a properly completed certificate of title unless the title is being qualified in some way (Practice Note, Law Society *Gazette*, March 1995). A lender's solicitor who does go behind a certificate of title would be putting himself or herself on notice. The lender might subsequently have a difficulty holding the borrower's solicitor liable on foot of the certificate of title. Since the activation of the certificate of title procedure, no major litigation has arisen in the courts concerning the matter. This means that practitioners are unclear as to how a court will react to a certificate of title in any particular circumstance. Statistically, this is not too surprising as, for every 100 mortgages, perhaps over 95 of the borrowers repay with no difficulty.

As a result of the Certificate of Title system the onus and responsibility for the correct preparation, execution, stamping, and registration of the mortgage document lies with the borrower's solicitor. Thus, it is important that the solicitor follows the instructions received from the lending institution to the letter and, if not in a position to comply with the lending institution's requirements, the solicitor must refuse to utilise the loan cheque for the borrower's benefit or to part with it until the matter has been clarified or the lending institution has waived the offending requirement.

The Conveyancing Committee of the Dublin Solicitors Bar Association confirmed that it received a number of queries regarding a new requirement by some lenders requesting an updated s 72 declaration when returning a certificate of title for a re-mortgage. It is the opinion of the committee that this is not an unreasonable request (albeit a new requirement). It may indeed be the case that the circumstances have changed since the original purchase and therefore the Committee feels that as a matter of practice a s 72 declaration should be included with the certificate of title for a re-mortgage (see the summer 2009 edition of *The Parchment*).

9.7.2.5   Guidelines and agreement

The guidelines and agreement for the certificate of title documentation (2011 edn) sets down time limits that are of benefit to solicitors. Lenders have agreed to furnish deeds on ATR within ten working days of a written request, or if the deeds are with another party, within ten days of the lender coming into possession of the deeds. Redemption figures will be furnished within a similar time frame. Importantly the lenders have agreed to give redemption figures for all loans secured by the property and if after completion the redemption figure quoted is inadequate to redeem the loans the lender will not withhold the discharge but will be free to pursue other remedies against the borrower. This is an important development as the failure of some lenders to stand over their redemption figures was a point of contention between solicitors and lenders for many years. See the Practice Note in the April 2012 *Gazette* which demonstrates the efforts of the Conveyancing Committee to have non-qualified or unconditional redemption figures issued by a particular lender.

The lenders have agreed to release the solicitor from his or her undertaking in writing within ten days of lodgement of title with the lender. The lenders have also agreed to provide a discharge within one month of receipt of payment. There is also a new procedure for resolving delays.

9.7.2.6   Delays

In the November 2010 *Gazette* the Conveyancing Committee issued a Practice Note addressing lenders' failure to honour redemption figures and/or failure to issue vacates and/or delays in issuing vacates, issuing deeds on ATR, issuing redemption figures, or releasing solicitors from their undertakings within the agreed time periods. The Committee have provided sample letters that may be used where these breaches of the Certificate of Title Guidelines and Agreement arise. These sample letters are available on the members' area of the Law Society website and may be adapted and used by practitioners. The four scenarios where the letters may be used are:

1. delays in issuing vacates (paragraph 23(a)—within one month of receipt of payment or the request (for vacate) whichever is the later);

2. delays in issuing deeds on ATR (paragraph 4(a)—within ten working days where the lender has possession of the deeds, or paragraph 4(b)—within ten working days of the deeds coming into the possession of the lender);

3. delays in issuing redemption figures (paragraph 5(b)—within ten working days of the solicitor's written request);

4. delays in releasing solicitors from their undertakings (paragraph 21(d)—within ten working days of the solicitor furnishing deeds to the lender).

The four sample letters are a reminder, a warning, a formal customer complaint, and lastly a formal complaint. See the Conveyancing Committee Practice Note in the January/February 2012 *Gazette* explaining the process for using this complaints process.

9.8   Acting for the Lending Institution

9.8.1   INTRODUCTION

For many years there was no agreed Certificate of Title system for commercial lending agreed between the lenders and the Conveyancing Committee of the Law Society. The Committee did however offer advice to solicitors on how to deal with lenders seeking certificates in commercial transactions (see Practice Note, Law Society *Gazette*, January/February 2004).

Following a significant surge in claims on solicitors' professional indemnity insurance, attributed to commercial undertakings, the Law Society decided to introduce new regulations in 2010 prohibiting certain undertakings by solicitors to lenders and prohibiting solicitors from acting for both lender and borrower in commercial property transactions. Previous regulations had already tightened up the position in relation to undertakings somewhat by restricting solicitors from giving undertakings in relation to transactions in which they have an interest.

The Solicitors (Professional Practice, Conduct and Discipline—Secured Loan Transactions) Regulations, 2009 (SI 211/2009) came into force on 1 September 2009. They restrict the giving of undertakings to mortgagees in secured loan transactions in which the solicitor, or a person closely connected, is beneficially interested. This restriction will apply unless the solicitor has given specified notice and the bank or other person has acknowledged receipt of the notice and consented to the solicitor providing the undertaking. A solicitor cannot avoid the requirements of the Regulations by arranging his or her interests so that they are held through the means of a company, a partnership, or a trust. See Practice Notes in the Law Society *Gazette* of July 2009, August/September 2009, and June 2013. While this restriction originally applied to both residential and commercial loan transactions it now applies only to residential loans because SI 366/2010 has since prohibited borrowers' solicitors from giving undertakings to lenders in commercial loan transactions.

The Solicitors (Professional Practice, Conduct and Discipline—Commercial Property Transactions) Regulations, 2010 (SI 366/2010) prohibit the giving of undertakings to lenders in commercial property transactions except in very limited circumstances. These regulations apply from 1 December 2010.

Following on from those regulations the Law Society deemed it necessary to provide guidance and assistance to its members on how they might best implement and incorporate the new regulations in practice. Thus the Society issued precedent forms and guidelines for commercial mortgage lending. This *Commercial Mortgage Lending Law Society Approved Forms* pack (2010 edn) contains an undertaking and two forms of certificate of title which are approved for use depending on the particular lending scenario. There are three alternate transaction types which are complex and should be considered carefully when a lender seeks an undertaking or certificate of title from a borrower's solicitor. Such solicitors should be careful not to breach the Regulations and to only use the recommended forms in appropriate circumstances. Solicitors are prohibited by law from acting for both borrower and lender in the same commercial property transaction and there is no exception to this.

It is more usual in commercial transactions for lending institutions to engage their own solicitor to investigate title. This is mainly because the sums of money in question are significantly larger than in the case of residential lending and because the lending institution is not precluded by law from passing on all of its legal costs and outlay to the borrower in the context of the transaction. It is important to read the terms of any letter of loan offer very carefully, particularly with a commercial loan, as, in addition to the usual conditions, the letter often contains a specific paragraph to the effect that all legal fees in relation to the creation of the security as well as the enforcement of same, if this becomes necessary, will be paid by the borrower. In this manner, the lender ensures that it does not have to carry any of its own legal costs. If such a condition is included in the loan offer it is important for the borrower and the borrower's solicitor to quantify the costs and to factor them into the overall cost of the transaction as these costs will invariably have to be discharged on completion.

If the lender has engaged its own solicitor, then that solicitor is invariably given very specific instructions as to how to act in relation to the mortgage and the security. The solicitor may be required to carry out a full investigation of the title or alternatively to rely on a certificate of title from the borrower's solicitor.

9.8.2   NO INVESTIGATION OF TITLE

The lender's solicitor may be told by the lender to accept a certificate of title from the borrower's solicitor and not to enquire further in relation to the title. The lender's solicitor will attend completion with the loan cheque and obtains the certificate of title and title documents in return. At completion the lender's solicitor will only examine the certificate of title to ensure that:

(a)   it has been properly completed, is absolute and unqualified (unless otherwise agreed) and has not been altered; and

(b)   the certifying solicitor is covered by professional indemnity insurance.

After completion, the lender's solicitor will attend to stamping and registration. Previously each lending institution had its own standard certificate of title for commercial transactions. This certificate of title was more detailed and onerous than the Law Society certificate of title agreed for residential lending (see Practice Note, Law Society *Gazette*, January/February 2004). However since 1 December 2010 a borrower's solicitor may only give one of the recommended forms of certificate of title contained in the *Commercial Mortgage Lending Law Society Approved Forms* pack (2010 edn). See **9.8.4**.

The lender's solicitor will also need to ensure that the borrowers have complied with the provisions of the Family Home Protection Act, 1976, as amended in relation to the creation of the mortgage, and that the deed in the purchaser's/borrower's favour is properly executed and should be registered in the Land Registry or Registry of Deeds without difficulty.

Some supplemental documents may be required by a particular lender such as a power of attorney from the borrower, etc and these will be requested by the lender's solicitor. The lender's solicitor will also require a cheque or lending institution draft to cover the stamp duty and registration fees payable and, in some cases, his own fees and outlay. Once this cheque has been tendered, and on receipt of all of the title documents and certificate of title, he will release the loan cheque to the borrower's solicitor and no further examination or investigation of the documents will be carried out.

9.8.3   INVESTIGATION OF TITLE

Alternatively, a lender's solicitor may be instructed to carry out a full and detailed investigation of the title offered as security. Normally this will result in a three-way closing involving the solicitor for the vendor, solicitor for the borrower, and solicitor for the lending institution. In such instances the lender may seek a certificate of title from its own solicitor. The borrower's solicitor should not sign or approve the lender's solicitor's certificate of title and neither a borrower nor a borrower's solicitor should confirm that the bank's solicitor's interpretation of title matters is correct. See the Practice Note in the April 2012 *Gazette*.

9.8.4   WARNING: UNDERTAKINGS IN COMMERCIAL LOAN TRANSACTIONS

Over the past few years the Law Society has introduced a number of regulations to prevent solicitors from giving undertakings to lenders in commercial loan transactions.

As noted earlier the Solicitors (Professional Practice, Conduct and Discipline—Secured Loan Transactions) Regulations, 2009 (SI 211/2009) came into force on 1 September 2009. This restricts the giving of undertakings to mortgagees in secured loan transactions in which the solicitor, or a person closely connected, is beneficially interested. The restriction applies unless the solicitor has given specified notice and the bank or other person both acknowledged receipt of the notice and consented to the solicitor providing the undertaking. A solicitor cannot avoid the requirements of the Regulations by arranging his or her interests so that they are held through the means of a company, a partnership, or a trust. See Practice Notes in the Law Society *Gazette* of July 2009 and August/September 2009.

From 1 December 2009 undertakings given on or after that date by solicitors to lenders in commercial loan transactions, where the solicitor acts either for the borrower alone or for the borrower and the lender jointly, are no longer covered by the minimum terms and conditions of professional indemnity insurance cover that solicitors are obliged by law to hold. (See the Solicitors Acts, 1954 to 2008 (Professional Indemnity Insurance) (Amendment) Regulations, 2009 (SI 384/2009).) Effectively anything other than a principal private residence or a not for letting holiday home is commercial property for the purpose of the Regulations. Buy to let properties are classed as commercial property. The Law Society also issued an *e-bulletin* on 14 December 2009 reminding practitioners that there is no agreed form of Undertaking and Certificate of Title for commercial properties and the Society expressed the view that in commercial transactions the best practice is for the financial institutions to retain their own solicitor to ensure that their security is in order. The Society recommended that all solicitors and lenders apply best practice of a three-way closing system for commercial loan transactions. In the August/September 2010 *Gazette* the Law Society Conveyancing Committee warned of the dangers of loan funds in commercial cases being released directly to the borrower and advised practitioners not to give commercial undertakings even if insured to do so. This warning was given in light of the decision by the Law Society Council to introduce a ban on solicitors giving undertakings to lending institutions in commercial mortgage lending.

The Society restricted the giving of commercial property undertakings to lenders in virtually all circumstances. The Solicitors (Professional Practice, Conduct and Discipline—Commercial Property Transactions) Regulations 2010 (SI 366/2010) prohibit the giving of undertakings to lenders in commercial property transactions except in very limited circumstances. These regulations apply from 1 December 2010. The Law Society *Gazette* of

October 2010 contains a Practice Note outlining the new procedures. The Law Society Conveyancing Committee also published a booklet entitled *Commercial Mortgage Lending Law Society Approved Forms* (2010 edn) comprising forms and guidelines which should be consulted. See **9.8.1** and also chapter 4 of the Law Society *Complex Conveyancing Manual* (2nd edn) published by Bloomsbury Professional.

9.9   Borrowing by a Company

When acting on behalf of a borrowing company or for a lender in a commercial loan transaction it is crucial to remember the provisions of the Companies Act 2014, ss 408 and 409 (previously Companies Act, 1963, s 99) which dictate that unless a notice of the charge created by a company is lodged within 21 days of the date of its creation with the Companies Registration Office the charge will be void against the liquidator or any creditor of the company. Accordingly, it is essential to ensure that a Companies Office Form C1 is completed by the borrowing company on the occasion of completing the loan transaction and is filed with the Companies Registration Office as quickly as possible after the completion of the transaction and, in any event, within 21 days (see Practice Note, Law Society *Gazette*, January/February 2002 re the 1963 Act provisions and Practice Note, Law Society *Gazette*, December 2015 re the 2014 Act requirements). The alternative is a two-stage procedure (introduced by the 2014 Act) whereby a notice of intention to create a charge, Form C1A, is filed and followed within 21 days by a confirmation of creation of that charge in Form C1B. Priority under the two-stage procedure is determined by the time and date of the filing of Form C1A, hence it accords priority to the pending charge. Priority under the one-stage procedure is determined by the date and time of filing of the Form C1. All filings are required to be made online using the www.core.ie e-filing system.

The Land Registry frequently insists upon the production of a note from the Companies Registration Office verifying that the provisions of the Companies Act have been complied with before it will complete the registration of any charge created by a limited liability company as a burden on a folio. This procedure serves as a useful reminder to comply with the provisions of the Companies Act but, unfortunately, it cannot be relied upon as the reminder will often come outside the 21-day period and accordingly, too late to be of any real help. A court application can be made for an extension of time but it is by no means certain that the court would grant such an application. Another option is to have the charge re-executed and to lodge the C1 (or C1A and C1B) relating to that new charge within the correct period. When acting for a borrower company it is essential to ensure that the company has the requisite power to borrow money and to give security in respect of the borrowing and loans. The solicitor should also ensure that the company seal is brought to the completion ceremony along with the requisite number of authorised signatories who must be in attendance to countersign the seal. It is not unusual to find that the various company resolutions which are required to give effect to the borrowing and to the sealing of the mortgage documentation will be passed at the closing ceremony itself and, accordingly, when the mortgage is being completed, it is wise to ensure that a quorum of the company is present so that the requisite resolutions may be passed.

It should be noted that there are many provisions in the Companies Act 2014 which restrict the power of companies to secure loans, the most notable of which are ss 82 and 238–239 (previously 1963 Act, s 60 and the 1990 Act, s 31); however such transactions can be validated by the Summary Approval Procedure (SAP) which replaced the previous 'whitewash' procedures.

9.10   Insuring the Property

In every case where a lending institution is advancing money on the strength of title to property it will insist on being satisfied that the premises have been covered for structural insurance. It will also insist that its interest has been noted on the insurance policy and that the policy will not fail, lapse, or be allowed to be cancelled unless it (the institution) receives advance notice in writing of the cancellation which is pending and an opportunity to put its own insurance in place or to call in the loan. In general, the lending institution will only oblige the borrower to insure the structure. Once the structural integrity of the premises has been secured, the lending institution will not oblige the borrower to insure his contents or to insure against flooding or personal injury or accident. As a result of this it is important that the solicitor points out to the borrower that the insurance which the lending institution requires is basic insurance alone and it is not necessarily comprehensive enough to meet or satisfy the requirements of the borrower himself or herself. The solicitor should also advise borrowers of the workings of the 'average' clause under which an insurance company may claim that because the borrower is underinsured, it will only make payment of a proportionate amount of any claim which is made on the policy, such proportion being directly equivalent to the proportionate amount of underinsurance as assessed by the institution.

9.11 Indemnity Bond

One further element of insurance which frequently arises is the indemnity bond. In situations where a borrower is obtaining a loan in excess of 75–80 per cent of the value of the property being offered as security the lending institution may oblige the borrower to take out an indemnity bond to cover the excess. This is an insurance company bond which guarantees to the lending institution that it will not suffer or be at a loss as a result of the fact that the loan being granted exceeds 75–80 per cent of the purchase price and is for an amount higher than the institution would ordinarily advance. In times of property recession, when the value of real property is not rising and interest rates are high, an institution may find that it has advanced too big a loan to a borrower who cannot meet the repayments. By the time the lending institution has succeeded in repossessing the property, selling and paying all of the fees and outlays which it had incurred in doing so, the proceeds of sale may be insufficient to repay the mortgage with accrued interest and to cover all of the legal costs of the repossession and the costs of the sale. This may result in the lending institution suffering an overall loss on the transaction and in such cases it calls on the insurance company under the indemnity bond to make good that loss. The premium payable for an indemnity bond is invariably charged to the borrower. It is a one-off premium and the borrower receives no direct benefit for the fact that the indemnity bond has issued other than that he or she would not receive a loan in excess of 75–80 per cent of the purchase price if the indemnity bond was not in place.

9.12 Bridging Finance

If the loan cheque will not be available for completion the purchaser may require a bridging loan. This loan will 'bridge' the gap between completion and the issue of the loan cheque. The purchase may be completed and when the loan cheque issues the bridging loan is discharged.

In such circumstances, the borrower's solicitor will issue an undertaking to the bank/building society giving the bridging loan to the effect that he or she will hold all of the deeds and documents of title relating to the property on trust and to the order of the bank/building society once the sale has been completed. The undertaking will also confirm that he or she will use all money obtained from the bank/building society solely with the aim of acquiring a good and marketable title to the premises in question, and it will also contain a provision to the effect that, as soon as the loan cheque becomes available and the mortgage is completed, the bridging account will be cleared out of the proceeds of the loan cheque itself. The undertaking which is required varies from case to case depending on the lending institution one is dealing with, the creditworthiness of the borrower, and the amount of the loan relative to the purchase price. Some lending institutions require an undertaking to furnish the net process of the loan, allowing the solicitor to deduct his or her fees and outlays from the loan cheque before making the necessary payment.

If a solicitor is being pressed to furnish an undertaking in relation to the full amount of the loan it is important for him or her to check that the full amount of the loan will issue. On occasions, the lending institution makes certain deductions from the loan cheque and these will result in a situation where the solicitor is unable to comply with his or her undertaking. He or she should ensure that his or her client puts him or her in funds for the stamp duty and registration fees, as these may not be deducted from the loan cheque in such circumstances.

Never allow a borrower to take up a bridging loan or a bridging facility unless absolutely certain that he or she will be in a position to obtain the loan cheque in the reasonably foreseeable future and repay the bridging loan. It is important for the borrower's solicitor to check that the borrower is in a position to comply with all of the requirements of the lending institution before the bridging facility is drawn down or that he or she will be in a position to comply with such requirements in the immediate future.

In recent years it is rare that a loan cheque would not be available for completion and thus it is more usual for bridging to be obtained to bridge the gap between the purchase of a new house and subsequent sale of the old house.

Most borrowers have nightmares when they hear the word 'bridging loan'. However, it is fair to say that bridging finance is a useful facility and when used correctly by a solicitor is an important tool of his or her trade.

9.13   Equity Release Schemes

Certain lending institutions offer packages whereby those over 65 or 70 can raise capital on their residences by way of loan or sale of a share therein. These equity release schemes are by their nature complex and may be difficult for some elderly people to comprehend without effective and clear legal advice. The schemes can be broadly divided into two types:

(a)   lifetime mortgage schemes allowing the borrower to mortgage an interest in their home without any liability to repay during their lifetime; and

(b)   home reversion schemes enabling the borrower to sell an interest in their home while retaining a right of residence for their lifetime.

In a Practice Note in the Law Society *Gazette* in May 2001, the Conveyancing Committee warned practitioners acting for clients availing of these schemes to take particular care to advise their clients of all the conditions therein, many of which differ from those in the usual standard residential loan documentation, including those relating to the interest rate charged, the involvement of executors and beneficiaries, and the events which will allow the lender/investor to call in the loan and sell the property.

In the June 2003 *Gazette*, the Conveyancing Committee issued a more detailed Practice Note. This expressed serious concerns about some of the requirements and provisions which the Committee felt were more relevant to commercial property mortgages and which were more stringent than those imposed in other jurisdictions. The Committee pointed out that it will continue to offer criticism of mortgage packages where they contain *excessive restrictions or provisions which are not in the interest of clients or are just not fair*. In the Committee's view, certain provisions of the scheme were not fair, reasonable, or necessary, while obligations requiring borrowers to waive aspects of their privacy were objectionable and quite unnecessary. The Conveyancing Committee did point out that equity release schemes are a useful method of releasing 'dead capital' tied up in residential property.

In May 2008 the Conveyancing Committee issued guidelines together with a checklist in order to assist practitioners when asked to advise a client in relation to an equity release scheme. The Committee recommended that solicitors exercise extreme caution when advising clients with regard to these schemes and expressed the opinion that such schemes should only be used as a last resort where, for example, the need for money is compelling and there is no option available to the client.

9.14   Enforcement

9.14.1   INTRODUCTION

The most obvious remedy available to a mortgagee when the mortgagor falls behind in his or her repayments is to sue him or her for the amount outstanding. This remedy, however, does not provide satisfactory relief where a mortgagor becomes unable to meet the repayments and the amount outstanding continues to grow.

The following is a very brief outline of some of the other remedies available to mortgagees in the event that the mortgagor defaults on the terms of the mortgage.

9.14.2   COURT ORDER FOR POSSESSION FOLLOWED BY SALE

The mortgagee has power to sell the property without the intervention of the court but only with the mortgagor's consent. The mortgagee's statutory power of sale previously arose under the Conveyancing Act, 1881, s 19. This section is now repealed and replaced with s 100 of the 2009 Act. Also, under s 97, a mortgagee shall not take possession of the mortgaged property without a court order unless the mortgagor consents in writing. Section 98 deals with abandoned property and allows the mortgagee to apply to court for an order authorising possession.

9.14.3   APPOINTMENT OF A RECEIVER

It is common for mortgages to contain provisions giving the mortgagee the right to appoint a receiver. The duty of the receiver is to manage the property so as to protect the mortgagee's interest therein. The receiver would also apply the rents and profits from the property towards discharging the debt owed to the lending institution. This remedy is most usually adopted when the property is a business, for example a shop or restaurant. The appointment of a receiver is now governed by s 108 of the 2009 Act.

APPENDIX 9.1

Solicitor's Undertaking (2011 Edition)

This is a true copy of the form of Undertaking agreed by the Law Society of Ireland with the Lending Institutions named in the Guidelines and Agreement (2011 Edition)

 **Law Society of Ireland**

**RESIDENTIAL MORTGAGE LENDING
SOLICITOR'S UNDERTAKING**

LAW SOCIETY APPROVED FORM (2011 EDITION)

To: _____

("the Lender" its transferees, successors and assigns)

MY/OUR CLIENT(S) _____

("the Borrower")

ADDRESS(ES) _____

_____

PROPERTY (Note (i)) _____

_____

_____

("the Property")

BEING

Registered Title

☐　　All of the lands in Folio　　　　County

☐　　Part of the lands in Folio　　　　County

Unregistered Title

☐　　All of the lands described in Deed dated _____ made in favour of _____
　　　(e.g. the current owner) registered in the Registry of Deeds on

☐　　Part of the lands described in Deed dated _____ made in favour of _____
　　　(e.g. the current owner) registered in the Registry of Deeds on

YOUR REF/ACCOUNT NO. _____

In consideration of the Lender agreeing to the drawdown of a loan facility in respect of the Property before the Lender's mortgage security has been perfected and subject to the payment through me/us of the loan cheque(s) or the loan proceeds I/we, the undersigned solicitor(s) for the Borrower, **HEREBY UNDERTAKE** with the Lender as follows:

1.   Good Title

Save for any qualification on title as agreed in writing with the Lender as set out in the Schedule hereto, to ensure, where the Borrower is acquiring the Property, that the Borrower will acquire good marketable title to it, or, where the Borrower already owns the Property, to satisfy myself/ourselves that such Borrower has good marketable title to it. (Note (ii)).

2.   Execution of Security Documents

To ensure, prior to completion (Note (iii)) that:

a)   the Borrower has executed a mortgage deed/charge in the Lender's standard form as produced by the Lender (the "Mortgage") over the Property (and, if required by the Lender, that any non-owning Borrower has joined in the Mortgage),

b)   a deed of confirmation is executed by all necessary parties where the circumstances render such a deed appropriate, and

c)   all the provisions of the Family Home Protection Act, 1976, the Civil Partnership and Certain Rights and Obligations of Cohabitants Act, 2010 and any Act amending, extending or replacing those Acts are complied with in respect of the Mortgage and any such deed of confirmation,

so that on completion the Mortgage ranks as a first legal mortgage/charge on the Property (Note (iv)) AND (if applicable)

d)   the Borrower has executed the Lender's standard form of life policy assignment, if specified in the facility letter/letter of offer (the "Letter of Offer") provided that the standard form is furnished to me/us by the Lender in the form in which it is to be signed prior to the drawdown of the loan

e)   a guarantee in the Lender's standard form is executed, if specified in the Letter of Offer and if furnished by the Lender to me/us prior to the drawdown of the loan.

3.   In Funds

To ensure, prior to negotiating the loan cheque(s) or the proceeds thereof that I am/we are in funds to discharge all stamp duty and registration fees.

4.   Loan Proceeds in Trust

Pending compliance with Clauses 1, 2 and 3 above, to hold the loan proceeds in trust for the Lender.

5.   Stamping, Registration & Furnishing Deeds to the Lender

A.   Stamping

Within the time prescribed by law to lodge the purchase deed/transfer for stamping and to deal expeditiously with all related queries and issues raised by the Revenue Commissioners.

B.   Registration

(i)   As soon as practicable, but in any event within four months (or such longer period as may be agreed in writing by the Lender, such agreement not to be unreasonably withheld) following receipt of the purchase deed/transfer duly stamped:

  (a)   To lodge the purchase deed/transfer and the Mortgage in the appropriate Registry so as to ensure that the Lender obtains a first legal mortgage/charge on the Property; and

  (b)   To furnish the Lender with the Land Registry dealing number (and consent to inspect the dealing if requested) and/or to confirm to the Lender in writing the date of lodgement in the Registry of Deeds.

(ii)   To ensure, where the Borrower already owns the property, that Clause 5 B(i) above is complied with in respect of the Mortgage within four months of completion.

C.   Furnishing Deeds to the Lender

As soon as practicable following registration to furnish to the Lender the following:

(i)   my/our Certificate of Title in the Law Society's standard form,

(ii)   all deeds and documents to the Property, stamped and registered as appropriate,

(iii)   the original Mortgage or, if Land Registry title, the counterpart Mortgage (if available) and an up-to-date copy folio of the Property showing the Mortgage registered as a burden thereon, and

(iv)   any deed of confirmation or life policy assignment which I/we have had executed and any guarantee which I/we have obtained pursuant to Clause 2 hereof.

To the extent to which the Lender has indicated that it will attend to stamping and registration or any work referred to above this part of the Undertaking shall be deemed to be amended accordingly.

6. **Holding Documents in Trust and Other Requirements**

Pending compliance with Clause 5:

    a)   to hold all title documents of the Property in trust for the Lender;

    b)   to advise in writing, if requested by the Lender, on progress concerning the stamping and registration of the purchase deed/transfer and the Mortgage.

7. **Certified Copy Mortgage**

If Clause 5 has not been complied with within the time therein specified, to furnish the Lender with a certified copy of the executed Mortgage within 5 working days of receipt of the Lender's written request.

Authority

I/We confirm that I/we have the Borrower's irrevocable authority to give this Undertaking and, where applicable, the prior consent of the Borrower's spouse or civil partner to give this Undertaking.

Extent of Undertaking

This Undertaking is given by me/us in my/our sole capacity as solicitor(s) for the Borrower and not as solicitor(s) for or as agent/quasi agent of the Lender. It relates to Matters of Title and represents the sum of my/our obligations to the Lender in relation to this loan transaction. I/We have no responsibility for any matter of a non-title nature except insofar as any of the matters set out in this Undertaking may be deemed to be matters of a non-title nature.

SCHEDULE

Qualifications on Title (if any) agreed in writing with the Lender

Dated this _____ **day of** _____

SIGNATURE _____

NAME OF SOLICITOR SIGNING _____
(Note (v))

STATE WHETHER PRINCIPAL/PARTNER
OR AUTHORISED SOLICITOR _____

NAME OF FIRM _____

ADDRESS OF FIRM _____

_____

*   Where it has been specifically agreed with the Lender that the funds shall issue by way of electronic funds transfer direct to the client account of the Borrower's solicitor(s), please tick (and initial) the boxes and insert the details of that account

Tick	Initial

Name & Address of Bank   _____

Bank Sort Code   _____

Solicitor's Client Account Name   _____

Solicitor's Client Account Number   _____

My/Our agreement to electronic funds transfer is subject to the Lender providing to my/our Bank sufficient detail and information to allow me/us to identify the Borrower.

NOTES :

(i)   The description of the Property should be taken from the Letter of Offer and must accurately identify the Property to enable the Lender to identify it by reference to the description in the Letter of Offer.

(ii)   In this Undertaking **"good marketable title"** means a title of a quality commensurate with prudent standards of current conveyancing practice in Ireland. The latter entails, where the Property is being acquired, that the purchase was effected on foot of the current Law Society's Conditions of Sale and/or Building Agreement. It also entails that the investigation of the title to the Property was made in accordance with the current Law Society Requisitions on Title together with any additional Requisitions appropriate to the Property and that satisfactory replies have been received. When the Property is already owned by the Borrower, the title shall be so investigated that if the said Requisitions had been raised, satisfactory replies would have been obtained.

In this Undertaking **"Matters of Title"** means only such matters as relate to the title to the Property in the context of a conveyancing transaction and does not include any matters relating to the condition of the Property, the suitability or otherwise of the Borrower or any other matter (including the form or efficacy of the Mortgage).

Any dispute as to the quality of any title or as to whether or not any matter constitutes a Matter of Title (within the foregoing definitions) may be referred for a ruling to the Conveyancing Committee of the Law Society of Ireland, but without prejudice to the right of either party to seek a determination by the Court on the issue.

(iii)   In this Undertaking **"completion"** means the payment of the loan proceeds (including by way of negotiation of the loan cheque) in or towards the discharge of the purchase price of the Property or in or towards the discharge of any encumbrance on the Property.

For the avoidance of doubt, completion shall not be deemed to have occurred for the purposes of this Undertaking for so long as the loan cheque or loan proceeds are held in trust for the Lender.

(iv)   Where the Lender is a Building Society within the meaning of the Building Societies Act, 1989 and any Act amending, extending or replacing that Act, any prior mortgage or charge must be redeemed prior to or contemporaneously with the creation of the Mortgage.

(v)   The Undertaking must be signed by a **Partner** or, in the case of a sole practitioner, by the **Principal** or other solicitor duly authorised in writing on behalf of the firm by either of the foregoing.
(**Note:** Where signed by the latter, the original of the written authority in question MUST be attached to this Undertaking or a copy certified by a solicitor other than the solicitor so authorised).

CLIENT(S) RETAINER AND AUTHORITY

To _____

Solicitor(s)

of _____

I/We irrevocably authorise and direct you to give an undertaking in the form and containing the information set out overleaf (including an undertaking to lodge with the Lender the title deeds of the Property) to

(Name of Lender) _____

and in consideration of your giving the foregoing undertaking, I/we hereby undertake that I/we will not discharge your retainer as my/our solicitor(s) in connection with the foregoing matter unless and until I/we have procured from the Lender your effective release from the obligations imposed by such undertaking and I/we hereby indemnify you and all your partners and your and their executors, administrators and assigns against any loss arising from my/our act or default. I/we irrevocably authorise the Lender to make my/our loan cheque payable to you or to transfer the proceeds of this loan to you by electronic funds transfer.

Dated the _____ **day of** _____

Signed by the Borrower   _____

in the presence of   _____

CONSENT PURSUANT TO FAMILY HOME PROTECTION ACT 1976 OR CIVIL PARTNERSHIP AND CERTAIN RIGHTS AND OBLIGATIONS OF COHABITANTS ACT 2010

I, _____ the lawful spouse/civil partner of the above named Borrower

DO HEREBY GIVE MY PRIOR IRREVOCABLE CONSENT for the purposes of the Family Home Protection Act, 1976 (as amended) or the Civil Partnership and Certain Rights and Obligations of Cohabitants Act, 2010 to the foregoing retainer and authority of my said spouse/civil partner and to the within undertaking to be given by my spouse's/civil partner's solicitor(s).

I acknowledge that it has been recommended to me that I should obtain independent legal advice with regard to the legal implications of giving this irrevocable consent. Where I have chosen not to take such advice, I declare that I did so voluntarily.

The Property is not adversely affected by section 5 of the Family Law Act, 1981, the provisions of the Judicial Separation and Family Law Reform Act, 1989, the Family Law Act, 1995, the Family Law (Divorce) Act, 1996, or the Civil Partnership and Certain Rights and Obligations of Cohabitants Act, 2010.

Dated the _____ **day of** _____

Signature of Spouse or Civil Partner _____

Name of Spouse or Civil Partner in BLOCK CAPITALS _____

Witness _____

(Solicitor)

Address of Witness _____

_____

APPENDIX 9.2

Certificate of Title (2011 Edition)

This is a true copy of the form of the Certificate of Title agreed by the Law Society of Ireland with the Lending Institutions named in the Guidelines and Agreement (2011 Edition)

Law Society of Ireland

RESIDENTIAL MORTGAGE LENDING CERTIFICATE OF TITLE

LAW SOCIETY APPROVED FORM (2011 Edition)

To: _____

("the Lender", its transferees, successors and assigns)

NAME(S) OF BORROWER(S) _____

_____

("the Borrower")

ADDRESS OF PROPERTY _____

_____

("the Property")

YOUR REF/ACCOUNT NO. _____

As Solicitor(s) for the Borrower, I/We have investigated the title to the Property and I/We hereby certify that the Borrower has good marketable title to the Property (save as set out in the **First Schedule** hereto), the description of which agrees with that stated in the Lender's Letter of Offer for the tenure specified in the **Second Schedule** hereto, free from any mortgage, charge, lien or incumbrance and any lease or tenancy, except for your Mortgage/Charge which is in the form prescribed by you (the **"Mortgage"**).

We hereby certify that the Mortgage ranks as a first Legal Mortgage/Charge over the Property.

All the documents evidencing the Borrower's title to the Property including the Mortgage are properly listed in the **Third Schedule** hereto and are furnished herewith.

My/Our Firm currently holds Professional Indemnity Insurance Cover with a qualified insurer as defined under under Statutory Instrument No. 617 of 2007 (as amended) for a sum which is in excess of the amount being advanced to the Borrower.

I/We as Solicitor(s) for the Borrower, am/are giving this Certificate for the benefit of the Lender, having regard to (1) the current Guidelines and Agreement published by the Law Society, to be followed when completing Certificates of Title for Lenders and (2) the current conveyancing recommendations of the Law Society.

This Certificate is being given by me/us in my/our sole capacity as Solicitor(s) for the Borrower and (other than as specifically set out herein) it relates only to Matters of Title.

This Certificate does not purport to certify anything in relation to the standard contents of the Mortgage executed by the Borrower. In particular, it does not certify that the Mortgage or any other document produced by the Lender in connection with the Loan complies with the requirements of the Consumer Credit Act 1995 or the European Communities (Unfair Terms in Consumer Contracts) Regulations 1995.

Signature: _____

Name of Solicitor signing: _____

State whether Principal/Partner: _____

Name of Firm: _____

Address of Firm: _____

_____

Dated this _____ **day of** _____ **20**_____

In this Certificate of Title **"good marketable title"** shall mean a title of a quality commensurate with prudent standards of current conveyancing practice in Ireland. The latter entails, where the Property is being acquired, that the purchase was effected on foot of the current Law Society's Conditions of Sale and/or Building Agreement. It also entails that the investigation of the title to the Property was made in accordance with the current Law Society Requisitions on Title, together with any additional requisitions appropriate to the Property and that satisfactory replies have been received. When the Property is already owned by the Borrower, the title shall be so investigated that, if the said requisitions had been raised, satisfactory replies would have been obtained.

In this Certificate, **"Matters of Title"** means only such matters as relate to the title to the Property in the context of a conveyancing transaction and does not include any matters relating to the condition of the Property, the suitability or otherwise of the Borrower or any other matter (including the form or efficacy of the Mortgage).

Any dispute as to the quality of any title or as to whether or not any matter constitutes a Matter of Title (within the foregoing definition) may be referred for a ruling to the Conveyancing Committee of the Law Society of Ireland but without prejudice to the right of either party to seek a determination by the Court on the issue.

FIRST SCHEDULE
Qualifications on Title (if any)
(as previously agreed in writing with the Lender)

SECOND SCHEDULE
Tenure

THIRD SCHEDULE
See Schedule of Documents attached hereto.

Approved Guidelines and Agreement (2011 Edition)

This is a true copy of the Guidelines & Agreement (2011 Edition) agreed by the Law Society of Ireland with the Lending Institutions named herein

Law Society of Ireland   **RESIDENTIAL MORTGAGE LENDING**

LAW SOCIETY APPROVED GUIDELINES AND AGREEMENT (2011 EDITION)

GUIDELINES AND AGREEMENT TO BE FOLLOWED BY SOLICITORS AND LENDERS WHEN COMPLYING WITH SOLICITOR'S UNDERTAKING, COMPLETING CERTIFICATE OF TITLE AND ADMINISTERING THE AGREED CERTIFICATE OF TITLE SYSTEM (LAW SOCIETY APPROVED FORMS (2011 EDITION))

The following matters are agreed between the Law Society of Ireland and the Lending Institutions listed herein.

Operative Date of new 2011 Edition of Agreed Documents

1. The new 2011 edition of the agreed forms of Solicitor's Undertaking (the "Undertaking"), Certificate of Title (the "Certificate of Title") and these Guidelines and Agreement (the "Guidelines") shall be used for all residential property mortgage loan transactions approved on or after 2nd April 2012 and the Guidelines shall apply in respect of such transactions. The 2011 edition of the Undertaking, Certificate of Title and the Guidelines are collectively referred to herein as the "Agreed Documents".

Agreement not to Alter

2. (a) It is agreed that the Lenders will use the Agreed Documents only as a suite of documents and will not change the content or format of the documents so that solicitors will not be obliged to check if any change has been made. To emphasise this aspect it has been agreed that each of the Agreed Documents will be headed with the statement that "This is a true copy of the form of Undertaking/Certificate of Title/Guidelines and Agreement (as appropriate) (2011 Edition) agreed by the Law Society of Ireland with the Lending Institutions named in the Guidelines and Agreement (2011 Edition)".

    (b) It is agreed that any alterations to or revisions of the Agreed Documents necessitated either by future legislation or changes in conveyancing practice shall be introduced only by the Conveyancing Committee of the Law Society in consultation with the Lenders.

    (c) No solicitor shall modify the Undertaking or the Certificate of Title without the prior written approval of the Lender to the modification.

Roles and Responsibilities

3. (a) The responsibility of the certifying solicitor is limited to Matters of Title only. The solicitor should ensure that there will be compliance with any requirements specified in the conditions in the Lender's Letter of Offer (the "Letter of Offer") insofar as they relate to Matters of Title.

    (b) Borrowers' solicitors do not act for Lenders.

    (c) All matters which are not related to title shall be the responsibility of the Lenders. These matters include but are not limited to:
    • credit worthiness of Borrowers,
    • loan repayment arrangements,
    • property valuations, and
    • all insurance matters.

    (d) It is a matter for the Borrower to comply with all conditions in the Letter of Offer before the loan cheque is requisitioned. The Borrower will be instructed by the Lender to contact the Lender directly regarding insurance, valuation and any other matter not of a title nature.

    (e) While the Guidelines acknowledge that the Borrower's solicitor has no responsibility to the Lender to explain the conditions of the Letter of Offer to the Borrower this does not affect the solicitor's duty to his/her client in that regard. In those cases where it is a Lender's practice to furnish the Letter of Offer directly to the solicitor or to the client with a recommendation that it be completed in the solicitor's presence, it is acknowledged by the Lender that the solicitor shall have no responsibility to the Lender to explain the conditions to his/her client. This however does not affect the solicitor's duty to his/her client to explain the said conditions.

(f)   In general terms, the Agreed Documents require that the certifying solicitor will, *inter alia,*
- carry out proper investigation of title to the Borrower's property,
- attend to the execution of the relevant purchase and mortgage documentation including, where applicable, deeds of confirmation and assignments of Life Policies,
- stamp and register the Borrower's purchase deed(s) and register the Mortgage,
and
- furnish to the Lender a duly completed Certificate of Title together with all relevant documents fully scheduled as soon as practicable.

(g)   Practitioners should read the Agreed Documents carefully as they set out requirements, *inter alia,* in relation to non-owning spouses or civil partners, deeds of confirmation and rights of residence. Practitioners particularly should note that because of the nature of an exclusive right of residence, a deed of release will be required prior to execution of the Mortgage (but the exclusive right of residence may be reconstituted thereafter).

Deeds on Accountable Trust Receipt

4.   Where a Borrower's title deeds are required on accountable trust receipt for a purpose (to be stated by the requesting solicitor):

(a)   If a Lender is in possession of the title deeds, the Lender agrees to make the deeds available to the requesting solicitor within 10 working days of the receipt of the request.

(b)   If a Lender is in control but not in possession of a Borrower's title deeds, e.g. because the title deeds are held by another solicitor on accountable trust receipt, the Lender shall call for the immediate return of the title deeds to the Lender and the Lender agrees to make the deeds available to the requesting solicitor within 10 working days of the title deeds coming into its possession.

(c)   The solicitor's request for the title deeds on accountable trust receipt shall be in writing and contain sufficient detail to enable the Lender identify the Property.

(d)   It is the responsibility of the solicitor to obtain the Borrower's irrevocable retainer and authority to take up the title deeds on accountable trust. Lenders may require evidence of the retainer and authority and the solicitor should produce a copy if requested. Where this is a requirement of the Lender (and provided that the request is made within the time period specified in sub-paragraph 4(a) above), time under sub-paragraph 4(a) above will not run against the Lender until evidence of the retainer and authority has been produced.

Redemption Figures

5.   Where a Borrower is selling or re-mortgaging his/her property and the Borrower's solicitor requests redemption figures, it is agreed that:

(a)   the request shall be in writing and shall contain sufficient detail to enable the Lender identify the relevant property and to furnish the redemption figures;

(b)   the redemption figures shall be furnished to the requesting solicitor as soon as practicable and in any event no later than 10 working days of the request being made;

(c)   in answering a request for such redemption figures the Lenders shall furnish redemption figures for all loans that are secured by the relevant property;

(d)   if, after completion, the redemption sum quoted by the Lender is found to be inadequate to redeem the loan(s) the Lender shall not withhold the release/discharge/vacate (see paragraph 23 below) but shall be free to pursue any other remedies against the Borrower that are available to the Lender.

Signature of Undertaking

6.   (a)   The Undertaking must be signed either by a partner or principal. In exceptional circumstances and without prejudice to paragraph 26 hereof, if a partner or principal is temporarily unavailable it may be signed by a solicitor duly authorised in writing by a partner or principal to sign such Undertakings.

(b)   Such signature by an authorised solicitor shall bind the partners or principal only.

(c)   The foregoing has been agreed with the Lenders to facilitate instances where the partner or principal is temporarily unavailable. Neither partners nor a principal should appoint an authorised solicitor to sign Undertakings other than to facilitate temporary unavailability of partners or a principal.

(d)   Before signing the Undertaking, the solicitor should ensure that the Borrower(s) sign(s) the form of Retainer and Authority endorsed on such Undertaking and obtain the prior consent of a spouse or civil partner to the giving of the Retainer and Authority when applicable.

Title

7.   (a)   The title must be Freehold, or Leasehold with an unexpired term of at least 70 years, unless the solicitor is satisfied that the lessee has a statutory right to purchase the fee simple under the Ground Rents legislation. If Land Registry title, it must be either absolute or good leasehold.

(b)   The Property must be free from encumbrances to ensure that the Lender shall have a first legal Mortgage/Charge.

(c)   The solicitor must insert a description of the Property on page 1 of the Undertaking. The description of the Property must accurately identify the Property to enable the Lender to identify the Property by reference to the description in the Letter of Offer. The solicitor should also indicate whether title to the Property is registered or unregistered. Where registered, the folio number should be included.

Stage Payment Loans

8.   The Law Society has already advised solicitors that stage payment transactions are undesirable in view of the potential difficulties they create for both purchasers and their solicitors. Practitioners are reminded of the terms of the various practice notes issued by the Conveyancing Committee expressing its disapproval of such form of house purchases. If, however, despite this advice, the Borrower is willing to make such payments to a builder/developer who is registered with HomeBond, Premier or such alternative or additional scheme as may be approved by a Lender as appropriate in advance of title vesting in the Borrower, and the Lender has specifically agreed to advance funds for the purpose of making such stage payments, the following qualification should be inserted in the Schedule to the Undertaking:

"The Property is being purchased by stage payments. Stage payments up to the limits covered by the HomeBond, Premier [or specify an alternative Lender-approved scheme as appropriate] are to be released in advance of title vesting in the Borrower and the Supplemental Stage Payments Undertaking set out in the LAW SOCIETY APPROVED GUIDELINES AND AGREEMENT (2011 EDITION) shall be deemed to be incorporated in this Undertaking".

The Supplemental Stage Payments Undertaking reads as follows:

"Property being Acquired - Stage Payments to Builder/Developer

Where stage payments are being paid to the builder/developer, to ensure:

(a)   that a valid and enforceable fixed price contract has been exchanged to obtain good marketable title to the Property upon completion of the construction thereof and the completion of the purchase formalities

(b)   that the Property is registered with HomeBond, Premier or such alternative or additional scheme as may be approved by a Lender as appropriate and

(c)   that prior to payment of any stage payment which the Lender may agree to lend in excess of the amount covered by HomeBond, Premier or such alternative or additional scheme as may be approved by a Lender as appropriate, title to the Property (including the right to immediate possession) is unconditionally vested in the Borrower and that there is compliance with all the requirements of clause 2 of the SOLICITOR'S UNDERTAKING LAW SOCIETY APPROVED FORM (2011 EDITION)"

N.B. Not all Lenders will advance stage payments on the basis of the foregoing. Solicitors are cautioned to check with the individual Lender.

Consideration

9.   Where the consideration is expressed in the Letter of Offer, the same consideration should be expressed in the purchase deed/building agreement. If there is any discrepancy, this must be brought to the attention of the Lender prior to drawing down the loan cheque. The amount of the loan may be reduced in the event of such a discrepancy.

Mortgage

10. (a)   There must be no restrictions on mortgaging the Property. Any necessary consent from a housing authority, for example, must be obtained and compliance with any condition procured.

     (b)   The Borrower's signature on the Mortgage (including any non-owning spouse or civil partner or other person who may be required to join in the Mortgage) and (subject to paragraph 15 hereof) any other security documents must be made in the presence of and witnessed by a solicitor.

Declaration of Identity

11. For "once off" properties or those not forming part of a housing estate, there must be with the title a declaration of identity declaring that the Property and its essential services (e.g. septic tank and well etc.) are entirely within the boundaries of the lands the subject matter of the Lender's security. If any such services are not within the boundaries of such lands, then a grant of easement must be furnished unless a prescriptive right thereto is established and this is verified by an appropriate statutory declaration.

Qualifications on Title

12. Any intended qualification of the Certificate of Title must be specifically agreed in writing with the Lender prior to furnishing the Undertaking and should be set out in the Schedule to the Undertaking. It may or may not be acceptable to the Lender. Where the Lender agrees to accept any qualification it shall be understood that the responsibility for explaining the nature of the subject matter of the qualification to the Borrower rests with the solicitor and the acceptance of the qualification shall not be taken to imply any responsibility or liability to the Borrower on the part of the Lender.

Family Home/Shared Home

13. If title to the Property vests in the sole name of one spouse or civil partner, and if the Family Home Protection Act, 1976 or the Civil Partnership and Certain Rights and Obligations of Cohabitants Act, 2010 applies, a prior consent to the Mortgage must be completed, signed and dated by the Borrower's spouse or civil partner.

     (Note: Even if the Property will not become a family home or a shared home vesting in sole name until immediately after completion it is, nonetheless, recommended that the prior consent is signed by the relevant spouse or civil partner as possession may have been taken informally or partially beforehand. To avoid doubt, it is prudent to get the consent completed in any such case).

Other Interests / Deed of Confirmation

14. (a)   There must be no person other than the Borrower with any estate or interest, beneficial or otherwise, in the Property and this must be confirmed by a statutory declaration of the Borrower. (Some Lenders may require such a declaration prior to drawdown).

     (b)   If there is any such person with any such estate or interest by reason of making a contribution to the purchase price or otherwise howsoever, that person should, after the Borrower signs the Mortgage, execute a Deed of Confirmation so as to supplementally mortgage any such estate or interest to the Lender. (The confirmation is non recourse i.e. it does not of itself impose a liability on the beneficiary to repay). Where appropriate the beneficiary's spouse or civil partner should sign his/her prior consent to the Deed of Confirmation.

     (c)   If there is a right of residence the person entitled thereto must sign a Deed of Confirmation except in the event of such right being an exclusive right - in which event the right of residence must be released prior to the execution of the Mortgage (but such right may be reconstituted thereafter).

     (d)   It should be noted that a sole Borrower's spouse or civil partner, although signing the prior consent under the Family Home Protection Act, 1976 or the Civil Partnership and Certain Rights and Obligations of Cohabitants Act, 2010 may be a beneficiary nonetheless because of e.g. direct or indirect financial contribution(s). If there is any doubt in this respect, the beneficiary should, after the Mortgagor signs the Mortgage, execute a Deed of Confirmation so as to supplementally mortgage any such estate or interest to the Lender. (The confirmation is non recourse i.e. it does not of itself impose personal liability on a beneficiary to repay).

     (e)   Without prejudice to the foregoing paragraph 14(d), if the Lender requires that the non-owning spouse or civil partner joins in the Mortgage there should be compliance with this requirement provided that the Lender notifies this requirement in advance of drawdown of the loan.

Assignments of Life Policy and Guarantees

15. (a)   Some Lenders may furnish Borrower's solicitors with deeds of assignment of life policy for execution at completion. Where this is done, the solicitor should ensure each relevant document is executed, witnessed and dated in order to comply with clause 2(d) of the Undertaking.

(b)   It is the responsibility of the Lender to furnish the Borrower's solicitor prior to completion with the assignment of life policy in the form in which they wish to have it executed and with the relevant policy details inserted. Borrowers' solicitors are not obliged to insert the details of the life policy in the schedule to the life policy assignment.

(c)   If a guarantee is furnished to the Borrower's solicitor, the solicitor should ensure the relevant document is executed on its face in order to comply with clause 2(e) of the Undertaking but shall not advise the guarantor on the effect of the guarantee and shall not witness it.

Independent Legal Advice

16.   Any

(i)   spouse signing the Family Home Protection Act, 1976 Consent or any civil partner signing a consent pursuant to the Civil Partnership and Certain Rights and Obligations of Cohabitants Act, 2010; or

(ii)   non-owning spouse or civil partner joining in the Mortgage; or

(iii) person signing the Deed of Confirmation or consent thereto;

must (a) receive independent legal advice and furnish written confirmation that such independent legal advice has been given or (b) after receiving legal advice from the Borrower's solicitor of the serious implication of not taking such advice and subject to the requirements of the Lender if specified in the Letter of Offer sign an explicit waiver of the right to be so advised in the form produced by the Lender.   A copy of such confirmation or waiver should be placed with the title deeds.

Searches

17.   Searches must include those against the Borrower and, when a purchase is completed in advance of the Mortgage, searches must be updated to the date of the Mortgage.

Before Releasing Loan Proceeds

18.   Before releasing the loan proceeds the solicitor shall

- ensure that all security documents have been executed; and
- be in funds to discharge all stamp duty and registration outlays in connection with the purchase and mortgage transaction; and
- be satisfied that he or she will be in a position to issue the Certificate of Title to the Lender without qualification (save for any qualification agreed by the Lender in writing prior to completion); and
- be satisfied that his or her Professional Indemnity insurance cover exceeds the amount of the loan and, if a solicitor intends to have the Undertaking signed by an authorised signatory, he or she should ensure that the Professional Indemnity insurance cover provides for this.

Electronic Funds Transfer

19.   It should be noted that some Lenders may offer an Electronic Funds Transfer facility for payment of the loan funds. In such cases the Lender will include the approved wording in its pre-printed form of Undertaking requiring the insertion of the relevant solicitor's client account details. Where an Electronic Funds Transfer is agreed the Lender shall provide same day written confirmation to the solicitor's bank containing sufficient detail and information so as to identify the Borrower to the solicitor.

Lodging the Purchase Deed/Transfer and the Mortgage with the Property Registration Authority

20.   The purchase deed/transfer (when stamped) and the Mortgage/Charge must be lodged for registration in the Land Registry or Registry of Deeds (as appropriate) within the time frame set out in the Undertaking. It is recognised that there may be legitimate reasons for delays in lodging such deeds for registration. If these arise, the solicitor should explain the cause of delay to the Lender.

Furnishing of Title Deeds and Certificate of Title to the Lender

21.   (a)   When the stamping and registration of the purchase deed/transfer and the Mortgage/Charge has been completed, the solicitor should furnish to the Lender the documents set out in clause 5(c) of the Undertaking within the time frame set out in the Undertaking.

(b)   All Certificates of Title shall be signed by a partner or principal.

(c)   All documents accompanying the Certificate of Title should be fully scheduled in the interest of efficiency and a quick response from the Lender.

(d)   Upon compliance by the solicitor with clause 5 of the Undertaking, the Lender shall release the solicitor from the Undertaking in writing within 10 working days.

Resolving Delays in Complying with the Undertaking

22. (a) If a solicitor needs an extension of time for the completion of any action he or she had undertaken to carry out in the Undertaking, he or she should write to the Lender setting out the reason for the delay. The Lender shall not unreasonably disallow a reason given for delay.

(b) A Lender concerned that the solicitor has not met the time limits set out in the Undertaking for the completion of certain actions by the solicitor should, in the first instance, write to the solicitor drawing his/her attention to the overdue actions. The solicitor should respond within 10 working days to such letter in writing either by confirming that the outstanding actions are completed or by specifying a good reason or reasons preventing the completion of the action. The Lender shall not unreasonably disallow a reason given for delay.

(c) Where a solicitor does not resolve such delays to the satisfaction of the Lender and arising from that the Lender intends to complain to the Law Society, the Lender will notify the solicitor of its intention to so do and shall, before making such a complaint, afford the solicitor at least 10 working days to complete the outstanding actions or to furnish an explanation as to why he/she cannot complete them.

(d) Complaints by Lenders to the Law Society will be made on the authority of a manager of the Lender not below the rank of Senior Manager or equivalent.

(e) Nothing in the Guidelines shall be interpreted as restricting or postponing any remedy the Lender may have against a solicitor where the Lender reasonably believes that a breach by a solicitor of the Undertaking may result in financial loss to the Lender or to the security it relies on or the priority of such security being adversely affected.

Releases, Discharges and Vacates

23. It is acknowledged that delays in lodging completed Certificates of Title with title deeds on behalf of a Borrower may occur due to delays in obtaining a vacate of the Borrower's previous mortgage or a vacate of a mortgage on title belonging to a previous owner of the relevant property. In order to eliminate this possible source of delay, the Lenders agree that:

(a) on payment of the sum requested to redeem a Borrower's outstanding mortgage and a written request to release the Mortgage, a release/discharge/vacate (as appropriate) will be furnished to the requesting solicitor within one month of receipt of payment or the request whichever is later;

(b) if the Mortgage to be released or discharged covers other property not being released or if the Lender does not wish to release the Borrower's covenant to repay the loan, the Lender will execute a deed of partial release or a partial discharge, provided a draft of such partial release or partial discharge (with map as appropriate) satisfactory to the Lender is provided by the Borrower's solicitor.

Resolving Delays on the Part of Lenders

24. (a) A solicitor concerned that a Lender has not met the time limits set out in paragraphs 4, 5, 21(d) or 23 of the Guidelines for the provision to him or her of any of the items described therein should, in the first instance, write to the Lender drawing its attention to the fact that the items are overdue. The Lender shall respond within 10 working days to such letter either by furnishing the outstanding item or by specifying in writing a good reason or reasons for the delay in the provision by the Lender of the item. The solicitor shall not unreasonably reject a reason given by a Lender for such delay.

(b) Where a Lender does not furnish the outstanding item or provide an explanation for delay to the satisfaction of the solicitor and, arising from that, the solicitor intends to make a complaint to the Lender, the solicitor will notify the Lender of his/her intention to do so and shall, before making such a complaint, afford the Lender at least 10 working days to furnish the outstanding item or such explanation.

(c) A complaint made by a solicitor to a Lender under this paragraph 24 will be treated by the Lender as a customer complaint to which, at a minimum, the procedure set out in Provision 10.9 of the 2012 Consumer Protection Code issued by the Central Bank of Ireland http://www.centralbank.ie/regulation/processes/consumer-protection-code/Documents/Consumer%20Protection%20Code%202012.pdf ("Provision 10.9") will apply.

(d) A solicitor shall not refer the matter giving rise to complaint to the Financial Services Ombudsman unless the complaint has not been resolved as provided for in paragraph d) of Provision 10.9.

(e) Nothing in the Guidelines shall be interpreted as restricting or postponing any remedy a solicitor or a client of a solicitor may have against a Lender where the solicitor or the client reasonably believes that the failure of the Lender to furnish an item described in paragraphs 4, 5, 21(d) or 23 of the Guidelines may result in financial loss to the solicitor or the client or which may affect the ability of either of them to fulfil their contractual obligations to any third party in respect of the property to which the outstanding item relates.

Frequency of Reminders

25. (a)   Lenders should not send solicitors requests for reports on progress as to stamping, registration of title and security at unreasonably close intervals.

     (b)   For normal cases, the solicitor should not expect a reminder from the Lender to provide confirmation of lodgement for registration in the appropriate registr(y) (ies) of the purchase deed/transfer and Mortgage until a date occurring 6 months after completion or thereabouts.

     (c)   If the solicitor lodges the purchase deed/transfer and Mortgage for registration and provides the dealing number or confirmation of lodgement in the Registry of Deeds (as appropriate) to the Lender within 6 months of completion, the solicitor should not (for normal cases) expect a reminder from the Lender to furnish an up-date on the progress of registration until a date occurring 6 months or thereabouts after such confirmation of lodgement.

     (d)   The Lender may need to correspond with the Borrower's solicitor more frequently in exceptional cases. Such exceptional cases include (i) where the Borrower is in default of its obligations to the Lender under the loan; (ii) where the Lender anticipates it may incur a financial loss in connection with the loan; (iii) where the Lender considers the security or its priority in respect of the security to be adversely affected or likely to be so; (iv) where the solicitor has been in serious breach of any Undertaking given by him or her to the Lender; or (v) where the solicitor has not responded to requests for information from the Lender or has furnished unsatisfactory responses to the Lender. The Guidelines should not be interpreted as limiting the Lender's rights and remedies in these and other exceptional cases.

     (e)   Solicitors should respond promptly and fully to such requests from Lenders for reports on stamping and registration of title and security provided they are made in accordance with this paragraph 25.

Accepting Undertakings

26. (a)   A Lender shall not refuse to accept an Undertaking or accountable trust receipt for title deeds from a solicitor without good objective reason.
     (b)   It is the solicitor's responsibility to obtain the Borrower's irrevocable retainer and authority in respect of any undertaking.
     (c)   Lenders may have policies concerning the acceptance of Undertakings from solicitors where there is a perceived conflict of interest.

Participating Lenders

The following Lending Institutions (referred to throughout the Guidelines as "the Lenders" and each a "Lender" which expression shall include any other financial institution which uses the Agreed Documents) have agreed to the matters contained herein in respect of utilising the 2011 edition of the Agreed Documents in relation to residential mortgage lending:

1. ACC Bank
2. A.I.B. Bank
3. Bank of Ireland
4. Bank of Scotland plc (including the former Bank of Scotland (Ireland) Limited).
5. EBS Limited
6. ICS Building Society
7. Irish Bank Resolution Corporation (including the former Irish Nationwide Building Society)
8. KBC Bank
9. National Irish Bank
10. Permanent TSB
11. Ulster Bank Ireland Limited (including the former First Active plc).

Dated the 2nd day of April, 2012

Excerpt from 2012 Consumer Protection Code issued by the Central Bank of Ireland ("Provision 10.9")

_____

COMPLAINTS RESOLUTION

10.8   When a *regulated entity* receives an oral *complaint*, it must offer the *consumer* the opportunity to have this handled in accordance with the *regulated entity*'s *complaints* process.

10.9   A *regulated entity* must have in place a written procedure for the proper handling of *complaints*. This procedure need not apply where the *complaint* has been resolved to the complainant's satisfaction within five *business days*, provided however that a *record* of this fact is maintained. At a minimum this procedure must provide that:

   a)   the *regulated entity* must acknowledge each *complaint* on paper or on another *durable medium* within five *business days* of the *complaint* being received;

   b)   the *regulated entity* must provide the complainant with the name of one or more individuals appointed by the *regulated entity* to be the complainant's point of contact in relation to the *complaint* until the *complaint* is resolved or cannot be progressed any further;

   c)   the *regulated entity* must provide the complainant with a regular update, on paper or on another *durable medium*, on the progress of the investigation of the *complaint* at intervals of not greater than 20 *business days,* starting from the date on which the *complaint* was made;

   d)   the *regulated entity* must attempt to investigate and resolve a *complaint* within 40 *business days* of having received the *complaint*; where the 40 *business days* have elapsed and the *complaint* is not resolved, the *regulated entity* must inform the complainant of the anticipated timeframe within which the *regulated entity* hopes to resolve the *complaint* and must inform the *consumer* that they can refer the matter to the relevant Ombudsman, and must provide the *consumer* with the contact details of such Ombudsman; and

   e)   within five *business days* of the completion of the investigation, the *regulated entity* must advise the *consumer* on paper or on another *durable medium* of:
       i)   the outcome of the investigation;
       ii)   where applicable, the terms of any offer or settlement being made;
       iii)   that the *consumer* can refer the matter to the relevant Ombudsman, and
       iv)   the contact details of such Ombudsman.

10.10   A *regulated entity* must maintain an up-to-date log of all *complaints* from *consumers* subject to the *complaints* procedure. This log must contain:
   a)   details of each *complaint*;
   b)   the date the *complaint* was received;
   c)   a summary of the *regulated entity's* response(s) including dates;
   d)   details of any other relevant correspondence or *records*;
   e)   the action taken to resolve each *complaint*;
   f)   the date the *complaint* was resolved; and
   g)   where relevant, the current status of the *complaint* which has been referred to the relevant Ombudsman.

CHAPTER 10

SEARCHES

10.1 Introduction

10.1.1 WHAT ARE SEARCHES?

Searches are enquiries carried out, usually by a purchaser's or mortgagor's solicitor, on the transfer of an interest in property. Searches are carried out in government and local government offices and they are intended to check the ownership of a property, what liabilities, charges, or other burdens or encumbrances affect it, and to obtain details regarding its planning and related matters. They also enquire into the status of the vendor or mortgagor which might affect ownership of the interest being transferred.

Any items disclosed as a result of the searches which adversely affect the property, its ownership, or the status of the vendor/purchaser will need to be brought to the attention of the purchaser/mortgagee and possibly also the lender.

10.1.2 WHY CARRY OUT SEARCHES?

10.1.2.1 Introduction

The basic conveyancing principle of the bona fide purchaser for value without notice was previously set out in s 3 of the Conveyancing Act, 1882. Section 3 of the 1882 Act has now been repealed by the Land and Conveyancing Law Reform Act, 2009 ('the 2009 Act') and it is replaced by s 86 of the Act. Section 86 contains a slightly different wording but retains the same basic principle of the bona fide purchaser for value without notice.

Section 86(1) states as follows:

> *A purchaser is not affected prejudicially by notice of any fact, instrument, matter or thing unless—*
>
> (i) *it is within the purchaser's own knowledge or would have come to the purchaser's knowledge if such inquiries and inspections had been made as ought reasonably to have been made by the purchaser, or*
>
> (ii) *in the same transaction with respect to which a question of notice to the purchaser arises, it has come to the knowledge of the purchaser's counsel, as such, or solicitor or other agent, as such, or would have come to the knowledge of the solicitor or other agent if such inquiries and inspections had been made as ought reasonably to have been made by the solicitor or agent.*

Thus, in order for a purchaser to have the protection afforded by the law to a bona fide purchaser for value the purchaser must carry out reasonable enquiries. The doctrine can only apply after such enquiries and inspections have been made, as ought reasonably to have been made, by the purchaser. It follows without question that there is a clear obligation on solicitors acting for purchasers and lenders in conveyancing transactions to carry out all searches relevant to the transaction in question.

An additional reason why searches are carried out is to ensure that the purchaser obtains 'good marketable title' to the property in accordance with the Contract for Sale and as required under the Certificate of Title system for residential mortgage lending.

10.1.2.2 Law Society standard conditions

The standard Law Society General Conditions of Sale and Objections and Requisitions on Title contain clauses relevant to searches.

The Searches Schedule of the Contract for Sale provides for the listing of any negative searches which are being furnished by the vendor's solicitor to the purchaser. It was the recommended practice for the vendor's solicitor to furnish an up-to-date negative search, which relates only to unregistered property, on the vendor covering the period from when he acquired an interest in the property up to the current date. These negative searches have now been replaced by the official search. See **10.2.7**.

General condition 19 provides that the purchaser shall be furnished with the searches (if any) listed in the Searches Schedule and any searches already in the vendor's possession which are relevant to the title on offer. In practice vendors' solicitors may decline to furnish any searches and can be reluctant to give the searches in their possession, however, purchasers' solicitors should try to insist on the vendor furnishing reasonable searches in accordance with conventional practice and as provided for in general condition 19.

General condition 19 of the Contract for Sale also provides that the vendor must explain and discharge any acts appearing on searches covering the period from the date stipulated or implied in the contract for the commencement of the title to the date of actual completion. However, where the special conditions in the contract provide that the title shall commence with a particular instrument and then pass to a second instrument or to a specified event, the vendor shall not be obliged to explain and discharge any act which appears on a search covering the intermediate period (between such particular instrument and the date of the second instrument or specified event) unless the same goes to the root of the title.

Requisition 13 of the standard Law Society Objections and Requisitions on Title provides that a purchaser will make searches where necessary in the following offices and registers:

(a)   Registry of Deeds;

(b)   Land Registry;

(c)   judgments;

(d)   bankruptcy;

(e)   sheriff;

(f)   Companies Registration Office; and

(g)   Planning Office.

Any act appearing on the result thereof must be explained and/or discharged by the vendor prior to completion.

While it is extremely important to carry out such searches it is equally important, having regard to the increasing cost of such searches, that solicitors do not make or require unnecessary searches for any transaction. Thus, it is vital that solicitors know the appropriate searches for each type of transaction.

10.2   Types of Searches

The following sets out the most likely searches to be made in a typical conveyancing transaction. Law searchers are usually engaged to do this work but many searches can now be made online and thus can be done directly by solicitors. The advantage of using a firm of law searchers is that the firm will have professional indemnity insurance. Solicitors should periodically check the level of this insurance to ensure it is adequate to cover any potential claim. Using law searchers may mean a time delay in getting the results whereas doing the search directly online means the information is current and immediate, however, there is no other party to fall back on if a search is not done correctly.

10.2.1 JUDGMENTS OFFICE SEARCH

10.2.1.1 Introduction

A judgment search involves a search on two registers in the central office of the High Court. It will show any judgment against the vendor in the last five years (Money Judgments Register) and any lis pendens (Lis Pendens Register), ie proceedings indicating a dispute over the title of the property or the registration of a charge on it may be pending.

Strictly speaking a Judgments Office search should only be against the Lis Pendens Register but law searchers will generally also search against the Money Judgments Register and it is recommended practice to search against both (see Practice Note Law Society *Gazette* August/September 2014).

10.2.1.2 Money Judgments Register

Where a judgment appears it presents the possibility of a judgment mortgage being registered against the property under s 116 of the 2009 Act. This was previously provided for by the Judgment Mortgage (Ireland) Act, 1850 which has now been repealed. The judgment itself does not affect the lands until a judgment mortgage is registered. A judgment mortgage registered after the closing of the sale will not catch any interest of the former owner as he or she has none. Prior to the 2009 Act all his or her interest in the property passed to the purchaser on payment of the balance of the purchase money on completion.

In *Tempany v Hynes* [1976] IR 101 the Supreme Court held that a purchaser of registered land took the land free of a judgment mortgage registered against the vendor post contract. This was because the Registration of Title Act, 1964, s 71(4) provides that such a charge is subject to 'all unregistered rights' affecting the vendor's interest at the time of registration of the judgment mortgage. The purchaser, it was held, had such an unregistered right under the contract.

See also *Re Murphy and McCormack* [1928] IR 479; [1930] IR 322.

Section 117(3) of the 2009 Act now provides that a judgment mortgage is subject to any right or incumbrance affecting the judgment debtor's land, whether registered or not, at the time of its registration. Section 130 amends the Registration of Title Act, 1964 by providing that registration of a judgment mortgage in the Land Registry operates to charge the estate or interest of the judgment debtor subject to—

(i) *the burdens, if any, registered as affecting that estate or interest,*

(ii) *the burdens to which, though not so registered, that estate or interest is subject by virtue of section 72,*

(iii) *all unregistered rights subject to which the judgment debtor held that estate or interest at the time of registration,*

and with the effect stated in section 117 of the said 2009 Act.

Section 52 of the 2009 Act also provides that the entire beneficial interest passes to the purchaser on the making of an enforceable contract for the sale or other disposition of land. The purchaser is deemed to acquire an interest in the property that will have priority over any judgment mortgage registered against the vendor's interest in the property after the making of such an enforceable contract. Taken together these sections ensure that a judgment mortgage registered after execution of the contract will not affect the property; however there is the practical difficulty of having the judgment mortgage removed.

Where a vendor has judgments registered against him or her and no action has been taken to convert any such judgments into judgment mortgages, a purchaser's solicitor is not entitled to require that any such judgments be vacated. However registration of the purchaser's title should be treated as a matter of priority and consideration should be given to lodging a priority entry if the title is registered (see **14.8**). Where a loan is being provided under the Certificate of Title system (see **9.7.2**) the purchaser's solicitor does not act for the lender and therefore owes no duty to the lender to inform it if any money judgments appear on searches against the purchaser/borrower. However, under the undertaking, the mortgage must be registered as a first legal charge so any judgment mortgages registered before registration of the purchaser's title must be cleared.

10.2.1.3   Lis Pendens Register

Where a lis pendens is disclosed the purchaser is on notice of the proceedings and if he proceeds with the transaction he or she will be bound by the outcome of such proceedings. Thus, any lis pendens must be dealt with prior to completion. However a lis pendens against unregistered land will not bind a purchaser without actual knowledge of it unless it has been registered in the Central Office of the High Court within five years before the making of the conveyance to the purchaser (s 125 of the 2009 Act). This is because a lis pendens can only be registered in the Judgments Office of the Central Office and in the Land Registry. There is no provision for registering in the Registry of Deeds. A lis pendens against registered land will remain on the register until cancelled. It would be highly inadvisable to close a transaction where a lis pendens appears on a search at closing unless the litigation in respect of which the lis pendens is registered does not affect the land. This may be difficult to determine as the third party plaintiff, who caused the lis pendens to be registered, may claim that it does affect the particular property.

It is difficult to ascertain the precise legal position in relation to lis pendens and registered land. The reason for this is as follows. Section 69 of the Registration of Title Act, 1964 sets out the burdens that may be registered as affecting registered land and these include lis pendens. The logical consequence is that if a lis pendens is not registered on the folio it cannot affect registered land. It is, however, the practice to make a search on the Lis Pendens Register when buying or lending on registered land.

Sections 120–126 of the 2009 Act now govern the Lis Pendens Register in the Central Office of the High Court (previously s 10 of the Judgments (Ireland) Act, 1844 which has now been repealed).

10.2.2   SHERIFF'S OFFICE SEARCH

There are two types of Sheriff's Office search: bills of sale Sheriff's Office search and revenue Sheriff's Office search. The sheriff has a legal right to seize the goods of a debtor on foot of a decree Fi Fa or equivalent. Previously this did not include real (freehold) property. Thus, the searches only needed to be carried out in respect of leasehold property. Section 133 of the 2009 Act provides that the power of the sheriff to seize a tenancy is abolished except in relation to a tenancy of land that is used wholly or partly for the purpose of carrying on a business. Thus for wholly residential property it was no longer necessary to do a Sheriff's Office search (see Practice Note, Law Society *Gazette*, March 2012).

The sheriff did not have a right to obtain possession. He merely had a right to sell. It was the purchaser from a sheriff who obtained a right to possession. A purchaser from a sheriff might have to sue for possession. The sheriff's right to execute only related to the legal estate in a property.

However the position has now changed with the enactment of the Fines (Payment and Recovery) Act, 2014 which came into force on 11 January 2016 (SI 6/2016). This provides that recovery orders for fines over €500 may be made by the court and such orders will appoint the sheriffs, including Revenue sheriffs to collect the fine. The Minister may also approve other persons to carry out the functions under the Act which are vested in the sheriffs or such other persons as 'receivers'. The powers granted by this legislation to the sheriffs to recover fines exceed those previously vested and most importantly the sheriffs have the power to seize and sell property belonging to the fined person. Property is defined in s 8(16) as land or personal property. Sheriffs have the power to enter, demand and take possession, manage, dispose of, retain and otherwise deal with, insure, and inspect any books and documents relating to the property.

Thus under this legislation sheriffs or 'receivers' have power to seize and take possession of real property and no distinction is made between residential or commercial property. However s 133 of the 2009 Act has not been repealed. While this limits the sheriff's power to seize a tenancy to commercial property and may prevent the exercise of such powers in relation to residential property, where there is a Part 4 or other tenancy in exist-ence, the safer option is to carry out a Sheriff's Office search for all property, whether resi-dential or commercial, freehold or leasehold.

10.2.3 PERSONAL INSOLVENCY AND BANKRUPTCY SEARCHES

A Bankruptcy Office search is only appropriate in the case of individuals, as a company cannot be made bankrupt. If the vendor has been made bankrupt he cannot deal with the property, as all his property will have vested in the Official Assignee. The certificate of the vesting of his estate in the Official Assignee must be registered in the Registry of Deeds or the Land Registry. If there is a voluntary deed on title a bankruptcy search must be made against the donor if the deed is less than five years old. If the donor is declared bankrupt within five years there is a presumption that it is void unless it can be shown that the donor was, at the date of the disposition, able to meet his debts without recourse to the property (s 59 of the Bankruptcy Act, 1988).

If the donor is made a bankrupt within three years of the deed, then the deed is void as against the official assignee (this was previously two years). If after three years and still within five years the donor is made bankrupt, the deed is void unless the donor can estab-lish that he or she was solvent at the time of the deed without relying on the property (Bankruptcy Act, 1988, s 59 as amended by s 154 of the Personal Insolvency Act 2012). A deed of this nature will accordingly require a statutory declaration by the donor (referred to in practice as a declaration of solvency) confirming that the transfer to the donee was effected for natural love and affection without any intent to defraud his or her creditors and for the purpose of conferring a benefit upon the donee and that in doing so the donor was solvent and able to meet his or her other creditors without the benefit of the property transferred. In addition a bankruptcy search will be required.

If, in fact, a transfer from the donee to another party has taken place within three years then previously an indemnity bond for the value of the property from an insurance com-pany was required to protect the purchaser from the possibility of the original donor be-coming bankrupt within the three-year period. However, a Practice Note in the April 1998 Law Society *Gazette* advises that a bond should not now be required once a declaration of solvency is produced by the donor. This Practice Note is based on case law on the 'old' bankruptcy rules, to the effect that within the three-year period the deed is void only as against the official assignee. Until the official assignee is appointed on the bankruptcy of the donor, the deed is merely voidable. A purchaser from a donee, within this three-year period, is protected provided they have no notice of the bankruptcy of the original donor. This is accomplished by carrying out a bankruptcy search. Therefore, a purchaser from a donee is protected, even within the three-year period, provided that the donor was not bankrupt at the time of the deed from the donee to the purchaser. It should be noted that the Personal Insolvency Act, 2012 increased the previous period of two years in s 59 of the Bankruptcy Act, 1988 to three from 3 December 2013 (see SI 462/2013).

In January/February 2016 the Conveyancing Committee recommended that when carry-ing out bankruptcy searches, practitioners also ensure that searches are carried out on the new registers set up pursuant to the personal insolvency legislation. The recommendation is that personal insolvency/bankruptcy searches are carried out on the following registers:

– a bankruptcy search on the Register of Irish bankruptcies maintained at the Office of the Examiner of the High Court

– Register of EU Personal Insolvencies held at the office of the Official Assignee

– Register of Debt Relief Notices

– Register of Protective Certificates

– Register of Debt Settlement Arrangements

– Register of Personal Insolvency Arrangements

10.2.4 PLANNING OFFICE SEARCH

A Planning Office search is carried out on the property. This search is usually carried out regardless of the type of property being sold or the title. It may be carried out by both the vendor and purchaser prior to contract; the vendor so as to provide assistance in determining if the warranty in general condition 36 of the contract needs to be limited, and the pur-chaser so as to determine, *inter alia*, if the planning history of the property is in order. However if, for example, the purchaser is buying the property for development or re-development he or she will likely have an architect and an engineer checking all aspects of the planning prospects of the property and these investigations may be much more intensive than a normal planning search which may then not be required.

The planning search will generally reveal, *inter alia*,

(a)   the zoning of the area;

(b)   any road widening proposals;

(c)   any prior applications for planning permission in respect of the property, any refusals or appeals of permission, any application for building bye-law approval, and any other entries in the Planning Register in respect of the property;

(d)   any enforcement action taken or warning notices served;

(e)   whether the property is a protected structure or any conservation order has been made;

(f)   whether any sterilisation agreement has been entered into relation to the property.

Some local authorities will furnish a planning search on payment of a fee, however in other areas a firm of law searchers will need to be engaged. It should be noted that some law searchers only search back five years unless instructed otherwise. It is important to note that some local authorities do not show enforcement proceedings in a general planning search and thus it is important to specify exactly what information is being sought about the property and the exact period for which the search should be undertaken. Until recently many of the planning registers were not well maintained and precise information can be patchy and in some cases missing entirely.

It is important that this search is carried out pre-contract and the purchaser told of the results. The search may then need to be updated for closing. It is vital that, if possible, a planning search covers the planning history of the property since 1 October 1964, the date of the coming into force of the Local Government (Planning and Development) Act, 1963.

A computer planning search may now be done in some areas. It is necessary to be careful doing this type of search as the computer will only search against the exact information furnished, eg if searching against 'Anne Ryland' it will not automatically search against 'Ann Ryland'. The name must be precise as there is a double charge for each name check, which makes the search expensive.

A planning search, however, will not disclose the existence of any unauthorised developments unless the local authority has served an enforcement or warning notice or unless an application has been made for retention permission. The assistance of an architect or engi-neer will be required to determine if the position on the ground corresponds with what was lodged in the planning office. If there are no enforcement proceedings or notices served this does not mean that the property has been built in accordance with planning. Local au-thorities do not carry out checks on whether properties have been built in accordance with planning as a matter of routine. If retention permission has been granted a purchaser will need to ensure that the drawings and plans on foot of which the retention permission was granted correspond with what in fact was built. No certificate of compliance is required because the retention permission itself is a confirmation of compliance.

The search will only reveal the planning history of the specific property in question. It will not disclose details about other developments in the area where the property is situate. For example, it will not reveal a proposed motorway scheme, that a factory is being built next door, or that a planning application has been made to convert the premises across the road into a chip shop. As a result a purchaser should be advised to personally attend the local authority offices to carry out an inspection of the Planning Register or to make enquiries of people in the area. Locals will tend to know what is planned in a particular area and developments occurring which could affect the amenities of the locality. This will allow the purchaser to determine if there are any proposed developments, for example a meat factory, in the immediate area of the property that might affect his decision to purchase. Alternatively it may disclose restrictions on the future development of the property that might affect his decision to purchase (see Practice Note, Law Society *Gazette*, November 1984).

For further information on planning searches see the Law Society CLE Series of Seminars on Planning Law by John Gore-Grimes and Patrick Sweetman, dated 2 December 1998.

10.2.5 ENVIRONMENTAL SEARCHES

Purchasers are advised to carry out searches to establish if the property is listed as a proposed special area of conservation or national heritage area. Lists of all proposed sites are maintained by each local authority. An examination of these searches is outside the scope of this chapter. Again for further information on these searches see the Law Society CLE Series of Seminars on Planning Law by John Gore-Grimes and Patrick Sweetman, dated 2 December 1998.

10.2.6 COMPANIES OFFICE SEARCH

A Companies Office search arises when the vendor is a company. It also arises in the case of apartments, as the management company will need to be searched against. It is not necessary to carry out such searches on companies which appear on prior title. A Companies Office search will disclose the status of the company, ie has it been struck off the register or does it still exist. It will disclose all charges on the assets of the company and whether it is in receivership, examinership, or liquidation. The end of the search is as important as the body of the search itself because this lists unregistered and recently registered documents. An entry of 'C.1.' or 'CHC' must be noted as they disclose that the company has created a charge and a certificate of registration of the charge has been received by the Companies Office but has not yet been registered. Confirmation should be sought that the charges do not affect the property being sold. Alternatively, confirmation that the charges have been discharged is required. If a floating charge is disclosed a purchaser will require a certificate from the company secretary that the charge has not crystallised, in other words, that it has not become a fixed charge on the property, and also a letter from the owner of the floating charge (usually a lending institution) confirming that it has not crystallised.

The Companies Office search should be carried out before contracts are exchanged to ensure that the company has not been struck off the register. In recent years the Companies Office has been very proactive in striking off companies, including some very prominent ones, for failure to make annual returns.

In June 2010 the Law Society Business Law Committee recommended in the *Gazette* that where Companies Office searches are being carried out by law searchers they should be requested to do the search at the CRO, either at the counter, or online using the CRO web-search facility rather than from the service providers' own database which would not be up to date.

10.2.7 REGISTRY OF DEEDS SEARCH

10.2.7.1 Generally

A Registry of Deeds search is carried out when the title being offered is unregistered, ie the title documents are registered in the Registry of Deeds. It is a search to find out what deeds have been registered affecting the particular property. The name of the person to be searched against, the premises affected, and the dates to be searched must be furnished.

There were previously a number of different official Registry of Deeds searches: negative search, common search, and hand search. Also the Registry of Deeds had a Names Index and a Lands Index, however, the Lands Index is deemed to have been closed on 31 December 1946 by virtue of s 46 of the Registration of Deeds and Title Act, 2006 ('the 2006 Act'). Now the only index operating is the Names Index (also known as the Index of Grantors) and it is on this index that searches are made. The former common and negative searches have been replaced by one type of search; the official search.

10.2.7.2 Official searches

An official search is made by an official Registry of Deeds searcher and the results are certified by the Registry. The application form is prescribed as is the certificate of the result. These are forms 11 and 12 in the Schedule to the Registration of Deeds Rules, 2008 (SI 52/2008).

10.2.7.3 Hand searches

The second type of search is a hand search. This may be made by any member of the public but is usually made by a firm of law searchers who will have professional indemnity insurance ensuring that any loss as a result of an error made by them will be covered. Hand searches ensure that it is possible to carry out searches right up to the date of actual completion of the purchase.

10.2.7.4 Importance of correct instructions for search

In relation to these searches it is important to ensure that a correct and full description of the property is given and also that the correct spelling of the parties' names is given. Regardless of the type of search it is vital that the requisition for the search includes all descriptions by which the land is or was previously known. If in doubt always include alternative descriptions and all alternative spellings. The reason for this is that if searching against 'Katherine Mullins', any acts of 'Kate' or 'Katie' Mullins will not show. It is for this reason that requisition 13.2 asks if the vendor has ever executed any document in relation to the property in the Irish equivalent or any other variant of his name.

10.2.7.5 Period of search

The general practice is to search back a minimum of 15 years; however, if the vendor has owned the property for 30 years then the search should be against the vendor for that period of 30 years. Each party on title during that 15-year period must be searched against. Where possible, solicitors should be practical about the length of title shown and accordingly the period in respect of which searches are made.

A Registry of Deeds search must be carried out against all parties on title for the appropriate period. The appropriate period is the *date of the deed* to the person to the *date of the registration of the deed* where the person disposes of their interest in the property ie the subsequent deed. To re-iterate: the relevant period to search is from the date of the deed when the person acquired their interest in the property to the date of registration of the subsequent deed when they disposed of their interest.

For example, if B buys from A on 5 May 1952 (registered on 14 May 1952) and then sells to C on 1 July 1963 (registered on 7 August 1963) who, in turn, sells on to D on 8 February 1978 (registered on 3 March 1978) and, on 13 June 1999, D executes a contract selling the property to the present client E then, if the 1952 deed is given as the root of title, the following searches should be made in the Registry of Deeds:

(a) against B from 5 May 1952 to the date of the registration of his deed to C on 7 August 1963;

(b) against C from 1 July 1963 to the date of the registration of his deed to D on 3 March 1978; and

(c) against D from 8 February 1978 to the date of completion of the purchase.

For the purposes of this example we are presuming that the 1963 and 1978 deeds are not good roots of title and that we must go back to the 1952 deed to establish good title.

If the purchaser E is obtaining a mortgage it is also necessary to search against him (E) from the date of the contract, ie the date he acquired a beneficial interest in the property, 13 June 1999, to the date of completion.

10.2.7.6 Death on title

The appropriate period is somewhat different if there is a death on title.

If there is a death on title the period to search against the testator is extended. The search must be up to the date of registration of the assent to the beneficiary. If there is no assent the period to search against the testator is up to the date of registration of the subsequent conveyance for value.

If an executor has been appointed the period to search against the executor is from the date of the testator's death to the date of registration of the assent. If the assent has not been registered the search should be up to the date of registration of the subsequent conveyance for value. The beneficiary should be searched against from the date of death of the deceased to the date of registration of the conveyance for sale disposing of his or her interest in the property.

Where there is no will and an administrator is appointed, the period to search against the administrator is from the date of the grant of administration to the date of registration of the assent. If the assent has not been registered the search should be up to the date of registration of the subsequent conveyance for value. The beneficiary should be searched against from the date of death to the date of registration of the conveyance for sale disposing of his or her interest in the property.

In other words, when there is a grant of probate the search against the personal representative must be from the date of death and when there is a grant of administration intestate the search against the personal representative must be from the date of the grant. Any documents that appear on the searches must be explained and, where necessary, discharged or released.

10.2.8 LAND REGISTRY SEARCH

A Land Registry search is carried out when the title being offered is registered in the Land Registry. The search will disclose all details on the folio, ie the current registered owner, the nature of the title (ie whether absolute, good leasehold, or possessory), any dealings pending and any encumbrances appearing (eg any cautions or inhibitions registered on the folio). If there is a letter after the number of the folio this must be given as there may be a number of different folios with the same number. For example, Folio 12345, Folio 12345F, Folio 12345L, and Folio 12345R are all different folios.

A Land Registry search will not disclose all necessary information about the property as there are certain burdens which can affect registered property without registration (s 72 Reg-istration of Title Act, 1964). These include easements and *profits à prendre* unless created by express grant or reservation after the first registration of the land, certain tenancies, rights of those in actual occupation, rights excepted from the effect of registration, and rights acquired or in the course of being acquired under the Statute of Limitations, 1957.

10.2.9 PRIORITY ENTRY (SEARCHES)

Section 108 of the Registration of Title Act, 1964, as amended by s 66 of the Registration of Deeds and Title Act, 2006 and rules 160 onwards of the LR Rules, 2012 provide for official searches in the Land Registry. The rules in relation to priority entry (previously called priority searches) (rules 161 and 162) are particularly important. This search has the added advantage that when the Registrar issues the search he puts an inhibition on the folio. This inhibits all dealings for a period of 44 days, save the dealing by the party on whose behalf the search was made, ie usually the purchaser or mortgagee. After the 44 days a further priority search may be applied for; however, this does not continue the previous period. Any applications lodged during the 44 days will be registered before the new 44-day period begins. This search is not commonly done but is recommended where there is a reason to be apprehensive about the financial status of the vendor or where the transaction involves a property of significant value. In some instances use of a priority entry may not be feasible. For example registration of a priority entry in a building estate could cause chaos by preventing registration of the ownership of purchasers of other units.

In a Practice Note in the August/September 2013 Law Society *Gazette* the Conveyancing Committee confirmed that there should not be a bank requirement for a priority search as an automatic requirement in every case and that it is a judgement call for each individual solicitor to make in each case. This position applies whether the solicitor is a panel solicitor acting for the bank or otherwise.

10.2.10 ADDITIONAL SEARCHES

Additional searches include searches of the Derelict Sites Register, Private Residential Tenancies Board Register, Register of Dangerous Buildings, Register of Fire Safety Certificates, and Register of Multi-Storey Buildings. A further type of search is a bills of sale search which deals with personal chattels, fixtures, and crops. This search will be necessary if, for example, the sale includes expensive equipment or shop contents. These additional searches are not dealt with here. For additional information see the lecture by Patrick Sweetman dated 27 February 1998 as part of the Law Society CLE Series of Four Seminars on Essential Conveyancing for Practitioners.

10.3 Who Carries Out Searches?

Searches should be prepared by a recognised firm of law searchers with an appropriate level of indemnity insurance. Previously it was thought that searches carried out by solicitors were not acceptable (see Practice Note, Law Society *Gazette*, June 1983) however this was during a time when the information was not available directly and immediately to solicitors. It is now possible for a knowledgeable and experienced conveyancer to do some searches themselves at a reduced cost. For example many solicitors would be hesitant about carrying out a planning search but have no difficulty accessing up-to-date folios via the Land Registry's landdirect.ie service.

10.4 When are Searches Carried Out?

As stated at **10.1.2.1** the purchaser must make appropriate enquiries in order to be afforded the protection offered by the law to a bona fide purchaser for value. This involves making the appropriate searches prior to completion in order to determine that the title is unencumbered and that other matters such as planning are in order. Generally these searches are carried out prior to completion; however, a prudent conveyancer, bearing in mind the principle of caveat emptor, may also wish to carry out some searches prior to contract. The vendor may also need to carry out searches pre-contract in order to properly fulfil his or her duty of disclosure to the purchaser. The vendor has a duty of disclosure in relation to defects on title, rights, and liabilities that affect the property and also notices served on the vendor in relation to the property. The vendor may be unable or unwilling to furnish his or her solicitor with certain information about the property or himself or herself and in these circumstances searches may need to be carried out in order to comply with the duty of disclosure. For example, the vendor may have several judgments against him or her but may not know if these have been converted into judgment mortgages. In relation to title matters this duty of disclosure will be limited by the period of title being offered to the purchaser. For example if title skips from the root of title to a deed for value 15 years old, the vendor does not have a duty of disclosure in relation to the period of intermediate title which is being skipped.

As a general rule most searches are carried out post contract and prior to completion. However it must be borne in mind that searches may reveal something about a property that might cause a purchaser to decide not to proceed with the transaction. Equally searches done pre-contract by a vendor's solicitor might reveal some fact which the vendor was unaware of and which might impact on the purchase. Hence the necessity for particular searches to be done; the viability and the cost implications must be judged on a case-by-case basis depending on the parties and the particular transaction.

An exception arises when the purchaser is also mortgaging the property and the completion of the mortgage occurs after completion of the purchase. In that instance the lender will require the searches to be updated to the date of completion of the mortgage. The Law Society Certificate of Title documents for residential mortgage lending (2011 edn) require that searches must include those against the borrower and, when a purchase is completed in advance of the mortgage, the searches must be updated to the date of the mortgage. The main reason lenders require such searches to be updated is to check the possibility of a judgment mortgage being registered against the property and gaining priority though case law and the new provisions in the 2009 Act show that a lender or purchaser need not be concerned with any judgment registered as a judgment mortgage after the contract or completion of the purchase. This is dealt with in more detail at **10.2.1.2.**

10.5 What to do with the Result of Searches?

The result of the various searches carried out will disclose information in relation to the vendor and/or the property. It may be necessary for the purchaser's solicitor to disclose some of that information to his or her client as it may affect the client's decision to purchase. Alternatively, the purchaser's solicitor may require the vendor's solicitor to confirm that the information or 'acts' appearing on the search do not affect the property being purchased by the client (see Practice Note, Law Society *Gazette*, December 1997). For example, if the Registry of Deeds search discloses a charge on the property the vendor's solicitor will be required to furnish a discharge on closing, or if the planning search discloses that the property is sterilised but the client wishes to build then this will obviously impact on his or her decision to purchase. Alternatively, if the search result throws up a mortgage on the property next door then the vendor's solicitor will confirm that this 'act' does not affect the property in sale. The vendor's solicitor will also need to state that this 'act' affects the property next door. Hence it is not enough for a vendor's solicitor to certify that an 'act' does not affect the property being sold. He or she must also state what property it does affect or be able to show reasonable grounds for believing that it is not the property the subject of the transaction.

The purchaser's solicitor makes the searches where necessary in the relevant offices and registers and any act appearing on the results thereof must be explained and/or discharged by the vendor prior to closing. The type of explanation usually offered by the vendor's solicitor is that the act appearing 'does not affect' the property in question. If this is the case the vendor's solicitor should state what the act does affect. The explanation must be noted on the result of the search, signed, and dated by the vendor's solicitor.

Any encumbrance affecting the property must be discharged and there must be no other transaction in relation to the property that would adversely affect the title being offered to the purchaser.

10.6 Sets of Searches

10.6.1 GENERALLY

The following sets out the searches that ought reasonably to be required in a general residential conveyancing transaction.

Some of these searches, as listed, are required only if the purchaser is mortgaging the property. The Law Society Certificate of Title documents for residential mortgage lending (2011 edn) require that searches must include those against the borrower from the date of the contract to the date of closing and, if the purchase is completed in advance of the mortgage, the searches must be updated to the date of the mortgage.

10.6.2 SECOND-HAND HOUSES

10.6.2.1 Freehold registered title

When buying a property with a freehold registered title (Land Registry):

The purchaser will require:

(a) Land Registry search against the freehold folio;

(b) judgment search against vendor;

(c) sheriff's search against the vendor;

(d) either bankruptcy and personal insolvency search (if the vendor is an individual) or Companies Office search (if the vendor is a body corporate) against vendor; and

(e) planning search against the property.

In addition, the mortgagee will require:

(i) up-to-date Land Registry search against the folio (unless the mortgage is contemporaneous with the completion of the purchase); and

(ii) judgment and either bankruptcy search or Companies Office search against borrower and any guarantor of the mortgage.

Note

A hand search in the Registry of Deeds is not required.

10.6.2.2 Leasehold registered title

When buying a property with a leasehold registered title (Land Registry):

The purchaser will require:

(a) Land Registry search against the leasehold folio;

(b) judgment search against vendor;

(c) sheriff's search against the vendor;

(d) either bankruptcy and personal insolvency search (if the vendor is an individual) or Companies Office search (if the vendor is a body corporate) against the vendor; and

(e) planning search against the property.

In addition, the mortgagee will require:

(i) up-to-date Land Registry search against the folio (unless the mortgage is contemporaneous with the completion of the purchase); and

(ii) judgment and either bankruptcy search or Companies Office search against borrower and any guarantor.

Notes

There is no necessity for a Registry of Deeds search, or a search against the freehold folio.

10.6.2.3   Freehold Registry of Deeds title

When buying a freehold property with unregistered title (registered in the Registry of Deeds):

The purchaser will require:

(a)   official search against all parties on title for the appropriate period;

(b)   hand search against vendor from the date to which the official search is made up to date of closing;

(c)   judgment search against vendor;

(d)   sheriff's search against the vendor;

(e)   bankruptcy and personal insolvency search (if the vendor is an individual) or Companies Office search (if the vendor is a body corporate) against vendor; and

(f)   planning search against the property.

In addition the mortgagee will require:

(i)   hand search against borrower from date of contract;

(ii)   official search in the Registry of Deeds against the vendor to date of completion of mortgage (unless the mortgage is contemporaneous with the completion of the purchase);

(iii)   judgment search against borrower; and

(iv)   bankruptcy search or Companies Office search against borrower and any guarantors.

Notes

The general practice is to search back a minimum of 15 years, ie to the root of title or the document from which title is being deduced. Where possible solicitors should be practical about the length of title shown and accordingly the period in respect of which searches are made. If there is a voluntary conveyance on title a bankruptcy search should be made against the donor.

10.6.2.4   Leasehold Registry of Deeds title

When buying a leasehold property with unregistered title (registered in the Registry of Deeds):

The purchaser will require:

(a)   official search against all parties on title for the appropriate period;

(b)   hand search against vendor from the date to which the official search is made up to date of closing;

(c)   judgment search against vendor;

(d)   sheriff's search against the vendor;

(e)   bankruptcy and personal insolvency search (if the vendor is an individual) or Companies Office search (if the vendor is a body corporate) against vendor; and

(f)   planning search against the property.

In addition the mortgagee will require:

(i)   hand search against borrower from date of contract;

(ii)   official search in the Registry of Deeds against the vendor to date of completion of mortgage (unless the mortgage is contemporaneous with the completion of the purchase);

(iii) judgment search against borrower; and

(iv) bankruptcy search or Companies Office search against borrower and guarantors.

Notes

The general practice is to search back a minimum of 15 years, ie to the root of title or the document from which title is being deduced. Where possible solicitors should be practical about the length of title shown and accordingly the period in respect of which searches are made.

If there is a voluntary conveyance on title a bankruptcy search should be made against the donor.

10.6.3 HOUSING ESTATES/NEW HOUSES

10.6.3.1 Freehold or leasehold registered title

When buying a new house where the title is freehold or leasehold and registered in the Land Registry:

The purchaser will require:

(a) Land Registry search against the folio;

(b) bankruptcy and personal insolvency search (if the vendor is an individual) or Companies Office search (if the vendor is a body corporate) against registered owner;

(c) judgment search against vendor;

(d) sheriff's search against vendor;

(e) certificate of the developer's solicitor that there are no adverse dealings pending registration, affecting the folio (only required if there are dealings pending); and

(f) planning search against the property.

In addition the mortgagee will require:

(i) judgment search against the borrower;

(ii) bankruptcy search or Companies Office search against borrower and any guarantors; and

(iii) sheriff's search against borrower (leasehold only where the property is used partly for the purpose of carrying on a business).

Notes

There is no necessity to obtain a Companies Office search against companies appearing on title other than the vendor, the management company (if any), and any company providing a structural defects indemnity or other guarantee.

If the vendor is different from the builder there is no necessity to do searches against the builder unless some of the purchase money is being released to the builder or his agent (Practice Note, Law Society *Gazette*, October 1985) or the builder is providing a structural defects indemnity or other guarantee. If the building agreement is with the builder, a Companies Office search should be made pre-contract to ensure that the builder company has not been dissolved.

Where planning permission was obtained a year or so before the sale and a recent certificate of compliance is being provided relating to such permission then a planning search may not be necessary unless required by the lender.

10.6.3.2 Freehold or leasehold Registry of Deeds title

When buying a new house, where the title is freehold or leasehold and is unregistered (registered in the Registry of Deeds):

The purchaser will require:

(a)   Registry of Deeds official search against all parties on title for the appropriate period;

(b)   judgment search against vendor;

(c)   bankruptcy and personal insolvency search or Companies Office search against vendor;

(d)   sheriff's search against vendor; and

(e)   planning search against the property.

The mortgagee will require:

(i)   hand search against borrower from date of contract to date of delivery of mortgage;

(ii)   judgment search against borrower;

(iii)   bankruptcy search or Companies Office search against borrower and any guarantors; and

(iv)   sheriff's search against borrower (leasehold only where the property is used partly for the purpose of carrying on a business).

Notes

The general practice is to search back a minimum of 15 years, ie to the root of title or the document from which title is being deduced. Where possible, solicitors should be practical about the length of title shown and accordingly the period in respect of which searches are made.

If there is a voluntary conveyance on title a bankruptcy search should be made against the donor.

There is no necessity to obtain a Companies Office search against companies appearing on title other than the vendor, the management company (if any), and any company providing a structural defects indemnity or other guarantee.

If the vendor is different from the builder there is no necessity to do searches against the builder unless some of the purchase money is being released to the builder or his agent (Practice Note, Law Society *Gazette*, October 1985) or the builder is providing a structural defects indemnity or other guarantee. If the building agreement is with the builder a Companies Office search should be made pre-contract to ensure that the builder company has not been dissolved.

Where planning permission was obtained a year or so before the sale and a recent certificate of compliance is being provided relating to such permission then a planning search may not be necessary unless required by the lender.

CHAPTER 11

PLANNING

11.1   The Planning Authority

11.1.1   INTRODUCTION

Prior to the coming into force of the first significant Planning Act, the Local Government (Planning and Development) Act, 1963 ('the 1963 Act'), planning control was exercised in a number of ways.

In rural areas there was little or no need for planning control. In urban situations, however, when grants of land were demised by way of lease, the freehold owner sought to keep some control over the future development of the land by way of covenant that within a specified period the lessee had to erect a building thereon of a certain height and to a certain standard. Much of the development of Georgian Dublin and, later, Victorian Dublin was governed in this way. Prime examples are the development of Mountjoy Square and the surrounding area where Lord Gardiner was a wealthy landowner, Merrion Square, which at the time of its development was regarded as the outskirts of Dublin, and Fitzwilliam Square, where the Earl of Pembroke owned extensive holdings. Further out, Lord Proby owned the lands around Blackrock and the Longford De Vesci Estate were landlords near Dun Laoghaire.

Another influence was the Wide Street Commissioners who laid down certain standards and were responsible for, obviously, widening the main thoroughfares in the centre of the city, principally Westmoreland Street, D'Olier Street, O'Connell Street, and the surrounding areas.

The Public Health (Ireland) Acts from 1878 onwards laid down minimum standards governing matters of public health in relation to construction, eg drainage, sewerage, standards for habitable dwellings, etc. The Town and Regional Planning Acts, 1934 and 1939 sought to put development on a more formal footing and, under these Acts, two types of permission: a general permission and a special permission, were available for development purposes.

11.1.2   PLANNING AND DEVELOPMENT ACT, 2000

The Planning and Development Act, 2000 revised and and consolidated in one Act all nine Planning and Development Acts (Acts of 1963, 1976, 1982, 1983, 1990, 1992, 1993, 1998, and 1999) enacted since 1963 and introduced a sustainable development philosophy to the Irish planning system.

The Planning and Development Act, 2000 was passed on 28 August 2000. The Act came into force piecemeal but is now fully in force. This Act extensively reformed and consolidated Irish planning law. Among other changes, it included radical new measures in relation to housing supply, in particular the provision of social and affordable houses. It was the first complete review of the planning code since the 1963 Act, and caused major controversy.

The purpose of this Act is set out in its title as follows:

An Act to revise and consolidate the Law relating to Planning and Development . . . to provide in the interests of the common good, for proper planning and sustainable development including the provision of housing; to provide for the licensing of events and control of funfairs. . . . and to provide for matters connected therewith.

The concept of sustainable development appears for the first time in a Planning Act.

However, the Act itself does not set out specific sustainability objectives to put into development plans. Instead, the idea seems to be that development plans should be infused with sustainable development concerns. In other words it will be a matter for each regional authority to ensure that the old development plan assesses the sustainability criterion. John Gore-Grimes in *Key Issues in Planning and Environmental Law* (Butterworths, 2002) p 469 gives a good definition of sustainable development as follows:

'Sustainable development is development which meets the needs of the present without compromising the ability of future generations to meet their own needs. It is achieved by ensuring that environmental concerns are taken into account in all aspects of the planning process so that development progress is not achieved at the expense of environmental quality.'

Indeed this book is, in general, an excellent and practical planning guide for conveyancers.

The Act at s 4(2)(a) allows for the provision of planning regulations and the regulations now in force are given in the list that follows.

John Gore-Grimes' second book in this area, *Planning and Environmental Law in Ireland* (Bloomsbury Professional, 2011) which substantially updates his previous text, is essential reading for practitioners in this area; in particular chapter 12, paras 1033–82 which looks specifically at planning from a conveyancing perspective.

The Act of 2000 has in itself been amended several times and various regulations issued as follows:

• the Planning and Development (Amendment) Act, 2002 which dealt with, amongst other issues, social and affordable housing conditions (see **11.5.7.1**) and abolished withering permissions as they apply to planning permissions obtained for residential permissions affected by Part V of the 2000 Act. These have been replaced by a levy. See requisition 26.3B of the requisitions on title, **11.8.2.8**;

• the Planning and Development Regulations, 2002 (SI 70/2002) which modified details required on OS maps when plans are being submitted for planning permission;

• the Planning and Development (No 2) Regulations, 2002 (SI 149/2002) which prescribed a fee for licences for fingerpost direction signs for tourist accommodation;

• the Planning and Development Regulations, 2003 (SI 90/2003) which made changes to the minimum floor areas for accommodation required for eligible people under s 100(1)(a) of the Planning and Development Act, 2000;

• the Planning and Development (Regional Planning Guidelines) Regulations, 2003 (SI 175/2003) which set out a number of procedural requirements in relation to the preparation of regional planning guidelines by regional authorities, including the taking into account of the National Spatial Strategy. They came into effect from May 2003;

• the Planning and Development Act, 2000 (Certification of Fairground Equipment) Regulations, 2003 (SI 449/2003) which dealt with matters of procedure, administration, and control in relation to applications for, and grants of, certificates of safety for funfair equipment. The Regulations came into effect from 1 October 2003;

• the European Communities (Environmental Assessment of Certain Plans and Programmes) Regulations, 2004 (SI 435/2004) which transposed into Irish law the Strategic

Environmental Assessment (SEA) Directive (Directive 2001/42/EC) on the assessment of the effects of certain plans and programmes, except land-use planning, on the environment. The Regulations came into force on 14 July 2004;

- the Planning and Development (Strategic Environmental Assessment) Regulations, 2004 (SI 436/2004) which transposed into Irish law the Strategic Environmental Assessment (SEA) Directive (Directive 2001/42/EC) on the assessment of the effects of certain plans and programmes on the environment, in so far as the Directive relates to the Planning and Development Regulations, 2005 (SI 364/2005) which amended the Planning and Development Regulations, 2001 to provide that a shop changing its use to an off-licence would require planning permission, amended the provisions in relation to peat extraction to facilitate consideration of the need for the environmental impact assessment of projects which are likely to have significant effects on the environment and also amended Parts I and II of Schedule 5 of the 2001 Regulations;

- the Planning and Development (Strategic Infrastructure) Act, 2006 ('the 2006 Act') which provided for the introduction of a 'strategic consent process' for strategic infrastructure of national importance provided by statutory bodies and private promoters. It also provided a range of supporting measures, including the restructuring of An Bord Pleanala and, in particular, for the provision of a strategic infrastructure division which now handles decisions for all major infrastructure projects. Most interestingly, the 2006 Act for the first time enabled planning authorities to refuse permission to developers on the basis of his or her past history of non-compliance with planning permissions. In effect, this means that such an applicant is required to apply to the High Court if he or she wishes to have any decision to refuse permission overturned. In effect, therefore, this amendment reverses the onus of proof: the developer rather than the planning authority will have to prove that such a decision to refuse permission is not warranted;

- the Planning and Development Regulations, 2006 (SI 685/2006) which provided for revised procedures to enhance public participation in the environmental impact assessment of projects having transboundary environmental impacts;

- the European Communities (Environmental Impact Assessment) (Amendment) Regulations, 2006 (SI 659/2006) which provided for revised procedures to enhance public participation in the environmental impact assessment of projects having transboundary environmental impacts;

- the Planning and Development Regulations, 2007 (SI 83/2007) and the Planning and Development (No 2) Regulations, 2007 (SI 135/2007). The former Regulations set out planning exemptions for micro-renewable energy technologies for domestic houses and came into effect from 28 February, 2007 and the latter which came into force on 31 March 2007 provided for a transitional period up to 1 June 2007 to ensure that there would be no excessive invalidations due to the changeover to the new arrangements. This 'grace period' only relates to the validation of applications; all the other provisions of the Regulations came into effect on 31 March 2007. Among the other amendments made by SI 135/2007 are provisions aimed at improved data protection for users of the planning system;

- the Planning and Development (Amendment) Regulations, 2008 (SI 256/2008) and Planning and Development Regulations, 2008 (SI 235/2008) which built upon the planning exemptions for certain micro-renewable energy technologies in the domestic sector that were announced in February 2007;

- the Planning and Development Regulations, 2008 (SI 235/2008) which give effect to new exempted development provisions in respect of renewable technologies for industrial buildings, business premises, and agricultural holdings. The Regulations provide exemptions for wind turbines, met masts, combined heat and power (CHP) plants, solar panels, and biomass boiler units, subject to certain conditions, across each of the sectors. The Regulations came into effect from 2 July 2008. See **11.4.1** for exemptions;

- the Planning and Development (Regional Planning Guidelines) Regulations, 2009 which dealt with regional planning matters;

- the Planning and Development (Amendment) Act, 2010 ('the 2010 Act'), ss 1–4, 26, 28–29, 37, 42, 46, 53–56, 58, 64, 66, 68, 70–71, 73, and 81 were commenced by SI 405/2010 on 19 August 2010. The commencent date for ss 32, 33, and 50A under SI 451/2010 was 28 September 2010 and ss 23A and C, 41A, 41B, and 49 were commenced on 23 March 2011 by SI 132/2011. The Act amended and extended the Planning and Development Act, 2000, and amended the Transport (Railway Infrastructure) Act, 2001 and provided for related matters. It provided that development plans shall contain relevant information to show that the development plan and the housing strategy are consistent with regional planning guidelines and the national spatial strategy 2002–2020. Post the Act development plans must also contain mandatory objects for the promotion of sustainable settlement and transportation strategies in urban and rural areas. It also makes provision in relation to the duration of planning permission. Under the 2010 Act planning permission can be refused by a planning authority where the applicant has previously carried out substantial unauthorised development or has been convicted of an offence under the 2000 Act. It also increases the penalties for offences and provides for the taking in charge by the local authority of housing/residential areas;

- in addition, one of the most important changes introduced in the 2010 Act is that it will no longer be possible to obtain retention permission for unauthorised developments which would have required an EIA. The Act now contains a substitute consent procedure and the circumstances in which one can extend the life of a planning permission are extended. A planning permission may now be extended on one occasion only for up to a further five years. Application to extend must be applied for before the expiry of the original permission. An extension may be granted where a development has not gone ahead due to commercial, economic, or technical considerations beyond the control of the applicant. For a full understanding of these changes, an examination should be made of the judgment of the European Court in Case C-215/06 *Commission v Ireland,* in which, in June 2008 the ECJ ruled that the Irish retention permission system did not comply with the EIA Directive. In addition, see the lecture given by Garrett Simons, SC at the Planning and Environmental Law Conference 2010, entitled 'The EIA Directive and the Planning and Development (Amendment) Act 2010' pp 87–105. See also *Farrell and Forde v Limerick Co,* 17 June 2009, High Court (unreported);

- the Planning and Development Regulations, 2010 (SI 406/2010) prescribed the information to be included in applications under the Planning and Development (Amendment) Act, 2010, ss 42 and 42A for extending the appropriate period as regards particular permissions, the commencement date for which was 19 August 2010;

- the Multi-Unit Developments Act, 2011 established a new statutory framework for multi-unit developments including dealing with transfer of common areas to the property management company and the management of such areas by the company and the effective internal governance of the company. See **11.9.14**;

- the Planning and Development (Amendment) Regulations, 2011 (SI 262/2011);

- the Planning and Development Act 2000 (Strategic Development Zone) (Amendment) Order, 2011 (SI 243/2011);

- the Planning and Development (Strategic Environmental Assessment) (Amendment) Regulations, 2011 (SI 201/2011), the purpose of which was to amend the Planning and Development (Strategic Environmental Assessment) Regulations, 2004 (SI 436/2004) (SEA), see earlier, which was on the assessment on the effects of certain plans and programmes on the environment;

- the European Communities (Amendment to Planning and Development Regulations) Regulations, 2011 (SI 464/2011);

- the Planning and Development (Amendment) Act, 2010 (Commencement) (No 2) Order, 2011 (SI 475/2011) which appointed 21 September 2011 as the day on which certain provisions of the Planning and Development Amendment Act, 2010, namely s 6, s 10(f), s 12(d), s 14(c), s 23(b), s 50(c), s 57, s 72, and s 80 come into operation;

- the Planning and Development (Amendment) (No 2) Regulations, 2011 (SI 454/2011) the primary purpose of which was to amend the exempted development provisions of the

Planning and Development Regulations, 2001 (SI 600/2001) which have been updated and amended by subsequent statutory instruments as set out earlier. The principal change in these regulations is that the exempted development threshold for draining of wetlands is being reduced from 20 hectares to 0.1 hectares on foot of a decision of the European Court of Justice (Case C–66/06) of 20 November 2008. Other drainage is being reduced to 2 hectares and some other land reclamation activities, eg removal of field boundaries, are being exempted from the planning system as they will be subject to a new consent system under the Department of Agriculture, Fisheries and Food. In addition, new planning exemptions are being introduced in respect of portable waste disposal compactors, agricultural rain water harvesting, temporary advertisement signs for local commercial events, and the exemption in relation to paving of gardens is being amended. The fee payable for a s 254 licence for placing an advertisement structure on a public road was reduced;

• the Planning and Development (Amendment) Regulations, 2012 (SI 116/2012);

• the Planning and Development Regulations, 2013 (SI 219/2013) commenced on 25 June 2013. It amends Class 41 of the Second Schedule, Part 1 of the Regulations substantially in relation to the carrying out of the developments under Part III of the Building Control Regulations—construction or erection of an external fire escape or water tank, activities under s 55 of the Waste Management Act, and s 70H5 of the Water Services Act, 2007 (as amended by the 2012 Act);

• European Union (Environmental Impact Assessment and Habitats) (s 181 of the Planning and Development Act 2000) Regulations, 2013 (SI 403/2013);

• the Planning and Development (Amendment) (No 2) Regulations, 2013 (SI 520/2013);

• the Electoral, Local Government and Planning Act, 2013. The purpose of this Act was to give effect to Council Directive 2013/1/EU and to amend the European Parliament Elections Act, 1997, to amend the Electoral Act, 1992, the Referendum Act, 1994, the Electoral Act, 1997, the Planning and Development Act, 2000, and the Local Government Act, 1991 and to provide for related matters in particular Part 8; s 28 deals with the Planning and Development sections of same;

• the Planning and Development Regulations, 2013 (SI 584/2013), (SI 424/2013), and (SI 272/2013); these were the Commencement Orders to the above Act;

• European Union (Environment Impact Assessment and Habitats) (ss 181 of the Planning and Development Act 2000) Regulations, 2013 (SI 493/2013);

• the Planning and Development (Amendment) Regulations, 2015 (SI 264/2015). These Regulations amend the Planning and Development Regulations 2001–2014 and impose an obligation on event organisers and Local Authorities to hold a pre-application consultation meeting;

• European Union (Environmental Impact Assessment) (Planning and Development) Regulations, 2014 (SI 543/2015). These Regulations deal with EIAs;

• the Planning and Development (Amendment) (No 2) Regulations, 2015 (SI 310/2015) which commenced on 16 July 2015 deal with applications to An Bord Pleanala under s 37L of the Act, ie quarries;

• the Planning and Development (Amendment) (No 3) Regulations, 2015 (SI 387/2015). These Regulations amend the Planning and Development Regulations 2001–2015 by making necessary technical amendments to planning application requirements and substitute the reference to vacant land use with land or structure which is not in use.

The above list, while extensive, does not include every piece of leglisation and in addition, it must be remembered that significant amendments to the planning leglisation have been made by 'non planning' leglisation, eg the Housing (Miscellaneous Provisions) Act, 2004, the Water Services Act, 2007, the Harbours (Amendment) Act, 2009, or the Compulsory Purchase Orders (Extension of Time Limits) Act, 2010. For further information on such leglisation see *Irish Planning Law Factbook*, edited by Berna Grist and James Macken (Thompson Roundhall). Indeed for a general overall background to the planning process this factbook is very good and easy to use.

11.1.3   DEFINITION

'Planning authority' is defined in the 2000 Act, s 2(1) as:

(a) *In the case of a county, exclusive of any borough or urban district therein, the council of the county,*

(b) *In the case of a county or other borough, the corporation of the borough, and*

(c) *In the case of an urban district, the council of the urban district,*

and references to the area of the Planning Authority shall be construed accordingly, and shall include the functional area of the authority (Dublin Corporation is now Dublin City Council).

In 1993 Dublin County Council was replaced by three new administrative counties which are known as Fingal, Dun Laoghaire/Rathdown, and South Dublin. Each of these has a separate council.

11.1.4   FUNCTIONS OF A PLANNING AUTHORITY

In general, the main functions of a planning authority are:

(a) to prepare and revise development plans: 2000 Act, Part II, ss 9–17;

(b) to make decisions on individual applications for planning permission: 2000 Act, Part III;

(c) to use powers of enforcement to ensure compliance with the requirement to obtain planning permission or to comply with the terms and conditions of any permission issued: 2000 Act, Part VIII, ss 151–164;

(d) to be party to any appeal against a decision made by it whether to grant or refuse permission: 2000 Act, Part VI(1), chapter III;

(e) maintenance of the public register: 2000 Act, Part I, s 7;

(f) to examine environmental assessment: 2000 Act, Part X, ss 172–177;

(g) to make compensation, which arises where planning permission is refused or conditions attached to a planning permission restrict future development of the property: 2000 Act, Part XII, chapters I–III, ss 183–201;

(h) to develop land itself; the development must not be in material contravention of its own development plan: 2000 Act, Part XI, ss 178–182;

(i) to acquire land, Part XIV, ss 210–223;

(j) to control development on the foreshore, Part XV, ss 224–228;

(k) to exercise authority re areas of special amenities Part XIII, ss 202–209;

(l) to exercise powers re housing supply, Part V, ss 93–101; (See also CLE lecture by Patrick Sweetman, 'Planning and Development Act 2000, Book IX', given in March 2001.) and

(m) to exercise powers on architectural heritage, Part IV, ss 51–92.

11.2   Planning Register

11.2.1   INTRODUCTION

Section 7 of the 2000 Act requires a planning authority to keep a planning register in which all relevant planning information is recorded. It extends considerably, ss 8 and 41 of the 1963 Act, and SI 349/1989 and SI 84/1994, for example: s 7(2)(d), (f), (g), (h), (i), (o), (p), (z) (discussed later). Not all of the changes are for the better. Note, in particular, s 7(3), where the planning authority has an obligation to make entries and corrections '*as soon as may be*', whereas, under the 1963 Act, it had to do so within seven days. There is no guarantee that a planning register is up to date. Further, no sanctions are imposed on a local authority which does not keep its register up to date. Section 248 of the 2000 Act allows the information to be provided in electronic form. Under s 8, the local authority can require a member of the public to provide them with information within a two-week period (previously 14 days) after it has been requested.

The register, which incorporates a map (s 7(4)) is available for inspection to members of the public at the offices of the planning authority during office hours (s 7(6)). A certified copy of an entry in the register is regarded as *prima facie* evidence of the entry without proof of signature or producing the register itself. A fee must be paid to obtain such a copy (s 7(9)).

Planning authorities are required to publish a weekly list of all planning applications received, not later than the third working day following that week: Local Government (Planning and Development) Regulations, 1994 (SI 86/1994) ('the 1994 Regulations'), Art 30. This list is required to be displayed at the planning office and in each public library for not less than two months beginning on the day on which it is made available.

11.2.2   CONTENTS OF THE PLANNING REGISTER

The planning authority is obliged to enter the following matters:

(a)   any application for permission whether for development, retention of development, or for outline permission. Please note (see **11.2.1**) details of such applications are no longer required to be entered within seven days of receipt;

(b)   where an environmental impact statement was submitted in respect of an application, s 172 provided that the Minister may prescribe information to be contained in the environmental impact statement. This will require regulations;

(c)   where development, to which an application relates, comprises or is for the purposes of an activity in respect of which an integrated pollution control licence, or a waste management license is required, or a licence under the Local Government (Water Pollution) Act, 1977, is required in respect of discharges from the development (this is a new requirement);

(d)   where the development to which the application relates would materially affect a protected structure, or is situated in an area declared to be an area of special amenity, under s 202

(e)   the complete decision of the planning authority in respect of any such application, including any conditions imposed, and the date of the decision;

(f)   the complete decision on appeal of the Board in respect of any such application, *including any conditions* imposed (this latter point is a new requirement) and the date of the decision (the italic words are new);

(g)   where the requirements of s 34(6) in regard to the material contravention of the development plan have been complied with (this is a new element of the register which helps the collection of evidence for a judicial review);

(h)   particulars of any declaration made by a planning authority under s 5 (this relates to a declaration and referral on development and exempted development and is a new requirement);

(i)   particulars of any application made under s 42 to extend the appropriate period of permission;

(j)   particulars of any decision to revoke or modify a permission in accordance with s 44 (s 44 only applies where the development plan has been amended, and the proposed development no longer applies to it);

(k)   particulars under s 45 of any order, any decision on appeal, or of any acquisition notice for compulsory acquisition of land for open space;

(l)   particulars of any notice under s 46 requiring the removal or alteration of any structure, or requiring discontinuance of any use, or the imposition of condition on the continuance thereof, including the fact of its withdrawal, if appropriate (this is a new requirement);

(m)   particulars of any agreement made under s 47 (see requisitions on title 26.11—sterilisation) for the purpose of restricting or regulating the development or use of the land;

(n)   particulars of any declaration issued by the planning authorities under s 57 (works affecting the character of protected or proposed protected structures) including the details of any review of this declaration;

(o)   particulars of any declaration issued by the planning authority under s 87 (development and special planning control area) including the details of any review of this declaration (this is a new requirement);

(p)   particulars of any notice under s 88 in respect of land in an area of special planning control, including, where such notice is withdrawn, the fact of its withdrawal (this is a new requirement);

(q)   particulars of any certificate granted under s 97 (this is development to which s 96, the provision of social and affordable housing does not apply and is a new requirement);

(r)   particulars of any warning letter issued under s 152 including the date of issue of the letter and the fact of its withdrawal if appropriate;

(s)   the complete decision made under s 153 on whether an enforcement notice should issue, including the date of the decision;

(t)   particulars of any enforcement notice issued under s 154, including the date of the notice and the fact of its withdrawal, or that it has been complied with if appropriate;

(u)   particulars of any statement prepared under s 188 concerning a claim for compensation under the 2000 Act;

(v)   particulars of any order under s 205, requiring the preservation of any tree or trees including the fact of any amendment or revocation of the order;

(w)   particulars of any agreement under s 206 for the creation of a public right of way over land;

(x)   particulars of any public right of way created under s 207;

(y)   particulars of any information relating to the operation of a quarry provided in accordance with s 261 (this is a new requirement); and

(z)   any other matters as may be prescribed by the Minister.

11.2.3   THE REGISTER FROM A CONVEYANCER'S POINT OF VIEW

Section 6 of the Planning and Development (Amendment) Act, 2010 which amends s 7 extends somewhat matters which must be included, mainly relating to substitute consent and EIAs but there are serious lacunae still in its completeness.

It is vital to realise that, despite this extensive list, there are several matters which are not included in the register, so it alone cannot be relied upon to accurately represent the situation as it actually is. It would be better if all registers were amalgamated into one (eg the Derelict Sites Register and any other register or record which the local authority or planning authority is statutorily bound to maintain), so that an examination of the planning register would give solicitors, planners, architects, a full picture not just of the permissions applied for and granted, sterilisation orders made, and all other planning-related matters, but also all environmental issues, for example whether or not a commencement notice has been served, whether or not a fire certificate has issued, etc. Conveyancers, when requesting a search from their law searchers, should request a search not only of the Planning Register, but also of the Building Control Act Register, and the Derelict Sites Register.

The importance of the necessity, given earlier, in every conveyancing transaction to carry out planning office searches at pre-contract stage cannot be over emphasised. It has long been accepted that the purchaser's solicitor should make a planning search before the exchange of contracts, and this is universally done. However, a solicitor acting for a vendor should also make a planning search before preparing a Contract for Sale. This has been reiterated many times by the Conveyancing Committee and at various Law Society Continuing Professional Development (CPD) lectures. In his seminal CPD lecture, 'Planning and Development Act, 2000, Book IV', John Gore-Grimes explains that if a vendor's solicitor fails to make such a search, and it transpires that a notice has been served under the Planning and Development Act, the vendor may well be in breach of the obligation provided in the Law Society's General Conditions of Sale, (general condition 35) which requires a vendor to disclose notices. General condition 35, in requiring the vendor to disclose notices, does offer some comfort to the purchaser but it specifically excludes notices, being the contents of a development plan. A notice which the vendor is required to disclose under general condition 35 is one *'in respect of the subject property, and affecting same at the date of sale'*. Apart from the making of pre-contract planning searches, when acting both for a vendor and a purchaser, it is now widely accepted within the profession that a solicitor should raise pre-contract enquiries on planning and any other matters to be dealt with by the client. To assist in this, the Law Society has issued pre-contract questionnaires for both vendor and purchaser.

11.3 Development Plan and Development

Part II, ss 9–17 of the 2000 Act deals with development plans, local area plans, regional planning guidelines, and ministerial guidelines and directives. Section 9 requires every planning authority to make a development plan every six years (previously, every five) which relates to the whole functional area of the authority. Section 9(4) and (5) now requires that regard must be had to the development plans of adjoining planning authorities. This is an attempt at a more integrated planning policy. Section 10(1) defines a development plan as follows:

> *a development plan shall set out an overall strategy for the proper planning and sustainable development of the area of the development plan, and shall consist of a written statement and a plan or plans indicating the development objectives for the area in question.*

It must contain a written statement with a map indicating the local authority's objectives as well as certain mandatory objectives (see s 10(2)(a)–(m)). What it may contain is set out in the first schedule to the Act (s 9(3)). The Minister is given power to add additional objectives which shall, or may, be incorporated in development plans (s 9(4)). Unlike s 19(2) of the 1963 Act, there is no distinction between urban and rural authorities in relation to objectives.

11.3.1 REVIEW AND VARIATION OF DEVELOPMENT PLAN

Review and variation of development plans are a major part of general planning law but are not within the remit of this chapter and thus will not be discussed here in any detail. If further information is required on this see ss 11–15 of the Act. In short, a planning authority, not later than four years after the making of a development plan, must give notice of its intention to review its existing development plan, and prepare a new one for its area.

That notice invites submissions and observations to be submitted to the planning authority within a specified period, which shall not be less than eight weeks (s 11(2)(b)). The planning authority then goes through a consultation procedure which can involve oral hearings, written submissions, and liaison with interested bodies.

11.3.2   DEVELOPMENT

Development is defined in s 3(1) of the 2000 Act, as follows:

> *'Development' in this Act means, save where the context otherwise requires, the carrying out of any works on, in, over, or under land or the making of any material change in the use of any structures or other land.*

There are two distinct parts to the definition of development, although they are not always exclusive and sometimes overlap. One refers to the carrying out of 'works' and the other refers to the making of any 'material change of use'.

'Works' are defined in s 2 of the 2000 Act as *'including any act or operation of construction excavation, demolition, extension, alteration, repair or renewal . . . .'* 'Alteration', also defined in s 2, includes 'plastering or painting or the removal of plaster or stucco, or the replacement of a door, window or roof which materially alters the external appearance of the structure so as to render such appearance inconsistent with the character of the structure or of neighbouring structures'. Since the 2000 Act, it also applies in relation to a protected structure or proposed protected structure where any act of operation involves the application or removal of plaster, paint, wallpaper, tiles, or other material to or from the surface of an interior or exterior of such a structure.

'Unauthorised structure' means a structure other than a structure which was in existence on 1 October 1964, or a structure, the construction, erection, or making of which was subject to permission for development granted under Part IV of the 1963 Act, or under s 34 of the 2000 Act, or which exists as the result of the carrying out of exempted development. Clearly therefore, any structure erected before 1 October 1964 is not an unauthorised structure.

'Unauthorised development' is for the first time interpreted in s 2 of the 2000 Act as meaning 'in relation to land, the carrying out of any unauthorised works, (including the construction, erection, or making of any unauthorised structure) or the making of any unauthorised use'. This interpretation does not make any reference to unauthorised development prior to 1 October 1964, because it does not have to—the essence of the interpretation refers to 'unauthorised works', 'unauthorised structure', and 'unauthorised use', all of which phrases respectively, do make reference to:

(a)   works commenced on or after 1 October 1964;

(b)   structures in existence on 1 October 1964; and

(c)   use commenced on or after 1 October, 1964. Therefore, unauthorised development can only have taken place after 1 October 1964.

'Unauthorised works' are also interpreted by s 2 of the 2000 Act. It means any works carried on, in, over, or under land commenced on or after 1 October 1964, being development other than exempted development or development which is the subject of a permission granted under Part IV of the 1963 Act or under s 34 of the 2000 Act being a permission which has not been revoked, and which was carried out in compliance with that permission or any condition to which that permission is subject. Re the onus of proof, where unauthorised development is disputed, and for the seeking of discretionary relief see *Wicklow Co Co v Jessup & Smith*, 8 March 2011 (unreported).

There is no clear definition of 'use'; rather it is stated negatively. Section 3(2) specifies cases which are to be treated as a material change of use. These include:

(a)   any structure, tree, or other object on land used for the exhibition of advertisements;

(b) placing or keeping vans, tents, or other objects for the purpose of caravanning or camping or the sale of goods;

(c) storage of caravans or tents; and

(d) the deposit of parts of vehicles, builders' waste, industrial waste, or old metal.

Section 3(3) also states that a material change of use arises where a single dwelling is sub-divided into two or more dwellings. If the use has remained the same since 1 October 1964, the use is an established use. If the use has changed since 1 October 1964, and permission for a new use was obtained from the local authority, it is a permitted use.

A change of use, by itself, does not constitute development. The change of use must be material. In other words, the degree of the change must be material.

There is a general principle that to constitute a material change of use, the use must be substantially different from the previous use. In practice, whether there has been such a change of use is one of fact and degree. Similarly, there is no definition of 'material change of use' in the 2000 Act and there is a considerable body of case law on what constitutes a material change of use within the meaning of the 1963 and 2000 Acts.

O'Sullivan and Shepherd, *Irish Planning Law and Practice* points out that the following tests have been suggested:

(a) Is the change physical rather than mental? (A change in the character of the land, say, from residential to commercial or from agricultural to quarry.)

(b) Is the change substantial? Can its effect be measured?

(c) Is the change one to be taken into account because of its impact on the environment or its increased traffic or demand for services?

There should be a comparison between the present use and the previous use of the lands. If the present use is for a quite different purpose then there is a material change. A material change of use would be if a dwellinghouse is changed entirely into barristers' chambers. However, if an engineer decided to work from home and used one room of his house as an office, did not invite clients there, or employ staff, or have a business plate outside then there would not be a material change of use. Another example often given is of a farm shop for the sale of surplus produce from the farm. Such a use would be ancillary. There would be a material change of use if the shop included items not produced on the farm.

A material change of use may also happen through the intensification of an existing long established use. The type of questions to be asked to ascertain whether there has been intensification would include:

(a) Has there been a change from the kind of products previously made?

(b) Is the production method more intense either by an increase in the workforce or the use of more modern machinery?

(c) Has there has been an increase in traffic, noise, or pollution?

(d) Has the area of activity increased or differed?

This latter question is often raised in relation to extracting stone from quarries and a substantial body of case law has built up in relation to quarrying operations. These are fully detailed in *O'Sullivan and Shepherd*.

An added complication is where there is permission for a particular use but it has been underutilised. Its subsequent, more efficient, expanded use might not amount to intensification. Again, a lot would depend on the actual facts and the application of the questions listed earlier. An example is *Cusack and McKenna v Minister for Local Government*, 4 November 1980, High Court (unreported) where the plaintiffs commenced using a portion of a residential house for their solicitors' practice without obtaining planning permission. Prior to this the premises had been used for a dentist's practice and then for residential flats. Planning permission was not required for the dental practice as that was prior to October 1964. The plaintiffs claimed that there was not a material change of use from a dentist's practice to a solicitor's practice or, if it was development, it was exempted as it was a material change of use within the same class (both uses for the office) and therefore exempt under the 1977 Regulations. However, at the time the plaintiffs purchased the premises they were used entirely for residential purposes. McWilliam J found on the facts that there was an intervening residential use and therefore any subsequent change was unauthorised. Such a change would be material as a dental practice and a solicitor's practice had nothing in common.

In assessing whether there has been a material change of use an examination will be made not only as to the use itself but also as to its effects. See *Cork Corporation v O'Connell* [1982] ILRM 505 and *Mahon v Trustees of the Irish Rugby Football Union* [1997] 3 IR 1369.

'Unauthorised use' means, in relation to land, use on or after 1 October 1964, being a use which is a material change of use of any structure or other land, being a development other than an exempted development or development which is subject to a permission granted under Part IV of the 1963, or s 34 of the 2000 Act, being a permission which has not been revoked which was carried out in compliance with that permission or any condition to which that permission is subject. Section 2 of the 2000 Act defines the word 'use' in relation to land, as not including the use of the land by the carrying out of any works thereon. Therefore, clearly, a use which existed prior to 1 October 1964 is not an unauthorised use if it is still in existence.

Section 3 of the 2000 Act has been amended and extended by ss 7–10 of the 2010 Act to give effect to the co-ordination of land use plans.

11.3.3   ESTABLISHED USE, ABANDONED USE, RESUMPTION OF ABANDONED USE

Where a use was established prior to 1 October 1964 and no enforcement action was taken by the planning authority in the following five years, it was authorised under s 2 of the 1963 Act, so long as it continued uninterrupted. There is a similar provision in the 2000 Act, except that the period is seven years (s 157(4) of the 2000 Act).

There are cases where an established use may be deemed to be discontinued or abandoned. Its subsequent resumption at a later date could constitute development for which permission would be required. There is no clear test as to when a resumption of an abandoned use is regarded as a material change of use. In *Dublin County Council v Tallaght Block Company Ltd* [1982] ILRM 534, the principle was stated that where a previous use of land had ceased for a considerable period of time with no clear intention of resumption then one was entitled to assume that the previous use had been abandoned so that when it was resumed its resumption constituted a material change of use.

A test to apply as to whether a use had been discontinued is to ask:

(a)   Has there been an actual cessation of activity?

(b)   Is there clearly an intention not to resume that activity?

Hence there has to be the intention to abandon the use. This may be determined from circumstantial evidence, and there has to be the actual cessation as well.

11.4   Exempted Development

11.4.1   INTRODUCTION

The relevant legislation is:

• Local Government (Planning and Development) Act, 1963 (as amended);

• Local Government (Planning and Development) Regulations, 1977 (SI 65/1977);

- Local Government (Planning and Development) Regulations, 1994 (SI 86/1994);

- Local Government (Planning and Development) Regulations, 1995 (SI 69/1995);

- Local Government (Planning and Development) Regulations, 1996 (SI 100/1996);

- Local Government (Planning and Development) Regulations, 2000 (SI 181/2000);

- Planning and Development Act, 2000 Local Government (Planning and Development) Regulations, 2001 (SI 600/2001);

- Local Government (Planning and Development) Regulations, 2007 (SI 83/2007);

- Local Government (Planning and Development) Regulations, 2008 (SI 235/2008);

- Planning and Development (Amendment) (No 2) Regulations, 2011 (SI 454/2011). See **11.1.2**.

- the Planning and Development Regulations, 2013 (SI 219/2013).

Exempted development is development where an applicant is exempt from the obligation to obtain planning permission. This occurs in the following circumstances:

(a)   where development took place before the commencement of the 1963 Act, ie 1 October 1964;

(b)   where the Planning and Development Act, 2000, s 4 (as amended by s 17 of the Environment (Miscellaneous Provisions) Act, 2011) provides that certain types of development are exempt;

(c)   where the Minister exercised his power pursuant to the 1963 Act, s 4(2) in making regulations providing classes of development to be exempted development. The Minister made exempted development regulations in 1977, which were then re-placed by the 1994 Regulations;

(d)   where the Minister exercises his power pursuant to the 2000 Act, s 4(2)(a) in mak-ing regulations providing classes of development to be exempted development, eg the Minister made exempted development regulations in 2000 which were then replaced by the 2001 Regulations and so on.

Exemption Regulations are an ongoing event and the latest Regulations should always be reviewed. Consideration should also be given to non planning legislation which also cre-ates exemptions, eg the Roads Act, 1993 or the Dublin Docklands Development Authority Act, 1997.

The courts have interpreted the exemptions quite strictly in the past. In the Supreme Court decision of *Pillion v Irish Cement Ltd*, 26 November 1986, High Court (unreported), the Chief Justice took the view that developers who avail of the exempted development status are in a special or, in a sense, privileged category as they are not subject to the views or opposition of other persons. It was held that the exempted development regulations *'should by a court be strictly construed in the sense that for a developer to put himself within them he must be clearly and unambiguously within them in regard with what he proposes to do'*. See also *Cunningham v An Bord Pleanala and Others* (2013) IEHC 234.

11.4.2   DEVELOPMENT PRIOR TO 1 OCTOBER 1964

Development, except for those listed in the 1963/2000 Acts themselves that commenced before 1 October 1964, does not require planning permission as it was in existence prior to the commencement of the 1963 Act.

11.4.3   EXEMPT DEVELOPMENT UNDER S 4 OF THE 2000 ACT

Section 4(1)(a) to (l) of the 2000 Act, provides a number of categories of development where an applicant is exempt from the obligation to obtain planning permission. Certain restrictions apply to these exemptions and it is important to know if any of the exemptions provided in legislation have been restricted in any way. Section 4 of the 2000 Act made significant changes to s 4 of the 1963 Act. These are summarised below.

(a)   Agricultural exemption, turbury, and initial planting of forestry, are removed from the agricultural exemption because of the significant impact which they have on land and on the surrounding land. Note, the definition of 'agriculture' now includes the training of horses and rearing of bloodstock (s 4(1)(a)). 'Agriculture' is defined in s 2.

(b)   The replacement of broad leaf high forest by conifer species is no longer exempted. Conifer species are environmentally unfriendly to wildlife and vegetation excepting foxes and badgers (s 4(1)(i)).

(c)   Development by a council or county in its own functional area is exempt. If a planning authority acts outside its own functional area, it is subject to the full rigours of the planning process, unless it is acting for, on behalf of, or as an employee of the other planning authority, where the work is being carried out. Development carried out on behalf of, or jointly, or in partnership with, a local authority is exempt. Obviously, therefore, this means not only development carried out by a local authority itself, but by its contractors. Local authority development in construction of a new road, or maintenance or improvement of an existing road development carried out by a local authority or statutory undertaker re inspecting, repairing, renewing, altering, or removing sewers, mains, pipes, cables, overhead wires, including the excavation of a street or other land for that purpose (s 4(1)(b) to (g)). Note however, Part XIII of the 2000 Act contains a number of restrictions on local authorities carrying out development.

11.4.3.1   Internal and external works: s 4(1)(h)

This is one of the most important exemptions provided for in the 2000 Act. The exemption is divided into two parts, internal and external works:

(a)   where development consists of the carrying out of works for the maintenance, improvement, or other alterations of any structure being works which affect only the interior of the structure; or

(b)   which do not materially affect the external appearance of the structure so as to render such appearance inconsistent with the character of the structure or the neighbouring structures.

Internal works

Works which affect only the interior of the structure, such as a partition wall or alterations to an internal layout, do not require permission.

If the interior of the building is listed for preservation in the development plan then the exemption in relation to internal works will not apply: Local Government (Planning and Development) Act, 1976, s 43(1)(c).

External works

Works which do not materially affect the external appearance of the structure so as to render it inconsistent with the character of the structure or the neighbouring structures are exempt. The question of whether development is consistent with the structure or the neighbouring structures can be a vexed one. See *Cairnduff v O'Connell* [1986] IR 73, and *Dublin Corporation v Bentham* [1993] 2 IR 58.

Section 57 of the Planning and Development Act, 2000 provides that the carrying out of works to a protected structure shall be exempt development only if those works would not materially affect the character of the structure or any element of the structure which contributes to a special architectural, historical, archaeological, artistic, cultural, scientific, social, or technical interest.

11.4.3.2 Uses incidental to the enjoyment of a dwellinghouse: s 4(1)(j)

This exemption applies only to the use of any structure or other land within the curtilage of a dwellinghouse. There is no Irish definition of 'curtilage' but the Scottish case of *Sinclair-Lockhart's Trustees v Central Land Board* 1951 SC 258 described curtilage as the ground which is used for the comfortable enjoyment of a house or other building. This exemption was examined in the Supreme Court decision of *Dublin Corporation v Moore* [1984] ILRM 339. In this case the parking of ice-cream vans was not incidental to the enjoyment of the dwellinghouse. The parking of a private car is incidental to the enjoyment of a dwellinghouse.

11.4.4 EXEMPT DEVELOPMENT UNDER THE 2001 REGULATIONS

11.4.4.1 Introduction

The Minister has the power pursuant to the 2000 Act, s 4(2)(a) to make regulations providing any class of development to be exempted development.

The 1977 Regulations, which were replaced by the 1994 Regulations, as amended by the 2000 Regulations provided that certain classes of development were exempt from obtaining planning permission. These in turn were consolidated by the Planning and Development Regulations, 2001 and all amendments thereto.

While the previous Regulations have been replaced, they are still relevant to development which occurred during their lifespan. For example, particular exempted classes such as swimming pools and golf courses were exempt under the 1977 Regulations, Third Schedule classes 26 and 27 respectively, but were not exempt under the 1994 or subsequent Regulations. However, Art 12 of the 1994 Regulations (Art 11 of the 2001 Regulations, see also Arts 207 and 208) provided that any development that was exempt under the previous Regulations continued to be exempted development, provided the development commenced prior to the coming into operation of the 1994 Regulations, ie 16 May 1994.

If there is a serious doubt as to whether a development is exempt under s 5 of the 2000 Act any person may on payment of a fee request in writing from the local authority a declaration confirming the position which declaration is required to issue within four weeks of the receipt of the request.

11.4.4.2 Second Schedule: generally

While additional exemptions have been issued the majority are still to be found in the Second Schedule of the 2001 Regulations (as amended and extended by (the Planning and Development (Amendment) Regulations, 2013) which is divided into four parts, all of which deal with classes of exemptions and restrictions. While a large number of different types of exemptions are provided, it is important to know and to remember that the Regulations have provided, in Arts 9 and 10, a list of restrictions to the provided exemptions (dealt with at **11.4.6**). When examining an exemption one must always refer back to the restrictions both in the second column (see later) and to Arts 9 and 10 to make sure that the exemption is in fact applicable in the circumstances. For example, Class 1 under column 1 provides that 'the extension of a house, by the construction or erection of an extension (including a conservatory) to the rear of the house, or by the conversion for use as part of the house of any garage, store, shed, or other similar structure attached to the rear or to the side of the house' is exempt. However, under column 2, there are extensive conditions and limitations listed to this exemption at 1 to 7.

11.4.4.3 Second Schedule, Part I: General

The Second Schedule, Part I deals with exemptions under the heading 'General'. Part I contains a column on the left containing the exemption and a column on the right specifying conditions and limitations to the exemption. Part I is the largest part of the Second

Schedule, containing 55 classes of exemption. Part I: General is further divided into the following sections:

(a)   development within the curtilage of a dwellinghouse (classes 1–13);

(b)   development consisting of change of use (class 14);

(c)   temporary structures and uses (classes 15–20);

(d)   development for industrial purposes (classes 21–22);

(e)   development by statutory undertakers (classes 23–32 including a new Class 29A under the 2013 Regulations);

(f)   development for amenity or recreational purposes (classes 33–37);

(g)   miscellaneous development (classes 38–61).

When examining these exemptions it is also important to check through the restrictions listed in Arts 9 and 10 to make sure that the exemption is not removed by virtue of some subsection of that article. An example of this would be if the proposed extension were to be added to a building which is located within an architectural conservation area as listed in the development plan (see Art 9(1)(a)(xii)).

By examining Part I, Class 1: General of the Second Schedule, it is apparent this exemption relates to extensions to the rear of a dwellinghouse and to the conversion of a garage, store, shed, or similar structure attached to the rear or the side of a dwellinghouse.

Prima facie, this type of development does not require planning permission as long as the conditions and limitations in column 2 are complied with. An examination of column 2 provides that such extensions are limited in size to less than 40 square metres where the house has not been extended previously. Therefore if a 20 square metre extension was erected in 1980, there is only provision for a 20 square metre extension now (s 1(a)). Further, in column 2(1)(b), the height of the extension is restricted and the extension may not reduce the private open space to less than 25 square metres (column 2(5)). If there is less than a 25 square metre private open space in the first instance, as often is the case in the inner city, mews developments, and new townhouses, then this exemption will not apply at all.

Class 14 of Part I of the Second Schedule provides six circumstances where development consisting of a change of use from one specified use to another specified use would be exempt. These changes of use exemptions largely encourage uses that the planning authorities are in favour of, such as the change of use of two or more dwellings to be used as a single dwelling of any structure previously used as a single dwelling. This exemption encourages the conversion from flats to single dwellings. Class 50 (a) and (b) deal with the demolition of habitable houses.

11.4.4.4   Second Schedule, Part II: Advertisements

The Second Schedule, Part II deals with exemptions under the heading 'advertisements'. The definition of advertisements may be found in s 2 of the 2000 Act. Article 6(2)(b) of the 2001 Regulations provides that development consisting of the use of a structure or other land for the exhibition of advertisements of a class specified in column 1 of Part II of the Second Schedule is exempted development provided that the limitations and conditions in column 2 are complied with. Again, the restrictions provided in Art 9 must be examined against these exemptions.

By examining Part II Class 1: Advertisements, of the Second Schedule, it is apparent that this exemption related to advertisements exhibited on business premises relating to the business, or other activity carried on, or the goods or services provided on those premises. There are nine conditions/limitations provided in column 2 that must be complied with. These relate to size, illumination, height, position, and location. Further, the restrictions in Art 9 must be examined against this exemption. The definition of 'business premises' may be found in the 2001 Regulations, Art 5(1) and also should be examined in light of this exemption as hotels and state authority buildings are included within the definition. There are 18 classes of exemption in Part II: Advertisements.

11.4.4.5 Second Schedule, Part III: Rural

Article 6(3) of the 2001 Regulations provides for the rural development exemptions. These are provided for in Part III of the Second Schedule. These exemptions apply to areas outside the county boroughs, urban districts, specified towns, and the excluded areas under s 9 of the Local Government (Reorganisation) Act, 1985. These exemptions are subject to the restrictions listed in Art 9 and to the conditions and limitations provided in column 2.

Part III, Class 1 of the Second Schedule provides an exemption for the temporary use of any land for the placing of any tent or caravan or for the mooring of any boat, barge, or other vessel used for the purpose of camping. There are four limitations/conditions attached to this exemption in column 2. Only one tent/caravan may be placed within 100 metres of another tent/caravan, the length of stay is restricted to ten days, no commercial use or advertisement is permitted, and no tent/caravan shall be placed within 50 metres of a public road unless the land is enclosed by a wall, bank, or hedge or combination thereof having an average height of 1.5 metres.

11.4.4.6 Second Schedule, Part IV: Use Classes

Article 10 of the 2001 Regulations provides that development which consists of a change of use within any one of the classes specified in Part IV of the Second Schedule and does not involve carrying out any works except works which are exempted, shall be exempted development. This exemption is subject to the proviso that the development will not contravene a condition attached to a planning permission or be inconsistent with a use specified in a permission. The planning conditions attached to a permission should be examined in order to make sure that no restrictions on the use have been imposed. Article 10 does not include the provision that these exemptions are subject to the restrictions in Art 9.

Part IV of the Second Schedule headed 'Classes of Use' contains 11 classes. Clause 1 of Part IV only contains one use, ie use as a shop. The use of a shop, which is defined under the 1977 Regulations, varies widely, but was revised and restricted in Art 8 of the 1994 Regulations to include: retail sale of goods, post office, sale of tickets for travel agency, hairdresser, display of goods for sale, hiring of domestic goods or articles, launderette/dry cleaners and reception of goods to be washed, cleaned, or repaired. The definition of 'shop', further defined by Art 5(1)(a) to (i) of the 2001 Regulations, specifically excludes funeral homes, hotels, restaurants, pubs, sale of hot food off the premises, or any use to which Classes 2 or 3 of Part IV of the Second Schedule applies. Within this class, one can change the use from post office to travel agency without obtaining planning permission, but cannot change from a post office to a funeral home.

Pursuant to Art 10(2)(b), nothing in any class in Part IV shall include any use as an amusement arcade, motor service station, sale, leasing or display for sale/leasing of motor vehicles, taxi business or hire of motor vehicles, scrap yard or breaking of vehicles, or for the storage of minerals. Any one of these uses requires planning permission.

11.4.5 FURTHER EXEMPTIONS FOR USES: ART 10

Article 10 actually provides for three specific exemptions for change of use. These exemptions are not subject to the restrictions in Art 6 and include the use of not more than four bedrooms in a dwellinghouse as overnight accommodation, provided that the same would not contravene a condition attached to a planning permission or be inconsistent with a use specified in a permission. A shop or restaurant provided in a building occupied by or under the control of the State for visiting members of the public is also exempt under Art 10.

It should be noted that exemptions relating to change of use may be found in three places in the 2001 Regulations:

(a) Part I of the Second Schedule: General, Class 14: see **11.4.4.3**.

(b) Article 10; and

(c) Part IV of the Second Schedule—Use Classes: see **11.4.4.6**.

11.4.6 RESTRICTIONS TO THE EXEMPTED DEVELOPMENT CLASSES IN PARTS I, II, AND III OF THE SECOND SCHEDULE

Article 9 of the 2001 Regulations provides that development to which Art 9 relates (ie Parts I, II, and III of the Second Schedule) shall not be exempted for the purposes of the Acts in a number of circumstances. The restrictions should be examined in detail against each exemption claimed, but the main restrictions are found in Art 9(1)(a).

1. If the development would:

(a) contravene a condition attached to a planning permission. Often, planning authorities attach a condition that the exempted development provisions in the 2001 Regulations do not apply, particularly in mews/townhouse developments, as they consider that the development potential of a site has reached its maximum. The legality of such conditions has not been tested;

(b) consist of the formation, laying out or material widening of a means of access to a public road, the surfaced carriageway of which exceeds four metres in width;

(c) endanger public safety by reason of a traffic hazard or obstruction of road users. Note some signs or illuminated advertising could cause a traffic hazard;

(d) with the exception of the exemption relating to porches (Part I, Class 7 of the Second Schedule), development which brings the building line forward of the front wall of the building on either side, or beyond a building line specified in the development plan or the draft plan for the area;

(e) consist of works under a public road other than connection to wired relay broadcast service, sewer, water/gas main, electricity supply line or cable or works to which Classes 25, 26, or 31(a) specified in column 1 in Part I of the Second Schedule relate;

(f) cause interference with a view or prospect of special amenity or special interest which is listed in the development plan or the draft variation or draft new plan;

(g) consist of the excavation/alteration/demolition (other than peat extraction) of places/caves/sites/features or other objects of archaeological/geological/historical interest, which are listed for preservation in the development plan, draft variation or draft new plan;

(h) consist of the extensions, alterations, etc of an unauthorised structure or an unauthorised use in a structure. If there is anything unauthorised about a building in terms of planning then all the exemptions in relation to Parts I, II, and III are lost;

(i) consist of the alteration/extension/demolition of a building or other structure listed for preservation in the development plan, draft variation, or draft new plan. If a building is listed for preservation in the development plan the exemptions relating to extensions, etc do not apply. Note that this restriction does not apply to an alteration consisting of painting any previously painted part of such a listed building or structure; therefore planning permission is required only the first time a listed building is painted;

(j) consist of the fencing or enclosure of any land habitually open to or used by, the public, during the ten years preceding such fencing or enclosure for recreational purposes or as a means of access to any seashore, mountain, lakeshore, river bank, or other place of natural beauty or utility;

(k) obstruct any public right of way;

(l) further to the provisions of s 82 of the Act, consist of, or comprise the carrying out of works to the exterior of a structure, where the structure concerned is located within an architectural conservation area in a development plan for the area, or pending the variation of the development plan, or the making of a new development plan, in the draft variation of the development plan, or the draft development plan, and the development would materially affect the character of the area.

2. In an area to which a special amenity order relates, if such development would be development:

(a) of class 1, 3, 11, 16, 21, 22, 27, 28, 29, 31 (other than paragraph (a) thereof), 33(c) (including the laying out and use of land for golf or pitch and putt, or sports involving the use of motor vehicles, aircraft, or firearms), 39, 44, or 50(a) specified in column 1, of Part 1 of Schedule 2; or

(b) consist of the use of a structure or other land for exhibition of advertisements of class 1, 4, 6, 11, 16, or 17 specified in column 1 of Part II of the Second Schedule or the erection of an advertisement structure for the exhibition of any advertisement of any of the said classes, or

(c) of class 3, 5, 6, 7, 8, 9, 10, 11, 12, or 13 specified in column 1 of Part III of the said schedule, or

(d) of any class of parts 1, 2, or 3 of schedule 2, not referred to in sub-paragraphs (i), (ii), and (iii) where it is stated in the order made under s 202 of the Act that such development shall be prevented or limited.

3. If it is development to which Part 10 applies, unless the development is required by, or under, any statutory provision (other than the Act, or these Regulations) to comply with procedures for the purpose of giving effect to the Council Directive.

4. If it consists of the provision of, or modifications to, an establishment, and could have significant repercussions on major accident hazards.

5. Sub-article 1(a)(vi) shall not apply where the development consists of the construction by any electricity undertaking of an overhead line or cable not exceeding 100 metres in length for the purpose of conducting electricity from a distribution or transmission line to any premises.

11.4.7 REFERENCE TO AN BORD PLEANALA UNDER THE 2000 ACT, S 5

Where a question arises as to what in any particular case is or is not exempted development, the question shall be referred to and decided by An Bord Pleanala. An appeal lies against the decision of the Board within four weeks of the date of decision or longer period if the court allows. Sometimes where enforcement proceedings are initiated by the local authority in relation to unauthorised development they will be adjourned pending a reference to the Board as to the status of the development. The court has absolute discretion whether to adjourn the proceedings or not.

11.4.8 APPLICATION OF EXEMPT DEVELOPMENT REGULATIONS TO CONVEYANCING SOLICITORS

While it is vital that conveyancing solicitors understand what is and is not exempted development, and can find their way through the legislation. But it is never their responsibility to decide what is, or what is not, exempted development. In other words, where there is the slightest doubt whether or not a development complies with, or does not comply with, the exempted Development Regulations or s 4 of the 2000 Act, the services of an architect or other suitably qualified person, must be employed and he should furnish either a declaration or certificate clearly setting out the grounds which bring the development under the exempt development categories (see **11.4.4**). It is very important when acting for the vendor that you ask your client whether or not they are aware of any exempted developments on any part of the premises. Similarly, when acting for a purchaser, the solicitor should specifically request the purchaser (either himself, or request his architect) to check the premises being purchased to see if there are any additions or extensions which might conceivably come within the exempted development provisions, or which may indeed require planning permission and then to deal with this appropriately in a special condition (see **11.10.8**).

11.4.9   NEW HOUSES AND EXEMPT DEVELOPMENTS

In a substantial number of instances developers in the course of building houses, especially during the boom years, made variations in reliance on the exempted developments regulations. For example, variations involving the addition of extensions, conversion of attic space, and revision of internal layout.

Planning permission must be implemented in its entirety or not at all. Implementation entails the construction of a dwellinghouse in accordance with the plans lodged and on foot of the planning permission issued. Therefore, where a developer seeks to carry out alterations or extensions in reliance of the exempted development regulations it is essential that the house is first fully completed in accordance with the full planning permission. Only then should the extension or the additional work be carried out.

The Conveyancing Committee of the Law Society published a guideline in the Law Society *Gazette*, December 2002 in relation to new houses and exempted development. They advised that solicitors acting for purchasers where such extensions or alterations are carried out after the house has been built should get an architect's certificate of compliance in the usual form and a further opinion stating that the extension or works comprising the exempted development are in accordance with the Building Control Act and Regulations pertaining thereto (see **11.9**).

11.5   Application for Planning Permission

11.5.1   WHY APPLY FOR PLANNING PERMISSION?

Section 32 of the 2000 Act imposes the general obligation to obtain permission and is basically a restatement of the provisions of s 24 of the 1963 Act, as amended. It states that, subject to the other provisions of this Act, permission shall be required under this Part: '*in respect of any development of land not being exempted development, and; in the case of development which is unauthorised, for the retention of that unauthorised development*'. Section 32 of the 2000 Act does make some changes to s 24 of the 1963 Act; for example, in contrast to the provisions of s 24(a) of the 1963 Act, there is no statement in s 32 stating that there is no obligation to obtain permission in respect to a development commenced before 1 October 1964. However, in the absence of a reference to development commenced before 1 October 1964, s 32 does not mean that it necessary to apply for retention permission in respect of developments commenced or completed before 1 October 1964.

Planning permission is required for all development of land which has been carried out since 1 October 1964 and which is not exempted development, or for the retention of unauthorised structures. Further, any person who carries out such a development without obtaining the required planning permission, or in contravention of a permission granted, is guilty of a criminal offence (see the 1963 Act, s 24 as amended by the 1976 Act, s 3(1); by the 1992 Act, s 20(4), and by the 2000 Act, Part VIII, s 151).

The definition of development in s 3(1) of the 2000 Act is vital. Before proceeding to apply for permission, any good solicitor should satisfy himself or herself as to whether or not permission is required at all. If the development contemplated is not one which requires permission, development should be commenced, as an unnecessary application may permit the planning authority to impose unwelcome conditions or to curtail the operation or activities of the development in some way and it may not be possible to argue at a later date that the application was not necessary. Further, the application should be restricted to those aspects of the development which require permission, ie if it is intended to change the use of only part of a building the entire should not be brought into question or, in the case of retention or continuance, only the unauthorised development should be made the subject of the application.

11.5.2 WHO MAY APPLY?

There is nothing in any of the Planning Acts or Regulations which actually specifies who may apply for planning permission. However there is some case law on the point which suggests that the legislature intended to restrict the class to the owner or occupier of the land, or someone acting with their authority. See *Frescati Estates Ltd v Marie Walker* [1975] IR 177 where Henchy J laid down the following rule:

> 'an application . . . to be valid must be made either by or with the approval of a person who is able to assert sufficient legal estate to enable him to carry out the proposed development or so much of the proposed development as relates to the property . . . '.

11.5.3 PROCEDURE TO APPLY FOR PLANNING PERMISSION

Part III of the 2000 Act deals with the making of applications for planning permissions, decisions on those applications, and related matters. See also Part 4 of the 2001 Regulations as substituted by Art 8 of the 2006 Regulations. They should be read and followed with great care, as the decision of the planning authority may be set aside as having been made without jurisdiction where the applicant has failed to comply with the requirements of the legislation. Compliance with this part of the Act (ss 32–47 inclusive, and s 50) is a pre-condition of the exercise of a planning authority's discretion to grant or refuse permission. However, a minor error would not make it invalid as it would be unduly harsh on a developer if a grant for planning permission could be invalidated for some minor infraction of the Regulations, especially as the planning authority is empowered to, and virtually always does, request further information to remedy any further default in the content of an application. The legislation should be consulted for the correct procedure to be followed in relation to notices etc.

11.5.4 WHO MAY COMMENT ON THE APPLICATION?

Any person or body may make submissions or observations in writing to a planning authority on a particular application. In recent times local communities, often through the vehicle of a residents' association, have become more active in this regard. Section 34(3) gives for the first time in Irish planning law, statutory recognition to submissions and observations made to a planning authority on planning applications. In effect, the planning authority must take into account written submissions or observations made by third parties on the planning application. So, in addition to the application itself, the planning authority shall have regard to any information relating to the application furnished to it by the applicant in accordance with the Planning Regulations. Note, Art 29(1) limits the time in which such a submission or observation must be made to within the period of five weeks beginning on the date of receipt by the authority of the application. The mandatory contents of the submission or observation are set out at Art 29(1)(b).

11.5.5 TIME PERIODS

Article 30 sets out the minimum period for determination of a planning application as not until *'after a period of five weeks beginning on the date of receipt of an Application has elapsed'*. While the planning authority must make the decision on the application not earlier than five weeks from its receipt, it must not make it later than eight weeks beginning on the date of receipt by the planning authority of the application, ie 56 days (see s 34(8) of the 2000 Act). Section 34(8) is designed to increase the efficiency of the planning control system—the previous nine Planning Acts used days, weeks, and months, so there was a variation in time periods anywhere from 52 to 69 days. Under the new Act, it is a clear 56 days beginning on the date of the receipt of the application. Further, where additional information is sought the planning authorities will have an additional four weeks, not two months as previously, to decide on an application other than for applications where an EIS is required; a material contravention case; a case involving risk of major accident or where the application is of such a nature that if a major accident occurred it could result in serious consequences, and the planning authority are bound to seek technical advice. If a decision does not issue within the eight-week period, permission is deemed to have been granted by default on the last day of that period (see s 34(8)(f)). The eight-week period may be extended (and generally is) by the planning authority requesting further information on aspects of the application or by consenting (at the request of the applicant, generally prompted by the local authority) to an extension of time for the consideration of the application up to a stated date (see s 34(9)). There is no statutory time limit to the number of time extensions which may be conceded, but some authorities restrict it to just one. The provisions in relation to default planning permission will not apply to developments which require an EIA.

Section 251 of the 2000 Act introduced changes to time limits to take account of public holidays and office closures over the holiday period (as did Art 29A of the 2006 Regulations) and s 72 of the 2010 Act amends s 251 of the Act extending the time frame provisions to plans and guidelines. As time limits are of crucial importance in applications special care should be taken and the most recent Acts and/or regulations consulted directly.

The 2000 Act inserted a new provision in relation to planning applications at s 35, in that, for the first time, a local authority could refuse planning permission for past failures to comply with previous permissions.

Article 37 allows for the withdrawal of planning applications by notice in writing at any time before the giving of the decision of the planning authority.

Section 34(1) provides:

(a)   that where an application is made to a planning authority in accordance with permission regulation for permission for the development of land, and

(b)   all requirements of the Regulations are complied with,

the authority may decide to grant the permission subject to, or without conditions, or to refuse it. When dealing with any such application, the planning authority is restricted to considering the proper planning and sustainable development of the area, regard being had to the provisions of the development plan, the provisions of any special amenity area order relating to the said area, any European site or other area prescribed for the purposes of s 10(2)(c), where relevant the policy of the government, the Minister, or any other minister of the government, and the matters referred at s 34(4), and any other relevant provision or requirement of this Act, and any regulations made thereunder. At the time of writing, the relevant regulations are the Planning and Development Regulations, 2001 (SI 600/2001).

Section 34 goes on to provide that s 34(1), together with the following subsections which deal with conditions, applies *mutatis mutandis* to determinations by An Bord Pleanala. In other words, the planning authority is restricted to considering the proper planning and the development of the area of its authority. The consideration of any irrelevant factor renders a decision invalid.

Section 34(6), which is rarely invoked, allows the planning authority to grant planning permission for development which would materially contravene the provisions of the development plan, but lays down a strict procedure for this. If a planning authority grants permission in material contravention of the plan without following this procedure, its decision may be quashed in proceedings for judicial review.

An Bord Pleanala, on the other hand, may, at its discretion, grant planning permission for development which would materially contravene the provisions of the development plan. Although An Bord Pleanala is obliged to have regard to the provisions of the development plan, it is not under any statutory duty to give effect to its objectives.

11.5.6   POWER TO IMPOSE CONDITIONS

Section 34(4) of the 2000 Act gives the planning authorities both a general power to attach conditions, and, without prejudice to the general power, express authorisation for certain enumerated conditions. There is an excellent commentary on conditions by John Gore-Grimes in his lecture (CLE) 'Planning and Development Act, 2000' given on 23 February 2001, Book Two, pp 96–109. The general power to impose conditions is not without limits, and is subject to a number of limitations laid down by case law. See *Killiney and Ballybrack Development Association Ltd v Minister for Local Government* (1978) 112 ILTR 691, and the *State (Abenglen) v Dublin Corporation* [1982] ILRM 590. The conditions enumerated in s 34(4) are as follows:

(a)   *The conditions imposed must be for a planning purpose and not for any ulterior one.* See *Dunne Ltd v Dublin County Council* [1974] IR 45, where Pringle J expressed the opinion that a condition attached to a planning permission requiring that houses be constructed so as to provide sound insulation against aircraft noise was *ultra vires*, because the matter could have been more appropriately dealt with by Building Regulations which the Minister has power to make under s 86 of the 1963 Act.

(b)   *The condition must be fairly and reasonably related to the development permitted.* This question very often arises in the case of a condition imposed under s 26(2) (a). See *State (FHP Properties SA) v An Bord Pleanala* [1989] IRLM 98; and *British Airports Authority v Secretary of State* 1979 SC 200.

(c)   *Conditions must not be unreasonable.* A condition attached to a grant of permission may be held by the courts to be void for 'unreasonableness' where it is one which 'no reasonable authority acting within the four corners of their jurisdiction could have decided to impose': *Westminster Bank Ltd v Minister of Housing and Local Government* [1971] AC 508. The question is whether the decision 'flies in the face of fundamental reason and common sense': *State (Keegan) v Stardust Compensation Tribunal* [1987] ILRM 202; [1992] ILRM 237.

There are many types of conditions which may be imposed. Conditions for requiring roads, open spaces, car parks, sewers, water mains, or drains in excess of the immediate needs of the proposed development, conditions restricting the occupation of buildings, conditions requiring matters to be agreed, etc.

Certain basic criteria are set out in the Development Management Guidelines 2007 at para 2.4.2.13.

11.5.7   CONDITIONS IN PLANNING PERMISSIONS FROM A CONVEYANCING POINT OF VIEW

While it is true to say the conveyancers must specifically concern themselves with the financial conditions in planning permissions (see **11.10.4**) it is absolutely essential that all conditions are carefully read, including pre-development conditions, and the consequences of all conditions explained to the client.

Further, it should be carefully considered *when* any queries in relation to any condition should be raised, that is to say whether they should be raised pre contract or post contract. As a general rule the sooner a query is raised and dealt with the better.

In recent times there has been considerable controversy about the imposition of discriminatory planning conditions, for example conditions which limit the occupancy of a dwelling to a certain class of person. Solicitors are concerned in particular with the legitimacy of such conditions, their vague manner, and above all how it is possible to confirm compliance. See **11.5.7.1**.

11.5.7.1 Practice Notes on compliance with planning conditions

Conditions re sight lines

The Conveyancing Committee of the Law Society published guidelines in relation to conditions in planning permission re sight lines in the Law Society *Gazette*, November 2003.

A number of local authorities are imposing conditions in planning permissions requiring the applicant to secure sight lines at the entrance of a house site from the public road. In some cases, the applicants, anticipating the requirement, have offered to provide the necessary sight lines in the application itself so there was nothing on the face of the planning permission to alert anyone of the requirement. The Committee pointed out that, in at least one case, the applicant offered to reduce the height of the hedge (with the permission of a neighbour who owned the land in question) but no thought was given to what was to happen when the hedge grew again. In another case, the applicant (again with the permission of a neighbour) confirmed that an arrangement had been made to provide an appropriate sight line. In that case the neighbour did not really understand what was required of him and the planning authority in question did not clarify the position. It is not satisfactory that planning authorities in some cases do not deal with the long-term implications.

It seems clear that conditions like this are going to cause problems for architects and engineers who may be asked to certify compliance. It will also obviously cause problems for conveyancing solicitors. Solicitors who are advising clients in relation to the purchase of a property subject to such a condition will have to advise the client very carefully, particularly if the condition is not going to be properly dealt with. In such circumstances, solicitors should point out that they are likely to have a problem certifying title and that there is a clear risk that there will be problems on reselling. The Committee advised that such advice should be confirmed in writing. In addition, when acting for a client purchasing a site with the benefit of a planning permission, it is yet another reason to advise clients to have the position regarding the planning permission checked out by a competent person. The Committee clearly doubted the wisdom for solicitors to brief an architecture/engineer on behalf of their clients in such situations but did recognise that from time to time solicitors will find that they will have to do this. The Committee feels that such a briefing should be in general terms rather than trying to anticipate all the issues that could arise. However, the issue of sight lines and other easements could be addressed by asking the surveyor to review whether the house, its access and any facilities, such as a septic tank or percolation area or water supply can be provided without passing over or acquiring rights over land in the ownership of any third party.

Of course, the practical problem here is that an applicant who already owns a site and has received a grant of planning permission subject to such a condition might not realise the full implications of such a condition and might have the house built before realising that there may be a problem. Compliance with the condition may be impossible because it would require the applicant to acquire land perhaps from both adjoining owners to provide the necessary lines of sight. Arguably, the planning authority should not grant permission until the applicant satisfies it that the applicant has such legal rights or perhaps ownership necessary to enable it to comply with any such condition. Planning authorities are ready do this routinely in relation to easements for drainage if a site cannot be drained without a grant of easements over property in the ownership of third parties.

The solicitors faced with such a situation should give the following advice. The best solution is for the client to buy the necessary land so as to put himself in a position of being able to comply with a planning condition and to provide a sight line in a permanent way. If this is not possible or practical (which it will not be in the majority of cases) the client should acquire a grant of easements which will enable him to comply properly with the condition. Any grant of easements should be registered on the title of the grantor. If none of this is possible, solicitors should advise clients they will have to qualify title in a manner which may not be acceptable to a lender and that the property may not be resalable without the problem being regularised. The law agent of one of the main lenders for housing has indicated that a qualification of a certificate of title would not be acceptable if it indicated that the condition about the provision of sight lines in the planning permission had not been complied with. The Committee went on to say that it suspected other lenders would take a similar position. Further they added that an informal arrangement or letters from friendly neighbours are simply not sufficient. They ended their note by saying that they intended to make representation to all relevant parties to try to have a more consistent and reasonable practice applied. Meanwhile this is a very dangerous situation for conveyancing solicitors which needs to be approached very carefully.

General planning conditions

The Conveyancing Committee of the Law Society in the Law Society *Gazette*, July/August 2002 decided to make general recommendations re compliance with planning conditions as there were an increasing number of queries relating to them. This Practice Note substituted that published in April 1987.

The recommendations they made were as follows:

(a) Conveyancers dealing with second or later purchases of residential houses, where there is a certificate of the local authority that the roads and services are in charge, should not concern themselves with enquiries as to the compliance with bonding and financial conditions in a planning permission, however see caveat to this set out in the August/September 2015 *Gazette* 'Letters re Roads and Services in Charge' which acknowledged that a local authority letter or a solicitor's certificate given in a previous transaction may no longer reflect the up-to-date position. It is therefore the recommendation of the Conveyancing Committee that an up-to-date certificate from the vendor's solicitor or an up-to-date local authority letter with accompanying identifying map should be obtained. Solicitors are reminded that they should not give certificates about roads and services (including roads, lanes, footpaths, sewers, and drains) abutting and servicing the property having been taken in charge except where this has been verified by an inspection of the local authority records or their own personal knowledge. Where in a residential housing estate there is a requirement under the planning permission for the provision of a bond or the payment of financial contributions and or levies by instalments, and where the estate has not been taken in charge conveyancers should only be concerned with the provision of the bond or with the payment of contribution of the subject house.

(b) The foregoing recommendations only apply to dwellings forming part of an estate and built at the same time as the development. They do not apply to one-off houses or infill developments.

(c) If the solicitor for a purchaser is on notice of a particular difficulty of the taking in charge of roads and services by the local authority then he should advise his client and consider qualifying his certificate of title. Obviously the matter should be raised as a pre-contract enquiry and the client advised before contracts are exchanged so that a decision can be reached as to whether or not to proceed. The provisions of the Planning and Development Act, 2000, s 180 which require the local authority to take the roads and services in charge in certain circumstances may assist in resolving the difficulty.

(d) The foregoing recommendations do not change the obligations on a purchaser's solicitor to seek evidence that there is in fact planning permission on the house and where appropriate to seek a certificate of opinion from an architect or engineer that the house has been built in accordance therewith and in accordance with the Building Control Act, 1990 (if pre-2014 regulations apply) and obtain a copy of the certificate of compliance (if post 1 March 2014 regulations apply). See **11.9**.

(e)   Where a condition in any planning permission states *'before any development commences the applicant shall submit to the local authority proof/evidence of compliance with . . .'* conveyancers need not obtain written proof or confirmation from the local authority where there is in existence a certificate or opinion from a suitably qualified architect or engineer confirming compliance with all conditions attaching to said planning permission/Building Regulations.

The committee went on to remind practitioners that it is unreasonable for them to insist now on being furnished with documentation which it was not the practice to furnish at the time of a previous investigation of title.

Conditions re residence or employment of applicant in planning authority area requirement

A number of local authorities are imposing conditions in planning permissions requiring the applicant to be resident or in full-time employment in the planning authority area. The reason for this is to ensure that the dwellings are suitably restricted to meet local growth needs.

The Conveyancing Committee of the Law Society in the Law Society *Gazette*, November 2003, published a guideline in relation to such conditions requiring residence or employment of an applicant in the planning authority area.

The problem arises from the fact that some planning permissions have a condition requiring confirmation from a solicitor that the dwellings have been sold in accordance with this condition. The Committee in their guideline unanimously agree that it is not acceptable that solicitors should be asked to certify matters in relation to the residence or place of work of their clients. They suggest that these are matters which the clients/applicants for planning permission can easily satisfy the local authority directly by way of completing their own certificate or statutory declaration. They go on to advise that purchasers' solicitor faced with requests to complete a certificate confirming their client's residence or place of employment should take the following steps:

(a)   advise their clients to write to the local authority applying for a waiver or a variation of this condition in the planning;

(b)   give their clients a copy of the Practice Note for enclosure with their application for a waiver/variation;

(c)   advise their clients to offer their own certificates and/or statutory declarations to verify the facts required by the local authority.

A number of developers have successfully appealed against the residency restrictions imposed on planning applications for some of the Wicklow towns, eg for projects in Rathcoole and Rathdrum. One of the successful appeals was a €20 million new town centre development for the Wicklow town of Rathdrum planned by Rathdrum Properties Limited.

However, where developers appealed on a separate issue to that of the residency condition An Bord Pleanala did not choose to alter this type of permission. Interestingly, in one case at least, An Bord Pleanala's inspector pointed out that where lands are zoned for residential use, it would not be reasonable to impose an occupancy condition. This would suggest that the Board would view appeals in such circumstances favourably but equally would suggest that the opportunities for developers to avail of An Bord Pleanala's liberal approach will be restricted in the smaller towns to the lands which are zoned for residential development.

Conditions re social/affordable housing

The Conveyancing Committee of the Law Society in the Law Society *Gazette*, December 2003, published a guideline in relation to conditions in planning permission re social/affordable housing.

They dealt with the query as to whether independent evidence, in addition to an architect's opinion on compliance in the usual form, is required to vouch compliance with the condition in a planning permission imposing a social/affordable housing requirement pursuant to Part V of the Planning and Development Act, 2000 (as amended).

Essentially they recommend that where an architect is prepared to furnish an architect's opinion on compliance in the usual form being either the form recommended for use by the Conveyancing Committee or the approved form as used by members of the RIAI (which forms address conditions attaching to the relevant planning permissions) then there is no necessity to require production of independent evidence with such a condition. They go on to say that there is no basis for distinguishing such a condition from the other conditions attaching to the planning permission.

However, if the architect is not prepared to certify compliance with the social/affordable housing condition, and qualifies his opinion or certificate of compliance to exclude that condition, that the purchaser's solicitor should require independent evidence of compliance, preferably by way of a letter from the planning authority.

This was reiterated in a Practice Note in the August/September 2010 *Gazette*. The Conveyancing Committee confirmed that Part V (social and affordable housing obligations to local authorities) can, by agreement with the local authority in an appropriate case, be satisfied wholly or partially by payment of monies. The Committee state that an agreement entered into by the developer with the planning authority pursuant to a Part V condition is not to be treated as a financial condition for conveyancing purposes even if the agreement requires the payment of monies. The Part V condition is satisfied when the developer enters into the agreement with the planning authority. As the condition is not a financial condition it does not come within the exclusions in the standard architect's opinion on compliance with planning.

11.5.8 SEVERANCE OF CONDITIONS

In *Bord na Mona v An Bord Pleanala and Galway County Council* [1985] IR 205 Keane J said:

'On principle, it seems wrong that a planning permission should be treated as of no effect simply because a condition attached to it, which is nothing to do with planning considerations, is found to be ultra vires. Again, if a condition of a peripheral or insignificant nature attached to a permission is found to be ultra vires, it seems wrong that the entire permission should have to fall as a consequence. But where the condition relates to planning considerations and it is an essential feature of the permission granted, it would seem equally wrong that the permission should be treated as still effective although shorn of an essential planning condition.'

11.5.9 PLANNING PERMISSION BY DEFAULT

Planning permission or approval may be obtained by default where the planning authority fails to give notice to an applicant of its decision on an application which complies with the Regulations, within a specified time period, referred to as 'the appropriate period' (see s 34(8)(f)). The decision by the planning authority to grant the permission or approval is regarded as having been given on the last day of that period.

In most cases the planning authority has a period of eight weeks in which to make its decision, unless a request for further information is made, or the applicant is required to publish a fresh notice of this application, both of which have the effect of extending the period by a further two months from the date of compliance or notice. The 2010 Act has extended the period to a further 12 weeks to remedy any failure by the local authority to make a decision.

The default procedure results in a decision to grant planning permission or approval only where the planning authority does not give notice to the applicant of its decision within the 'appropriate period'.

The default procedure results in a 'decision to grant' planning permission or approval so that an order of *mandamus* compelling the planning authority to issue a grant of planning permission has to be obtained before development may commence.

'A default permission' may be appealed to An Bord Pleanala, provided that they have made submission or observations on the planning application in question (see s 37(1)(a)) in the same manner as a decision to grant planning permission or approval made within the appropriate period. The default procedure cannot operate to produce a decision which is a material contravention of the development plan, as an order of mandamus 'cannot issue to compel the planning authority . . . to consider an application to do something which would be illegal if done' *per* Walsh J in *State (Pine Valley Developments Ltd) v Dublin County Council* [1982] ILRM 169.

Similarly, a default permission cannot issue where the planning authority does not have sufficient information to determine whether a proposal is in material contravention of the development plan or not. See **11.5.5**.

11.5.10 REASONS FOR DECISION

The planning authority is obliged to state its reasons for refusing planning permission or approval or for the imposition of conditions attaching to a grant of permission or approval: see s 34(10) of the 2000 Act. There is no statutory requirement to provide reasons for the granting of planning permission by the planning authority. It is not clear whether the planning authority has a duty to give all reasons for the refusal of permission. It appears it may extend the reasons for refusal on a second similar application: see *State (Dino Aprile) v Naas UDC* [1985] ILRM 510.

11.5.11 GRANT OF PERMISSION

Where the planning authority decides to grant a permission, it is obliged to make the grant '*as soon as may be*' after the decision, see s 34(11)(b).

In the case of a permission by default, it is obliged to make the grant as soon as may be after the period available for a third party appeal has expired; the applicant may be expected not to want to appeal against a default permission. Where an appeal is taken but withdrawn or dismissed by the Board for having been abandoned or as being vexatious, the planning authority is required to make the grant as soon as may be after the appeal has been withdrawn or dismissed. If the Board, having considered an appeal, issues a direction to the planning authority for the attachment, amendment, or removal of any condition or conditions, the planning authority is required to make the grant as soon as may be after the giving by the Board of the direction (see s 34(11)).

Note, the grant of planning permission or approval does not entitle a person to carry out any development which requires other licences or permits or is otherwise unlawful.

11.5.12 PERMISSIONS FOR RETENTION OF STRUCTURES OR CONTINUANCE OF USE

The provisions of Part III of the 2000 Act apply in the same way as to the other permissions discussed and consequently the application procedure and the power of the planning authority and An Bord Pleanala to determine applications are identical. It follows, therefore, that the planning authority is not entitled to take into account the prior existence of the unauthorised structure or use in deciding whether to grant or refuse permission, as this is 'a matter which the statute has excluded from the range of its consideration'.

The 2010 Act provides that it will no longer be possible to obtain a retention planning permission for an unauthorised development which would have required an EIA. The Act contains substitute consent procedures which have a wide scope and which allow regularisation of otherwise defective planning permissions.

11.6 Planning Appeals

11.6.1 INTRODUCTION

Planning appeals are a major part of general planning law but are not within the remit of this chapter and thus will not be discussed here. If further information is required on this, note the rules and procedures for making an appeal are set out in Part VI, chapter III, of the 2000 Act, ss 125–146 inclusive and chapter 2 of Part 7 of the Planning and Development Regulations, 2001 (SI 600/2001). Amendments to Part 7 are contained in ss 14–30 of the Planning and Development (Strategic Infrastructure) Act, 2006.

11.7 Enforcement

The remedies available to the local authority (and in some instances to third parties) under the planning code are set out in the following paragraphs. It should be noted that the time limits set out for those remedies run not only from grants of permission, but also from grants of retention permission.

11.7.1 ENFORCEMENT PROCEDURE UNDER THE 2000 ACT

Part VIII of the Planning and Development Act, 2000 (comprising ss 151–164 inclusive) has completely changed the enforcement procedures under the 1963 Act (ss 31–33, 35, and 36). Part VIII was not affected by the Planning and Decelopment (Amendments) Act, 2002 but the scope of s 156 was enlarged by the 2006 Planning and Development (Strategic Infrastructure Act.

The enforcement of planning control in the 1963 Act was virtually ineffective. Sections 26 and 27 of the 1976 Act and ss 19 and 20 of the 1992 Act were introduced to make planning control more effective and, to a certain degree, this did happen. The structure of the planning enforcement system remains the same in that it is still substantially based on the enforcement notice and the planning injunction.

However, the 2000 Act has introduced a much more streamlined enforcement regime. There are three enforcement mechanisms:

- criminal prosecution;
- the enforcement notice procedure or enforcement action;
- the planning injunction.

The 2010 Act has strengthened the enforcement provisions of the 2000 Act. Local authorities are mandated to issue warning letters, enforcement notices, or take proceedings under s 160 of the 2000 Act in cases of unauthorised development unless there are compelling reasons not to do so. This applies from 5 October 2010. The fines for non-compliance with enforcement notices are considerable.

11.7.2 CRIMINAL PROSECUTION

Section 151 states:

a person who has carried out, or is carrying out, unauthorised development is guilty of an offence.

Sections 156–159 deal with penalties, provisions for prosecution of offences, and the fact that fines imposed are payable to the planning authority. A person convicted of an offence may be ordered to pay the costs of the planning authority in the investigation of the offence, and in the case of the planning injunction, provision is made that the costs may be awarded to either the planning authority or to the person making the application (see s 156).

11.7.3   THE ENFORCEMENT NOTICE PROCEDURE

11.7.3.1   Section 152—warning letter

The warning letter is generally the first part of the enforcement procedure. However, it is possible that an enforcement notice can be issued without being preceded by a warning letter. Where representation is made in writing to a planning authority by a person that unauthorised development may have been, is being, or may be carried out, and it appears to the planning authority that the representation is not vexatious or without substance or foundation or, it otherwise appears to the authority that unauthorised development may have been, or is being carried out, then the planning authority shall issue a warning letter to the owner, occupier, or other person carrying out the development. It may also give a copy at that time or thereafter, to any other person, who in its opinion may be concerned with the matters to which the letter relates. Once the local authority reaches a decision that a letter written by a member of the public is well founded, they do not have any discretion, but must issue a warning letter, unless they consider it a matter of a trivial nature. Under s 152(3), the planning authority shall do so as soon as may be but not later than six weeks after receipt of the representation. However, failure to issue a warning letter will not prejudice the issue of an enforcement notice, or any other decision to take an enforcement action. The warning letter shall contain the information set out at s 152(4). This is a new procedure not previously provided for in the planning legislation.

11.7.3.2   Section 153—decision on enforcement

This provides for one type of enforcement notice for all types of unauthorised development, not the five notices and warning notices set out under previous legislation. This is a new section, and it provides that the planning authority shall investigate subsequent to the issue of a warning letter, and shall make a decision (unfortunately, the time period for this is defined as 'as soon as may be') as to whether or not to serve an enforcement notice, and shall include the reasons for the decision in the planning register entry. Because there is no time limit put in place between the issue of a warning letter and the completion of the investigations which the planning authority consider necessary, it effectively gives absolute discretion to the planning authority as to whether or not to issue an enforcement notice.

11.7.3.3   Section 154—the enforcement notice

Section 154(3)(a) no longer makes it compulsory to serve the notice on the owner and occupier of the relevant lands as was previously the case (see also s 154(13)). Now it may be served on any other person who in the opinion of the planning authority may be concerned with the matters to which the notice relates.

Section 154(4) is a new provision which states that the enforcement notice takes effect as and from the date of service thereof.

Section 154(5) deals with the contents of an enforcement notice.

Section 154(12) states that an enforcement notice shall have effect for ten years from the date of its service.

Section 154(13) states that the validity of an enforcement notice cannot be questioned by reason only that the person or other persons not being the person served with the enforcement notice was not notified of the service of the enforcement notice.

11.7.3.4   Section 155—issue of enforcement notice in cases of emergency

The procedures for issuing an enforcement notice in normal circumstances as can be seen from above are detailed and elaborate, presumably in the hope that if a problem exists it can be dealt with at an early stage and that the complainant is kept fully aware of all decisions being made. Here, however, if the local authority is of the opinion that the situation is urgent it can serve an enforcement notice without the need for a warning letter.

11.7.3.5   Section 156—penalties for offences/onus of proof and defences

Rather unusually, the frequency with which the amounts and the terms of the years to be served are changed, are dealt with here and not in the Regulations. The maximum penalty for conviction on indictment for offences under ss 58(4), 63, 151, 154, 205, 230(3), 239, and 274 is €10 million, and/or two years' imprisonment.

Section 156(2) provides increased penalties for continuing offences.

Section 156(6) reverses the onus of proof of prosecutions for an offence under ss 151 and 154. The presumption that the subject matter of prosecution was development and was not exempted development can only be rebutted where the contrary is shown by the defendant. It is not a defence that a person has applied for, or has been granted permission for retention of an unauthorised development since the initiation of the enforcement proceedings, the date of sending of a warning letter, or the date of service of an enforcement notice in a case of emergency. Under s 156(7) it is a defence to a prosecution under ss 151 or 152 where the defendant can show that he took all reasonable steps to secure compliance with an enforcement notice under s 154.

11.7.3.6   Section 157—prosecution of offences/time limits

This section provides that a planning authority may take summary proceedings for offences created under the Act whether or not the offence was committed in its area. Offences under ss 147 and 148 (declaration by members of the Board of certain interests and requirements affecting members of the Board who have certain beneficial interests) cannot be instituted except with the consent of the Director of Public Prosecutions.

In particular, note s 157(4)(a)(i) which increases the five-year time limit previously introduced by s 19 of the 1992 Act to a seven-year limit. For a discussion on the problems with the five-/seven-year limit, see **11.8.2.13**.

11.7.4   SECTION 160—PLANNING INJUNCTIONS

Section 160 restates with some amendments s 27 of the 1976 Act. There are some differences. Most importantly, s 160 allows an application to be made for an injunction where 'an unauthorised development has been, is being, or *is likely to be* carried out or continued'. (This allows the court to grant an injunction not just to past and present unauthorised development, but also to potential unauthorised development; thus, it allows the court to grant *quia timet* relief in circumstances which the Supreme Court decided were not permissible in *Mahon v Butler* [1997] 3 IR 369.) An application for a planning injunction may be made either by a planning authority or any other person, whether or not that person has an interest in land. The granting of a planning injunction is entirely at the discretion of the court. Section 160(2) is new in that it allows the court to make positive orders for the carrying out of works. Section 160(5)(a)–(d) now allows relief to be sought from the High Court or the circuit court where the rateable valuation of the land which is the subject of the application does not exceed €200, or is so determined by the circuit court. Section 160(6)(a)(i), (ii) states that the relevant period is now seven years instead of five as prescribed by s 27 of the 1976 Act (as inserted by s 19 of the 1992 Act). However, this does not apply where the development concerns the ongoing use of land, and this provision is new. Section 161 deals with costs of applications for injunctions and prosecutions. It allows for fines to be paid to the planning authority, and provides for costs and expenses as incurred by the planning authority in investigating and prosecuting the matter to be paid to them also. This is consistent with the 'polluter pays' principle, and is mirrored in s 159.

Section 162 is new. It provides that in any proceedings for an offence under this Act, the onus for proving the existence of any permission granted under Part III shall be on the defendant.

Finally, in relation to enforcement it should be noted that any development required to be carried out on foot of an enforcement notice, or an order under s 60 (see earlier), does not require planning permission. This provision was omitted in relation to development carried out pursuant to an order under s 27 of the 1976 Act.

11.7.5   ENFORCEMENT FROM A CONVEYANCING PERSPECTIVE

One of the most important questions which the previous paragraph raises for conveyancers is whether a purchaser's solicitor can be happy with the fact that an unauthorised development was completed, either in the case where no planning permission existed, more than seven years since the works first commenced, or, where the planning permission was granted, seven years after the expiration of the life of the planning permission (see **11.12.3**), being five years or such extended time as allowed by the planning authority, or under s 42 of the 2000 Act. Unlike the bye-law amnesty discussed at **11.9.1**, there is no full planning amnesty although unauthorised developments are immune from general enforcement proceedings under planning legislation after seven years, or seven years from the expiration of the planning permission. These are subject to some exceptions—those unauthorised developments remain unauthorised developments. Serious disadvantages stem from this (see **11.8.2.13**).

11.7.6   TIME LIMITS FOR ENFORCEMENT PROCEDURES POST 2000 ACT

Nature of Breach of Planning Code	*Enforcement Procedure*	*Time Limits*
No permission obtained	enforcement notice	7 years from the date the development is carried out
No permission obtained	planning injunction	7 years from date of commencement of the development
Development being or likely to be carried out without permission or in breach of permission	warning notice	Does not apply once the development is completed
Fear of removal of a tree, feature or other thing the preservation of which is required by a condition in a permission	warning notice	No time limit
Development not carried out in conformity	enforcement notice	7 years from expiration of life of permission (life of permission usually 5 years)
Non-compliance with a permission or a condition therein	planning injunction	7 years from the expiration of the life of the permission (life of permission usually 5 years)
Non-compliance with a condition in a permission within time limit specified therein	enforcement notice	7 years from the date specified in the permission
Non-compliance with a condition in a retention permission within time limit specified therein	enforcement notice	7 years from the date specified in the permission

Nature of Breach of Planning Code	Enforcement Procedure	Time Limits
Non-compliance with a condition in a permission which does not specify a date for compliance	enforcement notice	7 years from date for completion specified in a 'latest date' notice which must be served within life of permission (life of permission usually 5 years)
Non-compliance with a condition in a retention permission which does not specify a date for compliance	enforcement notice	7 years from date for completion specified in a 'latest date' notice which must be served within 5 years from date of retention permission
Non-compliance with a condition in a retention permission which does not specify a date for compliance	enforcement notice	7 years from date for completion specified in a 'latest date' notice which must be served within 5 years from date of retention permission
Unauthorised use	warning notice	7 years from day on which unauthorised use first commenced
Unauthorised use	planning injunction	7 years from day the unauthorised use first commenced. Ten years from the date of service

11.8 Planning Requisitions

11.8.1 INTRODUCTION

Planning requisitions on title have traditionally been raised post contract. However, there was always a practice amongst solicitors when dealing with commercial property, to raise planning requisitions on title pre contract. This practice is increasingly followed in all conveyancing transactions particularly, but not exclusively, in townhouse and apartment developments, and was recommended by John Gore-Grimes in a CLE lecture on the 1996 edition (revised) of the Law Society's Requisitions on Title.

The Law Society Requisitions on Title dealing with all planing matters should be sent pre contract to the vendor's solicitors. See also the regulations/requirements re DACs at **11.9.8**, Fire Services Act etc. However, it would be prudent for a purchaser's solicitor to also at least consider raising additional requisitions re architectural conservation areas, areas of special planning control, strategic development zones, landscape conservation orders, sociable and affordable housing, taking estates in charge, Habitats, Birds, Natural Heritage Areas Directives, environmental matters, and multi-storey buildings. This list is by no means exhaustive. Where a solicitor is acting for a vendor it is important to ensure that these requisitions on title are answered before the contract is prepared, preferably by sending them in duplicate to the vendor client and having him or her respond to them in writing and returned. It is always best to anticipate planning problems and try to solve them before entering into a contract.

The Conveyancing Committee of the Law Society has issued a recommendation in the Law Society *Gazette*, May 2003 in relation to pre-contract enquiries, re protected habitats.

See also 'Pre-Contract Enquiries/Requisitions re Habitats Directive' in John Gore-Grimes' *Planning and Environmental Law in Ireland* (Bloomsbury, 2011), p 1063. Where there is a prospect that there is a sensitive habitat in an area or that an environmental protection is in place he suggested that the following requisitions be raised pre contract and where there are replies in the affirmative more detailed enquiries should be made:

(a) Is any part of the property designated as a natural heritage area, special area of conservation or special conservation protection area?

(b) If not, is the vendor aware of any proposal for any such designation affecting the property?

(c) Has any order been made, notice served, or agreement entered into under the Wildlife Acts, 1976 and 2000 affecting any part of the property?

See 'General Requisitions re Environmental Matters' in John Gore-Grimes' *Planning and Environmental Law in Ireland* (Bloomsbury, 2011), pp 1059–66.

The updated requisitions 26.5 and 31 'Environmental', see later, are a good guide to what should be asked as a minimum.

While it is true that these requisitions are generally not appropriate for residential property in the middle of urban areas and would rarely be necessary in the case of other residential properties, unless a significant landholding is involved, this is not always the case: certain properties in Ballsbridge Dublin, an urban area, adjoining the River Dodder have been designated a conservation area. Requisition 26 relates to planning and there is a provision at the beginning of the requisitions on title whereby any reference to any Act shall include any extension, amendment, modification, or re-enactment thereof and any regulation, order, instrument made thereunder and for the time being in force. There is no need for the full citation of the Planning Acts.

11.8.2 PLANNING REQUISITIONS

The Law Society Objections and Requisitions 2015 are the present tequisitions in force and thus, that is what will be discussed shortly, but there may be some references made to the 2001 requisitions where this would be of assistance in understanding the present requisitions. There is a helpful explanatory memorandum issued by the Law Society in relation to the new requisitions setting out what changes have been made and crucially why. See, *Requisitions 2015—Explanatory Memorandum*.

11.8.2.1 Development requisition 26.1

The main change to this requisition is the numbering.

Requisition 26.1 states:

Has there been in relation to the property any development (including change of use or exempted development) within the meaning of the Planning Act on or after the 1st of October 1964.

The purpose of this requisition is to establish whether the premises were developed pursuant to planning permission since 1 October 1964 or whether the premises were built prior to that date. Given the length of time and wide meaning of the word 'development' in the Planning Acts, in the majority of cases, there has been substantial development. It is, of course possible, and it will be clear from the title documents, if a building was constructed prior to 1 October 1964. In such a case it is likely that the building was erected on foot of the Town and Regional Planning Acts, which precede the current planning code. Generally, the planning documentation in such a case would be retained with the title deeds, but it is not required to have evidence of compliance by way of an architect's certificate (see general condition 36 of the Law Society's General Conditions of Sale). Even where it is clear from the title that the premises were built prior to 1 October 1964, this requisition must still be raised. It is possible that further development has taken place by way of addition, alteration, change of use, or demolition since this date.

It is vital that a purchaser's solicitor checks the permissions against the planning search obtained prior to contract to ensure that nothing shows up on the search which has not been furnished. It is also important to check the reference numbers on the permission or the grant of permission or on the building bye-law approval and/or Fire Safety Certificates etc to ensure that these are the same numbers referred to in the architect's certificate/ opinion. Care should be taken in checking conditions precedent in a planning permission to ensure that they have been complied with before the development commences.

In many situations, such as sales by liquidators, receivers, mortgagees in possession, or personal representatives who have no knowledge of the property, this requisition will be precluded by contract.

Alternatively the planning warranty will apply. See Law Society, Practice Note, June 2014 *Gazette* issued by the Conveyancing Committee in relation to 'Conditions of Sales by re-ceivers/mortgagees'.

11.8.2.2 Grant of planning permission: requisition 26.2.a

Requisition 26.2 provides:

In respect of all such developments furnish now (where applicable):

a. grant of planning permission

Requisition 26.2.a requires a vendor to furnish copies of all relevant planning permission obtained since 1 October 1964, unless the contract special conditions provide to the con-trary. The purchaser must ensure that he receives a copy of the grant of permission and not a decision to a grant which may subsequently have been appealed.

11.8.2.3 Outline planning permission and grant of approval: requisition 26.2.b

Where a grant of approval has issued on foot of an outline planning permission it is neces-sary to obtain both the outline permission and the grant of approval. The outline permis-sion may contain conditions which were not carried through in the grant of approval, but which nevertheless apply and must be complied with. Further, the life of the planning permission is calculated from the date of grant of the outline permission not from the date of grant of approval. Since the 2000 Act, grants of approval no longer issue; the appropri-ate grant issuing subsequent to an outline permission is now termed a grant of permission. For further information on requisitions relevant to outline permission see John Gore-Grimes' *Planning and Environmental Law in Ireland* (Bloomsbury, 2011), p 1052.

11.8.2.4 Building bye-law approval: requisition 26.2.c

Building bye-laws are no longer relevant for works completed before 13 December 1989, provided the local authority did not serve a notice in relation to any such works before 1 December 1992. If no copy of the building bye-law approval is available, a purchaser should be prepared to accept a statutory declaration confirming that the works were car-ried out before 13 December 1989 and, as such, are deemed to comply with building bye-laws by virtue of the Building Control Act, 1990, s 22(7). The declaration must also state that no notice was served before 1 December 1992. Note, however, that special condition 36(b) of the General Conditions of Sale does require the vendor to furnish a copy of such bye-law approval so that, if it is not available, the position should have been covered by the vendor in the special conditions of the contract. Building bye-laws still apply to works carried out after 13 December 1989 and before 1 June 1992.

11.8.2.5 Evidence of compliance with the financial conditions: requisition 26.2.d

The usual means of establishing compliance with financial conditions is by the production of a letter from the local authority confirming that the sum required has been paid or that the appropriate bond is in place. However, under the 2001 edition of the Law Society Conditions of Sale, a vendor may instead produce formal confirmation from the local authority that the roads and services have been taken in charge. This is acceptable as evidence in lieu of receipts for financial contributions and/or the lodgement of bonds. However, see Law Society *Gazette*, Practice Note, July–August 2015 which is discussed further later, for the need for said letter to be recent.

Where financial conditions fall due for payment on a phased basis, a purchaser is only concerned to ensure that the payment has been paid up to the date when the house was first sold by the developer. (See Practice Notes, Law Society *Gazette*, April 1987 and July 2011.)

11.8.2.6   Certificate or opinion from an architect or engineer: requisition 26.2.e

It is necessary to furnish a certificate/opinion from an architect or engineer stating that the permission/approval relates to the property and that development has been carried out in conformity with the permission/approval and with the building bye-law approval (if applicable) and that all conditions other than financial conditions have been complied with.

The vendor will have contracted to give this certificate unless the general conditions of the contract have been varied by special condition. The Law Society has approved the format of certificates of compliance: see Law Society *Gazette*, March 1995. These certificates also contain provisions for exemptions and exceptions and these must be carefully checked and, if found, must be notified to the client. If the exemptions and exceptions are fundamental it is necessary, where a solicitor is also certifying title, to qualify the certificate of title by drawing the lender's attention to the specific exemptions or exceptions referred to in the architect's certificate.

The General Conditions of Sale do not define 'architect' or 'engineer'. The purchaser should establish, in an appropriate case by pre-contract enquiry, the qualifications of the architect or engineer who will give the certificate or should seek a condition in the Contract for Sale that the certificate to be given will be made by a person whose qualifications are recognised in accordance with Law Society recommendations and that the architect's certificate will be in a format approved by the Law Society: see Law Society *Gazette*, November 1994. The position regarding the qualification of the person giving the certificate/opinion has been somewhat clarified by the Building Control Act 2007, ss 13–27 and regulations arising therefrom. See **11.11.3.1.** Note, however, that the Law Society recommends that it is unreasonable for solicitors to insist on being furnished with documentation which it was not the practice to furnish at that time. It appears that the practice of furnishing architect's/engineer's certificates/opinions or declarations of compliance became general conveyancing practice in or about the year 1970. The Law Society now recommends that solicitors should only insist on such certificates or declarations on dwellinghouses built since 1 January 1975. Certificates are not required in relation to the original construction of a dwellinghouse built before this date. The exemption does not apply to any extensions to dwellinghouses or commercial properties, in other words in any other circumstances, a certificate is required as usual. However, in such a case a special condition must appear in the contract, varying general condition 36.

11.8.2.7   Exempted developments: requisition 26.2.f

Requisition 26.2.f provides:

> *In respect of exempted developments, in each case state the grounds upon which it is claimed that the development is an exempted development and furnish a certificate/opinion from an architect/ engineer in support of such claim.*

It has long been the practice to produce a certificate to confirm that a development was exempt. However, this requisition was only first introduced in the 1996 edition of the Law Society Requisitions on Title. Even if it appears at first sight that works are exempt a careful purchaser should seek such a certificate. This is because virtually every exemption has limitations placed on it. For example, it may be immediately obvious that an extension to a dwelling is less than 40 square metres, but it is not so obvious that the height restriction set out in the 2001 Regulations (Class 1, limitation (4)(c)) is complied with or, indeed, that the area of open space in the rear garden has not been reduced below 25 square metres (Class 1, limitation (5)). Even where all of the conditions placed on the exemptions have been met it is necessary to consider the general restrictions on exemptions in the 2001 Regulations, Art 9.

The Second Schedule, Part I of the 2001 Regulations (as amended) lists the classes of exemptions with limitations attached and it is very important to look at the definitions contained in Art 6 and the restrictions in Art 10 when dealing with changes of use. This is really an area beyond the solicitor's field of expertise and it is why it is essential to obtain an architect's certificate of compliance in relation to this.

This is a requisition which must be raised because a planning search will not disclose any information in relation to exempted developments. Further, replies to this requisition should be very carefully made. It is eminently possible, given that the planning history of the premises may go back to 1 October 1964 that your own client will not know the planning history of the premises. You are further handicapped in the giving of your replies due to the present inadequacies of the planning register, ie searches will not in many cases reveal everything that has occurred. The best method to protect yourself is to adopt the procedures as laid out by John Gore-Grimes in an old, but still relevant, CLE lecture 'Essential Conveyancing for Practitioners', Lecture 5, p 18, given in July 2001. These procedures are as follows:

(a) make a planning search before allowing a purchaser to sign a purchase contract or before preparing a sale contract for a vendor;

(b) show that search to the client and ask for explanations for any acts appearing thereon;

(c) send out to your client a pre-contract questionnaire along the lines of that attached to the 2009 Contract for Sale issued by the Law Society, expanding where you believe it necessary on the planning queries;

(d) carefully check the contract to see if there are any planning exclusions, or whether the planning warranty at condition 36 has been excluded altogether; in such case it will invariably be essential to employ an architect/engineer to examine the house and to examine the planning file in order to report fully;

(e) on all occasions when acting for a purchaser send out before exchange of contract pre-contract requisitions relating to planning and environmental matters;

(f) where there is even the smallest planning defect, and you are acting for a lending institution as well as the purchaser, list the defect in the certificate of title.

11.8.2.8 Withering permissions: requisition 26.3

Requisition 26.3 provides:

a. Is the permission a permission which would have withered but for the provisions of Section 4 of the Planning and Development (Amendment) Act 2002.

b. If the said permission is a permission which would have withered in the circumstances outlined in paragraph a. above, please state whether a levy has been paid or is still payable to the planning authority in the sum of 1% of the sale price if the sale price is equal to or in excess of €270,000.00 or 0.5% of the sale price if the sale price is less than that amount.

c. Please furnish local authority receipt for payment of the levy (if applicable).

d. If it is stated that no levy is payable, please state the reasons.

A 'withering permission' is one granted for residential development on foot of an application for planning permission lodged after 25 August 1999 and before the planning authority incorporated its housing strategy into its development plan.

Under s 96(15) of the Planning and Development Act, 2000, the permission withered on 31 December 2002 or two years from the date of the permission, whichever would have been the later.

However, by virtue of s 4 of the Planning and Development (Amendment) Act, 2002 the life of such a 'withering permission' was extended so as to have the normal life of a planning permission (usually but not always five years, see **11.12.3**).

At first glance, this requisition looks to be 'redundant', however, dwellings built on foot of a permission which would have withered but for the 2002 Act were made subject to a levy of 1 per cent of the sale price, if such sale price was equal to or in excess of €270,000 or 0.5 per cent of the sale price, if such sale price was less than that amount.

Requisition 26.3 asks if the planning permission for the property in sale was a withering permission and if so asks for evidence of payment of the applicable levy.

11.8.2.9   Developments completed after 1 November 1976: requisition 26.4

Requisition 26.4 provides:

> *In respect of developments completed after the 1st of November 1976 furnish now evidence by way of statutory declaration of a Competent Person that each development was completed prior to expiration of the permission/approval.*

The provisions of the Local Government (Planning and Development) Act, 1982, s 2(2)(v) set down time limits within which the development must be substantially completed. (Under the 2000 Act, s 40 is the relevant section.) This requisition on title seeks confirmation that the development was completed within the life of the planning permission. Frequently, this may be established from the title documents, for example, if there was a lease or conveyance with a building covenant and a certificate of compliance endorsed thereon. In addition, the architect's certificate of compliance should be dated and would have been given upon completion of the property.

Where the planning permission has expired and no extension has been obtained under s 4 of the 1982 Act (see also Arts 40 and 41 of the 2001 Regulations, and s 42 of the 2000 Act as amended) and it is not clear from the title documents when a development was substantially completed, then a purchaser will seek a statutory declaration to confirm that the development was completed within the life of the permission.

If the development is not completed within the time limit it is an unauthorised structure and, consequently, the requisition is of importance. Note that this requisition is, as indicated, only relevant as and from 1 November 1976.

11.8.2.10   Special Amenity Areas: requisition 26.5

Requisition 26.5 provides:

Is the property or any part of it:

a.   *Situate in*
   - *an architectural conservation area*
   - *an area of special planning control*
   - *an area of special amenity*
   - *a landscape conservation area*
   - *a strategic development zone*

or other area designated under the Planning Acts for any specific purpose or objective.

b.   *Subject to any actual or proposed designation of all or any of the property whereby it would become liable to compulsory purchase or acquisition for any purpose under the Planning Acts.*

c.   *A protected structure or proposed protected structure as defined in the Planning Acts.*

d.   *Subject to any tree preservation orders.*

This requisition now includes reference to additional designated areas under the Planning Acts and there is also a reference at requisition 26.5.c and d to protected structures and tree preservation orders. It is a matter for the purchaser to satisfy himself on these matters by inspection of the planning register. This requisition is a very good reason why a planning search should be made by a vendor's solicitor pre contract. A vendor might very well forget that years ago the facade of the dwelling in sale was the subject of a preservation order. Under the Planning Acts, where such orders are made, the local authority is required to register them in the planning register established under s 8 to the 1963 Act (s 7 of the 2000 Act) save for the special amenity areas order. A search in the planning register will not reveal if a special amenity order has been made under the 1963 Act, s 42(1) (as amended by s 40(a) of the 1976 Act and Part XIII of the 2000 Act). A special enquiry therefore will have to be made of the vendor and, if acting for a purchaser, a special enquiry will have to be made to the local authority by letter to ascertain if a special amenity order is in existence. Under condition 35(b) of the Contract for Sale, a vendor is not required to furnish details of the contents of the development plan other than actual or proposed designation for compulsory acquisition and the onus is on the purchaser to carry out a planning office search before entering into the contract. Accordingly, frequently the answer to this requisition is *'this is a matter for the purchaser'*.

However, where a notice has been served on the vendor or is otherwise known to the vendor, not being a notice in relation to the contents of the development plan, the vendor is obliged to furnish details: see general condition 35 of the General Conditions of Sale.

A vendor's solicitor will therefore need to do wider searches than the standard planning search in addition to taking full and detailed instructions from the vendor in relation to each and every element of this requisition.

11.8.2.11   Unauthorised development: requisition 26.6

Requisition 26.6 provides:

a.   *Is there any unauthorised development as defined in the Planning Acts.*

b.   *Has any warning notice or enforcement notice been served by the planning authority, or is the Vendor aware of any proposal to serve any such notice.*

c.   *Have any proceedings been initiated or threatened by any party alleging any breach of planning.*

d.   *Has any written request or acquisition notice been served on the Vendor (or to the Vendor's knowledge, on any predecessors in title) indicating the planning authority's intention to acquire the property or any part of it or is the Vendor aware of any proposal to serve such a request or notice.*

Under requisition 27.6 it is necessary to ascertain whether there is any unauthorised development as defined in the Planning Acts. Section 2 of the 2000 Act defines 'unauthorised structure'. That definition is difficult and refers back to permissions granted under the Town and Regional Planning Act, 1934. For conveyancing purposes, an unauthorised structure may be taken as being any structure erected after 1 October 1964, which was not built on foot of, and in accordance with, a planning permission obtained under the current planning code and which is not an exempt development.

11.8.2.12   Retention permission: requisition 26.7

Requisition 26.7 provides:

If there is any such unauthorised development furnish prior to closing:

a.   *A retention permission for such development and*
b.   *(Save where the retention permission relates only to a change of use and there were no conditions attached to said permission or was granted in respect of a private house more than ten years ago) satisfactory evidence of compliance from an architect/engineer that the drawings submitted on the application for retention correctly show the structure(s) as built and that the conditions (if any) attached to the retention permission have been complied with.*

c. *If applicable, satisfactory evidence from an architect/engineer that the development substantially complies with the Building Bye-Laws or with the Regulations made under the Building Control Acts 1990 to 2014.*

d. *If the unauthorised development is such that Part XA of the Planning and Development Act 2000 as amended applies, provide copies of the substitute consent.*

If there is any such unauthorised development it is necessary to furnish prior to closing a retention permission. If there is an unauthorised structure and there is no qualification of general condition 36 of the contract, then the vendor is in breach of that warranty and is open to an action for breach of contract by the purchaser. It is likely to prove extremely difficult to complete the sale of the property until such time as that matter is resolved. The purchaser may be prepared to agree that the vendor make an application for retention permission but if that retention permission issues subject to conditions which adversely affect the value of the property, then the purchaser would be entitled to compensation (or to rescind). The purchaser is under no obligation to wait until such time as the retention permission issues (which usually takes a minimum period of three months, but realistically is more like six) and could serve an appropriate notice under general condition 40 of the Contract for Sale thereby rescinding the contract or, in the alternative, might pursue an action against the vendor for breach of contractual warranty.

In the event of unauthorised development it is also necessary to furnish satisfactory evidence of compliance from an architect/engineer with the conditions in the said retention permission, see requisition 26.7.c.

Where a retention permission is sought and granted it is still essential to have a confirmation from an architect/engineer that the drawings submitted on the application for a retention permission correctly show the development as built and that the conditions of the retention permission have been complied with. This, of course, would not be required where the retention relates only to a change of use and there were no conditions attached.

If applicable, under requisition 26.7.c satisfactory evidence from an architect/engineer that the development substantially complies with the bye-laws or with the regulations made under the Building Control Act, 1990 should also be provided or as required re the latter under the 2014 Regulations.

Building bye-laws would only be relevant in the areas where they apply. The opinion of compliance with the Building Regulations where applicable (pre 1 March 2014) should be in the Law Society-approved format.

Section 19 of the 1992 Act gives some comfort in that the planning authority has a five-year period to use certain enforcement procedures against an unauthorised development. Section 19 of the 1992 Act also provides that a warning notice in relation to any unauthorised use of the land shall not be served after the expiration of a period of five years beginning on the date from which such unauthorised use first commenced (Part VIII of the 2000 Act, s 157(4)(a)(i) has increased this period to seven years).

However, there is a time limit for s 24 prosecutions under the 2000 Act. While s 19 of the 1992 Act (s 157(2)(a) of the 2000 Act) gives certain comfort to conveyancers, it does not make the unauthorised development authorised and there are certain disadvantages.

11.8.2.13 Disadvantages/problems of relying on the 'seven-year rule'

A planning authority has a period of seven years in which to issue enforcement proceedings. The seven years start to run where no permission has been granted from the date that the development is deemed to have been completed (in this regard it should be noted that completed is not an absolute term and there can be disagreement about that date, not least as completed in this context does not mean 'fully completed') and where permission has been obtained from the expiration of the planning permission. Therefore where the permission has a five-year life span which is the norm, then the planning authority cannot take enforcement proceedings after 12 years. It should be noted therefore that whether the planning permission, if same exists to begin with, has an extended life span, of say eight years, it will be 15 years before a planning authority will be precluded from taking action. Whatever time period applies, an unauthorised development remains an unauthorised development; all the 'seven-year rule' does is prevent the local authorities from taking enforcement proceedings. There are disadvantages/problems attaching to reliance on this rule, which may be summarised as follows:

(a)   In the event of subsequent compulsory acquisition unauthorised developments thereof may not attract compensation.

(b)   There is an almost automatic entitlement to compensation under the planning legislation in circumstances where premises have been destroyed by fire and for some reason planning permission to rebuild is refused. However, this is only the case where the premises were, in the first instance, authorised by grant of planning permission.

(c)   In certain instances water connections may be refused where the development requiring same is unauthorised. (See s 259 of the 2000 Act.)

(d)   In a situation where an original development was an unauthorised development it may be difficult to obtain permission for further development or redevelopment of that property.

(e)   A development which would otherwise be an exempted development will not be such if same would consist of or comprise the extension, alteration, repair, or renewal of an unauthorised structure or a structure, the use of which is an unauthorised use (see 1994 Regulations, Art 10(1)(a)(viii); Art 9(1)(a)(viii) of the 2001 Regulations).

(f)   Most important is the problem experienced by banks and building societies when they are told that the property (or perhaps a part of it which represents a significant part of the purchase price) is a non-conforming development. Many such institutions do not permit any qualification to their certificate of title unless first agreed with them and such agreement may in fact be difficult to obtain and, if agreed, must be in writing. Thus, if a purchaser signs a contract which includes a clause disclosing an unauthorised development more than five years/seven years old and relies on s 19 of the 1992 Act (s 157(4)(a)(i) of the 2000 Act) a purchaser's solicitor should, prior to the execution of contract, confirm that the lending institution will accept a qualification on the certificate of title. Therefore, a major problem with relying on the seven-year period is that, due to the planning defects, the property becomes less marketable as a prospective purchaser will find it difficult to obtain loan approval unless the defect is of an extremely minor nature. If such is the case it would still be prudent for a purchaser's solicitor to inform the lending institution of the defect and qualify the undertaking in writing.

(g)   Under s 246, the Minister has the power to make regulations for additional fees to be paid to the planning authority. These include fees for the making of submissions or observations in respect of planning permissions, fees for requests and declarations under s 5, fees for the granting of licences or certificates under ss 231, 239, and 254, but most importantly in this instance, the Minister may prescribe that a fee is payable to the authority for an application for retention permission which shall be in an amount which shall be related to the estimated cost of the unauthorised development, or the unauthorised part thereof as the case may be. This means that the Regulations may provide for fees for retention permission to be set at a percentage of the estimated cost of the development, and the memorandum accompanying the Bill of 1999 gives as an example '10 per cent of the cost' of constructing a building. This is a particularly self-defeating provision, because it is, after all, in the interests of the planning system as a whole that a retention permission should be encouraged rather than discouraged, unless of course, the authority is dealing with a developer who has deliberately created an unauthorised development hoping that the planning authority, as a matter of expediency, will issue a retention permission rather than order the removal of the unauthorised development and its reinstatement.

Given the length of time since planning legislation, and the increasing number of properties with 'irregularities' in their planning history, and the problems already discussed with s 19 of the 1992 Act (s 157 of the 2000 Act), it is clear that it is more than time for an introduction of a full amnesty on planning matters similar to the building bye-laws amnesty introduced by the Building Control Act, 1990, s 22(7). Indeed both the Law Society and the Law Reform Commission have strongly advocated this but at the time of writing no cognisance has been taken of such recommendations. Until such an amnesty is brought about vendors' solicitors must take great care when drafting contracts and/or deleting or amending general condition 36. If deleting general condition 36 in its entirety consider the loss to the vendor of 36.f which provides some protection for a vendor. Thus it may be more prudent to simply amend rather than delete.

Requisition 26.7.d is a new requisition and it seeks information on any substitute consent issued pursuant to Part XA of Planning Development Act, 2000 as amended in respect of any unauthorised development.

11.8.2.14 Present use of property: requisition 26.8

The purpose of requisition 26.8 is to establish whether the current use or uses are authorised. Obviously, this is a matter of fact in each case. A vendor's solicitor should ensure that he gets full instructions in relation to current uses, particularly where there is more than one. In a private dwellinghouse it may be that part of the property was used as a dentist's surgery or in a commercial building there may be a number of uses and the purchaser will need to know what is the prime use and what ancillary uses apply.

11.8.2.15 Use since 1 October 1964: requisition 26.9

Requisition 26.9 asks whether the property has been used for each of the uses in requisition 26.8 without material change continuously since 1 October 1964.

If the answer to this is 'no' then there has been a development within the meaning of the Planning Acts and the vendor will be required to produce the appropriate planning permission. Obviously, if no planning permission has been obtained then see requisition 26.5 at **11.8.2.10**. The only means of rectifying the position would be to discontinue the unauthorised use or obtain permission for continuance of such use. It is wise in such circumstances to consider the principles of intensification of user and the abandonment of use. Consider also that the change of use may comprise an exempt development under the 1994 Regulations (now the 2001 Regulations) in which case it is not 'unauthorised use' within the meaning of s 2 of the 1963 Act (now s 2 of the 2000 Act) and, accordingly, might be said not to be 'a material change'.

11.8.2.16 Applications under Planning Acts and building bye-laws: requisition 26.10

Requisition 26.10 provides:

Give particulars of any application for permission and/or approval under the Planning Acts and the building bye-laws and state the result thereof.

While requisition 26.10 could cover permissions referred to in other requisitions, its real purpose is to obtain details of any applications for planning permission where no decision to grant permission has issued or has been refunded or a permission granted has not been acted upon. The purchaser seeks information in relation to any such application or permission. These may have some use to the purchaser if they are still within their time limit, but if in the ordinary case the permissions have not been acted upon and are more than five years old they may be ignored. The requisition also requests the vendor to produce notification of refusal. This could be of importance to a purchaser who, for example, wished to have a residential property changed into a play school, and in those circumstances where the planning file already discloses a refusal for such change of use.

As building bye-laws have been replaced by the Building Control Act, 1990 and the regulations thereunder, they are only relevant in this context if building bye-law approval was obtained, issued on foot of an application lodged with the local authority prior to 1 June 1992. There is no time limit within which works must be completed on foot of a building bye-law approval.

11.8.2.17 Agreements with planning authority: requisition 26.11

Requisition 26.11 provides:

a. *Has any agreement been entered into with the Planning Authority pursuant to Section 38 of the 1963 Act (now s 47 of the 2000 Act) restricting or regulating the development or use of the property.*

b. *If so furnish now a copy of same.*

This requisition has been expanded to include a question on whether any agreement has been entered into with the planning authority pursuant to s 47 of the Planning and Development Act, 2000 as the requisition previously referred only to s 38 of the Local Government (Planning and Development) Act, 1963.

Section 38 of the 1963 Act is one of those matters which will be disclosed in the local authority planning register. Sterilisation agreements may be made under the provisions of s 38 of the 1963 Act, as extended by s 39 of the 1976 Act and now s 47 of the 2000 Act restricting or regulating the development or use of property. The point about s 38/s 47 is that they are drafted in such a way so that it is intended that these sterilisation agreements may be enforced against successors in title. In this way they are somewhat akin to restrictive covenants. They normally arise where the planning authority is prepared to grant permission for the development of one part of the landowner's holding on condition that another portion of his holding is sterilised so that there will be no further development of that other portion in the future (exempted or otherwise) for the period of the sterilisation. Clearly it is vital that a purchaser knows whether the plot of ground he is buying has been sterilised in such a manner. Details of any such s 38/s 47 agreement must be registered on the planning register. A purchaser who has carried out his planning search should be aware of the situation.

11.8.2.18 Application for compensation: requisition 26.12

Requisition 26.12 provides.

a. *Has there been any application for an award of compensation under the Planning Acts?*

b. *If so, furnish now a copy of same.*

A purchaser is also concerned to know whether any compensation has been paid by the planning authority by reason of refusal to grant permission. The Local Government (Planning and Development) Act, 1990 provides that where any such compensation is paid no development may be carried out on the land in question until such time as the compensation is refunded to the local authority (compensation is dealt with under the 2000 Act at Part XII, in relation to the above requisition, s 190).

11.8.2.19 Registration of statement of compensation: requisition 26.12.c

Requisition 26.12.c asks:

Has the statement of compensation been registered on the Planning Register under Section 72 of the 1963 Planning Act, Section 9 of the Local Government (Planning and Development) Act 1990 or Section 118 of the Planning and Development Act 2000 prohibiting development of the property under Section 189 of the Planning and Development Act 2000.

This subsection (c) has been expanded to include reference to a statement of compensation having been registered under s 72 of the 1963 Act or s 118 of the 2000 Act.

Subsection (d) is a new section and simply seeks details of any such statement of compensation registered on the planning register if such statement was disclosed in the reply to requisition 26.12.c.

Where compensation is paid the local authority is required to enter the details on the planning register, so that a purchaser who has made his enquiries in this regard will be aware of the position before contracts are exchanged. If his solicitor knows the purpose for which his client requires the land and that purpose is frustrated by a refusal or by permission which contains onerous conditions, the client must be advised as to what compensation may be claimed and this, of course, will have a very considerable bearing on the purchase price offered, that is if the matter is to proceed at all. A solicitor should never become involved in quantifying the amount of compensation since clearly this is a matter for valuers. Of course, should it have issued prior to contract, general condition 35 applies.

11.8.2.20 Development prior to 13 December 1989: requisition 26.13

Requisition 26.13.a provides:

a. *If any development was carried out prior to 13 December 1989 and Building Bye-Law approval was either not obtained or not complied with furnish now declaration that the development was completed prior to 13 December 1989 and that no notice under Section 22 of the Building Control Act 1990 was served by the building control authority between 01 June 1992 and 01 December 1992.*

b. *Has there been any development carried out since 13 December 1989 with the benefit of Building Bye-Law approval.*

c. *If so, furnish now copy of same and draft architect's/engineer's opinion of compliance.*

Essentially this requisition has not substantially changed but has merely been made clearer in that the old subsection (b) has been broken down into two subsections (b) and (c).

Requisition 26.13 is drafted widely enough to capture all works requiring building bye-law approval whether or not they are exempted development.

The Building Control Authority could only serve a notice under the Building Control Act, 1990, s 22 where it considers the works constitute a danger to public health or safety. Unfortunately, there is no public register which may be inspected to see whether any such notice was served.

11.8.2.21 Development after 13 December 1989: requisition 26.13.b and c

Requisition 26.13.b states:

Has there been any development carried out since 13 December, 1989 with the benefit of Building By-law approval. If so, furnish now a copy of same and draft engineer's/architect's opinion of compliance.

Under requisition 26.13.b a purchaser will require production of a building bye-law approval where the works have been carried out in a building bye-law area between 13 December 1989 and 1 June 1992 or on foot of a bye-law approval applied for prior to 1 June 1992 and will require an architect's certificate of compliance with such building bye-law approval.

When no building bye-law approval has been obtained, a purchaser will require a certificate from an architect to the effect that the works have been carried out in substantial compliance with building bye-laws in force at the date of construction and that had building bye-law approval been applied for, in the view of the architect, it would have been granted. Under the Law Society General Conditions of Sale a purchaser is not required to accept such certificate unless the special conditions so provide, although the fact of accepting such certificate is well established.

11.8.2.22 User of property from 1 October 1964: requisition 26.14

Requisition 26.14 states:

Furnish now a Statutory Declaration by a competent person evidencing user of the property from 1 October 1964 to date.

In this requisition the purchaser is asking for a statutory declaration by a competent person evidencing user of property from 1 October 1964 to date. Inevitably the answer is 'vendor declines'. There are immense practical difficulties, particularly as more and more time passes, of obtaining somebody competent to give a declaration which dates back to 1964. However, a purchaser seeking to rely on an established use dating pre-1964, for example where a house has been divided into a number of residential units, will insist upon appropriate evidence confirming such established use.

11.8.3 BUILDING CONTROL ACTS, 1990 TO 2014 AND ANY REGULATIONS. ORDER, OR INSTRUMENT THEREUNDER (REFERRED TO COLLECTIVELY AS 'THE REGULATIONS'): REQUISITION 27

Requisition 27 states:

1. *Is the property or any part thereof affected by any provisions of the regulations.*

2. *If it is claimed that the property is not affected by the regulations state why. Evidence by way of a statutory declaration of a competent person may be required to verify the reply.*

3. a. *Has a commencement notice been given to the building control authority in respect of the property.*
   b. *If so, furnish now a copy of same.*

4. a. *If a commencement notice was lodged with the building control authority on or after 01 March 2014 and Part IIIC of the Building Control Regulations 1997 (as inserted by the Building Control (Amendment) Regulations 2014) ('Part IIIC') applies, furnish now a copy (or certified copy if the certificate on the building control authority register is not accessible to the public) of the certificate of compliance on completion in the form prescribed by the Building Control (Amendment) Regulations 2014, together with evidence that it was registered by the building control authority.*
   b. *If a commencement notice was lodged with the building control authority on or after 01 March 2014 and Part IIIC does not apply, furnish now a certificate that the property is exempt from the requirements of Part IIIC and a certificate/opinion of compliance by a competent person confirming that all necessary requirements of the regulations have been met.*
   c. *If the property is affected by the regulations and neither of the circumstances described in a. or b. above apply, furnish now a certificate/opinion of compliance by a competent person confirming that all necessary requirements of the regulations have been met.*

5. *If the property is such that a fire safety certificate or a revised fire safety certificate or a disability access certificate or a revised disability access certificate or a regularisation certificate is one of the requirements of the regulations and the Building Control (Amendment) Regulations 2014 do not apply:*
   a. *Furnish a copy of the fire safety certificate or the revised fire safety certificate or the disability access certificate or the revised disability access certificate or the regularisation certificate.*
   b. *Confirm that no appeal was made by the applicant for such certificate(s) against any of the conditions imposed by the building control authority in such fire safety certificate, revised fire safety certificate, disability access certificate, revised disability access certificate or regularisation certificate.*

6. a. *Has any enforcement notice under section 8 of the Building Control Act 1990 as amended been served.*
   b. *If so, furnish now a copy of the notice and a certificate/opinion of compliance made by a competent person.*

7. *If any application has been made to the district court under section 9 of Building Control Act 1990 as amended furnish details of the result of such application.*

8.   *a.*   *Has any application been made to the circuit court or the high court under section 12 of the Building Control Act 1990, as amended.*

      b.   *If so, furnish a copy of any order made by the court and evidence of any necessary compliance with such order by a certificate / opinion of a competent person.*

The Building Regulations are a code of practice to ensure that structures/buildings are built according to the best code of practice and that the layout takes best advantage of fire escapes, sound control, ventilation, hygiene, drainage and waste disposals, stairways, ramps and guards, fuel and energy conservation in the interest of health, safety, and welfare of the users of these buildings. Whether or not there has been compliance is a task for the engineer/architect, not the solicitor.

This requisition is very similar to the old requisition but the title of it has been expanded to include the Building Control Acts and Regulations up to 2014.

11.8.3.1   Commencement Notices pre and post 1 March 2014

Requisition 27.4.a has been broken down into two categories of developments.

One, where a commencement notice was lodged on or after 1 March 2014 (see requisition 27.4.a. In which case, Part IIIC of the Building Control Regulations, 1997 (as inserted by the Building Control (Amendment) Regulations, 2014) applies. If post that date, then the 'new' regime applies, ie the new form of commencement notice, assigned certifiers, builder, building owner, competent person, and/or design certifier applies.

It should be noted here, in particular, that a surveyor for a purchaser of an apartment, for example, can no longer only consider the apartment but must also consider the apartment block itself.

The only requirement in relation to the new Building Regulations is that a copy of the statutory certificate of compliance (or a certified copy, if the certificate of compliance on completion on the Building Control Authority's register is not accessible to the public) together with evidence that it was registered by the Building Control Authority will be furnished.

Two, where the commencement notice was lodged pre that date; the 'old' regime applies. (See requisition 27.4.c.) In such cases the usual certificate/opinion on compliance by a competent person is required.

The requisition actually now provides purchasers with a very useful checklist as to what is required on closing depending on which category of development the property falls into.

Requisition 27.5 has been expanded from dealing solely with fire safety certificates to include reference to disability access certificates and any other certificates that may be required, eg a revised disability access certificate.

Requisition 27.8.a contains a new reference to the Circuit Court.

11.8.4   SAFETY HEALTH AND WELFARE AT WORK (CONSTRUCTION) REGULATIONS 1995, 2001 AND 2003, 2006–2013, AND 2013 (EACH THE 'SAFETY REGULATION'): REQUISITION 28

The requisition states:

1. *Has any construction work been undertaken by the client at or in the property where the construction stage was subsequent to 01 March 1996 (construction work, client and construction stage each meaning as defined in the Safety Regulations in force at the relevant time).*

2. *If so, furnish now copy safety file or confirm where the safety file containing the information required by the relevant Safety Regulation in force at the date of such work is available for inspection.*

The Regulations set out in this requisition were designed to promote safety, health, and welfare at construction sites. The wording of the requisition has been changed to bring further clarity to what is being asked. The Regulations require, among other things, the maintenance of a safety file. This replaces the previous requirement that a copy of the safety file be furnished at requisitions stage and the original safety file on completion. While is it true that most of the obligations under the Regulations only apply during the construction phase, a purchaser's solicitor to which the regulation applies will want to ensure that the safety file is available if a claim is made post acquisition and of course also should any further work be done to the building.

The requisition was updated to take account of legislative updates and also that a copy of the safety file be made available at requisition stage or confirmation of where it can be made available for inspection. The file is generally very large and full of drawings and technical documents. Thus, it is usual that they are now prepared in soft copy only and such a soft copy could be made available to a prospective purchaser. It is the purchaser's architect or engineer, not the solicitor, who is the appropriate person to review and comment on the sufficiency of the documents contained in the safety file while undertaking any pre-contract building survey.

The purchaser's solicitor only needs to know that the file exists and not the contents of same (see Law Society Practice Note, 1 November 1999).

The vendor's solicitor therefore needs to ensure that such a file exists and be able to produce a copy or refer to where the copy may be read. Given, especially during past economic booms, a certain laxity in keeping of records, the vendor's solicitor may well find that the safety file was not well maintained or maintained at all. Thus, the vendor's solicitor would need to establish as soon as possible in the conveyancing process the position regarding the file. There is little that can be done if the records do not exist.

11.8.5 NEWLY ERECTED PROPERTY: REQUISITION 29

Requisition 29 asks:

1. *Furnish now.*
   a. *Draft assurance.*
   b. *Draft site map.*
   c. *Draft statutory declaration of identity by the Vendor's architect or other competent person confirming that the entire of the property as shown on the site map and the rights of way easements and the services relating thereto form part of the lands to which the Vendor has shown title.*
   d. *Draft indemnity in relation to roads footpaths sewers and all services.*
   e. *Draft indemnity in relation to defects.*
   f. *Evidence of registration with Home Bond, Premier or alternative policy/scheme together with a copy of the policy document.*

2. *At closing hand over:*
   a. *Original assurance duly completed and a certificate of compliance with the building or other covenants endorsed thereon.*
   b. *Architect's statutory declaration of identity in accordance with 29.1.c.*
   c. *Indemnity under seal in relation to roads footpaths sewers and all services.*
   d. *Indemnity under seal in relation to defects.*
   e. *Architect's certificate confirming that all buildings have been erected within the confines of the site as per the deed map.*
   f. *The final certification with Home Bond, Premier or alternative policy/scheme.*

3. *If the property is registered land furnish in addition certified copy of the assurance.*

This requisition effectively provides a checklist for what is required on closing in relation to newly erected property. There have been very few changes to this requisition and those that have been made, were made to delete requirements in relation to documents which are now obsolete, eg memorials, PD Forms, Floor Area Certificates.

It does however, list Home Bond alternatives which reflects the entry into the market of such alternatives (see requisition 29.2.f).

11.8.6   FIRE SERVICES ACTS, 1981 AND 2003 ('THE FIRE SERVICES ACTS'): REQUISITION 30

Requisition 30 asks:

1. a. *Have any notices been served under the Fire Services Acts.*
    b. *If so, furnish now copies of same.*
    c. *Are there any proceedings pending under the Fire Services Acts.*

2. a. *Has the property ever been inspected by the fire authority for the functional area within which the property is situate.*
    b. *If so, what were its requirements.*

3. *Furnish architect's/engineer's certificate of substantial compliance with any such notices or requirements.*

Requisition 30 is a pre-contract requisition and any purchaser who buys a premises which is open to the public, or a flat, is liable to have a notice served on him by the fire officer and it is often a costly business to comply with the fire officer's requirements. Before purchasing any such property the client should be advised to check with the fire officer to ensure no notices have been served and that no notices are contemplated. However, while this letter should be sent, it is conveyancers' experience that no response is received.

This requisition makes enquiries as to whether any notice has been served or whether any proceedings are pending under the Fire Services Acts, 1981 and 2003, but in reality, the information can only be obtained from the vendor client. Thus, once again, the vendor's solicitor should seek this information from the client as early as possible in the conveyancing process.

Requisition 30.2 enquires as to whether the property has been inspected by the fire officer and whether the requirements of the fire officer have been complied with. The requisitions on title also enquire as to whether there are any outstanding requirements of the fire officer which have not been complied with and request the certificate from the fire office authority confirming compliance with any work which the fire officer requires to be done. Obtaining these certificates from the fire officer is a very difficult matter. It is important to serve at least one month's notice on the fire authority, both in respect of the applications for a new licence and for applications for renewals.

There is a misconception that the Fire Services Acts, 1981 and 2003 applies to residential dwellinghouses. The Acts do not apply to residential dwellinghouses other than flats and duplexes and the reply in cases of residential dwellinghouses is always 'not applicable'. Nevertheless, in cases where the Fire Services Acts do apply the non-compliance with the fire services notices incurs heavy penalties and possible court proceedings. Under the requisition, apart from asking whether any notices have been served, the vendor is asked to furnish copies of the same and to state whether or not proceedings are pending.

11.8.7   ENVIRONMENTAL: REQUISITION 31

This requisition states:

1. a. *Is the property a European Site as defined in the Planning and Development Acts 2000 to 2014.*
    b. *If so, give full particulars.*

2. *Is the Vendor aware of any European Site in the vicinity of the property which designation restricts any activity or use of the property.*

3. *Has any notice, certificate, order, requirement or recommendation been served upon or received by the Vendor or has the Vendor notice of any intention to serve any notice relating to the property or any part of it under or by virtue of or pursuant to any 'Environ mental Laws' (meaning all laws (whether criminal, civil or administrative) including common law, statutes, regulations, statutory instruments, directives, bye-laws, orders, codes and judgements having the force of law in Ireland concerning environmental matters, control and prevention of pollution, protection or preservation or improvement of the environment).*

4. *If so, furnish copies, with evidence of compliance therewith.*

5. a. *Is the Vendor aware of any breach of any Environmental Laws in respect of the property.*
   b. *If so, give full particulars.*

6. *Has any permit, licence or consent issued under Environmental Laws in respect of the property or any activity carried out therein.*

7. *If so, furnish copies, with evidence of compliance therewith.*

8. *Is the Vendor aware of any form of waste as defined under the Waste Management Acts 1996 to 2011 (and including any noxious, deleterious, harmful or polluting matter) in the property which will not be removed by the Vendor prior to completion of the sale.*

9. *If so, provide details.*

Under the Law Society's Contract for Sale 2009 (revised) edition the purchaser is, pursuant to general condition 16, *'deemed to buy with full notice of the actual state and condition of the subject property'*. It should, however, be noted that under general condition 35 a purchaser may seek to rescind the sale if the purchaser is sure that the vendor, prior to the sale, failed to notify the purchaser of a relevant notice or information.

Requisitions 31.1 and 31.2 are two new requisitions to find out if the property is designated as a 'European Site' or if there is one in the vicinity. Whatever about the former, it is not always going to be possible to establish the position re the latter. To understand this requisition, it requires to be cross-referenced with various sections of the most recent consolidation of the Planning and Development Acts, 2000–2014, but briefly, it appears to be designed to capture special areas of conservation and proportion as designated by the Habitats Directive and/or Birds Directive.

Requisition 31.3 previously referred to the European Communities Act, 1972 and to a range of laws and rules referred to as the 'Environmental Rules'; it is now referred to as 'Environmental Laws' and gives a revised description of the range of types of law covered by the new reference which is extensive.

Requisitions 31.6–9 seek information on any permit, licence, or consent issued under any environmental laws and in particular, requisitions 31.8 and 31.9 seek to obtain information on any waste in the property which will not be removed by the vendor prior to completion. Please note that the definition here, under the Waste Management Acts, 1999–2011, is very wide and is not merely hazardous waste.

Requisition 31.7 requires not only copies of consents but that evidence of compliance with that consent is furnished.

In short, the vendor is required to confirm that no notice, certificate, order, requirement, or recommendation has been served upon him or her or that the vendor has not been notified of any intention to serve such notice etc under the various environmental statutes and regulations listed, as updated. If the vendor has been served with copies these should be furnished to the purchaser and, if notices etc require work to be carried out, this question also must be answered, if necessary with a certificate from a competent person.

The problem for vendors' solicitors, in general, with this requisition but in particular re 31.2, is that few vendors will be aware in dwellinghouse situations of breach of any environmental controls in respect of their property. If a vendor is aware of such breach he is asked to give full particulars. It should be stressed, however, that this chapter deals with requisitions on title only for residential sale and very different criteria attach to a sale of farmlands, factory lands, or industrial premises.

This highlights, once again, the importance of a vendor's solicitor taking detailed instructions as to any item which may be caught by this requisition. A conveyancer can never assume that just because it is a residential sale the requisition does not apply.

From a purchaser's perspective, if there is any risk, then this clearly is a pre-contract issue and, while difficult, it is for the purchaser's solicitor to decide whether a more detailed pre-contract enquiry should be carried out.

11.8.8   LOCAL GOVERNMENT (MULTI-STOREY BUILDINGS) ACT, 1988 ('THE 1988 ACT'): REQUISITION 35

Requisition 35 states:

1.   *Is the property or any part of the property a multi-storey building within the meaning of the 1988 Act or does it form part of a development in which there is a multi storey building with which it shares a common management company.*

2.   *If so, is it governed by:*
     A.   *The regulations as defined in requisition 27 or*
     B.   *The 1988 Act.*

3.   A.   *If the answer to 1. above is 'no' because the entire building was constructed prior to 01 January 1950, furnish now a statutory declaration by a person who can prove satisfactorily that the building was so constructed.*
     B.   *If the answer to 2.b. Above is 'yes', reply to requisitions 4. To 9. below.*

4.   A.   *Has a notice been served by the local authority under section 2(2) of the 1988 Act.*
     B.   *If so, furnish now a copy of same.*
     C.   *Whether or not such a notice has been served and the construction of the building was completed prior to 14 November 1988 furnish now a certificate from a competent person in accordance with section 3(a) or a declaration in accordance with section 3(b) of the 1988 Act.*

5.   *Where a certificate has been submitted to the local authority pursuant to section 3 of the 1988 Act:*
     A.   *State whether or not the same is in accordance with the appropriate form provided for in the regulations made and in force under the 1988 Act.*
     B.   *Furnish now a copy of the said certificate.*

6.   A.   *Has any work been carried out to the building which might nullify the effect of a certificate furnished in accordance with section 3 and require a further certificate in accordance with section 5 of the 1988 Act.*
     B.   *If so, furnish now a certified copy of such certificate.*

7.   *If the building is a multi-storey building the construction of which was not completed prior to 14 November 1988, furnish now a certified copy of the certificate in the prescribed form submitted to the local authority pursuant to section 4 of the 1988 Act.*

8.   *Have any notices been served under the 1988 A which have not yet been complied with.*

9.   *Where any certificate has been submitted to the local authority under the 1988 Act furnish a letter from the local authority confirming that the certificate has been placed on the register.*

11.8.8.1

The Local Government (Multi-Storey Buildings) Act, 1988 ('the 1988 Act') came into effect on 14 November 1988 and it affects all multi-storey buildings which were not completed on or before 1 January 1950. As defined in the Act, a multi-storey building is a building comprising five or more storeys and a basement is regarded as a storey. The Act applies to such buildings whether residential, apartments, office blocks, hotels, or any other buildings.

From 1 June 1992 the provisions of the 1988 Act ceased to have effect except in cases coming within the transitional provisions of the Building Control Act, 1990, s 2(2). Multi-storey buildings started at 1 June 1992 with the benefit of building bye-law approval or, in the event of building bye-law approval not having issued, but the plans for building bye-law approval having been lodged, will require the usual certificates and must comply with the 1988 Act. In the event of planning permission having issued for multi-storey buildings where no building bye-law approval or plans have been lodged, the provisions of the 1988 Act will not apply and the buildings must be erected in accordance with the Building Regulations. If work is commenced on a multi-storey building after 1 June 1992 and before 1 August 1992, no fire safety certificate was required under the Building Regulations. In June 2015 the Conveyancing Committee published two sets of pre-contract enquiries on the Society's website covering sales of units in multi-unit developments, one being an updated set of the existing pre-contract enquiries dealing with units in developments that are subject to the MUD Act, 2011, and the other being a new set of pre-contract enquiries for units in developments that are not subject to the Act. Only developments that have the required residential elements are subject to the Act.

Solicitors acting for prospective vendors of such units are advised to familiarise themselves with the requirements of these enquiries with a view to equipping themselves to answer the enquiries when received. Some of the information required, particularly that relating to the appointment of managing agents, insurance, service charge, sinking funds, house rules, and voting rights, should have been provided to the vendor as a member of the owners management company (OMC). If the vendor cannot produce this information it should be available from the OMC and they or their agents should be sent a copy of the pre-contract enquiries as soon as possible.

11.8.8.2

Requisition 35.1, which asks whether the property in sale is a multi-storey building, ie a five-storey building including basement, with which it shares a common management company built since 1 June 1950, appears quite simple. However, what is a factual question has caused problems in that difficulties have arisen on the definition of what is and what is not a storey. Where any dispute arises counsel's opinion should be sought.

11.8.8.3

If the building is a multi-storey building, is it governed by: (a) the Regulations as defined in requisition 35, or (b) the 1988 Act.

The point of requisition 35.2 is to establish whether the building is covered by the 1988 Act or whether it is governed by the Building Control Act, 1990. The provisions of the 1988 Act ceased to have any effect from 1 June 1992 except for cases coming within the transitional provisions of the Building Control Act, 1990, s 2(2). Effectively the provisions of the 1988 Act have been fully replaced by the Building Control Act, 1990, together with the regulations made thereunder.

Each local authority is required by the 1988 Act to prepare and maintain a register of multi-storey buildings located in its area. This refers to five-storey buildings, including basements, completed after 1 January 1950. The local authorities are compelled to serve notice on the owners of multi-storey buildings requiring them to furnish a certificate in accordance with s 3 of the 1988 Act, and there is an obligation on the local authority to take follow-up action to ensure that the relevant certificate is submitted. This obligation on the local authorities' part to seek certificates only relates to multi-storey buildings which were completed between 1 January 1950 and 14 November 1988 when the Act came into force. Once an owner is served with a notice by the local authority, the owner is obliged to furnish a certificate to the local authority in one of the forms referred to in s 3 of the Act. Once an owner has been served with a notice all arrangements associated with submitting the certificate, including engaging a competent person to carry out works to be certified and submission of certificate are the responsibility of the owner. The certificate must cover the entire building and a certificate relating to a part of a building only is meaningless. Where a multi-storey building is completed after commencement of the 1988 Act (14 November 1988) and before the coming into force of the Building Control Act, 1990, there is an automatic duty on the owner to apply for a certificate and this must be done before the building or any part of it is occupied. Local authorities who own multi-storey buildings are not excluded from the provisions of the Act. If no notice was served there is no obligation under the Act.

Section 3 of the Act sets out the various kinds of certificates which the owner of a building may furnish to the local authority. There are several different certificates depending on the building's characteristics:

(a)   The first certificate specifies that the building is not a specified building as defined in the Act.

(b)   If the building is a specified building, the certificate can certify either:
(i)   that the building is built in accordance with the appropriate codes of practice and standards;
(ii)   that the occupiers of the building and the persons in its vicinity will not be exposed to risks related to robustness of the building unduly in excess of those which would be present in the building which is covered at (i) above;
(iii)   all reasonable actions have been taken to minimise, as far as is practical, the risks of accidental damage to the building.

(c)   The Act requires one appraisal and one certificate in respect of each building and there is no continuing requirement to submit further certificates on a regular basis, save under the provisions of s 5, which requires that no action be carried out which would nullify a certificate under s 3 without the prior submission of a further certificate.

(d)   A competent person to sign the said certificate has been defined by s 1 of the Act. In practice nearly all buildings completed before the coming into force of the 1988 Act have been served with a notice by the relevant authority, and in almost all cases the relevant certificates have been deposited with the local authority and are available for inspection. This obligation since the passing of the Act is on the owner of the buildings to file a multi-storey Building Act Certificate with the local authority and experience has shown that in almost all cases this has been done. Since the passing of the Building Control Act, 1990, and as and from 1 June 1992, save and except for the transitional provisions already referred, there is no need to file any certificate with the local authority and the architect's certificate of compliance dealing with the Buildings Regulations is sufficient.

(e)   The onus is placed on a competent person, usually a chartered engineer with structural engineering experience, to make an appraisal of an existing building for a response to accidental overload is a complex task involving detailed examination and the exercise of a large degree of engineering judgment. The Act provides for severe penalties for certificates which are inaccurate, or in any way misleading. In some cases engineers carrying out the appraisal have formed the opinion that the building could have insufficient robustness or resistance for accidental damage. In some cases they have also concluded the amount of disturbance to the building by opening up joints etc to meet the necessary inspections to ascertain the position would be excessive. For example, Harcourt House and Canada House on the corner of St Stephen's Green and Earlsfort Terrace were cases where a certificate could not be signed without very considerable expenditure being incurred in rendering the building sufficiently robust to the resistance for accidental damage. The purpose of the Act is to ensure that reasonable action is taken to make a building safe, if this is required.

11.8.8.4

The first part of requisition 35.3 requires a statutory declaration to be produced in a case where a multi-storey building was constructed prior to 1 January 1950. In obvious cases, this declaration is rarely furnished, but in cases where the completion of the building was in or about 1 January 1950 a declaration should be insisted upon. The second part of this requisition states that if the building is a multi-storey building built from 1 January 1950, answers must be furnished to requisitions 35.4–35.9 (inclusive).

11.8.8.5

In relation to requisition 35.4.it would be extremely rare that a local authority would not by now have served a notice on the owner of the multi-storey building requesting the submission of a certificate in respect of any building completed prior to 14 November 1988. Therefore part (b) of this requisition merely asks for a copy of the local authority's notice. Such notice may not always be available but the most important document is the certificate signed by a competent person in accordance with s 3(a), or a declaration in accordance with s 3(b), of the 1988 Act. Requisition 4(c) requests either a s 3(a) certificate or a s 3(b) declaration as to whether or not the local authority has served a notice on the owner of any building completed before 14 November 1988. The fact that the local authority omitted to request a certificate in an appropriate case does not relieve the owner of the building from obtaining such a certificate.

11.8.8.6

Requisition 35.5 refers to s 3 of the 1988 Act which came into force in 1990 under the 1988 Act setting out the prescribed form of certificate. Requisition 5(a) asks if the certificate is in the prescribed form and 5(b) asks for a copy of the certificate.

11.8.8.7

In relation to requisition 35.6(a), please note only one certificate issues only in respect of each building. However, there is an exception provided for in s 5 of the 1988 Act. If work has been carried out which effectively nullifies the certificate which has already been furnished in accordance with s 3, a further certificate is required under s 5 and the requisition calls for the production of this additional certificate.

11.8.8.8

In relation to requisition 35.7, as stated earlier, any building completed after 14 November 1988 does not require the local authority for the area to serve a notice requesting a certificate. These certificates must be submitted by the owner/developer to the local authority before any part of the building is occupied.

11.8.8.9

In relation to requisition 35.8, the local authority is entitled to serve notices under the 1988 Act requiring certain works to be carried out to ensure that the building is robust. This requisition requires the vendor to produce such notices (if any) which have been served.

11.8.8.10

The purpose of requisition 35.9 is to establish evidence of compliance with the 1988 Act. The register is a public register and any person is entitled to inspect it and to certify that the certificate has been submitted to the local authority and that the certificate, if such be the case, has been placed on the register.

John Gore-Grimes delivered an excellent CLE lecture *'Planning Issues in Relation to Convey-ancing Transactions'* on 20 November 2004 giving a very practical checklist for conveyancing practitioners in relation to requisitions on pp 65–123.

11.9 The Building Control Acts of 1990 and 2007, Building Control Regulations, 1997–2015, and Building Regulations, 1997–2015

11.9.1 INTRODUCTION

The Building Control Act, 1990 and amendments thereto, ie the Building Control Act, 2007, and the regulations made under the Acts are referred to collectively as 'Building Control Regulations and Building Regulations'.

The relevant legislation is:

- Building Control Act, 1990;

- Building Control Regulations, 1991 (SI 305/1991);

- Building Regulations, 1991 (SI 306/1991);

- Building Control (Amendment) Regulations, 1994 (SI 153/1994);

- Building Regulations (Amendment) Regulations, 1994 (SI 154/1994);

- Building Control Regulations, 1997 (SI 496/1997);

- Building Regulations, 1997 (SI 497/1997);

- Building Control (Amendment) Regulations, 2000 (SI 10/2000);

- Building Regulations (Amendment) Regulations, 2000 (SI 179/2000);

- Building Regulations (Amendment) (No 2) Regulations, 2000 (SI 249/2000);

- Building Regulations (Amendment) (No 3) Regulations, 2000 (SI 441/2000) (Class 9 exemption extended);

- Building Regulations Advisory Body Order, 2002 (SI 2/2002);

- Building Regulations (Amendment) Regulations, 2002 (SI 284/2002);

- Building Regulations (Amendment) (No 2) Regulations, 2002 (SI 581/2002) (Part F);

- Building Regulations Advisory Body Order, 2002 (Amendment) Order, 2003 (SI 62/2003);

- Building Control (Amendment) Regulations, 2004 (SI 85/2004);

- European Communities (Energy Performance of Building) Regulations (SI 872/2005);

- Building Control (Amendment) Regulations, 2006 (SI 115/2006);

- European Communities (Energy Performance of Building) Regulations (SI 666/2006 and SI 243/2012);

- Building Control Act, 2007, which became law on 1 April 2007, amends the Building Control Act, 1990 by strengthening enforcement powers of local building control authorities, and by revising procedures for the issue of FSCs and introducing DACs it widens the right of building control authorities to seek an order from the High Court or Circuit Court to stop work on certain buildings and introduces the option for the authorities to bring summary prosecutions for all building code offences in the District Court and it also increases the maximum penalties for breaches of the national Building Regulations (see **11.9.13**). It also deals with registration of titles of certain building professions, eg architects (see **11.11.3.1**) and finally, it was the method of legal transportation of relevant parts of the EU Mutual Recognition of Qualifications Directive 2005/36 EC of September 2005;

- European Communities (Energy Performance of Buildings) (Amendments) Regulations, 2008 (SI 229/2008);

- Building Regulations (Part L Amendment), 2008 (SI 259/2008);

- Building Regulations (Part G Amendment), 2008 (SI 335/2008);

- Building Control (Amendment) Regulations, 2009 (SI 351/2009) (changes to fire safety Certificates and providing for Disability Access Certificates). See the Practice Note in the Law Society Gazette August/September 2010 re disability access certificates (DACs) arising under this SI which came into force on 1 January 2010 and see **11.9.8.2**;

- Building Regulations (Part F Amendment) Regulations, 2009 (SI 556/2009);

- Building Regulations (Part H Amendment) Regulations, 2010 (SI 561/2010). These regulations amend Part H of the Building Regulations, 1997 re drainage and waste water disposal and, essentially, updates the standards and incorporates guidance on emerging sustainable technology. The operative date of 1 June 2011 is subject to the transitional exemption for construction works for which planning permission or approval is applied on or before 31 May 2011 provided substantial work has been completed by 31 May 2012. See **11.12.3** for 'what is substantial work';

- Building Regulations (Part M Amendment) Regulations, 2010 (SI 513/2010). These regulations, which came into force on 1 January 2012 subject to the transitional period cited therein, amended Part M, Art 11, and Art 13 of the Building Regulations, 1997 and essentially deals with the approach, access, and sanitary facilities in existing buildings which were extended;

- Building Regulations (Part L Amendment) Regulations, 2011 (SI 259//2011). These regulations, which came into force on 1 December 2011 subject to the transitional arrangements cited therein, amended Part L of the Second Schedule to the Building Regulations, 1997–2008 and essentially deals with conservation of fuel and energy by setting higher thermal performance/insulation standards for new domestic buildings;

- Building Control (Prescribed Bodies and Courses) Regulations, 2012 (SI 341/2012). These regulations updated the prescribed bodies and courses, in relation to 'who is an architect'. See **11.11.3.1**.

- Building Regulations (Part A Amendment) Regulations, 2012 (SI 138/2012). These regulations were required to ensure consistency with the Euro Codes which are a set of harmonised structural design codes for building and civil engineering works which are now in force generally across EU Member States;

- Building Regulations (Part D Amendment) Regulations, 2013 (SI 224/2013). These regulations apply to works and buildings commencing on or after 1 July 2013 and amended Part D of the Second Schedule of the Building Regulations, 1997–2012 and lay down harmonised conditions for the marketing of construction products throughout the EU;

- Building Control (Amendment) Regulations, 2013 (SI 80/2013). These regulations have been revoked partly as they contained an error but mainly as changes (which have now been incorporated into the 2014 Regulations) to the forms of architects and other certifiers' certificates were negotiated by the certifiers' respective institutions;

- Building Control (Part D Amendment) Regulations, 2013 (SI 224/2013). These regulations amend Part D of the Second Schedule to the Building Regulations 1997–2012 by revising the definition of 'proper materials';

- Building Control Regulations, 2014 (SI 9/2014). These regulations, which came into operation on 1 March 2014, revoked and replaced SI 80/2013 as listed earlier. The Regulations apply to any development where a commencement notice is filed after 1 March 2014. They apply to the design and construction of a new dwelling, to any extension to a dwellinghouse involving a floor area of more than 40 square metres, and works where a fire safety certificate is involved. Effectively, this means to nearly any type of commercial building, including retail industrial offices etc. The key changes are to the statutory certificates.

In short, the Regulations require greater accountability in relation to compliance with Building Regulations in the form of statutory certification of design, construction, lodgement of compliance documentation, mandatory inspections during construction, and validation and registration of certificates, eg Regulation 7 amends Art 9 of the Principal Regulations to provide for an amended form of commencement notice from 1 March 2014, The form is set out in the Second Schedule to the Regulations. This must be signed by the owner of the works. In addition, it should be noted that if the extension is greater than 40 square metres, or the works require an application for a fire safety control certificate, the commencement notice must now include considerably more detail than previously and be signed by the building owner. See below for a list.

At completion stage the assigned certifier is required to submit the following to the Building Control Authority:

- A certificate of compliance signed by the builder (at Part A) and by the assigned certifier (at Part B);

- Plans, calculations, specifications, and particulars showing how the completed building has achieved compliance with the Building Regulations either when the certificate of compliance on completion is submitted or at an earlier date;

- An inspection plan as implemented by the assigned certifier in accordance with the Code of Practice.

The Building Control Authority then, having reviewed the papers, validates the certificate and if it is in order places it on the register within 21 days.

As the Regulations prohibit the opening occupation or use of a building until a certificate of compliance on completion has been filed and registered by the Building Control Authority, compliance with the Regulations is vital for building owners, purchasers, or prospective tenants. The Regulations had no impact on certificates re planning which continue to be required in one of the existing forms.

See Law Society update 15/05/2014 'Update on Building Control Regulations, 2014' and 'Certificates of Compliance with Building Regulations' 6th June 2014 and an article by Andrew Ramsey 'Positive Change' in the Autumn 2014 *Surveyors Journal* Vol 4 Issue 3.

- Building Control (Amendment) (No 2) Regulations, 2014 (SI 105/2014). These regulations apply to a limited range of public and privately owned buildings classified as, first, second, or third level places of education, hospitals, or primary care centres. The Regulations set out an alternative but equivalent means of complying with the requirements under the Building Control Regulations, 1997–2014 by assigning a person to inspect and certify the works (the assigned certifier). The alternative means applies only to projects in the following circumstances; where planning permission, if applicable, has been obtained before 1 March 2014, contract documents have been signed before 1 November 2014 and a valid commencement notice has been lodged with the Building Control Authority, no later than 1 March 2015.

- Building Control (Part J Amendment) Regulations, 2014 (SI 122/2014). These regulations provide for the detection and warning of carbon monoxide in dwellings.

- Building Control (Part J Amendment) Regulations, 2014 (SI 133/2014). These regulations amend Part E (Sound) of the Second Schedule to the Building Regulations, 1997 in respect of new dwellings or extensions. Their purpose is to protect occupants from noise. They also amend Art 13 of Building Regulations, 1997 to ensure that Part E applies to an existing building or part of a building which undergoes a material change of use to a dwelling.

- Building Control (Amendment No 2) Regulations, 2014 (SI 105/2014). These regulations, which came into being on 28 February 2014, are of limited application, relating only to buildings intended for use in first, second, or third level education or hospitals or primary care centres.

- Building Control (Part K Amendment) Regulations, 2014 (SI 180/2014). These regulations amend Part K (Stairways, Ladders, Ramps and Guards) of the Second Schedule to the Building Regulations, 1997 and update the Technical Guidance Documents relating to Part K.

- Building Control (Part E Amendment) Regulations, 2014 (SI 606/2014).By the Revised Building Control Act of 2014 there was an administrative consolidation of the Building Control Act, 2007, see earlier). It was prepared by the Law Reform Commission in accordance with its function under the Law Reform Commission Act, 1975 (3/1975) to keep the law under review and to undertake revision and consolidation of statute law. All Acts up to and including the Water Services Act, 2014 (44/2014), enacted 28 December 2014, and all statutory instruments up to and including the Health Insurance Act, 1994 (Section 11E(2)) (No 5) Regulations, 2014 (SI 621/2014), made 22 December 2014, were considered in the preparation of this revision,

- Building Control (Amendment) Regulations, 2015 (SI 243/2015). The Regulations provide for revision in certain cases of the fee specified in Part A of the Fifth Schedule to the Principal Regulations in respect of an application for a DAC or a revised DAC.

- Building Control (Amendment) Regulations, 2015 (SI 365/2015) came into force on 1 March 2014. These regulations essentially amend SI 9/2014 following a review of the operations introduced under that statutory instrument during its first twelve months in operation. Article 5 clarifies the point that an owner intending to build a dwelling for their own use may take on the role of builder for building control purposes and sign the statutory forms which would usually be signed by the builder.

Articles 9 and 20F of the Principal Regulations are revised to give the owner of works involving the construction of a new single dwelling, or a single unit development, or a domestic extension, the facility to opt out of the requirement to obtain statutory certificates of compliance signed by a registered construction professional. A homeowner who wishes to avail of this facility must, when submitting the commencement notice, sign and submit the new form of 'Declaration of Intention to Opt Out of Statutory Certification' now included in the Second Schedule to the Principal Regulations. The homeowner in such circumstances is no longer required to provide the following compliance documentation specified under Art 9 of the Principal Regulations:

- the preliminary inspection plan prepared by the assigned certifier [Art 9(1)(b)(i)(IV) refers];

- a certificate of compliance (design) [Art 9(1)(b)(ii)(I) refers];

- a notice of assignment of person to inspect and certify works (assigned certifier) [Art 9(1)(b)(ii)(II) refers];

- a certificate of compliance (undertaking by assigned certifier) [Art 9(1)(b)(ii)(III) refers];

- a certificate of compliance (undertaking by builder) [Art 9(1)(b)(ii)(V) refers];

- a certificate of compliance on completion, and accompanying documents.

For the avoidance of doubt, a homeowner who opts out of the statutory certification process as outlined above is required, prior to the commencement of works, to submit a commencement notice accompanied by:

- a Declaration of Intention to Opt Out of Statutory Certification;

- such plans, calculations, specifications, and particulars as are necessary to outline how the proposed dwelling or domestic extension will comply with the relevant requirements of the Second Schedule to the Building Regulations; This will typically include, but will not be confined to, general arrangement drawings; a schedule of compliance documents, as designed or to be prepared at a later date; the online BCMS assessment of the proposed approach to compliance (Art 9(1)(b)(i) of the Principal Regulations refers);

• a Notice of Assignment of Builder (Art 9(1)(b)(ii)(IV) of the Principal Regulations refers);

• a fee of €30 (Part V of the Principal Regulations refers);

The effect of the above changes to Arts 9 and 20F is that the statutory forms of certification signed by builders and registered construction professionals are no longer mandatory in the case of a new single dwelling, or a single unit development, or a domestic extension.

Finally, Art 21 of the Principal Regulations has been amended to provide for reference to be made on the public register where a homeowner has declared their intention to opt out of statutory certification.

The 1991 Building Control Regulations, which came into force on 1 June 1992, were superseded by the 1997 Regulations, which came into force on 1 July 1998. The purpose of the Regulations is to promote observance of the Regulations by supplementing the basic powers of inspection and enforcement given to Building Control Authorities by different sections of the Building Control Act, 1990, as amended.

Briefly put, the Regulations do so in two ways:

1. by requiring commencement notices of works (change of use) to be lodged (see **11.9.6**); and

2. by requiring an FSC (see **11.9.8**).

Prior to the Building Control Act, 1990, such controls as existed arose by virtue of building bye-laws made under the Public Health (Ireland) Act, 1878, s 41, the Public Health (Amendment) Act, 1890, s 23, and the Dublin Corporation Act, 1890, s 33. Unlike the Building Control Act, which replaced building bye-laws, building bye-laws did not apply throughout the country; nor indeed were they obligatory; they were made in the following areas only: Bray UDC, Dublin Corporation, Dublin County Council, Dun Laoghaire Corporation, Cork Corporation, Galway Corporation, Limerick Corporation, and Naas UDC.

In areas where local authorities had made building bye-laws it was necessary to obtain a building bye-law approval before carrying out structural works or other works involving draining, sewerage, disposal, etc. Such an approval could not be obtained retrospectively. Therefore, technically, the absence of a building bye-law approval was a defect which could not be cured other than by demolishing the structure.

Accordingly, in such a situation it became established practice to accept the certificate of an architect confirming that the works complied with the building bye-laws as of the date the works were carried out, that in the opinion of the architect bye-law approval would have been granted if it had been applied for, and it is not uncommon to come across such architects' opinions on title (see Law Society *Gazette*, March 1986).

The Conveyancing Committee of the Law Society in the Law Society *Gazette*, May 2001 drew the attention of practitioners to a practice by Dublin Corporation in relation to retention of building bye-law records. Dublin Corporation notified the committee that all building bye-law records including decision documents prior to 1975 were no longer available. This in itself can cause problems where they were not kept with the title documents. The corporation also advised them that while records of decision documents since 1975 are available there are no drawings attached as it was not the policy of the corporation to retain drawings except for a brief period after the granting of the bye-law approval. If the documentation is not with the title deeds and they are now required, conveyancers are left in the position of trying to obtain either a record of the decision or plans depending on the circumstances from the original architect, if there was an architect involved in the original development. Even where there was such an architect it is not uncommon to find they have not also kept a copy of the approval or plans.

Section 22(7) of the Building Control Act, 1990 abolished the necessity to obtain bye-law approval from 1 June 1992. The effect of this is that there is no longer any need to obtain bye-law approval for development in areas where bye-law approval was required. The Building Control Authority had six months from 1 June 1992 to object to developments which were carried out prior to 13 December 1989. If no notice was served before 1 December 1992 in respect of works carried out prior to 13 December 1989 the works are deemed to have been built in accordance with the bye-law. However, building bye-laws are relevant in relation to works carried out between 13 December 1989 and 1 June 1992 and works carried out pursuant to bye-law approvals applied for prior to 1 June 1992.

Time Period	Building Bye-Laws	Amnesty re Building Bye-Laws	Building Regulations
From 1890 to 1 June 1992	Building bye-laws apply. Possibility of amnesty if conditions met	Amnesty applies if conditions met: work carried out prior to 13 December 1989 AND no notice served by local authority by 1 December 1992	Building Regulations do not apply
Prior to 13 December 1989	Building bye-laws apply. Possibility of amnesty if conditions met	Amnesty re bye-laws if conditions met: work carried out prior to 13 December 1989 AND no notice served by local authority by 1 December 1992	Building Regulations do not apply
From 13 December 1989 to 1 June 1992	Building bye-laws apply. No possibility of amnesty	Amnesty re bye-laws does not apply. Architect's cert or BBL approval necessary	Building Regulations do not apply
Post-1 June 1992	Building bye-laws apply if works carried out pursuant to bye-law approvals applied for prior to 1 June 1992	Amnesty re bye-laws does not apply	Building Regulations apply unless works carried out pursuant to bye-law approval applied for prior 1 June 1992

11.9.2 INTRODUCTION TO THE BUILDING CONTROL ACT, 1990

The Building Control Act, 1990 had three main purposes:

(a) to replace the existing system of building bye-laws (applicable in particular areas) with a national building control system;

(b) to improve the regulation of building standards by providing for additional matters including energy conservation, the needs of the disabled, the efficient use of resources, and the encouragement of good building practice. In particular, the Act enabled the Minister to make fire safety a central feature of Building Regulations; and

(c) the designation of a range of local authorities and building control authorities provides for the alignment of existing fire authorities (under the Fire Services Act, 1981) with building control authorities.

Thus, the Building Control Act, 1990 and amendments thereto—Building Control Act 2007 and the regulations made under it (as listed at **11.9.1**) provide a statutory basis for the making and administration of regulations for control of building. It constitutes a system for regulating building works and lays down minimum standards for design, construction, workmanship, materials, etc. Different standards apply depending on the use of the building.

The Building Control Act, 1990 set out a new system to regulate building practice. The new framework provided the Minister for the Environment with the power to make Building Regulations. The Act imposes a duty on everybody to comply with these regulations. The Regulations are a code of practice to ensure that structures are built to that code.

The Regulations are divided into various sections dealing with different aspects of building practice, from structure and fire, to conservation of fuel and energy.

The Department of the Environment has issued technical guidance documents in relation to each section which sets out technical buildings methods for use in the construction of buildings. The guidance documents refer to several hundred codes of practice, standards, or other technical references. However, there is no legal obligation to comply with the standards set out in the technical guidance documents although doing so certainly constitutes *prima facie* compliance with the Regulations.

11.9.3 APPLICATION AND COMMENCEMENT

The main provisions of the Building Control Act, 1990 came into force on 1 June 1992. From that date all works for the erection of buildings or the material alteration or extension or change of use of existing buildings must comply with the Regulations unless the works are covered by any of the exemptions specified later.

Statutory instruments updating Building Control Regulations have been and will continue to be periodically updated and have considerably evolved since 1992 (see **11.9.1)** and thus care should be taken that, at any point in time, the most recent Building Regulations are consulted eg SI 9/2014, Building Control (Amendment) Regulations, 2014 which substantially amends and extends commencement notices and, in general, strengthens control of building works.

11.9.4 EXEMPTIONS FROM THE BUILDING CONTROL ACT, 1990

The Building Control Act is similar to the Planning Acts in that certain classes of development are exempt. Below are some key exemptions;

(a) works commenced before 1 June 1992 or works carried out on foot of a building bye-law approval application which was made prior to 1 June 1992: Building Regulations, 1991, Art 7;

(b) alterations to buildings which do not affect the structural or fire safety aspects of the building: see Building Regulations, 1997, Art 11(1);

(c) detached domestic garages with a floor area not exceeding 25 square metres (originally 23 square metres as per Building Regulations, 1991, Art 6(1)(h) and, by virtue of the Building Regulations (Amendment) Regulations, 1994, Art 6(1)(i) increased to 25 square metres) and height of not more than three metres or, in the case of a pitched roof, four metres: see Building Regulations, 1997, Third Schedule, Class 1;

(d) single-storey detached buildings in the grounds of a dwellinghouse with a floor area not exceeding as above, initially 23 square metres and, since 1994, 25 square metres, a height of not more than three metres or, in the case of a pitched roof, four metres, and used exclusively for recreational or storage purposes as opposed to use for trade or business or human habitation: Building Regulations, 1997, Third Schedule, Class 2;

(e) single-storey extensions to existing dwellings ancillary to a dwelling and consisting of a conservatory, porch, car port, or covered area with a floor area not exceeding 25 square metres (or two square metres in the case of a porch) and a height less than three metres or, if a pitched roof, four metres: see Building Regulations, 1991, Art 6 and Building Regulations, 1997, Third Schedule, Class 3;

(f)   certain temporary structures: see Building Regulations, 1991, Art 6(1)(e)–(h); Building Regulations, 1997, Third Schedule, Classes 11, 12, 13;

(g)   a single-storey glasshouse where not less than three-quarters of its total external area is comprised of glass and it is used solely for agriculture and it is detached from any other building: see Building (Amendment) Regulations, 1994, Art 6(1)(l), Building Regulations, 1997, Third Schedule, Class 4;

(h)   a single-storey building which is detached from any other building and which is a building used solely for agriculture and is used exclusively for the storage of materials or products, for the accommodation of plant or machinery, or in connection with the housing, care, or management of livestock and is a building where the only persons habitually employed are engaged solely in the care, supervision, regulation, maintenance, storage, or removal of the materials, products, plant, machinery, or livestock in the building and which does not exceed 300 square metres in floor area: see Building Regulations, 1991, Art 6(1)(m), Building Regulations, 1997, Third Schedule, Class 5;

(i)   the design or construction of a building which is carried out by or on behalf of a Building Control Authority or material change of use of a building in the possession of a Building Control Authority where the building or works will be situated within the functional area of the Building Control Authority concerned (see Building Control Act, 1990, s 4)

However, please note that the Building Control (Amendment) (No.2) Regulations 2015 (SI 365/2015) amended Art 6 of the Regulations by removing the general exemption from Building Control Regulations undertaken by a local authority within its own functional area.

(j)   the Regulations do not apply to a building for mining or, quarrying, other than a house or building used as offices, laboratories, or showrooms, a building the construction of which is subject to the Explosives Act, 1875, a building subject to the National Monuments Acts, 1930–1994, a building constructed for and used by the Electricity Supply Board as its generating transmission or distribution station, a temporary dwelling as defined by the Local Government (Sanitary Services) Act, 1948: see Building Control Regulations, 1994, Art 6(1)(a)–(d), Building Regulations, 1997, Third Schedule, Classes 6–10. The exemption relating to the Electricity Supply Board has been amended by Building Regulations (Amendment) (No. 3) Regulations, 2000 (SI 441/2000);

(k)   lighthouses: Building Regulations, 1997 Third Schedule, Class 14;

(l)   Article 8 of the Building Regulations, 1997, which operates from 1 July 1998, creates a new emphasis in relation to certain buildings themselves as opposed to works to buildings. These buildings are exempt from the Regulations if they come within one of the classes set out in the Third Schedule, provided that they comply with the conditions attaching to the relevant class.

11.9.5   COMMENCEMENT NOTICES

When a development is subject to the Building Regulations, the nature of the development determines the level of control under the scheme. For all works and uses to which the Building Regulations apply a commencement notice must be submitted to the Building Control Authority when a proposed development is likely to be commenced, thus enabling it to consider whether it will inspect such a development and determine whether or not it complies with the Regulations. At the time of writing the most recent regulation setting out the requirements re a commencement notice is SI 9/2014, Building Control

(Amendment) Regulations, 2014 which substantially amends and extends commencement notices. From a conveyancing perspective, while it is preferable that a commencement notice be obtained, and it is an offence to carry out works without the appropriate notice, the action lies against the person who carried out the works and no action lies against the property or any subsequent owner. Therefore, while it should be obtained, it is not absolutely essential that a copy of the commencement notice served on the local authority be obtained by the purchaser's solicitor as the purchaser clearly had no obligation to serve the notice. However, it is possible that it could be claimed that a lack of a commencement notice renders the entire planning and building process void ab initio. While that case has not yet been made by a local authority, it is a possibility and thus where possible a copy of the notice should be obtained by a purchaser's solicitor. However, the Conveyancing Committee is of the view that solicitors should not be unduly concerned in relation to whether a commencement notice or 'seven-day' notice has been given to the Building Control Authority.

However, since the 2014 Regulations <u>if a notice was not served (as opposed to not being available) it will need to be carefully investigated, as</u> there are now, under the new regulations, significant consequences if a commencement notice is not served as no final certificate of compliance on completion can be filed, and, without this, opening, occupying, or using the building is an offence. Commencement notices are thus now more 'relevant' to conveyancers and indeed <u>the time when</u> a commencement notice is filed electronically will be very relevant as the 2014 Regulations only apply where the notice is filed on or after 1 March 2014.

If however the works do not commence within 21 days of the lodgement of the commencement notice a new notice has to be and can be submitted, but as there is no retrospective 'filing' of a commencement notice or provision to retrospectively comply with requirements it is not only an offence not to submit a notice but also to commence works and it may well affect the marketability of a property.

Further, unlike before the 2014 Regulations, the public will have access to the website, subject to copyright restrictions re professional designers.

See requisition 27.4.a of the requisitions on title.

11.9.6   EXEMPTIONS FROM THE NEED TO SERVE COMMENCEMENT NOTICES

The following developments are some of the exemptions from the need to serve commencement notices:

(a)   works exempt from the requirement to comply with the Building Regulations;

(b)   works carried out by a Building Control Authority in its own area;

(c)   Garda stations, military barracks, courthouses, and certain other buildings for officers of the State, and certain works carried out for national security reasons (Building Control Regulations, 1997, Art 6);

(d)   provisions of services, fittings, and equipment to a building not involving a material alteration; and

(e)   exempt development under the Planning Acts except:

(vi)   where a fire safety certificate is required, or

(vii)   for material alterations (other than minor works) in a shop or office or industrial building;

(f)   constructions of certain single-storey buildings for a domestic house such as a detached house, tool shed, conservatory, glass house, etc. Note, however, as with many exemptions, there are limits on the dimensions/size.

The exemptions are periodically updated and the most recent regulations issued in relation to same should always be consulted.

11.9.7 DEFINITIONS

It should be noted that the definition of terms, as with all legislation, is vital but particularly with planning legislation, as same can be very narrowly construed or, broadly stated, which can sometimes cause even more uncertainty, eg 'substantially completed': see **11.12.3**.

Definitions of 'an institutional building', 'an industrial building', 'a flat', 'a shopping centre', etc may be found in the Building Regulations, 1997, Art 5(4). In particular, note the definition of 'flat' which was amended in the 1994 Regulations and in the 1997 Regulations and is now defined as a separate and self-contained premises constructed or adapted for residential use and forms part of a building from some other part of which it is divided horizontally, ie duplex apartments are clearly flats under this definition.

Definitions are periodically updated and thus, again the most recent regulations should always be consulted.

11.9.8 FIRE SAFETY AND DISABILITY ACCESS CERTIFICATES

11.9.8.1 Fire Safety Certificate

The Fire Safety Act, 1981 and that of 2003 apply and The Building Control Act and Regulations and amendments thereto apply. See also requisition 30 of the requisitions on title.

By virtue of Arts 11 and 12 of the Building Control Regulations, 1997, it is mandatory to obtain a fire safety certificate ('FSC') before work commences on a development to which Part 'B' of the Regulations apply, since the relevant part of the Building Control Act, 1990 came into force on 1 August 1992.

In effect, it applies to virtually all buildings except single dwellings. Applications for FSCs are made to the Building Control Authority. The required application form and full information must be submitted or the application will be treated as invalid. The precise information is set out in the Regulations but ranges from location maps to specification of construction and material.

The Building Control Authority has two months to issue an FSC, unless an extension of time is agreed in writing between the FSC and the Building Control Authority. The certificate may be refused, or issue, with or without conditions and as with planning decisions, same may be appealed to An Bord Pleanala. Surprisingly, however, there is no obligation on the Building Control Authority to follow up on the FSCs with any inspection of the works, either before or during construction.

The Building Control Authority is required to maintain a register in respect of applications and decisions made and this should contain details of the applicant, the work and the decision, and the outcome of any appeal.

The Building Control (Amendment) Regulations, 2009 (SI 351/2009) ('the 2009 Regulations') came into force on 1 January 2010 and amendments thereto (see earlier list) included a significant new provision which imposed a prohibition on opening, operating, or occupying a building unless an FSC has been granted by the Building Control Authority in respect of the building. Any breach of this prohibition is an offence and any person so breaching it is liable to prosecution under the Building Control Act, 1990 as amended. See Practice Notes of the Conveyancing Committee in the Law Society *Gazette,* April 2010 and August/September 2010 for further details.

11.9.8.2 Disability Access Certificate

The 2009 Regulations and amendments thereto also introduced a completely new system to toughen the provisions for dealing with access for people with disability. The provisions imposed a prohibition on opening, operating, or occupying buildings unless an FSC and also a Disability Access Certificate (DAC) had been granted by the Building Control Authority in respect of the building. A breach of this prohibition is an offence. The need for a DAC applies to any new building, or an existing building, where significant revision or changes are made to it. General condition 36(d) of the Law Society Contract for Sale provides that copies of, *inter alia*, all FSCs should be furnished. A solicitor acting for a purchaser should ensure that, where appropriate, a special condition is included in the contract to provide that general condition 36(d) shall be deemed to include a DAC.

In any event the architect or other party issuing one of the agreed forms of certificates of building compliance with Building Regulations required (or as appropriate if under the 2014 Regulations) to be furnished under general condition 36(e)(ii) will need to be satisfied that the DAC has issued where required and that any conditions thereof have been complied with. The certificate of compliance need not make specific reference, however, to the DAC and the vendor's solicitor should consider all of these factors before issuing contracts for sale.

Note that the Fire Services Act, 1981 and that of 2003 are unaffected by the Building Control Act and all of the enforcement powers of a fire officer under the Fire Services Act remain.

As at the time of writing, the most current regulations affecting DAC or RDAC are the Building Control (Amendment) Regulations, 2015 (SI 243/2015) which revise the fees in certain cases.

11.9.9 APPLICATION FOR FIRE SAFETY CERTIFICATE

The application for a fire safety certificate must be in the prescribed form and be accompanied by a detailed plan showing compliance with the fire regulations and particulars of the proposed use. Any application which does not contain the necessary information is invalid. The Fire Regulations are comprehensive and must be complied with. The application is almost as demanding as an application for planning permission and requires a lodgement of plans, floor plans, elevations, and calculations to show that the proposal does comply with the Fire Regulations. It should be lodged at the same time as the application is made for a planning permission to try and save time. The Building Control Authority keeps a register of applications for fire safety certificates. If the application is accepted by the Building Control Authority it sends out a receipt to the applicant and the Building Control Authority has a two-month period in which to make its decision, either to grant permission with or without conditions or to refuse permission. A refusal, or grant of permission imposing conditions, must provide reasons. If the authority fails to reach a decision within that time a default procedure, akin to that applicable to a planning application, applies, whereby the certificate must automatically issue to the applicant. Again, as with a planning application, there is a procedure whereby an applicant may appeal to An Bord Pleanala against the decision of an authority either in part or in its entirety.

Again, the Building Control Authority may or may not inspect the development but it has wide powers if the developer proves uncooperative. It is an offence to carry out works or make a material change of use without first obtaining a fire safety certificate.

11.9.10 EXEMPTIONS TO THE REQUIREMENT TO OBTAIN A FIRE SAFETY CERTIFICATE

As with exemptions from planning itself, there are many exemptions from the requirements to obtain a fire safety certificate, eg building works (which have obtained or applied for Building Bye-Law Approval, prior to 1 June 1992) and commenced before 1 August 1992, single dwellings excluding flats, works which are exempt from having to lodge a commencement notice, certain buildings used exclusively for agricultural purposes, works carried out in compliance with a notice under s 20 of the Fire Services Act 1981 as amended by the 2003 Act or minor works which are defined as works consisting of the installation, alteration, or removal of a fixture or fitting or works of a decorative nature.

Exemptions from this are periodically updated and the most recent regulation issued in relation to fire safety certificates should always be consulted.

11.9.11 DISPENSATIONS/RELAXATIONS

An application to the authority for dispensations or relaxations of Building Regulations may be made. If no decision is made by the authority within two months the dispensation or relaxation is deemed to have been granted: see Building Regulations 1997, Art 14. There is an appeal procedure if an applicant is dissatisfied with the authority's decision, the appeal again lying to An Bord Pleanala. The Minister for the Environment also has power to dispense with or relax any regulations in respect of any particular class of building operation, works, or material alteration, subject to such conditions as he deems appropriate. Thus, once again, it is important to check the most up-to-date regulations.

11.9.12 ALTERATION OR EXTENSION OF EXISTING BUILDINGS

The Building Regulations apply to all material alterations (not being repair or renewal) or extensions of existing buildings, in that all works done must comply with the Regulations. In addition, the alteration or extension cannot result in a new or greater contravention of the Regulations.

11.9.13 LIABILITY, PENALTIES, AND ENFORCEMENT

Failure to comply with any requirements of the Building Control Act or the Regulations is an offence (see s 17). Fines of up to €50,000 and/or a term of imprisonment not exceeding two years, may be imposed for failure to comply with the Regulations or failure to comply with an enforcement notice. If the offence is committed by a company with the consent or contrivance of, or is attributable to any neglect on the part of, any director, manager, or secretary of that company, that person shall also be guilty of that offence.

Enforcement notices may be served by the authority on the owner of the building or any other person involved in the works. It may set out the works required to ensure compliance with the Regulations or may prohibit the use of a building or part of it until these works are done. The authority has power to enter a building and carry out the remedial works if the enforcement notice is not complied with and may recover the costs from the owner or the person who carried out works in breach of the Regulations as a simple contract debt. The authority also has power to enter buildings to inspect them and any plans or documents relating to the works and to take samples of materials being used (see Building Control Act, 1990, ss 7–8).

There is a limitation period of five years from completion of the works or change of use after which no enforcement notice may be served, see s 8(2) of the 1990 Act. The Act also provides for a procedure similar to the planning injunction under s 27 of the Planning Act, 1976 (as amended by the 1992 Act), and s 160 of the 2000 Act whereby the authority may seek a High Court order requiring alterations, the making safe of any structure, the discontinuance of works, or prohibiting the use of a building where the authority considers that there is substantial risk to health or safety. There is no time limit on this action being taken.

The Building Control Act, 1990 (see s 21) specifically prohibits the taking of any civil proceedings for contraventions of the Act or the Regulations. However, the Act does impose strict liabilities on designers and builders for which they may be held liable in contract or tort to their client or third parties without proof of negligence against them.

The Building Control Act, 2007 came into force on 1 March 2008. This Act amended the Building Control Act, 1990 by enhancing enforcement procedures by the local authority and increasing fees. Two new provisions relate to enforcement notices served under the Building Control Acts, 1990 and 2007. The enforcement notice now requires a person on whom the notice is served to pay the costs and expenses incurred by the local authority in relation to the investigation and detection of the building control matters, the issue of any warning, and also the service of the notice; the costs and expenses of employees, consultants, and advisors are also included (s 8(4), as amended). Section 9, as amended by the Building Control Act, 2007, inserts a new provision which allows for the court to order the applicant who has applied to the District Court to annul, modify, or alter an enforcement notice to pay the costs and expenses of the Building Control Authority measured by the court, in:

(a) appearing and adducing evidence at the hearing, including costs of employees and consultants' costs; and

(b) the costs and expenses reasonably incurred in the investigation and detection as regards the enforcement notice, where the Building Control Authority has not already recouped that sum.

A number of changes have also been incorporated into s 12 of the Building Control Act, 1990 by the Building Control Act, 2007 in relation to building control injunctions, and enhancing enforcement procedures by the local authority and increasing fees.

There has been an administrative consolidation of the Building Control Act, 2007 in 2014—see earlier. All Acts up to and including the Water Services Act, 2014 (44/2014), enacted 28 December 2014, and all statutory instruments up to and including the Health Insurance Act, 1994 (section 11E(2)) (No 5) Regulations, 2014 (SI 621/2014), made 22 December 2014, were considered in the preparation of this revision.

11.9.14 MULTI-STOREY BUILDINGS

The Local Government (Multi-Storey Buildings) Act, 1988 does not apply to buildings commenced after 1 June 1992, save where built on foot of a building bye-law approval applied for on or before that date. The 1988 Act does still apply to multi-storey buildings constructed between 1 January 1950 and 1 June 1992. 'Single-storey buildings' is defined in the Building Regulations, 1997, Art 5 as a building consisting of a ground storey or a basement storey only. Further, the same article goes on to define a basement storey as a storey which is below the ground storey or, where there is no ground storey it means a storey the top surface of the floor of which is situate at such a level or levels that some point in its parameters is more than 1.2 metres below the level of the finished surface of the ground adjoining the building in the vicinity of that point.

The Multi-Unit Developments Act, 2011 referred to at **11.1.2**, was enacted on 24 January 2011. The Act established a new statutory framework for multi-unit developments, but most importantly it introduced a court-based dispute resolution mechanism for both new and existing developments. There is a very comprehensive Practice Note in relation to the effect of this Act on existing developments by the Conveyancing Committee of the Law Society in the Law Society *Gazette,* November 2011. There have been several statutory instruments arising from the Act, eg:

(a) SI 95/2011 (which selects 1 April 2011 as the commencement date for ss 1–13, 15–31, 33, 34 and Schedules 1, 2, and 3 of the Act);

(b) SI 96/2011 (which prescribes certain classes of persons whose name may be put on the register for architects: see **11.11**);

(c) SI 97/2011 (prescribes the forms to be used for the purposes of s 30 of the Act, ie restoration to the register of a company struck off for being an owner's management company and prescribes a fee of €300: it commenced on 1 April 2011);

(d) SI 112/2011 (which relates to the nomination of chairpersons of mediation conferences in the event the parties do not agree on the chairperson, ie the person will be appointed by the court and will be either a practising barrister or solicitor of not less than five years' standing or a person nominated by one of the bodies prescribed by the order).

Requisition 35 of the requisitions on title should be consulted as this provides a useful checklist as to what is required.

11.10   Planning Warranty

11.10.1   INTRODUCTION

General condition 36 of the Law Society General Conditions of Sale 2001 (revised) edition is entitled 'Development' and deals with the question of planning matters generally. General condition 36, which is the only warranty contained in the Contract for Sale, provides a purchaser with a warranty by the vendor that all developments on or to the property since 1 October 1964 comply with all the requirements of the Planning Acts and, where applicable, building bye-laws and Building Control Regulations. The warranty does not cover/extend to building bye-law approvals in respect of development or works carried out prior to 13 December 1989.

The warranty goes further in that if a planning permission has been implemented then the vendor warrants that the conditions expressly notified with any permission by any competent authority in relation to and specifically addressed to any development or works were substantially complied with. See the article by John Gore-Grimes in the Law Society *Gazette* of June 2007 which outlines solicitors' responsibilities under general condition 36.

General condition 36 is divided into six sections: (a), (b), (c), (d), (e), and (f).

11.10.2   GENERAL CONDITION 36(A)

11.10.2.1   Generally

Where general condition 36(a) is left intact, ie not varied or deleted in the special conditions, it puts the vendor in the position of furnishing a warranty that the planning permission in relation to the property is fully in order and that there has either been no development whatsoever since 1 October 1964 that requires planning permission, building bye-law approval, or building control approval or that all necessary planning permissions and building bye-law approvals/building control approval have been obtained and the conditions contained therein have been complied with. Since the Building Control (Amendment) Regulations, 2009 (SI 351/2009), general condition 36(d) shall be deemed to include a disability access certificate (DAC). It is recommended that a solicitor acting for a purchaser ensures that where appropriate, a special condition is included in the contract to specifically provide that general condition 36(d) shall be deemed to include a DAC. However, just as architects' certificates of compliance with building control do not specifically refer to fire safety certificates, this is also the position with DACs.

It would not be untrue to say that the drafting of contracts and in particular those special conditions relating to planning, are becoming one of the most difficult elements of conveyancing for practitioners. This is because it is extremely difficult for a vendor to stand over the warranty given in general condition 36, as it is both so extensive and covers such a length of time. The warranty extends back to cover development of works executed since 1 October 1964, 50 years ago, and there is a pressing need for a general planning amnesty that a development is planning compliant after a reasonable period of time, at least in relation to residential properties, not dissimilar to s 22(7) of the Building Control Act. See **11.9.1**. There is a very good article on this issue in the August/September 2012 Law Society *Gazette* by Joseph Thomas, who is a member of the Law Society's Conveyancing Committee tasked with dealing with planning matters.

The warranty at condition 36(a)(1)(ii) warrants that if a planning permission had been implemented, the conditions expressly notified with any such permission by any competent authority in relation to and specifically addressed to any development or works were complied with substantially, for example when an engineering department of a local authority issues requirements which are notified with a planning permission, the vendor is warranting compliance with same even where they are not specifically incorporated in the permission. A vendor must be satisfied that no competent authority issued conditions with any planning permission which were not incorporated in the condition. If the vendor is in any way unsure of the position the appropriate special condition should be inserted in the contract to vary the warranty.

The full significance of condition 36(a) must be appreciated by all vendors, who must disclose any planning irregularity in the special conditions of the contract. Failure to do so will leave the vendor open to an action for breach of warranty, apart from the fact that it may be extremely difficult to compel the purchaser to complete the sale. It is a very significant warranty as it basically calls on the vendor to stand over all planning matters in relation to a property for a period of time in excess of 49 years. Where the vendor is simply unaware of the planning history of the property the warranty in general condition 36 should be restricted to cover only the period in respect of which the vendor has the appropriate knowledge. The importance of this condition is highlighted by a marginal note in the printed General Conditions of Sale (2009 edn) which reads:

> *In cases where property is affected by an unauthorised development or breach of Condition/Conditions in a permission/approval amounting to a non-conforming development or where the Bye-Law Amnesty covered by section 22(7), Building Control Act, 1990 is relevant, it is recommended that same be dealt with expressly by Special Condition.*

If it later transpires that matters are not as warranted in condition 36(a), the purchaser could have a right of action against the vendor for breach of warranty, which in turn could have serious financial implications for a vendor long after the transaction may have been completed: see general condition 48.

The Law Society Conveyancing Committee advises that the full vigour of the rest of general condition 36 will continue to operate even if part of the condition is varied by special condition (see Law Society *Gazette*, September 1993). Refer to Practice Note in Law Society *Gazette*, May 2000, pertaining to blanket exclusion of general condition 36.

11.10.2.2 Breach of warranty

If the extent of the warranty has not been limited by the vendor prior to the execution of contracts and the vendor is subsequently found to be in breach of it, a purchaser is in a strong position. Patrick Sweetman, in a CLE lecture entitled 'Property Transactions/Liabilities under Planning and Environmental Law' given on 1 December 1992 succinctly puts it as follows:

The consequences of a breach of this warranty could be that:

1. the purchaser would have a right of action in damages for breach of warranty;

2. the purchaser may be able to walk away from the contract;

3. even if the purchaser wishes to complete the sale, substantial delays will be incurred, so that the vendor will remain responsible for the property and will not receive the balance of proceeds until either the planning breach is resolved (normally by obtaining a retention planning permission) or the parties agree to terms of settlement.

General condition 51(d) of the Contract for Sale provides for submission to arbitration of disputes as to the materiality of any matter for the purpose of general condition 36(a) (ie breach of the planning warranty). Arbitration may take considerable time and it may suit the parties to agree to set aside an agreed sum, being a portion of the consideration, and to close the sale, leaving the planning issue to be decided subsequently. The purchaser accepting such a situation would need to satisfy himself as to the worst possible scenario arising from the planning breach and ensure that sufficient sums are retained to cover it.

Often no monetary payment would be sufficient to safeguard a purchaser's position, for example if there was a dispute as to whether a particular use was an established use since 1 October 1964. A purchaser would be unlikely to take the risk that continuance of use of permission might be granted, as he could be left with a property utterly useless to his requirements.

Hence the importance of a vendor's solicitor fully advising the vendor of the extent and importance of this warranty and that all developments, bearing in mind that 'development' as defined in the Planning Acts includes material change of use, are disclosed to the solicitor to enable the context of the warranty to be limited to when drafting the contract.

11.10.2.3 Building bye-law approval

Section 22(7) of the Building Control Act, 1990 provides that no enforcement action will be taken, and building bye-law approval will be deemed to have been granted, in respect of all works carried out prior to 13 December 1989 unless the local authority served a notice before 1 December 1992, stating the works constituted a danger to public health or safety. Therefore, it is not necessary for a purchaser to concern himself or herself with building bye-laws in respect of works carried out prior to 13 December 1989 unless such a notice was served. However, appropriate evidence must be produced to show that the works were carried out prior to 13 December 1989 and that no notice was served. This is usually given by way of a statutory declaration by the vendor. If this amnesty is being relied upon it is advisable to insert an appropriate special condition in the Contract for Sale to bring this to the purchaser's attention.

11.10.2.4 Extensions

Many house extensions and garage conversions are exempt developments. Previously, if the property was in an area where building bye-laws apply, the works lost their exempt status by reason of the Local Government (Planning and Development) Regulations, 1977 (SI 65/1977), Art 11(1)(a)(iv) if no building bye-law approval was obtained or the works did not comply with the bye-law approval. However, those regulations have been revoked and replaced with the Local Government (Planning and Development) Regulations, 2001 (SI 600/2001) so that, provided the works are exempt under the 2001 Regulations and amendments thereto, eg the Planning and Development (Amendment) Regulations, 2008 (SI 256/2008) and the Planning and Development Regulations, 2008 (SI 235/2008) respectively such previously unauthorised development now enjoys exempt status.

11.10.3 PRODUCTION OF DOCUMENTATION

General condition 36(d) requires production of all permissions and approvals, fire safety certificates and, if available, commencement notices under the Building Regulations. The words 'if available' are inserted in the light of the Law Society recommendation that a solicitor should not insist on production of a commencement notice (or post 1 January 2010 a seven-day notice) if it is not readily available (see Conveyancing Committee recommendation in The Law Society *News*, November 1994 and August/September 2010 *Gazette* and/or chapter 7 of the *Conveyancing Handbook*, paras 7.59 and 7.60).

In addition a special condition should be included to cover the disability access certificates as same is not currently covered by general condition 36(d).

11.10.4 FINANCIAL CONDITIONS

General condition 36(e)(1) requires that a vendor shall on or prior to completion furnish to the purchaser evidence of compliance with financial conditions. Alternatively, the vendor may provide formal confirmation from the local authority that the roads and services abutting the said property have been taken in charge by it without requirement for payment of money. This is, in effect, an extension of the Law Society's Recommendation (issued with the *Gazette*, May 1987) in relation to second-hand houses in housing estates. The recommendation states that where solicitors are dealing with a second or later purchase of residential houses where the roads and services are in charge of the local authority, then they should not be concerned with enquiries as to compliance with financial conditions in a planning permission, unless the purchaser's solicitor is on notice of some problem. If a solicitor is acting for the first purchaser buying a newly constructed house in a housing estate, he is only entitled to obtain copies of receipts for financial payments required to be paid up to the date of completion of the purchase. However, the present proviso that, in order to avail of such alternative, the roads and services must be taken in charge '*without requirement for payment of monies in respect of the same*' induces a complication. The parties to the contract will not necessarily know whether the local authority requires payment of money in respect of the taking in charge. Thus, as a matter of practice, if the local authority issues a letter confirming that the roads and services have been taken in charge and that letter makes no mention of payment of money, then such a letter will usually be accepted as satisfactory evidence of compliance with financial conditions. Please note, however, in relation to the date of the letter, the Conveyancing Committee warning of the danger of accepting 'old letters' (see **11.12.2.3**).

Further, in relation to letters of compliance with financial contributions, it is commonplace for a local authority to agree to accept payment of financial contributions from a builder/ developer by way of stage payments. Thus, if the property is purchased in the early stages of a large development, often the only evidence of compliance with the financial conditions will be a letter from the local authority confirming that the stage payments have been discharged to date because the next payments do not become due until a later date. If the property is sold, for example, six years later, a purchaser may seek evidence that the entire financial contribution has been paid, which may or may not be available. Thus it has become common practice that the purchaser's solicitor will now request evidence, normally by way of a letter from the planning authority confirming that all financial payments were made and, in practice, most vendor's solicitors, although under no obligation to do so, will write to the local authority for such confirmation before finalising the contract document.

There is a Law Society recommendation of April 1987 (Law Society *Gazette*) where it is recommended that it is only necessary to produce letters confirming compliance with financial conditions up to the date of the first purchase of the dwellinghouse, and frequently a vendor's solicitor will refer a purchaser's solicitor to said recommendation. However, it cannot be repeated often enough, that a vendor relying on this recommendation, or indeed any other, in relation to general condition 36 must insert the appropriate special condition in the contract. Note this recommendation applies only to housing estates and not to one-off houses on individual sites or, indeed, to commercial property. (See also Conveyancing Committee Recommendation (Law Society *Gazette*, February 1989) which provides that a solicitor may certify either from his own personal knowledge or from an inspection of the local authority records that the roads and services are in charge of the local authority.)

Section 180 of the 2000 Act is a new provision, and deals with taking charge of building estates. It requires planning authorities to take housing estates in charge where requested by a majority of the residents or the developer, once the estate is complete. It applies to development which includes the construction of two or more houses etc. It must have been completed to the satisfaction of the planning authority. This section applies to a development in respect of which a permission was granted under s 34 of the 2000 Act, or under Part IV of the 1963 Act, which means that estates already in existence qualify to be taken in charge provided that they comply with the conditions of s 180. If however, the estate is unfinished, the obligation to take it in charge does not arise during the seven-year period when enforcement action may be taken by a planning authority to ensure completion of the estate. If, however, enforcement proceedings have not been taken within the seven-year period, the planning authority shall take the estate in charge where requested to do so by a majority of qualified persons who own or occupy the houses in question. The procedure is initiated under s 11 of the Roads Act of 1993. See CLE lecture by Patrick Sweetman 'Planning and Development Act, 2000', Book IV.

In recent times, possibly due to the economic climate, developers' solicitors have been asking purchasers' solicitors to accept an undertaking in relation to compliance with financial conditions in planning permissions. See the Practice Note, Law Society *Gazette*, July 2011. However, in the current economic environment, there are developments where the funds are not available to discharge the development contributions due in respect of an individual unit, otherwise than out of the proceeds of sale. The Law Society have taken cognisance of this reality (see July 2011 Practice Notice re undertakings to pay development contributions) and propose as follows.

In those circumstances, and provided the purchaser's solicitor receives confirmation from the planning authority as to the amount of the development contribution payable in respect of the individual unit (taking into account any indexation and possible interest due in respect of late payment), and that there are sufficient funds out of the net proceeds of sale to discharge that amount (which may involve the consent of the bank, specifying the sum it will accept to discharge its security), then the purchaser's solicitor can accept an undertaking from the solicitor for the vendor to:

1. Retain the specified amount out of the proceeds of sale, and

2. Forthwith, following completion of the sale, pay such sum to the planning authority in exchange for written confirmation from the planning authority that all financial conditions of the planning permission, insofar as they relate to the particular unit, have been complied with, and

3. Furnish such confirmation to the purchaser's solicitor immediately upon receipt.

However, this is a very dangerous area and should be given considerable thought before proceeding. Indeed, in relation to undertakings in general and planning see also the Practice Note of the Complaints and Clients Relations, Guidance and Ethics Committee of March 2011 entitled 'Notice to all practising solicitors—undertakings.' See also **11.12.2.3.**

11.10.5 CERTIFICATES/OPINIONS

General condition 36(e)(2) requires the production of a certificate or an opinion on compliance with planning and bye-law requirements from an architect or an engineer or other person professionally qualified to so certify or opine. The Conveyancing Committee of the Law Society has set out recommended criteria in relation to the qualifications of the persons offering certificates or opinions on compliance and these are contained in the Law Society's Practice Note in the January/February 2010 *Gazette*. However, the General Conditions of Sale do not define 'architect' or specify who is competent to certify or opine and, accordingly, the identity and qualifications of a person who will approve compliance with planning and building control requirements should be established by the purchaser before contracts are exchanged. The Building Control Act, 2007 which came into effect on 1 March 2008, provides, *inter alia*, that the use of the titles 'architect', 'quantity surveyor', and 'building surveyor' will be confined to persons with recognised qualifications and experience whose names are entered on a statutory register. The relevant register will be administered by (a) the RIAI in the case of architects and (b) the Society of Chartered Surveyors (SCS) in the case of quantity surveyors and building surveyors.

General condition 36(e)(2) also provides that the certificate or opinion to be furnished must confirm that all conditions expressly notified with the permission by a competent authority, and especially directed to and materially affecting the property or any part of it, have been substantially complied with. The standard RIAI/Law Society Forms of Opinion cover these conditions, unless specifically excluded, and in such a case it is necessary to get an additional certificate from a third party to show compliance. If a vendor is agreeing to give a certificate covering such conditions issued by a competent authority, he must first check that his architect/engineer will be in a position to do so. It is not unusual in major commercial developments for planning conditions to specifically require the agreement or compliance with the requirements of the competent authority and that the architect in overall charge will generally refer in the opinion of compliance to a certificate of subcontractors confirming compliance, for example, with a fire officer.

Never in any of these certificates/opinions will there be a reference to compliance with financial conditions in any permission. Neither the RIAI Forms of Opinion nor the Law Society Specimen Certificates of Compliance cover such conditions so that conveyancers dealing with second-hand property must delete this condition by an appropriate special condition unless they obtain a supplemental certificate from an architect or engineer covering the point. If a vendor is agreeing to give a certificate containing this provision, he should first check that an architect or engineer is in a position to do so.

In relation to second-hand houses bought before 31 December 1975, the Law Society has recommended that, as it was not the practice at that time to furnish an architect's certificate of compliance, a purchaser's solicitor should not insist on one now (see Practice Note, Law Society *Gazette*, January/February 1993). However, three points should be noted. If a vendor seeks to rely on this recommendation there must be a restriction placed on the warranty contained in general condition 36(a) by inserting an appropriate special condition. Further, the recommendation relates to second-hand houses built prior to 31 December 1975 only. It does not relate to any other type of property. The planning permission should, of course, always be obtained.

General condition 36(f)(i)(ii) which is new to the 2001 contract, provides that where the vendor has furnished certificates or opinions on compliance, *the vendor shall have no liability* on foot of the warranties expressed in general condition 36(a) or (b) in respect of any matter with regard to which the architect's certificate/opinion is erroneous or inaccurate unless the vendor was aware at the date of sale that same contained any material error or inaccuracy. If subsequent to the date of sale and prior to completion thereof, it is established that any such certificate or opinion is erroneous or inaccurate, then, if the vendor fails to show that before the date of sale the purchaser was aware of the error or inaccuracy, or that same is no longer relevant or material, or that same does not prejudicially affect the value of the subject property, the purchaser may by notice given to the vendor rescind the sale.

11.10.6 BUILDING CONTROL ACT, 1990

General condition 36(b) warrants that the provisions of the Building Control Act, 1990 and the regulations thereunder have been complied with. The warranty is to the effect that where the provisions of the Building Control Act or the regulations thereunder apply to the design or development of the property or any activity in connection therewith, that there has been substantial compliance with the Act and Regulations. The vendor is required to produce a certificate or opinion by an architect or a professionally qualified person competent to certify compliance confirming such substantial compliance with general condition 36(e) (ii).

If such warranty is excluded in the general conditions of sale, a purchaser should satisfy himself or herself as to compliance with the Regulations prior to exchange of contracts by way of pre-contract enquiries. The Law Society has issued a standard set of requisitions on title in relation to same (see Planning Requisitions on Title at **11.8**).

11.10.7 CONTINUANCE OF WARRANTY

General condition 36 should be read in conjunction with general condition 48, which provides that all obligations and provisions under the contract which are not implemented by a deed of assurance and which are capable of continuing or taking effect after completion shall ensure and remain in full force and effect. Thus, a purchaser would have a remedy against the vendor even where the planning difficulty only came to light after the sale had been completed. Patrick Sweetman, in a CLE lecture on 'Planning Law', on 20 April 1999, gives a series of examples of the appropriate wording in drafting a special condition which will protect the vendor from the full rigours of the warranty in general condition 36 and yet not be so complex or all excluding so as to put off a purchaser or seriously affect the purchase price.

11.10.8 SAMPLE SPECIAL CONDITIONS

The following is a sample special condition to insert in the Contract for Sale where a purchaser is buying property conditional upon planning permission being obtained:

'(a) The sale is conditional upon the purchaser obtaining planning permission for the erection of one dwellinghouse in accordance with the plans and specifications whereof details of which will be submitted to the local planning authority within one month from the date hereof. The purchaser agrees to expeditiously process the application and to deal as soon as practicable with any request for additional information or query which may be required to be lodged or addressed by or with (insert local authority) or on application by An Bord Pleanala as the case may be.

(b) The closing date shall be twenty-eight days after the grant of a final permission acceptable to the purchaser either from (insert local authority) or An Bord Pleanala in the event of an appeal by a third party or the purchaser to An Bord Pleanala.

(c) If within one month from the date of a refusal of a grant of planning permission from (insert local authority) or An Bord Pleanala as the case may be and the fact shall have been notified to the vendor then the purchaser may rescind the agreement whereupon the vendor shall the return the deposit to the purchaser without interest, costs or compensation and the purchaser shall return the title deeds and all the other papers furnished therein.

(d) If within one month from the issuing of a grant of planning permission from (insert local authority) or An Bord Pleanala which shall have been granted subject to conditions which are unacceptable to the purchaser and that fact shall have been notified to the vendor within seven days of the issuing of the grant of permission then the purchaser may rescind this agreement whereupon the vendor shall then return the deposit to the purchaser without interest, costs or compensation and the purchaser shall return the title deeds and all the other papers furnished therein.

And the contract shall be deemed to be at an end.'

See also **6.3.6.3** for a further example of this type of special condition.

The following are some sample special conditions which might be inserted into a contract in order to protect the vendor from the full rigours of the warranty in general condition 36. Obviously, the precedent special condition will need to be amended to reflect the actual circumstances re planning, bye-laws, Building Regulations, etc for each and every development. One method of drafting a planning special condition is to state very simply what development occurred in date order, what element of the planning code was not complied with, list any possible exemptions, amnesties, or Law Society recommendations which may assist, provide proof (if applicable) of same (see declaration at **11.12.4**) and finally, amend or delete, as appropriate general condition 36.

11.10.8.1   Example 1

Problem

A vendor in Dublin built an extension to his house of less than 23 square metres in 1982. No application for bye-law approval was sought or obtained.

Answer

This fact should be stated in simple terms in the special conditions. If the vendor is able to furnish an architect's certificate in the form recommended by the Conveyancing Committee of the Law Society confirming compliance with bye-laws as at the date of construction then the special condition should indicate such a certificate will be forthcoming.

Specimen draft clause

'The vendor constructed an extension less than 23 square metres to the premises in sale in or about 1982. No application for bye-law approval was made or obtained at the time. The vendor shall furnish on closing architect's certificate in the form recommended by the Law Society confirming that from his inspection the works substantially comply with bye-laws as at the time of construction. No requisition, objection or enquiry shall be raised by the purchaser in relation to said extension. General condition 36 is amended in this respect.'

If the vendor is not able to furnish such an architect's certificate then, as the extension was built prior to 13 December 1989, the amnesty under the Building Control Act, 1990, s 22(7) applies and the extension is *'deemed to comply unless notice was served prior to 1 December 1992 that the works constituted a danger to public health or safety'*. In such circumstances the vendor should offer a statutory declaration stating when the works were carried out and that no notice was served. An example of this is set out as follows:

Specimen draft clause

'The vendor constructed in or around 1982 an extension to the premises in sale which said extension is less than 23 square metres. No application for bye-law approval was sought or obtained. The vendor relies on the benefit afforded by section 22(7) of the Building Control Act, 1990 and shall furnish on closing statutory declaration of vendor stating when the works were carried out and that no notice was served on the vendor by the local authority in relation to said premises as at 1 December 1992. The purchaser shall accept said statutory declaration and no further requisition, objection or enquiry shall be raised in relation to same. General condition 36 is amended in this respect.'

11.10.8.2 Example 2

Problem

A downstairs wc/cloakroom was installed under the stairs of an existing house in March 1990 in the Dublin area. No bye-law approval was sought and no planning permission was obtained.

Answer

Special conditions in the contract should state this fact. As the work was done between 13 December 1989 and 1 June 1992, it is necessary for the vendor to furnish an architect's certificate to say that no bye-law approval was sought, but there was substantial compliance. This is another example similar to above and the Law Society recommended form should be used. It would also be advisable to have a statutory declaration from the vendor confirming when the work was carried out.

The difference between this example and example 1 is that the vendor cannot avail of the amnesty under the Building Control Act, 1990, s 22(7). Hence as bye-law approval was required and not obtained, technically a retention permission is required. However, it should be noted that the work was carried out in March 1990 which was before the coming into force of the Building Control Act, 1990 on 1 June 1992.

Previously the vendor could have relied on the protection offered by the Local Government (Planning) and Development Act, 1992, s 19 but this Act was repealed by the Planning and Development Act, 2000. The position is now covered by s 157(4) of this Act whereby no warning letter or enforcement notice can be issued after seven years from the date of commencement of the development. The vendor should give a statutory declaration to this effect. See **11.12.4**.

Specimen draft clause

'A downstairs wc/cloakroom was installed in the premises in sale in or around March 1990. No bye-law approval was sought. The vendor shall furnish an architect's certificate stating that no bye-law approval was sought at the time the work was carried out but as far as he/she is able to ascertain from an inspection now of the work there was substantial compliance with the bye-laws in force at the time. The vendor shall also furnish a statutory declaration stating when the work was carried out and that the vendor has received no warning letter or enforcement notice from the local authority or Planning Authority and the vendor relies on section 157 (4) of the Planning and Development Act, 2000 in this regard. General condition 36 is hereby amended.'

11.10.8.3 Example 3

Problem

A three-storey residential house with a basement portion had been used continuously as an office since 2006. No planning permission was obtained for change of user of this portion of the house.

Answer

State the fact in the special conditions. As the user has been there for more than seven years the planning authority cannot issue a warning letter or enforcement notice nor make an application to the High Court or circuit court for a planning injunction. Now, s 157(4) and s 160 of the Planning and Development Act, 2000 apply.

The difference between examples 1 and 2 and example 3 is that the 'development' consists of a change of use for which no permission was obtained. Example 1 and example 2 relate to 'developments' consisting of works carried out.

A suitable special condition in the contract would be as follows:

Specimen draft clause

'The basement portion of the premises in sale has been used continuously as offices since 2006. No application was made for planning permission for change of use. The vendor will furnish a statutory declaration stating when said use was commenced and confirming that he has received no notice from the local authority or planning authority in relation to same nor has any planning injunction been obtained. The vendor relies on the benefit afforded by section 157(4) of the Planning and Development Act, 2000. The purchaser purchases the said premises with full knowledge of the position and no objection, requisition or enquiry shall be raised in relation thereto. General condition 36 is amended in this respect.'

11.10.8.4 Example 4

Problem

A house was constructed in 1973. No architect's certificate was available.

Answer

State the fact in the special conditions. Furnish planning permission and bye-law approval and refer to Practice Note Law Society *Gazette*, January/February 1993. Special condition should state the facts and refer to Law Society recommendation and that general condition 36 is varied accordingly.

11.10.8.5 Example 5

Problem

A Warehouse was built in 1973. Planning permission was given but no architect's certificate was available.

Answer

The vendor should be advised to engage the services of an architect who should attend at the planning office and inspect the plans on foot of which the planning permission issued (and bye-law approval if the warehouse was situated in an area to which bye-laws applied). This is unlikely to be possible in the major urban areas. The architect should then make a visual inspection of the building as constructed and furnish a certificate of compliance. If no architect's certificate is forthcoming the purchaser must be put on notice in the special conditions of the contract. The recommendation of the Conveyancing Committee set out in January/February 1993 Practice Notes of the Law Society *Gazette* relates only to private residential property. As the warehouse was constructed post 1 October 1964, planning permission was required (as well as bye-law approval if in a bye-law area) and an architect's certificate must be furnished as it is a non-residential building.

11.10.8.6 Example 6

Problem

Retention permission was obtained.

Answer

A special condition should draw attention to the retention permission. It is important to check that you are in possession of the grant of permission for the retention of the unauthorised development and not the notification of decision to grant permission. This is because there could have been an appeal before the grant issued or the possibility of a change in the conditions in the grant (this is unlikely but still a possibility). A retention permission should be treated in the same way as an ordinary planning permission in that an architect's opinion should be furnished confirming compliance with the conditions in the retention permission. The opinion of the architect should state that he/she prepared the plans which were lodged with the application for retention permission and he/she confirms the plans lodged on foot of which the retention permission issued reflect the present building. If the retention is for use only with no condition attached then a vendor's declaration is appropriate.

There may also be conditions attached to that retention permission and if that is the case the architect's opinion must state those conditions have been met. If is not usual but should there be a condition in the planning permission which requires financial contribution/payment then the vendor must furnish a receipt in discharge of that condition.

11.10.8.7 Example 7

Problem

A vendor constructed an extension of 20 square metres to the rear of a dwellinghouse in 1996 and in 2000 added a conservatory to the rear of the house measuring 16 square metres.

Answer

At the time the extension was constructed in 1996 the limit for exempted development was 23 square metres and hence there was no problem in relation to that extension. Now the total floor area of the extension and the conservatory total 36 square metres. However SI 181/2000 (which came into force on 22 June 2000) amended Part 1, Second Schedule, Class 1 of the 1994 Regulations which relates to dwellinghouses. In this case the extension of 2000 taken together with the previous extension in 1996 does not exceed 40 square metres in total and the vendor has confirmed to you that the area of private open space at the rear is not less than 25 square metres. It should be noted that an extension includes a conservatory.

Specimen draft clause

'A ground floor extension to the rear of the dwellinghouse was constructed in 1996 which said extension had a floor area of 20 square metres. In 2000 the vendor constructed a conservatory to the rear of the dwellinghouse which has a floor area of 16 square metres. The vendor shall furnish an architect's opinion that the works carried out in 1996 and 2000 were exempt from planning permission and further thereof an architect's opinion on compliance with building regulations (if 2014 regulations apply this would need to be amended accordingly) in relation to said extensions shall be forthcoming.'

11.10.9 CONSEQUENCES OF NON-DISCLOSURE

As previously stated at **11.10.2**, in view of the warranty in general condition 36, non-disclosure of any problem prior to the signing of contracts may have serious consequences.

The most serious is the rescission of the contract by the purchaser and proceedings issued for the return of the deposit and any damages. It is very likely, by that stage, that the vendor client will have already entered into a binding contract for the purchase of another house based on the proceeds of the sale of the problem property being available by a certain date. In turn, the vendor is caught in not having the funds to complete his own purchase and, at the very least, is exposed to a claim on the interest of the balance due as per the provisions of his contract to purchase.

Another consequence of a breach of warranty is an action for damages by the purchaser based on the diminution of market value of the property, as a result of the planning situation not being in order. Again, this may have consequences for the vendor who would be relying on receiving a certain sum of money for the property to enable him to purchase an alternative property. In the worst case scenario he may sue his solicitor for negligence in such a case.

A further consequence is that the purchaser may insist on retention permission being obtained before completing the purchase. Retention permission has the same time intervals as an application *de novo* and the same time period for appeals. It could add at least another three months to the completion date as well as the expense involved in the application, the architect's certificate, and the vendor's exposure in the meantime under his contract for the purchase of the alternative house.

If acting for the purchaser a pre-contract planning search would have revealed information regarding any planning application. In particular a survey report on the structure of the house will also have commented on the existence of any extension or user. This has the benefit of drawing the purchaser's attention to it and will allow the raising of further enquiries pre contract. If the special conditions have not been amended the purchaser, in addition, has the benefit of the warranty.

Even where a vendor has revealed planning problems and they have been dealt with in the special conditions by his solicitor, there might still be a problem and it is then up to the purchaser and his advisors to assess the situation and ascertain whether it may be rectified and at what cost and whether a renegotiation of the purchase price is required.

However, a further problem then arises in that the purchaser's solicitor is often required to furnish a certificate of title to the purchaser's lending institution and any problem in relation to planning must be brought to the attention of the lending institution's advisors prior to contract and their written requirements obtained. The borrower/purchaser may not be in a position to comply with them before proceeding. While naturally a certificate of title is better not qualified, there are occasions, particularly in relation to planning, where it is necessary to do so and there is an excellent review on same by Patrick Sweetman at a CLE lecture on 'Planning Law' dated Tuesday 28 April 1999 which, while an 'old' lecture, is still relevant.

11.11 Architects' Certificates of Compliance

11.11.1 INTRODUCTION

It is now a standard requirement for conveyancers acting for a purchaser of a property that the development conforms to the Planning Acts, Building Bye-laws, and all Building Regulations.

The practice of seeking certificates of compliance with planning permission was gradual but became everyday practice in the early 1970s: see Law Society *Gazette*, December 1979, June 1980, August 1989, May 1990, January/February 1993, and January/February 2010.

11.11.2 WHY IS AN ARCHITECT'S CERTIFICATE OF COMPLIANCE REQUIRED?

The need for architects' certificates of compliance was also partly brought about by the spread of lending by building societies to the country where previously house lending had been largely dealt with by local authorities under the Small Dwellings Acts. The tighter enforcement of the Planning Acts and the Fire Services Acts was a further reason why people became more careful and, indeed, such documentation became an element of title.

11.11.3 WHO SHOULD CERTIFY COMPLIANCE?

Until the commencement of the Building Control Act, 2007, which regulated the use of the titles 'architect', 'quantity surveyor', and 'building surveyor', came into effect on 1 May 2008, there was uncertainty as to the qualifications and training of an architect who could certify compliance. See **11.11.3.1**. However, conveyancers who constantly deal with certificates dated pre 1 May 2008 must still understand the old position.

Pre 2008 the Conveyancing Committee of the Law Society recommended that it was reasonable for solicitors to accept certificates or opinions on compliance from:

(a)   persons with a degree or diploma of degree standard in architecture, eg a Bachelor of Architecture;

(b)   persons who have been in practice as architects on their own account for ten years;

(c)   chartered engineers;

(d)   persons with a degree in civil engineering;

(e)   persons who have been in practice on their own account as engineers in the construction industry for ten years;

(f)   qualified building surveyors;

(g)   persons from another jurisdiction in the European Union whose qualification is entitled to recognition in Ireland under the Architects' Directive.

See Patrick Sweetman and Eammon Galligan, 'Planning—recent developments in conveyancing practice' *Irish Planning and Environmental Law Journal* (1994) Vol 1 No 4, at p 38. See also the Law Society *Gazette*, Practice Notes, June 2007 and January/February 2010. The latter contains a practice briefing entitled *'Who should certify compliance in 2010?'* This Practice Note sets out the current position and recommends that certificates of compliance or certificates of opinion be accepted from:

(a)   persons who are on the register of architects;

(b)   persons who have been in practice as architects or engineers on their own account for ten years;

(c)   qualified engineers practising in the construction industry;

(d)   qualified building surveyors practising in the construction industry;

(e)   persons from another jurisdiction in the European Union whose qualification is entitled to recognition in Ireland under the Architects' Directive.

Occasionally certifiers may be asked to provide confirmation or verification of the adequacy of their professional indemnity insurance. Most architects tend to resist giving details of their insurance unless this is sought by their own client or is part of their conditions of engagement.

It is the duty of solicitors to exercise caution in relation to the qualifications of a person from whom they will recommend acceptance of certificates of compliance. The reason for this is obvious—if a solicitor advises the client to accept a certificate of compliance in relation to a development, eg a house or house extension, from a person who is not adequately qualified and a problem arises, the solicitor will almost certainly be sued for negligence on the basis that he or she should not have accepted the certificate from a person who is not adequately qualified and indeed insured.

Thus when advising a client on a house purchase transaction regarding any material point such as whether a certificate of compliance relative to a house or an extension is in an acceptable form or is given by a person with an acceptable qualification, solicitors should apply a threefold test:

(a) In the solicitor's own opinion is the particular package in order and in accordance with good conveyancing practice?

(b) Will it be acceptable under the rules or guidelines for the bank or building society from whom the client is borrowing?

(c) Will it be acceptable to most other solicitors if the property were to be put up for sale again in the near future?

If the answer to any of these questions is in the negative, a solicitor normally advises his or her client not to accept the situation and advises the client not to proceed with the transaction unless the difficulty is resolved.

If a query arises over the qualification of a person giving a certificate, the solicitor should take care to make it clear that he or she is not making the decision but is advising the purchaser, and that the final decision as to whether or not to proceed with the purchase is the client's responsibility. Most purchasers, particularly those borrowing, tend to be cautious and accept their solicitor's advice, but some will take a commercial judgement and proceed despite what the solicitor perceives as a problem. Obviously, if a client decides to proceed despite the solicitor's concern, it is imperative for the solicitor to confirm the advice in writing. A solicitor should also bear in mind that, while the Law Society will assist and advise its members in regard to such practice, none of this can absolve the individual solicitor from his or her responsibility to the client. In other words, each solicitor must look at each individual case on its own merits.

11.11.3.1 The Building Control Act, 2007 and registration of the title 'architect'

Part 3 of the Building Control Act, 2007 (ss 13–27) provides statutory protection of the titles 'architect', 'quantity surveyor', and 'building surveyor' provided they are on the appropriate register. In short, it established an agreed internationally recognised professional standard against which all persons calling themselves architects will have been measured by restricting the lawful use of the title to suitably qualified persons whose names are entered on a statutory register established in accordance with the provisions of Part 3 of the Act.

The registration system is administered by the Royal Institute of Architects of Ireland (RIAI). The Act also specifies criteria for automatic eligibility for admission to the architects' register.

It provides for the setting up of an admissions board, a technical assessment board, and a professional conduct committee. Part 3 further provides for an appeals board to determine appeals against decisions of any of the aforementioned boards or committee, with an ultimate right of appeal against decisions of the appeals board to the High Court. Finally, Part 3 provides for payment of a registration fees, the appointment of a registrar, and for fines or penalties for misuse of the title of 'architect'.

Section 15 sets out the detailed criteria for registration of persons who are nationals of EU Member States, and the European Economic Area (EEA) in accordance with EU obligations. It includes nationals or residents of States which are members of the World Trade Organization.

Section 16 provides for application for recognition of qualifications by a further category of persons from Member States who are eligible to apply to the Admissions Board for registration under EU Directive 2005/36/EC (Chapter 1, Title III). It sets out the procedures for assessment of such applications, including the procedures for interview by the Board, or the undertaking of an aptitude test/adaptation period, where such is considered necessary. The Board must make its decision on the application within a three-month period of the date of receipt of a valid application. There is provision for extending the period for assessment by one extra month in specified cases.

Routes to registration/RIAI membership are as follows:

- Route A—Prescribed Qualifications (14)(2)(a)(I)—People who have a prescribed qualification in architecture and who have passed a prescribed postgraduate examination in Professional Practice. A prescribed degree is one which has been approved by the Minister for the Environment, Community, and Local Government in accordance with the Building Control Act, 2007 and therefore applies only to Irish qualifications.

- Route B—RIAI Membership (14)(2)(b)—People who have acquired all or part of the qualification requirements in another jurisdiction.

- Route C—Prescribed Qualification and experience assessment (14)(2)(a)(II)— People who have a prescribed qualification in architecture and who have acquired seven or more years of postgraduate practical experience.

- Route D1—The Automatic Recognition (15)(1)(a); D2—The General System (16(1))— EU/EEA applicants who meet the requirements of Chapter III of Directive 2005/36/EC on the Recognition of Professional Qualifications. D3—Recognition for the purpose of providing services on a temporary and occasional basis (60)(1). D4—Recognition of Decisions made by other Member States.

- Route E—Technical Assessment (14)(2)(h)—People applying for Technical Assessment under s 14(2)(h) of the Building Control Act, 2007 who must have been performing duties commensurate with those of an architect for ten or more years prior to 1 May 2008 in the State.

- Route F—The Register Admission Examination (14)(2)(f)—To pursue this route a person must have seven years' practical experience commensurate with that of an architect in the state, be at least 35 years of age, and have passed a prescribed register admission examination.

- Route M—Minister's List (14)(2)(d)—Be a person in respect of whom a notice in writing dated 7 January 1997, 13 March 1997, or 11 June 1997 was sent by the Minister whether to the person or to an organisation representing the person in the matter stating that the person was successful in his or her application to be included in relevant list.

- Route P—Distinguished Practice (14)(2)(i)—The RIAI is empowered to grant authorisation to use the title architect to individuals whose work in the field of architecture is especially distinguished and who are Irish citizens.

For further and updated information on application standards for RIAI membership for Irish nationals with Irish qualifications, EEA and Swiss nationals with qualifications from EU States other than Ireland, and architects with qualifications from non–EU States see the RIAI website at www.riai.ie.

The register system was welcomed by conveyancers as it has removed the uncertainty for practitioners in this area who now, post the enactment of the Act, will be unlikely to accept a certificate from someone who is not on the register. See also the Building Control (Prescribed Bodies and Courses) Regulations, 2012 (SI 341/2-012).

11.11.4 STANDARD FORMS OF COMPLIANCE

Following the introduction of the Building Regulations, 1991 (SI 306/1991) and the Building Control Regulations, 1991 (SI 305/1991) the Royal Institute of Architects in Ireland (RIAI) issued a set of five Standard Forms of Opinion on Compliance for use by its own members. The Incorporated Law Society has recommended that the March 1993 edition of these forms is acceptable. Forms 1, 2, and 3 concern compliance with Building Regulations. Form 4 concerns compliance with planning permission and or exemption from Planning Control and Form 5 concerns compliance with planning permission and/or building bye-law approval. See also the Law Society *Gazette,* August/September 1997. An additional Form 1A was issued in March 1997. Form 1A concerns compliance of an apartment dwelling with Building Regulations. Further the Conveyancing Committee subsequently agreed with the Institution of Engineers of Ireland and with the Association of Consulting Engineers in Ireland on the format of a certificate of compliance with Building

Regulations for completion by a structural/civil chartered engineer in cases only where a lead architect is appointed to the project. This certificate was published in the *Conveyancing Handbook* in appendix 8 at pp A8.1 to A8.5 (BR SE 9101). The most recent architect's certificate to be agreed by the Royal Institute of the Architect of Ireland and the Law Society is a Form 1B which relates to an architect's opinion on compliance of an apartment dwelling with Building Regulations for use where a professional architectural service has been provided at the design and construction stage of a relevant building or works was issued in June 2001. See the Conveyancing Committee's Guideline in the Law Society *Gazette*, May 2002.

The Law Society has produced its own forms of certificates of compliance dated 7 May 1993 (see Law Society *News*, published November 1993). There are two forms dealing with compliance with planning requirements and building bye-laws, one for full service and the other for part only service, and two which concern compliance with planning and Building Regulations (full service and part service only).

RIAI recommends to its members that they use its standard forms. Other certified professions generally follow the Law Society version.

The RIAI suggests that persons accepting forms from its members should check that the persons completing the forms are in fact members of the Institute and that the form carries the RIAI membership stamp. It also recommends that the original printed form be used rather than photocopies as this makes it very much easier to check that no amendments or alterations have been made to standard wording.

Frequently certificates of compliance are offered which are neither in the RIAI format nor the Law Society format. The RIAI form is often adopted without incorporating the definitions contained in the original version. This of course renders the document unintelligible. Care should be exercised when one is offered a form which is not in the RIAI or Law Society formats to ensure that it covers the essential information.

In relation to RIAI opinions on compliance see also the Conveyancing Committee's warning in the Law Society *Gazette*, April 2006. The Committee pointed out that it is open to RIAI members to use the online version of the pre-printed forms of opinions on compliance by downloading them from the RIAI website. However, practitioners must ensure that the downloaded online version contains endorsements as follows:

• On the front page after 'by registered RIAI members only', insert 'and it is warranted by the signatory that the standard text of this digital document is unaltered'.

• On the last page at the signature after 'registered member of the Royal Institute of the Architects of Ireland', insert 'who warrants that the standard text of this digital document is unaltered'.

In the Law Society *Gazette*, November 2001, the Conveyancing Committee issued a warning in relation to IEI/ACEI certificates of compliance. The Conveyancing Committee had previously agreed with the Institution of Engineers of Ireland and with the Association of Consulting Engineers in Ireland on the format of a certificate of compliance with Building Regulations for completion by a structural/civil chartered engineer in cases where a lead architect is appointed to the project. This certificate was published in the *Conveyancing Handbook* in appendix 8 at pages A8.1 to A8.5 (BR SE 9101). A prominent warning was published in the handbook on the front page of the specimen certificate of compliance to the effect that this form was intended for use only by a consulting engineer in the situation where a lead architect had also been appointed to the project. Despite this warning, this form is being offered by some vendors in relation to projects where no architect has been involved as the sole evidence of compliance with both planning and Building Regulations. The form has not been designed to meet this type of situation and under normal circumstances should not be used or accepted in connection therewith. The Committee proceeded to confirm that the form relates only to compliance of Building Regulations and a further certificate of compliance with planning should always be obtained from the lead architect appointed to the project. It is suggested therefore that in projects where the consulting engineer leads the project, one or other of the specimen forms of compliance at pp 7.41–7.52 of the *Conveyancing Handbook* be utilised with appropriate adaptations.

The Conveyancing Committee updated its precedent certificates of compliance to include reference to the Building Control Acts and the Building Regulations made thereunder and the Planning Acts currently in force.

Following the Building Control (Amendment) Regulations, 2014 and the Building Control (Amendment) (No 2) Regulations, 2014 there are new forms; Commencement Notices, Certificate of Design, Notice of Assignment of Person to Inspect and Certify Works (Assigned Certifier), Certificate of Compliance (Undertaking by an Assigned Certifier), Notice of Assignment of Builder, Certificate of Compliance (Undertaking by Builder), the two-part Certificate of Compliance on Completion (Part A by the builder and Part B by the assigned certifier.

It appeared that the likely result of this legislation is that it would no longer be possible for a builder or person building their home by direct labour to build without an architect, chartered engineer, or building surveyor designing the structure, monitoring it being built in accordance with the inspection plan submitted with the commencement notice, and certifying on completion that the building complies with the Building Regulations. However, the 2015 Regulations (SI 365/2015) have confirmed that such a person can opt out of the Regulations. Obviously this was never of major concern to commercial projects as these are not undertaken anyway without design teams. Thus, it was and is of more relevance to residential conveyancers.

Solicitors for purchasers of new houses or apartments will require a copy of the certificate of compliance on completion. Generally, they will accept a copy of the certificate of compliance on completion as signed and registered together of course with proof of its registration as sufficient compliance with the Building Regulations. It must be checked as with all planning documentation that it applies to the property being purchased. If it is not clear on the face of it the assigned certifier will need to certify that it does apply.

As the documents filed with the Building Control Authority will only be retained for six years it is important to ensure the copy certificates are kept carefully with the title deeds as after that time replacements will not be obtainable.

As always, certificates of compliance with planning will of course still be needed but all references to compliance with Building Regulations or (certificates of compliance with Building Regulations) as appeared in the old certificates will be omitted in relation to buildings where the new regulations apply and all that will be required is a copy or certified copy of the certificate of compliance on completion on the proscribed form as registered with the Building Control Authority. See **11.11.4**.

See the recommendation of the Conveyancing Committee in the Law Society *Gazette* of June 2014, where the Committee advised practitioners in what circumstances they should seek a certificate of compliance for individual houses, residential units in multi-unit developments, and extensions.

11.11.5 WHAT IS THE ESSENTIAL INFORMATION?

The following is a checklist of the requirements for a certificate of compliance. At the very least it should:

(a) specify the qualifications of the persons who will give the certificate;

(b) specify the means of knowledge of the person giving the certificate (ie details of the inspection and knowledge of the plans, drawings, and all the particulars on foot of which the planning permission and fire safety certificate issued);

(c) confirm that the planning permission and fire safety certificate relate to the development being conveyed;

(d) confirm that the design of the development is in substantial conformity with the Building Regulations (where the Building Control (Amendment) Act, 2014 does not apply, ie where the commencent notice was filed after 1 March 2014 as will increasing be the case);

(e) confirm that the development is in substantial compliance with the planning permission;

(f) where the planning permission covers a large development of which works being certified form part and that larger development has not yet been completed, confirm that the general conditions of the planning permission have been substantially complied with in so far as it is reasonably possible up to the date of the issue of the certificate;

(g) not contain any qualifications or exceptions which are not generally acceptable in practice such as those that are in the RIAI forms. When necessary independent evidence of compliance with matters excluded from forms of certificate should be obtained;

(h) be dated and signed; and

(i) be an original.

If pre the 2014 Regulations, it is fundamental in certifying compliance with the Building Regulations that the issue of the design of the works be dealt with. Where the certifier did not design the building a further certificate should be obtained from an appropriate person certifying compliance with the design elements. Also, copies of certificates upon which the certificate relies should be appended (see Practice Note, Law Society *Gazette*, August/September 1997). However see Practice Note, Law Society *Gazette*, March 2013 which rows back on this first recommendation.

See Law Society *Gazette* June 2014 on 'Certificates of Compliance with Building Regulations' and also a very good lecture by Suzanne Bainton at a CPD updates lecture in Kilkenny on 21 November 2014, 'Implications for Conveyancing'. In theory building bye-laws may still apply to some larger developments and, in particular, to housing estates where application for building bye-law approval was made prior to 1 June 1992. These are becoming increasingly rare. The form of architect's certificate which certifies compliance with planning requirements and building bye-laws for a house in a new housing estate is set out in the Law Society *Gazette* of November 1979, as amended by the *Gazette* of June 1982. It is still offered in some cases and, indeed, is perfectly acceptable. Where a home extension which would be an exempted development was built without building bye-law approval, because building bye-law approval could not be issued retrospectively, the Law Society has issued a recommendation in the *Gazette* of March 1986, re the certificate to be accepted.

Where a property has been purchased with the assistance of a bank or building society loan, the purchaser's solicitors are frequently required to give a certificate of title. That certificate will generally have to show 'a good marketable title' has been obtained by the purchaser and that all current conveyancing recommendations of the Law Society have been followed.

Where an architect's certificate or opinion is not in the RIAI standard format or in the form prescribed by the Law Society a solicitor may not be in a position to give the certificate of title sought.

A purchaser's solicitor should agree the format of the architect's certificate to be produced on completion and the qualification of the person who will give that certificate before signing a contract, otherwise a dispute may arise as to the form of certificate to be produced and a purchaser may find himself unable to satisfy his lending institution as to the existence of a good marketable title or, at least, could be compelled to accept a certificate which is less than it should be.

Where, in the architect's certificate of compliance, there are references to confirmations it was considered vital that they are actually obtained. See Law Society *Gazette*, August/September 1997. This Practice Note is, to quote the new recommendation in the Law Society *Gazette* of March 2013, 'no longer appropriate'. The Committee now recommends that where an architect's certificate of compliance confirms compliance with the Building Regulations and confirms that in coming to this opinion on compliance, reliance has been placed by the architect on confirmations received from other professionals, such as structural engineers, fire engineers, mechanical and electrical engineers, and so on, it is not necessary for the purchaser's solicitor to see such confirmations and the solicitor can rely on the architect's certificate of compliance itself. Further, if an architect's certificate is furnished and there are references to copies of the confirmations being attached, it is recommended that purchaser's solicitors should seek to have these words deleted, unless, of course, the confirmations are actually provided. Even where copies of the confirmations are provided, it is advised that solicitors do not review the confirmations (but of course should review the architect's certificate) and should it be necessary make it clear that they are relying on the architect's expertise in that regard.

11.11.6 INTEGRATED POLLUTION CONTROL (IPC) LICENSING

The recent introduction of Integrated Pollution Control Licensing under the Environmental Protection Agency Act, 1992 will necessitate a whole new set of enquiries in the conveyancing process where activities licensable by the Agency are concerned. The Law Society has not yet adopted a standard form of requisitions on title or conditions to accommodate the new Integrated Pollution Control (IPC) regime. Some of the significant features from the conveyancing perspective have been outlined by Patrick Sweetman in 'Recent Developments in Conveyancing Practice' *Irish Planning and Environmental Law Journal* (1994) Vol 1, No 3 and more recently in a paper by Tom Flynn BL at the Planning and Environmental Law Conference 2010 entitled 'The Implications of the New Planning and Development (Amendment) Act 2010' (see requisition 31 of the requisitions on title).

11.11.7 CERTIFICATES OF COMPLIANCE WITH RETENTION PERMISSION

Where a retention permission has been applied for and obtained it is still necessary for a purchaser to seek for confirmation by way of a letter of opinion by a suitably qualified person that the drawings submitted for the retention application correctly showed the actual structure for which permission to retain was applied for. If there are conditions to the grant of permission to retain, the certifier should go on to deal with these in the usual way. No certificate of compliance should be required where the permission related only to the retention of a change to use, where no conditions were attached. However is it reasonable to accept a title in a case where permission to retain an extension to a dwellinghouse was obtained more than ten years ago and no certification of compliance is available? The Conveyancing Committee in the Law Society *Gazette* of May 2000 (see also November 1997 *Gazette*) take the view that in the light of the provisions of the 1992 Act, it is reasonable for the solicitor not to require certified compliance in such a case unless there is an evident problem. When acting for a vendor in such a case a solicitor preparing a contract should put in a special condition putting the purchaser on notice of the position and providing that no requisition or objection shall be made due to lack of certification. In that way, before signing a contract, a purchaser has an opportunity of getting advice on the matter and, if necessary, getting advice from an experienced architect or engineer (see requisition 26.7).

11.12 Analysis of Planning Documentation

11.12.1 INTRODUCTION

The first thing to establish when examining planning documentation is what type of planning document is being looked at. This simple instruction is not always so simply complied with as there are several types of planning permissions which unfortunately all look very similar as, indeed, their names are equally similar. Therefore it is important to look very carefully at the document being held. Some of the various types of planning documentation are set out in the following paragraphs.

11.12.1.1 Outline planning permission

The grant of an outline planning permission does not authorise development. It is an agreement in principle and requires a grant of approval (post the 2000 Act, grant of permission) on foot of the outline permission before development may commence. The nature and character of outline planning permission have been changed substantially by s 36 of the 2000 Act (discussed later). However, given that conveyancers will of course be looking at planning permissions which issued before the new Act it is necessary to go into some detail on what those provisions in relation to outline permission were before addressing the changes wrought in same. For a fuller discussion on the special characteristics applying to planning permission and the necessary requisitions, see John Gore-Grimes' *Planning and Environmental Law in Ireland* (Bloomsbury, 2011), pp 1052–3.

Article 3 of the Local Government (Planning and Development) Regulations, 1994 defined it as permission for development subject to the subsequent approval of the details. It established the *principle* of the acceptability of the development and could not be subsequently reassessed by the planning authority. The grant of outline permission in effect bound the planning authority to grant the development subject to conditions regulating the details of the proposal when an application consequent on such outline permission was made.

This arose from the statement of Barrington J in *State (Pine Valley Developments Ltd) v Dublin County Council* [1982] ILRM 169, who summarised the law as follows:

(a)   a full permission in respect of which detailed plans must be lodged and on foot of which, if granted, the development may immediately commence;

(b)   an outline planning permission in which the applicant seeks approval in principle for the proposed development, which, if granted, does not authorise the commencement of development until the applicant has obtained an approval; and

(c)   an approval which is a detailed approval by the planning authority of the development permitted in principle under the outline permission and which authorises the developer to commence the development.

It followed from this that the outline permission set the parameters within which the planning authority had to consider the application for an approval and that it was not open to the planning authority at the approval stage, to reopen matters which have already been granted under the general terms of the outline permission.

It therefore appeared that outline permission, followed by an approval, was equivalent to a full permission. Thus, a developer having obtained his outline permission has gone a certain length of the road and when he applied subsequently for an approval, the planning authority was only concerned with the detail whereby the developer proposed to complete the development already approved in principle by the planning authority. However in recent times in particular (see *Irish Asphalt Ltd v An Bord Pleanala* [1996] 2 IR 179) it had been decided that if there was a significant change in planning circumstances the planning authority could reconsider its decision. The court had more or less determined that outline permission could be effectively overturned at approval stage or substantially. So the situation on what exactly a developer was entitled to expect from such permission was unclear.

The main value of outline planning permission (prior and post the 2000 Act) is that, at a relatively low cost (in terms of the designer's fees at least), it allows the principle of the development to be established and sets the parameter within which the planning authority must consider an application for subsequent approval. This type of planning permission is particularly valuable in the case of large sites where development may take place over a long period of time and whose precise architectural details could not be formulated at an early stage. In such cases it establishes the acceptability of the overall concept and allows for a series of approval applications to be lodged for individual sections as the proposal is further clarified.

Prior to the 2000 Act full planning permission could be obtained in two ways as set out as follows:

Method one: Outline Permission	Method two: No Outline Permission
Notification of *decision* to grant outline permission;	Notification of *decision* to grant permission;
Notification of *grant* of outline permission;	
Notification of *decision* to grant approval;	
Notification of *grant* of *approval*.	Notification of *grant* of *permission*.

Therefore, when given a grant of permission/approval one knows whether outline has issued by looking at the wording. If it says approval then a grant of outline permission has issued and must be obtained.

Post the 2000 Act, grants of 'approval' ceased to issue.

Section 36 cures the uncertain status of an outline permission created by previous planning legislation and case law as outlined earlier. It provides the basis in primary legislation for outline permission where previously this was dealt with only in regulations. An outline permission does not authorise the carrying out of the development to which the permission relates until the subsequent *permission* has been granted under the Act 2000. As a result of these new provisions the word *'approval'* will disappear from the planning vocabulary (see earlier).

In particular the provisions at subsection (3)(a) and (b) should be noted:

(a)   *Where outline permission has been granted by a planning authority, any subsequent application for permission must be made not later than three years beginning on the date of the grant of outline permission, or such period, not exceeding five years, as may be specified by the planning authority.*

(b)   *The outline permission shall cease to have effect at the end of the period referred to in paragraph (a) unless the subsequent application for permission is made within that period.*

The section continues on, however to give the planning authority discretion to extend the life of the outline permission from three to five years. Outline permissions are in a special category in relation to the time limit of duration of the permission (see **11.12.3**). In general under s 40, the duration of a planning permission is limited to five years. Section 41 of the Act provides that the planning authority or the Bord may, having regard to the nature and extent of the development, and any other material considerations, specify the period in excess of five years during which the permission will be effective. Section 42 provides that a planning authority may, in relation to an application as regards to a particular permission, extend the normal five-year period by such additional period as the authority considers requisite to enable the development to which the permission relates to be completed, subject to certain requirements. However s 40(1)/(2) does not apply to outline permissions.

Section 36(4) provides an important amendment which greatly strengthens the value of an outline permission by providing that the planning authority will not be able to refuse permission at the subsequent application on the basis of a matter agreed by the planning authority when the outline permission was granted, provided that the authority are satisfied that the proposed development is within the terms of an outline permission. Subsection (5) provides that no appeal can be brought to the Bord under s 37 against the decision of a planning authority to grant permission consequent on the grant of outline permission in respect of any aspect of the proposed development which was decided in the grant of outline permission. The time for the third-party objector to make an objection was by making a submission or observation on the outline permission after the date of lodgement and before the date of the decision and appealing the outline permission after the decision within the four-week period.

The provisions at s 36(4) and (5) will be particularly welcome for developers in circumstances where they have obtained outline planning permission as it significantly limits the opportunity of the planning authority to revisit matters decided in the course of the grant of outline permission when considering an application for full planning permission. Likewise, having outline planning permission will limit the ability for appeals to be brought against decisions on an application based on the previous outline planning permission. This is a significant change to the pre-existing position.

The Planning and Development Regulations, 2001, Art 21 places restrictions on outline applications in that they may not be made for permissions for retention of the development or for development which would consist of or comprise the carrying out works to protected structures or a proposed protected structure, or development which comprises or is for the purposes of an activity requiring an integrated pollution control licence or waste licence. Article 22 goes on to list the contents of planning applications generally.

11.12.1.2 Notification of a decision to grant permission/approval

A notification of a decision to grant permission/approval is *not* a full permission. Essentially it is a notice of intention to grant permission/approval (post 2000 Act, permission only). During a period of four weeks (prior to the 2000 Act, one month) beginning on the date of the making of this decision the applicant may appeal it or some conditions in it, to An Bord Pleanala. Where there is no appeal, the planning authority will formally give the grant of permission at the end of the appeal period. The applicant must not commence work until the final grant of planning permission issues.

11.12.1.3 Notification of grant of permission/approval

This is the actual planning permission.

11.12.1.4 Notification of grant of permission on appeal

After the notification of decision to grant permission issues, if it is appealed to An Bord Pleanala, the applicant will receive either the grant of permission with or without whatever conditions the Board considers appropriate or, if the Board so decides, a refusal of permission.

11.12.1.5 Notification of permission for retention

This application would be made where an unauthorised development has taken place and permission is sought to retain it. These circumstances would occur, for example, where no planning permission had ever been granted, or it had been granted but the building had not been erected in compliance with it, or there was an unauthorised use. One of the merits of this type of planning, unlike a proposed development, where its effect can only be gauged from drawings, is that its actual impact is evident and calculable. This approach should not be relied upon in order to avoid seeking planning permission before starting work as there is no guarantee permission for retention will be granted, or even if it is it may issue with conditions which the applicant will not like, eg the applicant may be required to carry out costly modifications. Note permission for retention does not automatically absolve the owner from prosecution if enforcement action has already been taken against him or her (see **11.7**).

11.12.2 PLANNING DOCUMENTATION CHECKLIST

Once it is decided what type of planning permission exists the following checklist should be applied:

- Is it a final grant? Bear in mind it could be a final grant but as per s 34(13) a person is not entitled to carry out the development permitted solely by reason of the permission as general conveyancing issues may conflict, eg a dispute as to ownership or rights of way.

- Does it relate to the property in question? If there are any doubts about this check with the architect's certificate of identity which should tie in the planning permission with the property.

- What is the expiry date of the planning permission (ie is the planning permission still alive?) (See **11.12.3**.)

- Was the property substantially completed within the lifespan of the planning permission? (See **11.12.3**.)

- Check the conditions attached to the planning permission. The Planning and Development Act, 2000, s 34(4) sets out various types of conditions which a local authority may include in a planning permission. That is not to say that the local authority is in any way restricted to those conditions. However, the general power to impose conditions is not without limits and is subject to a number of limitations laid down by case law. It may impose any conditions it considers appropriate in the context of the proper planning and development of the area, provided, of course, that they are reasonably related to the application made. Although this section is similar to s 26(2) of the 1963 Act there are some new conditions. Note that the conditions which dealt with the provision to collect financial contributions are no longer in the start of this section but are dealt with under ss 48 and 49 of the Act of 2000. The types of conditions may be divided into roughly five categories. These sections deal with development contributions and supplementary development contribution schemes. A series of guidelines for conveyancers re various types of conditions have been issued by the Conveyancing Committee of the Law Society (see **11.5.7**).

11.12.2.1 Conditions regulating development works

For example, in the context of housing estates it is quite common to find a condition which provides that certain houses not be built. This should be watched carefully, as the planning site number and the subsequent house number are not always the same and it is unfortunately not unheard of for a developer to erect houses which the planning permission required to be omitted. Therefore an architect's certificate certifying the identity of the particular property may be required.

Another example of a condition which may be imposed is that which would require that part of the larger development be ceded to the local authority and conveyancers, on notice of this requirement from reading the conditions, should ensure that it has been complied with.

11.12.2.2 Conditions precedent

Conditions precedent are obviously conditions which must be complied with before a development may proceed. A typical example is conditions requiring that steps be taken to protect trees or preserve open spaces. It could be very important in certain cases, even on one-off small dwellinghouses, whether the house is subject to a tree preservation order—see s 205 of the Planning and Development Act, 2000.

Another example would be the building of spine roads. Check whether an architect's certificate may cover these conditions or whether a third party, for example, the local authority, has to confirm it in writing. In other words, when on notice that a condition precedent has not been complied with, it is *not* sufficient to rely on the production of an architect's opinion on compliance. Each situation has to be examined on its own merits.

11.12.2.3 Financial conditions

There are essentially two main types of financial conditions although the Planning and Development (Amendment) Act, 2002 introduced a third type of financial condition 'a levy' (see **11.12.3**).

The first, 'development contributions', was set out under ss 48 and 49 of the 2000 Act. They were designed to ensure that there is some transparency in connection between the amounts collected from developers from infrastructural works and infrastructural works carried out by the local authority with these monies. These sections deal with the inclusion of contributions as conditions attached to planning permissions.

The local authority often requires a developer to make a contribution towards the provision of services for the development—in large-scale developments the financial condition may be expressed as a certain sum per house/industrial unit. The purchaser's solicitor should insist on receiving evidence from the local authority that the development contributions have been paid or, if developments are being paid in instalments, then paid in respect of the property being furnished. Post-Celtic Tiger, many developers are discharging same in instalments and what the purchaser's solicitor may accept in such circumstances and in particular the wording of any undertaking from the vendor's solicitor is set out by the Conveyancing Committee in the Practice Note 'Undertaking to pay development contributions', Law Society *Gazette*, July 2011. It states that the vendor's solicitor must undertake:

(i)   to retain the specified amount out of the proceeds of sale; and

(ii) forthwith following the completion of the sale to pay such sum to the planning authority in exchange for written confirmation from the planning authority that all financial conditions in so far as they relate to the particular property have been complied with; and

(iii) to furnish such confirmation to the purchaser's solicitor immediately upon receipt.

The second type of condition relates to cash deposits or guarantee or bond for the satisfactory completion of the common areas within the development prior to the local authority taking them in charge. See s 34(4)(g) of the Planning and Development Act, 2000.

This condition may be made in the form of an indemnity bond or cash lodgement or guarantee from a body approved by the local authority.

Bonds are often arranged in stages so that a bond may be obtained covering only a portion of the development. However, provided that the developer furnishes evidence that the financial conditions have been complied with for the particular property, they may safely proceed (see Law Society *Gazette*, Practice Notes, April 1987 and July 2011).

With regard to bonds in relation to roads and services the architect's certificate will not show whether these have been complied with and a receipt from the local authority must be obtained or a letter from the local authority confirming compliance. See Law Society *Gazette*, Practice Note, July–August 2002.

In relation to such letters, ie re roads and services, bear in mind that a road which had previously been thought to be or was 'in charge' can have its status changed. For example, there could be a new development providing a new means of access to the property and closing off a previous access or a right of way extinguishing a public right of way under ss 12 and 13 of the Roads Act, 1993.

Therefore, old letters re same or old solicitors' certificates should be carefully considered and an up-to-date certificate obtained from the vendor's solicitor and/or if appropriate an up-to-date letter from the local authority, see Law Society *Gazette*, Practice Note, July/August 2015. This recommendation is reflected in the 2015 edition of the requisitions on title.

It is not prudent to accept an undertaking that such securities are in place and the Conveyancing Committee in the Practice Note referred to earlier (July 2011) has recommended that such an undertaking is not accepted and purchasers' solicitors should require that such security be in place to the satisfaction of the local authority prior to completion of a purchase and that same is vouched for by a local authority.

Since the introduction of the Planning and Development (Amendment) Act, 2002, Part V (social and affordable housing) obligations to local authorities can by agreement with the local authority be satisfied wholly or partly by cash payments. It should be noted that such agreements are not, for conveyancing purposes, financial conditions. See Law Society

Gazette, August/September 2010, Conveyancing Committee Practice Note entitled 'Development Contributions and Part V Agreements'. See **11.5.7.1**.

11.12.2.4   Conditions restricting future development

Conditions restricting future developments are increasingly common, especially in urban areas where the size of gardens being sold with dwellinghouses, for example townhouses, is limited.

Frequently there is a prohibition against what would normally be exempt development on such a property provided it fell within the criteria, eg conservatories. Another example would be in relation to commercial property where there is a prohibition on advertising signs or a direction in relation to shop fronts. It is absolutely vital to alert the client to the existence of such a condition as the Local Government (Planning and Development) Regulations, 1994, Art 10(1)(a)(i) (under the 2001 Regulations, Art 9) which provides that any development referred to in the Second Schedule will not be exempt if it contravenes a condition attaching to a permission under the Acts or is inconsistent with the use specified in a permission. Another typical condition, particularly on the east coast, restricts the use of a property to members of the family of the applicant. This occurs in cases where a farmer wishes to develop a site on part of his farm and the local authority does not wish to encourage linear development. In the past, by reason of the absolute wording of the condition, problems arose because no lending institution would lend on the security of the property. This clearly gave rise to problems in financing the construction of the dwelling. In addition, of course, it made it impossible to sell the house.

Where such a condition is encountered an application for a new planning permission to free the property of this condition may be made. Local authorities noting all of the previously discussed problems nowadays tend to provide that the house when first constructed on a site be occupied by an applicant or member of his or her family.

11.12.2.5   Conditions incorporating previous permissions

When an alteration to or a revision of an existing permission has been obtained the revised planning permission often incorporates the terms of the earlier permission. Clearly in such a case it is necessary to obtain a copy of the earlier permission and the terms of same should be read very carefully.

11.12.3   HOW LONG DOES A PLANNING PERMISSION LAST?

The Local Government (Planning and Development) Act, 1982, s 2 provided for a limit on the life of a planning permission (s 40 under the 2000 Act). The standard duration for a planning permission is five years from the date of the grant of the permission by the planning authority or An Bord Pleanala. A longer period may be allowed if the development is complex. (See s 41.) Note that the time runs from the granting of the permission (not the date of the notification to grant). The decision of the planning authority on an application for approval/permission may be appealed to An Bord Pleanala, and this is a fact which should be taken into account.

If planning permission expires and an application for a new permission of the same development is made, the planning authority may refuse permission or attach significantly different conditions. This may happen if planning policies required for the proper planning and development of the area have changed in the interim. Prior to 1982, the situation in relation to the life of a planning permission was somewhat complex.

The current position is:

(a)   From 1 November 1982 the average life of a planning permission is five years (see (d)).

(b)   For planning permission granted between 1 November 1976 and 31 October 1982 it was seven years from the grant or until 31 October 1987, whichever was the earlier date.

(c)   For planning permission granted before 1 November 1976 the property had to be completed by 31 October 1983; if not, it was an unauthorised development and in need of a retention order.

(d)   Withering permissions: Section 96(15) of the 2000 Act. A withering permission is one granted for residential development on foot of an application made after 25 August 1999 and before the local authorities housing strategy is incorporated in its development plan. Under the 2000 Act the permission withered/or will lapse on 31 December 2002 or two years from the date planning permission was granted whichever is the later in respect of so much of the development, the external walls of which have not been completed.

The Planning and Development (Amendment) Act, 2002 extended the time limit. Such permissions now have the normal life of a planning permission, usually five years. However, as the Conveyancing Committee in its Guideline in the Law Society *Gazette*, January/February 2003 states 'there is a price to be paid' for this.

Dwellings built on foot of a permission that would have withered but for the 2002 Act will be subject to a levy of 1 per cent of the sale price if equal to or in excess of €70,000 or 0.5 per cent of the sale price if less than that amount. There are however provisions in the 2002 Act to prevent this levy being passed on to a purchaser. The levy will not apply to any planning permission for four or less dwellings, or for housing on land of 0.1 hectares or less. Nor will it apply to dwellings the external walls of which are completed within two years from the date of the permission or by 31 December 2002, whichever is the later.

The Committee points out that the purchaser's solicitor, when acting in the purchase in a dwelling erected on foot of a permission that would have withered but for the 2002 Act and which does not come within the exemptions, must obtain a receipt from a planning authority confirming payment of the levy in respect of that dwelling prior to or on completion of the purchase. See the article by John Gore-Grimes in the Law Society *Gazette*, January/February 2003 entitled 'Change of plan'.

This provision is clearly designed to allow planning authorities to impose social/affordable housing conditions in developments which are being constructed on foot of planning permissions issued before the housing strategy is in place. There is great uncertainty as to how the provisions will operate in practice and they could result in major delays in completing residential schemes, while the developer goes back to the planning authority for a new planning permission. See the article by Patrick Sweetman 'Recent Developments in Conveyancing Practice' in *Irish Planning and Environmental Law* Vol 7, No 4.

These time limits are subject to two exceptions:

(a)   under the Local Government (Planning and Development) Act, 1982, s 3 (s 41 of the 2000 Act) the planning authority has the power to grant permission for a period of more than five years; and

(b)   if the five-year period established with the Local Government (Planning and Development) Act, 1976, s 29 had been extended to a date later than that provided for, the later date applies.

In certain circumstances the planning authority may extend or reduce (rare) the period of validity over a planning permission (s 41) but only where substantial work has been carried out during the lifetime of the permission and the planning authority is satisfied that the development will be completed in a reasonable time.

Under the Local Government (Planning and Development) Act, 1987, s 4 (s 42 of the 2000 Act) provision is made for the extension of these time limits where substantial works were carried out during the relevant period and a further extension where failure to carry out the works during the extended period was due to circumstances outside the control of the developer; 'substantial' is unfortunately not defined: it is suggested that substantial works comprise either works which show an intention of completing the scheme or alternatively works which would be an eyesore or otherwise contrary to good planning or development if left unfinished. See *Frenchurch Properties Ltd v Wexford County Council* [1991] ILRM 769, where it was held that a planning authority is entitled to have basic views and policies regarding what is in a general sense 'substantial works'. It may amount perhaps to as much as 40 to 50 per cent of the development but the planning authority must decide each case on its merits and much would depend on the size and scale of the development, ie a small proportion of works being required have been carried out in a larger development. In this particular case, Lynch J decided that the manufacture of a floor slab and steelworks off the site was works within the definition because these items were especially made and could not be used otherwise.

Finally, bear in mind that, notwithstanding the grant and any remaining duration, planning permission may be altered or revoked. This is rare but does occur. Section 44 sets out when and how a local authority may do so and potential compensation and s 44(6)–(7) sets out the appeal procedures.

11.12.4 A GENERAL APPROACH TO A PLANNING QUESTION

Every practitioner approaches the checking of any planning issue in their own way. The following is just one possible approach to a planning question, which while very simplistic, gives a student or a new practitioner a frame of reference to assist them.

11.12.4.1 Checklist

Consider in relation to the original building/use and each extension/change of use (in date order of occurrence):

Is there:

1. Planning permission?

2. (a) Building bye-law approval or (b) Compliance with Building Regulations?

3. An architect's certificate of compliance with one and two? Remember, as per the 2014 Regulations and requisition 27.4.a, an architect's certificate of compliance re Building Regulations may not be required (if post the 2014 Regulations) but rather a copy of the certificate of compliance on completion together with proof of its registration is sufficient evidence of compliance with the Building Regulations.

1. In relation to planning, any development must have planning permission or be exempt from the same

Sources of exemptions are as follows:

• pre 1963 (1/10/1964);

• s 4 of the 1963 Act and 2001 Act;

• under the 1977 Regulations;

• under the 1994 Regulations;

• under the 2000 Regulations;

• under the 2001 Regulations;

• under the 2007 Regulations;

• under the 2008 Regulations (SI 256 and SI 235);

• under the 2011 Regulations; and

• under the 2013 Regulations.

See **11.4**.

If it is not exempt and no planning permission has been obtained there are three possibilities:

1(a) Apply for retention permission

There are some problems with this; it can take a long time to process the application, and retention permission may be refused. If retention permission is granted, it might be with conditions that do not suit. An application for retention does not, as was sometimes thought, mean that the application opened up the question of enforcement and thus the local authority could, should the application for retention be refused, start enforcement proceedings—see *Fingal Co Co v William P Keeling and Sons Ltd* [2005] 2 IR 108. The decision in this case that a developer was not estopped from claiming that a development was in fact an exempted development merely by reason of having made an application for retention permission was made on the basis that to allow the estoppel would in effect deprive the developer of a right of law simply because he was exercising another right. Therefore, once the requisite time limit has passed and immunity has been gained, ie seven years in the case of a development with no permission and generally 12 years in the case of a development with permission, the local authority cannot commence enforcement proceedings even if a subsequent application for retention permission is refused.

1(b) Rely on 'seven-year rule'

Section s 157(4)(a)(i) of the 2000 Act sets out what has become commonly known as 'seven-year rule'. It does not say that an unauthorised development becomes authorised after seven years. It merely says that the local authority after a period of seven years may not serve an enforcement notice or take proceedings. However, this has certain consequences, which must be explained to a client (see **11.8.2.15**).

1(c) Demolish unauthorised development/cease the unauthorised use

2. Bye-law approval or compliance with Building Regulations

2(a) If there is no bye-law approval

Check that the property is situate in an area where building bye-laws applied (see **11.9.1**) because, if it is not, then obviously this did not have to be obtained.

If it is in such an area, and was not obtained, then see if it is now possible that an architect will certify that while bye-law approval was not obtained, the development would have complied if it had been applied for. (See Law Society *Gazette*, March 1986 and **11.9.1**.)

See if the Bye-Law Amnesty applies. Section 22(7) of the Building Control Act, 1990 abolished the necessity to obtain bye-law approval from 1 June 1992. The Building Control Authority had six months from 1 June 1992 to object to developments which were carried out prior to 13 December 1989 and provided no notice was served before 1 December 1992, the works will be deemed to have been built in compliance with the bye-laws (see **11.9.1**).

Please note: it is the usual practice to accept a vendor's declaration in relation to same. The sample declaration that follows also incorporates a paragraph re the five-/seven-year rule:

STATUTORY DECLARATION

I,   of   aged eighteen years and upwards DO SOLEMNLY AND SINCERELY DECLARE as follows:

1. The property to which this Declaration relates is   (hereinafter called 'the Property').

2. I say that I purchased the Property on the   day of   20

3. During the course of my ownership of the Property I have not received any Enforcement or other Notices under the Local Government (Planning and Development) Acts 1963 to 1992 from the Planning Authority or any other person.

4. I say that Section 22 of the Building Control Act, 1990 has been explained to me and I say that the works carried out by me to the Property were carried out prior to the 13th of December 1989. **[Please note this paragraph deals with the Bye-Law Amnesty.]**

5. I say that no Notice has been served on me from the Building Control Authority in connection with works carried out to the Property within six months of the 1 June 1992 stating that the works constituted a danger to public health or safety. **[Please note this paragraph deals with the Bye-Law Amnesty.]**

6. I say that Section 19 of the Local Government (Planning and Development) Act, 1992/Section 157(4)(a) of the Local Government (Planning and Development) Act, 2000 has been explained to me and I say that as the 'works' to the Property had been completed for more than five years/seven years, it is my opinion that the Planning Authority are precluded from serving Enforcement Notices under the aforesaid Planning Act. It is also my opinion that the local authority is also precluded, in the circumstances from serving Warning Notices under Section 26 or Enforcement Notice under Section 37 of the 1976 Planning Act/Section 152 of the Local Government (Planning and Development) Act, 2000. **[Please note that this paragraph deals with the 'seven-year rule'.]**

I make this solemn Declaration conscientiously believing the same to be true from facts within my own knowledge and belief and for the benefit of

DECLARED before me .... (name of commissioner/practising solicitor in capitals)

a commissioner for oaths / practising solicitor

by .... and ....

[who is personally known to me]

[or: who is identified to me by ....

who is personally known to me]

at ....

in the City/County of...

this .... day of .... 20....

_____

Commissioner for Oaths / Practising Solicitor

I certify to my knowledge of the Deponent

Solicitor

This precedent declaration covers both the Bye-Law Amnesty and the seven-year rule. It is possible that both may not apply at the same time. However, building bye-laws are still relevant in relation to works carried out between 13 December 1989 and 1 June 1992 and works carried out pursuant to bye-law approval applied for before/prior to 1 June 1992.

2(b) Compliance with Building Regulations

In relation to compliance with Building Regulations, if they have not been complied with there is no 'solution', 'amnesty', 'five-year rule', etc which would apply whether or not the development in question is pre or post Building Regulations, 2014, ie where the commencement notice is filed before or after 1 March 2014.

3. Architect's certificate of compliance

In relation to all developments (including those that are exempt and in relation to those that have retention permission, see **11.11.7**) an architect's certificate of compliance with planning/bye-laws/Building Regulations is required (in this regard, consider the changes to said compliance arising from the 2014 Regulations). However, note in relation to residential properties there is a Law Society recommendation (Law Society *Gazette* of January/February, 1993) which states that prior to 1 December 1975, as it was not the practice to obtain architect's certificates of compliance, it is recommended that these are not sought now in relation to residential properties only.

Problem	Possible 'Solutions'		
NO PLANNING AND DEVELOP-MENT IS NOT PRE-63 OR EXEMPT FROM PLANNING	Apply for Retention Permission	Utilise 5/7 year rule. See s 157(4)(a)(i) 2000 Act. See **11.8.2.13**	Demolish/cease unauthorised use
NO BYE-LAW	Did Bye-laws apply? See **11.9.1**	If development was prior to 13/12/89 Bye-law amnesty s 22(7) of the Building Control Act, 1990, if applicable. See **11.9.1**	If development was between 13/12/89–1/6/92 obtain 'retro-spective' Archi-tect's Certificate. See **11.9.1** and Law Society *Gazette*, March 1986
NON-COMPLIANCE WITH BUILDING REGULATIONS	No 'Solution'		
NO ARCHITECT'S CERTIFICATE OF COMPLIANCE WITH PLANNING OR EXEMPTION THEREFROM OR BYE-LAWS	Obtain Architect's Certificate	If development was pre 1/12/75 on a residential property, utilise Law Society recommendation. See Law Society *Gazette*, January/ February 1993	
NO ARCHITECT'S CERTIFICATE OF COMPLIANCE WITH BUILDING REGULATIONS	Obtain Architect's Certificate	If the commencement notice was filed post 1/3/2014, a copy of the certificate of compliance as signed and registered together with proof of its registration is sufficient evidence of compliance with the Building Regulations assuming it clearly identifies the property in sale.	

11.12.4.2 Conclusion

It is vital to realise and explain to the client that in relation to all of the points already made, any 'solution', 'amnesty', 'five-/seven-year rule', 'Law Society Recommendation' etc which may apply does not mean that the vendor is in compliance with planning. Therefore, as the planning is not absolutely perfect, general condition 36 will have to be amended or deleted. Some examples of the appropriate special conditions, which must of course be adapted to the particular circumstances of any conveyance are included at **11.10.8**.

11.13   Building Energy Rating (BER) Certificates and Display Energy Certificates (DEC)

The Building Energy Rating System was introduced into Irish law on 1 January 2007 by virtue of the EC Energy Performance of Buildings Regulations, 2006 (SI 666/2006). The purpose of a BER certificate is to give an objective scale of comparison for the energy demand and performance of a building. It is issued by the Sustainable Energy Authority of Ireland (SEAI). It is essentially a calculation of a property's energy performance which has been described as being akin to a litre per kilometre for a car. The certificate gives a written report and a graph of the energy performance of a property, ranging from A1 (most efficient) to G (least efficient). The report provides advice and information on what steps could be taken to improve energy efficiency.

There are two types of BER: a provisional BER certificate and a full BER certificate. The former would be used where the vendor is selling a property where the house or building has not yet been built and in those cases the provisional BER must be given to the purchaser's solicitor before the building contract is exchanged and, when the building has been completed, a full BER must be provided to the purchaser's solicitor.

A BER certificate only has a ten-year life span, and thus, any BER certificate that is more than ten years old is an invalid certificate.

Initially, the provision of a BER certificate was confined to dwellings but the EU Energy Performance in Buildings Directive 2001/91/EC applies to all buildings and the requirement for a BER was introduced on a phased basis:

1. All new buildings for which planning permission was applied for on or before January 2007 require BER certificates.

2. New non-domestic buildings for which planning permission was applied for before 1 July 2008 require BER certificates.

3. All existing buildings (this includes dwellings and other buildings) which are offered for sale or letting on or after 1 January 2009 require BER certificates. In short, a vendor now must provide a BER certificate for all buildings to the purchaser or to the tenant before contracts are exchanged or before the lease is signed as the case may be.

4. All new dwellings (even when not for sale) must have a BER certificate before they are occupied, see SI 243/2012. This should assist in determining compliance with Part L of the Building Regulations, ie whether the building is in compliance with Building Regulations in terms of energy efficiency. This SI revokes earlier regulations contained in SI 666/2006, SI 229/2008, and SI 591/2008. Part 3 of these regulations set out the requirements in relation to the production of BER certificates, s 10 with the issuing of same for dwellings, and s 11 deals with the issuing of BER certificates for buildings other than dwellings. In addition, s 12 sets out the new requirements for advertising of BER certificates. Section 32 of the SI goes on to deal with the penalties for a person found guilty of an offence under the Regulations, and provides that such person is liable on summary conviction to a class A fine. For the purpose of the Regulations 'agent' under s 15(1) means any person who acts for or represents a person who: commissions the construction of a new building, offers a building for sale, or offers a building for letting. As solicitors can, therefore, be agents of such persons it is very important that it is ensured that the BER information is inserted into any advertisement relating to a property for sale or rent, including catalogues, brochures, websites, etc. See the Law Society Practice Note, January/February 2013 on Mandatory Advertising of BER.

5. From 9 January 2013, large public service buildings publicly and privately owned which exceed 500 square metres, frequently visited by the public, are required to exhibit a Display Energy Certificate (DEC), in a prominent place clearly visible to the public. The purpose of the DEC is to encourage public authorities to adopt environmentally responsible and efficient use of energy in buildings.

Under the legislation there is a positive legal obligation to have an assessment completed and, if this is not done, then the property owner is liable on summary conviction to a Class A fine or imprisonment for a term not exceeding three months or both. See s 25 of the Energy Performance of Building Regulations, 2006 (SI 666/2006) as amended by s 32 of SI 243/2012 (Regulation 15.1). Oddly enough, there is no obligation to follow any recommendation in the advisory report issued, merely that a BER certificate and advisory report is obtained. While the marketability of the property may be affected where the rating is low, the non-existence of the BER certificate does not affect 'good marketable title'. However, the purchasers' solicitors should ensure that a full BER certificate and advisory report is produced pre contract or before a lease is signed, as the case may be, and the vendors' solicitors should list this in the document schedule and send a copy with the contracts for sale.

11.14 Domestic Septic Tanks

Strictly speaking this is not a planning issue per se but under s 4 of the Water Services Act, 2007 as inserted by s 70D of the Water Services (Amendment) Act, 2012 a person who sells a premises connected to a 'domestic waste water treatment system' which includes a septic tank is obliged to furnish a valid certificate of registration in respect of same to the purchaser of the premises. Thus, the vendor's solicitors should seek this from the client as early in the conveyancing process as possible.

The purchaser must, post closing, inform the relevant Water Services Authority of the change in ownership. However, it is not the usual practice for the purchaser's solicitors to do this but rather to inform the client that they must do so. See Law Society Practice Note, April 2015 *Gazette* re 'Change of ownership of domestic septic tanks'.

11.15 Building Control (Carbon Monoxide Detection Bill) 2014

This Bill, which at the time of writing has not yet been passed, will require the vendor or landlord of a new or existing dwellinghouse or his/her agent, before placing the property on the market for sale or letting, to secure a certificate confirming that the requirements under the legislation have been complied with. This requires the installation of carbon monoxide detection devices.

The local authority may demand this from an owner, lessor, or an agent acting on behalf of such an owner or lessor and failure to provide the certificate within 28 days shall be an offence.

Once this Bill is passed, assuming no amendments, the vendor's solicitor should seek the certificate from the client as early in the conveyancing/letting process as possible.

CHAPTER 12

NEW HOUSES

12.1   Introduction

This chapter deals with the purchase of a new house in the course of construction, and related conveyancing matters.

When acting in the purchase of a new house, a solicitor should be aware that the procedure differs substantially from a conveyancing transaction involving the purchase of a second-hand property. This is best illustrated in the following table.

New houses	Second-hand houses
At contract stage there is usually a site only or, at most, a partially completed house on a site. The site value itself will be a fraction of the overall transaction value. Also there may or may not be services in situ to include, eg sewers, water and electricity mains, etc.	An existing dwellinghouse with all the usual services attached is being purchased and, on closing, a letter of charge from the local authority to this effect will usually be furnished.
The vendor is usually a limited liability company with all the attendant risks and requirements inherent in purchasing from such a company.	The vendor is usually a private individual.
The new house is built to certain specific standards, ie in accordance with the building agreement and also with plans and specifications furnished. Caveat emptor does not apply to new houses.	The doctrine of caveat emptor applies: see general condition 16 of the Contract for Sale. It is imperative to advise the purchaser in writing to have the property independently surveyed by a qualified architect/surveyor pre-contract.
The closing date depends on the completion of the structure and may vary from two weeks to 18 months from the date of signing the contract.	The closing date is usually four or five weeks from the date of signing the contract.
The deposit may be paid directly to the builder if he is a member of HomeBond or other similar scheme, which provides insurance cover for the deposit and any stage payment subject, however, to certain time and financial limitations: see IHBA purchasers' Protection Pledge. Although abolished since June 2007 stage payments may apply to one-off houses.	The deposit is held as stakeholder by the vendor's solicitor pending the legal completion of the sale. Stage payments do not arise.

New houses	Second-hand houses
Stamp duty is paid by the purchaser at the ad valorem (the standard) rate currently 1 per cent up to €1,000,000 and excess over €1,000,000 at 2 per cent.	Stamp duty is paid by the purchaser at the ad valorem rate currently 1 per cent up to €1,000,000 and excess over €1,000,000 at rate of 2 per cent.
Normally the builder/developer will purchase a large area of land with a specific title, be it registered or unregistered. The builder then sells on the individual plots or sites with the title for the sites being based on a certified copy booklet of title documents. Most building estates are based on common titles, ie a booklet of title is produced, and the title being common to each house, certified copies only of the title are produced.	With second-hand houses there is usually one specific title relating to that house.
Two contractual documents are provided, ie the building agreement and the Contract for Sale of the site.	One contractual document only is provided: the Contract for Sale.

12.2   What is Involved in the Contract to Purchase a New House?

In a usual housing development/building estate, a builder will be selling a number of plots of land to different purchasers. It is usual for the builder to enter into two agreements with each potential purchaser, one an agreement for the transfer of the site or plot of ground, ie the Contract for Sale, and the other a building agreement under which the purchaser employs the builder to build a house on the site. The documentation and procedures involved in selling each plot will normally be standardised.

The builder's solicitor sends each purchaser's solicitor a set of documentation immediately instructions have been received.

A sample of the documentation, which is usually supplied by the builder with the initial letter to the purchaser, is as follows:

(a)   building agreement in duplicate;

(b)   Contract for Sale in duplicate (often referred to as agreement for transfer/ conveyance) in duplicate;

(c)   HomeBond documentation or documentation under the Premier Guarantee Scheme or other similar scheme;

(d)   booklet of title including certified copy title documents and draft documents and the planning permission, draft architect's certificate of compliance with planning permission and the Building Regulations, indemnity under seal concerning roads and services;

(e)   house plans and specifications;

(f)   copy tax clearance certificate in the absence of a CG50A;

(g)   copy site location map (usually stated to be for identification purposes only);

(h)   declaration of identity;

(i)   draft deed of assurance;

(j) commencement notice under the Building Regulations; Note the new require-ments depending on whether the Comencement Notice was lodged either on or after 1 March 2014. See Planning **chapter 11**;

(k) fire safety certificate (only for new apartments and duplexes); and

(l) provisional BER certificate and advisory report.

When a purchaser agrees to purchase a new house, the building itself is not generally completed. The Law Society Standard Contract for Sale relates to the proposed sale of a property already in existence and imposes no obligation on the vendor to build anything on the property, and it is therefore inadequate to protect the purchaser. What is usually involved in a new house transaction is an agreement to sell the site together with an agree-ment to build a house on that site. These two agreements may be in the form of one or two separate contracts. Should the vendor's solicitor only supply the standard Contract for Sale, the purchaser's solicitor should check that it contains these two basic elements of agreement and the warranties contained in the building agreement (structural defects warranty and preservation of common law rights), failing which the entire building agree-ment should be incorporated into the Contract for Sale by way of special condition. Es-sentially therefore there are two contractual agreements entered into by the purchaser of a new house with the builder/developer. These are respectively:

(a) the building agreement; and

(b) the Contract for Sale/agreement for transfer/conveyance.

12.3 The Building Agreement

12.3.1 INTRODUCTION

The building agreement currently used by almost all practitioners is one that was originally approved and agreed in 1987 between the Law Society and the Construction Industry Federation (the CIF). This was amended in 2001. This has always been considered to be the most important contractual document in a new house conveyancing transaction. It sets out the obligations and responsibilities of both parties in some detail. Succinctly put, the building agreement deals with the bricks and mortar of the house. It sets out how, when, and in what manner the builder must build the house and how much, and when, the purchaser must pay for the house.

The builder is called 'the contractor' in the document and the purchaser is called 'the em-ployer'. The employer is employing the contractor to construct a new house according to certain plans and specifications and also subject to various general conditions, which are dealt with at **12.3.5**.

As with the Law Society Standard Contract for Sale, which has been dealt with in **chapter 6**, any of the general conditions 1–17 in the building agreement may be amended or deleted. However, when acting for the employer/purchaser any amendments to the general conditions may only be made with the written consent of the contractor's solicitor. If any such amendments are not allowed, the implications of leaving the building agree-ment intact must be explained to the purchaser. It is vital that the purchaser's solicitor should carefully examine the building agreement to note if the builder's solicitor has made any amendments or variations to it. Certain conditions may have been added by the contractor's solicitor, which would be unacceptable, for example:

(a) a condition allowing for forfeiture of the deposit; or

(b) a condition providing for a scrivenery fee to be paid to the contractor's solicitor in the event of the employer not proceeding.

Many building contractors' solicitors added additional conditions to the standard building agreement which were unfair and unreasonable and house purchasers were told that these conditions were non-negotiable. When faced with the option of losing a house they wished to buy, many purchasers had no choice but to accept these onerous conditions in the building agreement. The Law Society Conveyancing Committee urged the Director of Consumer Affairs to take action under reg 8(1) of the European Communities (Unfair Terms in Consumer Contracts) Regulations, 1995 (contained in SI 27/1995) to tackle these onerous and unfair terms and conditions. Proceedings were issued using 15 sample conditions provided mainly by the Law Society, and an application was made by the Director of Consumer Affairs to prohibit the use of these conditions in contracts and to limit the ability of builders to collect stage payments. The application for a declaratory order was heard in the High Court on 5 December 2001 and judgment was given on that day. The 15 terms prohibited from building agreements are contained in the first schedule to a High Court order dated 20 December 2001 and are reproduced at **12.3.2**. The court order, record no 229SP/2001, provides as follows:

'1. That no person or body shall use or, if appropriate, continue to use in Building contracts any terms in the form of the terms as identified or any term which is intended to, or does in fact have like effect, the said term having been adjudged by the Court to be unfair terms pursuant to the provisions of the European Communities (Unfair Terms in Consumer Contracts) Regulations, 1995.

2. Without prejudice to the issue of the propriety or impropriety of stage payments or interim payments in any such contract no such building contract providing for such stage or interim payment shall provide for any interim payment such as will exceed the percentages specified in the Irish Homebuilders Association Code of Practice, being the percentages set out in the Second Schedule of the Order, and reproduced below, or which exceed the extent and value of works carried out at the date specified for such payment. No Building Agreement shall provide for stage or interim payments which will exceed the following percentages:

Booking Deposit	4%
Contract Deposit	11%
Interim payment at joist level	25%
Interim payment at roof level	25%
Interim payment at internal plastering stage	25%
Completion payment	10%'

Significantly, the order not only prohibits the use, or, if appropriate, the continued use in building agreements of any of the 15 terms listed in the order, but it also prohibits the use of 'any term that is intended to, or does, in fact, have like effect'.

In the March 2016 edition of the Gazette the Conveyancing Committee reminded practitioners about the implications of including unfair terms in building contracts for new houses. The practice note states that any breach of the Regulations would be considered as a complaint by the Law Society's Complaints and Client Relations Committee and, if any such complaint is upheld, it may be deemed to be misconduct and, if so found, will be dealt with accordingly.

12.3.2 UNFAIR TERMS

The 15 terms are as follows:

12.3.2.1 Term 1

The employer hereby acknowledges that this building agreement and the Contract for Sale between the employer and of even date hereto constitutes the entire agreement between the parties and hereby admits that he/she has not entered into this building agreement or the aforementioned Contract for Sale in reliance on any other warranty or representation whether verbal or in writing. The employer further admits and agrees that he/she will not seek to enforce this building agreement without a similar enforcement of the aforementioned Contract for Sale.

12.3.2.2 Term 2

If the employer shall fail to pay any installment of the contract price or the balance of the contract price within 14 days of the same becoming due for payment, then without prejudice to any other right which the contractor may have at law or in equity, the contractor shall be at liberty to rescind this agreement by giving either directly or through his solicitors to the employer or the employer's solicitor seven days' notice in writing of such rescission and on the expiration of such notice the contractor shall be entitled to resell the site with the works thereon whether by way of private treaty or public auction and at such price as the contractor may determine upon giving seven days' prior written notice to the employer's solicitors. Any deficiency realised on such sale shall be payable by the employer and shall be recoverable as liquidated damages, but any excess realised on the sale shall belong to and be the sole property of the contractor. Any notice under this condition shall be effectively given if sent by post or delivered by hand to the employer or his solicitors at his or their last known address. Where such notice is sent by post, the notice shall be deemed to have been served on the day after the date of such posting.

12.3.2.3 Term 3

If the employer shall prior to the payment of any instalment of the contract price or the balance of the contract price make or raise any objection to or make any claim or demand in respect of the works or in any wise appertaining thereto or the materials or workmanship thereof or in respect of the area of measurements or dimensions of the site or in respect of any other matter whatsoever arising out of this agreement which the contractor shall either be unable or unwilling to remove or comply with any planning or building regulation requirement or if the compliance with any planning condition or local authority requirement shall cause delay in the completion of the works or other developments in the estate of which the site forms part, then notwithstanding any negotiations, litigation or attempt to remove, comply with or satisfy the same and notwithstanding anything contained in clauses 11, 12, and 13 hereof, the contractor shall be at liberty to rescind this agreement by giving either directly or through his solicitor to the employer or the employer's solicitor seven days' notice in writing of such rescission and on the expiration of such notice this agreement shall be at an end and neither party hereto shall have any claim against the other save that the contractor shall be bound to refund to the employer all monies actually paid by the employer to the contractor or the contractor's solicitor in return for all documents furnished to him. Any notice under this condition shall be effectively given if sent by post or delivered by hand to the employer or his solicitor at his or their last known address. Where such notice is sent by post, the notice shall be deemed to have been served on the day after the date of such posting.

12.3.2.4 Term 4

There shall also be excluded from the contractor's liability pursuant to sub-clauses (a) and (b) of clause 8 any defects (patent or otherwise) which occur before the employer enters into possession of the works or pays the balance of the contract price (whichever shall first occur) unless the existence of any such defect has been acknowledged in writing by the contractor.

12.3.2.5 Term 5

On receipt by the employer or his solicitor of notice from the contractor that the works have been completed, the employer shall be entitled to submit one snag list to the site foreman only within seven days of the completion notice. If the said snag list is not submitted within this period, the purchaser wholly relinquishes his right to submit the said snag list. The employer shall not submit a second snag list and shall include in the first snag list all items which he regards or considers as outstanding in the works.

In the event of this agreement or contract of even date in relation to the sale of site being rescinded or repudiated, the employer shall surrender any interest that he might have in the site and shall return all documentation in relation thereto. The purchaser shall not be entitled to possession of the premises or the site thereof until completion of both this agreement and the contact for sale of even date.

12.3.2.6   Term 6

The time period mentioned in general condition 4(c) is hereby amended from 14 days to seven days.

12.3.2.7   Term 7

The contractor may determine this contract by notice in writing to the employer and recover from the employer payment for all work executed and for any loss sustained by the contractor resulting from such determination with interest at the rate of 15 per cent per annum from the date upon which payment became due of the losses incurred up to the date of actual payment which sums are to be paid to the contractor.

12.3.2.8   Term 8

Notwithstanding clause 4(c) hereof:

- If the employer shall not pay the balance of the contract price on the closing day, the contractor may (unless this agreement shall first have been rescinded or become void) give to the employer or his solicitor notice in writing to complete the sale and pay the balance of the purchase price.

- Upon service of such notice, the employer shall complete the sale and pay the balance of the contract price within 14 days after the day of such service (excluding the day of service) in respect of such period time shall be of the essence of the contract (but without prejudice to any intermediate right of rescission by the contractor).

- If the employer does not comply with such notice within the said period (or within any extensions thereof which the contractor may permit), he shall be deemed to have failed to comply with these conditions and his deposit shall be absolutely forfeited to the contractor and the contractor shall be at liberty to re-sell the property without notice to the employer either by public auction or private contract and the deficiency (if any) arising on such re-sale (after giving credit for the deposit so forfeited) and all expenses and costs attending the same or an attempted re-sale shall be made good and paid by the employer as liquidated damages.

12.3.2.9   Term 9

The purchaser shall procure that the premises to be erected in pursuance of the building contract is erected in accordance with the provisions of the said building contract within 18 months from the date of execution of the building contract. In default of compliance with this provision and unless the within sale shall have been completed within the said period, interest shall accrue on the unpaid balance of the purchase price from the end of the 18 month period until completion of the within sale. In the event of the erection of the premises not being completed within a period of two years from the date hereof due to the default of the purchaser, then and in that event the vendor shall be entitled to rescind this agreement and to forfeit the deposit and in this respect time shall be deemed to be of the essence. In the event of the vendor rescinding the within contract, the vendor shall pay to the purchaser 75 per cent of all sums paid by the purchaser to the building contractor under the building contact, and the purchaser shall assign the benefit of the building contract to the vendor subject to the vendor indemnifying the purchaser against all further obligations of the purchaser under the building contract.

12.3.2.10 Term 10

The employer shall not assign or part with the benefit of this agreement or his interest in site without the previous consent in writing of the contractor. The contractor is entitled to assign the benefit of this agreement and the employer acknowledges this. General Condition 9 is modified accordingly.

12.3.2.11   Term 11

The vendor reserves the right to modify materials specifications and to vary dimensions of the site and building during construction.

12.3.2.12   Term 12

The contractor shall not be liable to the employer in respect of any loss, expenses, costs or otherwise incurred as a result of any delay howsoever caused in completing the works referred to in clause A hereof.

12.3.2.13   Term 13

It is further agreed between the parties hereto that any delay by the contractor or employer in completing the aforementioned work or works shall not operate so as to delay the closing date.

12.3.2.14   Term 14

The contractor shall endeavour to keep all extras ordered by the employer when supplied free from damage injury or dirt but it is hereby agreed that the contractor shall not be responsible for any damages of the same or other materials or work ordered by the employer when supplied.

12.3.2.15   Term 15

If any part of the sum demanded by the contractor for extras is not paid within five days from the date of the demand, then interest shall be payable by the employer to the contractor on a day-to-day basis at the rate of 20 per cent per annum from the date of demand to the date of payment.

It is, therefore, vital that solicitors acting for both builders and purchasers of new houses must examine each and every special condition in the building agreement and test it for compliance with this court order.

It is important to point out that no issue at all was taken by any party to the proceedings with any of the terms of the standard Law Society building agreement. The purchaser should be made aware of the Law Society recommendation set out in the Law Society *Gazette*, October 1992, which states that the inclusion of special conditions in a building agreement which limits a purchaser's rights may result in the purchaser's solicitor being unable to certify title for a lending institution, as many loan approvals contain a condition that only the standard form of building agreement may be used without amendments thereto.

As the building agreement will have been drawn up by the builder's solicitors on the strict instruction of their client, it may often contain provisions which operate against the interest of the purchaser. It is important therefore that the full effect of all of its clauses is pointed out to the purchaser pre-execution.

12.3.3   BREACH OF UNFAIR TERMS ORDER

Notwithstanding the preceding terms, various solicitors for builders have continued to use some of these terms in building agreements. This has led to complaints from various solicitors for purchasers who see little point in the High Court making such orders if they can be ignored.

The Law Society say that it is unreasonable to expect purchasers to go to the High Court to try to have the High Court order enforced as, in practice, if a builder wants to insist on a particular term being used he can refuse to sell to anyone who objects and a purchaser will frequently see little point in losing a house because of some clause which has been declared to be unfair but which might not necessarily impinge on his own contract. In the event of a builder becoming aware of an objection he may choose to sell to somebody else rather than get involved in litigation. Ultimately, responsibility falls on the solicitor for the builder who drafts the building agreement and the question arises as to whether such a solicitor is in breach of the court order by including such terms in a building agreement. If so, is there a remedy against such a solicitor to prohibit him from doing so, without having to return to the High Court to enforce the order?

The Law Society Complaints and Client Relations Services Committee (formerly known as the Registrars Committee) has now agreed to deal with complaints about solicitors who draft building agreements containing terms which are in breach of the High Court order and will, in future, be prepared to hold, where such allegations are proved, that such breach amounts to misconduct and be dealt with accordingly. Such solicitors may now be more inclined to explain to their clients that the unfair terms may not be included in building agreements because it may mean that the solicitor will be found guilty of misconduct and be subject to discipline by the Law Society as a result.

12.3.4 MAIN PROVISIONS

The main provisions of the building agreement are set out in the following paragraphs.

12.3.4.1 Definition section

This should be read carefully.

12.3.4.2 Covenant to build

The builder undertakes to build and completely finish the house to a certain reasonably high standard, and in accordance with the plans and specifications furnished, and also in accordance with conditions 1–17 dealt with at **12.3.5**. In order that the purchaser may ensure the quality of the house, the contract should provide that the house be built to some plan or specification, or in a similar fashion to an already existing showhouse.

The plans generally mean a house plan and a site layout plan and contain detailed dimensions of the property and should be checked pre contract. Specifications generally deal with the standard of work, the materials, and finish to be used in the construction of the house.

The purchaser should study the plans and specifications carefully as they form a specific part of the contractual relationship between the parties. These are architectural documents usually drawn up by the builder's architect and the builder is contractually bound to complete the new house in accordance with it. The solicitor for the purchaser should not take it upon himself or herself to advise on the plans and specifications which, in the capacity as solicitor for the purchaser, he or she is neither trained nor expected to advise on. If the purchaser is unable to understand the plans the purchaser should be directed, in writing, to engage the good offices of an architect or engineer to assist the purchaser. Frequently the plans and specifications may differ from what the purchaser thinks he or she is getting and any discrepancy should be clarified pre contract. The purchaser should also be advised in writing to have an architect physically inspect the property to ensure that the premises being constructed on site conform to the details set out in the plans and specifications. At **12.3.5.16** is a sample letter to a proposed purchaser of a new house explaining items of concern that may arise during the transaction.

12.3.4.3 Completion period

The completion of the house will depend very much on the size of the house to be built and its location in the building estate. General conditions 12(a)–(e) deal more particularly with the completion requirements.

12.3.4.4   Method of payment

Like the Standard Contract for Sale, the building agreement provides for a deposit (usually 10 per cent of the overall price of the property) to be paid at contract-signing stage, and for payment of the balance at a specified time. In reality most new house purchasers will have already paid a booking deposit on site either directly to the builder or to the builder's auctioneer as a holding deposit. If this is the case, then the balance only of the 10 per cent deposit will be due and payable by the purchaser at contract-signing stage. The whole question of deposits is dealt with at **12.11**, but in the interim see the Irish Home Builders Association purchaser-protection pledge. It should be noted that this document has not received the approval of the Law Society Conveyancing Committee. It is essentially a pledge by the builder to take the property off the market for an agreed period of time and not to deal with any other party during that period. The purpose of the agreement is to eliminate gazumping.

In addition, the payment clause provides for stage payments, which are payments made by the purchaser at various intervals throughout the transaction to fund the building works as they are carried out. There are generally three interim stage payments involved after the contract deposit is paid, at wall plate-joist level, at roof level, and at the internal plastering stage. The purchaser of a new house involving stage payments must be made aware of his or her liability under the building agreement for such payments and must ensure that funds are available to meet the interim payments when required. Where the purchaser is obtaining a loan this will involve drawing down the loan in a number of stages. The lending institutions require an interim stage payment certificate by an architect or engineer confirming that the particular stage of construction has been reached. The architect must also confirm that regular inspections of the house have been carried out before the purchaser is allowed to draw down the loan to meet the stage payments, and that the work to date has been carried out in compliance with planning permission and the Building Regulations. This certificate will also contain details of the value of the work carried out to date.

The Law Society has always strongly disapproved of stage payments (see **12.11.6**) and requested the Director of Consumer Affairs to call for a complete ban on them in the application to the High Court under reg 8(1) of the European Communities (Unfair Terms in Consumer Contracts) Regulations, 1995. The director did not seek an outright ban on stage payments and applied for a declaration that stage or interim payments which exceed the value of the actual work done, or goods supplied by the builder, are inherently unfair to a consumer and that the limits contained in the Irish Homebuilders code of practice are fair, reasonable, and balanced to both sides. The High Court did not give a ruling on whether stage payments are proper or not and gave an order in the terms sought by the director (see **12.3.1**).

The Law Society long campaigned against the system whereby builders extracted payments from buyers of new houses as the houses go up. It denounced the system as unfair and anti-consumer. On 21 February 2007 the Minister of State at the Department of the Environment wrote to the Law Society to say that agreement has been reached with the construction industry representatives to end the practice of stage payments in housing estates. Contracts or agreements entered into after 30 June 2007 for estate housing cannot include provisions for the making of stage payments or interim payments. See *Gazette*, March 2007. However, stage payments can still apply for one-off houses or specially commissioned houses even after June 2007.

12.3.4.5   Loan clause

There is a standard loan clause in the building agreement, which provides for written loan approval to issue by a certain date. It is essential that this clause be amended to allow that the loan approval conditions must be of such a nature that the purchaser can reasonably comply with them.

The usual clause to be inserted to amend this standard condition reads as follows: 'Upon Terms reasonably within the powers of procurement of the purchaser'. It is very important to check the written terms and conditions of the loan approval carefully to ensure the purchaser can comply with them. Where there is a loan clause the amount of the loan must be specified in the contract. In stage payment transactions, the solicitor must give a qualified undertaking to the lending institution. (In the case of a second-hand property, a solicitor who gives a certificate of title undertakes to furnish an architect's certificate that the property in question has been erected in accordance with the planning permission granted. In the case of a house in the course of construction, a solicitor cannot undertake this, and where the lending institution is paying out the loan by instalments, the solicitor's undertaking should be amended accordingly. If the undertaking is not amended, and if a solicitor pays out a loan cheque or any instalment of a loan to a client before the house is completed, he or she is at risk if there is any failure to comply with the planning permission granted.)

12.3.5 GENERAL CONDITIONS

The general conditions in the building agreement are set out in the following paragraphs.

12.3.5.1 Possession of site: condition 1

The builder must remove all rubbish, debris, scaffolding, and unused materials from the site pre-closing and leave the site clear and fit for human habitation. The purchasers should be advised to check that this is in fact the case pre closing.

12.3.5.2 Materials: condition 2(a) and (b)

If the contractor is unable to obtain the materials described in the plans similar materials may be used.

12.3.5.3 Employer's choice of materials: condition 2(e)

The purchaser must notify the contractor within 14 days of the choice of materials to be used in the house, eg tiles, kitchen fittings, fireplaces, etc.

12.3.5.4 Local and other authorities' requirements: condition 3

Condition 3 provides that the dwellinghouse will be built in accordance with all necessary planning permissions and in compliance with the Building Regulations. The solicitor should ensure that this condition is contained in the building agreement and that the onus is on the builder to see that these requirements are met, as otherwise the purchaser may have difficulties in obtaining local authority services.

12.3.5.5 Interest: condition 4(a)–(e)

Penalties are imposed upon the purchaser for not closing the purchase on time to include:

(a) interest being charged at the rate of 4 per cent per annum above the current bank rates;

(b) the contractor may suspend carrying out the works; or

(c) the contractor has an option to repudiate the contract.

There is no provision allowing for forfeiture of the deposit in the building agreement. The remedies available to the builder are as set out earlier. The purchaser's solicitor should check to see that a forfeiture clause has not in fact been added by the contractor's solicitor, and should point out to the purchaser that interest will be payable at the rate specified in the contract if completion is delayed unreasonably.

12.3.5.6   Insolvency of the contractor: condition 5

The building agreement may be terminated in the event of the bankruptcy of the builder. Condition 5 does not provide for the bankruptcy of the purchaser and it is common practice to provide for this in the building agreement by the insertion of an appropriate clause.

12.3.5.7   Price variation clause: condition 6

If the building agreement states that the cost to the purchaser of building the house will increase with current costs of labour and materials the condition should, if possible, be deleted by the purchaser who will wish to have a fixed price contract. The builder's solicitor may, however, insist on reinstating the condition. If it is left intact the contract price may be varied by the builder to reflect increases/decreases in the cost of labour, materials, and fuel provisions, VAT, etc.

12.3.5.8   Insurance: condition 7

Under the Law Society Standard Contract for Sale the risk of damage to the property remains with the vendor until completion and the building agreement reflects this by providing that the builder remains at risk and must insure the premises up to the date of legal completion against fire and personal injury and for the usual perils under public liability etc.

12.3.5.9   Liability for defects: condition 8(a) and (b)

Under the terms of the standard building agreement the builder must remedy any major structural defects within a period of 18 months post completion and must remedy any minor defects for a period of six months post completion. These obligations run parallel to the purchaser's rights under HomeBond and are in fact of wider application as HomeBond has financial limits. It is important to retain conditions 8(a) and (b) in the building agreement in order to give the purchaser as many avenues of redress as possible against the builder. For this reason the building agreement must be sealed (not merely signed) by a builder company.

12.3.5.10   Notice of alleged defects: condition 8(c)

Written notice of any alleged defects must be submitted to the builder within the relevant periods referred to in the condition. It is important to note that the lending institutions require the borrowers to have adequate 'course of construction' insurance in place prior to advancing any stage payments on foot of the loan. On completion of the dwellinghouse the purchaser is required to take out full insurance. It is important to advise the purchaser of the necessity of effecting insurance in a situation where ownership of the site is transferred to him or her on payment of the balance of the site fine but prior to the completion of the dwellinghouse in a typical stage payment transaction.

12.3.5.11   Limitations on builder's liability: condition 8(d)

Condition 8(d) sets out the limitations on the builder's liability under condition 8(a) and (b). The builder will obviously wish to limit his liability as much as possible by providing that the following defects are excluded from the structural defects warranty:

(i)   hair cracks in plaster works;

(ii)   defects or damage in paint work or decoration;

(iii) normal shrinkage or expansion of timber;

(iv)   defects in plaster work or damage occurring in the works by reason of the operation of any central heating system;

(v)   damage or defects caused by negligence or abuse on the part of the employer, his servants, agents, licensees, or invitees;

(vi)   damages or defects caused by fair wear and tear;

(vii)   items covered by a separate guarantee issued to the employer by any manufacturer; and

(viii) consequential loss arising as a result of any defect or the remedying thereof.

Consequential loss within the meaning of condition 8(d)(viii) is stated in condition 14(d) to include any cost or expense in respect of the alternative accommodation, transport or storage of furniture, loss of wages, salaries earnings or benefits, or damages for temporary inconvenience.

These exclusions are normally accepted in practice; however, the purchaser's solicitor should, if possible, seek to have 8(d)(i) and 8(d)(viii) deleted for the better protection of the purchaser.

These exclusions on liability are similarly excluded from the HomeBond Agreement, which, in addition, excludes liability for any defects consequent upon the installation of a lift or a swimming pool in or about the dwelling.

12.3.5.12 Common law rights: condition 8(e)

This is a most important condition as it stipulates that the common law rights of the purchaser are confirmed provided the contractor does not delete or exclude them in the building agreement. In addition to the specific guarantees regarding structural defects outlined in the maintenance agreement under condition 8(a) and (b), there is an implied warranty that the common law rights of the purchaser are guaranteed by the builder if condition 8(e) is left intact.

The implied warranties at common law in relation to a new house are:

(a) The contractor will carry out the work in a good and workmanlike manner.

(b) The contractor will supply good and proper materials.

(c) The building will be reasonably fit for the purpose required, ie fit for human habitation.

These will be dealt with under the heading 'Structural Defects' at **12.10**.

12.3.5.13 Services: condition 10

Condition 10 provides that the builder shall ensure that all the estate services will be provided for and laid as soon as possible to a standard acceptable to the local authority. In most building estates an indemnity bond is payable to the local authority by the contractor in order that the roads, sewers and all other services will be taken in charge by the local authority at a later date (see **chapter 11**). In the interim, the contractor who agrees to maintain the services until they are so taken in charge provides the purchaser with an indemnity under seal. Conditions in the planning documentation will provide details of the financial requirements placed on the contractor.

12.3.5.14 Completion date: condition 12(a)

Condition 12(a) should be read in conjunction with the definition in section A (iii) of the building agreement. In order for legal completion to take place, the builder must have previously served a completion notice on the purchaser or on his or her solicitor confirming the completion of the house in accordance with the terms of the building agreement. Normally there is a 14-day period during which the purchaser is obliged to attend on site or have his or her architect/engineer attend on site to arrange a thorough inspection of the property and to draw up a list of defects, called a 'snag list', which sets out the minor problems or defects which have to be remedied before the sale may close. This list should be furnished to the builder and the defects should be remedied before the final payment is made. Notwithstanding minor defects, the purchaser may be forced to close and may be liable for interest for any delays. It is wise for solicitors not to become too involved in disputes between a purchaser and builder where the defects complained of are of a very trivial nature. Any condition in a building agreement limiting a purchaser to one snag list is deemed to be an unfair term.

12.3.5.15 Arbitration: special condition 12(d)

Condition 12(d) provides that in the case of any dispute as to the existence or nature of a defect the experts, as defined, may decide whether it is major or minor. They may not, however, deal with any other aspects of the dispute. Other types of building agreements may be encountered in practice, particularly in the case of 'one-off' houses. See Law Society *Gazette*, July/August 1992, which details the procedures to be followed when the Standard Building Agreement is not used.

12.3.5.16 Sample initial letter to client purchasing a new house

Company
Solicitors,
Co. Clare,
15 May 20.

Mr and Mrs
Loughville,
County Clare.

Re PURCHASE OF 4, CARNALLY WOODS, ENNIS, Co CLARE.

Dear Mr and Mrs,

We note your recent instructions to act on your behalf in the proposed purchase of the above-mentioned premises for the sum of €360,000. We received the contract documentation from the solicitors acting for the vendor/builder and we enclose the following for your consideration:

1. The building agreement

The building agreement is probably the most important document when dealing with a new house. In short, it provides details of how and what the builder is to build and how he is to be paid for doing so.

2. The agreement for transfer/Contract for Sale

The agreement for transfer relates to the plot of ground on which the house will be built. It deals with technical matters such as the title to be shown.

3. Specimen deed

This is a sample of the deed, which will transfer the ownership in the site in due course to you. You will be obtaining a freehold interest, subject to various exceptions and reservations and also subject to certain covenants.

We shall be going through the Building Agreement, the Agreement for Transfer and the deed with you in detail at our appointment. If you have any queries in relation to any of these documents perhaps you might please make a note of them and we shall deal with your query then.

4. Site plan and specifications

The specification should set out in exact detail what materials, fittings and standards the builder is going to use in the construction of your house. The house plan should set out not just the proposed floor plan but also quite a lot of other details. It has been the increasing practice of builders to use plans and specifications of a general and vague nature. It is not unknown for them to contain inaccuracies and sometimes the plans are not even for the correct house. You should read through them carefully and examine the plans and compare them with the show house, if there is one. You should ensure that these accurately represent what you believe you are buying. We as your solicitors are not in a position to offer you advice on the plans and specifications. You should seek advice from a qualified architect/engineer in relation to the plans and specifications in order to satisfy yourself that they are in order and to establish whether or not you have any further requirements. When carrying out his inspection, after construction works are complete, the architect will be able to verify that the plans and specifications are strictly adhered to. It is advisable that your architect should attend on site on a number of occasions during construction of the house to ensure that all is proceeding in compliance with the plans and specifications. If you intend making any alterations to the original plans you should ensure that the necessary planning permission is obtained for any proposed development. The following items are often omitted from the plans and specifications:

(a) details of finish

(b) allowances for wallpaper, fireplaces, sanitary ware

(c) extent of tiling in bathroom and kitchen

(d) boundary walls and fences.

Please make a note of any omissions, which we can deal with.

5. Copy planning permission

Much of this is of a technical nature and on closing we will require a certificate of compliance from the builder's architect confirming that all conditions in planning permissions have been complied with. We will also be seeking an architect's opinion on compliance with the Building Regulations. We would recommend that you read through the planning permission carefully and address any questions that you may have to your architect/engineer. In addition you should attend the offices of the planning department with control for the area in which the property is situated. There you should check the development plan for the area to satisfy yourselves that there is no major motorway proposal, industrial development, etc proposed in close proximity to the development of which your house will form part. Should any such matters arise the decision will naturally rest with you as to whether or not you wish to proceed. We will be engaging an independent firm of law searchers to carry out a planning search but this is no substitute for a detailed search in the planning department as recommended above.

6. Deposit

In the case of a new house it is normal for the purchaser to pay a booking deposit to the builder or his auctioneer in order to secure the house. When executing the contract, the balance deposit (usually 10 per cent of the total purchase price) becomes payable by the purchaser. The balance of the purchase monies will be payable on completion. We will forward the balance deposit to the builder's solicitors with a request to hold it as stakeholder and not to release it until such time as the property has been completed. What this means, in effect, is that we will request the builder's solicitor not to pay the deposit over to the builder until such time as the house is completed. Please note that in the event of their failing to hold the deposit as stakeholder and, in the event of the builder going into liquidation or running into financial difficulties, then you could lose all monies paid with no guarantee of recovery.

We have caused a search to be made against the builder in the Land Registry and in the Companies Registration Office and this search discloses that the property is held subject to a bank mortgage. The builder's solicitor has refused our request to have the mortgage redeemed at this stage. Thus the bank that holds this mortgage would have a prior claim over yours should the builder go into liquidation prior to the completion of the sale to you. If you are prepared to pay over the deposit, notwithstanding the risk, you might please let me have your written confirmation of your instructions by return of post.

You should note that in most cases the vendor's/builder's solicitor will not hold the deposit as stakeholder and it is usually paid over directly to the builder once it is received by his solicitor thus leaving the purchaser's deposit and or stage payments (if applicable) at considerable risk. We would strongly advise that you do not hand over any further monies except through these offices.

We have not as yet received information as to whether the builder is a member of Home-Bond. This scheme provides some measure of protection for deposits in the event of the fraud or insolvency of the builder up to a certain amount. It also provides structural defects indemnity.

Yours faithfully,

Solicitors

12.4   The Contract for Sale/Agreement for Transfer/Conveyance

12.4.1   INTRODUCTION

The second contract document utilised in the sale of a new house is referred to variously as the Contract for Sale or the agreement for transfer/conveyance. The Contract for Sale of the site is usually the standard Law Society Contract for Sale that has been dealt with already in **chapter 6**.

This document deals with the physical location of the site, its dimensions and boundaries. Most importantly, it deals with the title to the site. It usually refers to the property as a plot of ground as no house will have been completed at this stage. Sometimes a builder's solicitor may attempt to exclude the general conditions of the Contract for Sale where reliance is placed upon a building agreement solely, incorporating some special conditions dealing with title. The format of the certificate of title clearly expresses that the 'purchase was effected on foot of the current Law Society's conditions of sale and/or building agreement'. The Conveyancing Committee is of the view that to preclude any such conditions en bloc would prevent the purchaser's solicitor giving a certificate of title. For the avoidance of any doubt, the committee has confirmed that the use of the wording 'conditions of sale and/or building agreement' in the certificate of title documentation was intended to mean that the conditions of sale are required in relation to the purchase of a second-hand property, and both the conditions of sale and building agreement are required in relation to the purchase of a newly constructed property or property in the course of construction.

In July/August 2002 the Law Society issued a Practice Note which advised of the increased practice of builder's solicitors issuing documents which are an amalgam of excerpts from the standard building agreement and Contract for Sale. While in practical terms the sale of a new dwelling is a single transaction as far as the client is concerned, from the legal perspective these are two separate transactions.

The Law Society Conveyancing Committee consistently reminds practitioners that in a new house transaction the standard documents should be used, that is the building agreement and the Contract for Sale. This avoids delay for the vendor as he is not obliged to deal with queries in relation to the minutiae of a non-standard document. It also allows the purchaser's solicitor to give an unqualified certificate of title to the lending institution. As stated earlier, the standard certificate of title requires the purchaser's solicitor to certify that the property was acquired 'on foot of the current Law Society conditions of sale and/or building agreement'. In recent months, the Conveyancing Committee has received an increasing number of queries from solicitors acting for purchasers who are being offered contracts for the sale of the sites, which are not based on the ideal situation where the builder is the owner of the land and in a position to execute an assurance of the sites to the purchasers of the houses. An example is:

Title furnished was a conveyance of unregistered land to AB, a third party. A special condition stated as follows: 'The vendors warrant that they have sufficient interest under a licence and option agreement with AB to enter into this Contract for Sale. The purchaser shall accept the same and not call for the vendor to be registered as owner of the site or for AB to join this agreement. The purchaser shall not call for or be furnished with a copy of the licence and option agreement.'

While these arrangements vary in detail, their basis is that the builder has an entitlement to call upon the landowner to execute an assurance of the site to the purchaser, as a nominee of the builder, at the builder's request. Difficulties may arise if the builder is seeking stage payments and the arrangement with the landowner only entitles the builder to call for an assurance of the sites when the houses have been completed.

Historically, the landowner entered into licences with the builders, entitling them to go in on the owner's land and build houses. The builders entered into contracts with the purchasers to build houses on the land. When the houses were satisfactorily completed, the builders were entitled to call on the owner to execute an assurance of the land on which the houses had been built to the purchasers. In some of the cases that have been brought to the notice of Committee, the builder is declining to furnish any evidence of the arrangements that the builder has with the landowner. In the absence of such evidence, a requirement for any stage payment places the purchaser's solicitor in considerable difficulties.

While the Conveyancing Committee is unhappy with some of these arrangements, it is satisfied that, in certain circumstances, they are just about acceptable. As long as deposits are of such a level that they are protected by the HomeBond or similar schemes, or are held by the builder's solicitors on trust or as stakeholder, and as long as purchaser's solicitors are entitled to obtain assurances of the site as soon as the first of any stage payments are made, then the purchasers do have a minimum level of protection.

Solicitors have expressed concern about their position in relation to the provision of undertakings and certificates of title to lending institutions. This should not present a difficulty as long as the purchaser's solicitor gets a transfer of the title on payment of the first stage payment, and the title is otherwise in order. A solicitor should not, of course, pay any stage payment without getting the transfer of title. In stage payment cases the Conveyancing Committee recommended in a Practice Note in the June 2013 *Gazette* that a solicitor who has drawn down the first tranche of a mortgage loan on completion of the mortgage is only obliged to certify the title as of that date. This includes certifying that the planning is in order at that date and this may include getting an interim opinion on compliance with the planning permission if any development has taken place at that stage.

As far as the closing of the transaction is concerned, as long as the purchaser's solicitor is presented with a valid deed of assurance from the landowner, that will be sufficient to ground the solicitor's Undertaking and Certificate of title. The particular difficulties that arose in this situation when the stage payment system operated no longer apply after 30 June 2007. Agreement was reached with the construction industry representatives to end the practice of stage payments in housing estates from that date. These difficulties will however continue to arise for one-off houses.

As usual, any amendments or additions to the standard documentation should be dealt with by way of special condition.

To briefly summarise, the Contract for Sale deals with the following.

12.4.2 PARTIES

The vendor is the builder/landowner and the purchaser is the client.

12.4.3 CLOSING DATE

The closing date is usually the completion date of the dwellinghouse by reference to the building agreement. Normally, the purchaser will be liable to pay the balance of money due for both the site and the house when the house is constructed, and title to the site shall not pass until that day. In a stage payment transaction it is vitally important that provision be made in the Contract for Sale that the vendor will transfer ownership of the site to the purchaser on payment of the balance site fine together with the first stage payment due under the building agreement. The lending institutions will not advance any money to the purchaser unless and until such time as the purchaser has title to the site. Failure to provide for the transfer of ownership of the site to the purchaser in advance of completion of construction could seriously hinder the purchaser client's ability to draw down funds on foot of his or her loan to meet his or her obligations under the building agreement and may necessitate him or her obtaining bridging finance.

12.4.4   PURCHASE PRICE

The consideration in the Contract for Sale will be the value of the site. Usually the purchase price for the site is a mirror of what the builder paid for the entire estate, ie if the builder bought ten sites for €1,000,000, the purchaser's site value is €100,000. The site value is generally a fraction of the overall value of the transaction.

12.4.5   THE PROPERTY

The particulars and tenure of the Contract for Sale will contain a full legal description of the property and will include reference to a map attached to the contract with the site boundaries outlined by an architect/engineer. Since the site boundaries may not have been 'pegged out' by the builder at contract stage it is important that the site map is submitted to the purchaser for approval before the contract is signed. Discrepancies may often arise between the size of the site or location of the site on the map and this should be dealt with pre contract. Unless the map furnished is a Land Registry approved scheme map any other map furnished is usually stated to be for identification purposes only. Always advise the purchaser to have the site location and boundaries checked by himself or herself and an architect. Ensure that a Land Registry approved scheme map is obtained on completion.

In November 2004, the Conveyancing Committee of the Law Society issued a Practice Note in relation to Land Registry approved scheme maps. Frequently a purchaser's solicitor in a new house transaction is required by the contract to accept an undertaking on closing from the vendor's/builder's solicitor in respect of the Land Registry scheme map and closes the purchase based only on a copy map provided for identification purposes. The Committee advises that the purpose of this practice is to limit the builders' exposure to the cost of amending Land Registry scheme maps accordingly as the development proceeds. From a conveyancing point of view this is completely unacceptable. The acceptance of such a condition in a contract means that a purchaser's solicitor cannot proceed following closing to stamp and register the client's title or the lender's mortgage, where applicable. In registration terms it places the purchaser's and lender's priority in jeopardy and, if accepted by the borrower's solicitor, places that solicitor in breach of the obligations under the undertaking given to the lender.

The Conveyancing Committee are of the view that no solicitor should expose their purchaser client in this matter to the risks associated with a building going into liquidation or otherwise going out of business in circumstances where a development may be unfinished and where the architect or engineer has not provided Land Registry approved scheme maps for the client's site. The Land Registry introduced a new method for the registration of transfers of sites in schemes which applies to all applications lodged after 10 May 2005. Two features of the initiative are the approval of scheme maps and the transfer of sites.

12.4.6   THE DOCUMENTS SCHEDULE

The vendor's/builder's documents of title to the site will be set out in the documents schedule. The title to the site must commence with a good root of title. The title to the site will be either a Land Registry title with an official copy folio and filed plan or an unregistered title where certified copies only of the title documents will be furnished.

12.4.7 SPECIAL CONDITIONS

There will usually be a considerable number of special conditions. It is, for example, generally stipulated that the deed of transfer/conveyance shall be in the form prepared by the vendor's/builder's solicitor and that no amendments or alterations shall be permitted to the said transfer. The deed of transfer/conveyance normally reserves certain rights to the vendor and should be inspected pre contract.

The special conditions usually provide that the title shall consist of the booklet of title and that no further documents shall be called for or supplied. This, of course, will not preclude any requisition being raised regarding any document which is omitted (or subsequently found to be omitted) and which goes to the root of title.

The task of the solicitor for the purchaser of a new house is to ensure that the vendor's/builder's title is a good and marketable one, and that the identity of the property is in order. The architect ascertains that the position of the site as per the contract map or deed map is in accordance with the physical location and boundaries of the site on the ground and approves the site map.

The solicitor's task is to ensure at all times that he or she has read the title in detail and is able to negotiate the deletion of any special conditions in the Contract for Sale that are unacceptable to the client or to the client's lending institution.

In many instances where the builder is not the owner of the lands the solicitor may find the Contract for Sale will provide that the builder undertakes to procure the execution of the deed by the site owner (who is usually the developer) by the closing date. This occurs where the developer of a housing estate and the builder of each house are different parties. Very often land is purchased by a company that develops that land as a housing estate and then enters into a licence agreement with a builder to build blocks of houses on that estate. Under the terms of the licence agreement, the developer undertakes to sell each site to those purchasers who are nominated by the builder.

If the house is not completed at contract stage and only the Standard Contract for Sale is being furnished by the vendor's solicitor it should be sufficient protection for the purchaser to add in the following special condition:

'The vendor shall prior to the closing date construct and complete in a good substantial and workmanlike manner a habitable dwellinghouse in accordance with the plans and specifications signed by the parties prior to the execution hereof and subject to general conditions numbered 1–17 in the 2001 edition of the Law Society Building Agreement and in accordance with all planning permission and Building Control Regulations. The purchaser is also given the structural defects warranty and his common law rights are preserved.'

It is, however, highly recommended that in all new house transactions, a building agreement and a Contract for Sale are provided and as stated previously this is expressly required in the Undertaking and Certificate of Title for residential mortgage lending.

12.4.8 ONE-OFF NEW HOUSES

Practitioners are reminded that purchasers of a standalone, new dwellinghouse, even if it is completed at the date of the contract, are entitled to the benefit of the general warranties contained in the Building Agreement. Practitioners should insist on a building agreement being furnished or alternatively that a special condition is inserted into the Contract for Sale similar to that above. Again the Undertaking and Certificate of Title will require that a separate building agreement and Contract for Sale be executed and, if this is not the case, the Undertaking and Certificate of Title will need to be qualified.

12.5   Stamp Duty and New Houses

12.5.1   GENERALLY

All deeds executed after 15 December 1999 must comply with the Stamp Duties Consolidation Act, 1999 ('the 1999 Act').

Section 29 of the 1999 Act applies to a conveyance on sale combined with building agreement for a dwellinghouse or apartment.

The stamp duty position relating to the purchase of what is in effect a new house or apartment depends on the nature of the contracts entered into. The deed may be giving effect to a contract to purchase:

(a)   a site with a connected building agreement;

(b)   a partially completed house; or

(c)   a completed house.

Prior to 8 December 2010 certain reliefs from stamp duty applied in relation to new houses for both first-time purchasers and owner-occupiers. Investors always paid stamp duty on the total price at the full ad valorem rate. The reliefs applicable to owner-occupiers depended on whether the floor area of the new house/apartment was less than or greater than 125 square metres and also whether the conveyance was of a newly completed house or a sale of a site together with a contract to build a new house, essentially whether the house was completed or not.

The Finance Act, 2011 confirmed changes to the stamp duty regime in the purchase of new houses and apartments. These changes included a new rates schedule for these residential properties as follows:

Current rate of stamp duty on residential property:

Stamp duty €1,000,000 @ 1%

Excess over €1,000,000 @ 2%.

The Finance Act, 2011 provided *inter alia* for the abolition of certain reliefs and exemptions in relation to the purchase of residential property. The following stamp duty reliefs for new houses and apartments were abolished with effect from 8 December 2010:

1.   Section 91A SDCA 1999—Exemption from stamp duty for the purchase of a new house or apartment not exceeding 125 square metres by an owner-occupier.

2.   Section 92 SDCA 1999—Relief for purchase of a new house or apartment where the floor area exceeds 125 square metres by an owner-occupier.

3.   Section 92B SDCA 1999—Exemption for purchase of a house or apartment by a first-time purchaser.

12.5.2   PURCHASE OF SITE WITH CONNECTED BUILDING AGREEMENT

12.5.2.1   Section 29 SDCA

Section 29 charges stamp duty when a site is being sold and, in connection with the sale, a house or an apartment has been, is being, or is to be built on that site. The stamp duty charge arises only where the sale of the site and the building of the house or apartment are part of an arrangement or are connected in some way. Stamp duty in such cases is paid on the aggregate of the consideration paid for:

(a)   the site; and

(b)   the construction works, that is the consideration paid in respect of building the house/apartment on the site.

At the time the deed giving effect to the purchase of the site is made the construction work may not have commenced or they may have been commenced and not have been completed. In any event because the deed is giving effect to a contract to purchase a site the deed must only recite the consideration provided for in the contract to purchase the site.

Example

X entered into a contract to buy a site from Y a vendor/developer, for €50,000. A Building Agreement was also entered into with Y whereby Y undertook to build a house on the site for X for €150,000. Y would not have sold the site to X if X had not entered into the Building Agreement. After the construction works were completed a deed giving effect to the purchase of the site was executed. Though the deed recited a consideration of €50,000, the stampable consideration is €200,000. As the property is residential property the stamp duty applicable is €2,000 (€200,000 @ 1 per cent).

Section 29 applies to the acquisition of a site where there is an arrangement to build a house on the site. Section 53 of the 1999 Act deals with similar provisions where a lease is granted with a connected agreement to build residential property (usually an apartment).

12.5.2.2   Exemptions from s 29

Section 29 does not apply to the following:

(a)   The purchaser is buying the site and it can be shown that there is no connection or arrangement between the purchase of the site and the building of a house or apartment on that site, eg where a person buys a site and employs a builder unconnected with the sale of the site.

(b)   Transfers or leases of sites on which the transferee will build a house by his or her own labour. However, if the Revenue Commissioners are not satisfied with the genuineness of a particular transaction it is open to them to invoke the anti-avoidance provisions contained in s 29(3) dealt with at **12.5.2.5**.

(c)   Purchase of a partially completed house (discussed in more detail later).

(d)   Purchase of a completed new house (discussed in more detail later).

(e)   The rules set out in s 29 and s 53 do not apply to non-residential property, eg stocks, marketable securities, offices, factories.

(f)   Simpliciter, in the case of a new house, s 29 and s 53 apply if the building agreement and the Contract for Sale are connected in some way. Section 29 and s 53 do not apply if there is no connection between the building agreement and the Contract for Sale.

Purchase of a partially completed house

Where a person enters into a contract for the purchase of a partially completed building and where it is shown to the satisfaction of the Revenue Commissioners that there is no connection between the sale of the partially completed house and the employment of the builder chosen to complete the construction work, stamp duty will be based on the amount paid for the partially completed house. The deed giving effect to this contract must recite the consideration provided for in the contract.

Example

A decides to build a house for his daughter on his own land using direct labour. After the building works had been commenced A ran out of money. All building work ceased. Sometime later A agreed to sell the partially completed house to C for €330,000. C employs his own builder to complete the house. The deed giving effect to the contract will recite a consideration of €330,000. As there is no connection between the sale of the partially completed house and the builder chosen to complete the house this section (s 29) does not apply. The stampable consideration is €330,000 and, as the property being transferred is residential property the stamp duty payable is €3,000 (€330,000 @ 1 per cent).

Purchase of a completed new house

Section 29 does not apply where the contract is a contract to purchase a new house, which has already been completed. In these circumstances there can be no connection or arrangement between the sale of the site and the building agreement. Where the deed is giving effect to a contract to purchase a completed new house the deed must recite the consideration provided for in the contract.

Example

X builds a house on his land in 2016. As soon as the house is built he sells it for €295,000. The deed will recite a consideration of €295,000 and, as the property being sold is residential property, the stamp duty payable is €2,950 (€295,000 @ 1 per cent).

12.5.2.3   Definitions: s 29(1)

This provision is self-explanatory.

12.5.2.4   Charge to stamp duty: s 29(2)

Stamp duty is chargeable where land is being sold and, in connection with that sale, a house or an apartment has been, is being, or is to be built on that land. The stamp duty charge arises only where the sale of the land and the building of the house or apartment or part of an arrangement are connected in some way.

The question of the existence of the arrangement, in so far as the transfer of the site and the building of the house or apartment on that land are concerned, will be determined by the facts in each case.

12.5.2.5   Anti-avoidance measure: s 29(3)

Where the building of a house or apartment has commenced prior to the execution of the instrument affecting the sale (ie the deed of transfer) such house or apartment will be deemed to be within the category of houses or apartments, which are built, being built, or to be built for the purposes of s 29(2).

12.5.2.6   Leases: s 53

Section 53 applies to a lease combined with building agreement for dwellinghouse or apartment.

Section 53 is similar to s 29 except that it applies where a 'lease' rather than a 'conveyance' is made of land combined with an agreement to build residential property (usually an apartment).

12.5.3   NEW DWELLINGHOUSES AND APARTMENTS WITH FLOOR AREA COMPLIANCE CERTIFICATES

12.5.3.1   General: s 91A of the SDCA

Section 91A of the 1999 Act provided for an exemption from stamp duty for any instrument giving effect to the first purchase of a new house or apartment upon its erection to first-time buyers and owner-occupiers as defined, and who occupied the house or apartment as his or her only or main place of residence for the specified period. The exemption only applied where there was a valid floor area compliance certificate (FACC) in respect of the house or the apartment. This FACC was issued by the Department of the Environment Heritage and Local Government pursuant to s 91A of the 1999 Act for stamp duty purposes. They were only issued in respect of newly constructed houses or apartments which met the required building standards and where the new house/apartment was within specified floor area limits (not less than 38 square metres and did not exceed 125 square metres).

The FACC confirmed that the floor area of the house was within the specified limits and complied with the standards set down by the Minister for the Environment, Heritage and Local Government and that the house was built strictly in accordance with the plans submitted to the department. The house/apartment must be constructed in compliance with the Building Regulations, 1991 including any amendments thereto.

The exemption was subject to clawback provisions.

This exemption has been abolished with effect from 8 December 2010 and this section is no longer effective. The Revenue online drop-down stamp duty window retains the option of availing of the floor area compliance certificate relief although it is now only of historic interest.

12.5.3.2 The 'rent a room' scheme

The 'rent a room' scheme was introduced in the Finance Act, 2001. Under the scheme, the gross annual rental income of less than €10,000 (including any sums paid for food, laundry, or similar goods and services) is exempt from income tax where a room or rooms in a person's principal private residence is let as residential accommodation.

12.5.3.3 Clawback of relief: s 91(2)(c)

If any person derives rent from the use of the house or apartment within the specified period the relief will be clawed back. Because the relief is clawed back in the guise of a penalty imposed on the purchaser there is no need to return the original instrument for restamping. The exception to this is there is no clawback of the relief where rent is received by the person in occupation of the house, on or after 6 April 2001, for the letting of furnished accommodation in *part* of the dwellinghouse or apartment. The clawback amounts to the difference between the higher stamp duty rates and the duty paid and it becomes payable on the date that rent is first received from the property.

12.6 Booklet of Title

12.6.1 INTRODUCTION

It is customary for the vendor's solicitor to send a booklet of title evidencing the builder's title when sending the contract documentation to the purchaser's solicitor. The Law Society Conveyancing Committee has stated that the vendor's solicitor is under an obligation to furnish a proper booklet of title containing an index or list of contents, with all pages numbered, having all maps properly coloured, clearly printed, and containing a full set of searches against the title. The committee advises solicitors acting for purchasers to reject any booklet, which does not reach an acceptable standard. Negative searches must always be furnished in the case of an unregistered title. Certified copies only of the title deeds are contained in the booklet of title and these must be properly investigated in the usual manner by the purchaser's solicitor and care must be taken to ensure that a proper root of title is available. The Law Society *Gazette* of July 2006 contains a Practice Note dealing with booklets of Land Registry title on CD-ROM for new houses. This does not endorse the practice but states that good practice is as follows:

(a) The purchasers' solicitors are entitled to obtain the documentation in hard copy at any time.

(b) All closing documents must be in hard copy.

(c) The procedure is only appropriate to Land Registry cases and particularly new developments.

(d) The furnishing of documentation by this method should be by agreement only and should not be imposed.

(e) When issuing a booklet of title on CD-ROM, the vendor's solicitor's initial letter should contain the following sentence: 'You are entitled to receive a hard copy of this booklet of title immediately on request'.

The booklet of title might include the following documentation. This sample list applies to a registered title and is not exhaustive.

12.6.2 SAMPLE DOCUMENTATION

1. Official certified copy folio and filed plan. This will contain details of the vendor's title. The registered owner should be 'the vendor' in the Contract for Sale.

2. Copy extract from memorandum and articles of association of the vendor company.

3. Copy certificate of incorporation of the vendor company. Note: in townhouse and apartment developments it is usual to include the memorandum and articles of association together with the certificate of incorporation of the management company to whom the common areas are transferred on completion.

4. Copy decision to grant planning permission and final grant of planning permission and/or outline planning permission and grant of approval. The builder of a new house must have obtained planning permission and complied with the Building Regulations and these are sent with the contracts.

5. Draft architect's certificate or opinion of compliance with planning permission and architect's opinion of compliance with the Building Regulations. These have been dealt with in **chapter 11** and care should be taken in reading the planning documentation to ensure that all the Law Society recommendations in relation to planning are complied with.

6. Copy commencement notice in relation to all works commenced after 1 June 1992. If the commencement notice was lodged with the Building Control Authority on or after 1 March 2014 a copy (or certified copy if the certificate on the building control register authority register is not accessible to the public) of the certificate of compliance on completion in the form prescribed by the Building Control (Amendment) Regulations, 2014, together with evidence that it was registered with the Building Control Authority must be obtained.

7. In the alternative where a commencement notice was lodged after 1 March 2014 and Part IIIC of the Building Regulations, 2014 do not apply, in such cases a non-statutory form of compliance from a competent person certifying compliance with all necessary requirements of the Building Regulations and that the property is exempt from Part IIIC is required. In the case of a new apartment or duplex a fire safety certificate must be obtained.

8. Copy letter or receipt from the local authority in respect of all financial contributions contained in the planning permission. If the planning documentation provides for the lodgement of a bond, evidence of payment of the same together with approval thereof by the planning authority should be included in the booklet of title. Note, however, that the purchaser will only be entitled to receive receipts in respect of all financial contributions due up to the date of closing.

9. Draft deed of conveyance/transfer.

10. Draft family law declaration.

11. Draft company secretary's certificate

12. Draft declaration of identity.

13. Approved Land Registry scheme map.

14. Final BER certificate and advisory report.

15. Disabiliy Access Certificate.

12.6.3 ORIGINAL OBJECTIONS AND REQUISITIONS ON TITLE

A set of requisitions on title with replies endorsed by the vendor will normally be included in the booklet of title. The purchaser's solicitor should check these carefully to see if additional requisitions should be raised. This may be restricted by the special conditions of the Contract for Sale as the time limit for raising such requisitions may be reduced from 14 days to a lesser period. It is not acceptable for the builder's solicitor to say that the purchaser's solicitor cannot raise any additional requisitions. He or she is obliged to do so despite any special condition to the contrary.

12.6.4 SECTION 72 DECLARATION

Section 72 of the Registration of Title Act, 1964 lists the burdens which, whether they are registered or not, affect registered land. The vendor provides the usual s 72 declaration confirming that none of the burdens listed in s 72 affects the land. It is preferable to obtain the long format of the statutory declaration, which recites s 72 in full.

12.6.5 DRAFT DECLARATION OF IDENTITY

A declaration of identity is usually prepared by the vendor's architect, and is provided to confirm that the property in sale is contained within the 'sold land' for which title is shown. The declaration must state that the site that the client wishes to purchase is wholly situate within the boundaries of the vendor's folio. It is also important to establish that all of the easements and services are within the boundaries of the folio and that the folio abuts on to the public roadway. This declaration should in all cases be shown to the purchaser in order that the location of his or her site may be carefully checked in relation to the map. The declaration should deal with all of the matters raised in requisition on title 23.2.d and f.

See sample declaration of identity as follows.

DECLARATION OF IDENTITY

Development at Lucan Heights, Co. Dublin.

I, HUGO LIPPI R.I.A.I. Architect of Donnybrook, in the City of Dublin aged 18 years and upwards do solemnly and sincerely declare as follows:

1. I am the Principal in the firm of D.A. Vinci, Architects and have been retained by Darius Property Company Limited in connection with its development of the lands at Lucan Heights, Co. Dublin being the lands comprised in Folio 11124F of the Register of Freeholders County of Dublin.

2. Site 1–41 inclusive form part of the development referred to at paragraph 1 above.

3. I have inspected the Land Registry map of Folio 11124F County Dublin and I say that the roads, footpaths, sewers and services abutting on and servicing the sites referred to at paragraph 2 above and leading to the public roadway are constructed entirely within the boundaries of the lands comprised in said Folio 11124F County Dublin.

4. That the map attached to the transfer to the purchaser in respect of the sites referred to at paragraph 2 above is identical in all respects to the Scheme Map for the development lodged in the Land Registry.

5. That all the sites referred to at paragraph 2 above are entirely situate within the boundaries of said Folio 11124F of the Register of Freeholders County Dublin.

6. All roads on the estate will be taken in charge by Dublin South County Council in accordance with the terms and conditions of the planning permission.

7. I make this solemn Declaration from facts within my own knowledge and for the benefit and satisfaction of the purchasers of the site numbers referred to at paragraph 2 above (and their mortgagees and assigns) conscientiously believing the same to be true and by virtue of the Statutory Declarations Act, 1938.

DECLARED before me.................................
A commissioner for oaths/practising solicitor
(Name of commissioner/practising solicitor in capitals)
By the said HUGO LIPPI
(Who is personally known to me)
(Or: who is identified to me by.....................
Who is personally known to me)
At................ in the City of Dublin
This   day of   20

_____
COMMISSIONER FOR OATHS/PRACTISING SOLICITOR

12.6.6 INDEMNITY IN RESPECT OF ROADS AND SERVICES

The builder will usually agree in the building agreement to construct the roads and kerbs in the development and to maintain the services. The danger for the purchaser is that the builder may default on this obligation and may go into liquidation before making the required financial contributions to the local authority. The planning permission will oblige the builder to complete the roads to the local authority's standard and, when all the financial contributions are discharged, the local authority will then take the roads and services in charge. Pending the taking in charge of the roads, footpaths, and services by the local authority the builder will issue an indemnity to the purchaser agreeing to maintain these until they are taken in charge. The draft indemnity is usually contained in the booklet of title (see requisition 23.1.d).

The purchaser's solicitor must also ensure that the deed of transfer to the purchaser contains the necessary easements, which the purchaser will need to reach the public highway from the property, and also those required so that the drains to the property can reach the public sewers. See sample indemnity as follows.

INDEMNITY RE ROADS AND SERVICES

THIS INDEMNITY made the   day of   20 , between Darius Property Company Limited having its registered office at 1 Tigris Avenue, Lucan, County Dublin (hereinafter called 'the vendor') of the One Part and   of   (hereinafter called 'the purchaser' of the Other Part).

WHEREAS:

1. Site No. Lucan Heights, Lucan, County Dublin is being transferred by the vendor to the purchaser.

2. The vendor is responsible for the construction and maintenance of the roads, sewers, water mains, public lighting, open spaces and landscaping works (hereinafter called 'the services') abutting on and servicing the said site until such time as the said services are taken in charge by the appropriate local authority.

3. Now the vendor hereby undertakes with the purchaser his/her/their executors, administrators, mortgagees and assigns:

a. That until such time as the said services are taken in charge by the local authority to construct (to a standard acceptable to the local authority) maintain and repair the services fronting and abutting on and servicing Site No. Lucan Heights, Lucan, County Dublin and to discharge the local authority charges on the taking over thereof and to indemnify and to keep indemnified the purchaser(s) his/her/their executors, administrators, mortgagees and assigns from and against all costs and claims, charges, demands and expenses in connection with the repair maintenance and taking over of the said services.

b. To take all reasonable steps to ensure that the said services are taken in charge by the appropriate local authority as soon as possible.

IN WITNESS WHEREOF the common seal of Darius Property Company Limited was affixed hereto the day and year herein WRITTEN.

PRESENT when the Common Seal
of Darius Property Company Limited
was affixed hereto.

12.6.7   INDEMNITY RE FOOTPATHS, KERBS, AND GRASS MARGINS

The purchaser's solicitors are often anxious to get an indemnity in relation to footpaths, kerbs, and grass margins, which matters are not usually covered in the indemnity provided by the builder/vendor. Therefore, an additional indemnity may be furnished dealing with these wherein the builder/vendor agrees to maintain and repair the footpaths, kerbs, and grass margins fronting and abutting on and servicing the site until they are taken in charge by the local authority or, alternatively, they may be covered by the insertion of the words 'footpaths, kerbs and grass margins' in the indemnity re roads and services above. The indemnity may be assigned to a subsequent purchaser of the new house if the roads and services are still not in charge.

12.6.8   FAMILY LAW DECLARATION/CERTIFICATE

When buying a new house a solicitor's certificate is usually furnished confirming that the property is not a family home/shared home within the meaning of the Family Home Protection Act, 1976 (as amended) or the Civil Partnership and Certain Rights and Obligations of Cohabitants Act, 2010. This may be acceptable where the vendor/builder is a company. However, where the vendor/builder of a new dwellinghouse/apartment is an individual it would be advisable for a purchaser to obtain a family law declaration sworn by that individual. While it may appear relatively straightforward for a solicitor to certify that a disposition is not affected by the provisions of the Family Home Protection Act, 1976 or the Civil Partnership Act, 2010 it is impossible to certify that any disposition is not reviewable or that proceedings have not been commenced or threatened by the vendor's spouse or civil partner or by a qualified cohabitant. Accordingly the vendor's solicitors may find themselves in personal difficulties if the certificate in question turns out to be incorrect. The solicitor should always check that the family law declaration/certificate is signed and dated.

Sample Family Law Certificate is as follows (Solicitor's Headed Paper)

RE: Hammurabi Developments Limited to Alexander Susa
Site 14, Lucan Heights, Lucan, County Dublin.

Dear Sirs,

As solicitors for Hammurabi Developments Limited, the registered owners of the lands known as Lucan Heights, being part of the lands comprised in Folio 11124F of the Register County of Dublin we hereby certify as follows:

1. That the site known as Site 14, Lucan Heights, Lucan, County Dublin consists of a plot of ground with a newly constructed dwellinghouse thereon which has never been resided in by a Director or a Member of Hammurabi Developments Limited and has never been occupied and is therefore not a family home within the meaning of the Family Home Protection Act, 1976 as amended by the Family Law Act, 1995.

2. That the property is not a shared home within the meaning of the term 'shared home' in Section 27 of the Civil Partnership and Certain Rights and Obligations of Cohabitants Act, 2010 (the 2010 Act).

3. That the provisions of the Family Law Act, 1981–1995 do not apply in that no Director of Hammurabi Developments has entered into an agreement to marry within the past three years, which has been terminated.

4. That the property is not subject to any application or order under the Judicial Separation and Family Law Reform Act, 1989, the Family Law Act, 1995 ('the 1995 Act') or the Family Law (Divorce) Act, 1996 ('the 1996 Act') or the 2010 Act and that the assurance of the property is not a disposition for the purposes of defeating a claim for financial relief (as defined in Section 35 of the 1995 Act, Section 37 of the 1996 Act and Section 137 of the 2010 Act).

Yours faithfully,

Solicitor

The booklet of title may contain other ancillary documents. It must be read in its entirety by the purchaser's solicitor and, once that has been done, the normal investigation of title procedure should be followed.

12.6.9   REQUISITIONS ON TITLE

12.6.9.1   Newly erected property

In a new house transaction, a set of requisitions on title with replies thereto is generally included in the booklet of title, which is sent with the contract documentation. The purchaser's solicitor should check the special conditions of the Contract for Sale to ensure that there is no prohibition against raising requisitions on title and that general conditions 17 and 18 have not been deleted.

Requisition 29 in the 2015 edition of the Law Society Objections and Requisitions on Title deals with newly erected property as follows.

12.6.9.2   Documents to be furnished

Requisition 29.1 provides that the following documentation should be furnished.

Draft assurance: requisition 29.1.a

In the case of newly erected property it is usual for the vendor's solicitor to furnish the draft assurance and site map for approval. This is different from the normal practice where the purchaser's solicitor prepares the draft assurance and submits it to the vendor's solicitor for approval. The draft deed should be checked to see the extent of the exceptions and reservations contained in it. It should also be checked in relation to any rights of way over the estate roadways reserved in favour of the purchaser. The deed of assurance will also include details of all other easements and rights in relation to pipes, drains, wires, cables, etc on, under, or over the property and statutory acknowledgement and undertaking for safe custody of title documents and all other reservations, covenants, conditions, and restrictions or any rights of any kind.

Draft site map: requisition 29.1.b

Previously in relation to registered land it was the practice to have a scheme map approved in the Land Registry and to have a copy of the Land Registry approved map attached to the deed of transfer. The draft map had to be checked to see whether it had the Land Registry stamp of approval as a scheme map endorsed thereon. Unless the map attached to the purchaser's deed of transfer conformed exactly to the scheme map which was lodged, the Land Registry would not affect registration of the purchase deed. It was important that the solicitor advised the purchaser client to examine the map carefully to ensure that the site being purchased was the site on the map attached to the draft deed (see **12.4.5**).

The practice in relation to scheme maps was amended in respect of all applications lodged in the Land Registry after 10 May 2005. The Land Registry will assign plan numbers to the sites on the scheme map and the plan numbers will be printed on a separate page referred to as a 'legend'. The legend will give the road names and site numbers of each site together with the relevant plan number. The original scheme map and a copy of the legend will be returned to the applicant.

This new facility enables practitioners to include the plan number and scheme map reference in the transfer. It is no longer necessary to lodge a map with the transfer where the scheme map has been approved. The site will be pre-mapped and its plan number will appear on the legend.

Land Registry mapping requirements must be strictly adhered to.

Draft statutory declaration of identity: requisition 29.1.c

Requisition 29.1.c provides that the following should be furnished:

> *Draft statutory declaration of identity by the vendor's architect or other competent person confirming that the entire of the property as shown on the site map and the rights of way, easements and the services relating thereto form part of the lands to which the vendor has shown title.*

The purchaser must receive a comprehensive declaration of identity dealing with the property, the access, and the services. The declaration of identity in relation to new house purchase is generally contained in the booklet of title. It requires the architect to confirm that the site in sale is wholly situate within the boundary of the folio when the title is registered in the Land Registry. In the case of unregistered title the architect must confirm that the site is wholly situate within the lands comprised in the title documents. The architect must further certify that the rights of way, all the easements, and services are entirely within the lands owned by the grantor. It is customary to get confirmation in the declaration of identity that the site abuts on to the public roadway. This declaration should be shown to the purchaser so that the location of his or her site may be carefully checked in relation to the map.

Draft indemnity in relation to roads, footpaths, sewers and all services: requisition 29.1.d

General condition 10 of the building agreement contains provisions in relation to roads, footpaths, sewers, and services to be provided by the builder and the taking in charge of these services by the local authority in due course. No reference is made in this condition to kerbs, grass margins, or open spaces. The builder normally issues an indemnity to the purchaser containing an undertaking to maintain the roads, footpaths, and services pending their taking in charge. Where the builder is also the landowner this indemnity will be included as a covenant on the part of the landowner in the deed of assurance. The planning permission will usually contain a requirement for the lodgement of a bond or other security for the taking in charge of the estate.

Draft indemnity in relation to defects: requisition 29.1.e

The indemnity in relation to defects is generally contained in the building agreement: see general condition 8(a), (d), and (e).

Evidence of registration with HomeBond, Premier, or alternative policy scheme together with a copy of the policy documents: requisition 29.1.f

The purchaser should receive the HomeBond/Premier or alternative insurance policy documents and certificate of insurance (registration) with the contract documentation.

The certificate of insurance (final certification) must be handed over on completion and the purchaser should refuse to close if it is not available.

12.6.9.3 Documents to be handed over on closing

Under requisition 29.2 the following documentation should be handed over on closing:

Original assurance: requisition 29.2.a

Original deed of assurance duly completed with a certificate of compliance with the building or other covenants endorsed thereon.

The deed should be completed by all parties and should have the Land Registry approved map annexed thereto. It should be checked to see if the certificate of compliance with the building covenant is on the deed and is signed and dated. The stamping of the deed will be a matter for the purchaser and details of the vendor's PPSN/tax reference number (together with those of all parties to the deed) must be provided. E-stamping and payment of stamp duty online is now mandatory since 1 July 2011. In relation to the Land Registry approved map schemes and deeds of transfer please note **14.2.8.3**.

Architect's statutory declaration of identity in accordance with requisition 29.1.c: requisition 29.2.b

As dealt with earlier the declaration should state that the house is situated within the confines of the site as shown on the map attached to the deed and that all the roads and services are situated within the lands comprised in the folio or maps attached to the title deeds.

Indemnities under seal in relation to roads, footpaths, sewers, and all services and in relation to defects: requisition 23.2.c and d

The original indemnity regarding roads and services and the structural defects indemnity (if not contained in the building agreement) should be furnished. If made by a company it should be under seal and the sealing should be in accordance with the articles of association of the company.

Architect's certificate: requisition 23.2.e

Architect's certificate confirming that all buildings have been erected within the confines of the site as per the deed map.

It may be that this is already included in the declaration of identity. It must be checked carefully because of the many inaccuracies that arise in relation to maps.

The final certificate with HomeBond, Premier or alternative policy /scheme. 29.1.f

The insurance certificate (registration) and certificate of insurance (final certification) under the HomeBond scheme.

This requisition provides for the HomeBond/Premier or other Insurance policy/scheme documentation to be handed over on completion. The certificate of insurance (final) is an extremely important document for the purchaser, particularly in relation to structural defects indemnity cover for ten years. If this form is not available the transaction should not be closed.

Registered land: requisition 29.3

If the property is registered land furnish an additional certified copy of the assurance.

A certified copy of the deed of transfer should be obtained, as it will contain details of the exceptions and reservations and cross-indemnities. In the event of a future sale, if this copy deed has not been kept with the title, a certified copy deed will not have to be bespoken from the Land Registry thus preventing delays.

12.7 Documents Required on Completion

12.7.1 CHECKLIST OF DOCUMENTS REQUIRED ON COMPLETION

The following is a list of documents normally required on completion of a new house transaction. The documents will vary on occasion.

(a) Deed of assurance to the purchaser duly sealed by the vendor (where the vendor is a company) with certificate of compliance with the building covenant (if any) endorsed. The type of deed will depend on the nature of the title in question whether registered or unregistered. In the case of a new house the deed will be either a deed of transfer or deed of conveyance. In the case of a new apartment the purchase deed will usually be a long lease.

(b) Booklet of title duly certified as at the closing date.

(c) Declaration of identity.

(d) Extract from memorandum and articles of association of vendor company showing its power to sell and its sealing requirements and the certificate of incorporation.

(e) Final grant of planning permission.

(f) Architect's certificate confirming that the house has been built in accordance with the planning permission furnished and architect's opinion of compliance with the Building Regulations and that all conditions therein have been complied with. These should be in the approved RIAI or Law Society formats.

(g) Letters from the local authority confirming compliance with the financial conditions contained in the planning permission.

(h) E-discharge/release/vacate or partial release/vacate of any mortgage or charge, which affects the property and appropriate Property Registration Authority fees if applicable.

(i) Indemnity in respect of roads, services, and public lighting under seal.

(j) Indemnity under seal in respect of kerbs, open spaces, and grass margins.

(k) Structural defects guarantee under seal and providing for the purchaser's common law rights or guarantee (if contained in the building agreement they should be under seal).

(l) HomeBond/Premier or alternative policy/scheme documentation to include certificates of insurance (registration) and (final) (if not already furnished).

(m) Family law declaration of the vendor or vendor's solicitor certificate.

(n) Keys of the property or letter for keys.

(o) PPS numbers or tax reference numbers of the vendors for the stamp duty return.

(p) Company secretary certificate as per requisition 18.3.c(5).

(q) Searches.

(r) Final BER certificate and advisory report (note this must be produced before and not at completion).

12.7.2 COMPLETION DOCUMENTS FOR REGISTERED LAND

The following documents are in addition to those listed at **12.7.1**:

(a) Up-to-date certified copy folio and filed plan.

(b) Certified copy s 72 declaration (long version).

(c)   Undertaking by vendor to discharge Land Registry queries.

(d)   Certificate of no dealing pending or certificate that the dealings do not affect the property.

(e)   Land Registry approved map or filed plan.

(f)   Certificate from the estate architect that a scheme map has been lodged and that the Land Registry has approved the transfer map.

12.7.3   ADDITIONAL DOCUMENTS FOR UNREGISTERED LAND

(a)   Official search against all parties on title.

(b)   Certified copies or original of documents of prior title.

(c)   Statutory acknowledgement and undertaking for safe custody of prior title deeds.

(d)   Land Registry compliant map for first registration application.

12.8   Miscellaneous Matters

12.8.1   C2 OR TAX CLEARANCE CERTIFICATE

The builder's solicitors should ensure that their client is in a position to furnish either a C2 or a tax clearance certificate expiry date.

Assuming that the builder's tax affairs are in order there should be no problem in obtaining a tax clearance certificate. The procedure is that the Department of the Environment sends the builder a stamped application form for this certificate (known as a TC1). The builder then fills in all relevant details including tax number. The Collector General issues a clearance certificate known as a TC2. The clearance certificate is dated and specifies the expiry date of the clearance certificate, which is usually one year later than the date of this certificate. There is provision in recent finance legislation giving the builder the option of producing a tax clearance certificate as an alternative to obtaining a capital gains tax clearance certificate. If such certificate is available the purchaser will be exempt from deducting the 15 per cent withholding tax and will not require a CG50A certificate.

12.8.2   OPTIONAL EXTENSIONS/GARAGE CONVERSIONS/ CONSERVATORIES

Some builders provide in the house plans for the possibility of an extended kitchen, utility room, garage conversion to family room, conservatory, etc. It is vital in such circumstances that, before contracts are signed, the vendor's solicitor in writing should confirm that the contemporaneous construction of such extras does not increase the net internal habitable floor area so as to infringe the requirements specified in the floor area compliance certificate and bring the house outside the permitted floor area limits and is not in breach of the planning permission obtained.

The purchaser should arrange to have the works carried out post closing.

12.9   The Deed of Assurance

12.9.1   INTRODUCTION

The Contract for Sale in a new house transaction normally provides that the purchase deed will be in a certain form, a specimen of which will usually be contained in the booklet of title. The deed deals with the title to the site and the location of the site on which the new house will be built. It also sets out the necessary easements and covenants in schedules to the deed. If the title is registered a specimen deed of transfer will be provided or, alternatively, for unregistered titles a deed of conveyance will be furnished.

Note: a lease of a new house is void under the provisions of the Landlord and Tenant (Ground Rents) (No 1) Act, 1978.

Under the terms of the standard purchase deed the site owner sells the site to the purchaser and the consideration expressed is usually the value of that site, normally called the site fine; the purchaser in turn covenants to build a house on that site.

12.9.2 THE DEED—REGISTERED LAND

A sample 2010 deed of transfer for building estates has been prepared by the Law Society Conveyancing Committee.

Because part only of the vendor's property is being transferred the deed will be in the form of a transfer of part.

12.9.2.1 Definitions section

The estate

The estate relates to the vendor's land of which the building estate is comprised and will normally refer to a folio when dealing with registered land or to the deed of assurance whereby the vendor acquired title in the case of unregistered land.

The sold land

The sold land is what the purchaser buys. It is described more fully in the first schedule to the deed.

The retained property

The retained property is everything on the estate other than the land purchased by the purchaser, ie all of the lands originally owned by the vendor other than the sold land.

The parties/owners

The vendor should be the registered owner(s) of the property in fee simple of the property and not the builder if these are two different parties.

The purchaser's name is usually left blank on the specimen deed that is submitted to the purchaser's solicitor by the vendor's solicitor, and should be inserted by the purchaser's solicitor having first confirmed all details with his client.

The operative words

A Land Registry transfer would usually use the words 'AB the registered owner as beneficial owner hereby transfers' in the operative part of the deed.

The consideration

Where there is a building covenant then the consideration is the site value as contained in the Contract for Sale.

Capacity

Although it is not a Land Registry requirement it is necessary to have the vendor transfer in the capacity as beneficial owner so that the purchaser will have the benefit of the covenants implied by those words (see **chapter 8**).

12.9.2.2   Statutory certificates

The usual statutory certificates incorporated in the deed may include a certificate pursuant to s 238 of the Companies Act, 2014 (formerly s 29 of the Companies Act, 1990) (where applicable).

12.9.2.3   Easements rights and privileges and reservations: the second and third schedules

The vendor may require rights over the sold lands. Such rights are known as reservations because they are retained from the land sold. These will be set out in a schedule to the transfer/conveyance. The words used should make it clear which land is benefited and the precise nature of the right concerned. If it is a right of way, is it with all kinds of transport at all times?

The purchaser should be granted rights of way over the sewers, drains, and roads that are not included in the sold land and that form part of the estate. The easements, rights, and privileges contained in the second schedule of the specimen deed of transfer are rights required by the purchaser for the necessary enjoyment of the sold land. Prior to the Land and Conveyancing Law Reform Act, 2009 it was normal to restrict these rights to those roads and services that were then in existence or which would be constructed within 21 years from the date of the deed to avoid infringing the rule against perpetuities. Section 16(d) of the Land and Conveyancing Law Reform Act, 2009 has now abolished the rule against perpetuities.

The solicitor must be able to explain to the client the effects of these reservations and the circumstances in which they remain in force. It is no longer necessary to include words of limitation when reserving easements by deed ('to his heirs, successors, assigns', etc) by virtue of s 67(1) of the 2009 Act.

12.9.2.4   Covenants: the fourth schedule

Apart from the covenant to build, the deed may contain certain covenants by the purchaser for the benefit of the rest of the estate. The usual types of covenants are those listed in the fourth schedule. The purchaser may be required to enter into covenants as to the use of the sold land; for example, the use of the sold land may be restricted to a residential user. It is common for a covenant to be inserted providing for the house to be painted every three years and specifying the quality of paint required to be used. Any unusual covenants should be brought to the attention of the purchaser and his or her lending institution.

It is provided in the specimen deeds in the appendices that the vendor has laid out the estate in plots for development as a residential estate and has caused a common form of transfer to be prepared and used in the sale of each plot. This is to enable any subsequent purchaser of the house to sue the subsequent purchaser of an adjoining house on the estate to enforce these covenants notwithstanding that there is no direct contractual relationship between them.

12.9.3   THE DEED—UNREGISTERED LAND

A sample 2010 edition of the deed of conveyance has been prepared by the Law Society Conveyancing Committee. The deed of assurance for unregistered land is in basically the same format as the deed of transfer, except that the appropriate words of grant, for example 'hereby assign' or 'hereby grant and convey', are used. Because the vendor is normally selling part only of the property, and certified copies only of the prior title will be furnished, it is customary to include in the deed the vendor's undertaking for the safe custody and production of the original deeds. See paragraph 'H'. The original title deeds being retained by the vendor are listed in the sixth schedule.

12.9.4 THE BUILDING COVENANT

It is important to ensure that the certificate of compliance with the building covenant is endorsed on the original deed of transfer/conveyance on the completion of the sale. Failure to do so may result in problems arising in a subsequent resale of the property. The certificate of compliance must be signed and dated.

The deed of transfer will be executed in duplicate. There will be an original and a counterpart deed, one of which is returned to the vendor's solicitor in due course.

12.10 Structural Defects

12.10.1 INTRODUCTION

In most new house transactions things generally go smoothly, the sale closes, and the client happily takes up possession of the new residence. However, a solicitor must be prepared for situations where the client may revert to the solicitor concerning physical problems with the new home, ie there may be structural or other defects or faults in the house which have only come to light after closure.

In this event there are three possible avenues of action to pursue against the builder on behalf of the client:

(a)   an action at common law against the builder;

(b)   an action against the builder for breach of contract; or

(c)   recourse to the National House Building Guarantee Company Ltd pursuant to the HomeBond insurance scheme or Premier or similar insurance scheme.

12.10.2 COMMON LAW

At common law the purchaser of a new house under a building agreement—provided there are no specific warranties or guarantees which might cancel out the common law rights—is entitled to have his or her home built:

(a)   in a good and workmanlike manner;

(b)   using good and proper materials; and

(c)   fit for human habitation.

There are rights contained in every building agreement and, if the builder is in breach of any of these common law obligations, the purchaser may pursue him or her at common law through the courts for negligence. The purchaser's rights to issue proceedings last for a period of six years, usually from the date when the defect became apparent.

The Standard Building Agreement contains, at clause 8(e), a provision, which guarantees the purchaser's common law rights. The usual clause is:

'Nothing in this Agreement or in any collateral or ancillary document shall deprive the employer of his rights of Common Law which are hereby confirmed.'

This is to ensure that any warranties or maintenance agreements contained in the contract do not override the purchaser's common law rights. It is vital to ensure that this clause is in the building agreement before the purchaser signs.

As may be seen from the definition of these common law rights, the wording is very broad and is deliberately so to enable judges to define, in certain specific cases or actions, the liabilities or responsibilities of the builder defendant. The rights are vital and ongoing and arguably may be termed the vanguard of the purchaser's action against the builder.

Where the building agreement is executed under seal the purchaser can sue the builder for breach of its terms for a period of 12 years (Statute of Limitations, 1957, s 11).

12.10.3 BREACH OF CONTRACT

As seen previously, under the terms of the building agreement, the builder is obliged to complete the new house to a certain high standard with good and proper materials strictly in accordance with plans, specifications, and planning permission and building regulations. If the builder fails to abide by the terms of the building agreement, he would obviously be in breach of contract and normally a civil action ensues from this. The civil action will normally combine breach of the common law rights as noted earlier, together with breach of the terms of the building agreement.

Most building agreements contain a maintenance agreement, whereby the builder undertakes to rectify any major structural defects arising over a said period, usually 18 months (see condition 8(a)(i)); this contractual warranty runs parallel with the NHBGS Home-Bond scheme. Usually the builder will exclude certain minor defects from the ambit of this structural defects warranty. Again, if there are problems with the house, he or she may be in breach of the warranty and therefore in breach of the contract as aforesaid.

The builder may, in addition, undertake to repair minor defects, which appear within six months from closing, and this basically comprises an after-sale service for minor defects (see condition 8(a)(ii) of the building agreement). However, condition 8 contains a number of exclusions and it is important to point these out to the purchaser before he or she signs the building agreement.

12.10.4 HOMEBOND

12.10.4.1 Introduction

The third possibility of action that a purchaser of a defective house has is a remedy under HomeBond Insurance Services Limited ('HomeBond Insurance').

HomeBond Insurance provides new home purchasers with insurance cover, underwritten by Allianz plc. Where the builder is registered with the National House Building Guarantee Company Limited ('the Company') the property will have the benefit of the HomeBond scheme. HomeBond Insurance will indemnify the policyholder for a period of ten years after the effective date on the certificate of insurance (final certification) in respect of the repair of major damage caused by building defects in the original construction carried out pursuant to the building contract. HomeBond Insurance will also indemnify the policyholder for a period of five years from the effective date specified in the certificate of insurance (final certification) for the cost of complete or partial rebuilding or rectifying work as a result of ingress of water caused to the housing unit by defects and the cost of repairing and making good any defects in chimneys and flues causing an imminent danger to the health and safety of occupants, subject to the exclusions and conditions contained in the HomeBond insurance policy document.

The terms and ambit of the scheme are set out in section 1 of the HomeBond insuring agreement. This document incorporates the definitions, insuring agreement, exclusions, conditions, certificates, and any endorsements for the full details of indemnity. It is important to read this document to the purchaser so that he or she is aware of the builder's/developer's and the purchaser's/policyholder's own obligations under the scheme. Upon the issue of the certificate of insurance (final certification) the Company agrees that it shall become bound to the purchaser in the terms of the HomeBond policy document.

The certificate of insurance (final certification) is issued by HomeBond Insurance to the policyholder on or following satisfactory structural completion of each new housing unit.

12.10.4.2 Processing a complaint

The procedure for processing a complaint, claims, and enquiries is set out in HomeBond policy document section 6. On discovery of any occurrence or circumstance that is likely to give rise to a claim under any section of the policy the policyholder must give immediate written notice to HomeBond Insurance. The policyholder must take all responsible steps to prevent further loss or damage, and must submit in writing full details of the claim and supply all correspondence, reports, plans, certificates, specifications, quantities, information, assistance, and cooperation as may be required including the completion of any claim form required. The HomeBond policy document is entered into at contract stage when both it, and the certificate of insurance (registration), are furnished with the contract documents by the builder's solicitor to the purchaser. The HomeBond policy is an insurance contract between the policyholder and Allianz plc, entered into by the developer on the policyholder's behalf and it is based on the details provided to Allianz by the developer.

The certificate of insurance (registration) is issued by HomeBond Insurance to the policyholder to signify acceptance of each housing unit for the insurance as detailed in the policy document.

12.10.4.3 The purchaser's obligations

The purchaser's obligations are set out in section 6 of the HomeBond policy document. The purchaser is obliged to send written notice to the member/builder as soon as possible after the appearance of any defect:

(a) in the case of any major defect within the meaning defined in the HomeBond policy document at section 1.3 not later than the end of the tenth year from the date of issue of the certificate of insurance (final certification) by the Company; and

(b) in the case of other defects within the meaning defined therein, ie in section 1.2 (lesser defects) such as remedial works in respect of smoke penetration from the chimney breasts to the habitual areas of the dwelling causing an imminent danger to the health and safety of occupants or water penetration through the main structural elements of the house, roof flashings or roof valleys of the dwelling, caused by a defect in the design, workmanship, materials or components of the waterproofing elements of the waterproof envelope within each housing unit, the claim must be made within five years from the date of the issue of the certificate of insurance (final certification).

The financial limits on liability are set out in section 2 of the HomeBond policy document.

12.10.4.4 Successors in title

Neither the member/builder nor the Company has any liability to any successor in title of the purchaser named in the agreement who has acquired title after the owner of the dwelling for the time being knew, or should have known, of the major defect or where reasonable examination by a competent surveyor, architect, or engineer would have disclosed the major defect.

12.10.4.5 Financial limit: section 2

The limit of the Company pursuant to the HomeBond agreement in relation to any major defect or number of defects is €200,000 in relation to any one housing unit or the reconstruction cost for the housing unit whichever is the lesser. Arguably this amount is quite small in the overall context of the remedying of a major defect on a modern house when costs and professional fees etc are taken into account. This amount has been exceeded in some cases.

In relation to structural defects, as with deposit protection, there are both time limits and financial limits in place and these must be pointed out to an intending purchaser.

12.10.4.6 Cumulative liability of HomeBond

The total liability of the Company in respect of any one member (subscribing developer) or builder is limited to €2 million for structural defects irrespective of the nature of the liability or how it arises. See HomeBond policy document, section 2 (1.1, 1.2, and 1.3).

12.11 Deposits

12.11.1 HISTORICAL BACKGROUND

The payment of deposits by the purchaser to either the builder or to the builder's solicitor has long been a matter of concern both to the purchaser and to the purchaser's solicitor. It is usual, in the case of a new house purchase for the purchaser, to be required to pay a booking deposit directly to either the builder or the builder's auctioneer/agent to secure the house. In practice these booking deposits are very often paid to the builder or selling agent on site. When the number of new houses coming on the market was at an all time high purchasers were prepared to pay a considerable booking deposit before even consulting their solicitor and, of course, did so entirely at their own risk. A further deposit is paid on the signing of the contract and, in some areas outside Dublin, various stage payment deposits are payable throughout the construction period for one-off houses.

It has generally been accepted that the builder is entitled to receive the deposits and use them to fund the development. These deposits, when paid to a builder's solicitor, are not held as stakeholder but are paid over to the builder and are taken into the builder's cash flow.

12.11.2 'SUBJECT TO CONTRACT'

Because many booking deposits are paid before a contract is entered into, the purchaser ranks as an unsecured creditor in the event of the subsequent insolvency of the builder. Any booking deposit paid by a purchaser on site or elsewhere should be paid on the usual 'subject to contract' terms and should state that it is not intended to be a written memorandum for the purposes of s 51 of the Land and Conveyancing Law Reform Act, 2009. This, however, rarely happens and the deposit is at risk until formal contracts are signed.

12.11.3 PURCHASER PROTECTION PLEDGE

The purchaser may have signed a purchaser protection pledge. This is a code of practice initiated by the Irish Home Builders Association (IHBA) and the Construction Industry Federation (CIF). It provides that upon receipt of a booking deposit paid to a member of the IHBA, the member will issue a contract to the purchaser at the price agreed between the purchaser and the member when the booking deposit was paid. It places a responsibility on the purchaser's solicitor to return the completed contract and balance deposit within three weeks from the date of issue of the contract. This pledge may provide peace of mind to a purchaser concerned that the builder may sell on the house to another purchaser.

If consulted by a purchaser before a booking deposit has been paid, a solicitor should advise that such deposit should not be paid directly to the builder unless some evidence is forthcoming that the deposit is covered under the National House Building Guarantee Scheme (ie HomeBond insurance is available).

Practitioners are reminded that in order for the purchaser to avail of the protection afforded by HomeBond, the deposit cheque should be made payable to the party registered under the HomeBond insurance scheme. Where booking deposits are paid to an agent, or to someone other than the person so registered, confirmation should be given by the builder's solicitor that this money has been passed on to the registered party. The purchaser's solicitor should ensure that the original HomeBond policy document and certificate of insurance (registration) are in their possession before releasing the cheque to the builder's solicitor. If these are not available, confirmation should be furnished by the builder's solicitor that any deposit will be held by them as stakeholder until the original issues and is in the purchaser's solicitor's possession. It is important to remember that booking deposits or any other contract deposits are not covered under the HomeBond insurance scheme if paid before the registration of the dwelling in respect of which the payment is made (condition 1.1 of the HomeBond policy document).

If the builder is not covered by HomeBond, the purchaser's solicitor should advise the client to pay the deposit through the solicitor's office to the builder's solicitor to be held by them as stakeholder pending completion. It is unlikely however that the builder's solicitor will agree to this.

12.11.4 *ROCHE V PEILOW*

Prior to the Supreme Court decision in *Roche v Peilow* [1985] IR 232 it was accepted as good conveyancing practice for purchasers' solicitors to advise clients in writing of the risks involved in paying deposits to builders or their solicitors. Clients were to be advised in writing that all deposits paid over—even those paid through the builder's solicitors—would be released immediately to the builder and would not be held as stakeholder. They were further advised that in the event of a builder becoming insolvent there was little chance of their deposits being recovered because the client would rank as an unsecured creditor. Most builders borrow very substantial amounts when buying development land. Their borrowings are generally secured by a fixed legal charge or mortgage in favour of a lending institution that will have priority in an insolvency situation. On signing the contract to purchase a new house the purchaser acquires an equitable right only. This equitable right ranks second to any fixed charge on the site. It may be protected in some small measure by registering the contract in the relevant registry but this procedure is rarely adopted.

To reiterate—it was accepted that any solicitor who followed the previously outlined standard conveyancing practice was protected in any subsequent negligence action by simply showing that the client had been warned in these respects. However, in the case of *Roche v Peilow* it was held that to follow what had been accepted as standard conveyancing practice to date was no longer acceptable.

Briefly the facts of *Roche v Peilow* are as follows. Mr and Mrs Roche consulted their solicitor, Mr Peilow, concerning the purchase of a new house in Cork. They were given the usual written advice concerning the risk to their deposit in the event of the builder going into liquidation. Nevertheless, they decided to proceed. It was the practice in Cork, as indeed it still is in respect of one-off houses, to adopt the stage payment system. The Roches paid an initial deposit followed by stage payment deposits totalling 75 per cent of the overall purchase price before completion. None of the advice conveyed to Mr and Mrs Roche dealt with the possibility of the site being encumbered with a mortgage. In fact, there was a prior equitable mortgage by deposit in favour of a bank affecting the site. Prior to completion, the builder went into liquidation. The purchasers lost their deposit and sued Mr Peilow for negligence. The High Court held that Mr Peilow had advised them correctly having followed standard conveyancing practice. On appeal to the Supreme Court it was held that Mr Peilow was guilty of negligence. The only way in which the equitable mortgage in favour of the bank would have been discovered was by the solicitor making a Companies Registration Office search prior to execution of the contract. It was not at that time the practice to make such searches until before completion. The Supreme Court held that Mr Peilow was negligent because he had not, prior to the client signing the contract, made searches in the Companies Registration Office to see whether or not the land was encumbered. If this search had been carried out and the existence of the equitable mortgage made known to Mr and Mrs Roche they might not have proceeded with the purchase.

Both Henchy J and McCarthy J in their decision stated that to blindly follow standard conveyancing practice simply because it was standard conveyancing practice was inadequate and Mr Peilow was negligent for so doing. This has implications, of course, which extend far beyond deposits.

12.11.5 THE RECOMMENDED PROCEDURE FOR DEPOSITS

Arising from *Roche v Peilow* it is recommended that solicitors should now adopt the following procedures where either: (1) the deposit is not being held as stakeholder by the vendor's solicitor, or (2) the deposit is not guaranteed under HomeBond:

(a)   advise the client at the very first opportunity that any deposits paid to the builder are at risk and that the client ranks as an unsecured creditor and will probably lose the deposit if the builder goes into liquidation;

(b)   request the builder's solicitor to hold the deposit as stakeholder. If this is done the transaction may proceed just as for a second-hand house purchase and the following procedures may be ignored;

(c)   if the builder's solicitor refuses to hold the deposit as stakeholder then, prior to signing the contract, the following searches must be made by the purchaser's solicitor:

    (i)   registered land (where the builder is a company): Companies Registration Office search, Land Registry search, Judgments Office search, and a planning search;

    (ii)   registered land (where the builder is an individual): Land Registry search, Judgments Office search, Bankruptcy Office search, and a planning search;

    (iii)   unregistered land (where the builder is a company): Registry of Deeds search, Companies Registration Office search, Judgments Office search, and a planning search;

    (iv)   unregistered land (where the builder is an individual): Registry of Deeds search, Judgments Office search, Bankruptcy Office search, and a planning search;

(d)   when the results of the searches become available, if they disclose no prior legal or equitable mortgage (highly unlikely) the client may be advised that, although he or she runs the risk of some financial loss and suffering and considerable inconvenience should the builder become insolvent, he or she should at least be able to exercise his or her equitable right in respect of the site;

(e)   if the results of these searches disclose a prior legal or equitable mortgage (which is highly likely), it must be sent to the builder's solicitor seeking an explanation of all acts appearing, together with a request to discharge all such acts pre contract or the mortgagee could be asked to join in the purchase deed. If this request is turned down, the purchaser's solicitor could ask for a letter of undertaking from the mortgagee agreeing that the mortgage will be discharged in consideration of a specific sum. It is unlikely that the mortgagee will issue such letter;

(f)   when a reply is received from the builder's solicitor the purchaser's solicitor should write to the purchaser in the following terms:
    (i)   explain that the builder insists on receiving the deposit and that it will not be held as stakeholder;
    (ii)   state that the deposit will be lost in the event of the builder becoming insolvent and stressing the inadvisability of entry into the transaction;
    (iii)   advise on all mortgages and, if such is the case, the amount required by the financial institution to release these mortgages should the builder run into trouble;
    (iv)   ask the purchaser to issue clear instructions if the deposit is to be released; and
    (v)   always obtain clear written instructions from the client authorising the solicitor to proceed despite the warnings concerning the risk posed by the existence of the encumbrance.

12.11.6   STAGE PAYMENTS OUTSIDE THE HOMEBOND INSURANCE SCHEME

12.11.6.1   Generally

The Law Society has never approved of stage payments and has issued many Practice Notes outlining its disapproval. Contracts entered into after 30 June 2007 for new houses in a housing estate will not include provisions for the making of stage payments or interim payments. The practice of stage payments for housing estates where the builder is a member of the Irish Home Builders Association ceased on 30 June 2007. This does not apply to one-off or specially commissioned houses. While the protection afforded by the Home-Bond scheme offers increased protection to purchasers' deposits it cannot protect purchasers from the difficulties and problems which would arise if the builder were to become insolvent, after stage payments were made on or above the limits set out in the scheme and before a transfer of title has been executed in the purchasers' favour. Accordingly, the Law Society Conveyancing Committee, in its Practice Note in the *Gazette* of June 1996, advised practitioners that in order to protect their purchaser clients they should ensure that title to the site should pass from the builder/developer to the client on the occasion of the making of the first stage payment outside the protection offered by HomeBond. The purchaser's solicitor should either get the deed of transfer/conveyance or alternatively confirmation from the builder's solicitor that it has been executed and that it will be held in trust pending completion.

In practice it was the requirement of all lending institutions in areas where the stage payment system operated to insist on the purchaser's/borrower's solicitor obtaining the deed of transfer to the purchaser before the first draw down of the loan.

See **12.3.1** for details of the application to the High Court in December 2001 in relation to *inter alia* stage payments.

12.11.6.2 The stage payment system

In areas where the stage payment system operated, legal title passed to the purchaser on payment of the balance of the site fine and the first stage payment as stipulated in the building agreement. The deed of assurance together with all title documents (save planning) were handed over to the purchaser's solicitor who proceeded to stamp and register the deed in the normal course. As the construction of the house had not been completed, it followed that both the architect's certificate of compliance with planning permission and HomeBond certificate of insurance (final certification) were not available.

When the house was completed, the purchaser's solicitor received a completion notice from the builder's solicitor. On receipt of this notice the purchaser was advised to arrange an inspection of the house by an architect/engineer and to obtain a snag list. When all matters outlined in the snag list were resolved, the final stage payment was made to the builder's solicitor at which stage the purchaser's solicitor was furnished with the planning documentation and the certificate of insurance (final certification).

12.11.7 HOMEBOND DEPOSIT PROTECTION

Although the warnings and ground rules set out in *Roche v Peilow* still apply in certain circumstances, the plight of purchasers and their solicitors has been ameliorated somewhat with the introduction of deposit bonding through the HomeBond scheme.

12.11.7.1 Background to HomeBond

The National House Building Guarantee Scheme was established in 1978 by the Construction Industry Federation with the approval of the Department of the Environment. Initially, the scheme provided a guarantee in respect of major structural defects to purchasers of new houses purchased within the terms of the scheme. It failed to guarantee the solvency of builders during the course of construction leaving purchaser's deposits open to serious risks, particularly in view of the increasingly high booking deposits and stage payments sought by builders. On 25 January 1995, the scheme was upgraded and extended with the introduction of loss of deposit cover on the insolvency of builders as an extension of the existing structural defects cover. It now provides an insuring contract between the policy holder/purchaser and Allianz plc.

HomeBond Insurance, in addition to providing structural defect insurance, also provides deposit and stage payment cover for new houses and apartments. Once the certificate of insurance (final certification) has issued HomeBond Insurance provides financial cover for the loss of money deposited for the construction or purchase of a new house or apartment.

12.11.7.2 HomeBond policy document and certificate of insurance (registration)

The HomeBond Insurance policy document replaces the guarantee agreement. The new certificate of insurance (registration) is a document issued by HomeBond Insurance to signify acceptance of each housing unit for the insurance as detailed in the policy document. Ensure that the purchaser gets the original certificate of insurance and not a photocopy; the original may have been sent to another prospective purchaser.

The purchaser, on receiving the HomeBond policy document, becomes bound by all of its terms and conditions. The HomeBond policy document and certificate of insurance (registration) sets out the level of cover in relation to deposits, major structural defects, the general limits on HomeBond's liability, exclusions and conditions, and claims procedures. It also contains a definition section. The purchaser should be given a copy of this document to become familiar with its contents.

12.11.7.3 Stage payment cover—HomeBond policy document, section 1.1

The HomeBond insurance scheme, while improving the lot of the purchasers of a new house in relation to both structural defects and deposits, has both financial and time limits to the cover provided. The HomeBond policy document also reduces the liability of the Company towards its members. Potential purchasers should be warned of the shortcomings of the scheme in relation to these limitations.

Where the final certification has not issued, if due to insolvency, examinership, or fraud the developer does not commence work or fails to complete work on a housing unit after work has commenced HomeBond Insurance will have the option to pay the additional costs required to complete the housing unit and the policy will be cancelled with immediate effect or to refund the loss of money paid by the policyholder to the developer as part payment for the construction of the housing unit and the policy will be cancelled with immediate effect.

Indemnity provided under section 1.1 of the policy is provided only for the following periods of time:

(a) where the certificate of insurance (final certification) has not issued in respect of the housing unit then a claim must be submitted within two years;

(b) where the certificate of insurance (final certification) has been issued in respect of the housing unit, a claim must be submitted within six months of the effective date on the certificate of insurance (final certification).

The financial limits are contained in section 2 of the HomeBond policy document.

Section 2(1.1) provides that the amount payable by the company in relation to any dwelling is limited to a maximum of 50 per cent of the purchase price, subject to a limit of €100,000 for any one housing unit.

In each case, the amount of any payment by HomeBond is reduced to take into account any value allowances or credits, which are either due or have been received by the purchaser.

The certificate of insurance (final certification) is defined in the insurance policy document and is issued by HomeBond Insurance on or following satisfactory structural completion of each housing unit. It is a vital document for both the member and the purchaser and should be kept safe.

Stage payment cover is available only for a limited period of time:

(a)   where a certificate of insurance (final certification) is issued, any claim for stage payment cover must be submitted within six months of the date of issue of such notice;

(b)   where no certificate of insurance (final certification) notice has issued, the claim for stage payment cover must be made within two years of the effective date stated on the certificate of insurance (registration).

The purchaser may make a written request to the Company for an extension of any of the above time limits and the Company has discretion to extend such time limits for a further six months. Delays in relation to the completion of new houses are not uncommon and the two-year period is often passed, quite often because of problems arising in relation to planning matters. The purchaser should apply for an extension if there is any possibility of the time limits expiring.

12.11.7.4 Booking deposits and HomeBond

Booking deposits do not appear to be covered by the HomeBond Insurance policy scheme. It is specifically stated in section 1.1 of the agreement that 'we are only liable in respect of monies paid by the policyholder to the developer after the effective date stated on the Certificate of Insurance (Registration). No cover is available in relation to a stage payment paid before the date of registration of the dwelling in respect of which such stage payment has been paid.'

12.11.7.5 Present position re deposits

The perils occasioned by the case of *Roche v Peilow* are to a large extent dissipated with the introduction of the HomeBond scheme. Nowadays, most lending institutions will not issue loan approval unless HomeBond covers the new house. The purchaser's solicitor should warn clients that if they hope to obtain a building society loan in due course the builder should be registered with HomeBond, especially if it is a one-off house. Nevertheless, booking deposits remain at risk, as they are not covered by the scheme. Where the stage payment system operates the Conveyancing Committee strongly recommends that solicitors for purchasers of new houses should protect their clients if the amount of the stage payment exceeds the limit of the indemnity. They should do this by ensuring that the title to the site passes from the builder to the purchaser on the occasion of the making of any stage payments outside the protection offered by the scheme. If the combination of the deposit and the stage payment exceed the level of cover provided in the HomeBond Insurance policy document the purchaser's solicitor is exposed to the decision in *Roche v Peilow* and may become exposed to a negligence action in the event of the builder becoming bankrupt or going into liquidation.

CHAPTER 13

FIRST REGISTRATION

13.1   Introduction

13.1.1   SYSTEMS OF REGISTRATION

In Ireland there are two systems of registration:

(a)   registration of deeds; and

(b)   registration of title.

Under the registration of deeds system, the existence of any document relating to land may be registered in the Registry of Deeds. This was formerly done by the filing of a memorial but since 1 May 2008 a prescribed form is filed. This form (and formerly the memorial) need contain only certain information as to the contents and nature of the document, the document itself being returned to the person making the registration. This mode of registration affords certain security to purchasers and mortgagees, but, except in the case of a judgment mortgage, it does not add any validity to the document itself, or to the title of which it forms part. A purchaser or mortgagee could ascertain by searching in the Registry of Deeds that such a document existed, but nothing more. On each and every transaction with any land the title must be fully investigated, and every document considered as to its validity, construction, and legal effect. This system is considerably different from the registration of title system.

Section 36 of the Registration of Deeds and Title Act, 2006 and rule 6 of the Registration of Deeds Rules, 2008 provide for the prescribed forms.

The essential differences between the registration of deeds and registration of title systems are as set out in the following table:

Registry of Deeds	Land Registry
Existence of documents noted	The effect of the document noted
Registration gives no validity except in a case of a judgment mortgage	Registration gives validity to the effect of a document
Title must be fully investigated—not conclusive of ownership	Title and folio conclusive (except for enquiry as to s 72 burdens)
Title not guaranteed by State	Title guaranteed by State
Property is identified by complex descriptions of parcels and map of varying standards, which may conflict, attached to individual deeds.	The foundation of the system of registration or title is an accurate and complete map (subject to the 'general boundaries rule'). All registered holdings are separately identified by a plan number.

This chapter deals solely with first registration under the registration of title system, ie first registration of title in the Land Registry that was formerly dealt with under the registration of deeds system. **Chapter 14** sets out how registered land is dealt with after it has completed first registration.

13.1.2   REGISTRATION OF TITLE

The registration of title system is operated by the Land Registry under the control of the Property Registration Authority. It is regulated by the following provisions:

- Registration of Title Act, 1964 (in force 1 January 1967);

- Registration of Deeds and Title Act, 2006;

- Land and Conveyancing Law Reform Act, 2009;

- Civil Law (Miscellaneous Provisions) Act, 2011 (s 37 in force 2 August 2011);

- Land and Conveyancing Law Reform Act, 2013 (s 1 in force 24 July 2013);

- Land Registry and Registry of Deeds (Hours of Business) Order, 1964 (SI 164/1964);

- Compulsory Registration of Ownership (Carlow, Laoighis and Meath) Order, 1969 (SI 87/1969);

- Registration of Title Act, 1964 (Compulsory Registration of Ownership) (Longford, Roscommon and Westmeath) Order, 2005 (SI 605/2005);

- Registration of Deeds and Title Act, 2006 (Commencement) Order, 2006 (SI 271/2006) (in force 26 May 2006);

- Registration of Deeds and Title Act, 2006 (Commencement) (No 2) Order, 2006 (SI 511/2006) (in force 4 November 2006);

- Registration of Deeds and Title Act, 2006 (Establishment Day) Order, 2006 (SI 512/2006) (in force 4 November 2006);

- Registration of Deeds and Title Act, 2006 (s 66) (Commencement) Order, 2007 (SI 537/2007) (in force 1 September 2007);

- Registration of Deeds and Title Act, 2006 (Commencement) Order, 2008 (SI 1/2008) (in force 1 May 2008);

- Registration of Title Act, 1964 (Compulsory Registration of Ownership) (Clare, Kilkenny, Louth, Sligo, Wexford and Wicklow) Order, 2008 (SI 81/2008) (in force 1 October 2008);

- Registration of Title Act, 1964 (Compulsory Registration of Ownership) (Cavan, Donegal, Galway, Kerry, Kildare, Leitrim, Limerick, Mayo, Monaghan, North Tipperary, Offaly, South Tipperary and Waterford) Order, 2009 (SI 176/2009) (in force 1 January 2010);

- Land and Conveyancing Law Reform Act, 2009 (Commencement) Order, 2009 (SI 356/2009) (in force 1 December 2009);

- Registration of Title Act, 1964 (Compulsory Registration of Ownership) (Cork and Dublin) Order, 2010 (SI 516/2010) (in force 1 June 2011);

- Land Registration Rules, 2012 (SI 483/2012) (in force 1 February 2013);

- Land Registration Fees (Order), 2012 (SI 380/2012) (in force 1 December 2012);

- Land Registration Rules, 2013 (SI 389/2013) (in force 1 November 2013);

- Land Registration (Fees) (Amendment) Order, 2013 (in force 28 January 2013);

In this chapter and **chapter 14**:

> 'the 1964 Act' refers to the Registration of Title Act, 1964;

> 'the 2006 Act' refers to the Registration of Deeds and Title Act, 2006;

'the 2009 Act' refers to the Land and Conveyancing Law Reform Act, 2009;

'the Authority' means the Property Registration Authority established under s 9 of the 2006 Act;

'the LR Rule' or 'the LR Rules' refers to the Land Registration Rules, 2012 to 2013 unless otherwise stated;

'Form' or 'Forms' refers to the Schedule of Forms to the Land Registration Rules, 2012 to 2013 unless otherwise stated.

13.1.3   ACCESSING INFORMATION

The Authority has controlled and managed the Land Registry and the Registry of Deeds since 4 November 2006, which was the establishment day.

The Authority has published a set of Practice Directions in relation to various types of applications and they are available on its website (www.prai.ie), which also contains a range of additional information with latest news and publications. The Authority's website (www.landdirect.ie) allows account holders to inspect folios and the Land Registry map, search the register, map and indices (and indeed search the index of names in the Registry of Deeds), make applications for certified copy documents, track progress of applications, and prepare applications for registration. All of these can be done online.

In addition to standard land law texts, the following deal specifically with registration: McAllister, *Registration of Title in Ireland* (1973); Fitzgerald, *Land Registry Practice* (2nd edn, 1995); and Deeney, *Registration of Deeds and Title in Ireland* (2014).

13.1.4   FIRST REGISTRATION

First registration means entering in the register, for the first time, the title to lands theretofore unregistered. 'The applicant for registration must be either in possession or in receipt of the rents and profits of the property', McAllister, *Registration of Title in Ireland* (1973) p 30, the principle being that which applied in the Landed Estates Court, ie 'A person seeking a declaration of title is bound to show possession in accordance with that title' (*Re Vandeleur* 49 1LTR 206).

See paragraph 2, Form 1 and Form 2 of the LR Rules which requires a statement to the following effect:

'I am in undisputed possession (or, in receipt of the rents and profits) of the property and there is no person in occupation of it, or any part of it, adversely to my estate therein.'

At present approximately 93 per cent of the landmass of the State and about 90 per cent of the titles are registered in the Land Registry. The Authority estimates that there are in excess of 200,000 properties whose titles remain to be registered in the Land Registry at this time. The majority of these titles are in Dublin and Cork. In 2015 the Land Registry had an intake of 13,722 (net of rejections) first registration applications, of which 9,630 being by solicitor's certificate in Form 3 of the LR Rules (ie 70 per cent), with the balance requiring a full investigation of title.

This chapter will deal with compulsory registration and first registration based on documentary title and also first registration based on adverse possession.

13.2   Compulsory Registration

13.2.1   SECTION 23 OF THE 1964 ACT

Section 23(1) of the 1964 Act provides that registration of freehold land is compulsory where:

(a)   land has been at any time sold or conveyed to or vested in any person under any of the provisions of the Land Purchase Acts or the Labourers Acts;

(b)   land is acquired, after 1 January 1967 by a statutory body;

(c)   the Minister for Justice has by order extended compulsory registration to any county or county borough.

Section 23(2) provides that registration of a leasehold interest shall become compulsory:

(a)   where the interest is acquired after 1 January 1967 by a statutory body; and

(b)   where the Minister for Justice has by order extended compulsory registration to any county or county borough.

Under s 107(7) of the National Asset Management Agency Act, 2009, ss 23 and 25 of the 1964 Act do not apply to NAMA or a NAMA group entity.

13.2.2   SECTION 24 OF THE 1964 ACT

Under s 24 of the 1964 Act the Minister for Justice and Equality may by order provide for compulsory registration in any county or county borough. In an area to which this section applies the registration of ownership shall, if not already compulsory, become compulsory in the case of freehold land, upon a conveyance on sale and in the case of a leasehold interest, on the grant or assignment on sale of such an interest. 'Conveyance on sale' and 'assignment on sale' mean an instrument on sale for money or money's worth by virtue of which there is conferred or completed a title in respect of which an application for registration as owner may be made, and include a conveyance or assignment by way of exchange where money is paid for equality of exchange and also include any contract, agreement, condition, or covenant affecting the property comprised in the conveyance or assignment and entered into or made as part of, or in association with, such conveyance or assignment. It does not include conveyances or settlements in consideration of marriage. The reason for confining the compulsory provisions to where there has been a sale is because of the presumption that the title has been investigated on the sale.

A lease granted on sale is compulsorily registrable if executed on or after the appropriate date in the relevant county as well as an assignment on sale of a lease. Section 3 of the 1964 Act as amended by s 50 of the 2006 Act and s 127 of the 2009 Act defines a 'leasehold interest' as follows:

> *an estate in land under a lease for a term of years of which more than twenty-one (or such other number as may be prescribed) are unexpired at the date of registration, not being a term for securing money . . .*

No shorter term has been prescribed to date and if and when this occurs rule 115(2) of the LR Rules would be amended also. The Authority maintains, *inter alia*, a register of leasehold interests (s 8(1)(ii) of the 1964 Act). An issue can arise where a lease is compulsorily registrable (on foot of a grant or assignment) and has a term of 25 years, for example, but an application for registration is not made promptly and is lodged after the term is less than 21 years. In such a case the Authority would not be in a position to register the title of same. Section 25 provides that if such a lease is not registered, no title vests in the party holding under such lease. In such a case if a mortgage was granted on a lease for 25 years where the lease was for example dated on or after 1 June 2011 in relation to property in Dublin or Cork (ie compulsorily registrable) and the lease was presented for registration over four years later (ie when the unexpired residue of the term of the lease did not exceed 21 years) then the Authority could not open up a leasehold folio for same nor register the mortgage. Great care should be exercised by solicitors for lending institutions in cases such as these to ensure prompt registration.

A vesting certificate issued either under s 22(1)(a) of the Landlord and Tenant (Ground Rents) (No 2) Act, 1978 (consent case) or under s 22(1)(b) of the No 2 Act (arbitration case) is deemed (s 22(3) of the No 2 Act) to be a 'conveyance on sale' for the purpose of s 24 of the 1964 Act and is therefore subject to compulsory registration. A conveyance or assignment on sale of a title where the vendor claims to have acquired title by long possession executed after the appropriate date is compulsory registrable. Whether a conveyance comes within the definition of an instrument on sale for money or money's worth would be a matter of interpretation and it would not be a matter for the Authority to decide, it would be a matter for the solicitor for the purchaser to decide and ultimately the courts, eg if there was a nominal consideration or it was a conveyance under ss 3, 4, or 5 of the Multi-Unit Development Act, 2011.

Note in divorce or separation cases if a conveyance or assignment is in consideration of the premises this would seem to take it out of the category of conveyance on sale but if a money consideration is included this would clearly be caught by the conveyance on sale rule (note the Law Society Practice Note, 'Compulsory registration and family law related assurances', Law Society *Gazette*, April 2012).

13.2.3   AREAS PRESCRIBED UNDER S 24

Counties Meath, Laois, and Carlow as of 1 January 1970;

Counties Longford, Roscommon, and Westmeath as of 1 April 2006;

Counties Clare, Kilkenny, Louth, Sligo, Wexford, and Wicklow as of 1 October 2008;

Counties Cavan, Donegal, Galway, Kerry, Kildare, Leitrim, Limerick, Mayo, Monaghan, North Tipperary, Offaly, South Tipperary, and Waterford as of 1 January 2010; and

Counties Cork, Dun Loaghaire-Rathdown, Fingal and South Dublin, and the cities of Dublin and Cork as of 1 June 2011.

Therefore as of 1 June 2011 compulsory registration applies to all counties.

13.2.4   AMENDMENT TO S 24

Under s 53 of the 2006 Act, s 24 of the 1964 Act was amended and the Minister is able to provide for compulsory registration not only to a specified area, including a local government area within the meaning of s 10 of the Local Government Act 2001, as previously but also to:

• specified land; or

• specified land in a specified area.

However, as stated earlier, compulsory registration applies to all counties since 1 June 2011.

In addition, a new s 24(2A) was added which allows the Minister to extend by order the type of dispositions to which compulsory registration will apply. Up until now, when registration becomes compulsory, it applies in the case of freehold land to a conveyance on sale and, in the case of leasehold land, to a grant or assignment on sale of such an interest. The new s 2A provides that an order under the section may extend compulsory registration to other types of disposition, for example succession or gifts inter vivos or even a mortgage. This type of extension will likely be necessary eventually to ensure the completion of the Irish Land Register and the closing of the Registry of Deeds. Neither of these new provisions has been exercised by the Minister to date.

Active consideration is being given to the acceleration of completion of the Irish Land Register by Authority-led first registrations and other initiatives (the 'Property Registration Authority Strategic Plan 2016–2018: Objective 1').

13.2.5   EFFECT OF NON-REGISTRATION

The legal effect of non-registration where registration is compulsory (under both ss 23 and 24) is set out in s 25 of the 1964 Act as amended by s 128 of the 2009 Act. All such conveyances and assignments must be registered within six months, or such later date as the Authority, or, in the case of its refusal the court, may allow. If such conveyance/assignment is not registered, no title vests in the party holding under such a conveyance or assignment. On registration the title relates back to the date of execution of the conveyance/assignment and any dealings with the land before the registration have effect accordingly. See McAllister, *Registration of Title in Ireland* (1973 edn) p 47. Under s 3(6) of the Housing (Miscellaneous Provisions) Act, 1992 where a housing authority is, by virtue of s 23 of the 1964 Act, required to register the ownership of a house in respect of which a shared ownership lease is granted by it, s 25 of the 1964 Act shall apply as if the reference to six months in the said s 25 were a reference to 18 months. Under s 107(7) of the National Asset Management Agency Act, 2009, ss 23 and 25 of the 1964 Act do not apply to NAMA or a NAMA group entity.

13.2.6   SUMMARY

Registration is compulsory therefore in the following circumstances:

- Where freehold land has been at any time sold and conveyed to or vested in any person under any of the provisions of the Land Purchase Acts. Where land has been purchased under the Land Purchase Acts prior to 1 January 1892, application is to be made by the successor in title to the purchaser. Where land has been purchased under the Land Purchase Acts on or after 1 January 1892 the Department of Agriculture and Food (Lands Division; formerly the Land Commission) lodges the fiat (purchase agreement) or vesting order (both referred to as schedules) for registration in the Land Registry.

- Where freehold land has been at any time sold and conveyed to or vested in any person under any of the provisions of the Labourers Acts, 1883 to 1962 (usually vesting orders of cottage plots).

- Where freehold land or a leasehold interest is acquired after 1 January 1967 by a statutory authority. This includes bodies such as the ESB and local authorities.

- Freehold land, upon a conveyance on sale executed on or after the operative date and in the case of a leasehold interest, on the grant or assignment on sale of such an interest executed on or after the operative date in the relevant counties as set out in **13.2.3**.

- Under s 126(3) of the 1964 Act 'Provision shall be made by general rules for the registration, without cost to the parties interested, of all titles recorded under the Record of Title (Ireland) Act, 1865, and care shall be taken in such rules to protect any rights acquired in pursuance of such recording. Until registration that Act shall apply thereto as if this Act had not been passed.' See rules 23 and 24 of the LR Rules. There can hardly be many of these titles outstanding as only about 800 were recorded. The entry on the register of such recorded property does not occur until an application is made for such registration under a disposition thereof. See rules 23(2) and 83 of the LR Rules.

- Under s 82(3) of the Housing Act, 1966; where a housing authority makes a vesting order under this section in relation to property acquired under the provisions of s 81 of the 1966 Act it must be registered in the Land Registry.

- Land sold or leased under s 90 of the Housing Act, 1966, if not already compulsorily registrable, is made compulsorily registrable; s 92(1).

13.3   First Registration Based on Documentary Title

The following are the requirements to be met for first registration based on documentary title.

13.3.1 STATEMENT OF TITLE

Rule 15(1)(a) and 16(2)(a) of the LR Rules provides for a statement of title in first registration applications except under rules 19(3), 19(4), 20(1), 21, and 22, ie:

A concise statement of the title giving in chronological order a summary of the documents and the events and facts on which the applicant's claim to the property is based, commencing with a good root of title and which shall form part of Form 1 (or Form 2).

The statement of title is now required to be part of Form 1 or Form 2 (Schedule Part 3)— see **13.3.4**.

Often a mere list of the documents lodged (a form of schedule of documents) is presented as a statement of title but this is not acceptable. The statement should be an accurate and concise summary in chronological order of all the documents on title and the effect it is claimed the said documents and events have on the title. It should specifically identify the root of title, and if the root is an assignment of a leasehold interest or a conveyance of a fee farm grant, the lease or fee farm grant should be recited and lodged (see s 56(2) of the 2009 Act) and that title should be traced to the applicant. Identification of the root of title can be made by stating that a specified deed is the 'root of title' or that 'title commences with' a specified deed. Pre-root documents should not be listed in the statement of title if the title is based on a good root (however if the root of title recites a deed that creates a s 69 burden that continues to effect the title the said deed should also be lodged as should a pre root deed that contains an indemnity regarding a fee farm rent). A statement of title should enable the Authority to get a clear picture of the title to the property including any defects in the title.

'The applicant should give full information on any points regarding which a well-advised purchaser should raise requisitions.'

See Fitzgerald, *Land Registry Practice* (2nd edn) para 22.6.

As per paragraph 3 of Form 1 and Form 2 (see **13.3.4**) the title should if possible commence with a good root of title (see **13.3.2.2**). A good root of title in relation to a leasehold interest (or a fee farm grant interest) under rule 19(1) would be an assignment (or a conveyance in the case of a fee farm grant) made not less than 15 years prior to the date of the application (and that otherwise would be a good root) together with the lease (or the fee farm grant). If a good root of title is not available it should commence with the available root of title and all the title documents in the applicant's possession or control should be lodged (see Note 3 of Form 1 and Form 2).

It should be noted that while the Land Registry accept a 15-year old assignment or conveyance (in the case of a fee farm grant) to be a good root of title (accompanied with the lease (or the fee farm grant)) in general conveyancing practice the lease or fee farm grant is itself the root of title for leasehold or fee farm grant interests. See **4.7** and in particular **4.7.5.1** for a list of good roots of title.

In most cases you will be applying under rule 19(1) of the LR Rules. However if you are applying under rule 19(2) of the LR Rules you should state specifically that you are applying under same and provide evidence of the valuation of the property, eg auctioneer's certificate (see **13.3.2.2**).

Note that paragraph 3 of Form 1 and Form 2 of the LR Rules refers to the statement of title and provides: 'The facts specified in the statement of my title are true and accurate.'

13.3.1.1 Example of statement of title in a first registration application

The following is an example of a statement of title involving two titles, a freehold and leasehold, and a merger of the leasehold in the freehold. In both cases the title commences with a good root of title. If a good root is not available it should commence with the available root.

Schedule

Part 3

Rule 15(1)(a) and 19(1) of the Land Registration Rules.

Freehold

1. **Good Root of Freehold Title.** By conveyance for value dated 1 October 1980 Peter Ormsby conveyed *inter alia* the property to Stuart Enterprises Limited in fee simple subject to *inter alia* the lease specified in paragraph 6 below.

   Stuart Enterprises Limited was incorporated in the State as evidenced by the duplicate Certificate of Incorporation lodged.

   Its power to acquire hold and dispose of property and the requirements for sealing documents is evidenced by a copy of the Memorandum and Articles of Association lodged.

2. By conveyance for value dated 9 January 2008 Stuart Enterprises Limited conveyed *inter alia* the property to Bernard Smith in fee simple.

3. Bernard Smith died testate on 10 November 2009 and by his Will (Probate of which issued to his son Thomas Smith on 3 February 2010) he devised *inter alia* the property to his son Thomas absolutely.

4. By assent dated 4 March 2010 Thomas Smith assented to the vesting of *inter alia* the property in himself in fee simple.

5. By conveyance for value dated 9 September 2013 Thomas Smith conveyed the property to Jeremiah Cronin in fee simple subject to the lease specified at item 6 below but with the intent that same would merge in the freehold as Jeremiah Cronin was also entitled to the leasehold interest.

Leasehold

6. By lease dated 8 June 1954 Paul McGrath demised the property the subject of this application to Andrew Cummins for 150 years from 25 March 1954 at the yearly rent of £60.

7. Leasehold title commences with an assignment for value dated 12 October 1997 whereby Dennis Connolly assigned the leasehold interest to Liam Murphy. (See note earlier at **13.3.1** re what documents the Land Registry accept as being a good root of leasehold title.)

8. By mortgage dated 12 October 1997 Liam Murphy mortgaged the property to the Governor and Company of the Bank of Ireland.

9. By receipt dated 15 August 2007 endorsed on the said mortgage the Governor and Company of the Bank of Ireland vacated the mortgage specified at item 8.

10. By assignment for value dated 3 June 2010 Liam Murphy assigned the leasehold interest to Jeremiah Cronin.

11. By virtue of the conveyance specified at item 5 of the freehold title the lease has ceased by merging in the freehold.

13.3.2   TITLE TO BE SHOWN

'The title sought by the Land Registry for first registration should, broadly speaking, be what a willing purchaser, acting under competent professional advice, could properly be advised to accept, and it should be prepared for registration as if it were being prepared for examination by a purchaser's solicitor.'

See Fitzgerald, *Land Registry Practice* (2nd edn) para 22.6.

The title to be shown should be a period of at least 15 years commencing with a good root of title (s 1 of the Vendor and Purchaser Act, 1874, which provided for 40 years, was repealed and replaced by s 56 of the 2009 Act). Where the title originates with a fee farm grant or lease, production of the fee farm grant or lease is required. While the Land Registry accept a 15-year old assignment or conveyance (in the case of a fee farm grant) to be a good root of title (accompanied with the lease (or the fee farm grant)) in general conveyancing practice the lease or fee farm grant is itself the root of title for leasehold or fee farm grant interests. See **4.7** and in particular **4.7.5.1** for a list of good roots of title.

It may be necessary to go back significantly more than 15 years to find a good root of title. There is no definition of a good root in the 2009 Act but *Williams on Title* (23rd edn) pp 651–2 defines it as:

'An instrument of disposition dealing with or proving on the face of it without the aid of extrinsic evidence the ownership of the whole legal and equitable estate in the property sold containing a description by which the property can be identified and showing nothing to cast doubt on the title of the disposing parties.'

Sections 33(4) and 40(4) and 40(5) of the 1964 Act provide that the Authority shall approve the title presented. Titles are examined in accordance with rule 18 (see **13.3.2.1**). Therefore it is for the Authority to decide if a root of title identified is or is not a good root and whether or not to approve the title applied for.

In relation to roots of title see **4.7** and for examples of good and bad roots see **4.7.5.1** and **4.7.5.2**.

13.3.2.1   Rule 18 of the LR Rules

Rule 18 of the LR Rules provides that an application under rules 14 or 17 shall be examined by or under the supervision of the Authority who shall direct such searches, advertisements, notices, and enquiries as it may deem necessary. The Authority may in any case dispense with or modify the official examination of title, or it may accept what it considers to be a good holding title and take such indemnity as it deems necessary. No evidence of title should be called for that could not be required on a sale of the property under an open contract. A 'good holding title' is less than a marketable title because of the lack of documentary evidence or because of defective documentary evidence and it would be supported by long and undisturbed possession. It is open to the Authority to approve a qualified or possessory title if satisfied that an absolute title is not warranted on the basis of the proofs lodged.

13.3.2.2   Rule 19 of the LR Rules

Rule 19 of the LR Rules gives the Authority discretion to modify the examination of title.

Rule 19(1) of the LR Rules provides that:

The title to be shown by the applicant may commence with a disposition of the property made not less than 15 years prior to the date of the application that would be a good root of title on a sale under a contract limiting only the length of title to be shown.

See s 56 of the 2009 Act.

Rule 19(2) of the LR Rules provides where the market value of the property is shown to the satisfaction of the Authority to be less than €1,000,000 the title to be shown by the applicant may commence 'with a conveyance or assignment on sale made not less than 12 years prior to the date of the application' that would be a good root of title as described earlier. If an application is being made under rule 19(2) of the LR Rules the applicant should state specifically that he or she is applying under the same and provide evidence of the valuation of the property (eg auctioneer's certificate).

Rule 19(3) of the LR Rules is dealt with at **13.3.16**.

Rule 19(4) of the LR Rules provides that Form 3 procedure is also available where a statutory authority acquires property where the purchase money or compensation paid does not exceed €1,000,000. Rule 19(3) refers to a sale whereas this sub-rule has a broader scope. See also **13.3.16**.

Rule 19(5) of the LR Rules: Where the title of the applicant has been examined:

(a) by the conveyancing counsel of a court on a sale or purchase of the property under an order of the court; or

(b) by a practising barrister or solicitor on a sale or mortgage of property,

the Authority may dispense with, or modify as it thinks fit, the official examination of title. Note that first registration will not be effected on production of legal opinion solely. Form 1 or Form 2 (Part 3 of the Schedule being the statement of title is not necessary: see rules 15(2) and 16(3)) and all documents in the applicant's possession relating to the title should be lodged: rules 15(1)(b) and 16(2)(b) of the LR Rules. In these cases the applicant should request the Authority either to dispense with the examination of title or alternatively modify its examination consistent with the opinion received. The net result can be to expedite the whole process of registration. Generally, rule 19(5) is not appropriate in multi-title or multi-property applications.

Rule 19(6) of the LR Rules provides that there is provision for a title to be referred for legal opinion either generally or on specified matters. The legal opinion may be furnished in Form 3, adapted as the case may require. Note 'legal opinion' is defined in rule 2 of the LR Rules as meaning 'the opinion of a practising barrister or practising solicitor' (formerly, the LR Rules 1972 only provided for an opinion of counsel).

13.3.3   ALL ORIGINAL DEEDS AND OTHER DOCUMENTS

The general requirement is lodgement of the original documents of title. Rules 15(1)(b) and 16(2)(b) of the LR Rules, stipulate that 'all original deeds and all documents in the applicant's possession, or under his control relating to the title' should be lodged. Note also rules 15(3) and 16(6) which provide:

> *The Authority shall not be on notice of any matter disclosed in any document lodged which bears a date prior to the date of the document identified as the root of title.*

If Form 1 or Form 2 (statement of title in Schedule Part 3) identifies a good root of title then only the documents relating to the title and commencing with a good root should be lodged (see **13.3.4**).

An applicant whose property has been carved out of a larger property, and who lodges certified copies of deeds prior to his conveyance/assignment is normally required to lodge or arrange for the lodgement of the original deeds to have them suitably marked under s 95 of the 1964 Act and rule 154 of the LR Rules, and to prove that they were not the subject of an equitable deposit or lien. If there is difficulty in producing the originals of such prior deeds of title, the practitioner could lodge, if such was the case, a certificate that they were produced to him or her as solicitor for the purchaser at the closing of the sale, or the practitioner could certify, if such was the case, as solicitor for the applicant, that he or she has satisfied him or herself that they were not the subject of an equitable lien at the time of closing.

Note requisitions 20.4, 20.5, and 20.6 of the 2001 edition of the Law Society's Standard Objections and Requisitions on Title.

The following paragraph appears in Glover, *Advising on Title*, p 159.

> 'Production of the abstracted deeds and documents is necessary, not only to verify the abstract but also to ascertain that they have not been deposited by way of mortgage: see Oliver v Hinton [1899] 2 Ch 264. If the deeds are deposited at the vendor's bank, a letter should be required from the bank manager stating that the bank has no charge.'

13.3.3.1   Deeds held on equitable deposit

Where an application for first registration is lodged for registration and the documents are held by a financial institution on equitable deposit, the possibility of termination of the lien on the documents once registration is completed should be taken into account. In such instance a release of the lien could be lodged eg a letter from the bank stating that the bank has no charge. An application can be made to have the lien protected by means of a caution (see **14.8.3**).

13.3.3.2   Lost title deeds

Application for first registration where the title deeds have been lost or destroyed is quite a common problem but fortunately it can be surmounted in most cases.

First, an approach should be made to any solicitor or solicitors who were involved in the sale, purchase or mortgage of the property. They may have copies of the title documents or sufficient of them to enable the title to be reconstructed. Ideally, certified copies of the title documents should be procured or plain copies together with the relevant certified copy memorials/application forms thereof from the Registry of Deeds. Application forms replaced the memorial from 1 May 2008 under s 36 of the 2006 Act and rule 6 of the Registration of Deeds Rules, 2008; see **13.1.1**.

In the case of leasehold property, an approach could be made to the landlord to whom the rent is paid. The landlord may be in a position to supply a copy of the counterpart lease. By ascertaining the changes of ownership and a certificate from the General Valuation Office showing the various occupiers may be of assistance in this regard, memorials/application forms of the missing deeds can be located. If the memorials/application forms contain sufficient information then they will on their own be accepted. Local knowledge may also be utilised to ascertain the changes in ownership and then astute searching in the Registry of Deeds may produce the necessary memorials/application forms.

If the title relates to an old lease or fee farm grant, the original of which is not forthcoming the Authority would not generally be concerned about the absence of the originals. If the fee farm grant is a conversion grant that converts a lease for lives renewable forever into a fee farm grant the Authority will not seek the original or copy lease.

If the property has passed under a will then a copy of the will and probate may be obtainable from the Probate Registry or from the National Archives.

Attempting to base a title on long possession when the title documents are missing is not satisfactory (see **13.4**).

If the property was known to have been the subject of a settlement, then it may be necessary to have recourse to the courts to have the trusts of the settlement declared. However, see *Cummins v Hall and Cummins* [1933] IR 419. It may be possible, as in the case of a marriage settlement, to trace first from the settlor, and then from the husband and wife in the settlement, and also from the children, and relying on possession of the property, and the service of notices by the Land Registry, to make title.

Where the applicant is unable to locate an original deed or deeds it is essential for them to establish that the deed was lost or destroyed whilst in proper custody. A full factual statutory declaration or affidavit exhibiting the best secondary evidence of the deed, dealing with the loss of the deed, the person in whose custody the deed was last known to be, and indicating the extent of searches made to locate it should be lodged. Searches and enquiries should be made in all places where such documents are likely to be including banks and other financial institutions, solicitors' offices, and so forth. The applicant should exhibit and lodge copies of all correspondence relating to such efforts to trace the missing deed with the affidavit. The applicant and his or her solicitor should also lodge an undertaking to produce the lost deed in the event of it being subsequently discovered. It should be clear from the affidavit that the deed has not been deposited with any person or with any bank or corporation, by way of lien or security for monies or otherwise and that there is no valid claim by any person to its custody. The affidavit should contain an undertaking by the applicant to indemnify the Authority and the State against all losses and/or damages arising from effecting his registration as owner on the Register with absolute title (or good leasehold title); see rules 17 and 18 of the LR Rules.

In addition an insurance bond may be required (in the name of the Authority and the State or assigned to the Authority and the State), as may an advertisement in the Law Society *Gazette* and perhaps also in a newspaper. An applicant should await Land Registry direction regarding the same.

A sample affidavit in relation to missing title deeds can read as follows:

> 'With regard to such of the documents of title referred to in paragraph x hereof as are not forthcoming, I say that same have been lost or destroyed. The person in whose custody such documents were last known to be was   . I have caused searches and enquiries to be made in all places where such documents were likely to be, including banks, solicitors' offices and so forth to trace said documents, but have been unable to obtain any information as to their whereabouts and I verily believe the said documents have been irretrievably lost or have been inadvertently or accidentally destroyed; that they have not been deposited with any person, or with any bank or corporation, by way of lien or security for monies lent or otherwise, and that there is no valid claim by any person to their custody. I refer to correspondence relating to such efforts to trace the missing documents upon which marked. I have endorsed my name previously to swearing this application. In the event of any of such documents being subsequently found, I hereby undertake to lodge them in the Land Registry. I hereby undertake to indemnify the Property Registration Authority and the State against all losses and/or damages arising from effecting my registration as owner on the Register with absolute title (or good leasehold title) on the basis of the proofs lodged.'

A personal indemnity is not necessary if an insurance bond is lodged (in the name of the Authority and the State or assigned to them with the consent of the insurer).

See further **14.5.3** re lost deed of transfer.

13.3.4 FORM 1 OR FORM 2

An application for first registration based on documentary title, save under rules 19(3) or (4) or 20(1), 21, or 22, shall be by application in Form 1 (freehold) or Form 2 (leasehold). Form 1 and Form 2 include the relevant paragraphs of the affidavit of discovery and a Form 16 is not required in these cases (see rule 47 of the LR Rules). Only the prescribed Form 1 and Form 2 are acceptable for first registration applications lodged since 1 February 2013. Paragraph 3 of Form 1 and 2 reads 'and to the schedule of documents lodged herewith, which is a list of all documents relating to the **title** in my possession or under my control'.

Paragraph 7 of Form 1 and Form 2 now reads:

> 'The contracts, abstracts, counsel's opinions, requisitions, replies, deeds, wills and other documents referred to or lodged with said application and produced in the proceedings thereunder are all the documents in my possession or under my control relating to the title to the said property **commencing with a good root of title**.'

Coupled with rule 15 and 16 (see **13.3.3**) this means that on applications for first registration based on documentary title, only the documents relating to the title and commencing with a good root of title should be lodged. Pre-root documents should not be lodged (see **13.3.1** re leases, fee farm grants, and deeds that create burdens that still effect the property) and, if lodged, the Authority shall not be on notice of any matter disclosed in them: see rule 15(3). In this regard it will be essential that a statement of title (Schedule Part 3 of Form 1 or 2) should if possible commencing with, and clearly identify, a good root should be lodged (see **13.3.1**) as per paragraph 7 of Form 1 and Form 2.

If the title does not commence with a good root of title paragraph 7 of Form 1 or Form 2 should be suitably amended as should the statement of title and all the title documents in the applicant's possession or under his control relating to the title (see rule 15(1)(b)) should be lodged and rules 15(3) and 16(6) shall not apply (see **13.3.3**). As compulsory registration applies to the whole country (see **13.2.2**) it may often occur that registration is compulsory where a good root of title is not available (eg where property has been held on trust for some time or has never moved out of a family).

In view of the fact that Form 1 and Form 2 now contain the relevant averments of Form 16, Form 1 and Form 2 is to be made by the applicant or in the cases of a company by the secretary or law agent. It may be made by a director with personal knowledge of the facts deposed and duly authorised to make the affidavit for and on behalf of the company (this should be stated specifically in Form 1 or Form 2: see Note 9, Form 1 and Note 11, Form 2). It may also be made by the liquidator.

It is becoming increasingly common that Form 1 or Form 2 in a first registration application is made by receivers including statutory receivers. The receiver may have been appointed under a mortgage by a company or an individual. Most commonly receivers make a Form 1 or a Form 2 application on behalf of an individual. As stated an application for first registration in Form 1 or Form 2 should in the first instance be made by the person who is entitled to be registered as owner. It appears that this is done on the basis that the receiver is an agent of the mortgagor or under a power of attorney as per the mortgage deed. It does not appear that a receiver even when appointed as attorney can make an oath on behalf of the applicants. Even if he or she has such power it does not appear that he or she would have the necessary knowledge of the facts required in relation to the affidavit of discovery averments of Form 1 or Form 2 (ie the averments formerly required in Form 16). The averments in Form 1 or Form 2 (which includes the affidavit of discovery averments contained in Form 16) require to be made by the applicant. The Authority adopts the following approach:

(a) The averments in Form 1 or Form 2 (which includes the affidavit of discovery averments formerly contained in Form 16) require to be made by the applicant.

(b) The solicitor is asked to show how the receiver as receiver can make Form 1 or Form 2 affidavit.

(c) If the receiver has such a power he or she may not have the necessary knowledge of the facts required in relation to the affidavit of discovery averments of Form 1 or Form 2 (ie the averments formerly required in Form 16).

(d) If the solicitor makes a case

   (i) That it is not possible for the applicants to make Form 1 or Form 2;

   (ii) That receiver has the power to make a Form 1 or a Form 2 affidavit;

   (iii) Form 3 is not an option;

   (iv) The Authority will consider same.

   If for example it is shown that the applicants cannot be contacted and are not cooperating with the receiver and it is also shown that the receiver has been appointed agent for the applicants the Authority may accept a Form 1 or a Form 2 made by the receiver subject to it containing an averment by the receiver that he or she has the necessary means of knowledge (unambiguous averment with no qualification).

13.3.5 FORM 16 AFFIDAVIT OF DISCOVERY

Section 93 of the 1964 Act, as amended by the 2006 Act, provides that where the Authority has to investigate title 'an affidavit shall be produced to the effect that, to the best of the deponent's knowledge and belief, all deeds, wills, instruments of title, and incumbrances affecting the title, and all facts material to the title, have been disclosed to the Authority'. Rule 47 of the LR Rules states that this affidavit shall, unless an application form is prescribed that includes the relevant averments, be in Form 16. Note that Form 1 and Form 2 (see **13.3.4**) now contain the relevant paragraphs of Form 16 and in these cases it is not necessary to lodge a separate Form 16.

The requirement to lodge all deeds and documents in the applicant's possession, including contracts for sale, and the opinion of counsel is to be noted. Care is to be taken to ensure that what is averred is correct. It often transpires when searches are made in the Registry of Deeds that the property is subject to mortgages or leases which have not been disclosed. The Authority may require updating of Form 1 or Form 2 prior to completion of a first registration application.

13.3.6 SEARCHES

Rules 15(1)(b) and 16(2)(b) of the LR Rules, require lodgement of any searches relating to the title in the possession of the applicant. On examination of the title in the Land Registry directions for searches are included in the rulings on title: see rule 18 of the LR Rules.

13.3.6.1 Registry of Deeds

While the rule states that all searches relating to the title in the possession of the applicant should be lodged, in straightforward documentary applications, full Registry of Deeds searches in the first instance should be lodged. The Registry of Deeds search should commence with the root of title and should cover all parties on title from then to date (may commence with roots at least 15 years or 12 years old—see **13.3.2.2**). The applicant may already have searches from previous transactions and these can be lodged; however all gaps in the searches should be closed.

While it is not an Authority requirement please note the Law Society Practice Note (Law Society *Gazette*, January/February 2013). It is the recommendation of the Conveyancing Committee that it is good conveyancing practice when lodging applications for first registration (whether same was previously compulsory or not) that the conveyance/assignment/ other assurance of unregistered title would first be registered in the Registry of Deeds before lodging it in the Land Registry, in order to preserve priorities pending registration in the Land Registry.

Common or verified hand searches should be lodged. The search is to be made in the Index of Names against all parties, and should include alternative names and spellings as appear from the title documents. The search is to be made from the day before the relevant deed to the day after the date of registration of the memorial/application form of the next subsequent deed; in the case of death, up to the end of the next calendar year. Personal representatives are to be searched against from the date of death up to the day after the registration of the memorial or application form of the assent or the next deed of sale. Search against beneficiaries (where there are no personal representatives) from the date of death. Search against trustees, on trust for or with a power of sale, from the date of death. The search should be made against all descriptions of the property, old and new. Originals of searches are required to be lodged. However, where the application property has been carved out of other property, copies of searches relating to the parent holding are acceptable. Faxed or e-mailed searches are to be followed by the originals. All acts appearing on the Registry of Deeds searches will need to be explained and certified.

13.3.6.2 Judgment Office

A Judgment Office search against all parties on title for past five years is required. All acts appearing will need to be explained. It is the existence of a lis pendens that is of interest, not money judgments, which have to be registered as a judgment mortgage to effect land: see **14.15.1**. This search should also include a search in the Register of Lis Pendens maintained in the Central Office of the High Court: s 121 of the 2009 Act.

13.3.6.3 Companies Registration Office

A Companies Registration Office Search is required against an applicant company and in an appropriate case against all, companies on the title for debentures, liquidators, receivers, change of name, equitable deposit, undertaking, etc. The appointment of a receiver crystallises a debenture and therefore state whether any debenture has crystallised or not.

13.3.6.4   Central Bank

Under the Irish Collective Asset-management Vehicles Act 2015 an Irish Collective Asset-management Vehicle (ICAV) can register with the Central Bank or if it was formerly registered under the Companies Acts can de-register with the Register of Companies and register with the Central Bank. Therefore searches in the Central Bank are required (in a similar manner to searches in the Companies Office see **13.3.6.3**) (see also the PRA Legal Office Notice 2 of 2015 for further on ICAVs).

13.3.7   BURDENS

The Authority is required to enter all burdens (s 34 of the 1964 Act) which appear from an examination of the title to affect the freehold interest (see s 41 re leasehold interests) by virtue of s 69 of the 1964 Act, as extended, except such interests which affect without registration by virtue of s 72 of the 1964 Act, as extended. (See **14.12**.) Note that s 3 of the 1964 Act provides that 'lease' includes 'an agreement for a lease'. Such interests will be registered as burdens on Part 3 of the new folio if they are disclosed in the application documents or searches. The plot the subject of the lease or agreement for a lease should be marked on the application map. It is to be noted that 'powers to charge' in debentures are registrable burdens. Court orders are registrable burdens by virtue of s 69(1)(h) of the 1964 Act. A subject right of way created prior to a first registration application is a burden which affects without registration by virtue of s 72(1) of the 1964 Act. However a 'notice of the existence' of such interest may be entered on the register under s 72(3). In such instance the property the subject of the right of way could be marked on an appropriate map (see **14.2.8**). Such a note of existence of a right of way is not mapped on the Land Registry map but reference is made to the map in the relevant instrument. See the Conveyancing Committee Practice Note 'Easements and *profits à prendre* created by express grant prior to first registration' (Law Society *Gazette*, July 2015) which recommends that practitioners apply for the registration of such a right of way under s 72(3) of the 1964 Act and retain a copy of the relevant deed with the title deeds for future reference. Note also the Law Society Practice Note. 'Registration of easement on a leasehold folio' (Law Society *Gazette*, November 2012) which advises solicitors to read through the s 72 burdens very carefully (and especially where it appears that the land was only newly registered on foot of a first registration application) to make sure that there were no easements created by express grant before the first registration of the land, and which are not shown on the folio as a burden or as a s 72(3) note, but which would be a burden under s 72(h) and would need to be disclosed in the s 72 declaration. The Practice Note also recommends that the long form s 72 declaration be used and a precedent is available in the member's area of the Law Society website. Where a Contract for Sale is on the title it may give rise to a caution and the applicant's solicitor may be advised as to the availability of the same.

13.3.8   APPURTENANT RIGHTS

If registration of appurtenant rights is required, the title thereto must be shown and a map complying with Land Registry mapping requirements lodged. See s 82 of the 1964 Act and rule 3(6)(c)(i) and rule 25(2) of the LR Rules. However, practitioners should note that a conveyance of land includes and conveys with the land any appurtenant rights attached to the land. See s 71 of the 2009 Act which replaces s 6 of the Conveyancing Act, 1881 and also see ss 37 (1) and 44(1) of the 1964 Act which provide that on registration of a person as owner of land all rights appurtenant to the land vest in the said owner. If the servient tenement is registered land, the assent of the registered owner to the registration of the interest as a burden on the servient folio should be enclosed: s 69(2) of the 1964 Act.

As stated s 72(3) of the 1964 Act allows for registration of a note of the existence of an easement. Notice will be in the following form:

'Notice pursuant to Section 72(3) of the Registration of Title Act 1964 that part of the property described herein is subject to a right of way more particularly described in Instrument No. D . . . in favour of . . .'

For easements or *profits à prendre* acquired by prescription see chapter 3 of the Law Society *Complex Conveyancing Manual* (2nd edn) published by Bloomsbury Professional and Law Society *Gazette,* July 2011. The Civil Law (Miscellaneous Provisions) Act, 2011 which came into operation on 2 August 2011 ('the 2011 Act') amended *inter alia* s 35 of the 2009 Act and the 1964 Act, in so far as they related to the acquisition of easements and profits by prescription. The 2011 Act provides for an application to be made directly to the PRA under a new s 49A of the 1964 Act (for uncontested claims) without the necessity of obtaining a court order (rule 46 and Form 68 of the LR Rules).

13.3.9   MINES AND MINERALS

The usual note that the registration does not extend to the mines and minerals will generally be entered on first registration: rule 28 of the LR Rules and especially rule 28(1). Rule 28(1) provides that:

Where, on an application for first registration of the ownership of property, no evidence is adduced as to the ownership of the mines and minerals therein or such ownership is not proved to the satisfaction of the Authority or it appears from any document, or otherwise, that all or any of the mines or minerals are severed from the property, a note shall be entered in the Register to the effect that the registration does not extend to the mines and minerals or to such of them as are so severed.

This mines and minerals note will not be entered where the root of title is a Land Commission conveyance and charging order prior to 1891 which does not reserve or except the mines and minerals. It should be noted that it is possible to make a first registration application in respect of mines and minerals and to effect registration of the same (McAllister, *Registration of Title in Ireland* (1973) pp 60–64 and Fitzgerald, *Land Registry Practice* (2nd edn, 1995) para 22.21).

13.3.10   MAP

Rules 15(1)(c) and 16(2)(c) of the LR Rules, require lodgement of 'an application map, unless the application otherwise sufficiently identifies the property on the registry map'. See **14.2.8.1**. Land Registry mapping requirements are set out in Practice Direction 'Mapping Practice' which is available on the mapping page of the Authority website www.prai.ie. Mapping requirements for multi-storey developments are also available online.

Care should be taken to ensure that the application property is wholly within the bounds of the descriptions, measurements, and maps contained in or endorsed on the relevant documents of title and that the property entirely comprises unregistered land. A search of the LR digital map should be conducted as early as possible and this search can be done online at www.landdirect.ie.

It is advised that in all cases when you are taking initial instructions from a client in relation to registered or unregistered property you should in the first instance check the Authority's digital map, with the applicant present, to ascertain whether the property is registered or unregistered, to check the boundaries of same, and ascertain whether they conflict with registered boundaries and in the case of registered land to check the ownership and burdens etc on the folio.

Difficulties in identifying the subject property may arise for a variety of reasons. For example, the subject property does not conform to ordnance survey detail or such detail may have changed. Older title maps might not be to scale and may only be sketch maps or drawings. Occasionally, there may be no maps on prior title and the parcels clause may contain only a physical description, locating the property by reference to adjoining lands and features. Depending on the facts of the particular case, one or more of the following may be required:

(a) A declaration of identity, from the applicant's architect or surveyor, confirming, if such be the case, that the subject property, as marked on the application map, is wholly comprised within the boundaries shown on title maps.

(b) A declaration, from the applicant's architect or surveyor, explaining the absence of ordnance survey detail and specifying the physical features on the ground that are represented by the boundary lines shown on the application map.

(c) A valuation office extract, showing a list of rated occupiers since 1950, together with a copy of the valuation office map.

(d) The names and addresses of adjoining owners/occupiers for service of notices.

(e) Indemnity.

(f) Corroborating affidavit.

13.3.11   DEALING WITH PROPERTY THE SUBJECT OF A FIRST REGISTRATION APPLICATION PENDING IN THE LAND REGISTRY

It often transpires that property the subject of a first registration application in the Land Registry is conveyed or assigned on prior to registration. As the date of registration of a first registration application is the date of settling by the Land Registry official (rule 51 of the LR Rules) the Land Registry will treat the application as a fresh application and the usual affidavits in Forms 1 or 2 of the LR Rules, as amended, should be enclosed as should further searches. In the interim the property remains unregistered land. The property, if freehold, should be conveyed rather than transferred but words of limitation are no longer necessary in a conveyance of freehold land on or after 1 December 2009: s 67 of the 2009 Act. In the case of leasehold land, a deed of assignment for the residue of the term etc should be used rather than a transfer. If the conveyance or assignment is lodged separately in the Land Registry by the purchaser's solicitor, reference should be made to the pending dealing number and consideration should be given to the pending dealing being taken over by the purchasing solicitor. Consent of the vendor's solicitor will be required.

Under s 58 of the 2006 Act, s 51 of the 1964 Act was amended. It provides that the word 'transfer' shall include a lease and thus when a registered owner of land leases the land or any part of it the lessee shall be registered as owner of the leasehold interest in the land. Such a lease is no longer deemed to confer an unregistered leasehold interest and therefore for leases of registered land dated on or after 26 May 2006, Form 16 and searches are not required and the interest can be transferred on by the person entitled to be registered as owner. In turn no Form 2 or searches are required. Such leases or transfers on are no longer registrable in the Registry of Deeds and registration is as of the date of lodgement not settling (rule 58 of the LR Rules).

Note also the different way registered and unregistered property was previously mortgaged. A charge is the appropriate method of registering a mortgage of registered land: s 62(2) of the 1964 Act. The normal procedure for mortgaging unregistered property prior to 1 December 2009 was by way of conveyance or demise with a proviso for redemption and the usual declaration of trust of any nominal reversion. If a mortgage of unregistered land dated prior to 1 December 2009 was by way of charge the mortgagee did not have the Conveyancing Act powers and the Land Registry could not register the ownership of the charge. Under s 89 of the 2009 Act a legal mortgage of both registered and unregistered land may now only be created by a charge by deed from 1 December 2009.

See the Conveyancing Committee Practice Note 'Status of unregistered title while first registration is pending' (Law Society *Gazette*, December 2014) which reminds practitioners that as the title remains unregistered the title should be investigated in the usual manner, that the purchaser's solicitor should have sight of the vendor's application for first registration in the Land Registry together with any rulings and responses thereto, that the vendor may not be described as 'the person entitled to be the registered owner', and that the deed of assurance to the purchaser and any mortgage or other relevant document should first be registered in the Registry of Deeds. In addition, when drafting the application for first registration the purchaser's solicitor may take into account the existing statement of title but the decision to do so should be based on the quality of that statement of title.

13.3.12 DEVELOPMENT SCHEMES

13.3.12.1 First registration

In the case of development schemes, whether they are industrial or housing estates or office blocks or apartments, where the title is unregistered or where there are multiple unregistered titles, consideration should be given to applying for first registration as it is more convenient to produce a folio to intending purchasers than to have to produce a booklet or booklets of title to each individual purchaser or lessee.

The property in the scheme will typically have been acquired from the several owners of estates and interests in the various properties. A typical application would be for first registration of No's 1 to 7 Main Street. Consideration could be given in a suitable case to the feasibility of dividing up such application into separate first registration applications. Such an approach has the advantage of allowing registration to proceed in respect of portions where the title is straightforward. Statements of title (see **13.3.1.1**) must be provided in respect of each interest on the title to each portion, eg fee farm grantor's interest, grantee's interest, lessee's interest, sub-lessee's interest. The statements of title should clearly and precisely show the title to each interest in each plot. All searches should be related to each interest in each plot. A multi-title map in appropriate cases, in addition to the application map, should be marked and lodged on an appropriate Land Registry compliant map with a distinctive colour for each title acquired and separate reference should be made to each coloured property on this map in the statement of title. Commonly the various deeds will contain either descriptions, measurements, or may have maps of varying quality endorsed. Where possible lodgement of an architect's declaration of identity confirming that the property the subject of the first registration is wholly comprised within the bounds of the relevant documents of title as shown in the descriptions, measurements, and maps contained in or endorsed on the various deeds is useful and will expedite matters. All contracts for sale on title should be lodged. Of particular relevance will be special conditions, if any. An original legal opinion dealing fully with the titles of the various interests in the various application properties and setting out the difficulties, if any, arising is useful (see **13.3.2.2**). In this regard the curative effect of title registration should be borne in mind in relation to defects in title, which may come to light on examination of the title and are ruled upon.

13.3.12.2 Companies

Development scheme applications are usually made on behalf of companies. In this regard care should be taken to lodge the following (see also **14.17**):

(a) affidavit in Form 1 or Form 2 to be made by secretary or law officer or, if made by a director, evidence that he is authorised and has the necessary means of knowledge to make the affidavit;

(b) original certificate of incorporation to be lodged unless the company is already the registered owner of other land;

(c) the memorandum and articles of association to be lodged for evidence of power to acquire and sell the property and to affix the seal;

(d)   Companies Registration Office search to be lodged against the applicant company and in a suitable case against all companies on the title (see **13.3.6.3**) and in the case of ICAVs searches in the Central Bank (see **13.3.6.4**);

(e)   certificate of registration of charge in the Companies Registration Office pursuant to s 409 of the Companies Act, 2014 (formerly s 99 of the Companies Act, 1963) to be obtained and lodged. If such certificate is not lodged a note to such effect will be entered in the register under rule 106 of the LR Rules.

In relation to the execution of deeds by a foreign company without the use of a seal note s 64(2)(b)(iv) of the 2009 Act provides that an instrument executed after 1 December 2009 is a deed if it is executed in the following manner:

if made by a foreign body corporate, it is executed in accordance with the legal requirements governing execution of the instrument in question by such a body corporate in the jurisdiction where it is incorporated.

Note also rule 74(5) of the LR Rules states:

On a disposition made by a foreign body corporate where a certificate is lodged from a lawyer from the country in question or who has sufficient knowledge of the laws of the country in question, that the deed was executed in accordance with the legal requirements governing execution of the instrument in question by such a body corporate in the jurisdiction where it is incorporated, the Authority shall be entitled to assume that the deed was duly executed by the body corporate.

13.3.12.3   Leases/Sub-leases

An issue arises where first registration of, for example, a block of apartments is applied for. This could be in relation to a freehold interest or a leasehold interest. The applicant grants leases or sub-leases of the apartments prior to making an application for first registration and continues to grant them on an ongoing basis while the application is pending registration. The date of registration of a first registration is the date of settling (rule 51 of the LR Rules) and burdens which include leases or sub-leases as the case may be have to be registered as burdens on the new folio opened: ss 34 and 41 of the 1964 Act. The normal Land Registry query in such a case is to request an up-to-date Form 1 or 2 prior to settling setting out all the leases or sub-leases granted to date (Schedule Part 2) together with certified copies of these leases. All the leases are then registered as burdens on the new folio opened. Difficulties can arise as certified copies of the leases are often not easily available and leases continue to be granted. The Land Registry now offers an option in these cases. An up-to-date Form 1 or 2 setting out the relevant details of all the leases or sub-leases granted to date should be lodged. Relevant details include the date of each lease or sub-lease, the names and addresses of the parties, property description, commencement date, and term of years and rent. The LR then registers the following entry on the new folio to be opened in the applicant's name:

'The leases listed in Instrument Number D2016LRXXXXXXA made between the registered owner herein as lessor and the lessees therein for the term of years and at the rent specified in each lease affecting the various parts of the property herein being the premises demised by each of the said leases.'

When the various leases are lodged for registration they will be registered as burdens on the applicant's folio in the normal manner.

13.3.13   TITLE TO BE REGISTERED

See Fitzgerald, *Land Registry Practice* (2nd edn) para 1.6 and McAllister, *Registration of Title in Ireland* (1973) pp 32–4.

13.3.13.1   Absolute title

The title normally applied for and registered is absolute and it is the policy of the Authority to register with absolute title whenever this is possible. Absolute title can be given where the title is approved by the Authority (ss 33(4) and 40(4) of the 1964 Act). The effect of registration with an absolute title is to vest in the person so registered an estate in fee simple in the land (or the leasehold interest) together with all implied or express rights, privileges or appurtenances attached or appurtenant thereto (ss 37 and 44 of the 1964 Act).

13.3.13.2 Good leasehold title

Leasehold title where the title to the leasehold interest is approved by the Authority but where the lessor's title has not been established will be registered as good leasehold (s 40(5) of the 1964 Act). An absolute title will not be registered for a leasehold unless the title to the freehold estate and any intermediate leasehold interest that may exist is approved by the Authority (s 40(4) of the 1964 Act). Registration with a good leasehold title shall not affect or prejudice the enforcement of any right adverse to or in derogation of the title of the lessor to grant the lease but, save as aforesaid, shall have the same effect as registration with an absolute title (s 45 of the 1964 Act).

However please note the following:

- In most instances the title to be applied for will be 'Good leasehold'; leasehold title where the title to the leasehold interest is approved by the Authority but where the lessor's title has not been established will be registered as 'Good leasehold' (s 40(5) of the 1964 Act).

- In order to register a title as absolute, the title of the lessor (and the freehold estate and any intermediate interest) to make the lease must be approved by the Authority (see s 40(4) of the 1964 Act).

  'If the applicant applies for an absolute title to the leasehold he should lodge, in addition to the deeds and documents of the leasehold title, normal conveyancing evidence of both the freehold and any intermediate leasehold titles' Fitzgerald, *Land Registry Practice* (2nd edn, 1995) para 22.5.

- In practice it is unlikely that the applicant will have all the relevant original title deeds for the freehold and any intermediate leasehold interests. In these cases the Authority accept the following:

  (a) Form 2 should apply for 'absolute title'.

  (b) The statement of title lodged (Part 3 of the Schedule of Form 2) should deal not only with the leasehold interest but should also fully set out the title of the freehold and any intermediate leaseholds commencing with a good root in relation to each title.

  (c) Certified copies of the documents of title of the freehold and any intermediate leasehold interests set out in the statement of title should be lodged. This usually takes the form of the booklet of title the original lessee received from the lessor.

  (d) Registry of Deeds searches against the relevant parties who held the freehold title and any intermediate leasehold titles from the day before the date of the root of title to the date after the lease was registered in the Registry of Deeds and all acts explained.

  (e) Judgment Office searches for the last five years against the persons holding the freehold title and any intermediate leasehold titles.

13.3.13.3 Qualified title

A title registered subject to specific limitations entered on the register is called a qualified title (ss 33(5) and 40(6) of the 1964 Act, as amended by ss 56 and 57 of the 2006 Act). Such a registration could only be made where, on an application for registration with absolute title, the Authority is satisfied that the title can be established for a limited period only or subject to certain reservations; (a) arising before a specified date, eg root less than permitted length; or (b) arising under a specified instrument, eg covenants in a missing fee farm grant; or (c) otherwise particularly described in the register. Registration with a qualified title shall have the same effect as registration with an absolute title, save that registration with a qualified title shall not affect or prejudice the enforcement of any right appearing by the register to be excepted (s 39 of the 1964 Act and in relation to leaseholds see s 47 of the 1964 Act). It does not in any way denote a defective title. Sections 56 and 57 of the 2006 Act amended ss 33 and 40 of the 1964 Act to allow for applications for first registration with qualified title. Therefore applicants are able to apply for qualified title ab initio subject to stated reservations that will appear on the register. It is the intention of Government that the extension of title registration should now be accelerated to ensure that the State will have a complete land register. This could mean that a title might have to be registered about which title there are certain reservations or the title can only be established for a limited period. For example if you only have a ten-year root in relation to a property that has a market value in excess of €1,000,000, this amendment allows you to apply for registration subject to a qualification regarding the short root. This qualification will be cured by time (see rule 39 of the LR Rules and **14.4.13**).

Rule 19(3) and 19(4) of the LR Rules which provides for a Form 3 (see **13.3.16.3**) allows a solicitor to certify title subject to certain reservations.

13.3.13.4 Possessory title

If in an application for registration the Authority is not satisfied that either an absolute or qualified title is warranted, it may register the applicant as owner with a possessory title (ss 33(6) and 40(7) of the 1964 Act). Where registration of title is not compulsory, a possessory title will not be registered without the consent of the applicant. It may be given where the title is clearly doubtful and defective, for example where the applicant has not accounted for all interests and rights arising on the title or title may be dependent upon actual occupation of the land or upon receipt of the rent and profits issuing out of the land and not necessarily upon documentary proof. Registration with a possessory title shall not affect or prejudice the enforcement of any right adverse to or in derogation of the title of that person and subsisting or capable of arising at the time of registration but, save as aforesaid, shall have the same effect as registration with an absolute title (s 38 of the 1964 Act and in relation to leaseholds see s 46 of the 1964 Act). A possessory title can be applied for ab initio: see Forms 1, 2, and 5.

13.3.14   FREEHOLD

An application for first registration in the freehold register should generally comprise:

- an affidavit in Form 1 of the LR Rules to be made by the applicant. A common error is the omission of Part 2 of the Schedule (incumbrances) to Form 1: rule 14 LR Rules;

- statement of title: rule 15(1)(a) which is in Part 3 of the Schedule to Form 1;

- schedule of documents. This is required in view of the large number of title documents usually lodged in first registration applications: rule 15(1)(d);

- application map: rule 15(1)(c);

- all original deeds and other documents relating to title: rule 15(1)(b);

- all searches in the applicant's possession: rules 15(1)(b) and 18 of the LR Rules;

- fees: rule 11(1)(b). Currently the Land Registry fee for first registrations is €500;

- Form 17 rule 11;

- if there is a mortgage to be registered a certificate by the solicitor for the mortgagee to the effect, if such be the case, that there have been no acts affecting the property or the mortgage by the mortgagee since the date of the mortgage;

- where the documents disclose a purchaser's prior tenancy or other interest in the application property, the prior tenancy is to be dealt with, with a view to merging the same or having it noted as a burden on the folio. It will usually be indicated by a small consideration in the deed. The title to the tenancy interest has to be investigated;

- first registration applications made under order of the court. It is to be noted that s 21 of the 1964 Act relates to registered land only. Where a court order is lodged, relating to unregistered land declaring that the applicant is entitled to an estate in fee simple free from encumbrances or directing the Authority to register the applicant as full owner etc the solicitor will be informed that the court order in respect of unregistered land does not come within s 21 of the 1964 Act and that an application in Form 1 of the LR Rules together with the title documents (including the court order) may be lodged.

13.3.15 LEASEHOLD

The general requirements are similar to those for freehold and are set out above (see rule 16 of the LR Rules). Form 2 is used instead of Form 1. (See **13.3.11** in relation to s 58 of the 2006 Act.)

In most instances the title to be applied for will be good leasehold. (See **13.3.13.2.**)

Burdens or rights of way created in leases are not as a matter of practice registered on a leasehold folio, being considered obligations and liabilities incident to the registered interest. (Sections 44(3)(c) and 72(1)(h) of the 1964 Act.)

Note: if the unexpired residue of the term granted in the lease does not exceed 21 years, see **13.2.2**.

Where the lease was carved out of registered property prior to 26 May 2006, then pursuant to s 70 of the 1964 Act and rule 115 of the LR Rules, the title to the lease must be registered simultaneously with the registration of the lease as a burden. Any such lease is deemed to confer an unregistered leasehold interest and any dealings therewith up to the date of its registration in the Land Registry (including a mortgage) should be in the manner appropriate to unregistered property. If the applicant is an assignee of the leasehold interest, Forms 2 and 16 etc should be lodged, together with the original lease and a certified copy thereof and all assignments. The original lease is returned to the applicant's solicitor on completion. If the applicant is the original lessee of the interest Form 2 is not required, but the other documents as set out earlier should be lodged.

See **14.12.10** in relation to lease burdens on folios.

13.3.16 CERTIFICATE IN FORM 3

The modified form of application for first registration of title in Form 3 of the LR Rules is appropriate if there is a recent sale (ie dated in the last two years) where the consideration does not exceed €1,000,000. If the solicitor can vouch for the title of the purchaser (or has given a certificate of title to a lending institution) then this modified form of first registration should be considered.

13.3.16.1 Situations in which Form 3 may not be appropriate

Form 3 may not be appropriate in the following circumstances:

(a) where the title is based on a voluntary conveyance/assignment or assent on death;

(b) where any part of the prior title is based on possession;

(c) where the conveyance/assignment is over five years old;

(d) where the title is subject to any unexplained rents or covenants;

(e) where superior, intermediate, or lower estates or interests have been acquired and merger or forfeiture is claimed;

(f) where the interest being conveyed/assigned is a lessee's interest under a renewable lease;

    (g) where the property being conveyed or assigned forms a portion of property comprised in a fee farm grant or lease in respect of which it is stated that rent has been apportioned;

    (h) where a step in prior title is impossible or erroneous;

    (i) where the solicitor who makes the Form 3 application has a beneficial interest in the property.

13.3.16.2 Form 3

The current Form 3 is provided for under rule 19(3) of the LR Rules 2012 as amended by rule 5 of the LR Rules, 2013. This revised Form 3 applies from 1 November 2013 (see **13.3.16.3**) and can also be used for applications under rule 19(4) of the LR Rules. Note, in both instances the difference from rule 19(2) which relates to current value: see **13.3.2.2**. Rule 19(3) and paragraph 8 of Form 3 allow for application for registration with an absolute, qualified, or good leasehold title as follows:

- If a solicitor investigates a title and certifies it, the Land Registry will not investigate it. The Land Registry will accept a properly executed certificate.

- The certifying solicitor must be the investigating solicitor, in person. The certificate should only be furnished where the practitioner can absolutely vouch for the title of the applicant. Certificates in Form 3 must be made and signed by the individual solicitor who investigated the title and not by or in the name of the firm.

- The application map must comply with Land Registry mapping requirements (see **14.2.8.1**). See especially **13.3.10**. Particular care should be taken to ensure that the application property is wholly within the bounds of the descriptions, measurements, and maps contained in or endorsed on the relevant documents of title. Also ensure by way of Land Registry mapping search under rule 160(1)(b) of the LR Rules or by inspection of the Land Registry map (which can be done online) that the property marked on the application map comprises unregistered land and does not conflict with registered land.

- Burdens to be registered should be set out fully at paragraph 8. This is a common omission. The solicitor must set out in paragraph 8 of Form 3 the burdens which by virtue of s 69 of the 1964 Act (as extended) (see **14.12.4.1**) appear from his investigation of the title to affect the interest, except those burdens which affect without registration by virtue of s 72 of the 1964 Act, as extended.

- The certificate in Form 3 should be lodged for registration without delay. Ideally the certificate of the solicitor with the deed of conveyance or assignment should be lodged within one month of execution. In the case of a delay in doing so, it may be necessary for the Land Registry to call for a fresh certificate or even call on the applicant to furnish the title documents for inspection, eg if the delay is more than two years. If the certificate and deed are more than five years old, a full application for first registration in Forms 1 or 2 under rules 14, 15, (or 16) of the LR Rules will be necessary.

- The rule 19(3) procedure is not appropriate where the vendor's title is based on possession. See paragraph 6 of Form 3.

- A conveyance or assignment must not have contradictions within the document. If the title is recited, it must be consistent with the interest and property assigned or conveyed.

- Difficulties arise if a grantee already has an interest in the property and he is now acquiring a superior interest to merge with the one he already has. See paragraph 7 of Form 3. The Land Registry will insist on full title to the prior interest if an absolute title is sought. The grantee takes as a constructive trustee for those entitled to the prior interest. JCW Wylie deals with this point in his book *Irish Land Law* at para 9.063. As set out in paragraph 7 the solicitor must certify that the interest conveyed/assigned by the conveyance/assignment specified is not an enlargement of a prior interest. For instance a conveyance of the freehold in a 2013 deed where the purchaser is already the owner of the leasehold and where merger is required is an enlargement (whereas if merger is not required then a Form 3 could be used and the lease registered as a burden on the new freehold folio opened) as is a 2013 conveyance by one joint owner (or tenant in common) to the other joint owner (or tenant in common). Whereas, if the deed conveys the freehold and also assigns the leasehold to the applicant, there is no question of enlargement. The question here is, is the whole interest the subject of the application also the subject of the conveyance/assignment on sale.

- An attested copy of a lease or of a fee farm grant should be lodged where appropriate. Note where Form 3 procedure is used in relation to the original lessee the original lease should be lodged.

- Searches are not required by the Land Registry. However the purchaser's solicitor should make searches in the Registry of Deeds, Judgments Office, Companies Office, or Central Bank (where appropriate) against not only the vendor and his predecessors but also against the purchaser up to and including the date of the certificate. Such searches should be made against the purchaser because he may well have dealt with the property prior to lodgement of the application for first registration or he may have suffered a judgment to be registered as a judgment mortgage against his interest. The certifying solicitor should ensure that he has clear title on first registration in accordance with his certificate. The Authority will conduct continuation searches from the date before the date of the Form 3.

Form 3 certificate is not appropriate in the case of problematic unregistered titles and should not be used to hide or attempt to rectify a defect on title. If a problem subsequently arose with the title the State could seek a remedy from the solicitor who certified.

In some Form 3 cases, in relation to a leasehold interest where the superior title (freehold and any intermediate leasehold interests) is not registered, solicitors may inadvertently certify absolute title and when queried accept good leasehold. In other cases, the certificate has been properly considered. The Authority, where absolute leasehold title is certified, raise the following query:

'In view of Section 40(4) of the Registration of Title Act 1964 as amended, and the provisions of Section 57(1) of the Land and Conveyancing Law Reform Act 2009, please confirm that you have examined and satisfied yourself of the title to the freehold and any intermediate interests, and that as a result of your investigation of these titles you are satisfied that the leasehold title acquired is absolute. Alternatively, please confirm that the title to be registered is good leasehold.'

Note prior title documents should not be lodged except as specified in **13.3.16.4**.

13.3.16.3 Form 3 as amended by the 2013 Rules

FORM 3

Application for first registration where purchase money or compensation does not exceed €1,000,000 (Rule 19(3) and (4))

LAND REGISTRY

County

1. I, (*insert solicitor's name*) am the solicitor for (*insert full name and address of the applicant*) who is applicant for registration as owner.

2. I have investigated the title to the property described in the conveyance dated the   day of   , (*or, other instrument*) lodged herewith. The property in or over which the estate or interest acquired by the conveyance (*or, other instrument*) exists is shown on the application map lodged herewith edged red and lettered.

3. As a result of my investigation of the title, I certify that the conveyance (*or, instrument*) conveyed (*or, vested*) the fee simple in the property (*or*), the lessee's interest in a lease dated the   day of   , from   to   in the property for   years from (*commencement date*)   , an attested copy of which is lodged herewith, (*or,*

other right acquired in the property) in the applicant, free from any adverse rights, restrictive covenants or incumbrances, except those subject to which the conveyance (*or, instrument*) expressly conveyed the property.

4. I certify that (save for the mortgage set out in paragraph 8) the said property remains free from any adverse rights, restrictive covenants or incumbrances (other than those already referred to at paragraph 3 hereof) and that there is not at the date of this certificate any transaction which affects or may affect the said property other than as stated herein.

5. The purchase money of (*or*, the compensation for) the property did not exceed €1,000,000. The whole of it had been paid to the person (*or* persons) entitled thereto or authorised to give receipts therefor.

6. I certify that the prior title is not based on possession.

7. I certify that the interest conveyed/assigned is not an enlargement of a prior interest held by the applicant in the property.

8. I apply for registration of the applicant as owner with absolute title (*or* qualified title (qualified as to   )) (*or* good leasehold title) and for the registration as burdens of (the mortgage dated   between   and   ) and the following rights appearing from the said conveyance (*or*, instrument) to affect the ownership.

Dated the   day of   20   .

Signed:

Note: The legal opinion set out in rule 19(6) may be furnished in Form 3, adapted as the case may require.

13.3.16.4 What should the applicant lodge?

- Form 3 dated within one month of lodgement;

- original deed of conveyance/assignment;

- mortgage (if any);

- in leasehold, attested copy of lease and, if a fee farm grant, an attested copy of the fee farm grant;

- if the title is subject to burdens (s 69) created in prior deed, attested copy of the deed;

- map acceptable to the Authority;

- Form 17;

- fees of €130.

13.3.17 VESTING CERTIFICATE

A vesting certificate may issue under s 22(1)(a) of the Landlord and Tenant (Ground Rents) (No 2) Act, 1978 (No 2 Act) (consent case—Form E) or under s 22(1)(b) of the same Act (arbitration case—Form F). Applications for first registrations where there is a vesting certificate on title are subject to the same procedure as set out earlier (see **13.2.2**).

The fee simple title to be shown in arbitration cases can commence with the vesting certificate and title to be traced from there in the normal way. The fee simple title in consent cases can commence with the vesting certificate provided the other documents lodged or any relevant folios do not cast any doubt on the title. The leasehold title should be investigated in all cases to establish the lessee/applicant's title and to ascertain any burdens or charges to be registered on the new freehold folio.

Section 29 of the No 2 Act preserves the security of a charge on a previous leasehold interest. It is therefore necessary to disclose such mortgage and to apply for its registration on the new freehold folio to be opened.

Section 28 of the No 2 Act as amended by s 77 of the 2006 Act provides for covenants which continue in force following the acquisition of the fee simple and which affect the lands without registration under s 72(1) of the 1964 Act.

When dealing with long residential leases of dwellings practitioners should check with their client and in the case of doubt with the ground rents section of the Land Registry to ascertain whether or not the fee simple was acquired under the No 2 Act. Frequently the document will not have been registered in the Registry of Deeds and will not be associated with the title deeds. Often it will be lost and in such case an official duplicate can be obtained from the ground rents section.

When preparing such first registration application the title to the freehold interest is to be traced from the date of the vesting certificate. The title to the leasehold title will be investigated by the Land Registry in all cases to establish the lessee's or applicant's title and to ascertain any burdens or charges to be registered on the new freehold folio. Accordingly, the usual requirements as to lodgement of all original deeds, statement of title, and searches apply to the leasehold title. The forms to be lodged and fees to be lodged will depend on whether or not the freehold and leasehold interests are registered or unregistered.

When an application is made for registration of a title on foot of a vesting certificate, merger of the leasehold interest is required by the Authority in all cases. This is so, as an intention to merge must be imputed to the lessee who avails of his right under the No 2 Act to enlarge his interest into a fee simple. The No 2 Act does not deal expressly with the issue of merger. Section 29 which provides that a mortgage or charge affecting the lessee's interest is deemed to be a mortgage or charge on the fee simple implies that merger has occurred without any express declaration of merger. If the two interests, freehold and leasehold, are unregistered, merger is effected on the issue of the vesting certificate. If one only title is registered, merger takes place with effect from the date of settling of the application for registration. In any dealing with the property after the vesting certificate issues (and prior to its registration in the Land Registry) it would appear to be good practice, to avoid any doubt, to draft the relevant deed as if merger had not taken place ie convey the freehold interest in the vesting certificate and assign the leasehold interest and include a declaration to merge the leasehold in the freehold.

13.4   First Registration of Title Based on Possession

13.4.1   INTRODUCTION

There are two distinct elements to an application to the Land Registry for first registration based on possession:

(a)   possession for the required statutory period will have to be proved; and

(b)   the title against which possession is claimed will have to be identified.

Often applications are lodged which deal with possession for the statutory period only and little or no effort is made to identify the title against which adverse possession is claimed. Applications are merely made for registration of an unencumbered freehold with no further explanation.

Applications for first registration based on possession are not to be confused with applications under s 49 of the 1964 Act (see **14.6**). That section of the Act relates to adverse possession of registered land only. The land in that case is already registered (freehold or leasehold) and the applicant would be claiming the acquisition of the interest of the registered owner by adverse possession. The form of application for first registration based on possession is Form 5 of the LR Rules and for adverse possession of registered land is Form 6 of the LR Rules. When making an application based on possession it is suggested that the first matter to investigate is whether the property in question comprises registered or unregistered land. The Land Registry digital map should be checked to see if the property intended for registration is already registered. If so a s 49 application should be made (see

Practice Direction 'Title by Adverse Possession to Registered Land' on the Authority's web-site www.prai.ie). A mapping search (see rule 160 of the LR Rules and **14.2.9**) (this search can be conducted online: see **13.3.10**) may be carried out to establish the position and this is an opportune time also to establish that the plot in question does not conflict with the boundaries of already registered property or otherwise. It often transpires that after lodge-ment the Land Registry finds that the property is already registered or partly registered and this may conflict with averments in Form 5.

Possession of land implies actual occupation of the land, and/or receiving the rents and profits out of lands and generally performing those acts of ownership in relation to the lands that are consistent with the interest claimed. Of necessity this involves dispossession of the owner. The Irish courts have interpreted this liberally in favour of the dispossessed owner. It is for the applicant to prove the facts on which he or she bases his or her claim and it is a matter for the Authority to decide whether on the facts proved, the title sought has been established. Each case is considered on its own merits in relation to adverse pos-session. See also the law as set out in various court cases (see **13.4.3**).

Where there is more than one layer of dispossession each should be dealt with separately (eg father goes into possession to dispossess the freeholder owner, the father dies, and one of his next of kin dispossesses the other next of kin or the persons entitled on testacy).

It is suggested that full inquiries are made with the applicant prior to Form 5 being com-pleted (see **13.4.15**) and these inquiries should include all the relevant matters set out in the standard rulings of title set out in **13.4.21**).

If an applicant can prove possession for the statutory period but there is difficulty proving the title against which adverse possession is claimed, it is open to the applicant to apply for possessory title ab initio. It is also open to the Authority to offer such possessory title at an early stage. This will be considered by the Authority based on the evidence lodged, eg rural areas are less problematic than city areas with pyramid titles. In this regard s 50(2) of the 1964 Act provides possessory title can be converted on registration of a transfer for valu-able consideration or other disposition for value when the land has been registered for 15 years (see rule 37 of the LR Rules). In these cases the Authority shall, if satisfied that the registered owner is in possession and after giving such notices, if any, as may be prescribed, register the title as absolute (or good leasehold). While this is not the answer to all the problems associated with registration with a possessory title it certainly could be useful in many cases (eg if the applicant did not intend to mortgage or sell the property in the near future or if the applicant is a local authority and the property is unlikely to be disposed of, eg acquired for road widening).

13.4.2   STATUTORY PROVISIONS

13.4.2.1   Statute of Limitations, 1957

Section 13 of the Statute of Limitations, 1957 sets out certain limitation periods as follows:

State property:	30 years.
Foreshore:	60 years or 40 years in certain circumstances.
Person (other than State authority):	12 years.

However, the claims of persons entitled to the estates of deceased persons dying after 1 January 1967 may be barred after six years under s 45 as amended by s 126 of the Succes-sion Act, 1965. Under s 49, as amended by s 127 of the 1965 Act, this period is extended by a further period of three years in the case of shares of persons under a disability. But, legal personal representatives are not barred except after the full period of 12 years. See *Gleeson v Feehan and anor* 1991 ILRM 783.

Section 14 sets out when the right of action is deemed to accrue for present interests and s 15 deals with future interests in land. Extreme care is exercised by the Authority when dealing with limitation periods in future interests.

Section 18 states:

> *No right of action to recover land shall be deemed to accrue unless the land is in the possession (in this section referred to as adverse possession) of some person in whose favour the period of limitation can run.*

Section 24 provides:

> *Subject to . . . at the expiration of the period fixed by this Act for any person to bring an action to recover land, the title of that person to the land shall be extinguished.*

(A subsequent acknowledgement cannot revive.)

Part III deals with extension of limitation periods, for example (Chapter II) persons under disability where the limitation period is up to 30 years.

Under s 99(2) of the 2009 Act s 34 'does not apply to a mortgagee who takes possession of land under a court order under section 97 or section 98'.

Under s 51 if a person in possession acknowledges the title of the owner during the limitation period, 'The right of action shall be deemed to have accrued on and not before the date of the acknowledgement'. Section 58 provides that acknowledgement 'shall be in writing and signed by the person making the acknowledgement'.

In the absence of fraud, mistake, or disability, a right of action for the recovery of land is barred following adverse possession by another for the duration of the statutory period. Time runs from the date the right of action accrues.

13.4.2.2 1964 Act

The 1964 Act makes no reference to applications for first registration based on possession.

13.4.2.3 LR Rules

Rule 17 of the LR Rules provides for applications for first registration based on possession or where the applicant has no documents of title in his or her possession or under his or her control. The title to be shown must be based on 'adverse possession' under the Statute of Limitations, 1957. Such applications shall be made in Form 5 of the LR Rules (see **13.4.15**).

13.4.2.4 Capital Acquisitions Tax Act, 2003

The certificate required by s 62(2) of the Capital Acquisitions Tax Consolidation Act, 2003 as amended by s 128 of the Finance Act, 2008 (formerly s 146 of the Finance Act, 1994) or, if appropriate, a solicitor's certificate in the form prescribed by s 62(7) of the Capital Acquisitions Tax Consolidation Act, 2003 as amended by s 128 of the Finance Act, 2008 (formerly s 128 of the Finance Act, 1996) should always be lodged in all applications based on possession. This is one of the most common omissions in lodgement of these cases and causes undue delay. Note that the Revenue usually require a copy of the applicant's grounding affidavit (Form 5) prior to their issuing the certificate. The Authority cannot accept an application without this certificate and it should always be enclosed on initial lodgement.

The procedure requires the applicant or his or her agent to make a declaration in Revenue Form CA 12 that no charge to tax arose in the period from the date of registration of the registered owner or 28 February 1974 (whichever is later) to the date of registration of the applicant. See Richard Grogan's article 'A Conveyancing Disaster Waiting to Happen', Law Society *Gazette*, April 1995.

There is special provision made in s 62(7) for minor boundary amendments, certain low value transactions, and statutory authorities, for certification by the solicitor in Revenue Form IT 76. This form can be used where the market value at the time of application does not exceed €2,540, the area does not exceed 500 metres, and the application is not part of a series of related applications affecting a single piece of ground exceeding these limits, and the IT 76 is lodged directly in the Land Registry.

All other cases continue to require a certificate in Form CA 12 and the considerations in Richard Grogan's article referred to earlier continue to apply.

Whilst a certificate CA11 for deaths or gifts on title is no longer required after 3 April 2010, the requirement to furnish a CA12 still remains.

13.4.3   THE LAW

It is necessary in the case of applications for first registration based on possession to set out in some detail the case law in this area which forms the basis of the decision of the Authority dealing with the application.

13.4.3.1   Adverse possession

The concept of adverse possession does not surrender itself easily to precise or brief definition. It is essential to be clear however as to the difference between adverse possession and non-adverse possession and perhaps that is the best way to understand it. Treatment over the years has been varied and the concept has developed through case law both in the English and Irish courts. For example it was held that the possession which founds a claim of adverse possession must be open, unconcealed and, it may be added, unequivocal: *Convey v Regan* [1952] IR 56. Generally, it can be said that there is no adverse possession where acts relied upon are equivocal and not inconsistent with the enjoyment of the lands by the owners. An equivocal act claimed as adverse possession, eg the grazing of cattle or other animals on lands, is sometimes claimed as a ground for ownership of lands based on long possession. In *Browne v Fahy*, 25 October 1975, High Court (unreported), Kenny J held that the acts of possession relied on did not amount to adverse possession because they followed from permissible grazing and were not inconsistent with the enjoyment of the lands by the owners. Later in the case of *Murphy v Murphy* [1980] IR 183 the Supreme Court again emphasised that the question of whether or not the person in possession of land was in adverse possession is ultimately a question of fact. In that case the claimant had farmed his mother's land for many years and had mortgaged them to a bank. It was held he had acquired title:

> 'Before the year 1833 the common law had engrafted the doctrine of non-adverse possession on to the earlier Statute of Limitations so that the title of the true owner was not endangered until there was possession clearly inconsistent with recognition of his title, i.e., adverse possession, and so there had to be an ouster. The doctrine of non-adverse possession was abolished by the Real Property Limitation Act, 1833, in which the words "adverse possession" were not used . . . . The use of the words "adverse possession" in the Act of 1957 does not revive the doctrine of non-adverse possession which existed before 1833. In section 18 of the Act of 1957 adverse possession means possession of land which is inconsistent with the title of the true owner: this inconsistency necessarily involves an intention to exclude the true owner, and all other persons, from enjoyment of the estate or interest which is being acquired. Adverse possession requires that there should be a person in possession in whose favour time can run. Thus it cannot run in favour of a licensee or a person in possession as a servant or caretaker or a beneficiary under a trust . . . .' (Kenny J in *Murphy v Murphy* [1980] IR 183 at 202)

13.4.3.2   *Animus possidendi*

Animus possidendi is required and this may be defined as 'the intention to acquire the property and involves the necessity to exclude the true owner'. See the Practice Direction 'Title by Adverse Possession to Registered Land' on the Authority's website, www.prai.ie, which discusses the subject in detail.

'Adverse possession depends on the existence of animus possidendi and it is the presence or absence of this state of mind which must be determined. Where no use is being made of the land and the claimant knows that the owner intends to use it for a specific purpose in the future, this is a factor to be taken into account. The principle has relevance only insofar as that when this factor is present it is easier to hold an absence of animus possidendi.' (Barron J in *Seamus Durack Manufacturing Ltd v Considine* [1987] IR 677 at 683)

In *Murphy v Murphy* [1980] IR 183 it was held by the Supreme Court that for possession to be adverse it must involve the intention by the occupier to exclude the owner from the enjoyment of the estate or interest. The case is cited as authority for the proposition that, to succeed in a claim for adverse possession, it is necessary to show that the true owner was dispossessed and that the squatter's use and occupation of the lands was made with the intention of acquiring possession. In *Feehan v Leamy* [2000] IEHC 118 in finding that the defendant did not have the necessary *animus possidendi* to dispossess the plaintiff Finnegan J drew an analogy with the defendant in *Leigh v Jack* [1879] 5 Ex D 264, citing the following passage of Cockburn CJ at p 271:

'I do not think that any of the defendant's acts were done with a view to defeating the purpose of the parties to the conveyances: his acts were those of a man who did not intend to be a trespasser or to infringe another's rights. The defendant simply used the land until the time should come for carrying out the objective originally contemplated.'

On the balance of probability Finnegan J found that the defendant's state of mind was that litigation was pending and dragging on in relation to the lands which were lying idle and ungrazed. He had been a witness in that litigation and must have been aware of the proceedings. When questioned by gardai after an altercation with a fencing contractor in 1998 he said that the lands belonged to a man in America. This answer, he held, 'indicates to me the absence of the necessary animus possidendi—an intention to preclude the true owner and all other persons from enjoyment of the estate or interest which is being acquired'. Summarising, he held that the 'defendant has failed to satisfy me on the evidence that he has dispossessed the plaintiff and also, insofar as he was in possession of the lands, that he was in possession of the same with the necessary animus possidendi'.

'The basis of the principle seems to be that when a trespasser seeks to oust the true owner by proving acts of unauthorised and long continued user of the owner's lands, he must show that those acts were done with animus possidendi, and he must show this unequivocally. It is not, in my view, enough that, the acts may have been done with the intention of asserting a claim to the soil, if they may equally have been done merely in the assertion of a right to an easement or a profit-à-prendre. When the acts are equivocal—when they may have been done equally with either intention—who should get the benefit of doubt, the rightful owner or the trespasser? I think it should be given to the rightful owner.'

See *Convey v Regan* [1952] IR 56 quoted by Clarke J in *Dunne v Iarnroid Eireann—Irish Rail & anor* [2007] IEHC 314. In this case Clarke J, in applying *Convey v Regan*, was

'satisfied that, where the extent of use of lands in respect of which adverse possession is claimed are consistent equally with establishing an easement or profit-à-prendre as with full ownership, then it is appropriate to infer the lesser rather than the greater entitlement'.

Clarke J asked the following questions:

'1. Is there a continuous period of twelve years during which Mr. Dunne was in exclusive possession of the lands in question to an extent sufficient to establish an intention to possess the land itself rather than to exercise grazing rights or the like over it. 2. Is any contended for period of possession broken by an act of possession by CIE. If so time will only commence to run again when that act of possession by CIE terminates.'

13.4.3.3   Possession

'As to possession, it must be considered in every case with reference to the peculiar circumstances. The acts, implying possession in one case, may be wholly inadequate to prove it in another. The character and value of the property, the suitable and natural mode of using it, the course of conduct which the proprietor might reasonably be expected to follow with a due regard to his own interests—all these things, greatly varying as they must, under various conditions, are to be taken into account in determining the sufficiency of a possession.' (*The Lord Advocate v Lord Lovat* (1880) 5 App Cas at p 288, cited with approval by Costello J at first instance in *Murphy v Murphy*, at p 193 and by Gilligan J in *Keelgrove Properties Ltd v Shelbourne Developments Ltd*, unreported, (2003 No 6598P) 8 July 2005)

'In order to defeat the title of the original landowner, I am of opinion that the adverse user must be of a definite and positive character and such as could leave no doubt in the mind of a landowner alerted to his rights that occupation adverse to his title was taking place. This is particularly the case when the parcel of land involved is for the time being worthless or valueless for the purposes of the original owner.' (*Doyle Administratrix ad Litem of James Doyle deceased v O'Neill* (1995) IEHC 4, O'Hanlon J 13 January 1995)

'1. In the absence of evidence to the contrary, the owner of land with the paper title is deemed to be in possession of the land, as being the person with the prima facie right to possession. The law will thus, without reluctance, ascribe possession either to the paper owner or to persons who can establish a title of claiming through the paper owner.

2. If the law is to attribute possession of land to a person who can establish no paper title to possession, he must be shown to have both factual possession and the requisite intention to possess ("animus possidendi").

3. Factual possession signifies an appropriate degree of physical control. It must be a single and conclusive possession, though there can be a single possession exercised by or on behalf of several persons jointly. Thus an owner of land and a person intruding on that land cannot both be in possession of the land at the same time. The question what acts constitute a sufficient degree of exclusive physical control must depend on the circumstances, in particular the nature of the land and the manner in which land of that nature is commonly used or enjoyed.' (Slade LJ in *Powell v McFarlane* (1979) 38 P&CR 452 quoted with approval by Clarke J in *Dunne v Iarnroid Eireann–Irish Rail & anor* [2007] IEHC 314 (7 September 2007))

13.4.3.4   Intention of the true owner

'In order to defeat a title by dispossessing the former owner, acts must be done which are inconsistent with his enjoyment of the soil for the purpose for which he intended to use it: that is not the case here, where the intention of the plaintiff and her predecessors in title was not either to build upon or to cultivate the land, but to devote it at some future time to public purposes.' (*Leigh v Jack* (1879) 5 ExD 264, Court of Appeal, Bramwell LJ p 273 quoted by Egan J in *Lord Mayor, Aldermen and Burgesses of the City of Cork v Lynch* [1995] 2 ILRM 598)

'As I understand the judgment of Barron J. it is to the effect that it might be inferred that a person, knowing that the paper title owner had no present use for the land but had a future use for it, might occupy it, not for the purposes of possessing it absolutely, but rather for the purposes of making temporary use of it until such time as the future purpose came on stream. In those circumstances the possessing party might not have a sufficient intention to dispossess the owner.' (Clarke J in *Dunne v Iarnroid Eireann–Irish Rail & anor* [2007] IEHC 314 (7 September 2007) referring with approval to *Seamus Durack Manufacturing Ltd v Considine* [1987] IR 677, Barron J, p 683)

The decision in *Leigh v Jack* [1879] 5 Ex D 264 has been construed as the court having laid down a special rule that a squatter cannot dispossess a true owner unless the squatter's use of the disputed land is inconsistent with the true owner's purpose for it. This approach has been followed by the Irish Courts: *Lord Mayor, Aldermen and Burgesses of the City of Cork v Lynch* [1995] 2 ILRM 598 (property required for road widening); *Dundalk Urban District Council v Conway* 15 December 1987, High Court (unreported) (council's use of land to run sewer not affected by occupation of claimant); and, more recently, *Feehan v Leamy* [2000] IEHC 118. Despite the view expressed in *Seamus Durack Manufacturing Ltd v Considine* [1987] IR 677 that it may be too broadly stated, the principle outlined in *Leigh v Jack* still applies in this jurisdiction. Accordingly, in circumstances where it has been established that the owner, while having no present use for the land, has a specific purpose in mind for its use in the future and if the ousted owner demonstrates that the use by the squatter or claimant is not inconsistent with their ultimate intention in respect of the property, registration will be refused. Such issue is properly a matter for the court and not the Land Registry.

13.4.3.5 Acts by paper owner that stop statute from running

Possession of land implies actual occupation of the land, and/or receiving the rents and profits out of lands and generally performing those acts of ownership in relation to the lands that are consistent with the interest claimed. Of necessity, this involves dispossession of the owner. The Irish courts have interpreted this liberally in favour of the dispossessed owner. See *Feehan v Leamy* [2000] IEHC 118 (29 May 2000) as to whether the defendant had dispossessed the plaintiff; on the evidence, Finnegan J found that the plaintiff had not discontinued possession, in that having acquired the lands he enforced his entitlement to possession by seeking and obtaining interlocutory relief against the defendant:

> 'The plaintiff here at no time had any cattle or other animals on the land and did not require same for grazing. The only use to which he put the land was to visit it on a number of occasions each year when he would park his car and, standing on the road or in the gateway, look over the hedge or gate into the same . . . . Insofar as the plaintiff's title is concerned the presumption is that it extends to the centre of the road and so when standing at the gate looking into the lands the plaintiff was in fact standing on his own lands . . . . the plaintiff was exercising all the rights of ownership which he wished to exercise in respect of the lands pending the determination of litigation. I find as a matter of fact that he was not dispossessed.

> An owner or other person with the right to possession of land will be readily assumed to have the requisite intention to possess, unless the contrary is clearly proved. This, in my judgment, is why the slightest acts done by or on behalf of an owner in possession will be found to negative discontinuance of possession.' (Slade LJ in *Powell v McFarlane* [1979] 38 P&CR 452 quoted with approval by Clarke J in *Dunne v Iarnroid Eireann–Irish Rail & anor* [2007] IEHC 314 (7 September 2007)

> 'It is, therefore, important to emphasise that minimal acts of possession by the owner of the paper title will be sufficient to establish that he was not, at least at the relevant time of those acts, dispossessed. The assessment of possession is not one in which the possession of the paper title owner and the person claiming adverse possession are judged on the same basis. An owner will be taken to continue in possession with even minimal acts. A dispossessor will need to establish possession akin to that which an owner making full but ordinary use of the property concerned, having regard to its characteristics, could be expected to make. It is not, therefore, a question of weighing up and balancing the extent of the possession of an owner and a person claiming adverse possession. Provided that there are any acts of possession by the owner, then adverse possession cannot run at the relevant time.' (Clarke J in *Dunne v Iarnroid Eireann–Irish Rail & anor* [2007] IEHC 314)

However it is not clear whether the views of Clarke J represent current Irish law on the subject. According to Nicholas McNicholas in his article 'Recent Developments in Adverse Possession' *Bar Review*, December 2007 'It would appear to be a novel formulation and hitherto unexplored.' In view of the uncertainty the view of Clarke J has to be treated with some caution.

13.4.4   TITLE CLAIMED

An application for first registration based on possession will not be acceptable if full efforts have not been made to ascertain the nature of the title against which adverse possession is claimed. The applicant cannot solely and simply swear a Form 5 affidavit claiming long undisturbed possession or absence of documents or being in receipt of the rents and profits and then relying on the Statute of Limitations, 1957 proceed to state that he is not aware of any fact whereby his title may be called into question and apply for registration of an unencumbered freehold.

Currently many applications are lodged in such an unprepared format and are badly researched (if at all) and in such cases standard preliminary rulings issue or in some instances there is no choice but to reject the application. See examples of such sample rulings at **13.4.21** and explanatory comments.

Section 50 of the 2006 Act, amends the definition of a 'leasehold interest' in s 3 of the 1964 Act to read 'the right or interest of a person who has barred under the Statute of Limitations 1957, the right of action of a person entitled to such leasehold interest'. This amendment brings adverse possession applications in relation to unregistered leasehold interests into line with adverse possession applications in relation to registered land pursuant to s 49 of the 1964 Act and was brought into operation on 26 May 2006. This amendment overturned *Perry v Woodfarm Homes Limited* [1975] IR 104. Therefore, as and from 26 May 2006 applications for first registration based upon adverse possession of an unregistered leasehold interest can be considered by the Authority on lodgement of the necessary proofs and after the usual enquiries and notices. The applicant, if successful, can then be registered as owner of a leasehold folio. A copy of the lease should be lodged.

Registration with absolute title is usually applied for but registration with possessory title may only be offered after an examination of the application and where sufficient proofs are not forthcoming. The same obstacles to registration with an absolute title would still obtain in the future if an application to convert such possessory title was made. However note **13.4.1** in relation to s 50(2) of the 1964 Act and conversion of title. Before such registration with possessory title is made the effect of s 38 of the 1964 Act would be pointed out to the solicitor for the applicant.

In applications in relation to a leasehold interest registration would be made with good leasehold title (unless the freehold and any intervening head leasehold are registered with absolute title or unless these superior titles are proved). Again possessory title might be offered as mentioned earlier.

13.4.4.1   Valuation Office

If the fee simple ownership cannot be shown, a certificate from the General Valuation Office records showing the occupiers and immediate lessors of the property from 1960 (or going back sufficiently in time to establish the factual situation), together with a General Valuation Office map to which the entries on the certificate or extract may be related, is required. See standard ruling 8 in **13.4.21**.

It is important to note that the Valuation Office certificate does not prove title but may show evidence to support the application. The Valuation Office certificate has columns for, *inter alia*, plot number, occupiers, immediate lessors, and description of tenement.

- The plot number column relates to the plot number on the Valuation Office map and the property should be edged red on same. Note that sometimes a plot number can be subdivided, eg plot 2.1, 2.2, etc.

- The occupiers column should ideally reflect the occupation as claimed by the applicant (see sample ruling 12 in **13.4.21**).

- The immediate lessors column is to be noted and same should be fully explained by the applicant (see sample ruling 11 in **13.4.21**).

• The description of tenement column gives as per its heading a description of the tenement, eg land or house and garden. It is most useful if it says 'in fee' which, while not conclusive, evidences a freehold.

13.4.5 ADJACENT PROPERTY OWNED BY THE APPLICANT

Property (whether registered or unregistered) owned by the same applicant in the area might assist as may reference to recently registered properties held under the same title in the same area. However on occasion too much reliance is placed and too much information given on the documentary title owned by the applicant with insufficient concentration on the property the subject of the application. There is often a good reason why the subject property did not form part of the relevant unregistered property or folio in the first instance (see **13.4.7**).

If the applicant owns leasehold property adjacent to the property the subject of the adverse possession application the issue of encroachment will have to be considered. While there is a presumption that the encroached plot is annexed to their lands on termination of the lease, the plot must be regarded as having accrued to the landlord's reversion together with the demised premises. This applies whether the title of the dispossessed owner of the encroached plot is freehold or leasehold. In the encroachment case of *Battelle v Pinemeadow Limited* [2002] IEHC 120 Finnegan J found that the title acquired by the plaintiffs is the title by encroachment, ie the right to possession of the premises in dispute against the fee simple owner for the unexpired term of their lease of the plaintiff's premises. The freeholder's entitlement to the land in reversion upon expiration of the lease remains undisturbed. The interest acquired is not a registrable interest. It is merely a right to remain in possession until the expiration of the lease. Evidence of a contrary intention on the lessee's part may rebut the presumption as the presumption is one of fact and not of law. See also *King v Smith* [1950] 1 All ER 553, Wylie's *Landlord and Tenant Law* (2nd edn) para 28.11; Brady and Kerr, *The Limitation of Actions* (2nd edn) pp 124–7; and LRC, *Report on Title by Adverse Possession*, 67–2002.

The presumption could be rebutted by proving that the encroached upon property was used independently of the leasehold premises and therefore the normal adverse possession rules apply in relation to the actual title of the encroached upon property. It is also open to an applicant to prove that the encroached upon property was always intended by the parties to the lease to be part of his lease and therefore encroachment does not arise (this would only be relevant where the landlord also owned the encroached upon property).

In all such cases the Authority will raise the issue of encroachment (see sample ruling 3 in **13.4.21**). It is open to the applicant to make a case rebutting the presumption quoting authorities. Each case will be decided on its merits. If the presumption cannot be rebutted the application cannot proceed.

13.4.6 OVERHOLDING ON LEASE OR TENANCY

Issues that arise include whether the lease was renewed or replaced on expiry? Has rent been paid subsequent to the expiry of the lease? Had the applicant/lessee a right to a renewal of the lease either under the terms of the lease or under statute? Has the lessee a right to enlarge his interest under the Landlord and Tenant Acts? Also in relation to a tenancy, was the tenancy in writing and, if so, when it terminated? If the tenancy is in writing there is no adverse possession: s 17(2) of the 1957 Act does not apply. This is dealt with in the Law Reform Commission *Report on Land Law and Conveyancing Law (1) General Proposals* (LRC 30–1989) paras 54 and 55. The relevant case is *Sauerzweig v Feeney* [1986] IR 224. The right of action of the owner of the superior interest (freehold) would accrue one year after expiry of the lease or tenancy.

13.4.7   AREAS LEFT OUT OF LAND COMMISSION VESTINGS

Frequently applications are made on the basis that certain areas of land were left out in error when property was vested in the applicant's predecessors by the Land Commission. While this may be a possibility it is often not the case. These areas of land were often left out of Land Commission vestings deliberately as the Land Commission only vested tenanted land and these areas for various reasons were not tenanted land. Rocky areas of land (fox coverts) were no use for farming and would not be the subject of tenancies and would therefore be left out of Land Commission vesting's even where the tenant owned all the land surrounding same. The same applies to groups of trees, ie copses. A third instance is trees that lined a road. The landlord would have retained rights to the trees. The farmer would not have taken this land on a tenancy as he could not use same and therefore the property would not have been vested by the Land Commission. In these cases the applicant may own all the land adjoining the road except for a strip of trees adjacent to the road itself. A final example is the old farmhouse. The farmer would have taken the property on a tenancy but not an agricultural tenancy. Therefore the property would not have been vested by the Land Commission even though all the surrounding land was. The issue then is whether the farmer continued to pay rent and to whom or did the farmer buy out the freehold, maybe without any evidence in writing. Comprehensive inquiries should be made in relation to the history of the property and also the name and address of the local landlord or his successors.

13.4.8   SUCCESSIVE SQUATTERS

Since a squatter has a title based on his possession which is good against everyone except the disposed owner, he can pass this title to others. Thus a squatter in the process of disbarring the true owner by adverse possession, eg ten years' possession, can pass his interest in the land **by deed** to someone else who can add the ten years' possession to his own, ie after another two years' possession he completes the acquisition of ownership by adverse possession. (*Asher v Whitlock* (1865) LR 1 QB 1; *Willis v Earl Howe* [1893] 2 Ch 545.) See Wylie, *Irish Land Law* (3rd edn) para 23.21. See also Fitzgerald, *Land Registry Practice*, (2nd edn) para 11.14.

13.4.9   ADVERSE POSSESSION AND FEE FARM RENTS

Fee farm rents are treated as incumbrances on the land like 'rentcharges' (ss 2(7)(a) and 18(4)(a) The Statute of Limitations, 1957). Non-payment of a fee farm rent for 12 years bars the right to recover the rent (*Wright v Redmond* [1936] 70 ILTR 227). Wylie, *Landlord and Tenant Law* (2nd edn) para 28.02 states it also extinguishes the grantor's title and with it the covenants enforceable by him (Wylie, 'The effect of non-payment of a fee farm rent', Western Law Gazette (Dli), Winter 1993 p 50). The Authority view is that while the fee farm rent is barred there is no case law to confirm the view re covenants and conditions. In practice if the covenants and conditions relate only to the rent then the fee farm grantor's interest is extinguished. However if the fee farm grant is a conversion grant (The Renewable Leasehold Conversion Act, 1849) that converts a lease for lives renewable forever into a fee farm grant it should be noted that the covenants and conditions in the lease continue to effect the property. The Authority will also consider the situation based on the facts of the individual application if a case is made that the covenants and conditions relate also only to keeping buildings in repair.

13.4.10   ADVERSE POSSESSION AND TRUSTEE APPLICANTS

To acquire title by adverse possession *specific persons* must:

• dispossess the original owner;

• and those specific persons must enter into possession, excluding the true owner and all others;

- and exercise such acts of ownership, use, and enjoyment to amount to exclusive possession;

- with an intention of acquiring the title of the original owner; and

- in a manner inconsistent with the title of the original owner.

In cases where the applicants are trustees for say a sporting club, they usually cannot meet these requirements.

Where a *prima facie* case of adverse possession by the trustees of say a sporting club has been shown for in excess of the statutory period the issue to be addressed is in whom the legal interest now vests. It cannot vest in the sporting club as it is not a legal entity. It also cannot vest in individual trustees as the trustees themselves have not been in adverse possession. Each case will have to be considered on its merits.

13.4.11   ADVERSE POSSESSION AGAINST A COMPANY

An issue can arise where adverse possession is claimed against a company but the company is dissolved prior to the completion of the limitation period of 12 years. Under s 28(2) of the State Property Act 1954:

> where a body corporate is dissolved . . . all land which was vested in or held in trust for such body corporate immediately before its dissolution . . . shall, immediately upon such dissolution, become and be the property of the State, subject however to any incumbrances or charges affecting the land immediately before such dissolution.

Section 31 of the State Property Act, 1954 enables the Minister for Finance, if he considers it proper to do so, to waive his interest in property which has vested in the State under s 28(2) of the Act. He may waive the right of the State to such property in favour of such person and on such terms (whether including or not including the payment of money) as he thinks proper having regard to all the circumstances of the case. Note, under s 13(1) of the Statute of Limitations, 1957 the limitation period for the State is 30 years:

> Subject to paragraphs (b) and (c) of this subsection, no action shall be brought by a State authority to recover any land after the expiration of thirty years from the date on which the right of action accrued to a State authority or, if it first accrued to some person through whom a State authority claims, to that person.

13.4.12   ADVERSE POSSESSION AGAINST THE STATE

As stated the limitation period for State owned property is 30 years. However, issues can arise as to the appropriate limitation period where the property devolves to the State as ultimate intestate successor (s 73(1) of the Succession Act, 1965) prior to the completion of the limitation period in relation to a deceased owner. See issue re property of companies at **13.4.11**.

Note *O'Hagan (personal representative of Alice Dolan (decd)) v Grogan* [2012] IESC 8, Supreme Court, 16 February 2012. It relates to a case where the Chief State Solicitor took out administration of an estate where he had the consent of the AG to take it out.

The issue related to which time limit for the taking of action applied, ie whether under s 1(a) of the Statute of Limitations, 1957 (the State authority—30 years) or s 13(2)(a) (12 years). The question was whether the Chief State Solicitor came under the definition of a State authority. The Supreme Court found that the Chief State Solicitor was not a State authority and the limitation period was 12 years.

However Mr Justice Finnegan did go on to state:

> 'The wording of the consent of the Attorney General and of the Letters of Administration Intestate issued in this case reflect that procedure—the grant is made to the Chief

State Solicitor as nominee for and on behalf of the State. It is quite clear that the person entitled to bring or defend proceedings on behalf of the estate is the Chief State Solicitor to whom representation has been granted. This will remain the position until an assent is executed to a Minister of State pursuant to the provisions of the State Property Act 1954. The Minister of State being a State authority could then maintain proceedings. As the Chief State Solicitor can be called upon at any time to execute an assent in favour of a State authority (normally the Minister for Finance) it does not appear to be necessary to construe Attorney General widely to enable the State's interest to be protected where representation issues on behalf of the State to the Chief State Solicitor. For this reason also I would not extend the definition of State authority.'

13.4.13   VESTING CERTIFICATES

As stated in **13.3.17** the leasehold title has to be investigated in all cases. If the applicant is claiming the leasehold based on adverse possession then the normal Land Registry requirements will apply in relation to this interest.

13.4.14   SUMMARY OF LAND REGISTRY REQUIREMENTS

To acquire title by adverse possession the applicant must:

- firstly, establish the nature of the interest claimed in the property;

- secondly, show how that interest has devolved to the applicant;

- specific persons must dispossess the true (paper) owner;

- those specific persons must enter into possession;

- exclude the true owner and all others;

- exercise such acts of ownership, use, and enjoyment to amount to exclusive possession;

- with an intention of acquiring the title of the true owner;

- in a manner inconsistent with the title of the true owner.

Further, the names and addresses of persons formerly entitled to the freehold (or leasehold) and against whom adverse possession is claimed should be furnished. Full information within the applicant's knowledge or procurement concerning them should be given.

Where the applicant further claims in succession to others this must also be comprehensively dealt with.

If the application is being made for registration in the freehold register, a full freehold estate (fee simple) must be shown. The best evidence of such title is a deduction from a documentary title for the statutory period of 15 years, commencing with a good root of title where the applicant shows:

(a)   the identity of the person who was entitled to the property at the date of the dispossession;

(b)   the nature of that person's interest at the date of such dispossession, ie evidence to establish that the interest was freehold and not leasehold;

(c)   sufficient acts of dominion to show that the possession was adverse.

Generally such evidence is rarely furnished and in such applications (particularly in rural areas where the matter of pyramid title does not arise) sufficient proofs of unequivocal acts of ownership, of user and enjoyment, and dealing with the property over a long period must be lodged in order to show a reasonable presumption of an absolute title in fee simple. Where details of the owner whose title is claimed to be barred are not forthcoming, a minimum period of 30 years' possession is required to establish title, since any owner might be a person under a disability. Any evidence of title, receipts for purchase money, or correspondence, should be lodged. Genuine efforts must be made to locate the freehold title. If it is held in fee simple, the owner thereof may be barred. If it is in settlement, the applicant will not be entitled to registration.

Reference to registered title owned by the same applicant might assist as this may refer to recently registered properties held under the same title in the same area.

13.4.15 FORM 5

The form includes the following.

Paragraph 1 must describe the property the subject of the application in unambiguous terms. The description should identify the property by location (ie townland, barony, street, house number in street, avenue, drive, etc, parish, county) or reference may be made to a schedule to the form where such description is contained. The application should be accompanied by a map of the property drawn to acceptable professional standards on a Land Registry compliant map (see **13.3.10** and **14.2**). This map must also be referred to in the description of the property and linked to the same. Most importantly, it must be averred that such map correctly shows the boundaries of the property which is the subject of the application. This is one of the most common causes of difficulty. Often, after rulings or inquiries from the Authority the application map has to be significantly amended which might call into question all the averments made in Form 5. The application should in every case identify the lands or premises by reference to the application map. Various recitals etc of the schedules to deeds, documents, etc will be of no use if they do not in turn refer to the map or if they cannot be readily equated with the application map. In addition, a search of the Land Registry digital map should be conducted to see if the property is registered. Application maps lodged often include half the roadway. It is hardly possible to establish exclusive possession to the half roadway and such portion should be excluded from the application.

Paragraph 2 sets out the full facts of the case in support of the applicant's claim (ie the facts upon which the averment in paragraph 1 is based). Paragraph 2(a) a description of how the occupation began and the facts to support the claim. Paragraph 2(b) the title against which adverse possession is claimed should be set out. It is suggested that each and every one of the issues mentioned in the sample rulings (set out in **13.4.21**), and all and any other pertinent information where relevant to the specific application, should be addressed prior to drafting up the affidavit, swearing of the same, and lodgement of the application in the Land Registry. Naturally some of the issues will not be relevant for certain cases (eg urban property) but are designed to assist submission of a properly constituted and comprehensively researched application. Failure to address these matters will inevitably mean a lengthy delay in the processing of the application and some of these rulings will be raised in any event. Particular attention should be paid to the notes to Form 5 and also the notes contained in paragraph 2 of the same.

The remainder of the form contains standard averments which are essential.

13.4.16 TREATMENT OF CASE BY THE AUTHORITY

On receipt of the application in the Land Registry the Authority will almost always require further or additional proofs and will raise further rulings with the lodging solicitor. By virtue of rule 18 of the LR Rules searches, newspaper notices, other notices, and enquiries may be directed as are deemed necessary in the circumstances of the case. Corroborating affidavits by a party with knowledge of the facts, perhaps a neighbour or senior solicitor practitioner with knowledge of the facts relating to old estates in the locality, may be called for in a suitable case. The Authority may call for an indemnity if it is deemed necessary. For example this can arise when the whereabouts of some of the notice parties is unknown or cannot be established. However an indemnity cannot be used as a substitute for title.

13.4.17 APPLICANT DIES PRIOR TO FIRST REGISTRATION

Where the applicant dies prior to completion of the registration on lodgement of an application, in Form 1 of the LR Rules by the personal representative of the original applicant (grant being extracted and lodged), and where it is confirmed that it is intended to effect his or her registration as personal representative in order to sell the property in the course of administration of the estate of the original applicant the Authority will consider registering the personal representative. The applicant would be required to consent to the registration of an inhibition restricting all dealings with the property by the registered owner save in the administration of the estate of the original applicant.

13.4.18 NOTICES SERVED

Rule 50 of the LR Rules prescribes the service of notices of the proposed registration. That rule allows for notices to be served on such persons as the Authority may direct. In practice, the Authority serves notice on all identified/necessary notice parties including adjoining/adjacent owners and such others as are deemed appropriate or necessary. The period allowed for reply/objection etc is usually 21 days. It may be deemed appropriate to direct service of notice in a newspaper circulating in the area, the newspaper with the greatest circulation, or in another county or country.

13.4.19 OBJECTIONS

Notices specify that any objection to the proposed registration should disclose a valid legal ground. Where an objection discloses *prima facie* a valid ground (the objection is normally required to be on affidavit) the objector is informed that the matter is being taken up with the applicant's solicitor and that a copy of the affidavit of objection will be forwarded to the applicant's solicitor. The Authority often suggests to an objector that solicitor's advice should be obtained. If a request is made for a copy of the applicant's grounding affidavit a copy may be forwarded (usually the Authority seeks the consent of the applicant). However, the Authority has to take care to ensure that 'personal data', within the meaning of the Data Protection Acts, 1988 to 2003, in relation to any party referred to in the grounding affidavit is redacted. The same applies to potentially defamatory statements or allegations of a criminal nature. In such cases provision of a summary of the contents of the grounding affidavit of the applicant would be considered as an alternative (the same issues may also arise in relation to the affidavit of objection).

The response to the objection is then notified to the objector or objector's solicitor. Supplementary affidavits by the applicant are usually required to deal with objections and for substantiation of the applicant's claims.

The following would not be regarded as valid grounds of objection:

    (a)   occasional social visits on holiday periods (*McEneaney v McEneaney* (1920) 54 ILT and SJ 199);

    (b)   payment of rates, rents, annuity, and outgoings on the lands;

    (c)   where relatives abroad send monies from time to time to help out or for repairs to the house;

    (d)   working on the lands of itself (eg a person working on the lands may sell stock at a fair or mart and hand over the price to another person on the lands who may perhaps be exercising control or acting as owner of the lands); or

    (e)   long continued cutting of turf from the bog of another owner is not sufficient: see *Convey v Regan* [1952] IR 56.

The Authority does not allow arguments and counter arguments to run for too long. Where there is clear conflict between the averments of the applicant and objector, the Registry is not the appropriate forum to resolve such conflict and registration cannot proceed, as the matter has to be dealt with by the court. Where an objector has stated his case on affidavit and the grounds of objection are *prima facie* valid the applicant will be informed that the case should be withdrawn and failure to do so will result in a formal refusal. In these circumstances the applicant may sometimes request a refusal in order to facilitate an appeal to court.

When a decision is made reasons are given to the unsuccessful party and they are informed that an appeal lies to the court under s 19(1) of the 1964 Act. A formal Authority ruling refusing registration will be obtained if the application is not withdrawn voluntarily.

13.4.20 REPLIES TO RULINGS

All replies relating to matters of fact should be on affidavit sworn by the applicant. Matters of interpretation or clarification may be certified by a solicitor.

13.4.21 SAMPLE RULINGS

Comments in relation to these rulings are in italics.

1. How is it shown that the title acquired by the applicant is an unencumbered fee simple rather than a lesser interest (eg an interest under a long lease or a lease subject to a nominal rent in respect of which rent may not have been paid? If it is a limited freehold then that is all that can be barred and will not be registered. See JCW Wylie and Una Woods, *Irish Conveyancing Law* (3rd edn) para 14.81.

   If the title acquired by the applicant is leasehold this leasehold title will have to be proved, eg copy of the lease.

2. The names and addresses of persons formerly entitled to the freehold (or leasehold) and against whom adverse possession is claimed should be furnished. Full information within the applicant's knowledge or procurement concerning them should be given.

   When the whereabouts of some of the notice parties is unknown (when it is established that sufficient effort has been made to locate), an indemnity will be sought, under the seal of the applicant, indemnifying the Authority and the State against all losses, damages or compensation, arising from effecting the applicants' registration as full owner on the Register of Freeholders (or Leaseholders) with absolute title (or good leasehold title) on the basis of the proofs lodged.

   The following sample rulings are designed to elicit the information necessary to comply fully with ruling 1 and above and to assist the practitioner to construct the application in a manner that will facilitate the application being progressed in a timely manner.

3. It appears from the affidavit lodged that the applicants are the persons entitled to the lessee's interest under a lease of the adjoining property and that they encroached on lands adjoining their lands. There is a presumption that the encroached plot is annexed to their lands and on termination of the lease the plot must be regarded as having accrued to the landlord's reversion together with the demised premises. This applies whether the title of the dispossessed owner of the encroached plot is freehold or leasehold. The interest acquired is not a registrable interest. It is merely a right to remain in possession until the expiration of the lease. Evidence of a contrary intention on the lessee's part may rebut the presumption. See *King v Smith* [1950] 1 All ER 553 and *Battelle v Pinemeadow Limited* [2002] IEHC 120. See also JCW Wylie, *Landlord and Tenant Law* (2nd edn) para 28.11, Brady and Kerr, *The Limitation of Actions* (2nd edn) pp 124–7 and Law Reform Commission, *Report on Title by Adverse Possession* LRC 67–2002.

4. Where details of the owners whose title is claimed to be barred are not forthcoming, a minimum of 30 year's possession is required to establish title, since any such owners might be a person under a disability.

5. Where the applicant claims in succession to others, he must show also who they were, how they acquired their interests, and how their interests devolved to the applicant. All deeds, probates, assents, unproved wills, etc, must be lodged, and full details provided of next of kin, heir at law (if relevant), and relicts of persons who died intestate or whose wills are unproved. Deaths should be evidenced by production of death certificates. If he or she claims to have acquired some of those interests by adverse possession, the names and addresses of those against whom he or she claims should be furnished. State, also, the circumstances (eg emigration, marriage, hospitalisation, or otherwise), of the departure of each such person from the property. (Refer also to the notes to paragraph 2(a) Form 5 Land Registration Rules.)

6. State the names and addresses of all persons known to the applicant, who would, but for the Statute of Limitations, have any interest in the property or who might be concerned with the property in any way.

7. Describe the facts relied upon in support of the applicant's claim to have acquired the full fee simple interest in the property, eg evidence that the applicant was not a licensee and was in adverse possession to the fee simple owner and not to a leaseholder, tenancy, life tenant, or other interest less than a fee simple.

8. Has the applicant or his predecessors ever paid any rent to any person in respect of the property? When was the last such payment made? State the name and address of the person to whom such rent was paid and the names and addresses of his or her successors in title and of his or her solicitors or other agent acting for them in the matter.

    Circumstantial evidence leading to the conclusion that the title is freehold may be taken subject to notices etc . . . but a claim that 'rent has not been paid' will not suffice without further evidence.

9. If rent was paid under a tenancy agreement, was such agreement in writing? If so, please lodge a copy of the same. State the nature of the terms of the tenancy. How is it shown that such tenancy terminated?

10. Lodge a certificate from the General Valuation Office records showing the occupiers and immediate lessors of the property from 1960 (or going back sufficiently in time to establish the factual situation), together with a General Valuation Office map to which the entries on the certificate or extract may be related.

    A copy of the General Valuation Office map is the most reliable map as the entries may be readily related to it. In the alternative, a letter from the General Valuation Office referring to an exhibited map and specifying the VO Lot No would be acceptable.

    If, after exhaustive efforts, the fee simple ownership cannot be shown an extract from the Valuation Office and Valuation Office map showing the occupiers and immediate lessors from the earliest date may be of benefit but is not conclusive.

11. Explain any relationship of landlord and tenant appearing on the certificate and any notation thereon that differs from the applicant's account of the occupation of the premises.

12. Say how the applicant acquired from each person appearing as occupier or immediate lessor on the certificate and state the addresses of any such persons whose interest has not been shown to have been acquired by the applicant other than under the Statutes of Limitations. In the case of any of them who are deceased, state the names and addresses of their representatives or successors.

13. Confirm, if such be the case, that the property was never subject to any proceedings under the Land Acts.

    Consider inspection of Land Commission estate map and obtaining a schedule of areas in rare appropriate cases.

14. Confirm that the freehold of the property herein was not vested in the Irish Land Commission.

15. Lodge a letter from the Land Commission/Department of Agriculture confirming whether or not the property was the subject of Land Commission proceedings.

16. Please state the name and address of the current owner of the landlord's estate. Is he or she a life tenant, a fee simple owner, or owner of some estate less than the fee simple?

    If, for instance, the landlord's estate was the subject of a settlement then the Statute of Limitations does not run against a remainderman until that remainderman's right of action accrues. Therefore the most the applicant in such circumstances could have acquired is an estate pur autre vie and would accordingly be unable to show acquisition of a full freehold and registration could not be effected.

17. State the names and addresses of the present representatives, agents, solicitors, and successors of the previous landlord.

18. Who were the original landlords of this area prior to the Land Purchase Acts? State the names and addresses of the present successors of such landlords. State the names and addresses of the present owners of any property formerly occupied by such original landlords.

19. Is the property securely bounded or fenced off from all adjoining property? When and by whom were the fences erected? What is the age, nature, and condition of such fences?

20. If the property has not been fenced in, the applicant's claim to sole and exclusive possession cannot be established. Applicants in such circumstances cannot establish that they have excluded the rightful owner from the property. The dealing should be withdrawn.

21. Some of the boundary does not appear to be OS detail. Produce photographs of these portions of the boundary along with a copy of the application map or a diagram upon which the location from which each photograph was taken and the direction of the shot is marked.

22. What is the age, nature and condition of the buildings, if any, on the property? By whom and in what manner and for what purpose are they used?

23. Is the property part of a bog? Has any person claimed turbary rights on the property? Has peat ever been extracted therefrom for any purpose? Could peat be extracted therefrom?

24. State the names and addresses of the owners and/or occupiers of all land adjoining the property herein so that notice of the application may be served on them.

25. Has the applicant and his predecessors in title been living on the property since commencement of possession by them? Have any other persons been living on the property?

26. State the use to which the applicant and his predecessors have put the property. State what acts of ownership were performed by them, what use and enjoyment they made of the land and how such acts of ownership and use and enjoyment amounted to exclusive possession. Has the property been used by any other person for any purpose since commencement of possession by the applicant or his predecessor?

    It is not sufficient to say that the applicant and his or her predecessors exercised exclusive possession over the property.
    Note also, for example, that if the applicant's possession is attributable to a right of grazing or other right in respect of the property, then he or she cannot claim to be in adverse possession to the legal owner.

27. How, precisely, did the applicant, or his predecessor, take up possession of the lands? Describe the acts by them that constituted the taking of possession by them. When, precisely, was such possession taken?

Where it transpires that entry into possession for example was as a licensee then such possession could not be adverse to the licensor and so prima facie the application must fail unless it could be shown the licence was revoked or determined otherwise.

28. How is it shown that the applicant had and continues to have and that the applicant's predecessors had *animus possidendi*?

   This is the intention to acquire the property and involves the necessity to exclude the true owner.

29. Has the property been acquired by the applicant or his predecessor for use in conjunction with other property in the applicant's possession? If so, please indicate the location of such property and describe the applicant's title thereto. The question of 'encroachment' may require to be considered.

30. As the property or portion thereof was formerly a schoolhouse, there is a probability that it was held under a long lease. What information have you on this? Have you made enquiries concerning the existence of such a lease from the Department of Education, the diocesan and parish trustees, and the Commissioners of Public Works? How is it shown that such lease has expired or otherwise determined? Was the school a Catholic or a Protestant school? Who were the trustees of such school? Furnish the names and addresses of the current successors of such trustees. How did the applicant acquire from them? Specify the diocese and parish to which the school belonged. state the name and address of the relevant bishop, parish priest or rector, diocesan trustees, and parish trustees.

31. The land is described on the map as woodland. Are there trees on the land? Who planted the trees? Has any timber been harvested? If so, when and by whom? State exactly what acts of ownership have been performed by the applicant and his predecessors.

32. Lodge all documents of title in the applicant's possession of control relating to the property.

   Any evidence of title, receipts for purchase money, correspondence, etc should be lodged.

33. Lodge corroborating evidence on affidavit by an independent person relating to the possession of the applicant and his/her predecessors in title.

   Corroborating affidavits may be called for in suitable cases.

34. Please lodge an indemnity, under the seal of the applicant, indemnifying the Property Registration Authority and the State against all claims, losses, damages, or compensation, arising from registration of the applicant as owner with absolute title of the property on the basis of the proofs lodged.

   Raised if the applicant is unable to fully address rulings, eg if applicant is unable to identify the identity of the paper owner or names and addresses of neighbours or title to the property.

35. It is hardly possible to establish exclusive possession of the roadway included within the boundary of the map lodged. Such portion must be excluded from your application.

36. Lodge a verified personal search in the Judgments Office for any lis pendens etc, for the past five years against the applicant and any of the applicant's predecessors who were in possession or appear on the title during any part of the last five years.

37. Lodge a common search or verified hand search on the Registry of Deeds Index of Names only, for all acts affecting the lands by the applicant and each of the applicant's predecessors, from the day prior to the date of commencement of the interest or possession of each such person to the date of registration of the disposition of the interest of such person or the last day or the year in which such person died, or the latest date. The description of the land in such search should include the name of the townland, barony, and county in which the land is situate and, also, any additional or alternative name by which the land has been described. All alternatives of the names of persons searched against should, also, be specified in the searches.

It may also be necessary for searches to be lodged against persons stated to be the dispossessed owners to ascertain the title involved etc.

38. Explain any acts appearing on the above searches.

39. Lodge a certificate by the Revenue Commissioners pursuant to s 62(2) of the Capital Acquisitions Tax Consolidation Act, 2003, as amended by s 128 of the Finance Act, 2008 (formerly s 146 of the Finance Act, 1994) or, if appropriate, a solicitor's certificate in the form prescribed by s 62(7) of the Capital Acquisitions Tax Consolidation Act, 2003, as amended by s 128 of the Finance Act, 2008 (formerly s 128 of the Finance Act, 1996).

13.5   Cautions against First Registration

Section 96 of the 1964 Act and rules 30 and 31 of the LR Rules deal with cautions against first registration (for cautions in general see **14.8**). The applicant must have such an interest as entitles him or her to object to a disposition without his or her consent, or must be an incumbrancer, and must be claiming otherwise than under an instrument registered in the Registry of Deeds. If the instrument under which he or she is claiming is registered in the Registry of Deeds then such registration is sufficient protection.

The application should be made in Form 7 of the LR Rules supported by an affidavit in Form 8 of the LR Rules, paragraph 2 of which states concisely the documents or facts which show that the cautioner has an incumbrance on the property or is entitled to object to a disposition of it without his consent. The Schedule of Form 7 should describe the property affected by the caution by reference to a Land Registry compliant map and should set out details of the applicant's interest and the name and address of the applicant for service of notice. The affidavit may be made by the applicant or his or her solicitor (rule 30(2) of the LR Rules).

The effect of a caution against first registration is that the cautioner is entitled to notice of any application that may be made for registration of an owner of such lands.

If an application for first registration is made, then notice in Form 19 of the LR Rules is served on the cautioner. If the cautioner objects to the registration, the Authority would consider same. However, the Authority's duty is to prevent a registration being effected, which would defeat the right of the cautioner before the respective rights of the cautioner and the applicant for first registration have been decided, either by agreement or by the court.

If a person lodges a caution without reasonable cause he or she shall be liable to make compensation, recoverable as a simple contract debt, to any person damaged thereby (s 96(3) of the 1964 Act).

CHAPTER 14

DEALINGS WITH REGISTERED LAND

14.1 Introduction

Chapter 13 dealt with the difference between registered and unregistered land, first registration of title in the Land Registry, and the relevant statutory provisions. This chapter explains how registered land is dealt with after registration in the Land Registry.

14.1.1 WHAT IS A REGISTER OF TITLE?

A register of title is, essentially, a list of owners of land, with particulars (by reference to the Land Registry map) of the properties owned and of the charges and restrictions affecting them. Legal validity is given to this list by statute (Registration of Title Act, 1891 which was repealed and replaced by the 1964 Act; which in turn has been further amended by the 2006 Act and the 2009 Act) and it is kept constantly up to date by the entry of all changes affecting any of its component parts. The register is conclusive as to the title therein, and purchasers or chargees for value are protected against errors or mistakes made by the Authority. There are compensation provisions in the Act and rules.

Persons desiring to deal in any way with registered land (ie land registered in the Land Registry) are therefore afforded direct and up-to-date information as to the ownership of the land and the burdens and notices affecting it. In practical terms, for example on the closing of any conveyancing transaction, this is by means of a recent certified copy folio and title plan (this is the term used to describe the individual plans of registered properties) brought up to date by appropriate searches (see **14.13.9.2**).

14.1.2 CONCLUSIVENESS OF TITLE

Under s 31(1) of the 1964 Act, the register is conclusive evidence of the owner's title as appearing thereon. This means that the register is conclusive evidence of any rights, privileges, or appurtenances noted as belonging or appurtenant to the property or of any burdens entered as affecting the same. So far as persons dealing for value with a registered owner are concerned, the importance of the subsection lies in the fact that it abrogates the equitable doctrine of notice in relation to such transactions. A purchaser for value who becomes registered as new owner is not affected by anything that does not appear on the register (other than the burdens mentioned in s 72 of the 1964 Act, as amended: see **14.12.4.2**).

It should be clearly noted, however, that the objective of the 1964 Act is the protection of persons acquiring an interest in property for value. A volunteer has no such protection under the Act.

14.1.3   TITLE SUBJECT TO EQUITIES/POSSESSORY TITLE

A registered freehold title 'subject to equities' arose under s 29(3) of the Registration of Title Act, 1891 (formerly called the Local Registration of Title Act, 1891 but subsequently altered by the Registration of Title Act, 1942). These were repealed by the 1964 Act—see McAllister, *Registration of Title*, p 8.

Agricultural land bought out under the Land Purchase Acts was registered 'subject to equities' because owing to the large number of transactions involved, the Land Commission could not examine the title of a purchaser to his or her previous 'tenant' interest in the land. The fee simple vested in him or her by the Commission was deemed to be a graft on his or her previous interest, and the equities subject to which his or her registration as owner was effected were those arising by virtue of this fact.

Under s 26(3) of the 1964 Act such registrations are made with 'possessory title' and under s 35, a title registered 'subject to equities' is deemed to be a 'possessory title'.

A note in the folio to the effect that the title is 'subject to equities' or 'possessory' means that the title of the registered owner has not been established. Note that 'possessory title' is not always synonymous with a title vested under the Land Acts and registered 'subject to equities'. A 'possessory title' may also arise in a first registration application (see **chapter 13**), but this is rare. For the effect of a possessory title, see **13.3.13.4**. It follows that any transaction affecting registered freehold land where the title is not absolute, or a registered leasehold where the title is not noted as absolute or good leasehold (where the lease is old enough), should be approached with caution (ss 36–39 and 43–47 of the 1964 Act).

14.1.4   BASIS OF REGISTERED TITLE

When acting for a purchaser of registered property, or indeed in any dealing with such property, a solicitor must ensure that he or she has up-to-date certified copies of the folio and title map (with certified copy of the lease in a leasehold title). The register, ie the folio, has to be read in conjunction with the Land Registry map and, in the case of a leasehold interest, with the lease (see s 44(3)(c) of the 1964 Act). Where covenants etc are contained in a fee farm grant or any rights referred to in any document and registered as such, the documents need to be inspected. Each entry in the folio should be carefully considered.

14.1.5   APPEALS AND REVIEW

The decisions of the Authority are reviewable. Section 19 of the 1964 Act permits the court to determine issues in dispute either on appeal from a decision of the Authority (s 19(1)) or by reference where the Authority has a doubt in a matter of a question of law or fact. The jurisdiction of the court will be altered by the Civil Liability and Courts Act, 2004, s 46 which amends s 18 of the 1964 Act when that section comes into force.

The Authority is also amenable to judicial review under Order 84 of the Rules of Superior Court, 1986 (see *Crumlish v Registrar of Deeds and Titles* [1991] ILRM 37) and is an 'organ of the State' for the purpose of the European Convention on Human Rights Act, 2003.

14.1.6   RECTIFICATION

While s 31 of the 1964 Act provides for the conclusiveness of the register as to the owner and the burdens appearing thereon, s 32 (as amended by s 55 of the 2006 Act) provides that any mistakes or errors originating in the Land Registry may be rectified by:

(a)   the Authority with the consent of the registered owner and all interested parties upon such terms as may be agreed in writing by the parties; or

(b)   the Authority where it is of the opinion that the error can be rectified without loss to any person after giving such notices as may be prescribed; or

(c)   the court upon such terms as to costs or otherwise as it thinks just.

Section 120 of the 1964 Act (as amended by s 69 of the 2006 Act) provides for the payment of compensation by the State in the case of error, fraud, or forgery. The amendment changed the method whereby the level of compensation was determined by the Registrar. This procedure had been adversely criticised by the courts. There is no provision for such determination by the Authority and if a claim for compensation is not settled an application may be made to the court.

14.1.7   ESTATES

It is important to note that registration is made of the ownership of an estate or interest in the land. It follows therefore that while one interest may be registered in the Land Registry, the title to another estate or interest in the same land may be unregistered or registered in a different register. The normal rules of unregistered conveyancing apply to the unregistered interest, including the necessity to register any assurance in the Registry of Deeds.

For instance, see **14.12.10** and note the comment on the lease registered as a burden at entry number (1).

14.1.8   TYPES OF FOLIO

A folio may represent the registration of:

(a)   freehold land and numbered, eg folio DN1234 or DN1234F;

(b)   leasehold land and numbered, eg DN1234L; or

(c)   subsidiary interests (see the 1964 Act, s 8(b)) and numbered, eg DN1234S.

It is important to note that DN1234, DN1234F, DN1234L, and DN1234S all represent registrations within the county of Dublin of entirely different interests and properties and care must be exercised in using the correct number and letter if there is one.

14.1.9   DEALINGS

14.1.9.1   Form 17

All applications for registration are required to be accompanied by Form 17 of the LR Rules (rule 11). Form 17 of the LR Rules is an important document in which the applicant or the solicitor is required to specify the actual registration required. The form is available to download from the Land Registry website (www.prai.ie) and may be completed online at www.landdirect.ie. The advantage of completion online is that the format is self-correcting, will calculate the fee due online, and will issue a dealing reference number immediately (documents still have to be lodged in the normal manner and the date of lodgement will be the date of settling: see **14.1.9.2**);

Form 17 is used to capture relevant information at the point of lodgement and as the information on the form is used as the basis of registration, it is imperative that correct information be entered on the form. The Law Society has confirmed that the reference in Form 17, to the fact that the lodging solicitor is 'the solicitor for the applicant' is not a derogation from or relaxation of the agreed position under the certificate of title system and that borrowers' solicitors are only discharging their undertaking and not specifically acting on behalf of the lender. (Practice Note, Law Society *Gazette*, June 2004.) However, for the purpose of dealing with the Land Registry and its requirements, the lodging solicitor is treated as solicitor for all applicants under the application. The practical effect of this is that all queries will issue to the lodging solicitor and it is that solicitor's responsibility to respond to them.

14.1.9.2   Date of lodgement/registration

See rules 58, 61, and 62 of the LR Rules for priority of dealings lodged.

In most cases, the date of registration is the date of lodgement (rule 60). See rule 51 for the date of registration consequential on an examination of title of unregistered interests (eg first registration applications). The said date is the day on which the draft folio or the draft entry is finally settled in the Registry.

However, if due to some fundamental defect, the documents are returned with Registry requisitions, the date of lodgement is of no significance. The date of registration will be then the date of relodgement of the documents, if they are in order.

Rule 61 provides that in certain cases a deed may be returned for amendment. However, registration will then proceed as of date of relodgement.

However, if a query arises in relation to stamp duty, rule 62 provides that the deed may be taken up on giving an undertaking as to relodgement and, when relodged, will suffer no loss of priority.

14.1.9.3   Registration queries

Often queries are issued by the Registry. Note the provisions of rule 183 of the LR Rules which permit the Authority after notice to treat as abandoned any dealing or application which is not being pursued. This power, however, is not generally exercised except after service of a specific notice warning of the proposed application of the rule.

14.1.9.4   Common omissions

A large percentage of applications for registration have to be rejected because of basic omissions. This results in extra work for the Land Registry and in loss of priority and additional expense for the practitioner. The following checklist sets out many of the most common omissions.

(a)   Are the correct fees enclosed and is the cheque signed?

(b)   Has stamp duty been impressed on the deed or if the deed is executed on or after 30 December 2009 is a paper stamp certificate attached to the deed (for e-stamping see **16.12**)?

(c)   Is a suitable Authority compliant map enclosed where required for subdivision or description?

(d)   Is the *original* or *official Probate Office copy* grant or probate/administration enclosed?

(e)   Are the correct transmission forms lodged?

(f)   Is the jurat complete in the affidavits lodged?

(g)   Does the charge fully and unambiguously describe the property charged?

(h)   Is the correct folio number quoted in the deed?

(i)   Is the execution of the deed witnessed?

(j)   Has an assent to the registration of charges/burdens been incorporated in the deed or is a Form 48 assent enclosed?

(k)   Where the parent folio is subject to a charge, is a partial release lodged in respect of a transfer of part or a lease?

(l)   Is the Form 17 signed by the solicitor personally and are all scheduled documents enclosed?

Note: this list is not exhaustive and responsibility for ensuring that the documents presented for registration are in order rests with the applicant.

14.1.9.5   Land Registry fees

Applications to the Registry must be accompanied by the correct fee (1964 Act, s 14 and LR Rules, rule 11(1)(b)).

Completion of the application form online will reduce difficulties with fees calculation as this will be done automatically. However, it will still be necessary to be familiar with the fee structure to ensure that clients are correctly advised as to outlays.

See the Land Registration (Fees) Order, 2012 and the Land Registration (Fees) (Amendment) Order, 2013.

14.2   Land Registry Mapping

14.2.1   REFERENCES

Sections 84 and 85 of the 1964 Act as amended by ss 61 and 62 of the 2006 Act and ss 86 to 89 of the 1964 Act; rules 2, 8, 29, 121, 139 to 142, 146, 147, 160, and 165 of the LR Rules.

See the Authority's Practice Direction 'Mapping Practice' and the related 'Practice Guide 2014' on the Authority website (www.prai.ie).

14.2.2   DIGITAL MAP

At present there are circa 2.14 million registered titles covering approximately 2.8 million land parcels shown on the Land Registry maps, together with various rights of way, pipelines, etc. The Land Registry map comprised 32,000 paper map sheets on a variety of scales, projections, and map series which were digitised.

The Land Registry digital maps are based upon the OSi, Irish Transverse Mercator (ITM) co-ordinate reference system and are updated on an ongoing basis as the OSi updates its own maps.

The Land Registry digital map is available for inspection online at www.landdirect.ie to account holders and is also available for non-account holders. Customers can ascertain online whether property is registered or unregistered and, if registered, can inspect the relevant folio. On a purchase or sale, boundaries of registered property can be confirmed with the client in the practitioner's own office and even in relation to unregistered property ordnance survey boundary detail is available.

14.2.3   FUNCTION OF A MAP

Property is best described not only by a verbal reference to its situation (for example, area, townland, barony, and county) but also by reference to a map accurately delineating the location and extent of the property. Land Registry legislation provides for the description of property not only by reference to the folio (being a written record of the title), but also by reference to a Land Registry map which may now, by virtue of s 84 of the 1964 Act as substituted by s 61 of the 2006 Act, be any map which the Authority considers satisfactory and which may be in an electronic or paper form or partly in one form and partly in the other form as may be prescribed. Rule 146 of the LR Rules prescribes the form of Registry maps.

14.2.4   ACCURACY

The Land Registry does not accept responsibility for the accuracy of maps presented to it. That responsibility rests solely with the applicant.

On presentation of a map with a dealing for registration, the Land Registry will return the map if it conflicts with existing Registry data and will point out the discrepancy with the Registry's records. In effect, the Land Registry asks the applicant to sort out with the owner of the adjoining lands the ownership of the relevant strip of property.

See **14.2.11** as to conclusiveness of registered boundaries.

14.2.5   CONFLICT

If there is no existing Registry data (in the case of a first registration where adjoining lands are not yet registered) the first applicant will be registered as owner of all the property shown on this map. If, on the subsequent application for first registration by an adjoining owner, a conflict of boundaries arises, the Authority will leave it to the applicant to sort the situation out. This may entail either a deed of rectification where the parties agree, or a court application in default of agreement. The matter rests with the applicant.

14.2.6   CURRENT EDITION OF MAP

In an effort to keep its data as up to date as possible the Land Registry always insisted that any maps submitted to it for registration must be drawn on the current edition of the largest scale available for the area in question. With the Land Registry map now in digital format it is updated with new OSi (Ordnance Survey Ireland) data as it becomes available. In relation to application maps see **14.2.8**.

14.2.7   TITLE PLANS

A title plan (or title map) is an individual print-out of the plans contained in a folio and is issued in hard copy format based on the scales published by OSi (scale of 1/5,000, 1/2,500 and 1/1,000). They can also be printed at 1/500 and 1/10,000. The title plan in conjunction with the folio recognises in principle that a proper definition of property should consist of a visual and a verbal description.

Note in relation to title plans:

1.   It is printed on an A3-sized sheet of paper regardless of map scale.

2.   Details printed along the right-hand column and lower section of the A3 page include the following: folio number, title plan application number, and the date the map was printed, north point, scale bar, and map scale (representative fraction).

3. The map area itself is edged by a border with the ITM co-ordinates printed at the lower left and upper right corners of the neat line.

4. The property boundary itself is highlighted in the appropriate tenure type colour with a light dotted colour infill, or the property is hatched and filled if the property is subject to a leasehold or sub-leasehold burden. The plan reference is printed in black regardless of the tenure type.

5. Burdens, rights of way, wayleaves, and pipelines are not lettered.

6. The automated production system is designed to fit each Registry plan (or number of plans if more than one plan exists on the folio) to a single A3 page at a standard metric map scale. Sometimes this will result in the 'title plan' being printed at a smaller map scale than that published by OSi.

See **14.2.8.2** re special registration map.

14.2.8   REQUIREMENTS FOR MAPS LODGED FOR REGISTRATION

14.2.8.1   Generally

The definition of an 'application map' is contained in rule 2 of the LR Rules. Application map means (a) a map in paper form or in electronic form issued by the Authority, (b) such other map in paper form or electronic form as the Authority may allow, on which is identified, in such manner as the Authority may direct, a property the subject of an application for registration. The Land Registry mapping practice and requirements are set out in Practice Direction 'Mapping Practice' and also the related 'Practice Guide 2014' available at www.prai.ie. Note also the appendices including those on development schemes and multi-storey buildings. Boundaries submitted for registration must be clearly defined (see rule 15(1)(c) and 16(2)(c) of LR Rules (for first registration applications) and rule 56 (for all other applications)).

The following are the requirements in respect of maps lodged for registration:

(i)   a 'Land Registry compliant map' which is an ITM map published by Ordnance Survey Ireland with ITM co-ordinates shown on the upper right corner and the lower left corner;

(ii)   Land Registry ITM title plan maps are also acceptable unless the scale is too small to accurately draw the boundaries;

(iii) computer-generated maps (OSi licensed) displaying ITM co-ordinate referenced maps;

(iv)   special registration map (see **14.2.8.2**).

14.2.8.2   Special registration map

Where the scale of the ITM title plan is too small to mark boundaries, application can be made for an ITM 'special registration map' from the Registry to issue on the next largest published scale, 1/2,500 or larger scale of their choice up to 1/500 scale. Special registration maps may also be requested for marking properties for first registration applications.

Note smaller scale 'title plan' maps (see **14.2.7**), may not be suitable for registration purposes where they are printed at 1/5,000 or 1/10,000 scale because the smaller scale hard-copy maps may not be large enough to plot accurately new non-OSi detail. As an alternative to ordering a 'title plan' and to ensure that practitioners can select a hard copy that is suitable for registration purposes, www.landdirect.ie account holders can order a 'special registration Map' (SRM) online. When using the SRM facility in www.landdirect.ie, account holders will have the facility to select the area of interest and select a suitable map scale at which they wish to print the SRM. SRMs may also be requested for marking properties for first registration applications.

14.2.8.3 Development schemes and maps

Practitioners dealing with developers and multi-storey buildings should familiarise themselves with the procedures in these cases, which will include housing schemes, office parks, and large-scale commercial developments. These are set out in documents available on the Authority website (www.prai.ie). See the Practitioners Guide 2014 'Mapping Procedure for Registration of Development Schemes' (appendix 3) and 'Mapping Requirements for Multi-Story Developments' (appendix 5(a) and (b)).

Scheme maps must be plotted from site surveys and must clearly show the reference number by which each holding—or part of holding—is to be identified in subsequent dealings and correspondence.

To ensure that the boundaries submitted for registration reflect the applicant's intentions, it is recommended that:

(a) boundary corners be unambiguously defined and clearly marked on the ground *before any survey is carried out*; and

(b) maps submitted for registration be prepared and certified by competent land surveyors.

Before the first application to transfer or lease a site from within the scheme is lodged, the solicitor for the vendor should send a drawing of the development to the Land Registry for approval:

• drawings can be lodged as a CAD file which must also be accompanied by a computer-generated hard copy;

• an original OSi 'Land Registry compliant map';

• a computer-generated map;

• an original Registry ITM co-ordinate 'title plan';

• an original Registry ITM co-ordinate 'special registration map';*

• an original Registry ITM co-ordinate 'official map search' Map'.*

* The scale of the SRM and official search map must be printed at the OSi published scale for the area *or*, if necessary, at one of the available large scale options—1/1,000 or 1/500 scale.

1/5,000 and 1/10,000 scale maps may not be acceptable for subdivision purposes in hard-copy form, regardless of whether they are original OSi or original Registry maps, unless the new property is entirely bounded by OSi topographic detail.

Where a development involves separate registration of apartments, flats, floors, retail units, etc, floor plans must be submitted to the Land Registry to provide a version of the plans that will become the Land Registry map to enable registrations to take place. Where a number of multi-storey blocks are involved in a single development scheme each property should be clearly and unambiguously identifiable within its correct block.

The boundaries of each site in the scheme must be clearly shown in red. The site numbers must be shown in black ink. All individual parcels of land within the scheme area must be identified in this way. Where the property to be registered comprises more than one parcel, as for example a dwelling having a separate garage, parking area, dustbin, or storage site, each of these parcels must be given distinguishing references on the scheme map. Unless different references are given for separate parcels, difficulties will arise in the interpretation of applications.

Accurate mapping is the foundation of any registration system and purchasers of houses or commercial units which are part of larger developments must bear in mind the particular difficulties arising from the provision of maps and plans meeting the Land Registry standards. These standards are set out in great detail in documents and briefings on www.prai.ie.

The original scheme map will be stamped approved and returned to the applicant.

Agreements between vendors and purchasers can now proceed based on the approved scheme map.

In any case involving a subdivision of a plot, surveyors and engineers must be fully up to date with the latest Registry requirements particularly in relation to large developments. The purchaser will require the proper maps and approved plans on closing and endless queries will be avoided by ensuring that the site map and, in the case of larger developments, approved scheme maps are in place on issue of contract documentation. Invariably, as developments proceed there may be adjustments. These must be flagged to the conveyancer well in advance and proper provision made.

The Law Society has drawn attention to the practice of inserting in contracts a requirement that sales be closed on foot of identification maps only. This practice is viewed as unacceptable (Practice Note, Law Society *Gazette*, November 2004). Land Registry approved scheme maps are required for registration purposes and registration will not proceed on any application in the absence of such a map.

14.2.9 MAPPING SEARCH

Section 107(2) of the 1964 Act and rule 160 of the LR Rules provide for the making of an official search including a mapping search. The mapping search may reveal the following information:

(a) whether the title to the property is registered or not; and

(b) who is the registered owner of the property.

The mapping search should be made in the manner described by Form 89 of the LR Rules. The application should be accompanied by a suitable map, with the relevant property outlined thereon in red, together with the prescribed fee. A suitable map is one on which the location of the property can be clearly ascertained so as to enable the search to be conducted accurately, eg Land Registry filed plan, largest scale map published by OSi. Customers may conduct a property search online and obtain folio numbers for properties that are registered in the Land Registry. There is no fee charged for this facility, a fee is charged when folio(s) are inspected. However, account holders can also apply for an 'official search' where the Land Registry maps are maintained in digital format. Any person may apply for an official search by selecting the area required using the official search function in www.landdirect.ie at any Land Registry office.

Section 107(2) also provides for the issue of a certificate of the result of a search in Form 92 of the LR Rules.

14.2.10 COLOURING

The colourings on the Land Registry maps usually denote the following

Red	freehold property
Green	leasehold property
Purple	subleases
Brown	sub-subleases or turbary
Yellow	rights of way and wayleaves
Blue	pipeline

Note: further information is available in the 'Practitioners Guide 2014', appendix 9 'Legends and Symbols on Registry Maps' on the Authority website (www.prai.ie).

14.2.11 CONCLUSIVENESS OF BOUNDARIES

Section 85 of the 1964 Act, as substituted by s 62 of the 2006 Act, provides that registered land is to be described by reference to the Registry maps (defined in s 84 of the 1964 Act as substituted by s 61 of the 2006 Act) on which the lands are included, but neither the identification by reference to a Registry map nor the description in a register is conclusive as to boundaries or extent of the property: s 85(2).

Section 87 of the 1964 Act enables landowners who have reached agreement on the boundary between their properties to make an entry to that effect on the folio and on the Land Registry map. Section 87(2) provides 'An entry in pursuance of this section *shall be conclusive only as between the parties* to the application and their respective successors in interest, and shall not operate to confirm the title to the lands the boundaries whereof are settled.' The boundary of lands about to be registered may also be made conclusive on agreement by the parties or by submission of a court order. See also s 86 of the 1964 Act. An entry in the register of the conclusiveness of a boundary is made by stating that physical boundaries of the property are along a specified line on the Registry map, eg that the boundary is the face or centre of a fence or wall or one side or other of a stream or drain along a specified line shown on the map.

Section 85 of the 1964 Act as substituted by s 62 of the 2006 Act provides that the description of land on a Registry map shall not be conclusive as to its boundaries or extent unless there is an entry to that effect on the folio. The boundaries on the Registry map are therefore what are usually referred to as 'general boundaries'. The precise line of the property boundary is undetermined. The Registry map does not indicate whether it includes a hedge or wall or a ditch or runs along the centre of a wall or fence or its inner or outer face, or how far it runs within or beyond it, or whether or not the land registered includes the whole or any portion of an adjoining road or stream. Where registration is made to the centre of a road or stream, the map is not to be taken as conclusive evidence that such portion of the same is included in the property. However the non-conclusive boundary system does not dispense with the requirement that the location of the physical features must be accurately defined on the application map within the limitations of the original scale of the map. See 'Pushing the Boundaries' on p 36 of the Law Society *Gazette*, November 2011.

14.2.12   AREAS

The mapping officials of the Land Registry will not check to see that the area given in any deed lodged with them corresponds with the area as completed from the map submitted for registration. If there is an obvious error the applicant's attention will be drawn to the same. However, it is for the applicant to ensure that the area in the deed corresponds with the property shown on the map itself. Areas must be supplied in the following cases:

• every first registration where the area exceeds 1 hectare;

• every transfer of part where the existing folio records an area;

• any other application where the applicant requires the area to be recorded on the folio.

Any folio may have the area inserted on request of the registered owner/applicant or his solicitor if area is in the instrument or if a suitable certificate by an engineer, architect, or qualified surveyor is furnished. See **14.2.11** re conclusiveness of boundaries and extent.

14.2.13   SUBDIVISION APPLICATION

As to applications for a new folio for part of registered land not involving a change of ownership, see Practice Note, Law Society *Gazette*, August 1989.

From time to time the need arises for an application to the Land Registry by a registered owner for the opening of a new folio for part of his or her registered land, separate from the rest, but not involving a change of ownership. For example, he or she may want to have the dwellinghouse and ground attached to it on a separate folio, or he or she may want a new folio for a site on which he or she proposes to build a new dwellinghouse.

The Land Registry will accept a simple application in the format set out in the example that follows. A formal transfer is not necessary or appropriate as it is not a transfer of part to another person.

The map attached to the application must comply with Land Registry mapping requirements: see **14.2.8.1**. The appropriate fee of €40 (Item 19 LR (Fees) Order, 2012) should be paid.

The following form of application may be used:

LAND REGISTRY

Application for a new folio for part of registered land not involving a change of ownership.

County:_____Folio:_____

I_____ the registered owner of the lands described in Folio . . ., of the Register of County   hereby apply for the opening of a new folio in respect of that part of my said lands specified in the Schedule hereto.

SCHEDULE

Part of the townland of_____described in Folio_____

County_____containing (area)_____ being the lands edged in red and marked with the letter 'B' on the map annexed

hereto_____

Dated this_____day of_____20

Signed by the said

_____

_____the registered owner, in the presence of:

To: The Property Registration Authority,

Land Registry.

14.3   Ownership

14.3.1   TYPES OF OWNERSHIP

Section 27 of the 1964 Act was repealed by the 2009 Act. The Authority can register:

(a)   an owner of freehold land, namely a fee simple or a fee farm grantee's interest; and

(b)   an owner of a leasehold interest, namely the person in whom the interest is vested in possession.

The Authority can no longer register a limited owner in the case of settled land (either freehold or a settled leasehold interest), ie a tenant for life (Settled Land Act, 1882, s 2), or a person having the powers of a tenant for life (Settled Land Act, 1882, s 58). The trustees of the trust in land (see s 19 of the 2009 Act which sets out who are trustees of land) should apply for registration as owners. However it was estimated that between 7,000 and 8,000 folios had registered limited owners. Under rule 145 of the LR Rules the following entry (Form 85) was made on folios registered in the name of a limited owner: 'The title is subject to the provisions of the Land and Conveyancing Law Reform Act, 2009.' The trustee(s) can also apply for registration as owners: see rule 66 and Form 86 of the LR Rules. Form 86 includes an application for an inhibition.

The repeal of s 27 of the 1964 Act abolishes the distinction between 'limited' and 'full' owners. All owners will be registered simply as 'owners'. Section 127(a) of the 2009 Act amends s 3(1) of the 1964 Act to state that 'owner' includes full owner.

Under s 18 of the 2009 Act a minor can no longer hold a legal interest in land. Therefore where land is vested in a minor, he or she can no longer apply for registration as owner. A trust in land exists and application for registration should be made by the trustees: see s 19(1)(c) of the 2009 Act. Special care should be taken where the registered owner is described as an infant or minor for registrations made prior to 1 December 2009. This clearly indicates that the owner is under a disability unless evidence is forthcoming as to his or her majority. Again under rule 145 of the LR Rules the following entry (Form 85) may be made on folios registered in the name of a minor or infant 'The title is subject to the provisions of the Land and Conveyancing Law Reform Act, 2009.' The trustee(s) can also apply for registration as owners. See rule 66 and Form 86 of the LR Rules. Form 86 includes an application for an inhibition.

To clarify, a life tenant or a minor cannot apply for registration as and from 1 December 2009. The application should be made in the name of the trustees. In addition where a life tenant or a minor is currently registered as a full owner and are so described in the folio the only persons who can deal with the property are the trustees.

In relation to settlements and trusts see the practice direction 'Trusts of Land' (published 1 February 2012) available on the Authorities website www.prai.ie. It sets out the procedures and forms necessary to register trusts and settlements in the Land Registry (see also the Law Society Practice Note, 'Registration of trusts and settlements', Law Society *Gazette*, December 2013).

14.3.1.1   Settlements and trusts chart for applications lodged prior to 1 December 2009

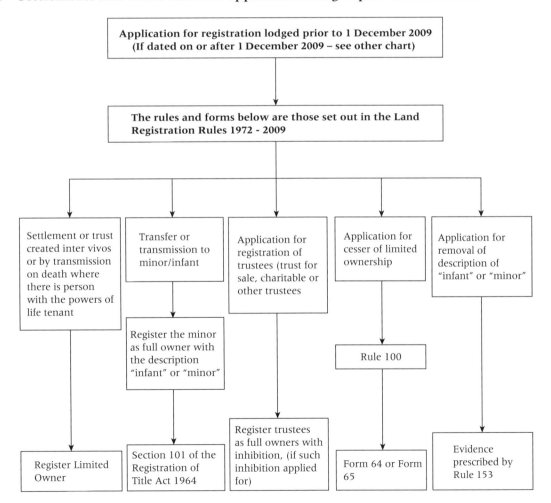

14.3.1.2   Settlements and trusts chart for applications lodged on or after 1 December 2009

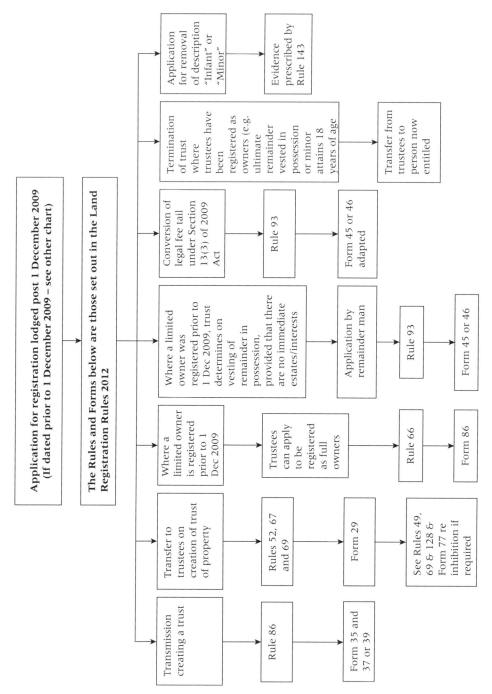

14.3.2   APPLICATION

It is important in framing an application to be clear what registration is applied for. It occasionally happens, particularly in transmission applications, that the forms are followed blindly.

14.3.3   WAYS OF REGISTERING

Ownership of registered land is effected on foot of the following applications:

   (a)   first registration: see **chapter 13**;

   (b)   deed of transfer: see **14.5**;

(c)   operation of law, eg survivor of joint tenants, or successor of limited owner: see **14.7**;

(d)   operation of statute, eg the 1964 Act, s 49: see **14.6**;

(e)   transmission on death: see **14.7**; and

(f)   court order: see rule 118 of the LR Rules.

14.4   Conversion of Title

14.4.1   'SUBJECT TO EQUITIES'

Property purchased by the tenant farmers under the Land Purchase Acts was compulsorily registrable on the freehold register by virtue of the Registration of Title Act, 1891, s 23. The Land Commission vested the fee simple in the property in the tenant farmer by means of a conveyance, vesting order, or a fiated purchase agreement. Application for registration was made by the Land Commission.

The prior title of the tenant farmer was not investigated and so the freehold was vested in the *ostensible tenant* as a graft on his or her previous tenancy or other interest. To give effect thereto he or she was registered under s 29 of the 1891 Act *'subject to equities'* in order to preserve the interest of any other person who had a title or right to the property. For instance, he or she might only have had a life interest, or an interest in remainder, or conceivably no title thereto at all. There may also have been a mortgage or a right of residence, maintenance, and support on the previous interest. If so, the equity note would protect same.

14.4.2   TITLE POSSESSORY

The Registration of Title Act, 1891 was repealed and replaced by the 1964 Act. Under s 35 of the 1964 Act property which was subject to equities on 1 January 1967 (the date the 1964 Act came into operation) is deemed to be a possessory title. Property purchased under the Land Purchase Acts is compulsorily registrable under s 23 of the 1964 Act and under s 26 of the 1964 Act the purchaser is registered with possessory title instead of subject to equities. However, the effect of both notes is the same. Where the note appears on the register the effect is that the register is *not by itself* sufficient evidence of the title to the lands See also s 38 of the 1964 Act.

The word 'possessory' will appear in Part II of the folio as follows:

Part II—Ownership

Title—Possessory

14.4.3   DISCHARGE/CONVERSION

How may the equities be discharged or the title converted to absolute? Section 50 is the relevant section of the 1964 Act and the relevant rules are 32–42 of the LR Rules inclusive. The relevant forms are 10–15 inclusive. A distinction is to be drawn between land purchased under the Land Purchase Acts and land registered with a possessory title on first registration.

14.4.4   LAND PURCHASED UNDER THE LAND PURCHASE ACTS

Land purchased under the Land Purchase Acts is registered pursuant to the 1964 Act, s 26(1) or the Registration of Title Act, 1891, s 29.

14.4.5   TENANTED LAND

'Tenanted land' means land where the purchasers of the fee simple from the Land Commission under the Land Purchase Acts had a previous interest in the land purchased—generally a yearly tenancy. Tenanted land is often referred to as a 'holding'.

John Smith was registered as full owner in 1995 under a vesting order from the Land Commission. He was, of course, registered with possessory title. It is now desired to have the title converted to absolute title. To do so, the title which existed prior to first registration in 1995 must be fully investigated and application made to the Authority. Rule 35 of the LR Rules is the appropriate rule and Form 11 and Form 12 of the LR Rules are the appropriate forms. If there was a disposition 15 years old and the investigation shows same to have been in order then title may commence therewith. To bring the disposition within rule 35(2)(a) it must have been prior to first registration and 15 years old.

Rule 35 reads as follows:

(1)   *Every other application for the conversion of a possessory title into an absolute title in the case of property purchased under the Land Purchase Acts shall show the title to the property that existed prior to such purchase.*

(2)   *Where the Authority so permits, the title to the tenancy*
   (i)   *may commence with a disposition thereof made not less than 15 years prior to the date of the application, or*
   (ii)   *may be deduced for a period of not less than 30 years prior to the application, whether based on possession or otherwise.*

(3)   *The application shall be made by affidavit in Form 11 or 12, with such modifications therein as the case may require, according as the applicant does or does not rely on opinion of counsel.*

Suppose John Smith's father (Peter) died testate on 6 June 1991 and by his will dated 3 April 1985 left his lands to his widow Mary for life (she elected to take under the will—s 115 of the Succession Act, 1965) and then to his son John absolutely subject to a legacy charged on John's estate only of £500 in favour of his other son Thomas. John was appointed sole executor and probate of the will was granted to him on 31 August 1993.

If at the date of the application to convert the title to absolute, Mary was still alive, the trustees of the trust in land would be entitled to be registered as owner (see s 19 of the 2009 Act which sets out who are trustees—in this case it would appear to be Mary the life tenant (s 1(1)(a)(i)) and any trustee appointed under the will or may be the personal representative (s 19(1)(b))).

If Mary Smith had died and the legacy had been discharged, then paragraph 3 of Form 11 would read:

'Peter Smith, my father, who was then tenant of the property died testate on 6 June, 1991 and Probate of his will dated 3 April 1985 was granted to me on 31 August 1993. By his Will he devised all the property described in the said folio in the words following:

I leave my farm at … to my wife Mary for life and then to my son John absolutely subject to a legacy of £500 in favour of my son Thomas.

My mother, Mary Smith elected to take under the will and died on the 8 August 1992 and I beg to refer to evidence of her election and her death certificate lodged herewith and upon which pinned together and marked with the letter 'B' I have endorsed my name prior to the swearing hereof.

I paid my brother Thomas his legacy of £500 and I beg to refer to a receipt therefore upon which marked with the letter 'C' I have endorsed my name prior to the swearing hereof.'

Note paragraph 4 Form 11. All documents affecting the title (including evidence of the election of Mary to take under the will) must be lodged.

The Land Registry would direct Registry of Deeds searches against John and Mary Smith.

Note that the Succession Act, 1965, s 54, which amended s 61 of the 1964 Act, would not apply to the will of Peter Smith as he was not a registered owner.

If the applicant is relying on legal opinion (rule 35(3) of the LR Rules) the application should be made in Forms 12 of the LR Rules. However, note also rule 36(2)(a) of the LR Rules where the Land Registry may dispense with an official examination of the title, where the same has been examined by a practising barrister, on the occasion of a disposition for valuable consideration. The opinion, together with the evidence of title on which it is based, must be lodged with the application. Such application may be furnished in Form 3 of the LR Rules, adapted as the case may require.

Under rule 36(2)(b) of the LR Rules, where in the course of the investigation of title it appears desirable that the title should be referred to counsel for an opinion generally or on a specific matter, such opinion may also be furnished in Form 3 adapted as the case may require. This rule is stated to be analogous to rule 19(6) in a First Registration application. See **13.3.2.2**.

14.4.6   THIRTY-YEAR RULE

If John Smith was registered as full owner under the Land Purchase Acts on 1 March 1975 (more than 30 years ago), the Authority *may* convert a possessory title into an absolute one on the registration of a disposition or transmission on death by virtue of the 1964 Act, s 50(3)(a).

By virtue of rule 32 of the LR Rules such a title may be converted to absolute on lodgement of an affidavit in Form 10 of the LR Rules.

14.4.7   TWELVE-YEAR RULE

Under the 1964 Act, s 50(3)(b): where

(i)   *the title registered is or is deemed to be possessory, and*

(ii) *the ownership of land had been registered for over twelve years, and*

(iii) *an application is made for registration of a transfer for valuable consideration or other disposition for value, and*

(iv) *a registered transfer for valuable consideration has been made after first registration of the land but not less than twelve years prior to the application,*

the Authority may convert the title to absolute.

Under rule 33 of the LR Rules, if there was a transfer for valuable consideration registered not less than 12 years prior to the application then, on lodgement of an affidavit in Form 10 of the LR Rules, the Authority *may* convert the title to absolute.

14.4.8   FORM 13

See rule 34 of the LR Rules. A solicitor acting for a purchaser or a statutory authority where the value of the property does not exceed €1,000,000 may, under this rule, give a certificate in Form 13 of the LR Rules to the effect that he or she has investigated the title to the tenancy existing prior to first registration and that same is in order.

14.4.9   UNTENANTED LAND

'Untenanted land' means a parcel of untenanted land provided by the Land Commission. In many cases the purchaser had no previous interest in the land purchased. Untenanted land is often referred to as a parcel. The Land Commission would acquire a parcel which became available and would allot it to surrounding owners to be consolidated with their holdings. Such parcels would be subject to the same trusts, rights, and equities as affected the 'holding'. The purchasing tenant would sign a purchase agreement with the Land Commission. Under the Land Act 1923, s 31(a) advances were made by the Land Commission for the purchase of a parcel by a person, being the tenant or proprietor of an uneconomic holding. The purchase agreement would show that the purchase was Class A and in paragraph 14 would show the holding with which it was to be consolidated.

To discharge the equities on the parcel one would commence with such purchase agreement and then move to the equities, rights, or trusts of the holding. Endorsed on such purchase agreement is the *fiat* of the Land Commission, and it is the *fiat* that vests the property in the tenant purchaser.

However, even in the absence of a purchase agreement, the parcel would be subject to any trusts that affected the holding (see McAllister, *Registration of Title*, p 74) Sometimes, instead of a fiated purchase agreement, the Land Commission vests the parcel in the tenant purchasers by means of a vesting order. Obtain a copy of the vesting order together with copies of the other Land Commission documents such as a temporary convenience letting agreement. The 30-year rule, 12-year rule, and notes on Form 13 apply in this case also.

14.4.10   EXCHANGE

If John Smith, registered owner of Folio X County Mayo, exchanged his Mayo holding for lands in County Kildare then the trusts, rights, and equities of the Mayo holding attach to the Kildare holding. So, in order to convert the title of the Kildare holding to absolute it will be necessary to examine the title of the Mayo folio. The fiated purchase agreement in respect of the Kildare folio will show that the purchaser came within the Land Act, 1923, s 31(b) and will show the lands given in exchange.

14.4.11   OTHERS

Section 31(f) of the Land Act, 1923 reads:

> *Any other person or body to whom in the opinion of the Land Commission an advance ought to be made . . .*

Therefore, a person with no holding, or who gives no property in exchange, may have obtained an advance to purchase a parcel from the Land Commission. The title commences with the fiated purchase agreement.

Whether the property is a holding or a parcel the same rules and forms are applicable, so the title to a parcel may be converted in the same manner as a holding.

The foregoing sections of the 1964 Act and Rules and Forms of the LR Rules apply also to untenanted land.

14.4.12   LANDS NOT PURCHASED UNDER LAND PURCHASE ACTS

For the conversion of possessory title into absolute freehold or good leasehold where the property has not been purchased under the Land Purchase Acts, see the 1964 Act, s 50(2)(a), (b), and (c) and rules 37, 38, 40, 42, and 43 of the LR Rules. See also McAllister, *Registration of Title*, p 79 and Fitzgerald, *Land Registry Practice*, pp 400 and 401.

These possessory titles are registered in first registration applications. An applicant proves that he or she is in possession of a freehold or leasehold, but is unable to prove a title such as would merit registration with absolute freehold or good leasehold.

Under s 50(2)(a) of the 1964 Act, where the title registered is possessory, an application for the registration of a transfer for valuable consideration or other disposition for value shall be accompanied by (rule 37(1) of the LR Rules):

    (a)   all documents relating to the title in the applicant's possession or control; and

    (b)   a Form 14 of the LR Rules.

If the Authority is satisfied, the possessory title will be converted to absolute.

Under s 50(2)(c) of the 1964 Act where the land has been registered for 15 years, with a possessory title, the Authority shall, in any case to which paragraph (a) applies (ie on an application for registration of a transfer for valuable consideration), if satisfied that the registered owner is in possession and after giving such notices, if any, as may be prescribed (rule 38 of the LR Rules), register the title as absolute in the case of freehold land or as good leasehold in the case of leasehold land. There is no need to lodge all documents relating to the title as set out in s 50(2)(a) of the 1964 Act.

Under rule 37(3) of the LR Rules an application to convert a possessory title into an absolute title, in a case to which s 50(2)(a) does not apply (ie not on an application for registration of a transfer for valuable consideration, eg voluntary transfer), shall be made in the Form 15 of the LR Rules.

14.4.13 QUALIFIED TITLE

Section 50(2)(a) of the 1964 Act and rule 39 of the LR Rules provides that an application for registration of a transfer for valuable consideration or other disposition for value (such as a charge for the repayment of money advanced) of such property registered with a qualified title (see **13.3.13.3**) shall be accompanied by such documents, if any, as may relate to the matters excepted from the effect of registration, together with a Form 14 of the LR Rules. The application shall be accompanied by evidence of the title of the registered owner to the estate or interest excepted in the register from the effect of registration or by such other evidence as the applicant relies on in proof that the estate or interest so excepted has been extinguished or has otherwise ceased to affect the property. In the case of a qualification as to time (eg a root that would be a good root except for time) the fact that the root would now be a good root could form the basis of the application.

14.5 Transfers

14.5.1 WHO MAY TRANSFER BY DEED OF TRANSFER?

Title to registered land may be transferred by:

    (a)   the registered owner(s) who may also act through an attorney duly appointed: see s 17 of the Power of Attorney Act, 1996 (formerly s 46 of the Conveyancing Act, 1881) and rule 55 of the LR Rules (see the Authority's Powers of Attorney Act, 1996 Legal Office Notice 3/2010 on www.prai.ie);

    (b)   the registered limited owner(s) used to be able prior to 1 December 2009 to transfer the full ownership either by:

        (i)   exercising their statutory powers under the Settled Land Acts: see Form 24 of the LR Rules 1972 (deleted rule 31 LR (No 2) of the Rules 2009); or

        (ii) joining with all persons having an interest in remainder (who had to be *sui juris*).

Note, however, that:

- in the case of the assignment of the limited estate only, the assignee was merely noted on the register as such; and

- in the case of the transfer of a remainder interest by a person entitled in remainder, no registration of ownership could be made. It was open to the transferee to apply for the registration of an inhibition to protect his or her interest.

- on or after 1 December 2009 a limited estate is no longer a legal estate (s 11 of the 2009 Act) and the legal estate vests in the trustees of the trust who are set out in s 19 of the 2009 Act. A trustee of land has the full power of an owner to convey or otherwise deal with land (s 20 of the 2009 Act). Therefore on or after 1 December 2009, where a limited ownership is already registered only the trustees can transfer the land (in relation to forms to be used in relation to settlements and trusts: see **14.3.1.1** to **14.3.1.2**);

- trustees with a power of sale. As and from 1 December 2009, the trustees of a trust in land includes trustees with a power of sale (s 19(1)(b)(ii) of the 2009 Act) and notice of the trust is not entered on the register: s 92 of the 1964 Act;

(c) registered owner of a charge exercising power of sale. Section 62(6) of the 1964 Act, as amended by the 2009 Act, deals with the effect of the registration of the ownership of a charge on registered land. It shall now operate as a 'legal mortgage under Part 10 of the Land and Conveyancing Law Reform Act, 2009'. Previously it operated 'as a mortgage by deed within the meaning of the Conveyancing Acts'. Section 100(2) of the 2009 Act provides that in the case of a mortgage executed on or after 1 December 2009 the power of sale shall not become exercisable without a court order granted under subsection (3) unless the mortgagor consents in writing to such exercise not more than seven days prior to such exercise. This provision cannot be contracted out of in the case of a housing loan mortgage: s 96(3) of the 2009 Act (see further on power of sale **14.13.2**). Please note the Authorities Legal Office Notice 1 of 2015 'Transfers executed by both receiver and chargee in exercise of power of sale' and **14.7.4** and **14.7.5** in relation to receivers. The transfer deed must give effect to *either* a transfer by the receiver as attorney or agent of the registered owner of the lands, *or* a transfer by the owner of the charge that overreaches the estate or interest of the registered owner of the land. It certainly cannot do both. A transfer deed must be in only one prescribed Form that is appropriate to the nature of the transaction;

(d) personal representative of deceased registered full owner by sale (s 61 of the 1964 Act, as amended by s 50 of the Succession Act, 1965) or in due course of administration of the estate; rule 87 and Form 40 of the LR Rules;

(e) persons entitled to be registered (s 90 of the 1964 Act as substituted by s 63 of the 2006 Act);

(f) companies acting by liquidator or receiver or statutory receiver (s 149 of the National Asset Management Agency Act, 2009);

(g) transfer expressly authorised by statute, eg by county Registrar under Landlord and Tenant (Ground Rents) Act, 1967 or by the Authority by vesting certificate under the Landlord and Tenant (Ground Rents) (No 2) Act, 1978;

(h) transfer by NAMA or a NAMA group entity under s 142 of the National Asset Management Agency Act, 2009;

(i) transfer under order of court; and

(j) granting a lease. Section 58 of the 2006 Act amended s 51 of the 1964 Act and provides that the word 'transfer' shall include a lease.

14.5.2 DEED OF TRANSFER

14.5.2.1 Generally

The 2009 Act amends s 51(2) of the 1964 Act and deletes 'or in such other form as may appear to the Authority to be sufficient to convey the land'. Thus, the Land Registry can only accept transfers of registered land in the prescribed form. See rules 52 and 67 and Forms 19 and 21–31 of the LR Rules, 1972. The discretion exercised by the Land Registry previously is amended. Where applications are in improper form or substance the Authority may refuse registration absolutely or with modifications (rule 53 of the LR Rules).

It is important to note that the deed of transfer or lease does not vest the land in the transferee. It only confers, as against the transferor, an equity to be registered (s 51(2) of the 1964 Act).

The essentials of a deed of transfer of registered land are set out in the following paragraphs. The essentials of a deed of lease of registered land do not differ significantly from a lease of unregistered land except in so far as the description of the property should of course refer to the folio number and county, refer to an appropriate map, and contain an assent to the registration of the lease as a burden on the superior interest. A prescribed form of lease of registered land is set out in Form 31 of the LR Rules.

14.5.2.2 Stamp duty

The Authority shall not proceed with registration of any document if there are reasonable grounds for suspecting that stamp duty or the correct amount of stamp duty has not been paid unless satisfactory evidence is produced by the applicant (s 104 of the 1964 Act as substituted by s 64 of the 2006 Act).

Appropriate duty must be paid, if not exempt.

Previously all deeds of transfer and leases had to bear a 'particulars delivered' stamp, with two exceptions: transfers of an interest under the Family Home Protection Act, 1976, s 14 or under s 106B of the Taxes Consolidation Act, 1997 as inserted by s 121 of the Finance Act, 2008 and further amended by s 64 of the Finance Act, 2011. PD stamps are no longer required after 30 December 2009.

Since December 2009 the stamp certificate is a separate A4 size paper document which must be attached to the instrument to denote that the instrument has been stamped. See Stamp Duty (E-Stamping of Instruments) Regulations, 2009 (SI 476/2009) and PRA Legal Office Notice 2/2010 e-Stamping of Deeds (Instruments)—Revenue Commissioners.

14.5.2.3 Date

Generally, the view taken by the Registry is that the deed should be dated on or after the date of registration of a transferor who is registered as owner. An obvious exception would be a transfer by a person entitled to be registered (s 90 of the 1964 Act, as substituted by s 63 of the 2006 Act).

14.5.2.4 Parties

The names of the parties should be clearly set out in their correct form. The identity and capacity of the person transferring should be set out. The prescribed form requires the transferor to be identified as 'the registered owner', but if transferring in another capacity this should be stated, eg:

'the person entitled to be registered'

'the personal representative of N, the deceased registered owner'

'the registered owner of a charge registered at Entry No . . . in exercise of his power of sale'.

Furthermore, appropriate words to introduce the covenants for title in s 80 of the 2009 Act (formerly s 7 of the Conveyancing Act, 1881) may then be inserted: eg 'as beneficial owner', 'as settlor', 'as mortgagee', 'as personal representative', etc.

14.5.2.5 Operative words

Words of transfer:

Appropriate operative words of transfer must be used. The forms in the rules use the following formulae:

'hereby transfers all the property comprised in folio......County......to CD' (see Form 19) or, if a transfer of part only of a folio,

> 'hereby transfers the part of the property described in folio……County……specified in the Schedule hereto to CD' (see Form 21)

Property

The deed must clearly and unambiguously identify the property intended to be transferred by reference to the folio either in the body of the deed or in the schedule and, if only part of the property is affected, by reference to an application map (see **14.2.8**) unless it may be clearly identified by description (rules 56 and 29 of the LR Rules).

Words of limitation

No words of limitation (eg 'in fee simple' or 'and his heirs' or 'successors' as the case may be) are necessary to effect the registration of the transferee as tenant of the fee simple (s 123 of the 1964 Act). Note that prior to 26 May 2006, s 123 only applied to *transfers* of freehold land. Other instruments required such words: see McAllister, *Registration of Title*, p 100 and Wylie, *Irish Land Law*, para 6.054. However, since the coming into effect of s 70 of the 2006 Act on 26 May 2006, such words of limitation are not required in the case of grants or reservations of easements or *profits à prendre* of registered freehold land. It should also be noted that under s 67 of the 2009 Act words of limitation are no longer required for conveyances of freehold unregistered land from 1 December 2009.

Transferees

The name of the transferee(s) must be set out clearly and correctly in the form required to be shown on the register. In the case of an incorporated body, the name in the deed should correspond to the name on the certificate of incorporation and on the company seal.

Co-ownership

If the parties are taking as joint tenants this should be stated in the deed: see note in Form 19 and other transfer forms. Note, under s 30 of the 2009 Act from 1 December 2009 any conveyance, or contract for a conveyance, of land held in a joint tenancy, or acquisition of another interest in such land by a joint tenant without the written consent of the other joint tenants is void both at law and in equity unless such consent is dispensed with under s 31(2)(e).

If taking as tenants in common this must be specified and the shares in which each is taking should be clearly set out (see rule 63 of the LR Rules) and again see note in Form 19 and other transfer forms.

Transfer to use

The prescribed forms formerly contained two examples of the necessity to employ a transfer to uses in *freehold* land:

(a) creation of a power of revocation (see Form 23 of the LR Rules 1972); or

(b) settlement creating a life estate in favour of the settlor (see Form 30 of the LR Rules 1972).

However, the Statute of Uses (Ireland) Act, 1634 was repealed by the 2009 Act and under s 11(2) of the 2009 Act a fee simple with a power of revocation is retained as a legal estate. A power of revocation will no longer be created by means of a 'use' but rather by reservation as and from 1 December 2009. Form 23 of the LR Rules is the prescribed form of transfer creating a power of revocation and the power of revocation will be protected by an inhibition rather than by registration as a s 69 burden (note that if the old Form 23 is used on or after 1 December 2009 the legal estate will vest in the nominal trustee). Also Form 30 of the LR Rules 1972 has been replaced by Form 29 of the LR Rules, ie a transfer to trustees.

14.5.2.6 Reservations, burdens, and covenants

Reservations, burdens, and covenants may be inserted where required, eg easements, mutual or otherwise, covenants as to the use and enjoyment of the retained or transferred land, covenants as to payment of rent and indemnity in a transfer of a leasehold (see note 5 of Form 19) or, if necessary, a statutory acknowledgement and undertaking under s 81 of the 2009 Act (formerly s 9 of the Conveyancing Act, 1881), may be inserted if the deed also conveys or assigns unregistered land. If an easement is created by express reservation, the transferee formerly had to fully execute the deed; however, from 1 December 2009 a reservation will operate fully whether or not the grantee has executed the conveyance (s 69 of the 2009 Act). Other burdens if correctly created and listed in s 69 of the 1964 Act (see **14.12.4.1**) may be registered. If a burden is required to be registered, an assent by the transferee to its registration as a burden under s 69(2) should also be incorporated in the deed.

14.5.2.7 Address

An address in the State must be supplied for the transferee (s 106 of the 1964 Act).

14.5.2.8 Certificates

With the introduction of e-stamping revenue certificates (formerly set out in Revenue Leaflet SD10B) are no longer required.

It should be noted that the Land Registry will not raise queries in relation to revenue certificates if the deed is stamped or has a stamp certificate attached therto.

14.5.2.9 Execution

By transferor

Previously the deed was expressed to be 'SIGNED SEALED AND DELIVERED' by the transferor; however, s 64 of the 2009 Act abolished the need for sealing by an individual as and from 1 December 2009. The signature must be attested (rule 54 of the LR Rules). See rule 74(4) of the LR Rules regarding the sealing of documents by corporate bodies and also s 64(2)(b)(ii), (iii) and (iv) of the 2009 Act. See also amended Form 19 of the LR Rules.

By transferee

Execution by the transferee is normal but is specifically required in appropriate cases to give effect to relevant certificates, eg the Finance Act certificates or to an assent to registration of burden (need only be signed).

Express grant

If there is a grant of easements or rights by the transferee, the transferee must also sign and deliver the deed, and his or her signature must also be attested.

Marksman

In the case of execution by a mark of a blind or illiterate person or of an infirm person, see rule 54 of the LR Rules. Note that an affidavit of attesting witness in Form 20 may be called for at any time. If the required averments are set out in the attestation clause and the witness is a solicitor, the affidavit may not be called for, eg:

'Signed and delivered

by the said John Smith

by affixing his mark after

the deed was read over to him

and understood by him in

the presence of:

Name

Solicitor'

Attestation

Only one witness is required: name, address, and description should be given. As stated earlier, an affidavit of attesting witness in Form 20 may be called for.

Foreign companies

Section 64(2)(b)(iv) of the 2009 Act provides that a seal is no longer necessary for a foreign company. This gets round a problem the Land Registry had in relation to foreign corporations which did not have seals and rule 77(4) of the LR Rules, 1972.

As and from 1 December 2009 whether the deed was executed prior to or on or after that date the Land Registry will require a certificate or opinion from a lawyer from the country in question (Practice Note on foreign lawyers opinion Law Society *Gazette,* March 2001), that the deed was executed in accordance with the legal requirements governing execution of the instrument in question by such a body corporate in the jurisdiction where it is incorporated (see **14.17.2**). As and from 1 February 2013 (see Rule 74(5) of the LR Rules) the certificate required is from a lawyer from the country in question, or who has sufficient knowledge of the laws of the country in question, that the deed was executed in accordance with the legal requirements governing the execution of the instrument in question.

Companies with a corporate seal

Rule 74(4) of the LR Rules should be noted. Where it is shown that the seal has been affixed in the presence of the specified officers, the Authority will generally raise no query as to execution by the company.

For execution by liquidator or receiver, see **14.17.3** and **14.17.4**.

14.5.3   LOST TRANSFER OF REGISTERED LAND

If a transfer of registered land is lost or destroyed, the Authority may effect registration on an order from the court directing it to act on a copy thereof: *Application of Patrick Foley* [1951] 85 ILTR 61; *Re Registration of Peter Gallagher* [1911] 45 ILTSJ 269; *Nally v Nally* [1953] IR 19.

However, in *Gardiner v Irish Land Commission* [1976] 110 ILTR 21, an application before Butler J, the Land Judge, for a direction to register on foot of a photostat copy of a deed of settlement, the learned judge referred to the decision of Madden J in *Re Gallagher* and of Kingsmill Moore J in *Nally v Nally* and other cases, and stated that it was clear that it is the practice to receive in evidence, and to act upon a copy of an original document which is shown to have been lost.

The Authority may now act on a copy deed in any case where evidence on affidavit is produced, which exhibits and identifies a copy of the lost deed and which clearly shows that:

(a)   the original deed was duly executed;

(b)   the parties to the deed subsequently acted on it according to its tenor; and

(c)   it has been lost or destroyed.

Unless it is also clearly shown that the original deed was duly stamped, the copy tendered must be stamped as an original.

See further in relation to lost deeds under **13.3.3.2**.

14.6   Long Possession of Registered Land: s 49

14.6.1   GENERAL

Applications for possession under the 1964 Act, s 49 are covered in:

• McAllister, *Registration of Title*, pp 92–9;

• Fitzgerald, *Land Registry Practice*, chapter 11;

• Deeney, *Registration of Deeds and Title in Ireland*, chapter 41

• Brady and Kerr, *The Limitation of Actions* (2nd edn), chapters 4 and 5;

• Land Registry Practice Direction 'Adverse Possession—Title by Adverse Possession to Registered Land' on Land Registry website www.prai.ie.

The Registration of Title Act, 1891 stipulated that there could be no acquisition of title by mere adverse possession without an order of the court. The application to the court was by notice of motion and grounding affidavit of the applicant: see s 52 of the 1891 Act. Section 49 of the 1964 Act now applies to titles acquired by possession.

Section 49 reads:

1. *Subject to the provisions of this section, the Statute of Limitations, 1957, shall apply to registered land as it applies to unregistered land.*

2. *Where any person claims to have acquired a title by possession to registered land, he may apply to the Authority to be registered as owner of the land and the Authority, if satisfied that the applicant has acquired the title, may cause the applicant to be registered as owner of the land with an absolute, good leasehold, possessory or qualified title, as the case may require, but without prejudice to any right not extinguished by such possession.*

3. *Upon such registration, the title of the person whose right of action to recover the land has expired shall be extinguished.*

4. *Section 24 of the Statute of Limitations, 1957, is hereby amended by the substitution for 'Section 52 of the Act of 1891', of 'Section 49 of the Registration of Title Act, 1964'.*

By virtue of this section such applications are not made to the court; they are made to the Authority, ie to the Land Registry. They are made under rule 45 of the LR Rules and Form 6 of the Schedule of Forms to the said rules should be used. Paragraphs 3, 4, and 5 are similar in content to the affidavit of discovery in Form 16. Under the 1964 Act, s 93, an affidavit of discovery is required in any case where an examination of title is involved. Form 6 contains the essentials of Form 16 to satisfy the section.

13.4 deals with first registration of title based on adverse possession. **13.4.2** sets out the relevant statutory provisions, and **13.4.3** sets out the case law on adverse possession.

14.6.2   FORM 6

Form 6 is used for s 49 applications and not for the first registration of property based on adverse possession where a Form 5 is used (see **13.4**) (under the LR Rules 1972 Form 5 was used in both cases).

Where application is made in respect of part of property in a folio, an application map should be lodged. The map should be referred to in the application as correctly showing the boundaries of the property. Paragraphs 1 and 5 of Form 6 contain averments proving the essentials on which the application is based; whether it was sole and exclusive occupation or sole receipt of the rents and profits and that no acknowledgement of title was given, if such be the case, that there is no person interested in the proceedings who is not *sui juris*, and that there are no proceedings pending in any court relating to the property.

Paragraph 2 sets out the facts upon which the averment in paragraph 1 is based and is the part of the affidavit which seems to present the most difficulty. The notes to the said paragraph should be carefully read and understood and read as follows:

> 'Describe how the occupation began and set out such facts as are relied upon in support of the applicant's claim to have established his/her title, e.g., deliberate squatting with intention to acquire the property; taking possession as one of the next-of-kin of a deceased owner against the personal representative of such owner, other next-of-kin, etc.; uses made of the property; the persons against whom he/she claims to have acquired his title (registered owner or his/her successors), departures or dispossessions, relevant deaths; next-of-kin, addresses for service of notices, etc.'

The facts should be set out clearly and precisely in chronological order.

Some practitioners are inclined to omit paragraph 2 and expect a registration on foot of the general statement in paragraph 1. Paragraph 1 is most important in that it proves that the occupation is 'exclusive' and 'beneficial' and the 'length of time' relied on and that there were 'no acknowledgements'. Paragraph 2 contains the details of the occupation. All documents upon which the application depends should be exhibited. If the applicant is claiming through a tenant, then the nature of the tenancy, and full particulars thereof, and the name of the tenant should be set out.

14.6.3 EXAMPLE

Let us say that John Smith wishes to make an application under s 49 of the 1964 Act and that the following are the facts:

Peter Smith the registered full owner died intestate on 1 January 1970 survived by his widow Mary and four children, namely Patrick, Thomas, Margaret, and Elizabeth, and has no issue of a predeceased child. Mary, the widow who was married once only, died testate on 1 March 1978 and devised and bequeathed her share to Patrick. The will was never proved. Thomas and Margaret had permanently left the lands prior to the death of their father—Thomas to go to America and Margaret to marry.

Thomas had never communicated with home and Margaret is now deceased leaving a family. Elizabeth left home in 1977 to enter a convent and is still alive. Patrick remained on the property all his life and died on 1 June 1996 a widower and by his will left the lands to his son John, the applicant. His will was proved by the applicant.

On such facts paragraph 2 would be drafted thus:

> 'Peter Smith, the registered owner and my grandfather, died intestate on 1 January 1970 survived by his widow Mary and four children, namely Patrick, Thomas, Margaret and Elizabeth. He was not survived by any other child or by the issue of a predeceased child. Representation was never raised to his estate and I beg to refer to his death certificate upon which marked with the letter 'A' I have endorsed my name prior to the swearing hereof.

> Mary Smith, my grandmother, who was married once only, died testate on 1 March 1978 and by her will, which was never proved, she left her share in the property to my father Patrick Smith. I beg to refer to the original of the said will when produced and I beg also to refer to the death certificate of Mary Smith upon which marked with the letter "B" I have endorsed my name prior to the swearing hereof.

> My uncle Thomas had emigrated to America prior to my grandfather's death and he never communicated with his family with the result his whereabouts, if he is still alive, are unknown.

> My aunt Margaret had left the property prior to my grandfather's death and married John Browne. She went to reside with him at Ballybeg and died on 6 January 1994 leaving her husband and two children surviving her. (Set out the names and addresses if possible to enable the Land Registry to serve notice if considered necessary or prudent.)

> My aunt Elizabeth left the property in 1977 to enter the convent. Her name and address is Sister Mary, Convent of Mercy, Rathfarnham, Dublin 16.

My father, Patrick Smith, remained on the property all his life and died testate on 1 June 1996 a widower and Probate of his will was granted to me on 6 March 1997. By his will he left the property to me in the words following:

"To my son John I leave my farm of land at Carrowbeg".'

Note: the affidavit should contain the usual assent under the Succession Act and the second and fourth paragraph of Form 34 of the LR Rules. Section 54 of the Succession Act, 1965 does not apply to the will of Patrick Smith as he was not a registered owner.

Note: the Status of Children Act, 1987 applies to all wills made on or after 14 June 1988 and to all deaths intestate on or after that date and should be considered if necessary.

14.6.4 NOTICES

Service of notices on persons whom the applicant claims to have statute-barred is carried out by the Land Registry. In the foregoing example, notices would probably be served on Elizabeth and the family of Margaret. The service of notices is at the discretion of the Land Registry. If any of them lodged an objection then the validity of same would be examined by the Land Registry. If the objection does not contain valid legal grounds the objector would be so informed. On the other hand if the objector did show cause, then the applicant would be so informed and the Authority would refuse to register the applicant. An appeal lies to the court by either applicant or objector against the decision of the Authority (see s 19 of the 1964 Act).

14.6.5 OBJECTIONS

The following are not regarded as valid grounds of objection:

    (a)   occasional social visits and holiday periods;

    (b)   payment of rates, rents, annuities, and outgoings on lands;

    (c)   sending home money from time to time to help out or for repairs to the house;

    (d)   never released his or her interest in the property.

14.6.6 EVIDENCE OF DEATH

The Land Registry will normally require evidence of the deaths of persons who remained on the lands. Usually evidence of the deaths of persons who permanently left is not required, unless, of course, such deaths are relevant to the title. In the case of persons who remained on lands it should be proved whether they died testate or intestate and the relevant grant (if any) exhibited. It should be emphasised that the full facts relied on should be set out in paragraph 2.

Unproved wills may be accepted, in certain cases, by the Land Registry where the testator is a long time dead, or where his or her interest was a partial one, and the property was left to the applicant or a predecessor in title. However, the affidavit should also set out the names and addresses of the persons who would have been entitled if the testator had died intestate. Notices may be served on them. If the unproved will creates a settlement or charges the property with legacies, the Land Registry may require its admission to probate.

14.6.7 ESTATES OF DECEASED PERSONS

The Succession Act, 1965, s 126 substituted the Statute of Limitations, 1957, s 45 and reduced to six years the period applicable in the case of claims to the estate of a deceased.

However, the obiter dicta of McMahon J in *Drohan v Drohan* [1984] IR 311 cast a doubt whether a personal representative was barred after the expiration of six years. The

Supreme Court in *Gleeson v Feehan* [1993] 2 IR 113 held that the limitation period of six years laid down by the amended section does not apply to an action by the personal representative of a deceased registered owner seeking recovery of such land. The relevant period in the latter case is 12 years (s 13(2) of the Statute of Limitations, 1957).

In his decision in *Gleeson* Finlay CJ adverted to a contention by the defendants that this interpretation would lead to an unjust anomaly, in that the right of the next-of-kin to claim a share in the estate of the deceased was barred six years after the death of the deceased by virtue of s 45 as amended. He went on to reserve a concluded view until the matter arose in a case in which it was necessary to determine it, but observed that there was authority for the proposition that the right of a next-of-kin accrues at the date at which the particular property comes into the hands of the personal representative (p 789). McCarthy J was the only other judge who referred to this point and he adopted the Chief Justice's observations.

The Supreme Court later revisited the case of *Gleeson v Feehan* in *Gleeson v Purcell* [1997] 1 ILRM 522. The following quotation of Keane J at p 537 is instructive:

> 'It is, however, clearly contrary to elementary legal principles to treat the persons entitled to the residuary estate of a deceased person as being the owners in equity of specific items forming part of that residue, until such time as the extent of the balance has been ascertained and the executor is in a position either to vest the proceeds of sale of the property comprised in the residue in the residuary legatees or, where appropriate, to vest individual property in specie in an individual residuary legatee. Precisely the same considerations apply to the rights of a next-of-kin in relation to the estate of a person who dies intestate. Until such time as the extent of the residue after payment of debts available to the beneficiaries is ascertained, there is no basis in law for treating them as entitled in equity to any specific item forming part of the estate.'

Among the other findings noted in the headnote are:

(a)   The next-of-kin have a right, in the nature of a chose in action, to payment to them of the balance of the estate after the debts have been discharged. The right may be enforced against the personal representative . . . he does not hold the property for his own benefit . . . he is properly regarded as a trustee who must perform the duties of his office in the interests of those who are ultimately entitled to the deceased's property, whether as beneficiaries or creditors, and not in his own interest.

(b)   In the instant case, the possession of the lands (prior to the grant of representation) was at all times adverse to the title of the President of the High Court, the true owner, whose title was extinguished by s 24 of the statute. Therefore no estate or interest could be vested by anyone in the next-of-kin, regardless of whether they were in or out of possession. The grant of letters of administration could not revive the title to the land which had been extinguished.

14.6.8   CO-OWNERSHIP

Section 125 of the Succession Act, 1965 altered the law as regards acquisition by two or more persons entitled jointly or in common to a share in the land of a deceased. When they enter on a property of a deceased, they do so, for the purpose of the Statute of Limitations, as joint tenants, not only as against those not in possession but also as between themselves. In *Maher v Maher* [1987] ILRM 582, O'Hanlon J determined the nature of the rights acquired by the next-of-kin of an intestate registered owner, where some, but not all of them, enter into or remain in possession of his land without taking out a grant of representation. He held that all those in possession held both their own distributive shares and those of the absent next-of-kin jointly.

The judge applied the principle of the Succession Act, 1965, s 125 retrospectively. The decision did not follow the previous authorities and was quoted with approval in *Gleeson v Feehan* and *Gleeson v Purcell*. In the latter case, Keane J went on to hold, on the facts of that case, that where a stranger (in this case, the non-marital son of a daughter of the registered owner) enters into possession with the next-of-kin in possession, the stranger also holds the property as joint tenant against the other next-of-kin and may acquire the title by survivorship. This point had been conceded by the parties.

14.6.9   BAILIFFS

The rule that 'once a bailiff always a bailiff' applies when a person holds in a fiduciary capacity on behalf of children and persons of unsound mind in the case of deaths on title before 1 January 1967. In respect of later deaths, the rule was abolished by the Succession Act, 1965, s 124 (note: Brady and Kerr, *The Limitation of Actions* (2nd edn) refers to a continuing non-trustee bailiffship (p 158)). Also the position of the bailiff of a person of unsound mind who remained in possession and later left the lands on committal to an institution would apparently be governed by the Succession Act, 1965, s 127 which reduces the time within which an action must be brought to three years following recovery.

14.6.10   APPURTENANT RIGHTS

The acquisition of easements and *profits à prendre* lies in prescription not in limitation; see ss 33–40 of the 2009 Act. However, the Land Registry has adopted a pragmatic approach when applications are received on folios with rights appurtenant to the holding. The rationale for this is explained in McAllister, *Registration of Title*, p 98; in the great majority of cases, the applicant is a family member who has some beneficial interest in the land and its appurtenances. The applicant is therefore registered as owner of the folio as it stands. In the case of a stranger, a new folio is opened, without the appurtenances. For easements or *profits à prendre* acquired by prescription see chapter three of the Law Society *Complex Conveyancing Manual* (2nd edn) published by Bloomsbury Professional and Law Society *Gazette*, July 2011 which outlines the role played by the Law Society Conveyancing Committee resulting in amending the onerous effect of Part 8 of the 2009 Act as it relates to the registration of prescriptive easements and *profits*. The 2011 Act amended the 2009 Act and the 1964 Act. The main purpose of the amendment is to permit the Authority to register easements and *profits* without a court order where there is no disagreement between the parties concerning entitlement to an easement or *profit*.

14.6.11   LEASEHOLDS AND TENANCIES

An applicant may be registered as owner of a leasehold folio for the residue of the term of the lease but without prejudice to any right not extinguished by such possession (s 49(2) of the 1964 Act).

14.6.12   POSITION PENDING REGISTRATION

It is important to note that, where rights under the statute have been acquired or are being acquired, such rights are included among the burdens which affect registered land without registration (s 72(1)(p) of the 1964 Act). Consequently, a squatter could not and would not need to apply for a caution to protect his or her interest.

14.6.13   CAPITAL TAXES

See **13.4.2.4**.

14.7   Change of Ownership on Death

Change of ownership on the death of a registered owner may occur as follows:

(a)   transfer on sale by personal representative;

(b)   registration of survivor(s) of joint tenants;

(c)   note of death;

(d)   registration of successor of a limited owner; and

(e)   transmission on the death testate/intestate of a registered owner.

14.7.1   SALE BY PERSONAL REPRESENTATIVE

Transfer on sale by personal representative(s) of registered property which devolves on them on the death of the registered full owner.

The personal representative of a deceased registered owner may sell the property to a bona fide purchaser for value (see Succession Act, 1965, ss 50(1), 51(1), and definition at s 3).

The documents to be lodged are:

(a)   Form 17 required under rule 11(2) of the LR Rules;

(b)   fees (see current Fees Order);

(c)   transfer duly stamped or with a stamp certificate attached; and

(d)   grant of representation—original or office (ie official) copy.

However, where personal representatives purport to sell in the course of administration of the estate many years after the death of the deceased, note *Joseph Shiels v Frank Flynn* [1975] IR 296 and *Finbarr Crowley v John Flynn* [1983] ILRM 513.

On a death intestate between 1 June 1959 and 1 January 1967, where the devolution of the property was not subject to Part IV of the Registration of Title Act, 1891 and a right of dower arises in favour of the widow, her concurrence should be sought (see *Re McMackin* [1909] 1 IR 374).

14.7.2   REGISTRATION OF SURVIVOR(S) OF JOINT TENANTS

See rule 94 of the LR Rules. The appropriate evidence should be lodged in a Form 47 of the LR Rules together with a Form 17 and fees of €40 (Item 19 of LR Fees Order, 2012) identifying the deceased registered joint owner with the person named in an exhibited death certificate, grant of representation such as probate or letters of administration, or other proof of death. Form 47 is required to be on affidavit unless made by the solicitor for the applicant (see Note 4 of Form 47).

14.7.3   NOTE OF DEATH

The Administration of Estates Act, 1959 provided for the devolution of all property on the personal representative.

Accordingly, *on the death after 1 June 1959* of the registered owner of *any* property, his death may be noted in accordance with rule 92 of the LR Rules.

The note of death replaced a procedure whereby the personal representative of a deceased registered owner was registered as full owner with an inhibition prohibiting dealing, except in the administration of the estate of the deceased registered owner (Land Registration Rules, 1937, rule 88). There is now no provision for this type of registration but it may be considered to facilitate an urgent sale of the property.

14.7.4 REGISTRATION OF SUCCESSOR OF A LIMITED OWNER

On or after 1 December 2009 a limited estate is no longer a legal estate (s 11 of the 2009 Act) and the legal estate vests in the trustees of the trust who are set out in s 19 of the 2009 Act. A trustee of land has full power of an owner to convey or otherwise deal with land (s 20 of the 2009 Act); see **14.3.1** and **14.5.1**. Current registrations of limited owners are overridden by the 2009 Act. Registration of a successor to a registered limited owner can now occur:

- where the limited owner (life estate) dies prior to 1 December 2009; or

- where the limited owner dies on or after 1 December 2009.

Where the registered limited owner died prior to 1 December 2009, see rule 93 of the LR Rules and Forms 45 and 46 of the Schedule of Forms to the said Rules. Where the registered limited owner dies on or after 1 December 2009 and where the remainderman is entitled to the legal estate (no intermediate interests) the trust will be regarded to have ended and remainderman regarded as being entitled in fee simple in possession. Form 45 or 46 should be lodged.

Note the foregoing only applies if the remainderman is entitled to the legal estate (no intermediate interests) as it is no longer possible for a person entitled to an intermediate interest (eg life estate) to apply for registration as limited owner. If there is such an intermediate interest the trustee(s) can apply for registration as owners; see rule 66 and Form 86 of the Rules. Form 86 includes an application for an inhibition, see **14.8.4.3**. It should also be noted that the trustee(s) can also apply for registration as owner even where the current registered limited owner's interest has not determined, eg life tenant is still alive.

Form 45 is used as follows:

(a)   where the settlement was created by the will of a registered owner who died on or after 1 June 1959 and registration of the limited owner thereunder is made on or after 1 January 1967 (commencement of Succession Act, 1965);

(b)   where the settlement was created by the personal representative and the persons claiming on the death of a registered owner who died on or after 1 June 1959 and registration of the limited owner is effected on or after 1 January 1967 (commencement of Succession Act, 1965).

Form 46 is used in all cases where Form 64 is not appropriate, eg:

(a)   where the settlement was created by deed by a registered owner; or

(b)   where the settlement was created by the personal representative and the persons claiming on the death of a registered owner and registration of the limited owner was effected prior to 1 January 1967 (commencement of the Succession Act, 1965); or

(c)   where the settlement was created by the will of a registered owner and registration of the limited owner was effected prior to 1 January 1967 (commencement of the Succession Act, 1965); or

(d)   where the settlement was created by the will of a registered owner who dies prior to 1 June 1959; or

(e)   where the settlement was created by the personal representative and the persons claiming on the death of a registered owner who died prior to 1 June 1959 and registration of the limited owner is effected after 1 January 1967 (commencement of the Succession Act, 1965).

14.7.5 TRANSMISSIONS OF OWNERSHIP ON DEATH OF REGISTERED OWNER

For transmission of ownership on death of registered owner, see:

(a)   s 61 of the 1964 Act which was amended by s 54 of the Succession Act, 1965 and further amended by the 2009 Act (under which s 61(1) and (3)(b) were repealed);

(b)   ss 109–114 of the 1964 Act;

(c)   rules 85–91 and 94 of the LR Rules;

(d)   rule 93 of the LR Rules;

(e)   Forms 33–44 of the LR Rules;

For further reading see McAllister, *Registration of Title*, chapter V and Fitzgerald, *Land Registry Practice*, chapter 6.

The principal statute dealing with this is the Succession Act, 1965.

14.7.6   LEGISLATIVE HISTORY

Prior to the enactment of the Registration of Title Act, 1891, freehold property on the death of a testate owner in fee simple devolved on his devisee; and on the death of an intestate owner in fee simple it devolved directly on the heir-at-law. The rules of law relating to special occupancy, tenancy by the curtsey, and dower were also relevant.

14.7.6.1   Registration of Title Act, 1891 (formerly called the Local Registration of Title Act, 1891)

Most of the freehold land of which the ownership was registered under the Registration of Title Act, 1891 had been purchased by the occupying tenants under the various Land Purchase Acts. The great majority of the purchasers under these Acts were yearly tenants whose interest devolved as a chattel real. To change the mode of the devolution when the tenant acquired the freehold under the Land Purchase Acts would have caused hardship and confusion.

To ensure that the tenant's interest should continue to devolve as a chattel real, notwithstanding his acquisition of the freehold, special provisions were inserted in the Act, amending the law of property relating to the devolution of freehold land so acquired. They are contained in Part IV of the Registration of Title Act, 1891.

Section 19 of the Labourers Act, 1936, applied the provisions of ss 84 and 85 of the Registration of Title Act, 1891 to the fee simple interest purchased by tenants under the Labourers Act, 1936.

14.7.6.2   Succession statutes

The Intestate Estate Act, 1954 (repealed by the Succession Act, 1965), or the earlier one of 1890 may still need to be considered in certain cases.

Administration of Estates Act, 1959

Sections 6 and 7 of the Administration of Estates Act, 1959 in respect of estates of persons dying after 1 June 1959 made certain real estate devolve on the personal representative to hold in trust for the devisee or heir-at-law as the case may be. The Administration of Estates Act, 1959 was repealed by the Succession Act, 1965.

Succession Act, 1965

By virtue of Part II of the Succession Act, 1965 real and personal estates of a deceased person which do not cease on his death vest in his personal representative to be held in trust for the persons entitled thereto, and Part VI of the Succession Act, 1965, lays down the rules of intestate succession. These provisions apply in respect of estates of persons dying on or after 1 January 1967.

By virtue of the Succession Act, 1965, s 54(2) which inserted s 61(3) into the 1964 Act, the administration of an estate of a deceased registered owner is a matter for the personal representative and lodgement of an application for registration made by a person who claims to be entitled to property of a deceased registered owner accompanied by an assent or transfer by the personal representative in the prescribed form shall authorise the Authority to register such person as owner.

The foregoing is a brief summary of some substantive amendments to the law relating to the devolution of real estate and is set out only for the purpose of indicating the procedure necessary to obtain registration of the successor of a registered owner.

14.7.7 TRANSMISSIONS

14.7.7.1 Generally

Prior to 1 January 1967 (the date on which both the 1964 Act and the Succession Act, 1965 came into operation) the Registrar fully examined any application which dealt with the transmission of registered land on the death of the registered owner thereof. In the case of a testacy the Registrar examined the will of a deceased registered owner to ensure that the application was in accordance therewith. In the case of an intestacy it was incumbent on the Registrar to be satisfied that the interest of all the persons who became entitled on the death intestate of the registered owner had been accounted for.

Note rule 85 and Forms 33 and 34 in the Schedule of Forms to the LR Rules.

By virtue of the Succession Act, 1965, s 54 which inserted s 61(3) into the 1964 Act the Authority has no responsibility to examine the will of a deceased registered owner in order to satisfy itself that its terms are being properly interpreted and implemented if the registered owner dies on or after 1 June 1959 (s 61(8) of the 1964 Act). Similarly, it has no responsibility to ensure that the claims of all those who became entitled on the death intestate of the registered owner have been satisfied, if the registered owner dies on or after 1 June 1959. In both cases, be it the testacy or intestacy of a deceased registered owner, the Authority *must act* on the assent of the personal representative.

The notes to the transmission forms in the Schedule to the Rules should be read where the death occurred after 1 June 1959 as well as paragraph 3 of the Authorities Practice Direction 'Devolution and Transmission' (updated 1 February 2013).

14.7.7.2 Trustees of the settlement (testacies)

Section 19 of the 2009 Act sets out the persons who are trustees of a trust in land. Section 19(1)(b)(iv) of the 2009 Act provides that in the case of a trust created by a will the testator's personal representative or representatives are the persons who are the trustees of the trust in land if there is no relevant person(s) of the other paragraphs of s 19(1)(b). Under s 21 of the 2009 Act a conveyance to a purchaser of a legal estate or legal interest in land (see s 11 of the 2009 Act) by a person or persons specified in subsection (2) overreaches any equitable interest so that it ceases to affect that estate or interest, whether or not the purchaser has notice of the equitable interest. Section 21(2) of the 2009 Act states that persons specified shall in general (ie in the case of a strict settlement, a trust including a trust for sale of land held by persons in succession or land vested in or held on trust for a minor) be at least two trustees (this complies with previous safeguards in s 39 of the Settled Land Act, 1882) or a trust corporation. A single trustee can be registered as owner but a purchaser from same would not have the protection of s 21.

14.7.7.3 Transmissions on death of person entitled but not registered as owner

The Rules do not explicitly prescribe the forms to be used in the case of a transmission on the death of a person who, at the time of his death, was entitled to be registered as owner. It is, therefore, doubtful whether the provisions of the 1964 Act, s 61(3)(a) and (c) as amended by the Succession Act, 1965, s 54 apply to such transmissions. However, the general provisions regarding assents in the Administration of Estates Act, 1959, s 20 and the Succession Act, 1965, s 52, do, of course, apply.

If, therefore, the person entitled died on or after 1 June 1959 an assent in writing by his or her personal representative operates to vest the property in the person entitled.

If, however, the deceased died before 1 June 1959 an assent by his or her personal representative was ineffective to vest an interest, and a transfer from the personal representative to the person entitled on the death would be required unless the applicant is a devisee.

In either case an affidavit by the personal representative is required showing:

(a)   full disclosure of all the persons becoming entitled to any interest in the property; and

(b)   that the personal representative makes no claim against the property for the funeral and testamentary expenses and debts of the deceased person.

Such averments may be provided in the same documents as the assent, or may be given in a separate Form 34.

14.7.8   MISCELLANEOUS

14.7.8.1   Assents by personal representatives

The Administration of Estates Act, 1959 gave the power to the personal representative to vest any land of a deceased person dying testate or intestate after 1 June 1959 in the person entitled thereto by means of an assent in writing (s 20) and authorised the Registrar (now the Authority) to register the person named in such assent (s 22(3)).

Prior to the said Act an assent was not effective to pass an interest in land and was appropriate only in the case where a devisee was to be registered. (The interest passed by virtue of the devise.)

These provisions were re-enacted by the 1964 Act, s 61(3) as inserted by the Succession Act, 1965, s 54 which provided in addition that, in the case of an application accompanied by an assent in the prescribed form:

> *it shall not be the duty of the Authority, nor shall it be entitled to call for any information as to why any assent or transfer is or was made, and it shall be bound to assume that the personal representative is or was acting in relation to the application, assent or transfer correctly and within his powers.*

14.7.8.2   Chain of executorship

Prior to the Succession Act, 1965 the executor of a sole or last surviving executor was the executor of the original testator. Because of the Succession Act, s 19 such a chain does not arise in the case of an executor who died after 1 January 1967. However, it continues to apply in respect of an executor who was such by reason of a chain of executorship arising before the Succession Act came into operation, ie where the executor whose death created the chain died before 1 January 1967.

14.7.8.3   Proving executors

Where probate is granted to one or some of several persons named in the will as executors, whether or not power is reserved to the others to prove, the proving executors alone may exercise the powers of a personal representative.

On the death of the last proving executor, a dealing by a surviving executor who has not proved is not to be registered unless and until he or she produces a grant to his or her testator.

However, it should be noted that where an executor extracts a grant of probate, reserving the rights of another executor or other executors, such other executor(s) may extract a grant while the first executor is still alive, and this grant is called a grant of double probate.

It seems therefore, that where the rights of other executor(s) are reserved, a search in the Probate Office should be made to ascertain if a grant of double probate has issued.

14.7.8.4   Where personal representative is a company

Where the personal representative is a company or corporation such as a bank the person authorised by the company or corporation may swear affidavits for registration purposes. If the company divests itself of the property by an assent or transfer, such assent or transfer must be under the seal of the company or corporation: rule 74(4) of the LR Rules but see **14.5.2.9**.

14.7.8.5   Personal representatives as trustees

It is to be noted that in cases where the property of a deceased owner vests in his or her personal representative, while the latter is not an express trustee for the persons beneficially entitled, he or she is a trustee, and all incidents of trusteeship attach to his or her office.

However, on sale by a personal representative to himself, whether or not through a nominal trustee, registration will proceed after notice to the beneficiaries if they are all *sui juris*.

See the comments of Keane J in *Gleeson v Feehan* [1993] 2 IR 113 referred to at **14.6.7**. See also, in relation to trustees, **14.7.4**.

14.7.8.6   Grants of limited duration

If a grant of representation is of limited duration, eg during the minority of a person, the Authority must be satisfied that the grant was in full force and effect at the date of execution of assent or transfer. A certificate to this effect from the solicitor may be accepted in the Land Registry.

14.7.8.7   Impounded grants

If a grant of representation is impounded by the Probate Office, the operation of the grant while so impounded is suspended.

14.7.8.8   Dispensing with raising further representation

The court has power under the 1964 Act, s 61(7) to dispense with the raising of further representation to a deceased registered owner in certain circumstances.

An application under s 61(7) of the 1964 Act is made by notice of motion and supporting affidavit, which bearing appropriate Land Registry fees are lodged with the Land Registry's Court Registrar in the case of proceedings in the High Court or with the county Registrar in the case of proceedings in a Circuit Court.

14.7.8.9   Forms to be used for transmission applications.

14.7.8.10 sets out the appropriate forms to use in relation to transmission applications in the Land Registry. The Authority previously had two separate flowcharts for pre 1959 and post 1959 transmissions. Only one flowchart is now required. It is a guide to which form(s) should be used where the death occurred pre 1959 or post 1959 and in the case of post 1959 whether the person died testate or intestate; whether the personal representative is also the applicant; and whether the applicant takes beneficially or as trustee. Where three forms are mentioned two options are available; an assent and application can be lodged or a transfer from the personal representative can be lodged. The forms lodged should be strictly in the prescribed form and should be accompanied by the original or official copy of the probate or letters of administration, Form 17 and fees of €130 (Item 17 LR Fees Order, 2012).

14.7.8.10 Chart of transmissions as per the Land Registration Rules 2012

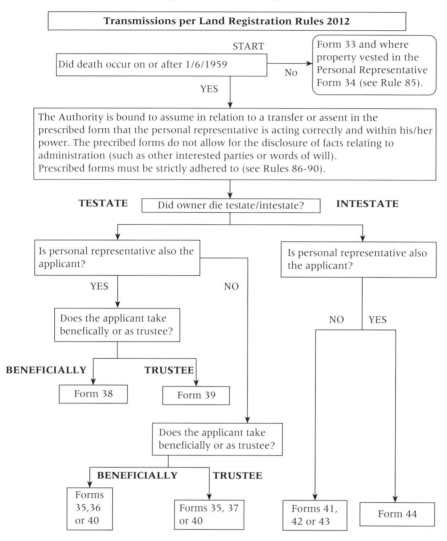

If the personal representative is an applicant in addition to another party (or parties) it is preferable to answer 'No' to the question 'Is the personal representative also the applicant?' and proceed accordingly. This results in the lodgement of one assent and one application which is a better option on the basis of simplicity and clarity. The alternative would require two separate applications; one relating to the interest of the personal representative and the other relating to the interest of the other applicants.

14.8   Cautions, Inhibitions, and Priority Entry (Search)

14.8.1   GENERAL

Persons holding unregistered interests in registered land or registered charges may protect them by registering cautions or inhibitions or by applying for a priority entry.

Indeed a caution may even be lodged by a person claiming an interest in unregistered land (1964 Act, s 96) requiring notice of any application for first registration of the land (see rules 30 and 31 of the LR Rules and **13.5**).

Cautions and inhibitions are governed by ss 96 and 97 of the 1964 Act, s 98 of the 1964 Act, as amended by the 2009 Act, and s 121 of the 1964 Act and rules 30, 31, 49, 69, 122–136 (inclusive) of the LR Rules. The responsibility for a caution rests with the applicant: s 97(5) of the 1964 Act. An inhibition is registered by the Authority or by court order.

For further information on cautions, inhibitions, and priority searches, see McAllister, *Registration of Title*, chapter VII and Fitzgerald, *Land Registry Practice*, chapter 10.

Under s 195 of the National Management Agency Act, 2009 where NAMA or a NAMA group entity has acquired a bank asset, a lis pendens, caution, or inhibition registered on or after 30 July 2009 shall be of no effect against NAMA, a NAMA group entity, or a person who acquires that bank asset from NAMA or a NAMA group entity, even if it is registered against the title to any registered land that forms part of the bank asset unless the party registering it has secured or secures an order under s 182(2).

14.8.2   DIFFERENCE BETWEEN CAUTIONS AND INHIBITIONS

14.8.2.1   Introduction

The distinction between cautions and inhibitions may sometimes be confusing and may not be apparent from an inspection of the entry in the register, eg an entry restricting dispositions for value by the registered owner except after notice to some party may either be a caution *or* an inhibition.

The main differences arise from:

    (a)   interests protected;

    (b)   form of application for registration; and

    (c)   liability for compensation.

14.8.2.2   Interests protected

The types of interest generally protected are set out in detail later under the relevant heading. As a rule of thumb, the proper use of a *caution* is for the temporary protection of unregistered rights pending their conversion into registered interests by registration. Unregistrable rights that cannot be converted into registered rights by registration should be protected by an *inhibition*. See **14.8.3.2** for examples of the use of a caution and **14.8.4.6** for the use of an inhibition.

14.8.2.3   Form of application

Application for a caution is made in Forms 70 and 71 to the effect that 'no dealing in the land is to be had on the part of the registered owners until notice has been served on the cautioner'. The governing section is s 97 of the 1964 Act.

An inhibition is registered:

    (a)   on foot of a court order; or

    (b)   by the Authority,

on the application of any person interested in any registered land. Application is in Form 76 (the suggested texts of the entries are set out in Form 77) and the governing section is s 98 of the 1964 Act.

14.8.2.4   Liability

Liability is perhaps the most important distinction. Sections 96(3) and 97(5) of the 1964 Act specifically provide that any person lodging a caution without reasonable cause is liable to make compensation to any person damaged by such registration. There is no such provision in relation to inhibitions, except for general compensation provisions under s 120 of the 1964 Act as amended by s 69 of the 2006 Act.

14.8.3   CAUTIONS

14.8.3.1   General

A caution is a requisition to the Authority requiring notice to be given to the cautioner before a registration is made under any disposition by the registered owner of the registered land or a registered charge. Its purpose is to obtain notice of dealings by the registered owner and to ensure that the cautioner has an opportunity of asserting his or her unregistered right against the registered owner, in the event of the latter trying to evade his or her obligation, before it is defeated by the registration of someone who on registration would not be bound by it, ie a purchaser for value.

In relation to cautions against first registration, see **13.5**.

A caution may only be entered against dealings by the registered owner. No caution entitles a cautioner to a warning of dealings by other persons with the land. Its proper use is for the temporary protection of unregistered rights pending their conversion into registered interests under instruments lodged in the Registry for that purpose, or pending litigation, or agreement. Its effect is therefore that of a delaying action.

A caution is not entered in the register unless the cautioner has shown by affidavit that he has, *prima facie*, an equity enforceable against the registered owner. A purchaser or mortgagee would not be safe in taking a transfer or charge from an owner against whom a caution has been entered, until the caution has been withdrawn, or the consent of the cautioner to the registration of the purchaser or the charge obtained.

As already set out a caution is a restriction on disposition by the registered owner *without notice* to a person who claims 'any right in, to or over registered land or a registered charge' (s 97(1) of the 1964 Act).

Section 3(1) of the 1964 Act defines 'right' as including 'any estate, interest, equity or power' over lands.

A caution entitles a cautioner to notice of dealings by the registered owner only and not in respect of dealings other than by the *registered owner*, eg a judgment mortgage, etc.

A caution against registered land is entered on Part II of the folio. A caution against a registered charge is entered on Part III of the folio.

14.8.3.2   Rights which may be protected by caution

The following are examples of rights which may be protected by caution:

(a)   the right of a purchaser of lands under a Contract for Sale (the caution can only be registered to affect the part of the property which is the subject of the contract);

(b)   the right of a mortgagee under an agreement to give a charge on lands;

(c)   a right under any unregistered instrument or facts as would disclose an interest in the lands or a particular registered charge on the lands;

(d)   the right of next-of-kin on intestacy or persons entitled under the will of a deceased owner to an interest in lands (but see the judgment of Keane J in *Gleeson v Feehan* [1993] 2 IR 113); and

(e)   the right of a person who claims he has provided all or part of purchase money for the lands.

14.8.3.3   Exceptions

Cautions are not given:

(a)   in respect of rights which are immediately capable of registration as burdens under s 69 of the 1964 Act as amended: see **14.12.4**; or

(b)   in respect of rights which affect without registration under the s 72 of the 1964 Act as amended: see **14.12.4.2**.

14.8.3.4 Other rights that may be protected

However, a caution may be used as a temporary protection of an unregistered right or equity pending its conversion into a registered interest or pending litigation, actual or contemplated. For example, the correct registration in respect of an s 69 burden is normally the registration of the burden. But, if the consent of the registered owner to such registration has not been given, the owner of the right in question could apply for a caution pending litigation to force the registered owner to give his consent.

14.8.3.5 Map

If the right of the cautioner relates to a specific identifiable part of the property, such part should be identified in accordance with rule 56 of the LR Rules and the caution will be limited to affect such part only. See **14.2.8.1** re application map requirements.

14.8.3.6 Evidence to support caution

The evidence necessary to support a caution is not as stringent as the evidence necessary to support an inhibition.

The cautioner must show by affidavit that he has *prima facie* a right enforceable against the registered owner, ie he or she must aver that he or she has such a right as would be suitably protected by a caution.

A person lodging a caution without reasonable cause is responsible for making compensation to any person damaged thereby (s 97(5) of the 1964 Act), whereas in the case of the registration of an inhibition, the Authority takes responsibility for making the entry.

14.8.3.7 Dealings affected by cautions and applications to discharge cautions

Whenever (a) an application for discharge of the caution is made by the registered owner, or (b) a dealing by the registered owner is lodged, a warning notice is sent to the cautioner in Forms 73 or 74 and the cautioner must then reply *and* take whatever action is considered necessary to establish such right (see rule 123(2) of the LR Rules).

If the cautioner does not reply to the warning the caution will lapse and registration of the dealing should proceed and the caution would probably be cancelled (rule 127 of the LR Rules).

If the cautioner replies to the warning requesting the continuance of the caution, or objecting to the registration of the dealing on the grounds that it would defeat the cautioner's interest in the lands, or that proceedings are about to be issued or are pending in relation to the matter, such facts and evidence would probably be called for.

It is not the function of the Authority to decide between the merits of the 'equity' of the cautioner and the 'equity' of the person in whose favour the dealing has been made.

In general, if the dealing is a transfer to a volunteer, such volunteer will be registered and the caution will be left standing on the folio, since a volunteer will take subject to any unregistered rights affecting the interest of the transferor including the unregistered right of the cautioner (ss 52(2), 55(2), 64(4)(a), 68(2), and (3) of the 1964 Act). But, if the dealing is for value, registration will be stayed pending litigation by the cautioner to establish his or her right. If proceedings are not instituted within a reasonable specified time, the dealing may be registered and the caution cancelled.

Similarly, on application to discharge a caution on the grounds that the right does not exist, the cautioner would probably be allowed a reasonable time to establish his or her right by litigation.

A caution may be withdrawn at any time against the whole or part of the property to which it relates or, alternatively, a cautioner may consent to a specified dealing (see rule 126 of the LR Rules).

14.8.3.8 Application procedure

(a) Lodge a requisition for caution in Form 70 of the schedule of forms supported by affidavit in Form 71 (rule 122(1) and 122(3) of the LR Rules).

(b) Notice of the entry of a caution will be sent by the Authority to the registered owner of the property or charge to which it relates. The notice will be in Form 72 (rule 122(4) of the LR Rules).

(c) The registered owner may apply (stating the grounds) to have same discharged. If so, a notice in Form 74 (rules 123 and 124 of the LR Rules) is sent to cautioner.

(d) If a dealing of which the cautioner requires notice is presented for registration without the consent of the cautioner, notice in Form 73 is sent to the cautioner (rule 123 of the LR Rules).

(e) The cautioner may appear to a warning notice in Form 73 or Form 74, for the purpose of obtaining a stay on registration of the dealing referred to in the notice or where the warning is sent on the application of the registered owner, for the purpose of obtaining the continuation of the caution. The grounds must be stated (rule 125(1) and 125(2) of the LR Rules).

(f) The Authority may appoint a day and time for the parties to attend (rule 125(3) of the LR Rules).

(g) The Authority makes a ruling (rule 125(4) of the LR Rules).

(h) Where the time given in the warning notices (Form 73 or 74) has expired the caution will be cancelled, unless the Authority otherwise directs (rule 127 of the LR Rules).

(i) For absolute or conditional consent of cautioner to a dealing, see rule 126(2) of the LR Rules.

14.8.4 INHIBITIONS

14.8.4.1 Object

Section 92 of the 1964 Act provides that notice of a trust shall not be entered on the register subject to the provisions of the Act. The 1964 Act goes on to provide at s 98 for the registration of inhibitions.

The object of an inhibition is, like that of a caution, to protect unregistered rights against registrations under dispositions for value that would defeat them. A caution protects by enabling the cautioner to prevent such a registration; it always throws on him or her the onus of taking the action necessary to prevent the unregistered right that conflicts with his or her own from being converted by registration into a legal interest in the land. An inhibition may also by its terms impose on the inhibitor the onus of preventing the registration applied for; it does so when the inhibition is against registrations under dealings without notice to him or her. But it is usually in the form of a restriction on registration that prevents all registrations, except those made in compliance with its terms as entered in the register, and so imposes on the applicant for registration the onus of seeing that the registration applied for complies with the terms on which registration may be made; for, if it does not, the registration is refused.

14.8.4.2 May be specific

An inhibition may restrict registration for a specified time; it may make registration conditional on some consent, approval, or order, being given or made, or on the happening of some event; it may restrict registrations except those under instruments of a specified character; or it may restrict registration under specified instruments. When such an inhibition by way of specific restriction appears in the register, the onus is on every applicant for registration either of complying with its terms or of getting it removed from the register, before he or she may be registered. No action by the inhibitor is necessary. An inhibition by way of specific restriction gives, therefore, more complete and permanent protection than a caution and is the appropriate method of protecting the unregistered rights of beneficiaries under trusts in land against dispositions in breach of trust by registered trustee owners (see **14.8.4.3**). Such an inhibition is expedient when a trustee is registered.

An inhibition is usually a restriction of all dealings for value by a person except with the consent of specified persons or within a specific time. An inhibition is the proper machinery to protect rights that may not mature for years.

14.8.4.3   Trusts

It is obvious that the restriction that should be entered on the registration of a trustee as owner must depend on the trusts on which the property is held; and in framing the terms of a restriction its object must be borne in mind; it is to protect the beneficiaries from the registration of an ownership, charge, or other burden, under a disposition for value by the trustee owner, which, if made, would defeat the unregistered rights of the beneficiaries by reason of the provisions of ss 52, 55, 64(4) and 68(2), and (3) of the 1964 Act.

Inhibitions are suitable for the protection of persons entitled under trusts. Under s 11 of the 2009 Act the only legal estates capable of being created or disposed of are a freehold estate and a leasehold estate. All other interests or estates take effect as an equitable interest only. Therefore, for example, where a life estate is created in freehold land a trust will come into operation under Part 4 of the 2009 Act and the legal interest will vest in the trustees. Any interest of a life tenant or a remainderman is an equitable interest only and such interests are capable of being protected by means of a suitable inhibition. See **14.7.4**.

A restriction against registration under a voluntary disposition is unnecessary, for a voluntary transferee from a trustee owner is, notwithstanding registration, affected by and subject to all the unregistered rights that affected his or her transferor.

Note that a restriction against registrations under a disposition that a trustee owner may make in exercise of the powers under the trust instrument is improper; no entry should restrict or limit the powers vested in a trustee for the purpose of enabling him or her to discharge the duties under the trust.

Under s 20 of the 2009 Act, subject to the duties of a trustee, and any restrictions imposed in the instrument creating the trust, a trustee of land has the full power of an owner to convey or otherwise deal with it. Where the trustees have powers of disposition, no entry should restrict their powers. In such cases, the restriction should be against dispositions other than those authorised. For example, if land is conveyed to trustees upon trust for sale, the trust does not authorise a mortgage or lease. On their registration the inhibition entered should restrict registration under any dispositions for value except transfers on sale; and, if the consent of some other person to the sale is required by the trust, except with that consent. If the trustees are expressly precluded from disposing of the land then the restriction to be entered on the registration of the trustees should be one that will prevent any disposition for value during the duration of the trust. If the power of appointing new trustees is vested in some person other than the trustees, further protection may be secured by also inhibiting any registration without notice to that person. Cases also occur where the persons ultimately entitled for their own benefit are known and ascertained. In such cases the inhibition may also, if desired, inhibit any registration without notice to them or some of them.

14.8.4.4   'Charitable trusts'

Part 4 of the 2009 Act, Trusts of land, does not apply to land held directly for charitable purposes: see s 18(9) of the 2009 Act. Charitable trusts are dealt with by the Law Reform Commission in 'Charitable Trust Law: General Proposals' (LRC CP 36–2005), 'Consultation Paper on Legal Reform of Charities' (LRC CP 38–2005), and 'Report Charitable Trusts and Legal Structures for Charities' (LRC 80–2006). See also Charities Act, 2009.

A considerable amount of registered land is held by trustees on trusts for education, religious, parochial, and public purposes, technically called charitable. In these cases the trust may be effectively protected by the entry of a restriction against registration under any disposition by the registered owners without prior notice to the secretary, or other person in administrative control of the educational, diocesan, parochial, or other organisation, for which the property is held. This gives the organisation effective supervision over all the transactions of its trustee owners; for, on receipt of notice of an application for registration under a disposition by them, it is the duty of the person in administrative control to see that the transaction is one sanctioned by the organisation; that it is authorised under the trust; and, where necessary, that the sanction of the Charities Regulatory Authority (formerly the Commissioners of Charitable Donations and Bequests, s 82 of the Charities Act, 2009 commenced 16 October 2014) has been obtained. If it is unauthorised, it is his or her duty to obtain a stay on registration in the same way, and for the same purposes, as a stay obtained by a cautioner.

14.8.4.5   General

Section 98 of the 1964 Act, as amended by the 2009 Act, provides that an inhibition may be entered on the register:

(a)   on foot of a court order; or

(b)   by the Authority on application of any person interested in any registered land or charge after making such enquiries and notices as may be considered necessary.

The entry may inhibit any dealing with the lands or charge for a time, or until the occurrence of an event specified, or except with the consent or notice to some specified person, or until further order.

Care should be taken in an application for entry of an inhibition that dealings with the property are not unduly restricted (see rule 131(1) of the LR Rules).

The entry of an inhibition under a court order will state that it is made pursuant to such order (rule 136 of the LR Rules).

An inhibition may be withdrawn or modified at the request of all persons appearing on the register to be interested in it.

For procedure on application for registration of inhibitions and their discharge, see rules 128–136 of the LR Rules.

14.8.4.6   Purpose and grounds for inhibition

As already stated, the object of an inhibition, like that of a caution, is to protect unregistered rights against registrations under dispositions that would defeat them.

An inhibition is usually a restriction on all dealings for value by a person except with the consent of specified persons or within a specified time. A voluntary disposition could not defeat or postpone unregistered rights (see ss 52(2), 55(2), 64(4)(a), 68(2), and (3) of the 1964 Act).

Inhibitions are suitable for the protection of persons entitled under *trusts* (see **14.8.4.3** and **14.8.4.4**).

The onus is on the applicant for registration, who may be a trustee under any of the preceding heads, to apply for the appropriate form of inhibition to protect the trusts (see s 92 and rules 49, 64, 69, and 128 and Form 77 of the LR Rules).

Inhibitions may *also* be entered on foot of:

(a)   priority entry under s 108, as amended by s 66 of the 2006 Act, and rule 162 and Form 93 of the LR Rules (see **14.8.5**);

(b) in bankruptcy matters where the relevant court registrar furnishes a copy of a petition of bankruptcy or petition for arrangement (see s 103(2) of the 1964 Act). Such inhibition is for a period of three months only, but may be extended by court order;

(c) the right of some person to the exclusive use of registered property other than a dwellinghouse for life. Note, however, that an exclusive right of residence, which is a burden registrable under s 69 of the 1964 Act, would not be protected by inhibition (see s 81 of the 1964 Act);

(d) the unregistered right of a person arising on the disposition by way of transfer or charge of the remainderman's interest under a registered settlement;

(e) the provisions of s 121 of the 1964 Act where a mistake has been made in registration;

(f) option to purchase; Professor Wylie draws attention to the case of *Midland Bank Trust Co Ltd v Hett, Stubbs and Kemp* [1979] Ch 384, [1978] 3 WLR 167 where solicitors were held negligent for failure to register an option to purchase;

(g) where a restraint order under the Criminal Justice Act, 1994, s 25 is made, notice of the order is served on the Authority which enters an inhibition;

(h) on foot of a court order; whether pleaded as a principal or ancillary relief in for example, family law proceedings or under the Jurisdiction of Courts and Enforcement of Judgments Act, 1998 or in Mareva or other injunctive proceedings.

14.8.4.7 Evidence to support inhibition

The evidence necessary to support an inhibition is more stringent than that to support a caution.

If the consent of the registered owner is provided, a statement of the facts showing the nature of the unregistered right should be provided (rule 129 of the LR Rules). Such statement is not necessary if the deed indicates the trust, eg transfer to diocesan trustees.

If the consent of the registered owner is not provided, the applicant for an inhibition must establish his or her right to have the inhibition entered (rule 130 of the LR Rules). The instrument (if any) creating the right must be lodged.

When satisfied that there is, *prima facie*, a case for entry of the inhibition, notice is served, as prescribed by rule 131 of the LR Rules. The inhibition is not entered until all objections are considered.

The sole duty of the Authority is to determine whether a person claiming as inhibitor has *prima facie* a right or interest which warrants its protection by entry on the register. If there is a conflict as to the existence of a right or interest claimed, or if two or more applicants make conflicting claims, the duty of the Authority is confined to staying registration pending the determination by the court of the matters in dispute.

14.8.4.8 Procedures in respect of inhibitions

The procedures in respect of inhibitions are as follows:

(a) entry of inhibition on consent of registered owner: rule 129 of the LR Rules;

(b) application for inhibition where there is no consent: rule 130 on Form 76 of the LR Rules;

(c) procedure on application for entry of an inhibition: rule 131 of the LR Rules;

(d) procedure on objection to inhibition: rule 132 of the LR Rules;

(e) an application for modification or discharge of registered inhibition: rule 133 and Forms 79 and 80 of the LR Rules;

(f) application in anticipation of dealing inhibited without Authority's order or approval: rule 134 of the LR Rules.

14.8.5 PRIORITY ENTRY

14.8.5.1 Application for priority entry

Priority entry replaces the previous priority search under s 108, as amended by s 66 of the 2006 Act, and rules 161–163 and Forms 193, 94, and 95 of the LR Rules. See also Practice Direction 'Priority Entries' (updated 1 February 2013) on the Authority website (www.prai.ie).

A priority entry may be applied for by a person who has entered a contract to purchase, or taken a lease of or lent money on the security of a charge on registered land. The priority entry should only affect the property the subject of the contract. Where part only of a folio is affected, a map should be lodged or other sufficient identification in accordance with rule 56 of the LR Rules. The fee payable is €40 for each folio involved (item 28, LR Fees Order, 2012).

An application in Form 93 must be lodged together with a map (if required) and the prescribed fee. The Form should be suitably amended where only a part of the folio is affected. The application must confirm that the notice in Form 94 was served on the other party to the contract.

The following entry (Form 95) is entered on the relevant folio if the application is in order:

> 'The [part of the] property [shown as Plan] is subject to the priority to be conferred by section 108 of the Registration of Title Act 1964 as substituted by section 66 of the Registration of Deeds and Title Act 2006.'

The priority entry protects the intended purchaser, lessee, or chargee for 44 days from the date of registration (rule 162(1)) (formerly 21 days).

On occasion lenders may require a priority entry to be made. The Conveyancing Committee is of the view that this should not be an automatic bank requirement in every case and that it is a judgement call for each individual solicitor to make in each case. This position applies whether the solicitor is a panel solicitor acting for the bank or otherwise. See Law Society Gazette Practice Note, August/September 2013.

14.8.5.2 Lodgement of other dealing during the priority period

Such dealing(s) if they are *prima facie* in order must be accepted for registration. If the transaction protected by the priority entry is not lodged within the priority period it loses the priority conferred by the priority entry. The pending dealing may then be registered. Determination of the priority will be arrived at on the expiry of the period of the priority entry (ie 44 days from the date of registration of the priority entry). A second or further priority entry in respect of the same transaction covers a new priority period. It does not revive or continue the period of priority of the first priority entry. An applicant for registration on a folio showing an unexpired priority entry is to be notified of the existence of such entry and to be referred to rules 162 and 163 of the LR Rules. On the termination of a priority entry, when the transaction protected by the priority entry is not lodged for registration, the date of registration of any other pending dealing affecting the property and lodged during the priority period is the date of lodgement in the Registry (rule 58 of the LR Rules).

14.8.5.3 Lodgement of dealing protected by priority search

To obtain the priority given by s 108(2) of the 1964 Act, as amended, the applicant must lodge his or her application for registration within the priority period. The registration is made as of the date of lodgement and the priority entry is cancelled.

14.9 Family Home Protection Act, 1976, the Family Law Acts, and the Civil Partnership and Certain Rights and Obligations of Cohabitants Act, 2010

See Practice Directions 'The Family Home and Family Law Acts' and 'Civil Partnership and Certain Rights and Obligations of Cohabitants Act, 2010' on the Authority's website at www. prai.ie. See also **14.11.1**. The Family Home Protection Act, 1976 (1976 Act) originally provided in s 3(1) that a conveyance of the family home by one spouse without the prior consent of the other spouse was void. Since the coming into operation of s 54(1)(b) of the Family Law Act, 1995 (FLA 1995), such a conveyance is voidable only. This provision is mirrored in s 28 of the Civil Partnership and Certain Rights and Obligations of Cohabitants Act, 2010 (2010 Act) in relation to alienation of an interest in a 'shared home' by one partner.

Note that a conveyance made as a result of an enforceable agreement (eg a mortgage) made before the marriage/partnership, will not be void or voidable (s 3(2) 1976 Act and s 28(2) 2010 Act). Similarly a conveyance made to a bona fide purchaser for full value and without notice (as per s 3 1976 Act and s 28 of the 2010 Act), will not be void or voidable (s 3(3) 1976 Act and s 28(3) 2010 Act).

The Authority's view is that it is the purchaser's solicitor who is primarily responsible for compliance with the 1976 and the 2010 Acts. He or she has the means of knowledge and opportunity (inspection and requisitions on title) to ensure compliance. A purchaser has a duty to make full enquiries on the matter. In *Somers v Weir* [1979] IR 94 Gannon J said that the provisions of s 31(1) of the 1964 Act (establishing the conclusiveness of the register) afford a sufficient protection of the vendor and the intending purchaser in relation to all prior transactions affecting the registered ownership as appearing on title. (See also *Guckian v Brennan* [1981] IR 478.) The court also held that 'the duty of ensuring that any instrument of transfer is valid and effective, so as to enable a transmission of ownership to be duly registered, falls upon the Registrar (Authority) at the time of the registration'. Since the commencement of the FLA 1995 and since the commencement of the 2010 Act, ie 1 January 2011, all that would be required is that the Authority be satisfied that no proceedings have been commenced, and no statement made, such as referred to in s 3(8)(c) and (d) of the 1976 Act, as inserted by s 54 of the FLA 1995 and s 28(12) and (13) of the 2010 Act in respect of the conveyance lodged for registration.

In the case of a mortgage application it is the responsibility of the lending institution to ensure that the rights of any spouse in actual occupation of the property have been safeguarded; s 54(1)(b)(ii) of the FLA 1995 and s 28 of the 2010 Act.

Before registration the following matters will be checked by the Authority:

- that there is no entry on Part III of the relevant folio as to a statement of invalidity under s 3(8) of the 1976 Act, as amended or s 28(12) of the 2010 Act, by the parties to the deed, and no such dealing pending; and

- that there is no lis pendens on the folio as per s 3(8) of the 1976 Act as amended or s 28(13) of the 2010 Act, and no such dealing pending.

If an entry relating to either of these matters appears on the folio the matter will be drawn to the attention of the lodging solicitor and registration stayed. Otherwise, no consents, statutory declarations, or certificates will be requested by the Authority, but if lodged these will be filed with the instrument.

However, it should be emphasised that the solicitor acting for a transferee or mortgagee should ensure compliance with the 1976 Act and the 2010 Act.

14.9.1   NOTICE UNDER S 12 OF THE 1976 ACT AND S 36 OF THE 2010 ACT

Registration of a notice of marriage/civil partnership is effected by lodging an affidavit or declaration:

    (a)   identifying the property of the owner-spouse/partner;

    (b)   identifying the interest the owner-spouse/partner has in same; and

    (c)   proving the marriage/civil partnership.

No fee is payable on registration of the notice.

On lodgement of a disposition of the property subject to such notice of marriage/civil partnership notice is served by the Authority and any objection is considered on its merits.

The Law Society has recommended that it is good practice to have such notices removed from the register when they no longer apply, eg on change of ownership (Practice Note, Law Society *Gazette*, December 2003). This can be done by lodging a form of application adapted from Form 57A where the spouse/civil partner who registered the notice consents; in other cases Form 57B should be adapted and appropriate evidence of non-application of the notice adduced (see **14.14**).

14.9.2   PROPERTY ADJUSTMENT ORDERS

Property adjustment orders under ss 9 and 18 of the FLA 1995 and ss 14 and 22 of the Family Law (Divorce) Act, 1996 or under s 118 or 131 of the 2010 Act are registrable as burdens under the 1964 Act, s 69(1)(h).

It follows that to ensure such orders are registered correctly, full details of the registered title are correctly set out in the order of the court, including correct folio number(s) and county, and, if part only of a registered title is affected, a map in accordance with Land Registry requirements must be furnished. Care should be taken to ensure that proper particulars of title are included in the pleadings (see Practice Direction, Law Society *Gazette*, October 2001).

Sections 74 and 75 of the Civil Law (Miscellaneous Provisions) Act, 2008 insert new subsections in s 9 and 14 (mirrored in s 118(5) of the 2010 Act) which provide that the Authority, on being satisfied that a property adjustment order has been complied with or discharged, shall cancel the entry made in the register. Rule 103 of the LR Rules (also deals with the 2010 Act) provides that an application for cancellation of a property adjustment order may be made in Forms 59A, 59B, or 59C of the said Rules. See 'Property Adjustment Order LR' Legal Office Notice 2 of 2009 on the Authority website www.prai.ie.

The Authority shall cancel the entry on lodgement of any one of the following proofs:

* where the property is transferred on foot of the property adjustment order. Application to be made by solicitor's certificate in Form 59A or by the beneficiary in Form 59B (affidavit);

* where the consents of the affected parties are furnished confirming that the terms of the order have been satisfied. Application to be made in Form 59C. The form may be embodied in a deed of transfer;

* production of certificate from the court Registrar confirming that the terms of the property adjustment order have been complied with in so far as the property is concerned. The relevant folio number, county, and entry number should be specified in the certificate.

The 2008 Act also inserts new subsection (8) to s 18 of the FLA 1995 and s 22 of the Family Law (Divorce) Act, 1996 (see also s 131(10) of the 2010 Act) which provide that where a property adjustment order which has been registered is varied, discharged, suspended, or revived by a subsequent order and the subsequent order is duly lodged for registration, the Authority shall amend or cancel the entry made in the register. Such orders must specify the relevant folio number, county, and entry number and set out clearly the amendment or cancellation to be effected. Any amendments are to be effected by the cancellation of the original burden and the registration of the subsequent order in the terms of the order furnished.

14.9.3   LIS PENDENS

If proceedings are instituted to declare a conveyance void, a lis pendens may be registered: see **14.16**. If the deed is declared void by the parties or their successors in accordance with the 1976 Act or the 2010 Act, a statement to this effect may be entered in the register.

14.9.4 TRANSFER INTO JOINT NAMES

Section 14 of the 1976 Act and s 38 of the 2010 Act facilitated the transfer of the family/ shared home into joint names by providing that no registration fees or stamp duty are payable on a transfer from the owning spouse/civil partner into the names of both spouses/ civil partners.

14.10 Land Certificates and Certificates of Charge

The Authority previously issued land certificates and certificates of charge but these have now been abolished. Section 73 of the 2006 Act provides that land and charge certificates cease to function as certificates as of 1 January 2010 (the Authority ceased to issue same on 1 January 2007).

During the period 1 January 2007 to 31 December 2009 a person who claimed to hold a lien on registered land or registered charge created by deposit or possession of a land certificate or certificate of charge could have applied to the Authority for registration of the lien (pursuant to s 73(3) of the Registration of Deeds and Title Act, 2006) which lien was deemed for the purposes of s 69 of the 1964 Act to be a burden which may be registered as affecting registered land. As of 1 January 2010 it is no longer possible to create an equitable mortgage on registered land. Any reference on a folio to a land certificate or certificate of charge may be ignored.

14.11 Prohibition Notes

14.11.1 SECTION 59(2) OF THE 1964 ACT

Section 59(2) of the 1964 Act provides that 'it shall be the duty of the Authority to note upon the register in the prescribed manner the prohibitive or restrictive provisions' of any enactment prohibiting or restricting the alienation, assignment, subdivision, or subletting of land and further provides that such provisions shall be burdens under s 72 of the 1964 Act, though not registered. Under s 13 of the 1976 Act and s 37 of the 2010 Act the provisions of s 59(2) do not apply to the 1976 Act or Part 4 (shared home) of the 2010 Act (see **14.9**).

A variety of prohibition notes appears in Part III of folios.

14.11.2 HOUSING ACT, 1966, S 90

The consent of the local authority named in the entry to transfers, subdivisions, and mortgages is required.

By the Housing Act, 1988, s 17 where consent under s 90 has been given to a charge, additional consent to a further charge between the parties will not be required, nor will a separate consent be necessary to the exercise of the statutory power of sale thereunder. Section 26(1) of the Housing (Miscellaneous Provisions) Act, 1992 further amended s 90: see new s 90(12)(b); once consent to a sale has been given, no further consent is required.

14.11.3 LABOURERS ACT, 1936, S 17

Consent during the specified period to transfers, subdivisions, and charges is required. Section 17 of the Labourers Act, 1936 has been amended by the Housing Act, 1966, s 98.

14.11.4   STATUTORY AUTHORITIES

Where the registered owner is, for example, a local authority, health board, etc, usually the consent of the relevant Minister is required for disposals. The relevant governing legislation should be checked.

14.12   Burdens

14.12.1   INTRODUCTION

The 1964 Act makes provision for two classes of burden that affect registered land. Section 69(1) sets out the class of burdens that may be registered as affecting registered land. Section 72(1) sets out the class that affects without registration. Both classes have been extended by various enactments (see **14.12.4**). Notice of any s 72 burden may be entered on the register under s 72(3) of the 1964 Act.

For further information on burdens, see McAllister, *Registration of Title*, chapter VI and Fitzgerald, *Land Registry Practice*, chapters 12 and 13.

As s 72 (as extended) burdens will not be evident on examination of a registered title, a declaration is taken up on closing of a transaction as to the applicability of such burdens to the property (see the Conveyancing Committee of the Law Society revised precedent long form s 72 declaration, and the October 2013 Law Society *Gazette* briefing note. See also the Practice Note in the November 2012 *Gazette* which recommended that the long form of this declaration should be executed.) This 'section 72' declaration is not a document required by the Land Registry and should be retained with the title documents. Care should be exercised to take full and correct instructions from clients in relation to the contents of such a declaration.

14.12.2   CONCLUSIVENESS OF THE REGISTER

As set out at **14.1.2**, the register is conclusive evidence of the title of the owner as appearing on the folio and conclusive evidence of, *inter alia*, the burdens appearing thereon.

14.12.3   REGISTRATION AND DISCHARGE

The creation and registration of the various types of burden are discussed extensively in McAllister, *Registration of Title* and Fitzgerald, *Land Registry Practice*.

Provision is made for discharge or modification by rule 101 and Forms 57A and 57B and for cancellation on merger by rule 104. Discharge may also occur by operation of the Statute of Limitations (see **14.14** in relation to discharges generally).

14.12.4   EXTENSIONS TO SS 69 AND 72

14.12.4.1   Section 69(1) of the 1964 Act as extended

(a)   any incumbrance on the land existing at the time of the first registration of the land;

(b)   any charge on the land duly created after the first registration of the land;

(c)   any rentcharge (not being a rentcharge to which, though not registered, the land is subject under s 72) or fee farm or other perpetual rent issuing out of the land;

(d)   any power to charge land with payment of money, whether created or arising before or after the first registration of the land;

(e)   any trust for securing money created or arising after the first registration of the land;

(f)   any lien on the land for unpaid purchase money;

(g)   any lease where the term granted is for a life or lives, or is determinable on a life or lives, or exceeds 21 years (*or such other period as may be prescribed*) (inserted by s 59 of the 2006 Act), or where the term is for any less estate or interest but the occupation is not in accordance with the lease;

(h)   any judgment or order of a court, whether existing before or after the first registration of the land;

(i)   any judgment mortgage, recognisance, State bond, inquisition, or lis pendens, whether existing before or after the first registration of the land;

(j)   any easement, *profit à prendre* or mining right created by express grant or reservation after the first registration of the land;

(jj)   any easement or *profit à prendre* where the Authority is satisfied, pursuant to s 49A, that there is an entitlement to such an easement or *profit à prendre* (inserted by s 42 of the Civil Law (Miscellaneous Provisions) Act, 2011);

(k)   any covenant or condition relating to the use or enjoyment of the land or of any specified portion thereof;

(kk)   a freehold covenant within the meaning of s 48 of the Land and Conveyancing Law Reform Act, 2009 Act (inserted by s 129 of the 2009 Act);

(l)   any estate in dower;

(m)   any burden to which s 54 of the Forestry Act, 1946 relates;

(n)   any right of the Land Commission or a local authority to lay pipelines for whatsoever purpose and any right ancillary thereto;

(o)   a power to appoint an estate or interest in the property exercisable within a period not exceeding a life or lives in being and 21 years thereafter;

(p)   a power of distress or entry;

(q)   a right in the nature of a lien for money's worth in or over the property for a limited period not exceeding life, such as a right of support or a right of residence (whether an exclusive right of residence or not);

(r)   a burden created by statute or under a statutory power that is not one of the burdens to which, though not registered, registered land is subject under s 72;

(rr)   an agreement under s 18 of the Wildlife Act, 1976, which provides that it shall be enforceable against persons deriving title to the relevant land under a party to the agreement (inserted by s 66 of the Wildlife Act, 1976);

(rrr)   a judgment opening proceedings referred to in Art 3(1) of Council Regulation (EC) No 1346/2000 of 29 May 2000 on insolvency proceedings (inserted by Regulation 4 of European Communities (Personal Insolvency) Regulations, 2002 (SI 334/2002));

(rrrr)   an order under s 18(1) of the Wildlife (Amendment) Act, 2000 (inserted by s 73 of the Wildlife (Amendment) Act, 2000);

(s)   any such other matter as may be prescribed, eg protected structure s 7 of the Local Government (Planning and Development) Act, 1999.

In addition:

• rule 107 of the LR Rules—crystallised charge;

• s 19 of the National Monuments (Amendment) Act, 1987;

• s 5 of the Housing (Miscellaneous Provisions) Act, 1992—improvement work on houses;

- s 73(3)(d) of the 2006 Act—lien re deposit of land certificate or certificate of charge (can no longer be applied for: see **14.10**);

- s 17 of the Nursing Homes Support Scheme Act, 2009—charging order.

14.12.4.2 Section 72(1) as extended

(a) estate duty farm tax and interest payable on farm tax (s 21(6) of the Farm Tax Act, 1985), succession duty, gift tax, and inheritance tax (s 113 of the Capital Acquisitions Tax Consolidation Act, 2003), former crown rents, tithe rentcharges, and payments in lieu of tithe or tithe rentcharge, residential property tax (s 107(6) of the Finance Act, 1993);

(b) land improvement charges and drainage charges;

(c) annuities or rentcharges for the repayment of advances made under the provisions of any of the Land Purchase Acts on account of purchase money;

(d) rights of the Land Commission or of any person under a vesting order, vesting fiat, final list, or transfer order made or published under the Land Purchase Acts;

(e) rights of the Land Commission upon the execution of an order for possession issued under s 37 of the Land Act, 1927;

(f) rights of the public or of any class of the public;

(g) customary rights, franchises, and liabilities arising from tenure;

(h) easements and *profits à prendre*, unless they are respectively created by express grant or reservation after the first registration of the land;

(hh) any wayleave which is a wayleave to which this section applies (inserted by s 43 of the Gas Act, 1976);

(i) tenancies created for any term not exceeding 21 years (*or such other period as may be prescribed*) (inserted by s 60 of the 2006 Act) or for any less estate or interest, in cases where there is an occupation under such tenancies;

(j) the rights of every person in actual occupation of the land or in receipt of the rents and profits thereof, save where, upon enquiry made of such person, the rights are not disclosed;

(k) in the case of land registered with a possessory, qualified or good leasehold title, all rights excepted from the effect of registration;

(l) a perpetual yearly rent (in this section referred to as the superior rent) which is superior to another such rent (in this section referred to as the registered rent) registered as a burden on registered land and which, as between the said registered land and the registered rent, is primarily payable out of the registered rent in exoneration of such land;

(m) the covenants and conditions contained in the deed or other document creating the superior rent, in so far as those covenants and conditions affect such land;

(n) a purchase annuity payable in respect of a cottage which is the subject of a vesting order under the Labourers Act, 1936;

(o) restrictions imposed by s 21 of the Labourers Act, 1936, on the mortgaging or charging of cottages purchased under that Act;

(p) rights acquired or in course of being acquired under the Statute of Limitations, 1957;

(q) burdens to which s 59 or s 73 applies;

(r) covenants which continue in force by virtue of s 28 of the Landlord and Tenant (Ground Rents) (No 2) Act, 1978 (inserted by s 28 of the Landlord and Tenant (Ground Rents) (No 2) Act, 1978).

The text of the Conveyancing Committee Practice Note, 'Registration of easement on a leasehold folio', in the November 2012 *Gazette* should be read carefully when making enquiries about s 72 burdens and the Committee recommends that the long form s 72 declaration be used so that clients can be properly advised about what such a declaration entails.

14.12.5 MAPPING

It must be noted that a suitable map (see **14.2.8.1**) is required for registration of any burden affecting part of property (rule 56 of the LR Rules). Also note the particular requirement in rule 121 of the LR Rules which relates to the registration of easements and *profits à prendre*. Not only must the part of the servient tenement the subject of the easement be shown, the dominant tenement must also be identified.

14.12.6 PERSONS ENTITLED TO BE REGISTERED

Section 90 of the 1964 Act as substituted by s 63 of the 2006 Act provides that persons entitled to be, but not as yet, registered, may transfer, charge, or create a lien on the property, and since 26 May 2006, grant a lease or create an easement or a *profit à prendre*.

Similarly, since 26 May 2006, the Minister for Agriculture, Food and the Marine has powers previously conferred on the Land Commission relating to rights of ownership.

14.12.7 PRIORITY

See s 74 of the 1964 Act and rules 98, 99, and 100 of the LR Rules in relation to the priority of registered burdens; and note the position of judgment mortgages in s 71(2) of the 1964 Act, as amended by s 130 of the 2009 Act. In summary, s 69 burdens rank, inter se, as of date of registration; s 72 burdens rank, inter se, as of date of creation; registered s 69 burdens rank in priority to subsequently created s 72 burdens; s 72 burdens rank in priority to subsequently registered s 69 burdens. See the special provision in s 75 of the 1964 Act for further advances on foot of a charge for present and future advances. Section 111(1) and (2) of the 2009 Act replicates s 75 of the 1964 Act for a mortgage for future advances.

14.12.8 ASSENT

No burden will be registered (except by order of the court) if not accompanied by an assent by the registered owner or person authorised by rule 96 (see s 69(2) of the 1964 Act). If the assent is not incorporated in the instrument creating the burden, it may be given in Form 48 (and rule 97) by such person or by his or her solicitor duly authorised.

14.12.9 WORDS OF LIMITATION

Since 26 May 2006, in order to create or convey a fee simple interest in a hitherto unregistered incorporeal hereditament, eg an easement or *profit* of registered freehold land, no words of limitation are required. This followed the amendment of s 123 of the 1964 Act by s 70 of the 2006 Act. Prior to that date, it was necessary to limit the property to the grantee in fee simple or to his or her heirs as the former s 123 only applied to the transfer of freehold registered land. See McAllister, *Registration of Title*, p 100 or Wylie, *Irish Land Law*, para 6.054. Note: in relation to words of limitation see s 67 of the 2009 Act and **14.5.2.5**.

14.12.10 LEASE BURDEN

The following entries may appear on Part III of a freehold folio:

(1) 18 January 1966   Lease dated 31 day of October 1965 from Good Houses

No 823/1/1966   Limited to John Daw of the part of the property edged green
and numbered 12A on the plan thereof on the Registry Map
(O.S. 22/10) Term 300 years from 29 September 1965. Rent
£20.

(2) 29 January 1971   Lease dated 31 day of October 1970 from Good Houses

No 98/1/1971   Limited to John Black of the part of the property edged green
and numbered 12 on the plan thereof on the Registry Map
(O.S. 22/10). Term 300 years from 25 September 1970. Rent
£20.

Note: The title to this lease is registered on Folio 25868L

Note the lease registered as burdens at (1) and (2) above.

The lease at (1) in this example was registered as a burden under s 45(g) of the Registration of Title Act, 1891. It was not compulsory to register the title thereto on a leasehold folio. Any assignment or mortgage etc thereof would be registered in the Registry of Deeds.

The lease at (2) in this example was registered as a burden under s 69(1)(g) of the 1964 Act and it was compulsory under s 70 of that Act and rule 123 of the LR Rules, 1972 (now rule 115 of the LR Rules, 2012) simultaneously to apply for registration of the title thereto, which was registered on folio 25868L. It is a registered title and all dealings therewith should be registered on that folio.

Note also that a lease may be registered as a burden without an ownership under a first registration of a freehold or a superior leasehold interest if no application for opening a new folio is lodged. See **13.3.15**.

14.12.11 RELEASE OF BURDENS

The appropriate form is Form 57A or 57B, as appropriate. See the general discussion at **14.14** and for further guidance refer to the Authorities Practice Direction 'Burdens—Cancellation of Burdens' which is available on the Authority website (www.prai.ie).

14.13 Charges

Charges are dealt with in the 1964 Act, s 62 of the 1964 Act, as amended by s 73 of the 2006 Act and the 2009 Act, ss 63 and 64 of the 1964 Act, s 64 of the 1964 Act, as amended by s 73 of the 2006 Act and the 2009 Act, and ss 65, 66, and 67 of the 1964 Act. See also rules 105–109 of the LR Rules and Forms 49–57B of the LR Rules. See also McAllister, *Registration of Title*, p 185 *et seq*, Fitzgerald, *Land Registry Practice*, chapter 9, and Wylie, *Irish Land Law*, chapter 12.

14.13.1 SECTION 69(1)(B)

Section 69(1)(b) of the 1964 Act provides that any charge on land *duly created* after first registration may be registered as affecting registered land.

14.13.2 CREATION

In order to see how a charge on registered land may be duly created it is necessary to revert to s 62 of the 1964 Act, as amended by s 73 of the 2006 Act and the 2009 Act, which provides, *inter alia*:

> *(2) There shall be executed on the creation of a charge, otherwise than by will, an instrument of charge in the prescribed form but, until the owner of the charge is registered as such, the instrument shall not confer on the owner of the charge any interest in the land.*

> *(6) On registration of the owner of a charge on land for the repayment of any principal sum of money with or without interest, the instrument of charge shall operate as a legal mortgage under Part 10 of the Land and Conveyancing Law Reform Act, 2009, and the registered owner of the charge shall, for the purpose of enforcing his charge, have all the rights and powers of a mortgagee under such a mortgage, including the power to sell the estate or interest which is subject to the charge.*

Section 62(7) of the 1964 Act was repealed by Schedule 2 Part 5 of the 2009 Act. This referred to applications to the court by the registered owner of a charge for possession. See *Start Mortgages Ltd & Ors v Gunn & Ors* [2011] IEHC 275 (Dunne J) which found that the repeal of s 62(7) means a mortgagee cannot apply for possession under s 62(7) of the 1964 Act if proceedings have not been commenced prior to 1 December 2009 or if the mortgagee has acquired a right to apply for an order pursuant to s 62(7) by 1 December 2009. See further *Kavanagh & Anor v Lynch & Ors* [2011] IEHC 348 (Laffoy J). The *Start Mortgages* case is understood to be under appeal. However the repeal of s 62(7) of the 1964 Act has no effect on a transfer under a power of sale or as mortgagee in possession under s 62(9) (see further on power of sale **14.5.1**). Section 1 of the Land and Conveyancing Law Reform Act, 2013 clarified the law in relation to mortgages created prior to 1 December 2009. Subsection (2) provides that the statutory provisions apply and may be invoked or exercised by any person as if the provisions had not been repealed by the 2009 Act. Subsection (3) provides that the amended provisions apply and may be invoked or exercised by any person as if these provisions had not been amended by the 2009 Act while subsection (5) provides that this does not apply to proceedings initiated before 24 July 2013 (ie the date the section came into operation).

Section 62(2) of the 1964 Act was amended (s 8(3) of the 2009 Act) by the deletion of 'or an instrument in such other form as may appear to the Authority to be sufficient to charge the land, provided that such instrument shall expressly charge or reserve out of the land the payment of the money secured'. Thus the Authority can only accept a charge in the prescribed form: rules 52 and 105 and Forms 49–53 of the LR Rules. Rule 105 prescribes several forms of charge. The Form 50 is a prescribed form for a charge for future or present and future advances. The deed must be one page only with any mortgage conditions filed on a separate document. Form 49 is the prescribed form of charge for principal sums.

Section 89(1) of the 2009 Act commenced on 1 December 2009 and provided that a legal mortgage of land may only be created by a charge by deed. The old methods of creating a legal mortgage over unregistered land, by conveyance or demise, in the case of freehold land, or by sub-demise or assignment, in the case of leasehold land, were abolished. Accordingly all lending institutions will be reviewing their mortgage documentation to ensure that a document which is intended to create a legal mortgage over land is made in the correct form.

As of 1 February 2013, Form 51 is the prescribed form of charge for present and future advances (formerly of the LR Rules 2011) and Form 52 is the prescribed form for a specific charge for present and future advances arising on the creation of a commercial mortgage or debenture (formerly Form 115 of the LR Rules 2011).

If a mortgage of registered land dated prior to 1 December 2009 contained only a conveyance or demise or an assignment or sub-demise with a proviso for redemption (ie mortgaged as if unregistered land) is submitted, it will be returned unregistered and the solicitor will be referred to s 62(3) (which was deleted by the 2009 Act). Under s 89 of the 2009 Act such a mortgage will not create a legal mortgage in either registered or unregistered land.

14.13.3 REGISTRATION

A charge for present and future advances is by far the most common form of charge. The charge for present and future advances may be stated not to exceed a specific amount but is not usually limited. See Forms 50, 51, and 52 of the LR Rules and **14.13.2**.

A charge of this type will appear on the folio in the following form.

Date	)	Charge for present and future
Inst. No.	)	advances repayable with interest.
		A.B. is the owner of this charge.

Where the charge for present and future advances is not to exceed a specific amount this will be stated in the entry.

See s 75 of the 1964 Act regarding the priority of future advances.

14.13.4 STAMPING

As and from 7 December 2006 charges no longer require stamping (see **16.5**). Previously the amount of stamp duty was entered on the register and if the maximum duty was paid this was noted. Rule 116 of the LR Rules, 1972 provided for the notation in the register of increased stamping on charges for present and future advances, and has been rescinded by the LR (No 2) Rules, 2009. However, where the cumulative advance does not exceed the stamping threshold or the deed is dated on or after 7 December 2006, no further registration appears necessary. However, if the lending institution insists, a notation may be made on the register in the following form 'Note: see Instrument Number X'.

14.13.5 CONTENTS OF THE DEED

The requirements that apply to a deed of charge in relation to date, parties, description of the property, and execution etc are provided for in the prescribed forms of charge (see **14.13.2**).

The covenants for title in s 80 of the 2009 Act (formerly s 7 of the Conveyancing Act, 1881) may be introduced by the use of 'as beneficial owner' in Forms 50–52.

If part of the property is to be charged, an appropriate map (rule 56 of the LR Rules) should be referred to in the deed and lodged (see **14.2.8.1**).

14.13.6 COMPANIES REGISTRATION OFFICE

Under rule 106 of the LR Rules where a charge is created by a registered company, and a certificate of the registration of the charge in the Companies Registration Office is not produced on making application to the Registry for registration of the charge, a note as to such non-production will be entered on the register (see s 409 of the Companies Act, 2014 formerly s 99 of the Companies Act, 1963).

14.13.7 COLLATERAL CHARGE

Where a charge collateral to another charge was lodged in the Land Registry, it had to be accompanied by the primary security to evidence the duty paid. Note charges no longer require stamping and therefore entries on the register will no longer refer to same.

14.13.8 DEBENTURES/FLOATING CHARGES

The case of *Mono Food Equipment Ltd,* 21 May 1986, High Court (unreported), which was a reference by the Registrar of Titles to the High Court, decided that registration of the crystallised charge as a burden on registered land is a prerequisite to the exercise by the receiver of the powers conferred on her or him in the debenture. Thus where a floating charge has crystallised, and the charge has not been secured on the registered property, the registration of the floating charge on the register is provided for under rule 107 of the LR Rules (see **14.17.4**).

Such a charge will appear in the register as follows (ie Form 55 of the LR Rules):

Date	)	Crystallised charge arising on the
Inst. No.	)	appointment of ....
		as receiver of ....
		by Deed of Appointment dated......
		day of............ 20 ....made between
		...............of the one
		part and............... of the
		other part under Debenture dated......
		...... day of...... 20 ...... Made between
		...... of the one part and
		...... of the other part.

14.13.9 CHARGES AND LEASES

See *George Maloney v Paul O'Shea and anor* [2013] IEHC 354.

14.13.9.1 Creation of lease on folio the subject of a charge

Prior to the coming into force of the 2009 Act the law on the power of a mortgagor to grant a lease of mortgaged lands was governed by s 18 of the Conveyancing Act, 1881. A mortgagor had a statutory power to grant a lease of mortgaged land subject to same not having been excluded by the terms of the mortgage. A lease granted in contravention of such a condition is void against the mortgagee and the mortgagee is not bound by it. Section 112 of the 2009 Act changed the law for mortgages created after 1 December 2009. This section provides that a mortgagor while in possession of mortgaged land may as against every other incumbrancer lease the land with the consent in writing of the mortgagee, which consent shall not be unreasonably withheld. A lease made without such consent is voidable by the mortgagee who establishes that the lessee had actual knowledge of the mortgage at the time of granting of the lease and the granting had prejudiced the mortgagee. In the case of registered land the Authority now requires, if the mortgagee has not joined in the lease, the consent of the owner of the registered charge to the creation of the lease or in the alternative a deed of postponement or partial discharge. See paragraph 7.1 of the

Authorities Practice Direction, 'Leases'. See also the Conveyancing Committee's Practice Note 'Consent required for registration of leases as a burden on charged land', Law Society *Gazette*, January/February 2014.

14.13.9.2 Lease burden registered on a folio subject to a charge

If a charge is registered on a folio (parent folio) and a lease burden is registered as a burden on that folio after the date of the registration of the charge (whether the title of the lease has been registered on a leasehold folio or not) practitioners acting for the owners of the leasehold interest (or a charge or other burden thereon) should ensure that either the charge has been released in relation to the property the subject of the lease or a priority note has been registered on the parent folio indicating that the lease burden ranks in priority to the charge.

If the registered owner of the charge on the parent folio sells the parent folio exercising its power of sale under s 62(9) of the 1964 Act, all puisne burdens on the parent folio will be cancelled under s 62(10) of the 1964 Act. This includes any lease burdens ranking in priority after the charge where the charge has not been released in relation to the property the subject of the lease. If a leasehold folio has been opened in relation to the lease it will be closed whether or not there are charges or other burdens registered on Part 3 of the leasehold folio. It is the Authority's practice to serve notice on the owners of burdens after they have been cancelled under s 62(10). In this regard it is now the Authority's practice to register a note on Part 1A of leasehold folios in the following terms: 'This lease is registered as a burden on the lessor's folio(s) referred to above and ranks in priority set down by Section 74 of the Registration of Title Act 1964 as amended. As between this lease burden and prior charges registered on the lessor's folio(s), (if any) the provisions of Section 62(10) of the aforementioned Act apply.'

A solicitor acting for a purchaser of a leasehold folio (irrespective of whether the title is absolute or not) should not merely inspect the leasehold folio but should also inspect the parent folio (if the lessor's title is registered) and ensure him/herself that there is no charge registered in priority to the lease burden relating to the leasehold folio or, if there is, that the charge has been released in relation to the property the subject of the lease. One cannot merely inspect the leasehold folio and depend on the conclusiveness of the register. The register is conclusive (s 31 of the 1964 Act) and that includes both the parent folio and the leasehold folio and the leasehold folio cannot be considered in isolation from the parent folio.

14.14 Discharges

The procedures in the following paragraphs may be adapted to suit the release or discharge of any burden on the register. For further guidance refer to the Land Registry Practice Direction 'Burdens—Cancellation of Burdens' on the Authority's website (www.prai.ie).

14.14.1 CHARGE PAID

The proper person to release a charge is the registered owner thereof or his personal representative. This may be done by:

(a) a requisition for discharge of a charge in Form 57A of the LR Rules. This form does not contain a receipt clause and does not of itself show that the charge has been paid but a bona fide purchaser for value will be protected (see McAllister, *Registration of Title*, p 196); or

(b) on foot of a receipt or release of the owner of the charge or burden (s 65 of the 1964 Act); or

(c) if the owner is a building society, by a vacate (Building Societies Act, 1976, s 84(5)); or

(d) by a receipt under seal (Housing Act 1988, s 18(2)).

14.14.2 DISCHARGE/RELEASE BY THE OWNER OF CHARGE OR BURDEN

Where the ownership of a charge or burden is registered on the folio, the registered owner of the charge or burden may give an effective release or discharge of it. The folio should be examined to see that there is no notice on the folio affecting such ownership, eg by way of caution or to ensure that the ownership of the burden has not become fragmented or apportioned between a number of folios.

The ownership of the charge or burden may be registered on another folio, eg on the subsidiary register maintained under s 8(b) of the 1964 Act (viz. ownership of incorporeal hereditaments held in gross or such other matters as may be prescribed—see s 83 of the 1964 Act and rules 186–189 of the LR Rules) *or* on another folio of the register, eg in the case of a dominant tenement enjoying easements and *profits* (not held in gross). In this case, the relevant folio should be examined carefully to ensure that the owner of it has full disposing power, that there are no cautions, inhibitions, or other notices, that the interests of mortgagees and persons with burdens on the title are gathered in, where necessary, and in cases where the ownership of the charge or burden is apportioned between a number of folios due to subdivision, that all interests are gathered in.

NAMA acquisition schedules are registered on the subsidiary register maintained under s 8(b) of the 1964 Act (see Legal Office Notice No 2/2011 'NAMA—Registration of National Asset Management Agency Acquisition Schedules').

Also see the earlier reference to Form 57A, s 65 of the 1964 Act and McAllister, *Registration of Title*, p 196. It may be appropriate to insert a receipt clause in Form 57A where a charge is being discharged or released on payment of all sums due.

14.14.3 EDISCHARGES

The system of eDischarges was introduced in March 2009. eDischarges is the first tangible element of eConveyancing in Ireland. This new online system enables lending institutions to request the cancellation of registered charges by electronic means without the need to submit any paper to the Authority. This secure transparent and user-friendly system has significantly reduced many of the inefficiencies and inherent delays experienced when mortgages were redeemed in the paper environment. An up-to-date list of all participating lenders is published on the eDischarges web portal (www.eregistration.ie).

No fee is charged for an eDischarge while release or discharge in paper format attracts a €40 fee: see L R Fees Order (paragraph 8(f) and Item 19 of the schedule). See also the Authority's Practice Direction 'eDischarges (Applications in electronic form for the cancellation of charges)'.

The following should be noted in relation to this system:

• eDischarges are lodged by the lender.

• An online application is completed and submitted electronically—there is no paper in the process.

• There is electronic third-party notification of the completion of the discharge to solicitors whose e-mail address is supplied by the lodging party.

• The system is 'automated' not 'automatic'—the Authority continue to sign off on the cancellation of charges from the register.

• eDischarges will only deal with full discharges of registered charges.

14.14.4   RECEIPT UNDER S 18

Where all money has been fully paid, a housing authority shall, and any other mortgagee may, issue a receipt under seal which will be sufficient proof of the satisfaction of the charge: Housing Act, 1988, s 18(2). (See also Practice Note, Law Society *Gazette*, November 1990.)

It should be endorsed on the original, counterpart, or certified copy of the charge. A receipt not so endorsed but clearly referring to the charge and identifying the lands charge may also be acceptable, but otherwise Form 57A or 57B of the LR Rules should be used. Similar provision is made in relation to unregistered land.

14.14.5   NO RELEASE FORTHCOMING

Sometimes a release may not be obtained as, for example, where the owner of the charge is dead and no representation is raised to the estate. If the charge was in fact paid, the applicant should lodge an application in Form 57B of the LR Rules setting out:

(a)   death of the owner of the charge;

(b)   no representation raised;

(c)   full facts relating to the payment of the charge: any receipt or evidence of payment should be exhibited; if no receipt etc is available, a corroborative affidavit of some witness should be lodged (if available); and

(d)   names and addresses of persons entitled on death of owner of charge. (Notices will be served on them by the Registry.)

14.14.6   NO OWNERSHIP OF CHARGE REGISTERED

If a charge is registered on first registration of property or on discharge of equities/conversion of title, the ownership of the charge may not be registered (eg original charge not lodged). If discharge of such a charge is required, the ownership of it must be proved (rule 44 of the LR Rules). It must be established that the person/body releasing is entitled to the benefit of the charge. This will necessitate inspection of the instrument of charge. In Form 57B applications it must also be established who is entitled to ownership of the charge and notices served in appropriate cases.

In the case of banks and other financial institutions cancellation may proceed on lodgement of:

1.   an original release of the charge;

2.   an up-to-date certificate of 'no acts' by the mortgagee; and

3.   the original mortgage (which must always be produced).

14.14.7   CHARGE STATUTE BARRED

If it is claimed that the charge no longer affects the folio by virtue of the Statute of Limitations, 1957, an affidavit in Form 57B of the LR Rules should be lodged by the registered owner or his personal representative.

The averment at paragraph 3 must show that:

(a)   no payment was made on foot of principal;

(b)   no payment was made on foot of interest;

(c)   no claim was made in respect of the charge; and

(d)   no acknowledgement was given.

Note, in addition, the facts shown must constitute a *prima facie* case that claims are barred under the statute, viz.:

(a) that the appropriate limitation period has expired since the date the charge became payable (see Statute of Limitations, ss 36 and 40, generally 12 years); and

(b) that the owner of the charge was not under a disability.

If the registered owner is dead, the name(s) and address(es) of his or her personal representative(s) or, if no representation raised, his or her next-of-kin should be set out. If he or she is not dead, the name(s) and address(es) of all notice parties should be supplied.

See Notes to Form 57B.

14.14.8 BURDENS

In general, the principles discussed in the preceding paragraphs would apply to *all* registered burdens: but see rules 113 and 114 of the LR Rules in relation to judgment mortgages: and see rule 104 of the LR Rules in relation to cancellation of burdens on merger.

Rule 104 provides for the cancellation of burdens where the registered owner of a burden becomes the registered owner of the property on which it is a burden. Note the rule is discretionary and the burden may only be extinguished and cancelled in the register following notice to all interested parties and where no objection is received.

In view of the judgment of the High Court in the case of *Stepstone Mortgage Funding Limited v Mary Tyrrell* [2012] IEHC 139, which was delivered on 30 March 2012, particular care is taken with easements and other burdens that are appurtenances to other lands. In that case, the court held that the order for possession obtained by the owner of a charge included the folio lands and the appurtenant rights of way and easements, which were registered on that folio when the charge was created and when the plaintiff was registered as owner of the charge. The court found in this case that the Authority acted in error in cancelling appurtenant rights on acquisition of the dominant and servient tenements by the same owner. As a result of this case rule 104, which was previously rule 112 of the LR Rules 1972, provides that notice is to be served on all interested parties.

14.15   Judgment Mortgage

14.15.1 GENERALLY

See the Authority's Practice Direction 'Judgment Mortgages' on its website at www.prai.ie.

Previously a judgment mortgage was registered by lodgement of an affidavit prescribed by the Judgment Mortgage (Ireland) Act, 1850, s 6 and s 71 of the 1964 Act.

Part 11 of the 2009 Act replaces with substantial amendments the Judgment Mortgage (Ireland) Acts, 1850 and 1858 which are repealed as of 1 December 2009. The substantive provisions of Part 11 have been drafted on the basis that the detailed requirements as to registration, including the forms which should be used in future, will be prescribed by statutory instrument. Section 115 of the 2009 Act defines 'creditor' as including 'an authorised agent and any person authorised by the court to register a judgment mortgage on behalf of a judgment creditor'. Section 116 of the 2009 Act provides that a creditor who has obtained a judgment against a person may apply to register a judgment mortgage against that person's estate or interest in land and such a judgment mortgage shall be registered in the Land Registry or Registry of Deeds. Section 71 of the 1964 Act is amended by s 130 of the 2009 Act. Rule 110 of the LR Rules provides that an application for registration of a judgment mortgage shall be in Form 60. Note Rule 110 and Form 60 have been amended (as of 1 February 2013) by rule 3 of the LR Rules, 2013 with reference to judgments of the Supreme Court. Rule 111 of the LR Rules provides for a statement by the applicant re property owned by judgment debtor. See also Forms 61, 62, and 63 of the LR Rules.

Note in relation to the prescribed Form 60:

- It must be strictly complied with.

- It does not include the amount of the judgment or costs.

- It must include thereon a certificate that the particulars of the judgment described therein are correctly signed by the proper officer of the court in which the judgment was obtained.

- The property and the estate or interest of the judgment debtor in same must also be identified as per rule 111 of the LR Rules, as amended.

- Where the judgment creditor is a company the opening paragraphs of Form 60 should read:

  '*I, EF aged 18 and upwards, of ... ... the creditor within the meaning of Section 115 of the Land and Conveyancing Law Reform Act 2009 make oath and say as follows:–*

  1. AB did on the   day of obtain a judgment in the   court against CD of   in the above entitled Action or matter'.

- It is a matter for the applicant to ensure that the person making the affidavit is authorised and the Land Registry will make no inquiries re same.

- The address of the debtor to be inserted in paragraph 1 of Form 60 is the address as at the time of the judgment and not the current address.

As and from 1 December 2009 a judgment mortgage irrespective of when obtained can only be registered by lodging the Form 60.

Under the Bankruptcy Act, 1988, s 51, a judgment mortgage will not be effective if bankruptcy or winding up occurs within three months following registration of that judgment mortgage.

14.15.2 DUTY OF AUTHORITY

The duty of the Authority in registering the application for registration of a judgment mortgage in Form 60 of the LR Rules is ministerial only and it has no power to refuse to accept the application (*Re Phelan* [1912] IR 91). However, it is open to the registered owner or any other person interested to apply to have the judgment mortgage cancelled on the basis that the deposit and the notice thereof does not create a valid burden or that the judgment mortgage is not a valid burden.

An issue previously arose when details of the amount of the judgment and costs were included in the judgment affidavit. This issue would also arise if the amount of the judgment and costs were included in Form 60. Where costs are awarded 'to be taxed in default of agreement', it would appear that if there is no agreement, costs should be waived for the purposes of registration or registration delayed until taxed. In *Re Field's Estate* (IR R 11 Eq 456) costs were waived for the purpose of registration and the affidavit of judgment was registered. When the costs were taxed, a fresh affidavit was registered, apparently registering the full judgment with costs. It was held that the registration of the judgment was valid where the costs were waived, but the judgment for costs was invalid as there could not be two registrations of the same judgment against the same lands. Of course, an award of costs may be registered as a judgment mortgage in its own right, eg in a family law matter or in injunctive proceedings. However, once costs have been waived for registration purposes, it may not be possible to register them later.

14.15.3 RELEASE

See rules 113 and 114 of the LR Rules generally regarding release of a judgment mortgage.

Also an application to discharge may be made if the judgment mortgage no longer affects the lands, eg if it is statute barred. Adapt Form 57B of the LR Rules and note the special limitation period under s 47(c)(iii) of the Statute of Limitations, 1957. Section 119 of the 2009 Act clarifies the operation of s 32 of the Statute of Limitations, 1957 in relation to judgment mortgages and confirms the current law (s 47(c)(iii) of the 1957 Act). It adds a subsection (3) to that section: 'In the case of a judgment mortgage, the right of action accrues from the date the judgment becomes enforceable and not the date on which it is registered as a mortgage.' See also **14.15.5**.

14.15.4 INSPECTION

Note the provision in rule 159 of the LR Rules allowing inspection of judgment mortgage affidavits or an application for registration of a judgment mortgage under rule 110 so long as it is not cancelled.

14.15.5 CASES

Pim v Coyle [1907] 1 IR 330: A voluntary transferee is not protected, because he or she takes no interest in the property until he or she is registered as owner and, consequently, a judgment mortgage registered after the date of the deed of transfer, but before registration thereof, will take priority.

Re Murphy and McCormack [1928] IR 479, [1930] IR 322: A purchaser for value is protected. After completion of the sale, the registered owner has no beneficial interest, whereas the purchaser had an unregistered right, enforceable against the registered owner, and any person.

Re Strong [1940] IR 382, 386: The Supreme Court held a purchaser of registered land is entitled to have cancelled from the register a judgment mortgage which was registered before the purchaser's deed, but after the entire purchase money has been paid.

The question still arose as to what was the position where a contract was signed and a deposit paid, but the sale had not been completed when the judgment mortgage was registered.

Section 52 of the 2009 Act deals with the passing of interest. It states that 'The entire beneficial interest passes to the purchaser on the making, after the commencement of this Chapter, of an enforceable contract for the sale or other disposition of land' subject to any provision to the contrary in the contract. This restores the orthodox position from the majority view in *Tempany v Hynes* [1976] IR 101 which held that the beneficial interest passes only to the extent that the purchase money has been paid.

14.15.6 CO-OWNERSHIP

Under s 33(3) of the 2009 Act on or after 1 December 2009 registration of a judgment mortgage against the estate or interest in land of a joint tenant does not sever the joint tenancy either in registered or unregistered land. If the joint tenancy remains unsevered, the judgment mortgage is extinguished upon the death of the judgment debtor: subsection (3). Under the old law with respect to judgment mortgages it appeared that severance did occur where the interest was in unregistered land but did not where it was registered land. See *Judge Mahon & Ors v Lawlor & Ors* [2008] IEHC 284 (Laffoy J).

14.15.7 COMPANIES

Under the Companies Act, 1963, s 102, when a judgment mortgage was obtained against a limited company, the judgment creditor was required to cause two copies, certified by the Land Registry as true copies 'of the affidavit required for the purpose of registering the judgment as a mortgage', to be delivered to the company within 21 days after the date of registration. The company was required to then, within three days, deliver one copy to the Registrar of Companies. The Land Registry was also required to deliver a copy of the said affidavit to the Registrar of Companies as soon as may be. This section was not amended by the 2009 Act but the affidavit referred to in s 102 would appear to apply to the application for registration of a judgment mortgage in Form 60 (affidavit).

Section 413 of the Companies Act, 2014 replaced s 102 of the Companies Act, 1963 as and from 1 June 2015. There is no provision in s 413 requiring the Authority to forward a copy of the judgment mortgage application form to the Registrar of Companies. Therefore in the case of applications for registration of a judgment mortgage lodged on or after 1 June 2015 copies of the application form will not issue to the Registrar of Companies. There remains the requirement for the prescribed particulars in the prescribed form, together with the relevant judgment mortgage document (Form 60, 60A, or 60B of the LR Rules, 2012–2013, see s 413(4)), to be received by the Registrar of Companies within 21 days from the date on which notification by the Authority of the judgment mortgage's creation is received by the judgment creditor (s 413(3)).

14.15.8 ADMINISTRATION OF ESTATES

Rule 72 of the LR Rules provides that on application by a purchaser from the personal representative of a deceased registered owner for registration, the purchaser may apply for cancellation of notice of the deposit of an affidavit of judgment as a mortgage on the estate or interest of a person who has a beneficial interest in the property under the will or intestacy of the deceased owner.

14.15.9 JUDGMENTS CAPABLE OF REGISTRATION

Judgments of the Superior Courts (Supreme Court, Court of Appeal, and High Court), the Circuit Court and the District Court for a liquidated sum (ie judgments which require the payment of a sum of money) are capable of being registered as judgment mortgages.

14.15.10 FOREIGN JUDGMENTS

Judgments obtained abroad, outside EU Member States, are not generally capable of registration as judgment mortgages. However, the High Court has jurisdiction to make enforcement orders, in respect of foreign judgments, made by courts of competent jurisdiction, for payment of fixed money sums. The order of the High Court may include protective measures, such as an injunction preventing the defendant reducing the value of his or her assets in the State below a sum sufficient to discharge the foreign judgment. Where the assets include registered land, which are specified in the order, such an order would be registrable as a burden. See s 69(1)(h) of the 1964 Act.

Since 1988, there has been legislation in place giving effect to the Brussels Convention 1968 (as amended), for the enforcement of judgments in civil and commercial matters throughout EU Member States. The Jurisdiction of Courts and Enforcement of Judgments (European Communities) Act, 1988 (as amended by Jurisdiction of Courts and Enforcement of Judgments Act, 1993), was repealed and consolidated by the Jurisdiction of Courts and Enforcement of Judgments Act, 1998. Except for Denmark, enforcement of judgments of Member States is now governed by the Brussels I Regulation of 2002 (Council Regulation [EC] No 44/2001). This is given effect to in the European Communities (Civil and Commercial Judgments) Regulations, 2002 (SI 52/2002).

In relation to judgments obtained prior to 10 January 2015, if a judgment creditor wishes to enforce a judgment in Ireland, which was obtained in the national courts of another EU Member State, an application for recognition and enforcement of that judgment must first be made to the master of the High Court. The master will deal with such application in accordance with Brussels I Regulation. An application for registration of a judgment mortgage, in respect of a judgment obtained in another EU Member State, is now provided for under rule 4 of the LR Rules, 2013 (from 1 February 2013) which inserted a new rule 110A into the LR Rules, 2012 which provides that the application shall be made in the Form 60A and shall be accompanied by:

- an official copy of the relevant judgment; and

- an official copy of the order of the Master of the High Court declaring the judgment enforceable.

In relation to judgments obtained from 10 January 2015 note that the Brussels I Regulations were revoked and replaced by the European Union (Civil and Commercial Judgments) Regulations, 2015 (SI 6/2015). The Regulations of 2015 transpose the amended Brussels I Regulation, which was amended under Regulation (EU) No 1215/2012 of the European Parliament and of the Council, generally referred to as 'Brussels I Regulation (recast)', into Irish law as and from 10 January 2015. Although Denmark did not take part in the adoption of the Regulation and is not bound by it, Denmark has agreed to implement the contents of the amending Regulation. Under the Brussels I Regulation (recast), an enforcement order of the Master of the High Court is no longer required in respect of civil and commercial judgments obtained in courts of Member States of the European Union. However, under Art 37 of Regulation (EU) No 1215/2012, a party who wishes to invoke in a Member State a judgment given in another Member State shall produce, in addition to a copy of the judgment, the certificate pursuant to Art 53 from the court of origin. The certificate referred to in Art 53, which issues from the court of origin where the original judgment was obtained, should accompany the official copy judgment. The Art 53 certificate is in a form prescribed by Annex 1 of the Regulation. It gives full details of the judgment and bears the court stamp. An Enforcement Order of the Master of the High Court is not required and will not be called for. New Land Registration and Registration of Deeds Rules will be made in due course to reflect these changes. In the interim, judgments accompanied by Art 53 certificates should be regarded in the same way as judgments accompanied by an Enforcement Order from the Master of the High Court. Prescribed forms that are adapted by substituting references to the Enforcement Order of the Master of the High Court with references to Art 53 certificates may be accepted in both Land Registry and the Registry of Deeds. Rule 52(2) of the Land Registration Rules, 2012 and rule 6(1) of the Registration of Deeds Rules, 2008 refer.

Since 21 October 2005 under regulation 7 of European Communities (European Enforcement Order) Regulations, 2005 (SI 648/2005), which implemented into Irish law Regulation (EC) No 805/2004 of the European Parliament and of the Council of 21 April 2004 creating a European Enforcement order for uncontested claims:

Where a judgment, court settlement or authentic instrument on an uncontested claim has been certified as a European Enforcement order in a Member State of origin, that Judgment, court settlement or authentic instrument, as the case may be—(a) shall be of the same force and effect as a judgment of the High Court, and (b) may be enforced by the High Court, and the proceedings taken on it, as if it were a judgment of that Court.

Therefore to register such a foreign judgment (EU countries except Denmark) there is no longer any need to acquire an order of the master of the High Court. An application for a European enforcement order shall be made to the court which delivered the judgment on the uncontested claim: regulation 8(1) of 2005 Regulations. This situation is now provided for under rule 4 of the LR Rules, 2013 (from 1 February 2013) which inserted a new rule 110B into the LR Rules, 2012 which provides the application shall be made in the Form 60B and shall be accompanied by:

- official copy of the relevant judgment;

- official copy of the European enforcement order certificate; and

- where necessary, a transcription of the European enforcement order cetificate or a translation thereof in Irish or English.

14.15.11 PRIORITY OF JUDGMENT MORTGAGE AND CHARGES

In a decision of Carroll J (*Re the Registration of Title Act, 1964, s 19 between ICC plc (applicant) and M J Gleeson & Co Ltd (respondents)*, 18 February 1992, High Court (unreported)) it was held that the payment of loan money pursuant to a loan agreement created an equitable charge which predated the registration of judgment mortgage against the borrowers. When the judgment mortgages were registered, they took subject to that equitable charge. The priority of the charge should be protected by a note on the register that it had priority over the registered judgment mortgages.

Section 117(3) of the 2009 Act provides that the judgment mortgage is subject to any right or incumbrance affecting the judgment debtor's land, whether registered or not, at the time of its registration. In relation to registered land see s 71(2)(c) of the 1964 Act as substituted by s 130 of the 2009 Act.

14.16   Lis Pendens

14.16.1 GENERALLY

Section 121 of the 2009 Act provides for keeping the register of lis pendens in the prescribed manner, which is already maintained in the central office of the High Court. Under s 121(4), a lis pendens already registered under the 1844 Act and not vacated when this legislation comes into force will continue to have effect as if the 1844 Act had not been repealed. It will be deemed to form part of the register to be maintained under s 121(1). This will avoid the Courts Service having to re-enter it in a new register. Section 121(2) provides that the following may be registered as a lis pendens: any action in the Circuit Court or the High Court in which a claim is made to an estate or interest in land (including such an estate or interest which a person receives, whether in whole or in part, by an order made in the action) whether by way of claim or counterclaim in the action; and any proceedings to have a conveyance of an estate or interest in land declared void.

Note rule 119 and Form 64 of the LR Rules.

Under s 195 of the National Asset Management Agency Act, 2009 where NAMA or a NAMA group entity has acquired a bank asset, a lis pendens, caution, or inhibition registered on or after 30 July 2009 shall be of no effect against NAMA, a NAMA group entity, or a person who acquires that bank asset from NAMA or a NAMA group entity, even if it is registered against the title to any registered land that forms part of the bank asset unless the party registering it has secured or secures an order under s 182(2).

See the 1964 Act, s 69, rule 119, Forms 64 and 65, and McAllister, *Registration of Title*, p 215.

A lis pendens is an entry made on the folio to the effect that litigation is pending in relation to the lands.

The only suit that may be registered as a lis pendens is one to recover or charge the land the subject of the suit. This would encompass proceedings to have a deed declared void, for example, a 'conveyance' of the family home without the prior consent of the non-owning spouse.

An application in Form 64, as amended, is to be accompanied by a certificate of the proper officer of the High Court of the existence of the cause or proceedings which is registered in the Central Office of the High Court, which must be a suit to recover or charge the property.

14.16.2 APPLICATION FOR DISCHARGE

Under rule 119(3) of the LR Rules an application for discharge shall be made by lodging in the LR a certificate in Form 33 as provided by rule 5 of order 72A of the Rules of the Superior Courts, (the Act of 2009) 2010 by the proper officer in the Central Office of the High Court that the lis pendens has been cancelled on the Register of Lis Pendens maintained in the Central Office of the High Court (or alternatively where the lis pendens was registered prior to 1 December 2009 by lodging an order of the court directing its cancellation on the register, or by lodging a transfer made in pursuance of an order for sale by the court in which the lis pendens may be, or by lodging the consent of the person on whose application it was registered as a burden). In old cases long in abeyance the Registry may accept a release from the plaintiff, his or her personal representative or, if no representative, the persons entitled to the assets of the plaintiff.

14.16.3 UNREGISTERED LAND

The Judgments (Ireland) Act, 1844 provided a system of registration whereby an action against a landowner might be registered as a lis pendens; previously, once a suit was instituted, any person subsequently dealing with the land took subject to all the rights and liabilities which might be declared in the suit, whether or not he or she had notice of the suit. Since then a lis pendens cannot affect a purchaser of unregistered property unless the lis pendens is registered in the Central Office of the High Court. This office contains two registers. One is a Register of Money Judgments and the other is a Lis Pendens Register. Non-practitioners are frequently confused by the fact that an ordinary search against the Lis Pendens Register is called a judgment search. They expect a judgment search to be against the Register of Money Judgments but if a judgment search is ordered from a firm of law searchers they will only search on the Lis Pendens Register unless it is specified that the search should include money judgments. As seen in **14.16.1** under s 121 of the 2009 Act such a lis pendens will be deemed to be part of the new Register of Lis Pendens.

14.16.4 REGISTERED LAND

To affect registered land a lis pendens must be registered on the folio. It is not settled as to whether a purchaser of registered land should do an ordinary judgment search. Some practitioners say that there should be no need to search on the Lis Pendens Register in the Central Office, since to affect registered land a lis pendens must be on the folio. It is, however, fairly widespread practice to make a judgment (lis pendens) search when buying registered land and this is probably the safest thing to do. If a person bought registered land and searched only on the folio and there was an act on the Lis Pendens Register which he or she had not searched then it is imperative that he or she procures himself or herself to be registered as owner before the lis pendens is registered on the folio.

14.16.5 LIS PENDENS AND UNREGISTERED TRANSFERS

In *Coffey v Brunel Construction Ltd* [1983] IR 36 a litigant registered a lis pendens on a folio against a registered owner. The purchasers of the property had paid all the purchase money but the deed of transfer had not been registered. The Supreme Court held that the transferees had an unregistered right to the full beneficial interest and that the lis pendens was not entitled to priority over such unregistered right as there was no provision of the Act which prevented the prior right or estate of the transferees in the registered land from retaining, in accordance with equitable principles, its predominance over the lis pendens registered later.

Note s 52 of the 2009 Act which states: 'the entire beneficial interest passes to the purchaser on the making of an enforceable contract for the sale or other disposition in land.' The effect of this provision is that a purchaser under s 52 acquires full beneficial interest in the property which will have priority over any lis pendens registered after the date of the contract.

14.17   Corporate Bodies

13.3.12.2 dealt with some Land Registry requirements re companies, but note also the following.

14.17.1   FIRST REGISTRATION OF OR TRANSFER TO A COMPANY

If a company has not already been registered as owner of registered land, evidence of its incorporation must be lodged on first registration by a company and on registration of a transfer to a company.

For an Irish company:

(a)   if registered under Companies Acts, certificate of incorporation is required (rule 74(1) of the LR Rules); and

(b)   if not so registered, evidence of its incorporation, eg by charter or statute, must be produced.

For a foreign company the evidence is:

(a)   a certificate from the Companies Registration Office pursuant to the European Communities (Branch Disclosure) Regulations, 1993 (SI 395/1993) that the particulars required by the Companies Act 1963, s 352 have been delivered will suffice;

(b)   otherwise (if the company has not established a place of business or a branch within the State), relevant documentary proof of incorporation (with certified copies for retention) and, if necessary, duly authenticated translations may be lodged; or

(c)   alternatively, a statement or certificate (with authenticated translation) by a recognised authority on the corporate law of the domicile of the company, ie the law by which it was incorporated, that it is a corporate entity in accordance with such law, is acceptable (McAllister, *Registration of Title*, p 112).

Note **13.3.6.4** and Office Notice 2 of 2015 available on the Authority's website in relation to an Irish Collective Asset-management Vehicle (ICAV). The evidence the Authority requires is a certified copy of the registration order from the Central Bank and in the case of a converted company the certificate of de-registration of the company.

The correct name of the company, as in the certificate of incorporation and as set out on its seal must be used in all cases. While the general principle is that a grant to a company in any other than its true name is void, an error in the name will not render a grant bad, if the name given is sufficient to identify the intention of the transferor and to clearly distinguish the transferee from others. However, use of the correct name is clearly advisable and will avoid queries from the Registry.

14.17.2   TRANSFER BY A COMPANY

See rule 74(3) of the LR Rules in relation to *ultra vires* rule.

Every limited company must, under the Companies Act, have its name engraved on its seal. If the seal does not make an impression on the paper and/or is illegible, a query will be raised by the Registry.

The name of the company, on the register, recited in the deed and appearing on the seal must correspond precisely (allowing for the accepted abbreviations).

Every deed of transfer must be sealed and the sealing requirements are as follows:

(a)   Irish company, registered under Companies Act: where the seal appears to have been affixed in the presence of and attested by the secretary, deputy secretary, or a director, the Authority will be entitled to assume that the deed was duly executed by the company (rule 74(4) of the LR Rules), in the case of a transfer of *registered* land. It is quite common for such persons to omit the necessary identification (as secretary etc). If so, the matter must be dealt with as at (b) below.

(b) Other corporate bodies, and all companies conveying unregistered land, must affix a seal and execute the deed in accordance with their governing regulations. Evidence of compliance will be required by the Authority.

(c) Foreign companies: if the company has a corporate seal and is empowered to use it, it must be affixed to the deed and evidence of compliance with the company's governing regulations must be lodged (with authenticated translations where necessary).

For further on foreign companies see **13.3.12**.

14.17.3   COMPANIES IN LIQUIDATION

If a company is in liquidation this should be recited in the deed, and the name of the company should be set out as 'A B Ltd (in liquidation)'.

14.17.3.1   Transfer and execution by company

The corporate status of the company subsists until it is dissolved. The liquidator has power to sell the property of the company and to execute in the name of and on behalf of the company all deeds and to use when necessary the company seal (s 627(3) of the Companies Act, 2014 formerly s 231 of the Companies Act, 1963).

Unless the property has vested in the liquidator under s 614 of the Companies Act, 2014, formerly s 230 of the Companies Act, 1963, the property remains vested in the company and a transfer must be by, or in the name of, the company.

Requirements for execution of the deed are as follows:

(a) Property vested in company: The seal of the company should be affixed by or in the presence of the liquidator. The liquidator should also join in the deed to give receipt for purchase money.

(b) Property vested in liquidator (s 614): Transfer should be by liquidator and executed as such.

The following documents must also be lodged:

(a) members'/creditors' voluntary winding up: copy of resolution for winding up and of appointment of liquidator, certified by company secretary; or

(b) winding up by court: office copy of court order winding up company and appointing liquidator; or

(c) s 614: office copy of vesting order.

14.17.3.2   Disclaimer of onerous leasehold property by a liquidator

Under the Companies Act, 2014, ss 615 and 616 (formerly s 290 Companies Act, 1963) the documents to be lodged in the Land Registry are:

(a) office copy of court order giving liberty to disclaim;

(b) office copy of notice of disclaimer;

(c) office copy of vesting order pursuant to s 616(3)–(5) stating in whom the disclaimed property is to vest; and

(d) application by solicitor for liquidator to close leasehold folio and cancel lease burden (where applicable).

14.17.4 COMPANY IN RECEIVERSHIP

The name of the company should be set out in the deed as 'A B Ltd (in receivership)'.

Before the receiver may exercise the powers conferred under the debenture, where the property is not specifically charged in the debenture, the crystallised charge must be registered on the folio, if not already registered. See rule 107 of the LR Rules and **14.13.8**.

Documents to be lodged:

(a)   original debenture and appointment of receiver;

(b)   certified copies of above;

(c)   assent to registration (Form 48);

(d)   certificate re Companies Act, s 409 (see rule 106); and

(e)   fee.

On lodgement of the deed of transfer, the crystallised charge may be released in Form 67A. Note that unlike a transfer under a power of sale (s 62(10) of the 1964 Act) puisne burdens are not cancelled.

14.17.5 EXECUTION OF DEED OF TRANSFER

The Supreme Court dealt with the execution of deed by receivers in *IDA v Moran* [1978] IR 159. The court held that:

(a)   by reason of the powers vested in the receiver by the debenture and the provisions of the Conveyancing Act, 1881, s 46, the execution of the conveyance by the receiver in his own name was effective to vest in the purchaser the company's fee simple estate in the lands assured by the receiver; and

(b)   the company's articles of association did not require the grant by the company of a power of attorney to be authorised by the company in general meeting.

Kenny J set out *obiter* 'the usual and better practice' in executing such deeds:

(a)   the receiver writes the name of the company;

(b)   underneath this he or she writes words that indicate that the name of the company was written by the receiver as attorney of the company under power of attorney given by the debenture; and

(c)   he or she then executes the deed in his or her own name.

It will also be necessary to show that the articles of association contained at the date of the debenture a provision corresponding to art 80 of Table A of the Companies Act, 1963 and to show that this article was not otherwise qualified in the articles. Article 80 of Table A has been replaced and amended by ss 40(1) and 158 of the Companies Act, 2014

As to receiver and judgment mortgages, see judgment mortgages at **14.17.8**.

14.17.6 PROPERTY OF DISSOLVED COMPANY

Section 28 of the State Property Act, 1954 provides that where a company has been dissolved, all property (other than property held in trust) automatically vests in the State. The waiver of the right of the State in respect of registered land is by deed of transfer from the Minister for Finance (1954 Act, s 31).

14.17.7 CHARGES

The requirements for execution of charges are essentially the same as discussed earlier for transfers. See rule 74(3) of the LR Rules in relation to *ultra vires* rule.

Under rule 106 of the LR Rules, where a certificate of registration of a charge in the Companies Registration Office under s 410(1) of the Companies Act, 2014 (formerly s 99 of the Companies Act, 1963) is not produced, a note to that effect is entered on the register.

For a charge created by a debenture to be registrable on registered land, it must contain a specific charge on a specified folio in accordance with s 62 of the 1964 Act, as amended by s 73 of the 2006 Act and the 2009 Act. While the debenture, in this case, may constitute a floating charge over the other assets of the company, in so far as the registered land is concerned it is a fixed charge and the debenture holder has all the powers conferred by s 62(6) of the 1964 Act as amended.

Where no specific charge is created, see **14.13.8** and **14.17.4** for discussion of registration of the charge when it crystallises.

14.17.8 JUDGMENT MORTGAGES

14.17.8.1 Company as creditor

Where the creditor is a joint stock banking, or other company or corporate body, the application for registration in Form 60 (see **14.15.1**) should be made by an authorised agent; see s 115 of the 2009 Act. The Form 60 in these cases should simply describe the person making the form as the creditor within the meaning of s 115 of the 2009 Act. The Authority's function is purely ministerial.

See the Authority's Practice Direction 'Judgment Mortgages' on the Authority's website (www.prai.ie).

14.17.8.2 Company as debtor

See **14.15.7**.

14.17.8.3 Validity

Note the provisions of s 619(3) of the Companies Act, 2014 (formerly s 284(2) of the Companies Act, 1963, as amended by the Bankruptcy Act, 1988, s 51(2)) in relation to the invalidity of a judgment mortgage registered within three months prior to the winding up of a company.

CHAPTER 15

REQUISITIONS ON TITLE

15.1   Introduction

Requisitions on title are a set of queries raised by the purchaser after the Contract for Sale has been signed—as part of the post-contract investigation of title. The vendor is 'required' to respond to them. In the definition section of the Law Society Contract for Sale requisitions are defined as follows:

> '"Requisitions" include Requisitions on the title or titles as such of the Subject Property and with regard to rents, outgoings, rights, covenants, conditions, liabilities (actual or potential), planning and kindred matters and the taxation issues material to such property.'

The purpose of requisitions on title is to ensure that the purchaser receives title in accordance with the Contract for Sale. It does not enable the purchaser to have a 'second bite of the cherry' in respect of matters which were overlooked at the time the contract was being signed.

The Law Society has recently issued a third edition standard form of Objections and Requisitions on Title (3rd edn, issued in 2015) which the vast majority of solicitors use. Where the standard form is not used the requisitions should be specific and relevant to the purchaser. Care should be taken to avoid raising queries which put the purchaser on notice of an issue which would not otherwise have affected him (See Wylie and Woods, *Irish Conveyancing Law* (3rd edn) para 15.19. See also **15.2.2**).

'Objections' are dealt with at **15.3**.

While the standard form is called 'Objections and Requisitions on Title', the requisitions extend well beyond matters of title. They may be grouped into three categories:

(a)   requisitions on title;

(b)   requisitions on non-title matters; and

(c)   a conveyancing checklist.

Many of the requisitions serve as a reminder to the vendor of particular documents required/various matters to be completed on or before the closing of the sale.

This may be illustrated by choosing three different requisitions:

(a)   Requisition 20(1) requires a vendor to furnish an assent by the personal representative if any person on the title died after 31 May 1959. This is purely a title matter.

(b)   Requisition 1.4 asks whether the property is registered under the HomeBond, Premier, or other policy/scheme. This does not relate to the title.

(c)   Requisition 16.3 relates to the furnishing of a capital gains tax clearance certificate (CG50A) where the consideration exceeds the current capital gains tax threshold.

By law, it is a matter for the vendor to furnish this on or before closing or, in the event of the vendor failing to do so, the purchaser must lodge 15 per cent of the purchase price with the Revenue and account for the transaction.

Many of the requisitions are extracted from the standard set and are raised at pre-contract stage.

Many practitioners are of the opinion that the current requisitions on title are too long and too cumbersome and this argument has been considered by the Conveyancing Committee of the Law Society. The view of the Committee is that it is better to have all the requisitions so as to alert practitioners to the different problems which may arise. Further, the requisitions are in themselves a great source of legal information. Where possible the relevant statutory provisions are quoted and this enables the practitioner to refer to source law where necessary.

The purchaser raises requisitions on title by sending two sets to the solicitor for the vendor, on the basis that the vendor's solicitor will keep one copy with replies endorsed and return the other copy with replies endorsed to the solicitor for the purchaser.

When sending the requisitions to the vendor's solicitor the purchaser's solicitor should delete any of the requisitions which do not apply to the transaction, ie these requisitions should not be raised. For example, if the property is registered title the requisitions relating to the Registry of Deeds should be deleted.

In certain circumstances a vendor's solicitor may furnish requisitions on title with replies without the necessity of the purchaser raising them. The main examples of this are where the requisitions together with the replies are included in a booklet of title for a new house or in cases where the solicitor for the vendor is using the CORT requisition system (computer system for raising and replying to requisitions).

Where the purchaser's solicitor is not satisfied with the response to a requisition they can raise further queries, known as rejoinders, arising from the replies received.

The Conveyancing Committee recommend that practitioners retain the original requisitions and replies with title documents to a property when lodging them with the lending institution when certifying title. Where the original requisitions and replies are lodged together with original title deeds with the Land Registry in support of a first registration application a copy of the requisitions and replies should be retained with the remaining title documents. They are then available for the solicitor instructed in the next transaction (Conveyancing Committee Practice Note, Law Society *Gazette*, November 2015).

15.2   Time Limits

General conditions 17 and 18 of the Contract for Sale set out the time limits and procedures in relation to the raising of requisitions on title and the replies thereto.

15.2.1   GENERAL CONDITION 17

General condition 17 provides:

> *The purchaser shall, within fourteen Working Days after the later of (i) the Date of Sale or (ii) the delivery of the copy documents of title in accordance with Condition 7, send to the vendor's solicitor a written statement of his Objections (if any) on the title and his Requisitions. Any Objection or Requisition not made within the time aforesaid and not going to the root of the title shall be deemed to have been waived. The vendor's Replies to any Objections or Requisitions shall be answered by the purchaser in writing within seven Working Days after the delivery thereof and so on toties quoties, and, if not so answered, shall be considered to have been accepted as satisfactory. In all respects time shall be deemed to be of the essence of this Condition.*

The requisitions on title are raised after the contract has been signed by both parties and after a copy of the title documents has been furnished to the purchaser's solicitor.

The purchaser must raise his or her requisitions on title within 14 days after the delivery of title to him or her. Time is of the essence in this regard with the exception of where an objection or requisition goes to the root of title. Where requisitions have been raised out of time (and not going to the root of title) the vendor should mark any replies 'without prejudice'.

When replying to the requisitions on title, a vendor's solicitor should ensure that the replies are those of the vendor and are accurate. Some solicitors go through each reply individually with their client while other solicitors use a checklist which they work from. Either way, it is of utmost importance to ensure that the vendor has confirmed the replies and that they are accurate. Otherwise, the vendor's solicitor runs the risk of being sued for negligence or fraud. In *Doran v Delaney* [1998] IESC 66 (9 March 1998) the Supreme Court found that the vendor's solicitors had a duty of care to the purchaser in replying to requisitions. In this case the vendor's solicitor knew that there had been a dispute with the adjoining owner as regards access to the property but was instructed by his client that the dispute had been resolved. The reply to the requisition asking whether there was any litigation pending or threatened was 'Vendor says none'. The reply to the requisition enquiring if there was any dispute with adjoining owners was 'Vendor says no'. The solicitor did not ascertain from the vendor the terms upon which the dispute had allegedly being settled. In fact the matter had not been settled. It is the duty of the prudent solicitor to make further enquiries and not rely on the client's replies if there is any reason to doubt the accuracy of the reply. The Supreme Court held that whilst there was no contractual relationship between the plaintiffs and the solicitors for the vendors a duty of care existed. Keane J, at p 76 of his judgment, stated that the vendor's solicitor 'assumes at least some responsibility for the information given in reply and cannot be exonerated from responsibility solely on the ground that he or she is simply transmitting the vendor's instructions'. Moreover, if anything unusual arises in the replies to the requisitions on title the purchaser should be informed.

15.2.2   GENERAL CONDITION 18

General condition 18 provides:

> *If the purchaser shall make and insist on any Objection or Requisition as to the title, the Assurance to him or any other matter relating or incidental to the Sale, which the vendor shall, on the grounds of unreasonable delay or expense or other reasonable ground, be unable or unwilling to remove or comply with, the vendor shall be at liberty (notwithstanding any intermediate negotiation or litigation or attempts to remove or comply with the same) by giving to the purchaser or his solicitor not less than five Working Days notice to rescind the Sale. In that case, unless the Objection or Requisition in question shall in the meantime have been withdrawn, the Sale shall be rescinded at the expiration of such notice.*

Wylie and Woods, *Irish Conveyancing Law* (3rd edn) para 15.28 states as follows:

'Condition 18 makes this clear by requiring the purchaser to make "and insist" on the objection or requisition. Thus, in substance, several steps must take place under Condition 18, ie:

(1)   The purchaser makes the objection or requisition.

(2)   The vendor decides he is unable or unwilling to remove or to comply with it.

(3)   He communicates this unwillingness to the purchaser.

(4)   The purchaser refuses to withdraw it.'

The standard Law Society form of requisitions covers almost every conceivable aspect of conveyancing and it is rarely necessary to raise further requisitions on title. The rules governing the raising of requisitions on title were formulated at a time when there were no standard requisitions and where every solicitor raised his or her own. These rules still have relevance today in respect of the additional requisitions which solicitors tend to add on to the printed form. (See Wylie and Woods, *Irish Conveyancing Law* (3rd edn) para 15.18 *et seq*.)

The following general principles should be applied to requisitions on title:

(a) Requisitions on title should be specific and should not be used by the purchaser or his solicitor to embark upon a general 'fishing' expedition for information, eg 'Have all the material facts in connection with the title been disclosed?' The vendor should always decline to answer such a wide-ranging requisition.

(b) Requisitions should not be raised about matters of no concern to the purchaser.

The basic conveyancing rule is that trusts should be kept off the title. A purchaser's solicitor should avoid asking requisitions which would disclose a trust (not otherwise identifiable from the documents of title).

Wylie and Woods, *Irish Conveyancing Law* (3rd edn) at para 15.36 states:

'The general rule is that the vendor must answer satisfactorily all proper [ie those which are not too vague or general] requisitions, otherwise he may be held not to have shown a good title to the property.

Technically this rule probably applies only to requisitions relating to the "title", so that the vendor may be entitled strictly not to reply to other requisitions, such as those seeking general information about the property, on the ground that these are not concerned with the title deduced by the vendor.'

15.3 Law Society Objections on Title

Page 2 of the requisitions on title provides for any objections which a purchaser's solicitor may wish to make. An objection is a specific matter which, in the opinion of a purchaser's solicitor, needs to be resolved to enable the vendor to complete the contract in accordance with the terms of the contract. Objections usually are raised on the grounds that something in the title is seriously defective.

It is a device that should be used very sparingly. If a purchaser's solicitor is aware, prior to the signing of the contract, of a serious defect in the title he or she should not let his or her client sign until the position has been clarified. There are two main reasons for clarifying the position first. It is difficult to explain to a client that he or she was allowed to sign a contract where there was a problem on the title. The client is locked in and cannot buy another property, until the position has been clarified. Further, there may be difference of opinion between the vendor's solicitor and the purchaser's solicitor as to whether there is a defect.

15.4 Law Society Requisitions on Title

The following paragraphs work chronologically through the Law Society's Standard Requisitions on Title (2015 edn) excluding those requisitions which have been dealt with elsewhere in this manual. The requisitions are printed on the left-hand column and the vendor replies in the right-hand column.

15.4.1 REQUISITION 1: PREMISES

15.4.1.1 Requisition 1.1: Chattel property

General condition 46 of the Contract for Sale warrants that, at the closing of the sale there will be no encumbrances affecting chattel property included in the sale. Accordingly, this requisition is of the checklist variety because of the warranty the vendor has already given and the vendor would have clarified this in the non-title information sheet.

15.4.1.2 Requisition 1.2: Boundaries

Requisition 1.2 enquires as to which of the boundaries belong to the property and which are party. A buyer must bear in mind the limits placed on the vendor's obligation in this regard under general condition 14 of the Contract for Sale. In particular, general condition 14 states that the vendor 'shall not be required to define exact boundaries, fences, ditches, hedges or walls or to specify which (if any) of the same are of a party nature'.

The Land and Conveyancing Law Reform Act, 2009 ('the 2009 Act') has introduced specific provisions dealing with party structures. Section 44 provides that on or after 1 December 2009 if your client owns a property or land they can carry out works to a party structure for the following reasons:

- to comply with a notice or order served on them;
- to carry out development for which planning permission has been granted or which is exempted development;
- to preserve a party structure; and
- to carry out other works which would not cause inconvenience or damage to their neighbour, or even if it does cause damage and inconvenience, that it is reasonable for them to still do those works.

Section 45 of the 2009 Act contains a comprehensive definition of what exactly a party structure is. It also provides for the situation where the parties have not been able to reach agreement in relation to the works. If this is the case they can then apply to court for an order authorising the carrying out of the works (a 'works order'). The court can order the carrying out of the works on such conditions as it thinks are necessary. Party structures include any arch, ceiling, ditch, fence, floor, hedge, partition, shrub, tree, wall, or other structure which divides the properties. It includes structures which are in or on the adjoining building, or unbuilt—on land or those which straddle the boundary line.

15.4.1.3 Requisition 1.3: Boundary arrangements

Requisition 1.3 enquires as to whether there are any agreements in relation to the repair and maintenance of the boundary fences and also enquires as to whether there are any disputes with adjoining owners.

If there is a dispute with an adjoining owner the vendor should not sell the property until the dispute has been resolved.

15.4.1.4 Requisitions 1.4 and 1.5: HomeBond, Premier or other alternative policy/scheme

Both HomeBond and Premier schemes have similar features. The insurance lasts for a period of ten years in respect of major structural defects. A purchaser is entitled to the benefit of the certificate of insurance. The guarantee extends to the successors in title of the original purchaser. However, it does not extend to properties which have major structural defects which exist at the time of transfer from one owner to another.

It is a pre-contract matter as to whether a house is covered by any building insurance scheme. The vendor does not warrant under the general conditions that the house is covered by the scheme. In appropriate cases, this should always be checked out pre contract. In practical terms, a purchaser should have the property surveyed before the contract is signed. He or she will be advised not to go ahead with the transaction if his or her survey discloses a major structural defect.

While many lending institutions insist on new houses being registered under the Home-Bond insurance scheme or other insurance scheme before they will provide finance, the fact that a house is not registered in the scheme does not in any way make it unsaleable. It is merely a matter to be pointed out to a purchaser and for the purchaser to take up with his lending institution.

15.4.2 REQUISITION 2: SERVICES

15.4.2.1 Requisition 2.1: Supply of services

Drainage, waste water treatment systems (eg septic tank), water, electricity, and gas are matters which should have been addressed by a buyer before signing the contract. This is also dealt with in the non-title information sheet at pp 5 and 6 of the Contract for Sale.

It is too late to discover, after the contract has been signed, that there is a problem in relation to the services.

This requisition has been expanded in the current edition of the requisitions to obtain more detailed information for registration of domestic waste water treatment systems (in light of new requirements in this regard) and on the type of water supply and water services licence where applicable. Under s 70D of the Water Services (Amendment) Act, 2012 a vendor of a property connected to a domestic waste-water treatment system (including a septic tank) is obliged to furnish a valid certificate of registration in respect of the treatment system on or before closing. Property owners are obliged to ensure that the system does not, or is not likely to constitute a risk to human health or the environment. There is also a duty not to create a nuisance through noise or odour (See the Conveyancing Committee Practice Note in the March 2013 *Gazette)*. After completion of a sale the purchaser (and not the solicitor) is obliged to notify the relevant water services authority of the change of ownership (by e-mail to support@protetourwater.ie or post to Protect our Water, PO Box 12204 Dublin). See Conveyancing Committee Practice Note, Law Society *Gazette*, April 2015.

15.4.2.2 Requisitions 2.2 to 2.5: Access to property

Access to the property in sale is very much a pre-contract matter. Again this is dealt with in the non-title information sheet. It is too late to discover at requisitions stage that the property being bought is landlocked! The requisition asks whether the services 'abutting *and* servicing' the property have been taken in charge. In a new development it is of utmost importance to clarify whether or not the roads and services have been taken in charge.

Because of the expense of obtaining certificates from local authorities, the requisition asks for a letter from the local authority or the vendor's solicitor could give a certificate where he or she is satisfied that the roads and services abutting the property in sale are taken in charge by the local authority. The wording of the current requisition ensures that it is a certificate from the current vendor's solicitor that is required. This is to ensure that older certificates provided in previous transactions are not relied upon as 'in charge' roads may have been re-designated (due to a new development leading to a new means of access and closing an existing one off or abandonment or extinguishment of a public right of way by the local authority pursuant to s 12 and s 73 of the Roads Act, 1993). The Conveyancing Committee advise against solicitors providing such certificates unless verified by an inspection of the local authority records or personal knowledge (see Conveyancing Committee eZine Article, Issue 64, August 2015).

While the requisitions look for an indemnity under seal or an assignment of that indemnity, in many cases these are worthless. For example, a builder may have formed a company for the purpose of developing a particular development. This company gives an indemnity to the purchasers. When the development has been completed, the builder liquidates the company. Unfortunately, the indemnity is of little value after the company has been liquidated.

Because there is no warranty as to access to the property in the Contract for Sale, no local authority letter, no solicitor's certificate, or no indemnity will be forthcoming if the property is landlocked.

15.4.3 REQUISITION 3: EASEMENTS AND RIGHTS

15.4.3.1 Requisition 3.1: Services passing over property

Requisition 3.1 deals with pipes, drains, sewers, etc which pass over other property and which serve the property being sold. It has been expanded at 3.2.a to include turbary rights or other *profits à prendre*.

In the housing estate situation the standard transfer or conveyance will include a grant of the necessary easements. In other cases it will not be so clear.

15.4.3.2 Requisition 3.2: Rights affecting property

Requisition 3.2 relates to rights affecting the property in sale. General condition 15 of the Contract for Sale requires that

> *The vendor shall disclose before the Date of Sale, in the Particulars the Special Conditions or otherwise, all easements, rights, reservations, exemptions, privileges, covenants, restrictions, rents, taxes and liabilities (not already known to the purchaser or apparent from inspection) which are known by the vendor to affect the Subject Property and are likely to affect it following completion of the Sale.*

Subject to this, the purchaser buys subject to any rights which may affect the property where apparent from inspection or where known to the purchaser (general condition 16 of the Contract for Sale, ie the caveat emptor condition). In order to protect his or her client, a vendor's solicitor should always check this matter with his or her client. For example, in the town situation a sewer pipe may have been placed at the rear of the houses rather than on the adjoining roadway. A purchaser is entitled to know that a sewer pipe is passing under his or her garden or back yard. If there is a manhole there it may be argued that the sewer line was obvious from inspection.

Section 35 of the 2009 Act provides that easements or *profits à prendre* acquired by prescription will only arise on registration of a court order. An enquiry should be raised regarding any court orders made and not yet registered or any proceedings initiated in this regard. Section 35 of the 2009 Act and the Registration of Title Act, 1964 were amended by s 37 of the Civil Law (Miscellaneous Provisions) Act, 2011 relating to the registration of easements and *profits* acquired by prescription. The amendments permit the Property Registration Authority (PRA) to register easements or *profits* without a court order where there is no disagreement between the parties concerning entitlement to the easement or *profit à prendre*. Parts 12 and 13 also grant the PRA the power to register easements and *profits à prendre* without a court order if the land in question is being registered for the first time.

By virtue of s 69 of the Registration of Title Act, 1964 easements and *profits à prendre* created by express grant or reservation prior to the first registration of the servient tenement are not capable of registration as a burden on the newly opened folio and are instead s 72 type burdens (non registrable). The Conveyancing Committee recommend the entry of a notice on the register of the existence of the easement or profit. See the Practice Note issued by the Committee in the Law Society *Gazette*, July 2015 for the recommended procedure.

15.4.4 REQUISITION 4: OBLIGATIONS/PRIVILEGES

15.4.4.1 Requisition 4.1: Appurtenant rights

Requisition 4.1 relates to roads, paths, drains, boundary walls etc used in common with other people. The vendor is required to disclose his or her rights and obligations in respect of any appurtenant rights and to furnish any agreements relating to the user in question (this will need to be clarified pre contract.) There are many instances where there is a common entrance or possibly a shared septic tank or a shared facility of one sort or another. Also, there may be written agreements dealing with the respective common user and where there are written agreements these form part of the documents of title and must be furnished.

15.4.5   REQUISITION 5: FORESTRY

Requisition 5 should be deleted unless the property in sale has commercial trees growing on it.

15.4.5.1   Requisitions 5.1 to 5.5: Timber felling

The requisition asks if there is felling licence in existence and for details of any unfulfilled conditions under the Forestry Acts. The felling of trees, originally governed by s 37 of the Forestry Act, 1946 is now governed by the Forestry Act, 2014, specifically s 7 and Part 4. Basically, an application is made to the Minister for Agriculture, Food and the Marine for a licence to fell.

15.4.5.2   Requisition 5.3: Forestry grants

Requisition 5.3 relates to the grants which are available for the private planting of forestry. In particular, 5.3.b requires details of any outstanding grant payments which remain. Clearly, if a commercial forestry was being purchased the question of outstanding grants would need to be clarified pre contract so as to enable a buyer to know exactly what he or she was getting for his or her money. Requisition 5.3.c requests the official Departmental indemnity form in respect of any existing grant.

This requisition also asks for details on any agreement affecting the right to fell trees of any breach or proceedings arising under the relevant legislation.

15.4.6   REQUISITION 6: FISHING

Again, requisition 6 should be deleted unless the property in sale includes a water course or portion of a water course. The requisition covers two distinct scenarios:

1.   one dealing with fishing licences; and
2.   where a third party has a fishing right over the property in sale.

Because rights and reservations are carried forward where old folios are broken up, fishing rights often appear on folios in respect of property which no longer has any connection with a water course. The standard conveyancing practice is to ignore such fishing rights.

The difference between a reservation and a charge should be noted. A reservation is something which is reserved out of the folio (ie it does not form part of the folio).

Accordingly, when a purchaser's solicitor sees a note on the folio that fishing rights or sporting rights are reserved to someone he or she is on notice of this and buys subject to the reservation.

The requirement for an affidavit to confirm non user of a fishing right (not granted by deed but by prescription) for the past 20 years is no longer relevant as s 35 of the 2009 Act as amended provides that easements or *profits* à *prendre* acquired by prescription will only arise on registration of a deed or court order. It is important to check that no court order has been made or no proceedings have been initiated.

This requisition now asks if there is any related easement exercised in connection with any right to fish.

For a detailed examination of the law in relation to fishing rights see Peter Bland, *The Law of Easements and Profits à Prendre* (2015).

15.4.7   REQUISITION 7: SPORTING RIGHTS

Similarly, this requisition is divided into two sections: one dealing with sporting licences and the other dealing with sporting rights to which the property might be subject.

When land was being purchased from the landlords through the Land Purchase Acts the sporting rights were reserved to the landlords. Section 18 of the Land Act, 1965 provided that such sporting rights would cease to exist if they had not been exercised for 12 years. The procedure for cancelling the rights from the folio depends on whether the sporting rights are reserved to the Land Commission or to a private individual. In either case an advertisement must be inserted in the local newspaper of the proposed application to have the sporting rights removed from the folio.

It would not be normal conveyancing practice to remove sporting rights from folios.

The requirement for an affidavit to confirm non user of a sporting right (not granted by deed but by prescription) for the past 12/20 years is no longer relevant as s 35 of the 2009 Act as amended provides that easements or *profits à prendre* acquired by prescription will only arise on registration. Such registration may arise on foot of a deed, court order, or as a result of an application to the Registrar of Titles. It is important to check that no court order has been made or no proceedings have been initiated. See the provisions of the 2011 Act earlier at **15.4.3.2**.

This requisition now asks if there is any related easement exercised in connection with any sporting right.

15.4.8   REQUISITION 8: POSSESSION

Condition 21 of the Contract for Sale provides that the vendor must give vacant possession of the property in sale. Accordingly, this is merely a reminder to the vendor of this fact.

15.4.9   REQUISITION 9: TENANCIES—COMMERCIAL AND RESIDENTIAL

15.4.9.1   Generally

Requisition 9 relates to cases where vacant possession is not being handed over on closing. Normally, if a property is let on a short-term letting a vendor will obtain vacant possession before putting the property up for sale. Therefore, in the majority of cases, this requisition relates to investment properties where the tenant or tenants have rights of tenure pursuant to the Residential Tenancies Act, 2004 or the Landlord and Tenant Acts.

Conditions 22 and 23 of the Contract for Sale deal with property which is let. Condition 22 provides that, prior to the sale, the vendor shall furnish evidence of the nature and terms of the letting together with copies of any notices in the vendor's possession served by or on the lessee. Condition 23 warrants that there has been no change in the terms or conditions of the lease, other than those disclosed to the purchaser.

The requisition looks for details of the tenancy including the commencement date and the gale days. It asks that if a deposit has been retained by the landlord, will it be refundable to the tenant. It also enquires as to whether the tenant may have a claim for compensation in the future or have a claim for improvements. The request for information regarding any other agreement between the landlord and tenant, details on how rent is paid, and confirmation from the tenant where no deposit is paid are recent additions to this requisition. These are all matters which should be dealt with prior to the signing of the contract to ensure the purchaser is aware of all details pertaining to the tenancy.

One of the purposes of the requisitions is to determine whether the tenant has a right to a new lease under the Residential Tenancies Act, 2004 or the Landlord and Tenant Acts. Again, this is a matter which should be clarified prior to the signing of the contract. A purchaser must be clearly advised as to the tenant's rights.

15.4.9.2   Requisition 9.1.d: Renunciation of tenant's rights

Requisition 9.1.d deals with the case where a tenant may contract out of his or her rights to a new lease where the property involved is wholly and exclusively an office.

Section 4 of the Landlord and Tenant (Amendment) Act, 1994 permitted renunciation where the terms of the tenancy provided for the use of the tenement wholly and exclusively as an office. Prior to the commencement of the tenancy, the tenant executes, whether for or without valuable consideration, a valid renunciation of its entitlement to a new tenancy in the tenement and receives independent legal advice in relation to the execution of title renunciation. Section 47 of the Civil Law (Miscellaneous Provisions) Act, 2008 has now extended the right to waive renewal rights to all business users.

15.4.10 REQUISITION 10: TENACIES—RESIDENTIAL ONLY

15.4.10.1 Residential Tenancies Act

These requisitions look for information regarding registration with the Private Residential Tenancies Board (PRTB), whether there are any disputes before the PRTB, and whether notice has been served by the landlord.

For a detailed examination of the Residential Tenancies Act, 2004 see Law Society of Ireland, *Landlord & Tenant Law* (6th edn) chapter 6.

15.4.10.2 Landlord and Tenant (Amendment) Act, 1980

This requisition seeks to obtain information on any long occupation equity leases under the Landlord and Tenant (Amendment) Act, 1980, as amended.

15.4.10.3 Housing (Private Rented Dwellings) Acts, 1982–1983

Again, requisition 10.9 is a specialist requisition which should be deleted where vacant possession is to be handed over. The requisition requires the vendor to furnish the relevant documentation, such as the tenancy agreement, certificate of registration with the local authority, certificate of registration of changes in the terms of the tenancy, and certified copy of any court order, rent tribunal, or rent officer decision on the rent.

15.4.11 REQUISITION 11: OUTGOINGS

15.4.11.1 Rates

Rates are a charge on property and the purchaser must be satisfied that at the closing of the sale the rates are paid up to date, or that credit is given in the apportionment account for the unpaid rates.

Because there are no rates payable on private dwellings the purchaser should not insist on obtaining details of the rateable valuation. General condition 27(b) of the contract provides for apportionment of the outgoings including any rent payable out of the property.

15.4.11.2 Requisitions 11.2–11.3: Revaluation

The Commissioner of Valuation has a right in any year to revalue premises. The ratepayer has a right of appeal in respect of the revaluation.

The purpose of these two requisitions is to identify if the property is likely to be revalued or if matters have gone a step further and a revaluation has been carried out.

15.4.11.3 Requisition 11.4: Remission of rates

Requisition 11.4 enquires as to whether there is any remission of the rates in force.

15.4.11.4 Requisition 11.5: Section 32 Local Government Reform Act, 2014

This new requisition deals with commercial rates under s 32 of the Local Government Reform Act, 2014. This Act obliges a landlord to notify the rating authority of a transfer of a tenant's interest. Where this does not occur and the tenant does not discharge rates on assignment, the landlord is liable for up to two years of the arrears of rates. The issue here is that the tenant's arrears of rates become a charge on the landlord's interest on an assignment. The advice given by the Conveyancing Committee is that landlord clients should be advised to seek arrears of rates before consenting to an assignment (See Conveyancing Committee Practice Note, Law Society *Gazette*, August/September 2014. It is important to ensure there is no charge under the Act where there has been an assignment of a lease post 1 July 2014.

15.4.11.5 Requisition 11.6: Water and refuse collection charges

Requisition 11.6 enquires as to whether there are separate water charges or refuse collection charges payable in respect of the property in sale. It requires the vendor to identify the party to whom the payments are made and to identify if there are any agreements or contracts in relation to the payment. The vendor's solicitor should seek confirmation from the local authority that there are no environmental waste charges outstanding.

15.4.11.6 Requisitions 11.7 to 11.10: Other outgoings

This is a catch-all requisition to cover any other outgoings, including rent charges, which a property may be liable to. A distinction must be made between outgoings which affect the property and outgoings which affect the individual. For example, electricity and telephone charges are not outgoings which affect the property.

The object of the requisitions is to identify any outgoing which will become the responsibility of the purchaser after the closing of the sale and in respect of which the arrears will become the responsibility of the purchaser unless he or she ensures that the vendor has paid the outgoings to date.

15.4.12 REQUISITION 12: NOTICES

General condition 35 of the Contract for Sale states:

Where prior to the Date of Sale:

(a)   any closing, demolition or clearance order or

(b)   any notice or any other notice (other than such other notice, details of which are to be entered on the Planning Register pursuant to the requirements of Planning Legislation) for compulsory acquisition

made or issued by or at the behest of a Competent Authority in respect of the Subject Property and affecting same at the Date of Sale has been notified or given to the vendor (whether personally or by advertisement or posting on the Subject Property or in any other manner) or is otherwise known to the vendor, or where the Subject Property is, at the Date of Sale, affected by any award or grant, which is or may be repayable by the vendor's successor in title then, if the vendor fails to show

(i)   that, before the Date of Sale, the purchaser received notice or was aware of the matter in question or

(ii)   the matter in question was apparent from inspection of the Development Plan or the current published Draft Development Plan for the area within which the Subject Property is situate

(iii) that same is no longer applicable or material or

(iv) that same does not prejudicially affect the value of the Subject Property or

(v)   that the subject thereof can and will be dealt with fully in the Apportionment Account the purchaser may by notice given to the vendor rescind the Sale.

The purchaser's rights are clearly set out in condition 35. In all cases a vendor's solicitor should check with his or her client if he or she has received any notices in relation to the property. This check should be made before the contract is issued and again at the requisitions stage. If a purchaser becomes aware, as a result of the reply to the requisitions, of the existence of some notice which was not dealt with at contract stage, then, depending on the gravity of the notice and when it was served, he or she may well have a right of rescission.

The 3rd edition of the Requisitions 2015 extends the list of legislation to all Acts of relevance enacted since the 2001 edition, eg Local Government Acts, Civil Partnership and Certain Right and Obligations of Cohabitants Act, 2010, Finance (Local Property Tax) Acts etc.

15.4.13 REQUISITION 13: SEARCHES

15.4.13.1 Generally

General condition 19 of the Contract for Sale provides as follows:

> *The purchaser shall be furnished with the searches (if any) specified in the Searches Schedule and any searches already in the vendor's possession, which are relevant to the title or titles on offer. Any other searches required by the purchaser must be obtained by him at his own expense. Where the Special Conditions provide that the title shall commence with a particular instrument and then pass to a second instrument or to a specified event, the vendor shall not be obliged to explain and discharge any act which appears on a search covering the period between such particular instrument and the date of the second instrument or specified event, unless same goes to the root of the title. Subject as aforesaid the vendor shall explain and discharge any acts appearing on Searches covering the period from the date stipulated or implied for the commencement of the title to the date of actual completion.*

The purpose of requisition 13 is twofold:

(a) to obtain the searches to which the purchaser is entitled under general condition 19; and

(b) to give such information to the purchaser's solicitor to enable him or her to make the appropriate searches in the particular case.

While requisition 13.3.a enquires as to whether the vendor ever committed an act of bankruptcy or has been adjudicated a bankrupt, a purchaser's solicitor should never rely on the reply to this but should make his or her own searches. The new edition of the requisitions introduces requisition 13.3.c to obtain information in respect of a vendor's personal insolvency arrangement pursuant to the Personal Insolvency Act, 2011 where applicable. The registers listed in which searches are carried out have been extended to include those relevant to EU personal insolvency legislation. Searches are not limited to the registers listed. See **chapter 10** for an in-depth discussion regarding the appropriate searches to be carried out. When acting for a vendor it is good practice to make searches at the time initial instructions are given. A solicitor should not find that he or she is not in a position to deal with an act which appears in the purchaser's search which is produced at or near the closing date. For example, a vendor may have obtained a second mortgage from a lending institution and, having repaid it, totally forgotten about it.

In practice, searches rarely disclose matters which are not already known to the purchaser's solicitor. However, there is the occasional transaction where they are vital.

15.4.13.2 Requisition 13.4

Because of the dangers of something unexpected appearing on the searches, a vendor's solicitor should never undertake to explain and discharge anything which might appear in the purchaser's search. He or she should insist on the search being produced at or prior to the closing. The reply usually given to this requisition is 'noted'.

15.4.14   REQUISITION 14: INCUMBRANCES/PROCEEDINGS

Condition 8(c) of the Contract for Sale provides that:

> the vendor shall, prior to or at the completion of the Sale, discharge all mortgages and charges for the payment of money . . . which affect the Subject Property.

The exception to this is where a mortgagee is selling the property under a power of sale contained in the mortgage. Here, a purchaser takes free from any mortgages or charges which rank in priority after the mortgage under which the power of sale is being exercised.

15.4.14.1   Requisition 14.1: Mortgages

Requisition 14.1 asks for details of mortgages or charges which affect the property. The most common mortgage or charge will be in respect of the vendor's borrowing from a lending institution to finance his or her acquisition of the property. With the introduction of the eDischarge system the vendor, on closing, will furnish a notice of completion of the cancellation of a charge or an up-to-date folio (or an undertaking in this regard) and not a discharge where there is full redemption of a charge in respect of registered land and the lender is participating in the eDischarge system. See **chapter 9** for more details on this system.

Property transferred under a family settlement may have rights of residence, support, and maintenance, or be subject to monetary payments to family members.

15.4.14.2   Non principal place of residence (NPPR)/household charge

Despite the abolition of the NPPR charge, any unpaid charge (including late payment fees and interest) is a charge on the property for a period of 12 years from the due date for payment of the charge. Therefore, the purchaser should obtain a certificate of discharge or a certificate of exemption from NPPR. Section 4 of the Local Government (Charges) Act, 2009 sets out the exemptions which include the sole or main residence and where the owner is incapacitated due to long-term physical or mental infirmity. A receipt for payment of the NPPR charge or a declaration by the vendor is not sufficient. Requisition 14.2.a seeks either the certificate of exemption or discharge where relevant for each liability date (31 July 2009; 31 March, 2010; 31 March 2011; 31 March 2012; 31 March, 2013). It also asks for a declaration from each owner on each liability date where the property did not meet the definition of residential under the relevant Act (the Local Government (Charges) Act, 2009). For example, a vendor provides a declaration with supporting evidence for each liability date where he is selling a derelict dwelling unsuitable for use as a dwelling that he purchased in 2000.

Currently, where the NPPR liability was not paid since 31 July 2009 the tax payable (together with interest and penalties) on an original charge of €200 per year is €7,230.

The household charge has been abolished with any outstanding amounts now forming part of the Local Property Tax. In any event, a certificate of discharge, waiver, or exemption is required in respect of the liability date—1 January 2012 and requisition 14.2.b is seeking this. Similarly, the owner on the liability date can provide a declaration that the property did not meet the definition of residential property as set out in the Local Government (Household Charge) Act, 2011. Similarly to NPPR, exemptions include an incapacitated owner and where the liability date falls after the date of death of the owner and the grant of representation has not issued before the liability date. A waiver applies to unfinished housing estates.

A sale for the purposes of both the NPPR and the household charge includes a voluntary transaction and a compulsory purchase order (CPO).

15.4.14.3   Requisition 14.2.c: Local Property Tax (LPT)

Revenue issue LPT clearance in respect of crystallised liabilities only. Any uncrystallised liabilities not paid by the vendor before the completion of sale (includeing a voluntary transaction and CPO) is a charge on the property for an indefinite period. The discharge of LPT is now an integral part of the conveyancing process.

This requisition asks, where the property is liable to LPT, for confirmation from Revenue's online system that there is no outstanding LPT. This confirmation is required together with, where relevant, a declaration by the owner at each liability date setting out why LPT is not payable.

Specific clearance is required (in addition to general clearance) where the agreed sale price is in a higher valuation band than was declared in the LPT return by the vendor and the increase in value cannot be explained by a general increase of prices in the area or does not meet:

    (a)   the Allowable Valuation Margin condition (as set out at section 4.2.1 of the Revenue's Guidelines for the Sale or Transfer of Ownership of a Relevant Residential Property—the 'Guidelines');

    (b)   the Expenditure on Enhancements condition (as set out at section 4.2.2 of the Guidelines); or

    (c)   the Sales of Comparable Properties condition (as set out at section 4.2.3 of the Guidelines).

If specific Revenue clearance is required the vendor needs to confirm that application has been made for same and that it will be produced on or before closing.

See **chapter 16** for an in-depth discussion of LPT.

15.4.14.4 Requisition 14.2: Grants

Requisition 14.3 relates to grants which the vendor or his or her predecessor in title may have obtained. The purchaser's solicitor must satisfy himself or herself as to the nature of any grant and whether or not any conditions had been attached to the grant which might affect the title to the premises (in general practice these are rare).

15.4.14.5 Requisition 14.4: Judgments

There may be judgment mortgages affecting the property. Prior to the abolition of land certificates it was important to note that a judgment mortgage may have been registered against a property in the Land Registry without the production of the land certificate. Since 1 January 2010, this is no longer an issue as land certificates have no effect. An up-to-date official or certified copy folio should be obtained or a Land Registry search carried out to ensure the title is in order.

While the law is clear on the position in relation to judgment mortgages registered after the sale has been closed, prior to the enactment of s 52(1) of the 2009 Act this was not so in respect of the period from the signing of the contract to the closing of the sale. Because of the decision in *Tempany v Hynes* [1976] IR 101 there was a fear that any judgment mortgage registered between the signing of the contract and the closing of the sale might catch the vendor's interest. Section 52(1) of the 2009 Act reverses the decision in *Tempany v Hynes* and provides that the entire beneficial interest will pass to the purchaser on the making of an enforceable contract for the sale of land.

It should be noted that registering a judgment mortgage differs from registering a judgment in the Judgments Office. The registration of a judgment in the Judgments Office is basically a form of publication of the judgment. This type of registration does not affect the vendor's title.

15.4.14.6 Requisition 14.5: Litigation

Before issuing the Contract for Sale a vendor's solicitor should have satisfied himself or herself that no litigation is pending. He or she should enquire fully as to the position from the vendor. The basic rule is that a court will not force a purchaser to 'buy a law suit'.

If there is a problem a vendor should be advised not to sell.

In particular, the vendor's solicitors should be aware of the decision in *Doran v Delaney* [1996] 1 ILRM 490 and [1998] IESC 66. Here, a vendor's solicitor was held personally liable for failing to reply correctly to this particular requisition.

15.4.14.7   Requisition 14.6: Contributions

Prior to the enactment of the 2009 Act requisition 14.6 was an important requisition. The courts recognised that various persons other than the legal owner of the property may have acquired an equitable interest in it by virtue of a direct or indirect financial contribution. Section 21(1) of the 2009 Act now provides that a conveyance to a purchaser by the owner of the legal estate or interest overreaches any equitable interest in land, whether or not the purchaser has notice of the equitable interest, unless it is protected by registration prior to the date of the conveyance. If pre-closing searches reveal such a registered interest the claimants must join in the deed to the purchaser.

15.4.15   REQUISITION 15: VOLUNTARY DISPOSITION/BANKRUPTCY

This requisition now asks if there is a voluntary disposition on title.

15.4.15.1   Generally

There are two time periods which have to be examined when dealing with the Bankruptcy Acts. These are the three-year rule and the five-year rule. In the context of deeds being set aside the Conveyancing Act (Ireland), 1634, s 10 was of relevance. (See Practice Note in the Law Society *Gazette*, April 1998.) The 2009 Act has now repealed the 1634 Act but s 10 is restated in an amended format in s 74.

15.4.15.2   The three-year rule

Under the three-year rule, if a settlor or transferor is adjudicated bankrupt within three years of the date of the deed, then that deed is void as against the official assignee. It is the same as if the deed had never been executed and the property vests in the official assignee. This occurs regardless of the motive of the parties to the transaction. See Part 4 of the Personal Insolvency Act, 2012, which amended s 59 of the Bankruptcy Act, 1988.

15.4.15.3   The five-year rule

Where the deed is more than three years old, but less than five years old then, if the transferor is adjudicated bankrupt, the deed would be void unless the transferor could establish that at the date of the deed he or she was able to pay his or her debts without having recourse to the property comprised in the transfer.

It is interesting to note that if a transferor dies he or she may not subsequently be adjudged bankrupt and the Bankruptcy Act, 1988, s 59(1)(a) and (b) would not apply.

15.4.15.4   2009 Act, s 74

Section 74 of the 2009 Act provides as follows:

> *any voluntary disposition of land made with the intention of defrauding a subsequent purchaser of the land is voidable by that purchaser . . .*

It also provides that any conveyance of property made with the intention of defrauding a creditor or other person is voidable by any person thereby prejudiced: s 74(3). There is no time limit on an application under s 74 and nor is there a requirement that the transferor be adjudicated bankrupt in order for it to apply. However, in order for a gift to be voidable under s 74, it is necessary to establish that it was done with the intention of defrauding a subsequent purchaser, a creditor, or other person. The deed may not be set aside against a subsequent bona fide purchaser for value without notice. This includes a mortgagee.

Accordingly, in order to become a bona fide purchaser for value without notice a purchaser must obtain either:

(a) a statutory declaration from the disponer that the disposition was made bona fide for the purpose of benefiting the disponee but without fraudulent intent to delay. hinder, or defraud; or

(b) confirmation from the vendor that he or she is not aware of any such fraudulent intent to delay, hinder, or defraud.

In reality, if a person is executing a deed with fraudulent intent he or she will, more than likely, complete a statutory declaration stating that the disposition was made bona fide and without fraudulent intent!

15.4.16 REQUISITION 16: TAXATION

Requisition 16 covers estate duty, capital acquisitions tax, probate tax, and capital gains tax.

15.4.16.1 Requisition 16.1: Estate duty

The vast majority of currently practising solicitors qualified after estate duty was abolished on 1 April 1975 and are unfamiliar with it. Very basically, under the Finance Act, 1975, s 47 estate duty was abolished in respect of anyone who died after that date. Requisition 16 is only relevant where the deceased died before the abolition of estate duty and where, under the estate duty code, the payment of the duty was deferred until the death of the life tenant and a reversionary interest arose. In this situation Form A(X) is used in place of the Inland Revenue Affidavit Form CA24.

15.4.16.2 Requisition 16.2: Capital Acquisitions Tax (CAT)

The 2010 Finance Act abolished CAT as a charge on property received as a gift or on inheritance except where the title to the property depends on a claim of possessory title. In that case a certificate of discharge from CAT is required. By virtue of s 62(2) of the Capital Acquisitions Tax Consolidation Act, 2003, no application may be made to the Land Registry in respect of any property without first furnishing a certificate from the Revenue Commissioners confirming that there is no outstanding tax due on the property.

The certificate is known as a form CA12 and is required in all cases when a s 49 application is made for first registration of title based on adverse possession. This procedure ensures that any liability relating to gifts and inheritances which may not have been disclosed to the Revenue must be discharged to register the title. A self certification option is available where the value does not exceed €19,050 in value and 5 hectares in area or a value of €127,000 where the applicant is a statutory authority.

15.4.16.3 Requisitions 16.3 to 16.16: Capital Gains Tax (CGT)

Basically, this is a reminder requisition in that if a CGT tax clearance certificate is available the purchaser pays the entire consideration to the vendor, but if it is not available 15 per cent of the purchase price must be deducted and paid to the Revenue Commissioners. The clearance certificate will be available where (a) the vendor is resident in the State; (b) there is no capital gains tax; or (c) the capital gains tax due has been paid. Since the coming into force of the Finance Act, 2007, where a CG50A is required and not produced on closing, the purchaser must deliver an account of the consideration paid by him or her to the vendor, and the amount deducted from the consideration, within 30 days after the date of the payment of the consideration and remit the amount deducted by him or her to the Collector-General. If the purchaser does not do this, the Revenue Commissioners can assess him or her for the amount due, including any interest due because of late payment. The certificate of clearance cannot be issued retrospectively, ie after the sale closes. Therefore, under no circumstances should a vendor's solicitor undertake to obtain a certificate or should a purchaser's solicitor accept such an undertaking. This obligation ensures that non-residents pay any liability to CGT. Where a non-resident vendor does not have sufficient funds to pay any CGT due the Revenue will issue the CGT clearance certificate on foot of an undertaking by a solicitor acting on behalf of the non-resident vendor to discharge the CGT liability from the sale proceeds.

The capital gains tax clearance certificate must be furnished in all sales where the purchase price currently exceeds €1,000,000 (for houses and apartments) and €500,000 otherwise.

See the Taxation Committee Practice Note, Law Society *Gazette*, June 2014 'CGT Clearance Certificates' for agreed procedures with the Revenue Commissioners where the transaction does not fall within the normal transaction described earlier, eg simultaneous signing and closing of contract, consideration paid by instalments.

15.4.16.4 Requisition 16.7/8: Stamp duty

All stamp duty returns and all payment of stamp duty must be made online with a stamp certificate issuing once the filing of return and payment of stamp duty is completed. The E-stamping of Instruments (Amendment) (No 2) Regulations, 2011 removed the optional ability to file paper forms in place of electronic returns from 1 June 2011 except in very specific circumstances. This requisition asks for the information required to stamp a deed—the vendor's tax number, and property ID number all duly vouched. In practice these are provided at contract stage. Recently Revenue have confirmed that the tax type will no longer be required in the majority of cases (see Law Society eZine, January 2016).

Requisition 16.8 provides for the furnishing of a draft apportionment form where there is 'mixed' property involved in the sale. In practice, because of the different implications it is better to agree the apportionment prior to the signing of the contract.

15.4.16.5 Requisition 16.5: Probate tax

Probate tax was introduced by the Finance Act, 1993. It applied in all cases where a deceased died after 17 June 1993. It was abolished on 6 December 2000.

In the majority of cases, probate tax was paid before the grant of probate or administration to a deceased's estate was obtained. The danger area is where an estate is willed to a testator's spouse for life with remainder to a third person. No probate tax becomes payable until the surviving spouse (the life tenant) dies. The amount of probate tax payable is ascertained at the date of death of the first dying spouse. Therefore probate tax is charged on property for 12 years and a certificate of clearance should be obtained in one particular situation—where there is a death on title after 17 June 1993, and before 6 December 2000 leaving a surviving spouse inheriting a life interest that will cease or has ceased within the last 12 years. The Certificate of Discharge from Probate Tax is the PT2.

15.4.16.6 VAT

VAT is now dealt with pre contract. Requisition 16.10 requires that all documents pursuant to the contract and the VAT Consolidation Act, 2010, as amended be handed over on closing. The Law Society has issued a standard set of pre-contract VAT enquiries. See **chapter 16**.

15.4.17 REQUISITION 17: NON-RESIDENT VENDOR

The Revenue Commissioners have power to direct the purchaser to deduct income tax at the standard rate (currently 20 per cent) before paying the purchase money to a non-resident vendor. Once no direction under s 644(2) of the TCA 1997 has been made the money may be paid to the vendor's solicitor. Section 644 provides for a charge to tax under Case IV of Schedule D on gains from a disposal deriving its value from land (eg shares).

The aim is to prevent a scheme which removes profits from the scope of income tax to a CGT charge which is generally a lower effective rate of tax.

Solicitors should note the Income Tax Act, 1967, ss 200 and 201 which provide that the agent of a non-resident person may be liable for income tax and capital gains tax owed by the non-resident client.

The concern for solicitors is that they may be deemed the agent of a non-resident client for capital gains tax purposes. While the legal position is arguable, the safer course of action is to obtain the client's authority to hold sufficient funds to clear any tax liability. The solicitor can release the funds when the CGT is paid (if a liability arises), a return is made, and a Revenue letter of no audit is received.

15.4.18 REQUISITION 18: BODY CORPORATE VENDOR

The purpose of requisition 18 is to ensure that the company is in a position to sell and that no steps have been taken to wind up the company. Furthermore, the purchaser must be made aware of all charges affecting the property and any breach of ss 238 and 239 Companies Act, 2014 (previously s 29 or s 31 of the Companies Act, 1990). This requisition sets out a number of points:

(a) Has the company power to sell the property? (Check the memorandum of association.)

(b) What are the requirements for the sealing of documents by the company? (Check the memorandum of association.). Both (a) and (b) are relevant not only to the current vendor but any other body corporate on title.

(c) What charges affect the assets of the property?

(d) Are there steps currently being taken to wind up the company?

(e) Has any floating charge crystallised so as to affect the assets of the company?

(f) Has an arrangement within the meaning of the Companies Act, 1990, s 29(1)(a), (b) been entered into which would have an effect on the property in sale? (Section 29 provides that certain transactions between the company and connected parties are voidable by the company.)

The Companies Act, 2014 has repealed the Companies Act, 1990. Section 238 replaces s 29 of the Companies Act, 1990. The new section is very similar to the existing s 29.

Section 238(1) states that:

a company shall not enter into an arrangement—

(a) where a director of the company or its holding company or a person connected with such a director acquires or is to acquire one or more non-cash assets of the requisite value from the company;

(b) where the company acquires or is to acquire one or more non-cash assets of the requisite value from such director or a person so connected;

unless the arrangement is first approved by a resolution of the company in general meeting and, if the director or connected person is a director of its holding company or a person connected with such a director, by resolution general meeting of the holding company.

A non-cash asset is now defined in the new Act as of the requisite value if it is not less than €5,000 but exceeds €65,000 or 10 per cent of the company's relevant assets.

Section 238(3) provides that where there is an arrangement entered into in contravention of the section then that arrangement will be avoidable at the instance of the company unless:

(a) there is restitution of any money or other asset;

(b) any rights are acquired bona fide for value and without actual notice of the contravention; or

(c)   the arrangement is affirmed by a resolution of the company in general meeting, within a reasonable time.

Section 239 replaces s 31 of the Companies Act, 1990. It is similar to the old provision in that it provides that the company shall not make a loan or quasi loan to a director, a director of a holding company, or to a person connected with such a director or enter into a credit transaction as creditor, or enter into a guarantee or provide any security in connection with a loan, quasi loan, or credit transaction. The old s 34 validation procedure has been dispensed with and the Summary Approval Procedure (SAP) can be used to validate any transaction or arrangement that would otherwise be prohibited by s 239. The SAP does not require an independent accountant's report (this was almost impossible to provide).

Any transaction affected by s 239 is void if it has not been validated by SAP and hence the need for requisition 18.6.a and b.

15.4.19   REQUISITION 19: LAND ACTS, 1965 TO 2005

While ss 12 and 45 of the Land Act, 1965 have been repealed this requisition deals with any remaining requirements under these Acts—any vesting orders providing for consolidation with the property sold, any land purchase annuities in excess of €200, and any Land Registry requirements for first registration in cases where there were outstanding consents pursuant to ss 12 and 45 in transactions prior to 4 November 2005.

15.4.20   REQUISITION 20: UNREGISTERED PROPERTY

15.4.20.1   Generally

Until 1959 the personal estate of a deceased vested in his or her personal representatives but his real property passed directly either under his or her will or to his or her heir-at-law. Property registered in the Land Registry was deemed to be personal property and did not pass to the heir-at-law.

The Administration of Estates Act, 1959 provided that real property also vested in the personal representatives of the deceased. Therefore, in respect of any person who died after 31 May 1959, the personal representatives had to pass title to the beneficiary. This is done by way of assent. Without an assent, the beneficiary does not have title. There is one exception to this. If the beneficiary and the personal representative are one and the same person, then an assent is not necessary: *Mohan v Roche* [1991] 1 IR 560. However, it is good conveyancing practice to always do an assent.

15.4.20.2   Requisition 20.2: Compulsory registration

Requisition 20.2 deals with the situation where the registration of the vendor's title was compulsory prior to the date of the contract. It may also arise in relation to property originally vested in the Commissioners of Church Temporalities in Ireland. Section 23 of the Registration of Title Act, 1964 provides for compulsory registration in respect of certain titles (see Brendan Fitzgerald, *Land Registry Practice* (2nd edn) pp 381–3).

Compulsory registration also applies to lands acquired by a statutory authority since 1 January 1967 and to lands sold, conveyed, or vested under the provisions of the Land Purchase Acts, the Labourers Act, 1936 and the Housing Act, 1966.

General condition 29 of the Contract for Sale provides:

> *If all or any of the Subject Property is unregistered land the registration of which was compulsory prior to the Date of Sale the vendor shall be obliged to procure such registration prior to completion of the Sale.*

15.4.20.3   Requisition 20.3: Future compulsory registration

Requisition 20.3 deals with the situation where, by virtue of the transaction, the registration of the title will become compulsory (for sale of property in all counties/sale to a local authority, etc).

15.4.20.4   Requisitions 20.4 to 20.6: Title documents

The Contract for Sale, at general condition 34, provides that where title documents relate to property being retained by the vendor certified copies only will be given over to the purchaser on closing and requisitions 20.4, 20.5, and 20.6 deal with this.

Where deeds are subject to an equitable mortgage and part only of the property is being purchased, the purchaser's solicitor must be satisfied that the mortgagee is aware of the sale and consents to it. For example, a solicitor could have retained certified copies of the title documents and sent the originals to a lending institution. If he or she is selling a part of the property, he or she will be handing over the certified copies only, and the consent of the mortgagee could easily be overlooked.

15.4.20.5   Requisition 20.6: Safe custody and production

Requisition 20.6 deals with the undertaking for safe custody and production of documents. Where a vendor is selling part of the holding, this undertaking should be included in the conveyance to the purchaser. Under the Conveyancing Act, 1881, s 9(3) the benefit of the acknowledgement passes to any subsequent owner of the property. Accordingly, a subsequent purchaser of the property does not require to include an acknowledgement in the conveyance to him or her but it is usual to do so.

Under the provisions of the Conveyancing Act, 1881, s 9 any person giving a statutory acknowledgement and undertaking for safe custody and production is bound to produce the documents on demand for inspection and is further bound to furnish copies or to attend court with the originals.

Section 84 of the 2009 Act outlines the current position regarding production and safe custody of documents and is a replica of s 9 of the Conveyancing Act, 1881. Section 58(6) of the 2009 Act states that such acknowledgements and undertakings are furnished at the purchaser's expense where the purchaser requires them. This is subject to the terms of the Contract for Sale.

15.4.21   REQUISITION 21: IDENTITY

The purchaser's rights in relation to the identity of the property are determined by condition 14 of the Contract for Sale. This condition is dealt with in the context of the Contract for Sale. If there is any doubt as to the identity of the property, the purchaser should satisfy himself or herself in that regard prior to the signing of the contract.

15.4.22   REQUISITION 22: REGISTERED PROPERTY

15.4.22.1   Generally

As to registered property, see **chapter 14**.

Under condition 13(c) of the Contract for Sale, the vendor is obliged to furnish an official or certified copy of the Land Registry folio written up to date (or as near as is practicable up to date) together with the Land Registry map or file plan. With the introduction of the land direct online facility an out-of-date folio is not acceptable in practice. A copy of a certified copy folio written up to date is required. Where there is a transfer of part of the land a duly marked map complying with Land Registry mapping requirements is required.

If a vendor produces an up-to-date folio without file plan and an old folio with a file plan, then, if the new folio shows no changes from the old folio, the file plan cannot have changed either. Again, under the contract, the vendor agrees to furnish a s 72 declaration and agrees to furnish sufficient evidence to enable the purchaser to discharge the equities so as to enable the purchaser to convert the title to absolute. The vendor is not obliged to discharge the equities prior to closing. Under the Land Commission system, the Land Commission registered as owner of the holding the person who was in possession of the land.

As that person might not have been the owner of the land, the Land Commission registered him or her on the basis that the interest of anyone else who had a claim on the land was protected. Land purchase annuities are automatically cancelled where the sum payable is less than €200 per annum (s 2 of the Land Act, 2005). Pursuant to s 5 of the same Act a certificate from the Minister for Agriculture certifying that all annuities are paid to date is required to enable the Registrar to register certain transactions.

The Conveyancing Committee advises that an official Land Registry copy of a burden instrument should be provided as evidence of the contents of a burden registered. Where a purchaser is willing to accept a copy of the relevant deed of transfer creating the burden this must be supported by a certificate from the vendor solicitor confirming that all the covenants and conditions affecting the property are comprised in this deed. A solicitor should only provide this certificate if it is within his own personal knowledge of the title. (Conveyancing Committee Practice Note, Law Society *Gazette*, February 2014.)

15.4.22.2 Requisition 22.2.c: Mapping queries

Requisition 22.2.c requires the vendor to give an undertaking to discharge Land Registry mapping queries. It does not require the vendor's solicitor to do this. A vendor's solicitor should never give such an undertaking. It also requires the vendor to undertake to cover the payment of Land Registry mapping fees.

15.4.22.3 Requisition 22.2.e: Section 72 declaration

This requisition has been expanded to provide that the s 72 declaration shall contain an additional paragraph so that the vendor declares that there have been no deaths or voluntary dispositions on title within the previous 12 years. As the Finance Act, 2010 has abolished capital acquisitions tax as a charge on property received as a gift or inheritance, this addition is no longer necessary.

15.4.22.4 Requisition 22.4: Dealings pending

Requisition 22.4 enquires as to dealings pending; a purchaser's solicitor should not rely on the reply to this requisition but should do his or her own independent Land Registry search (together with all other appropriate searches). The Conveyancing Committee of the Law Society has recommended against the practice of a purchaser's solicitors seeking a certificate of no dealings pending from the vendor's solicitor where all property in the folio is being purchased, as third parties may have lodged a dealing that a vendor's solicitor is unaware of. It is only recommended where part of a folio is the subject of the transaction.

Requisitions 23–27, 28–31, and 35 are dealt with in other chapters (requisitions 23–25—Family Home, **chapter 7**; requisitions 26–27, 30, 31, and 35—Planning, **chapter 11**; requisition 29—New Houses, **chapter 12**).

15.4.23 REQUISITION 28: SAFETY, HEALTH AND WELFARE AT WORK (CONSTRUCTION) REGULATIONS, 1995, 2001 AND 2003, 2006 TO 2013 ('SAFETY REGULATIONS')

These regulations were introduced for the purpose of improving safety procedures on building sites. Since then there have been various safety, health, and welfare regulations enacted.

From the conveyancing perspective, the solicitor is not concerned with the actual implementation of the Regulations on any particular building site. However, the Regulations provide for the appointment of supervisors at appropriate stages to look after the safety aspects both of the design and the construction of the works. The supervisor is obliged in appropriate cases to prepare a safety file in respect of the works. It is this safety file that the conveyancers are concerned with.

Requisition 28.1 enquires as to whether construction work as defined by the Regulations has been carried out after March 1996 and requisition 28.2 requires that a copy of the safety file be handed over at requisition stage or confirmation that the safety file containing the required information (as per safety regulations in force at time work was carried out) is available for inspection.

The safety file should contain a record of all work carried out on the premises after March 1996. A solicitor should not be concerned with the contents of the file but merely its existence. It may well be that a purchaser's architect or engineer may want to inspect the file before the signing of the contract. A solicitor should not hold himself or herself out as being competent to advise on the contents of the safety file.

(See Conveyancing Committee Practice Note, Law Society *Gazette*, November 1999 p 33 'Safety Files and Once off Houses'.)

For a detailed description of the Safety, Health and Welfare Regulations see chapter 13 of the Law Society *Complex Conveyancing Manual* (2nd edn) published by Bloomsbury Professional.

15.4.24 REQUISITION 32: FOOD AND FOOD HYGIENE

This requisition requires evidence of registration from the relevant competent authority, evidence of relevant approval, compliance with conditions undertakings or requirements relating to such registration or/and approval, and details of any inspections or notices served in this regard. When purchasing a premises to which the Food Hygiene Regulations or the EC (Hygiene of Foodstuffs) or EC (Food and Feed Hygiene) Regulations relate, requisition 32 should be raised pre contract. This was confirmed by Clarke J in *Kelleher & Kelleher v Don O'Connor practising as Don O'Connor company* [2010] IEHC 313.

The Food Hygiene Regulations, 1950 (SI 205/1950) have been amended by Regulation (EC) No 852/2004 (as amended) and the Food Safety Authority of Ireland Act, 1998. The EC (Hygiene of Foodstuffs) Regulations, 2006 (as amended) and the EC (Food and Food Hygiene) Regulations, 2009 (as amended) require that all food businesses must be registered with the supervising competent authority, eg for those businesses supervised by the HSE (eg restaurants, caterers, supermarkets, wholesale operators) a food business operator is obliged to notify the HSE of each establishment under its control. Approval of the competent authority or official agency of the Food Safety Authority is also required. Changes to a food business (eg change of proprietor, the type of food being handled, the amount of food being produced) must also be notified to the competent authority. Furthermore, a food business is obliged to comply with operational and structural hygiene standards contained in Annex II to Regulation (EC) No 852/2004. The definition of 'food business' is very wide.

For further information see also chapter 12 of the Law Society *Complex Conveyancing Manual* (2nd edn) published by Bloomsbury Professional.

15.4.25 REQUISITION 33: LEASEHOLD/FEE FARM GRANT PROPERTY

As mentioned in relation to pre-contract enquiries (**chapter 4**), general condition 10 of the Contract for Sale deals with various matters in relation to this type of property.

15.4.25.1 Requisition 33.1: Lessor's title

This requisition looks for evidence of the title of the lessor to grant the lease/fee farm grant to the vendor or his or her successor in title.

Section 57(2) of the 2009 Act provides that if a lease or sub-lease is for more than five years, the purchaser can insist on the production of a copy of the conveyance to the vendor (if he holds a fee simple interest) or the superior lease and any assignment to the vendor (if he holds a leasehold title). If the lease is for full market value the purchaser can also look for 15 years' title. General condition 10(a) of the General Conditions of Sale will need to be amended as this condition provides that a purchaser is precluded from investigating the title of the grantor. Therefore, if a purchaser's solicitor is in doubt as to the right of the grantor to grant the lease, he or she must enquire about this, prior to the signing of the contract (note that general condition 10(a) does not cover fee farm grants). However, the special conditions in the contract will normally provide that the title shall commence with the particular deed. Therefore, in relation to a fee farm grant, the purchaser's solicitor will not be entitled to go behind the deed under which the title being produced commences.

15.4.25.2 Requisition 33.2: Covenants and conditions

Requisition 33.2 provides for evidence of the observance and performance of the conditions contained in the lease or fee farm grant. Under general condition 10 of the Contract for Sale, it is provided that the production of the receipt for the last gale of rent shall be accepted as conclusive evidence in relation to payment of the rent and in respect of the performance of all covenants and conditions contained in the lease. Section 59(2) and (3) of the 2009 Act reiterates this by re-enacting s 3(4) and (5) of the Conveyancing Act, 1881 and provides that unless the contrary appears the purchaser must assume that all covenants and provisions of the tenancy have been performed and observed to date on the production of the receipt for the last payment of rent due.

15.4.25.3 Requisition 33.3: Notices

Requisition 33.3 enquires as to whether any notices have been served by the landlord in respect of the property.

15.4.25.4 Requisition 34.4: Breach

Requisition 33.4 enquires as to whether there has been any breach of the covenants and conditions of the lease or fee farm grant.

15.4.25.5 Requisition 33.7: Nominal rent

Requisition 33.7 deals with the situation where the rent payable is nominal. The position in relation to nominal rent is covered by general condition 10(b)(iii) of the Contract for Sale and sets out that where the rent is not a rack rent, the vendor shall be obliged to furnish a statutory declaration indicating that no notices or rent demands have been served on or received by the vendor for six years and that the vendor has complied with the covenants (other than those in respect of the payment of rent) and the conditions contained in the lease and that he or she is not aware of any breaches thereof either by himself or herself or by any of his or her predecessors in title.

The vendor must furnish a sum in respect of unpaid rent for at least six years in the case of a lease or 12 years in the case of a fee farm grant.

15.4.25.6 Requisition 33.9: Consent to assignment

Requisition 33.9 relates to the consent of the landlord to the assignment of the property. Again, the question of the consent to assignment is covered by general condition 10(b)(iv) of the Contract for Sale.

Condition 10(b)(iv) provides that where the lease requires the landlord's consent to alienation and, if same has been refused or has not been procured, or if such consent is issued subject to a condition which the purchaser, on reasonable grounds, refuses to accept, either party may rescind the sale by seven days' prior notice to the other.

15.4.26 REQUISITION 34: ACQUISITION OF FEE SIMPLE

This requisition deals with the acquisition of fee simple by way of three alternative procedures.

15.4.26.1 Requisitions 34.1–6. Acquisition of fee simple under the Landlord and Tenant (Ground Rents) Act, 1967 (1967 Act), as amended

Requisition 34.1 asks if the vendor has taken any steps to acquire the fee simple under the 1967 Act. If the vendor has not taken any steps to acquire the fee simple then the remainder of the requisition is irrelevant. Likewise, if he or she has completed the acquisition of the fee simple the requisition is irrelevant. The requisition deals with the situation where the vendor is, at the time of the sale, in the process of acquiring the fee simple and asks that the application complies with either ss 9, 10, or 15 of the 1967 Act and is not restricted by s 16 of the 1967 Act. It also asks for a copy of any draft conveyance in connection with the application.

15.4.26.2 Requisition 34.7: Acquisition of fee simple under Part III of the Landlord and Tenant (Ground Rents) (No 2) Act, 1978 (1978 Act)—Vesting certificate in Land Registry

Where the application for the vesting certificate is with the consent of the landlord the vendor must consent to the issue of the vesting certificate in the purchaser's name. If the application is by way of Land Registry arbitration then the vendor must authorise the Land Registry to continue the arbitration on behalf of the purchaser and the purchaser must also apply to the Land Registry to have this done.

Normally, a vendor will include a special condition in the contract in any case where the acquisition of the freehold has not been completed. (See specimen special conditions in **chapter 5**.)

Requisition 34.9 covers the situation where the vesting certificate has been issued by the Land Registry but its registration has not been completed.

15.4.26.3 Requisition 34.13: Acquisition of fee simple by other means

Requisition 34.13 deals with the situation where the fee simple has been acquired other than by way of vesting certificate or under the 1967 Act. This requisition deals with, for example, the position where an application is made before the county Registrar to acquire the freehold of property under the Landlord and Tenant (Ground Rents) Act, 1967 where the property in question is not a dwellinghouse.

Requisition 35 has been dealt with in the Planning chapter, **chapter 11**.

15.4.27 REQUISITION 36: NEW OR SECOND-HAND PROPERTY IN A MANAGED DEVELOPMENT TO WHICH MULTI-UNIT DEVELOPMENTS ACT, 2011 (MUD ACT) APPLIES

This requisition should be raised pre contract and should only be raised at requisition stage where they were not raised pre contact. These complex requisitions set out the documentation required pre-closing (these are furnished with the Contract for Sale/building agreement) and the documentation required on closing when the transaction involves a new or second-hand property which is part of a management scheme. A management scheme is required where the local authority will not be taking the common areas in charge. The developer incorporates a management company generally limited by guarantee and with no share capital and prior to the Multi-Unit Developments Act, 2011 ('MUD Act') entered into a contract with the management company to transfer the common areas to it usually on the sale of the last unit in the development. The unit owners become shareholders in the company and pay a service charge to it for the repair, maintenance, and insurance of the common areas.

Management schemes are now governed by the MUD Act. In cases where no units in a development have been sold before April 2011 the developer is obliged to transfer the common areas to an owners' management company (OMC). Where units had been transferred prior to April 2011 the MUD Act imposed a statutory obligation on the developers to transfer the common areas to OMCs. The requisitions seek evidence that the OMC is registered as owner of the common areas and reversionary interests. Other information required includes details regarding the service charge and how it is apportioned, managing agents' details, legal representation, sinking fund, claims, proposed works, house rules, and insurance details. Where the property was not sold prior to 1 April 2011 a copy of the required certificate and contract pursuant to the MUD Act (s 3(1)) is required. Where the property was sold prior to or after 1 April 2011 and the development stage has ended, the statutory declaration (as per ss 11 and 12) and written confirmation regarding Schedule 3 documents must be provided. The requisition asks for confirmation that the OMC have been notified of the change of ownership and that the service charge has been paid.

For precedent pre-contract enquiries regarding MUD see the precedents section/Conveyancing Committee on the Law Society website (members area).

Pre-contract enquiries have been dealt with in **chapter 6**. For further information regarding the MUD Act, 2011 see also chapter 6 of the Law Society *Complex Conveyancing Manual* (2nd edn) published by Bloomsbury Professional.

15.4.28   REQUISITION 37: NEW OR SECOND-HAND PROPERTY IN A MANAGED DEVELOPMENT TO WHICH THE MULTI-UNIT DEVELOPMENTS ACT 2011 (MUD ACT) DOES NOT APPLY

It is of utmost importance to raise these requisitions at pre-contract stage when the purchase involves a second-hand managed property (as noted earlier). Again these requisitions are required where not raised pre contract. The requisition asks if services are provided by a management company and full details of the management of the company including membership, accounts, voting rights, service charge, managing agents, insurance, work proposals, and claims are required. Where the common areas and reversionary interest have been assured to the management company a copy of the assurance is required. Where this has not occurred, a copy of the relevant contract is required. The requisition asks for confirmation that OMC have been notified of the change of ownership and that the service charge has been paid.

15.4.29   REQUISITION 38: TAX-BASED INCENTIVES

Various Acts have introduced different tax-based incentives. The requisition has been drafted in general terms to cover any tax benefit which may attach to a property being purchased.

Clearly, if a property being purchased has a tax benefit for the purchaser this will have to be clarified fully pre contract.

Requisition 38.3 requires the vendor to hand over all documentation necessary to transfer the allowances to the purchaser. This documentation should all have been agreed pre contract. Tax-based incentives include certain industrial buildings, toll roads/bridges, farm buildings, multi-storey car parks, etc. These reliefs are being phased out.

15.4.30   REQUISITION 39: THE NAMA ACT

Requisition 39.1 asks if the property in sale is affected by any easement or profit arising under s 144 of the National Asset Management Agency Act (NAMA) Act, 2009. This section gives rise to statutory easements in favour of NAMA over lands retained by a disponer. Requisition 39.2 asks if any notice has been published or served under s 160 of the Act—this section gives compulsory acquisition powers to NAMA. Requisition 39.3 asks if the property is 'relevant land' as defined by s 172(1) of the Act and if there is any requirement to notify NAMA of any 'dealing' in the property, or any previous dealing on title, as defined in s 172. Requisition 39.4 asks if any party on title is a person prohibited from acquiring an interest in the property. A prohibited person includes a debtor or party connected with a debtor (s 172(3)). If a prohibited person is acquiring an interest confirmation is required that it is a person not in default within the meaning of the Act. Section 39(5) asks if an application under s 211 of the Act has been made (this is relevant where a sale should have been notified) and asks the vendor to disclose circumstances whereby the current sale or any prior transaction might hinder NAMA in acquiring an 'eligible bank asset' or impair the value of such an asset or rights which NAMA or a group entity would have acquired but for this transaction or a previous transaction. Pursuant to s 211 the relevant court may declare the disposition to be void if in the court's opinion it is just and equitable to do so. In deciding whether it is just and equitable to make a declaration the court shall have regard to the rights of any person who has in good faith and for value acquired an interest in the asset the subject of the disposition.

Where the property in sale is subject to a charge or mortgage that has been transferred to NAMA pursuant to the NAMA Act, the vendor is required to obtain the prior approval of NAMA before proceeding with any proposed sale. The approval may be subject to conditions that must be adhered to. This approval is a pre-contract issue (the contract may be subject to obtaining this approval). A draft of the release should be sought at requisition stage (See Conveyancing Committee Practice Note, Law Society *Gazette*, August/September 2013 'Sales of property where NAMA is the chargeholder').

15.4.31 REQUISITION 40: LICENSING

15.4.31.1 Introduction

Licensing is a substantial area of law and a solicitor needs to be familiar with it before embarking on the sale or purchase of licensed premises.

A purchaser's solicitor should always raise requisition 40 with the vendor's solicitor prior to the signing of the Contract for Sale. The existence of the licence is of crucial importance to the transaction. The purchaser needs to be aware of any issues affecting the licence before entering into a contract. Licensing has always been a minefield for solicitors. The authorities decided to use the same form for two different types of licence. The danger is that, instead of having a publican's licence, the vendor may have a hotel licence. In the main, licences granted prior to 1902 are ordinary seven-day publican's licences. Up to 1902 publicans' licences were issued on demand. However, in 1902 a law was introduced prohibiting the issue of new licences but that law introduced a new type of licence, namely the hotel licence. The same form is used for hotel licences granted after 1902 as is used for ordinary licences granted prior to 1902.

To compound matters, there are various premises trading as ordinary licensed premises which obtained hotel licences after 1902 and ceased to be hotels.

Searches may be carried out in the Circuit Court Office to ascertain what type of licence attaches to the premises. Such searches are not always successful. The District Court records may be missing or may not have been kept correctly. The Customs and Excise Office which issues the licence may also have details and it may be worth doing a search there. A further search which may be carried out is that in the Register of Licences in the Public Records Office. The register, which goes back to the nineteenth century, gives details, for each year, of all the licensees in the area and the type of licences which they held.

15.4.31.2 Requisitions 40.1 and 40.2: Type of licence

The purpose of requisitions 40.1 and 40.2 is to identify the type of licence attached to the premises. A purchaser's solicitor will want to see the licence when the contract is being signed and by the requisition stage should be aware of the type of licence.

15.4.31.3 Requisitions 40.3 and 40.4

Assuming that the licence was granted prior to 1902, then once it states on the face of it that it is an ordinary publican's licence, the purchaser knows that it cannot be a hotel licence. If it was granted after 1902 further enquiries would be necessary.

15.4.31.4 Requisition 40.5: Special and general exemptions

Special and general exemptions are two types of exemptions granted by the District Court enabling a licence holder (subject to different conditions in each case) to serve drink during prohibited hours. A special exemption is for a one-off event where a general exemption remains in force until the next annual licensing court. Section 5(4)(b) of the Intoxicating Liquor Act, 1927 (as amended) provides that the court may impose conditions on such an exemption as it sees fit. The Intoxicating Liquor Act, 2008 provides for further conditions that may be attached to the grant of special exemption orders. Practitioners should be aware of any conditions attached to exemptions and advise their clients accordingly.

15.4.31.5 Requisition 40.6: Conditions attached

Requisition 40.6 enquires as to whether there are any conditions or restrictions or qualifications attaching to the licence or agreed with any authority and requires details of them.

15.4.31.6 Requisition 40.8: Plan of property

Requisition 40.8 looks for a plan of the property showing the exact extent of the area covered by the licence. If an application has been made to the Circuit Court in respect of the premises, then a map will have been lodged in the Circuit Court Office. Otherwise there will not be a map available. If there is no map available the licence extends to the bounds of the 'house' specified on the licence. For further information, see Constance Cassidy, *Cassidy on the Licensing Acts* (3rd edn).

15.4.31.7 Requisition 40.10: Changes to property

Requisition 40.10 deals with any changes which have been made to the property since the licence was granted and whether a court order was obtained to incorporate alteration to the property. Although the requisition simply requires the production of the order, s 39 of the Intoxicating Liquor Act, 2000 requires the order to be presented to the Revenue Commissioners within 12 months of its issuance before they will grant the new licence for the existing licensed area and new licensed area. This is a matter which should be checked out pre contract. The vendor's solicitor needs to know the position before he or she prepares the Contract for Sale. Since most premises obtained their licences prior to the 1902 Act, it means that most licensed premises are in excess of 100 years old. Most properties will have had some changes to them in the course of 100 years. If no application has been made to the court to cover the changes to the premises, then the position must be dealt with by a special condition in the Contract for Sale. It is important to advise clients of the consequences of entering into a binding contract without an order to extend having been granted.

15.4.31.8 Requisition 40.11: Undertakings given

Requisition 40.11 enquires as to whether any undertakings were given by the original applicant to the court when the licence was first granted. These may still be relevant.

15.4.31.9 Requisitions 40.14 to 40.16: Convictions and endorsements

Requisitions 40.14 to 40.16 deal with convictions and endorsements on the licence. For the law on convictions and endorsements, see Constance Cassidy, *Cassidy on the Licensing Acts* (3rd edn).

In particular, requisition 40.16 asks if there has at any time been an application for an order under s 30 of the Intoxicating Liquor Act, 1927 (as amended) directing that any offences recorded should cease to be recorded. This enquiry relates to applications made at any time within the past ten years.

15.4.31.10 Requisition 40.17: Pending summons

Requisition 40.19 enquires about prosecutions pending against the vendor for alleged breaches of the Licensing Acts. Prior to the Courts (No 2) Act, 1986 this was an extremely important matter. Prior to then, if a licensee had three endorsements recorded within a certain period the licence was automatically forfeited. There was therefore a danger that a conviction prior to the closing of the sale could result in the licence being lost. Because of the discretion granted by the Courts (No 2) Act, 1986 this is less likely to happen now.

15.4.31.11 Requisition 40.19.a and b: Closing

Requisition 40.19.a looks for the handing over of the licence to the purchaser on closing while the vendor will normally endorse the licence (see order 77 of the District Court Rules).

While requisition 40.19.b requests the vendor to attend at the court, there is no provision in the General Conditions of the Contract for Sale requiring him to so attend.

15.4.31.12 Requisitions 40.20 and 40.21: Fire safety requirements

Requisitions 40.20 and 40.21 deal with notice to the fire officer and compliance with any requirements of the fire officer given at the previous annual licensing court.

15.4.31.13 Requisition 40.22: Drug trafficking legislation

Requisition 40.22 seeks information on any convictions of the vendor under drug trafficking legislation and enquires about any resulting revocation of the vendor's licence.

15.4.32 REQUISITION 41: RESTAURANT/HOTEL

As mentioned in relation to requisition 40 a new category of licence known as a hotel licence was created by the Licensing (Ireland) Act, 1902, s 2(2).

Section 2(2) provides for the granting of a licence 'for an hotel, which expression shall refer to a house containing at least ten apartments set apart and used exclusively for the sleeping accommodation of travellers, and have no public bar for the sale of intoxicating liquors'.

Under the Intoxicating Liquor Act, 1960, s 19 there was provision for the holder of a hotel licence granted under s 2(2) of the 1902 Act to apply to the Circuit Court enabling the hotel to have a public bar. (The applicant had to extinguish an ordinary seven-day licence.)

Requisition 41.1 enquires as to whether there is a hotel licence attached and whether there is a public bar in the premises. If there is a public bar, the vendor is asked to furnish evidence of his or her entitlement to have such a bar.

Requisition 41.2 enquires as to when the court order granting the hotel licence was made.

Requisition 41.3 enquires as to the number of rooms ('apartments') at present used for accommodation. If the licence was granted under s 2(2) of the 1902 Act then there is the minimum requirement of ten rooms but if there is a bar on the premises, having been granted pursuant to s 19 of the 1960 Act, then the hotel must have 'at least ten, or, if situate in a County Borough (which expression shall be deemed for the purposes of this section to include the Dublin Metropolitan District), twenty apartments set apart and used exclusively for the sleeping accommodation of travellers'.

Requisition 41.4 deals with registration of the hotel with Failte Ireland. Section 20 of the Intoxicating Liquor Act, 1960 states:

An application for a certificate for the renewal of a licence in respect of which effect was given to subsection (1) of section 42 of the Tourist Traffic Act, 1952, or which was granted after the passing of this Act by virtue of paragraph (2) of section 2 of the Act of 1902 shall not be granted unless it is shown to the satisfaction of the Court hearing the application for the grant of the certificate that the hotel is registered in the register of hotels kept by Bord Failte Eireann.

If the premises are not registered with Failte Ireland then they are not entitled to have a licence.

Requisition 41.7 deals with restaurant certificates. Section 12 of the Intoxicating Liquor Act, 1927 provides for the issue of restaurant certificates. The holder of a restaurant certificate is entitled to apply to the District Court for special exemption orders entitling the premises to trade outside the prohibited hours.

A restaurant certificate is not transferable. However, it attaches to the premises and remains current until the next annual licensing court.

For further reading see Constance Cassidy, *Cassidy on the Licensing Acts* (3rd edn), Karl Dowling and Brendan Savage, *Civil Procedure in the District Court*, and Marc McDonald, *Hotel Restaurant and Public House Law*.

15.4.33   REQUISITION 42: SPECIAL RESTAURANT LICENCE

A special restaurant licence is a type of licence created by the Intoxicating Liquor Act, 1988. The definition given in s 7(1) of the Act is as follows:

In this Act 'Special Restaurant Licence' means a licence granted by the Revenue Commissioners pursuant to a Certificate of the Circuit Court given under Section 8 of the Act to a person in respect of a restaurant of which he is the owner and occupier authorising, subject to the provisions of the Act,

(a)   *to supply intoxicating liquor for consumption on those premises; and*

(b)   *the consumption of the intoxicating liquor on those premises, if, in each case, the intoxication liquor is:*
   (i)   *ordered by or on behalf of a person by whom a substantial meal has been ordered;*
   (ii)   *supplied in either the waiting area or the dining area of the restaurant;*
   (iii)   *consumed in the waiting area of the restaurant before the meal by the person for whom the meal has been ordered, or consumed by that person in the dining area of the restaurant either during the meal or at any time not later than thirty minutes after the meal has ended; and*
   (iv)   *paid for at the same time as the meal is paid for provided always that suitable beverages other than intoxicating liquor (including drinking water) are also available for consumption.*

Section 16(1) provides that a restaurant in respect of which a special restaurant licence has been granted shall not contain a bar. The standards for this type of licensed premises are set out in the Special Restaurant Licence (Standards) Regulations, 1988 (SI 147/1988).

15.4.34   REQUISITION 43: DANCING, MUSIC, AND SINGING

15.4.34.1   Public dance licences

These are governed by the Public Dance Hall Act, 1935. There are two types of licence, namely: an annual licence and a temporary licence. A temporary licence is for a period not exceeding a month and an annual licence runs from one annual licensing court to the next (September to September). A public dancing licence is not transferable. If a property changes hands, the new purchaser will have to apply for a new licence. However, as a public dancing licence may have conditions attached, the purchaser will need to see these. This is an issue to be attended to pre contract.

15.4.34.2 Public music and singing licences

These are governed by the Public Health Amendment Act, 1890. The need to obtain such licences only arises in areas where the relevant local authority has passed a resolution applying the Act to its area. Licences are granted annually. A licence may be transferred from a vendor to a purchaser by making application to the District Court.

Requisition 43.2 enquires as to whether there is a music and singing licence attached to the property and asks for production of the original on closing.

Requisition 43.3 enquires as to whether there are any conditions or undertakings which may be attached to the licence.

For a detailed discussion of the law relating to public dance halls and music and singing licences, see James Woods, *The District Court Practice and Procedure in Civil Licensing and Family Law Proceedings*.

There were changes made to the intoxicating liquor licensing District Court procedures by the Intoxicating Liquor Act, 2008 requiring the issuance of a certificate by the District Court before the grant of a new wine retailer's off-licence by the Revenue Commissioners. This is requested at Requisition 43.1.b. Other amendments include the setting out of the grounds on which the District Court may refuse the grant of a certificate in respect of a new off-licence, the requirements in applying for the new off-licence, and the power of the court to impose certain conditions on the grant of the certificate. For a more in-depth discussion on the 2008 Act see the Law Society *Gazette,* December 2009. See also Karl Dowling and Brendan Savage, *Civil Procedure in the District Court.*

15.4.35 REQUISITION 44: DOCUMENTS REQUIRED ON CLOSING

Requisition 44 sets out the documents which the purchaser requires in order to complete the sale. These will be different in every case. While the requisitions look for various documents such as family law declarations etc it is good practice to list these in requisition 44 so as to have an immediate checklist to hand both for the vendor's solicitor and for the purchaser's solicitor. Where solicitors have an exhaustive list of closing requirements on their word processors, they should delete all the unnecessary items from that list before completing requisition 44.

In relation to the procedures for closing the sale see **chapter 6**.

Specimen requisition 44 (for registered property):

1. Such documents as arise from the foregoing requisitions.

2. Executed transfer.

3. PPS/tax number of vendor and LPT ID number for stamp duty return.

4. Section 72 declaration (in the long form as recommended by the Conveyancing Committee).

5. Family law declaration.

6. Official copy folio and title plan.

7. Copy folio showing cancellation of mortgage/discharge of mortgage in favour of XY together with relevant Land Registry fees or undertaking to redeem mortgage and furnish discharge and relevant fees/copy folio.

8. Letter re roads and services.

9. CGT clearance certificate (Form CG50A).

10. Clearance Certificate CA 12 if adverse possession or first registration application being made to the Land Registry.

11. Original planning permission documentation together with certificate of compliance with both planning permission and the Building Control Act regulations.

12. Original BER certificate and advisory report.

13. Specific LPT clearance (if required).

14. Receipt for environmental waste.

15. Notice of assignment to the rating authority.

16. The keys, alarm code, and vacant possession.

17. Non-principal private residence certificate of discharge/certificate of exemption.

18. Certificate re waste water treatment system.

Specimen requisition 44 (for unregistered property):

1. Such documents as arise from the foregoing requisitions.

2. Original title documents pursuant to Contract for Sale together with stamp duty certificate where relevant.

3. Executed conveyance/assignment.

4. PPS/tax number of vendor and LPT ID number for stamp duty return.

5. Family law declaration for current transaction and all deeds on title since 1976.

6. Original mortgage with vacate endorsed thereon duly registered in the Registry of Deeds or undertaking to redeem mortgage and furnish registered vacated mortgage.

7. Letter re roads and services.

8. CGT clearance certificate (CG50A).

9. Original planning permission documentation together with architect's certificate of compliance.

10. Architect's opinion of compliance with the building regulations.

11. Original BER certificate and advisory report.

12. NPPR certificate of discharge/certificate of exemption.

13. Receipt for environmental waste.

14. Notice of assignment to the rating authority.

15. Statutory declaration of non-severance of joint tenancy.

16. Statutory declaration of non-breach of covenants in the lease and non-demand for rent.

17. Specific LPT clearance.

18. Certificate re waste water treatment system.

19. The keys, alarm code, and vacant possession.

20. Application for first registration (Forms 1, 2, or 3).

21. Land Registry compliant map for first registration.

CHAPTER 16

CONVEYANCING AND TAXATION

16.1   Introduction

This chapter deals with the various taxation issues that may arise in a typical conveyancing transaction. Any or indeed all of the following taxes may have to be considered by both the vendor's and the purchaser's solicitor when consulted to sell or buy a property on behalf of a client, namely stamp duties, capital gains tax, capital acquisitions tax, charges arising under the Local Government (Charges) Act, 2009, the Local Government (Household Charges) Act, 2011, The Finance (Local Property Tax) Act, 2012, Water Charges as provided for under the Environment (Miscellaneous Provisions) Act, 2015, or VAT.

In the April 2016 edition of the Gazette the Conveyancing Committee advised, in cases where records required for conveyancing transactions are maintained only online, it is the online record that is conclusive and can be accepted by a purchaser's solicitor. A purchaser's solicitor may accept a photocopy, coloured copy, print out or review the online record, for example LPT online record, BER certificates or NPPR certificates of exemption. There is no need for either a purchaser's or a vendor's solicitor to certify a copy as being a copy of the original.

16.2   Conveyancing Taxation Checklist

16.2.1   CAPITAL GAINS TAX

Does the consideration exceed €1,000,000 in the case of houses and apartments or €500,000 in all other cases? If it does a clearance certificate pursuant to s 980 of the Taxes Consolidation Act, 1997, is required by a purchaser's solicitor. Alternatively, 15 per cent from the purchase price must be deducted and paid to the Revenue Commissioners (withholding tax) where such clearance certificate is not provided by the person disposing of the asset.

16.2.2   STAMP DUTIES

Stamp Duty is a duty charged on certain written documents known as 'instruments'. With the exception of the CREST share transfer system, where no document exists, the general rule is that there is no exposure to stamp duty. If assets can be transferred without the use of a document, stamp duty can be avoided on the transaction.

16.2.3   CAPITAL ACQUISITIONS TAX (CAT)

Prior to 3 April 2010 s 60 and s 61 of the Capital Acquisitions Tax Consolidation Act, 2003 provided that CAT was a charge on property for 12 years. However since 3 April 2010, it is no longer a charge on property.

However, an exception was made for applications made to the Property Registration Authority (Land Registry) to register property held by way of adverse possession; this is the only remaining instance where a certificate of discharge from CAT is required. Under s 62(2) of the Capital Acquisitions Tax Consolidation Act, 2003, a clearance certificate of discharge from CAT (Form CA12) should be obtained for such applications before a title based on adverse possession will be registered. A self-certification option is available for small properties which come within prescribed limits of value and are not part of a larger property.

16.2.4   THE FINANCE (LOCAL PROPERTY TAX) ACT, 2012

This Act governs the application of Local Property Tax (LPT) to residential property as defined. LPT is due and payable by the person who is liable on the liability date and the amount on which LPT is chargeable is the market value that the property could *reasonably* be expected to fetch on a sale in the open market on the valuation date.

16.2.5   THE LOCAL GOVERNMENT (CHARGES) ACT, 2009 (NPPR) AND THE LOCAL GOVERNMENT (HOUSEHOLD CHARGES) ACT, 2011

In essence these provided for an annual local government charge of €200 on non-principal private residences, such as investment/rental properties, vacant investment properties, and holiday homes, and an annual charge of €100 on residential property respectively. The appropriate receipts or certificates of exemption had to be produced to the purchaser on completion. Whilst both of these charges are now abolished they still remain a charge on property and will remain so for 12 years. In the case of the NPPR charge the purchaser's solicitor should ensure that the relevant certificate of discharge, or a certificate of exemption, is obtained at closing from the local authority. A receipt or declaration made by the vendor is not sufficient. However a declaration can be provided where the property does not come within the ambit of the Act.

The household charge was abolished on 1 January 2013. Any outstanding household charge plus interest and penalties unpaid on 1 July 2013 will be converted into LPT of €200 due and payable on that date. It may be collected and pursued by the Revenue through the LPT system

16.2.6   WATER CHARGES

Water charges are provided for under the Environment (Miscellaneous Provisions) Act, 2015 which commenced on 1 January 2016. The Law Society in a Practice Note in the December 2015 edition of the *Gazette* advise that it will be necessary to advise vendors' solicitors to notify vendors at the initial instruction stage of a sale transaction that they will have difficulty acting in the sale if the vendor does not wish (whether as a matter of principle or otherwise) to pay any charges due to Irish Water in respect of the property. The definition of 'sale' includes a voluntary transfer.

If the vendor does not provide before the completion of the sale either a certificate of discharge from Irish Water confirming that any such charge has been paid or a statement from Irish Water that any such charge is not a liability of the vendor then the vendor's solicitor shall, before completing the sale, request such statement from Irish Water. In this situation the vendor's solicitor should submit a request on headed notepaper to Irish Water setting out the name of the vendor and the address of the property. A scanned signed copy of this letter may be submitted electronically to Irish Water.

Irish Water will aim to issue such certificate within five working days of receiving the request. Section 48(5) provides that the vendor's solicitor shall withhold from the net proceeds of sale remaining (if any), after the discharge of all mortgages and other liabilities relating to the sale the amount (if any) set out in the statement provided to the solicitor and remit same to Irish Water within 20 working days of the completion of the sale of the dwelling.

Section 48(7) provides that Irish Water shall provide a receipt to the vendor's solicitor in respect of the amount remitted to it and s 48(8) provides that a receipt provided under s 48(7) shall be in full and final settlement of any obligation imposed on the vendor's solicitor under this section.

Where there is no sale of the property and in the event that there are no 'net proceeds' available to pay the water charges, the vendor's solicitor shall notify Irish Water of this within 20 working days. Irish Water have confirmed per the Department of the Environment, Community and Local Government that Irish Water will acknowledge receipt of such a notification and that no further action is required by the solicitor. The Department has confirmed to the conveyancing committee of the Law Society that where this situation arises there are no implications for the purchaser of the property (that is, there is no provision for a charge on the property) in so far as the liability for unpaid charges would remain with the vendor. It would remain for Irish Water to pursue the vendor for these unpaid charges by other means.

This reflects the position as of May 2016 however the future of water charges is now uncertain.

16.2.7 VAT

The manner in which value added tax (VAT) is levied upon property transactions was dramatically altered with the introduction on 1 July 2008 of a new VAT on the property system. The manner in which the new rules are applied to the sale of freehold and 'freehold equivalent interests' are examined in detail later in this chapter. Given the complexity of this new VAT on property system and its potential fundamentally to affect the financial position of the vendor and the purchaser, it is imperative that both the solicitors acting for the vendor and the purchaser are apprised of the VAT position at a pre-contract stage. In order to assist practitioners in this regard, the Conveyancing and the Taxation Committees of the Law Society jointly issued VAT pre-contract enquiries which were first posted on the Law Society website in May 2009 and may be accessed by logging onto the member's area of that website. As these enquiries are updated on a regular basis, practitioners should ensure that the most up-to-date version available on the website is used in each individual transaction. Although the enquiries are to be raised by the purchaser's solicitor, in a joint Practice Note issued in the May 2009 *Gazette*, the Conveyancing and Taxation Committees stated that it was their view that the enquiries would prove a useful tool for the vendor's solicitor in establishing the VAT position in each individual transaction, thereby assisting the vendor's solicitor in correctly drafting the Contract for Sale. It is, therefore, advisable that, on receiving instructions regarding the sale of the property, the vendor's solicitor would liaise with the vendor and, if necessary, the vendor's taxation advisor, in order to complete the questionnaire. The purchaser's solicitor should carefully consider the responses to the enquiries received from the vendor and ensure that the purchaser is fully aware of the VAT implications of the transaction. On completion, the purchaser's solicitor ought to seek confirmation from the vendor's solicitor that the replies to the enquiries are still accurate and correct. As the enquiries are comprised of a series of very detailed questions regarding the VAT history of the property, it is strongly advised that, unless the solicitor in question is an expert in VAT or the transaction is a straightforward one, the vendor should be advised to engage the services of a VAT specialist or a tax advisor. Equally, the purchaser's solicitor, if he or she does not feel competent to analyse the information furnished by the vendor and advise on the consequences of the same for the VAT treatment of the transaction, ought to advise the purchaser to seek specialist assistance.

16.2.8 PROBATE TAX

Was there a death on title between 18 June 1993 and 6 December 2000 where the surviving spouse inherited a life interest that will now cease or has ceased within the last 12 years? If there was, a clearance certificate of discharge from probate tax (PT2) must be obtained from the vendor. Probate tax was abolished with effect from 6 December 2000. However if a spouse received a limited (life) interest in property with the remainder to a third party after the death of the spouse the probate tax was deferred or postponed until after the death of the surviving spouse. It was deferred until the remainder interest crystallised, ie on the death of the surviving spouse, and becomes a charge on the property for a period of 12 years once it has crystallised on the life tenant's death.

16.3 Stamp Duties

16.3.1 INTRODUCTION

The current law relating to stamp duty is principally contained in the Stamp Duties Consolidation Act, 1999 ('the SDCA, 1999') which became law on 15 December 1999, and subsequent amending Finance Acts. Prior to this the law of stamp duty was found *inter alia* in the Stamp Act, 1891 and substantive amendments were made in subsequent Finance Acts. Stamp duty is a tax on 'instruments'. That is to say on various types of written documents, and not on transactions. If there is no instrument or document to stamp then no stamp duty can arise unless the legislation provides otherwise. When dealing with the question of whether a stamp duty exposure arises the first question that needs to be asked is, 'is there a document?' These documents are referred to as 'instruments' in the stamp duty code. Not every instrument is liable to stamp duty. To be liable an instrument must be listed under one of the headings in Schedule 1 to the SDCA, 1999 which contains a list of those instruments liable to stamp duty. The documents listed in this Schedule are usually referred to as 'heads of charge'. The three main heads of charge being: *conveyance on sale, lease, and mortgage*. Schedule 1 also specifies the appropriate rates of duty, which may be ad valorem or fixed, applicable to each instrument.

16.3.1.1 Ad Valorem

When a document is charged to stamp duty at the ad valorem rate, the value of the property is subject to stamp duty based on the appropriate table of rates and will depend on the type of the property whether residential or non-residential. Currently the rate of stamp duty applicable to residential property is 1 per cent where the consideration does not exceed €1,000,000 and 2 per cent on any excess over €1,000,000. A flat rate of 2 per cent applies to all non-residential/commercial property.

16.3.1.2 Fixed

When a document is charged to stamp duty at the fixed rate, stamp duty of €12.50 is payable. For example, a duplicate or counterpart lease.

16.3.2 THE MANDATORY NATURE OF STAMP DUTY, THE FINANCE ACTS 1991 AND 2012, AND PENALTIES

With effect from 1 November 1991 the payment of stamp duty became mandatory. Prior to this date the payment of both ad valorem and fixed duties was voluntary. This was so because although a liability arose to stamp instruments the Revenue did not have any method of enforcing the payment of duty. Section 2(3) of the SDCA, 1999 provides that an instrument which is subject to stamp duty must be stamped within 30 days after it is first executed. The Finance Act, 1991 is of importance to solicitors because it created a number of obligations and imposed a duty of disclosure on professional advisors and their clients in relation to the payment of stamp duty. Penalties were imposed for late stamping of instruments chargeable to duty, and surcharges were imposed where property had been undervalued in returns to the Revenue Commissioners. The Finance Act, 2012 (the 2012 Act) introduced a range of changes in the administration of stamp duty that came into effect on 7 July 2012 in respect of instruments executed on or after that date. The provisions of the 2012 Act are now contained in ss 8, 14, 16, and 127 to 134A of the SDCA, 1999. In addition to the fact that the payment of stamp duty is compulsory (s 2) and that late payment of stamp duty will give rise to interest (s 14), ss 127 to 134A of the SDCA contain a number of provisions/penalties to help to ensure that returns are filed on time through the Revenue Online System (ROS) for instruments which are chargeable to stamp duty. Section 8 of the SDCA, 1999 provides for a penalty of €3,000 for failing to file a return, setting out all of the relevant information. Section 8A of the SDCA, 1999 provides that all facts and circumstances affecting the liability to stamp duty or affecting the amount of duty are to be fully disclosed to the Revenue Commissioners in the returns. This section puts the onus on a person to bring to the attention of the Revenue Commissioners all the facts and circumstances affecting the liability of an instrument to stamp duty and these must be stated in the instrument itself. In some cases it will not be practicable for the instrument to contain all relevant facts and circumstances. In such cases it is permissible to set out any facts or circumstances not set out in the instrument in an accompanying statement. This statement is not required to be delivered to the Revenue where the instrument is stamped under the e-stamping system.

Evidence in relation to the chargeability of an instrument to duty must be retained by an accountable person for audit purposes for six years from the date of stamping of the instrument under the e-stamping system should the Revenue wish to examine it. In addition s 128A provides that an accountable person is obliged to retain records relating to a stamp duty liability or to a relief or exemption claimed for a period of six years from the date a stamp duty return is filed or the date the duty is paid, whichever date is the later. The 2012 Act introduced new fixed penalties on each accountable person for failure to file a stamp duty return. The obligation would appear to apply to solicitors involved in the preparation and filing of stamp duty returns on behalf of clients.

These penalties apply to instruments executed on or after 7 July 2012. Section 8A provides for a penalty of €3,000 where an incorrect electronic or paper return relating to an instrument is filed with the Revenue in circumstances where the person is aware that the facts filed are incorrect.

Section 8B provides for a penalty of €3,000 where an accountable person fails to cause an electronic or paper return relating to an instrument to be filed before the time specified in s 2(3) of the SDCA that is before the expiration of 30 days after the first execution of the instrument.

Section 8(3) provides that in the case of fraudulent or negligent execution of an instrument where facts affecting liability are not fully set forth in the instrument a penalty of €1,265 applies together with the amount of difference of duty. This penalty applies to a person 'employed or concerned in or about preparation of the instrument'. This applies to solicitors and any other professional advisor to any parties executing instruments that may be liable to stamp duty.

The penalties outlined in ss 8 and 134A SDCA must be considered carefully by all practitioners. There is no de minimis threshold on the application of these penalties which could theoretically apply even where there is no stamp duty payable on the unfiled return.

Section 15 of the SDCA, 1999 reiterated the provisions of the Finance Act, 1991 in relation to surcharges imposed where the value of the property is understated to the Revenue Commissioners. This section has however been abolished in respect of instruments executed on or after 7 July 2012. For such instruments where an undervaluation of property is included in the stamp duty return filed under the e-stamping system, penalties relating to the filing of an incorrect return will be incurred (s 134A).

16.3.2.1 Penalties for late filing of returns: The Finance Act, 2012

Section 14 of the SDCA, 1999

An instrument that is chargeable to stamp duty must be duly stamped within 30 days after its first execution otherwise penalties for late filing will be imposed (s 2 and s 14 of the SDCA, 1999 refer). Where the correct amount of stamp duty is not paid within the time limit set down in s 2 of the SDCA, that is, if the deed is stamped after 30 days from the date of first execution of the instrument under s 14 SDCA, 1999 interest is payable at the rate of 0.0219 per cent per day or part of a day. The 2012 Act did not change the specified return date for the filing of stamp duty returns, which is 30 days after first execution, nor was the rate of late filing interest (0.0219 per cent) changed. The Revenue has confirmed that they will continue to accept returns filed up to 44 days after first execution in line with previous practice.

Section 14A of the SDCA, 1999: late filing of returns

The penalty regime for stamp duty has undergone a very substantial change since the Finance Act, 2012 became law on 7 July 2012. A self-assessment regime was introduced and, for instruments executed on or after that date, a new late filing surcharge was introduced. Solicitors must continue to file e-stamping returns as previously. The e-stamping system will ensure that returns for instruments executed on or after 7 July 2012 will be treated automatically on a self-assessed basis. Adjudication was abolished and the Revenue will no longer examine instruments prior to stamping and the stamp certificate will issue immediately after the return is lodged, provided all charges are paid. The new system of penalties include tax geared surcharges for late filing of returns, tax geared penalties for failing to file a return, and a number of other penalties that will not be dealt with in this text.

The new surcharge is based on a percentage increase of the stamp duty payable and is subject to a grading of the surcharge by reference to the length of the delay in filing the stamp duty return as well as being subject to an overall cap on the level of the surcharge.

The surcharge

For instruments executed on or after 7 July 2012 a new late filing surcharge applies equal to 5 per cent of the unpaid duty where the stamp duty return is filed after the specified return date (44 days) subject to a maximum of €12,695. Where the stamp duty return is filed later than 92 days of the date of execution of the instrument a late filing surcharge of 10 per cent of the unpaid duty applies subject to a maximum of €63,485. The surcharge is not a penalty and therefore forms part of a stamp duty charge. Late filing interest is charged on the amount of the original stamp duty liability plus the surcharge amount. Eamon Scally has written an excellent article on the changes in the stamp duty regime following the Finance Act, 2012 under the heading 'Shifting sands' in the Law Society *Gazette*, January/February 2013 which should be consulted.

On 1 June 2011 it became mandatory to file stamp duty returns online using the Revenue Online Service (ROS) subject to very limited exceptions. Payment of stamp duty must also be made online from that date by ROS or in limited cases payment can be made by electronic fund transfer (EFT).

Section 134A SDCA, 1999 Penalties: Solicitors' liability and obligations

In cases of fraud or negligence penalties will also apply. A voluntary conveyance must be brought to the attention of the Revenue by ticking the relevant box in the return. Failure to do so will result in a presumption of negligence or of acting deliberately under s 134A SDCA, 1999. Tax geared penalties apply in addition to a fixed penalty of €1,265 in instances of fraud and negligence. The penalty is determined by the number of defaults by the person, whether the category of default is deliberate, careless (failure to take reasonable care) but not deliberate, the level of cooperation, and whether a prompted or unprompted qualifying disclosure is made. The penalty can be 100 per cent of the underpayment.

If an error is neither deliberate nor careless, action must be taken without undue delay on spotting the error to rectify same to prevent it being treated as a deliberate action.

Other obligations to be aware of include s 129 SDCA, 1999, which provides that any person who enrols, enters, or registers an instrument that is not properly stamped will incur a penalty of €630.

Mitigation of penalties under s 1065 of the Taxes Consolidation Act (TCA), 1997 applies to stamp duty penalties.

Pursuant to s 128 SDCA, 1999 there is an obligation to produce documents, provide information, and permit access to Revenue officials. Failure to comply is an offence under s 1078 TCA. Section 129A SDCA, 1999 provides an obligation to retain records of a true return for six years from the date the tax was paid or return made. This is subject to a penalty of €3,000 for failure to comply. Failure to produce records where a relevant person (including a solicitor) is retaining records on an accountable person's behalf can lead to a penalty of €19,045 plus €2,535 per day until compliance. Employees of a relevant person can also be held liable (s 128B SDCA, 1999). There is a defence of legal professional privilege to s 128A but not to s 128B.

It is advisable to retain a record of the stamp duty return (which has been approved by your client) for auditing purposes for four years from the stamping of the instrument. Unfortunately the drop boxes selected in the return are not shown in the printed version and this issue has been brought to the attention of the Revenue by the Law Society Taxation Committee.

16.3.2.2 Effect of a document not being stamped

Section 127 of the SDCA provides that if an instrument is not duly stamped:

(a) Such instrument cannot be used as evidence in court in civil or arbitral proceedings until any duty and penalties are paid. An unstamped document can be produced in criminal proceedings;

(b) It will not be acceptable to the Land Registry when applying for registration of ownership; and

(c) A purchaser is not obliged to accept an unstamped deed. In fact an unstamped deed is not a good link in a chain of title.

Prior to the Finance Act, 2012 instruments that had been adjudicated were considered to be duly stamped but instruments that had been 'straight stamped' were not considered to be duly stamped.

Section 127 of the SDCA has been amended by the 2012 Act so that all instruments executed on or after 7 July 2012 and stamped using the e-stamping system are considered to be duly stamped. This change will be of considerable benefit to solicitors who otherwise would have to satisfy themselves as to the sufficiency of the stamping of documents. Solicitors will have to ensure that instruments executed before 7 July 2012 (unless bearing an adjudication stamp) have been duly stamped.

16.3.2.3 Categories of stamp duties

Ad valorem duty and revenue certificates in deeds

'Ad valorem' is a Latin term meaning 'by value' and is used to describe a rate of stamp duty that is proportionate to the value of the transaction involved. Schedule 1 to the SDCA, 1999 identifies the rate of duty applicable to various instruments, whether ad valorem, fixed, or exempt from duty. Prior to 7 July 2012 the amount of duty applicable to a particular instrument often depended on that instrument containing a particular certificate. The concept of certification in deeds was introduced in the Finance Act, 1910. Under this Act lower rates of stamp duty were introduced for property transactions under a certain value and, in the absence of what became commonly known as a 'Finance Act certificate', the maximum rate of duty was payable.

Certification in deeds was subsequently expanded to identify:

(a) the type of property being transferred under a deed, for example whether residential or non-residential;

(b) the nature of the transaction involved;

(c) whether an exemption from stamp duty applied; or

(d) whether a relief from stamp duty could be claimed.

The rationale behind certification in deeds was that the maximum rate of stamp duty would be chargeable unless the correct certification to support the lower rate or exemption being claimed was used. It should be noted that prior to 7 July 2012 the insertion of an incorrect certificate was an offence (SDCA, 1999, s 17). With effect from 7 July 2012 however there is no longer a requirement for the inclusion of such certificates in stampable instruments. Section 17 SDCA has been abolished in respect of instruments executed on or after that date.

As stamp duty certificates are no longer required in deeds the Conveyancing Committee of the Law Society in the December 2015 edition of the *Gazette* recommends that solicitors obtain a written record of instructions as to stamp duty. A suggested precedent record sheet is available on the[1] precedent page in the members' area of the website (www.lawsociety.ie/Solicitors/Practising/Precedents). This may then be retained on file by way of a future record, in addition to the copy printout available from the Revenue e-stamping system.

16.3.2.4 The charge to stamp duty—Territoriality

Stamp duty is a charge on certain written documents known as instruments which are listed under one of the headings as specified in Schedule 1 to the SDCA, 1999 and which is executed in the State or which relates to property situate in the State. 'Instrument' is defined in s 1 as including every written document. The most usual types of instruments on which stamp duty arises are deeds effecting transfers of lands or dwellinghouses, by conveyance, transfer, assignment, or lease. Once a document exists, it then becomes important to determine if it is possible for an exposure to stamp duty to arise. There must be a link between the document and Ireland. Territoriality is decided by ascertaining whether the document:

(a) is executed in the State; or

(b) relates to Irish property; or

(c) relates to something done or to be done in the State.

If the document is linked to Ireland in one or more of these ways, it will be exposed to Irish stamp duty. The nationality or residence of the parties to the instrument is irrelevant for stamp duty purposes, If any instrument listed in Schedule 1 of the SDCA, 1999 is executed in the State or relates to property situate in the State or relates to any matter or thing done or to be done in the State then it is chargeable to stamp duty.

A document is regarded as executed in the State if the formalities required to make it a legally effective document are completed in Ireland. For stamp duty purposes executed means signed.

16.3.2.5 Conveyance on sale

Once a document exists and that document is within the Irish territorial limits indicated earlier, an exposure to stamp duty will arise if the document is one of those listed in the First Schedule to the SDCA. As previously stated the documents listed in this schedule are referred to as 'heads of charge'.

The amount of stamp duty payable on any instrument depends on the purpose of that instrument. A document is chargeable to stamp duty if it comes within the heads of charge contained in the SDCA, 1999, as amended. The most common heads of charge, that is the basic categories of stamp duty, together with examples of how stamp duty is calculated under the head, are set out in the following text. The two main heads of charge for conveyancers include a conveyance on sale and a lease. A mortgage is no longer a head of charge.

Some of the heads of charge are subject to ad valorem duty and some of them are exposed to fixed type duty. Whether the stamp duty is charged at the ad valorem rates or the fixed duty rates depends on how the transaction evidenced or recorded in the instrument is classified. Conveyances on sale of shares are exposed to stamp duty at the rate of 1 per cent. Conveyances of Policies (for more than two years and with an Irish risk) are exposed to stamp duty at the rate of 0.1 per cent.

The most important head of charge in stamp duties is the 'conveyance on sale' head which deals with the sale of real property (houses, commercial premises, factory, farms, etc), and these are exposed to stamp duty at the ad valorem rate. Property is defined in s 1 of the SDCA, 1999 to include

> *every instrument, and every decree or order (including a decree or order for, or having the effect of an order for, foreclosure) of any court or of any commissioners, whereby any property, or any estate or interest in any property, on the sale or compulsory acquisition of that property or that interest is transferred to or vested in a purchaser, or any other person, or any other person on such purchaser's behalf or by such purchaser's direction.*

Thus, any document that is used to convey or transfer property to include houses, land, etc will attract stamp duty at the ad valorem rate. For a 'Conveyance' to be a Schedule 1 SDCA instrument it must be either 'on sale' or operate as a 'voluntary disposition' under s 30 SDCA.

To be 'on sale' there must be parties competent to contract, mutual assent, property, a vendor/donor and purchaser/donee, and a price or consideration.

Consideration for stamp duty purposes can take the form of cash, shares, satisfaction of debt, assumption of liabilities, or an exchange of property.

In addition the following instruments are treated as a conveyance on sale:

- a declaration of trust by a vendor in favour of a purchaser;

- a release by a life tenant of his life interest to the remainderman;

- a release by the remainderman of his remainder interest to the life tenant;

- the grant of an option.

16.3.2.6 Rates of stamp duty

There are five categories of rates. The first two are as follows:

(a) Conveyance on sale of residential property. This is dealt with at **16.4.2**.

(b) Conveyance on sale of non-residential property. The rates are set out at **16.3.2.7**. These rates apply to conveyances on sale not covered in (a) or in any other head of charge provided in the legislation. This head of charge applies in situations involving non-residential elements of a conveyance on sale containing mixed residential and non-residential property.

The remaining three categories of rates of stamp duties relate to conveyances on sale of stocks and marketable securities, policies of insurance, and CREST transfers on sale and are not dealt with in this text.

16.3.2.7 Rates of stamp duty on conveyance on sale or lease premiums of non-residential property for instruments executed after 6 December 2011

In the case of non-residential property, the rate of stamp duty is 2 per cent. This rate applies to instruments executed on or after 6 December 2011. This single rate of 2 per cent applies to the entire amount of the consideration attributable to non-residential property.

Aggregation

As a single rate of 2 per cent now applies to non-residential property, aggregation is no longer relevant in determining the stamp duty liability where a transaction forms part of a larger transaction or of a series of transactions involving non-residential property.

Non-residential property is any property other than residential property, stocks or marketable securities, or policies of insurance. It includes sites, offices, factories, shops, public houses, land, and goodwill attached to businesses.

16.3.2.8 Finance Act (transaction) certificates

This was the first form of certification introduced for stamp duty purposes and one that practitioners will be most familiar with. Originally this certificate dealt solely with the amount or value of the transaction but later it also identified whether the property was residential or non-residential in nature. The rationale for this certificate was to prevent the breaking up of a larger transaction into a number of smaller transactions in order to avoid a higher rate of duty. However for instruments executed on or after 7 July 2012 these certificates are no longer required to be included and s 17 of the SDCA has been abolished.

As they are no longer required in deeds, the Law Society Conveyancing Committee recommended in a Practice Note in the December 2015 *Gazette* that solicitors should obtain a written record of instructions as to stamp duty. A suggested precedent record sheet is available on the precedent page in the members' area of the website (www.lawsociety.ie/Solicitors/Practising/Precedents). This may then be retained on file by way of a future record in addition to the copy printout available from the Revenue e-stamping system.

16.3.2.9 Negligence provisions and the professional advisor

As discussed earlier, various Finance Acts have increased the scope of offences in the context of tax evasion, in particular for the professional advisor to a transaction. Any advisor who is involved in aiding and abetting a taxpayer to evade tax will be guilty of a criminal offence.

Similarly, money laundering legislation can impose a liability upon advisors who are not connected with such transactions, and in certain circumstances even if the advisor is not involved, failure to make the appropriate reports of a transaction may render the advisor liable.

Section 8 of the SDCA, 1999 in particular is relevant. Under s 8, there is an onus to bring to the attention of the Revenue the full facts and circumstances affecting the liability of an instrument to stamp duty. If these are not included in the instrument then the additional information must be disclosed in an accompanying statement. If the statement is incorrect, then any person employed or concerned in or about making the statement, will be responsible with the parties to the instrument for the breach of duty. Thus, s 134A provides for a penalty of €1,265 plus a tax geared further penalty where a person acts deliberately or carelessly in relation to the execution of an instrument in which:

(a)   All the facts and circumstances affecting the liability of the instrument to duty are not disclosed in the instrument or in a statement to which s 8(2) applies.

(b)   The delivery of an incorrect electronic or paper return under the e-stamping system,

(c)   The failure to deliver an electronic or paper return under the e-stamping system;

which gives rise to an underpayment in the amount of stamp duty due and payable. Professional advisors who are unsure as to whether certain facts are relevant may express to the Revenue their uncertainty and, provided the uncertainty expressed is genuine and not a tactic to evade or avoid stamp duty, a prosecution for negligence or fraud may be avoided.

Expression of doubt: s 8C of the SDCA

This section allows an accountable person, who is in doubt about the application of stamp duty to an instrument, to lodge a letter of expression of doubt with the Revenue. If the expression of doubt (EOD) is accepted by the Revenue as genuine, late filing interest will not apply to any duty payable on resolution of the doubt.

A letter of EOD must be clearly identified as a letter of expression of doubt and must meet certain additional criteria to be valid and must:

(a)   set out full details of the facts and circumstances affecting the stamp duty liability of the instrument;

(b)   make reference to the provisions of the law giving rise to the doubt;

(c)   identify the amount of stamp duty in doubt in respect of the instrument to which the expression of doubt relates;

(d)   be accompanied by any relevant supporting documentation;

This letter may be lodged with the Revenue at the Stamp Duty Office, Dublin Castle.

Both the letter of EOD and the electronic or paper return relating to the instrument must be lodged before the expiration of 30 days after the first execution of the instrument.

The Revenue has enhanced the right to reject the expression of doubt under s 8C(4) SDCA, 1999, which contains a non-exhaustive list of grounds on which the expression can be rejected. The Revenue may reject an EOD as not being genuine. Section 8C sets out situations where an expression of doubt will not be accepted by the Revenue to include:

(a)   where the Revenue have issued general guidelines on the matter;

(b)   where the Revenue are of the opinion that the matter is otherwise sufficiently free from doubt as not to warrant an EOD; or

(c)   where the Revenue are of the opinion that the accountable person was acting with a view to the evasion or avoidance of duty.

The Revenue will notify the accountable person if an expression of doubt is not accepted as genuine. On receipt of the notification, an amended return must be filed together with payment of the additional duty and interest. A right of appeal exists against the decision to reject the expression of doubt.

16.3.2.10 Stamp duty on documents

Section 64 of the Registration of Deeds and Title Act, 2006 amends s 104 of the Registration of Title Act, 1964. After the commencement of this section on 4 November 2006 the Registrar no longer has a 'duty' to check the stamp duty on each deed but may now proceed to register a deed unless there are 'reasonable grounds for suspecting' that stamp duty, or the correct amount of stamp duty, has not been paid.

16.4   Residential Property

Residential property is defined in s 1 of the SDCA, 1999 as a building or part of a building that, at the date of the instrument of conveyance or lease, was used or was suitable for use as a dwelling, or was in the course of being constructed or adapted for use as a dwelling. It includes also the normal domestic outhouses, garden, etc up to one acre. A rate of 1 per cent applies on the conveyance on sale or lease of residential property where the consideration does not exceed €1,000,000. Any excess over €1,000,000 is liable to stamp duty at the rate of 2 per cent.

16.4.1   RATES OF STAMP DUTY

Prior to the Finance Act, 2011 the rate of stamp duty applying to residential property depended on whether the residential property was a new or second-hand house or apartment, and the category of person buying it, ie whether a first time buyer or an owner occupier, or an investor. This is no longer the case. The rates have changed regularly over the last three years and the rates applicable are as stated earlier.

16.4.2   RESIDENTIAL PROPERTY RATES OF STAMP DUTY

The stamp duty regime for residential property was substantially amended and simplified by the Finance Act, 2010. The amount of stamp duty payable depends on the price/consideration paid or the market value where the price paid is less than the market value of the property.

Aggregate Consideration	Rate of stamp duty
Aggregate Consideration not exceeding €1,000,000	1%
Excess over €1,000,000	2%

Sample

Edwin purchases a house for €1,500,000.

The stamp duty payable is calculated as follows:

First €1,000,000	@ 1%	€10,000
Excess €500,000	@ 2%	€10,000
Total stamp duty		€20,000

'Residential property' is defined in s 1 of the SDCA, 1999 as a building or part of a building which, at the date of the execution of the conveyance or lease was used or was suitable for use as a dwelling. It also includes curtilage (that is the normal domestic outhouses, yard, or garden) up to one acre exclusive of the site of the residential property.

16.4.2.1 Aggregation

Aggregation applies in determining the stamp duty liability where a transaction forms part of a larger transaction or of a series of transactions involving residential property. The stamp duty liability is calculated on the basis of the aggregate consideration. The duty is then apportioned between the separate properties that are transferred by separate instruments and the apportionment is pro rata to the consideration for each property.

Where two or more residential properties are transferred as part of one or more connected transactions and the combined consideration exceeds €1,000,000, each of the instruments is stamped on the combined consideration valuation, that is, the instruments cannot be stamped separately to avail of the lower rate.

16.4.2.2 The rent-a-room scheme

Under the rent-a-room scheme, there was no claw back of the first-time purchaser's or owner-occupancy relief where rent was derived from the provision of fully furnished residential accommodation in part of the house while the owner-occupier or first-time purchaser continues to occupy the remaining part of the dwellinghouse or apartment as his or her only main residence. The scheme was introduced to encourage house owners to provide residential accommodation by renting out rooms in their own houses/apartments.

Claw back does occur if rent is obtained from the letting of the house other than in the circumstances already noted. The claw back amounts to the difference between the higher stamp duty rates and the duty paid. It becomes payable on the date that rent is first received from the property, if let within two years of the current purchase. If the house is let for example in the first year after the date of acquisition full claw back of stamp duty will result. It is not proportioned.

Under the rent-a-room scheme, the gross annual rental income of less than €10,000 is exempt from tax where a room or rooms in a person's principal private residence is let as residential accommodation. Furthermore, availing of this scheme will not adversely affect stamp duty relief on purchase of principal private residence, principal private residence capital gains tax relief on disposal, or mortgage interest relief.

The Finance (No 2) Act, 2000 and the Finance Act, 2001 make provision for the claw back of stamp duty in certain cases where a property or its owner ceases to meet the requirements set down by the Act in order to qualify for stamp duty relief. The Revenue Commissioners have confirmed to the Conveyancing Committee of the Law Society that it is not necessary for a subsequent purchaser to ascertain if any of the conditions giving rise to a claw back have occurred. A subsequent purchaser has no responsibility in relation to this relief (Practice Note, Law Society *Gazette*, May 2001).

If anyone derives rent from the property (other than the owner occupier) a penalty is charged which is equal to the amount of stamp duty that should have been charged together with interest (0.0322 per cent per day) from the date when rent is first received to the date the penalty is paid.

The person receiving the rent must notify the Revenue within six months from the date of the first receipt. The form of notification to the Revenue, which should be completed in conjunction with the payment of the claw back and interest (if any), is set out later in this paragraph. As the claw back is in the form of a penalty payable by the purchaser who originally obtained the benefit of the exemption or reduced rate of stamp duty, there is no need to re-present the original instrument for stamping where a claw back is incurred.

The sample form to notify the Revenue of receipt of rent or payment in the nature of rent to be filled in where relief was granted under ss 91, 91A, 92, 92A, and 92B SDCA, 1999 and rent was received subsequently within a period of two years from the date of execution of the document, as recommended by the Law Society is reproduced below.

Advice of Receipt of Rent or Payment in the Nature of Rent Claw Back of Stamp Duty Exemption/Relief granted under Section 91; 91A; 92; 92A; and 92B of the Stamp Duties Consolidation Act, 1999

This notification should be accompanied by (i) copy of the deed of conveyance/ lease, including related contracts, in respect of which exemption/relief was granted, and (ii) payment of penalty.

Part 1—Notification of Payment

(To be completed by the person who receives the rent or payment in the nature of rent other than rent in consideration of the provision, on or after 1 April 2004 in respect of section 91A, of furnished residential accommodation in part of the house/apartment)

(1) Stamp Duty Ref No: ....

     Name of recipient (in block capitals):..

     Address of recipient:..

     ....

     ....

     ....

(2) Address of Property subject of claw back: ....

     ....

     ....

     ....

(3) Date of receipt of first rent ....

(4) If recipient is not the owner state name ....

     and address of the owner:..

(5) Signature of Recipient:...

     Status of Recipient: .... Owner/Agent

     Date: _____

Part 2: Calculation of Claw Back and Penalty

(The penalty comprises the amount of stamp duty to be clawed back and any interest due*)

Calculation of Claw Back

(a)   Total purchase price: €_____

(b)   Less any Value-Added Tax: €_____

(c)   Net purchase price [(a)–(b)]: €_____

(d)   Amount of duty payable on net purchase price

had exemption/relief not been granted €_____

(e)   Less any stamp duty already paid: €_____

(f)   Amount of claw back [(d)–(e)]: €_____

Calculation of Interest due

(g)   From   / / to / /   €_____

Total amount due (amount of claw back plus interest [(*f*) + (*g*)]: €_____

16.4.3   NEW HOUSES AND APARTMENTS

The stamp duty implications of dealing with new houses and apartments are dealt with in **chapter 10** and are currently exactly the same as the rates applicable to second-hand residential property.

16.4.4   MIXED USE PROPERTY

16.4.4.1   Apportionment (s 45 of the SDCA, 1999)

Section 45 of the SDCA sets out how the consideration for a sale is to be apportioned in certain circumstances.

If the property being purchased is partly residential and partly non-residential, ie mixed use property, the consideration should be apportioned between the residential and the non-residential elements and the relevant rate of stamp duty applied to each portion of the consideration: ss 45(2) and 52(5) of the SDCA, 1999. The consideration must be apportioned on a just and reasonable basis between the residential and non-residential elements of the property. The vendor must provide a form headed 'Apportionment Statement' which should be retained by the purchaser's solicitor.

For such instruments, where an incorrect apportionment is included in the stamp duty return filed under the e-stamping system, penalties relating to the filing of an incorrect return will be incurred (see s 14(a)).

In a mixed use property situation the residential property part of the transaction is not aggregated with the non-residential portion for the purposes of determining the appropriate rate of duty. The consideration should be apportioned between the residential and non-residential elements on a just and reasonable basis and each type of property is to be separately certified to the applicable threshold and the appropriate rate of duty is chargeable in respect of each of the residential and non-residential parts of the transaction.

16.4.4.2   Apportionment details

Apportionment details are required (a) where a mixed use property is sold for one consideration or (b) where the sale of a wholly residential property or a mixed use property forms part of a larger transaction or a series of transactions. A suggested format for the furnishing of apportionment details is set out below. Whilst this will no longer be presented to the Revenue it should be retained on file in the event of a Revenue audit. In the case of (b), the aggregate consideration (including that portion attributable to contents) should also be apportioned where necessary as between the residential element and non-residential element comprised in the larger transaction or series of transactions.

These details are delivered under s 8(2) of the Stamp Duties Consolidation Act, 1999—as required by s 16(2) of the Stamp Duties Consolidation Act, 1999—because the property in question consists partly of an interest in residential property.

Re: Conveyance/Lease Dated:

Parties:

Apportionment by the Vendor(s)/Lessor(s):

In relation to the above-mentioned sale/lease:

  1. I/We state that the 'aggregate consideration'*is: €_____

  2. I/We estimate the 'residential consideration'**to be: €_____

  3. The basis for the estimate at 2 above is as follows:

....

....

....

Signed: _____ Date: _____

Signed: _____ Date: _____

Apportionment by the Purchaser(s)/Lessee(s):

In relation to the above-mentioned sale/lease:

• I/We state that the 'aggregate consideration'*is: €_____

• I/We estimate the 'residential consideration'**to be: €_____

• The basis for the estimate at 2 above is as follows:

....

....

....

Signed: _____ Date: _____

Signed: _____ Date:_____

Note: Any other facts or circumstances affecting the liability of the instrument to stamp duty should be disclosed, unless contained in the deed.

Where the property is mixed, that is part residential and part non-residential, for example living quarters over a shop or a farm sold together with the farmhouse, the residential rate of stamp duty will apply only to the residential element.

The apportionment form is available on the Revenue website.

Sample calculation

Darragh buys a building for €1,200,000 (net of VAT). It comprises a retail shop at ground floor level and a residential apartment overhead that he will live in. The amount of consideration attributable to the residential apartment is €300,000 and the shop is €900,000.

*As that term is defined in section 45(2)/52(5) of the Stamp Duties Consolidation Act, 1999.

**As that term is defined in section 16(1) of the Stamp Duties Consolidation Act, 1999.

The stamp duty on the deed is:

The stamp duty on the deed is:

Retail shop	€900,000 @ 2%	€18,000
Residential apartment	€300,000 @ 1%	€3,000
Total stamp duty		€21,000

Total stamp duty on shop and apartment is €21,000.

The apportionment details form set out earlier would have to be completed.

16.4.4.3   Anti-avoidance—asset splitting (s 45A SDCA, 1999) Simultaneous transactions

Before the Finance Act, 2005 the stamp duty rate on a dwellinghouse could be reduced by splitting the transaction. This arose where a house or an apartment is purchased by more than one purchaser and each purchaser takes a separate conveyance or transfer of the house or apartment in order to avail of the lower rate of stamp duty. Generally where there are a number of sales between two parties at or about the same time, irrespective of whether there is a single contract or several contracts, there is a strong presumption that each individual conveyance must form part of a larger transaction or of a series of transactions. The Finance Act, 2005 introduced an anti-avoidance provision with effect from 3 February 2005. Section 45A of the SDCA, 1999 was introduced to counter attempts at avoidance where a house or an apartment is purchased by more than one purchaser and each purchaser takes a separate conveyance or transfer of an interest in the house or apartment in order to avail of lower stamp duty rates. It provides that if an existing interest in a dwellinghouse is transferred by more than one instrument executed within a period of 12 months, the instruments will be deemed to form part of a larger transaction. In addition if the 'first transfer' of an interest in a dwellinghouse (occurring before or after 1 March 2005) is followed by a 'subsequent transfer' of other interests in the same dwellinghouse within a 12-month period the transferee of the first transfer will be liable to a claw back penalty together with interest at the rate of 0.0219 per cent per day from the date of execution of the instrument to the date the claw back is paid. The purpose of the section is to state beyond any doubt that the stamp duty on such conveyances or transfers will be determined on the basis of the value of the whole house or apartment for instruments executed on or after 5 November 2007. This section also extends to gifts made in a similar manner.

16.4.5   STAMP DUTY ON CONTENTS AND FIXTURES

Generally, stamp duty is not paid on the purchase of house contents, carpets, curtains, etc which will pass by delivery and are not included in the deed of assurance. Section 45A of the SDCA, 1999 as amended provides that the contents of residential property are not taken into account in determining the rate of stamp duty on the consideration attributable to that residential property. However, the total consideration must be apportioned on a bona fide basis between the contents and the property. The contents pass by delivery so no stamp duty is payable. In the event that the Revenue makes a finding that the property element has been undervalued, the Revenue has a right to seek surcharges.

16.4.6   STAMP DUTY EVASION

The Conveyancing Committee of the Law Society has, in various Practice Notes to the profession, pointed out the sanctions that will be incurred by solicitors who engage in stamp duty evasion on behalf of their clients. They advise that practitioners should be aware that apportionment of sale consideration in transactions relating to the sale of residential properties inclusive of contents should be made on the basis that realistic and correct values are attributed to such contents based, if necessary, on valuations from reputable auctioneers. Any apportionments made on the basis of spurious or excessive valuations of contents in such transactions clearly constitute evasion and are in breach of Revenue guidelines. Practitioners are also reminded of the powers available to the Revenue Commissioners to impose substantial financial penalties and other sanctions not only against the parties involved in such transactions but also against their solicitors and other professional advisors. The Law Society also condemns the practice on the part of purchasers' solicitors of engaging in and assisting in the practice of deliberately inflating the sale price of properties in excess of their real price to facilitate purchasers seeking and obtaining increased loans to finance purchase of property. This practice is not in accordance with good conveyancing practice and also constitutes fraudulent and unprofessional conduct, which would render practitioners assisting in such practice liable to serious sanctions by the Law Society.

16.5 Mortgage Head of Charge

Previously where property was purchased with the aid of a mortgage, stamp duty was chargeable on both the deed of assurance and on the mortgage deed.

However, there is no stamp duty payable for mortgage deeds executed on or after 7 December 2006. The mortgage head of charge in Schedule 1 to the SDCA, 1999 is abolished. Mortgage deeds covered by these provisions include primary collateral, additional, and equitable mortgages together with transfer of mortgages. This also applies to further advances made on or after 7 December 2007 in relation to existing mortgages.

16.6 Lease Head of Charge

The Lease head of charge applies to the creation of leases and not to the assignment of pre-existing leasehold interests which are stampable under the conveyance on sale head of charge. Stamp duty under the lease head of charge consists of two distinct charges:

(a) duty on any premium paid for the granting of the lease; and

(b) duty on the rent payable on the lease.

Both of these charges to stamp duty can, and frequently do, arise on the same transaction. The duty chargeable on the premium is at the rate for residential or non-residential property as appropriate. The rate of stamp duty on rent depends on the length of the term of the lease in question. A lease is chargeable to stamp duty under paragraph 3 of the 'Lease' head of charge in the SDCA, 1999.

16.6.1 RENT

The rate of stamp duty payable on rents depends on whether the lease is of residential or non-residential property. A lease for any indefinite term, or not exceeding 35 years, of a house or apartment is exempt from stamp duty where the annual rent does not exceed €30,000 per year. In all other cases the rate of stamp duty is determined by the term or length of the lease and the rent paid.

The rate of stamp duty payable on leases is as follows:

1. Where the lease does not exceed 35 years, or is indefinite (and the annual rent exceeds €30,000) stamp duty is chargeable at the rate of 1 per cent of the average annual rent.

2. Where the lease exceeds 35 years but does not exceed 100 years, stamp duty is chargeable at the rate of 6 per cent of the average annual rent.

3. Where the lease exceeds 100 years, stamp duty is chargeable at the rate of 12 per cent of the average annual rent.

In all cases duty is rounded down to the nearest euro.

If there is a rent review clause in the lease, an additional fixed duty of €12.50 is payable.

16.6.2   PREMIUM

In addition to any rent, a lease may also provide for the payment of a premium also known as a 'fine'. This is usually a one-off capital payment payable to the landlord by the tenant as part of the consideration for granting the lease. It is paid at the commencement of the lease. Where both a premium and a rent are paid stamp duty is payable on both. The rate applicable to premiums is essentially the same as the ad valorem rate applicable to conveyances on sale. The rate reliefs and exemptions have changed frequently over the years.

16.7   Conveyance by Way of a Sub Sale

The provisions relating to sub sales are contained in the SDCA, 1999, s 46. The relief applies in the situation where the owner of property X contracts to sell property to Y, and no deed of assurance has been executed on foot of the contract: then, prior to completion of this contract Y agrees to sell the property or part of it, to a sub purchaser Z) and, therefore, another contract exists between the purchaser Y for the further sale of the same property or part of it to a sub purchaser Z. If, by the direction of the purchaser Y the vendor X conveys the property directly to the sub purchaser Z, stamp duty is payable on the consideration paid by the sub purchaser Z, that is, on the conveyance to the sub purchaser Z only on the amount of the consideration passing between the sub purchaser Z and the purchaser Y irrespective of whether it is greater or smaller than the consideration paid to the vendor X. The legislation allows for a chain of sub-purchasers to be involved. As the conveyance is between the original vendor and the sub-purchaser the co-operation of the vendor is required for this relief to operate.

Sample sub sale:

Alan contracts to sell his house in Donnybrook to Bob for €500,000. Before the property is conveyed to him Bob contracts to sell the same property to Christian for €600,000. Under Bob's direction, Alan conveys the property by a single conveyance on sale directly to Christian, with Bob joining in to transfer any beneficial interest he may have. Stamp duty is charged on the conveyance on sale to Christian only in respect of the consideration of the €600,000 paid by Christian to Bob.

The property is residential.

Stamp duty is payable as follows:

€600,000 @ 1% is €6,000.

Stamp duty payable is €6,000.

Consanguinity relief was not available in relation to a sub sale (SDCA, 1999, s 46(5)).

16.7.1   EXCHANGES OF PROPERTY

The law concerning exchanges is now contained in the SDCA, 1999, s 37 which provides that where an exchange of immovable property (that is land and buildings) is effected, full ad valorem stamp duty will be charged on the value of all the property being transferred. Previously, stamp duty was payable only on the inequality of value in the property which was the subject matter of the exchange. These provisions apply in cases where immovable property is exchanged for other immovable property. It also applies where some consideration was paid for example where the properties were of unequal value. In effect therefore, deeds of exchange are chargeable to stamp duty based on the value of lands and buildings therein conveyed. The value of any other property or any equality money paid is ignored. Where immovable property situate in the State is exchanged for foreign property immoveable or otherwise, stamp duty is payable on the value of the Irish property only.

16.7.2   DEEDS OF FAMILY ARRANGEMENT

Deeds of family arrangement are used when the beneficiaries under a will or the persons entitled to a share on intestacy decide to rearrange the benefits by means of substitution and exchange. Such deeds are executed by the beneficiaries, and the legal personal representative then proceeds to distribute and vest the property in the beneficiaries by means of a deed of assent which was exempt from stamp duty. However, where any beneficial interest passes under the terms of a deed of family arrangement, then full ad valorem stamp duty is payable. This category of instrument has sometimes been overlooked in relation to stamping, as the Land Registry is precluded from seeking production of same when registering transmissions on death by virtue of s 54(2) of the Succession Act, 1965 and s 61(3) of the Registration of Title Act, 1964. These sections provide that 'it shall not be the duty of the Registrar, nor shall he be entitled to call for any information as to why any assent or transfer is or was made and shall be bound to assume that the personal representative is or was acting in relation to the application, assent or transfer correctly and within his powers'. This has generated a mistaken belief that deeds of family arrangement in respect of registered land for deaths occurring on or after 1 July 1966 do not attract stamp duty because they do not have to be produced in order to vest good title in a beneficiary. This is not the case. Great care should be taken to ensure that they are fully stamped in accordance with the statutory provisions previously specified. Even though the deed of family arrangement, duly stamped, may not be produced to the Land Registry, it still forms part of the title deeds to the property and must be retained. In addition these deeds should be entered into within two years of the date of death to ensure that they do not constitute a disposal for capital gains tax purposes.

16.8   Fixed Duties

The fixed duty charge of €12.50 was abolished under the Finance Act, 2007 in respect of instruments executed on or after 2 April 2007 in relation to the following heads of charge in Schedule 1 of the SDCA, 1999:

> 'Conveyance or Transfer of any kind not already described in Schedule 1.'

> 'Exchange' (other than an exchange chargeable under s 37 of the SDCA, 1999. This section imposes a charge to ad valorem duty on exchanges involving immovable property.)

> 'Release or Renunciation of any property, or of any right or interest in any property (other than an instrument which operates as sale or a gift).'

> 'Surrender of any property or of any right or interest in any property (other than an instrument which operates as a sale or gift).'

There is no need to present such instruments to the Revenue prior to being lodged in either the Land Registry or the Registry of Deeds.

16.8.1   STAMP DUTY ON GIFTS—VOLUNTARY DISPOSITIONS INTER VIVOS: S 30 OF THE SDCA

A transfer by way of a voluntary gift inter vivos is chargeable to stamp duty in the same way as a transfer on sale with the market value of the property being substituted for the consideration.

Where property is transferred as a gift or for less than its full value, stamp duty is charged on the market value of the property transferred. This is the price that the property would make if sold on the open market. A voluntary disposition is not a conveyance on sale as there is no sale (SDCA, 1999, s 30). However it is chargeable to stamp duty as if it were a conveyance on sale and the market value of the property being conveyed or transferred determines the rate of duty payable. In the case of land and buildings, residential and non-residential, the rates of stamp duty in the case of a voluntary disposition are the same as those that apply to conveyances or transfers on sale. For instruments executed on or after 7 July 2012 where an incorrect apportionment is included in the stamp duty return filed under the e-stamping system penalties relating to the incorrect filing of a return will be incurred (see s 134A). Prior to 7 July 2012 s 30(3) of the SDCA, 1999 provided that a voluntary deed must be lodged for adjudication with the Revenue Commissioners. Adjudication is now abolished in respect of all instruments executed on or after 7 July 2012. The mode of valuing property for the purposes of the SDCA, 1999, s 30 is set out in ss 18 and 19. In the case of an instrument, which operates as a voluntary disposition inter vivos, all parties are accountable for the payment of stamp duty (s 30(1) and s 54(1)).

Section 8(5) of the SDCA imposes an obligation on all parties to a voluntary transfer to ensure that the Revenue are aware from the stamp duty return delivered under the e-stamping system that the transfer is by way of gift and the market value must be set out in the return. If the parties to the instrument fail to provide this information they are regarded as having acted deliberately for the purpose of s 134 A(2)(a) until the contrary is proven.

16.8.2 INFORMATION FROM PROPERTY REGISTRATION AUTHORITY

A new s 137A of the SDCA, 1999 was introduced by the Finance Act, 2010 to allow the Revenue to obtain information from the Property Registration Authority as might be required by the Revenue for the purposes of the SDCA, 1999. In addition, the Revenue are also required to furnish details to the Property Registration Authority, at such intervals and as requested, such information as might be required by the PRA to consider stamp duty in relation to documents presented for registration.

16.8.3 RESTING IN CONTRACT: S 31A OF THE SDCA

16.8.3.1 Licence agreements S31B and Agreements for more than 35 years: s 50A

The Finance Act, 2013 changed the previously used legitimate stamp duty avoidance scheme where instead of taking a conveyance or transfer of land, the full purchase price was paid by or on completion and the purchaser relied on the contract, that is the transaction 'rested on contract'. In that way no stamp duty was paid unless at some time in the future the purchaser sought a conveyance or transfer.

Section 31A of the SDCA as inserted by the Finance Act, 2013 provides that a charge to stamp duty will arise on a contract or agreement for the sale of an estate or interest in land in the State where 25 per cent or more of the consideration for the sale has been paid to the holder of the estate or interest. The charge will arise where a stamp duty return has not been filed and stamp duty paid in respect of a conveyance or transfer of the lands concerned within 30 days after that amount of consideration has been paid. This charge under s 31A applies to instruments executed on or after 13 February 2013. However, the charge will not apply where an instrument is executed solely in pursuance of a binding contract or agreement entered into before 13 February 2013.

A subsequent conveyance or transfer will not be chargeable to stamp duty.

The contract or agreement for sale is chargeable to stamp duty as if it were a conveyance or transfer of the estate or interest where a payment which amounts to 25 per cent or more of the consideration for the sale has been paid. The charge does not apply where, within 30 days of the date of the payment of 25 per cent or more of the consideration,

(a) a stamp duty return is filed in relation to a conveyance or transfer made in conformity with the contract or agreement for sale; and

(b) the stamp duty chargeable on the conveyance or transfer has been paid to the Revenue.

The Revenue will refund any duty paid on the contract if the contract is later rescinded or annulled. While this section does not specify the time limit for submitting claims for a refund, a four year time limit is provided by s 159A from the date the contract is stamped in respect of a valid claim for a refund. Interest may arise on the refund (s 159B of the SDCA).

Similarly this will also apply to licences given to builders by developers to enter on to lands to develop, that is to build houses, apartments, or other non-residential buildings or carrying out any engineering or other operations to adapt it for materially altered use. The stamp duty is assessed on the market value of the land. This is provided for in s 31B of the SDCA which provides that a charge to stamp duty will arise on certain licence agreements relating to land in the State under which the licensee is allowed to carry out development on that land and 25 per cent or more of the market value of the land is paid to the licensor, other than as consideration for the sale of all or part of the land. The charge under s 31B applies to instruments executed on or after 13 February 2013.

The charge will also apply where long leases greater than 35 years are created under an agreement for lease as provided for in s 50A.

The overall effect of these three sections is that contracts, building licences, and agreement for leases in excess of 35 years are to be treated as conveyances for sale/leases in certain circumstances.

16.9 Exemptions and Reliefs

Certain instruments are exempted from the charge to stamp duty or bear a reduced amount of stamp duty. Part 7 of the SDCA, 1999 lists both the instruments that are exempt from stamp duty and the reliefs from stamp duty available in certain situations. Prior to the termination of the adjudication process for instruments executed on or after 7 July 2012, in order to benefit from an exemption or relief the instrument may or may not have had to be presented for adjudication to the Revenue. For instruments executed on or after 7 July 2012 a self-assessed return must be filed under the e-stamping system in order to benefit from an exemption or relief.

If the exemption or relief is general then the instrument is not liable to stamp duty under any head of charge in Schedule 1.

The Finance Act, 2011 was enacted on 6 February 2011. It included, *inter alia*, the abolition of certain reliefs and exemptions from stamp duty on residential property. The following reliefs and exemptions were abolished with effect from 8 December 2010:

• s 83A SDCA, 1999—transfer of a site from a parent to a child;

• s 91A SDCA, 1999—exemption for purchaser of a new house or apartment not exceeding 125 square metres by an owner-occupier;

• s 92 SDCA, 1999—exemption for purchaser of a new house or apartment where the floor area exceeds 125 square metres by an owner-occupier;

• s 92B SDCA, 1999—exemption for purchaser of a house or apartment by a first-time purchaser;

• consanguinity relief on residential property and on all non-residential property (apart from agricultural property) from 31 December 2015 (see **16.9.7**).

The following are instruments of which a self-assessed stamp duty return must be filed under the e-stamping system in order to obtain the exemptions and reliefs available.

16.9.1   SECTION 79 SDCA ASSOCIATED COMPANIES

Conveyances and transfers of property between certain bodies corporate and instruments dealing with the reconstruction and amalgamation of companies are exempt from stamp duties (SDCA, 1999, ss 79 and 80 respectively). Section 79 of the SDCA, 1999 grants a relief from stamp duty on certain transfers of property between associated Irish and/or non-Irish associated companies under the conveyance on sale head only. The relief does not apply to the leasing of property between such entities. The relief also applies to voluntary dispositions and dispositions between all 'bodies corporate' which include industrial and provident societies, limited and unlimited companies, and foreign companies. Section 79 of the SDCA, 1999, contains claw back provisions providing that a claw back of the exemption will now apply if any of the three tests of ownership cease to be met within two years after the date the instrument is executed. The following conditions must be satisfied before the relief will be granted. The instrument in respect of which the relief is sought must convey or transfer a beneficial interest in property from one body corporate to another:

(a)   One company must own beneficially 90 per cent or more of the ordinary share capital of the other company, or a third company owns over 90 per cent of the ordinary share capital of both, directly or indirectly;

(b)   The company must be entitled to 90 per cent or more of the profits available for distribution to the shareholders of the other company;

(c)   The company must be entitled to 90 per cent or more of the assets available for distribution to the shareholders of the other company on its winding up.

It is further provided that stamp duty exemption will be denied between two companies in a 90 per cent relationship if the instrument or transfer is executed in pursuance of or in connection with any arrangement whereby any part of the consideration is to be provided or received by any person who or which is not a company in a 90 per cent relationship with either the transferor or the transferee though meeting all three tests.

In relation to stamp duty relief for company reconstruction and or amalgamations set out in s 80 of the SDCA, 1999, a self-assessed stamp duty return must be filed in relation to the instrument in respect of which the relief is claimed. Section 68 of the Finance Act, 2004 provides that in relation to the conveyance or transfer on sale head (immovable property) where this forms part of the transfer of an undertaking, the s 80 exemption will only apply if there has been an actual conveyance to the transferor company before the reconstruction or amalgamation.

16.9.2   LAND ACQUIRED BY APPROVED SPORT BODIES

Stamp duty is not chargeable on any conveyance, transfer, or lease of land to an approved sport body approved under s 235 of the Taxes Consolidation Act, 1997 where the land will be used for the sole purpose of promoting athletic or amateur games or sports. The relief is now contained in s 82B of the SDCA, 1999. A self-assessed stamp duty return must be filed under the e-stamping system in relation to the instrument in respect of which the exemption is sought.

16.9.3   TRANSFER OF STOCK OR MARKETABLE SECURITIES UNDER €1,000

The transfer of certain stock or marketable securities where the consideration paid is €1,000 or less qualifies for an exemption from the 1 per cent rate of stamp duty payable on stock transfer forms.

16.9.4 TRANSFERS BETWEEN SPOUSES/CIVIL PARTNERS/CERTAIN QUALIFIED COHABITANTS

The Civil Partnership and Certain Rights and Obligations of Cohabitants Act, 2010 ('the 2010 Act'), which came into effect on 1 January 2011, did not include any tax provisions, and the taxation measures required were published in the Finance (No 3) Act, 2011, which applies from 1 January 2011. The Act provided that the tax treatment of registered civil partners mirrors that of married couples. Section 96 of the SDCA, 1999 (as amended) provides that a conveyance or transfer or lease of any property between spouses/civil partners is exempt from stamp duty unless the transfer is a transfer referred to in s 46(1) to (4) of the SDCA (sub-sales), whether the property is transferred by a spouse/civil partner or spouses/civil partners of a marriage to either spouse/civil partner or to both spouses/civil partners of that marriage/civil partnership. If any other person is a party to the instrument the exemption does not apply. Section 14 of the Family Home Protection Act, 1976 (as amended) exempts from stamp duty an assurance of a family/shared home into the joint names of both spouses/civil partners. An application form of such assurance is also exempt from stamp duty. Also where any property, which is not a family/shared home, is transferred between spouses/civil partners the relevant deed of assurance is exempt from stamp duty. However, Registry of Deeds application forms of these assurances are liable to stamp duty at the rate of €50. These provisions are now contained in s 96 of the SDCA, 1999. The exemption from stamp duty will not apply if the property is transferred to any person other than a spouse/civil partner. Spouses/civil partners do not cease to be spouses/civil partners as a result of a deed of separation or a decree of judicial separation or on the dissolution of the civil partnership.

Section 97A of the SDCA exempts from stamp duty certain transfers of property between former cohabitants. All transfers of property from one cohabitant to his or her cohabitant made pursuant to an order under s 174 of the Civil Partnership and Certain Rights and Obligations of Cohabitants Act, 2010 are exempt from stamp duty. The exemption only applies to transfers between the cohabitants. If any other person is a party to the instrument the exemption does not apply.

16.9.5 CERTAIN TRANSFERS FOLLOWING THE DISSOLUTION OF MARRIAGE OR CIVIL PARTNERSHIP AND CERTAIN TRANSFERS BY QUALIFIED COHABITANTS

It is provided in s 97 of the SDCA, 1999 that certain conveyances following the dissolution of marriage or the dissolution of a civil partnership are not chargeable to stamp duty where the conveyance is on foot of certain specified court orders. Section 97 provides that stamp duty is not chargeable on an instrument by which property is transferred pursuant to:

(1) a relief order under s 23 of the Family Law Act, 1995 made following the dissolution of marriage; or

(2) an order under Part III of the Family Law (Divorce) Act, 1996; or

(3) where property is transferred between former spouses pursuant to a foreign court order or other determination to like effect made on or after 10 February 2000, which is similar to an order referred to at (1) or (2) above of a court under the law of another territory made or in consequence of the dissolution of a marriage, being a dissolution that is entitled to be recognised as valid in the State; or

(4) an order under Part 12 of the Civil Partnership and Certain Rights and Obligation of Cohabitants Act 2010.

After divorce, spouses cease to be such, and therefore enjoy an exemption from stamp duty only if the provisions of s 97 above apply. The exemption does not apply in relation to an instrument by which any part of or beneficial interest in the property concerned is transferred to a person other than the spouses concerned. If any other person is a party to the instrument the exemption does not apply.

Section 97A of the SDCA, 1999 provides for an exemption from stamp duty where a property is transferred pursuant to an order under s 174 of the 2010 Act by a cohabitant to his or her cohabitant. If any other person is a party to the instrument the exemption does not apply. This section applies to transfers made on or after 1 January 2011.

16.9.6   CONVEYANCES ON SALE AND VOLUNTARY DISPOSITIONS TO YOUNG TRAINED FARMERS

Section 81AA of the SDCA provides an exemption from stamp duty where agricultural land, including such farm buildings, farm houses, and mansion houses occupied therewith is conveyed/transferred to young trained farmers. The purpose of the relief is to encourage the transfer of lands into the hands of a younger more trained generation of farmers. The parties to the deed do not have to be related for the relief to apply. The relief applies to both conveyances on sale or voluntary dispositions executed after 2 April 2007, and has been extended to transfers executed on or before 31 December 2018. The relief although applying to both sales and gifts does not apply to leases or where a power of revocation exists. A power to revoke the transfer, whether it is contained in the instrument conveying or transferring the lands or otherwise, will disqualify the young trained farmer from the relief. To be a young trained farmer, an individual must show that he or she was under the age of 35 at the date of execution of the instrument and that he or she has completed one of the qualifying farming courses set out in Schedule 2B to the SDCA, 1999 and in s 81AA of the Act.

In order to qualify for the relief a self-assessed return must be filed under the e-stamping system in relation to the instrument in respect of which the relief is sought.

The relief also applies where the agricultural land is conveyed or transferred to joint owners where all satisfy the conditions for granting the relief (SDCA, 1999, s 81(4)). The only exception to this rule is where the land is being transferred into the joint ownership of a husband and wife or to a civil partner. In such cases only one of the spouses or civil partners must be a young trained farmer and meet the conditions set out earlier. The section provides a revised list of qualifications, establishments, and revision to the standards of those qualifications. This relief has now been extended to 31 December 2014. The Finance Act, 2007 included changes relating to education criteria and a simplified refund procedure governing the relief for young trained farmers contained in s 81AA of the SDCA, 1999. To qualify as a young trained farmer the minimum requirement will be a FETAC Level 6 Advanced Certificate in Agriculture, rather than a minimum number of hours training. The qualifying third level course titles are being updated.

Furthermore, if the farmer receives land, pays stamp duty, and subsequently qualifies as a young trained farmer, the farmer will be required to retain and farm the land for a period of five years from the date which the claim for a refund of duty is made to the Revenue. Also, there will be no requirement that a refund be made within a set time period.

It appears that the Minister has tightened up the minimum educational requirements for young trained farmers to ensure that only genuine farmers qualify for the relief. In addition where an EU Single Farm Payment (SFP) in respect of the land to be transferred has been received such a payment will also qualify for the exemption from stamp duty.

The definition of agricultural assets for the purposes of capital acquisitions tax in respect of gifts and inheritances now includes the EU SFP entitlement.

This effectively means that the entitlement can be counted as an agricultural asset in determining whether or not the individual will pass the so-called farmer test and in so doing qualify for a 90 per cent reduction in the taxable value of the gift or inheritance received.

Similarly, the EU SFP entitlement will qualify as an asset for capital gains tax and for retirement relief from capital gains tax provided that the farmer in question fulfils the other criteria attaching to the relief such as the minimum ten-year period of ownership.

16.9.7 CONSANGUINITY RELIEF

If parties to a transaction are related to each other they may qualify for a reduction in stamp duty. Stamp duty at the rate of one half the ad valorem or normal rate is chargeable where a relationship exists between the parties to the deed and this is known as consanguinity relief. This relief is available in the case of either a sale or a gift of property between certain related persons and the instrument is stamped at 50 per cent, the specified rate for such instrument. The relief is not available in relation to a lease or the transfer of stocks or marketable securities *nor is it available for residential property for instruments executed on or after 8 December 2010 or for non-residential property apart from agricultural land after 31 December 2015.*

In the case of farming land consanguinity relief continues to apply to instruments executed;

1. On or after 1 January 2015 and before 1 January 2016 in respect of transfers or conveyances of land by a person of any age; and

2. On or after 1 January 2016 and before 1 January 2018 in relation to transfers or conveyances of land but only where the individual transferring the land has not reached the age of 67 years at the date of the transfer or conveyance.

In addition the individual to whom the farmland is being transferred or conveyed must be an active farmer and must from the date of execution of the transfer or conveyance:

1. Farm the land for a period of not less than six years; or

2. Lease it for a period of not less than six years to an individual who will farm the land, or lease the land to a partnership or to a company whose main shareholder and working director farms the land on behalf of the company.

The person who farms the land (including the partners or working director in the case of a company), or the individual, to whom the land is leased, must:

(a) Be the holder of (or within a period of four years from the date of the deed of transfer/conveyance, become the holder of) a qualification set out in Schedule 2, 2A, or 2B of the SDCA, 1999; or

(b) Spend not less than 50 per cent of the individual's normal working time farming land including the land being transferred. The Revenue accepts that 'normal working time' approximates to forty hours per week. This will enable farmers with off-farm employment to qualify for the relief provided they spend a minimum of twenty hours per week working on the farm;

(c) The land must be farmed on a commercial basis with a view to the realisation of profits from the land.

In order to avail of the relief, each of the persons to whom the property is transferred must be related to each of the transferors to the required degree. The degree of relationship is mainly based on direct ancestry and extends to nephews and nieces but does not include cousins or in-laws. The relief is provided for in paragraph 15 in Schedule 1 to the SDCA, 1999, and the list of related persons who may qualify for consanguinity relief includes a lineal descendant, parent, grandparent, step-parent, husband or wife, brother or sister of a parent or brother or sister, or lineal descendant of a parent, husband or wife or brother or sister.

'Lineal descendant' is also now defined in s 1, in relation to a conveyance or transfer (whether on sale or as a voluntary disposition inter vivos), to include a person who, as transferee, is a child of the transferor. The 'child' would be interpreted in the context of the above definition and will also include a child as defined in s 2 of the Adoption Act, 2010. This would include as a relative for the purpose of consanguinity relief, a foster brother or foster nephew, foster uncle, etc.

16.9.8 FAMILY FARM TRANSFER RELIEF

Section 83B of the SDCA, 1999 provides for an exemption from stamp duty on certain transfers of farmland from a child to a parent in the context of certain family arrangements to which the provisions of s 599 of the Taxes Consolidation Act, 1997 apply for capital gains tax purposes. A child includes a child of a deceased child, certain nephews, nieces, and foster children. A self-assessed stamp duty return must be filed under the e-stamping system in order to obtain the exemption.

16.9.9 COMMERCIAL WOODLANDS

Section 95 of the SDCA, 1999 provides partial relief from stamp duty in respect of certain instruments relating to the sale or lease of lands on which commercial woodlands/trees are growing. The relief only applies to a sale or lease of land and is not available in the case of a gift.

The trees must be growing on a substantial part of the land. While 'substantial' is not defined in the legislation the Revenue will consider each case on its merit. A substantial part is regarded as not less than 75 per cent of the land. The woodlands must be managed on a commercial basis and with a view to making a profit.

The relief applies to the portion of the consideration which represents the value of the trees growing on the lands. An apportionment of the consideration between the land and the trees growing on the lands is required.

16.9.10 CHARITIES

Section 82 of the SDCA, 1999 provides an exemption from stamp duty for conveyances, transfers, and leases of lands which will be used for charitable purposes in the State or Northern Ireland to a body of persons established solely for charitable purposes or to the trustees of a trust so established.

The appropriate charity (CHY) number must be quoted on the instrument. If charity exemption status has not already been obtained an application form must be completed and the exemption status obtained.

On receipt of the CHY number a self-assessed stamp duty return must be filed under the e-stamping system to obtain the exemption.

16.9.11 TRANSFERS BY HOUSING AUTHORITY OR AFFORDABLE HOME PARTNERSHIP NOW STAMPABLE

Paragraph 3 of Schedule 1 to the Stamp Duty (E-stamping of Instruments) Regulations, 2009 (SI 476/2009) lists instruments that do not have to be stamped using the e-stamping system. They include instruments giving effect to the conveyance, transfer, or lease of a house, building, or land to or by a housing authority or the Affordable Homes Partnership (AHP).

However, with effect from 1 April 2011, s 64 of the Finance Act, 2011 (which amended s 106B SDCA, 1999):

(a) removed the stamp duty exemption that applied on the transfer of property by a housing authority or the AHP; and

(b) limited the stamp duty payable on such transfers to a maximum of €100.

As a result of these changes paragraph 3 of the Stamp Duty (E-stamping of Instruments) Regulations, 2009 (SI 476/2009) has been amended by the Stamp Duty (E-stamping of Instruments) (Amendment) Regulations, 2011 (SI 87/2011). These regulations now provide that only transfers to a housing authority or to the AHP do *not* have to be stamped.

Accordingly, any instrument executed on or after 1 April 2011 that gives effect to the conveyance, transfer, or lease of a house, building, or land by a housing authority or the

Affordable Homes Partnership must be stamped through the e-stamping system and any stamp duty, up to a maximum of €100, must be paid.

(See the Law Society *Gazette* Practice Note of June 2011.)

16.10 Adjudication

Section 20 of the SDCA, 1999 provides for the accountable person to include an assessment of the duty in the return filed in relation to an instrument under the e-stamping system and also enables the Revenue, in certain circumstances, to assess the amount of duty chargeable on an instrument. The Finance Act, 2012 abolished the requirement for adjudication for instruments executed on or after 7 July 2012. Prior to that, in order to benefit from an exemption or relief from stamp duty the instrument had to be presented to the Revenue for adjudication. Adjudication of an instrument for stamp duty purposes meant that the Revenue Commissioners determined the correct amount of stamp duty that owed on the instrument if any. The adjudication stamp will appear on many deeds executed on or before that date.

Adjudication is no longer possible in respect of instruments executed on or after 7 July 2012 nor can adjudication be requested by the Revenue or the taxpayer. For instruments executed on or after that date a self-assessed stamp duty return must be filed under the e-stamping system in order to obtain the exemption or relief.

Although the Revenue no longer retain the power to adjudicate documents, they have the power to require the taxpayer to produce the instrument together with such evidence (including statutory declarations similar to those routinely required in adjudicated transactions) as they deem necessary in order to establish that the instrument has been properly stamped. In addition the Finance Act, 2012 gave the Revenue new powers to inspect and require the production of documents held by, or on behalf of, an accountable person which are backed up with significant penalties for non-compliance.

16.11 Dealing with Agricultural Land

Significant changes have been made to the direct payment schemes by which farmers and others using agricultural lands receive subsidies related to that land. Practitioners are referred to the news piece by Oliver Ryan-Purcell, solicitor, which highlights the issues involved published in the November 2014 *Gazette* at p 10. In a Practice Note in the February 2015 edition of the *Gazette* practitioners dealing with farmland are advised that they should be aware of the information contained in a publication (CAP 2015; 'An Introduction to Direct Payments') available on the Department of Agriculture website at www.agriculture.gov.ie (follow CAP 2015 Direct Information Centre). This contains examples of what happens in commonly arising situations of sales, leases, gifts, and inheritances of land and entitlements during the transition from the existing single payment scheme to the new basic payment scheme and how in certain circumstances, the right to apply for payments under the basic payment scheme in 2015 (the 'allocation right') will transfer with land.

16.12 New Stamping System

16.12.1 E-STAMPING

The Revenue Commissioners commenced the operation of an e-stamping system on 30 December 2009 in accordance with SI 476/2009 entitled Stamp Duty (e-Stamping of

Instruments) Regulations, 2009. Details of the system, which also provides details for paying stamp duty, can be found on the Revenue website (www.revenue.ie).

The new system called e-stamping applies to every document that requires to be stamped. Each solicitor should register with the Revenue Online System (ROS) as, in order to use the e-stamping system, solicitors must be registered with ROS. Practitioners must also set up a Revenue debit instruction to authorise the online payment of stamp duty.

On 1 June 2011 it became mandatory to file stamp duty returns through ROS (subject to very limited exceptions) and to make payment of stamp duty through ROS.

On 1 June 2011, the e-stamping regulations were amended to remove the optional ability to file a paper form of stamp duty return as an alternative to an electronic stamp duty return. The Revenue have made regulations under s 17A of the SDCA, 1999 on mandatory electronic stamp duty returns and payment of stamp duty (Stamp d=Duty (E-stamping of Instruments) (Amendment) (No 2) Regulations, 2011 (SI 222/2011). The Revenue have made the following regulations in relation to the filing of self-assessed returns under the e-stamping system—The Stamp Duty (E-stamping of Instruments and Self-assessment) Regulations, 2012 (SI 234/2012).

The amended regulations allow the Revenue to exempt a person from having to pay and file electronically where they are satisfied that the person does not have the capacity to do so. Incapacity is limited to cases where there is insufficient access to the internet or where an individual is prevented by reason of age or physical or mental infirmity from filing and paying electronically. A person aggrieved by the failure of the Revenue to exempt them from having to pay and file electronically can bring an appeal to the Appeal Commissioners.

In order to file a stamp duty return through ROS it will be necessary to include the PPS number for individuals (or tax reference number for others) of all the parties to the document to be stamped even if the parties to the deed are non-resident. Practitioners should start collecting this information as soon as possible in all transactions involving the potential stamping of an instrument, and preferably before the instrument is executed (which should be verified where possible) to enable the instrument be stamped. Otherwise there is a real risk that late filing and interest charges will arise. Returns with incorrect PPS or tax reference numbers will be rejected by the Revenue.

The PPS number is an individual's unique reference number for all dealings with the public services including tax, education etc. However a PPS number does not become an individual's tax reference number until such time as it has been registered with the Revenue as that individual's tax reference number. Consequently if a PPS number is input into an e-stamping return before it is registered as a tax reference number with the Revenue, it will not be recognised by, and the return will be rejected by, the e-stamping system. In addition the Local Property Tax ID number is required since 30 November 2013 for residential property.

As most people are already registered for tax with the Revenue, the easiest way to check a tax reference number is to obtain a copy of recent correspondence from the Revenue to the client, for example a tax credit certificate or PAYE balancing statement, or a notice of assessment in the case of an individual.

As and from 7 December 2015 a tax reference type is no longer a mandatory field when completing an e-stamping return.

The main changes introduced under the new system include:

(a)   a comprehensive stamp duty return setting out all relevant particulars and information required to calculate duty and issue the stamp;

(b)   a new form of stamp;

(c)   a facility to stamp deeds online;

(d)   the extension of tax reference number requirements to apply to all instrument types;

(e)   more reliance by the Revenue on post-stamping checks and audits.

16.12.2 STAMP DUTY RETURNS

Stamp duty returns must be completed and filed electronically for every instrument executed on or after 1 June 2011, with a few exceptions. On execution of an instrument that requires stamping, the practitioner files a stamp duty return with the Revenue on behalf of the client together with any stamp duty payable. This return must be filed electronically or in paper format (the latter in limited circumstances only). The completed stamp duty return will contain all the information needed to calculate the stamp duty and to stamp the instrument. On receipt of the return and payment when validated by the Revenue, the Revenue electronically issues the practitioner with a stamp certificate which must then be printed and attached to the instrument to denote that it has been stamped. If a paper return is made the stamp certificate will issue in hard copy. The return will be used to generate the stamp.

The former foil/holograph stamp is replaced by the stamp certificate.

A stamp duty return should not be filed in the case of any of the following instruments:

1. An instrument creating a joint tenancy between spouses or civil partners to which s 14 of the Family Home Protection Act, 1976 applies.

2. A conveyance, transfer, or lease of a house, building or land by or to a Housing Authority or the Affordable Homes Partnership to which s 106B (Housing Authorities and Affordable Homes Partnership) of the SDCA applies.

3. A lease for any indefinite term or any term not exceeding 35 years to which paragraph (1) under the heading 'lease' in Schedule 1 to the SDCA applies, or an instrument to which s 108B (National Asset Management Agency) of the SDCA applies.

16.12.3 STAMP CERTIFICATE FORMAT

Each stamp certificate bears its own unique security number and other specific details that will associate it solely and clearly with one particular instrument only. The stamp certificate will need to be printed in paper form whether the return was submitted in electronic or paper format. Returns filed electronically, and completed correctly, will result in the immediate issue of a stamp certificate online in cases not subject to adjudication.

Returns filed in paper format will result in the issue of a stamp certificate by post some days later. A facility to amend details on a submitted return is provided for both electronic and paper returns.

An instrument is considered to be duly stamped when the stamp certificate is attached to it.

The stamp certificate contains the Revenue logo and the following elements:

(a) stamp certificate security number (stamp certificate ID). The security number will be alpha numeric and will always have 20 digits and be in the following format:

12-0123456-A12B-DDMMYY-A

(b) document ID number;

(c) date of instrument;

(d) parties' names;

(e) address and folio number (if registered) of the property;

(f) chargeable consideration;

(g) duty (including for leases the rental element) and all penalty amounts whether mitigated in full or in part;

(h) reliefs applied;

(i)   adjudication marker;

(j)   date of issue of stamp certificate;

(k)   counterpart marker.

Should a stamp certificate be lost or need to be verified, the e-stamping system will allow the Revenue to issue duplicate stamp certificates and to verify the authenticity of a stamp certificate.

Under the new system the instrument itself will not be presented to the Revenue before stamping except in certain cases, such as in refund applications, penalty mitigations, where additional information is required, or where the case is subject to an expression of doubt or the case is selected by the Revenue for assurance check or audit.

Even in cases where the instrument is presented the Revenue will use the return to calculate the duty payable and to generate a stamp certificate. Any instrument or documentation presented to the Revenue in support of the return will be sent back to the practitioner pending issue of the stamp certificate.

16.12.4 LOST DEEDS

Under the pre-ROS system a deed on which stamp duty had been paid was sometimes lost. It was then necessary to produce a substitute deed to prove the owner's title to the property. In such cases the Revenue would agree to stamp the substitute deed without the stamp duty being paid a second time, provided adequate evidence could be produced to show that the original deed was properly stamped. The claimant would usually have to produce a statutory declaration giving evidence in relation to the lost deed.

Under the e-stamping system a return is filed on ROS and a record of the return will be on record. The stamp certificate with its unique ID number and security code can be reprinted.

16.12.5. RECENT CHANGES TO E-STAMPING

In a Practice Note in the January 2016 edition of the *Gazette* the Law Society Taxation Committee outlined the changes made to e-stamping screens applicable since 7 December 2015 by the National Stamps Office which are as follows:

1.   A tax reference type for the parties to the instrument will no longer be required when completing an e-stamping return. However in a small number of cases (less than 1 per cent) the tax reference type may be sought by the e-stamping system for verification purposes.

2.   Re individuals: PPS Numbers received from the Department of Social Protection and not registered for any tax will continue to require registration by the National Stamp Duty Office (NSDP) prior to the number being used on an e-stamping return.

3.   Re foreign companies: foreign companies which are not (or were not at any time in the past) registered for tax will continue to have to apply to the NSDO for a tax reference number.

4.   The 'consideration' field on the ROS dropdown window has been increased to allow input of 11 digits preceding the decimal point (eg the system will in future accept a consideration up to a maximum of €99,999,999,999,00).

5.   The local authority 'field' in the Address Details section of the e-stamping return (for residential property) can now be amended where a change of address entry is made.

The above information and further information on tax reference numbers and other stamp duty issues is available on the Revenue website.

16.13 Capital Gains Tax

Capital gains tax (CGT) was introduced in 1974. It is a tax on the gain arising on the disposal of a capital asset by a chargeable person to include land, buildings, and shares in a company on or after 6 April 1974. Because it is a tax on disposals (ie not just a sale), gifts come within its scope. The standard rate of tax is currently 33 per cent. Various other rates apply, for example, a rate of 40 per cent applies to certain foreign life assurance policies and units in off shore funds, while rates of 12.5 per cent and 15 per cent apply to certain venture capital fund managers. Other rates apply in exceptional cases, for example windfall tax, which is charged at the rate of 80 per cent. In addition the Finance Bill, 2015 introduced a revised CGT relief for entrepreneurs, 'entrepreneur relief', which allows a reduced rate of 20 per cent CGT, which applies from 1 January 2016 in respect of chargeable gains arising on the disposal of chargeable assets. There is a lifetime chargeable gain limit of €1m, and the current standard rate of 33 per cent CGT applies to gains in excess of this amount.

Certain assets are excluded from the tax and some gains are relieved from the tax. There was an allowance for inflation, that is the base cost or purchase price is multiplied by an indexation factor. However, this relief known as indexation relief will apply only for the period of ownership of the asset up to 31 December 2002. Gains accruing to persons are chargeable to capital gains tax, whereas gains accruing to companies are generally chargeable to corporation tax (except in the case of development land). The Finance Bill, 2015 revised the provisions for CGT payable on the disposal of certain development lands which were zoned after 30 October 2009.

The taxation of capital gains is incorporated into the Taxes Consolidation Act, 1997 (the TCA, 1997) as amended by subsequent Finance Acts. Previously, it was governed by the Capital Gains Tax Act, 1975 and the Corporation Tax Act, 1976 as amended by the Capital Gains Tax (Amendment) Act, 1978 and subsequent Finance Acts. The Finance Act, 2012 introduced full self-assessment for chargeable persons and obliges the disponer or their agent to self-assess when making a tax return and the legislation allows for penalties where no self-assessment is made.

16.13.1 SCOPE OF CAPITAL GAINS TAX

Section 28 of the Capital Gains Tax Act, 1975 provides that tax shall be charged in respect of *chargeable gains* computed in accordance with the Act and accruing to a *person* on the *disposal* of *assets*. It is necessary for all of these four conditions to arise in order for a charge to capital gains tax to arise (subject to a limited number of exceptions). Since the introduction of the calendar tax year by s 77 of the Finance Act, 2001, this year of assessment now runs from 1 January to the following 31 December.

The tax year is divided into two periods for payment purposes as follows:

• initial period 1 January to 30 November both inclusive;

• later period 1 December to 31 December both inclusive.

The due date for payment of capital gains tax is now as follows:

• disposals in the initial period: tax is due by 15 December in the same tax year;

• disposals in the later period: tax is due by 31 January in the following tax year.

CGT can be returned as part of the income tax return or, where a tax return is not otherwise required, on a CGT return (Form CG1). The return must be submitted by 31 October in the year following the tax year in which the disposal is made.

If CGT is not returned and paid when due surcharges and penalties will apply.

16.13.2 PERSONS CHARGEABLE

A person's liability to capital gains tax generally depends on the following factors, namely domicile, residence, and ordinary residence and the location and type of the asset disposed of. Any person who is resident or ordinarily resident and domiciled in the State for a year of assessment is liable to tax or chargeable to tax on chargeable gains accruing on all disposals of chargeable assets made during that year. The same applies to a company in respect of the chargeable gains accruing to it for a chargeable period during which it resided in the State. In relation to a person who is resident or ordinarily resident in the State but is not domiciled, gains realised on disposals of assets situated outside the State and the United Kingdom are liable to tax only to the extent that the gains are remitted to this country and such gains are not chargeable to tax until so remitted. Everyone is liable to capital gains tax on the disposal of Irish land. Where someone is neither resident nor ordinarily resident in Ireland they are chargeable on gains on specified Irish assets only, for example land in Ireland.

16.13.2.1 Residence

A statutory definition of residence is set out in s 819(1) of the Taxes Consolidation Act, 1997 (TCA 1997).

Residence status for Irish tax purposes is determined by the number of days a person is present in the State during a given tax year. Section 819(1) sets out the two basic tests of residence. A person will be tax resident in the State in a tax year if:

(a) he or she is present in the State for a period amounting to 183 days or more in that calendar tax year—the current year test; or

(b) he or she is present in the State for 280 days taking the current and preceding calendar years together—the two-year test. An individual who is present in the State for 30 days or less in a tax year will not be treated as resident for that year unless he or she elects to be resident.

Up to the end of 2009 an individual was deemed to be present in the State for a day if he or she was in the State at the end of a day—midnight (a 'Cinderella' test). Effectively it was the nights spent in the State which were counted. From 2009 forward a taxpayer is 'present in the State' for a day if he or she is present at any time during that day.

16.13.2.2 Ordinary residence

Section 820(1) of the TCA, 1997 contains the definition of ordinary residence. This refers to an individual's pattern of residence over a number of tax years. If a person has been resident in the State for three consecutive tax years, he or she is regarded as ordinary resident for the beginning of the fourth tax year. Ordinary residence implies a greater degree of permanence than simply being resident. Once an individual becomes ordinary resident in the State he or she will remain ordinary resident until or unless he or she is non-resident for three consecutive years.

16.13.2.3 Domicile

The TCA 1997 does not contain a definition of domicile. This is because domicile is a common law legal term rather than a tax specific term. Under common law, every person must have a domicile. A person can have only one domicile at any particular time but cannot be without a domicile. There are three kinds of domicile:

1. Domicile of origin.

2. Domicile of choice.

3. Domicile of dependence.

It is broadly interpreted as meaning residence in a particular country with the intention of residing permanently in that country.

16.13.2.4 Assets

All forms of property wheresoever situate are assets for the purpose of capital gains tax. Assets include land, houses, other buildings, sites be they developed or green field and with or without planning permission, shares in a company, incorporeal property, for example, goodwill or an option, and any interest in property, including a lease. However, Irish currency is not an asset for the purpose of the tax, nor are prize bonds or lottery and gaming winnings or gains from the disposal of Irish government stocks or securities and gains from the disposal of one's principal private residence.

16.13.2.5 Disposals and date of disposal and acquisition

The disposal of an asset includes any transfer of ownership of the asset by way of sale, exchange, gift, or settlement on trustees. A part disposal occurs where less than the whole of an asset is disposed of or an interest in an asset is transferred, for example the granting of a lease at a premium. Disposals which are not made at 'arm's length', for example gifts, are deemed to have been made at market value.

The main rules for determining the time/date of disposal and acquisition for capital gains tax purposes are as follows:

1. For a disposal under an unconditional contract the date of disposal and acquisition is the date of the contract, and not the completion date.

2. Where the contract is subject to a condition, the date of disposal and acquisition is the date the condition is satisfied, not the completion date. A contract is conditional if a condition must be satisfied before an obligation to perform the contract arises. For example where the acquisition of land is subject to the purchaser obtaining planning permission, the time of the disposal and acquisition is the date the permission is obtained.

16.13.2.6 Indexation relief (adjustment for inflation): s 556 of the TCA, 1997

Each year up to 2003 the Revenue issued indexation factors which were based on the consumer price index and compensated for inflation. Indexation relief permitted the effects of inflation to be taken into account in computing chargeable gains. Indexation relief was not available for disposals made within 12 months of acquisition. If the expenditure incurred in acquiring or enhancing an asset was incurred more than 12 months before its disposal, the amount of that expenditure was adjusted to take account of inflation. The adjustment was made by multiplying the relevant item of allowable expenditure by a factor 'the multiplier' which reflects the change in the all items consumer index during the period since the asset was incurred and the year of assessment in which the disposal is made. A table of multipliers for the year ending 2002 is available. The indexation table is based on the tax year in which the asset was acquired (columns on the left side) and the tax year in which it was sold (top of the table). Assets owned at 6 April 1974 are deemed to have been disposed of and reacquired on that date. Thus if an asset was acquired before 6 April 1974, its market value on that date is used as the base cost. Indexation relief applies to all assets without exception but is restricted in the case of development land. However, no allowance for inflation will be allowed for future years of ownership from 31 December 2002, and indexation relief will apply only for the period of ownership of an asset up to 31 December 2002.

Example of indexation

Land is bought on 15 June 1980. This is in the tax year 1980–81. It is disposed of on 12 May 2000. This is in the tax year ending 5 April 2001. The indexation factor is 2.833. There is no indexation if you sell within 12 months of purchasing an asset.

The Finance Act, 2003 abolished inflation indexation with effect from 3 December 2002. The 2003 indexation factors are used for 2003 and later years, and have not been increased since 2003.

16.13.2.7 Annual personal exemption

There is an annual exemption of €1,270 per individual which is not transferable between spouses/civil partners. The first €1,270 of an individual's net gain (that is, gains less loss including losses brought forward from earlier years) are not chargeable. If either individual cannot utilise the exemption it cannot be transferred to the other. The annual exemption applies to individuals only—companies, trustees, or other non-corporate bodies are not entitled to it.

16.13.2.8 Sample computation of gain

The three main headings for CGT deductions are:

• the cost of acquisition together with any incidental costs;

• enhancement expenditure;

• incidental costs of disposal.

The amount of chargeable gain or an allowable loss is determined by deducting any allowable expenditure from the consideration received for the disposal.

The capital gain is the difference between:

(a)   the consideration for the disposal of the asset or the deemed consideration (for example market value in the case of a gift or disposal between connected persons); and

(b)   the cost of acquisition of the asset or its market value if not acquired at arm's length and any expenditure incurred on its which is reflected in the state of the asset at the time of disposal: expenditure to establish, preserve, or defend legal title. This may be adjusted to take account of inflation; and

(c)   the incidental costs of making the disposal, such as legal fees and selling costs may also be deducted.

Section 542 of the TCA, 1997 provides that where the disposal occurs by contract the date of disposal is the date of the contract and is not the date of the subsequent deed of assurance.

The following is a sample layout of a capital gains tax computation in relation to an asset:

Niall Murray—Capital Gains Tax computation for 2016.

Facts

Niall Murray a developer sold lands for €1,000,000 on 31 December 2015 paying costs of sale of €20,000. He had inherited the land in May 2006 at which time the land was valued at €400,000.

Sale proceeds		€1,000,000
Less		
Allowable costs of sale	€20,000	
Original cost/market value		
at date of acquisition	€400,000	
No indexation post 2003		
No enhancement expenditure.		
Base cost		€420,000
	Gain	€580,000
	Less annual allowance	1,270
	Taxable Gain	€578,730
Capital Gain Tax @ 33% €190,980.9		

Sample CGT layout for computation

TAX YEAR 31 December 20 .

1. Date of Disposal (generally the date of the Contract for Sale)

2. Description of Asset

3. Date of Acquisition

Computation.   €

4. Disposal consideration

Less

5. Incidental costs of Disposal (if any)

6. Net Disposal consideration (4-5)

Deduct allowable costs of sale	€
7 & 8. Original cost of acquisition of asset market value as at date of acquisition	X Multiplier INDEXED @ (X Multiplier)
Incidental costs of acquisition/purchase	Indexed to 2003
9 & 10. Enhancement expenditure	Indexed to 2003
	X Multiplier

11. Total indexed cost

12. Capital Gain/Loss after indexation (6-11)

13. Actual monetary gain (or loss)

14 & 15. Chargeable gain

14 & 15. Allowable loss

If these are any unused losses from previous year insert the amount here

Calculation of Capital Gains Tax payable

16. Total chargeable gains net of allowable losses

17. Less annual personal exemption €1,270

Less relief (if any)

Net Chargeable gain
Capital Gains Tax payable: Taxable gain @ 33%. (In 2016)

16.13.2.9 Incidental costs of disposal and acquisition

Incidental costs of disposal mean the expenditure wholly and exclusively incurred for the purposes of the disposal. The disposal consideration is the value of the consideration received on disposal for example the sale price in the case of a sale at arm's length. If the disposal is not made by a bargain at arm's length then the consideration is equal to its market value at the time of disposal. Any disposal proceeds received in foreign currency must be converted to Irish currency by reference to the rate of exchange at the time of the disposal. The following costs are allowable deductions when doing the capital gains tax computation and they may be deducted from the consideration received for the disposal:

(a)   the cost of acquisition of the asset and costs such as surveyors, estate agents, auctioneers' fees to include valuation fees, and costs in relation to the transfer for example stamp duty and legal fees;

(b)   expenditure incurred for the purpose of enhancing the value of the asset that is reflected in the state of the asset at the time of disposal; and

(c)   incidental costs of making the disposal, for example legal fees and advertising costs.

If the asset was acquired by inheritance on a death, by way of gift or on a transfer from a trust, it is the market value at the date of death, gift or transfer that is to be used. If the asset was acquired prior to 6 April 1974 the allowable cost to be entered in the computation is the market value as at 6 April 1974. In the case of a part disposal of an asset, only part of the original cost is allowed.

Items included in (a) and (b) may be adjusted to take account of inflation.

Note: on or after 2003, the multiplier is 1.

16.14   Enhancement Expenditure

Enhancement expenditure is the cost of additions to the asset, after the date of acquisition, which adds to the value of the asset and is reflected in the asset at the date of sale. Expenditure must be reflected in the state of the asset at the time of disposal. Interest paid is not an allowable deduction for capital gains tax purposes. Where enhancement expenditure has been incurred on an asset, the cost and each subsequent item of enhancement expenditure is treated as separate assets for the purposes of indexation relief. The chargeable gain is calculated as the difference between the various items of expenditure that is both original cost and enhancement expenditure as adjusted for indexation and the sale proceeds. Generally, expenditure qualifies as 'enhancement' if it includes an element of improvement, for example building a new garage, conservatory, landscaping, or an attic conversion is 'enhancement', whereas routine maintenance such as painting or rewiring a house is not. It also includes expenditure incurred to establish, preserve, or defend legal title. To be deducted the expenditure must not have proved futile or have wasted away before disposal.

It should be noted that deductions may only be made in respect of expenditure wholly and exclusively incurred in connection with the acquisition, enhancement, or disposal of an asset.

16.15   Losses

Where there is a loss on a disposal, it will generally be allowable if the gain on the same transaction would be chargeable. Special provisions apply in relation to development land.

16.15.1   DISPOSALS ON A DEATH

Death does not give rise to a capital gains tax liability. Section 573 of the TCA, 1997 deals with the passing of assets on a death. The assets, which a deceased person was competent to dispose of, are deemed to be acquired on his or her death by the personal representative or by the beneficiary at the market value at the date of death. The deemed transfer at market value at the date of death does not give rise to a chargeable disposal for capital gains tax purposes and accordingly, no liability will attach to the estate of the deceased in respect of any gains realised on the asset over his or her lifetime. The converse is also true in that no allowable losses are crystallised on a death. The base cost for the purposes of a subsequent disposal, by the personal representatives or by the beneficiaries, of an asset acquired on death will be the market value at the date of death, irrespective of when the death occurred and indexation relief is applied from the date of death to this base cost. If the death occurred before 6 April 1974, then the market value at 6 April 1974 will form the base cost. If the personal representative sells any property during the administration period, there may be a liability to capital gains tax—but only to the extent that the value of the property in question has increased between the date of death and the date of sale.

The distribution of property by the personal representative to the beneficiaries does not give rise to a capital gains tax liability.

Section 104 of the Capital Acquisitions Tax Consolidation Act, 2003 provides that if CGT and CAT payable on the acquisition of a property by way of gift or inheritance arise on the same property on the same event the person paying the CAT can credit the amount of CGT paid by the disponer (the person making the gift) against his CAT liability. The credit granted for CGT paid will cease to apply and there will be a claw back of the relief where the property the subject matter of the gift or inheritance is disposed of within two years.

16.15.2   DEVELOPMENT LAND

Development land means land, including a building, in the State which is disposed of for a price higher than its current use value. Special provisions apply to chargeable gains arising from disposals of development land (see ss 648–653 of the TCA, 1997). Development land is defined for capital gains tax purposes and the test relates to the value of the land rather than its use. The current use value is the value of land assuming it is unlawful to carry out development (other than development of a minor nature). The current use value may be defined as the value the land would have if no development other than development of a minor nature could be carried out in relation to the land. The special provisions include restrictions on indexation, roll over relief, and relief for losses.

16.15.2.1   Restriction on relief

In relation to development land, indexation relief is confined to the amount of the current use value of the land at the time of acquisition or at 6 April 1974, if acquired prior to that date. One can allow but cannot index the development value. Enhancement expenditure is allowed but cannot be indexed. Only those parts of incidental costs of purchase relating to the current use value can be indexed; the balance costs are allowed, but cannot be indexed. The rules relating to restriction of indexation and loss relief, and restriction of availability of roll over relief, which normally apply to the sale of development land, are specifically excluded from operation where the total sales consideration (not the amount of the gain) does not exceed €19,050 in any year of assessment. This special relief is restricted to an individual and is not available to a company.

Where an individual sells, for example, part of his or her garden to a builder who builds a house on it a charge to capital gains tax arises. Normally when an individual disposes of his or her principal private residence and a garden or gardens of up to one acre (excluding the site of the house), then any gain on such a disposal is exempt from capital gains tax. However where a dwellinghouse or garden or part of a garden is sold for greater than its current use value, then this constitutes the sale of development land and the principal private residence relief will only apply to the current use value. In general terms the difference between the consideration and the current use value is liable to capital gains tax.

16.15.2.2   Windfall gains tax

The National Asset Management Agency (NAMA) introduced a 'windfall gains tax' on certain capital gains. This tax is charged at a rate of 80 per cent in respect of a disposal of development land (and where both a rezoning and a disposal took place on or after 30 October 2009) and ending 31 December 2014. The Finance Act, 2010 widened the scope of the provisions by introducing a relevant planning decision which includes both a rezoning and a material contravention of a development plan. This change applies to decisions made on or after 4 February 2010.

A relevant planning decision will, in general terms, mean a change in the zoning of land from non-development land use to another development land use, including a mixture of such uses.

It also applies to a decision to grant permission for a development that would materially contravene a development plan. The 80 per cent rate is charged on the amount by which the land increased in value as a result of the relevant planning decision. The remainder of the gain will be taxed at the 33 per cent rate with effect from 7 December 2013.

The windfall tax will not apply in relation to gains derived from relevant planning decisions where:

(a) the disposal of land occurs as a result of a compulsory purchase order;

(b) the disposal is by a company in which NAMA owns any part of the ordinary share capital, or by a company which is an effective 75 per cent subsidiary of such company;

(c) the disposal is of a site of 0.4047 hectares or less whose market value at date of disposal does not exceed €250,000, other than where the disposal forms part of a larger transaction or of a series of transactions. This exemption applies regardless of whether planning permission has been granted for the disposal.

There are provisions included to ensure that the 80 per cent charge cannot be sidestepped by a transfer between connected persons.

The Revenue Commissioners can be contacted in order to provide full information as to the definitions above but it may be necessary to consult with the relevant local authority to establish if a relevant planning decision has been taken in any particular case.

16.15.3 EXEMPTIONS AND RELIEFS

16.15.3.1 Personal exemption

There is an annual exemption of €1,270 per individual which is not transferable between spouses or civil partners. A husband and wife and two civil partners are separate persons for capital gains tax purposes and their gains and losses should be computed separately. The residence status of each spouse or civil partner must be considered individually to decide whether or not that person is chargeable to capital gains tax. It is the first €1,270 of an individual's net gain (gains less losses, including losses brought forward from earlier years) that is exempt. The chargeable gains accruing to a married woman/civil partner in any year of assessment during which she is living with her husband/civil partner will be assessed on the husband/civil partner unless an application for separate assessment for capital gains tax purposes has been made. The relief only applies to individuals; companies, trustees or other non-corporate bodies are not entitled to it.

By virtue of the Finance (No 3) Act, 2011 the tax treatment of registered civil partners, which applies from 1 January 2011, mirrors that of married couples. Civil partners can be assessed jointly to CGT on chargeable gains accruing in a year of assessment during which they are living together, and the CGT will be assessed and charged on the civil partner who is the nominated civil partner.

16.15.3.2 Disposals of a site from a parent to a child

A capital gains tax exemption for the disposal of a site to a child of the transferor is provided for in s 603A inserted into the TCA, 1997. Section 603A of the TCA, 1997 has been extended by including the 'foster child' as defined at **16.15.4.1** in the definition of a child of a parent and this takes effect from 31 March 2006. No capital gains tax is payable on the disposal of a site from a parent to a child on or after 6 December 2000, where the site is valued at €500,000 or less, and the purpose of the transfer is to enable the child to build a principal place of residence on the land which the child will occupy as his or her only or main residence. If the value of the site exceeds €500,000, there is no provision for relief up to that amount so that capital gains tax is payable in the normal way. The word 'site' is not defined in s 603A, except by reference to 'land'. On a subsequent sale of the site (other than a disposal to a spouse or civil partner), the child pays capital gains tax on the site transfer unless he or she can show that a dwellinghouse was built on the site and he or she occupied it as his or her only or main residence for a period of at least three years. If the child disposes of the site without building the dwellinghouse and occupying it for at least three years the child must at that stage pay capital gains tax on the site transfer. The area of the site must not exceed 0.4047 hectare (one acre) exclusive of the area on which the house is to be built.

16.15.3.3 Principal Private Residence relief

Generally any gain arising on the disposal of the main residence of an individual is exempt from capital gains tax. Grounds up to one acre (exclusive of the site of the house) around the house are exempt. This exemption is contained in the TCA, 1997, s 604.

If there is more than one acre, then the acre to be taken into account is that which would be most suitable for occupation and enjoyment with the residence. The exemption is available if the dwellinghouse, or part of the dwellinghouse, was occupied by the individual as his or her only or main residence throughout the period of ownership, or under certain circumstances, as the sole residence of a dependent relative. In the case of a married couple/civil partners living together, only one house can qualify as the principal private residence of both spouses/civil partners. A person with two or more residences will nominate which one will qualify for relief and will agree this with the Revenue. There is full relief only where the owner has occupied the house throughout the period of ownership. Full relief may not be due if only part of the house has been used as the individual's residence, in which case an apportionment is made to arrive at the exempt portion of the total gain (partial relief) This may happen where the house is used partly for business purposes or where rooms in the house have been let.

However, availing of the rent-a -room scheme introduced by the Finance Act, 2001 will not affect an individual's full entitlement to Principal Private Residence relief on the subsequent disposal of the property.

There are special provisions in the legislation setting out certain circumstances in which the individual is deemed to have occupied the premises for example where the individual is required, because of work commitments, to reside outside the State or elsewhere in the State, principal private residence relief may be available, because of the 'deemed occupation' principle. However a period of the last 12 months before a principal private residence is sold is deemed to be the period of occupancy even though the individual may not have been actually living in it during that period. Periods of foreign or local employment will only qualify as periods of occupation if the individual occupies the residence both before and after the periods as their only or main residence and has no other house eligible for exemption. The relief does not apply where the house was acquired wholly or mainly for the purposes of making a gain on disposal.

16.15.3.4 House occupied by dependent relative

The principal private residence relief is also available to a gain arising on the disposal of a second dwelling owned by an individual and occupied without payment by a dependent relative as his or her principal private residence. A dependent relative is a relative of the owner or his or her spouse/civil partner who is either incapacitated by old age or infirmity from maintaining himself, or the widowed father or mother of the individual or his or her spouse/civil partner whether or not he/she is incapacitated by old age or infirmity.

16.15.3.5 Separated, divorced spouses and spouses inter vivos, and separated civil partners

Inter vivos disposals between spouses/civil partners are dealt with in the TCA, 1997, s 1028 which provides that no capital gains tax will arise on transfers between spouses/civil partners provided they are living together. In effect an inter vivos transfer between spouses/civil partners is ignored for tax purposes. When, at a further date, the transferee spouse/civil partner disposes of the asset, that spouse/civil partner will be deemed to have acquired the asset at the same time and for the same cost as the transferring spouse/civil partner.

Where assets are transferred between separated or divorced spouses in certain specified circumstances by virtue of, or in consequence of a deed of separation or an order made or following judicial separation or an order made under Part III of the Family Law (Divorce) Act, 1996, such disposal will not give rise to a capital gains tax liability (see ss 1030 and 1031 of the TCA, 1997). This relief now applies to civil partners under Part 12 of the 2010 Act which provides that a charge to capital gains tax does not arise where a person disposing of a civil asset is a former civil partner following a court order on the dissolution of the civil partnership. Similarly a charge to CGT does not arise where a person disposes of an asset to a former cohabitant as a consequence of a court order under Part 15 of the 2010 Act.

16.15.4 RETIREMENT RELIEF

16.15.4.1 Disposal of a business or farm within the family

Certain gains arising on the disposal of 'qualifying assets' by an individual who has attained the age of 55 years and has owned the assets for ten years or more may be exempt from capital gains tax if certain conditions are satisfied (see TCA, 1997, s 599). This relief is commonly referred to as 'retirement relief', but there is no requirement that the individual in question should actually retire. The amount of relief that will be available depends upon whether the assets are disposed of to the individual's children or alternatively, to third parties.

Up to 31 October 2013, irrespective of the amount of the consideration for the disposal, total relief from capital gains tax could be claimed by an individual aged fifty-five or over on the disposal to his or her child of the whole or part of his or her qualifying asset, for example farm or business assets or shares in the family company. A disposal to a niece or nephew who has worked full time on the farm or in the business for the previous five years similarly qualified for the relief.

The Finance Act, 2011 introduced measures to promote the early transfer of family farms. Full retirement relief from capital gains tax on transfers within the family will be maintained for individuals aged between 55 and 66 years. The Act introduced an upper limit of €3,000,000 on retirement relief for business and farm assets disposed of within the family where the individual transferring ownership is over 66 years. Where the market value of the asset disposed of to the child is more than €3,000,000 relief will be given as if the consideration was €3,000,000.

Unrestricted relief will continue to apply to individuals aged 55 or over but who have not attained the age of 66. The relief is clawed back where the child disposes of the asset within six years of the date of acquisition from his or her parent.

Section 71 extends the retirement relief of s 599 (disposals within the family of business or farm) by including along with the favourite nephew or niece provisions, a 'foster child'—same definition as appears in the capital acquisitions tax legislation.

For this purpose, the term 'child' includes not only the favourite nephew or niece but also includes a foster child who is defined as:

> (ii) *an individual (in this paragraph referred to as the 'first mentioned individual') who resided with, was under the care of and was maintained at the expense of the individual making the disposal throughout—*
>
> - *a period of five years, or*
> - *periods which together comprised at least five years*
>
> *before the first mentioned individual attained the age of eighteen years but only if such claim is not based on the uncorroborated testimony of one witness.*

Although the legislation now applies, and a 'foster child' can qualify for relief under these provisions, there must be corroborating evidence of his or her residence etc. For the future, we should advise clients in this situation to keep records of time, expenditure, and any other factors which might be regarded as evidence. This relief is now extended to the child of a deceased child and to a child as defined in s 2 Adoption Act, 2010. In the case of a nephew or a niece they must have worked full time in running or assisting in the running of the business concerned for a minimum of five years ending on the date of the disposal.

16.15.4.2 Disposal of a business or farm outside the family

The retirement relief provisions in s 598 of the TCA, 1997 were amended by subsequent Finance Acts. This section provides that from 1 January 2014 where the sale proceeds on the 'qualifying assets' do not exceed (currently) €750,000 total relief from capital gains tax may be claimed from gains accruing to an individual aged between 55 and 65 years on the disposal of the whole or part of his or her business assets or farm or shares in his or her family company, owned for ten or more years, subject to certain conditions.

The Finance Act, 2010 amended the retirement relief provisions. The amendments clarified the position that an individual can come within the scope of the retirement relief provisions on the proceeds of a disposal of shares pursuant to a qualifying redemption, repayment, or purchase by a family company of its own shares. Therefore the payments will fall within the scope of the €750,000 threshold relevant to CGT retirement relief.

The upper limit for retirement relief for business and farming assets transferred outside the family is reduced from €750,000 to €500,000 for individuals aged over 66 years. Where the individual disposing of the asset is 66 years or over and the consideration exceeds €500,000 marginal relief applies so as to limit the amount of CGT payable to one half the amount of the consideration and €500,000. Where the individual disposing of the asset is 66 years or over and the consideration does not exceed €500,000 relief is given in respect of the full amount of the CGT chargeable. The reduction of the amount to €500,000 given to individuals aged 66 or over applies to dispositions on or after 1 January 2014.

16.15.4.3 Retirement relief

The relief was extended to disposals of farmland which has been leased prior to disposal. To qualify, the land must:

- have been leased for no longer than five years prior to disposal;
- have been owned and used for farmland by the disponer for ten years prior to the initial letting; and
- be disposed of to the person leasing the land.

This charge applies only to disposals to individuals other than qualifying family members as no value cap is placed on the relief relating to qualifying disposals to a child/favourite niece/nephew/foster child as per **16.15.4.1**.

16.15.4.4 Relief for disposal of property purchased between 7 December 2011 and 31 December 2013

The Finance Act, 2011 introduced a new relief from capital gains tax in respect of properties purchased between 7 December 2011 and 31 December 2013. Where the property was held for more than seven years no capital gains tax will arise on any gain attributable to that seven-year period. The Revenue has confirmed that this relief is not extended beyond 31 December 2014.

16.15.4.5 Entrepreneur relief

The Finance Bill, 2015 introduced a new entrepreneur relief and provides for a reduced rate of CGT of 20 per cent in respect of a chargeable gain or chargeable gains arising on the disposal of certain business assets made by an individual on or after 1 January 2016 up to a lifetime limit of €1m.

The chargeable business must be owned by that individual for a minimum period of three years prior to the disposal of those assets.

The relief will not apply to disposals of chargeable business assets by companies or to disposals of development lands or a business consisting of dealing in or developing land, a business consisting of the letting of land or buildings, or holding investments.

Where the business is carried on by a private company, individuals seeking to qualify for the relief must own not less than 15 per cent of the shares of the company and at least 15 per cent of the shares to a holding company which owns 100 per cent of the company. The shareholder must be a full-time working director of the company for a minimum of three years prior to the disposal of the chargeable asset.

16.15.4.6 Certificates of clearance

Capital Gains Tax (withholding tax)

Section 980 of the TCA, 1997 as amended by subsequent Finance Acts contains provisions regarding capital gains tax clearance certificates. Section 980 provides that on the disposal of land and buildings in the State (including leasehold interests), mineral assets in the State, exploration/exploitation rights on the Irish continental shelf, unquoted shares deriving their value from these assets, goodwill of a trade carried on in the State where the consideration exceeds a certain amount (currently €1,000,000 for houses and apartments and €500,000 for all other properties), the person 'by or through whom' the payment is made (the purchaser or the purchaser's solicitor), must withhold and remit capital gains tax at 15 per cent unless the vendor produces a clearance certificate from Capital Gains Tax CG50A. This certificate does not indicate that the Revenue is satisfied with the CGT position; it merely provides that the purchaser need not deduct the 15 per cent withholding tax. This 15 per cent of the gross purchase consideration must be withheld and paid directly to the Revenue Commissioners regardless of whether a gain arises on the disposal of the asset in question. However, there is no need to deduct any tax unless the sale proceeds exceed either €1,000,000 in the case of houses and apartments and €500,000 in all other cases. Section 980 of the TCA, 1997 provides that the purchaser must deliver an account of the payment, and the amount deducted from the payment, within 30 days of the date of payment, and remit the 15 per cent to the Revenue. This also provides that if the 15 per cent has not been paid within the period of 30 days the Revenue can assess the purchaser for that amount. Where the 15 per cent is paid within the 30 days that amount will be allowed as a credit against the capital gains tax liability of the vendor.

The Revenue Commissioners under the TCA, 1997, s 916 must issue a clearance certificate with a copy to the purchaser if they are satisfied that the vendor is resident in the State or that capital gains tax is not payable or that capital gains tax chargeable in respect of the disposal (and any previous disposals) has already been paid. In the latter two instances, the vendor's solicitor must demonstrate to the vendor's Inspector of Taxes with supporting computation, payment and so on, that the relevant condition is satisfied. For example, in the case of an application by a non-resident vendor the solicitor must show that either no capital gains tax is payable, or, if tax is payable, the solicitor must attach a computation of the tax payable and pay any such tax together with any tax chargeable on any gain accruing in any earlier year on a previous disposal of the asset. *The grounds for the application must be clearly marked on the Form CG50 and only one of the three available options should be specified.* The clearance certificate is given on a Form CG50A. Anti-avoidance provisions are in place to ensure that this requirement is not avoided by negotiating a number of contracts, each for a consideration of less than €1,000,000 or €500,000. The provisions contained in s 980 apply to all sales whether by an Irish resident or by a non-resident. However, the legislation is principally enacted to ensure that capital gains tax is collected on sales of Irish property by non-residents. Tax deducted is treated as payment on account of the eventual capital gains tax liability.

When the consideration is of a kind from which the 15 per cent deduction cannot be made and the vendor does not produce a clearance certificate, the person acquiring the asset must, within seven days of the time at which the acquisition is made, notify the Revenue Commissioners in writing of the acquisition and give particulars of the asset acquired, the consideration for acquiring the asset, the market value of the consideration, and the name and address of the person making the disposal. In addition the person must pay to the Revenue Commissioners an amount of capital gains tax equal to 15 per cent of the market value. In all cases the vendor's solicitor must submit a Form CG50 applying for a CG50A immediately the contracts are signed and where the consideration exceeds €1,000,000 where a dwellinghouse or apartment is being sold or €500,000 when any other property is being sold.

Where the withholding tax of 15 per cent is withheld, the purchaser's solicitor should give a completed form CG50B to the vendor's solicitor, and when a receipt for the payment issues from the Revenue this should also be provided to the vendor's solicitor to facilitate the vendor in claiming the tax withheld as a credit against any capital gains tax that may be due.

16.15.4.7 Procedure for obtaining capital gains tax clearance certificates (CG50A)

Where the consideration of the disposal of certain assets exceeds €1,000,000 in the case of houses and apartments and €500,000 in all other cases, the person paying that consideration must deduct 15 per cent and remit it to the Revenue Commissioners unless the vendor produces a capital gains tax clearance certificate (Form CG50A). The assets in question are specified in s 980(2) of the TCA, 1997 and in **16.13.2.4**. In practice, the Revenue Commissioners will not issue a CG50A after the consideration has been paid and under no circumstances should an undertaking be accepted from a vendor's solicitor to produce a certificate after completion. An application for Form CG50A is made on Form CG50 which may be obtained from any tax office or downloaded from the Revenue website ('Application for Certificate under s 980(8) TCA 1997'). The form can be signed by the vendor or his/her or its agent and the completed form should be sent directly to the Inspector of Taxes who deals with the vendor's tax affairs at the correct tax office. The vendor's solicitor should apply for Form CG50 at the earliest possible time, and in the case of a sale immediately both parties have signed the contract. At the latest, applications should be made at least five working days in advance of the closing date. The availability of a clearance certificate in time for the closing date cannot be guaranteed if the 'five-day' rule is not observed. The following details must be completed in Form CG50:

(a) the name and address of the tax office that deals with the tax affairs of the vendor;

(b) the name, address, and tax reference number of the vendor (the PPS number);

(c) the consideration involved;

(d) a full description of the asset;

(e) the name and address of the person acquiring the asset;

(f) the date of the Contract for Sale with a copy of the contract attached;

(g) the date on which the vendor acquired the asset;

(h) the grounds for the application, for example 'resident', 'no tax payable', or 'tax paid' as appropriate;

(i) the signature of the vendor (and not the vendor's solicitor). The application form must be signed by the person chargeable (the vendor);

(j) the capacity in which application is made; and

(k) the proposed closing date of the sale.

A copy of the Contract for Sale should be sent with the form CG50.

The Law Society *Gazette* of July 2014 outlines the full procedures to follow when applying for Form CG50A, together with details of the various tax offices with addresses and telephone numbers and should be consulted. It also outlines situations that do not readily fall within the above procedures and the procedures to be followed, for example;

(a) Where the vendor is a builder/developer and is disposing of a newly constructed house;

(b)   Where the purchaser has signed the contract 'in trust';

(c)   The simultaneous signing of contract and closing of the sale;

(d)   Disposals where there is no contract;

(e)   Consideration payable by instalments;

(f)   Disposal by co-owners, partners in a partnership, cross-border mergers.

The clearance certificate will be available where:

1.   the vendor is resident in the State;

2.   there is no capital gains tax due on the disposal; or

3.   the capital gains tax due has been paid.

Sometimes a vendor will refuse to furnish Form CG50A arguing that a particular property was not liable for capital gains tax by reason of being the vendor's only or main residence. The legal position is quite clear. The question of whether a particular transaction is or is not liable to capital gains tax is not relevant. A purchaser is not required to make any enquiries about the vendor's tax liability and is not obliged to consider any information about it that may be given to him. All that is relevant is the amount of the consideration. If it exceeds a certain threshold (currently €1,000,000 for houses and apartments and €500,000 for all other property), the purchaser's solicitor must insist on getting Form CG50A or make the deduction prescribed by the Act from the amount of the purchase money paid. A solicitor should not offer or accept an undertaking to furnish CG50A.

16.15.4.8   New houses and capital gains tax

There is one exception to the rule that Form CG50A must be produced where all the relevant conditions apply, in order to avoid withholding tax. If the asset being sold is land on which a new house has been built or land on which a new house is in the course of construction other certificates can be used.

As an alternative to obtaining Form CG50A where the vendor (the builder) is disposing of a newly constructed house, production of any one of the following certificates will exempt the purchaser from deducting the 15 per cent withholding tax:

(a)   A copy current notification of determination issued to the vendor under the TCA, 1997, s 5311; (C2 Clearance Certificate—subcontractors);

(b)   A copy current tax clearance certificate issued to the vendor under ss 1094 and 1095 of the TCA, 1997; or for licence application; or

(c)   Copy current tax clearance certificate issued to the vendor for the particular purposes of the TCA, 1997, s 980.

If the appropriate tax clearance certificate Form CG50A or those referred to at (a), (b), and (c) above are not produced by the vendor, the person acquiring such asset is obliged on payment of the consideration to deduct 15 per cent of the consideration and remit that amount to the Revenue Commissioners.

16.15.4.9   Agents for foreign vendors

In the past a non-resident vendor has had to pay the capital gains tax withholding tax prior to completion. However, recently, the Revenue has introduced a practice of issuing form CG50A on foot of an undertaking from the solicitor acting for that non-resident vendor.

Section 980(8) of the TCA, 1997 provides that a non-resident vendor can obtain a capital gains tax clearance certificate (Form CG50A) where the capital gains tax payable on the disposal and any earlier disposals by him or her on the same asset) has been paid in full. If the vendor does not have sufficient funds to pay the liability in advance of the disposal the Revenue has confirmed that it will accept a written undertaking from the solicitor acting for the vendor to discharge the liability (and any earlier unpaid tax on his or her disposal of the same asset) from the sale proceeds of the transaction concerned.

The undertaking should be on the solicitor's headed notepaper, signed, and contain the name and address of the vendor, the PPS number, the amount for which the undertaking is given, and the date by which the payment will be made. It should be submitted with the application for the form CG50A.

A payment in satisfaction of an undertaking should be submitted without request, to the Revenue office which issues the CG50A and should be accompanied by a copy of the undertaking and the vendor's PPS number.

It is important to deal with the issue of obtaining Form CG50A in relation to a disposal by a non-resident vendor at the early stage of a transaction and not regard same as a mere completion item, in order to prevent the withholding tax applying. An individual, who is neither resident, nor ordinarily resident in the State, is chargeable to Irish capital gains tax on the disposal of certain 'specified Irish assets'. The specified assets are listed in the TCA, 1997, s 29 and are as follows:

(a)   land in Ireland;

(b)   minerals in Ireland or any rights, interests, or other assets in relation to minerals or searching for minerals; and

(c)   shares deriving their value or greater part of their value directly or indirectly from mining or from assets listed in paragraphs (a) and (b) above other than shares quoted on a stock exchange.

If a capital gains tax clearance certificate is required in respect of a disposal by a non-resident, the Inspector of Taxes will only issue the certificate if the capital gains tax liability has been discharged in full, or if the Inspector of Taxes is satisfied that no tax liability arises, or if a solicitor's undertaking is relied on as noted earlier.

Even where an inspector issues a certificate authorising payment of the proceeds in full, any Irish resident by or through whom the payment is made should be aware of the provisions of s 1034 of the TCA, 1997 which applies equally to income tax and capital gains tax.

Section 1034 of the TCA, 1997 provides that, in the case of a non-resident, capital gains tax can be assessed:

> in the name of any trustee, guardian or committee of such person, or of any factor, agent, receiver, branch or manager, whether such factor, agent, receiver, branch or manager has the receipt of the profits or gains or not, in like manner and to the like amount as such non-resident person would be assessed and charged if such a person were resident in the State and in the actual receipt of such profits or gains.

The Revenue interprets s 1034 widely as applying to any representative of any kind in Ireland. If an Irish resident solicitor acts as an agent for a non-resident vendor he or she needs to bear in mind that this may result in a tax liability under s 1034. The term 'agent' is not defined and, in light of the fact that the 'agent' can be assessed for the non-resident's capital gains tax liability, regardless of the fact that it is not in receipt of the proceeds of sale, solicitors should be particularly cautious in relation to this section. It would be prudent for a solicitor who is acting for a non-resident in the case of a disposal of a specified asset and who is in receipt of the sale proceeds, not to release the proceeds to his or her client until:

(a)   the relevant capital gains tax returns have been made to the Revenue Commissioners;

(b)   the outstanding capital gains tax has been paid;

(c)   a nil notice of assessment has issued; and

(d)   the Revenue Commissioners have issued a 'no audit' letter.

Essentially, the no audit letter is a letter which states that based on the information that is contained in the tax return for the non-resident, it is not intended to carry out an audit. It might be prudent for a solicitor to ensure that any tax is paid even though Form CG50A is not required. The January/February 2003 issue of the Law Society *Gazette* contains a briefing outlining the procedures to be observed when acting for a non-resident vendor. The Revenue has recently issued a statement relating to CGT Clearance Certificates (S56FA05). This section puts an existing Revenue practice on a statutory basis from 25 March 2005. A vendor may now claim a credit for tax paid to the Revenue by the purchaser where consideration takes a form other than money (eg an exchange of land) and the purchaser pays CGT withholding tax to the Revenue which is recovered from the vendor. In addition from 25 March 2005 certain bodies which are exempt from CGT (eg local authorities) are no longer obliged to provide a CGT clearance certificate.

16.15.4.10 Purchase in trust

Circumstances can arise where a purchaser does not want to reveal its identity to a vendor, or where this may not have been finally decided, say in the context of a group of companies. The Revenue has agreed that, notwithstanding note 7 of the existing Form CG50, the inclusion of 'in trust' details for the purchaser on the application form will not prevent the issue of a clearance certificate. The purchaser's solicitors must however furnish the name and address of the purchaser to the Revenue Office that issued the certificate immediately on the closing of the sale.

16.16 Capital Acquisitions Tax

Since 28 February 1974, gift tax is payable on certain gifts made during the lifetime of the donor. A gift is taken when a donee becomes beneficially entitled in possession to some property and does not give any or gives less than the full consideration for it.

Inheritance tax is charged on the taxable value of a taxable inheritance taken by a successor where the date of the inheritance is on or after 1 April 1975.

For the purpose of gift tax and inheritance tax, the relationship between the person who provided the gift or inheritance (the disponer) and the person who receives the gift or inheritance (the donee/beneficiary/successor) determines the maximum tax-free threshold, known as the 'group threshold'. Three group thresholds were introduced on 1 December 1999 in respect of gifts and inheritances. These thresholds are indexed by reference to the consumer price index.

The indexed group thresholds for the year 2016 are set out in the following table:

Group	Relationship to disponer	Amount
A	Child, stepchild, foster child, a natural adopted child, and a child adopted under the Adoption Acts, 1952 to 1991 or under a foreign adoption a grandchild, the minor child of a deceased child.	€280,000
B	Lineal ancestors and lineal descendants, brothers and sisters, and the child of a brother or sister.	€30,150
C	Any donee or beneficiary who does not come under group A or group B.	€15,075

16.16.1 THE CALCULATION OF GIFT TAX AND INHERITANCE TAX

All gifts and inheritances taken by a donee or beneficiary on or after 5 December 1991 which come within the same group threshold are aggregated to determine the amount of tax payable on the current gift or inheritance. This means that if an individual receives a gift or an inheritance on or after 5 December 2001, any prior gifts or inheritances received by that individual before 5 December 1991 will be completely ignored in calculating the tax. This change applies to gifts and inheritances taken on or after 5 December 2001. The rate of tax is currently 33 per cent (in 2016) and applies to both gift tax and inheritance tax for gifts or inheritances received on or after 6 December 2012.

16.16.2 CAPITAL ACQUISITIONS TAX CLEARANCE CERTIFICATES

Prior to 3 April 2010 capital acquisitions tax was a charge on the property comprised in the taxable gift or inheritance for a period of 12 years. The charge had priority over all other charges and interests created by the donee/successor.

Section 60 of the Capital Acquisitions Tax Consolidation Act, 2003 (the 'CAT Act'), gave the Revenue not only the right to follow the person accountable for tax but also a right against the property of which the benefit consists at the valuation date. This section also provided that tax due and payable in respect of a taxable gift or taxable inheritance was and remained a charge on the property of which the taxable benefit consists at the valuation date.

Because of this charge for tax on the property comprised in the benefit it was imperative for a solicitor acting for a purchaser to obtain from the vendor's solicitor a clearance certificate of discharge from CAT, particularly where the title showed a death within the last 12 years (s 61 of the CAT Act).

Section 147(1)(r) of the Finance Act, 2010 deleted ss 60 and 61 of the CAT Act with effect from 3 April 2010 being the date of the passing of the Finance Act, 2010. Certificates of clearance were obtained from the Revenue under the provisions of s 61 of the CAT Act as appropriate. Since 3 April 2010 CAT is no longer a charge on property in respect of which gift or inheritance tax is due to be paid and clearance certificates will no longer issue from the Revenue. This change to the legislation is retrospective in its application from 3 April 2010.

The Finance Act also abolished the concept of secondary liability for the tax due, except in the case of non-resident beneficiaries.

16.17 Certificates Relating to Registration of Title Based on Possession. Section 62(2) Capital Acquisitions Tax Consolidation Act, 2003 (Form CA12)

Despite the abolition of CAT being a charge on property, an exception was made in relation to applications to the Property Registration Authority (the PRA) to register property held by way of adverse possession.

Section 146 of the Finance Act, 1994 as amended by s 62(2) of the Capital Acquisitions Tax Consolidation Act, 2003 is of importance to practitioners and its provisions should be noted. This section provides that the Registrar of Titles in the Land Registry requires a clearance certificate of discharge from capital acquisitions tax (Form CA12) before applications for first registration and/or applications pursuant to s 49 of the Registration of Title Act, 1964 based on adverse possession can be considered and registered. The requirement also relates to applications based on solicitor's certificate in Form 3. This is the only remaining instance in which a certificate of discharge from CAT is required.

Section 146 of the Finance Act, 1994 applies to all applications for registration made on or after 11 April 1994. Section 146 provides that:

1. *After the passing of this Act a person shall not be registered as owner of property in a register of ownership maintained under the Act of 1964 on foot of an application made to the Registrar on or after the 11th day of April 1994 which is:*
   (A) Based on possession and

    (B)   *Made under the Rules of 1972, or any other rule made for carrying into effect the objects of the Act of 1964, unless the applicant produces to the Registrar a certificate issued by the Commissioners to the effect that the Commissioners are satisfied:*

        (1) *that the property did not become charged with gift tax or inheritance tax during the relevant period (defined as a period commencing on the 28 February 1974 and ending on the date registration was made).*

        (2) *That any charge for Gift Tax or Inheritance Tax to which the property became subject during that period has been discharged, or will (to the extent that it has not been discharged) be discharged within a time considered by the Commissioners to be reasonable.*

        (3) *In the case of an application for registration in relation to which a solicitor's certificate is produced for the purpose of Rule 19(3), 19(4) or Rule 35 of the Rules of 1972, the Registrar may accept that the application is not based on possession if the solicitor makes to the Registrar a declaration in writing to that effect.*

The procedure required the applicant or his/her agent to make a declaration in Revenue Form CA 12 that no charge to CAT arose in the period from the date of Registration of the registered owner or 28 February 1974 (whichever is later) to the date of registration of the applicant.

The application of the section to minor boundary amendments, certain low value transactions and statutory authorities was ameliorated by s 128 of the Finance Act, 1996. There is now provision in s 62 of the Capital Acquisitions Act, 2003 at subsections (7) and (8) for certification *by the solicitor* in Revenue Form IT 76.

The certificate is lodged directly to the Land Registry.

All other cases continue to require a certificate in form CA 12 and the considerations in Richard Grogan's article continue to apply.

Many tax problems can arise on even the most routine possessory title application to the Land Registry. When taking instructions in relation to such applications or when considering whether to extract representation on the death of a person on title the tax implications should be considered and the client should be duly advised.

To reiterate, the requirement to furnish a CAT clearance certificate to the Property Registration Authority for the registration of title based on adverse possession to certify that the property did not become charged to CAT during the relevant period or that any tax arising will be paid still remains despite the abolition of the requirement to obtain CAT clearance certificates.

16.18 The Local Government (Charges) Act, 2009 (NPPR Charge)

The NPPR charge was introduced by the Local Government (Charges) Act, 2009 ('the 2009 Act'). Section 3 of the 2009 Act applied an annual charge of €200 to the owners of all Irish non-principal private residences. The charge was payable to the relevant local authority. Liability to pay the charge was determined on the basis of ownership of the property in question on a single day each year. The date is called the 'liability date'.

For the year 2009, 31 July was the liability date. For the years 2010, 2011, 2012, and 2013, 31 March was set as the liability date. The charge must be paid within two months of the liability date. Liability falls on all co-owners of the property but payment by any one co-owner discharges the liability of all co-owners.

Residential property was defined in s 2 of the 2009 and the main type of residential property liable for the charge was private rented property, vacant property (except new but unsold property), apartments, flats, maisonettes, bedsits, and holiday homes.

If the property met with the definition of residential property and no exemptions applied then the NPPR charge was payable.

If the vendor was claiming an exemption from payment of the charge, s 8 of the 2009 Act provided that the owner of a residential property may apply to the relevant local authority for a certificate of exemption in relation to any liability date specifying the reason why the charge was not payable.

Exemptions from the charge included the following:

(a)   an individual's sole or main residence including a house where the individual is claiming a tax relief under the 'rent-a-room' scheme;

(b)   a building of particular heritage which is an 'approved building' by the Minister of the Environment, Heritage, and Local Government and the Revenue Commissioners;

(c)   a building forming part of the trading stock of a business (only if it has not previously been let or used as a dwelling);

(d)   a building occupied under a shared ownership lease;

(e)   a building leased to a housing authority or the Health Service Executive;

(f)   a mobile home;

(g)   properties which through judicial separation or divorce become the principal residence of the other spouse or civil partner;

(h)   the owner was incapacitated by long-term mental or physical infirmity and as a result was obliged to vacate his/her sole or main residence and to reside in a property not owned by him/herself;

(i)   the property was occupied rent free by a relative of the owner as their sole or main residence and the owner resided in a different sole or main residence located within 2 kilometres;

(j)   any year where the liability date falls after the date of death of the owner, and the grant of representation had not issued before the liability date.

Further exemptions may also apply.

Any unpaid NPPR charge is a charge on property for a period of 12 years. Section 7(1) of the 2009 Act provides that any charge or late payment fee due and unpaid by the owner of residential property shall be and shall remain a charge on the property. However, s 7(2) provides that the property shall not, as against a purchaser for full value or as against a mortgagee, remain charged with or liable to the payment of the NPPR charge after 12 years. The penalties in relation to this charge are particularly high.

16.18.1 REQUIREMENTS FOR CONVEYANCING SOLICITORS RE NPPR AS OUTLINED IN LAW SOCIETY GUIDELINES

If the vendor can claim an exemption on a particular liability date or where the charge or tax is paid and there is statutory provision for issuing a receipt, then the vendor must furnish on closing:

A certificate of exemption/waiver/discharge from the local authority for the years 2009, 2010, 2011, 2012, and 2013, as there is a statutory provision for them. If they are not obtained a purchaser cannot be certain that a property is not subject to a charge for any unpaid NPPR or household charge. Essentially in the case where an exemption applies the vendor may apply to the local authority for a certificate of exemption in relation to any liability date specifying the reasons the charge was not payable. On the other hand if the property meets the definition of residential property and an exemption does not apply then the NPPR tax is payable and the vendor must apply to the local authority for a certificate of discharge from the local authority for each liability date.

There are situations where the property does not come within the ambit of the 2009 Act because, for example, it does not meet the definition of residential property or relevant residential property (it is uninhabitable for example or is part of trading stock) in which case the Act does not apply and the property is not subject to the charge. This is not an exemption situation and a certificate of exemption is not necessary and will not issue from the local authority. In these situations the vendor's solicitor must provide on closing a statutory declaration of the vendor setting out the basis and giving the reasons why the property does not come within the ambit of the 2009 Act.

In view of the uncertainty as to when a statutory declaration as opposed to a certificate of exemption/waiver/discharge was required the Law Society issued a Practice Note in the January/February 2014 edition of the Law Society *Gazette* clarifying the position, see **16.18.5.8**.

16.18.2 NPPR CHARGE AND THE POSITION OF THE LEGAL PERSONAL REPRESENTATIVE

There was considerable confusion as to the position of a personal representative in relation to the NPPR charge. In particular, concerns were raised as to how property where the owner was deceased was to be treated where the grant of representation had not yet been granted. The Conveyancing Committee of the Law Society in a Practice Note in the March 2011 issue of the Law Society *Gazette* clarified the position as follows:

> 'It is only when a grant of representation issues in a deceased's estate that a personal representative becomes liable for the charge. Where there is a property whose owner is deceased there is no person meeting the definition of owner in the Local Government (Charges) Act until letters of administration or probate have been granted. Where letters of administration are required, the person who is granted administration becomes the owner for the purposes of the Act. In a Probate case, the executor becomes the owner on the issuing of the grant of probate. Only at that point does liability commence and liability lies with the owner that is the personal representative.'

There is no liability to the NPPR charge in a relevant year if the Grant of Representation has not issued by the liability date (ie 31 March).

The Local Government (Charges) Act, 2009 was amended by s 19 of the Local Government (Household Charges) Act, 2011 by inserting a new s 8A that transposes certain similar provisions of the 2011 Act into the 2009 Act. It provides that:

- A vendor's failure to pay the NPPR charge under the 2009 Act before completion of the sale is an offence carrying a Class C fine on summary conviction.

- The definition of 'vendor' includes an agent of the owner who receives the sale proceeds or part thereof on behalf of the owner, or who provides legal advice to the owner in a voluntary or below market value transfer. This will include a solicitor or auctioneer receiving a deposit or booking deposit on behalf of a vendor in the sale of a non-principal private residence. They will become liable to conviction of an offence and payment of a Class C fine if the sale is closed without the amount of any outstanding charge and arrears and late payment fees having been paid to the local authority.

- Section 8(4) of the 2009 Act (as inserted by the 2011 Act) provides that on or before the completion of a sale of residential property the vendor of that residential property shall, in respect of that residential property give to the purchaser a certificate of exemption or a certificate of discharge as may be appropriate in respect of each year in which a liability date fell since the date of the last sale of the property. A sale includes a voluntary transfer.

16.18.3 ABOLITION OF HOUSEHOLD CHARGES

Both the NPPR and the household charge dealt with at **16.18.4** were abolished with effect from 1 January 2014 and 1 January 2013 respectively. Nevertheless any unpaid NPPR or household charge remain a charge on property for a period of 12 years from the due date for payment of the charge after which a bona fide purchaser takes free of the charge. If a residential property is sold, the vendor is liable to pay all outstanding charges, late payment fees, and interest due before completion of the sale. 'Vendor' is defined to include a solicitor as agent of the owner who receives the proceeds of sale or provides legal advice to the owner. A sale includes a CPO or gift.

Therefore, despite the current abolition of both the household and the NPPR charges, vendors and their solicitors will still have to deal with both of these charges for a period of 12 years from the last due date.

Under the legislation, a vendor is obliged to give to the purchaser either a certificate of discharge, a certificate of exemption, or a certificate of waiver in respect of the NPPR charge. An up-to-date receipt or a declaration made by the vendor is not sufficient (except where the property does not come within the ambit of the 2009 Act). Applications for certificates in relation to the NPPR charge should be made to the NPPR section of the relevant local authority. The Law Society *Gazette* of 5 April 2012 sets out the procedures for applying for the relevant certificate regarding the household charge. The January 2014 edition of the *Gazette* sets out the requirements for certificates of waiver/exemption/discharge or declaration that legislation does not apply in respect of NPPR, household charge, and LPT.

16.18.4 THE LOCAL GOVERNMENT (HOUSEHOLD CHARGE) ACT, 2011

The Local Government (Household Charge) Act, 2011 (enacted 19 December 2011) introduced a new household charge set at €100 for 2012 as a temporary measure pending the introduction of the Local Property Tax. It was a €100 flat tax chargeable on 1 January 2012 and to be paid by 31 March 2012. Section 3 of the Act provided that in 2012 and in each subsequent year the owner as defined of a residential property shall pay an annual household charge to the relevant local authority. Section 4 set out a list of exemptions and waivers and s 9 dealt with applications for certificates of exemption or certificates of waiver. The provisions of s 9 mean, in effect, that certificates of waiver and certificates of discharge will be required in connection with sales of residential property.

Section 8 provided that any unpaid charge, late payment fee, or late payment interest due shall be a charge on the property to which it relates. This is important for conveyancing purposes as it will fall within the remit of general condition 8C of the General Conditions of Sale 2009 edition. As against a bona fide purchaser for value or a mortgagee, the property shall not remain charged after the expiration of 12 years from the date upon the amount owing fell due. Essentially the property is liable to the household charge if on the liability date (1 January 2012) the property met the definition of residential property and the vendor cannot claim an exemption or waiver.

The Conveyancing Committee in a Practice Note in the Law Society *Gazettes* of January/February 2012 and April 2012 issued guidelines to practitioners in relation to these new charges. Because the Act provided that the household charge is a charge on the property to which it relates, solicitors should, on or before closing a transaction, seek confirmation of whether the property in sale is liable to the charge and, if so, obtain a certificate of discharge of the statutory charge on the property to place with the title deeds. If it is claimed by a vendor that the property is not liable to the local authority household charge, the purchaser's solicitor should seek confirmation of this by way of either a certificate of exemption or a certificate of waiver, as appropriate. If the property does not meet the definition of residential property then the vendor must furnish a statutory declaration confirming this and giving the reason.

The vendor's solicitor should also keep a copy of the relevant certificate as evidence of the instructions of the client as it may be of assistance should the solicitor later be prosecuted under s 10(6). Section 10(6) makes it an offence for a person to contravene the Act and such person is liable on conviction to a Class C fine (up to €2,500). This person can by virtue of s 10(8) include, *inter alia*, a solicitor who receives the proceeds of sale on behalf of the owner or who provides legal advice to the owner in connection with the a voluntary or below market value transfer of the property. Section 10(8) provides that the definition of 'vendor' includes *inter alia* in relation to a residential property an agent of the owner.

Solicitors acting for a purchaser must ensure that a certificate of discharge will be available on closing.

The charge is not an item that is apportionable under the standard Contract for Sale. If the parties agree to apportion the charge, this should be dealt with by way of special condition in the Contract for Sale.

The household charge ceased to apply from 1 January 2013. Where the household charge for 2012 has not been paid prior to 7 July 2013 the arrears amount (including late payment penalties) has now increased to €200 and is included as part of the Local Property Tax liability in respect of the property. In effect the arrears of the household charge become a Local Property Tax charge and so becomes part of the outstanding 'crystallised' liability. In addition since 7 July 2013 these arrears are being collected by the Revenue rather than by the local authority. The statutory requirement to provide a certificate of discharge, exemption, or waiver from the household charge was repealed by s 73(3)(a) of the Local Government Reform Act, 2014 with effect from 27 January 2014. It is still possible to obtain a certificate of discharge or waiver or exemption from the household charge support unit by e-mail: support@householdcharge.ie, or by phone (1890) 357357.

Property owners can pay the €200 arrears by accessing the Revenue's online system using their PPSN/Tax registration number, LPT property ID number, and pin. Alternatively they can pay by cheque or postal order which should be sent to The Revenue Commissioners, LPT Branch, PO Box 1, Limerick. They should confirm that the payment is for household charge arrears. If the charge was paid after 1 July 2013 then it is a Local Property Tax and not household charge and the evidence of payment is the usual LPT printout.

16.18.5 LOCAL PROPERTY TAX (LPT)

The Local Property Tax (LPT) came into effect on 1 July 2013 following the passing of the Finance (Local Property Tax) Act, 2012 as amended by the Finance (Local Property Tax) Amendment Act, 2013. As the tax did not come into effect until July 2013, for that year, 2013, the LPT was payable for the last six months of the year and not the full 12 months as is now the case. Unless it is outside of the scope of the LPT charge or is exempt from the charge, all residential property as defined in the legislation that is sold after 1 May 2013 is chargeable to LPT in respect of that liability date.

Although the LPT is a tax on residential property, unlike the NPPR and the household charge the LPT is administered and collected by the Revenue Commissioners rather than the local authorities. In addition, the LPT, again unlike the NPPR and household charge, is not a fixed charge and is based on a self-assessment of the value of the property. The owner of the property on the valuation date is responsible for valuing the property, filing the return, and paying the tax. The liability and valuation date for the LPT for 2013 was 1 May 2013 and for subsequent years is 1 November in the preceding year.

A return must be made in respect of the LPT and failure to file a return can result in a penalty of up to €3,000 and late payment attracts interest at a rate of 0.0219 per cent in line with other taxes. In addition a €500 fixed penalty may be imposed on a vendor who does not provide information to a purchaser about the chargeable value of the property that he or she has disclosed to the Revenue. A vendor could also be liable for a separate penalty of the amount of the additional LPT that is payable for making a false statement to obtain a reduction in the LPT payable.

The LPT is as stated a self-assessed tax based on the value of the property. For properties valued at €1,000,000 or less the charge is 0.18 per cent of the value of the property. The Revenue has introduced a banded system details of which can be downloaded from the Revenue website (www.revenue.ie). In addition the Revenue provided in November 2015 a most helpful guide under the heading 'LPT Guidelines for the Sale or Transfer of ownership of a relevant residential property' which should be downloaded by all convey-ancing solicitors from the Revenue website.

The usual valuation rule applicable to LPT is that the chargeable value that applies in rela-tion to a valuation date continues to apply until the following valuation date. Thus, the chargeable value at 1 May 2013 covered the periods 2013, 2014, 2015 up to 31 October 2016. The chargeable value at 1 November 2016 covers the period 2016, 2017, 2018 up to 31 October 2019. Subject to one exception which is dealt with later this rule applies even where there is a sale during the valuation period.

As the value declared for the preceding valuation date applies for LPT purposes until the next valuation date, a vendor is required to provide a purchaser with details of the charge-able value/valuation band he or she declared in relation to the immediately preceding valuation date. This valuation is the relevant valuation for the next liability date, subject to the situation outlined below and to the vendor considering whether the valuation was honest and reasonable.

16.18.5.1   Example

A vendor values a property for LPT purposes on 1 May 2013 in the €250,001–€300,000 band (Band 5) and sells it for €305,000 in July 2014. The valuation band for the liability dates 1 November 2014 and 1 November 2015, on which the liability for 2015 and 2016 is based, will also be Band 5. If the property had been sold in July 2014 for €240,000 the valuation band would still be Band 5.

16.18.5.2   Sales of exempt property

Subject to one exception, there are no immediate implications arising from a sale of a property that was not a relevant residential property on the valuation date. Such a prop-erty is not potentially taxable until the following valuation date. The exception relates to the purchase of a property from a vendor who purchased the property in 2013 and who qualified for the 'first-time buyer' exemption provided for in s 8 of the LPT Act, 2012 as amended in respect of the years 2013 to 2016 inclusive. This exemption does not carry through to a subsequent purchaser. Thus a property acquired after 1 May 2013 and before 1 November 2013, 2014, or 2015 as the case may be from a person who qualified for relief under s 8 will become taxable in respect of subsequent liability dates in the first valuation period.

Example

A person qualifying for relief under s 8 of the 2012 Act purchases a second-hand property for €195,000 in March 2013. The house is sold in April 2014 for €203,000. The purchaser in April 2014 is taxable in respect of 2015 and 2016. In accordance with the usual valua-tion rule, the chargeable value at 1 May 2013 continues to be the chargeable value until the following valuation date of 1 November 2016. The purchaser should therefore make a return based on Band 3, ie €150,000 to €200,000.

16.18.5.3   Who is liable for payment of the LPT?

Section 11 provides that the liability to pay the LPT falls upon any person who

> *holds any estate, interest or right in a relevant residential property entitling the person to—*
>
> • *the immediate possession of such property for a period that may equal or exceed 20 years, or*
>
> • *the receipt of rents or profits of such property for a period that may equal or exceed 20 years.*

The owner of a residential property on the liability date (which is 1 May 2013 for the tax year 2013 and 1 November thereafter) is liable to pay the LPT. Joint owners will have a joint and several liability. In the case of properties leased for more than 20 years the tenant of the property is liable for the tax but in the case of properties leased for 20 years or less, the landlord is liable.

If a person has no legal title to the property but has acquired (or is acquiring) title by ad-verse possession he or she will be liable to LPT. Revenue have indicated that a person who has occupied a property on a rent free basis without challenge, and has a *prima facie* right to register title under the adverse possession legislation (which normally occurs after 12 years unchallenged occupation) will be the liable person.

Whilst the Revenue are conscious that difficulties can arise in terms of establishing the ownership of property, the LPT deals with this by placing the onus of proof on the tax-payer. Section 11 of the Finance (Local Property Tax) Act, 2012 (FLPTA, 2012) provides that the absence of documentary evidence of title to property shall not preclude an assess-ment and it will be presumed that a person, who is in occupation of a relevant residential property, or in receipt of the rents or profits, is a liable person.

The following is s 11 ss 3 reproduced in full to give an idea of the wide-reaching implica-tions of who is liable to pay the LPT:

> *Without prejudice to subsections (1) and (2) the following persons shall for the purposes of this Act be liable persons in relation to a relevant residential property (the 'property')*
>
> - *a person having an equitable or beneficial estate, interest or right in the property that entitles the person to the possession or receipt referred to in subsection 1(a) or (b)*
>
> - *a trustee that holds the property by an estate, interest or right in the property that entitles the Trustee or a beneficiary to the possession or receipt referred to in subsection 1(a) or (b)*
>
> - *a trustee or other person having a power to appoint in the property, an estate, interest or right that entitles a person to the possession or receipt referred to in subsection 1(a) or (b)*
>
> - *a person having an exclusive right of residence in the property for*
>   - *his or her life or the life or lives of one or more or*
>   - *a period that may equal or exceed 20 years*
>
> - *the personal representative of the estate of a person who was a liable person by virtue of any of the preceding provisions of this section*
>
> - *a person occupying the property with the right to be registered, pursuant to the Registration of Title Act 1964, in respect of any estate, interest or right that would entitle the person to the pos-session or receipt referred to in subsection 1(a) or (b).*

Subsection 4 provides:

> *For the avoidance of doubt-in a case where a person is a trustee as referred to in subsection (3) (b), that person shall, for the purposes of this Act, be a liable person in relation to the relevant residential property concerned notwithstanding that the one or more beneficiaries under the trust is or are, for the purposes for this Act, also a liable person or persons in relation to that property.*

What is clear from this is that there may, at any time be several liable persons all of whom are responsible to discharge the LPT and all of whom may be targeted by the Revenue. It is also clear from this that the provisions of the Act have implications for those involved in the administration of trusts and estates.

16.18.5.4 LPT and the legal personal representative and trustees

There is no doubt that a legal personal representative of a person who was subject to the charge is a liable person under s 11 of the Act.

The Act does not however specify that the liability does not arise until after a grant of representation has been extracted and so it is possible that an executor of an estate, who has power from the date of death of a deceased, may be liable for the charge from the date of death while an LPR of an intestate deceased would not be liable from that date.

However, the Finance (Local Property Tax) Amendment Act, 2013 in s 4 amends the pri-mary Act in relation to who is a liable person and creates a period of grace for the estate of an intestate deceased (or an estate where the executor has predeceased the deceased) for 12 months if no grant has been extracted in that time. Once the 12 months are up, then any person in occupation or in receipt of rent from the property is liable. The same provision is not available for the executor of an estate.

A deferral of the LPT is available to the LPR of an estate in circumstances where there is no grant of representation in the first 12 months after death, where the deceased himself had deferred the LPT, or where there was an outstanding liability to the charge as at the deceased's date of death.

In any event the LPT will be due for payment when the LPR is in a position to transfer the property to a beneficiary, distribute the proceeds from the sale of the property or, at the very latest, three years from the date of death of the deceased. In addition a trustee is liable for the payment as is a beneficiary entitled to possession.

The Revenue have suggested that where multiple parties are liable then they must all agree as to who should file the return and pay the tax.

16.18.5.5 Unpaid crystallised liabilities—LPT and solicitor's obligation

Section 123 of the Finance (Local Property Tax) Act, 2012 provides that any unpaid LPT, and interest, or other monetary penalty amount that is due and unpaid by a liable person shall be and remain a charge on the relevant residential property to which it relates, and shall continue to apply without a time limit until such time as it is paid in full. This was confirmed in s 126(1) of the 2012 Act as amended by s 12(e) of the Finance (Local Property Tax) (Amendment) Act, 2013 which provided that a vendor of residential property must, before completion of the sale of the property pay any LPT, penalties, and accrued interest due in respect of the property. These must be paid notwithstanding that a sale of the property is completed before the tax is payable. This statutory obligation on the vendor does not mean that the amount of the LPT already paid by the vendor cannot be apportioned between the vendor and purchaser on closing. The conveyancing committee of the Law Society in a Practice Note in the June 2013 edition of the *Gazette* confirmed that the apportionment between the vendor and purchaser of the LPT should be done except where an exemption from LPT applies. The precedent wording of the special condition dealing with the apportionment of LPT as between the vendor and the purchaser is dealt with at **6.2.9**. Therefore before a sale of residential property is completed, a vendor is required to pay upfront any unpaid LPT due in respect of a liability date falling before the date of the sale, even if, in the ordinary course of events, such liability would not yet be payable. The liability that has crystallised at this stage comprises unpaid LPT, accrued interest, and any penalty amount that has been imposed in relation to a vendor's self-assessment or a Revenue assessment. In addition, all outstanding returns must be filed. Any outstanding crystallised liability that is not paid by the vendor before the completion of the sale is a charge on the property. In addition where the household charge for 2012 has not been paid or has been part paid prior 1 July 2013 the arrears amount (including late payment penalties) has now been increased to €200 and is included as part of the LPT liability in respect of the property. In effect, the arrears of the household charge become an LPT charge and so become part of the outstanding crystallised liability. As from 1 July 2013 these arrears are being collected by the Revenue.

The LPT is a charge on property, however, unlike most charges to include the NPPR and the household charge that have a 12-year life span, there is no time limit for the LPT and the normal provisions of the Statute of Limitations will not apply. It is important therefore when dealing with a sale or transfer of a property to receive confirmation from the Revenue that same has been discharged. There is also a 'snitch clause' in the legislation in that a purchaser will be bound to inform the Revenue of vendors who have placed a much lower value on their property than the sale price. Offending vendors will be fined €500 if they refuse to reveal to the purchaser the band in which they valued the property for the purposes of the LPT. In turn the Purchaser must file a revised chargeable value return and valuation where it appears to him or her that the valuation declared by the vendor to the Revenue was too low given the circumstances at the valuation date. This penalty will be the amount of the additional LPT payable as a result of the correct value being declared, subject to a maximum penalty of €3,000.

It is important to be mindful of these points when acting in the administration of an estate and more particularly when acting for a vendor/purchaser in a conveyancing transaction.

16.18.5.6 Residential property and exempt property

It is important for a vendor's solicitor to determine if the property in sale meets the definition of residential property or relevant residential property as defined in the LPT Act. The Act defines residential property as 'any building or structure which is in use or is suitable for uses as a dwelling and includes any shed, outhouse, garage and other building or structure and any yard, garden or other land, appurtenant to or used and enjoyed with that building, save as so much of the yard, garden or other land that exceeds one acre shall not be taken into account for the purposes of this definition'.

'Relevant residential property' is defined as a building in the State that is a residential property on a liability date.

Sections 4–10 of the LPT Act set out a number of properties that will not be regarded as a relevant residential property for the purposes of the Act. An LPT exemption will be available for the following properties, some of which are limited in relation to time:

- Commercial property.

- A property vacated by the occupier for at least 12 months due to their long-term physical or mental infirmity, that is certified by a medical practitioner, or alternatively, where the medical practitioner—if it for less than 12 months—certifies that the person is unlikely to return and provided that the property is not occupied by another.

- Newly built, unoccupied, and unrented properties that are sold between 1 January 2013 and 31 October 2016. (This exemption no longer applies after 31 October 2016.)

- Residential property owned by a charity or similar body that is used solely or primarily to accommodate people with special needs.

- A residential property purchased or adapted for use as the main or sole residence of a permanently incapacitated individual who has received an award from the Personal Injuries Assessment Board or a court or who is a beneficiary under a trust established for that purpose.

- Property purchased by all owner occupiers to include a first-time purchaser in the 2013 calendar year shall not be relevant property for the years 2013, 2014, and 2015 provided certain criteria are met as provided for by s 8 of the Act. For example, the purchaser must occupy the house as their sole or main residence. These are exempt from LPT until the end of 2016. This relief applies where the property is purchased jointly with a spouse/civil partner or cohabitant who is not a first time buyer. The relief applies to both new and second-hand properties. If the property is subsequently sold within the exemption period, the tax will then become payable by the next purchaser for all future liability dates.

- Mobile homes, vehicles, and vessels.

- Houses in certain 'ghost estates' and other unfinished developments as listed in the schedule to the Finance (Local Property Tax) Regulations, 2013 (SI 91/2013).

- Residential properties having pyrite damage are exempt for a temporary period of at least three years. The Finance (Local Property Tax) (Pyrite Exemption) Regulations, 2013 (SI 147/2013) stipulated how properties are to be tested to establish whether they have been affected by a significant level of pyrite induced damage and providing for the issue of certificates by a competent person where this has been established.

- Registered nursing homes.

Where an exemption from LPT applies, and the LPT will, therefore, either not arise (for example in the case of new properties) or will not be apportioned between the parties (for example, where the purchaser is a first-time buyer), evidence of entitlement to the exemption should be furnished by the relevant party, if necessary in the form of a statutory declaration. It is possible to check online what the LPT status of a property is.

To recap:

1. If the property meets the definition of relevant residential property on a liability date, then the LPT is payable. Confirmation from the Revenue that the tax has been paid should be furnished by way of an up-to-date printout from the online Revenue system.

2. If the property did not meet the definition of relevant residential property on the liability date then the vendor should furnish a statutory declaration confirming this and giving the reason, together with a copy confirmation from the Revenue by way of a printout from Revenue online system (ROS) that there are no outstanding amounts of LPT payable (if applicable).

16.18.5.7 Conveyancing committee guidelines for LPT

In a Practice Note in the June 2013 edition of the *Gazette* the Conveyancing Committee provided guidelines for dealing with LPT in the context of including a special condition in the Contract for Sale dealing with the apportionment of LPT and providing for the amendment of general conditions 27 and 8(c) of the general conditions.

The Practice Note contained the following guidelines for practitioners:

The vendor should be advised to:

• Submit all outstanding LPT returns and print off their confirmation of payment if they are paying their LPT online.

• Pay all outstanding tax, interest, and penalties; this applies even if the tax is being paid by instalments.

• Advise those vendors who are paying LPT by deduction at source from salary that they will not be given credit for amounts paid during the year until their employers file P35s after the end of the relevant tax year. If they are selling within the tax year, they will have to pay the full amount of LPT for the year upfront before closing, and later claim a refund from the Revenue of any amount deducted at source. If they know they intend selling during the course of a particular year, they might prefer to alter their method of payment so as to avoid the inconvenience of such a double payment.

• It is recommended that a vendor would furnish a purchaser at the pre-contract stage with a note of the value band declared for a property by the vendor. Advise vendors to keep a copy of their returns for this purpose.

• Self-correct any return where there has been an under declaration of value.

• Provide the purchaser with such information about the tax arising on the previous valuation date as is relevant to the purchaser. This is usually given through a vendor's solicitor by providing the property history screen printout.

• Ascertain if the agreed sale price comes within the general clearance or whether specific clearance is required.

The purchaser should:

• Obtain any relevant information from the vendor. The Revenue suggest this includes the property ID, valuation band, basis for valuation, and details of any exemption claimed.

• Confirm that there is no outstanding tax, interest, or penalties.

• Where the property is sold within a valuation period consider whether the valuation declared by the vendor appears to have been reasonably and honestly made. If not, the purchaser's own estimate of the property's valuation should be used at the following liability date.

• Ascertain from the vendor if the agreed sales price comes within general clearance and if not, whether formal clearance has been obtained.

In a Practice Note in the October 2013 edition of the *Gazette* the Conveyancing Committee confirmed that it was successful in getting the Revenue to accept that purchasers must be given some assurance that the property they purchase is not subject to a charge in respect of a vendor's unpaid LPT where the value declared by the vendor on a LPT return is less than the subsequent sale price. The Revenue in November 2015 issued a publication 'Guidelines for the sale or transfer of ownership of a relevant residential property' which should be consulted by practitioners and is available on the Revenue website, www.revenue.ie/en/tax/lpt/sale-transfer-property.html. The Revenue will not issue a certificate of discharge for LPT and instead a system of general and specific clearance has been agreed to facilitate a purchaser to satisfy themselves that the property is not subject to a charge.

It is important to note that the clearance provisions are intended to facilitate purchasers. A purchaser is given an assurance that there is no charge on the property but the Revenue reserve the right to pursue a vendor for pre-sale liabilities where clearance has been obtained on the basis of false information or inadequate disclosure.

The assurance is provided in one of two ways:

1. General clearance—subject to three conditions

   This general clearance should cover the vast majority of sales. It is determined by a purchaser by reference to the online LPT status of the property. Revenue is not directly involved in this clearance process and will not issue written clearance if any one of the three conditions set out later applies. See section 4.2 of the Revenue guidelines for an outline of what this general clearance entails, and in particular, the details of the three conditions, any one of which, if met, will assure a purchaser that Revenue will accept that there is no charge on a property following a sale where it establishes after the sale that a vendor had under declared his or her LPT liability before a sale. The three conditions can be described as allowable valuation margin, expenditure enhancement to a property and sale of a comparable property.

   A practice note in the March 2016 issue of the Gazette outlines revised LPT guidelines on the sale and transfer of residential property as agreed between the Law Society and Revenue. These changes increase the number of cases where general clearance applies without having to refer the matter to the Revenue. This expanded the allowable valuation margin from 1 November 2015 in situations where the property is sold for €300,000 or less.

   (a) Allowable valuation margin

      This relates to the allowable margin by which the sale price of a property exceeds the valuation band/chargeable value declared for the property at the valuation date. See section 4.2.1 of the Revenue guidelines for the three levels of allowable margins set respectively for:

      (i) the first five valuation bands;

      (ii) the remaining 14 valuations; and

      (iii) the properties whose declared chargeable value exceeded €1,000,000 and;

      (iv) since 1 November 2015 there is a new general clearance condition where a property is sold for €300,000 or less general clearance applies regardless of what chargeable value was declared for the property. The allowable valuation margins by which the sale price/value exceeds the valuation band/chargeable value declared have been increased:

         – in relation to properties outside Dublin city and county from 15% to 25% and

         – in relation to properties in Dublin city and county from 25% to 50%.

(b)   Expenditure on enhancement to a property

This relates to whether or not a vendor has enhanced the value of the property since the valuation date by carrying out construction or refurbishment work. See section 4.2.2 of the Revenue guidelines in relation to adjustments of the margins referred to in section 4.2.1 by the value of construction and/or refurbishment carried out. Take note also that the vendor must produce receipts/verification of expenditure on construction and/or refurbishment. Since 1 November 2015 the above increased allowable margins are carried through to this condition (15% to 25% and 25% to 50%).

(c)   Sale of comparable properties

This relates to whether or not a vendor based the declared chargeable value on the valuation date on known and verifiable sales prices of comparable properties in the area. See section 4.2.3 of the guidelines for the rule and for the guidelines on deciding whether two properties are comparable and whether two properties are in a similar state of repair/condition. Prior to 1 May 2013 the time period within which there must be evidence of a sale of comparable property has been increased from six to nine months.

This general clearance is for the protection of a purchaser. Revenue reserve the right to pursue the vendor for any LPT liability attributable to a pre-sale under declaration.

2.   Specific Revenue clearance in certain circumstances

Revenue will provide specific written clearance on request from the vendor where the conditions specified in sections 4.2.1, 4.2.2, and 4.2.3 of the guidelines are not met, but the vendor nevertheless claims that the valuation made at the valuation date was made in good faith. See section 4.3 of the guidelines for all the conditions that apply and for a list of the supporting documentation that must accompany a request for clearance.

It should be noted that:

(a)   This request for clearance is conducted by secure email (pre-registration with the Revenue is required) using form LPT5 (which is confusingly called 'Application for General Clearance').

(b)   Application is made following agreement of the sale price but in advance of closing.

(c)   Revenue will either issue a written clearance (where satisfied that there was no under declaration of the chargeable value), which the vendor must furnish to the purchaser on or before closing, or make an assessment on the vendor (where not satisfied that the valuation band/chargeable value that was declared was reasonable), which then becomes part of the standard online clearance process and which should be paid online by the vendor in advance of closing and the usual evidence of payment produced to the purchaser on or before closing.

These issues are outlined in a Practice Note in the Law Society *Gazette* of October 2013.

16.18.5.8   Certificates of waiver/exemption/discharge or declaration that legislation does not apply: NPPR, household charge, LPT

The Law Society in a Practice Note in the January/February 2014 edition of the Law Society *Gazette* has clarified the circumstances in which certificates of waiver/exemption/discharge from the NPPR charge or the household charge must be obtained and when it is appropriate to obtain a declaration from a vendor as to the non-applicability of the relevant piece of legislation.

It appears to the committee that exemptions (from a charge or tax that would otherwise be due) are being confused with situations where the relevant Act does not apply at all. The Practice Note provides that it is necessary to distinguish between:

1.   Situations where the relevant legislation makes statutory provision for a specific exemption or waiver and provides for the issue of a certificate in relation to same or

where it provides for issue of a certificate of discharge following payment of the relevant charge or tax.

2. Situations where a property does not come within the ambit of the relevant legislation because, for example, it does not meet the definition of 'residential property' or 'relevant residential property' as set out in the different pieces of legislation (either because it is uninhabitable, is part of trading stock, and so on), in which case the relevant act does not apply and the property is not subject to the charge. This second situation is not an exemption situation and a certificate of exemption is not necessary and will not be issued.

In addition the committee clarifies the contents of its Practice Note published in the June 2013 issue of the *Gazette* referred to earlier which relates to cases that come within the ambit of the relevant legislation and where the legislation provides for a waiver or exemption in certain circumstances or where the charge or tax is paid and there is statutory provision for issuing a receipt, that is, cases described in 1. earlier. The committee confirms in its Practice Note that certificates of waiver/exemption/discharge should be obtained in those cases, as there is a specific statutory provision for them and, if they are not obtained a purchaser cannot be certain that a property is not subject to a charge for any unpaid NPPR or Household Charge. A declaration from a vendor as to entitlement to a waiver or exemption is not sufficient, and a receipt for payment by itself is not sufficient in these cases.

To deal with the situations described in 2. earlier, the committee's first Practice Note on NPPR published in the September 2009 *Gazette* recommended that a statutory declaration should be obtained if it is claimed that the charge does not apply. Although not repeated in subsequent Practice Notes, the committee understands that this has also become common practice in relation to cases where it is claimed that the household charge and the Local Property Tax do not apply, and the committee recommends this extension of this practice.

The committee has set out in a table the circumstances in which the various certificates or declarations are appropriate. It is reproduced in **Appendix 16.2** at the end of this chapter and it can also be accessed in the members' area of the Society's website by clicking on 'Committees', Conveyancing Committee', 'Resources' (in the box titled 'Additional information') and scrolling down the Resources page to click on 'Conveyancing guidelines'.

16.19 Value Added Tax

16.19.1 BACKGROUND

Value Added Tax ('VAT') was introduced into Ireland on 1 November 1972 as one of the conditions of Ireland's accession to the European Economic Community. Irish VAT legislation is embodied primarily in the Value Added Tax Consolidation Act, 2010 ('VCA') and various European Community regulations. (References to sections of the Act refer to the Value Added Tax Consolidation Act, 2010.) Many of the provisions of the VAT Act are supported or given effect by VAT Regulations.

VAT is a tax that all EU Member States must impose. All Member States, and all applicant States, must implement national VAT legislation in accordance with the Council Directive 2006/112/EC (the recast of the Sixth VAT Directive).

An EU Member State's own national VAT legislation may only vary from obligations set out in EU VAT legislation where derogation is permitted and has been granted. In the absence of a derogation a person may seek to rely on EU legislation where he or she feels national legislation has not properly reflected the EU provision.

16.19.2 HOW VAT OPERATES

VAT is a transaction-based tax, its fundamental principle being that VAT is paid on the *value added* at each stage of the chain from production to consumption.

VAT is levied at each stage in the chain (referred to as 'output' VAT). In order to tax the 'value added' by a supplier, the supplier can deduct from his or her output VAT, before payment, VAT charged to him or her on resale purchases, and most other business expenses (referred to as 'input' VAT).

Each supplier must file regular VAT returns on which the supplier's output VAT and input VAT are declared. If output VAT exceeds input VAT, payment of the difference must be made to the Revenue. If input VAT exceeds output VAT the difference will be repaid by the Revenue.

An example of the operation of the system can be seen from the following table:

Transaction	Price	23%	Input	Pays to
	Exc VAT	VAT	Credit	Revenue
	€	€	€	€
1 Manufacturer sells to wholesaler	300	69	(46) (say)	23
2 Wholesaler sells to retailer	400	92	(69)	23
3 Retailer sells to consumer	500	115	(92)	23
Total VAT paid				**69**

16.19.2.1 What is subject to VAT?

Irish VAT arises on:

(a) the supply of VATable goods or VATable services for consideration by a taxable person acting in that capacity when the place of supply is the State;

(b) the importation of goods into the State;

(c) the intra-Community acquisition (as defined) of goods made within the State.

Taxable services received in Ireland from EU and non EU suppliers are also subject to reverse charge VAT in Ireland (ie the trader is the accountable person and must self-account for the VAT).

16.19.2.2 Taxable goods and taxable services

Supplies of goods and/or services meeting the conditions mentioned earlier are subject to VAT unless the supplies are specifically exempted from VAT. The exemptions are listed in Schedule 1 to the VAT Act and include:

(a) medical care services;

(b) public transport services;

(c) social welfare services;

(d) education;

(e) activities of public radio and television bodies (excluding advertising);

(f) live theatrical and musical performances;

(g) fund-raising activities of certain non-profit making organisations;

(h) insurance and banking services together with related agency services;

(i) supply of stocks and shares and related agency activities.

16.19.2.3 Supply of goods and services: VCA Part 3 Chapters 1 & 3

In general, a supply of goods takes place where there has been a transfer of ownership of goods by agreement. Goods are defined (s 1) as all movable and immovable objects, but this does not include things in action, or money. References to goods include references to both new and used goods. The legislation also contains specific provisions which hold that certain transactions are regarded as being a supply of goods, eg electricity, gas, heat, refrigeration, and ventilation.

A self-supply of goods takes place when a person either appropriates goods from his or her business for a non-business use (eg takes goods from his or her shop for his or her own house) or, in the case of movable goods, applies the goods from a taxable to an exempt activity. A self-supply is also liable to VAT and the trader must charge himself or herself VAT based on the tax exclusive cost of acquiring or manufacturing the goods that have been self-supplied.

Certain transactions are regarded as not constituting a supply of goods. These include the transfer of ownership of goods as security for a loan (particularly relevant when mortgaging a property) and the transfer of ownership of goods in connection with the transfer of a business or part of a business.

A supply in relation to a service means:

> the performance or omission of any act or the toleration of any situation other than the supply of goods and other than a transaction specified in Section 20 or 22(2).

This provision is sufficiently wide so as to encompass VATable transactions which are not treated as a supply of goods for VAT purposes.

16.19.2.4 Place of supply of goods and services— VCA Part 4 Chapters 1 & 3

As stated earlier, only supplies of goods and services effected within the State can be subject to Irish VAT. It is essential, therefore, to determine the place where the supply of goods or the supply of services has taken place and the legislation provides a series of rules for determining where a supply of goods and where a supply of services takes place for VAT purposes. These rules include:

* immovable goods—where the goods are located;

* services connected to supplies of immovable goods—where the goods are located.

16.19.2.5 Rates of VAT— VCA Part 6 Chapter 1 and Schedules 2 & 3

Currently the rates applicable are:

(a)   zero: mostly food and drink, children's clothing and footwear, medicine (VCA s 46(1)(b) and Schedule 2);

(b)   4.8 per cent—supply of livestock (s 46(1)(d));

(c)   13.5 per cent—sale, maintenance and repair of property; tour guide services; short-term hire of cars, boats and caravans; general repair and maintenance services; certain personal services and certain flour-based bakery products (s 46(1)(c) and Schedule 3);

(d)   23 per cent—all goods and services not listed in the Schedules to the VCA (s 46(1)(a)) and including VAT on rental income;

(e)   9 per cent—this rate applies to restaurant and catering services, hotel and holiday accommodation, cinema/certain theatre and musical tickets/museum tickets, use of sporting facilities, hairdressing services, and certain printed matter.

16.19.3 ACCOUNTING FOR VAT

16.19.3.1 Basis of accounting for output VAT

When a trader is completing his periodic VAT return he or she must calculate the amount of output tax arising in the period. There are two bases under which output VAT may be calculated: the invoice basis and the cash receipts basis.

Invoice basis

Generally, under the invoice basis. a trader must pay output VAT to the Revenue based on the sales invoices issued (or which should have issued) in the VAT period, irrespective of whether the invoice has been paid or not. For supplies which do not require an invoice to be issued, VAT is due at the time the goods or services are supplied.

Cash receipts basis

Under the cash receipts basis, VAT is only payable to Revenue when the cash is received by the trader.

The cash basis is only available to traders whose turnover from the supply of goods or services to customers not registered for VAT exceeds 90 per cent of total turnover, or to traders whose annual turnover does not exceed €2,000,000.

The main advantage of the cash receipts basis over the invoice basis is that the trader only accounts for the output VAT when he himself has been paid whereas a trader on the invoice basis must pay over VAT at the due date whether or not he himself has been paid.

16.19.3.2 Issuing VAT invoices—VCA Part 9 Chapter 2

When a taxable person supplies taxable goods or services to a person who is in business (or to the State or a local authority or a body established by statute) a VAT invoice must be issued by the 15th of the month following the month in which the goods or services are supplied. The invoice must contain certain specified details including:

(a) the name, address, and registration number of the supplier;

(b) the name and address of the person to whom the supply is made;

(c) the date of issue of the invoice;

(d) a sequential number;

(e) the date on which the goods or services were supplied;

(f) a description of the goods or services supplied;

(g) the quantity or volume of goods supplied;

(h) the consideration exclusive of VAT for the supply; and

(i) the rate of VAT applicable to the supply.

Other details are required in relation to specific transactions; for example, when supplying most legal services to businesses based within the EU but outside Ireland, the customer's non-Irish VAT number must be included on the fee note and an indication that the recipient must account for the VAT arising on the supply. There is no requirement to issue an invoice for supplies to a private individual (ie a person not acting in a business capacity) but the supplier may issue an invoice if they so wish.

As mentioned, the requirement to issue an invoice is normally triggered by the completion of supply of the goods or services in question. It should be noted, however, that the receipt of a payment (for example, a deposit, pre-payment, or a retainer) in advance of completion of the supply is deemed to be a supply in that amount and therefore triggers an obligation to issue an invoice and account for VAT in relation to the amount received.

Example

ABC Limited agrees to sell the freehold to a new store to Retail Ltd for €1.5m. Under the sale agreement a deposit of €150,000 is payable in March 2016 (deposit paid to ABC Ltd, ie not held in escrow) and the sale will close in May 2016.

• The deposit is deemed to create a supply and so the invoice relating to the payment must be raised by 15 April 2016 at the latest.

• The invoice in respect of the balance is triggered when the sale closes in May 2016 and so must be issued by 15 June at the latest.

16.19.3.3 VAT returns

The majority of traders are required to file VAT returns for each two-month taxable period, those periods being based on a calendar year (ie January–February, March–April, May–June, July–August, September–October, and November–December).

Certain traders, rather than filing on a two-monthly basis, may be granted permission by the Collector General to file an annual return, a biannual return, a quarterly return, or a thrice annual return depending on the size of their annual VAT liability.

Returns must be completed and returned to the Revenue Commissioners by the 19th day of the month following the end of the filing period in question so, for example, the September/October return must be filed on or before 19 November. Filing is generally now electronic via ROS (Revenue Online Service).

The VAT charged by a person on the supply of goods or services (together with any VAT he is deemed to have charged) is known as 'output' tax. The VAT payable by a person on goods and services supplied to him is known as 'input' tax. When filing a VAT return, a person may claim credit for 'input tax' against 'output tax' arising, paying the excess only to the Revenue. If allowable 'input tax' in any accounting period exceeds the 'output tax', the person is entitled to a refund of the difference from the Revenue Commissioners.

Example

A solicitor bills fees of €5,000 (excl VAT @ 23 per cent) in the period March/April 2015. During that period he purchased a dictaphone system costing €200 (excl VAT @ 23 per cent). The VAT return will show the following:

		Price	VAT
		€	€
Output VAT	Supplies—fees	5,000	1,150
Less: Input VAT	Purchases—dictaphone	(200)	(46)
Net VAT payable			(1,104)

16.19.3.4 Input credit: VCA part 8 Chapter 1

Generally, a taxable person can obtain an input credit for any VAT borne on purchases of goods for resale and most business expenses when they relate to VATable supplies. However, an input credit is not allowed for the following:

(a) the provision of food, drink, accommodation, or other personal services supplied to the taxable person, his or her agent, or employee, eg VAT on hotel bills incurred while a solicitor is on circuit is not recoverable;

(b) entertainment expenses;

(c) the purchase, lease, or hire of cars and petrol otherwise than as stock in trade (except car hire firms, and driving schools). (A proportion of the VAT incurred on new cars purchased subsequent to 1 January 2009 with a CO_2 emission of less than 156g/km may also be reclaimed.)

Generally, a trader is prohibited from claiming input tax on costs associated with exempt sales. Therefore a trader who makes an exempt sale of property or an exempt letting will be prohibited from taking a deduction for VAT incurred on costs such as estate agents' fees, legal fees, and any costs incurred in preparing the property for sale.

16.19.3.5 Records

A taxable person must keep records in such form and containing such information as is necessary so that his liability to VAT (output VAT) and the credits (input VAT) to which he is entitled for taxable purchases can be checked. Records must be maintained for six years from the date of the transaction to which they relate.

Records relating to property transactions must be retained by a taxable person for the entire period that he or she holds an interest plus six years thereafter.

Revenue officials have powers enabling them to:

(a)   enter premises;

(b)   seek production of the relevant business records and inspect them;

(c)   make extracts or remove them for a reasonable period; and

(d)   seek assistance from any person on the premises.

Generally notice of any intention to inspect records is given.

16.19.4 FREEHOLD AND FREEHOLD EQUIVALENT INTERESTS

16.19.4.1 Introduction

With effect from 1 July 2008 the manner in which VAT is levied on property transactions was changed fundamentally. Here the rules applicable to the sale of freehold and freehold equivalent interests are examined. The rules governing lettings are examined in **Landlord and Tenant**, chapter 13.

The VAT rules (VCA s 94) apply to 'immovable goods' which is defined in s 2 as meaning 'land'. In reality this includes both land and any buildings on the land ('buildings' is also specifically defined and is essentially any prefabricated or like structure that has a roof and one or more rigid walls and a floor (except for greenhouses) which is designed to be accessed by humans and should not be mobile or portable).

As mentioned, these new rules apply to both freehold and freehold equivalent interests. A freehold equivalent interest is defined in s 2 of the VCA as 'an interest in immovable goods (other than a freehold interest) the transfer of which constitutes a supply of goods'. For example, a 150-year lease would be regarded as a freehold equivalent interest. Note: the initial definition of freehold equivalent included further categories which were subsequently removed by the Finance (No 2) Act, 2008; care is needed therefore in examining a transaction occurring between 1 July 2008 and 24 December 2008.

The new rules contain specific measures applicable to residential properties.

Obviously there was a stock of properties held on 1 July 2008. Specific transitional rules apply to these properties which for convenience are referred to hereafter as 'transitional properties' (VCA s 95).

The new rules will therefore be examined under the following areas:

1.   Sales—general provisions

2.   Special rules relating to sales of residential property

3.   The Capital Goods Scheme

4.   Special rules relating to sales of transitional property

5.   Interaction with Transfer of Business rules

6.   Miscellaneous topics.

16.19.4.2 Sales—general provisions

Essentially, sales of new properties (including properties which have been sufficiently redeveloped so as to render them new) which are completed on or after 1 July 2008 will be subject to the new rules. Since 1 July 2008, s 94 deals with sales of property.

You may recall that from a VAT perspective all sales of goods for consideration by a taxable person acting in that capacity are subject to VAT (s 3). However, s 94(2) operates by stipulating that the following sales of immovable goods are *not* subject to VAT:

- where the property has not been developed within a 20-year period prior to the sale;

- where the sale of completed immovable goods takes place more than five years from the date of the most recent completion;

- where it is a second or subsequent sale of completed immovable goods within five years of completion, the property has been occupied for at least 24 months post completion, and there has been no development since completion or if there was development that development was minor;

- where in the case of a building the building was completed more than five years prior to the sale and there has been development of the property within five years prior to the sale but that development was only minor.

In principal therefore sales not falling within these categories *are* subject to VAT at the reduced rate, currently 13.5 per cent.

There are a number of terms used earlier which are specifically defined.

(i) Development

'Development' in relation to any land is defined in s 2 as meaning:

(a) the construction, demolition, extension, alteration or reconstruction of any building on the land, or (b) the carrying out of any engineering or other operation in, on, over or under the land to adapt it for materially altered use.

(ii) Minor development

Minor development is development where:

(i) such development did not and was not intended to adapt the building for a materially altered use, and (ii) the cost of such development did not exceed 25% of the consideration for that supply.

(iii) Refurbishment

Refurbishment is defined as 'development on a previously completed building, structure or engineering work'.

(iv) Completed

'Completed' is defined in s 94(1) as meaning that

the development of those goods has reached the state, apart from only such finishing or fitting work that would normally be carried out by or on behalf of the person who will use them, where the goods can effectively be used for the purposes for which the goods were designed, and the utility services required for those purposes are connected to the goods.

(v) Occupied

'Occupied' is also defined by s 94(1) and means:

(a) occupied and fully in use following completion, where that use is one for which planning permission for the development of those goods was granted, and (b) where those goods are let, occupied and fully in such use by the tenant.

Joint option for taxation

Each of the categories noted earlier is not, as stated, subject to VAT. Section 94(5) however provides that where both the supplier and the purchaser are taxable persons within the State they can jointly opt to tax the transaction. *Note:* the provision refers only to purchasers who are 'taxable persons' which is essentially persons who are in business; the ability to opt is therefore not enjoyed by a buyer who is not in business.

In relation to a joint opt to tax:

- The agreement must be in writing.

- It must be entered into no later than the 15th day of the month following the month in which the supply occurs.

- The purchaser becomes the accountable person, ie the supplier does not charge the VAT rather the purchaser self-accounts (ie charges the VAT to themselves) under a reverse charge.

Why would the parties choose to tax a transaction that would otherwise be exempt from VAT?

In general no input VAT is deductible in connection with an exempt supply. Therefore where a sale of immovable goods is exempt from VAT the vendor cannot recover VAT incurred on estate agency fees, legal fees, tax advice, etc in connection with that sale.

Similarly, where the sale is exempt there is a loss of input credit in respect of any VAT incurred by the vendor on the acquisition and/or development of the property. This loss of deduction entitlement is addressed under the Capital Goods Scheme regime which was also introduced on 1 July 2008. In making an exempt supply the supplier may be required to make a Capital Goods Scheme claw back payment or may miss out on a Capital Goods Scheme repayment. The Capital Goods Scheme is examined later.

Sales subject to VAT

In light of the list of supplies of property that are not subject to VAT, the following are the key supplies of property that *are* subject to VAT at the reduced rate applies, currently 13.5 per cent.

- The first sale of a new or transformed* building within the first five years from completion will be subject to VAT.

- The second or subsequent sale of a new or transformed* building within the first five years following completion will also be subject to VAT unless the property has been occupied for a period of 24 months in that period.

- A supply of an incomplete property is subject to VAT (the five-year rule only applies to completed buildings).

- A supply of property which would be exempt from VAT but where both parties have exercised the joint option for taxation (see earlier).

- Generally sales of undeveloped property are not subject to VAT. However, s 94(3) provides that where a person supplies property to a person and in connection with that supply enters into an agreement with that person or somebody connected with that person.

* A transformed building is one which has been rendered 'new' through development.

- to carry out a development of that property then the sale is subject to VAT (see example 3 later in the paragraph).

Example 1

Sahel Ltd constructs two new retail units, the construction of which is completed on 1 July 2009.

Sahel Ltd concludes the sale of the freehold of Unit 1 to Gobi Ltd on 1 August 2009. Is this sale subject to VAT?

Yes. This is the first sale and it occurs within five years of completion so it is subject to VAT. In 2012 Gobi Ltd agrees to sell the unit. Is this sale subject to VAT?

No. This is a second sale within five years of completion but as it has been occupied for more than two years it is exempt.

Example 2

Sahel Ltd occupies the second unit from September 2009 using it as a depot. In October 2011 it finally secures a purchaser. Will the sale be taxable?

> Yes. This is the first sale of the unit so the 'occupancy' test does not apply. As the first sale is taking place within five years of completion it is subject to VAT.

Note: a property is commonly referred to as 'new' within that first five-year window from its completion.

Example 3

Clawail Ltd owns a site. It sought and obtained planning permission to build a number of retail units on the site. The company however no longer wishes to proceed with the development itself. No works of any kind have taken place on the site. Newbuild Ltd enters an agreement with Clawail Ltd under which it will develop and put the retail units on the market. The prospective purchaser will be required to (i) purchase the site from Clawail Ltd; and (ii) enter into a building agreement with Newbuild Ltd.

While the sale by Clawail Ltd would be of an undeveloped site (note planning permission of itself does not constitute development) s 94(3) will apply as the sale is connected with an agreement to subsequently develop the site.

Note: the extent of any works on a property is therefore crucial from a number of perspectives. Where the works are simply repairs and maintenance then they do not need to be considered further. Works that constitute development may render a property 'new' and therefore start a five-year window from completion (with the consequence that a sale within that window is likely to be subject to VAT). However, where the works are development but are only minor development then they are not regarded as commencing a five-year window.

Time of supply

The time of supply is obviously also an important date as it is the status of the property on that date that will determine its liability to VAT or not etc. It also dictates when any related invoice must be issued and when any VAT arising will be accounted for.

Under VAT rules a supply of goods takes place where there is a transfer by agreement of ownership of the goods. (Note the 'by agreement' requirement; special rules ensure a transfer under a compulsory purchase or as settlement of a debt are nevertheless subject to VAT.) Typically this will occur when the Contract for Sale is completed. Note it is not necessary that legal title be transferred; it is sufficient to trigger a supply that the purchaser has acquired the right to dispose of the property as owner. (Note also that any pre-payment/deposit paid and made available to the vendor will necessitate the charge of VAT where the supply of the property is liable to VAT.)

You will be aware that the Land and Conveyancing Law Reform Act, 2009 came into effect in December 2009. The following article issued by Revenue (from Tax Briefing 81) confirms its view that this Act does not change existing practice regarding the time of supply for VAT purposes.

Confirmation of the time of supply for VAT on property transactions

. . . The fact that this section provides that the beneficial interest in relation to land passes on the making (signing) of an enforceable contract has given rise to questions as to whether or not the section impacts on the time of supply (tax point) for VAT purposes in relation to property transactions. Revenue can confirm that there is no change in the existing position for the determination of the time of supply for property transactions.

The time of supply for property transactions is determined by s 3(1C) of the Value-Added Tax Act 1972 (as amended) which states:

For the purposes of this Act in the case of immovable goods "supply" in relation to goods shall be regarded as including—

(a) *the transfer in substance of the right to dispose of immovable goods as owner or the transfer in substance of the right to dispose of immovable goods.*

As s 52 of the Land and Conveyancing Law Reform Act 2009 does not confer on the purchaser the right to dispose of the property as owner, the time of supply for VAT purposes is unaffected by the introduction of the section.

Time of supply—(same criteria as previously).

The transfer of the right to dispose of property as owner is usually regarded as taking place when the Contract for Sale of the property is completed. In practice, this generally entails the payment of the full consideration due under the contract. In the more straightforward situation of a Contract for Sale, with a deposit being paid and the balance being paid on completion of the contract, the supply will be regarded as taking place on completion of the contract, with the payment or deposit received by the vendor before the supply is completed being subject to VAT in the hands of the vendor on receipt of payment.'

16.19.4.3 Sale of residential property

The general rules outlined earlier are varied in certain instances when the property in question is a residential property.

VCA s 94(8) specifically sets aside the provisions in subsection (2), ie the five- and two-year rules, and provides that the first supply of 'a dwelling' by the developer ('... *the person who developed the immovable goods in the course of a business of developing immovable goods ...*') or a person connected with the developer is subject to VAT providing that person was entitled to a deduction on the acquisition and/or development of the property.

Example

Cathbest Limited buys a site in 2009, obtains planning permission for three townhouses, and completes the construction of the houses on 30 September 2010. The market still being slow it rents out the houses and finally in October 2015 puts them on the market. They all sell by 31 December 2015.

Under the general rules as this is a first sale and it is taking place more than five years from completion the sale would be exempt. However, s 94(8) kicks in and the sale is specifically subject to VAT.

16.19.4.4 Capital goods scheme—general provisions—VCA Part 8 chapter 2

VCA s 2 defines a 'capital good' as 'developed immovable goods and includes refurbishment within the meaning of section 63(1) and a reference to a capital good includes a reference to any part thereof . . . 'Refurbishment' is defined as 'development on a previously completed building, structure or engineering work'.

A property which is also a capital good has a 'VAT life', being the adjustment period during which the owner of the property is required to continuously review his deduction entitlement which was exercised on the acquisition of that property. More importantly, a sale of such a property within this adjustment period may trigger a claw back or additional deduction depending on the particular circumstances and so the decision to opt to tax a sale is very much linked to the Capital Goods Scheme (CGS) status of that property.

The possible adjustment periods are as follows:

- the general adjustment period—20 intervals;

- refurbishment—10 intervals;

- long leases—various (see Law Society's Manual on Landlord and Tenant Law, chapter 13).

Initial interval	The 12 months immediately following the completion or purchase of the property is known as the 'initial interval'.
Second interval	The period from the end of the initial interval to the trader's financial year-end.
Third and subsequent intervals	Each successive period to the trader's next accounting year-end following the second or subsequent interval.

In the initial interval the use of the property is examined and if it is for fully taxable use, then all VAT is recoverable, if it is for fully exempt use, no VAT is recoverable and if it has a 'mixed use' (ie both a taxable and exempt use) then an element of the VAT incurred is deductible.

At the end of the initial interval an adjustment is performed to take account of any change in deductibility which occurred within 12 months of the acquisition of the property. This is fundamental to the intent of the Capital Goods Scheme, which is to try and link the amount of VAT deducted to the use of property over the VAT life of the property.

In each of the following intervals an adjustment is made *if* the taxable use of the property varies from the use in the initial interval (as adjusted).

Example 1

In June 2009 Trated Ltd purchases the freehold in a new building for €10m plus €1.35m VAT. This VAT is recoverable in full in 2009 if the building is used wholly for taxable purposes in that initial interval. For the remaining VAT life of the property, the VAT deduction entitlement of Trated Ltd must be reviewed under the Capital Goods Scheme.

The VAT life of a freehold interest is deemed to be 20 intervals therefore every interval the Capital Goods Scheme will consider one-twentieth of the VAT initially recovered, ie €1.35m ÷ 20 (€67,500).

In 2010 if Trated Ltd continues to use the property for taxable purposes no adjustment needs to be made in these years.

However, let us assume that in 2015 Trated Ltd creates a VAT exempt letting of 30 per cent of the property for a five-year period. That part of the property has therefore been moved to an exempt use and an adjustment will arise as a consequence. Trated Ltd will therefore have to pay an amount under the Capital Goods Scheme of €20,250 to Revenue ((€1.35m ÷ 20) × 30 per cent)) for the tax year 2015. For each subsequent interval that the exempt letting continues Trated Ltd will have to pay an amount of €20,250.

The Capital Goods Scheme works, in general, on the basis that the appropriate amount of deductible VAT is reclaimed upfront and an annual adjustment is made at the end of each succeeding year to the extent that the usage of the property varies from the usage in the initial interval when the input VAT was deducted. Generally speaking, where the annual taxable usage is less than the taxable usage in the initial interval then an amount of VAT is payable, which is, in effect, a claw back of a proportion of the VAT deducted in the initial interval. Where the annual taxable usage is greater than the taxable usage in the initial interval then an additional amount of VAT is deductible.

Example 2

The following example from Revenue's *VAT on Property Guide* illustrates a number of the key features of the Capital Goods Scheme and how variations in the trader's deductibility entitlement are handled by the CGS.

ABC Ltd acquired a property on 13 September 2010. Its accounting year ends 31 December. ABC Ltd claimed in full the VAT it incurred on the acquisition:

'Total tax incurred' = €1,350,000

'Base tax amount' = €67,500 (€1,350,000/20). This is the 'total tax incurred' divided by the number of intervals in the adjustment period.

However, when ABC Ltd reviewed its actual deductible entitlement for its initial interval it noted it was 80 per cent. It therefore had to review its deduction taken etc as follows:

'Total reviewed deductible amount' = €1,080,000.

'Reference deduction amount' = €54,000 (€1,080,000/20). This is calculated by dividing 'total reviewed deductible amount' by the number of intervals in the adjustment period and is used for any calculations required at the end of the second or subsequent intervals. The reference deduction amount is the same for the second and each subsequent interval.

Where the deductible amount for the second or any subsequent interval (known as the 'interval deductible amount') differs from this amount an adjustment will be required.

Second interval—no adjustment

For the second interval (which ends on 31 December 2011) ABC's taxable use was 80 per cent. (This is known as the 'proportion of deductible use' for the interval.) As this is the same as the use for the initial interval, no adjustment is required.

Third, fourth, and fifth interval—no adjustment

For the third (ending 31 December 2012), fourth (ending 31 December 2013), and fifth (ending 31 December 2014) intervals the 'proportion of deductible' use was still 80 per cent so adjustments are not required for those intervals.

Sixth and seventh interval—change in taxable use—VAT payable on adjustment

For the sixth interval (ending 31 December 2015) the 'proportion of deductible use' due to a change in ABC's business mix is reduced to 70 per cent. As this differs from 80 per cent (use during initial interval) an adjustment is required. In order to carry out the calculation ABC is obliged to calculate the 'interval deductible amount' which is the 'proportion of deductible use' for that interval multiplied by the 'base tax amount' c 67,500 × 70 per cent = c €47,250.

The adjustment is the difference between the 'reference deduction amount' and the 'interval deductible amount'—

C – D

(C = reference deduction amount; D = interval deductible amount)

€54,000 – €47,250 = €6,750.

As C is greater than D €6,750 is payable to Revenue as tax due for the taxable period following the end of the interval, which is January/February 2016.

For the seventh interval (ending 31 December 2016) the 'proportion of deductible use' was 70 per cent. Again, an adjustment is required—

C – D

€54,000 – €47,250 = €6,750

As C is greater than D €6,750 is payable as tax due for the taxable period following the end of the interval, which is January/February 2017.

Eighth and nine interval—no adjustment required

Trading mix changes again so that ABC's entitlement returns to 80 per cent. For the eighth (ending 31 December 2017) and ninth intervals (ending 31 December 2018) the 'proportion of deductible use' for the interval was 80 per cent, so no adjustment required.

Tenth interval—change in taxable use—VAT deductible on adjustment

For the tenth interval (ending 31 December 2019) the 'proportion of deductible use' changes again due to a further change in the business mix and ABC is now entitled to 95 per cent. As this differs from 80 per cent (use during the initial interval) an adjustment is required. Similar to the above, the 'interval deductible amount' is €67,500 × 95 per cent = €64,125

Adjustment for the interval—

C – D

€54,000 – €64,125 = –€10,125

As D is greater than C €10,125 is given as a VAT credit to ABC by the Revenue for the taxable period following the end of the interval, which is January/February 2020.

For the remainder of the intervals the 'proportion of deductible use' is 80 per cent which means there are no adjustments made at the end of all the intervals. The twentieth interval ends on 31 December 2029. After this date there are no further obligations under the scheme.

Interval	Amt Deducted	Total Rev Ded Amt	Adjustment	VAT
1	€1,350,000	€1,080,000	€270,000	Payable
	€67,500	= base tax amount		

Interval	Ref Deduction	Interval Deduction	Adjustment	VAT
2	€54,000	€54,000		
3	€54,000	€54,000		
4	€54,000	€54,000		
5	€54,000	€54,000		
6	€54,000	€47,250	€6,750	Payable
7	€54,000	€47,250	€6,750	Payable
8	€54,000	€54,000		
9	€54,000	€54,000		
10	€54,000	€64,125	–€10,125	Repayable
11	€54,000	€54,000		
12	€54,000	€54,000		
13	€54,000	€54,000		
14	€54,000	€54,000		
15	€54,000	€54,000		
16	€54,000	€54,000		
17	€54,000	€54,000		
18	€54,000	€54,000		
19	€54,000	€54,000		
20	€54,000	€54,000		

'Big swing'

Normally an adjustment (ie a payment or repayment of an amount of VAT depending on variation in usage) is made on an annual basis. An exception arises however where in any interval other than the initial interval the proportion of tax deductible differs by more than 50 per cent from the initial interval proportion of tax deductible then the owner of the property must perform an adjustment covering all of the remaining intervals, not just the current one.

Example

Trixy Limited incurs VAT of €400,000 when it acquires a property. As Trixy was engaged in fully VATable activities it recovered this VAT in full. The base tax amount is therefore €20,000—(€400,000/20) one-twentieth of the amount initially recovered.

If in year 10, the property is used for only 40 per cent taxable purposes (ie 60 per cent exempt purposes) then the adjustment which is made is in relation to not just year 10 but in respect of the entire remainder of the VAT life of the property.

The adjustment of €132,000 which must be paid to the Revenue is calculated as €20,000 × 60 per cent × 11 = €132,000. (Note: if Trixy's deduction moves from 40 per cent in the future then any adjustment is referenced to a base amount of €8,000 (€20,000 × 40 per cent) per interval thereafter.)

Note: a property can have a number Capital Goods Schemes open on it simultaneously. By way of example, say a building is constructed in 2010 and an extension is added in 2012 and then a mezzanine floor is added in 2018 there will be three CGSs open, a 20-year adjustment period for the construction, a ten-year adjustment period for refurbishment for the extension, and a further ten-year adjustment period for the mezzanine.

16.19.4.5   Capital Goods Scheme—interaction with sales

At the time of sale the first issue to be addressed from a VAT perspective is whether or not the sale is taxable.

If the sale is taxable (see earlier) then the vendor should review his CGS position for that property as he may be entitled to an additional deduction.

Example

Minx Limited incurs €400,000 VAT on the construction of a new building in 2009 but it cannot recover any of the VAT because it is engaged in a wholly exempt business. It continues to use the building for exempt purposes until it sells the building in 2013. This is the first sale following completion and is within five years so it is subject to VAT.

At the time of sale, say there are 15 intervals left. As the sale is VATable Minx Limited will be obliged to levy VAT at 13.5 per cent on the consideration. However, Minx Limited will also be entitled to a deduction of 16*/20ths of the input VAT (€300,000) under the CGS. It will claim this input VAT at the time of sale of the property.

*15 plus 1 as per the relevant formula in the legislation.

Where the sale of the property is exempt it is therefore necessary to determine whether or not it worthwhile for both parties to exercise a joint option for taxation in relation to the sale. Essentially this will depend on the CGS position of the property together with commercial considerations. In addition VAT incurred on the costs of sale of an opted sale is recoverable whereas it is not recoverable when that sale is exempt.

Example

Brush Ltd purchased a building in 2001 and the VAT incurred of €400,000 was recovered in full. Having used the building for taxable purposes since acquiring it the company sells the building in 2012 for €5m.

The sale is exempt from VAT. Brush Ltd and the purchaser now face a choice.

If both parties do not jointly exercise an option for taxation Brush will incur a VAT cost under the CGS. The VAT cost for Brush is €180,000 (400,000/20 × 10*).

(*The number of years remaining in the VAT life of the property is nine plus one as per the formula.)

Interval	Amt Deducted	Ref Deduction
Initial	€400,000	
2		€20,000
3		€20,000

Interval	Amt Deducted	Ref Deduction
4		€20,000
5		€20,000
6		€20,000
7		€20,000
8		€20,000
9		€20,000
10		€20,000
11		€20,000
12		€20,000
13		€20,000
14		€20,000
15		€20,000
16		€20,000
17		€20,000
18		€20,000
19		€20,000
20		€20,000

But what of the purchaser? If the purchaser agrees to jointly exercise an option for taxation he will incur VAT of €675,000 (€5m × 13.5 per cent), which may or may not be recoverable by him. If he does not agree then he does not incur this VAT.

The commercial dynamic then becomes clear. Obviously it should not be assumed that a purchaser will agree to a joint option for taxation even where he has a full deduction entitlement.

Where the purchaser does not have VAT recovery (or restricted recovery) it may be worth agreeing to uplift the price to €5m + €180k (ie the CGS adjustment cost the vendor will have to pay if the sale is not opted). This would still be cheaper than incurring €5m plus VAT of €675k if the sale is subject to a joint option for taxation.

Example

Take the earlier example but assume Brush Ltd was unable to claim any deduction when it built the property.

If the sale is exempt then Bush Ltd has no further CGS issue. However, if the sale is subject to a joint option for taxation then Brush Ltd will be entitled to a VAT deduction of €180,000 (400,000/20 × 9). Again the issue will turn on the purchaser's position.

16.19.4.6 Capital Goods Scheme—residential property

You recall that where a person applies a property (capital good) to a VAT exempt use it will trigger an adjustment under the Capital Goods Scheme and where the variation in the person's deduction entitlement swings by more than 50 per cent a full adjustment (rather than an interval by interval adjustment) is triggered. You might also recall that since 1 July 2008 lettings are exempt from VAT and that while the landlord has a right to opt to tax, an opt to tax is prohibited when it is residential accommodation.

VCA s 94(8)(c) varies the general rules above in the case of a developer and residential property with the effect that a developer who lets a residential property:

- will not incur a 'big swing' adjustment;

- will incur an adjustment payment on an interval by interval basis; and

- will always have to charge VAT on the sale of the property.

16.19.4.7 Supplies of transitional property

Prior to 1 July 2008 the sale of a freehold interest in a property was subject to VAT only where the following conditions were met:

- the property must have been developed post 1 November 1972;

- the vendor must have been entitled to an input credit in respect of his acquisition and/ or development of that property;

- the vendor must hold an interest and must be disposing of an interest in the property;

- the disposal must be in the course of furtherance of business.

Where these conditions were met the sale was subject to VAT at the 13.5 per cent rate. Where any one condition was not met then the sale was not subject to VAT. When VAT arose the vendor was responsible for levying this VAT. There was no joint opting to tax provision available.

VCA s 95 deals with the transitional measures which have been introduced to deal with interests in properties acquired pre 1 July 2008 and held on 1 July 2008.

'Interests' here include freehold interests and what were commonly referred to under the old regime as 'long leases', ie leases that were for a period of ten years or more (long leases and the transitional measures applying thereto are examined in **Landlord & Tenant**, chapter 13). Where a property was incomplete on 1 July 2008 then the new rules apply when that property is sold post 1 July 2008.

Note: s 95 contains specific provisions and so if a particular transaction does not fall within its remit the general rules as detailed in s 94 then apply.

VCA s 95(3) provides that in relation to freehold and freehold equivalent interests the following applies:

- Where the vendor was not entitled to deduct any VAT on the acquisition and/or development of the property prior to 1 July 2008 and there has been no development of that property on or after 1 July 2008 then the sale is *not* subject to VAT.

- Where the vendor was not entitled to deduct any VAT on the acquisition and/or development of the property prior to 1 July 2008 and there has been development of that property on or after 1 July 2008 but that development is minor then the sale is *not* subject to VAT.

- Where the transaction is not subject to VAT a joint option for taxation can be exercised. In relation to a joint option for taxation:

  - the agreement must be in writing;

  - it must be entered into no later than the 15th day of the month following the month in which the supply occurs;

  - the purchaser becomes the accountable person, ie the supplier does not charge the VAT, rather the purchaser self-accounts (ie charges the VAT to itself) under a reverse charge.

From the above, therefore, where the vendor was entitled to an input deduction, the specific measures of s 95 do not apply and so the new general rules detailed in s 94 do, ie:

- The first sale of a new or transformed (ie development works that have rendered it new) building within the first five years from completion will be subject to VAT. VAT at the reduced rate applies, currently 13.5 per cent.

- The second or subsequent sale of a new or transformed building within the first five years following completion will also be subject to VAT unless the property has been occupied for a period of 24 months in that period.

Example

Bush Ltd built a new retail unit in 2007 at a cost of €1m plus VAT. The work was complete in June 2007 and Bush Ltd opened for business on 1 July 2007. In December 2011 the company is being wound up and it agrees to sell the unit for €750k plus VAT. Is the sale subject to VAT?

The property was held on 1 July 2008 and is therefore a transitional property. As Bush Ltd would have been entitled to recover VAT on the build cost the new rules apply. Given that this is the first sale since completion and is within five years thereof the sale is subject to VAT.

If the sale was delayed to 30 July 2012 then it would be outside the five-year window and would be exempt. Vendor and purchaser may, however, jointly exercise an option for taxation in relation to the sale.

The special provisions of s 94(3) apply to transitional properties also so where a person supplies a transitional property to a person and in connection with that supply enters into an agreement with that person or somebody connected with that person to carry out a development of those goods then the sale is subject to VAT.

16.19.4.8 Capital Goods Scheme—transitional properties

Transitional properties (their development and subsequent work thereon) are capital goods for the purposes of the Capital Goods Scheme, ie they have a VAT life; however, certain of the obligations under the Capital Goods Scheme are set aside and certain specific measures are applied. These variations to the general rules can be summarised as follows:

- The adjustment period for freehold and freehold equivalent interests held on 1 July 2008 is a period of 20 years from the acquisition of that interest. Where the property has been developed post acquisition but prior to 1 July 2008 then the adjustment period is 20 years from the most recent development.

- There is no requirement to conduct the annual review normally required (but any development/refurbishment post 1 July 2008 would be subject to the normal CGS rules).

- If on or after 23 February 2010 a transitional property is used for the first time or there is a change of use in the property of more than 50 percentage points, the 'big swing' adjustment will apply.

- Where the person makes an exempt letting of a transitional property they are required to make a deductibility adjustment (s 95(4)(a) refers): see later regarding deductibility adjustments.

- There is no requirement to make a Capital Goods Scheme adjustment where the person exercises an option to tax or terminates an option to tax in respect of a letting of that property (but see later).

- Where a transitional property is sold within its adjustment period the Capital Goods Scheme *must* be considered. Where the sale is within the adjustment period applicable to the property then:

  - where a sale is exempt from VAT the vendor may incur a VAT payment adjustment under the Capital Goods Scheme;

  - where a sale is taxable the vendor will preserve his deduction entitlement and where he was entitled to recover less than 100 per cent he would be entitled to an additional deduction under the Capital Goods Scheme.

16.19.4.9 Transitional properties and exempt lettings

It was mentioned earlier that where an owner makes an exempt letting of a transitional property a CGS adjustment payment is not required. Rather the formula in s 95(4) is employed and a payment adjustment in accordance with this formula is required. The logic is the same as the CGS and a 20-year VAT life is also used; however, the deductibility adjustment is made upfront as a single payment.

In terms of determining whether the subsequent sale of a transitional property is taxable or not the vendor would still be regarded as having been entitled to a deduction even if he made an adjustment payment in accordance with the formula in s 95(4).

Having to make a lump sum adjustment payment is in sharp contrast with the situation where a property developer lets a non-transitional property (ie he does not avail of the landlord's opt to tax rules). Here a landlord will incur an adjustment payment on an interval-by-interval basis rather than a lump sum adjustment payment.

Tax Briefing 69 contains a Revenue concession on this issue but only for developers and only where the property in question is a residential property. Essentially a developer can avail of s 94(8)(c) and apply interval by interval adjustment payments rather than the lump sum adjustment payment.

Note: Prior to 1 July 2008 lettings of less than ten years were exempt from VAT. A landlord could choose to waive this exemption in which case VAT at the standard rate applied to the rents as they fell due. In general, when a landlord waived the waiver applied to all his lettings which were for periods of less than ten years.

A landlord with a waiver of exemption can cancel his waiver in which case all short-term lettings covered by the waiver will become exempt from VAT. The landlord will be required to perform a cancellation look-back, essentially comparing the VAT he has claimed with the VAT paid on rents and, if greater, he must refund the difference. In these circumstances the subsequent sale of the property will not be subject to VAT.

Under specific rules a landlord with a waiver of exemption in place may find that he will be required to treat the waiver in respect of individual properties as being deemed to have been cancelled. This arises in relation to lettings to connected persons who do not have 90 per cent recovery entitlement and where the rents on that lease do not meet a minimum threshold.

In terms of dealing with a sale by somebody who has/had a waiver, care is needed in particular to ascertain whether the waiver is live at the time of sale or whether it had been cancelled prior to the sale, both of which impact the VAT status of the property.

16.19.4.10 Sales as part of a transfer of a business

Where ownership of a property transfers as part of a transfer of business the supply is regarded as outside the scope of VAT (s 20(2)(c) applies).

While the sale itself may not be subject to VAT there may be obligations under the Capital Goods Scheme to be addressed.

The issue of deductibility of VAT incurred on the costs of the disposal can be complex and care is needed; an entitlement to deduction should not be presumed.

CGS adjustments—transfer in the period the property is regarded as 'new'

Where the property is new and where the transferor was entitled to a full deduction, then he has no CGS adjustment to contend with. If, however, he had a prior restricted deduction entitlement he will be entitled to a further deduction under the CGS as he is regarded as making a taxable sale.

The transferee is regarded as supplying the property to himself and he must therefore charge himself VAT, this being the amount of VAT that would have been charged to him if VAT had been charged by the transferor. If his deduction entitlement is less than 100 per cent he must pay over the difference to the Revenue.

Example

A Ltd agrees to sell its business (including its business premises) to B Ltd. Assume VAT of €400,000 would have been charged to B Ltd on the supply of the premises but for transfer of business relief.

B Ltd has 50 per cent recovery. B Ltd will be required to pay €200,000 to Revenue (400k – 200k) at time of the transfer.

The transferee starts a new 20-interval CGS (VAT life) from the date of acquisition.

CGS adjustments—transfer in the period the property is not regarded as 'new'

Unlike the previous scenario where the property is outside its 'new' period the transferee is regarded as stepping into the shoes of the transferor. He therefore takes on the existing CGS (VAT life) of the property (ie if there were, say, eight intervals left when sold the transferee will take on those remaining eight intervals).

Note: care is always required to establish whether a transaction qualifies for transfer of business or not. Where it does not then the vendor needs to establish whether or not he should charge VAT and if it is an exempt sale the parties need to agree or not on whether they will jointly opt to tax.

Transfer of a legacy lease as part of a transfer of business

Where a legacy lease transfers in connection with a transfer of a business and the transferor had an entitlement to deduct VAT incurred on the acquisition or development of the property and that transfer or assignment would be taxable in the absence of transfer of business then the transferee steps into the shoes of the transferor. There is no new 20-year life and the transferee is liable for CGS obligations for the remainder of the VAT life of the capital good.

Property transferring under transfer of business and impact on waiver cancellation

A cancellation of an existing waiver may be triggered by the sale of a property that is subject to transfer of business (s 96(12)). Where this occurs Revenue will give credit in calculating the cancellation sum as follows:

- Where the sale would have been taxable but for TOB, a credit is given for VAT at reduced rate, currently 13.5 per cent of the sales consideration.

- Where the sale would have been exempt but for TOB, a credit is given for the VAT taken on by the purchaser under the capital goods scheme, that is, the liability that would arise for the transferee if the transferee immediately diverted the property to an exempt use.

Transfers of let properties and transfer of business rules

The transfer of a let property may be regarded as being a transfer of a business or part thereof. Vacant units may qualify where it was let or partially let on a continuing basis but Revenue will not accept that the transfer of a vacant unit that has never been let qualifies. The following is an excerpt from Revenue's leaflet 'Transfer of Business' published in November 2015 (Annex 2 thereof) giving examples of transfers of property capable of being regarded as a transfer of a business ('TOB' being Transfer of Business).

- TOB applies to properties that are let at the time of transfer. For example, a developer developed a block of apartments with the intention of selling them on completion. The developer was unable to sell the apartments on completion and rented them for a period. The developer subsequently sold the block of apartments to an accountable person. TOB rules apply to this sale. However, if the developer had sold the same apartments to private individuals TOB would not apply.

- TOB applies where a property has been let on a continuing basis and is being sold to a tenant who is an accountable person.

- TOB applies where a portfolio of properties, some or all of which are let or have been let on a continuing basis, is being sold as one lot by one vendor to one purchaser, who is an accountable person. Where a similar portfolio of properties is being divided and sold to more than one purchaser or where a number of vendors are selling a portfolio of properties to a single purchaser, each sale should be treated separately in respect of TOB provisions.

- The sale of a mixed development, which includes some let units, some vacant units, some incomplete units and some development land, by a single vendor in one lot to a single purchaser is capable of TOB treatment. The appropriate CGS treatment should be applied to each portion of the development.

Vacant properties

- TOB applies in the case of a vacant property that was let or partially let on a continuing basis in the past.

- TOB applies where a vacant property was used for the purposes of a business in the past and has the necessary quality and attributes to be used for a similar business again immediately after transfer. For example, TOB applies to a factory that is vacant at the time of transfer but has all the necessary fixtures and fittings to be operated as a factory again following transfer.

16.19.4.11 Miscellaneous

Rent to buy

These are schemes whereby potential purchasers are attracted by initial periods of renting. It should be noted that as the conditions of these schemes can vary significantly; each should be examined on its own merits. Commonly however they feature:

- an upfront payment;

- the prospective purchaser renting the property for a defined period of time;

- at the end of the rental period they can exercise an option to purchase the property at an agreed price or walk away; and

- the final price paid will generally be net of the upfront payment and some or all of the rental payments.

Revenue eBrief 40/09 announced the Revenue's general position regarding rent-to-buy schemes. In such cases, a multiple supply occurs for VAT purposes. Essentially the Revenue views these agreements as being a multiple supply, ie two supplies being: (1) the granting of an option to purchase the property at an agreed price; and (2) the granting of a lease. The consideration for these supplies must therefore be apportioned between these two supplies and are taxed accordingly.

With regard to the option to purchase the VAT treatment will follow that of the underlying supply (ie if the option is granted on undeveloped land it is exempt from VAT, if the sale of the property would be subject to VAT then the option is also taxable).

Where the vendor is the person who developed the property, the sale will always be subject to VAT (special rules apply for sale of residential property).

Where the prospective purchaser exercises the option to buy the property, then if a discount is given for the option/rental payments already made this amount will not be treated as consideration for the taxable sale.

If the purchaser does not exercise the option to buy then no further issues arise.

Holiday homes

The renting out of holiday homes is subject to VAT. Traders may avail of the turnover thresholds. Where a trader was obliged to register for this activity then the sale of the property will follow the usual rules as outlined in earlier paragraphs (note it would not be regarded as residential property).

Traders in this business who do not exceed the registration turnover limits are entitled to elect to register for VAT. Where a trader who elected to register cancels that election there is a proportionate claw back of the VAT they deducted (based on a ten-year life, s 8 applies). Where the sale of a holiday property is not subject to VAT s 8 will apply, not the CGS, to the original acquisition/development. Any subsequent refurbishment would, however, be dealt with under the CGS.

Sale of property to a 'connected person' (s 64(8))

A 'connected person' is defined at VCA s 97(3) of the VAT Act. The usual rules, as outlined in this chapter, apply in the case of a sale of a property to a person connected with the vendor.

However, where the VAT arising on the sale price of the property (or the notional VAT in the case of a transfer to which VCA, s 20(2)(c) applies) is less than the 'adjusted VAT amount'* then a potential additional VAT liability, being the difference between the two amounts, arises for the vendor, which amount cannot be passed on to the connected purchaser.

$$\text{*'adjusted VAT amount'} = \frac{H \times N}{T}$$

Where:

H = total tax incurred on acquisition/development

N = number of full intervals remaining in the adjustment period

T = the total number of intervals in the adjustment period for that property

However, this VAT liability for the vendor, should it arise, can be avoided where the purchaser agrees, in writing, to be responsible for all CGS obligations as if the total tax incurred by the purchaser was equal to the total tax incurred by the vendor for the purpose of any subsequent adjustments by the purchaser under the Capital Goods Scheme.

Finance Act, 2015 introduced a new provision at section 64, subsection (8A), to apply a similar measure to supplies of incomplete properties between connected persons. In this scenario the liability is calculated as being the difference between the VAT incurred in relation to that capital good by the owner and the amount of VAT arising on the transfer (or VAT that would arise but for the operation of transfer of business rules). It is not clear that a similar relief to that available for completed buildings will apply to subsection (8A) (ie whereby the acquirer can agree to take on the remaining obligations).

Sale by receiver/mortgagee in possession ('MIP')

Where business property is disposed of by a receiver/MIP in satisfaction of a debt owed by the borrower, s 22(3) provides that the goods are deemed to be supplied by the borrower in the course of his business. However, s 76(2) provides that it is the receiver/MIP that is responsible for accounting to the Revenue any VAT arising on such sales.

Where the sale of a property would otherwise be exempt from VAT, a receiver/MIP can exercise the joint option to tax the sale (provided the receiver/MIP or borrower is not connected with the purchaser) subject to the normal criteria for exercising the joint option (s 94(7)).

The Finance Act, 2013 clarified the position relating to the application of the Capital Goods Scheme ('CGS') to the sale of property by receivers/MIPs. Where a receiver/MIP is appointed/takes possession of a property, then the borrower is obliged to furnish a copy of the CGS record to the receiver/MIP. From the date on which either the MIP takes possession or the receiver is appointed, the receiver/MIP is treated as if they are the capital goods owner of the property. This means that the receiver/MIP is responsible for all obligations of the borrower under the CGS from the date of appointment/date of taking possession (s 64(12A)).

In practice, it is often difficult for the receiver/MIP to obtain details of the VAT history of the property to allow them to comply with their obligations under the CGS. In such circumstances, the receiver/MIP can write to the Revenue district of the borrower to request further information.

16.19.4.12 Summary

When dealing with a freehold sale prior to 1 July 2008 it was a question of establishing whether the sale was taxable or not (sales being taxable only where the conditions were met). Responsibility to levy VAT fell on the vendor except in very limited instances when it shifted to the purchaser.

Since 1 July 2008 an additional dimension arises in that not only is it necessary to determine whether the sale is taxable or not but if it is not whether an opt to tax should be made or not.

Understanding the VAT 'history' of a property is critical to determining the appropriate application of VAT to a disposal. The pre-contract enquiries are designed to capture this history and are therefore critical to any property contract.

In addressing VAT on a sale therefore it is necessary to consider:

- Works

    - What works have been undertaken?

    - When were those works undertaken?

    - What were those works—do those works constitute development and, if so, when were they complete and would they be regarded as minor?

- Capital Goods Scheme

    - What is the property's adjustment period and how many intervals are left?

    - Would an option to tax avoid a claw back or unlock an additional deduction?

- Taxable or not?

    - First sale within five years of completion.

    - Second or subsequent sale within five years of completion—was it occupied, if so for how long?

    - Is the vendor operating a waiver—if so should the waiver be cancelled prior to sale?

- Opt to tax

    - Is the purchaser in a position to opt?

    - What is in it for the purchaser to opt?

- Accountability

    - Who must report the VAT (opt to tax shifts to purchaser)?

Warning: do not issue a VAT invoice earlier than is necessary otherwise you may needlessly accelerate the time VAT becomes due.

16.19.5 ADDENDUM

Extract from E-Brief 69/2008 issued by Revenue Commissioners

Frequently Asked Questions on 2008 VAT on Property

(These are now included as Appendix II to Revenue's publication 'VAT on Property Guide'.)

Note: some paragraphs from the original are excluded as they do not relate to topics covered in this text.

2. **Under Section 7A(1)(d)(iii) [now s 97(1)(d)(iii)] it is provided that a landlord's option to tax is terminated where the landlord and the tenant become connected persons after the lease has been granted. Upon a strict reading of the legislation this applies whether or not the tenant has the ability to recover at least 90% of VAT on input costs.**

Where a landlord and tenant become connected the landlord's option to tax is terminated. However, if the tenant is entitled to at least 90% deductibility in relation to the VAT on rents, the option to tax may remain in place. Similarly if the tenant sub-lets the property to a person who is connected to the landlord, the landlord's option is terminated. However, if the person connected to the landlord is entitled to at least 90% deductibility in relation to the VAT on rents, the option to tax may remain in place. Accordingly, in Example 17 VAT on Property Guide, the termination of the option would not arise if 'C' has at least 90% VAT recovery entitlement.

...

5. **Where a tenant carries out a refurbishment in say year fifteen of a twenty-year lease and the lease expires at the end of the twenty years without being renewed, is the tenant responsible for a capital goods adjustment in respect of the refurbishment when the lease expires?**

In the case described above there is no obligation on the tenant to make an adjustment since the lease simply expires. It is not assigned or surrendered. It should be noted that Revenue will examine cases where a tenant carries out a significant refurbishment approaching the end of the lease to see if in fact the refurbishment is for the benefit of the landlord and the issue of entitlement to input credit of the landlord, etc, would need to be considered.

6. **What is the VAT treatment of a premium/reverse premium payable by the tenant to his landlord on the surrender/assignment of a legacy lease on/after 1 July?**

The payment of a reverse premium to the landlord by the tenant on the surrender of a 'legacy' lease is not taxable: it is considered outside the scope of VAT. The consideration for the assignment/surrender of a legacy lease is based on the CGS amount as per Section 4C(7) [now VCA s 95(8)]. The position of premiums generally is set out in paragraph 4.11 of the VAT on Property Guide.

...

8. **Section 4C(11) [now VCA s 95(12)] provides that the adjustment period for an assigned or surrendered legacy leasehold interest in the hands of the assignee or person who makes the surrender is 20 years. The capital goods scheme operates by intervals. Can the Revenue explain how the capital goods scheme will work in relation to an assigned or surrendered legacy lease?**

Where a legacy lease is assigned/surrendered from 1 July onwards, the person who is assigning or surrendering the lease calculates the number of intervals remaining in the adjustment. This is calculated from Section 4C(11)(c) [now VCA s 95(12)(c)].

The adjustment period for the new owner (assignee/landlord) is advised by the assignor/surrendering tenant per section 4C(8)(b)(i) [now VCA s 95(9)(b)(i)], which will be the number of intervals remaining (being the number of intervals remaining in the latter's adjustment period, including that in which the assignment/surrender takes place).

Section 4C(8)(b) [now VCA s 95(9)(b)] provides that that the assignee/landlord is a capital goods owner for the purposes of Section 12E (now VCA Part 8 Chapter 2]. The initial interval runs for a full 12 months from the date on which the assignment and surrender occurs. The second interval (as per Section 12E) will end on the date of the end of the accounting year of the capital goods owner. (Example 1 in Appendix A illustrates how this operates in practice)

9. **In Section 12E(3)(a) [now VCA s 64(1)(a)] the adjustment periods for various classes of capital goods are set out. This sub section does not refer to shorter adjustment periods which will apply in the case of capital goods to which the transfer of business applies and legacy leases. The words 'in all other cases 20 years' give cause for concern. Can the Revenue confirm that different periods than those set out in Section 12E(3) [now VCA s 64(1)] can apply in the case of properties transferred under transfer of business rules and legacy leases?**

    The adjustment period for legacy leases for the person who holds the interest on 1 July is provided for in Section 4C(11) [now VCA s 95(12)]. For a person to whom a lease is assigned or surrendered post 1 July the adjustment period is provided for in Section 4C(8)(b)(i) [now VCA s 95(9)(b)(i)].

    In relation to a transfer of business there are two separate scenarios. If a transfer of business occurs during the period where the property is considered 'new' then the adjustment period is 20 intervals as per Section 12E(3)(a)(iii) [now VCA s 64(1)(a)(iii)] for the transferee and the 'total tax incurred' is the amount of tax that would have been chargeable on the transfer but for the application of Section 3(5)(b)(iii) [now VCA s 20(2)(c)] as per section 12E(3)(b)(ii) [now VCA s 63(1)].

    If the transfer occurs outside the period where the property is considered 'new' then Section 12E(10) [now VCA s 64(10(c)] provides that transferee will effectively 'step into the shoes' of the transferor and must make adjustments for the remainder of the adjustment period as provided for in Section 12E(10)(c) [now VCA s 64(10)(c)(iii)]. Where the transferee's accounting year ends on a different date to the transferor's, the transferee may align the end of the CGS intervals with his or her end of accounting year. See Regulation 21A of S.I. No. 548 of 2006—VAT Regulations 2006 (inserted by S.I. No. 238 of 2008—VAT (Amendment) Regulations 2008).

10. **Can a body that is considered outside the scope of VAT, such as local authority avail of the option to tax the sale of a transitional property under Section 4C(2) [now VCA s 95(3)]?**

    A local authority, or any other person or entity to the extent that their activities are outside the scope of VAT, cannot avail of the option to tax since they are not a 'taxable person' and therefore do not come within the provisions of Section 4C [now s 95] which only applies to immovable goods acquired or developed by a taxable person. Similarly the CGS will not apply to such a person since it only applies to taxable persons.

11. **When a person leaves a VAT Group and is either the landlord or the tenant of a person who remains a member, can the landlord avoid a deductibility adjustment by opting to tax the letting?**

    Yes, subject to the connected persons rule in Section 7A [now VCA s 97].

    ...

13. **More clarification is needed regarding the meaning of 'freehold equivalent'—What is the position of a lease for 50 years, for 70 years, for 80 years that do not fall foul of the '50% rule'?**

    The length of the lease is not of great importance. The amount of the payment and the nature of the payment(s) is the most significant issue. However, as a very general rule of thumb, leases of 75 years duration or longer are likely to be considered as 'freehold equivalent'.

    ...

16. **Will there be flexibility with the practical application of the CGS in regard to the first and second interval? For some businesses, the partial exemption calculation is a major task performed once a year—the application of the CGS would require partial exemption calculations**

throughout the year. Would it be acceptable to allow some flexibility in the timing of calculating the initial interval adjustment?

In practice this major task of calculating the partial exemption calculation is likely to be dealt with in Large Cases Division (LCD) and should be taken up by each business with LCD. In the majority of cases the proportion of taxable use should be readily identifiable by direct attribution. See paragraph 6.9 of the VAT on Property Guide. Revenue appreciate the practical application of the CGS may give rise in certain circumstances to some issues and some flexibility will be considered as these issues come to light.

For example, if the minimum VAT as calculated by the formula is €12,000 per year, the minimum amount for each taxable period is €2,000. Therefore €2,000 must be accounted for the in July/Aug VAT return.

18.   **Has the exclusion for supplies of immovable goods in the grouping provisions being removed?**

The exclusion has not been removed. The grouping provisions do not apply to the supply of immovable goods.

19.   **Can a person who carries on an exempt business avail of the joint option for taxation and is such a person subject to the CGS?**

Any person who carries on a business in the State (even an exempt business) is a 'taxable person'. The joint option for taxation is allowed when the sale is between taxable persons. The CGS applies to properties where VAT was chargeable on the acquisition or development of that property to a **taxable person.** This should not be confused with a person or body who is involved in activities that are outside the scope of VAT. (See Q10).

20.   **In relation to Section 12E(8) [now VCA s 64(7)]—are paragraphs (b)(i) and (b)(ii) separate exclusions?**

The conditions for the non-application of Section 12E(8)(a) [now VCA s 64(7) (a)] set out in (i), (ii) and (iii) of Section 12E(8)(b) [now VCA s 64(7)(b)] are not separate—they are cumulative. The taxpayer must satisfy the three conditions in order to avoid the CGS adjustment.

21.   **Does Section 12E(8) [now VCA s 64(7)] apply to 'legacy leases'?**

Yes. It is separate to the tax charge that arises on the assignment or surrender of a legacy lease under Section 4C [now VCA s 95].

22.   **Can Revenue confirm that, where a long lease that is subject to VAT is granted before 1 July 2008 (passing EVT, etc) and the landlord then disposes of the reversionary interest in that lease after 1 July 2008 in circumstances where Section 4(9) [now VCA s 93(2)] applies, the landlord will not suffer any CGS adjustment on that disposal of the reversion?**

A CGS adjustment will not apply in these circumstances.

23.   **Is VAT chargeable on the sale of commercial or residential 'transitional' property post cancellation of waiver after payment of cancellation sum?**

Generally no VAT due on sale but see Tax Briefing 64 in respect of sales by a developer/builder—otherwise no change in treatment intended under new rules.

24.   **When does development constitute 'refurbishment'? Is it subject to the 25% rule?**

Refurbishment is a concept within the CGS. Whenever a person carries out a development on a previously completed building, this constitutes a refurbishment and essentially 'creates' a capital good. The adjustment period for a refurbishment is ten intervals, the first of which begins when that refurbishment is completed.

If a property is sold, the 25% test and the materially altered test apply to determine whether or not a property is 'new'. For example, suppose a property was acquired in 1985 without VAT and developed at a cost of €1,000,000 + VAT €135,000 in Apr 2007 (the development was completed 5 July 2007). A further development was carried out in Jan 2008 (completed 18 Mar 2008) at a cost of €200,000 + VAT €27,000. Both developments constitute refurbishment and 'create' two separate capital goods with ten intervals for each capital good. The adjustment period for the first capital good (development completed 5 July 2007) begins on 5 July 2007. The adjustment period for the second capital good (development completed 18 Mar 2008) begins on 18 Mar 2008.

If the property is subsequently sold, it is necessary to determine whether or not the sale is taxable or exempt. This means looking at all development carried out in the five years before the sale occurs. The property is sold in Feb 2009 for €4,000,000. The total cost of the development (neither of which materially altered the property) in the previous five years is €1,200,000. Since this is more than 25% of the consideration for sale the sale is taxable.

If the property had been sold for €6,000,000 the cost of the development would not breach the 25% rule and so the sale would be exempt. In order to avoid a CGS claw-back (separate claw-back for each capital good), the joint option for taxation would have to be exercised.

Note—if the property is not sold there are simply two capital goods— each with an adjustment period of ten intervals. Neither of these capital goods is subject to the annual adjustment provisions under the CGS since the development which 'created' them was completed prior to 1 July 2008.

25. **If a developer disposes of a holiday cottage after 1 July 2008, what are the VAT implications for the developer and the investor? Is the investor entitled to recover VAT on the purchase price and let the property to the management company as the letting of a holiday cottage is a taxable activity?**

The position for such arrangements post 1 July 2008 is as follows. The developer charges VAT to the investor on the sale of the holiday home. As there is no distinction between long and short leases under the new system for VAT on property the granting of the lease from the investor to the management company is an exempt supply of a service. There is no entitlement to deductibility for the purchaser. However, the investor can choose to register for VAT and exercise the landlord's option to tax in accordance with Section 7A [now VCA s 97] and opt to tax the letting to the management company (assuming that the investor and the management company are not connected, or if connected the tenant is entitled to at least 90% deductibility). The investor must then charge VAT on the periodic rents to the management company at 21.5% over the term of the lease. The management company who are engaged in the provision of holiday accommodation are obliged to charge VAT at 13.5% (para (xiii)(b) Sixth Schedule) on the moneys received for providing the holiday homes to its customers.

...

27. **Where a property, in which there is a short-term letting that is subject to a waiver, is sold and the sale is subject to VAT Revenue have traditionally allowed the amount of VAT charged on the sale be included in the 'tax paid' for the purposes of the cancellation adjustment. Will this practice continue for waivers that are cancelled after 1 July?**

Yes, this practice will continue where VAT is chargeable on the sale of a property and the waiver is subsequently cancelled.

28. **A landlord creates a 25-year letting in a property on or after 1 July and the landlord's option to tax is exercised. Two years later the landlord**

sells the property. Can the transfer of business relief in Section 3(5)(b)(iii) [VCA s 20(2)(c)] apply to such a situation where the purchaser will continue to apply the landlord's option to tax?

Yes the transfer of business relief can apply where a landlord sells a property in which there is a sitting tenant and where the purchaser (landlord 2) will continue with the landlord's option to tax and charge VAT on the rents to the sitting tenant.

...

30. **What is the VAT treatment of a premium/reverse premium payable by a landlord to a tenant or a tenant to a landlord on or after 1 July in respect of leases created prior to 1 July?**

There are essentially four possible scenarios—

a) Long lease created prior to 1 July on which VAT was chargeable when created.

b) Long lease created prior to 1 July on which VAT was **not** chargeable when created.

c) Short lease created prior to 1 July where waiver of exemption did not apply (ie exempt lease).

d) Short lease created prior to 1 July where waiver of exemption did apply (ie landlord charges VAT at 21.5% on the rents).

In respect of (a) the VAT chargeable on the assignment or surrender of the lease is restricted to the amount specified in Section 4C(7) [now VCA s 95(8)]. (See question 6 above)

In respect of (b) and (c) no VAT is chargeable on the assignment or surrender of the lease in such cases.

In respect of (d) VAT is chargeable at 21.5% the payment on the assignment or surrender of the lease is linked to the taxable waived letting.

© Revenue Commissioners and reproduced with permission of the Revenue Commissioners.

16.20 Conveyancing Fees

The following is a list of conveyancing fees payable to the Property Registration Authority for both registered and unregistered transactions.

Land Registry fees

Land Registration (Fees) Order, 2012. These fees are effective from 1 January 2012.

1. **Fee scale for transfers on sale**

Value		Fee
€1	€50,000	€400
€50,001	€200,000	€600
€200,001	€400,000	€700
In excess of €400,000		€800

2. **Other registrations affecting registered land**

a. Voluntary transfers €130

b. Opening a new folio or subdivision of parent folio €75

c. Charge €175

d.	Transfer order	€130
e.	Transmissions on death	€130
f.	Section 49 application	€130
g.	First registration in Form 3	€130
h.	First registration other than application in Form 3	€500
i.	Caution/Inhibition	€40
j.	Priority entry	€40
k.	Release of burden/charge	€40
l.	Any other registration not specified above	€40

3. Other services

1.	Special registration map	€40
2.	Copy folio with file/title plan (sealed and certified)	€40
3.	Copy instrument, affidavit, order, or ruling	€40
4.	Names index search	€5
5.	Approval of scheme map (where lodged in electronic form)	€130
6.	Approval of scheme map lodged for the first time	€300
7.	Approval of revision of scheme map	€50

4. Miscellaneous

(a)	Administration fee on refused, abandoned, or withdrawn dealings	€50

Registry of Deeds fees

On 1 May 2008, the Registry of Deeds (Fees) Order, 2008 came into operation. The most commonly used applications are as follows:

1.	Registration of a deed/application form	€50
2.	Registration of a vacated mortgage	€20
3.	Resubmission of a deed and application	€20
4.	Certified copy memorial or application form	€20

The fees order can be viewed on the Authority's website at www.prai.ie.

All Registry of Deeds fees must be paid directly to the Registry of Deeds at Henrietta Street, Dublin 7.

Multiplier Table for Capital Gains Tax

Capital Gains Tax	Multipliers									
Year Expenditure Incurred	Capital Gains Tax Multiplier for Disposals Years ended 5 April 1993 to 31 December 2002									
	Y/e 5 April 1996	Y/e 5 April 1997	Y/e 5 April 1998	Y/e 5 April 1999	Y/e 5 April 2000	Y/e 5 April 2001	Short Y/e 31 Dec 2001	Y/e 31 Dec 2002	Y/e 31 Dec 2003	Y/e 31 Dec 2004 et seq/
1974/75	5.899	6.017	6.112	6.215	6.313	6.582	6.930	7.180	7.528	7.528
1975/76	4.764	4.860	4.936	5.020	5.099	5.316	5.597	5.799	6.080	6.080
1976/77	4.104	4.187	4.253	4.325	4.393	4.580	4.822	4.996	5.238	5.238
1977/78	3.518	3.589	3.646	3.707	3.766	3.926	4.133	4.283	4.490	4.490
1978/79	3.250	3.316	3.368	3.425	3.479	3.627	3.819	3.956	4.148	4.148
1979/80	2.933	2.992	3.039	3.090	3.139	3.272	3.445	3.570	3.742	3.742
1980/81	2.539	2.590	2.631	2.675	2.718	2.833	2.983	3.091	3.240	3.240
1981/82	2.099	2.141	2.174	2.211	2.246	2.342	2.465	2.554	2.678	2.678
1982/83	1.765	1.801	1.829	1.860	1.890	1.970	2.074	2.149	2.253	2.253
1983/84	1.570	1.601	1.627	1.654	1.680	1.752	1.844	1.911	2.003	2.003
1984/85	1.425	1.454	1.477	1.502	1.525	1.590	1.674	1.735	1.819	1.819
1985/86	1.342	1.369	1.390	1.414	1.436	1.497	1.577	1.633	1.713	1.713
1986/87	1.283	1.309	1.330	1.352	1.373	1.432	1.507	1.562	1.637	1.637
1987/88	1.241	1.266	1.285	1.307	1.328	1.384	1.457	1.510	1.583	1.583
1988/89	1.217	1.242	1.261	1.282	1.303	1.358	1.430	1.481	1.553	1.553
1989/90	1.178	1.202	1.221	1.241	1.261	1.314	1.384	1.434	1.503	1.503
1990/91	1.130	1.153	1.171	1.191	1.210	1.261	1.328	1.376	1.442	1.442
1991/92	1.102	1.124	1.142	1.161	1.179	1.229	1.294	1.341	1.406	1.406
1992/93	1.063	1.084	1.101	1.120	1.138	1.186	1.249	1.294	1.356	1.356
1993/94	1.043	1.064	1.081	1.099	1.117	1.164	1.226	1.270	1.331	1.331
1994/95	1.026	1.046	1.063	1.081	1.098	1.144	1.205	1.248	1.309	1.309
1995/96	—	1.021	1.037	1.054	1.071	1.116	1.175	1.218	1.277	1.277
1996/97	—	—	1.016	1.033	1.050	1.094	1.152	1.194	1.251	1.251
1997/98	—	—	—	1.017	1.033	1.077	1.134	1.175	1.232	1.232
1998/99	—	—	—	—	1.016	1.059	1.115	1.156	1.212	1.212
1999/00	—	—	—	—	—	1.043	1.098	1.138	1.193	1.193
2000/01	—	—	—	—	—	—	1.053	1.091	1.144	1.144
2001	—	—	—	—	—	—	—	1.037	1.087	1.087
2002	—	—	—	—	—	—	—	—	1.049	1.049
2003 et seq										1.000

Note: in the 'Year Expenditure Incurred' column, for all years to 2000/2001 inclusive, a year means a 12-month period commencing on 6 April and ending on the following 5 April. The 'Short year' 2001 covers the period 6 April 2001 to 31 December 2001. With effect from 1 January 2002 the Income Tax year is the calendar year, ie 2002 refers to the year ended 31 December 2002.

Indexation is not available on expenditure incurred within 12 months prior to the date of disposal. Indexation relief will *only* apply for the period of ownership of the asset up to 31 December 2002 for any disposals made on or after 1 January 2003.

CERTIFICATES OF WAIVER / EXEMPTION / DISCHARGE
OR DECLARATION THAT LEGISLATION DOES NOT APPLY:
NPPR, HOUSEHOLD CHARGE, LPT

TABLE

This is the table referred to in the practice note on the above topic published by the Conveyancing Committee in the January/February issue of the Gazette and it should be read in conjunction with that practice note. View the practice note on the Law Society website.

Where required, "Statutory Declaration" below means (except where otherwise indicated) a declaration of owner/vendor setting out the reason(s) why the relevant Act does not apply e.g. why the property does not meet the definition of "residential property" or, in the case of LPT, "relevant residential property", etc.

NPPR		
Local Government (Charges) Act 2009 ("2009 Act") as amended by Sections 19(f) and 19(j) of Local Government (Household Charge) Act 2011 ("2011 Act")		
Circumstances of owner/vendor ("V") and/or property	Is this a statutory exemption?	Required
A building not used or not suitable for use as a dwelling	No Does not meet the definition of "residential property" in S.2(1) of 2009 Act - Act does not apply	Statutory declaration – cover all liability dates
(a) An approved building under S. 482 of Taxes Consolidation Act 1997 i.e. in receipt of tax relief for expenditure on significant buildings and gardens (b) A building that forms part of the trading stock of a business and from which no income was derived since construction and which was never occupied as a dwelling (c) A building let by a Minister of the Government, a housing authority or the HSE (d) A building occupied under a shared ownership lease within the meaning of S.2 of the Housing (Misc. Provisions) Act 1992 (e) A building let by a body approved for the purposes of S.6 of the Housing (Misc. Provisions) Act 1992 (f) A building leased to a housing authority for performance of its functions under S.56 of Housing Act 1966 (g) A building leased to the HSE for performance of its functions under Health Act 2004 (h) A building to which Schedule 3 of Valuation Act 2001 applies – subject of or	No All are excluded by S.2(1) of 2009 Act from the meaning of "residential property" in S.2(1) of 2009 Act – Act does not apply	Statutory declaration - cover all liability dates

capable of rateable valuation		
A bedroom in shared accommodation	No Excluded by S.2(2) of 2009 Act from the meaning of "residential property" in S.2(1) of 2009 Act – Act does not apply	Statutory declaration – cover all liability dates
V's sole or main residence	Yes S.4(1)(a)(i) of 2009 Act + S.19(j) of 2011 Act substituted new S.8(1) in 2009 Act	Certificate of exemption for each liability date
Property partly occupied by V as sole or main residence and V entitled to tax relief under "rent-a-room" scheme	Yes S.4(1)(a)(ii) of 2009 Act + S.19(j) of 2011 Act substituted new S.8(1) in 2009 Act	Certificate of exemption for each liability date
Property comprised in discretionary trust and owner is a body corporate being an eligible charity	Yes S.4(1)(b) of 2009 Act + S.19(j) of 2011 Act substituted new S.8(1) in 2009 Act	Certificate of exemption for each liability date
V owns and occupies property 1 as sole or main residence on liability date, acquires property 2 within one year before liability date, property 2 becomes V's sole or main residence within 6 months after liability date	Yes S.4(2) of 2009 Act + S.19(j) of 2011 Act substituted new S.8(1) in 2009 Act	Certificate of exemption for each liability date
On liability date, divorced or judicially separated V owns property which is occupied by other party to the marriage	Yes S.4(4) of 2009 Act + S.19(j) of 2011 Act substituted new S.8(1) in 2009 Act	Certificate of exemption for each liability date
V incapacitated by long term mental or physical infirmity, obliged to vacate sole or main residence, residing in a property not owned by V	Yes S.4(5) of 2009 Act + S.19(j) of 2011 Act substituted new S.8(1) in 2009 Act	Certificate of exemption for each liability date
Property occupied free of rent by relative of V as sole or main residence, and V resides in a different sole or main residence provided that V's sole or main residence is located on same property or within 2 km	Yes S.4(6) of 2009 Act + S.19(j) of 2011 Act substituted new S.8(1) in 2009 Act	Certificate of exemption for each liability date
Any year where liability date falls after date of death of V and grant of representation has not issued to personal representative before liability date	Yes S.4(7) of 2009 Act as inserted by S.19(f) of 2011 Act + S.19(j) of 2011 Act substituted new S.8(1) in 2009 Act	Certificate of exemption for each liability date
All other cases where V owns residential property	No V must pay charge and any associated late payment for all liability dates	Re all liability dates:- (1) Receipt as evidence of payment (2) Certificate of discharge

Household Charge		
Local Government (Household Charge) Act 2011 ("2011 Act")		
Circumstances of owner/vendor ("V") and/or property	**Is this a statutory exemption or waiver?**	**Required**
A building not occupied or suitable for occupation as a separate dwelling	No Does not meet the definition of "residential property" in S.2(1) of 2011 Act - Act does not apply	Statutory declaration – cover all liability dates
(a) a building from which no income was derived since construction which has never been used as a dwelling and which forms part of the trading stock of a business (b) a building vested in a Minister of the Government, a housing authority or the HSE (c) A building owned by a body approved for the purposes of S.6 of the Housing (Misc. Provisions) Act 1992 (d) A building used wholly as a dwelling (other than part of a "mixed hereditament" as defined) and in respect of which local authority rates are payable (e) A bedroom in shared accommodation	No All are excluded by S.2(2) of 2011 Act from the meaning of "residential property" in S.2(1) of 2011 Act – Act does not apply	Statutory declaration – cover all liability dates
Property comprised in discretionary trust within the meaning of the Capital Acquisitions Tax Consolidation Act 2003	Yes S.4(1)(a) of 2011 Act + S.9(1) of 2011 Act	Certificate of exemption for each liability date
Owner is a body corporate beneficially entitled in possession and an approved body (eligible charity) within meaning of S.848A of Taxes Consolidation Act 1997 as inserted by S.45 of Finance Act 2001	Yes S.4(1)(b) of 2011 Act + S.9(1) of 2011 Act	Certificate of exemption for each liability date
V incapacitated by long term mental or physical infirmity, obliged to vacate sole or main residence, residing in a property not owned by V	Yes S.4(2) of 2011 Act + S.9(1) of 2011 Act	Certificate of exemption for each liability date
Any year where liability date falls after date of death of V and grant of representation has not issued to personal representative before liability date	Yes S.4(3) of 2011 Act + S.9(1) of 2011 Act	Certificate of exemption for each liability date
V of property entitled on liability date to payment of supplement under S.198(5) of Social Welfare Consolidation Act 2005 towards mortgage interest on that property	Yes S.4(4)(a) of 2011 Act + S.9(2) of 2011 Act	Certificate of waiver for each liability date
Property on liability date is situated in an unfinished housing estate (in a list prescribed by Minister) (for years 2012 and 2013 only)	Yes – for years 2012 and 2013 only S.4(5) of 2011 Act + S.9(2) of 2011 Act	Certificate of waiver for 2012 and/or 2013
All other cases where V owns residential	No	Re all liability

property	V must pay charge and any associated late payment fee and/or late payment interest for all liability dates	dates:- (1) Receipt as evidence of payment (2) Certificate of discharge

LPT		
Finance (Local Property Tax) Act 2012 ("2012 Act")		
Circumstances of owner/vendor ("V") and/or property	**Is this a statutory exemption or waiver?**	**Required**
Building or structure not in use as or not suitable for use as a dwelling	No Does not meet the definition of "residential property" in S.2 of 2012 Act or "relevant residential property" in S.2 and S.3 of Part 2 of 2012 Act - Act does not apply	Statutory declaration – cover all liability dates
Residential property fully subject to municipal rates (a building used wholly as a dwelling (other than part of a "mixed hereditament" as defined) and in respect of which local authority rates are payable)	No Excluded by S.4 of 2012 Act from definition of "relevant residential property" – Act does not apply	Statutory declaration – cover all liability dates
Sole or main residence has been vacated by V for at least 12 months by reason of long term mental or physical infirmity certified by a doctor, or, if vacated less than 12 months, doctor is satisfied V unlikely at any stage to resume occupation provided property is not occupied by any other person	No Excluded by S.5(2)(a) of 2012 Act from definition of "relevant residential property" – Act does not apply	Statutory declaration – cover all liability dates
Property is used exclusively for the care of individuals certified by a doctor as suffering from long term mental or physical infirmity and is registered under S.4 of Health (Nursing Homes) Act 1990	No Excluded by S.5(2)(b) of 2012 Act from definition of "relevant residential property" – Act does not apply	Statutory declaration – cover all liability dates
Newly constructed residential property - completed but not sold by person who built it or had it built, not occupied as a dwelling, has produced no income tax or corporation tax, and is trading stock of the person who built it or had it built	No Excluded by S.6 of 2012 Act from definition of "relevant residential property" – Act does not apply	Statutory declaration - – cover all liability dates
Special needs accommodation – owned by a charity or a body established by statute and property is used solely or primarily to provide accommodation to persons who by reason of old age, mental or physical disability require	No Excluded by S.7 of 2012 Act from definition of "relevant residential property" – Act does not	Statutory declaration – cover all liability dates

special accommodation or support to enable them live in the community	apply	
Second-hand residential property purchased in period 1st January 2013 to 31st December 2013, and purchaser (or a spouse, civil partner or co-habitant if purchased jointly) would have been entitled to mortgage interest relief had a qualifying loan been taken out, and property is occupied following purchase by the purchaser (or jointly with spouse, civil partner or cohabitant) as sole or main residence.	No. While described as "Exemption for first time buyers" in the Arrangement of Sections Part 2 and in the margin of the Act appearing at Section 8, the wording of Section 8 itself does not refer to an exemption. Excluded by S.8(1) of 2012 Act from definition of "relevant residential property" – Act does not apply [There is no provision in the 2012 Act for issuing certificates of exemption] [Applies for years 2013, 2014 and 2015 only] [S.8(1) ceases to apply in 2016 and also when first time buyer sells the property or ceases to occupy it as sole or main residence at any time after the purchase of the property and before 2016.]	Statutory declaration **of purchaser** – cover all liability dates
Purchase of new residential properties in period 2013 to 2016	No Excluded by S.9 of 2012 Act from definition of "relevant residential property" – Act does not apply	Statutory declaration **of purchaser** - cover 2013 and/or 2014 and/or 2015
Unfinished housing estates (in a list prescribed by Minister)	No Excluded by S.10 of 2012 Act from definition of "relevant residential property" – Act does not apply	Statutory declaration – cover all liability dates
All other cases where V owns residential property	No V must pay the local property tax for all liability dates, any penalties and any accrued interest	Re all liability dates:- Confirmation from Revenue (printout from online system) that there are no outstanding amounts payable

Conveyancing Committee

January/February 2014

Source: https://www.lawsociety.ie/Documents/committees/conveyancing/CertificatesOfWaiver-etc-notApply-JanFeb2014.pdf.

To view the Practice Note please visit: https://www.lawsociety.ie/Solicitors/Practising/Practice-Notes/Certificates-of-waiverexemptiondischarge-or-declaration-that-legislation-does-not-apply-NPPR-household-charge-LPT/#.U6lWy5RdXTo.

INDEX